The Norton Introduction to

PHILOSOPHY

Second Edition

GIDEON ROSEN
Princeton University

ALEX BYRNE
Massachusetts Institute of Technology

JOSHUA COHEN
Apple University; University of California, Berkeley

ELIZABETH HARMAN
Princeton University

SEANA SHIFFRIN
University of California, Los Angeles

W. W. NORTON & COMPANY, INC.
New York • London

W. W. Norton & Company has been independent since its founding in 1923, when William Warder Norton and Mary D. Herter Norton first published lectures delivered at the People's Institute, the adult education division of New York City's Cooper Union. The firm soon expanded its program beyond the Institute, publishing books by celebrated academics from America and abroad. By midcentury, the two major pillars of Norton's publishing program—trade books and college texts—were firmly established. In the 1950s, the Norton family transferred control of the company to its employees, and today—with a staff of four hundred and a comparable number of trade, college, and professional titles published each year—W. W. Norton & Company stands as the largest and oldest publishing house owned wholly by its employees.

Editor: Ken Barton
Assistant Editor: Shannon Jilek
Project Editor: Sujin Hong
Managing Editor, College Digital Media: Kim Yi
Production Manager: Eric Pier-Hocking
Media Editor: Erica Wnek
Media Assistant Editor: Ava Bramson
Marketing Manager, Philosophy: Michael Moss
Design Director: Hope Miller Goodell
Permissions Associate: Elizabeth Trammell
Permissions Manager: Megan Schindel
Composition: S4Carlisle Publishing Services
Manufacturing: LSC Communications—Crawfordsville

Permission to use copyrighted material is included in the Credits.

ISBN 978-0-393-62442-7

W. W. Norton & Company, Inc., 500 Fifth Avenue, New York, NY 10110
wwnorton.com

W. W. Norton & Company Ltd., 15 Carlisle Street, London W1D 3BS
1 2 3 4 5 6 7 8 9 0

Contents

PART I   PHILOSOPHY OF RELIGION

1   Does God Exist?   3

2   Is It Reasonable to Believe without Evidence?   63

PART II · EPISTEMOLOGY

3   What Is Knowledge?   133

4   How Can We Know about What We Have Not Observed?   159

5   How Can You Know Your Own Mind or the Mind of Another Person?   211

6   How Can We Know about the External World?   259

PART III   METAPHYSICS AND THE PHILOSOPHY OF MIND

7   Is Mind Material?   307

8   What Is Consciousness?   351

9   Are Things as They Appear?   405

PART IV   FROM METAPHYSICS TO ETHICS

PART V   ETHICS

14   What Is the Right Thing to Do?   671

15 Do Your Intentions Matter? 733

16 Which Moral Theory Is Correct? 784

17 Is Morality Objective?   844

18   Why Do What Is Right?   924

19   What Is the Meaning of Life?   973

PART VI   POLITICAL PHILOSOPHY

Preface

Philosophy is an ancient subject, and an important one. The great philosophers—Plato, Aristotle, Descartes, and the rest—have shaped the way people think about the world. Philosophy is also a peculiar subject. Philosophers focus on fundamental questions: Do we know anything at all? Does the material world exist? Are actions really right or wrong? In everyday life, and in every other academic discipline, we take the "obvious" answers to these questions for granted. In philosophy, we pause over these answers and subject them to exacting scrutiny.

Such scrutiny can be unsettling, making what was once familiar seem puzzling. As confident understanding gives way to perplexity, a tempting response is to turn away from the questioning that gives rise to it. In philosophy, we make it our business to face the perplexity head-on, and ask whether and how our basic assumptions about knowledge, existence, and morality can be defended.

Because philosophy focuses on fundamental questions of this sort, it can seem to operate at a great distance from life's practical concerns. In *The Clouds*, the great Athenian playwright Aristophanes portrays his contemporary Socrates as a manic babbler who spouts (and sells) manifestly useless nonsense. Such mockery can seem like the right response to people who spend their time puzzling over our basic assumptions when life constantly confronts us with urgent questions that need answers here and now.

We too feel the force of this dismissive stance, especially in those frustrating moments when we struggle to get a grip on the hardest philosophical questions. But we resist it. It is possible to live a life that is both engaged and reflective, focused simultaneously on practical concerns as well as on the basic assumptions that guide our thoughts and choices. Socrates famously said that "the unexamined life is not worth living." This is one of the great overstatements in the history of philosophy, but there is truth in it. Philosophical reflection can inform and enhance the value of any life. Philosophy is rooted in the deep—and deeply practical—human aspiration to live reflectively. In this book, we aim to keep faith with that aspiration and to provide readers with materials that will help them pursue it for themselves.

The Norton Introduction to Philosophy is designed for use in introductory courses in philosophy and as a resource for readers approaching the subject for the first time. Philosophy does not have a well-defined structure or settled boundaries—nothing is obvious—so composing an introductory book for this large field has required numerous editorial decisions. To explain the shape of the book, we would like to say a few words about our guiding editorial ideas.

We start from the premise that philosophy is best learned and taught from primary sources. The first formulations of great ideas and arguments are not just historically significant; they are rich with nuances that are easily lost as the ideas are distilled and refined by others. More importantly, to learn how to read a complex and nuanced philosophical text is (to a very significant extent) to learn how to do philosophy. The challenge in reading is to approach the text with the right mix of openness and critical scrutiny, and this is the same challenge students face with respect to their own ideas as they begin to do philosophy on their own. An introduction to philosophy should expose students to important philosophical ideas, while also helping them to read and think like philosophers. The best way to achieve this is to engage with the original texts.

That engagement, however, presents a challenge. The great books in the history of philosophy were not written for contemporary readers, and the important works of contemporary philosophy were not written for beginning students. In almost every case, the original texts assume more than anyone new to the subject can be expected to know.

The Norton Introduction to Philosophy is designed to address this challenge. The historical and contemporary selections in the book have been supplemented with substantial editorial materials that are designed to supply relevant background and to focus the readers' attention on central themes. But they are mainly designed to enable readers to approach philosophical texts as philosophers do: to restate the thesis in plain terms, to reconstruct the arguments, to illustrate them with fresh examples, and to engage with the arguments, sympathetically and critically. These supporting materials are informed by our belief that the central purpose in reading philosophy is not only to learn what other philosophers have thought but to work out what we should think, and thus to live more reflectively.

Most introductions to philosophy draw their materials exclusively from previously published books and articles. We have done something very different. Philosophy is not a collection of settled findings or a canon of established texts. It is a living subject. While contemporary philosophers engage directly with many of the issues that animated their predecessors, their approaches (and in some cases, their questions) are new, informed by recent developments in the sciences, in other scholarly disciplines, and within philosophy itself. To convey the current vitality of the discipline, we have commissioned 29 essays from contemporary philosophers specifically for inclusion in this book, 9 of which are new to the Second Edition.[1] In each case, the author was asked to write an essay on an active research problem in his or her field, and to present the issue in terms that

---

1. In addition to the 29 commissioned essays in this book, there are 5 more commissioned essays available online: Stewart Cohen, *Contextualism*; Ned Hall, *Causation and Correlation*; David Lyons, *Utilitarian Justification of the State*; Tim Maudlin, *Science and Metaphysics*; and Jonathan Wolff, *Equality as a Basic Demand of Justice*. See "Additional Essays" at digital.wwnorton.com/introphilosophy2.

someone new to the subject can understand. These commissioned essays are not neutral summaries or surveys. They are works of original contemporary philosophy cast in an idiom that any reader of this book will find accessible. Taken together, they paint a vivid (though inevitably partial) picture of what philosophers are doing now. They are:

Louise Antony, *No Good Reason—Exploring the Problem of Evil*
Nomy Arpaly, *Why Moral Ignorance Is No Excuse*
Elizabeth Barnes, *The Metaphysics of Gender*
Lara Buchak, *When Is Faith Rational?*
Alex Byrne, *Skepticism about the Internal World*
David Chalmers, *The Hard Problem of Consciousness*
Alan Hájek, *Pascal's Ultimate Gamble*
Elizabeth Harman, *Is It Reasonable to "Rely on Intuitions" in Ethics?*
Barbara Herman, *Impermissibility and Wrongness*
Rosalind Hursthouse, *Virtue Ethics*
Rae Langton, *Ignorance of Things in Themselves*
Penelope Maddy, *Do Numbers Exist?*
Sarah McGrath, *What Is Weird about Moral Deference?*
Martha Nussbaum, *Political Equality*
Sarah Paul, *John Doe and Richard Roe*
Gideon Rosen, *Numbers and Other Immaterial Objects*
T. M. Scanlon, *When Do Intentions Matter to Permissibility?*
A. John Simmons, *Rights-Based Justifications for the State*
Angela M. Smith, *Implicit Bias, Moral Agency, and Moral Responsibility*
Quayshawn Spencer, *Are Folk Races Like Dingoes, Dimes, or Dodos?*
Galen Strawson, *Free Will*
Sharon Street, *Does Anything Really Matter or Did We Just Evolve to Think So?*
Judith Jarvis Thomson, *Why Ought We Do What Is Right?*
Michael Tye, *The Puzzle of Transparency*
Jonathan Vogel, *Skepticism and Inference to the Best Explanation*
R. Jay Wallace, *Moral Subjectivism*
Roger White, *The Argument from Cosmological Fine-Tuning*
Timothy Williamson, *Knowledge and Belief*
Stephen Yablo, *A Thing and Its Matter*

In choosing materials for this book, we have been guided to a significant degree by a shared philosophical orientation. We are all trained in and identify with the so-called analytic tradition in philosophy, the dominant tradition in Anglo-American philosophy since the early twentieth century (and powerfully represented outside the Anglo-American world as well). Analytic philosophy does not have a well-defined method or a distinctive set of topics. Insofar as it is unified at all, it is so by an intellectual style that emphasizes clear, precisely stated theses and explicit arguments. Most of the modern selections we have included, and all of the newly commissioned essays, are in the analytical tradition.

Organization and Readings

The Norton Introduction to Philosophy includes 109 selections, more than any other text of its kind; of these, 81 are drawn from previously published work. These present central arguments and classic formulations of important problems from the most influential works in the history of philosophy, including Plato's *Republic*, Aristotle's *Nicomachean Ethics* and *Politics*, Descartes's *Meditations*, Kant's *Groundwork*, and Mill's *Utilitarianism*. Selections from previously published work have been edited for length and lightly annotated to supply definitions of key terms and needed background. Because our aim is to provide a text suitable for a first course in philosophy, we have omitted classic readings that assume substantial acquaintance with the field or are in other ways too challenging for beginners.

We have organized these selections into six major parts: Philosophy of Religion, Epistemology, Metaphysics and the Philosophy of Mind, From Metaphysics to Ethics, Ethics, and Political Philosophy. Each part is divided into chapters, and each chapter is headed by a question. Few of these questions will be familiar to students (e.g., Does God exist?), but others may be new (e.g., How Can the State Be Justified?). We title each chapter with a question to emphasize that philosophy is a form of inquiry, and that the first step in any inquiry is to ask the right questions.

We have focused on a selection of central topics in philosophy. To do them justice and to give a sense of competing perspectives, we had to exclude other rich and exciting parts of the field, including the philosophy of language, aesthetics, the philosophy of physics, the philosophy of mathematics, action theory, and the philosophy of biology. Work in these areas often presupposes the material covered here, and so we are confident that after working through this book, readers will be in a good position to approach these and other important topics.

That said, we should note that unlike many introductory texts, *The Norton Introduction to Philosophy* devotes substantial space to moral theory, metaethics, and political philosophy. These are areas that have been central to philosophy from its beginnings but not always represented in introductory texts on the ground that they are specialized subjects that require prior training. We disagree. Philosophical questions about the good life, the nature of morality, the demands of moral responsibility, and the requirements of justice provide a natural and compelling point of entry into philosophy.

To ensure that students read the primary texts as thoughtfully as possible, each chapter opens with an introduction that frames the questions in accessible and compelling terms and provides essential background about the essays and the arguments presented in them. Each primary text is followed by a "Test Your Understanding" section designed to help students determine whether they have read the text carefully. The answers to these questions are provided in the back of the book, so students can immediately gauge whether they have grasped the main ideas. Few of the more difficult essays in the book—18 in all—are accompanied by "Reader's Guides," which explain a central argument from the text in accessible terms.

For every reading in the book, there is a set of "Notes and Questions" to encourage students to analyze the arguments more carefully, to respond to problems raised by the text, to reply (on the author's behalf) to apparent counterexamples to central claims, and so on. Each chapter then closes with an "Analyzing the Arguments" feature, which prompts students to bring the readings into dialogue with one another. This closing section also points to problems that merit further study and, in many cases, to open questions of current interest.

The book begins with a brief guide to logic and argumentation, some guidelines for writing philosophy papers, and four brief personal essays on the nature and value of philosophy. And it concludes with an extensive discursive glossary in which technical terms are explained and illustrated, and in which some of the main issues that arise in the interpretation of these technical distinctions are addressed.

Despite its long history and the intrinsic difficulty of its problems, philosophy is that rare academic field in which it is possible for beginning students not only to learn the discipline but to practice it. Our hope is that this book will be especially useful for readers who approach the study of philosophy with a double aim: to understand the ideas of great philosophers past and present and to use those ideas as a resource in their own philosophical investigations.

Gideon Rosen, *Princeton University*
Alex Byrne, *MIT*
Joshua Cohen, *Apple University;*
University of California, Berkeley
Elizabeth Harman, *Princeton University*
Seana Shiffrin, *UCLA*
(November 2017)

Acknowledgments

Each of us loves philosophy. That common passion drew us together to work on *The Norton Introduction to Philosophy*. It sustained us through seven years, from conception to publication of the First Edition, and through the substantial revisions to this Second Edition. Before letting the book go, we want to acknowledge the many people who have helped us complete it.

First things first: we are very grateful to Roby Harrington, Director of the College Department at W. W. Norton, for initiating the project, and to Roby and our editors, Ken Barton and Pete Simon, for their philosophical and editorial insights, as well as their patience (and the limits on their patience). We are grateful, too, for the help of the other publishing professionals at Norton—Shannon Jilek, Assistant Editor; Sujin Hong, Project Editor; Megan Jackson, Permissions Manager; Hope Miller Goodell, Associate Design Director; Debra Morton Hoyt, Design Director; Eric Pier-Hocking, Production Manager; Michael Moss, Marketing Manager; and Erica Wnek, Media Editor, who assisted in simplifying the complex process of wrestling this large book to the ground.

We would like to thank Anand Krishnamurthy, Tobey Scharding, and Elyse Meyers for expert assistance in preparing the manuscript, and Robbie Hirsch for invaluable assistance with the glossary and illustrations. We would also like to thank the ancillary authors who created the ancillary resources for the Second Edition: Kevin McCain (University of Alabama at Birmingham), Danielle Hampton (Montclair State University), Richard Yetter Chappell (University of York), and Helen Yetter Chappell (University of York).

We also wish to thank the many instructors who offered us advice and feedback on early draft chapters. It is our firm hope that this book will be useful to teachers of philosophy everywhere, from the smallest colleges to the largest universities and beyond. The wise counsel of colleagues with widely diverse experience in the classroom has been invaluable in informing our choices at every stage.

In preparing the second edition we have benefited from the advice of Terry Capellini (Harvard University), Justin A. Capes (Flagler College), Jacob N. Caton (Arkansas State University), Jonathan Eric Dorsey (Texas Tech University), Alexander Guerrero (Rutgers University), John Gulley (Piedmont Virginia Community College), Derek Green (Oakland University), Eric W. Hagedorn (St. Norbert College), David Haig (Harvard University), Carol Hay (University of Massachusetts, Lowell), Carole Hooven (Harvard University), Dimiter Kirilov (George Washington University),

Amanda Lusky (University of Kentucky), Kevin McCain (University of Alabama at Birmingham), Steven McFarlane (University of Minnesota, Morris), Matthew McGrath (University of Missouri), Benjamin Morison (Princeton), Joshua Mugg (Indiana University Kokomo), Celeste Parisi (Apple University), Alejandro Pérez Carballo (University of Massachusetts, Amherst), Katherine Ritchie (City College of New York, CUNY), Tiger Roholt (Montclair State University), Quayshawn Spencer (University of Pennsylvania), Meghan Sullivan (Notre Dame), J. Robert Thompson (Mississippi State University), and Coleen P. Zoller (Susquehanna University).

We also owe a great debt to the philosophers (and philosophically minded friends) who took the time to read and review early draft chapters. They include Joseph Baltimore (West Virginia University), Yancy Dominick (Seattle University), Craig Duncan (Ithaca College), Heimir Geirsson (Iowa State University), Cody Gilmore (University of California, Davis), Deke Gould (Syracuse University), Christopher Grau (Clemson University), Jeff Foss (University of Victoria), Kevin Harrelson (Ball State University), Claire Horisk (University of Missouri at Chapel Hill), Michael Horton (University of Alabama), Peter Hutcheson (Texas State University), Kristen Intemann (Montana State University), Janine Jones (University of North Carolina at Greensboro), Andrew Melnyk (University of Missouri), Seyed Hossein Mousavian (Princeton University), Catherine Muller (University of Birmingham), Pam Spritzer, William Ramsey (University of Nevada, Las Vegas), Michele Reeves, Sharon Ryan (West Virginia University), Timothy Schroeder (The Ohio State University), Adam Sennet (University of California, Davis), Matthew Silverstein (New York University, Abu Dhabi), Matthew Strawbridge, Matthew Talbert (West Virginia University), James Stacey Taylor (The College of New Jersey), and Andreas Teuber (Brandeis University).

Thanks to the philosophers who responded to the publisher's initial survey about the introductory course: Christa Acampora (Hunter College and The Graduate Center, CUNY), Kendrick Adams (University of Arkansas Community College at Hope), David Aiken (University College Roosevelt, The Netherlands), Panos Alexakos (Santa Fe Community College), William Allbritton (Blinn College), Dawn Allen-Herron (University of Alaska Southeast), Torin Alter (University of Alabama), Kenneth Anderson (Oxford College of Emory University), Linda Anthony (Blue Mountain Community College), Mike Austin (Eastern Kentucky University), Karen Bardsley (Morehead State University), Carmine Bell (Pasco-Hernando State College), Joseph Bessing (Lehigh Carbon Community College), Carrie-Ann Biondi (Marymount Manhattan College), Daniel Bonevac (University of Texas at Austin), Marshell Bradley (Sam Houston State University), Alexandra Bradner (Kenyon College), Girard Brenneman (William Jewell College), Robert Brimlow (St. John Fisher College), Robert Briscoe (Loyola University, New Orleans), Michael Carper (Lindenwood University), Thomas Carroll (Middlesex Community College), Charles Cassini (Barry University), Daniel Christensen (Iowa Western Community College), William Clohesy (University of Northern Iowa), Kevin Coffey (New York University, Abu Dhabi), Charlie Coil (John Brown University), James Coleman (Central Michigan University), Juan Comesaña (University of Arizona), Sam Condic (University of Houston-Downtown), Elizabeth Cooke (Creighton University), Ron Cooper (College of Central Florida), Glen Cosby (Spokane Community College), Olga-Maria Cruz (Bellarmine University), Norman Cubbage (University of Louisville), Mike Cundall (North Carolina A&T State University), Margaret Cuonzo (Long Island University), Elaine Davis (Mississippi Gulf Coast Community College), Douglas Deaver (Santiago Canyon College), David Denby (Tufts University), Christian Diehm (University of Wisconsin-Stevens Point), Jill Dieterle (Eastern Michigan University), Dittmar Dittrich (Loyola University, New Orleans), Tyler Doggett (University of Vermont), Yancy Dominick (Seattle University), Cian Dorr (New York University), Karánn Durland (Austin College), JoAnne Dyson (Front Range Community College), M. Dominic Eggert (Vanderbilt University), Zoe Eisenman (Saint Xavier University), Gary Elkins (Toccoa Falls College), Linda Emmerson (Walla Walla University), Miguel Endara (Azusa Pacific University), Jonathan Evans (University of Indianapolis), Michael Fara (Princeton University), Dean Finley (Ozarks Technical Community College), Michael Fitch (Florida State College), Russell Ford (Elmhurst College), Roger Foster (Borough of Manhattan Community College, CUNY), Craig Fox (California University of Pennsylvania), Jonathan Gainor (Harrisburg Area Community College), Erik Gardner (University of Hawaii: Windward Community College), Bruno Garofalo (West Chester University), Aaron German (Eastern Kentucky University), Caryl Gibbs (Rose State College), Douglas Giles (Elmhurst College), Ron Glass (University of Wisconsin-La Crosse), Steven Godby (Broward College), James Grady (Vanderbilt University), Franz-Peter Griesmaier (University of Wyoming), Kevin Guilfoy (Carroll University), John Gulley (Winston-Salem State University), Dorothy Haney (Marywood University), Robert Hansen, Richard Hanson (University of Wisconsin-Washington Country), Gary Hardcastle (Bloomsburg University), Kate Harkins (Coconino Community College), Maralee Harrell (Carnegie Mellon University), Allan Hazlett (University of Edinburgh), Scott Hendricks (Clark University), Will Heusser (Cypress College), Travis Hicks (Merced College), David Hoekema (Calvin College), Kent Hoeffner (McLennan Community College), Mark Horton (Norwalk Community College), Robert J. Howell (Dedman College, Southern Methodist University), Clark Hutton (Volunteer State Community College), Creed Hyatt (Lehigh Carbon Community College), Debbie Ingle (Rose State College), William Jamison (University of Alaska Anchorage), Scott Jenkins (University of Kansas), Michael Jordan (Iona College), Thomas Keyes (Our Lady of the Lake University), Hye-Kyung Kim (University of Wisconsin-Green Bay), Boris Kment (Princeton University), Achim Koeddermann (State University of New York, Oneonta), Avery Kolers (University of Louisville), A. J. Kreider (Miami Dade College), Douglas Krueger (Northwest Arkansas Community College), Denny Kuhn (Hillsdale Free Will Baptist College), Safro Kwame (Lincoln University), Jennifer Lackey (Northwestern University), Philip LaFountain (Eastern Nazarene College), Michael Latzer (Gannon University), Stephen Leach (University of Texas-Pan American), Kenneth Locke (Glendale Community College), Jessica E. Logue (University of Portland), Paul Long (Metropolitan Community College-Maple Woods), Shannon Love (Old Dominion

University), William Lycan (University of North Carolina), Tim Maddox (Hardin-Simmons University), Adrianne McEvoy (Mansfield University), Michael McGlone (The University at Buffalo, SUNY), Marcia McKelligan (DePauw University), Jon Mandle (The University at Albany, SUNY), Don Merrell (Arkansas State University), Garret Merriam (University of Southern Indiana), Anthony Miccoli (Western State Colorado University), Daniel Milsky (Northeastern Illinois University), Marc Moffett (University of Wyoming), Brad Morris (North Dakota State University), John. G. Moore (Lander University), Mark Moyer (University of Vermont), John Mullen (Bethany College), Jennifer Mulnix (University of Massachusetts, Dartmouth), Daniel Musgrave (New Mexico Military Institute), Vasile Munteanu (College of Southern Nevada), Alan Nichols (Georgia Highlands College), Kathryn Norlock (Trent University), Suzanne Obdrzalek (Claremont McKenna College), Douglas Olena (Evangel University), Barry Padgett (Bellarmine University), David Palmer (Massachusetts Maritime Academy), John Pappas (Saint Joseph's University), Michael Patton (University of Montevallo), Richard Peddicord (Aquinas Institute of Theology), Emile Piscitelli (Northern Virginia Community College), Stephen Pluhacek (Michigan Technological University), Consuelo Preti (The College of New Jersey), David Przekupowski (Northeast Lakeview College), Richard Reilly (Blinn College), Ray Rennard (University of the Pacific), John Rettura (Lackawanna College), Jay Reuscher (Georgetown University), Victoria Rogers (Indiana University-Purdue University Indianapolis), Michael Rosenthal (University of Washington), Chad Russell (University of Mississippi), Nathan Sager (Mesabi Range Community College), Mark Sanders (Three Rivers Community College), John Sarnecki (University of Toledo), James Schaar (University of Minnesota, Crookston), Kevin Scharp (The Ohio State University), Stephen Schmid (University of Wisconsin-Rock County), Edward Schoen (Western Kentucky University), Sally Scholz (Villanova University), Stephen Scholz (St. Augustine's College), Emily Sedgwick (East Los Angeles College), Darin Senestraro (East Los Angeles College), Robert Sessions (Emeritus, Kirkwood Community College), Gail Shaughnessey (Cochise College), Warren Shrader (Indiana University South Bend), Ivana Simic (University of Florida), Jack Simmons (Armstrong Atlantic State University), Thomas Singleton (Spring Hill College), Robert Skipper (St. Mary's University), James Spence (Adrian College), Jeffrey Staudt (Washington State Community College), Robert Stecker (Central Michigan University), Roderick Stewart (Austin College), Todd Stewart (Illinois State University), Bill Stone (Northeast Mississippi Community College), Andrew Strauss, Kevin Sweeney (University of Tampa), Robert Sweet (Clark State Community College), James Swindler (Illinois State University), Ed Szymanski, Jr. (Valencia Community College), Matthew Tedesco (Beloit College), Carolyn Thomas (University of New Mexico), Debbie Thompson (Ozarks Technica Community College), Katherine Tietge (Ocean County College), Terry Toma (St. Louis Community College at Forest Park), Zev Trachtenberg (University of Oklahoma), Ariela Tubert (University of Puget Sound), Dale Turner (California State Polytechnic University, Pomona), Donald Turner (Hillsdale College), Zach VanderVeen (Vanderbilt University), Andrew Vassar (Northeastern

State University), Lorraine M. Victoria (Bucks County Community College), Steven Vogel (Denison University), Russell Waltz (University of North Carolina at Charlotte), Andrea Weisberger (University of North Florida), Scott West (Harford Community College), David White (St. John Fisher College), Glenn Whitehouse (Florida Gulf Coast University), Joel Wilcox (Barry University), Stephen Wilhelm (Metropolitan Community College), Melissa Willmore (Jefferson College), Anita Wilson (Bismarck State College), Marc Wilson (Treasure Valley Community College), Ted Zenzinger (Regis College), and Robert Zeuschner (Pasadena City College).

Thank you all.

Getting Started

Why Philosophy? Five Views

ALEX BYRNE

What is knowledge, and why is it valuable? These are characteristic philosophical questions, treated in Plato's *Meno* (see Chapter 3 of this anthology). And, as Socrates says in another of Plato's dialogues, the *Theaetetus*, wonder is where philosophy begins. Philosophers take something that seems of central importance—knowledge, justice, truth, religion, mind, matter—and ask what it is. They then go on to ask other questions about it. Why is knowledge valuable? Is any religion true? How should a just society be organized? Naturally, we can do the same with philosophy, too: What is philosophy, and why is it valuable?

Take the first question first. Philosophers love asking "What is *X*?" The problem is that they very rarely answer it correctly. They are very good at telling us what *X isn't*—Socrates, in *Meno*, explains why knowledge is not "true opinion." They often say helpful things *about X*—Socrates in effect points out that one can't know something that is false. But their attempts to say what *X is*—to give a *definition* of *X*—almost invariably fail. There is unlikely to be an exception when *X* = philosophy. Is philosophy, perhaps, the study of fundamental and general problems that relies on logic and argument? But there are fundamental and general problems in, for example, mathematics, history, and biology; and mathematicians, historians, and biologists certainly rely on logic and argument. Is it, then, the study of fundamental and general *philosophical* problems? Well, yes, but this is almost entirely unenlightening and so not the sort of answer that counts as a *definition*. Still, that doesn't mean we can't say anything helpful about philosophy. Something was already said in the first paragraph, and much more is said over the thousand pages in this anthology.

That is my rather disappointing nonanswer to the first question. What about the second question? What's the value in philosophy? (You might get this from a hostile relative, so it's good to be prepared.)

Will philosophy help you get into law school? True, philosophy majors have very high average LSAT scores, but that probably says more about the kind of person who chooses to major in philosophy than about any intellectual health benefits of the subject itself.

Does philosophy make you a better person? Some years ago, a philosopher with a spare afternoon crunched some data and concluded that ethicists (philosophers who study right and wrong) were *more* likely to steal library books than other philosophers. Even if that's mistaken, there is no evidence that ethicists are especially ethical. And similarly for philosophers in general: the philosophers I know are mostly fine and admirable people, but I cannot say that they exemplify the good life for humans more than hairdressers, telephone sanitizers, and everyone else.

In his 1912 book *The Problems of Philosophy*, the British philosopher Bertrand Russell wrote that a person "who has no tincture of philosophy goes through life imprisoned in the prejudices derived from common sense, from the habitual beliefs of his age or his nation, and from convictions which have grown up in his mind without the co-operation or consent of his deliberate reason." Philosophy, he continued, "removes the somewhat arrogant dogmatism of those who have never travelled into the region of liberating doubt, and it keeps alive our sense of wonder by showing familiar things in an unfamiliar aspect."

Is this at least part of the answer to the second question? You might not be persuaded if you don't find doubt particularly liberating and prefer the comfort provided by conventional wisdom. If you're determined to resist the appeal of philosophy, then the forces of logic are powerless to change your mind. But I hope you do see some value in keeping alive your sense of wonder. And if you do, then you are on your way to becoming a philosopher.

JOSHUA COHEN

Because you are reading these words, I know something about you. I know you have a very long book in front of you, with roughly half a million words: a book that is long in words and large in scope, with topics ranging from God and consciousness to knowledge and justice.

I do not *know* that you are reading it for an introductory philosophy course. But I assume you are. So you probably do not know much about philosophy. If you are like most people encountering philosophy for the first time, you are unsure what you will get from it. I took my first philosophy course in 1969, in the fall of my freshman year in college. The professor was a philosopher of science named Paul Feyerabend. I liked the course but was as uncertain about what to expect from philosophy when the course ended as I was when it started.

One thing is clear: what you get from reading philosophy depends on how hard you work at it. But how hard you work at it depends on what you expect to get from it. So what should you expect? Or more exactly, what can you reasonably expect to get from it, on the assumption that you work hard?

Four things.

First, philosophers think *carefully*. They simplify problems and address them one step at a time. That does not mean they get things right. But it does mean that if you work hard at the reading, you will get a better sense of how to wrestle with questions in an intellectually careful way.

Second, philosophers think *deeply*. When a philosopher hears that keeping promises is the right thing to do, he or she wants to know why. And not only why, but what does it mean that it is *right*? What is rightness? Why does rightness matter? And how does it fit into the world? Work hard at the readings, then, and you will get a better sense of how to think about fundamentals.

Third, philosophers think *critically*. As you will see, philosophers disagree with one another, and they sometimes disagree with received wisdom. But they do not simply disagree. They give reasons for their disagreement. Work hard at the readings, then, and you will get a better sense of how to rationally challenge settled assumptions and views you disagree with—and how to challenge yourself.

Fourth, philosophers think *ambitiously*. Look at the table of contents of this anthology. It does not cover every philosophical issue, but we have selected topics that are important—starting with God and ending with equality—and challenging. Work hard at the readings, and you will get a better sense of how to think about large, difficult topics.

That is a lot to expect. But that is the promise of philosophy: to think more carefully, deeply, and critically about issues that are genuinely worth thinking about. We have invested lots of time and energy in this book to deliver on that ambitious promise. We hope you get as much from it as we have given to it.

ELIZABETH HARMAN

I loved philosophy before I knew that the thing I loved was philosophy. What I loved were surprising questions and arguments for surprising conclusions. For me, these questions included: Is a red car in a dark garage still red? If the only way to save your daughter's life is to steal some medicine, is it okay to steal the medicine? If a man who's a barber shaves all and only those men who don't shave themselves, does he shave himself?

There are certain questions that philosophers have tended to think about—many of these questions are posed as the titles of chapters in this book—but philosophy can be *about* anything. Some philosophical questions are not surprising: Is there a God? How should people treat each other? When is a person blameworthy for her actions? What do we know? But within these questions—questions that are basic and central to ordinary human life—we may find surprising further questions: Should I believe in God because that's a *safe bet*? Must I give almost all my money away to fight famine and suffering in faraway places? If someone is wrong about what

How does philosophy work this magic? As a start, philosophical study instills crucial skills useful in all walks and aspects of life. It directs you to pay strict attention to the words an author uses, to investigate their meaning closely, and to pay the same critical attention to what arguments are given (or are missing) and exactly what they establish. You then must devote the same level of care to your own speech and argumentation. In a fairly short time, this practice will lead you to speak and write with greater precision and clarity.

The critical stance philosophical inquiry encourages can be illuminating. Philosophical training inclines you to keep asking and answering the question "why" and "how" with increasing sophistication and ever deepening humility as satisfying answers evade easy efforts. The challenging process helps you identify what you value. When you stop taking the way things are for granted and ask for justifications and explanations, you come to understand yourself and your circumstances better. In some cases, you come to cherish how things are. In other cases, you come to see that things could be different. That realization may be profoundly liberating.

Alongside developing a critical eye, philosophical study also demands that you learn to read and think charitably. When an author's argument appears to fall short of its ambition, it is not enough to identify the failure. You are trained to identify the author's aims, how you could read her effort in its best light, and what contribution you could make to her success. If her argument cannot succeed, there is pressure on you to show another approach that could supply better answers. The practice of charitable interpretation builds skills of mutual understanding and encourages creative and imaginative solutions.

The combination of critical and cooperative perspectives is a powerful cocktail, whether for an advocate, a planner, a counselor, a friend, a citizen, or for one's personal life. Honing your analytical abilities to make critical assessments, to communicate carefully, and to interpret others fairly will improve almost every aspect of your life, including your sense of comedy and your relationships with other people.

These priceless skills work a permanent, transformative effect on one's life. So does the exposure to philosophy's subject matter. The basic issues philosophy tackles involve questions that occur, in one form or another, to most people as early as childhood, such as: What is the connection between your mind and your body? What exists outside your mind, and is it possible to know you perceive it accurately? What makes for a good and meaningful life? How should I relate to other people? How should we live together?

These questions persist throughout one's life. Philosophical study offers structured, articulate ways to grapple with them. In learning how others have answered them, you are connected to other thinkers across history and geography. By elaborating your own answers, you construct and express your character and sense of the meaning of life. Perhaps philosophy's greatest contribution is to offer ideas absorbing and important enough to return to repeatedly over a lifetime of thought.

A Brief Guide to Logic and Argumentation

When a philosopher tackles a question, her aim is not just to answer it. Her aim is to provide an argument for her answer and so to present her audience with reasons for believing what she believes. When you read a philosophical text, your main job is to identify and assess the author's arguments. When you write a philosophy paper, your main job is to offer arguments of your own. And because philosophy is an especially reflective discipline—every question *about* philosophy is a philosophical question—philosophers have turned their attention to this phenomenon. What is an argument? What is a *good* argument? How can we tell whether an argument is a good one? The aim of this brief guide is to introduce some of the tools that philosophers have developed for answering these questions. But be warned: some of what follows is controversial, and many of the most important questions in this area remain wide open. It may be unsettling to discover that even at this elementary stage, philosophy raises questions that centuries of reflection have not resolved. But that is the nature of the subject, and you might as well get used to it.

1. WHAT IS AN ARGUMENT?

An **argument** is a sequence of statements. The last claim in the sequence is the *conclusion*. This is the claim that the argument seeks to establish or support. An argument will usually include one or more **premises**: statements that are simply asserted without proof in the context of the present argument but which may be supported by arguments given elsewhere. Consider, for example, the following argument for the existence of God:

ARGUMENT A

(1) The Bible says that God exists.

(2) Whatever the Bible says is true.

(3) Therefore, God exists.

Here the premises are (1) and (2), and statement (3) is the conclusion.

Now, anyone who propounds this argument will probably realize that his premises are controversial, so he may seek to defend them by independent arguments. In defense of (2) he may argue:

ARGUMENT B

(4) The Bible has predicted many historical events that have come to pass.

(5) Therefore, whatever the Bible says is true.

These two arguments may be combined:

ARGUMENT C

(6) The Bible has predicted many historical events that have come to pass.

(7) Therefore, whatever the Bible says is true.

(8) The Bible says that God exists.

(9) Therefore, God exists.

Here the premises are (6) and (8). Statement (7) is now an *intermediate conclusion*, supported by premise (6), and the conclusion of the argument as a whole is (9), which is in turn supported by (7) and (8). It can be useful to make all of this explicit by writing the argument out as follows:

ARGUMENT C, ANNOTATED

(6) The Bible has predicted many historical events that
     have come to pass.   [premise]

(7) Therefore, whatever the Bible says is true.   [from (6)]

(8) The Bible says that God exists.   [premise]

(9) Therefore, God exists.   [from (7), (8)]

All of this is trivial when the arguments are simple and neatly packaged. But when you are reading a philosophical text with an eye toward identifying the author's argument, it is extraordinarily important (and often quite difficult) to distinguish the author's premises—the propositions she takes for granted as a starting point—from her conclusions. Why is this important? If a statement is meant as a conclusion, then it is fair to criticize the author if she has failed to give a reason for accepting it. If, however, a statement is a premise, then this sort of criticism would not be fair. Every argument must start somewhere. So you should not object to an argument simply on the ground that the author has not proved her premises. Of course, you can object in other ways. As we will see, it is perfectly fair to reject an argument when its premises are false, implausible, or defective in some other way. The point is rather simply this: since every argument must have premises, *it is not a flaw in an argument that the author has not argued for her premises.*

> *Rules of thumb:* If a sentence begins with "hence" or "therefore" or "so," that is a clue that it functions as a conclusion. If a sentence begins with "Let us assume that ..." or "It seems perfectly obvious that ..." or "Only a fool would deny that ...," this is a clue that it functions as a premise.

Exercise: Consider the following passage. What are the premises? What is the main conclusion?

> Everyone knows that people are usually responsible for what they do. But you're only responsible for an action if your choice to perform it was a free choice, and a choice is only free if it was not determined in advance. So we must have free will, and that means that some of our choices are not determined in advance.

2. VALIDITY

An argument is **valid** if and only if it is *absolutely impossible* for its premises to be true and its conclusion false. In our examples, argument A is clearly valid. If the premises are true—if the Bible is infallible, and if the Bible says that God exists—then God must certainly exist. There is no possible situation—no possible world—in which the premises of the argument are true and the conclusion false. Argument B, by contrast, is clearly **invalid**. It is easy to imagine a circumstance in which the Bible makes many correct predictions about historical events while remaining fallible on other matters. When an argument is valid, we say that the premises **entail** or *imply* the conclusion, or, equivalently, that the conclusion *follows from* the premises.

   This concept of validity is a technical one, and some of its applications may strike you as odd. Consider:

ARGUMENT D
All philosophers are criminals.
All criminals are short.
Therefore, all philosophers are short.

ARGUMENT E
God exists.
Therefore, God exists.

ARGUMENT F
The moon is green.
The moon is not green.
Therefore, God exists.

It is easy to see that argument D is valid. The premises are *false*, but that is irrelevant. They *could* have been true, and any possible circumstance in which they *are* true is one in which the conclusion is also true. Argument E is also valid. Since the premise and the conclusion are identical, it is clearly impossible for the one to be true and the other false. To see that argument F is valid, note that it is obviously impossible for its premises to be true together—the moon cannot be both green and not green! But this means that it is impossible for the premises to be true and the conclusion false, and that is exactly our definition of validity.

As the examples show, a valid argument can be a *lousy* argument. Still, validity is an important property of arguments. Some disciplines—notably, mathematics— insist on valid arguments at every stage. In these areas, a good argument must be a **proof**, and a proof is a valid argument from premises known to be true. Philosophy, like most disciplines, does not insist on proof. Yet philosophers often aspire to produce valid arguments for their conclusions, and there is a good reason for this. Begin by noting that it is always possible to turn an invalid argument, or an argument whose validity is uncertain, into a valid argument by adding premises. Suppose a philosopher offers the following argument:

ARGUMENT G

I can imagine existing without my body. (I can imagine my feet slowly and painlessly disappearing, then my knees, then my legs. . . . As my body disappears, I lose all sensation. As my head disappears, everything goes black and silent because my eyes and ears have disappeared, but still I'm thinking about these strange events, and because I'm thinking, I must exist.)

Therefore, I am not my body.

It may be hard to say whether this is a valid argument, but we can easily turn it into an argument whose validity is beyond dispute:

ARGUMENT H

I can imagine existing without my body.

If I can imagine X existing without Y, then X is not Y.

Therefore, I am not my body.

A philosopher who offers argument G as a proof that human beings are not identical to their bodies probably has argument H in mind. She is probably tacitly *assuming* the premise that is missing in argument G but that H makes explicit. For philosophical purposes, it is often important to make these tacit assumptions explicit so that we can subject them to the bright light of scrutiny. *When you reconstruct the argument implicit in a philosophical text, you should set yourself the task of producing a valid argument for the author's conclusion from the author's stated premises, supplying any missing premises that might be necessary for this purpose, so long as they are premises that the author might have accepted.* If there are many ways to do this, you will find yourself with several competing interpretations of the argument. If there is only one sensible way of doing this (as with argument G), you will have identified the author's tacit assumptions. This is often a valuable step in your effort to assess the argument.

Exercise: Spot the valid argument(s):

(i) If abortion is permissible, infanticide is permissible.
Infanticide is not permissible.
Therefore, abortion is not permissible.

(ii) It is wrong to experiment on a human subject without consent.
Dr. X experimented on Mr. Z.
Mr. Z consented to this experiment.
Therefore, it was not wrong for Dr. X to experiment on Mr. Z.

(iii) I will not survive my death.
My body will survive my death.
Therefore, I am not my body.

(iv) Geoffrey is a giraffe.
If X is a giraffe, then X's parents were giraffes.
Therefore, all of Geoffrey's ancestors were giraffes.

Exercise: The following arguments are not valid as they stand. Supply missing premises to make them valid.

(v) Every event has a cause.
No event causes itself.
Therefore, the universe has no beginning in time.

(vi) It is illegal to keep a tiger as a pet in New York City.
Jones lives in New York City.
Therefore, it would be wrong for Jones to keep a tiger as a pet.

(vii) The sun has risen every day for the past 4 billion years.
Therefore, the sun will rise tomorrow.

Check your understanding. Some statements express *necessary truths*: truths that could not possibly have been false under any circumstances. The truths of pure mathematics are the best examples. There is no possible circumstance in which $2 + 3 \neq 5$, so "$2 + 3 = 5$" is a necessary truth. With this in mind, show that an argument whose conclusion is a necessary truth is automatically a valid argument.

3. SOUNDNESS

A valid philosophical argument is a fine thing. But if the premises are false, it cannot be a good argument. Good arguments, after all, provide us with reasons for accepting their conclusions, and an argument with false premises cannot do that. Recall argument D:

ARGUMENT D

(1) All philosophers are criminals.

(2) All criminals are short.

(3) Therefore, all philosophers are short

The argument is perfectly valid, but it obviously fails to establish its conclusion.

This means that when you evaluate a philosophical argument, it is never enough to show that the author's conclusions follow from her premises. You must also ask whether the premises are true. A valid argument with true premises is called a **sound** argument.

Check your understanding: Use the definitions of soundness and validity to show that if an argument is sound, its conclusion must be true.

4. HOW TO RECONSTRUCT AN ARGUMENT: AN EXAMPLE

One of the most important skills a philosopher can acquire is the ability to extract an explicit argument from a dense block of prose. There is no recipe for doing this: it is an art. Here we work through an example to illustrate one way of proceeding.

Assignment: Identify and assess the argument in the following passage.

> We see that things which lack intelligence, such as natural bodies, act for an end, and this is evident from their acting always, or nearly always, in the same way, so as to obtain the best result. Hence it is plain that not fortuitously, but designedly, do they achieve their end. Now whatever lacks intelligence cannot move towards an end, unless it be directed by some being endowed with knowledge and intelligence, as the arrow is shot to its mark by the archer. Therefore some intelligent beings exist by whom all natural things are directed to their end. (Thomas Aquinas, *Summa Theologica*, part I, question 2, article 3)

Step 1: Identify the Conclusion
When you seen an argument like this, your first job is to identify the main conclusion. Unsurprisingly, this will usually come at the end, though many writers will tell you at the start what the conclusion of the argument is going to be. (This is very helpful to the reader, and you should always do it in your own writing.) In this case, the main conclusion is helpfully marked by an explicit "therefore."

(Main conclusion)   Some intelligent beings exist by whom all natural things are directed to their end.

Step 2: Interpret the Conclusion

Now that you have identified the conclusion, your next job is to understand it. This can be difficult, especially when the text is old and the language unfamiliar. What is it for a being to be *intelligent*? What is a *natural* thing? In this case, the most pressing issue is to understand what it means for a natural thing to be "directed towards an end." As the context makes clear, a natural thing is anything that is not a person or an artifact—an animal or a plant, or perhaps a rock. What is it for such a thing to have an *end*? This is in fact a profound question, but to a first approximation, the end of a thing is its purpose or function. The *end* of the heart is to pump blood, the *end* of a worker bee is to supply food for the queen, and so on. The conclusion of the argument, reformulated in more familiar terms, is therefore this:

> (Main conclusion,   There is an intelligent being that ensures that
> reformulated)   natural objects perform their functions.

This illustrates a general point: when you analyze an argument, you are not required to employ the author's original words in every case. It is sometimes useful to supply more familiar words and grammatical constructions, provided they represent a plausible interpretation of the author's meaning. In this case, we have replaced Aquinas's talk of "ends" with talk of "functions."

Step 3: Reconstruct the Argument

Your next job is to reconstruct the argument for the main conclusion. What are the premises from which Aquinas argues? You might think that the first sentence states a premise: "We see that things which lack intelligence . . . act for an end." But as we read on, it becomes clear that this is, in fact, an intermediate conclusion. The first sentence, taken as a whole, is itself an argument.

> Unintelligent things always or nearly always act in the same way, so as to achieve
>   the best result. [premise]
> Therefore, unintelligent things perform a function.

This is an interesting argument, but the connection between the premise and the conclusion is obscure. As it stands, the argument is not clearly valid. But we can render it valid by interpolating an unstated premise:

(1) Unintelligent things always or nearly always act in the same way, so as to achieve the best result.

(2) If a thing always or nearly always acts in a certain way, so as to achieve the best result, then that thing performs a function.

(3) Therefore, unintelligent things perform a function.

This shows the value of making unstated premises fully explicit. The unstated premise (2) contains an important idea. The function of the heart is to pump blood.

How do we know? Because hearts almost always pump blood, and this is a benefit to the organism as a whole. In general, when we see a natural thing acting in a way that provides a benefit, we infer that its function (or one of its functions) is to provide that benefit. The second premise makes this assumption explicit.

When we turn to the next sentence, we have a puzzle. "Hence it is plain that not fortuitously, but designedly, do they achieve their end." This sentence begins with "hence," so we naturally assume that it is supposed to be a conclusion supported by what precedes it. If we pursue this interpretation, the argument will look like this:

(1) Unintelligent things always or nearly always act
    in the same way, so as to achieve the best result.   [premise]

(2) If a thing always or nearly always acts in a certain
    way, so as to achieve the best result, then that
    thing performs a function.   [premise]

(3) Therefore, unintelligent things perform a function.   [from (1) and (2)]

    Therefore, unintelligent things perform their
    functions by design (and not by accident).   [from ?]

The puzzle is that nothing in the argument appears to support this new conclusion. Why shouldn't natural beings perform their functions by accident rather than by design? Nothing in the text speaks to this question, and so it may be unclear whether Aquinas means this to be a new premise or an intermediate conclusion supported by what comes before.

Again, we can interpolate an unstated premise that will render the argument valid. Aquinas apparently finds it obvious that if a thing has a function, it must have been designed to perform that function. If this is right, then the complete argument up to this point runs as follows:

(1) Unintelligent things always or nearly always act
    in the same way, so as to achieve the best result.   [premise]

(2) If a thing always or nearly always acts in a certain way, so as
    to achieve the best result, then that thing performs a function. [premise]

(3) Therefore, unintelligent things perform   [intermediate conclusion,
    a function.   from (1) and (2)]

(4) If a thing performs a function, it does so by design.   [implicit premise]

(5) Therefore, unintelligent things perform their   [intermediate conclusion,
    functions by design.   from (3) and (4)]

The remainder of the argument is now straightforward. The next sentence states another premise.

(6) If an unintelligent thing performs a function by design,
   then there exists an intelligent being that ensures
   that it performs this function.   [premise]

And from this, Aquinas moves directly to his main conclusion:

(7) Therefore, there exists an intelligent being that ensures   [conclusion,
   that natural objects perform their functions.   from (5) and (6)]

What just happened? We took a dense philosophical text and we turned it into an explicit argument. Along the way, we did our best to make the author's unspoken premises explicit and to understand what they might mean. The result is a *reconstruction* of the original argument.

Step 4

We are now in a position to assess the argument as we have reconstructed it. We have two questions to ask: Is it valid, and are the premises true?

   Taking the second question first, we twenty-first-century philosophers will have doubts about premise (1)—Do *most* natural things really act so as to achieve the "best result"?—and also about premise (6). The heart of an animal performs a function. Must it have been designed by an intelligent being for that purpose? Certainly not; natural selection can do the job even if no intelligence is involved. So the premises of the argument are certainly open to question.

   But even if we waive this objection and suppose that the premises are true, there is a further problem. The conclusion (7) claims there is a *single* intelligent being that ensures that natural things perform their functions. But the premises only require that each natural thing be directed toward its end by some intelligent being or other. To see the difference, note that it is one thing to say that every clock has a designer and another to say that there is a single master-designer who is responsible for every clock. This means that we can accept Aquinas's premises and much of his reasoning without accepting his main conclusion. Even if every natural thing was designed by an intelligent being, it does not follow that a single intelligent being designed them all. Verdict: *Aquinas's argument, as we have reconstructed it, is not valid.*

   This brings up a very important point. We have given a reasonably careful reconstruction of Aquinas's argument, but despite our best efforts, the argument as we have reconstructed it is clearly *bad.* Now of course no one is perfect: good philosophers sometimes give bad arguments. But when you have produced a reconstruction of an argument by a good philosopher and the result is an argument that is clearly flawed, that is a sign that you may have misunderstood the original argument. The philosophers represented in this collection are all good philosophers, so you should approach their arguments with this in mind: *Before you dismiss an argument on the basis of your reconstruction of it, you should be sure that your reconstruction is the most charitable interpretation you can find.* A charitable reconstruction will present the argument in its best light. It may still involve mistakes, but they will not be gross and obvious mistakes. The most convincing way to object to a philosophical argument is to take the time to identify the best possible version of it, and then to show that *this* version of the argument is still no good.

Exercise: Provide a reconstruction of Aquinas's argument that does not commit the logical error mentioned above in the transition from (6) to (7).

5. FORMAL VALIDITY

Consider:

ARGUMENT I
Every number is an abstract object.
Abstract objects are not located in space.
So numbers are not located in space.

This is a concrete argument with a specific subject matter. It is about numbers, spatial location, and so on. But we can abstract from these specific features of the argument in order to focus on its *form*. One way to do this is to replace all of the subject-specific terms in the argument with *schematic letters*, leaving only the logical skeleton of the argument in place. In the case of argument H, this yields the following *schematic argument*.

Every F is a G.
Gs are not H.
So Fs are not H.

Once we have identified this schematic argument, it is easy to produce other arguments that exhibit the same form but concern an entirely unrelated subject matter. For example:

ARGUMENT J
Every whale is a mammal.
Mammals do not lay eggs.
So whales do not lay eggs.

In this case, it is clear not just that our original argument is valid but that any argument generated from it in this way must be valid. (The second premise in argument J is false, as every platypus knows. But that does not prevent the argument from being valid. If that puzzles you, review the definition of validity.) When an argument is an instance of a scheme all of whose instances are valid, the argument is said to be **formally valid**.

Note: An argument can be valid without being formally valid. Consider:

ARGUMENT K
Every crayon in the box is scarlet.
So every crayon in the box is red.

The underlying form of this argument is:

Every F is G.
So every F is H.

And it is obvious that many arguments of this form will not be valid. (*Exercise: Give an example.*) Of course, we can make argument K formally valid by adding the premise, "If a thing is scarlet, then it is red." As we have emphasized, this is always worth doing when you are analyzing a philosophical argument. And yet, the original argument is valid as it stands, since it is absolutely impossible for the premise to be true and the conclusion false.

Formal logic is the study of formally valid arguments. It aims to catalog the vast array of formally valid arguments and to provide general principles for determining whether any given argument has this feature. Formal logic is an intricate, highly developed subject at the intersection of philosophy and mathematics, and it can be extraordinarily useful for the student of philosophy. Here we list some examples of formally valid arguments along with their traditional names. In what follows, the schematic letters P, Q, and R stand for complete declarative sentences. For your amusement, we also include the standard symbolic representations of these forms of inference. Here "$\rightarrow$" means "if . . . then"; "$\sim$" means "it is not the case that"; and "$\vee$" means "or."

MODUS PONENS
If P then Q $P \rightarrow Q$
P P
———————————
Q Q

MODUS TOLLENS
If P then Q $P \rightarrow Q$
It is not the case that Q $\sim Q$
———————————
It is not the case that P $\sim P$

DISJUNCTIVE SYLLOGISM
Either P or Q $P \vee Q$
It is not the case that P $\sim P$
———————————
Q Q

HYPOTHETICAL SYLLOGISM

If P then Q	$P \rightarrow Q$
If Q then R	$Q \rightarrow R$
If P then R	$P \rightarrow R$

CONTRAPOSITION

If P then Q $\qquad\qquad\qquad\qquad\qquad\qquad\qquad\qquad$ $P \rightarrow Q$

If it is not the case that Q, then it is not the case that P $\qquad$ $\sim Q \rightarrow \sim P$

All of this may seem obvious, but it can sometimes be quite tricky to determine whether an argument is formally valid. Consider:

A person is responsible for a choice only if it is a free choice.

Every human choice is either caused or uncaused.

If a choice is caused, then it is caused either by prior events or by the agent himself.

If a choice is caused by prior events, then it is not free.

If a choice is uncaused, it is not free.

So a choice is free only if it is caused by the agent himself.

But no choice is caused by the agent himself.

So there is no such thing as a free choice.

So no one is ever responsible for his choices.

Is this a valid argument? You could stare at it for a while, and you might find yourself persuaded one way or the other. Or you could take a logic class and learn enough formal logic to settle the matter conclusively once and for all. One of the great advantages of formal logic is that it permits us to *prove* that an argument of this sort is valid by breaking it down into steps, each of which is indisputably an instance of a valid form.

6. A PUZZLE ABOUT FORMAL LOGIC

Apart from its utility as a tool, formal logic is a source of philosophical perplexity in its own right. Imagine a long row of colored squares on the wall in front of you. The left-most square (square 1) is bright red; the right-most square (square 1000) is bright yellow. The squares in between run from red on the left through orange in the middle to yellow on the right. But there are so many of them that they satisfy the following condition:

(1) Square n and square $n + 1$ are indistinguishable by ordinary means.

If you had a measuring device, you might discover that they differ slightly in color, but you can't tell them apart just by looking, no matter how hard you try. (If you don't think this is possible, get out your paint set and play around. It is easy to produce a sequence of colored patches running from red to yellow that satisfies this condition.)

We now note what appears to be an obvious fact:

(2) If two things are indistinguishable by ordinary means, then if one of them is red, so is the other.

If someone shows you a red rose and tells you, "I've got another rose that's indistinguishable from this one, but it's not red," you would know immediately that he was lying. It's built into our concept of *red* that if two objects look just alike to the naked eye in broad daylight, then either both are red or neither is.

From these two premises, it follows by modus ponens that:

(3) If square n is red, then so is square $n + 1$.

But now we're in trouble. For we can reason as follows:

(4) Square 1 is red.   [premise]

(5) If square 1 is red, then square 2 is red.   [3]

(6) So square 2 is red.   [4, 5, modus ponens]

(7) If square 2 is red, then square 3 is red.   [3]

(8) So square 3 is red.   [6, 7, modus ponens]

. . .

(1002) So square 999 is red.   [1000, 1001, modus ponens]

(1003) If square 999 is red, then square 1000 is red.   [3]

(1004) So square 1000 is red.   [1002, 1003, modus ponens]

But this is nuts. It was built into our description of the situation that square 1000 is not red; it is bright yellow!

What's gone wrong? If you look closely, you will see that this argument has only three premises. Two of them are stipulated as part of our description of the situation: square 1 is red, and adjacent squares are indistinguishable by ordinary means. The other premise is (2), the claim that there cannot be two indistinguishable things, one of which is red, the other not. The argument uses only one rule of inference: modus ponens. And this leaves us with only two responses to the paradox: either (2) is false and there is a sharp cutoff between red and "not red" somewhere in our series or modus ponens is not a valid rule of inference after all. What is the best response? The problem is called the *sorites paradox* (pronounced saw-*rye*-tees), and it remains unsolved.

7. WHAT MAKES AN ARGUMENT GOOD?

We have seen (see section 2 earlier) that valid arguments can be lousy arguments. The same goes for sound arguments. The question of God's existence is the most important question in the philosophy of religion. But it is easy to produce a sound argument that settles it:

ARGUMENTS L AND M
L: God exists.
    Therefore, God exists.
M: God does not exist.
    Therefore, God does not exist.

These arguments are both formally valid, and one of them has true premises. That means that *one of them is sound*. But neither of these arguments is a contribution to philosophy, and neither could possibly provide a reason for believing its conclusion. Why not?

The obvious answer is that these arguments are defective because they are **circular**—their conclusions are included among their premises—and that is certainly a defect. This might tempt us to say that an argument is good if and only if it is sound and noncircular. But this is not quite right. Consider:

ARGUMENT N
God knows when you will die.
Therefore, God exists.

This argument may be sound, and the premise is clearly *different* from the conclusion, so it is not circular. And yet it is perfectly useless for establishing its conclusion. One way to bring this out is to note that anyone who doubts the conclusion will *automatically* doubt the premise. We cannot imagine a reasonable person *coming to believe* that God exists by first believing that God knows when she will die, and then *inferring* the existence of God. If she believes the premise, she must *already* believe the conclusion.

This shows something important. In a good argument, the premises must be credible *independently* of the conclusion. It must be possible for someone who has not already accepted the conclusion to accept the premise first, and to do so reasonably. This point is sometimes put by saying that a good argument must not **beg the question**. Imagine that you are arguing with someone who doubts your conclusion. Now ask: Could this person reasonably accept my premises if he has not already accepted my conclusion? If not, then the argument is bad in this distinctive way.

It is worth stressing, however, that this idea is not completely clear. Suppose you have read about the platypus, but you are not sure that such things exist. (For all you know, the platypus may be extinct like the dodo or legendary like the hippogriff.) A friend may set you straight as follows:

ARGUMENT O

That thing in the bushes is a platypus.

So platypuses exist.

This is a valid argument, and if it is sound—if your friend really is pointing to a platypus—it might give you an excellent reason for accepting its conclusion. Argument O is thus a good argument: it does not beg the question.

Now suppose that you have been impressed by Descartes's famous suggestion that for all you know, there is no external world at all, and in particular that for all you know, you are a disembodied spirit whose experiences are hallucinations produced in your mind by a malicious demon.[1] At this stage, you are in the market for an argument to show that the material world—the world of rocks and trees and houses—really exists. Trying to be helpful, I hold up a rock and say:

ARGUMENT P

This rock in my hand is a material object.

So material objects exist.

Argument P has exactly the same form as argument O. Both are valid, and both may be sound. And yet it has seemed to many (though not to all) that given the context in which it has been presented, argument P begs the question. If you want to prove the existence of the material world to someone who doubts it, you can't just hold up a rock and say "Voilà!" Your interlocutor, after all, will not believe the rock is real.[2]

---

1. René Descartes, "Meditation I: What Can Be Called into Doubt," in his *Meditations on First Philosophy*, reprinted in Chapter 6 of this anthology.

2. Samuel Johnson (1709–1784) disagreed. As his biographer reports:

> After we came out of the church, we stood talking for some time together of Bishop Berkeley's ingenious sophistry to prove the nonexistence of matter, and that every thing in the universe is merely ideal. I observed, that though we are satisfied his doctrine is not true, it is impossible to refute it. I never shall forget the alacrity with which Johnson answered, striking his foot with mighty force against a large stone, till he rebounded from it—"I refute it *thus*." James Boswell, *Life of Johnson*, ed. G. B. Hill (Oxford University Press, 1935), Vol. 1, p. 471.

What is the difference between these two "proofs"? This is a difficult question. It is often easy to tell in practice when an argument begs the question—when it *presupposes* what it seeks to prove. But it is quite hard to provide a general rule for determining when an argument begs the question in this sense. This is one point at which our understanding of the contrast between good and bad arguments is incomplete.

8. NON-DEMONSTRATIVE ARGUMENTS

So far we have been discussing valid arguments and asking, in effect: What is the difference between a good valid argument and a bad one? We have seen that a good valid argument must be sound, and that it must not beg the question. And there is no doubt that philosophers have often sought to provide arguments of just this sort. But it would be a grave mistake to suppose that every worthwhile argument must fit this description.

Consider:

ARGUMENTS Q, R, S, AND T

Q: Everyone who has drunk hemlock has died soon afterward.
∴ If I drink this hemlock, I will die.

R: Despite years of looking, no one has ever seen a unicorn.
∴ Unicorns do not exist.

S: The cheese in the cupboard is disappearing.
We hear scratching sounds in the cupboard late at night.
There is a suspicious mouse-sized hole in the back of the cupboard.
∴ A mouse has come to live with us.

T: It's normally wrong to kill a person.
The bartender is a person.
∴ It would be wrong to kill the bartender.

By ordinary standards, these are all excellent arguments. If you are trying to give me reason to believe that unicorns don't exist, or that I will die if I drink the hemlock, or that a mouse has infiltrated the kitchen, or that I shouldn't kill the bartender, these arguments ought to do the trick. But of course *these arguments are not valid.* In each case, it is logically possible for the premises to be true and the conclusion false. Unicorns may be very good at hiding. I may be a biological freak immune to hemlock. The evidence in the kitchen may be a hoax cooked up by my roommates as a joke. The bartender might be a dangerous fiend who will destroy the world unless I shoot him, and so on.

Arguments such as Q, R, S, and T are called **non-demonstrative** arguments. (A *demonstration* is a valid proof, and since these arguments are not valid, they are not demonstrations.) A good non-demonstrative argument must have true premises, and it must not beg the question. But how do we distinguish a good non-demonstrative argument from a bad one? We have a developed theory of validity for demonstrative arguments; namely, formal logic. When it comes to non-demonstrative arguments, however, we have nothing comparable. The problem of formulating a general account of good non-demonstrative reasoning is one of the great open problems in philosophy. We cannot solve it here, but we can introduce some terminology that may be helpful.

Some non-demonstrative arguments exhibit a common form.

Inductive arguments take as premises a series of observations that exhibit a pattern, and then conclude that the pattern holds as a general rule. Argument Q is a very simple inductive argument. Its form appears to be this:

> In the past, events of type A have always been followed by events of type B.
> Therefore, in the future, events of type A will be followed by events of type B.

But it would be a mistake to suppose that every argument of this form is a good one. Consider:

> In the past, every time a presidential election has been held in the United States, the winning candidate has been a man.
> Therefore, in the future, every time a presidential election is held in the United States, the winning candidate will be a man.

As of 2017, the premise of this argument is true; but it would be silly to conclude that there will never be a female president on this basis. Philosophers have long hoped that there might be some sort of formal test for distinguishing the good inductive arguments from the bad ones, but that turns out to be impossible. (See Nelson Goodman's "The New Riddle of Induction" reprinted in Chapter 4 of this anthology.) The theory of statistical inference is an attempt to characterize the good inductive inferences in mathematical terms.

Abductive argument—also called **inference to the best explanation**—begins from some collection of settled facts, and then reasons backwards from these facts to the hypothesis that would best explain them. Arguments R and S are abductive arguments. Their general form is roughly this:

> Certain facts are observed. (The cheese is disappearing, etc.; no one has ever found a unicorn despite years of looking.)
> The best explanation for these facts is *H*. (There is a mouse in the kitchen; there are no unicorns.)
> *H* is a good explanation (and not merely the best of a bad lot).
> Therefore, *H* is (probably) true.

Many of the arguments that one finds in the natural sciences are abductive. Whenever the scientist defends a theory about unobserved objects or events by appeal to evidence, the argument takes roughly this form. (Think about the chemist's case for molecules or Darwin's case for evolution.) A theory of abductive argument will tell us what it is for a hypothesis to constitute the *best* explanation of the data, and it will identify the conditions under which it is reasonable to infer the truth of best explanation. This part of the theory of argumentation is even less well developed than the theory of inductive argument and remains an active area of research.

Argument T is neither inductive nor abductive. Indeed, there is no standard name for arguments of this sort. Their general form is roughly this:

Normally, *P*.
∴ *P*.

We know that cats normally have four legs; so if we are told that Felix is a cat, it is reasonable to infer that Felix has four legs—unless, of course, we have special information about Felix that would suggest that he might be an exception. Arguments of this sort may be especially important in ethics. Some writers hold that the general principles of ethics—unlike the laws of physics and mathematics—are not exceptionless rules but, rather, powerful but imperfect generalizations: rules that hold for the most part, but which tolerate exceptions. If that is so—and this is highly controversial—whenever we apply an ethical principle to a case in order to derive a verdict about how to act, our inference is of this nameless non-demonstrative form.

9. SOME GENERAL REMARKS ON ARGUMENTATION IN PHILOSOPHY

In some areas of inquiry—mathematics is the best example—the only good arguments are valid arguments. Suppose I want to argue for Goldbach's Conjecture: Every even number greater than 2 is the sum of two prime numbers.

If I have a lot of time on my hands, I might begin by checking some examples.

$$4 = 2 + 2 \checkmark$$
$$6 = 3 + 3 \checkmark$$
$$8 = 3 + 5 \checkmark$$
$$10 = 3 + 7 \checkmark$$

Impressed by the pattern but getting bored, I might program a computer to check some more examples, and if I do I can easily verify that:

(#) Every even number between 2 and 10 billion is the sum of two prime numbers.

And yet it would be a mistake by mathematical standards to treat this as an argument for Goldbach's Conjecture. It is always *possible* that some even number I have not checked provides a counterexample. The inference from (#) to Goldbach's Conjecture is not valid, and in mathematics the only good arguments are valid arguments.

Philosophy grew up with mathematics, and philosophers have sometimes held themselves to a similar standard, insisting that the only good philosophical arguments are (non–question begging) valid arguments from true premises. (Indeed, they have often insisted on valid arguments from *indisputably* true premises.) This remains the gold standard for argument in philosophy. Interesting arguments of this sort are often possible, and when they are possible, they are desirable. When you reconstruct the arguments of the philosophers for the purposes of evaluating them or when you give arguments of your own, it often makes sense to try for arguments of this sort.

And yet it is a mistake to suppose that philosophical arguments are only good when they are valid. As we have noted, the arguments that serve us well in science and in ordinary life—the arguments that persuade us that atoms and molecules exist or that it would be wrong to kill the bartender—are often non-demonstrative in character. There is no good reason to hold philosophy to a higher standard. But, of course, this leaves us in a difficult position, since as we have stressed, there is no accepted account of when a non-demonstrative argument is a good one.

Some Guidelines for Writing Philosophy Papers

Writing a good philosophy paper is a lot like writing a good paper in history, political science, literature, or biology. Yes, philosophy papers are a little different in that they require a particularly careful use of language and a particularly close examination of ideas and arguments. Still, a good philosophy paper is basically a good paper that happens to be about philosophy. So the guidelines we sketch here apply with equal force in other courses as well.

Generally speaking, a philosophy paper presents an argument in support of a thesis. Here are some examples of philosophical theses (as you will see, some are very broad and some are much narrower):

- Numbers are real.

- We cannot know that there are objects outside the mind.

- Van Inwagen's argument for the incompatibility of free will and determinism is unpersuasive.

- The best interpretation of Hume's theory of causation is as follows. (Here you supply your own interpretation of Hume's theory.)

- Moral convictions are nothing more than strongly held feelings.

- The ontological proof of God's existence is flawed because (here you state what you see as the principal flaw).

Although philosophy papers require careful, abstract, critical reasoning, they also have a personal side. You are saying what you think and trying to defend it. When you do that, you expose your ideas—thus yourself—to criticism. The only way to learn from writing a paper is to accept that vulnerability, be as clear as you can about what you think, and make the best case for your views. You can try to protect your ideas by obscuring them with a blur of words, but that defeats the purpose.

Writing a paper—with this blend of abstract reasoning and personal conviction—is best approached in a social way, as if you were in a dialogue with another person. So you should write with a particular reader in mind: a friend or a student in another class who wonders what you are working on. Write the paper as if you were directing your argument to this particular person. Your reader can, of course, only read your paper, not your mind. So you need to tell him or her what you are aiming to show in the paper, to consider where he or she will need some more explanation, to ask yourself where your reader might have some doubts about what you are saying, to articulate those doubts for your reader, and to try to answer them.

More specifically,

1. **State the main thesis** of your paper at the beginning, preferably in the opening paragraph. It is not bad to say something like: "I will argue that. . . ." (Although in some fields, using the first-person pronoun is frowned on, in philosophy it is encouraged: it is a straightforward method of conveying your perspective.) If you do not have a thesis, then get one. You are not expected to remain above the fray. Take a position!

2. **Take seriously the philosophers you are discussing.** The philosophers you are reading are not fools, even if their views or arguments are incorrect. Keep in mind that the readings in your course are the product of sustained reflection. The authors often distributed drafts of their manuscripts to other people who disagreed with them, and then tried to incorporate responses to objections. Their views may not be right, or fully coherent, or nice. But you can safely assume that they have greater depth and coherence than a first reading might suggest.

   A first step toward taking a philosopher seriously is to make your criticisms and points of agreement explicit, rather than simply expressing your approval or disapproval of what you have read. Suppose, for example, you think that David Hume's views on causation are wrong. Before you start writing a paper, you will first need to clarify your disagreement with Hume. Are you disputing his assumptions or the reasoning that leads from his assumptions to his conclusion? Then try to "argue against yourself": How would Hume respond to your criticism? This means that you will need to get "inside" his view and develop a sense of its internal integrity.

3. **Keep the writing focused.** Do not pad your paper with digressions from the main topic. For example, suppose you are examining Hobbes's argument that in a state of nature, with no political authority, we would all be at war with one another. You will need to explain why he thinks we need an authority to keep us from fighting each other. You should *not* also discuss his views on monarchy. Confine yourself to the aspects of Hobbes's view that are of immediate relevance to your thesis.

4. **Avoid sweeping generalities.** Forget such profundities as: "Since Plato, philosophers have sought out the meaning of justice," or "For millennia, human beings have searched for truth." (What about: "Man is born free, but is everywhere in chains"? If you are Jean-Jacques Rousseau, you are allowed to violate our guidelines.) By distracting from your point, such remarks subtract substance. Moreover, they suggest that you are unsure of what to say and are looking to fill space. So just get right to the point.

5. **Write clearly.** Philosophical ideas are often abstract and subtle, which makes it easy to get lost. You should therefore write short sentences, avoid very long paragraphs, and be sure to signal transitions. If a sentence occupies more than (say) five lines, find a way to divide it up; similarly, if a paragraph goes on for more than 20 lines. If your paper falls into sections, make sure to include a transition sentence or two between them. Assume that your reader is unfamiliar with philosophical vocabulary, which means that you will need to explain the philosophical terms in your paper. If possible, define them. At the very least, give examples of how the terms are used. Note that writing philosophy does not require esoteric words, or long words, or newly invented words. Nor do you need to strive to use different words to express the same concept within the same paragraph or page; indeed, it is helpful if you stick with the same term. Your papers need to focus readers' attention on the ideas you wish to express, not on the words you have chosen to express those ideas. As George Orwell (the author of *1984*) wrote, "Good prose is like a windowpane." Bad writing is a smudge on the window.

6. **Support assertions.** When you attribute a position to someone, provide some evidence for the attribution by citing relevant passages. You need not include quotations. As a general rule, you should only quote a passage if the passage plays an important role in your paper (say, it is a passage that you will want to be able to refer back to at various points in the argument) or if you think that there is some controversy about whether the philosopher held the view you are attributing to him or her. Your paper should not string together lots of quotations.

7. **Do not confuse philosophy with a debate team.** The point in a philosophy paper is not to win a competition but to isolate the truth of the matter. One good argument, explored in depth, beats three or four quick and dirty ones. Indeed, the best philosophy papers identify objections to the author's thesis and state those objections in the strongest way possible. Try to do this. It is an intellectual virtue to admit where the weaknesses of your argument lie rather than to pretend that your position faces no difficulties.

8. **Leave time for substantial revision and rethinking.** After you have written your first draft, put it aside for an hour or a day and then reread it for clarity, organization, and soundness. Does each argument contribute to the overall position? Is it directly germane to your thesis? Are the arguments presented

in a logical order? Could someone unfamiliar with the ideas or arguments you are discussing follow what you are saying? Edit your paper accordingly. If in the course of your revisions you find that you cannot respond to one of the objections that you have raised to your thesis, change your thesis and start over. The aim is not to defend your first thoughts on the topic but to defend your *considered* views, and these may well change during the process of writing. Expect to rewrite your paper more than once.

9. As part of your editing process, **read your paper aloud.** If it does not *sound* right, it will not read right. Rewrite any part of it that sounds unclear or weak in argumentation.

Part I

PHILOSOPHY OF RELIGION

Does God Exist?

When a philosopher tells you that he or she is going to prove that God exists (or that God does not exist) your first thought should be, "Wait! Stop! Before you say another word, tell me as clearly and as plainly as you can what you mean by the word 'God.'" Like most familiar words, the word "God" has many meanings, and each yields a different interpretation of the question "Does God exist?" Here are some of the most important possibilities.

Some Meanings of "God"

THE GOD OF SCRIPTURE AND TRADITION

We have ancient books about God and complex religious traditions built around them. One way to use the word "God" is to use it to mean *the figure described in one or another of these traditions.* In this view, when we ask whether God exists, we are asking whether there exists a being who did all or most of the things that God is said to have done in (say) the Hebrew Bible or the Koran. Atheists who answer "no" regard these stories as myths, as we now regard the ancient Greek and Roman myths, while theists in the relevant tradition regard them as true stories about a real being whom the stories more or less accurately depict.

THE GOD OF THE PHILOSOPHERS

Philosophers often use the word "God" to mean *an absolutely perfect being.* Anselm's famous **ontological argument** is not an argument for the historical accuracy of the Christian scriptures. It is an argument for the existence of a being *than which none greater can be thought.* A being of this sort would be perfect in all respects: perfectly powerful (omnipotent), perfectly wise (omniscient), perfectly good (omnibenevolent), and so on. When the word is used in this way, it is a contradiction to say that God is limited in some way. Even if the world was created by an immaterial spirit who loves mankind and ensures that justice is done in the next life, if that being is imperfect in any way, then that being *is not God* when the word is used in Anselm's sense.

GOD AS FIRST CAUSE; GOD AS DESIGNER

For some writers, the debate over the existence of God is a debate about the origin of the universe. In this view, when we ask whether God exists, we are asking whether the natural world owes its existence to a being that is not simply part of nature. A supernatural creator must presumably be immaterial, since it exists before any material thing exists. If it is to count as a designer, it must presumably be intelligent and very powerful. But it need not be perfect in every way, and it need not play the role in human history that God is said to play in (say) the Bible.

GOD AS A TRANSCENDENT SOURCE OF "MEANING"

If philosophy could establish the existence of a supernatural cause of the universe, that would be an amazing contribution to metaphysics. But it would not by itself have much religious significance. We can imagine someone saying, "Wow, that's fascinating. But unless this cosmic being plans to interfere with my life, I plan to ignore it. You've given me no reason to take this being into account or to live my life differently in light of its existence." Some writers use the word "God" to signify a being that no one could sensibly shrug off in this way. On this conception, to say that God exists is to affirm the existence of a being whose existence somehow manages to give meaning, purpose, directions, or limits to human life—a being that, by its very nature, merits devotion or obedience or even love.

Ground Rules in Philosophical Theology

These are rough sketches of some of the many meanings that philosophers have attached to the word "God." Which is the correct meaning? *This is a bad question.* It's like asking what the word "bat" really means, when we all know that it sometimes means a stick used in sports like baseball and sometimes a flying rodent of the order Chiroptera. Anselm seeks to establish the existence of God, by which *he* means a perfect being. You can object to his argument in many ways. But you should not object to it by saying, "By 'God' *I* mean the supernatural creator of the universe; Anselm has not proved the existence of a creator, so his argument is no good." When you review the arguments for and against the existence of God,

> Your first job is to figure out what the author means by the words in his or her text.
> Your second job is to determine what his or her argument is supposed to be.
> Your third job is to decide whether the argument establishes its conclusion.

Given these aims, it makes no sense to quibble with the author's terminological choices. You have more important things to do.

That said, it is possible to abuse the word. Occasionally someone will say, "I'm a religious person; I believe in God," and then go on to explain that she doesn't believe in anything supernatural. "When I say that God exists, I just mean to express my hope for human progress." There is no law against this sort of Humpty Dumptyish use of words. ("'When I use a word,' Humpty Dumpty said—in a rather scornful tone—'it means just what I choose it to mean, neither more nor less.'"[1]) But in philosophy this sort of idiosyncratic usage is a recipe for confusion. So avoid it. If you want to express your secular hope for the future of humanity, we have perfectly good words for that already. There is no need to co-opt the language of theology for your purposes.

One last potential source of confusion should be mentioned. It is surprisingly common in discussions of the existence of God for people to say that God is an *idea* or a *concept*. One hears this from atheists who mean to say that God is just a figment of the imagination. But one also hears it from professed theists who seem to think that it makes their position less controversial. This way of speaking is, however, seriously misleading. There may be such a thing as *the idea of God*. In fact there may be many such things: *your* idea of God, *my* idea of God, and so forth. These ideas are representations in the minds or brains of human beings, and for present purposes, no one denies their existence. It is, however, a grave mistake to confuse your idea of *X* with *X* itself. You would never confuse your idea of your mother with *your mother*. Your mother is a flesh-and-blood person with hands and feet who existed years before you existed. Your idea of your mother is—well, who knows exactly what it is? But it is obviously nothing like *that*. Similarly, your idea of God did not create the universe. Your idea of God is not omnipotent, even if it is the idea *of* an omnipotent thing. The debate over God's existence is a debate over the existence of a real being with extraordinary attributes. It is not a debate about the existence of an idea.

A Brief Taxonomy of the Arguments

However we understand the word, everyone agrees that, if God exists, God is invisible, intangible, and undetectable by means of scientific instruments. How then are we to approach the question of God's existence? In this book, we set aside arguments that depend on special revelation or on private religious experiences that are not widely shared. These arguments are important. But the main philosophical challenge has always been to ask whether God's existence can be established by philosophical reasoning informed by ordinary experience. This is the project of **natural theology**.

Some arguments proceed **a priori**. The most important is Anselm's ontological argument—one of the strangest and also one of the most difficult arguments in this

---

1. Lewis Carroll, *Through the Looking-Glass* (1871).

area. Think of it as a **reductio ad absurdum**. The atheist says, "A perfect being does not exist." But if he says this, he must understand the phrase "a perfect being," and whatever he understands must exist in his understanding, according to Anselm. So the atheist must agree that God exists in the understanding (i.e., in the mind). The only question is whether he exists in reality as well. Anselm then seeks to show that if God exists only in the understanding, God could have been greater than he is. But as God is a perfect being, this is absurd. And so it follows that God must exist both in the understanding *and in reality*. Almost every modern student of this argument rejects it, but there is no consensus about where the error lies. If you reject the argument, your job is not simply to show *that* it is unsound but to identify the source of the problem: the false premise, the invalid step. Be advised: this is very slippery material.

The remaining arguments all proceed **a posteriori**. The aim is to show that certain facts of observation and experiment constitute "evidence of things unseen." The **cosmological argument** begins with an observed causal or explanatory sequence in nature, and then argues that this sequence must have an *origin*—a first cause—that is not just another part of nature. Some versions assume that each such sequence must have a beginning in time. But the most sophisticated versions hold that even if the natural universe has always existed, there must still be something outside the world to explain why the world exists, and so to answer the question: "Why is there something rather than nothing?"

The most important arguments in recent natural theology begin with detailed observations drawn from the sciences. The **design argument** begins from the observation that the parts of plants and animals are brilliantly adapted to serve the purposes of the organisms whose parts they are. Before Darwin, the only serious explanations for this fact were theological, and even after Darwin, some versions of this argument are worth discussing. Darwinian arguments assume the existence of living things, but the first living thing must already have had parts that were adapted to benefit the whole. Thus, some writers argue that the existence of life itself constitutes evidence of God's existence.

There is of course a famous danger in such arguments. At any given stage in the history of science, there will be facts that science cannot explain. Given such a gap, a theist can say, "Aha! Science can't explain it. But it must have an explanation. So God exists!" The defect in arguments of this form should be clear. Science makes progress. What we cannot explain today, we may well explain tomorrow. So given an ordinary gap in our scientific understanding of nature, the rational response is not to posit a convenient **God of the gaps,** but rather to acknowledge that for now we just don't know, and perhaps to hope that ordinary science will solve the problem.

The most recent of the arguments for God's existence is crafted to evade this difficulty. The **cosmological fine-tuning argument** begins from a claim about the fundamental constants of nature: certain numbers—like the gravitational constant— that appear in the basic laws of physics. We do not know these laws in detail. But we know a bit about them, and what we know suggests the following: If the fundamental constants had been slightly different from what they are, stars and planets would not have formed, and life would never have arisen. This raises a question: Why do the constants have "life-permitting" values? And here (it is claimed) there can be no scientific explanation. The constants are aspects of the *fundamental* laws of nature. But a fundamental law—by definition—cannot be explained. (If it could, it would not be fundamental.) So the answer to our question, if there is one, cannot possibly come from science. Proponents of the argument regard the fact of "fine tuning" as a reason to believe that a divine first cause exists. Are they right? The argument is new. Unlike the other arguments discussed in this section, it is a creature of the late twentieth century. The science it assumes remains unsettled, and philosophers are not going to settle it from the armchair. The question for you is therefore conditional: *If* the physicists tell us that the fundamental constants of nature appear to be "fine-tuned," what would this show about the existence of God?

The Case for Atheism

Suppose the arguments for the existence of God are all no good. Would this vindicate the atheist? Not automatically. Our search for extraterrestrial life has so far turned up nothing. But this does not warrant the conclusion that no such life exists. To the contrary, at this stage, the only reasonable attitude on that question is **agnosticism**: a principled refusal to answer the question given the present state of the evidence. By parity of reasoning, the atheist who wishes to affirm with confidence that God does not exist needs a positive argument for this negative conclusion. What is it to be?

The most important argument for atheism is the **argument from evil**. The target is the God of the Philosophers. If there were a perfect being, there would be no unnecessary suffering in the world, since a good God would prevent unnecessary suffering if he could, and an omnipotent God could certainly prevent it. But there *is* unnecessary suffering: think of the animals injured in forest fires who suffer terribly before they die. And so, the argument concludes, there is no God. The argument is as old as theology, though it has been refined over the years. It has occasionally been offered as a knock-down *proof* of atheism. These days, however, it is generally understood as providing *evidence* for atheism—evidence that any credible form of theism must overcome. A theistic argument that attempts to meet this challenge is called a **theodicy**.

After you have read and discussed these arguments, it will be useful to step back. What have you been discussing? The existence of an invisible spirit—a being whose existence would be of absolutely fundamental importance, both for our understanding of the universe and for the conduct of our lives. How have you been approaching the question? By reading and thinking and talking. Have you made progress? One hopes so. Even if you have not settled the question, you have a clearer sense of what it would take to settle it. Familiar arguments that once seemed compelling may strike you as hopeless; unfamiliar arguments may strike you as promising. This encourages the thought that more work of this sort might bring the issue into sharper focus. Perhaps the most important point to stress is that philosophical progress in this area, as in others, does not always consist in marshaling knockdown arguments that "compel assent" from any rational creature, but rather in displaying the available positions and the best arguments for and against them. The questions addressed in this chapter are very old, as the classic selections from Anselm of Canterbury and Thomas Aquinas attest. The selection from William Paley illustrates how these questions were transformed by the rise of science. The contemporary selections from Roger White, Eleonore Stump, and Louise Antony show that progress is still being made.

Anselm of Canterbury (c. 1033–1109)

Anselm is one of the first important figures in the history of scholasticism—the effort to provide a philosophical foundation for Christian doctrine that incorporates the insights of Greek philosophy. His *Proslogion* (1077–78) is an extended meditation on the attributes of God, originally entitled *Fides quaerens intellectum*, or "Faith Seeking Reason."

THE ONTOLOGICAL ARGUMENT
from *Proslogion*

Chapter 2

THAT GOD TRULY EXISTS

Therefore, Lord, you who grant understanding to faith, grant that, insofar as you know it is useful for me, I may understand that you exist as we believe you exist, and that you are what we believe you to be. Now we believe that you are something than which nothing greater can be thought. So can it be that no such nature exists, since "The fool has said in his heart, 'There is no God' " (Psalm 14:1; 53:1)? But when this same fool hears me say "something than which nothing greater can be thought," he surely understands what he hears; and what he understands exists in his understanding, even if he does not understand that it exists [in reality]. For it is one thing for an object to exist in the understanding and quite another to understand that the object exists [in reality]. When a painter, for example, thinks out in advance what he is going to paint, he has it in his understanding, but he does not yet understand that it exists, since he has not yet painted it. But once he has painted it, he both has it in his understanding and understands that it exists because he has now painted it. So even the fool must admit that something than which nothing greater can be thought exists at least in his understanding, since he understands this when he hears it, and whatever is understood exists in the understanding. And surely that than which a greater cannot be thought cannot exist only in the understanding. For if it exists only in the understanding, it can be thought to exist in reality as well, which is greater. So if that than which a greater cannot be thought exists only in the understanding, then that than which a greater *cannot* be thought is that than which a greater *can* be thought. But that is clearly impossible. Therefore, there is no doubt that something than which a greater cannot be thought exists both in the understanding and in reality.

Chapter 3

THAT HE CANNOT BE THOUGHT NOT TO EXIST

This [being] exists so truly that it cannot be thought not to exist. For it is possible to think that something exists that cannot be thought not to exist, and such a being is greater than one that can be thought not to exist. Therefore, if that than which a greater cannot be thought can be thought not to exist, then that than which a greater cannot be thought is *not* that than which a greater cannot be thought; and this is a contradiction. So that than which a greater cannot be thought exists so truly that it cannot be thought not to exist.

TEST YOUR UNDERSTANDING

1. Anselm identifies God with "something than which nothing greater can be thought." Briefly explain this formulation.

2. "It is one thing for an object to exist in the understanding, and another thing to understand that an object exists [in reality]." Explain this distinction using examples of your own.

3. Anselm argues that even though the fool denies that God exists, God must exist in his understanding. Give the argument for this claim.

4. In Chapter 3, Anselm distinguishes between "things that can be thought not to exist" and "things that cannot be thought not to exist." Explain the distinction with examples.

READER'S GUIDE

Anselm's Ontological Argument

Anselm's goal is to prove the existence of God, by which he means *an absolutely perfect being*, a being so perfect that no greater being is conceivable. As Anselm puts it, God is "something than which nothing greater can be thought."

More specifically, Anselm's goal is to refute the "fool" (i.e., the atheist). Think of the atheist as someone who says: "I know what God is *supposed* to be, just as I know what the Loch Ness Monster is supposed to be. I just think that God, like the Loch Ness Monster, does not exist." Anselm's aim is to show that this combination of views is incoherent.

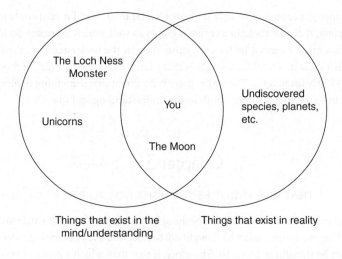

The Loch Ness
Monster

You

Undiscovered
species, planets,
etc.

Unicorns

The Moon

Things that exist in the   Things that exist in reality
mind/understanding

Figure 1

If you understand what God is supposed to be—as you do!—you have no choice but to concede that God exists.

A key premise is a general account of how thinking works. According to Anselm, whenever you think about an object—Donald Trump, the Loch Ness Monster—the thing you are thinking about must exist in your *understanding*. In particular, when you deny the existence of the Loch Ness Monster, you understand what you are saying and, according to Anselm, "what [you] understand exists in [your] mind." The interesting question about Nessie is therefore not "Does Nessie exist *at all*?" If you can ask the question, Nessie must at least exist in your mind. The question is rather "Does Nessie exist *in reality*?" Similarly, the interesting question about God is not "Does God exist at all?" If you can ask the question, God certainly exists in your mind. The question is whether God exists in reality.

Figure 1 is a way to picture the problem as Anselm sees it. Everything that exists falls into one of three categories. There are things that exist in the mind alone (e.g., Nessie); things that exist both in the mind and in reality (e.g., you); and things that exist in reality but not in the mind (e.g., undiscovered species).

The trick is to say where God belongs in this picture. Because we can think about God, he clearly belongs in the circle on the left. The atheist says that God belongs in the crescent on the far left along with Nessie. Anselm thinks that God belongs in the center with you.

This brings us to the decisive step in the argument. Anselm assumes as a premise that it is *greater* to exist in reality than in the mind alone. A painter may imagine an excellent painting. But if she can bring it into existence just as she imagined it, it will be better, more nearly perfect. In general, Anselm thinks that if X exists in the mind alone, then X would have been greater if X had existed in reality. This is a strange idea to us, but it is central to Anselm's argument.

If we grant this premise, we may reason as follows. We start by placing God at the far left along with Nessie. That gives us the world according to the atheist (Figure 2).

But then we notice that *that's impossible!* Everything in that crescent on the left is imperfect, since each such thing would have been better if it had existed in reality. But

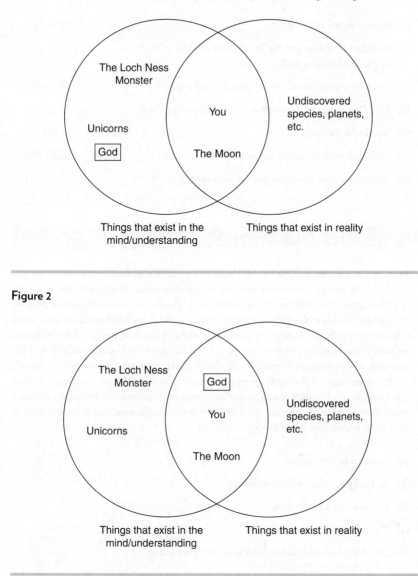

Figure 2

Things that exist in the
mind/understanding

Things that exist in reality

Figure 3

God is, by definition, absolutely perfect. If a thing could have been better, *it is not God.*
This means that the only place for God in the diagram is in the center (Figure 3). But this
is just to say that God exists in reality.

Here is one way to reconstruct Anselm's argument:

(0) God is an absolutely perfect being. [Definition]

(1) We can think about God. [Premise]

(2) Whatever we can think about exists in the mind. [Premise]

(3) So God exists in the mind.   [(2), (3)]

(4) So either God exists in the mind alone or God exists both
     in the mind and in reality.   [(4)]

(5) If X exists in the mind alone, then X is not perfect.   [Premise]

(6) So if God exists in the mind alone, God is not perfect.   [(5)]

(7) But God is perfect.   [(0)]

(8) So God does not exist in the mind alone.   [(6), (7)]

(9) So God exists both in the mind *and in reality*.   [(4), (8)]

NOTES AND QUESTIONS

1. *Anselm on "existence in the mind."* Anselm's argument assumes that whenever you
    think of X, X exists *in your mind*. But that is a peculiar idiom. It suggests that the mind
    is a place, populated with real things like Barack Obama, and also with shadowy unreal
    things like the Loch Ness Monster. One way to resist Anselm's argument is to reject
    this way of speaking. We might concede that when we think of the Loch Ness Monster,
    an *idea* of the monster exists in our minds. But we should not confuse our idea of the
    monster, which exists in the mind, with the monster itself, which does not exist at all.

    Some versions of the ontological argument do without this assumption. Say that
    a *perfection* is a property that any perfect being must possess. When a property is a
    perfection, it is always greater (in Anselm's sense) to possess that property than to
    lack it. Now consider the following argument:

    (1) God is a perfect being.

    (2) So God possesses every perfection.

    (3) Existence is a perfection.

    (4) Therefore, God exists.

    Exercise: Say where (if anywhere) this argument goes wrong.

2. *Gaunilo's perfect island.* An eleventh-century monk named Gaunilo presents a famous
    parody of Anselm's argument from *Proslogion 2*:

    > It is said that somewhere in the ocean is an island . . . which has an ines-
    > timable wealth of all manner of riches and delicacies [and which] is more
    > excellent than all other countries, which are inhabited by mankind, in the
    > abundance with which it is stored.
    >
    > Now if someone should tell me that there is such an island, I should easily
    > understand his words, in which there is no difficulty. But suppose that he
    > went on to say, as if by a logical inference: "You can no longer doubt that
    > this island, which is more excellent than all lands exists somewhere, since

you have no doubt that it is in your [mind]. And since it is more excellent not to be in the [mind] alone, but to exist both in the [mind] and in reality, for this reason it must exist [in reality]. For if it does not exist [in reality], any land which really exists will be more excellent than it; and so the island already understood by you to be more excellent will not be more excellent."

How might a proponent of the ontological argument distinguish Anselm's proof from Gaunilo's?

Note: Even if Anselm's argument cannot be distinguished from Gaunilo's parody, it is still important to say *where* these arguments go wrong. The parody may show us that there must be a mistake somewhere, but a satisfying response to Anselm must locate that mistake explicitly.

For Gaunilo's critique and Anselm's reply, see *Philosophy in the Middle Ages,* ed. A. Hyman and J. J. Walsh (3rd ed., Hackett, 2010).

3. *Two ontological arguments.* The selection presents two independent arguments. The argument of *Proslogion 2* relies on the distinction between *existence in the mind* and *existence in reality.* The argument of *Proslogion 3* relies on a rather different distinction between *things that can be thought not to exist* and *things that cannot be thought not to exist.*

What can Anselm mean when he says that God *cannot be thought not to exist*? After all, he says himself that the fool believes in his heart that there is no God. *Hint:* Distinguish the *psychological* claim that no one is capable of denying the existence of God from the *logical* claim that no one can *consistently* or *coherently* deny God's existence.

Thomas Aquinas (1225–1274)

Aquinas, the "Angelic Doctor," is one of the great figures in the history of Catholic philosophy and theology. His major works, *Summa Theologica* and *Summa contra Gentiles,* seek to provide the rational basis for those aspects of Christian doctrine that can be established without special revelation and to reconcile Christian doctrine with key insights of Aristotle.

THE FIVE WAYS
from *Summa Theologica*

Article 3. Whether God Exists

The existence of God can be proved in five ways.

The first and more manifest way is the argument from motion. It is certain, and evident to our senses, that in the world some things are in motion. Now whatever is in motion is put in motion by another, for nothing can be in motion except it is in potentiality to that towards which it is in motion; whereas a thing moves inasmuch as it is in act. For motion is nothing else than the reduction of something from potentiality to actuality.[1] But nothing can be reduced from potentiality to actuality, except by something in a state of actuality. Thus that which is actually hot, as fire, makes wood, which is potentially hot, to be actually hot, and thereby moves and changes it. Now it is not possible that the same thing should be at once in actuality and potentiality in the same respect, but only in different respects. For what is actually hot cannot simultaneously be potentially hot; but it is simultaneously potentially cold. It is therefore impossible that in the same respect and in the same way a thing should be both mover and moved, i.e., that it should move itself. Therefore, whatever is in motion must be put in motion by another. If that by which it is put in motion be itself put in motion, then this also must needs be put in motion by another, and that by another again. But this cannot go on to infinity, because then there would be no first mover, and, consequently, no other mover; seeing that subsequent movers move only inasmuch as they are put in motion by the first mover; as the staff moves only because it is put in motion by the hand. Therefore it is necessary to arrive at a first mover, put in motion by no other; and this everyone understands to be God.

The second way is from the nature of the efficient cause.[2] In the world of sense we find there is an order of efficient causes. There is no case known (neither is it, indeed, possible) in which a thing is found to be the efficient cause of itself; for so it would be prior to itself, which is impossible. Now in efficient causes it is not possible to go on to infinity, because in all efficient causes following in order, the first is the cause of the intermediate cause, and the intermediate is the cause of the ultimate cause, whether the intermediate cause be several, or only one. Now to take away the cause is to take away the effect. Therefore, if there be no first cause among efficient causes, there will be no ultimate, nor any intermediate cause. But if in efficient causes it is possible to go on to infinity, there will be no first efficient cause, neither will there be an ultimate effect, nor any intermediate efficient causes; all of which is plainly false. Therefore it is necessary to admit a first efficient cause, to which everyone gives the name of God.

The third way is taken from possibility and necessity, and runs thus. We find in nature things that are possible to be and not to be, since they are found to be generated, and to corrupt, and consequently, they are possible to be and not to be.[3] But it is impossible for these always to exist, for that which is possible not to be at some time is not. Therefore, if everything is possible not to be, then at one time there could have been nothing in existence. Now if this were true, even now there would be nothing in existence, because that which does not exist only begins to exist by something already existing. Therefore, if at one time nothing was in existence, it would have been impossible for anything to have begun to exist; and thus even now nothing would be

---

1. Aquinas speaks of "motion"—change of place—and then invokes a general theory of change due to Aristotle. According to this theory, a change occurs when something that is *potentially* F becomes *actually* F, as when something that is potentially hot becomes hot, or something that is potentially in Los Angeles comes to be in Los Angeles.

2. Following Aristotle, Aquinas distinguishes several kinds of cause. The **efficient cause** of an object or event is the thing whose activity brings that object into being or produces the event in question.

3. A thing that is "possible to be and not to be" is a **contingent being**: a thing that exists but could have failed to exist, or which fails to exist but could have existed. You are a contingent being, since you exist but could easily have failed to exist. A thing that exists and could not have failed to exist is a **necessary being**.

in existence—which is absurd. Therefore, not all beings are merely possible, but there must exist something the existence of which is necessary. But every necessary thing either has its necessity caused by another, or not. Now it is impossible to go on to infinity in necessary things which have their necessity caused by another, as has been already proved in regard to efficient causes. Therefore we cannot but postulate the existence of some being having of itself its own necessity, and not receiving it from another, but rather causing in others their necessity. This all men speak of as God.

The fourth way is taken from the gradation to be found in things. Among beings there are some more and some less good, true, noble and the like. But "more" and "less" are predicated of different things, according as they resemble in their different ways something which is the maximum, as a thing is said to be hotter according as it more nearly resembles that which is hottest; so that there is something which is truest, something best, something noblest and, consequently, something which is uttermost being; for those things that are greatest in truth are greatest in being, as it is written in [Aristotle's] *Metaphysics,* ii. Now the maximum in any genus is the cause of all in that genus; as fire, which is the maximum heat, is the cause of all hot things. Therefore there must also be something which is to all beings the cause of their being, goodness, and every other perfection; and this we call God.

The fifth way is taken from the governance of the world. We see that things which lack intelligence, such as natural bodies, act for an end, and this is evident from their acting always, or nearly always, in the same way, so as to obtain the best result. Hence it is plain that not fortuitously, but designedly, do they achieve their end. Now whatever lacks intelligence cannot move towards an end, unless it be directed by some being endowed with knowledge and intelligence; as the arrow is shot to its mark by the archer. Therefore some intelligent being exists by whom all natural things are directed to their end; and this being we call God.

TEST YOUR UNDERSTANDING

1. In the First Way, Aquinas claims that "whatever is in motion is put in motion by another." Briefly state the argument for this claim.

2. In the Second Way, Aquinas argues for the existence of a "first cause." Say what this means.

3. In the Third Way, Aquinas distinguishes between "things that are possible to be and not to be" (i.e., contingent beings) and necessary beings. Explain the distinction with examples.

4. True or false: In *The Five Ways,* Aquinas assumes that God is an absolutely perfect being.

READER'S GUIDE

Aquinas's Cosmological Arguments

Aquinas's first two Ways are versions of the cosmological argument, the basic idea of which has occurred to everyone who has ever wondered about God's existence. We find ourselves in a world of ordinary finite things: people, animals, rocks, and so on. Choose one and call it Alice (Figure 1).

Alice

Figure 1

We notice that in this world, ordinary things are caused to exist by other things. Animals and rocks always come to be from other things; they don't just pop into existence. So Alice must have had a cause, even if we cannot identify it. More specifically, Alice must have been caused to exist by *something else*, since (as Aquinas says) "there is no known case . . . in which a thing is found to be the efficient cause of itself." Call this cause Bob[4] (Figure 2).

Bob   Alice

Figure 2

Now if Bob is also an ordinary thing, it too must have had a prior cause. And so we come to think of Alice as the result of a process stretching backwards in time (Figure 3).

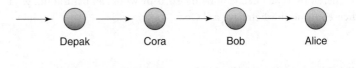

Depak   Cora   Bob   Alice

Figure 3

At which point we are naturally led to ask: How did this whole business get started? There are only three possibilities.

1. The causal chain that leads to Alice begins with an ordinary thing (or some collection of ordinary things) that just popped into existence, thereby constituting an exception to the rule that ordinary things can't do that (Figure 4).

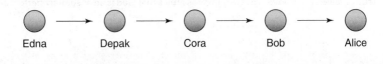

Edna   Depak   Cora   Bob   Alice

Figure 4

4. Of course, Alice might have had many causes. If that worries you, you can think of "Bob" as a name for Alice's many causes taken together.

Historically, almost every philosopher who has entertained this argument has rejected this possibility. The idea that "nothing comes from nothing"—that every thing that comes to exist is caused by something else—has been regarded as self-evident.[5] Aquinas does not even mention this possibility.

2. The causal chain that leads to Alice has no beginning. The universe of ordinary things has always existed; each thing has infinitely many causal antecedents (Figure 5).

Golda   Fareed   Edna   Depak   Cora   Bob   Alice

Figure 5

Aquinas explicitly rejects this possibility in an obscure passage:

> Now in efficient causes it is not possible to go on to infinity, because in all efficient causes following in order, the first is the cause of the intermediate cause, and the intermediate is the cause of the ultimate cause . . . Now to take away the cause is to take away the effect. Therefore, if there be no first cause among efficient causes, there will neither be an ultimate effect, nor any intermediate efficient causes, all of which is plainly false.[6]

The idea appears to be this: In this infinite universe, every cause along the road to Alice is an "intermediate cause." But there cannot be intermediate causes without first causes, since an intermediate cause is a cause that comes in between the first cause and the ultimate effect (Alice). A universe that includes intermediate causes without a first cause is thus impossible.

Why must an intermediate cause come between a *first* cause and the ultimate effect? Imagine an iron chain stretching from your hand out into space *forever*. Apart from the link in your hand, every link in the chain is an intermediate link. Why can't there be *causal* chains like this? Many people recoil at the idea. The underlying idea seems to be that intermediate causes borrow their causal *oomph* from their causes, and that causal oomph cannot be "on loan" at every stage. If Alice borrowed a dollar from Bob, who borrowed it from Cora . . . we can conclude that someone must have acquired this dollar in some other way. If causal *oomph* is like money, then the idea of an infinite causal chain will not do. But this argument is too metaphorical to assess. Suffice it to say that Aquinas's case for rejecting this possibility is inconclusive.

---

5. This principle is no longer regarded as self-evident. It seems easy to imagine a thing simply popping into existence. (It happens all the time in cartoons.) So if this is *impossible*, there must be some deep reason of physics or metaphysics why this is so. For example, the spontaneous emergence of a material thing from nothing at all might violate the principle of the conservation of energy. If you want to reject the possibility of a spontaneous uncaused beginning of the universe, you must cite and defend some such principle.

6. See page 14 of this anthology.

Which brings us to the third and final possibility:

3. The causal chain that leads to Alice begins with an extraordinary object: an *uncaused cause* (Figure 6).

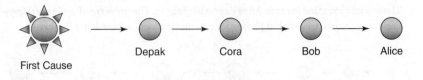

Figure 6

This first cause would have to be eternal, since if it came into existence, it would need a prior cause of its own. And it would have to be *supernatural*, since everything in nature comes into being from prior causes. Of course, nothing in this argument shows that this first cause must be intelligent or good or God-like in other ways. But that's no objection. Like each of the five Ways, this argument seeks to establish the existence of an entity with one of the attributes traditionally associated with God. The proof that the cosmic First Cause is also wise and good is a topic for another time.

NOTES AND QUESTIONS

1. *Aquinas on the uniqueness of God.* Aquinas's arguments are designed to establish the existence of a being that differs radically from ordinary objects in various important respects. The First Way starts from the fact that ordinary objects are moved and seeks to show that there is at least one object that is not moved. The Second Way starts from the fact that ordinary objects are caused and seeks to show that there is at least one thing that is not caused, and so on. In each case, Aquinas writes as if his argument shows something stronger, namely, that *exactly one* being possesses the remarkable property in question. The argument for this further claim is not explicit.

    Exercise: Reconstruct Aquinas's arguments in stages. First produce an argument for the conclusion that there is at least one being with the remarkable property in question. Then try to complete the argument by showing that there can be at most one such being.

    Note: Even if these arguments succeed in establishing the existence of a unique first mover, a unique necessary being, and so on, it would require further argument to show that a single being possesses all of these attributes. How do we know that the first mover established by the First Way is also the necessary being established by the Third Way? The Five Ways do not pretend to address this question. Aquinas's arguments for the unity of God are found elsewhere (e.g., *Summa Theologica,* part 1, question 11, article 3).

2. *The cosmological argument.* Aquinas's first two Ways are versions of the **cosmological argument,** one simple version of which runs as follows:

    (1) Every natural object is caused to exist.

    (2) No natural object causes itself to exist.

(3) So given any natural object *X*, there is a chain of objects leading up to X that contains *X*'s causes, the causes of *X*'s causes, and so on.

(4) This chain must have a first member. Call it *G*.

(5) *G* is not caused to exist by something else.

(6) So *G* is not a natural object.

(7) So there is at least one supernatural object.

This argument has two questionable premises: (1) and (4).

> *Against premise (1):* There is no reason to believe that every natural object has a cause. It is not contradictory to suppose that a thing might simply pop into existence for no reason; indeed, contemporary physics suggests that this sometimes happens. Nor is it contradictory to suppose that a natural object (say an atom) has always existed.
> *Against premise (4):* There may be good scientific reasons for positing a first event (the "Big Bang"). But the idea of a causal sequence that extends infinitely backwards in time is not absurd: time might have the structure of the number line, infinite in both directions.

A proponent of the argument must either defend these premises or reconfigure the argument so as to avoid them.

Exercise: Imagine how Aquinas might respond to these objections to premises (1) and (4).

For discussion, see William Rowe, *The Cosmological Argument* (Princeton University Press, 1975).

3. In his *A Demonstration of the Being and Attributes of God* (1705), Samuel Clarke gives a version of the cosmological argument that is explicitly designed to allow for the possibility of causal chains with no beginning. Here is a version of Clarke's argument.

> Whenever an object exists, there is always a sufficient explanation for its existence. This is sometimes called the Principle of Sufficient Reason. Now natural objects are all *dependent*. They can only exist if they are caused to exist by something else. With this in mind, consider the totality of dependent beings, a totality that includes every natural object. Call it Nature. Nature may be finite or infinite; it doesn't matter. By the Principle of Sufficient Reason, there is some explanation for its existence. But Nature is just a collection of dependent beings, so it can't explain its own existence. There must therefore be something outside of Nature that explains why Nature exists. But Nature includes every dependent being, so this further thing must be a "self-existent being": a being that is somehow capable of explaining its own existence. A supernatural self-existent being therefore exists.

In his *Dialogues Concerning Natural Religion* (pub. 1779), David Hume concedes that the existence of Nature must be explained but denies that the explanation needs to mention something outside of Nature.

> Did I show you the particular causes of each individual in a collection of twenty particles of matter, I should think it very unreasonable should

you afterward ask me what was the cause of the whole twenty. This is sufficiently explained in explaining the cause of the parts. (*Dialogues*, IX.9)

Exercise: Set out Clarke's argument explicitly, identify the premise to which Hume objects, and then evaluate Hume's objection.

William Paley (1743–1805)

Paley was known in his day both for his lucid contributions to theology, of which his *Natural Theology* (1802) is the most famous, and for his *Principles of Moral and Political Philosophy* (1785), which urged the reform of British law according to utilitarian principles.

THE ARGUMENT FROM DESIGN
from *Natural Theology*

Chapter I

STATE OF THE ARGUMENT

In crossing a heath, suppose I pitched my foot against a *stone*, and were asked how the stone came to be there, I might possibly answer, that, for any thing I knew to the contrary, it had lain there for ever: nor would it perhaps be very easy to shew the absurdity of this answer. But suppose I had found a *watch* upon the ground, and it should be enquired how the watch happened to be in that place, I should hardly think of the answer which I had before given, that, for any thing I knew, the watch might have always been there. Yet why should not this answer serve for the watch, as well as for the stone? Why is it not as admissible in the second case, as in the first? For this reason, and for no other, viz., that, when we come to inspect the watch, we perceive (what we could not discover in the stone) that its several parts are framed and put together for a purpose, e.g., that they are so formed and adjusted as to produce motion, and that motion so regulated as to point out the hour of the day; that, if the several parts had been differently shaped from what they are, of a different size from what they are, or placed after any other manner, or in any other order, than that in which they are placed, either no motion at all would have been carried on in the machine, or none which would have answered the use, that is now served by it. To reckon up a few of the plainest of these parts, and of their offices, all tending to one result:—We see a cylindrical box containing a coiled elastic spring, which, by its endeavour to relax itself, turns round the box. We next observe a flexible chain (artificially wrought for the sake of flexure) communicating the action of the spring from the box to the fusee. We then find a series of wheels, the teeth of which catch in, and apply to, each other, conducting the motion from the fusee to the balance, and from the balance to the pointer; and at the same time, by the size and shape of those wheels, so regulating that motion, as to terminate in causing an index, by an equable and measured progression, to pass over a given space in a given time. We take notice that the wheels are made of brass, in order to keep them from rust; the springs of steel, no other metal being so elastic; that over the face of the watch there is placed a glass, a material employed in no other part of the work, but, in the room of which, if there had been any other than a transparent substance, the hour could not be seen without opening the case. This mechanism being observed (it requires indeed an examination of the instrument, and perhaps some previous knowledge of the subject, to perceive and understand it; but being once, as we have said, observed and understood), the inference, we think, is inevitable; that the watch must have had a maker; that there must have existed, at some time and at some place or other, an artificer or artificers who formed it for the purpose which we find it actually to answer; who comprehended its construction, and designed its use.

I. Nor would it, I apprehend, weaken the conclusion, that we had never seen a watch made; that we had never known an artist capable of making one; that we were altogether incapable of executing such a piece of workmanship ourselves, or of understanding in what manner it was performed: all this being no more than what is true of some exquisite remains of ancient art, of some lost arts, and, to the generality of mankind, of the more curious productions of modern manufacture. Does one man in a million know how oval frames are turned? Ignorance of this kind exalts our opinion of the unseen and unknown artist's skill, if he be unseen and unknown, but raises no doubt in our minds of the existence and agency of such an artist, at some former time, and in some place or other. . . .

II. Neither, secondly, would it invalidate our conclusion, that the watch sometimes went wrong, or that it seldom went exactly right. The purpose of the machinery, the design, and the designer, might be evident, and in the case supposed would be evident, in whatever way we accounted for the irregularity of the movement, or whether we could account for it or not. It is not necessary that a machine be perfect, in order to shew with what design it was made: still less necessary, where the only question is, whether it were made with any design at all.

III. Nor, thirdly, would it bring any uncertainty into the argument, if there were a few parts of the watch, concerning which we could not discover, or had not yet discovered, in what manner they conduced to the general effect; or even some parts, concerning which we could not ascertain, whether they conduced to that effect in any manner whatever. For, as to the first branch of the case; if, by the loss, or disorder, or decay of the parts in question, the movement of the watch were found in fact to be stopped, or disturbed, or retarded, no doubt would remain in our minds as to the utility or intention of these parts, although we should be unable to investigate the manner according to which, or the connection by which, the ultimate effect depended upon their action or assistance: and the more complex is the machine, the more likely is this obscurity to arise. Then, as to the second thing supposed, namely, that there were parts, which might be spared without prejudice to the movement of the watch, and that we had proved this by experiment,—these superfluous parts, even if we were completely assured that they were such, would not vacate the reasoning which we had instituted concerning other parts. The indication of contrivance remained, with respect to them, nearly as it was before.

IV. Nor, fourthly, would any man in his senses think the existence of the watch, with its various machinery, accounted for, by being told that it was one out of many possible combinations of material forms; that whatever he had found in the place where he found the watch, must have contained some internal configuration or other; and that this configuration might be the structure now exhibited, viz., of the works of a watch, as well as a different structure. . . .

VII. And [he would be] not less surprised to be informed, that the watch in his hand was nothing more than the result of the laws of *metallic* nature. It is a perversion of language to assign any law, as the efficient, operative, cause of any thing. A law presupposes an agent; for it is only the mode, according to which an agent proceeds: it implies a power; for it is the order, according to which that power acts. Without this agent, without this power, which are both distinct from itself, the *law* does nothing; is nothing. . . .

VIII. Neither, lastly, would our observer be driven out of his conclusion, or from his confidence in its truth, by being told that he knew nothing at all about the matter. He knows enough for his argument. He knows the utility of the end: he knows the subserviency and adaptation of the means to the end. These points being known, his ignorance of other points, his doubts concerning other points, affect not the certainty of his reasoning. The consciousness of knowing little, need not beget a distrust of that which he does know.

Chapter II

STATE OF THE ARGUMENT CONTINUED

Suppose in the next place, that the person, who found the watch, should, after some time, discover, that, in addition to all the properties which he had hitherto observed in it, it possessed, the unexpected property of producing, in the course of its movement, another watch like itself; (the thing is conceivable;) that it contained within it a mechanism, a system of parts, a mould for instance, or a complex adjustment of laths, files, and other tools, evidently and separately calculated for this purpose; let us enquire, what effect ought such a discovery to have upon his former conclusion?

I. The first effect would be to increase his admiration of the contrivance, and his conviction of the consummate skill of the contriver. Whether he regarded the object of the contrivance, the distinct apparatus, the intricate, yet in many parts intelligible, mechanism by which it was carried on, he would perceive, in this new observation, nothing but an additional reason for doing what he had already done; for referring the construction of the watch to design, and to supreme art. . . .

II. He would reflect, that though, the watch before him were, *in some sense,* the maker of the watch, which was fabricated in the course of its movements, yet it was in a very different sense from that, in which a carpenter, for instance, is the maker of a chair; the author of its contrivance, the cause of the relation of its parts to their use. With respect to these, the first watch was no cause at all to the second: in no such sense as this was it the author of the constitution and order, either of the parts which the new watch contained, or of the parts by the aid and instrumentality of which it was produced. We might possibly say, but with great latitude of expression, that a stream of water ground corn: but no latitude of expression would allow us to say, no stretch of conjecture could lead us to think, that the stream of water built the mill, though it were too ancient for us to know who the builder was. Therefore,

III. Though it be now no longer probable, that the individual watch which our observer had found, was made immediately by the hand of an artificer, yet doth not this alteration in any wise affect the inference, that an artificer had been originally employed and concerned in the production. The argument from design remains as it was. Marks of design and contrivance are no more accounted for now, than they were before. In the same thing, we may ask for the cause of different properties. We may ask for the cause of the colour of a body, of its hardness, of its heat, and these causes may be all different. We are now asking for the cause of that subserviency to a use, that relation to an end, which we have remarked in the watch before us. No answer is given to this question by telling us that a preceding watch produced it. There cannot be design without a designer, contrivance without a contriver; order without choice; arrangement, without any thing capable of arranging; subserviency and relation to a purpose, without that which could intend a purpose; means suitable to an end, and executing their office in accomplishing that end, without the end ever having been contemplated, or the means accommodated to it. Arrangement, disposition of parts, subserviency of means to an end, relation of instruments to an use, imply the presence of intelligence and mind. No one, therefore, can rationally believe, that the insensible, inanimate watch, from which the watch before us issued, was the proper cause of the mechanism we so much admire in it, could be truly said to have constructed the instrument, disposed its parts, assigned their office, determined their order, action, and mutual dependency, combined their several motions into one result, and that also a result connected with the utilities of other beings. All these properties, therefore, are as much unaccounted for, as they were before.

IV. Nor is any thing gained by running the difficulty further back, i.e., by supposing the watch before us to have been produced from another watch, that from a former, and so on indefinitely. Our going back ever so far brings us no nearer to the least degree of satisfaction upon the subject. Contrivance is still unaccounted for. We still want a contriver. A designing mind is neither supplied by this supposition, nor dispensed with. If the difficulty were diminished the further we went back, by going back indefinitely we might exhaust it. And this is the only case to which this sort of reasoning applies. Where there is a tendency, or, as we increase the number of terms, a continual approach towards a limit, *there,* by supposing the number of terms to be what is called infinite, we may conceive the limit to be attained: but where there is no such tendency or approach, nothing is effected by lengthening the series. There is no difference as to the point in question (whatever there may be as to many points), between one series and another; between a series which is finite, and a series which is infinite. A chain, composed of an infinite number of links; can no more support itself, than a chain composed of a finite number of links . . . The machine, which we are inspecting, demonstrates; by its construction, contrivance and design. Contrivance must have had a contriver; design, a designer; whether the machine immediately proceeded from another machine, or not. . . .

The question is not simply, How came the first watch into existence? which question, it may be pretended, is done away by supposing the series of watches thus produced from one another to have been infinite, and consequently to have had no such *first*, for which it was necessary to provide a cause. This, perhaps, would have been nearly the state of the question, if nothing had been before us but an unorganised, unmechanised, substance, without mark or indication of contrivance. It might be difficult to shew that such substance could not have existed from eternity, either in succession (if it were possible, which I think it is not, for unorganised bodies to spring from one another), or by individual perpetuity. But that is not the question now. To suppose it to be so, is to suppose that it made no difference whether we had found a watch or a stone. As it is, the metaphysics of that question have no place; for, in the watch which we are examining, are seen contrivance, design; an end, a purpose; means for the end, adaptation to the purpose. And the question which irresistibly presses upon our thoughts, is, whence this contrivance and design. The thing required is the intending mind, the adapting hand, the intelligence by which that hand was directed. This question, this demand, is not shaken off, by increasing a number of succession of substances, destitute of these properties; nor the more, by increasing that number to infinity. If it be said, that, upon the supposition of one watch being produced from another in the course of that other's movements, and by means of the mechanism within it, we have a cause for the watch in my hand, viz., the watch from which it proceeded, I deny, that for the design, the contrivance, the suitableness of means to an end, the adaptation of instruments to an use (all which we discover in the watch), we have any cause whatever. It is in vain, therefore, to assign a series of such causes; or to alledge that a series may be carried back to infinity; for I do not admit that we have yet any cause at all of the phenomena, still less any series of causes either finite or infinite. Here is contrivance, but no contriver: proofs of design, but no designer. . . .

The conclusion which the *first* examination of the watch, of its works, construction, and movement suggested, was, that it must have had, for the cause and author of that construction, an artificer, who understood its mechanism, and designed its use. This conclusion is invincible. A *second* examination presents us with a new discovery. The watch is found, in the course of its movement, to produce another watch, similar to itself: and not only so, but we perceive in it a system of organisation, separately calculated for that purpose. What effect would this discovery have, or ought it to have, upon our former inference? What, as hath already been said, but to increase, beyond measure, our admiration of the skill, which had been employed in the formation of such a machine? Or shall it, instead of this, all at once turn us round to an opposite conclusion, viz., that no art or skill whatever has been concerned in the business, although all other evidences of art and skill remain as they were, and this last and supreme piece of art be now added to the rest? Can this be maintained without absurdity? Yet this is atheism.

Chapter III

APPLICATION OF THE ARGUMENT

This is atheism: for every indication of contrivance, every manifestation of design, which existed in the watch, exists in the works of nature; with the difference, on the side of nature, of being greater and more, and that in a degree which exceeds all computation. I mean that the contrivances of nature surpass the contrivances of art, in the complexity, subtlety, and curiosity of the mechanism; and still more, if possible, do they go beyond them in number and variety; yet, in a multitude of cases, are not less evidently mechanical, not less evidently contrivances, not less evidently accommodated to their end, or suited to their office, than are the most perfect productions of human ingenuity.

I know no better method of introducing so large a subject, than that of comparing a single thing with a single thing; an eye, for example, with a telescope. As far as the examination of the instrument goes, there is precisely the same proof that the eye was made for vision, as there is that the telescope was made for assisting it. They are made upon the same principles; both being adjusted to the laws by which the transmission and refraction of rays of light are regulated. I speak not of the origin of the laws themselves; but, such laws being fixed, the construction, in both cases, is adapted to them. For instance; these laws require, in order to produce the same effect, that the rays of light, in passing from water into the eye, should be refracted by a more convex surface, than when it passes out of air into the eye. Accordingly we find, that the eye of a fish, in that part of it called the crystalline lense, is much rounder than the eye of terrestrial animals. What plainer manifestation of design can there be than this difference? What could a mathematical instrument maker have done more, to shew his knowledge of his principle, his application of that knowledge, his suiting of his means to his end; I will not say to display the compass or excellency of his skill and art, for in these all comparison is indecorous, but to testify counsel, choice, consideration, purpose?

To some it may appear a difference sufficient to destroy all similitude between the eye and the telescope, that the one is a perceiving organ, the other an unperceiving instrument. The fact is, that they are both instruments. And, as to the mechanism, at least as to mechanism being employed, and even as to the kind of it, this circumstance varies not the analogy at all. For observe, what the constitution of the eye is. It is necessary, in order to produce distinct vision, that an image or picture of the object be formed at the bottom of the eye. Whence this necessity arises, or how the picture is connected with the sensation, or contributes to it, it may be difficult, nay we will confess, if you please, impossible for us to search out. But the present question is not concerned in the enquiry. It may be true, that, in this, and in other instances, we trace mechanical contrivance a certain way; and that then we come to something which is not mechanical, or which is inscrutable. But this affects not the certainty of our investigation, as far as we have gone. The difference between an animal and an automatic statue consists in this,—that, in the animal, we trace the mechanism to a certain point, and then we are stopped; either the mechanism becoming too subtile for our discernment, or something else beside the known laws of mechanism taking place; whereas, in the automaton, for the comparatively few motions of which it is capable, we trace the mechanism throughout. But, up to the limit, the reasoning is as clear and certain in the one case as the other. In the example before us, it is a matter of certainty, because it is a matter which experience and observation demonstrate, that the formation of an image at the bottom of the eye is necessary to perfect vision. The image itself can be shewn. Whatever affects the distinctness of the image, affects the distinctness of the vision. The formation then of such an image being necessary (no matter how) to the sense of sight, and to the exercise of that sense; the apparatus by which it is formed is constructed and put together, not only with infinitely more art, but upon the self-same principles of art, as in the telescope or the camera obscura. The perception arising from the image may be laid out of the question: for the production of the image, these are instruments of the same kind. The end is the same; the means are the same. The purpose in both is alike; the contrivance for accomplishing that purpose is in both alike: The lenses of the telescope, and the humours of the eye bear a complete resemblance to one another, in their figure, in their position, and in their power over the rays of light, viz., in bringing each pencil to a point at the right distance from the lens; namely, in the eye, at the exact place where the membrane is spread to receive it. How is it possible, under circumstances of such close affinity, and under the operation of equal evidence, to exclude contrivance from the one, yet to acknowledge the proof of contrivance having been employed, as the plainest and clearest of all propositions in the other? . . .

Chapter V

APPLICATION OF THE ARGUMENT CONTINUED

Every observation which was made, in our first chapter, concerning the watch, may be repeated with strict propriety concerning the eye; concerning animals; concerning plants; concerning, indeed, all the organized parts of the works of nature. As,

I. When we are enquiring simply after the *existence* of an intelligent Creator, imperfection, inaccuracy, liability to disorder, occasional irregularities, may subsist, in a considerable degree, without inducing any doubt into the question: just as a watch may frequently go wrong, seldom perhaps exactly right, may be faulty in some parts, defective in some, without the smallest ground of suspicion from thence arising, that it was not a watch; not made; or not made for the purpose ascribed to it. When faults are pointed out, and when a question is started concerning the skill of the artist, or the dexterity with which the work is executed, then indeed, in order to defend these qualities from accusation, we must be able, either to expose some intractableness and imperfection in the materials, or point out some invincible difficulty in the execution, into which imperfection and difficulty the matter of complaint may be resolved; or, if we cannot do this, we must adduce such specimens of consummate art and contrivance proceeding from the same hand, as may convince the enquirer of the existence, in the case before him, of impediments like those which we have mentioned, although, what from the nature of the case is very likely to happen, they be unknown and unperceived by him. This we must do in order to vindicate the artist's skill, or, at least, the perfection of it; as we must also judge of his intention; and of the provisions employed in fulfilling that intention, not from an instance in which they fail, but from the great plurality of instances in which they succeed. But, after all, these are different questions from the question of the artist's existence; or, which is the same, whether the thing before be a work of art or not: and the questions ought always to be kept separate in the mind. So likewise it is in the works of nature. Irregularities and imperfections are of little or no weight in the consideration, when that consideration relates simply to the existence of a Creator. When the argument respects his attributes, they are of weight; but are then to be taken in conjunction (the attention is not to rest upon them, but they are to be taken in conjunction) with the un-exceptionable evidences which we possess, of skill, power, and benevolence, displayed in other instances, which evidences may, in strength, number, and variety be such, and may so overpower apparent blemishes, as to induce us, upon the most reasonable ground, to believe, that these last ought to be referred to some cause, though we be ignorant of it, other than defect of knowledge or of benevolence in the author. . . .

TEST YOUR UNDERSTANDING

1. Paley argues that living things are like watches in one respect: both exhibit "contriv-ance" or "design." Say what this means.

2. "Nor is any thing gained . . . by supposing the watch before us to have been produced from another watch, that from a former, and so on indefinitely. . . . Contrivance is still unaccounted for." State the argument implicit in this passage.

3. True or false: Paley argues that the existence of rocks and stars proves the existence of God.

4. True or false: Paley considers and rejects Darwin's theory of evolution as an alternative explanation for apparent design in nature.

NOTES AND QUESTIONS

1. *Analogy and inference to the best explanation.* Paley's argument is sometimes taken to be an argument by analogy:

> Living things are like watches.
> Watches are the product of intelligent design.
> Therefore, living things are the product of intelligent design.

But arguments from analogy are notoriously weak. Consider:

> Living things are like watches.
> Watches are made in factories.
> Therefore, living things are made in factories.

It is more fruitful to view Paley's argument as an **inference to the best explanation**. Such arguments have the following general form:

> Some remarkable fact F is observed.
> The best (or perhaps the only) explanation for F is hypothesis H.
> Therefore H is (probably) true.

Exercise: Recast Paley's core argument in this form. Then explain why the extended analogy with watches provides important support for the argument.

2. *Paley and Darwin.* Paley argues that the only reasonable explanation for the observed "design" in nature is that living things were made by an intelligent creator. In this form, the argument was undermined by Darwin. Without appeal to supernatural causes, the theory of evolution by natural selection can explain why living things are well adapted to their environments. (Paley wrote before Darwin, so he cannot be faulted for failing to anticipate this alternative.) For a detailed Darwinian response to Paley, see Richard Dawkins, *The Blind Watchmaker* (W. W. Norton, 1986).

A version of Paley's argument nonetheless survives the Darwinian response. Darwin's theory explains why populations of living things change over time. But it does not explain the emergence of life itself. (This is not an objection to Darwin's theory: it was never meant to explain this process.) Moreover, we can be confident that the first living things exhibited remarkable "order and contrivance." Any creature capable of reproduction needs intricate systems for taking in food from the environment, copying its genetic material, and so on. So consider the first cell. It is like Paley's watch—an intricate contrivance that exhibits "apparent design." Why are *its* parts so brilliantly adapted to its needs? Modern biology has no answer. So Paley might insist: the only available explanation for this fact is intelligent design. It is reasonable to believe the best explanation. So it is reasonable to believe in intelligent design.

Exercise: Consider how the atheist might respond to this argument. In doing so, do not try to invent your own theory of the origin of life. That would be hopeless speculation, and it should not be necessary. Contemporary atheists believe that even in the absence of a positive scientific account of the emergence of life, it is unreasonable to posit an intelligent designer. This sort of atheist must reject at least one premise in this Paley-style argument. Identify the most vulnerable premise and say why it might be reasonable to reject it.

For a modern version of this argument, see Michael Behe, *Darwin's Black Box* (Free Press, 1996). For a response, see H. Allen Orr, "Darwinism vs. Intelligent Design (Again)," *Boston Review* (December 1996/January 1997).

Roger White (b. 1967)

White is Professor of Philosophy at the Massachusetts Institute of Technology. He specializes in epistemology and the philosophy of science.

THE ARGUMENT FROM COSMOLOGICAL FINE-TUNING

A high-security combination lock is wired up to nuclear warheads that threaten to destroy the whole world. The bombs will be detonated unless several dials are set to a very precise configuration of values. Miraculously, it turns out that the dials are delicately set within the tiny range that deactivates the bombs. Had they differed ever so slightly from their actual positions, all life would be gone. Is this just a lucky accident or might they have been adjusted that way on purpose?

The fanciful story is in certain respects analogous to the view presented by many contemporary physical cosmologists. We are told that our universe is "fine-tuned for life." What is meant is roughly the following. For life to have any chance of evolving, the universe must meet certain conditions. It turns out that these conditions are extremely stringent. Had the values of various physical constants differed ever so slightly from their actual values, the universe would not have been hospitable to life. It is said that these crucial constants could easily have taken different values. If we were to witness another Big Bang, the new universe it created would almost certainly be a rather boring one. It might collapse within seconds, or contain nothing but hydrogen, or nothing but black holes. There is only the tiniest chance that the crucial particle masses and force strengths would take the precise values required for life to emerge. While there is room for controversy over the details, the picture sketched here is widely endorsed by experts in the field. Our question is what philosophical implications this might have.

To say that our universe is "fine-tuned" in this sense is not to imply that there is a Fine-Tuner, an intelligent agent who had a hand in setting the values of the physical constants. It is just to say that these constants happen to fall in the narrow range required for life to exist. However, that our universe meets the stringent conditions for life has been taken as the basis for a contemporary version of the argument from design. There are many ways that such an argument can be developed in detail. I will consider just one way, which focuses on *explanation*. Here is an outline of the argument.

Fine-Tuning Argument (FTA)

1. If a fact E that we observe stands in need of explanation, and hypothesis H provides a satisfactory explanation of E that is better than any alternative explanation available, then E provides significant evidential support for H.

2. That our universe is hospitable to life stands in need of explanation.

3. That God adjusted the constants in order to allow for life to develop provides a satisfactory explanation for why our universe is life-permitting.

4. There is no comparably satisfying explanation of this fact available.

5. Therefore, that our universe is life-permitting provides significant evidential support for theism.

First, a couple of general points about this argument. The conclusion of this argument is not that there *is* a God, or even that all things considered it is most reasonable to believe that there is. The argument seeks only to establish an evidential connection between certain observed facts and theism. This makes the conclusion somewhat modest while far from trivial. Any assessment of theism will have to consider various considerations for and against. The FTA just focuses on one such consideration. Second, the FTA as presented here concerns the existence of God. Often, discussions of cosmological fine-tuning focus on the more modest *design hypothesis:* that some kind of intelligent agent or agents influenced the values of the constants. (Theism is a specific version of the design hypothesis.) It can make sense to frame the issue this way, as the attributes of God according to traditional theism go well beyond what is required to explain the fine-tuning facts. Nevertheless, our focus here is on an argument for the existence of God, and insofar as the data support the existence of a designer they will also support the existence of God, even if much more is involved in an assessment of theism.

Let's consider the premises in turn. Premise 1 states a general principle of evidential support, a version of what is called *inference to the best explanation.* The idea is a familiar one. Among the myriad facts that a detective is faced with, some stand out and compel her to ask "Why?" The plausibility of her case hinges on how well her hypothesis can explain these various clues. Similarly, we can't *see* electrons the way we do tables and chairs, and we weren't around to observe the origin of species. Why then should we believe in electrons or evolutionary theory? Because they provide the most satisfying explanation of certain striking facts that we do observe.

There is a distinction being appealed to here between facts that *stand in need* of explanation and those that don't. Some situations rightly compel us to ask *why* things are like so. We are compelled because we think there surely is some answer. For others, an appropriate response may be, "That's just the way things are." Suppose I spill some soapy water and it splatters in some arbitrary shape on the floor. It need not have landed in the very shape that it did. There are indefinitely many possible puddle shapes that might have been formed. But the fact that it landed in *this* very pattern does not strike us as in special need of explanation. The water had to land in some way, and this is just one of many ways it could have landed. While it is possible that there is more to discover here, nothing about the shape of the puddle compels us to seek further answers. It is a different matter when the soapy water is blown through a wire ring. Now a thin film of liquid forms a perfect sphere. Even without any understanding of chemistry and physics, we are compelled to ask why it formed in this way. We have no doubt that there is some deeper explanation for why this occurred than that it just turned out that way. It is scarcely credible to be told, "Well, it had to be in some shape, and on this occasion it happened to form a perfect sphere."

It needn't redound to the credit of a hypothesis that it can explain some fact that didn't strike us as needing explanation in the first place. We find some alphabet tiles scattered on the table reading "ANOW AWNVIUUEPOBN VNJSKNVJKEWN AJKFN." Might some undiscovered law of physics determine that they be arranged thus? More plausibly, might someone have arranged them to form a coded message? Perhaps. But their configuration gives us little reason to believe any such hypothesis, as their arrangement doesn't require much of an explanation in the first place. Finding the letters "O THAT THIS TOO TOO SOLID FLESH WOULD MELT THAW AND RESOLVE ITSELF INTO A DEW" is a different matter. It would be crazy to believe that the pieces happen to be arranged in this manner for no reason. Of course, in this case the obvious explanation is that someone arranged them in order to spell a line from *Hamlet*. To the extent that this gives a satisfying explanation, we have reason to suppose that it is true.

The last point to note concerning the principle is that the degree of support that a hypothesis enjoys depends on how it compares with alternative explanations. The papers on my desk are not where I left them. Why? They could hardly move around by themselves. Perhaps an intruder was rifling through my stuff. This might well explain it, although it leaves us with the question of how he managed to get into a locked room on the ninth floor when there are no signs of forced entry. I notice the window is slightly ajar. A simpler explanation might be that a gust of wind blew the papers out of place. Only insofar as this provides a satisfying explanation is the case for an intruder diminished. I notice further that my financial documents are all left in one pile. The intruder hypothesis may explain this in a way that the wind cannot. And this might make it the more plausible hypothesis despite its other difficulties.

Does the fact that the universe is suitable for life stand in need of explanation as premise 2 asserts? It is not easy to say in general how we assess whether something needs explanation. In most cases, it is just obvious. We don't need to apply some theory to see that spherical soap bubbles and meaningful strings of alphabet tiles require explanation. Rightly or wrongly, the cosmological fine-tuning argument strikes many scientists and philosophers the same way (including many with no sympathy for theism or any design hypothesis). If the fine tuning of the constants does not strike you this way, then this version of the FTA may have little appeal for you. While there isn't space here for a detailed argument that cosmological fine-tuning does call for an explanation, we can make some suggestive points. First, without some further explanation, the fine tuning of our universe is thought to be extremely *improbable*. If we were to witness a new Big Bang, we should firmly expect it *not* to produce anything like a universe with stable stars and planets and enough of the right elements for life. But while this is part of what makes something call for an explanation, it can't be the whole story. It is highly unlikely that by tossing a handful of alphabet tiles on the table, we will see the sequence "ANOW AWNVIUUEPOBN VNJSKNVJKEWN AJKFN," since there are trillions of possible sequences of that length. But this hardly calls for an explanation. Typically, those facts that do call for explanation involve some further significant feature that makes them stand out among the alternative possibilities. The spherical soap bubble is a *simple geometrical figure*; most possible shapes of water are irregular splatters. The line from *Hamlet* is *meaningful*; most such sequences are gibberish. Perhaps what makes a universe with *life* stand out is that it is *valuable*, morally and aesthetically. Most of the possible outcomes of a Big Bang are pretty bleak, just vast lifeless space with some simple atoms floating about. That against all odds we have the vast panoply of living creatures we find here can seem extraordinary.

Before turning to consider possible explanations of fine tuning, let's briefly consider a common suggestion as to why we shouldn't find it remarkable in the first place. It is sometimes said that we shouldn't be surprised that we find the constants to be fine-tuned for life, since if they weren't, we wouldn't be here to observe them. Since we couldn't observe the constants taking other than life-permitting values, there is nothing puzzling about the fact that we find them to be so. The following story illustrates what is unsatisfying about this response. You are standing before a firing squad with fifty rifles aimed in your direction. To your astonishment, as the guns blast, each bullet flies close by you, leaving you unharmed. Why did all the bullets miss? Was it just an accident? Surely this cries out for explanation if anything does. It cannot help to be told, "Well, if they hadn't all missed you wouldn't be alive to see it." While this is true, it does nothing to remove the mystery of how the bullets all managed to miss you. Whatever appeal this suggestion has seems to rest on the confusion of thinking that our observations of the fine-tuned constants are somehow *inevitable*, and hence not in need of any further explanation. It was not inevitable that we would observe the constants to be fine-tuned. What was inevitable was just that *if* we were to observe the constants at all, we would find them to be fine-tuned for life. But there was a slim chance that we or anyone else would be around to observe anything at all. That we are here to observe our good fortune remains as puzzling as ever.

If the fine-tuning facts do require explanation, can theism provide a satisfactory explanation, as premise 3 claims? Let's begin by considering the positive case before addressing some objections. We explain phenomena by appeal to the actions of rational agents all the time. Why do the letter tiles spell a line from *Hamlet*? Why were the dials set to the very combination that disabled the nuclear warheads? Why are the financial documents on my desk sitting in one pile? In each case, the answer is that an agent brought matters about on purpose. Many such explanations are utterly compelling, as good as any explanation of anything.

Of course, in each of the last three cases, it is a familiar *human* agent that we have in mind. While everyone must grant that there are overwhelmingly plausible explanations that appeal to human agency, numerous objections have been raised to explanations invoking *divine* agency. We will briefly look at just two of these. First, there is thought to be something suspiciously *too easy* about invoking acts of God to explain some puzzling phenomenon. An omnipotent being can bring about anything. So no matter what we find, we could in principle just point to it and say, "God did that." This gives rise to the suspicion that such appeals are in some sense *empty*. The worry is sometimes expressed in the slogan "Whatever can explain anything explains nothing."

But of course humans are capable of arranging letter tiles in any possible sequence, dials in any configuration, and papers in any order. No matter how we found the letters, we could in principle say, "Someone put them like that." This observation does nothing at all to diminish the force of the explanation when the letters form meaningful sentences. The grain of truth behind the emptiness complaint might be illustrated by the following story. We read that some stranger Jane Smith just won the lottery. "Aha," I say. "What are the odds of that, given the millions that bought tickets? I'll bet the lottery was rigged in her favor. That would explain why *she* won out of all those players." One way to see what is silly about my conspiracy theorizing is to note that if Bob Brown or Suzie Jones had won instead, I could just as well have invoked a similar explanation to account for his or her good fortune. But what goes wrong here is not just that I *could* propose such an explanation no matter how the lottery turned out. The problem is that such an explanation is no more or less compelling in the case of Jane Smith's winning than in any other. Her having won no more *stands in need* of explanation than any other possible outcome would. And this can only show that it does not require an explanation at all. For it can hardly be that no matter how the lottery turned out, we would have reason to suppose that it was rigged. The crucial point is that there is nothing about Jane Smith that I'm aware of that makes *her* having won rather than someone else especially striking. Someone had to win, and it could just as well have been Smith as anyone else. It would be a different matter if she had won the last three lotteries or if she had just taken a senior position at the lottery commission.

The charge of explanatory emptiness may carry some force if the observed features of the universe are no more in need of explanation than any other possible features, and if we were no less inclined to invoke divine design regardless of how the universe was. But the possible outcomes of a Big Bang do not equally call for an explanation. If instead of a universe suitable for life the Big Bang had yielded nothing but a bland, lifeless cosmic soup, it would not strike us as in urgent need of explanation. Here it is significant that the existence of living creatures has value in a way that other possible outcomes do not. It is not unlikely that a benevolent, rational being would prefer a universe hospitable to living creatures over, say, one containing nothing but thinly dispersed hydrogen atoms. Note that for the explanation to be compelling, it is not necessary that on the basis of theism one could *predict* that the universe will be suitable for life, let alone that there will be creatures much like us. Supposing that a human agent is arranging some letter tiles hardly allows me to predict that they will spell "O THAT THIS TOO TOO SOLID FLESH WOULD MELT THAW AND RESOLVE ITSELF INTO A DEW." There are billions of possible sentences that an agent might produce. We can't even be so sure that the letters will form a *meaningful* string. This agent might just shuffle them about in meaningless ways that strike her fancy. Nevertheless, arranging the letters in a meaningful way is a plausible purpose that an agent might have. And that is enough to make a far more satisfying explanation than supposing that they fell in this order by accident. Similarly, if the creation of life is a plausible purpose that a rational agent might have, then theism may provide a satisfactory explanation of the fine tuning of the constants, one that is far more satisfying than supposing that it just happened by accident.

A second objection notes that when we invoke *human* agency to explain things, we understand quite well *how* this might occur, as we understand how humans function.

Humans have brains, a nervous system, muscles, and limbs. We understand how such a being can manipulate wooden tiles or fiddle with dials. We haven't the faintest grip on how a being like God can "set" the physical constants to within some range of values. To invoke God, the objection goes, is just to introduce a mystery and not to make any explanatory progress.

We can first note that the explanatory force of our appeal to human agents does not crucially depend on our understanding of human physiology. Long before we had the faintest clue as to how our brains and bodies work, we could understand that human agents were responsible for various phenomena we observed. A short conversation with someone is enough to make it abundantly clear that there is a thinking agent behind the sounds coming out of her mouth. This is just by far the most satisfying explanation of my observations even if I have no idea whether brains even exist let alone how they work or how mental activity is related to a physical body, or anything of the sort. To further evaluate the force of the current objection, it is useful to consider a hypothetical case. David Hume imagined there being a voice booming from the sky for everyone in the world to hear. We can elaborate the story and suppose that we also see the clouds shuffle about to create messages in all the languages on Earth. The voice provides us with all sorts of extraordinary information that we can verify to be correct. It gives us a detailed explanation of a cure for cancer. It makes amazingly precise predictions about future events such as the exact time and location of every raindrop over the next week. We are able to converse with the mystery voice, and it appears to reveal knowledge and intelligence orders of magnitude beyond what any human could have. Now I hardly have a better grasp of how an agent might do all of this than I do of how an agent might "fine-tune" the constants to permit life. But this would do little to blunt my conviction that somehow, some kind of agent vastly more powerful and intelligent than any human is behind the voice from the sky. I can perfectly well understand *why* we hear a voice in the sky (some kind of extraordinary agent is speaking) without much understanding of *how* this is achieved. I can similarly understand why the universe is life-permitting (God or some extraordinary agent made it so) without much of a grasp of how this could be done.

Even if theism can provide a satisfying explanation for the fine-tuning facts, the force of the argument will be diminished to the extent that there are plausible rivals. The argument is perhaps most vulnerable at premise 4, which claims that there is no comparably satisfying explanation available. What might an alternative explanation look like?

The most interesting proposal is that our universe is just one of very many universes, one part of a large "multiverse." The constants on which life depends may vary randomly among the universes. Given a large enough number of universes, it is to be expected that at least one such universe will meet the conditions for life. To illustrate, suppose we take a handful of alphabet pieces and drop them on the table. The letters form a string of gibberish. We try it again. Another (different) string of gibberish. We try it again. We repeat the process trillions of trillions of times until eventually we find a line from *Hamlet*. Amazing? Hardly. This sort of thing is bound to happen sometime if you repeat the process enough times. Similarly, the supposition that there have been many random "attempts" at a fine-tuned universe would appear to give a satisfying account of what would otherwise seem extraordinary.

Should we suppose that there are multiple universes? Some argue that the observed fine tuning of the universe itself provides evidence for the existence of a multiverse, just as others see it as evidence of divine design. There is reason to be dubious of this inference. Suppose we tossed the letter tiles and they spelled out a line from *Hamlet* on the first try. Does our observation give us reason to suppose that these pieces have been tossed on the table many times before by others or that there are millions of people out there similarly tossing letter tiles? Surely not. Even if such a multi-toss hypothesis were plausible to begin with, the surprising outcome that we have observed does nothing to support the hypothesis further. The crucial point here is that while the occurrence of multiple tosses makes it likely that the letters will land in a meaningful sequence on some occasion, it is no more likely that we will find such a sequence on the one toss that we observe. Similarly with the universes. That there are other universes out there makes it no more likely that we will find the one universe that we observed to be fine-tuned. Putting the matter in terms of explanation, the answer to the question "Why is the universe that we observe fine-tuned?" is not "Because there are lots of other universes." Even if they are out there, these universes have no bearing on what goes on in the universe that we see. So arguably, our observations of a fine-tuned universe provide no evidence for the existence of other universes.

There could, however, be independent theoretical grounds to believe in a multiverse. Cosmologists are divided on whether there are such grounds. And even proponents of the multiverse admit that the matter is highly speculative. Still, it is worth considering how the FTA fares in the event that we do have reason to believe in a multiverse, independently of the fine-tuning data. In this case, it does seem that the FTA is undermined. However, I would suggest that it is not premise 4 that is threatened in this case but premise 2. The existence of a multiverse does not *explain* but rather *removes the need to explain* the fine tuning of our universe. Once we suppose there are many universes, it is to be expected that at least one of these will be fine-tuned just by chance. The question of why it is that *this* one, the one that we inhabit, is fine-tuned loses its urgency. Like Jane Smith's winning the lottery, our universe could just as easily be a lucky one as any other, and there is nothing about our particular universe that makes it stand in special need of explanation.

I have hardly scratched the surface of the possible defenses, rebuttals, and replies concerning the premises of this argument, not to mention the other ways we might frame the whole issue. But I hope to have conveyed some of the intuitive force of the puzzle about fine tuning as an argument for theism. The argument, I would suggest, carries considerable force, although the verdict may ultimately depend on the credibility of the multiverse hypothesis.

TEST YOUR UNDERSTANDING

1. The cosmological fine-tuning argument begins from the observation that the fundamental laws of nature appear to be "fine-tuned" to permit the existence of life. Say what this means.

2. Some facts "require explanation," and others do not. Give examples to illustrate the distinction.

3. Give an example of an improbable fact that does not require explanation.

4. True or false: According to White, the existence of God is the only possible explanation for the fact that the laws of nature are hospitable to the existence of life.

NOTES AND QUESTIONS

1. The worst arguments for the existence of God go like this: "Here is some marvelous fact. Science can't explain it. Therefore God exists." These arguments are bad because science makes progress. At any given stage in the development of science, there will be facts that science cannot explain. But in many of these cases, the explanation will be just around the corner, and even when it isn't, the success of science gives us reason to think that scientific explanation is possible in principle. When we are confronted with a fact that science cannot explain, the rational response is almost always, "Let's wait and see." Why isn't the cosmological fine-tuning argument just another appeal to this **God of the gaps**?

2. The scientific basis for the cosmological fine-tuning argument is controversial. The key premise is a claim about the *fundamental* laws of nature, but we do not know the fundamental laws, so any such claim is at best conjectural. For a review of some of the relevant facts, see Paul Davies, *Cosmic Jackpot: Why Our Universe Is Just Right for Life* (Penguin, 2006).

Louise Antony (b. 1953)

Antony is Professor of Philosophy at the University of Massachusetts, Amherst. She specializes in the philosophy of mind and epistemology. She is the editor, most recently, of *Philosophers Without Gods: Meditations on Atheism and the Secular Life* (Oxford University Press, 2007).

NO GOOD REASON—EXPLORING
THE PROBLEM OF EVIL

There are many different ways to conceive of the divine, but according to one familiar conception, common to Judaism, Christianity, and Islam, there is exactly one deity—God—and this deity is eternal, omnipotent (all-powerful), omniscient (all-knowing), and perfectly good. I'll use the term *theism* to denote the view that God, so conceived, exists. I'll call those who accept this doctrine *theists* and those who deny it *atheists.* Theists believe that God, this being who is perfect in all respects, has complete dominion over the world in which we live; most believe he created it. But therein lies a problem: Is *this* world the kind of world we would expect from a perfect being?

The issue is *suffering.* Our world is full of suffering; it seems woven into the fabric of life. Every sentient being on the planet suffers, some almost incessantly. Physical suffering is entailed by a natural order that requires some animals to kill others in order to live, and all animals, predator and prey alike, lead lives governed by urgent but frequently unsatisfied biological needs. Much of the physical pain we suffer is the result of disease or injury—to which all animals are constantly vulnerable—but some of it is the natural accompaniment to perfectly healthy processes, like menstruation and childbirth. Creatures who are capable of emotion experience emotional pain: terror, sadness, and confusion. Complex psychologies make available new forms of pain: dread, hopelessness, anxiety, depression, guilt, shame, compulsions, hallucinations, and delusions. The human need for social connection makes nearly inevitable for us the searing pain of loss. How can all of this be squared with the supposition that an all-powerful being set things up with the well-being of His creatures in mind?

Considerations like these constitute what's often called the *problem of evil,* a problem that is regarded by believers and nonbelievers alike as posing a deep challenge to theism. Many atheists will say that it is this problem that convinced them that there was no God,[1] and many theists will admit that they have struggled with the problem themselves. I'm going to argue in this essay that in the end, the atheists are right: the problem of evil—or, as I will refer to it, the *problem of suffering*[2]—constitutes a strong enough argument against theism to justify atheism. But I want also to show that the matter is a little more complicated than some atheists realize.

---

1. Noted Bible scholar Bart D. Ehrman has given several interviews in which he explains that it was his work on the problem of suffering, in connection with his book *God's Problem,* that led to the loss of his Christian faith: see www.npr.org/templates/story/story.php?storyId=19096131 (transcript of part of an interview with Terry Gross on the radio program *Fresh Air*). For a video interview with Ehrman, see www.amazon.com/dp/B00125OKXU/ref=dp-kindle-redirect?_encoding=UTF8&btkr=1. Several philosophers in my edited volume, *Philosophers Without Gods* (Oxford University Press, 2007), cite the problem of suffering as the cause of their rejecting religion. See, for example, the essays by Stewart Shapiro ("Faith and Reason, The Perpetual War: Ruminations of a Fool"), Walter Sinnott-Armstrong ("Overcoming Christianity"), Edwin Curley ("On Becoming a Heretic"), and David Lewis ("Divine Evil").

2. I think the other name is misleading. "Evil" suggests that the only issue is suffering caused by the deliberate acts of a malicious person. But as my little survey of suffering was meant to show, there is a great deal of pain in our world that was not caused by any human agent. Philosophers acknowledge this by dividing "evil" into two kinds: *moral* evil is pain caused by deliberate human actions; *natural* evil is pain caused by anything else. I think it is clearer to just speak of the problem of suffering.

The Logical Argument from Suffering

Some atheists argue that the mere existence of suffering shows conclusively that there is no God.[3] That is, they argue that the characteristics standardly attributed to God—specifically, his moral goodness and his omnipotence—are logically incompatible with the toleration of suffering. Hume, in his *Dialogues Concerning Natural Religion*, attributes reasoning like this to the ancient philosopher Epicurus, paraphrasing him thus:

> Is [God] able, but not willing? Then he is malevolent. Is he willing, but not able? Then he is impotent. Is he both able and willing? Whence then, is evil?

Now a series of rhetorical questions is not yet an argument, but it's pretty easy to see what Hume had in mind. Here's one way of reconstructing the argument:

THE LOGICAL ARGUMENT FROM SUFFERING

(1) No morally good being would allow suffering if he or she were able to prevent it. ["No Tolerance"]

(2) An omnipotent[4] being would always be able to prevent suffering.

(3) THEREFORE, if there were a morally good, omnipotent being, there would be no suffering.

(4) There is suffering.

(5) THEREFORE, there is no being who is both morally good and omnipotent.

This argument is valid, and many atheists find it completely convincing. But they shouldn't. The argument is not sound; its first premise is false. We can see this from everyday experience.

Consider the following case: A loving parent (who we will call "Parent") follows the guidance of child-care experts and disciplines his child ("Child") by allowing her to experience the "natural consequences" of her actions. On one occasion, Child leaves a favorite toy outside overnight, ignoring Parent's warning that doing so might result in damage to the toy. Indeed, there is a terrible rainstorm that night; the toy is buffeted by the winds and pelted by the rain. The next morning Child finds the toy in ruins, its delicate mechanism shattered. Child is disconsolate.

---

3. For example, Sam Harris and Neil deGrasse Tyson. See Harris's "There is No God (And You Know It)" at www.huffingtonpost.com/sam-harris/there-is-no-god-and-you-k_b_8459.html and DeGrasse Tyson's comments on religion at www.huffingtonpost.com/entry/neil-degrasse-tyson-talks-god-aliens-and-multiverses_us_561297abe4b0dd85030c97fc for representative statements.

4. Here, and in what follows, I'm going to treat omniscience as a power, and thus as included in omnipotence, just to make it easier to state the arguments.

Now let us suppose further that Parent foresaw all of this. He realized, when the storm first threatened, what damage it would do to the toy. Parent also knew how upset Child would be to find it ruined. Parent could have spared Child the pain—all he would have had to do was run out to the backyard and retrieve the toy before the storm hit—but he allowed it.

What's the verdict about Parent? I hope you will agree that Parent was not wrong to leave the toy where Child abandoned it. Parent's purpose in mindfully ignoring the toy was to teach Child a lesson—a valuable one—about the consequences of negligence. Had Parent intervened, he would have spared Child the pain of losing her favorite plaything, but at the cost of allowing her to persist in behavior that might eventually lead to much worse suffering down the road. Had Parent intervened, Child might have remained ignorant of important structural features of her world—like the strength of wind and the fragility of toys—that make it necessary to care for the things one values. Given the importance of this lesson for Child's future happiness, we might even go so far as to say that Parent actually had a *duty* to take the steps necessary to impart it.

Clearly then, the Principle of No Tolerance is false. There *are* circumstances in which a morally good being might choose to allow suffering that he or she could have prevented.

But maybe we were just careless in the phrasing of premise (1). Let's see if we can repair the logical argument by reformulating the first premise, to take account of the considerations that came to light in our story. Basically what emerged is that a morally good being might justifiably permit an instance of suffering that he could have prevented, as long as he had a *good reason* for doing so. So let's build that condition into our revised principle. That would gives us:

THE PRINCIPLE OF NO TOLERANCE UNLESS

(1*) No morally good being would allow suffering if he or she were able to prevent it *unless* he or she had a *good reason* to permit it.

This principle is much more plausible than No Tolerance, and it does protect the argument from mundane counterexamples such as our story of the damaged toy. But this revision marks the beginning of the end for the Logical Argument.

Notice that if we simply replace premise (1) with premise (1*), then the resulting argument is not valid—we cannot derive (3) from (1*) and (2). The Principle of No Tolerance Unless opens up a logical loophole. To close it, the atheist would have to add a premise like this:

NO GOOD REASON

(2.5) There is no good reason that a morally good, omnipotent being could have to allow suffering.

Putting all this together, we get what we could call "The Weakened Logical Argument":

THE WEAKENED LOGICAL ARGUMENT FROM SUFFERING

(1*) No morally good being would allow suffering if he or she were able to prevent it, unless he or she had a good reason to permit it. ["No Tolerance Unless"]

(2) An omnipotent being would always be able to prevent suffering.

(2.5) There is no good reason that a morally good, omnipotent being could have to allow suffering. ["No Good Reason"]

(3) THEREFORE, if there were a morally good, omnipotent being, then there would be no suffering.

(4) There is suffering.

(5) THEREFORE, there is no being who is both morally good and omnipotent.

Now we have a valid argument again, but we've strayed far from the original terms of the Logical Argument. The atheist was supposed to show that it was *inconceivable* how suffering could be tolerated by an omnipotent, morally good being, and she was supposed to do this by showing how the nonexistence of suffering could be derived from the theist's own conception of God. But No Good Reason goes well beyond the theist's definition. It makes a substantive claim about God's motives, and one that is by no means obviously true.

The theist will point out that even in the realm of the human, we are never in a position to say *for sure* that someone acted without good reason. They will point out—quite reasonably, I think—that we cannot tell from the superficial appearance of a situation what the moral facts are. Suppose you saw someone plunging a penknife into the throat of another person. There's no reason that could justify an action like that, right? Wrong! It *might* turn out that the "victim" was choking to death and needed an emergency tracheotomy, which the "assailant," who happened to be a surgeon, was fortunately able to perform. What this shows, the theist might argue, is that situations can turn out to be complicated in ways that one wouldn't have anticipated, and these complications can make a decisive difference to our understanding of the moral dimensions of the case.[5]

I think the atheist should concede that the Logical Argument is a failure; the theist does not violate logic in believing that there is a morally good, omnipotent being in a world that also contains suffering. But the failure of the Logical Argument doesn't mean that the problem of suffering has been solved. The atheist will note that while there is no *contradiction* in supposing that a morally good, omnipotent being would have a good reason for tolerating suffering, it is still very difficult to see what such a reason might be. If the atheist can show that there are *good grounds* for believing that no such reason exists, then she will have shown that there are good grounds for denying that God exists.

---

5. This is not the same strategy as one that is called *skeptical theism*. Proponents of this position contend that we human beings are *generally* unable to judge what is right and what is wrong because we may well be *forever* ignorant of important moral goods. In contrast, the strategy I'm outlining above takes for granted that we would be able to *recognize* a good reason if it were presented to us.

An Evidential Argument from Suffering

What the atheist needs to do, then, is modify her strategy. She can't show that the existence of suffering *proves* that there is no God, but perhaps she can show that the existence of suffering provides very good *evidence* that there is no God. She cannot say that the principle No Good Reason is *certainly* true, but perhaps she can give grounds for thinking that it is *very probably* true.[6] So let's consider the following argument:

AN EVIDENTIAL ARGUMENT FROM SUFFERING

(1*)　No morally good being would fail to prevent suffering if he or she were able to prevent it, unless he or she had a good reason to permit it. ["No Tolerance Unless"]

(2)　An omnipotent being would always be able to prevent suffering.

(2.5)　*Probably,* there is no good reason that a morally good, omnipotent being could have for failing to prevent suffering. ["No Good Reason"]

(3)　THEREFORE, if there were a morally good, omnipotent being, then *probably* there would be no suffering.

(4)　There is suffering.

(5)　THEREFORE, *probably* there is no being who is both morally good and omnipotent.

Let's see how this argument fares.

The atheist should start by explaining what it is for someone to have a "good reason" for permitting suffering. In our story, Parent's reason for allowing Child to suffer was that Parent wanted to teach Child an important lesson, and allowing her to experience the painful consequences of her own negligence was the only way to do it.[7] What makes this a *good* reason?

First of all, Parent acted on the basis of a morally laudable goal—sparing Child great pain and disappointment in the future. It's vital to our moral assessment of Parent's actions that we are able to endorse this goal as a good one. But it's also important that we can recognize it as *sufficiently* important to warrant the suffering that Parent allowed Child to endure. Suppose that the only reason Parent failed to retrieve the toy before the rains came was that Parent did not want to interrupt a story that his spouse was telling. In this case, I think, we would judge Parent harshly. While it is laudable

---

6. This may seem like a substantial concession, but it isn't. In every discipline besides mathematics, probability is sufficient. Physicists and chemists do not establish their results with perfect certainty. They show that they are highly probable given the evidence. If the atheist can show that the nonexistence of God is highly probable in the same sense in which the basic facts of chemistry are highly probable, the atheist wins.

7. Notice that we don't have to say that Child *deserved* to suffer *because* she acted negligently. This might have been the justification Parent used, but in this story it's not the reason for which Parent acted as she did. I've taken punishment out of the picture because it could only help the theist in explaining a small part of the suffering that we observe. It cannot possibly be God's reason for permitting the suffering of non-human animals. They are not morally responsible agents and so cannot be blamed for their actions.

to attend to a spouse's story without interruption, doing so is not important *enough*. The momentary frustration that someone might experience at having to postpone a punchline (and I take that seriously, I assure you!) is simply not comparable to the sadness Child will suffer when she discovers that her favorite toy is ruined. We also have to consider the *fairness* of Parent's action—it's important that Parent's goal is *Child's* well-being. It would be wrong for Parent to allow Child's toy to be ruined simply in order to show an older sibling what happens if you are negligent. Although teaching Sibling an important lesson is a morally laudable goal, Parent would not be justified in causing distress to *Child* in order to achieve it. That would be unjust.

So the first requirement that would have to be met for God to have a good reason for permitting the amount of suffering we observe in the world is that that reason would have to be very, very, *very* important, because we are talking about an *enormous* amount of suffering. Consider just the suffering of non-human animals. As I noted at the beginning, hunger, fear, exhaustion, and violence are a regular part of their everyday experience. What moral goal could justify the creation of a natural order where this is so? It could not be the imparting of an important lesson to the animals, because most if not all of them are incapable of the kind of reasoning they'd need to learn it and benefit from it. And it could not be the imparting of a lesson to *us*, because it would be unjust to make the non-human animals suffer in order to benefit the human ones.

Well, how about this as a surpassingly important moral goal: eternal bliss? Couldn't it be that the whole of earthly existence—including all the suffering—is a necessary part of God's plan to bring his creatures into eternal union with him in heaven?[8] I agree that eternal bliss would be a very, very, *very* important moral goal. And perhaps it could be part of the story (to finesse the question of justice) that the non-human animals get to go to heaven, too. But now we get to a different problem—what kind of "necessity" could there be that compels God to use suffering to achieve his goal?

Parent, recall, is constrained to pursue his morally laudable goal against a background of constraints that he did not choose and that he could not alter. He wants Child to live as healthy and as happy a life *as possible*, given the factors that structure human life. Parent cannot alter the physical and psychological contingencies that make it necessary for him to decide between the small, local suffering entailed by the loss of the toy and the potentially greater future suffering to which Child is vulnerable if she doesn't learn to take care of her things. Parent cannot alter the conditions under which material things decay, nor can he alter the laws of human psychology that make harsh experience not only the best but often the only possible teacher. Thus, while Parent could act to prevent that one particular bit of suffering, he cannot do so without exposing Child to the risk of greater suffering in the future. Parent cannot prevent Child's ever suffering at all.

All this is true for Parent, but none of it is true for *God*. God is not just any morally good agent—God is an *omnipotent* morally good agent. Parent's reason for permitting Child to suffer was that it was necessary in order for Child to learn a morally valuable lesson. But God has options that Parent didn't have. God *could* arrange things so that it

---

8. See Eleonore Stump, "The Problem of Evil," later in this chapter. See also Peter van Inwagen, *The Problem of Evil* (Oxford University Press, 2006).

never matters to Child's happiness whether she is responsible or not, maybe by assigning a Super Guardian Angel to follow Child around for the rest of her life, miraculously protecting toys, books, musical instruments, and anything else threatened by Child's carelessness. Alternatively, God could have altered Child's psychology so that she accepted without question the counsel of her Parent, without needing to experience the harsh consequences of ignoring it. In the same vein, God could simply arrange it so that, when the time comes, Child simply *knows* the consequences of negligence without having had to learn them from experience. Finally, God could have arranged for toys, and other precious things, to be made out of indestructible materials. In short, God cannot shift the blame in the ways that Parent can.

In what sense, then, could the suffering of non-human animals be *necessary* for God to achieve his aim of bringing human creatures to eternal bliss? It is plausible that it was *biologically* necessary for the emergence of human animals that there be a long—*really* long—period of evolution in our past, with all the suffering for prehistoric non-human animals that entails. But God, as an omnipotent being, can bend biology to his will. Indeed, what biology *is* is dependent on God's will—*he's* the one who makes the laws of biology in the first place. Facts of nature of the sort that constrain Parent and structure his choices are as nothing to an omnipotent being. It's very difficult to see what kind of "necessity" could force God to trade off suffering now for greater happiness later.

The theist might respond by saying that there *is* a kind of necessity that can constrain even an omnipotent being: *logical* necessity. No one, not even God, can make it the case both that there are spiders and that there are no spiders. (Tip: If *you* ever get to choose, go for no spiders.) That's because it's logically impossible for spiders to both exist and not exist. There simply is no such possible state of affairs. Not being able to bring about such a state of affairs seems consistent with God's being omnipotent, for it's hardly a limitation on his power to be unable to bring about a state of affairs that cannot—because logic says it cannot—be brought about.

But how does this help the theist? There are two possible ways. First, there is what's called the *free will defense*. According to this line of thought, free will is something of surpassingly important moral value. (Let's suppose that that is so.[9]) But in order for God to create beings with free will, he must refrain from interfering with the actions they freely choose to perform. Of course human beings, many times, choose to do things that cause suffering. God *cannot* prevent this suffering, because to do so he would have to ensure that we choose one way rather than another, and that would be the same thing as revoking our free will. So God has no choice in this matter—there is no possible situation in which God both grants us free will and ensures that we make good choices.

Much has been written for and against the free will defense.[10] One objection, which you likely will have anticipated, is that human free will cannot be a good reason for

---

9. One could ask, of course, what makes free will *so* valuable that it warrants all of the suffering it is supposed to entail. For discussion, see A. Plantinga, "The Free Will Defense," in his *God and Other Minds* (Cornell, 1967).

10. The free will defense is part of Peter van Inwagen's response to the problem of evil; see *The Problem of Evil* (Oxford University Press, 2006). Important criticisms of the free will defense have been made by William L. Rowe, "The Problem of Evil and Some Varieties of Atheism," *American Philosophical Quarterly* 16 (1979): 335–41, and David Lewis, "Evil for Freedom's Sake," *Philosophical Papers* 22 (1993): 149–72.

permitting the vast amounts of animal suffering that human beings had nothing to do with or the human suffering that is due to natural forces (think volcanoes, hurricanes, earthquakes) rather than to human choice. But maybe the strategy behind the free will defense (i.e., appealing to *logical* necessity as a source of "constraint" on even the omnipotent) can be employed to show us how God might have had a good reason for permitting even non-human-caused suffering.

Here's how the story might go: just as it may be difficult to give a moral assessment of a situation when we know little about it, it can be difficult to give a *logical* assessment of a situation when we know little about it. There can be coherent *descriptions* of a state of affairs that, once we know a bit more, turns out to be impossible. Consider poor Oedipus. Oedipus *thought* that the following described a possible state of affairs: "I will marry Jocasta, and I won't marry my mother." But as he discovered later, to his horror, there was no such possible state of affairs. Jocasta *was* his mother, so it was impossible for him to marry Jocasta and not marry his mother.[11] Similarly, the theist might continue, the descriptions we give of situations that we think are perfectly possible, and that God therefore could easily have brought about, may turn out to refer to situations that cannot possibly exist. It may seem to us that God could have designed human anatomy in such a way that childbirth was not painful to women. But that may only be because "women give birth without pain" looks like a self-consistent description. Maybe, if we knew all the facts, we would see that there is something about women, or childbirth, or pain that connects them necessarily, just as Jocasta turns out to be connected necessarily to Oedipus's mother. Maybe, in fact, *all* the laws of nature are connected in such a way that if God created *any* material world at all, he'd *have* to create one like this.

I think that the atheist has to concede, as she did earlier in our discussion of moral assessment, that we cannot be sure, from a surface description of a situation, that it has the features that it appears to have. But where has this concession gotten us? The atheist has already given up the *logical* argument from suffering; she admits that there *could be* a good reason for God to permit the suffering we observe around us. Right now we are concerned with what it is *reasonable* to believe, not with what is merely possible. Yes, the person stabbing someone with a penknife *could*, for all we've observed so far, be a surgeon performing a life-saving operation. But what are the *chances*?

If we were asked in the abstract "Could a loving Parent possibly allow his child's favorite toy to be ruined, when he could easily have saved it?" we might initially say no. But as soon as someone mentioned the possibility that Parent was trying to teach Child a lesson, we'd quickly change our mind. Yes, of course, we'd say—we didn't think of that. Parent might have had a good reason after all. Seeing the possible reason for it, we can easily see Parent's behavior in a different light.

But now let's suppose we get some *more* information. Child testifies, credibly, that Parent never warned her about the consequences of leaving her toy out in the rain, and that she, Child, didn't know what those consequences would be. Maybe Parent himself admits the truth of all this. Suppose, further, that you learn that there was, in fact, no rainstorm. Parent, it turns out, deliberately activated the sprinkler system and allowed it

---

11. In Sophocles's play *Oedipus the King*, Oedipus, who has been raised abroad by adoptive parents, returns as an adult to his hometown and unwittingly marries his biological mother.

to run throughout the night. Discoveries of this sort continue, and the more you learn, the more unsettled you become. It emerges that there have been a host of incidents throughout Child's short life in which Parent did things that good parents never do. Once, Child was beaten severely for setting the table incorrectly. Another time, Parent arranged for a neighbor to offer Child a type of luscious candy that Child had been specifically forbidden to eat; when Child (predictably) succumbed to temptation, Parent punished her by locking her out of the house, forcing her to sleep in a dangerous back alley where she was vulnerable to vermin and desperate drug addicts. In light of all this new evidence, you conclude that you were right in the first place: Parent is a very *bad* parent.

At this point, it would be grotesque for someone who wanted to defend Parent simply to point out that there is surely *some possible* reason a good parent might have had for doing all the things that Parent has done, and that perhaps Parent had no choice but to do the things he did. You don't deny that it is *possible* that such a reason exists—you cannot prove that it doesn't. It is, however, a *mystery* what such a reason could be. The details of the case raise particular sticking points, such as: How could an etiquette mistake warrant a *beating*? How could it be that Parent had *no* option but to expose Child to mortal danger? And since the danger is mortal, what greater good could the punishment serve? If Parent's defender cannot give us a substantive candidate reason, one that addresses these and the many other questions that can be raised about the case, then we are justified in concluding that *probably*, Parent is bad.

The situation, I contend, is the same with God. When we confront seriously the amount of suffering in the world (fawns dying in fires, children struck with painful illness, adults enduring pointless depression) and consider the way it is distributed (afflictions heaped disproportionately on the poor and the vulnerable), I think the rational conclusion to draw is that there is no good reason for it. A good reason would have to be one that involved a surpassingly important moral goal, where the achievement of that goal required, in a sense strong enough to constrain an omnipotent being, the mass of suffering we see in the world around us. It's not enough for the theist to insist that there *could* be such a reason or to point out that we haven't proved that there *couldn't* be such a reason: the theist has to show us what such a reason might be. And if the theist cannot? Then the Evidential Argument from Suffering succeeds.

TEST YOUR UNDERSTANDING

1. What's the difference between the *logical* argument from suffering and the *evidential* argument from suffering?

2. Does Antony accept the logical argument from suffering?

3. According to Antony, what's wrong with the following response to the problem of suffering? "Good parents sometimes allow their children to suffer in order to teach them important lessons. God allows us to suffer for the same reason."

4. True or false: According to Antony, theists can be satisfied with the conclusion that there *could be* a reason for God to allow suffering.

NOTES AND QUESTIONS

1. *The problem of animal suffering.* Most discussions of the problem of evil focus on the suffering of human beings. Antony follows William Rowe in emphasizing the suffering of animals as well. Rowe's example:

   > Suppose in some distant forest lightning strikes a dead tree, resulting in a forest fire. In the fire a fawn is trapped, horribly burned, and lies in terrible agony for several days before death relieves its suffering. So far as we can see, the fawn's intense suffering is pointless. (Rowe, "The Problem of Evil and Some Varieties of Atheism," *American Philosophical Quarterly* 16 [1979]: 338)

   This has the advantage of blocking most of the usual responses to the problem. Animal suffering cannot be justified on the ground that it is a consequence of the exercise of free will or because it serves to bring animals closer to God, since according to most theological traditions, animals do not possess free will and are incapable of union with God.

   Exercise: Construct a response to the argument from animal suffering on behalf of the theist. Any such response will point to a plausible, morally sufficient reason for God to allow animals to suffer.

2. *The free will defense.* According to the **free will defense**, God allows suffering because (a) it's good for human beings to possess free will, and (b) if we are to possess free will, God cannot prevent us from making bad choices and harming others. As Antony notes, this does not explain why God allows suffering due to *natural* causes. But we might ask whether the free will defense succeeds even in the limited task of explaining why God allows suffering due to human choices.

   Suppose Jones is about to attack Smith, and you pull Smith to safety at the last minute. You have frustrated Jones's plan. But have you interfered with his free *will*? No. Jones made his choice freely, and you did not prevent him from doing that. You simply protected Smith from the harm that Jones's free choice would have caused.

   Why doesn't God do likewise? Without limiting anyone's capacity for free choice, he could still protect the innocent from the evil choices of others (e.g., by putting an invisible shield around us that would prevent others from harming us without good reason). A good parent would certainly protect her child in this way if she could. But God doesn't do this. Isn't that compelling evidence that a good God does not exist?

   Question: Imagine what it would be like to live in a world in which we were protected from human evil in this way. Would such a world be worse in any way? If not, does this show that the free will defense fails on its own terms?

3. Consider the following response to Antony:

   > If God eliminated suffering altogether, human beings would not need one another. Children would not depend on their parents for their basic needs, since God would provide if the parents didn't. People would not depend on friends and family for care and compassion, since we only need care

and compassion because we suffer. God leaves us vulnerable to suffering because some of the most valuable human relationships are only possible if we are vulnerable. God lets us suffer because if he didn't, love and friendship (which involve care and compassion) would be impossible.

How might Antony respond?

Eleonore Stump (b. 1947)

Eleonore Stump is a Robert J. Henle Professor of Philosophy at St. Louis University. She specializes in medieval philosophy and the philosophy of religion. Her major works include a comprehensive study of the philosophy of Thomas Aquinas in *Aquinas* (2003) and *Wandering in Darkness: Narrative and the Problem of Suffering* (2010).

THE PROBLEM OF EVIL

The problem of evil traditionally has been understood as an apparent inconsistency in theistic beliefs.[1] Orthodox believers of all three major monotheisms, Judaism, Christianity, and Islam, are committed to the truth of the following claims about God:

(1) God is omnipotent;

(2) God is omniscient;

(3) God is perfectly good.

Reasonable people of all persuasions are also committed to this claim:

(4) There is evil in the world;

and many theists in particular are bound to maintain the truth of (4) in virtue of their various doctrines of the afterlife or the injunctions of their religion against evil. The view that (1)–(4) are logically incompatible has become associated with Hume in virtue of Philo's position in the *Dialogues Concerning Natural Religion*, though many other philosophers have maintained it.[2] . . . As other philosophers have pointed out, however, Philo's view that there is a logical inconsistency in (1)–(4) alone is mistaken.[3]

---

1. For a review of recent literature on the problem of evil, see Michael Peterson, "Recent Work on the Problem of Evil," *American Philosophical Quarterly* 20 (1983): 321–40. [Stump's note.]

2. David Hume's posthumously published *Dialogues Concerning Natural Religion* (1779) presents a wide-ranging critique of **natural religion:** the effort to defend theism on rational grounds. Philo is Hume's spokesman in the *Dialogues*.

3. Cf., e.g., Nelson Pike, "Hume on Evil," *The Philosophical Review* 72 (1963). [Stump's note.]

To show such an inconsistency, one would need at least to demonstrate that this claim must be true:

(5) There is no morally sufficient reason for God to allow instances of evil.

Since Hume, there have been attempts to solve the problem of evil by attacking or reinterpreting one of the first four assumptions. . . . [But] most attempts at solving the problem, especially recently, have concentrated on strategies for rejecting (5). . . . In this paper, I will develop in detail a solution of my own by presenting and defending a morally sufficient reason for God to allow instances of evil. . . .

II

. . . The problem of evil is generally presented as some sort of inconsistency in theistic beliefs, and (1)–(4) present the relevant theistic assumptions. And yet *mere* theists are relatively rare in the history of religion. Most people who accept (1)–(4) are Jews or Christians or Muslims. If we are going to claim that *their* beliefs are somehow inconsistent, we need to look at a more complete set of Jewish or Muslim or Christian beliefs concerning God's goodness and evil in the world, not just at that limited subset of such beliefs which are common to all three religions, because what *appears* inconsistent if we take a partial sampling of beliefs may in fact look consistent when set in the context of a more complete set of beliefs. I do not of course mean to suggest that an inconsistent set of propositions could become consistent if we add more propositions to it. My point is simple and commonsensical: that the appearance of inconsistency in a set of beliefs may arise from our interpretation of those beliefs, and our reinterpretation of them in light of a larger system of beliefs to which they belong may dispel the appearance of inconsistency. A more promising foundation for a solution to the problem of evil, then, might be found if we consider a broader range of beliefs concerning the relations of God to evil in the world, which are specific to a particular monotheism. . . .

In what follows I will focus on one particular monotheism, namely, Christianity; I do not know enough about Judaism or Islam to present a discussion of the problem of evil in the context of those religions. In fact, my account will not deal even with all varieties of Christian belief. Because my account will depend on a number of assumptions, such as that man has free will, it will present a solution to the problem of evil applicable only to those versions of Christianity which accept those assumptions. Christians who reject a belief in free will, for example, will also reject my attempt at a solution to the problem of evil.

Besides (1)–(4), there are three Christian beliefs that seem to me especially relevant to the problem of evil. They are these:

(6) Adam fell.

(7) Natural evil entered the world as a result of Adam's fall.

(8) After death, depending on their state at the time of their death, either (a) human beings go to heaven or (b) they go to hell.

It is clear that these beliefs themselves raise a host of problems, partly because they seem implausible or just plain false and partly because they seem to raise the problem of evil again in their own right. In this section I will consider worries raised by these beliefs themselves; in the next section I will argue that these three beliefs . . . provide a basis for a Christian solution to the problem of evil. . . . The applicability of this solution to monotheisms other than Christianity depends on whether they accept these beliefs.

It would, of course, make a difference to my solution if any of the beliefs added in (6)–(8) could be *demonstrated* to be false, and so I will devote this section of the paper primarily to arguing that though (6)–(8) are controversial and *seem* false to many people, they are not *demonstrably* false. The fact that the problem of evil is raised again by (6)–(8) in conjunction with (1)–(3) is also worrisome. If a solution to the problem of evil relies on (6)–(8) and (6)–(8) themselves raise the problem, the problem is not solved but simply pushed back a stage. If (6)–(8) are to serve as the basis for an effective solution, the appearance they give of being inconsistent with the existence of a good God must be dispelled; attempting to do so is my other main concern in this section. If I can show that these beliefs are not demonstrably false and are not themselves incompatible with belief in a good God, . . . it will then be possible for me in the next section to use (6)–(8) in my attempted solution to the problem of evil.

The Christian belief summarized as (8) appears to raise the problem of evil because it gives rise to questions such as these:

(Q1)   If an omnipotent God could bring it about that all human beings be in heaven and if a good God would want no human beings in hell, wouldn't a good, omnipotent God bring it about that all human beings be in heaven?

(Q2)   Even if an omnipotent God does not bring it about that all human beings be in heaven, how could a good omnipotent God allow any human beings to suffer torment in hell?

(Q3)   How could a good, just God decree that some human beings suffer torment for an infinite time for evils done during a finite human lifetime?

. . . I cannot do justice to these difficult questions in this paper; but . . . I can do enough, I think, to show that (8) can be interpreted in a way which significantly diminishes or dispels the appearance that it is incompatible with God's goodness.

To begin with, on Christian doctrine heaven should be understood not as some place with gates of pearl and streets of gold but rather as a spiritual state of union with God; and union with God should be understood to involve as a necessary (but not sufficient) condition the state of freely willing only what is in accordance with the will of God. This understanding of heaven . . . goes some way towards answering (Q1). If, as I think, . . . it is not logically possible for God to make human beings do anything freely, and if heaven is as I have described it, then it is not within God's power to ensure that all human beings will be in heaven, because it is not within his power to determine what they freely will.

An answer to (Q2) also can be sketched by looking more closely at the Christian doctrine being questioned. Hell is commonly regarded as God's torture chamber. . . . And yet even a cursory look at traditional Christian writings shows that this is a crude and simplistic account of the doctrine of hell. For example, Dante,[4] who has given perhaps the most famous Christian description of hell, includes as part of hell something like what Socrates was hoping for as otherworldly bliss:[5] a beautiful, bright place with green meadows and gentle streams in which the noblest and wisest of the ancients discuss philosophy.[6] This is part of Limbo, and on Dante's view it is in hell and fearsome. What makes Limbo awful is not physical tortures or spiritual torments, of which there are none, but rather the fact that the people there are separated from union with God and will always be so; and for Dante, I think, that is the fundamental awfulness of all the rest of the hell, too. . . .

On Dante's view, the essence of hell consists in the absence of union with God, a condition entailed by a person's psychological state which is a result of that person's free choices and which is naturally painful. (By a naturally painful psychological state I mean that human beings, in consequence of the nature they have, experience the state in question as painful. . . . Humiliation and grief seem to me examples of naturally painful psychological states.) On this view of hell . . . an answer to (Q2) might go along these lines. Everlasting life in hell is the ultimate evil which can befall a person in this world; but the torments of hell are the natural conditions of some persons, and God can spare such persons those pains only by depriving them of their nature or their existence. And it is arguable that, of the alternatives open to God, maintaining such persons in existence and as human is the best.

I am not arguing that this view of hell is the only one or even necessarily the right one for Christians to have; nor have I presented any argument for the account of human psychology on which this view is based. What I am claiming is that the view described here . . . has a place in traditional Christian theology and that a philosophical case could be made for it. For present purposes I will take the Dantean view as the Christian view of hell, and I will take (8) and all other talk of hell in this paper as referring to hell in the Dantean sense. . . .

The answer to (Q2), then, is also the answer to (Q3): on the Dantean view, hell is the natural state and, even understood as unending, it is arguably the best possible state of those whose free wills are not in conformity with the divine will, on the assumption that continued existence as a human being even with pain is more valuable than the absence of that pain at the cost of one's existence or human nature. . . .

The Christian belief in the fall of Adam, expressed in (6), has been interpreted in many ways. Some (but not all) of these interpretations are incompatible with the theory of evolution. . . . My solution, however, will rely on only a few elements which are common to many interpretations of (6) and not incompatible with the theory of evolution, namely, that

(6') (a) at some time in the past as a result of their own choices human beings altered their nature for the worse,

---

4. Dante Alighieri (1265–1321), Italian poet. Dante's *Inferno*, the first book of his *Divine Comedy* (1320), describes the poet's journey through hell.

5. Cf. Plato, *Apology* 41a–c, *Phaedo* 63b–c, 108a–c, 109b–114c. [Stump's note.]

6. *Inferno*, Canto IV. [Stump's note.]

(b) the alteration involved what we perceive and describe as a change in the nature of human free will, and

(c) the changed nature of the will was inheritable.

(6′) is compatible with the denial (as well as with the affirmation) that there once was a particular man named Adam who fell from a better to a worse state in consequence of a bad choice, but for the sake of convenience I will continue to refer to the events described in (6′) as "Adam's fall." Nothing in the theory of evolution entails the falsity of any part of (6′). . . .

Of course, the fact that the theory of evolution does not entail the falsity of (6) understood as (6′) does not rule out the possibility that (6) is demonstrably false for some other reason. The historical claim of (6′a) will strike many people as implausible, unsupported by evidence, the product of neurotic psychological forces, and so on. But although such reactions show that (6′) is controversial, they are of course not sufficient to show that (6′) is false. A more promising line of attack on (6′) involves (6′b) or (6′c). What a change in the nature of the will is supposed to be is unclear, but any sensible account of such a change would, it seems, have to be incompatible with the notion that such a change in the will is inheritable. A reply to this objection requires a closer examination of the traditional Christian understanding of the will and its post-fall alteration.

One of the classic expositions of this understanding is that given by Anselm[7]. . . . According to Anselm, human beings originally had wills disposed to will as they ought to will and an ability to preserve that disposition. This ability is what Anselm calls free will. On Anselm's view, free will is a strength. The capacity for either getting sick or staying healthy, Anselm would say, is not a strength, only the capacity to stay healthy is. Similarly, Anselm maintains that the ability to will what one ought to will or what one ought not to will is not a strength and cannot count as free will: only the ability to will what one ought to will is a strength and it alone is free will. Human beings in their pre-fall state could do evil because as finite beings they could be less than they had the strength to be. They could fail to use their strength to preserve the uprightness of their wills and so fall into evil. Adam's fall consists in such a failure. In consequence of past failure of this sort, human beings have lost their initial disposition to will what they ought to will and acquired instead a disposition to will what they ought not to will. This acquired disposition consists primarily of an inclination to will one's own power or pleasure in preference to greater goods; it was and is inheritable. Although human beings still have some sort of ability to do good after the fall, because of the disposition of their will they find it very difficult (but not impossible) to resist evil. To this extent, then, their free will (in Anselm's sense of "free will") is diminished.

The notion of a disposition of the will which is operative in this account needs to be understood in light of Anselm's unusual definition of free will. A free will is a will disposed to will the good and able to maintain such a disposition. In Aquinas's[8] development of Anselm's account, recognition of what is good is the job of reason; and the

---

7. Anselm of Canterbury (1033–1109), early medieval Christian philosopher and theologian.

8. Thomas Aquinas (1225–1274), medieval Christian philosopher and theologian.

righteous disposition of free will is a function of a right relationship among reason, the will, and desire.[9] For the will to be free, desire must be subject to reason, and reason must guide both the will and desire to what really is good. The post-fall disposition of the will is the result of a disordered relationship among these three. Desire is not subject to reason; often enough it governs reason instead. And rather than being guided by reason, the will tends to be moved by irrational desire, so that it wills an apparent or partial good rather than what is really or wholly good. This disordered relationship among reason, the will, and desire on Aquinas's view constitutes the change in the will produced by Adam's fall.[10] The original inclination of the will to will the good proposed by reason has been lost and replaced by an inclination to will what is sought as good by the appetites. These inclinations are inclinations of the will itself, not external constraints on the will; and they are only inclinations or tendencies. . . . Post-fall evil is voluntary, not compelled. On the other hand, this account lends plausibility to the claim that the altered disposition of the will is inheritable. What is said to be inherited is not a certain set of acts of will . . . but rather a weakened influence of reason and strengthened influence of appetite on the will, a loss of the will's natural inclination to follow reason. There is nothing obviously incoherent, as far as I can see, in supposing this change in the relationship of reason, will, and desire to be inheritable.

(6) also raises the problem of evil in [another way]:

(Q4)   Couldn't God have prevented the human race from inheriting this evil inclination of will after Adam's fall, by some miraculous intervention in human history if necessary?

. . . Without destroying any of his creatures, God could have prevented the transmission of a defective free will in any number of ways. He could have prevented procreation on the part of the defective people, for example, or he could miraculously have prevented the transmissible defect from actually being transmitted. But I think there are two things to be said against these alternatives. In the first place they constitute in effect the abrogation of God's first creation; they put an end to the first human beings God produced. If God were then to replace these human beings by others and they also corrupted their wills, God would then presumably replace them also, and so on, in what appears to be a series of frustrations and defeats inappropriate to a deity. It seems to me arguable that there is more power and dignity and also more love and care in restoring fallen humanity to a good state than in ending and replacing it. Secondly, Swinburne seems to me right in maintaining that what makes God's human creatures persons rather than pets is the ability to exercise their free will in serious choices.[11] If God immediately removed or prevented the consequences of any free choice eventuating in major evil, his creatures would not have that significant exercise of free will and would thus not be persons.

9. See, for example, Thomas Aquinas, *Summa Theologica* I, q. 82, articles 3–5, and q. 83, articles 1 and 3. [Stump's note.]

10. See, for example, *Summa Theologica* I–II, q. 82, articles 1 and 3. [Stump's note].

11. See Richard Swinburne, *The Existence of God* (Clarendon Press, 1979), pp. 200–24.

As for (7), it can be read in either of these two ways:

(7′) There were no diseases, tornadoes, droughts, etc. in the world until Adam's fall;

or

(7″) No person suffered from diseases, tornadoes, droughts, etc. until Adam's fall.

The weaker assumption, of course, is (7″), and it is all I need for my purposes here. The ways in which an omnipotent God might have brought about (7″) are limited only by one's imagination, and there is no need to specify any one of them here.

In this brief account of (6), (7), and (8), I cannot hope to have given either an adequate presentation of these doctrines or a sufficient answer to the questions they raise. But my sketchy treatment indicates, I think, both that none of these three beliefs is demonstrably false and that there are some reasonable arguments against the charges that (6) and (8) are themselves incompatible with God's goodness. Those results are enough to enable me to use (6)–(8) in an attempt to show how on Christian beliefs the existence of evil is compatible with the existence of an omnipotent, omniscient, perfectly good God.

III

According to the Christian beliefs summarized as (6), (7), and (8), all human beings since Adam's fall have been defective in their free wills, so that they have a powerful inclination to will what they ought not to will, to will their own power or pleasure in preference to greater goods. It is not possible for human beings in that condition to go to heaven, which consists in union with God; and hell understood in Dantean terms is arguably the best alternative to annihilation. A good God will want to fix such persons, to save them from hell and bring them to heaven; and as the creator of these persons, God surely bears some responsibility for fixing and saving them if he can. How is he to do so?

It seems to me clear that he cannot fix the defect by using his omnipotence to remove it miraculously. The defect is a defect in *free* will, and it consists in a person's generally failing to will what he ought to will. To remove this defect miraculously would be to force a person's free will to be other than it is; it would consist in causing a person to will freely what he ought to will. But it is logically impossible for anyone to make a person freely will something, and therefore even God in his omnipotence cannot directly and miraculously remove the defect in free will. . . .

If God cannot by his omnipotence directly fix the defect in free will, it seems that human beings must fix it themselves. Self-repair is a common feature of the natural world, but I do not think self-repair is possible for a person with post-fall free will. . . . To reform the will requires willing something different from what one previously willed; that is, it requires a change of will. But how to change the will is the problem in the first place. If we want to know whether a man himself can fix a defect in his will, whether he himself can somehow remove his tendency to will what he ought not to will, it is no help to be told that of course he can if he just wills to change his will. We know that a man *can* change his will for the better; otherwise his will would not be free. The problem with a defect in the will is not that there is an inability to will what one ought to will because of some external restraint on the will, but that one does not and will not will what one ought to will because the will itself is bent towards evil. . . . Self-repair, then, is no more a solution to the problem of a defective will than is God's miraculous intervention.

If God cannot and human beings will not fix the defect in their wills, what possible cure is there? Christianity suggests what seems to me the only remaining alternative. Let a person will that God fix his defective will. In that case, God's alteration of the will is something the person has freely chosen, and God can then alter that person's will without destroying its freedom. It is a fact well-attested in religious literature that people who find it next to impossible to will what (they believe) they ought to will may nonetheless find it in themselves to will that God alter their wills. Perhaps two of the most famous examples are the sonnet of John Donne in which he prays for God to overwhelm him so that he will be chaste and Augustine's prayers that God give him continence. The traditional formulation of the crucial necessary condition for a person's being a Christian . . . is that he wills God to save him from his sin; and this condition is, I think, logically (and perhaps also psychologically) equivalent to a person's willing that God fix his will. . . .

The fixing of a defective free will by a person's freely willing that God fix his will is, I think, the foundation of a Christian solution to the problem of evil. What sort of world is most conducive to bringing about both the initial human willing of help and also the subsequent process of sanctification?[12] To answer that question, we need to consider the psychological state of a person who wills God's help. Apart from the obvious theological beliefs, such a person must also hold that he tends to do what he ought not to do and does so because he himself wills what he ought not to will, and he must want not to be in such a condition. He must, in other words, have both a humbling recognition of himself as evil and a desire for a better state. So things that contribute to a person's humbling, to his awareness of his own evil, and to his unhappiness with his present state contribute to his willing God's help.

I think that both moral and natural evil make such a contribution. The unprevented gross moral evils in the course of human history show us something about the nature of man, and our own successful carrying out of our no doubt smaller-scaled evil wills shows us that we are undeniably members of the species. Natural evil—the pain of disease, the intermittent and unpredictable destruction of natural disasters, the decay of old age, the imminence of death—takes away a person's satisfaction with himself. It tends to humble him, show him his frailty, make him reflect on the transience of temporal goods, and turn his affections towards otherworldly things, away from the things of this world. No amount of moral or natural evil, of course, can *guarantee* that a man will seek God's help. If it could, the willing it produced would not be free. But evil of this sort is the best hope, I think, and maybe the only effective means, for bringing men to such a state.

That natural evil and moral evil, the successful carrying out of evil human wills, serve to make men recognize their own evils, become dissatisfied with things of this world,

---

12. Sanctification is the process of coming to will what God wills and so achieving union with God.

and turn to God is a controversial claim; and it is clear that a compelling argument for or against it would be very difficult to construct. To produce such an argument we would need a representative sample, whatever that might be, of natural and moral evil. Then we would need to examine that sample case by case to determine the effect of the evil in each case on the human beings who suffered or perpetrated it. To determine the effect we would have to know the psychological and moral state of these people both before and after the evil at issue (since the effect would consist in some alteration of a previous state); and we would have to chart their state for the rest of their lives after that evil because, like the effect of carcinogens, the effect of the experience of evil may take many years to manifest itself. Even with the help of a team of psychologists and sociologists, then, it would be hard to collect the data necessary to make a good argument for or against this claim. Hence, I am unable to present a cogent argument for one of the main claims of this paper, not because of the improbability of the claim but because of the nature of the data an argument for the claim requires. . . . Still, there is *some* historical evidence for it in the fact that Christianity has tended to flourish among the oppressed and decline among the comfortable, and perhaps the best evidence comes from the raising of children. The phrase "spoiling a child" is ambiguous in current parlance between "turning a child into a unpleasant person" and "giving a child everything he wants," and the ambiguity reflects a truth about human nature. The pains, the hardships, the struggles which children encounter tend to make them better people. Of course, such experiences do not invariably make children better; children, like adults, are also sometimes made worse by their troubles. But that fact would be a counterexample to the general claim about the function of evil in the world only in case it maintained that evil was *guaranteed* to make people better; and that is something this claim could not include and still be compatible with Christianity as long as Christianity is committed to the view that human beings have free will.

Someone may object here that the suffering of children is just what this attempted solution to the problem of evil cannot explain. In *The Brothers Karamazov,* Dostoevsky provides the most eloquent presentation this objection is likely ever to get, concluding with Ivan's passionate insistence . . . that even if the whole world could be saved for eternal bliss by the torture of one innocent child, allowing the torture of that child for that purpose would be horribly wrong.[13] I am in sympathy with the attitude Dostoevsky has Ivan express and in agreement with Ivan's conclusion. The suffering of children is in my view unquestionably the instance of evil most difficult for the problem of evil, and there is something almost indecent about any move resembling an attempt to explain it away. The suffering of children is a terrible thing, and to try to see it otherwise is to betray one's humanity. Any attempt to solve the problem of evil must try to provide some understanding of the suffering of children, but it must not lessen our pain over that suffering if it is not to become something monstrous and inhumane.

With considerable diffidence, then, I want to suggest that Christian doctrine is committed to the claim that a child's suffering is outweighed by the good for the child which can result from that suffering. This is a brave (or foolhardy) thing to say, and the risk inherent in it is only sharpened when one applies it to cases in which infants

---

13. Fyodor Dostoevsky (1821–1881), Russian novelist.

suffer, for example, or in which children die in their suffering. Perhaps the decent thing to do here is simply to sketch some considerations which may shed light on these hard cases. To begin with, it is important to remember that on Christian doctrine death is not the ultimate evil or even the ultimate end, but rather a transition between one form of life and another. From a Christian point of view, the thing to be avoided at all costs is not dying, but dying badly; what concerns the Christian about death is not that it occurs but that the timing and mode of death be such as to constitute the best means of ensuring that state of soul which will bring a person to eternal union with God. If children who die in their suffering thereby move from the precarious and frequently painful existence of this world to a permanently blissful existence in the other world and if their suffering was among part of the necessary means to effect that change, their suffering is justified. I am not trying to say here that the suffering which a child or any other person experiences is the only way in which that person could be brought to God. Rather, I am trying to avoid constructing the sort of explanation for evil which requires telling the sufferer that God lets him suffer just for the sake of some abstract general good for mankind. . . . It seems to me that a perfectly good entity who was also omniscient and omnipotent must govern the evil resulting from the misuse of . . . freedom in such a way that the sufferings of any particular person are outweighed by the good which the suffering produces *for that person*; otherwise, we might justifiably expect a good God somehow to prevent that *particular suffering* . . . by intervening (in one way or another) to protect the victim, while still allowing the perpetrator his freedom. . . . And since on Christian doctrine the ultimate good for persons is union with God, the suffering of any person will be justified if it brings that person nearer to the ultimate good in a way he could not have been without the suffering. I think that Christianity must take some such approach to the suffering or death of children. . . .

In all these hard cases, the difficulty of formulating a Christian position . . . will be diminished if we have clearly in mind the view of man Christianity starts with. On Christian doctrine, all human beings are suffering from the spiritual equivalent of a terminal disease; they have a defect in the will which if not corrected will cost them life in heaven and consign them to a living death in hell. Now suppose that we are the parents of a child with a terminal brain disease, which includes among its symptoms the child's rejecting the notion that he is sick and refusing to cooperate in any treatments. The doctors tell us that there are treatments which may well cure the child completely, but they hurt and their success is not guaranteed. Would we not choose to subject the child to the treatments, even if they were very painful? The child's suffering would be a terrible thing; we would and we should be grieved at it. But we would nonetheless be glad of the treatments and hope of a cure. And yet this example is only a pale reflection of what Christianity claims to be the case for all human beings, where the loss inflicted by the disease and the benefits of its cure are infinitely greater. If moral and natural evil contain an essential ingredient of a possible cure, surely the cure is worth the suffering such evil entails. . . .

Someone might also object here that this solution to the problem of evil prohibits us from any attempt to relieve human suffering and in fact suggests that we ought to promote it, as the means of man's salvation. Such an objection is mistaken, I think, and rests on an invalid inference. Because God can use suffering to cure an evil will, it does not follow that we can do so also. God can see into the minds and hearts of human beings and determine what sort and amount of suffering is likely to produce the best results; we cannot. . . . Furthermore, God as parent creator has a right to, and a responsibility for, painful correction of his creatures, which we as sibling creatures do not have. Therefore, since all human suffering is *prima facie* evil, and since we do not know with any high degree of probability how much (if any) of it is likely to result in good to any particular sufferer on any particular occasion, it is reasonable for us to eliminate the suffering as much as we can. At any rate, the attempt to eliminate suffering is likely to be beneficial to our characters, and passivity in the face of others' suffering will have no such good effects. . . .

V

I think, then, that it is possible to produce a defensible solution to the problem of evil by relying both on the traditional theological and philosophical assumptions in (1)–(4) . . . and on the specifically Christian doctrines in (6)–(8). Like other recent attempted solutions, this one also rests fundamentally on [an assumption of free will; namely,]

(9) Because it is a necessary condition for union with God, the significant exercise of free will employed by human beings in the process which is essential for their being saved from their own evil is of such great value that it outweighs all the evil of the world.

(9) constitutes a morally sufficient reason for evil and so is a counterexample to (5), the claim that there is no morally sufficient reason for God to permit instances of evil.

TEST YOUR UNDERSTANDING

1. One way to formulate the problem of evil is to note that the following four propositions can't all be true:

    (1) A perfect God exists.

    (2) Evil exists.

    (3) A perfect God would allow evil only if there were a morally sufficient reason to allow it.

    (4) There is no morally sufficient reason for God to allow evil.

    A solution to the problem must reject one of these propositions. Which one does Stump reject?

2. Stump's solution assumes that after death, human beings go either to heaven or to hell. What are heaven and hell for Stump?

3. According to Stump, what is the "morally sufficient reason for God to allow evil"?

4. Stump's solution to the problem of evil depends on controversial assumptions from Christian theology. Does Stump claim to have established these assumptions?

NOTES AND QUESTIONS

1. *The free will defense.* Stump's approach to the problem of evil is a version of what has come to be called the **free will defense** (see A. Plantinga, "The Free Will Defense," in his *God and Other Minds* [Cornell, 1967]). The key assumption of this approach is that free will is so valuable for human beings that even if God could eliminate human suffering by interfering with our free will, the benefit would not be worth the price.

Traditional versions of this view stumble on the problem of *natural evil*. It is one thing to say that God allows murderers to murder in order to preserve their capacity for free choice. But why would a good God permit the suffering caused by disease, natural disasters, and the like? God could eliminate this sort of suffering without interfering with anyone's free will. So why doesn't God do *that*?

Stump's version of the free will defense does not face this problem. Her focus is not on the free will of the person who *causes* the suffering, but rather on the free will of the person who endures it. Every person suffers from a "disease" of the will: we are disposed to oppose God's will. We cannot cure this disease ourselves. But God cannot cure it against our will without interfering with our freedom. According to Stump, God permits us to suffer—whether at the hands of other people or from natural causes—so that we will freely will that God repair this defect in our wills.

Question: In Stump's view, our suffering does not compel us to will that God help us. If it did, this willing would not be free. But it must somehow incline us to will God's help; otherwise, it would be pointless and God would not allow it. But then we might ask: If God can use suffering to incline our wills in the right direction, why can't he simply (and painlessly) cause our wills to be inclined in the right direction? When human doctors treat a disease, they sometimes have no choice but to use a painful treatment. But God is omnipotent. Whatever he can do by means of suffering, he can do directly. So wouldn't we expect a perfect God to incline our wills painlessly in his direction?

2. *The fall.* In Stump's account, human beings were not originally created with a disposition to oppose God's will. If they were, it would be fair to ask why a perfect God would create such defective creatures. Rather, human beings were originally disposed to align their will with God's, but as a result of the event symbolized by "Adam's fall," human nature changed for the worse. Any solution to the problem of evil that relies on this idea must explain how a good God could possibly have permitted this *heritable* change in human nature. It is one thing to say that Adam and Eve deserved punishment as individuals for their disobedience. It is quite another to explain why this punishment should take the form of a serious moral defect that was passed on to their children, and their children's children.

With this in mind, consider the following argument:

(1) God allows innocent human children to inherit a serious moral defect from their parents.

(2) A perfect God would not allow innocent children to inherit a serious moral defect.

(3) So God is not perfect.

Stump accepts (1). And (2) seems highly plausible. So how can Stump resist the conclusion that God is not perfect after all? Stump discusses this question on page 52. Explain and assess her grounds for rejecting (2).

Stump's recent views on the problem of evil are developed in her book *Wandering in Darkness: Narrative and the Problem of Suffering* (Oxford University Press, 2010). For critical discussion, see P. Draper's review in *Notre Dame Philosophical Reviews*, July 2011 (http://ndpr.nd.edu/news/wandering-in-darkness-narrative-and-the-problem-of-suffering/).

ANALYZING THE ARGUMENTS

1. *The attributes of God.* The traditional attributes of God—omniscience, omnipotence, perfect goodness, and so on—cry out for analysis. For some attributes, this is easy. To say that God is omniscient, for example, is to say that for every true **proposition** p, God knows that p is true. In other cases, the analysis raises interesting questions.

   Omnipotence. It is sometimes said that God's omnipotence consists in his ability to do *anything.* If God were omnipotent in this sense, God could make a triangle with four sides, or a free human being who was incapable of acting badly, or a world in which there is no God; but it is widely assumed that God need not be omnipotent in *that* sense.

   Exercise: Provide an account of God's omnipotence that does not have these implications. Your account should have the form: X is omnipotent if and only if . . .

   Perfect goodness. It is tempting to suppose that a perfectly good being is a being that always chooses the best available option. As applied to God, this entails that a perfect God would create the best of all possible worlds. But there is no such thing as the *best* possible world. No matter how excellent the world is—no matter how many happy creatures living in harmony with one another it contains—there might have been a better world containing more happy creatures living even happier lives. If this is right, we cannot say that God's perfect goodness consists in his choice to create the best of all possible worlds (since there is no such thing).

   Exercise: Provide an account of God's perfect goodness that avoids this problem.

2. *The God of the Philosophers.* The authors of our selections generally agree that there *could* be a perfect being. But it has occasionally been claimed that the idea of such a being is contradictory. Consider the following arguments:

   The paradox of omnipotence. A perfect being would be omnipotent. But there cannot possibly be an omnipotent being. Suppose that X is omnipotent and ask: Can X create a stone so heavy that she cannot move it? If she cannot create such a stone, then she is not omnipotent, because there is something she cannot do. But if she *can* create such a stone, then again, there is something she cannot do, namely, move the stone in question. So either way, there is something X cannot do. So X is not omnipotent.

   The paradox of moral perfection and omnipotence. A perfect being would be both perfectly good and perfectly powerful. But there cannot be a being that combines these attributes. A perfectly good being would be *essentially* good. It would be *impossible for her to sin.* But if X cannot sin, X is not omnipotent. (After all, *you* can sin, and an omnipotent being can do anything you can do.) So if X is perfectly good, X is not omnipotent.

The paradox of omniscience and omnipotence. A perfect being would be both omnipotent and omniscient. But it is impossible for a being to be both omniscient and omnipotent. To see why, suppose that *X* is both omniscient and omnipotent and suppose that *X* is on the brink of a decision: she must decide whether to destroy the moon or to leave it alone. If *X* is omnipotent, then *X* can choose either option. But if *X* is omniscient, then she knows exactly what she will do. But if she *knows* now that she will not destroy the moon, then it is settled now that she will not destroy it. And if it is settled now that she will not destroy it, it is not in her power to destroy it. So if *X* is omniscient, she is not omnipotent.

Exercise: Set out these arguments in full and identify a premise that the theist might reject. Then try to strengthen the argument so as to block this response.

3. *Inference to the best explanation in natural theology.* Proponents of **natural theology** maintain that the hypothesis of God's existence provides the best explanation of certain observed facts—the adaptation of organisms to their environments, the fine tuning of the fundamental constants, and so on—and that belief in God is therefore justified on scientific grounds. But even if the best *available* explanation for some observed fact posits God, this by itself cannot justify belief in God. After all, the best available explanation may be the best of a bad lot, and when it is, we should not accept it. Moreover, there is reason to believe that theological explanations are always *terrible* explanations by scientific standards.

   a. Unlike serious scientific explanations, the theological explanation is not *testable*. Scientists accept Einstein's theory of gravitation, for example, only because it makes detailed predictions that have been confirmed by experiment. The God hypothesis makes no predictions, so it is not acceptable by scientific standards. (For the claim that a scientific hypothesis must be testable, see K. Popper, *Conjectures and Refutations,* chapter 11 [Routledge and Kegan Paul, 1963].)

   b. Unlike serious scientific explanations, the theological explanation is thin. Scientists accept our current theory of fundamental physics because it provides a *detailed* account of how subatomic particles generate the phenomena we observe. By contrast, the God hypothesis tells us nothing about *how* God does what he is supposed to do, so it is not a serious hypothesis by scientific standards.

   c. Unlike serious scientific explanations, the theological explanation is *stalled*. Good scientific theories generate progressive research programs. They generate new theoretical questions, the answers to which motivate improvements in the theory: new lines of inquiry are opened up; new phenomena are identified. By contrast, the God hypothesis has not generated any *new* science, and it is unclear how it could. So it is not a serious hypothesis by scientific standards (see I. Lakatos, "Falsification and the Methodology of Scientific Research Programs," in *Criticism and the Growth of Knowledge,* ed. I. Lakatos and A. Musgrave [Cambridge University Press, 1970]).

Exercise: Say how the proponent of natural theology might respond to these objections.

4. *The argument from evil*

   a. *Is God a murderer?* The argument from evil begins from the premise that if there is
   an omnipotent and omniscient God, he *allows* innocent creatures to suffer and die
   when he could easily save them. But we can entertain a stronger premise: If there
   is an omnipotent and omniscient *creator* God, then God *knowingly causes* the slow
   and painful deaths of innocents and is thus a torturer and a murderer. God may not
   cause these deaths directly. But if God made the natural world and the laws that
   govern it, God causes them indirectly, and that is just as bad.

   Exercise: Say how the theist might respond to this challenge.

   b. *The problem of evil and the virtue of faith.* If there is a God, then God permits (and
   perhaps even causes) the deaths of millions of children every year from famine and
   disease. Many theists will grant this point and say, "While we do not understand how
   a good God could do this, still we have *faith* that God is good." This raises a moral
   question: Is this sort of faith a virtue? Imagine that a powerful dictator does these
   things, and suppose his subjects insist that even though they cannot comprehend
   his motives, they nonetheless have faith that he is good. We would not regard *this*
   faith as a virtue: we would regard it as a pitiable moral failing. Why is faith in the
   goodness of God any different?

Is It Reasonable to Believe without Evidence?

Suppose you have reviewed the arguments for and against the existence of God and found them wanting. Not only do they fail to *prove* that God exists (or that God does not exist): they fail to provide good, solid reasons for belief—reasons of the sort we often get in daily life and in the sciences even when proof is not in the cards. It's always possible that there are better arguments waiting to be discovered. But we do not have them yet, and that raises a question: Can it be reasonable to believe that God exists even though we cannot provide reasons for this belief? We sometimes use the word "faith" to describe a belief that we cannot defend by giving reasons. So we can also put our question like this: Is faith in God's existence ever reasonable?

The Problem of "Properly Basic" Belief

A negative answer would follow immediately from a general principle:

> You should not hold a belief unless you can support it by citing evidence or giving an argument.

This can sound extremely plausible. When you get caught up in arguments about the existence of God or any other controversial matter, it is easy to feel that if you cannot defend your position by providing reasons you have lost: your position has been shown to be unreasonable. Moreover, there are contexts in which the principle clearly applies. It *is* unreasonable to believe that the defendant is guilty of murder or that $835 \times 267 = 222{,}945$ if you cannot say anything in support of your opinion. So the only question is whether there are exceptions to the rule—special cases in which it is reasonable to hold a belief even though you cannot support it.

Alvin Plantinga calls beliefs of this sort **properly basic**. A belief is basic (for you) if you cannot defend it with an argument. A basic belief is *properly* basic if it's nonetheless reasonable for you to hold it. So we have three questions:

Are there any properly basic beliefs?

If so, what are the conditions under which a belief is properly basic?

And finally:

Does a belief in God satisfy those conditions?

An Argument for the Existence of Properly Basic Beliefs

A simple argument seems to show that there must be *some* properly basic beliefs. Take anything you believe; for example, $835 \times 267 = 222{,}945$. (Check the math if you have doubts.) In this case, you can give an argument by running through the calculation. But that argument will have premises. For example, the first step in the calculation is $5 \times 7 = 35$. You took this for granted when you did the math; you did not bother to argue for it. Of course, you could provide an argument for this assumption if you were pressed. But when you set out *that* argument, you will again find yourself relying on premises that you have not defended. And when you are pressed to defend *those* premises, and the premises upon which *they* depend, and so on, you will eventually reach a premise that you cannot defend. Why? Because you are a finite being and no matter how smart you are, you have only a finite number of arguments at your disposal. (*Exercise:* Reconstruct your reasons for believing that $7 \times 5 = 35$ and identify the assumptions that underlie this belief that you cannot prove.) So if you start with any belief you hold and turn the spotlight on the premises that support it, you will eventually arrive at premises that are basic for you.

Now we could say that these basic beliefs are all unreasonable simply because you cannot defend them. But then we will be forced to say that *all* of your beliefs are unreasonable. After all, an argument can only support its conclusion if we are justified in accepting its premises. So if there are no properly basic beliefs to get us started, our arguments will never get us anywhere. (Garbage in, garbage out.) This is an ancient argument for radical **skepticism**: the view that it is never reasonable to believe anything. But radical skepticism is very hard to take seriously. It clearly *is* reasonable for you to believe that $7 \times 5 = 35$. And that means the argument for skepticism must go wrong somewhere.

When Is a Belief Properly Basic?

Many philosophers (including Plantinga) take this to show that some of our beliefs must be properly basic. And this leads to one of the great unsolved problems in philosophy: *When* is a belief properly basic? When is it reasonable to believe a proposition we cannot support or defend by argument?

Some philosophers have held that a belief is properly basic when its denial is somehow unthinkable—absurd, incoherent, self-contradictory. This might explain why some basic principles of logic and mathematics are properly basic. But a belief in God will not count as properly basic on such a view, since the atheist's worldview is not unthinkable. Others have held that a belief is properly basic when it is psychologically impossible for a human being to doubt it. This might explain why our belief in the reality of the external world is properly basic, since no psychologically normal human being can doubt it for very long. It might also explain how beliefs about our own conscious mental states can be properly basic, since no one who is in pain can seriously doubt that she is in pain. But even if this were right it would be no comfort to the theist, since it is obviously possible for human beings to doubt the existence of God.

Epistemic versus Practical Reasons for Belief

One important tradition, represented here by Blaise Pascal and William James, approaches this question in a different way. To understand the approach, we need a distinction. Suppose you have been invited to interview for a terrific job, and you know two things about your prospects. On the one hand, you are one of five equally qualified candidates, all with the same skills and experience. On the other hand, you have just read a scientific study that shows that *confident* candidates— candidates who firmly believe they will get the job—are somewhat more likely to succeed than candidates who harbor doubts. Given all of this information, what should you believe about your prospects?

Two incompatible arguments suggest themselves:

1. You are one of five equally qualified candidates, so you probably won't get the job. Even if you can somehow work up some confidence—say, by looking in the mirror and repeating, "This job is *mine*. This job is *mine!*"—that would only improve your chances a little bit: from 20 percent to (say) 25 percent. So it is reasonable to believe that you won't get the job.

2. If you believe that you will get the job, you improve your chances, and that's what matters. A rational person does what she can to get what she wants (at least when her goals are permissible and the means are moral, as they are here). Just as it is reasonable to "dress for success" when that will give you an edge over the competition, it is reasonable for you to be confident, since that will also give you an edge. So it is reasonable for you to believe that you will get the job.

These conclusions sound contradictory. How can a single belief be both reasonable and unreasonable?

The answer is that words such as "rational" and "reasonable" are ambiguous. When we ask whether a belief is rational, we might be asking whether it is likely to be true given the evidence or whether it would be reasonable to hold it if one's sole concern were to believe the truth about the issue at hand. A belief that is rational in this sense is said to be **epistemically rational**. Alternatively, and much less commonly, we may be asking whether holding the belief will have good consequences. A belief that is rational in this sense is said to be **practically (or pragmatically) rational**. These two notions usually coincide. It is almost always beneficial to hold beliefs that are likely to be true given your evidence. But they occasionally come apart, as they do here. And when they do, it makes no sense to ask without qualification, "What is it rational to believe?" We must say which sort of rationality we have in mind. In this puzzling case, it is practically rational for you to believe that you will get the job, even though you have no good epistemic reason to believe this.

The Practical Rationality of Belief in God

Now if the word "rational" is ambiguous, then so is the notion of a properly basic belief. When we ask whether belief in God is properly basic, we could be asking whether an undefended belief in God is *epistemically* rational, but we could also be asking whether such belief is *practically* rational.

Pascal defends a positive answer to the second question. He admits that there are no good theoretical arguments for God's existence. But that does not show that religious belief is irrational in every sense. Pascal assumes that if there is a God, he rewards those who believe with "infinite felicity"—eternal and unsurpassable happiness. Pascal then gives a gambler's argument, analyzed in detail by Alan Hájek. Think of your belief in God as a lottery ticket that yields infinite happiness if God exists. How much should you be willing to pay for this ticket? Pascal argues that you should be willing to pay any finite amount for a chance to win this infinitely valuable prize, including whatever costs you would incur by believing in God and living a religious life. Pascal concludes that religious belief is practically rational even if the theoretical arguments are inconclusive.

We can think of this as a partial solution to our problem about properly basic beliefs. According to Pascal, it is practically rational to hold a belief that one cannot defend by argument when holding that belief is in your interest. Pascal does not say that such beliefs are epistemically rational. But he does think that a rational *person*—someone who aims to be both epistemically and practically rational—has no choice but to believe.

William James appeals to our practical interests in a different way. He begins by noting that the question of God's existence is very special. Like many questions, it cannot be settled on the basis of the available evidence. But in most cases of this sort, we are under no pressure to form an opinion. (Is the number of stars odd or even? No one needs an answer to that question.) When it comes to the existence of

God, however, the question is both *forced* and *momentous*. It is forced because at every moment, we must choose either belief or unbelief. (Agnosticism is a form of unbelief.) And it is momentous, James thinks, because *if* God exists, then a belief in God is of enormous value. James disdains Pascal's crass appeal to posthumous rewards and punishments. He thinks that an intellectual connection to God is profoundly valuable *here and now*: every moment one goes without it, one misses out on a great good.

Now an epistemological rule that forbids us from believing without evidence would cut us off from this great good. And for James, that is enough to show that such a rule must be rejected. Instead James says (in effect): When you are confronted with a forced and momentous question that you cannot resolve on intellectual grounds, then you may believe *what would best promote your legitimate interests as you understand them*. If you are inclined to take a risk (the risk of being wrong) in order to secure a benefit (intellectual contact with God), then you are free to take that risk. Anyone who says otherwise merely shows "his own preponderant horror of becoming a dupe."

Unlike Pascal, James is arguing that it may be both practically and epistemically rational to believe what one cannot prove. All theoretical inquiry, including science, is guided by values, the most important of which are love of truth and fear of error. Rationality does not tell us exactly how much weight to give these values. But it allows us to place *more* value on attaining truth than on avoiding error, especially when the truths in question are valuable for other reasons. And if you have values of this sort, it can be epistemically rational to believe what you cannot prove in the hope of achieving the benefits—both practical and intellectual—that come with being right.

This view has important implications. Suppose that you and I face a profound moral or religious question that cannot be settled by evidence and argument, and that we arrive at different answers because we have different values: you care more about truth; I care more about avoiding error. James's position entails that we may both be perfectly reasonable *even though neither of us can give the other a reason to change his mind*. There is a powerful tendency to suppose, in the heat of moral or religious debate, that anyone who disagrees with us must be either pigheaded or blind. But if James is right, there is another possibility. Your opponent may be perfectly reasonable, disagreeing with you only because she attaches different weights to the values that guide her intellectual life.

The Problem Restated

You may reject James's view, but that will not make the problem go away. Every epistemologist owes us an account of when it is rational to believe what we cannot prove or argue for. The selections below address this issue as it arises in the philosophy of religion. But as you read through the selections, you should bear this general problem in mind. The epistemology of religious belief is an important topic. But there are no special-purpose rules of religious epistemology. The principles of rationality that govern our beliefs about God also govern our beliefs in other areas. So you can always test a proposed defense of religious faith by extracting the principle that underlies it and applying that principle elsewhere. To repeat a point made earlier, we all know that it is *sometimes* unreasonable to believe what we cannot prove or defend by argument. If Seymour believes that the world will end on New Year's Eve 2035 but can provide no evidence whatsoever for his opinion, then Seymour is not 100 percent rational. The question is whether an ungrounded belief in God is like Seymour's belief in doomsday. And we cannot answer that question without a general principle that tells us when our basic beliefs are rational and when they are not.

Blaise Pascal (1623–1662)

Pascal invented the first mechanical calculator and made foundational contributions to physics and mathematics. His main contribution to philosophy—*Pensées*—was published posthumously in 1669 from fragments found among his papers.

THE WAGER
from *Pensées*

Unity when joined to the infinite does not increase it at all, any more than a foot when added to an infinite length. The finite annihilates itself in the presence of the infinite, and becomes a pure nothing. So does our mind when confronted with God, so does our justice before divine justice. Yet the disproportion between our justice and God's is not as great as that between unity and infinity.

The justice of God must be as enormous as his mercy. The justice he shows to the damned is less enormous and should shock us less than the mercy he shows to the elect.

We know that there is an infinite, and we are ignorant of its nature. Similarly, we know it is false that the series of numbers is finite, and it is therefore true that there is an infinite number, but we do not know what it is. It is false that it is even; it is false that it is odd; for by adding a unit the infinite does not change its nature. Yet it is a number, and every number is even or odd—this may be truly understood of every finite number.

Thus we can perfectly well recognize that there is a God, without knowing what he is. . . .

We know the existence and the nature of the finite, since we, like it, are finite and extended.

We know the existence of the infinite and we are ignorant of its nature, since it has extension like us, but does not have limits as we do.

But we do not know either the existence or the nature of God, because he has neither extension nor limits.

But by faith we know his existence, and in glory we shall come to know his nature.

Now I have already shown that one may quite well know the existence of a thing without knowing its nature.

Let us now speak according to our natural lights.

If there is a God, he is infinitely beyond our comprehension, since having neither parts nor limits he bears no relation to us. We are thus incapable of knowing either what he is or if he is. This being so, who will dare undertake to resolve this question? Surely not we, who bear no relation to him.

Who then will blame Christians for not being able to provide reasons for their belief, since they profess a religion for which they cannot provide a rational basis? In proclaiming it to the world they declare that it is "folly," and will you then complain that they do not prove it? If they were to prove it, they would not be keeping their word. This very lack of proof shows they do not lack sense. "Yes; but even if this excuses those who offer their religion in this way and takes away any blame for their putting it forward without reason, it does not excuse those who *accept* it without reason." Let us then examine this point. Let us say: either God is or he is not. But which side shall we incline towards? Reason cannot settle anything here. There is an infinite chaos which separates us. A game is being played at the far end of this infinite distance: the coin will come down heads or tails. How will you bet? Reason will not enable you to decide either way, or rule out either alternative.

So do not blame those who have made a choice, or say they have chosen a false path, for you know nothing of the matter. "No, but I will blame them for having made not *this* choice but *a* choice; for though the player who chooses heads is no more at fault than the other one, both of them are still at fault. The correct option is not to bet at all."

Yes, but you must bet. It is not voluntary; you are already involved. Which will you choose then? Look: since you must choose, let us see which is the less profitable option. You have two things to lose, the true and the good, and two things to stake, your reason and your will, your knowledge and your happiness. Your nature has two things to avoid, error and wretchedness. Since a choice must necessarily be made, your reason is no more offended by choosing one rather than the other. There is one point settled. But your happiness? Let us weigh up the gain and the loss in choosing heads, that God exists. Let us figure out the two results: if you win, you win everything, and if you lose, you lose nothing. So bet that he exists, without any hesitation. "This is splendid: yes, I must bet, but maybe I am betting too much." Let us see. Since there is an equal chance of gain and loss, if you stood merely to gain merely two lives for one, you could still bet. But suppose you had three lives to gain?

You would have to play (since you must necessarily play), and you would be foolish, since you are forced to play, not to risk your life to gain three lives in a game where there is equal chance of losing and winning. But there is an eternity of life and happiness. This being so, in a game where there were an infinity of chances and only one in your favor, you would still be right to wager one life in order to gain two; and you would be making the wrong choice, given that you were obliged to play, if you refused to bet one life against three in a game where there were an infinity of chances and only one in your favor, if the prize were an infinity of infinitely happy life. But the prize here *is* an infinity of infinitely happy life, one chance of winning against a finite number of chances of losing, and what you are staking is finite. This leaves only one choice open, in any game that involves infinity, where there is not an infinite number of chances of losing to set against the chance of winning. There is nothing to ponder—you must stake everything. When you are forced to play, you would have to be renouncing reason if you were to hang on to life rather than risk it for an infinite gain which is just as likely to come about as a loss which is a loss of nothing.

It is no use saying that it is uncertain whether you will win and certain that you are taking a chance; or that the infinite distance between the certainty of what you are risking and the uncertainty of what you stand to gain makes the finite good which you are certainly risking as great as the infinite gain that is uncertain. This is not how things stand. Every player takes a certain risk in exchange for an uncertain gain; but it is no sin against reason for him to take a certain and finite risk for an uncertain finite gain. It is just not true that there is an infinite distance between the certainty of what is risked and the uncertainty of the gain. There is, in truth, an infinite distance between the certainty of winning and the certainty of losing; but the proportion between the uncertainty of winning and the certainty of what is being risked corresponds to the proportion between the chances of winning and losing. From this it follows that if there are as many chances on one side as on the other, the game is being played for even odds. And hence the certainty of what you are risking is equal to the uncertainty of the possible gain, so far from being infinitely distant from it. There is thus infinite force in the position I am taking, when the stakes are finite in a game where the chances of winning and losing are equal and the prize is infinite.

This result has demonstrative force, and if human beings are capable of any truth, this is it.

"I confess it, I admit it, but is there not any way at all of seeing what lies behind the game?" Yes, Holy Scripture and the rest. "Yes, but my hands are tied and my mouth is gagged; I am being forced to wager and I am not at liberty. I cannot get free and my constitution is such that I am incapable of believing. So what do you want me to do?" What you say is true, but you must at least realize that your inability to believe comes from your passions. Since reason moves you to believe, and nevertheless you cannot, your task is not to convince yourself by adding on more proofs of God, but by reducing your passions. Your desired destination is faith, but you do not know the road. You want to cure yourself of unbelief, and you ask for remedies: learn from those who were tied like you and who now wager all they possess. These are people who know the road you would like to follow; they are cured of the malady for which you seek a cure; so follow them and begin as they did—by acting as if they believed, by taking holy water, by having masses said, and so on. In the natural course of events this in itself will make you believe, this will tame you. "But that is just what I fear." Why? What have you to lose? If you want to know why this is the right way, the answer is that it reduces the passions, which are the great obstacles to your progress. . . .

Now what harm will come to you if you make this choice? You will be faithful, honest, humble, grateful, a doer of good works, a good friend, sincere and true. Admittedly you will not dwell amid tainted pleasures, in glory and luxury, but will you not have others?

I tell you that you will be the gainer in this life, and that on every step you take on this path you will see such certainty of gain, and such emptiness of what you hazard, that you will finally know that what you have wagered for is something certain and infinite, and what you have given in exchange is nothing.

TEST YOUR UNDERSTANDING

1. Pascal likens the decision whether to believe in God to a bet. In an ordinary bet we choose a proposition; for example, "The Yankees will win the 2020 World Series." Then we specify the payoffs: how much you win if the proposition turns out to be true, and how much you lose if it turns out to be false. Represent Pascal's Wager as a bet in this sense.

2. Pascal insists that "you must bet." Why does he say this?

3. Pascal says that "unity when joined to the infinite does not increase it at all." Say what he means by this.

4. True or false: Pascal maintains that if you wager for God and lose, you will be no worse off than if you had wagered against God.

NOTES AND QUESTIONS

1. *A crash course in decision theory.* Pascal's argument assumes a (now) widely accepted theory of rational choice. The key idea is that a rational agent seeks to maximize the *expected utility* of his choices. Suppose you have been asked to bring the wine to a dinner party, and you have two choices: red or white. You do not know what's for dinner, but there are only two possibilities: beef or chicken. Many people have a slight preference for white wine with chicken and a strong preference for red wine with beef. If those are your preferences, we can represent your situation as follows:

	They serve chicken	They serve beef
Bring white	10	2
Bring red	7	10

Here the numbers represent (somewhat arbitrarily) the **utility** you attach to the outcome in question: how *good* that outcome is by your lights.

To determine what you should do in the situation, you need one more bit of information: how *likely* it is that they will serve chicken as opposed to beef. These probabilities are measured with numbers between 0 and 1. If you attach a probability of

1 to a proposition, you are sure that it is true; if you attach a probability of 0, you are sure that it is false. A probability of 0.5 means that you think the proposition is just as likely to be true as not.

The **expected utility** of bringing white wine is the sum of the utility of bringing white wine if they serve chicken and the utility of bringing white wine if they serve beef, each weighted by the appropriate probability. So suppose first that chicken and beef are equally likely. Then the expected utility of bringing white is 0.5(10) + 0.5(2) = 6, whereas the expected utility of bringing red is 0.5(7) + 0.5(10) = 8.5. Since the expected utility of bringing red is higher, that is what you should do. According to this account of rational choice—**standard decision theory**—*a rational agent always acts so as to maximize expected utility.*

But now suppose that in your long experience with your hosts, they have served chicken 90 percent of the time. In that case, the expected utility of bringing white is

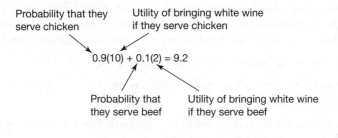

whereas the expected utility of bringing red is

$$0.9(7) + 0.1(10) = 7.3$$

In that case, you should bring white wine, even though you are risking the bad outcome in which you bring white and they serve beef. This makes sense because although this outcome is bad, it is unlikely. (For an introduction to decision theory, see M. Resnik, *Choices: An Introduction to Decision Theory* [University of Minnesota Press, 1987].)

2. *Representing Pascal's Wager as a decision problem.* You have two options—Believe in God or Don't believe—and there are two possibilities: God exists or God does not exist. To represent the Wager as a decision problem, we need to specify the utilities and the probabilities.

    Probabilities: Pascal seems to assume that for someone faced with this decision, the probability of God's existence must be ½. This is unwarranted, but it makes no difference. As we will see, so long as the probability of God's existence is not zero, Pascal's argument is unaffected.

    Utilities: Pascal assumes that if you believe in God and God exists, your reward is an unending blissful afterlife, the value of which is *infinite*—greater than any finite value. No ordinary finite number can represent an infinite value. So let us suppose that there is an *infinite* number ∞, greater than any finite number. *We must be very careful here.* The "arithmetic" of infinite numbers is a very tricky subject. But in fact we only need two assumptions about this infinite number for Pascal's purposes:

For any finite number n, $n + \infty = \infty$.
For any positive number n between 0 and 1, $n \times \infty = \infty$.

We may then represent the Wager as follows:

	God exists	God does not exist
Believe	∞	17 (or any finite number)
Don't believe	17 (or any finite number)	17 (or any finite number)

Exercise: Show that given these assumptions, you maximize expected utility by believing in God no matter what probability you attach to God's existence, provided that probability is not zero.

Exercise: Vary the finite utilities. Suppose that if God does not exist, then a religious life is somewhat worse than a nonreligious life (since one forgoes certain pleasures). Alternatively, suppose that a religious life is better than a nonreligious one, perhaps for the serenity it brings. Show that these variations all yield the same result: the finite values do not matter, so long as they are finite.

3. *The "many Gods" objection.* Pascal assumes that there are only two possibilities: either there exists a God like the Christian God who rewards believers with infinite happiness or there is no God at all. But in fact there are many other possibilities. For example, there might be a Perverse God who rewards nonbelievers with infinite happiness in heaven (much to their surprise!) while punishing religious believers with annihilation. This may not be likely, but it is possible. How does Pascal's Wager look if we take this possibility into account? You have two possible acts, Believe and Don't Believe, and there are three possible states of the world relevant to your decision:

	Christian God exists	Perverse God exists	No God exists
Believe	∞	17	17
Don't believe	17	∞	17

Exercise: Determine the expected utility of belief and nonbelief on the assumption that there is some nonzero chance that each of these possibilities obtains.

There are, of course, many other possibilities. There might be a Doubly Perverse God who rewards nonbelievers while *punishing* believers with infinite misery. There might be two Gods, A and B, each of whom rewards those who believe in him while punishing those who believe in his rival, and so on. It is useful to explore the implications of these possibilities for Pascal's reasoning.

Alan Hájek (b. 1962)

Hájek is Professor of Philosophy at the Australian National University. He works mainly in probability and decision theory.

PASCAL'S ULTIMATE GAMBLE

As you enter the casino, a host of gambling games vie for your attention—and cash. The first is especially simple. A coin you know to be fair will be tossed. If it lands heads, you win $1; if it lands tails, you lose $2. Should you play? Let's assume that all you care about here is money—you don't receive an additional benefit from the thrill of gambling, for example—and that you value equally each dollar gained or lost. Then it seems that you *should not play*: while there is an equal probability of losing and of winning, the magnitude of a loss would be greater than that of a win.

Then there is an announcement. It is now Happy Hour, and the game has suddenly changed: now, if the coin lands heads, you win $1; if it lands tails, you lose $1. Obviously this is an *improvement* for you—there is now a way the coin could land (tails) for which your payoff is better than it was before; otherwise your payoff is the same as before. Moreover, the new game seems *fair* to you—in the long run, you would expect to break even. You could rationally play the game but also rationally turn it down.

You have just engaged in three little exercises in *decision theory* (their respective upshots being that you *should not play* the first game, that the second game is an *improvement*, and that the second game is *fair*). Decision theory is an account of how probabilities and utilities (payoffs) associated with your various options together determine what it is rational for you to do. Soon we will see in more detail what the theory has to say about these gambles.

In his classic *Pensées*, Blaise Pascal contended that in an important sense, there is an ultimate gamble that we all face. We must choose whether to believe in God or not—in Pascal's words, whether to "wager that He is" or not. If we found some decisive argument that settled the matter of God's existence either way, then our job would be done: we should simply believe the conclusion of the argument. But this is not our situation according to Pascal: "God is, or He is not. But to which side shall we incline? Reason can decide nothing here."[1] However, he insists, reason *can* decide that we should *wager* that God exists. Pascal presents the problem of whether to wager that God exists as a *decision* problem, and he solves it with the same decision-theoretic machinery that one should deploy when faced with a gamble in a casino. Indeed, Pascal was one of the pioneers of that machinery, and his Wager is described by Hacking as "the first well-understood contribution to decision theory."[2] In short, Pascal maintains that one should wager for God because *it is the best bet*. And how good a bet is it? According to Pascal, *infinitely good*.

1. Blaise Pascal, *Pascal's Pensées*, trans. W. F. Trotter (London: J. M. Dent & Sons; New York: E. P. Dutton & Co., 1910).

2. Ian Hacking, *The Emergence of Probability* (Cambridge University Press, 1975).

A One-Minute Primer on Decision Theory

To understand the Wager, we will need to understand how to set up a decision problem and two fundamental principles of decision theory. In a decision problem, what you do and what the world does together determine what you get. If the problem is nontrivial, you have a choice of at least two actions, and there are at least two ways that the world could be—"states"—that are relevant to your fate and about which you are uncertain. We may represent this as a matrix, with rows corresponding to your possible actions and columns corresponding to the states. In each cell of the matrix we have a number, called a *utility*, that represents the degree to which you value the corresponding outcome—think of it as a payoff. For example, the original gamble in the casino confronted you with this decision matrix:

	Heads	Tails
Play	1	-2
Don't play	0	0

Here, -2 is the utility of your losing $2, and 0 is the utility of your neither losing nor winning money. The "Happy Hour" decision matrix is:

	Heads	Tails
Play	1	-1
Don't play	0	0

In *decisions under uncertainty,* you have to decide solely on the basis of utilities. Suppose you had to choose between playing the original gamble and the Happy Hour gamble, with the same coin toss determining the outcome. But now suppose that you have no idea whether the coin in question is fair. (This ignorance of probabilities makes this a decision under uncertainty.) You could not do worse in the Happy Hour gamble, and you could do better (if the coin lands tails), so it seems you should choose it. This is an instance of *dominance* reasoning. More generally, given two actions A_1 and A_2, say that A_1 *dominates* A_2 if each outcome associated with A_1 is at least as good as the corresponding outcome associated with A_2, and for at least one state, A_1's outcome is strictly better than A_2's. Dominance reasoning can be captured by the following principle of rationality: *Choose the dominant action if there is one.* Playing the Happy Hour game dominates playing the original game, so by the principle, you should play the Happy Hour game if you have to choose between them.

Now let's return to the opening examples, in which you know that the coin is fair. You thus have more information at your disposal than just the utilities: you also have *probabilities* for the various states. This makes each decision about whether to play or not a *decision under risk* (as opposed to a decision under uncertainty). For such a decision, a simple formula yields a figure of merit for each action, called the *expected utility* of the action: for each state, multiply its probability by the utility of the outcome associated with the action, then add these numbers. The centerpiece of decision theory is the rationality principle: *Choose the action of maximal expected utility if there is one.* The games we have described involve flipping a fair coin, so we know that the probability of heads and the probability of tails are both ½. The expected utility of playing the original game is therefore:

$$(½ \times 1) + (½ \times -2) = -½$$

which is less than the expected utility of not playing, 0. So you should not play. The expected utility of the Happy Hour game is

$$(½ \times 1) + (½ \times -1) = 0$$

the same as not playing. This reflects the fairness of the game—you could rationally play it or not. And when faced with a choice between the two games, you should choose the latter.

We now have two tools for solving decision problems. You can use dominance reasoning to solve certain decisions under uncertainty, although when it applies it can tell you only *what* to choose, not *how desirable* your choice is, and in particular not *how much better* it is than some alternative. Decisions under risk allow more nuanced treatment: the expected utilities of the alternative actions are numerical measures of their desirabilities.

Pascal's Gamble

Pascal presents you with a decision problem: Should you wager that God exists or not? First, we will look to the relevant passage of the *Pensées* to construct the decision problem as he conceived it. Then, we will use these decision-theoretic tools to solve it.

Pascal writes:

> Which will you choose then? . . . You have two things to lose, the true and the good; and two things to stake, your reason and your will, your knowledge and your happiness; and your nature has two things to shun, error and misery. Your reason is no more shocked in choosing one rather than the other, since you must of necessity choose. . . . But your happiness? Let us weigh the gain and the loss in wagering that God is. . . . If you gain, you gain all; if you lose, you lose nothing. Wager, then, without hesitation that He is.[3]

---

3. All quotes in English are from Blaise Pascal, *Pascal's Pensées*, trans. W. F. Trotter (London: J. M. Dent & Sons; New York: E. P. Dutton & Co., 1910). [Hájek's note.]

Your possible actions are to wager that God exists (for short: *wager for God*) or to wager that He doesn't (*wager against God*). There are two possible states: either He exists or He does not. We are not yet in a position to put numerical values on the utilities of the corresponding outcomes, but Pascal's qualitative characterization of them seems to be captured by the following:

	God exists	God does not exist
Wager for God	Gain all	Lose nothing = status quo
Wager against God	Misery	Status quo

This is informative enough for us to apply dominance reasoning—wagering for God dominates wagering against God, so it seems that you should wager for God.[4]

At this point, Pascal regards himself as having settled the question of *what* to choose. But he imagines an interlocutor replying: "Yes, I must wager; but I may perhaps wager too much." This invites the further question: What is wagering for God worth? So Pascal then goes on to determine *how desirable* that choice is, and in particular how much better it is than wagering against God. This requires a calculation of expected utilities, which in turn require probabilities.

So Pascal immediately makes a probabilistic assumption: "There is an equal risk of gain and of loss." As we would say it nowadays: the probability that God exists is ½. This appears to be a naïve application of the so-called classical theory of probability, according to which the probability of an event is equal to the number of outcomes in which the event occurs, divided by the total number of possible outcomes. (Thus, the classical probability that a die lands even is 3/6.) This theory finds its natural home in gambling games, and once again Pascal writes as if he is taking the gambling picture literally. To be sure, from a modern perspective this application of the theory appears particularly strained.[5] But bear with Pascal for now, for as we will see, he will soon relax this assumption.

Expected utilities also require utilities—what are they to be? In a startling move, Pascal makes the unit of utility a *life*:

---

4. This is too quick (Alan Hájek, "Blaise and Bayes," in *Probability in the Philosophy of Religion*, ed. Jake Chandler and Victoria Harrison [Oxford University Press, 2011]). Dominance reasoning may fail when the actions and states are not probabilistically independent of each other. This brings in complications that are beyond the scope of this essay. See also Hacking for a discussion of Pascal's dominance reasoning here (Ian Hacking, "The Logic of Pascal's Wager," *American Philosophical Quarterly* 9/2 (1972): 186–92; reprinted in *Gambling on God: Essays on Pascal's Wager*, ed. Jeff Jordan (Rowman & Littlefield, 1994). [Hájek's note.]

5. What probability should you give to my next car being blue (all over)? According to the classical theory, the answer is ½. After all, there are two possible outcomes: either it is blue or it is not blue, and in one out of these two outcomes the car is blue. What probability should you give to my next car being red? Again, the classical theory says ½. And so on for each different color. But that's absurd: these outcomes are mutually exclusive (the car can only be one color all over), so they cannot all have probability ½. [Hájek's note.]

> If you had only to gain two lives, instead of one, you might still wager . . . and you
> would be imprudent, when you are forced to play, not to chance your life to gain
> three at a game where there is an equal risk of loss and gain.

The metaphysics may be questionable, but the decision-theoretic reasoning is impeccable: the first hypothetical gamble has an expected utility of

$$\tfrac{1}{2} \times 2 \text{ lives} = 1 \text{ life}$$

so you could rationally stake one life to play it or not. (Compare the Happy Hour gamble.) The second hypothetical gamble has an expected utility of

$$\tfrac{1}{2} \times 3 \text{ lives} = 1\tfrac{1}{2} \text{ lives}$$

so you would be imprudent not to stake one life to play it. But according to Pascal, the *actual* gamble that you face is far more favorable than these:

> But there is here an infinity of an infinitely happy life to gain, a chance of gain
> against a finite number of chances of loss, and what you stake is finite. It is all di-
> vided; wherever the infinite is and there is not an infinity of chances of loss against
> that of gain, there is no time to hesitate, you must give all. And thus, when one is
> forced to play, he must renounce reason to preserve his life.

Measured in lives, a gamble that pays *infinity* (∞) with probability $\tfrac{1}{2}$ (and nothing otherwise) has an expected utility in lives of

$$\tfrac{1}{2} \times \infty = \infty$$

so all the more you would be imprudent not to stake one life to play it.

But notice how the probability $\tfrac{1}{2}$ plays no special role in this reasoning. We could replace it with any positive probability[6] p:

$$p \times \infty = \infty$$

This means the expected utility of wagering for God is infinite, *no matter how unlikely it is that God exists*, provided the probability of God's existence is greater than zero. And this in turn means that you should be prepared to stake not only one life to play such a gamble, but any finite amount ("what you stake is finite . . . you must give all"). In particular, you should be prepared to stake your reason, which presumably you value only finitely. We now have our answer to the question of what wagering for God is worth: *an infinite amount.* In Pascal's words, "our proposition is of infinite force."

---

6. I assume that p is not infinitesimal—a tiny number that is positive, but smaller than every positive real number. It is striking that Pascal explicitly makes this assumption, albeit in different words ("there is not an infinity of chances of loss against that of gain"). [Hájek's note.]

What does giving up your *reason* have to do with all this? That seems to come out of nowhere, but a subsequent passage helps us make sense of it. An imaginary interlocutor grants Pascal his conclusion ("I confess it, I admit it"), but plaintively admits being unable to do what is rationally required:

> I am forced to wager, and am not free. I . . . am so made that I cannot believe. What, then, would you have me do?

The problem is that it seems that you cannot believe in God at will. Yet this was supposed to be a *decision problem*, and you can choose only among actions that you are capable of performing. Pascal's advice to you is to suppress your passions, which are an obstacle to your belief, and in particular to engage in the practices of those who believe: "taking the holy water, having masses said, etc." In short, *act like a believer*; "this will naturally make you believe, and deaden your acuteness." The phrase that is translated here as "deaden your acuteness" is even more astonishing in French. Its literal meaning is "will make you a beast"; that is, something devoid of reason. And yet according to Pascal, this is a price worth paying; after all, it's a finite price for an option that has infinite expected utility.

There is some tension within these passages of Pascal's. He began by saying that "if you lose, you lose nothing"; but now he seems to admit that if you lose, you lose *something*, namely your reason. This threatens to undermine his argument that wagering for God *dominates* wagering against God. Yet it seems that in the end this does not matter, for he still has the argument from expected utilities. The utilities associated with wagering against God are finite, and whatever they are, they are swamped in the expected utility calculations by the infinite utility that you may gain by wagering for God—much as the probability that God exists did not matter, beyond its being positive. The expected utilities then apparently carry the day for wagering for God.

There is also some dispute among commentators about what the utility of "misery" is supposed to be. Perhaps Pascal, who was a Catholic, has in mind the doctrine of eternal damnation, in which case this utility may be *negative infinite*? But he writes: "The justice of God must be vast like His compassion. Now justice to the outcast is less vast . . . than mercy towards the elect." This suggests that "misery" is only finitely bad, "less vast" than the infinitude of the reward of salvation.

Let us summarize Pascal's reasoning in modern parlance.

P1. You should choose the action of maximal expected utility if there is one.

P2. The probability p that God exists is positive.

P3. The decision matrix is as follows, where f_1, f_2, and f_3 are finite utilities:

	God exists	God does not exist
Wager for God	∞	f_1
Wager against God	f_2	f_3

Conclusion 1: Wagering for God has infinite expected utility.
Conclusion 2: You should wager for God.

Conclusion 1 follows from the premises. The expected utility of wagering for God is

$$(\infty \times p) + f_1 \times (1-p) = \infty$$

And conclusion 2 seems to follow from conclusion 1 and the premises, since the expected utility of wagering against God is finite:

$$(f_2 \times p) + f_3 \times (1-p) = \text{some finite quantity}$$

which is less than the infinite expected utility of wagering for God. When philosophers speak of "Pascal's Wager," it is typically a version of this argument that they have in mind.

Objections

A host of objections to the Wager vie for our attention.[7]

OBJECTING TO P1

While P1 is enshrined in modern decision theory, it has met with considerable opposition. The Allais, Ellsberg, and St. Petersburg paradoxes, well known to economists, are thought by many to provide counterexamples to it. They all turn on intuitions that other factors besides expected utilities may determine choiceworthiness; for example, the *variance* of the utilities (a measure of how spread out the utilities are). Roughly, high-variance gambles are *risky* in the sense that they may with disturbingly high probabilities yield outcomes far worse than their expected utilities.

Indeed, in the St. Petersburg paradox, getting less than your expected utility is guaranteed. Imagine that you are offered the following gamble: a coin is tossed until it lands heads for the first time. The longer it takes, the better for you: your reward grows exponentially according to the number of tosses up to and including the first heads. Specifically, if it takes a total of n trials for the first heads to appear, you get 2^n dollars. Equating utility with dollar amount, the expected utility of the gamble is

$$(2 \times \tfrac{1}{2}) + (4 \times \tfrac{1}{4}) + (8 \times \tfrac{1}{8}) + \cdots = 1 + 1 + 1 + \cdots = \infty$$

Again, we have an *infinite* expected utility. Yet *every possible amount you could win is finite* ($2, or $4, or $8, or . . .). Thus, it seems that decision theory overvalues the gamble.

---

7. See Alan Hájek, "Pascal's Wager," in *Stanford Encyclopedia of Philosophy*, ed. Edward Zalta (http://platostanford.edu/archives/fall2008/entries/pascal-wager/), for more objections and more responses to objections than I can present here. [Hájek's note.]

In fact, most people would not pay more than $50 up front to play the gamble, much less an infinite amount. Offhand, this is a counterexample to P1: if you are like most people, you would prefer $100, say, to this gamble, even though the latter has far greater expected utility.[8] The apparent failure of decision theory's appeal to expected utilities here should make us wary of appealing to them in Pascal's Wager. Note that there is an *infinite* discrepancy among the utilities in Pascal's Wager, so the concern that expected utilities are a poor guide to choiceworthiness in high-variance gambles may have particular force.

OBJECTING TO P2

An atheist may insist that the probability that God exists is zero—perhaps citing some argument that an omnipotent, omniscient, omnibenevolent being is impossible. This is essentially to disregard entirely the first column of Pascal's decision matrix, so the decision comes down to a comparison of f_1 and f_3. If "losing your reason" comes at a cost, then it may be that $f_1 < f_3$; or if both are the utility of the "status quo," then $f_1 = f_3$. Either way, you are not required to wager for God after all.

Notice, however, just how strong the atheist's conviction needs to be in order to dispute P2. It will not suffice, for example, to think that the probability that God exists is one in a trillion, or one in a googol, or one in a googolplex—those numbers are positive and enough to give Pascal's argument a toehold. The atheism required is *absolute*. But many authors believe that this is really an extreme form of *dogmatism*, unwarranted by any evidence that we could ever get, and therefore *irrational*.

At the "[e]nd of this discourse," Pascal goes on to strengthen his claims about the benefits of wagering for God:

> Now, what harm will befall you in taking this side? You will be faithful, humble, grateful, generous, a sincere friend, truthful. Certainly you will not have those poisonous pleasures, glory and luxury; but will you not have others? I will tell you that you will thereby *gain in this life.* [my italics]

Then it surely does follow that you should wager for God (whether or not you are an atheist). But now the problem has only been shifted: many of us will not grant Pascal this strengthened claim; for example, those who value earthly pleasures rather more than Pascal does.[9] One of the great virtues of Pascal's Wager, its neutrality regarding the comparative sizes of $f_1, f_2,$ and f_3, has been lost.

OBJECTING TO P3

Pascal assumes that we all face the same decision problem. However, perhaps the payoffs are different for different people. Perhaps, for example, there is a predestined

8. There is a vast literature of replies to the St. Petersburg paradox; Martin (2008) surveys some of it. [Hájek's note.]

9. Alan Hájek, "Pascal's Wager," in *Stanford Encyclopedia of Philosophy,* ed. Edward Zalta (http://plato .stanfordedu/archives/fall2008/entries/pascal-wager/), discusses some more technical objections to P2: the probability of God's existence may be positive but *infinitesimal*; and it may be *imprecise* over an interval that includes zero. [Hájek's note.]

infinite reward for the Chosen, whatever they do, and finite utility for the rest, as Mackie suggests. But even granting Pascal this assumption, we may still dispute what that decision problem is.

Disputing the rows. Perhaps there is more than one way to wager for God, and the rewards that God bestows vary accordingly. Perhaps, for example, God does *not* reward those who wager for Him solely based on the mercenary considerations of the very kind that Pascal advocates, as James suggests. Or perhaps God rewards sincere inquiry rather than blind faith, a possibility mooted by Dawkins.

Disputing the columns. Here we come to the most famous objection to Pascal's Wager: the *many Gods objection*. Pascal envisages the God of Christianity. But the same considerations that he adduces apparently apply equally to other Gods. As Diderot writes, "An Imam could reason just as well this way," and Mackie extends the point to the Anabaptists, Mormons, and the worshippers of Kali or of Odin. Indeed, Cargile generates infinitely many alternative Gods: for each real number x, consider the God who prefers contemplating x more than any other activity and who rewards only those who believe in *him*. If Pascal is right that "reason can decide nothing here," then presumably it cannot decide among myriad theistic hypotheses. Perhaps, then, reason itself *requires* us to stay open-minded about all of them, dignifying each of them with at least some probability. But then there are multiple putative routes to infinite expected utility.

In response, some authors argue that the many Gods objection can be mitigated. For example, some of the rival Gods—Kali and Odin among them—do not bestow infinite rewards, so they may be dismissed from our calculations. Among those that do, we arguably should confine our attention to theistic hypotheses that are based on tradition or serious theology (Jordan), or that are in some sense the simplest (Lycan and Schlesinger).

DENYING THAT THE WAGER IS VALID

Now, grant for the sake of the argument all of Pascal's premises. Does it follow that you should wager for God? Earlier I said that Pascal's conclusion *seems* to follow from his premises, but does it really? No. To see why not, consider a different strategy. Toss a fair coin; if it lands heads, wager for God; if it lands tails, wager against God. What is the expected utility of this strategy? With probability ½, the coin lands heads, and then you will perform an action that has an expected utility of ∞, by Pascal's lights; with probability ½, the coin lands tails, and then you will perform an action that has some finite expected utility. So the expected utility of this strategy is

$$(\text{½} \times \infty) + (\text{½} \times \text{some finite utility}) = \infty$$

But notice how the ½ plays no special role in this reasoning. We could replace it with any positive probability p. Sounds familiar? Like a snake eating its own tail, Pascal's assumption of infinite utility for salvation returns to annihilate his own argument! Suppose you wager for God if the winning ticket in a million-ticket lottery is number 17; otherwise, you wager against God. This strategy has expected utility

$$(1/1{,}000{,}000 \times \infty) + (999{,}999/1{,}000{,}000 \times \text{some finite utility}) = \infty$$

And so it goes: *any* strategy for which you have *some* positive probability of winding up wagering for God has infinite expectation.

But isn't that any strategy whatsoever? For *whatever* you do, there is surely such a probability. Suppose you decide to have a beer. There is *some* positive probability that you will wind up wagering for God by the end of the beer. Multiply that probability by ∞, and you see that having a beer has infinite expected utility. Or suppose you do all you can to *avoid* wagering for God—you *express* your passions, you engage in the practices of those who *disbelieve*, and so on. Still, there is *some* probability that you will fail and wager for God nonetheless. Multiply that probability by ∞ and calculate the expected utility of doing everything in your power to *avoid* belief in God. Not only is Pascal's Wager invalid; it is invalid in the worst possible way. Far from establishing that you should wager for God, it "establishes" that every possible action you may undertake is equally good: everything you might do has infinite expected utility given Pascal's assumptions. "The first well-understood contribution to decision theory"? This looks more like *indecision* theory.[10]

Pascal's Final Sting in the Tail

It appears that Pascal's Wager runs aground. But perhaps Pascal has the last laugh. I have posed the problem that all actions that you may undertake have infinite expected utility as a problem for his Wager. But perhaps it is a problem for all of us.

The problem arose when we granted for the sake of the argument all of Pascal's premises. Very well then; let's *not* grant those premises. In fact, I invite you to be highly skeptical of each of them. By all means assign tiny probability to each of them. In fact, assign to the conjunction of them as small a probability *p* as you like, as long as *p* is positive. Go ahead and assume that there is some *minuscule but positive* probability that you should maximize expected utility *and* that God exists *and* that Pascal's decision matrix is correct. Sounds familiar? In doing so, you assign probability *p* to things being exactly as Pascal claims they are. But we know what follows: every action you may undertake has expected utility ∞. Why? Because *p* times ∞ equals ∞. So it isn't just by Pascal's lights that every action you may undertake is equally good. As long as you dignify Pascal's assumptions with at least *some* probability, that staggering conclusion is true by *your* lights as well.

But what's your alternative? To assign probability *zero* to his premises all being true? (Not one in a trillion; not one in a googol; not one in a googolplex; . . .) That seems like an extreme form of dogmatism, unwarranted by your evidence. To be sure, we have seen various ways of questioning the premises, of arguing against them. By all means question them, argue against them. But can you really justify giving them *no* credence

10. See Antony Duff, "Pascal's Wager and Infinite Utilities," *Analysis* 46 (1986): 107–9; and Alan Hájek, "Waging War on Pascal's Wager," *Philosophical Review* 112/1 (January 2003): 27–56, for versions of this argument and further refinements. See also George Schlesinger, "A Central Theistic Argument," in *Gambling on God: Essays on Pascal's Wager*, ed. Jeff Jordan (Rowman & Littlefield, 1994), for a tie-breaking principle that one might add to the Wager in response, and Hájek (2003) and (2011) for six reformulations of Pascal's Wager that render it valid. [Hájek's note.]

whatsoever, given your evidential situation? That seems like a sin against *theoretical rationality*. You may insist that this sin is preferable to the sin against *practical rationality* to which you are committed if you regard every action you may undertake as equally good. But it is surely a disquieting thought, to say the least, that as far as rationality is concerned, you appear to be a sinner whatever you do.

You may need that beer.[11]

REFERENCES

Maurice Allais, "Le Comportement de l'Homme Rationnel Devant le Risque: Critique des Postulats et Axiomes de l'École Américaine," *Econometrica* 21 (1953): 503–46.

James Cargile, "Pascal's Wager," *Philosophy* 35 (1966): 250–57.

Richard Dawkins, *The God Delusion* (Bantam Books, 2006).

Denis Diderot, *Pensées Philosophiques*, LIX, *Oeuvres*, ed. J. Assézat, vol. I (Garnier Frères, 1875–77).

D. Ellsberg, "Risk, Ambiguity and the Savage Axioms," *Quarterly Journal of Economics* 25 (1961): 643–69.

William James, "The Will to Believe," in *The Will to Believe and Other Essays in Popular Philosophy* (Dover Publications, 1956).

Jeff Jordan, "The Many Gods Objection," in *Gambling on God: Essays on Pascal's Wager*, ed. Jeff Jordan (Rowman & Littlefield, 1994).

William Lycan and George Schlesinger, "You Bet Your Life," in *Reason and Responsibility*, 7th ed., ed. Joel Feinberg (Wadsworth, 1989). Also in the 8th, 9th, 10th editions; in *Philosophy and the Human Condition*, 2nd ed., ed. Tom Beauchamp et al. (Prentice Hall, 1989); and in *Contemporary Perspectives on Religious Epistemology*, ed. Douglas Geivet and Brendan Sweetmar (Oxford University Press, 1993).

J. L. Mackie, *The Miracle of Theism* (Oxford, 1982).

Robert Martin, "The St. Petersburg Paradox," in *Stanford Encyclopedia of Philosophy* (Fall 2008 ed.), ed. Edward N. Zalta (http://plato.stanford.edu/archives/fall2008/entries/paradox-stpetersburg/).

TEST YOUR UNDERSTANDING

1. Hájek emphasizes that in assessing the force of Pascal's argument, it does not matter whether the probability of God's existence is ½ or 1/1,000,000. Explain the basis for this claim.

2. True or false: Hájek thinks that Pascal's Wager shows that we all have reason to cultivate a belief in God.

3. Briefly restate the many Gods objection to Pascal's Wager.

4. Construct an argument, using Hájek's assumptions, for the claim that tying your shoes has *infinite* expected utility.

---

11. I thank Gideon Rosen for many helpful suggestions. [Hájek's note.]

NOTES AND QUESTIONS

1. *Two pills.* You are offered a choice between a red pill that will grant you infinite, eternal happiness with a probability of 10 percent and a blue pill that will grant you the same reward with a probability of 99 percent. (If the pill doesn't work, it does nothing.) Hájek's principles entail that these options have the same expected utility. (*Exercise: Explain why.*) But intuitively, there is only one rational choice: it would be crazy to take the red pill; you should take the blue one. So consider the following modification of standard decision theory:

> When faced with several otherwise similar options, each of which might yield an infinite payoff, choose the act that has the highest probability of yielding that payoff.

Question: Does this new theory avoid Hájek's problem? Is it an acceptable theory of rational choice?

2. *The St. Petersburg game.* Suppose someone offers you the opportunity to play the following game. A fair coin will be flipped until it comes up heads. If it comes up heads on the first toss, you get \$2. If it comes up heads for the first time on the second toss, you get \$4. And in general, if the coin comes up heads for the first time on the nth toss, you get \$$2^n$. Now since the probability of the coin's coming up heads for the first time on the nth toss is $\frac{1}{2}^n$, anyone who plays this game has a 50 percent chance of winning \$2, a 25 percent chance of winning \$4, and so on. This means that the chance of winning more than \$16 is quite small: 1/16. And yet there is also a very small chance that you will win an astronomical sum. The expected value of the game is

$$(\tfrac{1}{2} \times \$2) + (\tfrac{1}{4} \times \$4) + \cdots + (\tfrac{1}{2}^n \times 2^n) \cdots$$

$$= \$1 + \$1 + \cdots + \$1 \cdots$$

$$= \infty$$

How much would you be willing to pay to play this game? Let's suppose you would be willing to pay \$20 and no more. Does this show that you are not an "expected utility maximizer"?

W. K. Clifford (1845–1879)

Clifford was a distinguished British mathematician famous for his contributions to geometric algebra. In addition to "The Ethics of Belief," his contributions to philosophy include an early defense of the view that consciousness emerges because the molecules that compose organic matter each contain a bit of preconscious "mind stuff."

THE ETHICS OF BELIEF

I. The Duty of Inquiry

A shipowner was about to send to sea an emigrant-ship. He knew that she was old, and not over-well built at the first; that she had seen many seas and climes, and often had needed repairs. Doubts had been suggested to him that possibly she was not seaworthy. These doubts preyed upon his mind, and made him unhappy; he thought that perhaps he ought to have her thoroughly overhauled and refitted, even though this should put him to great expense. Before the ship sailed, however, he succeeded in overcoming these melancholy reflections. He said to himself that she had gone safely through so many voyages and weathered so many storms, that it was idle to suppose she would not come safely home from this trip also. He would put his trust in Providence, which could hardly fail to protect all these unhappy families that were leaving their fatherland to seek for better times elsewhere. He would dismiss from his mind all ungenerous suspicions about the honesty of builders and contractors. In such ways he acquired a sincere and comfortable conviction that his vessel was thoroughly safe and seaworthy; he watched her departure with a light heart, and benevolent wishes for the success of the exiles in their strange new home that was to be; and he got his insurance-money when she went down in mid-ocean and told no tales.

What shall we say of him? Surely this, that he was verily guilty of the death of those men. It is admitted that he did sincerely believe in the soundness of his ship; but the sincerity of his conviction can in nowise help him, because *he had no right to believe on such evidence as was before him.* He had acquired his belief not by honestly earning it in patient investigation, but by stifling his doubts. And although in the end he may have felt so sure about it that he could not think otherwise, yet inasmuch as he had knowingly and willingly worked himself into that frame of mind, he must be held responsible for it.

Let us alter the case a little, and suppose that the ship was not unsound after all; that she made her voyage safely, and many others after it. Will that diminish the guilt of her owner? Not one jot. When an action is once done, it is right or wrong for ever; no accidental failure of its good or evil fruits can possibly alter that. The man would not have been innocent, he would only have been not found out. The question of right or wrong has to do with the origin of his belief, not the matter of it; not what it was, but how he got it; not whether it turned out to be true or false, but whether he had a right to believe on such evidence as was before him. . . .

It may be said, however, that . . . it is not the belief which is judged to be wrong, but the action following upon it. The shipowner might say, "I am perfectly certain that my ship is sound, but still I feel it my duty to have her examined, before trusting the lives of so many people to her." . . .

In the first place, let us admit that, so far as it goes, this view of the case is right and necessary; right, because even when a man's belief is so fixed that he cannot think otherwise, he still has a choice in regard to the action suggested by it, and so cannot escape the duty of investigating on the ground of the strength of his convictions; and necessary, because those who are not yet capable of controlling their feelings and thoughts must have a plain rule dealing with overt acts.

But this being premised as necessary, it becomes clear that it is not sufficient, and that our previous judgment is required to supplement it. For it is not possible so to sever the belief from the action it suggests as to condemn the one without condemning the other. No man holding a strong belief on one side of a question, or even wishing to hold a belief on one side, can investigate it with such fairness and completeness as if he were really in doubt and unbiased; so that the existence of a belief not founded on fair inquiry, unfits a man for the performance of this necessary duty.

Nor is that truly a belief at all which has not some influence upon the actions of him who holds it. He who truly believes that which prompts him to an action has looked upon the action to lust after it, he has committed it already in his heart. If a belief is not realized immediately in open deeds it is stored up for the guidance of the future. . . . No real belief, however trifling and fragmentary it may seem, is ever truly insignificant; it prepares us to receive more of its like, confirms those which resembled it before, and weakens others; and so gradually it lays a stealthy train in our inmost thoughts, which may some day explode into overt action, and leave its stamp upon our character for ever.

And no one man's belief is in any case a private matter which concerns himself alone. Our lives are guided by that general conception of the course of things which has been created by society for social purposes. Our words, our phrases, our forms and processes and modes of thought, are common property, fashioned and perfected from age to age; an heirloom, which every succeeding generation inherits as a precious deposit and a sacred trust, to be handed on to the next one, not unchanged, but enlarged and purified, with some clear marks of its proper handiwork. Into this, for good or ill, is woven every belief of every man who has speech of his fellows. An awful privilege, and an awful responsibility, that we should help to create the world in which posterity will live.

In the . . . supposed case which [has] been considered, it has been judged wrong to believe on insufficient evidence, or to nourish belief by suppressing doubts and avoiding investigation. The reason of this judgment is not far to seek; it is that . . . the belief held by one man was of great importance to other men. But forasmuch as no belief held by one man, however seemingly trivial the belief, and however obscure the believer, is ever actually insignificant or without its effect on the fate of mankind, we have no choice but to extend our judgment to all cases of belief whatever. Belief, that sacred faculty, which prompts the decisions of our will, and knits into harmonious working all the compacted energies of our being, is ours not for ourselves but for humanity. It is rightly used on truths which have been established by long experience and waiting toil, and which have stood in the fierce light of free and fearless questioning. Then it helps to bind men together, and to strengthen and direct their common action. It is desecrated when given to unproved and unquestioned statements, for the solace and private pleasure of the believer. . . . Whoso would deserve well of his fellows in this matter will guard the purity of his belief with a very fanaticism of jealous care, lest at any time it should rest on an unworthy object, and catch a stain which can never be wiped away.

It is not only the leader of men, statesman, philosopher, or poet, that owes this bounden duty to mankind. Every rustic who delivers in the village alehouse his slow, infrequent sentences, may help to kill or keep alive the fatal superstitions which clog his race. Every hard-worked wife of an artisan may transmit to her children beliefs which shall knit society together, or rend it in pieces. No simplicity of mind, no obscurity of station, can escape the universal duty of questioning all that we believe.

It is true that this duty is a hard one, and the doubt which comes out of it is often a very bitter thing. It leaves us bare and powerless where we thought that we were safe and strong. To know all about anything is to know how to deal with it under all circumstances. We feel much happier and more secure when we think we know precisely what to do, no matter what happens, than when we have lost our way and do not know where to turn. . . . It is the sense of power attached to a sense of knowledge that makes men desirous of believing, and afraid of doubting.

This sense of power is the highest and best of pleasures when the belief on which it is founded is a true belief, and has been fairly earned by investigation. For then we may justly feel that it is common property, and holds good for others as well as for ourselves. Then we may be glad, not that *I* have learned secrets by which I am safer and stronger, but that *we men* have got mastery over more of the world; and we shall be strong, not for ourselves, but in the name of Man and in his strength. But if the belief has been accepted on insufficient evidence, the pleasure is a stolen one. Not only does it deceive ourselves by giving us a sense of power which we do not really possess, but it is sinful, because it is stolen in defiance of our duty to mankind. . . .

And, as in other such senses, it is not the risk only which has to be considered; for a bad action is always bad at the time when it is done, no matter what happens afterwards. Every time we let ourselves believe for unworthy reasons, we weaken our powers of self-control, of doubting, of judicially and fairly weighing evidence. We all suffer severely enough from the maintenance and support of false beliefs and the fatally wrong actions which they lead to, and the evil born when one such belief is entertained is great and wide. But a greater and wider evil arises when the credulous character is maintained and supported, when a habit of believing for unworthy reasons is fostered and made permanent. If I steal money from any person, there may be no harm done by the mere transfer of possession; he may not feel the loss, or it may prevent him from using the money badly. But I cannot help doing this great wrong towards Man, that I make myself dishonest. What hurts society is not that it should lose its property, but that it should become a den of thieves; for then it must cease to be society. This is why we ought not to do evil that good may come; for at any rate this great evil has come, that we have done evil and are made wicked thereby. In like manner, if I let myself believe anything on insufficient evidence, there may be no great harm done by the mere belief; it may be true after all, or I may never have occasion to exhibit it in outward acts. But I cannot help doing this great wrong towards Man, that I make myself credulous. The danger to society is not merely that it should believe wrong things, though that is great enough; but that it should become credulous, and lose the habit of testing things and inquiring into them; for then it must sink back into savagery.

The harm which is done by credulity in a man is not confined to the fostering of a credulous character in others, and consequent support of false beliefs. Habitual want of care about what I believe leads to habitual want of care in others about the truth of what is told to me. Men speak the truth to one another when each reveres the truth in his own mind and in the other's mind; but how shall my friend revere the truth in my mind when I myself am careless about it, when I believe things because I want to believe them, and because they are comforting and pleasant? Will he not learn to cry, "Peace," to me, when there is no peace? By such a course I shall surround myself with a thick atmosphere of falsehood and fraud, and in that I must live. It may matter little to me, in my cloud-castle of sweet illusions and darling lies; but it matters much to Man that I have made my neighbours ready to deceive. The credulous man is father to the liar and the cheat; he lives in the bosom of this his family, and it is no marvel if he should become even as they are. So closely are our duties knit together, that whoso shall keep the whole law, and yet offend in one point, he is guilty of all.

To sum up: it is wrong always, everywhere, and for any one, to believe anything upon insufficient evidence.

If a man, holding a belief which he was taught in childhood or persuaded of afterwards, keeps down and pushes away any doubts which arise about it in his mind, purposely avoids the reading of books and the company of men that call in question or discuss it, and regards as impious those questions which cannot easily be asked without disturbing it; the life of that man is one long sin against mankind.

If this judgment seems harsh when applied to those simple souls who have never known better, who have been brought up from the cradle with a horror of doubt, and taught that their eternal welfare depends on *what* they believe; then it leads to the very serious question, *Who hath made Israel to sin?*

It may be permitted me to fortify this judgment with the sentence of Milton[1]—

> A man may be a heretic in the truth; and if he believe things only because his pastor says so, or the assembly so determine, without knowing other reason, though his belief be true, yet the very truth he holds becomes his heresy.

And with this famous aphorism of Coleridge[2]—

> He who begins by loving Christianity better than Truth, will proceed by loving his own sect or Church better than Christianity, and end in loving himself better than all.

Inquiry into the evidence of a doctrine is not to be made once for all, and then taken as finally settled. It is never lawful to stifle a doubt; for either it can be honestly answered by means of the inquiry already made, or else it proves that the inquiry was not complete.

---

1. *Areopagitica.* [Clifford's note.]
2. *Aids to Reflection.* [Clifford's note.]

"But," says one, "I am a busy man; I have no time for the long course of study which would be necessary to make me in any degree a competent judge of certain questions, or even able to understand the nature of the arguments." Then he should have no time to believe.

II. The Weight of Authority

Are we then to become universal sceptics, doubting everything, afraid always to put one foot before the other until we have personally tested the firmness of the road? Are we to deprive ourselves of the help and guidance of that vast body of knowledge which is daily growing upon the world, because neither we nor any other one person can possibly test a hundredth part of it by immediate experiment or observation, and because it would not be completely proved if we did? Shall we steal and tell lies because we have had no personal experience wide enough to justify the belief that it is wrong to do so?

There is no practical danger that such consequences will ever follow from scrupulous care and self-control in the matter of belief. Those men who have most nearly done their duty in this respect have found that certain great principles, and these most fitted for the guidance of life, have stood out more and more clearly in proportion to the care and honesty with which they were tested, and have acquired in this way a practical certainty. The beliefs about right and wrong which guide our actions in dealing with men in society, and the beliefs about physical nature which guide our actions in dealing with animate and inanimate bodies, these never suffer from investigation; they can take care of themselves, without being propped up by "acts of faith," the clamour of paid advocates, or the suppression of contrary evidence. Moreover there are many cases in which it is our duty to act upon probabilities, although the evidence is not such as to justify present belief; because it is precisely by such action, and by observation of its fruits, that evidence is got which may justify future belief. So that we have no reason to fear lest a habit of conscientious inquiry should paralyze the actions of our daily life.

But because it is not enough to say, "It is wrong to believe on unworthy evidence," without saying also what evidence is worthy, we shall now go on to inquire under what circumstances it is lawful to believe on the testimony of others; and then, further, we shall inquire more generally when and why we may believe that which goes beyond our own experience, or even beyond the experience of mankind.

In what cases, then, let us ask in the first place, is the testimony of a man unworthy of belief? He may say that which is untrue either knowingly or unknowingly. In the first case he is lying, and his moral character is to blame; in the second case he is ignorant or mistaken, and it is only his knowledge or his judgment which is in fault. In order that we may have the right to accept his testimony as ground for believing what he says, we must have reasonable grounds for trusting his *veracity*, that he is really trying to speak the truth so far as he knows it; his *knowledge*, that he has had opportunities of knowing the truth about this matter; and his *judgment*, that he has made a proper use of those opportunities in coming to the conclusion which he affirms. . . .

If a chemist tells me, who am no chemist, that a certain substance can be made by putting together other substances in certain proportions and subjecting them to a known process, I am quite justified in believing this upon his authority, unless I know anything against his character or his judgment. For his professional training is one which tends to encourage veracity and the honest pursuit of truth, and to produce a dislike of hasty conclusions and slovenly investigation. And I have reasonable ground for supposing that he knows the truth of what he is saying, for although I am no chemist, I can be made to understand so much of the methods and processes of the science as makes it conceivable to me that, without ceasing to be man, I might verify the statement. I may never actually verify it, or even see any experiment which goes towards verifying it; but still I have quite reason enough to justify me in believing that the verification is within the reach of human appliances and powers, and in particular that it has been actually performed by my informant. His result, the belief to which he has been led by his inquiries, is valid not only for himself but for others; it is watched and tested by those who are working in the same ground, and who know that no greater service can be rendered to science than the purification of accepted results from the errors which may have crept into them. It is in this way that the result becomes common property, a right object of belief, which is a social affair and matter of public business. Thus it is to be observed that his authority is valid because there are those who question it and verify it; that it is precisely this process of examining and purifying that keeps alive among investigators the love of that which shall stand all possible tests, the sense of public responsibility as of those whose work, if well done, shall remain as the enduring heritage of mankind.

But if my chemist tells me that an atom of oxygen has existed unaltered in weight and rate of vibration throughout all time, I have no right to believe this on his authority, for it is a thing which he cannot know without ceasing to be man. He may quite honestly believe that this statement is a fair inference from his experiments, but in that case his judgment is at fault. A very simple consideration of the character of experiments would show him that they never can lead to results of such a kind; that being themselves only approximate and limited, they cannot give us knowledge which is exact and universal. No eminence of character and genius can give a man authority enough to justify us in believing him when he makes statements implying exact or universal knowledge. . . .

What shall we say of that authority, more venerable and august than any individual witness, the time-honoured tradition of the human race? An atmosphere of beliefs and conceptions has been formed by the labours and struggles of our forefathers, which enables us to breathe amid the various and complex circumstances of our life. It is around and about us and within us; we cannot think except in the forms and processes of thought which it supplies. Is it possible to doubt and to test it? and if possible, is it right?

We shall find reason to answer that it is not only possible and right, but our bounden duty; that the main purpose of the tradition itself is to supply us with the means of asking questions, of testing and inquiring into things; that if we misuse it, and take it as a collection of cut-and-dried statements, to be accepted without further inquiry, we are not only injuring ourselves here, but by refusing to do our part towards the building up of the fabric which shall be inherited by our children, we are tending to cut off ourselves and our race from the human line.

Let us first take care to distinguish a kind of tradition which especially requires to be examined and called in question, because it especially shrinks from inquiry. Suppose that a medicine-man in Central Africa tells his tribe that a certain powerful medicine in his tent will be propitiated if they kill their cattle; and that the tribe believe him. Whether the medicine was propitiated or not, there are no means of verifying, but the cattle are gone. Still the belief may be kept up in the tribe that propitiation has been effected in this way; and in a later generation it will be all the easier for another medicine-man to persuade them to a similar act. Here the only reason for belief is that everybody has believed the thing for so long that it must be true. And yet the belief was founded on fraud, and has been propagated by credulity. That man will undoubtedly do right, and be a friend of men, who shall call it in question and see that there is no evidence for it, help his neighbours to see as he does, and even, if need be, go into the holy tent and break the medicine.

The rule which should guide us in such cases is simple and obvious enough: that the aggregate testimony of our neighbours is subject to the same conditions as the testimony of any one of them. Namely, we have no right to believe a thing true because everybody says so, unless there are good grounds for believing that some one person at least has the means of knowing what is true, and is speaking the truth so far as he knows it. However many nations and generations of men are brought into the witness-box, they cannot testify to anything which they do not know. Every man who has accepted the statement from somebody else, without himself testing and verifying it, is out of court; his word is worth nothing at all. And when we get back at last to the true birth and beginning of the statement, two serious questions must be disposed of in regard to him who first made it: was he mistaken in thinking that he *knew* about this matter, or was he lying? . . .

In regard, then, to the sacred tradition of humanity, we learn that it consists, not in propositions or statements which are to be accepted and believed on the authority of the tradition, but in questions rightly asked, in conceptions which enable us to ask further questions, and in methods of answering questions. The value of all these things depends on their being tested day by day. The very sacredness of the precious deposit imposes upon us the duty and the responsibility of testing it, of purifying and enlarging it to the utmost of our power. . . .

III. The Limits of Inference

The question, in what cases we may believe that which goes beyond our experience, is a very large and delicate one, extending to the whole range of scientific method, and requiring a considerable increase in the application of it before it can be answered with anything approaching to completeness.[3] But one rule, lying on the threshold of the subject, of extreme simplicity and vast practical importance, may here be touched upon and shortly laid down.

A little reflection will show us that every belief, even the simplest and most fundamental, goes beyond experience when regarded as a guide to our actions. A burnt child dreads the fire, because it believes that the fire will burn it to-day just as it did yesterday; but this belief goes beyond experience, and assumes that the unknown fire of to-day is like the known fire of yesterday. Even the belief that the child was burnt yesterday goes beyond *present* experience, which contains only the memory of a burning, and not the burning itself; it assumes, therefore, that this memory is trustworthy, although we know that a memory may often be mistaken. But if it is to be used as a guide of action, as a hint of what the future is to be, it must assume something about that future, namely, that it will be consistent with the supposition that the burning really took place yesterday; which is going beyond experience. Even the fundamental "I am," which cannot be doubted,[4] is no guide to action until it takes to itself "I shall be," which goes beyond experience. The question is not, therefore, "May we believe what goes beyond experience?" for this is involved in the very nature of belief; but "How far and in what manner may we add to our experience in forming our beliefs?"

And an answer, of utter simplicity and universality, is suggested by the example we have taken: a burnt child dreads the fire. We may go beyond experience by assuming that what we do not know is like what we do know; or, in other words, we may add to our experience on the assumption of a uniformity in nature. What this uniformity precisely is, how we grow in the knowledge of it from generation to generation, these are questions which for the present we lay aside, being content to examine [one] instance which may serve to make plainer the nature of the rule.

From certain observations made with the spectroscope, we infer the existence of hydrogen in the sun. By looking into the spectroscope when the sun is shining on its slit, we see certain definite bright lines; and experiments made upon bodies on the earth have taught us that when these bright lines are seen, hydrogen is the source of them. We assume, then, that the unknown bright lines in the sun are like the known bright lines of the laboratory, and that hydrogen in the sun behaves as hydrogen under similar circumstances would behave on the earth.

But are we not trusting our spectroscope too much? Surely, having found it to be trustworthy for terrestrial substances, where its statements can be verified by man, we are justified in accepting its testimony in other like cases; but not when it gives us information about things in the sun, where its testimony cannot be directly verified by man?

Certainly, we want to know a little more before this inference can be justified; and fortunately we do know this. The spectroscope testifies to exactly the same thing in the two cases; namely, that light-vibrations of a certain rate are being sent through

---

3. For extensive discussion, see Chapter 4 of this anthology.

4. René Descartes famously argued that the statement "I am, I exist" cannot rationally be doubted. See the selection from Descartes's *Meditations* in Chapter 6 of this anthology.

it. Its construction is such that if it were wrong about this in one case it would be wrong in the other. When we come to look into the matter, we find that we have really assumed the matter of the sun to be like the matter of the earth, made up of a certain number of distinct substances; and that each of these, when very hot, has a distinct rate of vibration, by which it may be recognized and singled out from the rest. But this is the kind of assumption which we are justified in using when we add to our experience. It is an assumption of uniformity in nature, and can only be checked by comparison with many similar assumptions which we have to make in other such cases.

But is this a true belief, of the existence of hydrogen in the sun? Can it help in the right guidance of human action?

Certainly not, if it is accepted on unworthy grounds, and without some under-standing of the process by which it is got at. But when this process is taken in as the ground of the belief, it becomes a very serious and practical matter. For if there is no hydrogen in the sun, the spectroscope—that is to say, the measurement of rates of vibration—must be an uncertain guide in recognizing different substances; and consequently it ought not to be used in chemical analysis—in assaying, for exam-ple—to the great saving of time, trouble, and money. Whereas the acceptance of the spectroscopic method as trustworthy has enriched us not only with new metals, which is a great thing, but with new processes of investigation, which is vastly greater. . . .

We may, then, add to our experience on the assumption of a uniformity in nature: we may fill in our picture of what is and has been, as experience gives it us, in such a way as to make the whole consistent with this uniformity. . . .

No evidence, therefore, can justify us in believing the truth of a statement which is contrary to, or outside of, the uniformity of nature. If our experience is such that it cannot be filled up consistently with uniformity, all we have a right to conclude is that there is something wrong somewhere; but the possibility of inference is taken away; we must rest in our experience, and not go beyond it at all. If an event really happened, which was not a part of the uniformity of nature, it would have two prop-erties; no evidence could give the right to believe it to any except those whose actual experience it was; and no inference worthy of belief could be founded upon it at all.[5]

Are we then bound to believe that nature is absolutely and universally uniform? Certainly not; we have no right to believe anything of this kind. The rule only tells us that in forming beliefs which go beyond our experience, we may make the assumption that nature is practically uniform so far as we are concerned. Within the range of hu-man action and verification, we may form, by help of this assumption, actual beliefs; beyond it, only those hypotheses which serve for the more accurate asking of questions.

---

5. An allusion to David Hume's famous argument in his *Enquiry Concerning Human Understanding*, Section X ("Of Miracles"), that since a miracle is, by definition, an event outside the ordinary laws of nature, it is never reasonable to believe in miracles on the basis of someone else's testimony. When someone tells you that a miracle occurred, there are two possibilities. Either a miracle did in fact occur and the laws of nature were violated or your informant is mistaken. But we only call something a law of nature if it is supported by a vast abundance of observations. So in any case of this sort, the only reasonable conclusion, given your evidence, will be that your informant somehow got it wrong.

To sum up:—

We may believe what goes beyond our experience, only when it is inferred from that experience by the assumption that what we do not know is like what we know.

We may believe the statement of another person, when there is reasonable ground for supposing that he knows the matter of which he speaks, and that he is speaking the truth so far as he knows it.

It is wrong in all cases to believe on insufficient evidence; and where it is presumption to doubt and to investigate, there it is worse than presumption to believe.

TEST YOUR UNDERSTANDING

1. True or false: According to Clifford, it is sometimes morally permissible to believe a proposition without good evidence.

2. Clifford contrasts two shipowners. Each believes that his ship is seaworthy despite evidence to the contrary and lets it sail. In the first case, the ship sinks. In the second, it arrives safely. The first shipowner is blameworthy because his action kills many people. Why is the second blameworthy according to Clifford?

3. True or false: According to Clifford, it is wrong to believe what other people tell you if you have not verified their claims for yourself.

4. Testimony aside, when is it permissible to hold a belief that goes beyond one's own personal experience in Clifford's view (e.g., a belief about the chemical composition of the sun)?

NOTES AND QUESTIONS

1. *Clifford on religious belief.* Clifford's essay is widely read as an attack on religious faith, though in fact Clifford says relatively little about religion.

   Exercise: Using premises drawn from Clifford's essay, construct an argument for the conclusion that it is morally wrong to believe that God exists.

2. *Rule consequentialism.* Jones has a boring job and no friends, but he has a hobby that keeps him amused. He stays up late thinking about dinosaurs and forming wild hypotheses about what they were like. Jones has no evidence for these hypotheses, but he sometimes believes them because it makes him happy. He never acts on his beliefs and never talks to anyone about them. According to Clifford, it is nonetheless wrong for Jones to do this. Why?
   Here is one way to reconstruct Clifford's argument:

   (1) Of all the rules we might adopt for forming beliefs, a rule that strictly prohibits believing without evidence would have the best consequences if it were generally adopted.

(2) An act is wrong if it violates a rule that would have the best consequences if it were generally adopted.

(3) So it is always wrong to believe without evidence, even if this is sometimes harmless.

Premise (1) is a factual claim. Clifford argues that if we tolerate sloppy thinking in any context, the rot will spread. We will make more mistakes. Society will become more credulous. And this will cause harm in the long run.

Question: Is this true? Can you formulate a rule that would allow belief without evidence in certain circumstances but which would not have these bad consequences?

Premise (2) is a version of **rule consequentialism,** a general approach to ethics according to which the rightness or wrongness of an act depends on its conformity to maximally beneficial general rules.

Question: Is rule consequentialism a plausible general theory? If not, can you reconstruct Clifford's argument without assuming it?

On rule consequentialism, see B. Hooker, *Ideal Code, Real World: A Rule Consequentialist Theory of Morality* (Oxford University Press, 2000).

3. *The uniformity of nature.* Clifford follows David Hume (see Chapter 4 of this anthology) in holding that our beliefs about things we have not personally observed are often formed by observing a pattern in our experience and then assuming that "the unknown is like the known."

A burnt child dreads the fire, because it believes that the fire will burn it to-day just as it did yesterday; but this belief goes beyond experience and assumes that the unknown fire of today is like the known fire of yesterday.[6]

Clifford calls the assumption that underlies this reasoning the uniformity of nature (UN). We can put it roughly as follows:

UN: If a pattern holds in my experience, then it holds generally.

The idea is that whenever we reason from observations to conclusions about things we have not observed, we take this principle for granted. The child in the example reasons as follows:

Evidence: In my experience, fire burns.
UN: If a pattern holds in my experience, it holds generally.
Conclusion: So fire always burns (even the fire I have not yet experienced).

---

6. See page 93 of this anthology.

This sort of reasoning is morally permissible on Clifford's view. When a child who has been burned forms the belief that fire burns by reasoning in this way, the resulting belief is based on "sufficient evidence."

But now focus on the child's (implicit) belief in the uniformity of nature. Is this belief based on "sufficient evidence"? Hume argued that our belief in this principle is not based on evidence at all. Very briefly, Hume's argument runs as follows:

a. A belief about the unobserved is based on evidence only if it results from a bit of reasoning that has UN as a premise.

b. Our belief in UN is a belief about the unobserved.

c. So our belief in UN is based on evidence only if it results from a bit of reasoning that has UN as a premise.

d. But our belief in UN cannot result from reasoning that has UN as a premise.

e. So our belief in UN is not based on evidence.

Question: How might Clifford respond to this argument? If he cannot, must he conclude that at least one belief—our belief in UN—is morally permissible even though it is based on no evidence whatsoever? (See Chapter 4 for an extensive discussion of this issue.)

William James (1842–1910)

James was trained as a physician and made important contributions to both philosophy and psychology. His *Principles of Psychology* (1890) established experimental psychology as a scientific discipline in the United States. His contributions to philosophy include *Pragmatism* (1907) and *The Meaning of Truth* (1909).

THE WILL TO BELIEVE

I have brought with me tonight something like a sermon on justification by faith to read to you,—I mean an essay in justification of faith, a defence of our right to adopt a believing attitude in religious matters, in spite of the fact that our merely logical intellect may not have been coerced. "The Will to Believe," accordingly, is the title of my paper.

I

Let us give the name of hypothesis to anything that may be proposed to our belief; and just as the electricians speak of live and dead wires, let us speak of any hypothesis as either live or dead. A live hypothesis is one which appeals as a real possibility to him to whom it is proposed. If I ask you to believe in the Mahdi,[1] the notion makes no electric connection with your nature,—it refuses to scintillate with any credibility at all. As an hypothesis it is completely dead. To an Arab, however (even if he be not one of the Mahdi's followers), the hypothesis is among the mind's possibilities: it is alive. This shows that deadness and liveness in an hypothesis are not intrinsic properties, but relations to the individual thinker. They are measured by his willingness to act. The maximum of liveness in an hypothesis means willingness to act irrevocably. Practically, that means belief; but there is some believing tendency wherever there is willingness to act at all.

Next, let us call the decision between two hypotheses an option. Options may be of several kinds. They may be:

- Living or dead;
- Forced or avoidable;
- Momentous or trivial;

and for our purpose we may call an option a genuine option when it is of the forced, living, and momentous kind.

1. A living option is one in which both hypotheses are live ones. If I say to you: "Be a theosophist[2] or be a Mohammedan," it is probably a dead option, because for you neither hypothesis is likely to be alive. But if I say: "Be an agnostic or be Christian," it is otherwise: trained as you are, each hypothesis makes some appeal, however small, to your belief.

2. Next, if I say to you: "Choose between going out with your umbrella or without it," I do not offer you a genuine option, for it is not forced. You can easily avoid it by not going out at all. . . . But if I say, "Either accept this truth or go without it," I put on you a forced option, for there is no standing place outside of the alternative. Every dilemma based on a complete logical disjunction, with no possibility of not choosing, is an option of this forced kind.

3. Finally, if I were Dr. Nansen[3] and proposed to you to join my North Pole expedition, your option would be momentous; for this would probably be your only similar opportunity, and your choice now would either exclude you from the North Pole sort of immortality altogether or put at least the chance of it into your hands. He who refuses to embrace a unique opportunity loses the prize as surely as if he tried and failed. *Per contra*, the option is trivial when the opportunity is not unique, when the stake is insignificant, or when the decision is reversible if it later prove unwise. Such trivial options abound in the scientific

1. The redeemer, a descendant of Muhammad whose coming is expected in some branches of Islam.

2. Theosophy is a system of esoteric doctrine associated in James's time with the mystical teachings of Mme. Blavatsky (1831–1891).

3. The Norwegian explorer Fridtjof Nansen (1861–1930) did not reach the North Pole on his famous journey of 1893, though he did come closer than anyone had come before.

life. A chemist finds an hypothesis live enough to spend a year in its verification: he believes in it to that extent. But if his experiments prove inconclusive either way, he is quit for his loss of time, no vital harm being done.

It will facilitate our discussion if we keep all these distinctions well in mind.

II

The next matter to consider is the actual psychology of human opinion. When we look at certain facts, it seems as if our passional and volitional nature lay at the root of all our convictions. When we look at others, it seems as if they could do nothing when the intellect had once said its say. Let us take the latter facts up first.

Does it not seem preposterous on the very face of it to talk of our opinions being modifiable at will? Can our will either help or hinder our intellect in its perceptions of truth? Can we, by just willing it, believe that Abraham Lincoln's existence is a myth, and that the portraits of him in McClure's Magazine are all of some one else? Can we, by any effort of our will, or by any strength of wish that it were true, believe ourselves well and about when we are roaring with rheumatism in bed, or feel certain that the sum of the two one-dollar bills in our pocket must be a hundred dollars? . . .

In Pascal's *Thoughts* there is a celebrated passage known in literature as Pascal's wager. In it he tries to force us into Christianity by reasoning as if our concern with truth resembled our concern with the stakes in a game of chance. Translated freely his words are these: You must either believe or not believe that God is—which will you do? Your human reason cannot say. A game is going on between you and the nature of things which at the day of judgment will bring out either heads or tails. Weigh what your gains and your losses would be if you should stake all you have on heads, or God's existence: if you win in such case, you gain eternal beatitude; if you lose, you lose nothing at all. If there were an infinity of chances, and only one for God in this wager, still you ought to stake your all on God; for though you surely risk a finite loss by this procedure, any finite loss is reasonable, even a certain one is reasonable, if there is but the possibility of infinite gain. Go, then, and take holy water, and have masses said; belief will come and stupefy your scruples. . . . Why should you not? At bottom, what have you to lose?

You probably feel that when religious faith expresses itself thus, in the language of the gaming-table, it is put to its last trumps. It is evident that unless there be some pre-existing tendency to believe in masses and holy water, the option offered to the will by Pascal is not a living option. Certainly no Turk ever took to masses and holy water on its account; and even to us Protestants these seem such foregone impossibilities that Pascal's logic, invoked for them specifically, leaves us unmoved. . . .

The talk of believing by our volition seems, then, from one point of view, simply silly. From another point of view it is worse than silly, it is vile. When one turns to the magnificent edifice of the physical sciences, and sees how it was reared; what thousands of disinterested moral lives of men lie buried in its mere foundations; what patience and postponement, what choking down of preference, what submission to the icy laws of outer fact are wrought into its very stones and mortar; how absolutely impersonal it stands in its vast augustness,—then how besotted and contemptible seems every little sentimentalist who comes blowing his voluntary smoke-wreaths, and pretending to decide things from out of his private dream! . . .

[As] that delicious *enfant terrible* Clifford[4] writes: "Belief is desecrated when given to unproved and unquestioned statements for the solace and private pleasure of the believer. . . . Whoso would deserve well of his fellows in this matter will guard the purity of his belief with a very fanaticism of jealous care, lest at any time it should rest on an unworthy object, and catch a stain which can never be wiped away. . . . If [a] belief has been accepted on insufficient evidence [even though the belief be true, as Clifford on the same page explains] the pleasure is a stolen one. . . . It is sinful because it is stolen in defiance of our duty to mankind. That duty is to guard ourselves from such beliefs as from a pestilence which may shortly master our own body and then spread to the rest of the town. . . . It is wrong always, everywhere, and for every one, to believe anything upon insufficient evidence."

III

All this strikes one as healthy. . . . Yet if any one should thereupon assume that intellectual insight is what remains after wish and will and sentimental preference have taken wing, or that pure reason is what then settles our opinions, he would fly quite as directly in the teeth of the facts.

It is only our already dead hypotheses that our willing nature is unable to bring to life again. But what has made them dead for us is for the most part a previous action of our willing nature of an antagonistic kind. When I say "willing nature," I do not mean only such deliberate volitions as may have set up habits of belief that we cannot now escape from,—I mean all such factors of belief as fear and hope, prejudice and passion, imitation and partisanship, the circumpressure of our caste and set. As a matter of fact we find ourselves believing, we hardly know how or why. . . . Here in this room, we all of us believe in molecules and the conservation of energy, in democracy and necessary progress, in Protestant Christianity and the duty of fighting for "the doctrine of the immortal Monroe," all for no reasons worthy of the name. . . . Our reason is quite satisfied, in nine hundred and ninety-nine cases out of every thousand of us, if it can find a few arguments that will do to recite in case our credulity is criticised by some one else. Our faith is faith in some one else's faith, and in the greatest matters this is most the case. . . .

As a rule we disbelieve all facts and theories for which we have no use. Clifford's cosmic emotions find no use for Christian feelings. . . . Newman,[5] on the contrary,

---

4. W. K. Clifford (1845–1879), English mathematician and philosopher, author of "The Ethics of Belief" (1877), excerpted in this chapter.

5. John Henry Newman (1801–1890) converted from Anglicanism to Catholicism and later became a cardinal of the Roman Catholic Church.

goes over to Romanism, and finds all sorts of reasons good for staying there, because a priestly system is for him an organic need and delight. This very law which the logicians would impose upon us—if I may give the name of logicians to those who would rule out our willing nature here—is based on nothing but their own natural wish to exclude all elements for which they, in their professional quality of logicians, can find no use. . . .

The state of things is evidently far from simple; and pure insight and logic, whatever they might do ideally, are not the only things that really do produce our creeds.

IV

Our next duty, having recognized this mixed-up state of affairs, is to ask whether it be simply reprehensible and pathological, or whether, on the contrary, we must treat it as a normal element in making up our minds. The thesis I defend is, briefly stated, this: *Our passional nature not only lawfully may, but must, decide an option between propositions, whenever it is a genuine option that cannot by its nature be decided on intellectual grounds; for to say, under such circumstances, "Do not decide, but leave the question open," is itself a passional decision,—just like deciding yes or no,—and is attended with the same risk of losing the truth.* . . .

VII

One more point, small but important, and our preliminaries are done. There are two ways of looking at our duty in the matter of opinion. . . . *We must know the truth; and we must avoid error,*—these are our first and great commandments as would-be knowers; but they are not two ways of stating an identical commandment, they are two separable laws . . . and by choosing between them we may end by coloring differently our whole intellectual life. We may regard the chase for truth as paramount, and the avoidance of error as secondary; or we may, on the other hand, treat the avoidance of error as more imperative, and let truth take its chance. Clifford exhorts us to the latter course. Believe nothing, he tells us, keep your mind in suspense forever, rather than by closing it on insufficient evidence incur the awful risk of believing lies. You, on the other hand, may think that the risk of being in error is a very small matter when compared with the blessings of real knowledge, and be ready to be duped many times in your investigation rather than postpone indefinitely the chance of guessing true. I myself find it impossible to go with Clifford. We must remember that these feelings of our duty about either truth or error are in any case only expressions of our passional life. . . . [H]e who says, "Better go without belief forever than believe a lie!" merely shows his own preponderant private horror of becoming a dupe. . . . For my own part, I have also a horror of being duped; but I can believe that worse things than being duped may happen to a man in this world: so Clifford's exhortation has to my ears a thoroughly fantastic sound. . . . Our errors are surely not such awfully solemn things. In a world where we are so certain to incur them in spite of all our caution, a certain lightness of heart seems healthier than this excessive nervousness on their behalf. . . .

VIII

And now, after all this introduction, let us go straight at our question. I have said, and now repeat it, that not only as a matter of fact do we find our passional nature influencing us in our opinions, but that there are some options between opinions in which this influence must be regarded both as an inevitable and as a lawful determinant of our choice.

I fear here that some of you my hearers will begin to scent danger. . . . Two first steps of passion you have indeed had to admit as necessary,—we must think so as to avoid dupery, and we must think so as to gain truth; but the surest path to those ideal consummations, you will probably consider, is from now onwards to take no further passional step.

Well, of course, I agree as far as the facts will allow. Wherever the option between losing truth and gaining it is not momentous, we can throw the chance of gaining truth away, and at any rate save ourselves from any chance of believing falsehood, by not making up our minds at all till objective evidence has come. In scientific questions, this is almost always the case; and even in human affairs in general, the need of acting is seldom so urgent that a false belief to act on is better than no belief at all. . . . Let us agree [then] that wherever there is no forced option, the dispassionately judicial intellect with no pet hypothesis, saving us, as it does, from dupery at any rate, ought to be our ideal.

The question next arises: Are there not somewhere forced options in our speculative questions, and can we (as men who may be interested at least as much in positively gaining truth as in merely escaping dupery) always wait with impunity till the coercive evidence shall have arrived?

IX

Moral questions immediately present themselves as questions whose solution cannot wait for sensible proof. A moral question is a question not of what sensibly exists, but of what is good, or would be good if it did exist. Science can tell us what exists; but to compare the worths, both of what exists and of what does not exist, we must consult not science, but what Pascal calls our heart. Science herself consults her heart when she lays it down that the infinite ascertainment of fact and correction of false belief are the supreme goods for man. Challenge the statement, and science can only repeat it oracularly, or else prove it by showing that such ascertainment and correction bring man all sorts of other goods which man's heart in turn declares. . . .

Turn now from these wide questions of good to a certain class of questions of fact, questions concerning personal relations, states of mind between one man and another. Do you like me or not?—for example. Whether you do or not depends, in countless instances, on whether I meet you half-way, am willing to assume that you must like me, and show you trust and expectation. The previous faith on my part in your liking's existence is in such cases what makes your liking come. But if I stand aloof, and refuse to budge an inch until I have objective evidence, until you shall have done something apt, as the absolutists say, . . . ten to one your liking never comes. . . . The desire for a certain kind of truth here brings about that special truth's existence; and so it is in innumerable cases of other sorts. Who gains promotions, boons, appointments, but the man in whose life they are seen to play the part of live hypotheses, who discounts them, sacrifices other things for their sake before they have come, and takes risks for them in advance? His faith acts on the powers above him as a claim, and creates its own verification.

A social organism of any sort whatever, large or small, is what it is because each member proceeds to his own duty with a trust that the other members will simultaneously do theirs. Wherever a desired result is achieved by the co-operation of many independent persons, its existence as a fact is a pure consequence of the precursive faith in one another of those immediately concerned. A government, an army, a commercial system, a ship, a college, an athletic team, all exist on this condition, without which not only is nothing achieved, but nothing is even attempted. A whole train of passengers (individually brave enough) will be looted by a few highwaymen, simply because the latter can count on one another, while each passenger fears that if he makes a movement of resistance, he will be shot before any one else backs him up. If we believed that the whole car-full would rise at once with us, we should each severally rise, and train-robbing would never even be attempted. There are, then, cases where a fact cannot come at all unless a preliminary faith exists in its coming. And where faith in a fact can help create the fact, that would be an insane logic which should say that faith running ahead of scientific evidence is the "lowest kind of immorality" into which a thinking being can fall. Yet such is the logic by which our scientific absolutists pretend to regulate our lives!

X

In truths dependent on our personal action, then, faith based on desire is certainly a lawful and possibly an indispensable thing.

But now, it will be said, these are all childish human cases, and have nothing to do with great cosmic matters, like the question of religious faith. Let us then pass on to that. . . . What then do we now mean by the religious hypothesis? Science says things are; morality says some things are better than other things; and religion says essentially two things.

First, she says that the best things are the more eternal things, the overlapping things, the things in the universe that throw the last stone, so to speak, and say the final word. . . .

The second affirmation of religion is that we are better off even now if we believe her first affirmation to be true.

Now, let us consider what the logical elements of this situation are in case the religious hypothesis in both its branches be really true. . . . So proceeding, we see, first that religion offers itself as a momentous option. We are supposed to gain, even now, by our belief, and to lose by our nonbelief, a certain vital good. Secondly, religion is a forced option, so far as that good goes. We cannot escape the issue by remaining sceptical and waiting for more light, because, although we do avoid error in that way if religion be untrue, we lose the good, if it be true, just as certainly as if we positively chose to disbelieve. . . . Scepticism, then, is not avoidance of option; it is option of a certain particular kind of risk. *Better risk loss of truth than chance of error,*—that is your faith-vetoer's exact position. . . . To preach scepticism to us as a duty until "sufficient evidence" for religion be found, is tantamount therefore to telling us, when in presence of the religious hypothesis, that to yield to our fear of its being error is wiser and better than to yield to our hope that it may be true. It is not intellect against all passions, then; it is only intellect with one passion laying down its law. . . . I simply refuse obedience to the scientist's command to imitate his kind of option, in a case where my own stake is important enough to give me the right to choose my own form of risk. If religion be true and the evidence for it be still insufficient, I do not wish, by putting your extinguisher upon my nature, . . . to forfeit my sole chance in life of getting upon the winning side,—that chance depending, of course, on my willingness to run the risk of acting as if my passional need of taking the world religiously might be prophetic and right. . . .

Now, to most of us religion comes in a still further way that makes a veto on our active faith even more illogical. The more perfect and more eternal aspect of the universe is represented in our religions as having personal form. The universe is no longer a mere *It* to us, but a *Thou*, if we are religious; and any relation that may be possible from person to person might be possible here. For instance, although in one sense we are passive portions of the universe, in another we show a curious autonomy, as if we were small active centres on our own account. We feel, too, as if the appeal of religion to us were made to our own active good-will, as if evidence might be forever withheld from us unless we met the hypothesis half-way. . . . This feeling, forced on us we know not whence, that by obstinately believing that there are gods . . . we are doing the universe the deepest service we can, seems part of the living essence of the religious hypothesis. If the hypothesis were true in all its parts, including this one, then pure intellectualism, with its veto on our making willing advances, would be an absurdity; and some participation of our sympathetic nature would be logically required. I, therefore, for one, cannot see my way to accepting the agnostic rules for truth-seeking. . . . I cannot do so for this plain reason, that *a rule of thinking which would absolutely prevent me from acknowledging certain kinds of truth if those kinds of truth were really there, would be an irrational rule.* . . .

I confess I do not see how this logic can be escaped. But sad experience makes me fear that some of you may still shrink from radically saying with me, *in abstracto*, that we have the right to believe at our own risk any hypothesis that is live enough to tempt our will. I suspect, however, that if this is so, it is because you have got away from the abstract logical point of view altogether, and are thinking (perhaps without realizing it) of some particular religious hypothesis which for you is dead. The freedom to "believe what we will" you apply to the case of some patent superstition; and the faith you think of is the faith defined by the schoolboy when he said, "Faith is when you believe something that you know ain't true." I can only repeat that this is misapprehension. *In concreto*, the freedom to believe can only cover living options which the intellect of the individual cannot by itself resolve; and living options never seem absurdities to him who has them to consider. When I look at the religious question as it really puts itself to concrete men, and when I think of all the possibilities which both practically and theoretically it involves, then this command that we shall put a stopper on our heart, instincts, and courage, and wait—acting of course meanwhile more or less as if religion were not true[6]—till doomsday, or till such time as our intellect and senses working together may have raked in evidence enough,—this command, I say, seems to me the queerest idol ever manufactured in the philosophic cave. Were we scholastic absolutists, there might be more excuse. If we had an infallible intellect with its objective certitudes, we might feel ourselves disloyal to such a perfect organ of knowledge in not trusting to it exclusively, in not waiting for its releasing word. But if we are empiricists, if we believe that no bell in us tolls to let us know for certain when truth is in our grasp, then it seems a piece of idle fantasticality to preach so solemnly our duty of waiting for the bell. Indeed we may wait if we will,—I hope you do not think that I am denying that,—but if we do so, we do so at our peril as much as if we believed. In either case we act, taking our life in our hands. No one of us ought to issue vetoes to the other, nor should we bandy words of abuse. We ought, on the contrary, delicately and profoundly to respect one another's mental freedom: then only shall we bring about the intellectual republic; then only shall we have that spirit of inner tolerance without which all our outer tolerance is soulless, and which is empiricism's glory; then only shall we live and let live, in speculative as well as in practical things.

TEST YOUR UNDERSTANDING

1. According to James, it is rational to believe a proposition in the absence of evidence when the option is *forced, live,* and *momentous* and when the question *cannot be resolved on intellectual grounds.* Explain these four conditions with examples.

2. True or false: James thinks that the option "Believe in God or don't" is live, forced, and momentous.

6. Since belief is measured by action, he who forbids us to believe religion to be true, necessarily also forbids us to act as we should if we did believe it to be true. The whole defence of religious faith hinges upon action. If the action required or inspired by the religious hypothesis is in no way different from that dictated by the naturalistic hypothesis, then religious faith is a pure superfluity, better pruned away, and controversy about its legitimacy is a piece of idle trifling, unworthy of serious minds. I myself believe, of course, that the religious hypothesis gives to the world an expression which specifically determines our reactions, and makes them in a large part unlike what they might be on a purely naturalistic scheme of belief. [James's note.]

3. James gives several examples in which it is permissible to believe a proposition even though the evidence for it is insufficient. Give an example of your own to illustrate James's position.

4. James holds that our intellectual lives are governed by two commandments: "Believe truth!" and "Shun error!" Explain why these are two distinct commandments.

NOTES AND QUESTIONS

1. *Clifford's moralism.* James's essay is a response to W. K. Clifford's "The Ethics of Belief" (1877), excerpted in this chapter. Clifford's main argument may be summarized as follows:

> Human beings are prone to superstition, prejudice, and other forms of thinking that lead us to believe on insufficient evidence. These tendencies are profoundly damaging. Belief is not a private matter. We act on our beliefs, and our actions affect the lives of other people. Irrational beliefs place other people at risk and are therefore morally wrong. Even when an individual belief is harmless, allowing yourself to believe without evidence is reckless. Intellectual laziness on your part contributes to intellectual laziness in society, which has manifestly bad effects. So we each have a moral duty to do our part to maintain intellectual standards by believing only what the evidence supports.

James does not respond directly to this moral argument. How should he respond to it? In answering the question, be sure to pose the sharpest version of Clifford's challenge. The religious view James endorses is vague and benign, but consider someone who has read James's essay and who has come to embrace a *violent* religion and the way of life it recommends, not because she has evidence for its truth, but rather as a free choice in the face of a live, forced, and momentous option. Is James committed to saying that this choice is every bit as reasonable as his own?

2. *James's self-refutation argument.* James argues that Clifford's position undermines itself:

> Our passional nature not only lawfully may, but must, decide an option between propositions, whenever it is a genuine option that cannot by its nature be decided on intellectual grounds; for to say, under such circumstances, "Do not decide, but leave the question open," is itself a passional decision—just like deciding yes or no—and is attended with the same risk of losing the truth.[7]

Clifford affirms the moral proposition that it is wrong to believe without evidence. But according to James, this proposition itself is not supported by evidence, so Clifford is wrong by his own lights in affirming it.

Exercise: Present an explicit formulation of this argument and say how Clifford might respond.

---

7. See page 101 of this anthology.

3. *James on the value of religious belief.* James holds that if there is a God, then the belief that God exists is of great value to the individual here and now, and not just in the afterlife. But what sort of value might he have in mind? Why are we better off in believing, as James puts it, that "perfection is eternal"?

Alvin Plantinga (b. 1932)

Plantinga, Professor of Philosophy at Calvin College, has been called "America's leading orthodox Protestant philosopher." He is the author of important studies in metaphysics (*The Nature of Necessity,* 1974) and epistemology (*Warrant and Proper Function,* 1993) and of numerous contributions to theology and the philosophy of religion.

IS BELIEF IN GOD PROPERLY BASIC?

Many philosophers have urged the *evidentialist* objection to theistic belief; they have argued that belief in God is irrational or unreasonable or not rationally acceptable or intellectually irresponsible because, as they say, there is insufficient evidence for it. . . . Many other philosophers and theologians—in particular, those in the great tradition of natural theology—have claimed that belief in God is intellectually acceptable, but only because the fact is there is sufficient evidence for it. These two groups unite in holding that theistic belief is rationally acceptable only if there is sufficient evidence for it. More exactly, they hold that a person is rational or reasonable in accepting theistic belief only if she has sufficient evidence for it—only if, that is, she knows or rationally believes some *other* propositions which support the one in question and believes the latter on the basis of the former. . . . The evidentialist objection is rooted in *classical foundationalism*, an enormously popular picture or total way of looking at faith, knowledge, justified belief, rationality and allied topics. This picture has been widely accepted ever since the days of Plato and Aristotle; its near relatives, perhaps, remain the dominant ways of thinking about these topics. We may think of the classical foundationalist as beginning with the observation that some of one's beliefs may be *based upon* others; it may be that there are a pair of propositions A and B such that I believe A *on the basis of B*. Although this relation isn't easy to characterize in a revealing and nontrivial fashion, it is nonetheless familiar. I believe that the word "umbrageous" is spelled u-m-b-r-a-g-e-o-u-s: this belief is based on another belief of mine: the belief that that's how the dictionary says it's spelled. I believe that $72 \times 71 = 5,112$. This belief is based upon several other beliefs I hold: that $1 \times 72 = 72; 7 \times 2 = 14; 7 \times 7 = 49; 49 + 1 = 50$; and others. Some of my beliefs, however, I accept but don't accept on the basis of any other beliefs. Call these beliefs *basic.* I believe that $2 + 1 = 3$, for example, and don't believe it on the basis of other propositions. I also believe that I am seated at my desk, and that there is a mild pain in my right knee. These too are basic to me; I don't believe them on the basis of any other propositions. According to the classical foundationalist, some propositions are *properly* or *rightly* basic for a person and some are not. Those that are not, are rationally accepted only on the basis of *evidence*, where the evidence must trace back, ultimately, to what is properly basic. . . .

Now many Reformed thinkers and theologians[1] have rejected *natural theology* (thought of as the attempt to provide proofs or arguments for the existence of God). They have held not merely that the proffered arguments are unsuccessful, but that the whole enterprise is in some way radically misguided. . . . The reformed rejection of natural theology is best construed as an inchoate and unfocused rejection of classical foundationalism. What these Reformed thinkers really mean to hold, I think, is that belief in God need not be based on argument or evidence from other propositions at all. They mean to hold that the believer is entirely within his intellectual rights in believing as he does even if he doesn't know of any good theistic argument (deductive or inductive), even if he doesn't believe that there is any such argument, and even if in fact no such argument exists. They hold that it is perfectly rational to accept belief in God without accepting it on the basis of any other beliefs or propositions at all. In a word, they hold that *belief in God is properly basic*. In this paper I shall try to develop and defend this position.

But first we must achieve a deeper understanding of the evidentialist objection. It is important to see that this contention is a *normative* contention. The evidentialist objector holds that one who accepts theistic belief is in some way irrational. . . . Here "rational" and "irrational" are to be taken as normative or evaluative terms; according to the objector, the theist fails to measure up to a standard he ought to conform to. There is a right way and a wrong way with respect to belief as with respect to actions; we have duties, responsibilities, obligations with respect to the former just as with respect to the latter. . . .

This "ethics of the intellect" can be construed variously; many fascinating issues— issues we must here forebear to enter—arise when we try to state more exactly the various options the evidentialist may mean to adopt. Initially it looks as if he holds that there is a duty or obligation of some sort not to accept without evidence such propositions as that God exists—a duty flouted by the theist who has no evidence. If he has no evidence, then it is his duty to cease believing. But there is an oft remarked difficulty: one's beliefs, for the most part, are not directly under one's control. Most of those who believe in God could not divest themselves of that belief just by trying to do so, just as they could not in that way rid themselves of the belief that the world has existed for a very long time. So perhaps the relevant obligation is not that of divesting myself of theistic belief if I have no evidence (that is beyond my power), but to try to cultivate the sorts of intellectual habits that will tend (we hope) to issue in my accepting as basic only propositions that are properly basic. . . .

[But] perhaps the evidentialist need not speak of duty or obligation here at all. Consider someone who believes that Venus is smaller than Mercury, not because he has evidence of any sort, but because he finds it amusing to hold a belief no one else

---

1. A Reformed thinker or theologian is one whose intellectual sympathies lie with the Protestant tradition going back to John Calvin (not someone who was formerly a theologian and has since seen the light). [Plantinga's note.]

does—or consider someone who holds this belief on the basis of some outrageously bad argument. Perhaps there isn't any obligation he has failed to meet. Nevertheless his intellectual condition is deficient in some way; or perhaps alternatively there is a commonly achieved excellence he fails to display. And the evidentialist objection to theistic belief, then, might be understood as the claim, not that the theist without evidence has failed to meet an obligation, but that he suffers from a certain sort of intellectual deficiency (so that the proper attitude toward him would be sympathy rather than censure).

These are some of the ways, then, in which the evidentialist objection could be developed; and of course there are still other possibilities. For ease of exposition, let us take the claim deontologically[2]; what I shall say will apply *mutatis mutandis* if we take it one of the other ways. The evidentialist objection, therefore, presupposes some view as to what sorts of propositions are correctly, or rightly, or justifiably taken as basic; it presupposes a view as to what is *properly* basic. And the minimally relevant claim for the evidentialist objector is that belief in God is *not* properly basic. Typically this objection has been rooted in some form of *classical foundationalism*, according to which a proposition *p* is properly basic for a person *S* if and only if *p* is either self-evident or incorrigible for *S* (modern foundationalism) or either self-evident or "evident to the senses" for *S* (ancient and medieval foundationalism). [Elsewhere] I argued that both forms of foundationalism are self-referentially incoherent and must therefore be rejected.

Insofar as the evidentialist objection is rooted in classical foundationalism, it is poorly rooted indeed: and so far as I know, no one has developed and articulated any other reason for supposing that belief in God is not properly basic. Of course it doesn't follow that it *is* properly basic; perhaps the class of properly basic propositions is broader than classical foundationalists think, but still not broad enough to admit belief in God. But why think so? What might be the objections to the Reformed view that belief in God is properly basic?

I've heard it argued that if I have no evidence for the existence of God, then if I accept that proposition, my belief will be groundless, or gratuitous, or arbitrary. I think this is an error; let me explain.

Suppose we consider perceptual beliefs, memory beliefs, and beliefs which ascribe mental states to other persons: such beliefs as

(1) I see a tree,

(2) I had breakfast this morning,

and

(3) That person is angry.

Although beliefs of this sort are typically and properly taken as basic, it would be a mistake to describe them as *groundless*. Upon having experience of a certain sort, I believe that

---

2. **Deontology** is the theory of duty or obligation.

I am perceiving a tree. In the typical case I do not hold this belief on the basis of other beliefs; it is nonetheless not groundless. My having that characteristic sort of experience... plays a crucial role in the formation and justification of that belief. We might say this experience, together, perhaps, with other circumstances, is what *justifies* me in holding it; this is the *ground* of my justification, and, by extension, the ground of the belief itself.

If I see someone displaying typical pain behavior, I take it that he or she is in pain. Again, I don't take the displayed behavior as *evidence* for that belief; I don't infer that belief from others I hold; I don't accept it on the basis of other beliefs. Still, my perceiving the pain behavior plays a unique role in the formation and justification of that belief; as in the previous case, it forms the ground of my justification for the belief in question. The same holds for memory beliefs. I seem to remember having breakfast this morning; that is, I have an inclination to believe the proposition that I had breakfast, along with a certain past-tinged experience that is familiar to all but hard to describe. . . . In this case as in the others, however, there is a justifying circumstance present, a condition that forms the ground of my justification for accepting the memory belief in question.

In each of these cases, a belief is taken as basic, and in each case properly taken as basic. In each case there is some circumstance or condition that confers justification; there is a circumstance that serves as the *ground* of justification. So in each case there will be some true proposition of the sort

(4) In condition C, S is justified in taking p as basic.

Of course C will vary with p. For a perceptual judgment such as

(5) I see a rose-colored wall before me,

C will include my being appeared to in a certain fashion. No doubt C will include more. If I'm appeared to in the familiar fashion but know that I'm wearing rose-colored glasses, or that I am suffering from a disease that causes me to be thus appeared to, no matter what the color of the nearby objects, then I'm not justified in taking (5) as basic. . . .

So being appropriately appeared to, in the perceptual case, is not sufficient for justification; some further condition—a condition hard to state in detail—is clearly necessary. The central point, here, however, is that a belief is properly basic only in certain conditions; these conditions are, we might say, the ground of its justification and, by extension, the ground of the belief itself. In this sense, basic beliefs are not, or are not necessarily, *groundless* beliefs.

Now similar things may be said about belief in God. When the Reformers claim that this belief is properly basic, they do not mean to say, of course, that there are no justifying circumstances for it, or that it is in that sense groundless or gratuitous. Quite the contrary. Calvin[3] holds that God "reveals and daily discloses himself to the whole workmanship of the universe," and the divine art "reveals itself in the innumerable and yet distinct and well ordered variety of the heavenly host." God has so

---

3. John Calvin (1509–1564), early Protestant theologian, author of the *Institutes of the Christian Religion*.

created us that we have a tendency or disposition to see his hand in the world about us. More precisely, there is in us a disposition to believe propositions of the sort *this flower was created by God* or *this vast and intricate universe was created by God* when we contemplate the flower or behold the starry heavens or think about the vast reaches of the universe.

Calvin recognizes, at least implicitly, that other sorts of conditions may trigger this disposition. Upon reading the Bible, one may be impressed with a deep sense that God is speaking to him. Upon having done what I know is cheap, or wrong, or wicked, I may feel guilty in God's sight and form the belief *God disapproves of what I've done.* Upon confession and repentance, I may feel forgiven, forming the belief *God forgives me for what I've done.* A person in grave danger may turn to God, asking for his protection and help; and of course he or she then forms the belief that God is indeed able to hear and help if he sees fit. When life is sweet and satisfying, a spontaneous sense of gratitude may well up within the soul; someone in this condition may thank and praise the Lord for his goodness, and will of course form the accompanying belief that indeed the Lord is to be thanked and praised. . . .

Of course none of these beliefs . . . is the simple belief that God exists. What we have instead are such beliefs as

(6) God is speaking to me,

(7) God has created all this,

(8) God disapproves of what I have done,

(9) God forgives me,

and

(10) God is to be thanked and praised.

These propositions are properly basic in the right circumstances. But it is quite consistent with this to suppose that the proposition *there is such a person as God* is neither properly basic nor taken as basic by those who believe in God. Perhaps what they take as basic are such propositions as (6)–(10), believing in the existence of God on the basis of propositions such as those. From this point of view, it isn't exactly right to say that it is belief in God that is properly basic; more exactly; what are properly basic are such propositions as (6)–(10), each of which self-evidently entails that God exists. It isn't the relatively high level and general proposition *God exists* that is properly basic, but instead propositions detailing some of his attributes or actions. . . .

We may say, speaking loosely, that belief in God is properly basic; strictly speaking, however, it is probably not that proposition but such propositions as (6)–(10) that enjoy that status. But the main point, here, is that belief in God or (6)–(10), are properly basic; to say so, however, is not to deny that there are justifying conditions for these beliefs, or conditions that confer justification on one who accepts them as basic. They are therefore not groundless or gratuitous.

A second objection I've often heard: if belief in God is properly basic, why can't *just any* belief be properly basic? Couldn't we say the same for any bizarre aberration we can think of? What about voodoo or astrology? What about the belief that the Great Pumpkin returns every Halloween? Could I properly take *that* as basic? And if I can't, why can I properly take belief in God as basic? Suppose I believe that if I flap my arms with sufficient vigor, I can take off and fly about the room; could I defend myself against the charge of irrationality by claiming this belief is basic? If we say that belief in God is properly basic, won't we be committed to holding that just anything, or nearly anything, can properly be taken as basic, thus throwing wide the gates to irrationalism and superstition?

Certainly not. What might lead one to think the Reformed epistemologist is in this kind of trouble? The fact that he rejects the criteria for proper basicality purveyed by classical foundationalism? But why should *that* be thought to commit him to such tolerance of irrationality? . . .

The fact that he rejects the Classical Foundationalist's criterion or proper basicality does not mean that he is committed to supposing just anything is properly basic.

But what then is the problem? Is it that the Reformed epistemologist not only rejects those criteria for proper basicality, but seems in no hurry to produce what he takes to be a better substitute? If he has no such criterion, how can he fairly reject belief in the Great Pumpkin as properly basic?

This objection betrays an important misconception. How do we rightly arrive at or develop criteria for . . . justified belief, or proper basicality? Where do they come from? Must one have such a criterion before one can sensibly make any judgments— positive or negative—about proper basicality? Surely not. Suppose I don't know of a satisfactory substitute for the criteria proposed by classical foundationalism; I am nevertheless entirely within my rights in holding that certain propositions are not properly basic in certain conditions. Some propositions seem self-evident when in fact they are not: that is the lesson of some of the Russell paradoxes.[4] Nevertheless it would be irrational to take as basic the denial of a proposition that seems self-evident to you. Similarly, suppose it seems to you that you see a tree; you would then be irrational in taking as basic the proposition that you don't see a tree, or that there aren't any trees. . . .

And this raises an important question—one Roderick Chisholm has taught us to ask. What is the status of criteria for knowledge, or proper basicality, or justified belief? Typically, these are universal statements. The modern foundationalist's criterion for proper basicality, for example, is doubly universal:

(11) For any proposition A and person S, A is properly basic for S if and only if A is incorrigible for S or self-evident to S.

---

4. Bertrand Russell (1872–1970) showed in 1902 that an apparently evident "axiom" of mathematics was in fact self-contradictory. The axiom states that whenever there exist some things, there exists a class that contains all and only those things as members. Russell was also, incidentally, a famously outspoken atheist.

But how could one know a thing like that? What are its credentials? Clearly enough, (11) isn't self-evident or just obviously true. But if it isn't, how does one arrive at it? What sorts of arguments would be appropriate? Of course a foundationalist might find (11) so appealing, he simply takes it to be true, neither offering argument for it, nor accepting it on the basis of other things he believes. If he does so, however, his noetic structure will be self-referentially incoherent. (11) itself is neither self-evident nor incorrigible; hence in accepting (11) as basic, the modern foundationalist violates the condition of proper basicality he himself lays down in accepting it. On the other hand, perhaps the foundationalist will try to produce some argument for it from premises that are self-evident or incorrigible: it is exceedingly hard to see, however, what such an argument might be like. And until he has produced such arguments, what shall the rest of us do—we who do not find (11) at all obvious or compelling? How could he use (11) to show us that belief in God, for example, is not properly basic? Why should we believe (11), or pay it any attention?

The fact is, I think, that neither (11) nor any other revealing necessary and sufficient condition for proper basicality follows from clearly self-evident premises by clearly acceptable arguments. And hence the proper way to arrive at such a criterion is, broadly speaking, *inductive*. We must assemble examples of beliefs and conditions such that the former are obviously properly basic in the latter, and examples of beliefs and conditions such that the former are obviously *not* properly basic in the latter. We must then frame hypotheses as to the necessary and sufficient conditions of proper basicality and test these hypotheses by reference to those examples. Under the right conditions, for example, it is clearly rational to believe that you see a human person before you: a being who has thoughts and feelings, who knows and believes things, who makes decisions and acts. It is clear, furthermore, that you are under no obligation to reason to this belief from others you hold; under those conditions that belief is properly basic for you. But then (11) must be mistaken; the belief in question, under those circumstances, is properly basic, though neither self-evident nor incorrigible for you. Similarly, you may seem to remember that you had breakfast this morning, and perhaps you know of no reason to suppose your memory is playing you tricks. If so, you are entirely justified in taking that belief as basic. Of course it isn't properly basic on the criteria offered by classical foundationalists; but that fact counts not against you but against those criteria.

Accordingly, criteria for proper basicality must be reached from below rather than above; they should not be presented as *ex cathedra*, but argued to and tested by a relevant set of examples. But there is no reason to assume, in advance, that everyone will agree on the examples. The Christian will of course suppose that belief in God is entirely proper and rational; if he doesn't accept this belief on the basis of other propositions, he will conclude that it is basic for him and quite properly so. Followers of Bertrand Russell and Madalyn Murray O'Hair[5] disagree, but how is that relevant? Must my criteria, or those of the Christian community, conform to their examples? Surely not. The Christian community is responsible to *its* set of examples, not to theirs.

---

5. Madalyn Murray O'Hair (1919–1995), founder of American Atheists.

Accordingly, the Reformed epistemologist can properly hold that belief in the Great Pumpkin is not properly basic, even though he holds that belief in God is properly basic and even if he has no full-fledged criterion of proper basicality. Of course he is committed to supposing that there is a relevant *difference* between belief in God and belief in the Great Pumpkin, if he holds that the former but not the latter is properly basic. But this should prove no great embarrassment; there are plenty of candidates. These candidates are to be found in the neighborhood of the conditions I mentioned in the last section that justify and ground belief in God. Thus, for example, the Reformed epistemologist may concur with Calvin in holding that God has implanted in us a natural tendency to see his hand in the world around us; the same cannot be said for the Great Pumpkin, there being no Great Pumpkin and no natural tendency to accept beliefs about the Great Pumpkin.

By way of conclusion then: being self-evident, or incorrigible, or evident to the senses is not a necessary condition of proper basicality. Furthermore, one who holds that belief in God is properly basic is not thereby committed to the idea that belief in God is groundless or gratuitous or without justifying circumstances. And even if he lacks a general criterion of proper basicality, he is not obliged to suppose that just any or nearly any belief—belief in the Great Pumpkin, for example—is properly basic. Like everyone should, he begins with examples; and he may take belief in the Great Pumpkin as a paradigm of irrational basic belief.

TEST YOUR UNDERSTANDING

1. What is it for a belief to be properly basic?

2. True or false: Plantinga holds that some beliefs about God are properly basic.

3. Plantinga argues that whether a belief is properly basic is not settled by the content of the belief, but also depends on the circumstances in which it is held. Explain the basis for this claim.

4. Plantinga suggests that certain theistic beliefs—like the belief that God is talking to me now—are strongly analogous to perceptual beliefs, like the belief that I am looking at a rose. List three important respects in which such beliefs are similar according to Plantinga.

NOTES AND QUESTIONS

1. *The Great Pumpkin problem.* Plantinga imagines an objector who says, in effect, "If a belief in God can be properly basic for you, why can't a belief in the Great Pumpkin be properly basic for me?" Let's consider a more sober version of the question. The ancient Greeks believed in many gods: Zeus, Athena, and so on. Let us suppose that

some of these beliefs were basic for them. Were these beliefs *properly* basic? Plantinga does not provide a theory of the conditions under which a belief is properly basic for a person. So we cannot answer by applying a general criterion. But we can ask: Is there *any* epistemologically relevant respect in which the basic religious beliefs of the ancient Greeks differed from the basic religious beliefs of a modern Protestant Christian like Plantinga? (Plantinga may say that his beliefs are *true* while theirs were not; but a belief can be properly basic without being true.)

Exercise: Try to construct a criterion of properly basic belief that answers this question. Such a criterion will take the form:

> *Belief B is properly basic for subject S if and only if . . .*

For Plantinga's detailed views, see *Warranted Christian Belief* (Oxford University Press, 2000). Would it be an objection to Plantinga's view if he were forced to say that the Greeks were justified in holding their religious beliefs as basic?

2. *The problem of disagreement.* If I'm looking at a rose in normal conditions, then the belief that I'm looking at a rose may be properly basic for me. But if someone comes up to me and says, "I'm sorry but *I* don't see a rose. You must be hallucinating," then I am no longer warranted in taking my belief as basic. I must suspend judgment until I can produce some evidence that my eyes are working properly or that his are not. This suggests a principle: *A belief is not properly basic for a person when that person is aware of other equally competent, equally informed people who reject it.* If this principle holds, then religious belief in our culture is not properly basic, since everyone is aware of intelligent, thoughtful atheists who deny that God exists.

Exercise: Say how Plantinga should respond to this argument.

Lara Buchak (b. 1981)

Buchak is Associate Professor of Philosophy at the University of California, Berkeley. She specializes in decision theory and the philosophy of religion.

WHEN IS FAITH RATIONAL?

Can it be rational to have faith? In order to answer this question, we need to have a firm grasp on what having faith actually means. In the first section of this essay, I give an analysis of faith. Faith is not "belief without reasons." Rather, to have faith in a claim is to be willing to *act* on that claim without further evidence and to remain committed to acting on that claim even when counterevidence arises. In the remainder of this essay, I consider when and why such faith is rational, and I argue that faith is rational in certain circumstances—indeed, in these circumstances, those who lack faith stand to miss out on important goods.

1. What Is Faith?

Let us begin with a few preliminaries.[1] First, this essay is about faith both in the mundane sense (you have faith that a friend is trustworthy or that a bridge will hold your weight) and in the religious sense (you have faith that God exists, or that God is asking you to take some action). The account here explains religious and mundane faith as instances of the same general attitude.

Second, although we talk both about what is it to have faith *in* someone and faith *that* something is the case, this essay will only give an account of the latter. (They are, of course, related: to have faith in someone requires having faith that some things are the case; for example, to have faith in a friend requires having faith that she is trustworthy.) Notice that only certain claims are candidates for faith at all. For example, while it makes sense to say that you have faith that a friend will quit smoking, it does not make sense to say that you have faith that a friend will continue smoking (assuming you think that smoking is bad). It is not that you *lack* faith that your friend will continue smoking; rather, this claim is not an appropriate object of faith at all. You can only have or lack faith in a claim that you have a positive attitude toward. Similarly, it does not make sense to say that you have (or lack) faith that $2 + 2 = 4$. You can only have or lack faith in a claim if you're not certain of the claim on the basis of your evidence alone: your evidence must leave it open that the claim is false.

Claims that will be particularly good candidates for faith, then, are claims concerning interpersonal, religious, or moral matters. For example, take the claim that my friend will keep my secrets. I care a great deal that this claim is true, and my evidence will always leave it open that the claim is false, since she could at any time decide not to keep one of my secrets. Or take the claim that God exists. Many people have a positive attitude toward this claim—they hope it is true—and while they may have some evidence in its favor (evidence from their experiences within a religious community, direct personal experiences, philosophical arguments, or the testimony of others), all of these sources typically leave some room for doubt. Similar points hold for particular instances of faith in Jewish and Christian texts: Abraham's faith that his descendants would be greater than the number of stars; Moses's faith that God would lead his people out of Egypt into the Promised Land; Paul's faith that Jesus was raised from the dead.

---

1. This essay draws heavily on L. Buchak, "Can It Be Rational to Have Faith?" in *Probability in the Philosophy of Religion*, ed. J. Chandler and V. S. Harrison (Oxford University Press, 2012), 225–47; and L. Buchak, "Faith and Steadfastness in the Face of Counter-Evidence," *International Journal for Philosophy of Religion* 81, 1–2 (2017): 113–33. See also L. Buchak, "Rational Faith and Justified Belief," in *Religious Faith and Intellectual Virtue*, ed. T. O'Connor and L. Goins (Oxford University Press, 2014), 49–73.

Preliminaries out of the way, we can now turn to the account of what it is to have faith that something is the case. Some people think that to have faith is to believe something without any evidence at all or even to believe something when the evidence is squarely against it. But these ideas don't fit with the way in which "faith" is used, both in interpersonal and religious contexts. So what is it to have faith?

Let us start with the observation that faith is tied to action. To have faith in a claim is to be willing to take risks on that claim. It is risky to tell your friend a secret, to dedicate your life to following God's commands, to leave Egypt to seek the Promised Land. One has a higher degree of faith in a claim to the extent that one is willing to take more risks on that claim.

But not every case of risk-taking will be an act of faith. Faith requires a willingness to act on the claim you have faith in without first looking for additional evidence. Furthermore, faith requires a willingness to continue to act, even if counterevidence arises. In the Christian Bible, when Jesus called Simon Peter and Andrew, they immediately stopped what they were doing to follow him—and Jesus's disciples continued to remain committed to him even after his death gave them some reason to think he was not the messiah they were looking for. (Simon Peter and Andrew were Jews, and first-century Jews did not expect their messiah to die.) Mundane faith works the same way. If you have faith that a particular person would be a good marriage partner, you will marry him and you will stick with him even if the marriage isn't what you expected. If you have faith that you will complete your college degree, you will continue in the program even after failing an exam.

Thus, you have faith in a claim if you are committed to taking risks on the claim without examining additional evidence and you would maintain that commitment even if counterevidence arose. More formally:

A proposition X is a *candidate for faith* for a person S if S cares that X holds and is uncertain that X holds on the basis of his evidence alone.

S has faith that X if and only if:

(1) S is willing to take a risk on X without looking for additional evidence; and

(2) S is willing to follow through on such risky actions even when he receives evidence against X.

To the extent that S is willing to perform riskier acts that express his faith and remain steadfast in the face of stronger counterevidence, he has a higher degree of faith that X.

To tell your secrets to a friend is to take a risk on the claim that she will keep your secrets: you gain something if she keeps the secrets and lose something if she doesn't. Whether you have faith in this claim is a matter of whether you are willing to tell your secrets without first double-checking that your friend is trustworthy and to continue to tell your secrets even if you overhear a piece of gossip that your friend is bad at keeping secrets.

So too for religious faith. People with faith that God is real act in ways that make sense on this assumption without waiting for more evidence, and they continue to act in these ways even when they encounter evidence and arguments against their belief. Someone might take these ways of acting to show that people with religious faith are dogmatic and irrationally confident in their beliefs; but on the present view, that is not what faith consists in. As we will see, you can be disposed to *act* faithfully in these ways even if your underlying beliefs are nondogmatic and responsive to evidence.

2. What Is Rationality?

Now that we know what faith is, we can begin to ask whether faith is rational.

There are two important senses of rationality that are relevant to the main question of this essay: rationality in what you believe, and rationality in what you do. Philosophers use formal tools for thinking about each kind of rationality.

In the case of rationality in what you believe (*epistemic rationality*), philosophers commonly think of belief not as an all-or-nothing phenomenon, but instead as a matter of degree. Your degree of belief in a claim—sometimes called your *credence*—can be thought of as the probability you assign to that claim. Degrees of belief must obey two requirements to count as rational. First, they must cohere with each other. You can't believe to degree 0.8 that it will rain and also believe to degree 0.8 that it won't rain. (If you're rational, your credences in X and not-X must add up to 1.) If you believe to degree 0.5 that it will rain tomorrow, then your credence that it will *either rain or snow* must be at least 0.5. (If you're rational, your credence in X *or* Y must be at least as great as your credence in X.)[2] Second, your degrees of belief must fit with the evidence you possess: if you live in a sunny climate and have no reason to suppose that today will be any different from previous days, then you cannot believe to a high degree that it will rain. Finally, your degrees of belief must be sensitive to new evidence: when the weatherman predicts rain, you must raise your degree of belief that it will rain. (If you're rational, then if you get some good evidence for X that you didn't have before, you should take it into account by raising your credence in X and lowering your credence in not-X.)

In the case of rationality in what you do (*practical rationality*), the rough idea is that to be practically rational, you must take the means that you believe will lead to your ends. Taking onboard the above idea that belief is a matter of degree, philosophers commonly hold that practical rationality is formalized by *decision theory*. According to decision theory, we can represent how much you value particular outcomes by a "utility" function that assigns high values to things you want a lot and lower values to things you want less. On the classical view, a rational individual must choose the act that maximizes **expected utility**, relative to his utility values and degrees of belief. Here, "expected" utility just means a weighted average: the utility

2. For an overview of some of the concepts in this section, see M. Resnik, *Choices* (University of Minnesota Press, 1987).

value of each outcome is weighted by the likelihood of getting that outcome, and the resultant values are summed.[3] In addition to the classical view, we will be concerned with a variant on the classical view that takes into account how an individual treats risk. According to the classical view, you simply average over all the possible utility values. This means that all equally likely scenarios weigh equally in your evaluation of an action. However, contra the classical view, it is plausible that you might care about making sure that things won't go too poorly, so that in thinking about the value of an act, you place more weight on what happens in worse scenarios; or someone else might care a great deal about making sure there's some chance that things go really well, so that he places more weight on what happens in better scenarios.[4] If you give more weight to worse scenarios than to better ones, we will say that you are *risk avoidant*.

3. When Is It Rational to Have Faith?

We can now turn to the question of when it is rational to have faith, keeping in mind the above criteria for rationality. It will help to focus on an example.

Let's say that Anna has known Bates for a long time, and he has proposed marriage.[5] She has abundant evidence that he is morally upstanding; thus she believes to a high degree that he is not capable of murder. However, he is currently under investigation for murder. If he is innocent, then he would make an excellent husband, but it would be a disaster to marry a murderer. She could accept his proposal or decline it and continue her fairly happy life, which is better than marrying a murderous Bates but worse than marrying an innocent Bates. (We may assume that marrying an innocent Bates is preferable even if Bates is *found* guilty and thrown in jail—his actual innocence is the basis for the risk Anna would take in marrying him.) If she has faith that Bates is innocent, what will she do? She will agree to marriage before the investigation is concluded and stick with the decision even if the investigation finds him guilty.

---

3. For example, if you think that the probability of rain is 0.5 and of not-rain is 0.5, and if the utility of getting wet is −3, the utility of staying dry but having to carry an umbrella is 1, and the utility of staying dry without having to carry an umbrella is 6, then the expected utility of not bringing an umbrella is $0.5(-3) + 0.5(6) = 1.5$, and the expected utility of bringing an umbrella is $0.5(1) + 0.5(1) = 1$. Thus, you should not bring your umbrella. For a brief introduction to decision theory, see Alan Hájek, "Pascal's Ultimate Gamble," in this chapter.

4. See L. Buchak, *Risk and Rationality* (Oxford University Press, 2013). In the example in footnote 2, if you place twice as much weight on what happens in the worst 50 percent of states than in the best 50 percent of states, then the *risk-weighted expected utility* of not bringing an umbrella is $0.67(-3) + 0.33(6) = 0$ and of bringing an umbrella is $0.67(1) + 0.33(1) = 1$. Thus, you should bring your umbrella. I note that the idea that risk avoidance is rational is controversial. Still, risk-weighted expected utility maximization is more descriptively accurate than expected utility maximization, so if one does not think that it is rational, then one can read this essay as a comment on how to act if one is in fact (irrationally) risk avoidant.

5. This example comes from the British television series *Downton Abbey*.

Anna's decision has the same structure as many cases of religious faith. Moses, we are to suppose, has interacted with God personally. He has ample reason to believe that God is trustworthy and cares about his people. God has told him to journey out of Egypt with his people. If such a journey would indeed be successful—if God will indeed lead his people to the Promised Land—then embarking on it would be the best thing for Moses and his people, but if it would not be successful, then embarking on it would be a disaster. He could embark on the journey or simply stay in Egypt. Moses had faith that God would lead his people to the Promised Land, so what did he do? He embarked on the journey without first verifying that it would be successful, and he stood firm even when the Egyptians pursued his people to the Red Sea.

The key question for this section is whether such faith is rational.

3.1   EPISTEMIC RATIONALITY

Let us begin with epistemic rationality. To be epistemically rational, Anna needs to have degrees of belief that are coherent and supported by the evidence. If Anna's evidence indeed supports a high degree of belief in Bates's innocence, and if her other degrees of belief cohere, then she will indeed be epistemically rational. So too with Moses: if his evidence indeed supports a high degree of belief in the truth of God's utterances[6]—in this case, that God will lead his people to the Promised Land—and if his other degrees of belief cohere, then he will indeed be epistemically rational.

Faith does not require either individual to alter his or her evidentially supported degrees of belief. More generally, faith does not require you to do anything "special" with your beliefs: it does not, for example, require you to believe a claim more strongly than the evidence suggests or to believe a claim in the absence of any evidence at all. Furthermore, faith does not require you to refrain from looking for evidence for purposes of knowing more about the world, nor does it ask you to ignore new evidence in regulating your degrees of belief. It simply means that your *decisions* won't depend on what new evidence comes in. Thus, as long as you meet the criteria for epistemic rationality—as long as your beliefs are coherent and respect the evidence—then you can have faith while remaining epistemically rational.

Anna's faith in Bates's innocence, for example, does not require her to ignore the evidence of his guilt as it comes in. Her degree of belief in his innocence may drop as the damning evidence accumulates. Her faith simply requires her to stick by her decision to marry him nonetheless: acting on the premise that he is innocent even when this action seems too risky given her degree of belief. Similarly for Moses: his faith does not require him to ignore evidence that the journey will be unsuccessful. When he approaches the Red Sea, his degree of belief that they will make it through alive might drop. His faith requires him to stay the course nonetheless.

---

6. Or in the claim that the utterer really is God.

As I've been emphasizing, faith is not belief without reasons. It is a commitment to action, even when you're not sure, and to seeing the action through, even when doing so seems too risky. Thus, faith is perfectly compatible with having beliefs that respect the evidence.

3.2 PRACTICAL RATIONALITY AT THE BEGINNING OF AN ACT OF FAITH

The question of practical rationality is more interesting, since faith requires a practical stance: take a risk without looking for more evidence, and stick with that risk even if evidence arises that makes it no longer seem like a good one. We will ask about each of these elements of faith separately: when is it practically rational (in the sense of maximizing utility) to stop one's search for evidence and make a decision, and when is it practically rational to stick with a decision even though new evidence no longer supports it?

Let us begin with the question of looking for further evidence. I will use the Anna and Bates example, but the reader is invited to keep in mind that analogous claims hold for Moses's case. To see whether Anna should answer Bates's proposal before hearing the verdict or instead wait, we compare her three options and the utility payoffs they yield under the four possible states[7]:

	Bates is actually innocent, and the investigation finds him innocent (Positive correct evidence)	Bates is actually innocent, and the investigation finds him guilty (Negative misleading evidence)	Bates is actually guilty, and the investigation finds him innocent (Positive misleading evidence)	Bates is actually guilty, and the investigation finds him guilty (Negative correct evidence)
A: Say yes to Bates ("the faithful act")	9	9	–1	–1
B: Say no to Bates	7	7	7	7
C: Wait for the verdict and then decide				

7. When assigning utility numbers, the actual numbers don't matter, just the relationship between them: so what these numbers represent is that Anna's life without Bates would be nearly as good as her life married to an innocent Bates, and much better than her life married to a murderous Bates.

I've labeled the states according to whether the evidence is *positive* or *negative* (whether it tells in favor of Bates's innocence or not) and whether it is *correct* or *misleading* (whether it tells in the direction of the truth). Let us assume that Anna's current degree of belief in the claim that Bates is innocent is high enough that A has a higher utility than B (otherwise, faith in the claim will already be irrational).[8]

How we fill in the last line of the matrix will depend on what Anna would do upon hearing the results of the investigation, which will depend on how she expects the investigation to affect her degrees of belief. If she thinks the evidence from the investigation will be weak compared to the rest of her evidence, either because she already has a *lot* of evidence about Bates's character or because the investigation itself is flawed (sloppily conducted or hopelessly corrupt), then she knows that even if she were to learn that the investigation found Bates guilty, this will not lower her degree of belief in his innocence very much. Thus, if she waits for the verdict, then whatever it is, she will still say yes to Bates and get the corresponding payoffs, minus whatever cost c there is to postponing the decision (not getting to be married as quickly, Bates's disappointment in her dithering, etc.):

	Bates is actually innocent, and the investigation finds him innocent (Positive correct evidence)	Bates is actually innocent, and the investigation finds him guilty (Negative misleading evidence)	Bates is actually guilty, and the investigation finds him innocent (Positive misleading evidence)	Bates is actually guilty, and the investigation finds him guilty (Negative correct evidence)
A: Say yes to Bates ("the faithful act")	9	9	−1	−1
B: Say no to Bates	7	7	7	7
C: Wait for the verdict and then decide	9 − c	9 − c	−1	−1

In this case, A (the faithful act) and C will yield the same payoffs, except that C might be worse if there are postponement costs. So, if there are no postponement costs, then A and C are equally choiceworthy, and if there are postponement costs, then A is to be preferred to C.

---

8. For example, if Anna is an expected utility maximizer, then she believes to a degree greater than 0.8 that Bates is innocent.

Thus, the first result is that *faith is rationally permissible if you know that whatever negative evidence you get, it won't be strong enough to discourage you from taking a risk on the faith claim—and faith is rationally required if, in addition, there are costs to postponing the decision.* If your evidence for a claim is already deep and convincing—even if it doesn't yield certainty—then you *may* have faith in that claim, and indeed you *must* have faith in that claim if there are costs to postponing the decision.

The more interesting case is the one in which a negative result from the investigation would lower Anna's degree of belief enough that marrying Bates would no longer be the utility-maximizing option. In this case, waiting for the verdict will lead to saying yes to Bates if the verdict is positive (innocent) and to saying no if the verdict is negative (guilty); therefore, the payoffs for waiting for the verdict are as follows:

	Bates is actually innocent, and the investigation finds him innocent (Positive correct evidence)	Bates is actually innocent, and the investigation finds him guilty (Negative misleading evidence)	Bates is actually guilty, and the investigation finds him innocent (Positive misleading evidence)	Bates is actually guilty, and the investigation finds him guilty (Negative correct evidence)
A: Say yes to Bates ("the faithful act")	9	9	−1	−1
B: Say no to Bates	7	7	7	7
C: Wait for the verdict and then decide	9 − c	7	−1	7

Under what circumstances should *A* be chosen rather than *C*? Notice that there are two potential benefits to saying yes to Bates rather than waiting. The first is that if the evidence is positive and correct, doing so yields 9 rather than 9 − c: this is the *potential benefit of acting now rather than later.* The second is that if the evidence is negative and misleading, doing so yields 9 rather than 7: this is the potential benefit of *not backing out on bad information.* There is also a potential benefit to waiting. If the evidence is negative and correct, doing so yields 7 rather than −1: this is the potential benefit of *backing out on good information.* How these benefits trade off against each other will depend on the likelihood of (i.e., Anna's degree of belief in) each of the states in which the benefits occur. And, using decision theory, we can say exactly when the benefits of saying yes to Bates now outweigh the benefits of waiting for more evidence.[9] Consider the following conditions:

(1) Anna is already fairly confident that Bates is innocent.

(2) If the investigation says that Bates is guilty, then (even though it will lower Anna's degree of belief enough to prefer saying no) it won't tell conclusively in favor of his guilt.

(3) Postponing the decision to marry Bates is costly OR Anna is risk avoidant.

Call conditions (1) and (2) the *credence conditions* and the elements of condition (3) the *value* and *attitude* conditions. When these conditions obtain, Anna is *rationally required* to have faith that Bates is innocent: she is rationally required to stop her search for evidence and decide to marry Bates.

On the side of the faithful act, we have the potential benefit of acting now (you might take the risk anyway, when it would have been at least as good to take it immediately) and the potential benefit of not backing out on bad information (you might be talked out of a risk that would have paid off); and on the side of waiting until more evidence comes in, we have the potential benefit of backing out on good information (you might be talked out of a risk that would not have paid off). If the cost of postponing the decision is high, then the potential benefits of the faithful act are higher, particularly if you are likely to get positive correct evidence—which is more likely if you already have a large body of positive evidence. If you are risk avoidant, then you require a higher degree of belief to take a risk; therefore, you are more easily talked out of taking a risk. Consequently, if the negative evidence wouldn't be conclusive, so that backing out on bad information and backing out on good information are both possible, you are in particular danger of the former. Negative evidence is less likely to be conclusive if the source of the evidence is unreliable or if you already have a large body of positive evidence.

Putting these facts together, the benefits of the faithful act are apt to outweigh the benefits of waiting for more evidence when you have a large body of evidence in favor of the proposition you are considering taking a risk on, the evidence that you might still encounter is sparse or unreliable, and either postponing the decision is costly or you are risk avoidant. And this is because when your evidential situation has these features, the benefits you stand to lose by getting more evidence (you won't act now, you might back out on bad information) outweigh the benefits you stand to gain by getting more evidence. We might say: faith guards against unnecessary dithering and misleading evidence.

Again, the credence conditions are more apt to obtain if Anna antecedently has a large body of evidence in favor of Bates's innocence. For example, if Anna has a long

---

9. For details, see Buchak (2012) and L. Buchak, "Instrumental Rationality, Epistemic Rationality, and Evidence-Gathering," *Philosophical Perspectives* 24 (2010): 85–120.

history of observing Bates's character, then even if the investigation says he is guilty, her degree of belief in his innocence will only drop somewhat, since the guilty verdict must be weighed against her own large body of evidence. Furthermore, if her evidence comes from many sources, then her degree of belief is more likely to remain high in the face of counterevidence. So, we can say more generally: a larger and more diverse body of evidence is more apt to make faith practically rational. An individual who commits prematurely is not rational, *but neither is an individual who insists on seeing all the evidence before committing.*

If Anna has no experience with Bates, it would be irrational for her to have faith in his innocence, but since she does, it would be irrational for her not to have faith. If you have no experience with your friend's character (or only negative experience), it would be irrational for you to have faith that she will keep your secrets, but if you have ample positive experience, it would be irrational for you not to have faith. If we accept the supposition that Moses had a long history of trusting God and had even interacted with him personally, then it would have been irrational for him not to have faith that God would lead his people to the Promised Land. If you have no evidence that God exists or no experience with a particular religion, then it would be irrational for you to have faith that God exists or to have faith in the claims of that religion,[10] but if you've had a series of religious experiences or if you are embedded in a religious community that has in your experience led to truth and flourishing, it would be irrational for you not to have faith. Similar points hold of reliance on testimony, which can be considered a special case of faith (faith that some testifier is telling the truth): it might not be rational to take the testimony of a stranger on faith, but it will be rational to take the testimony of someone who you know has a good track record or about whom you know other facts that imply he has access to the truth and honestly shares it. You must get evidence first, but you must not postpone acting forever.

3.3   PRACTICAL RATIONALITY DURING AN ACT OF FAITH

Let us now turn to the other requirement of faith: if Anna has faith that Bates is innocent, then she must stick with her decision to marry him, even if the verdict is that Bates is guilty. (If Moses has faith that God will lead his people to the Promised Land, then he must not turn back when Pharaoh's army pursues him.) Again, this case will only be interesting if a guilty verdict lowers her degree of belief enough to make her not want to risk marrying Bates. When will sticking with her decision anyway be practically rational?

This case has roughly the same features as the "more interesting case" above, with one twist. If the credence and attitude conditions are satisfied, then *before* Anna gets the evidence it will be rational for her to plan to stick with her decision no matter what

---

10. This stands in contrast to claims made by Pascal in "The Wager" and James in "The Will to Believe" (both excerpted in this chapter), at least on plausible interpretations of these authors.

the evidence says.[11] But if she learns that the verdict is that Bates is guilty, then she will, *upon hearing this*, want to back out of her commitment, and rationally so (in the sense that this action will be recommended by her new degrees of belief, given her utilities). Thus, there might be a conflict between what Anna should plan to do at an earlier time and what it would be rational for her to do at a later time after new information has come in, at least if we set her past plan aside. It looks like faith will tell Anna to stick with a plan it was rational for her to make given what she knew then, but which it would not be rational for her to make now given what she's learned. How can that ever be rational?

Recall one feature that made the don't-wait-for-more-evidence aspect of faith rational: faith guards against the possibility that misleading evidence will make one want to back out of a course of action that would actually be best. Such a safeguard is needed when one is apt to encounter evidence that will make one less sure of the claim one is taking a risk on, but will still leave one in a position in which that claim is highly probable. And one is more apt to encounter evidence of this form when one is engaged in a long-term risky project where a variety of "low-quality" evidence comes in that pushes one's degree of belief up and down. When one is engaged in a project on a long-enough timescale, and with irregular-enough evidence, one is apt to encounter misleading evidence. Thus, this feature also explains why remaining committed, despite counterevidence, is rational.

For example, take the claim that you will successfully complete the degree and training required for your career. Completing a degree takes years, and you can't be completely certain ahead of time you will finish (in part because doing so depends on your own efforts). You may begin with a high degree of belief—based on good evidence—that you will complete the degree. But during the time required to complete it, evidence will come in that will knock your degree of belief around. You do well as a freshman, and your degree of belief rises; you struggle as a sophomore, and your degree of belief plummets; you are praised by a professor, and your degree of belief rises again; and so forth. You won't be able to complete the degree if you drop out whenever your degree of belief is low enough to justify your doing so. You won't be able to complete it unless your commitment to completing it is resilient in the face of counterevidence.

Or consider again Moses's faith in the claim that God will lead his people to the Promised Land. Pharaoh at first refused to let Moses's people go; then he agreed; then he took back his agreement; then he agreed to let them leave Egypt; then he pursued them with his army; then God parted the Red Sea; then there was no food for the people to eat in the desert; then God gave them manna to eat; and so forth. Again, Moses wouldn't have been able to lead his people to the Promised Land if he turned back whenever his degree of belief was low enough to justify doing so—he needed a resilient commitment to completing the journey.

Other cases have this structure as well. Consider the claim that one's efforts toward justice will not be in vain, and the risk of dedicating one's life to such an effort: one

---

11. The choice between sticking with her decision and backing out is represented by the choice between *A* and *C* when $c = 0$. (There will be no costs to postponing the decision, because she has already made it, and all four possibilities are live, because we are asking about what, *before* she gets the evidence, she should plan to do in the future.)

will likely experience, in addition to successes, setbacks that make one reasonably doubt whether one's efforts aren't in vain. Or consider the religious adherent: he can expect to reasonably doubt when he encounters setbacks, when his expectations are thwarted, or when he encounters reasonable disagreement with an adherent of a different religion.

Even if you are rationally confident that the faith claim is true when you embark on a long-term risky project, if the project involves a long enough timescale, then you should ahead of time expect to encounter misleading evidence at some point. You can expect, even if the faith claim is in fact true, that at some point you will rationally doubt enough to want to back out of the project. Given this, in order to have the possibility of completing such a project at all, your commitment must be resilient: you must not waver when your degree of belief drops.

We might have thought that a rational person is someone who always does what makes most sense in light of his current information and his current preferences. But as these examples show, if you adopt a policy of always acting on your degrees of belief at a given time—if Anna adopts a policy according to which she will back out of her commitment to Bates if the verdict says he is guilty—then you will likely not be able to complete long-term risky projects at all, because you can expect to encounter misleading evidence at some point. If instead, you adopt a policy of making commitments and following through on them—if Anna maintains faith in Bates—then you will be able to complete these projects *if* the faith claim is true. Thus, faith allows us to adhere to an act over time—to complete a risky long-term project—in a way that is decoupled from evidence that the project will fail or isn't worth it. *Faith keeps us from being blown about by the changing winds of evidence.*

Of course, you do lose something by adopting faith: you leave yourself open to acting at particular times against what your evidence suggests. And you thus leave yourself more open to taking a bad risk. It is important to note that while faith recommends sticking with an action in the face of counterevidence, there are mechanisms for losing faith: if your degree of belief in the faith claim drops drastically, or stays low for a long period of time, or if your initial reasons for adopting faith are undermined, then it may be wise, all things considered, to give up the faith commitment. Rational faith is not blind, dogmatic faith: although someone who initially has faith should maintain that faith as the evidence starts to go against the claim in question, it can be rational to change one's mind if negative evidence keeps piling up. At some point, it could be rational for Anna to give up on Bates, and maybe even for Moses to give up on God. But in the meantime, especially if they start out with convincing and deep evidence, their faith can withstand a lot of negative evidence.

4. Conclusion

Faith is not belief without evidence or reason. To have faith in a claim is to be willing to take risks on that claim without looking for more evidence and to continue to take these risks even if you encounter evidence against the claim.

Such faith can be rational. In particular, embarking on an act of faith—acting without gathering more evidence—is rationally required when your evidence is strong and deep in that it justifies a high degree of belief in the claim in question, further evidence will not tell conclusively against it, and there are costs to postponing the decision or you are risk avoidant. Seeing the act through—maintaining your commitment to act even if you get evidence against the claim in question—is rationally required when your evidence is strong and deep in the above sense, when you are risk avoidant, and if you would rather allow for the possibility of completing long-term risky projects than act as you think best at every given time.

Taking these two points together, the rationality of faith arises from the possibility that you might get evidence that is misleading—evidence that talks you out of a risk that would have in fact paid off. Faith is a bulwark against misleading evidence. It is the attitude that allows you to start and finish risky long-term projects, particularly when these projects depend on claims about which you cannot be certain before acting.

TEST YOUR UNDERSTANDING

1. True or false: For Buchak, to have faith that God exists is to believe in God even though you have no evidence that God exists.

2. Briefly restate Buchak's account of what it means to have faith that a friend is trustworthy.

3. True or false: Buchak argues that it can be rational to retain your faith that God exists even when your evidence leads you to doubt that God exists.

4. True or false: For Buchak, a rational agent always acts so as to maximize expected utility.

NOTES AND QUESTIONS

1. *What is faith good for?* We can imagine rational creatures who never go in for faith in Buchak's sense. These creatures proportion their beliefs to their evidence, so their confidence goes up and down as new evidence comes in, and they make rational, utility-maximizing choices at every stage. Buchak's key idea is that we are better off than these creatures. Our capacity for faith makes it possible for us to undertake risky projects and follow through with them, even when it is foreseeable that at some point along the way, the prospects for success will look bleak. A utility maximizer will give up at that point; a faithful person will not. And according to Buchak, the faithful person is better off in such a case.

   Exercise: Choose an example from your own life in which you have persisted in a risky endeavor despite evidence that you would not succeed. Analyze the example in Buchak's way and say whether your faith was rational.

2. *Faith and morality.* Most of Buchak's examples of rational faith are cases in which the agent's faith justifies behavior that involves risk *to the agent but not to others.* Anna takes a risk when she places her faith in Bates and decides to marry him, but the risk is only a risk to her. But suppose Anna had children whom she might be placing at risk by marrying Bates. Could it be rational for Anna to have faith that Bates is innocent in such a case? And even if it could, would it be *morally decent* for her to do so?

Exercise: Say how Buchak might respond to the following claim:

> *Faith may be rationally permissible in many cases. But it is only morally permissible when it poses no significant risk to others. When the interests of others are at stake, we are morally required to abandon our risky projects when we lose confidence in the beliefs that underlie them.*

3. *Buchak on religious faith.* For a striking example of faith in Buchak's sense, consider the life of Mother Teresa. Mother Teresa's lifelong project of ministering to the poor in India was initially informed by a vivid sense that she was called by God to do this and that God was present with her. As was revealed only after her death, however, her sense of God's presence soon disappeared, never to return:

> In my soul I feel just that terrible pain of loss, of God not wanting me—of God not being God—of God not really existing. (Quoted in B. Kolodiejchuk, Ed., *Mother Teresa: Come Be My Light* [Doubleday, 2007], 192.)

Analyzing the case in Buchak's way, we can think of Mother Teresa as having had evidence for God's existence at the outset, and as having made a commitment to act on that belief *and to continue doing so even if evidence to the contrary emerged,* as it did.

Question: Was Mother Teresa's faith rational in Buchak's sense? Compare Mother Teresa with a religious believer who never had a vivid sense of God's presence but who chose to put her faith in God anyway and then lived a life doing similar good works. Does Buchak's analysis imply that this second believer was irrational, even though she did almost exactly what Mother Teresa did?

ANALYZING THE ARGUMENTS

1. *Belief and the will.* Philosophers often write as if belief were under our voluntary control. But is it? Take a **proposition** about which you currently have no opinion and no evidence; for example, the proposition that the number of hairs on your head is even. Now try to believe that proposition. Can you? (You can certainly *say* that you believe it, but can you summon up real *conviction*?) If not, does this show that it is always impossible to believe at will? And if it is impossible to believe at will, does that undermine the practical arguments for religious belief given by Pascal and James? For discussion of the general problem, see Bernard Williams, "Deciding to Believe," in *Problems of the Self* (Cambridge University Press, 1973).

2. *Practical reasons for belief and the value of faith.* Both James and Pascal provide what might be called *self-interested* reasons for believing that God exists. Many people find arguments of this sort unseemly. Religious faith is supposed by many to be a virtue (for which one might be admired) or a gift (for which one might be grateful). Do the defenses of faith in James and Pascal deprive faith of its value?

3. *Drawing the line.* As Plantinga notes, anyone who says that it is *sometimes* okay to believe without evidence must immediately concede that this is not *always* okay. (*Exercise:* Explain in vivid terms why this "anything goes" principle is unacceptable.) Any such view must therefore provide a principle that specifies the conditions under which evidence and argument are not required. A principle for this purpose must satisfy two conditions: It must be consistent with what we already know (e.g., that many of our scientific beliefs are reasonable, that superstitious beliefs are unreasonable, etc.), and it must be *nonarbitrary*: it must draw a principled line between the cases in which ungrounded belief is reasonable and the cases in which it is not. This is a notoriously difficult problem. As an exercise, begin the effort to identify such a principle. Make a list of some opinions you hold but cannot defend by means of argument. Determine which of those opinions you regard as reasonable upon reflection. Then try to articulate a principle that draws the line where you have drawn it. Is this principle plausible upon reflection? What does it imply about the various cases of religious belief discussed in the selections?

4. *Reasonable versus unreasonable belief.* The selections all presume a distinction between beliefs that are reasonable or justified and beliefs that are unreasonable or unjustified. Imagine that you are trying to explain this distinction to someone unfamiliar with it. Suppose she says, for example, "I don't see why it takes a fancy argument to show that it's okay for me to believe that God exists even if I don't have a shred of evidence. It's a free country. I can believe what I like!" This person needs an explanation of the difference between a *legally permissible belief* and a *reasonable belief.* An ideal account will take the form of an explicit definition:

   A belief is reasonable (warranted, justified) if and only if . . .

   But even if that is too much to ask, an informal explanation should be possible.

   Exercise: Imagine that you are addressing someone who does not understand the distinction between a reasonable belief and a belief that one is legally allowed to hold. What is the best way to put her in a position to understand this important contrast?

Part II
EPISTEMOLOGY

What Is Knowledge?

In 2008, Nicholas Evans, the author of the novel *The Horse Whisperer*, picked some wild mushrooms, sautéed them in butter, and served them to his family. They nearly died. The mushrooms were deadly webcaps, which contain the potentially fatal toxin orellanine. Evans's kidneys failed, and he later received a kidney transplant from his daughter.

Evans did not know that the mushrooms were poisonous. If he had known that, he would never have cooked them. This illustrates one way in which knowledge is valuable. Lack of knowledge can have serious, even fatal, consequences. Sometimes knowledge can save your life.

Propositional Knowledge, Personal Knowledge, Procedural Knowledge

The kind of knowledge Evans lacked was *propositional* (or *factual*) knowledge, where what follows the verb "to know" is a clause beginning with "that." You know that the earth is round, and you know that Evans wrote *The Horse Whisperer*. These clauses pick out what philosophers call **propositions,** things that can be *true* or *false*. That the earth is round is a true proposition; that the earth is flat is a false proposition. This is why the kind of knowledge reported by a statement like "You know that the earth is round" is called **propositional knowledge** (and also sometimes *knowledge-that*). This is the topic of the selections that follow and is the main subject matter of the branch of philosophy called **epistemology**—derived from the Greek word *episteme*, meaning "knowledge."

Propositional knowledge is not the only kind of knowledge, as the variety of grammatical constructions using the verb "to know" indicates. For example, in one construction the verb is followed by a noun (or noun phrase) that typically picks out a person or a place. Nicholas Evans knows Scotland: he is quite familiar with that country, having picked mushrooms there. He also knows Robert Redford, the director and star of the movie based on Evans's novel. We could paraphrase these claims by saying that Evans is acquainted with both Scotland and Redford. This sort of knowledge is accordingly called *acquaintance knowledge*, or *personal knowledge*.

Propositional knowledge is not a kind of personal knowledge. Someone can know that Paris is the capital of France without knowing Paris or France. What about the other way around? Could personal knowledge be a kind of propositional knowledge? That seems doubtful. If you read Michael Callan's lengthy *Robert Redford: The Biography*, you will acquire a lot of propositional knowledge about Redford but will not thereby know him. The case that propositional and acquaintance knowledge are quite different can be strengthened by noting that many languages distinguish them using different verbs, where English has only one. In French, for instance, *connaître* is used for acquaintance knowledge and *savoir* for propositional knowledge.

There are other notable constructions using the verb "to know." For example: Evans knows where Edinburgh is, knows who inspired the main character in *The Horse Whisperer*, and knows which actor directed the movie. These constructions seem to say something about Evans's propositional knowledge. If Evans knows where Edinburgh is, then he knows that it is in Scotland, or south of the Firth of Forth, or some other salient fact about its location, and similarly for the other two examples.

There is another related construction that is less clearly propositional: Evans knows how to cook mushrooms, how to tie his shoes, and how to write best sellers. These are examples of *knowledge-how*, or *procedural knowledge*. Is procedural knowledge a kind of propositional knowledge? One might think not, on the ground that reading Julia Child's *Mastering the Art of French Cooking* will give you lots of propositional knowledge about French cooking but is not guaranteed to prevent your soufflés from collapsing. It is a controversial matter whether knowledge-how is a kind of propositional knowledge, although not one taken up in the selections.[1]

Propositional Knowledge: Belief, Truth, and Justification

Now that we have the relevant kind of knowledge clearly in view, the task is to say something interesting about it. The traditional approach is to try to break knowledge down into its components, as one might study an engine by taking it apart.

One uncontroversial component of propositional knowledge is truth. When Evans picked the deadly webcaps, he believed that they were harmless. Indeed, he

---

1. For an argument that knowledge-how is a kind of propositional knowledge, see J. Stanley and T. Williamson, "Knowing How," *Journal of Philosophy* 98 (2001): 411–44.

presumably took himself to *know* that they were harmless. "I know that these are harmless," we can imagine him saying. But he *did not* know that the mushrooms were harmless, as they were not. You cannot know what is false: if *S* (a person) knows *p*, then *p* must be true.

Belief is a good candidate for another component of knowledge. If you know that the earth is round, then you will probably reply "The earth is round" if asked about its shape, be unconcerned when a ship disappears over the horizon, and so forth. That is, you will give every impression that you *believe* that the earth is round. Although the belief component is not as uncontroversial as the truth component (the selection by Timothy Williamson discusses one objection), it is widely accepted. So let us assume that if *S* knows *p*, then *S* must believe *p*.

So far, we have two components of knowledge: truth and belief. If *S* knows *p*, then it must be that (i) *p* is true, and (ii) *S* believes *p*. In other words, (i) and (ii) are **necessary conditions** for *S* to know *p*.

Necessary conditions need not also be **sufficient conditions**. Having four equal sides is a necessary condition for being a square: it is impossible to be a square without having four equal sides. But it is not a *sufficient* condition: having four equal sides does not guarantee being a square, as some rhomboids (which have four equal sides) are not squares. What about (i) and (ii)? Might they also be, taken together, a sufficient condition for knowledge? And if they are, then knowledge is just the two components of belief and truth added together. That is: *S* knows *p* if and only if (i) *p* is true, and (ii) *S* believes *p*.

However, as has been known since Plato's time, belief and truth are not sufficient for knowledge. Suppose someone buys a ticket for the lottery convinced that he will win because his fortune teller told him so, and by a fluke he does. He truly believed that he would win, but he did not *know* that he would win. As Plato puts it, knowledge is not "correct opinion"; as a contemporary philosopher might say, knowledge cannot be "analyzed" as true belief. What might another component of knowledge be?

The lottery winner has no *reasons* or *evidence* for his true belief that he will win. That is, his belief is not *justified*. Conversely, your true belief that the earth is round is justified—perhaps you read about its shape in a reliable textbook or a knowledgeable teacher told you that it is round. So this suggests that justification is another component of knowledge. Like the belief component, the justification component is also widely accepted. So let us assume that if *S* knows *p*, then *S* must justifiably believe *p*.

Now we have three necessary conditions for *S* to know *p*. If *S* knows *p*, then it must be that (i) *p* is true, (ii) *S* believes *p*, and (iii) *S*'s belief is justified. Might (i), (ii), and (iii) together be sufficient conditions for knowledge? And if they are, then knowledge is just the three components of belief, truth, and justification added together. That is: *S* knows *p* if and only if (i) *p* is true, (ii) *S* believes *p*, and (iii) *S*'s belief is justified.

What else could knowledge be? There is no obvious fourth component, so the received view used to be that knowledge simply is justified true belief.

Gettier's Counterexamples, and the Aftermath

All that changed with the publication in 1963 of Edmund Gettier's "Is Justified True Belief Knowledge?" Gettier presents a series of examples in which someone has a justified true belief but apparently does not know. These *Gettier cases* are commonly taken to refute the claim that (i), (ii), and (iii) are sufficient for *S* to know *p*.

Once you get the idea, Gettier cases are easy to construct. Here is one. Suppose that Evans believes that the mushrooms are harmless because he consulted the authoritative *Field Guide to Edible Mushrooms of Britain and Europe*. Because of a printer's error (most unlikely in a work of this kind), the photograph of deadly webcaps was captioned *Ceps*, a desirable type of edible mushroom. Evans's false belief that the mushrooms are harmless is justified: he knows that past editions of the *Field Guide* were accurate. Evans puts the mushrooms in a bag and takes them back to his kitchen. As far as he knows, these are his only mushrooms. He believes that the mushrooms in the bag are harmless and that they are in his kitchen. Evans makes a trivial deductive **inference** from the premise that the mushrooms in the bag in his kitchen are harmless, and he believes that there are some harmless mushrooms in his kitchen. Since Evans is justified in believing the premise, and the conclusion deductively follows from the premise, he is also justified in believing the conclusion. So Evans's belief that there are some harmless mushrooms in his kitchen is justified. By luck, it is also true: Evans's wife bought some mushrooms from the supermarket yesterday and put them in the refrigerator. Yet Evans does not *know* that there are some harmless mushrooms in his kitchen.

Gettier's paper immediately created an industry tasked with finding a fourth component of knowledge that, when added to truth, belief, and justification, would result in a sufficient condition. It proved very difficult, and the consensus is that no such fourth component was ever found. (For more details, see this chapter's "Reader's Guide," which follows the Gettier selection.)

Because of the apparent failure of this project (among other reasons), many philosophers have become skeptical that knowledge can be broken down into components. They accept that there are a variety of necessary conditions for *S* to know *p*, but they deny that these conditions are also jointly sufficient for *S* to know *p*. Prominent among them is Timothy Williamson, who champions a "knowledge-first" approach to epistemology. Knowledge, according to Williamson, cannot be analyzed as justified true belief plus some extra factor *X*; instead, knowledge should be taken as explanatorily fundamental in its own right. Inquiry always proceeds with *some* things being taken for granted, not needing a definition or analysis, and why can't knowledge be one?

Even if knowledge is unanalyzable, that does not mean we cannot discover anything interesting about it. Indeed, to say that truth, justification, and belief are necessary conditions for knowledge is already to say something interesting. And Williamson finds much more to say.

Many questions about knowledge remain. One is raised by Plato: Why is knowledge better than true belief, or "correct opinion"? If Evans had known that the mushrooms were poisonous, then he would not have cooked them. But he would not have cooked them if he had believed truly that they were poisonous, whether or not he also knew that they were poisonous. Plato suggests a (somewhat metaphorical) answer to that question: knowledge is "shackled" in the mind, whereas true belief has a tendency to "scamper away and escape." Williamson suggests a way to develop Plato's answer. Suppose Evans has a mere true belief that the mushrooms in his possession are poisonous because some overconfident friend told him that all mushrooms in Scotland are poisonous. Evans might well learn later that his friend is not to be trusted or that there are many edible mushrooms in Scotland. And if he does, he will give up his belief that the mushrooms are poisonous and perhaps will take them back to his kitchen and start sautéing. By contrast, if he knows that the mushrooms are poisonous, he is much less likely to change his mind.

Plato (429–347 BCE)

Plato is one of the most important figures in Western philosophy. He founded the Academy in Athens, which was a major center of learning in classical Greece, where he taught Aristotle (384–322 BCE). Plato's works typically take the form of dialogues, and nearly all of them feature his teacher Socrates (469–399 BCE).

MENO

SOCRATES: So can you name any other thing[1] where the people who claim to teach it, so far from being acknowledged as capable of teaching anyone else, aren't even recognized as knowing anything about it themselves—they're actually thought to be especially bad at the very thing they claim to teach!—meanwhile, the people who are acknowledged as decent men themselves can't make up their minds about whether or not it can be taught? And if they're so confused about it, do you think they could possibly be teaching it properly?

MENO: Absolutely not.

S: So if sophists[2] can't teach it, and people who are decent men themselves can't teach it, clearly nobody else could be teaching it?

M: No. I don't think so.

S: And if nobody's teaching it, then nobody's learning it, either?

M: That's right.

1. That is, any subject other than virtue, or being good.
2. Ancient Greek philosophers and rhetoricians who charged for their services.

s: And we already agreed that if there's something that nobody teaches, and nobody learns, then it's something that can't be taught?

m: Yes, we did.

s: And there's no trace, anywhere, of anyone teaching people how to be good?

m: Right.

s: And if there's no one teaching it, there's no one learning it?

m: Apparently not.

s: So it looks like being good is something that can't be taught?

m: It looks that way—if we've thought it through correctly; which makes me wonder, Socrates, if maybe there aren't even any good men at all! Or, how on earth *do* people become good, if and when they do?

s: Chances are, Meno, you and I are a couple of rather ordinary men. I'm afraid our teachers—Gorgias in your case, and in my case, Prodicus[3]—haven't educated us well enough. So we've definitely got to take a good look at ourselves and find out who's going to make us better, somehow or other. And I'm saying that with this search of ours in mind: what idiots we've been! How silly of us not to realize that it isn't always *knowledge* that's guiding people when they do things well and succeed in their affairs. That's probably why the answer keeps getting away from us—I mean, the discovery of how exactly good men become good.

m: How do you mean, Socrates?

s: Here's what I mean. We were right to agree that men who *are* good also always *do* good—weren't we? That's got to be right?

m: Yes.

s: And we were also right to agree that good men will do us good if they guide us in our affairs and "show us the way"?

m: Yes.

s: But the claim that you can only show people the way if you have wisdom—it looks like we were wrong to agree on that.

m: What makes you say that?

s: Well, I'll tell you. Look—suppose someone *knew* the way to Larissa[4] (or wherever) and was on his way there, and showing other people how to get there; obviously he'd be good at showing them the right way?

m: Of course.

s: And what about someone who had an *opinion* on how to get there—a correct opinion—but who'd never actually been there, and didn't know how to get there; wouldn't he be able to show them the way as well?

m: Of course.

s: And presumably as long as he has his correct opinion (about the same thing the other man has knowledge of), he'll be every bit as good at showing people the way? With his true belief, but without knowledge, he'll be just as good a guide as the man with the knowledge?

---

3. Gorgias and Prodicus were both sophists.

4. City in ancient (and present-day) Greece.

M: Yes, he'll be just as good.

S: In other words, true opinion is just as good a guide to right action as knowledge. There's the key fact that we kept leaving out, just now, when we were looking into the nature of being good. We said that wisdom was the only thing that can show us how to do things the right way. But that's not so. There's also true opinion.

M: Yes, it certainly looks like it.

S: So in other words, a correct opinion does just as much good as knowledge?

M: Except in one respect, Socrates. If you have knowledge, then you'll *always* be dead on target; but if you only have a correct opinion, sometimes you'll hit, and sometimes you'll miss.

S: What makes you say that? If you've always got the correct opinion, won't you always be "on target" as long as you've got your correct opinion?

M: Yes, good point . . . it seems that must be right; which leaves me wondering, Socrates: If that's the case, why on earth is knowledge so much more valuable than correct opinion, and why are they treated as two different things?

S: Well, you know why it is you're wondering about it? Shall I tell you?

M: Go ahead.

S: It's because you haven't pondered Daedalus's[5] statues. Maybe you haven't even got any up there in Thessaly.[6]

M: What have they got to do with it?

S: Well, they're the same: if they aren't shackled, they escape—they scamper away. But if they're shackled, they stay put.

M: What are you getting at?

S: If you own an original Daedalus, unshackled, it's not worth all that much—like a slave who keeps running away—because it doesn't stay put. But if you've got one that's shackled, it's very valuable. Because they're really lovely pieces of work. What am I getting at? My point is, it's the same with true opinions. True opinions, as long as they stay put, are a fine thing and do us a whole lot of good. Only, they tend not to stay put for very long. They're always scampering away from a person's soul. So they're not very valuable until you shackle them by figuring out what makes them true. (And that, my dear Meno, is a matter of remembering, as we agreed earlier.) And then, once they're shackled, they turn into knowledge, and become stable and fixed. So that's why knowledge is a more valuable thing than correct opinion, and that's how knowledge *differs* from a correct opinion: by a shackle.

M: You know, I bet that's pretty much right, Socrates.

S: Of course, I'm speaking as someone who doesn't have knowledge myself. I'm just guessing. But I certainly don't think it's only a guess that correct opinion and knowledge are two very different things. If there's anything at all I'd claim to know—and I wouldn't claim to know a lot—I'd certainly count that as one of the things I know for sure.

5. Mythological architect, inventor, and craftsman.

6. Region of Greece containing the city Larissa.

M: And you're quite right to, Socrates.

S: So tell me: Am I also right in saying that if true opinion is guiding you, it's just as good as knowledge at achieving the goal of any sort of action?

M: Yes, I think that's right as well.

S: So correct opinion is just as good a thing as knowledge and does us just as much good in our actions; and a man with correct opinions will do as much good as a man with knowledge?

M: Right.

S: And we agreed that that was a characteristic of a good man—doing good?

M: Yes.

S: So it isn't just knowledge that makes men good, and able to do their cities good, if and when they do; it's also correct opinion. In which case, given that neither one of those things—knowledge or true opinion—arises in people just by nature . . . or am I wrong about that? Do you think either of them comes to us naturally?

M: No.

S: So if neither of them comes naturally, it can't be people's nature that makes them good men?

M: No, it can't be.

S: And since our nature doesn't make us good . . . the next thing we asked was whether being good is something teachable?

M: Yes.

S: Right, and didn't we decide that being good is teachable *if* it's a kind of wisdom?

M: Yes.

S: And conversely, that it would have to be a kind of wisdom, if it's teachable?

M: Exactly.

S: And that if there are people teaching it, then it's teachable; but if there aren't any people teaching it, then it isn't teachable?

M: That's right.

S: And we've decided that there aren't any people teaching it?

M: We did.

S: So that means we've decided that it isn't teachable, and that it isn't a kind of wisdom?

M: Exactly.

S: But we're certainly agreeing that it's a good thing?

M: Yes.

S: And that what's good—what does us good—is the element that guides us and shows us the right way?

M: Absolutely.

S: And that there are only two things that can show us the right way: true opinion and knowledge. At least, that's what a person has to have, to show the way. I don't count things that come out right just by some stroke of luck. That's not a case of anything happening through human guidance. In any area where people show the way, those are the only possible guides: true opinion and knowledge.

M: I think that's right.

S: And since being good is something that can't be taught, it's no longer an option that it's knowledge?

M: Apparently not.

S: So of the only two things that are good, and that enable us to do good, that rules out knowledge: it seems it isn't knowledge that guides people in the civic and ethical sphere.

M: I agree.

S: So in other words it wasn't through having knowledge, or by being experts, that men like that were able to guide their cities—men like Themistocles[7] and the ones Anytus[8] was talking about. Of course! That's why they couldn't turn other people into the sort of men they were themselves—because it wasn't knowledge that made them the way they were.

M: That seems very plausible, Socrates.

S: So if it wasn't knowledge that made them the way they were, the only remaining possibility is that it was a sort of knack for having the right opinions. That's what statesmen must use to set their cities on the right path; and that means they're just like fortune-tellers and soothsayers, in terms of how close they are to having knowledge. Soothsayers are the same: when they're "inspired" they say plenty of things that are true; but they don't really know what they're saying.

M: Yes, that's probably right.

S: And isn't it right to call people "inspired" when they achieve lots of great things by what they say and do, without any understanding?

M: Absolutely.

S: So it makes sense to call those people inspired: the fortune-tellers and soothsayers; and poets and playwrights, too; and we'd be especially right to call statesmen inspired, and to say they're in a kind of trance, possessed by some divine spirit, when they achieve so many great successes by saying the things they say, even though they don't really know what they're talking about.

M: Absolutely.

S: And remember that women, Meno, call good men "inspired"; and in Sparta,[9] too, the highest praise for a good man is when they say, "That man's *inzpired*."[10]

M: And apparently they're right, Socrates. Mind you, Anytus here will probably get annoyed with you for saying so.

S: I don't care about that. We'll talk with him again some other time, Meno. As for us, here and now—if we've done a good job of our search for the truth, and if what we've said at each stage of our talk was right, then it turns out that being good is not something that comes to us naturally, or something that can be taught; instead, it seems it arises by gift of god, and without understanding, in the people who have it . . . unless, that is, there were a man, among good statesmen, who could also turn someone else into the sort of man he is himself. If there were such a man, they'd probably speak of him as being up here among the living just what Homer says Tiresias was among the dead. He says,

---

7. Athenian politician and military leader.

8. Athenian politician who makes an earlier appearance in the dialogue. He was one of the prosecutors of Socrates, who was tried and sentenced to death in 399 BCE.

9. City-state in ancient Greece.

10. Most editors think that Plato here imitated the Spartan dialect. [Translator's note.]

He alone has sense in the world below;[11]
the rest are flitting shadows.

A man like that would be the same thing here: something real, among mere shadows of what it is to be good.

M: I think that's quite right, and very nicely put, Socrates.

S: So by our line of reasoning, Meno, it appears that being good is a quality that comes to people, when it does, by gift of god. Of course, we really won't know for sure until we set aside the question of exactly how it comes to people and first try to find out what being good is, in itself.

But now it's time for me to go. And as for you, try to convince your host Anytus here about the things you've been convinced about yourself—try to calm him down. If you can do that, you may well be doing Athens a favour.[12]

TEST YOUR UNDERSTANDING

1. Socrates gives an example to show that "it isn't always *knowledge* that's guiding people when they . . . succeed in their affairs." What is this example?

2. Suppose you guess correctly that a coin flip comes up tails. According to Socrates, do you know that the flip comes up tails?

3. The dialogue gives a reason for thinking that correct opinion and knowledge are equally valuable. What is it? According to Socrates, do we think that they are equally valuable?

4. Does Socrates think that the possession of knowledge explains why someone is a good person?

NOTES AND QUESTIONS

1. The *Meno* is one of Plato's many dialogues featuring his teacher Socrates (469–399 BCE), and mostly concerns the questions of whether virtue can be taught and what virtue is. The selection is from the end of the *Meno*; earlier in the dialogue, Socrates raises the following puzzle:

> You can't try to find out about something you know about, because you know about it, in which case there's no point trying to find out about it; and you can't try to find out about something you don't know about, either, because then you don't even know what it is you're trying to find out about. (*Meno* 80e)

Exercise: Set out this puzzle more clearly. What is the solution?

11. Tiresias was a mythical blind prophet. The quotation is from Homer's ancient Greek epic poem *The Odyssey*.

12. Plato (not Socrates) means, if Meno (or anyone) could have "calmed Anytus down," he might not have prosecuted Socrates, which would have been the greatest possible favor to Athens. [Translator's note.]

2. Plato's main dialogue on knowledge is the *Theaetetus*, in which Socrates, a mathematician Theodorus, and his student Theaetetus discuss the question "What is knowledge?" (The following selection by Gettier refers to this dialogue in footnote 1, as well as to *Meno*.) One proposed definition is that knowledge is "true belief with an account" (*Theaetetus* 201d). As Gettier says in "Is Justified True Belief Knowledge?" this sounds rather like the "justified true belief" analysis of knowledge. After examining this suggestion at some length, Socrates ends up rejecting it. For a discussion of the dialogue and various interpretive controversies, see Timothy Chappell, "Plato on Knowledge in the *Theaetetus*," in *Stanford Encyclopedia of Philosophy*, ed. Edward Zalta (https://plato .stanford.edu/archives/win2013/entries/plato-theaetetus/).

Edmund Gettier (b. 1927)

Gettier is Professor Emeritus of Philosophy at the University of Massachusetts at Amherst. "Is Justified True Belief Knowledge?" is one of the most widely cited papers in contemporary philosophy.

IS JUSTIFIED TRUE BELIEF KNOWLEDGE?

Various attempts have been made in recent years to state necessary and sufficient conditions for someone's knowing a given proposition. The attempts have often been such that they can be stated in a form similar to the following[1]:

a. S knows that P   *IFF*[2]   (*i*) P is true,

(*ii*) S believes that P, and

(*iii*) S is justified in believing that P.

For example, Chisholm has held that the following gives the necessary and sufficient conditions for knowledge.[3]

b. S knows that P   *IFF*   (*i*) S accepts P,

(*ii*) S has adequate evidence for P, and

(*iii*) P is true.

1. Plato seems to be considering some such definition at *Theaetetus* 201, and perhaps accepting one at *Meno* 98. [Gettier's note.] (See page 139 of this anthology.)

2. **IFF** or **iff**: abbreviation for "if and only if."

3. Roderick M. Chisholm (1916–1999) taught at Brown University for many years and made influential contributions to epistemology and other subjects.

Ayer[4] has stated the necessary and sufficient conditions for knowledge as follows:

    c. S knows that P   *IFF*   (*i*) P is true,

                                         (*ii*) S is sure that P is true, and

                                         (*iii*) S has the right to be sure that P is true.

I shall argue that (a) is false in that the conditions stated therein do not constitute a *sufficient* condition for the truth of the proposition that S knows that P. The same argument will show that (b) and (c) fail if "has adequate evidence for" or "has the right to be sure that" is substituted for "is justified in believing that" throughout.

    I shall begin by noting two points. First, in that sense of "justified" in which S's being justified in believing P is a necessary condition of S's knowing that P, it is possible for a person to be justified in believing a proposition that is in fact false. Secondly, for any proposition P, if S is justified in believing P, and P **entails**[5] Q, and S deduces Q from P and accepts Q as a result of this deduction, then S is justified in believing Q. Keeping these two points in mind, I shall now present two cases in which the conditions stated in (a) are true for some proposition, though it is at the same time false that the person in question knows that proposition.

Case I

Suppose that Smith and Jones have applied for a certain job. And suppose that Smith has strong evidence for the following conjunctive[6] proposition:

    d. Jones is the man who will get the job, and Jones has ten coins in his pocket.

Smith's evidence for (d) might be that the president of the company assured him that Jones would in the end be selected, and that he, Smith, had counted the coins in Jones's pocket ten minutes ago. Proposition (d) entails:

    e. The man who will get the job has ten coins in his pocket.

Let us suppose that Smith sees the entailment from (d) to (e), and accepts (e) on the grounds of (d), for which he has strong evidence. In this case, Smith is clearly justified in believing that (e) is true.

    But imagine, further, that unknown to Smith, he himself, not Jones, will get the job. And, also, unknown to Smith, he himself has ten coins in his pocket. Proposition (e) is then true, though proposition (d), from which Smith inferred (e), is false. In our example, then, all of the following are true: (*i*) (e) is true, (*ii*) Smith believes that (e) is

---

4. A. J. Ayer (1910–1989) was one of the leading British philosophers of the past century.

5. **Entails**: logically implies.

6. The conjunction of two sentences "p" and "q" is the sentence "p and q."

true, and (*iii*) Smith is justified in believing that (e) is true. But it is equally clear that Smith does not *know* that (e) is true; for (e) is true in virtue of the number of coins in Smith's pocket, while Smith does not know how many coins are in Smith's pocket, and bases his belief in (e) on a count of the coins in Jones's pocket, whom he falsely believes to be the man who will get the job.

Case II

Let us suppose that Smith has strong evidence for the following proposition:

> f. Jones owns a Ford.

Smith's evidence might be that Jones has at all times in the past within Smith's memory owned a car, and always a Ford, and that Jones has just offered Smith a ride while driving a Ford. Let us imagine, now, that Smith has another friend, Brown, of whose whereabouts he is totally ignorant. Smith selects three place-names quite at random, and constructs the following three propositions:

> g. Either Jones owns a Ford, or Brown is in Boston;
>
> h. Either Jones owns a Ford, or Brown is in Barcelona;
>
> i. Either Jones owns a Ford, or Brown is in Brest-Litovsk.

Each of these propositions is entailed by (f). Imagine that Smith realizes the entailment of each of these propositions he has constructed by (f), and proceeds to accept (g), (h), and (i) on the basis of (f). Smith has correctly inferred (g), (h), and (i) from a proposition for which he has strong evidence. Smith is therefore completely justified in believing each of these three propositions. Smith, of course, has no idea where Brown is.

But imagine now that two further conditions hold. First, Jones does *not* own a Ford, but is at present driving a rented car. And secondly, by the sheerest coincidence, and entirely unknown to Smith, the place mentioned in proposition (h) happens really to be the place where Brown is. If these two conditions hold, then Smith does *not* know that (h) is true, even though (*i*) (h) is true, (*ii*) Smith does believe that (h) is true, and (*iii*) Smith is justified in believing that (h) is true.

These two examples show that definition (a) does not state a *sufficient* condition for someone's knowing a given proposition. The same cases, with appropriate changes, will suffice to show that neither definition (b) nor definition (c) do so either.

TEST YOUR UNDERSTANDING

1. Is Gettier arguing that belief, truth, and justification are not necessary for knowledge?

2. Is Gettier arguing that belief, truth, and knowledge are not sufficient for knowledge?

3. In Gettier's two examples, Smith is justified in believing a certain **proposition** P and reasons from P to another proposition Q, which Gettier says Smith does not know. Does Smith know P?

4. The second example relies on what logical principle?

   a. P-and-Q entails P.

   b. P entails P-or-Q.

   c. P entails not-not-P.

READER'S GUIDE

Gettier's Definition of Knowledge

The introduction to this chapter mentioned Gettier's counterexamples to the "justified true belief" (JTB) definition (or "analysis") of knowledge:

S knows p if and only if (i) p is true, (ii) S believes p, and (iii) S's belief is justified.

This guide discusses two of the many subsequent attempts to define knowledge. A *Gettier case*—an example refuting the JTB analysis—was given in the introduction. Here is one of Gettier's original cases from "Is Justified True Belief Knowledge?":

> Suppose that Smith and Jones have applied for a certain job. And suppose that Smith has strong evidence for the following conjunctive proposition:
>
> a. Jones is the man who will get the job, and Jones has ten coins in his pocket.
>
> Smith's evidence for (a) might be that the president of the company assured him that Jones would in the end be selected, and that he, Smith, had counted the coins in Jones's pocket ten minutes ago. Proposition (a) entails:
>
> b. The man who will get the job has ten coins in his pocket.
>
> Let us suppose that Smith sees the entailment from (a) to (b), and accepts (b) on the grounds of (a), for which he has strong evidence. In this case, Smith is clearly justified in believing that (b) is true.
>
> But imagine, further, that unknown to Smith, he himself, not Jones, will get the job. And, also, unknown to Smith, he himself has ten coins in his pocket. Proposition (b) is then true, though proposition (a), from which Smith inferred (b), is false. In our example, then, all of the following are true: (*i*) (b) is true, (*ii*) Smith believes that (b) is true, and (*iii*) Smith is justified in believing that (b) is true. But it is equally clear that Smith does not *know* that (b) is true; for (b) is true in virtue of the number of coins in Smith's pocket, while Smith does not know how many coins are in Smith's pocket and bases his belief in (b) on a count of the coins in Jones's pocket, whom he falsely believes to be the man who will get the job.[7]

---

7. See pages 144–45 of this anthology (Gettier's sentences have been relettered).

In this example—like the one in the introduction—someone has a justified true belief in some proposition *p*, but does not know *p*. That is, this example shows that conditions (i), (ii), and (iii) in the JTB analysis are not *sufficient* for knowledge. So another condition must be added to the JTB analysis:

> *S* knows *p* if and only if (i) *p* is true, (ii) *S* believes *p*, (iii) *S*'s belief is justified, and
> (iv) _____.

After the publication of Gettier's paper, philosophers tried for years to fill in the blank.[8] Following are two of the more instructive suggestions.

No False Premise

Smith does not know that the man who will get the job has ten coins in his pocket. He inferred that [(b), above] from the **premise** that Jones is the man who will get the job, and Jones has ten coins in his pocket [(a), above]. Although Smith has "strong evidence" for (a), and so is justified in believing it, that proposition is false, as Gettier says. This suggests that Smith does not know (b) because he *inferred it from a false premise*. (*Exercise*: Find the false premise in the Gettier case described in the introduction.) Perhaps, then, the blank should be filled in like this:

> (iv*) *S* does not infer *p* from a false premise.

Causation

Often the fact that such-and-such causally explains why someone believes that such-and-such. Why do you believe that John Adams was the second U.S. president? Because, or partly because, Adams *was* the second president. The fact that Adams was the second president caused the writing of "Adams was the second president" in various documents, later read by historians, who transmitted this information about Adams to the author of a history textbook that you read in high school. The fact that Adams was the second president stands at one end of this long causal chain, at the other end of which is the fact that you believe that he was the second president.

Since reading authoritative books is a way of knowing things, you *know* that Adams was the second president. Note, however, that this sort of causal chain, linking the fact believed to the believing of it, is *absent* in the case of Smith. The fact that the man who will get the job has ten coins in his pocket plays no role in the causal explanation of why Smith believes it. So an alternative suggestion for filling in the blank is:

> (iv**) *p* causes *S* to believe *p*.

Is either of these two suggestions ("No False Premise" and "Causation") correct? Consider the following example, due to Alvin Goldman:

> Henry is driving in the countryside with his son. For the boy's edification Henry identifies various objects on the landscape as they come into view. "That's a cow," says Henry, "That's a tractor," "That's a silo," "That's a barn,"

---

8. Sometimes (iii) is folded into (iv); the project is then described as one of filling in the blank in: *S* knows *p* if and only if (i) *p* is true, (ii) *S* believes *p*, and (iii) _____. This is the way Timothy Williamson puts it in his essay in this chapter.

etc. Henry has no doubt about the identity of these objects; in particular, he has no doubt that the last-mentioned object is a barn, which indeed it is. Each of the identified objects has features characteristic of its type. Moreover, each object is fully in view, Henry has excellent eyesight, and he has enough time to look at them reasonably carefully, since there is little traffic to distract him. ... [Now suppose] that, unknown to Henry, the district he has just entered is full of papier-mâché facsimiles of barns. These facsimiles look from the road exactly like barns, but are really just façades, without back walls or interiors, quite incapable of being used as barns. They are so cleverly constructed that travelers invariably mistake them for barns. Having just entered the district, Henry has not encountered any facsimiles; the object he sees is a genuine barn. But if the object on that site were a facsimile, Henry would mistake it for a barn.[9]

Henry says, pointing at the barn, "That's a barn." What he says is true. But his belief is true by a lucky accident, since he could easily have been looking at a fake barn. So (most philosophers agree), Henry does not *know* that that's a barn. Yet conditions (iv*) and (iv**) both appear to be satisfied: plausibly, Henry does not infer that that's a barn from a false premise, and the fact that that's a barn causes Henry to believe it. So adding either (iv*) or (iv**) to (i), (ii), and (iii) does not give a sufficient condition for knowledge.

This is only the beginning. Many more attempts were made (see the "Analyzing the Arguments" section later in this chapter for another one), and they all succumbed to counterexamples. Some philosophers (such as Timothy Williamson) think the moral is that knowledge cannot be broken down into components—it is *unanalyzable*.

For further reading, see Jonathan Jenkins Ichikawa and Matthias Steup, "The Analysis of Knowledge," in *Stanford Encyclopedia of Philosophy*, ed. Edward Zalta (https://plato.stanford.edu/archives/spr2017/entries/knowledge-analysis/).

NOTES AND QUESTIONS

1. Imagine you are looking at an animal in a field that looks exactly like a sheep. In consequence, you believe that there is a sheep in the field. How can you continue this example to turn it into a Gettier case (i.e., a case where you have a justified true belief that there is a sheep in the field, but do not know that there is a sheep in the field)?

2. Suppose you have bought a lottery ticket. The odds of your winning are a million to one. The winning ticket has been selected and it's not yours, but the number has not yet been announced on television. You are sure that you've lost. Do you *know* that you've lost? Assuming you do not know that you've lost, how does this case differ from Gettier's two examples?

9. Alvin Goldman, "Discrimination and Perceptual Knowledge," *Journal of Philosophy* 73 (1976): 771–91, esp. 772–73.

Timothy Williamson (b. 1958)

Williamson is Wykeham Professor of Logic at the University of Oxford. He is known for bringing formal methods to bear on traditional philosophical problems. He is also the author of many influential books and papers, including *Vagueness* (1994), *Knowledge and Its Limits* (2000), *The Philosophy of Philosophy* (2007), and *Modal Logic as Metaphysics* (2013).

KNOWLEDGE AND BELIEF

The most striking difference between knowledge and belief is that although there is false belief, there cannot be false knowledge. People once believed that the earth was flat. They believed falsely, because the earth was not flat. They did not *know* that the earth was flat, because knowing that the earth was flat would have required the earth to be flat. They *believed* that they knew that the earth was flat, but that was another of their false beliefs.

We can make the same point about a disagreement without even taking sides. Suppose that Mary believes that there is life on other planets, while John believes that there is no life on other planets. We do not know which of them is right, but we know that there are only two possibilities. Either there *is* life on other planets, in which case Mary believes truly while John believes falsely, so John has belief without knowledge, or there is *no* life on other planets, in which case Mary believes falsely while John believes truly, so Mary has belief without knowledge. Either way, one of them falsely believes that something is the case without knowing that it is the case, even if we cannot tell which of them it is.

Belief does not imply knowledge. What about the other way around: Does knowledge imply belief? It seems obvious that you could not know that the earth is round without believing that the earth is round. However, there are some tricky cases. Suppose that many years ago Kerry read a good history of China but has forgotten all about doing so. Now she enters a quiz. Some of the questions turn out to be on Chinese history, of which Kerry believes herself to be totally ignorant. Nevertheless, answers pop into her head. She regards them as random guesses, but nevertheless tries them out, since she has nothing better. They are all correct. In fact, her answers were caused by memory traces derived from the book. One hypothesis is that Kerry unconsciously knows those truths about Chinese history, because she remembers them, although she does not believe them. If so, knowledge does not imply belief. But that hypothesis has problems. Consider Terry, who also read a history of China many years ago and has forgotten all about doing so. When Terry enters the quiz, answers about Chinese history pop into his head, too, and he tries them out, too, for want of anything better, despite regarding them as random guesses. In fact, Terry's answers, too, are caused by memory traces derived from a book. However, all Terry's answers are wrong, because his book was a bad one, full of mistakes. The hypothesis that Terry unconsciously knows those falsehoods about Chinese history does not work, since false knowledge is impossible. If Kerry unconsciously knows the right answers, Terry unconsciously *believes* the wrong answers. But then, since Kerry is no less sincere than Terry, Kerry also unconsciously believes the right answers. Thus Kerry is not a convincing example of knowledge without belief. She may instead be an example of unconscious knowledge and belief without conscious knowledge or belief. That knowledge implies belief is a good working hypothesis.

The upshot so far is that knowledge implies true belief. But true belief does not imply knowledge. If Larry believes that the name of the capital of California starts with "S," he believes truly, since the capital is Sacramento. But if that belief rests only on his irrational belief that the capital is San Francisco, Larry does not *know* that the name of the capital begins with "S." Similarly, although either John or Mary has a true belief as to whether there is life on other planets, perhaps neither of them *knows* whether there is life on other planets, because neither of them has sufficient evidence for their belief.

Many philosophers have reacted to such examples by asking: What must be added to true belief to get knowledge? At one time a popular answer was justification, in the sense of blameless belief. The idea was that Larry's true belief that the name of the capital begins with "S" does not amount to knowledge because he deserves blame for irrationally believing that the name of the capital begins with "S"; his belief, although it happens to be true, is not justified. However, we can imagine a slightly different story, in which Barry is the victim of a massive hoax, so that he has strong misleading evidence that San Francisco is the capital. For example, that is what his high school teacher tells the class, everyone whom he asks confirms that it is, his classmates hack into his computer so that he cannot access websites that say differently, and so on. Barry's beliefs that San Francisco is the capital and that the name of the capital begins with "S" *are* blameless, and in that sense justified. Thus Barry has a justified true belief that the name of the capital begins with "S," but he still does not *know* that the name of the capital begins with "S." For he does not *know* that San Francisco is the capital, because that is false, and beliefs based on ignorance do not constitute knowledge. In his famous article "Is Justified True Belief Knowledge?" (see page 143) the philosopher Edmund Gettier used such examples to make just this point, that justified true belief is not always knowledge.

Gettier's 1963 article acted as a challenge to philosophers to find the "missing ingredient" that added to true belief would make knowledge. Many proposals have their supporters, but in each case they are greatly outnumbered by opponents. In effect, the aim is to find a solution to the equation

$$\text{Knowledge} = \text{true belief} + X$$

Typically, when someone proposes such an *X*, other philosophers soon find examples of knowledge without true belief + *X*, or of true belief + *X* without knowledge, either of which suffices to refute the equation. Although no argument refutes all such proposals at one shot, their track record looks increasingly poor. Rather than examine in detail various attempts to solve the equation, let us take a step back and consider the presupposition that it has a solution.

An analogy: Crimson is a specific type of red. Just as all knowledge is true belief but not all true belief is knowledge, so all crimson is red but not all red is crimson. Now consider the equation

$$\text{Crimson} = \text{red} + Y$$

We have no reason to expect this equation to have a useful solution. It asks for a property *Y* such that the crimson things are exactly those red things that have *Y*. The only natural suggestion is: *Y* = crimson. Crimson is indeed equivalent to red that is crimson, but as an account of crimson that is blatantly circular (all it tells us is that crimson implies red). Similarly, knowledge is indeed equivalent to true belief that is knowledge, but as an account of knowledge that is blatantly circular (all it tells us is that knowledge implies true belief). The attempt to analyze crimson as red plus other elements is wrongheaded. Why should the attempt to analyze knowledge as true belief plus other elements do better? Why should we try to explain knowledge in terms of belief rather than belief in terms of knowledge? What should we take as our starting point? In philosophy, as in the rest of life, where you start makes a big difference to where you end up.

There are specific reasons why philosophers have regarded belief as "simpler" or "more basic" than knowledge, and therefore as a better starting point for explanation. One reason is that, until recently, the dominant conception of mind was an *internalist* one. According to internalism, what mental states you are in is completely determined by what is going on internally to you, which for present purposes we can understand as: inside your head. Although an event outside your head can *cause* you to be in a specific mental state, as when a glass breaking causes you to have a corresponding experience, it does so by causing other events to occur in your head, and internalists say that the events in your head completely determine that you are having the experience, irrespective of what is going on outside your head. For them, any difference between two situations in your mental state implies a difference in what is going on in your head. Belief seems to fit this account much better than knowledge does. In one situation, a pilot knows that he is flying above the Atlantic. In another situation, without realizing it the pilot was put in a perfect flight simulator back at the airport and falsely believes that he is flying above the Atlantic; therefore, the pilot does not know that he is flying above the Atlantic. Thus the two situations differ in what the pilot knows. They do not seem to differ in what he believes. In both situations, he *believes* that he is flying above the Atlantic. By hypothesis, what is going on in the pilot's head is also the same in the two situations, in the sense that exactly the same microscopic descriptions apply. Consequently, his knowledge violates the internalist principle "No difference in mental state without a difference in the head," while his belief seems not to. The internalist diagnosis is that knowledge, unlike belief, is not a "pure" mental state. Rather, for internalists, knowing that one is flying above the Atlantic is a *mixture* of mental states such as believing that one is flying above the Atlantic with nonmental conditions, typically on the external environment, such as that one really is flying above the Atlantic. On that view, it is very natural to try to analyze knowledge into components such as belief and truth and perverse to try to analyze belief into components such as knowledge.

However, further reflection suggests that not even belief really fits the internalist model. Imagine a third situation, a perfect duplicate of the first except for being on a different planet, exactly like Earth but billions of miles from it. The Atlantic is not on that other planet—it is on Earth. Rather, the people on that planet have another ocean exactly like the Atlantic. They even spell its name "Atlantic," but that is *their* name for it. When *we* use the name "Atlantic," we refer to the ocean on Earth, not to the one on the other planet. Does the extraterrestrial pilot believe that he is flying above the Atlantic? If so, his belief is false, because he is not flying above the Atlantic; he is flying above another ocean billions of miles from the Atlantic. But he is no more mistaken about his position by billions of miles than the terrestrial pilot is (the one who really is flying above the Atlantic). Both of them know where they are. Thus the extraterrestrial pilot does *not* believe that he is flying above the Atlantic. In fact, neither pilot has any beliefs about the other's ocean at all, because he has no idea that there is any such ocean. Thus they differ in their beliefs, even though what is going on in their heads is exactly similar. More specifically, they differ in the *content* of their beliefs: the content of the terrestrial pilot's belief is that he is flying above the Atlantic; the extraterrestrial pilot also has a belief, but its content is different, because it is about a different ocean. More generally, the contents of mental states are *world-involving* in the sense that they essentially involve relations to things out there in the world, such as oceans.

Far from being "impurities," relations to the external environment are the point of the mental. With minds, we can get what we need by adjusting our behavior to what we know of a complex, changing environment. We perceive our surroundings and intentionally act on them. Thinking mediates between perception and action. Emotions, too, involve relations to the external environment. To treat the person whom you love or hate as inessential to your emotion is to forget that love and hate are essentially relations, not undirected qualities of feeling. Since mental states have this sort of world-involving function, no wonder they have world-involving contents. To abstract away from relations to the world in search of pure mind is like peeling layer after layer away in search of pure onion.

Belief is world-involving in its content. Knowledge is world-involving not only in its content but also in the way in which the knower is related to that content. Whether the pilot knows or merely believes that he is flying above the Atlantic depends in part on whether he *is* flying above the Atlantic. Given what was just said about the nature of mind, this extra dimension of world-involvingness in knowledge may make it more central to mind than belief is, not less.

When things go as they should with our cognitive faculties, such as perception and memory, we get knowledge. When something goes wrong, we get mere belief. "Knowledge" is a success term; "belief" is neutral between success and failure. The relation between believing and knowing resembles that between trying to be something and being it by intention. If you believe that you are popular, you may or may not *be* popular. Similarly, if you try to be popular, you may or may not *be* popular. But if you know that you are popular, you *are* popular. Similarly, if you are popular by intention, you *are* popular. Cases in which you believe truly that you are popular without knowing that you are popular correspond to cases in which you try to be popular and are popular, but not by intention; for example, you may be popular *despite* your embarrassing attempts to be popular. Just as it would be perverse to investigate the phenomenon of trying to be something without special reference to the phenomenon of being something by intention (the case when action goes well), so it is perverse to investigate the phenomenon of believing something without special reference to the phenomenon of knowing something (the case when cognition goes well). Malfunctioning must be understood in relation to good functioning. Misremembering must be understood in relation to remembering, misperceiving in relation to perceiving, and so on. All this suggests a knowledge-first methodology.

Defenders of a belief-first methodology may reply that once we start giving detailed causal explanations, success terms like "knowledge" are no longer useful, because they are irrelevant to a step-by-step analysis of a causal process. In explaining how an automobile engine works, at some point you have to specify the actual physical processes involved, and their effects do not depend on whether they are classified as functioning or malfunctioning. Similarly, they say, whether you drink from the glass does not depend on whether you *know* that it contains water; you will drink from it as long as you *believe* that it contains water (and desire water), whether or not your belief constitutes knowledge or is true. However, this simple picture faces several problems.

First, explanations of action in terms of mental states typically involve a time lag between the mental states and the completion of the action, during which feedback can occur. For example, a reporter decides to interview a politician involved in a scandal; she drives to his house and knocks on the door. The mental states "immediately behind" an action at a given instant, such as moving her hand a fraction closer to the door, are typically just those concerned with the execution of that stage of the action plan. The connection with the original reasoning that gave the action its point—"I want more embarrassing details for this story, and he can supply them, so I'll interview him"—is less direct. Once you have worked out an action plan, you need not keep referring back to the reasons for adopting it in the first place. When we seek to explain human action, our aim is typically to understand it in terms of the earlier reasoning that gave the action its point, so there is a time lag between the reasoning and the completion of the action. That allows for the difference between knowledge and mere belief to make a causal difference to whether the action is completed. For example, how the reporter reacts if her knock at the door is not answered may depend on whether she started with knowledge or mere true belief that the politician was at home. If she knew he was at home, she is likely to be more persistent, and so more likely to get the interview. If she merely had a true belief, she is likely to give up more easily.

Second, what *reasons* are available to you to act on depends on what you know, not on what you believe. If you know that the glass contains water, you may drink from it *because it contains water*. Your knowledge makes the fact that the glass contains water available to you as a reason to act on. If you believed falsely that the glass contained water, my explanation "You drank from the glass because it contained water" is automatically false. In cases of mere belief, we might say "You drank from the glass because *you believed that* it contained water." However, such a fact about your beliefs is not normally a reason on which you act, in the way in which you act on the fact that the glass contains water when you know. For the premise of your reasoning is normally something like "The glass contains water," not "I believe that the glass contains water." You are thirsty, so you think about the water, not about your beliefs. Moreover, the fact that *you believed that* the glass contained water is not what made drinking from it a good thing to do; what made it a good thing to do is the fact that the glass *did* contain water. Water quenches thirst; beliefs do not. A reason for drinking from the glass is a fact that makes drinking from it a good thing to do. But to act on a fact you must be aware of that fact, which is to know the fact. You need knowledge; not even blameless true belief is enough. For example, if your blameless true belief that the glass contained water were based on your blameless false belief that you could see the water, when it was a trick opaque glass with water in it, the fact that the glass contained water would be outside your awareness, since you lacked knowledge. Thus in order to act on a reason, you must *know* the fact that is the reason. For acting on reasons, what matters is knowledge, not belief.

But then how are we to explain the actions of the agent who has mere belief? The agent who merely believes acts *as if* on known facts. This agent is in a state that resembles knowledge in its immediate effect on action. If you did not know that the glass contained water, you were not in a position to act on the fact that it contained water (even if there was such a fact), but you could act as if on the fact that it contained water, if you believed that it contained water. Thus the central case is reason-giving explanation, in which we explain why an agent did something by citing facts known to the agent that made it a good thing to do, but the central case is surrounded by a mass of somewhat similar cases that deviate from it more or less because things went more or less wrong, in one way or another. That the agent has mere belief rather than knowledge is one common deviation. Another is that the agent merely tried to do something but did not succeed. These defective cases do not fit the original pattern, but we can nevertheless understand them as deviations from it.

Mere belief is to be understood as a deviation from knowledge. To believe is to be in a mental state similar to knowing in its immediate effects on action, but which differs from knowing in other respects. To work with such an account is to understand belief in terms of knowledge, rather than knowledge in terms of belief.

Mental life is a bewildering complex of interacting processes. The key to understanding the nature of these processes is to focus on what happens when things go right. For that, we need the notions of knowing and doing. Having seen the point of these processes, we must then go on to understand all the ways in which things can go more or less wrong. For that, we need the notions of believing and trying.[1]

TEST YOUR UNDERSTANDING

1. Does Williamson think that one could know p without believing p?

2. According to Williamson, knowing stands to believing as:

   a. succeeding stands to failing?

   b. remembering stands to misremembering?

   c. doing X by intention stands to trying to do X?

3. Williamson claims that there is no reason to suppose that the equation "crimson = red + Y" has "a useful solution." What does he mean? What is this analogy supposed to show?

4. Does Williamson endorse an "internalist" conception of mind?

NOTES AND QUESTIONS

1. Consider the following principle:

   Knowledge-internalism: Necessarily, if the brains of two people, S and S^*, are internally exactly the same (i.e., same neurons, connected in the same way, firing in the same pattern, etc.), then if S knows P so does S^*.

   Explain how Williamson's first example of the two pilots shows that knowledge-internalism is false.

2. Consider a similar principle for belief:

   Belief-internalism: Necessarily, if the brains of two people, S and S^*, are internally exactly the same (i.e., same neurons, connected in the same way, firing in the same pattern, etc.), then if S believes P so does S^*.

---

1. The knowledge-first approach advocated in this essay is developed at greater length in Timothy Williamson, *Knowledge and Its Limits* (Oxford University Press, 2000). [Williamson's note.]

Williamson's second pilot example is supposed to show that belief-internalism is false. How? Is this argument just as convincing as the one against knowledge-internalism?

3. Williamson discusses a potential counterexample to the claim that knowledge requires believing. How does he respond to this counterexample? Is his response convincing?

4. For more on Williamson's "knowledge-first" approach, see chapter 1 of *Contemporary Debates in Epistemology*, ed. M. Steup, J. Turri, and E. Sosa (Wiley-Blackwell, 2013).

ANALYZING THE ARGUMENTS

1. Knowing that this is the road to Larissa is better, somehow, than not knowing but truly believing that this is the road to Larissa. Why? Does Williamson's discussion of the connections between knowledge, action, and reason help to suggest an answer? Is knowledge also better than not knowing but truly believing on the basis of excellent evidence that this is the road to Larissa?

2. Often, if someone knows p, they can give reasons or evidence in support of p. For instance: "Bob's office light is on and he said he was coming into work today; that's my reason for believing that he's in his office." That might suggest that a **necessary condition** for knowing p is being able to give reasons or evidence in support of p. Give some examples to show that this suggestion is implausible. (You may find it helpful to look at the discussion of "properly basic beliefs" in the introduction to Chapter 2, "Is It Reasonable to Believe without Evidence?")

3. Consider the following analysis of knowledge (simplified from Robert Nozick, *Philosophical Explanations* [Oxford University Press, 1981], chapter 3):

    S knows p **iff** (i) p is true, (ii) S believes p, and (iii) if p had been false, S wouldn't have believed p.

    Explain why this analysis seems to get the right result in Gettier's example of Smith and Jones, described in the "Reader's Guide."

4. Saul Kripke objected to Nozick's analysis as follows (using the fake barn example given in the "Reader's Guide"):

    [Consider] Henry and the barn. Suppose . . . there is a real barn in the field Henry looks at, while unbeknownst to Henry counterfeit barns abound in the area, and but for the building of this real barn a counterfeit would surely have been built in its place. Henry naively judges that there is a real barn in the field, but the third condition is not satisfied (though the others are); had there been no genuine barn there, the counterfeit there in its place would have taken Henry in. So, according to Nozick's theory, Henry does not know that there is a barn in the field.

    So far so good, but now let us suppose that the barn is red. Suppose further that any counterfeit erected in its place would have been green. (We can suppose, if we wish, that for some chemical reason the cardboard in the counterfeit barns cannot be painted red. Alternatively, those who erected counterfeit barns definitely preferred green ones, or even definitely preferred a green one in this particular location.) Now consider Henry's true belief (thus satisfying the first two conditions) that there is a (genuine) red barn in the field. Now the third condition is satisfied. If there had not been a red barn in the field, then there would have been a green counterfeit, and Henry would not have believed that there was a red barn in the field. . . .[1]

---

1. Saul Kripke, *Philosophical Troubles* (Oxford University Press, 2011), 185–86.

How do you think Kripke's objection continues? *Hint:* The objection is related to the following plausible "closure" principle: if *p* entails *q*, and you know *p*, then you are in a position to know *q*. (Gettier appeals to a similar principle for justification in "Is Justified Belief True Knowledge?" on page 143 of this anthology.)

5. Can the barn example be modified so that Nozick's theory wrongly predicts that Henry does know that there is a barn in the field? *Hint:* The counterfeit barns are made of papier-mâché and (let's suppose) cannot be erected in fields that are especially boggy.

4

How Can We Know about What We Have Not Observed?

You're reading a book and the room is getting dark, so you flip the switch and the lights come on. This sudden illumination does not surprise you. You knew in advance that the lights would come on when you flipped the switch.

How did you know this? You did not know it **a priori**, independently of experience, in the way you know the truths of mathematics.[1] Someone who had never seen a light switch or anything like it could not possibly have known what would happen when you flipped the switch. So your knowledge in this case is **a posteriori**, or **empirical**: it somehow derives from your experience.

This is obvious, but it is also puzzling. After all, your knowledge that the lights would come on was knowledge of the *future*. It concerned an event—the illumination of the room—that you had not yet experienced. But how can experience provide us with information about the future? This is a special case of a more general problem. Experience by itself provides us with knowledge of the present. Together with memory, it provides us with knowledge of the past, or more precisely, of past events we happen to have observed. This does not include the future, obviously. But it also does not include those aspects of the past and present that we have not managed to inspect. *And yet we know a great deal about these things.* You know that there are people in Siberia right now, that the book in front of you will not explode when you turn the page, that dinosaurs once roamed the earth, and so on. All of this knowledge must be grounded in experience. But it is not the *direct* upshot of experience. And that sets our question: How can experience provide us with knowledge of things we have not experienced?

1. Sensory experience is certainly *useful* in mathematics. When you add up a column of numbers with pencil and paper, your knowledge of the result is based in part on your visual experience of the figures you have written down. But this sort of experience is not strictly necessary: you could, in principle, perform the calculations "in your head." If this is true in general, it shows that while much of our mathematical knowledge may be empirical, the truths of mathematics are nonetheless knowable a priori.

The Problem of Induction

Before we try to answer the question, we need to clarify it. We have framed the question as a question about knowledge. But as we will see as the discussion unfolds, there is a powerful tendency to back off from claims to "knowledge" when one is pressed—to say, "Okay, fine. Maybe I don't really *know* anything about the future." So it's important to emphasize that the problem is not really a problem about knowledge or certainty. The crucial starting point is the observation that our beliefs about the unobserved are not all on a par. If you believe that tomorrow's lottery numbers will be 4, 8, 15, 16, 23, and 34 because these numbers came to you in a dream, your belief may be real enough, but it is *totally unwarranted*. (Even if it's true, it's just a lucky guess.) Your belief that the sun will rise tomorrow, or the scientist's belief that there will be a solar eclipse on April 30, 2041, is very different: these beliefs are **justified**. Now when we ask how experience can provide us with "knowledge" of the unobserved, we are asking an epistemological question that is best put as follows: How can experience *justify* beliefs about things we have not seen? How can our observations make it *rational* for us to form beliefs about the unobserved? This is the most general statement of the **problem of induction**.

Enumerative Induction

Let's consider what ought to be a simple case. You have been sent to an uncharted planet to investigate the wildlife. You step out of your spaceship and before long you spot a bright blue beast in the middle distance. Careful scientist that you are, you write this down:

> Saw an animal. It was blue.

You turn over a rock and find a bluish worm, so you write:

> Animal 2. Also blue.

This continues:

> Animal 163. Blue.
> Animal 164. Blue again.

So far this is just a record of your observations, and if you are cautious, you will stick with facts of this sort for some time. But eventually, when you have collected many observations, you will make a leap:

> Therefore, the next animal I encounter will be blue.

In fact, you may infer a stronger claim:

Therefore, all (or most) of the animals on this planet are blue.

At this point, you have relied on your experience as a source of information about the unobserved.

The general form of this transition seems to be this:

Premise: In a large sample, all observed *F*s are *G*.
Conclusion: Therefore, all *F*s are *G* (or at least, the next *F* we encounter will be *G*).

This form of argument is sometimes called **enumerative induction**. There is little doubt that we often seem to reason in this way. More importantly, we think that this sort of reasoning is often justified. Enumerative induction is not just something that we quirky human beings happen to do: it is a rational procedure, or so we think. So this is a preliminary solution to our problem: experience justifies beliefs about the unobserved when those beliefs are supported by enumerative induction.

Hume's Problem

This brings us to the first great puzzle in the theory of inductive reasoning. Begin by noting that the inference from

In a large sample, all observed *F*s are *G*.

to

All *F*s are *G*.

is patently **invalid**: the premise does not guarantee the truth of the conclusion. No matter how many blue animals you have inspected, there is no contradiction in supposing that the animals you have *not* inspected are all pink, or purple, or some random hodgepodge of colors. But how can an invalid argument justify its conclusion? If there is nothing more to inductive reasoning, it seems bogus.

Of course, we can turn these inductive arguments into valid deductive arguments by supplying a missing premise:

UN: If all observed *F*s are *G*, then all *F*s are *G*.

Following John Stuart Mill, this is sometimes called the principle of the **uniformity of nature (UN)** (see Mill, *A System of Logic*, book 2, chapter 3). You may never have formulated it explicitly. But it would seem that whenever you go in for a bit of inductive reasoning, you take this principle or something like it for granted.

If we include UN as a premise, our inductive inferences will be valid.

Data:	All observed *F*s are *G*.
UN:	If all observed *F*s are *G*, then all *F*s are *G*.
Generalization:	Therefore, all *F*s are *G*.

But note: If *this* is the general form of inductive reasoning, our conclusions are justified only if we are justified in accepting UN. (This is an instance of a general rule: An argument justifies its conclusion only if the premises are independently justified.) And there's the rub. A famous argument due to David Hume appears to show that however natural this assumption may be, we can have no rational justification whatsoever for believing it.

Note first that UN is not a **necessary truth**. We can easily imagine situations in which it is false—situations in which the things you have not observed are very different from the things you have observed. (*Exercise:* Describe a world in which UN is wildly and systematically false.) From this it follows, Hume thinks, that UN cannot be justified a priori, since a priori reasoning can only disclose necessary truths like the truths of mathematics.

Note second that UN is itself a claim about the unobserved. It says that the unobserved things resemble the observed things in certain ways. And this means that UN cannot be justified directly by experience. We cannot *see* that things we have not seen resemble the things we have seen.

Note third that UN cannot possibly be justified by induction. If UN is a *premise* in every inductive argument, then any attempt to support UN by induction will be circular.

But these are the only ways to justify a belief, or so Hume seems to think. And if that is so, it follows immediately that our belief in UN cannot be justified. We accept this principle instinctively, and thank goodness we do: we would be paralyzed without it. Unfortunately, we have no reason to believe that it is true.

Let's be perfectly clear about what is at stake here. Science and common sense would be useless if they did not supply us with information about the unobserved. But all of our reasoning about the unobserved appears to presuppose UN or something like it. So if this assumption cannot be justified, our scientific and commonsensical beliefs about the unobserved are totally unwarranted. It is not just that we cannot be *certain* about these things. If Hume's argument as we have interpreted it here is sound, we have *no reason whatsoever* to believe that the sun will rise tomorrow, or that the lights will come on when we flip the switch, or that smoking causes cancer, because every argument for these conclusions involves a premise we have no reason to accept. This result is absurd, so there must be some mistake in the argument. The challenge is to find it.

Responses

The most straightforward response would be to provide an explicit argument for UN. You should try this. It is a profoundly instructive exercise. However, most philosophers take another tack. We were led to posit UN as a tacit premise in our inductive reasoning when we noticed that without it, our inductive inferences would be invalid. But why is that a problem? Valid inferences are infallible; when the premises are true, the conclusion *must* be true. But why shouldn't there be *good* inferences—inferences that justify their conclusions—that are also fallible? Recall the scientist who has examined thousands of animals on that distant planet and found every one of them to be blue. The evidence does not *guarantee* that the next animal she encounters will be blue. But surely the evidence *all by itself* makes it reasonable for her to believe this proposition. An inference of this sort—deductively invalid but cogent nonetheless—is called a **non-demonstrative inference**. If there can be cogent non-demonstrative inferences, Hume's problem as we have framed it disappears.

If we take this approach, we immediately face two problems. The first is to provide some explicit rules for distinguishing the good non-demonstrative arguments from the bad ones. There are plenty of bad arguments that fit the crude form given above; for example,

So far, I have not died.
Therefore I will never die.

So we need a better account of what distinguishes the good inductive arguments from the rest. But even if we had a test for sorting the inductive arguments into two categories—"good" and "bad"—there would still be a further question: Why is it *rational* to believe the conclusion of the "good" arguments, given that it is always perfectly possible for the premises to be true and the conclusion false?

P. F. Strawson argues that there are many forms of cogent inductive reasoning, and that there need be no simple account of what they all have in common. We as a society (or as a species) have adopted rules for reasoning: standards we bring to bear whenever we say that so-and-so is being unreasonable (superstitious, biased, incautious, insane). We cannot easily articulate those rules. We have mastered them implicitly, in much the same sense in which we have mastered the grammatical rules of English. It would be useful to make those standards explicit if we can. But even before we have done this, we can rely on our tacit mastery of these rules to judge whether an argument conforms to them. Now suppose we ask the larger question: "How do we know that our standards for assessing inductive arguments are the *right* ones? How do we know that an argument that is *cogent-by-our-standards* is really *cogent*?" According to Strawson, this is a silly question. To be a cogent argument—an argument that justifies its conclusion—*just is* to be an argument that meets our standards for cogency. There is no higher standard against which our shared standards might be measured.

The New Riddle of Induction

It is natural to assume that inductive reasoning must be governed by formal rules, analogous to the formal rules that govern deductive reasoning. In 1947, Nelson Goodman *proved* that this is not so. Real proofs are rare in philosophy, so this is a remarkable achievement. Goodman's paper shows that *for every good inductive argument, there is a bad inductive argument with exactly the same form.* Deduction is not like this. In many cases, a valid deductive argument will have a form every instance of which is valid. For example,

> All cats are animals.
> Fred is a cat.
> Therefore, Fred is an animal.

is of the valid form

> All *F*s are *G*s.
> *X* is an *F*.
> Therefore, *X* is a *G*.

But now suppose we are given a cogent inductive argument, say:

> In a large sample, every emerald we have examined has been green.
> Therefore, the next emerald we examine will be green.

We can extract a form from the argument by replacing the special-purpose words like "emerald" with schematic letters.

> In a large sample, every *F* is *G*.
> Therefore, the next *F* will be *G*.

Goodman's argument shows that whenever we do this, there will always be instances of resulting schema that are *clearly* no good.

Goodman's argument has a striking implication. You might have thought that it should be possible in principle to program a computer to reason inductively: to take the data derived from observation as input and spit out the conclusions that are supported by that data. Goodman—writing in 1947—does not mention computers. But his result entails that there is no general-purpose algorithm that will do this. Any mechanical system that learns from experience, as many now do, must include not just a formal rule, but also some sort of substantive constraint on the language in which the data are described—in effect, a constraint on what sorts of *words* can be substituted for *F* and *G* in the formal schema above. The *new* riddle of induction is the problem of explaining how this line is to be drawn.

Induction and Inference to the Best Explanation

It is an established scientific fact that the diversity of living things on Earth is the result of a long process of evolution driven mainly by natural selection. This is a fact about the unobserved. The theory of evolution tells a story about the diversification of life in the distant past, almost all of which took place before human beings were on the scene. How do we know what we know about the history of life on Earth? Not by direct observation, clearly. *And not by enumerative induction either.* It's not as if we have *observed* the emergence of new species in many cases, noticed that it is always driven by natural selection, and concluded that the unobserved cases must resemble the observed ones in this respect. This shows that there must be some way of arriving at knowledge of the unobserved that is not a matter of enumerative induction.

Gilbert Harman calls it *inference to the best explanation* (IBE). The idea is familiar from detective stories: we collect clues; we formulate hypotheses that would explain why the evidence is as it is; we notice that one candidate explanation is clearly better than the others, and eventually we conclude that the best explanation of our observations is (probably) true. Harman argues that enumerative induction is really a special case of IBE. When we notice that every observed emerald is green and conclude that all emeralds are green, we are in effect arguing as follows:

All observed emeralds are green.
The best explanation of this fact is that all emeralds are green.
Therefore (by IBE), probably all emeralds are green.

If this is correct, the old problem of induction dissolves. But of course new problems arise. There is the descriptive problem of saying what it means for one explanation to be "better" than another, and there is the justificatory problem of saying why it's reasonable to believe the best explanation. To get a feel for the justificatory problem, note that just as induction seems to presuppose the uniformity of nature, IBE seems to presuppose that nature is "simple"—that the simplest, most plausible story about the evidence yields a correct account of the universe as a whole. This is not a necessary truth. We can imagine badly behaved worlds in which the unobserved parts of the universe are messier and more complicated than our observations would lead us to suspect. (*Exercise:* Describe a world in which the simplest explanation for the observed facts is often false.) If we live in one of those worlds, IBE will lead us astray. The justificatory problem for IBE is to say why we are justified in assuming that our world is simple or well behaved. And here we face a problem exactly analogous to Hume's problem for induction. We cannot know this a priori, since this is not a necessary truth. We cannot know it by observation, since the claim is a claim about the unobserved part of the universe.

And we cannot know it by IBE, since any IBE argument for this conclusion would be circular. Harman does not address the justificatory question, but it is very much worth addressing. (For discussion, see Peter Lipton, *Inference to the Best Explanation* [Routledge, 1991].)

The Staggering Fact

You have existed for a brief time. Your experience has been confined to a tiny corner of an unfathomably vast universe. And yet you know (or think you know) a great deal about this universe. This staggering fact yields two questions that must be addressed together: "How do we reason about what we have not observed?" and "How, if at all, can this reasoning be justified?" The selections that follow seek to untangle the knots that arise as we think through these questions.

David Hume (1711–1776)

Hume, a Scottish philosopher, essayist, and historian, is a central figure in Western philosophy. His *Treatise of Human Nature* (1739), *An Enquiry Concerning Human Understanding* (1748), and *An Enquiry Concerning the Principles of Morals* (1751) have been profoundly influential. Many contemporary philosophical discussions in epistemology, metaphysics, and ethics are reactions to Hume's theories and arguments. Hume's *Dialogues Concerning Natural Religion* (published posthumously in 1779) is a classic attack on arguments for the existence of God.

SCEPTICAL DOUBTS CONCERNING THE OPERATIONS OF THE UNDERSTANDING
from *An Enquiry Concerning Human Understanding*

Section IV

PART I

All the objects of human reason or enquiry may naturally be divided into two kinds, to wit, Relations of Ideas, and Matters of Fact. Of the first kind are the sciences of Geometry, Algebra, and Arithmetic; and in short, every affirmation which is either intuitively or demonstratively certain.[1] That the square of the hypothenuse is equal to the square of the two sides, is a proposition which expresses a relation between these figures. That three times five is equal to the half of thirty, expresses a relation between these numbers. Propositions of this kind are discoverable by the mere operation of thought, without dependence on what is anywhere existent in the universe. Though there never were a circle or triangle in nature, the truths demonstrated by Euclid would for ever retain their certainty and evidence.

Matters of fact, which are the second objects of human reason, are not ascertained in the same manner; nor is our evidence of their truth, however great, of a like nature with the foregoing. The contrary of every matter of fact is still possible; because it can never imply a contradiction, and is conceived by the mind with the same facility and distinctness, as if ever so conformable to reality. That the sun will not rise tomorrow is no less intelligible a proposition, and implies no more contradiction than the affirmation, that it will rise. We should in vain, therefore, attempt to demonstrate its falsehood. Were it demonstratively false, it would imply a contradiction, and could never be distinctly conceived by the mind.

It may, therefore, be a subject worthy of curiosity, to enquire what is the nature of that evidence which assures us of any real existence and matter of fact, beyond the present testimony of our senses, or the records of our memory. This part of philosophy, it is observable, has been little cultivated, either by the ancients or moderns; and therefore our doubts and errors, in the prosecution of so important an enquiry, may be the more excusable. . . . They may even prove useful, by exciting curiosity, and destroying that implicit faith and security, which is the bane of all reasoning and free enquiry. The discovery of defects in the common philosophy, if any such there be, will not, I presume, be a discouragement, but rather an incitement, as is usual, to attempt something more full and satisfactory than has yet been proposed to the public.

All reasonings concerning matter of fact seem to be founded on the relation of Cause and Effect. By means of that relation alone we can go beyond the evidence of our memory and senses. If you were to ask a man, why he believes any matter of fact, which is absent; for instance, that his friend is in the country, or in France; he would give you a reason; and this reason would be some other fact; as a letter received from him, or the knowledge of his former resolutions and promises. A man finding a watch or any other machine in a desert island, would conclude that there had once been men in that island. All our reasonings concerning fact are of the same nature. And here it is constantly supposed that there is a connexion between the present fact and that which is inferred from it. Were there nothing to bind them together, the inference would be entirely precarious. The hearing of an articulate voice and rational discourse in the dark

---

1. A proposition is **intuitively certain** (or *self-evident*) if any fully rational being who understands it is in a position to know that it is true without further reasoning. An example might be: If *x* is greater than *y*, then *y* is less than *x*. A proposition is **demonstratively certain** when it can be derived from intuitively certain premises by a sequence of steps, each of which is clearly valid. Hume assumes that the truths of mathematics are all either intuitively or demonstratively certain.

assures us of the presence of some person: Why? because these are the effects of the human make and fabric, and closely connected with it. If we anatomize all the other reasonings of this nature, we shall find that they are founded on the relation of cause and effect, and that this relation is either near or remote, direct or collateral. Heat and light are collateral effects of fire, and the one effect may justly be inferred from the other.

If we would satisfy ourselves, therefore, concerning the nature of that evidence, which assures us of matters of fact, we must enquire how we arrive at the knowledge of cause and effect.

I shall venture to affirm, as a general proposition, which admits of no exception, that the knowledge of this relation is not, in any instance, attained by reasonings a priori; but arises entirely from experience, when we find that any particular objects are constantly conjoined with each other. Let an object be presented to a man of ever so strong natural reason and abilities; if that object be entirely new to him, he will not be able, by the most accurate examination of its sensible qualities, to discover any of its causes or effects. Adam, though his rational faculties be supposed, at the very first, entirely perfect, could not have inferred from the fluidity and transparency of water that it would suffocate him, or from the light and warmth of fire that it would consume him. No object ever discovers, by the qualities which appear to the senses, either the causes which produced it, or the effects which will arise from it; nor can our reason, unassisted by experience, ever draw any inference concerning real existence and matter of fact.

This proposition, that causes and effects are discoverable, not by reason but by experience, will readily be admitted with regard to such objects, as we remember to have once been altogether unknown to us. . . . Present two smooth pieces of marble to a man who has no tincture of natural philosophy; he will never discover that they will adhere together in such a manner as to require great force to separate them in a direct line, while they make so small a resistance to a lateral pressure. . . . [N]or does any man imagine that the explosion of gunpowder, or the attraction of a loadstone, could ever be discovered by arguments a priori. . . .

But the same truth may not appear, at first sight, to have the same evidence with regard to events, which have become familiar to us from our first appearance in the world, which bear a close analogy to the whole course of nature, and which are supposed to depend on the simple qualities of objects, without any secret structure of parts. We are apt to imagine that we could discover these effects by the mere operation of our reason, without experience. We fancy, that were we brought on a sudden into this world, we could at first have inferred that one billiard-ball would communicate motion to another upon impulse; and that we needed not to have waited for the event, in order to pronounce with certainty concerning it. Such is the influence of custom, that, where it is strongest, it not only covers our natural ignorance, but even conceals itself, and seems not to take place, merely because it is found in the highest degree.

But to convince us that all the laws of nature, and all the operations of bodies without exception, are known only by experience, the following reflections may, perhaps, suffice. Were any object presented to us, and were we required to pronounce concerning the effect, which will result from it, without consulting past observation; after what manner, I beseech you, must the mind proceed in this operation? It must invent or imagine some event, which it ascribes to the object as its effect; and it is plain that this invention must be entirely arbitrary. The mind can never possibly find the effect in the supposed cause, by the most accurate scrutiny and examination. For the effect is totally different from the cause, and consequently can never be discovered in it. Motion in the second billiard-ball is a quite distinct event from motion in the first; nor is there anything in the one to suggest the smallest hint of the other. A stone or piece of metal raised into the air, and left without any support, immediately falls: but to consider the matter a priori, is there anything we discover in this situation which can beget the idea of a downward, rather than an upward, or any other motion, in the stone or metal?

And as the first imagination or invention of a particular effect, in all natural operations, is arbitrary, where we consult not experience; so must we also esteem the supposed tie or connexion between the cause and effect, which binds them together, and renders it impossible that any other effect could result from the operation of that cause. When I see, for instance, a billiard-ball moving in a straight line towards another; even suppose motion in the second ball should by accident be suggested to me, as the result of their contact or impulse; may I not conceive, that a hundred different events might as well follow from that cause? May not both these balls remain at absolute rest? May not the first ball return in a straight line, or leap off from the second in any line or direction? All these suppositions are consistent and conceivable. Why then should we give the preference to one, which is no more consistent or conceivable than the rest? All our reasonings a priori will never be able to show us any foundation for this preference.

In a word, then, every effect is a distinct event from its cause. It could not, therefore, be discovered in the cause, and the first invention or conception of it, a priori, must be entirely arbitrary. And even after it is suggested, the conjunction of it with the cause must appear equally arbitrary; since there are always many other effects, which, to reason, must seem fully as consistent and natural. In vain, therefore, should we pretend to determine any single event, or infer any cause or effect, without the assistance of observation and experience. . . .

Nor is geometry, when taken into the assistance of natural philosophy, ever able to remedy this defect, or lead us into the knowledge of ultimate causes, by all that accuracy of reasoning for which it is so justly celebrated. Every part of mixed mathematics[2] proceeds upon the supposition that certain laws are established by nature in her operations; and abstract reasonings are employed, either to assist experience in the discovery of these laws, or to determine their influence in particular instances, where it depends upon any precise degree of distance and quantity. Thus, it is a law of motion, discovered by experience, that the moment or force of any body in motion is in the compound ratio or proportion of its solid contents and its velocity; and consequently, that a small force may remove the greatest obstacle or raise the greatest weight,

---

2. Now called "applied" mathematics: the use of mathematics in physics, engineering, and other sciences.

if, by any contrivance or machinery, we can increase the velocity of that force, so as to make it an overmatch for its antagonist. Geometry assists us in the application of this law, by giving us the just dimensions of all the parts and figures which can enter into any species of machine; but still the discovery of the law itself is owing merely to experience, and all the abstract reasonings in the world could never lead us one step towards the knowledge of it.

PART II

When it is asked, What is the nature of all our reasonings concerning matter of fact? the proper answer seems to be, that they are founded on the relation of cause and effect. When again it is asked, What is the foundation of all our reasonings and conclusions concerning that relation? it may be replied in one word, Experience. But if we still carry on our sifting humour, and ask, What is the foundation of all conclusions from experience? this implies a new question, which may be of more difficult solution and explication. . . .

I shall content myself, in this section, with an easy task, and shall pretend only to give a negative answer to the question here proposed. I say then, that, even after we have experience of the operations of cause and effect, our conclusions from that experience are not founded on reasoning, or any process of the understanding. This answer we must endeavour both to explain and to defend.

It must certainly be allowed, that nature has kept us at a great distance from all her secrets, and has afforded us only the knowledge of a few superficial qualities of objects; while she conceals from us those powers and principles on which the influence of those objects entirely depends. . . . But notwithstanding this ignorance of natural powers and principles, we always presume, when we see like sensible qualities, that they have like secret powers, and expect that effects, similar to those which we have experienced, will follow from them. If a body of like colour and consistence with that bread, which we have formerly eaten, be presented to us, we make no scruple of repeating the experiment, and foresee, with certainty, like nourishment and support. Now this is a process of the mind or thought, of which I would willingly know the foundation. It is allowed on all hands that there is no known connexion between the sensible qualities and the secret powers; and consequently, that the mind is not led to form such a conclusion concerning their constant and regular conjunction, by anything which it knows of their nature. As to past Experience, it can be allowed to give direct and certain information of those precise objects only, and that precise period of time, which fell under its cognizance: but why this experience should be extended to future times, and to other objects, which for aught we know, may be only in appearance similar; this is the main question on which I would insist. The bread, which I formerly ate, nourished me; that is, a body of such sensible qualities was, at that time, endued with such secret powers: but does it follow, that other bread must also nourish me at another time, and that like sensible qualities must always be attended with like secret powers? The consequence seems nowise necessary. At least, it must be acknowledged that there is here a consequence drawn by the mind; that there is a certain step taken; a process of thought, and an inference, which wants to be explained. These two propositions are far from being the same, *I have found that such an object has always been attended with such an effect, and I foresee, that other objects, which are, in appearance, similar, will be attended with similar effects.* I shall allow, if you please, that the one proposition may justly be inferred from the other: I know, in fact, that it always is inferred. But if you insist that the inference is made by a chain of reasoning, I desire you to produce that reasoning. The connexion between these propositions is not intuitive. There is required a medium,[3] which may enable the mind to draw such an inference, if indeed it be drawn by reasoning and argument. What that medium is, I must confess, passes my comprehension; and it is incumbent on those to produce it, who assert that it really exists, and is the origin of all our conclusions concerning matter of fact.

This negative argument must certainly, in process of time, become altogether convincing, if many penetrating and able philosophers shall turn their enquiries this way and no one be ever able to discover any connecting proposition or intermediate step, which supports the understanding in this conclusion. But as the question is yet new, every reader may not trust so far to his own penetration, as to conclude, because an argument escapes his enquiry, that therefore it does not really exist. For this reason it may be requisite to venture upon a more difficult task; and enumerating all the branches of human knowledge, endeavour to show that none of them can afford such an argument.

All reasonings may be divided into two kinds, namely, demonstrative reasoning, or that concerning relations of ideas, and moral reasoning, or that concerning matter of fact and existence. That there are no demonstrative arguments in the case seems evident; since it implies no contradiction that the course of nature may change, and that an object, seemingly like those which we have experienced, may be attended with different or contrary effects. May I not clearly and distinctly conceive that a body, falling from the clouds, and which, in all other respects, resembles snow, has yet the taste of salt or feeling of fire? Is there any more intelligible proposition than to affirm, that all the trees will flourish in December and January, and decay in May and June? Now whatever is intelligible, and can be distinctly conceived, implies no contradiction, and can never be proved false by any demonstrative argument or abstract reasoning a priori.

If we be, therefore, engaged by arguments to put trust in past experience, and make it the standard of our future judgment, these arguments must be probable only, or such as regard matter of fact and real existence according to the division above mentioned. But that there is no argument of this kind, must appear, if our explication of that species of reasoning be admitted as solid and satisfactory. We have said that all arguments concerning existence are founded on the relation of cause and effect; that our knowledge of that relation is derived entirely from experience; and that all our experimental conclusions proceed upon the supposition that the future will be conformable to the past. To endeavour, therefore, the proof of this last supposition by

---

3. By "medium" Hume means a further premise that connects the observed fact about the past ("Such an object *has* always been attended by such an effect") with the conclusion about the future ("Similar objects *will* be attended by similar effects").

probable arguments, or arguments regarding existence, must be evidently going in a circle, and taking that for granted, which is the very point in question. . . .

Should it be said that, from a number of uniform experiments, we *infer* a connexion between the sensible qualities and the secret powers; this, I must confess, seems the same difficulty, couched in different terms. The question still recurs, on what process of argument this *inference* is founded? Where is the medium, the interposing ideas, which join propositions so very wide of each other? It is confessed that the colour, consistence, and other sensible qualities of bread appear not, of themselves, to have any connexion with the secret powers of nourishment and support. For otherwise we could infer these secret powers from the first appearance of these sensible qualities, without the aid of experience; contrary to the sentiment of all philosophers, and contrary to plain matter of fact. Here, then, is our natural state of ignorance with regard to the powers and influence of all objects. How is this remedied by experience? It only shows us a number of uniform effects, resulting from certain objects, and teaches us that those particular objects, at that particular time, were endowed with such powers and forces. When a new object, endowed with similar sensible qualities, is produced, we expect similar powers and forces, and look for a like effect. From a body of like colour and consistence with bread we expect like nourishment and support. But this surely is a step or progress of the mind, which wants to be explained. When a man says, *I have found, in all past instances, such sensible qualities conjoined with such secret powers*; and when he says, *Similar sensible qualities will always be conjoined with similar secret powers*; he is not guilty of a tautology, nor are these propositions in any respect the same. You say that the one proposition is an inference from the other. But you must confess that the inference is not intuitive; neither is it demonstrative: Of what nature is it, then? To say it is experimental, is begging the question. For all inferences from experience suppose, as their foundation, that the future will resemble the past, and that similar powers will be conjoined with similar sensible qualities. If there be any suspicion that the course of nature may change, and that the past may be no rule for the future, all experience becomes useless, and can give rise to no inference or conclusion. It is impossible, therefore, that any arguments from experience can prove this resemblance of the past to the future; since all these arguments are founded on the supposition of that resemblance. Let the course of things be allowed hitherto over so regular; that alone, without some new argument or inference, proves not that, for the future, it will continue so. . . . My practice, you say, refutes my doubts. But you mistake the purport of my question. As an agent, I am quite satisfied in the point; but as a philosopher, who has some share of curiosity, I will not say scepticism, I want to learn the foundation of this inference. No reading, no enquiry has yet been able to remove my difficulty, or give me satisfaction in a matter of such importance. Can I do better than propose the difficulty to the public, even though, perhaps, I have small hopes of obtaining a solution? . . .

It is certain that the most ignorant and stupid peasants—nay infants, nay even brute beasts—improve by experience, and learn the qualities of natural objects, by observing the effects which result from them. When a child has felt the sensation of pain from touching the flame of a candle, he will be careful not to put his hand near any candle; but will expect a similar effect from a cause which is similar in its sensible qualities and appearance. If you assert, therefore, that the understanding of the child is led into this conclusion by any process of argument or ratiocination, I may justly require you to produce that argument; nor have you any pretence to refuse so equitable a demand. You cannot say that the argument is abstruse, and may possibly escape your enquiry; since you confess that it is obvious to the capacity of a mere infant. If you hesitate, therefore, a moment, or if, after reflection, you produce any intricate or profound argument, you, in a manner, give up the question, and confess that it is not reasoning which engages us to suppose the past resembling the future, and to expect similar effects from causes which are, to appearance, similar. This is the proposition which I intended to enforce in the present section.

SCEPTICAL SOLUTION OF THESE DOUBTS
from *An Enquiry Concerning Human Understanding*

Section V

PART I

Suppose a person, though endowed with the strongest faculties of reason and reflection, to be brought on a sudden into this world; he would, indeed, immediately observe a continual succession of objects, and one event following another; but he would not be able to discover anything further. He would not, at first, by any reasoning, be able to reach the idea of cause and effect; since the particular powers, by which all natural operations are performed, never appear to the senses; nor is it reasonable to conclude, merely because one event, in one instance, precedes another, that therefore the one is the cause, the other the effect. Their conjunction may be arbitrary and casual. There may be no reason to infer the existence of one from the appearance of the other. And in a word, such a person, without more experience, could never employ his conjecture or reasoning concerning any matter of fact, or be assured of anything beyond what was immediately present to his memory and senses.

Suppose, again, that he has acquired more experience, and has lived so long in the world as to have observed familiar objects or events to be constantly conjoined together; what is the consequence of this experience? He immediately infers the existence of one object from the appearance of the other. Yet he has not, by all his experience, acquired any idea or knowledge of the secret power by which the one object produces the other; nor is it by any process of reasoning, he is engaged to draw this inference. But still he finds himself determined to draw it: and though he should be convinced that his understanding has no part in the operation, he would nevertheless continue in the same course of thinking. There is some other principle which determines him to form such a conclusion.

This principle is Custom[4] or Habit. For wherever the repetition of any particular act or operation produces a propensity to renew the same act or operation, without being impelled by any reasoning or process of the understanding, we always say, that this propensity is the effect of Custom. By employing that word, we pretend not to have given the ultimate reason of such a propensity. We only point out a principle of human nature, which is universally acknowledged, and which is well known by its effects. . . . And it is certain we here advance a very intelligible proposition at least, if not a true one, when we assert that, after the constant conjunction of two objects—heat and flame, for instance, weight and solidity—we are determined by custom alone to expect the one from the appearance of the other. This hypothesis seems even the only one which explains the difficulty, why we draw, from a thousand instances, an inference which we are not able to draw from one instance, that is, in no respect, different from them. Reason is incapable of any such variation. The conclusions which it draws from considering one circle are the same which it would form upon surveying all the circles in the universe. But no man, having seen only one body move after being impelled by another, could infer that every other body will move after a like impulse. All inferences from experience, therefore, are effects of custom, not of reasoning.

Custom, then, is the great guide of human life. It is that principle alone which renders our experience useful to us, and makes us expect, for the future, a similar train of events with those which have appeared in the past. Without the influence of custom, we should be entirely ignorant of every matter of fact beyond what is immediately present to the memory and senses. We should never know how to adjust means to ends, or to employ our natural powers in the production of any effect. There would be an end at once of all action, as well as of the chief part of speculation. . . .

What, then, is the conclusion of the whole matter? A simple one; though, it must be confessed, pretty remote from the common theories of philosophy. All belief of matter of fact or real existence is derived merely from some object, present to the memory or senses, and a customary conjunction between that and some other object. Or in other words; having found, in many instances, that any two kinds of objects—flame and heat, snow and cold—have always been conjoined together; if flame or snow be presented anew to the senses, the mind is carried by custom to expect heat or cold, and to believe that such a quality does exist, and will discover itself upon a nearer approach. This belief is the necessary result of placing the mind in such circumstances. It is an operation of the soul, when we are so situated, as unavoidable as to feel the passion of love, when we receive benefits; or hatred, when we meet with injuries. All these operations are a species of natural instincts, which no reasoning or process of the thought and understanding is able either to produce or to prevent.

---

4. In Hume's English, a "custom" need not be a *social* custom, a way of doing things that differs from time to time and place to place. A custom is *any* acquired habit of the mind that does not result from reasoning.

TEST YOUR UNDERSTANDING

1. Explain Hume's distinction between "relations of ideas" and "matters of fact" using your own examples.

2. Say why "The future will resemble the past" is a "matter of fact" claim.

3. Explain Hume's claim that "all inferences from experience . . . are effects of custom, not reasoning."

4. Does Hume claim that these "inferences from experience" are irrational?

READER'S GUIDE

Hume on Induction

Hume's Question

We know (or think we know) a lot about the world around us. Hume wants to know how we come by that knowledge. His focus is our knowledge of the unobserved. He allows for the sake of argument that we can know about things we have personally seen and heard.[5] Still our knowledge seems to go well beyond this. You know that the Grand Canyon existed a hundred years ago. You know that the moon exists now (in the daytime) even though you cannot see it. You know that the sun will rise tomorrow, even though you cannot see the future, and so on. Hume wants to know how you know these things.

Some of your knowledge of the unobserved concerns what Hume calls **relations of ideas**. Every triangle has three sides: this you can know without examining a single triangle. According to Hume, you arrive at this sort of knowledge by inspecting your ideas and unpacking their definitions. You can tell just by reflecting on your ideas that the very idea of a triangle without three sides is self-contradictory. Since a proposition that entails a contradiction must be false, you can know **a priori** that every triangle has three sides, even the triangles you have not seen. (Hume thinks that all mathematical knowledge is like this; that's controversial.)

But this (boring) knowledge is not Hume's focus. In all of the interesting cases listed above, the thing you claim to know—for example, that the moon exists now, or that the sun will rise tomorrow—cannot be known a priori just by inspecting your ideas. These propositions concern matters of fact and real existence. Their denials are not self-contradictory. According to Hume, this means that if they can be known at all, they can be known only **a posteriori**: on the basis of experience. But of course they are not known *directly* through experience. Hence Hume's question: How do we arrive at our knowledge of unobserved matters of fact? (Note: Almost all scientific knowledge is knowledge of this sort. So we can take Hume to be asking, "How is science possible?")

Hume's Negative Thesis

Hume's central claim is that we do not arrive at our knowledge of unobserved matters of fact simply by reasoning from our observations. This is in keeping with a central theme in Hume's philosophy: that philosophers have vastly overestimated the role of reason in

5. For Hume's considered view on this question, see Chapter 6 of this anthology.

human life. Hume's claim is not just that ordinary sloppy thinkers arrive at their beliefs by non-rational methods. It is that even the best scientist—even an ideal scientist—cannot arrive at conclusions about the unobserved simply by reasoning from her observations. Put it this way: A creature with excellent vision, a perfect memory, and an ideal capacity for reasoning but with no other mental capacities would know *nothing* about the unobserved. She might know that the sun has risen in the past, but she will have no way of knowing that the sun will rise tomorrow, or that bread nourishes, or that the moon exists when we're not looking. This "perfectly rational being" would be the world's worst scientist.

Hume's Argument

A restatement of Hume's argument is given in the introduction to this chapter. In general, the argument is best thought of as a challenge. If you think that you can *reason* to the conclusion that the sun will rise tomorrow from your observations of the past, let's see the reasoning! Hume's central observation is that no list of observed facts can entail, all by itself, a prediction about an unobserved matter of fact. Suppose we could know on the basis of perception that the sun has risen every day for a billion years. Still there is no valid argument from this fact, by itself or in conjunction with other observed facts, to the conclusion that the sun will rise tomorrow. It is always *possible* that tomorrow will be different.

This means that any valid reasoning from our observations to claims about the unobserved must include a supplemental premise. Hume puts it as the claim that "the future will resemble the past," though of course he knows that this is only an approximate formulation. Hume's first important claim—contested by many later writers—is that whenever you move from observations about the past to claims about the unobserved, you rely on some such principle as an unstated premise. Hume's second important claim is that this premise cannot be the result of reasoning. It is not a **relation of ideas**: its denial is not self-contradictory. It cannot be inferred directly from our observations, since it is a claim about the unobserved. (It's the claim that the future *will* resemble the past.) And it cannot be the result of an inductive "inference from experience"—the sort of "reasoning" that supports our ordinary conclusions about the unobserved—since all such reasoning *assumes as a premise* that the future will resemble the past. Hume's conclusion: all of our "reasoning" about unobserved matters of fact relies on an assumption that is not the result of reasoning, observation, or any combination of the two.

Hume's Skeptical Solution

It is tempting to conclude from this that our scientific and commonsensical beliefs about the unobserved are all totally *irrational*, like our belief in ghosts and witches. (This position is called **inductive skepticism**.) That is not Hume's view. Ordinary and scientific beliefs about the unobserved depend on a *non-rational* aspect of our minds: our capacity to pick up on regularities and to form expectations on the basis of them. Hume calls the resulting expectations "custom or habit," but the tendency to form these expectations is (for Hume) a basic "hard-wired" feature of the human mind. This capacity is not required by reason, but it is not *contrary to reason* either. Moreover, it is totally *unshakable*. Philosophy can temporarily dazzle us into doubting the inferences we make from our observations. But nature instantly reasserts itself and stifles these doubts whether we like it or not. For Hume, there is simply no point in asking whether we are "justified" in relying on these unshakable tendencies of the human mind. We can do so happily and without violating any rules of epistemic hygiene, so long as we do not pretend that our conclusions are compelled by the evidence all by itself. The result is not that science is undermined, but rather that it is taken down a peg by being shown to depend, at its core, on assumptions that reason and experience cannot supply.

NOTES AND QUESTIONS

1. *Illustrating Hume's theory.* Hume gives a general account of how we come by our beliefs about unobserved "matters of fact," but most of his examples concern a special case: beliefs about the future. Choose an example that does not fit this mold—a belief about some past or present matter of fact that you have not personally observed. Give a Humean account of how you came by this belief and assess the merits of the account.

2. *Cause and effect.* Hume claims that all of our reasoning concerning unobserved matters of fact is "founded on the relation of cause and effect." But this is puzzling. People living near the ocean have always known that high tide is followed by low tide at certain intervals. These people experience a regularity and come to expect it to persist into the future, and this would appear to be a clear example of the sort of reasoning Hume has in mind. But over the centuries, most of these people have had no idea what *causes* the tides. That is a scientific discovery (due to Isaac Newton). So is Hume just wrong to say that reasoning about the unobserved always involves reasoning about causes? Hume's theory of causation is developed in section VII of his *Enquiry Concerning Human Understanding.*

3. *A reconstruction of Hume's skeptical argument.* There are many ways to extract an explicit argument from Hume's text. Consider the following possibility:

(1) A "matter of fact" claim about the future is justified only if it is supported by an inductive argument; for example, an argument of the form

> Data: In a large sample, all observed Fs are G.
> UN: If, in a large sample, all observed Fs are G, then in the future, all Fs will be G.
> Generalization: Therefore, in the future, all Fs will be G.

(2) An inductive argument of this form justifies its conclusion only if we are independently justified in accepting UN (the "uniformity of nature").

(3) UN is a "matter of fact" claim about the future.

(4) So UN is justified only if it is supported by an inductive argument.

(5) But UN is a premise in every inductive argument.

(6) So an inductive argument for UN would be circular.

(7) Circular arguments never justify their conclusions.

(8) So UN cannot be justified.

(9) So inductive arguments never justify their conclusions.

(10) So matter of fact claims about the future are never justified.

Does Hume accept the conclusion of this argument? If not, which premises or transitions would he reject?

Exercise: Never mind what Hume thinks. Is this a cogent argument? If not, choose one vulnerable premise or transition and say why it is mistaken. If so, defend the argument against a challenge to it.

P. F. Strawson (1919–2006)

Until his retirement in 1987, Strawson was the Waynflete Professor of Metaphysical Philosophy at the University of Oxford. His influential writings include seminal contributions to the philosophy of language ("On Referring," 1950), metaphysics (*Individuals*, 1959), and the interpretation of Kant's philosophy (*The Bounds of Sense*, 1966).

THE "JUSTIFICATION" OF INDUCTION
from *Introduction to Logical Theory*

7. What reason have we to place reliance on inductive procedures? Why should we suppose that the accumulation of instances of As which are Bs, however various the conditions in which they are observed, gives any good reason for expecting the next A we encounter to be a B? It is our habit to form expectations in this way; but can the habit be rationally justified? When this doubt has entered our minds it may be difficult to free ourselves from it. For the doubt has its source in a confusion; and some attempts to resolve the doubt preserve the confusion; and other attempts to show that the doubt is senseless seem altogether too facile. The root-confusion is easily described; but simply to describe it seems an inadequate remedy against it. So the doubt must be examined again and again, in the light of different attempts to remove it. . . .

Suppose that a man is brought up to regard formal logic as the study of the science and art of reasoning. He observes that all inductive processes are, by deductive standards, invalid; the premises never entail the conclusions. Now inductive processes are notoriously important in the formation of beliefs and expectations about everything which lies beyond the observation of available witnesses. But an *invalid* argument is an *unsound* argument; an *unsound* argument is one in which *no good reason* is produced for accepting the conclusion. So if inductive processes are invalid, if all the arguments we should produce, if challenged, in support of our beliefs about what lies beyond the observation of available witnesses are unsound, then we have no good reason for any of these beliefs. This conclusion is repugnant. So there arises the demand for a justification, not of this or that particular belief which goes beyond what is entailed by our evidence, but a justification of induction in general. And when the demand arises in this way it is, in effect, the demand that induction shall be shown to be really a kind of deduction; for nothing less will satisfy the doubter when this is the route to his doubts.

Tracing this, the most common route to the general doubt about the reasonableness of induction, shows how the doubt seems to escape the absurdity of a demand that induction in general shall be justified by inductive standards. The demand is that induction should be shown to be a rational process; and this turns out to be the demand that one kind of reasoning should be shown to be another and different kind. Put thus crudely, the demand seems to escape one absurdity only to fall into another. Of course, inductive arguments are not deductively valid; if they were, they would be deductive arguments. Inductive reasoning must be assessed, for soundness, by inductive standards. Nevertheless, fantastic as the wish for induction to be deduction may seem, it is only in terms of it that we can understand some of the attempts that have been made to justify induction.

8. The first kind of attempt I shall consider might be called the search for the supreme premise of inductions. In its primitive form it is quite a crude attempt; and I shall make it cruder by caricature. We have already seen that for a particular inductive step, such as "The kettle has been on the fire for ten minutes, so it will be boiling by now," we can substitute a deductive argument by introducing a generalization (e.g., "A kettle always boils within ten minutes of being put on the fire") as an additional premise. This manoeuvre shifted the emphasis of the problem of inductive support on to the question of how we established such generalizations as these, which rested on grounds by which they were not entailed. But suppose the manoeuvre could be repeated. Suppose we could find one supremely general proposition, which taken in conjunction with the evidence for any accepted generalization of science or daily life (or at least of science) would entail that generalization. Then, so long as the status of the supreme generalization could be satisfactorily explained, we could regard all sound inductions to unqualified general conclusions as, at bottom, valid deductions. The justification would be found, for at least these cases. The most obvious difficulty in this suggestion is that of formulating the supreme general proposition in such a way that it shall be precise enough to yield the desired entailments, and yet not obviously false or arbitrary. Consider, for example, the formula: "For all f, g, wherever n cases of $f \cdot g$,[1] and no cases of $f \cdot \sim g$,[2] are observed, then all cases of f are cases of g." To turn it into a sentence, we have only to replace "n" by some number. But what number? If we take the value of "n" to be 1 or 20 or 500, the resulting statement is obviously false. Moreover, the choice of any number would seem quite arbitrary; there is no privileged number of favourable instances which we take as decisive in establishing a generalization. If, on the other hand, we phrase the proposition vaguely enough to escape these objections—if, for example, we phrase it as "Nature is uniform"—then it becomes too vague to provide the desired entailments. . . .

Even if these difficulties could be met, the question of the status of the supreme premise would remain. How, if a non-necessary proposition, could it be established? The appeal to experience, to inductive support, is clearly barred on pain of circularity.

1. "$f \cdot g$" = "f and g."

2. "$f \cdot \sim g$" = "f and not g."

If, on the other hand, it were a necessary truth and possessed, in conjunction with the evidence for a generalization, the required logical power to entail the generalization, . . . then the evidence would entail the generalization independently, and the problem would not arise: a conclusion unbearably paradoxical.

9. I shall next consider a more sophisticated kind of attempt to justify induction: more sophisticated both in its interpretation of this aim and in the method adopted to achieve it. The aim envisaged is that of proving that the probability of a generalization, whether universal or proportional, increases with the number of instances for which it is found to hold. . . .

I state the argument as simply as possible; but even so, it will be necessary to introduce and explain some new terms. Suppose we had a collection of objects of different kinds, some with some characteristics and some with others. Suppose, for example, we had a bag containing 100 balls, of which 70 were white and 30 black. Let us call such a collection of objects a *population*; and let us call the way it is made up (e.g., in the case imagined, of 70 white and 30 black balls) the *constitution* of the population. From such a population it would be possible to take *samples* of various sizes. For example, we might take from our bag a sample of 30 balls. Suppose each ball in the bag had an individual number. Then the collection of balls numbered 10 to 39 inclusive would be one sample of the given size; the collection of balls numbered 11 to 40 inclusive would be another and different sample of the same size; the collection of balls numbered 2, 4, 6, 8 . . . 58, 60 would be another such sample; and so on. Each possible collection of 30 balls is a different sample of the same size. Some different samples of the same size will have the same constitutions as one another; others will have different constitutions. Thus there will be only one sample made up of 30 black balls. There will be many different samples which share the constitution: 20 white and 10 black. It would be a simple matter of mathematics to work out the number of possible samples of the given size which had any one possible constitution. Let us say that a sample *matches* the population if, allowing for the difference between them in size, the constitution of the sample corresponds, within certain limits, to that of the population. For example, we might say that any possible sample consisting of, say, 21 white and 9 black balls matched the constitution (70 white and 30 black) of the population, whereas a sample consisting of 20 white and 10 black balls did not. Now it is a proposition of pure mathematics that, given any population, the proportion of possible samples, all of the same size, which match the population, increases with the size of the sample. . . .

Conclusions about the ratio of a subset of equally possible chances to the whole set of those chances may be expressed by the use of the word "probability." Thus of the 52 possible samples of one card from a population constituted like an orthodox pack, 16 are court-cards or aces. This fact we allow ourselves to express (under the conditions, inductively established, of equipossibility of draws) by saying that the probability of drawing a court-card or an ace was 4/13. If we express the proposition referred to at the end of the last paragraph by means of this use of "probability" we shall obtain the result: The probability of a sample matching a given population increases with the size of the sample. It is tempting to try to derive from this result a general justification of the inductive procedure: which will not, indeed, show that any given inductive conclusion is entailed by the evidence for it, taken in conjunction with some universal premise, but will show that the multiplication of favourable instances of a generalization entails a proportionate increase in its probability. For, since matching is a symmetrical relation,[3] it might seem a simple deductive step to move from

I. The probability of a sample matching a given population increases with the size of the sample.

to

II. The probability of a population matching a given sample increases with the size of the sample.

II might seem to provide a guarantee that the greater the number of cases for which a generalization is observed to hold, the greater is its probability; since in increasing the number of cases we increase the size of the sample from whatever population forms the subject of our generalization. Thus pure mathematics might seem to provide the sought-for proof that the evidence for a generalization really does get stronger, the more favourable instances of it we find.

The argument is ingenious enough to be worthy of respect; but it fails of its purpose, and misrepresents the inductive situation. Our situation is not in the least like that of a man drawing a sample from a given, i.e., fixed and limited, population from which the drawing of any mathematically possible sample is equiprobable with that of any other. Our only datum is the sample. No limit is fixed beforehand to the diversity, and the possibilities of change, of the "population" from which it is drawn: or, better, to the multiplicity and variousness of different populations, each with different constitutions, any one of which might replace the present one before we make the next draw. Nor is there any *a priori* guarantee that different mathematically possible samples are equally likely to be drawn. If we have or can obtain any assurance on these points, then it is assurance derived inductively from our data, and cannot therefore be assumed at the outset of an argument designed to justify induction. So II, regarded as a justification of induction founded on purely mathematical considerations, is a fraud. . . .

10. Let us turn from attempts to justify induction to attempts to show that the demand for a justification is mistaken. We have seen already that what lies behind such a demand is often the absurd wish that induction should be shown to be some kind of deduction—and this wish is clearly traceable in the two attempts at justification which we have examined. What other sense could we give to the demand? Sometimes it is expressed in the form of a request for proof that induction is a *reasonable* or *rational* procedure, that we have *good grounds* for placing reliance upon it. Consider the uses of the phrases "good grounds," "justification," "reasonable," &c. Often we say such things as "He has *every justification* for believing that *p*"; "I have *very good reasons* for believing

---

3. A **relation** *R* is *symmetric* if and only if, whenever *x* bears *R* to *y*, *y* also bears *R* to *x*. For example, marriage is a symmetric relation, since whenever *x* is married to *y*, *y* is also married to *x*. Love, by contrast, is not symmetric, since there can be cases in which *x* loves *y* but *y* does not love *x*, alas.

it"; "There are *good grounds* for the view that *q*"; "There is *good evidence* that *r*." We often talk, in such ways as these, of justification, good grounds or reasons or evidence for certain beliefs. Suppose such a belief were one expressible in the form "Every case of *f* is a cause of *g*." And suppose someone were asked what he meant by saying that he had good grounds or reasons for holding it. I think it would be felt to be a satisfactory answer if he replied: "Well, in all my wide and varied experience I've come across innumerable cases of *f* and never a case of *f* which wasn't a case of *g*." In saying this, he is clearly claiming to have *inductive* support, *inductive* evidence, of a certain kind, for his belief; and he is also giving a perfectly proper answer to the question, what he meant by saying that he had ample justification, good grounds, good reasons for his belief. It is an analytic proposition that it is reasonable to have a degree of belief in a statement which is proportional to the strength of the evidence in its favour; and it is an analytic proposition, though not a proposition of mathematics, that, other things being equal, the evidence for a generalization is strong in proportion as the number of favourable instances, and the variety of circumstances in which they have been found, is great. So to ask whether it is reasonable to place reliance on inductive procedures is like asking whether it is reasonable to proportion the degree of one's convictions to the strength of the evidence. Doing this is what "being reasonable" *means* in such a context.

As for the other form in which the doubt may be expressed, viz., "Is induction a justified, or justifiable, procedure?," it emerges in a still less favourable light. No sense has been given to it, though it is easy to see why it seems to have a sense. For it is generally proper to inquire *of a particular belief*, whether its adoption is justified; and, in asking this, we are asking whether there is good, bad, or any, evidence for it. In applying or withholding the epithets "justified," "well founded," &c., in the case of specific beliefs, we are appealing to, and applying, inductive standards. But to what standards are we appealing when we ask whether the application of inductive standards is justified or well grounded? If we cannot answer, then no sense has been given to the question. Compare it with the question: Is the law legal? It makes perfectly good sense to inquire of a particular action, of an administrative regulation, or even, in the case of some states, of a particular enactment of the legislature, whether or not it is legal. The question is answered by an appeal to a legal system, by the application of a set of legal (or constitutional) rules or standards. But it makes no sense to inquire in general whether the law of the land, the legal system as a whole, is or is not legal. For to what legal standards are we appealing? . . .

11. It seems, however, that this way of showing the request for a general justification of induction to be absurd is sometimes insufficient to allay the worry that produces it. And to point out that "forming rational opinions about the unobserved on the evidence available" and "assessing the evidence by inductive standards" are phrases which describe the same thing, is more apt to produce irritation than relief. The point is felt to be "merely a verbal" one; and though the point of this protest is itself hard to see, it is clear that something more is required. So the question must be pursued further. First, I want to point out that there is something a little odd about talking of "the inductive method," or even "the inductive policy," as if it were just one possible

method among others of arguing from the observed to the unobserved, from the available evidence to the facts in question. If one asked a meteorologist what method or methods he used to forecast the weather, one would be surprised if he answered: "Oh, just the inductive method." If one asked a doctor by what means he diagnosed a certain disease, the answer "By induction" would be felt as an impatient evasion, a joke, or a rebuke. The answer one hopes for is an account of the tests made, the signs taken account of, the rules and recipes and general laws applied. When such a specific method of prediction or diagnosis is in question, one can ask whether the method is justified in practice; and here again one is asking whether its employment is inductively justified, whether it commonly gives correct results. This question would normally seem an admissible one. One might be tempted to conclude that, while there are many different specific methods of prediction, diagnosis, &c., appropriate to different subjects of inquiry, all such methods could properly be called "inductive" in the sense that their employment rested on inductive support; and that, hence, the phrase "non-inductive method of finding out about what lies deductively beyond the evidence" was a description without meaning, a phrase to which no sense had been given; so that there could be no question of justifying our selection of one method, called "the inductive," of doing this.

However, someone might object: "Surely it is possible, though it might be foolish, to use methods utterly different from accredited scientific ones. Suppose a man, whenever he wanted to form an opinion about what lay beyond his observation or the observation of available witnesses, simply shut his eyes, asked himself the appropriate question, and accepted the first answer that came into his head. Wouldn't this be a non-inductive method?" Well, let us suppose this. The man is asked: "Do you usually get the right answer by your method?" He might answer: "You've mentioned one of its drawbacks; I never do get the right answer; but it's an extremely easy method." One might then be inclined to think that it was not a method of finding things out at all. But suppose he answered: "Yes, it's usually (always) the right answer." Then we might be willing to call it a method of finding out, though a strange one. But, then, by the very fact of its success, it would be an inductively supported method. For each application of the method would be an application of the general rule, "The first answer that comes into my head is generally (always) the right one"; and for the truth of this generalization there would be the inductive evidence of a long run of favourable instances with no unfavourable ones (if it were "always"), or of a sustained high proportion of successes to trials (if it were "generally").

So every successful method or recipe for finding out about the unobserved must be one which has inductive support; for to say that a recipe is successful is to say that it has been repeatedly applied with success; and repeated successful application of a recipe constitutes just what we mean by inductive evidence in its favour. Pointing out this fact must not be confused with saying that "the inductive method" is justified by its success, justified because it works. This is a mistake, and an important one. I am not seeking to "justify the inductive method," for no meaning has been given to this phrase. *A fortiori*, I am not saying that induction is justified by its success in finding out about the unobserved. I am saying, rather, that any successful method of finding out about the unobserved is necessarily justified by induction. This is an analytic proposition. The phrase "successful method of finding things out which has no inductive support" is self-contradictory. Having, or acquiring, inductive support is a necessary condition of the success of a method.

Why point this out at all? First, it may have a certain, therapeutic force, a power to reassure. Second, it may counteract the tendency to think of "the inductive method" as something on a par with specific methods of diagnosis or prediction and therefore, like them, standing in need of (inductive) justification.

12. There is one further confusion, perhaps the most powerful of all in producing the doubts, questions, and spurious solutions discussed in this Part. We may approach it by considering the claim that induction is justified by its success in practice. The phrase "success of induction" is by no means clear and perhaps embodies the confusion of induction with some specific method of prediction, &c., appropriate to some particular line of inquiry. But, whatever the phrase may mean, the claim has an obviously circular look. Presumably the suggestion is that we should argue from the past "successes of induction" to the continuance of those successes in the future; from the fact that it has worked hitherto to the conclusion that it will continue to work. Since an argument of this kind is plainly inductive, it will not serve as a justification of induction. One cannot establish a principle of argument by an argument which uses that principle. But let us go a little deeper. The argument rests the justification of induction on a matter of fact (its "past successes"). This is characteristic of nearly all attempts to find a justification. The desired premise of Section 8 [pp. 179–80] was to be some fact about the constitution of the universe which, even if it could not be used as a suppressed premise to give inductive arguments a deductive turn, was at any rate a "presupposition of the validity of induction." Even the mathematical argument of Section 9 [pp. 180–81] required buttressing with some large assumption about the makeup of the world. I think the source of this general desire to find out some fact about the constitution of the universe which will "justify induction" or "show it to be a rational policy" is the confusion, the running together, of two fundamentally different questions: to one of which the answer is a matter of non-linguistic fact, while to the other it is a matter of meanings.

There is nothing self-contradictory in supposing that all the uniformities in the course of things that we have hitherto observed and come to count on should cease to operate to-morrow; that all our familiar recipes should let us down, and that we should be unable to frame new ones because such regularities as there were were too complex for us to make out. (We may assume that even the expectation that all of us, in such circumstances, would perish, were falsified by someone surviving to observe the new chaos in which, roughly speaking, nothing foreseeable happens.) Of course, we do not believe that this will happen. We believe, on the contrary, that our inductively supported expectation-rules, though some of them will have, no doubt, to be dropped or modified, will continue, on the whole, to serve us fairly well; and that we shall generally be able to replace the rules we abandon with others similarly arrived at. We might give a sense to the phrase "success of induction" by calling this vague belief the belief that induction will continue to be successful. It is certainly a factual belief, not a necessary truth; a belief, one may say, about the constitution of the universe.

We might express it as follows, choosing a phraseology which will serve the better to expose the confusion I wish to expose:

I. (The universe is such that) induction will continue to be successful.

I is very vague: it amounts to saying that there are, and will continue to be, natural uniformities and regularities which exhibit a humanly manageable degree of simplicity. But, though it is vague, certain definite things can be said about it. (1) It is not a necessary, but a contingent, statement; for chaos is not a self-contradictory concept. (2) We have good inductive reasons for believing it, good inductive evidence for it. We believe that some of our recipes will continue to hold good because they have held good for so long. We believe that we shall be able to frame new and useful ones, because we have been able to do so repeatedly in the past. Of course, it would be absurd to try to use I to "justify induction," to show that it is a reasonable policy; because I is a conclusion inductively supported.

Consider now the fundamentally different statement:

II. Induction is rational (reasonable).

We have already seen that the rationality of induction, unlike its "successfulness," is not a fact about the constitution of the world. It is a matter of what we mean by the word "rational" in its application to any procedure for forming opinions about what lies outside our observations or that of available witnesses. For to have good reasons for any such opinion is to have good inductive support for it. The chaotic universe just envisaged, therefore, is not one in which induction would cease to be rational; it is simply one in which it would be impossible to form rational expectations to the effect that specific things would happen. It might be said that in such a universe it would at least be rational to refrain from forming specific expectations, to expect nothing but irregularities. Just so. But this is itself a higher-order induction: where irregularity is the rule, expect further irregularities. Learning not to count on things is as much learning an inductive lesson as learning what things to count on.

So it is a contingent, factual matter that it is sometimes possible to form rational opinions concerning what specifically happened or will happen in given circumstances (I); it is a non-contingent, *a priori* matter that the only ways of doing this must be inductive ways (II). What people have done is to run together, to conflate, the question to which I is [an] answer and the quite different question to which II is an answer; producing the muddled and senseless questions: "Is the universe such that inductive procedures are rational?" or "What must the universe be like in order for inductive procedures to be rational?" It is the attempt to answer these confused questions which leads to statements like "The uniformity of nature is a presupposition of the validity of induction." The statement that nature is uniform might be taken to be a vague way of expressing what we expressed by I; and certainly this fact is a condition of, for it is identical with, the likewise contingent fact that we are, and shall continue to be, able to form rational opinions, of the kind we are most anxious to form, about the unobserved. But neither this fact about the world, nor any other, is a condition of the necessary truth that, if it is possible to form rational opinions of this kind, these will be inductively supported opinions.

TEST YOUR UNDERSTANDING

1. "Of course, inductive arguments are not deductively valid; if they were, they would be deductive arguments. Inductive reasoning must be assessed, for soundness, by inductive standards." Explain what Strawson means by this.

2. Explain Strawson's point in the following passage:

   > To ask whether it is reasonable to place reliance on inductive procedures is like asking whether it is reasonable to proportion the degree of one's convictions to the strength of one's evidence. Doing this is what "being reasonable" means in this context.

3. True or false: According to Strawson, there is a single master premise in all inductive reasoning—the uniformity of nature—which makes a substantive claim about what the world is like.

4. Does Strawson believe that there is such a thing as "the inductive method"?

NOTES AND QUESTIONS

1. *Strawson's appeal to "analyticity."* Strawson's account depends on the notion of an **analytic statement**. This concept is a descendant of Hume's notion of a "relation of ideas." It is sometimes explained by saying that an analytic statement is one that is true *simply in virtue of the meanings of the words that make it up.* Putative examples include "All bachelors are unmarried," "Red is a color," "If *x* is taller than *y*, then *y* is shorter than *x*," and so on. The crucial feature of analytic statements, for Strawson, is that they cannot meaningfully be called into question. Anyone who doubts that bachelors are unmarried and asks for a justification of this statement shows that he does not know what "bachelor" means. Similarly, Strawson suggests, anyone who doubts the rationality of induction shows that he does not know what the word "rational" means. The notion of analyticity played a central role in twentieth-century philosophy. It was famously attacked by W. V. Quine in "Two Dogmas of Empiricism" (in *From a Logical Point of View* [Harvard University Press, 1960]) and defended by Grice and Strawson in "In Defense of a Dogma" (*Philosophical Review* 65, 2 [1956]).

   Exercise: Assess Strawson's claim that

   > [I]t is an analytic proposition that it is reasonable to have a degree of belief in a statement which is proportional to the strength of the evidence in its favour; and it is an analytic proposition . . . that, other things being equal, the evidence for a generalization is strong in proportion as the number of favourable instances, and the variety of circumstances in which they have been found, is great. So to ask whether it is reasonable to place reliance on inductive procedures is like asking whether it is reasonable to proportion the degree of one's convictions to the strength of one's evidence. Doing this is what "being reasonable" means in this context.

In order to do this, try to describe a rational, competent speaker of English who has genuine doubts about the reasonableness of induction.

2. *Alternative inductive practices.* Suppose we come upon a tribe that forms beliefs about the future more or less as we do, with this exception: when they have an especially important question that they cannot answer by ordinary means, they kill a chicken and inspect its entrails for clues. (They have an elaborate set of rules for deriving predictions from the entrails of birds.) We want to know whether they are reasonable in following this method, so we start talking to them. They do not speak English, but their language has the word "gleeb" that we translate with our word "rational." (The translation works perfectly in every other context.) So we ask them, "Why is it *gleeb* to make predictions by inspecting the entrails of birds?" And they say, "What a funny question! You might as well ask why bachelors are unmarried: it is an analytic proposition that it is *gleeb* to make predictions by inspecting entrails."

Exercise: Explain the problem this case raises for Strawson's justification of induction and say how Strawson might reply.

Nelson Goodman (1906–1998)

Goodman was a central figure in the development of analytic philosophy in America. His books include *Fact, Fiction, and Forecast* (1955), a landmark study in epistemology and the philosophy of language, *Languages of Art* (1968), and *Ways of Worldmaking* (1978), which defends the bold thesis that there are many worlds, all equally real and all made by *us*.

THE NEW RIDDLE OF INDUCTION

from *Fact, Fiction, and Forecast*

1. The Old Problem of Induction

What is commonly thought of as the Problem of Induction has been solved, or dissolved; and we face new problems that are not as yet very widely understood. To approach them, I shall have to run as quickly as possible over some very familiar ground.

The problem of the validity of judgments about future or unknown cases arises, as Hume pointed out, because such judgments are neither reports of experience nor logical consequences of it. Predictions, of course, pertain to what has not yet been observed. And they cannot be logically inferred from what has been observed; for what *has* happened imposes no logical restrictions on what *will* happen. . . .

Hume's answer to the question how predictions are related to past experience is refreshingly non-cosmic. When an event of one kind frequently follows upon an event of another kind in experience, a habit is formed that leads the mind, when confronted with a new event of the first kind, to pass to the idea of an event of the second kind. The idea of necessary connection arises from the felt impulse of the mind in making this transition.

Now if we strip this account of all extraneous features, the central point is that to the question "Why one prediction rather than another?" Hume answers that the elect prediction is one that accords with a past regularity, because this regularity has established a habit. Thus among alternative statements about a future moment, one statement is distinguished by its consonance with habit and thus with regularities observed in the past. Prediction according to any other alternative is errant.

How satisfactory is this answer? The heaviest criticism has taken the righteous position that Hume's account at best pertains only to the source of predictions, not their legitimacy; that he sets forth the circumstances under which we make given predictions—and in this sense explains why we make them—but leaves untouched the question of our license for making them. To trace origins, runs the old complaint, is not to establish validity: the real question is not why a prediction is in fact made but how it can be justified. . . .

All this seems to me quite wrong. I think Hume grasped the central question and considered his answer to be passably effective. And I think his answer is reasonable and relevant, even if it is not entirely satisfactory. . . .

I suppose that the problem of justifying induction has called forth as much fruitless discussion as has any halfway respectable problem of modern philosophy. The typical writer begins by insisting that some way of justifying predictions must be found; proceeds to argue that for this purpose we need some resounding universal law of the Uniformity of Nature[1] and then inquires how this universal principle itself can be justified. At this point, if he is tired, he concludes that the principle must be accepted as an indispensable assumption; or if he is energetic and ingenious, he goes on to devise some subtle justification for it. Such an invention, however, seldom satisfies anyone else; and the easier course of accepting an unsubstantiated and even dubious assumption much more sweeping than any actual predictions we make seems an odd and expensive way of justifying them.

---

1. Many philosophers have supposed that inductive arguments are really *deductive* arguments with an unstated premise to the effect that the future will resemble the past. The simplest statement of this principle is this: If all observed Fs are Gs, then all Fs are Gs. The problem of induction in this tradition is to *justify* our acceptance of this principle. But there is a more serious problem. As stated, the principle is clearly false. (All observed emeralds have been observed; but there are many emeralds that have not been observed.) The more serious problem is to *state* a version of the principle that stands a chance of being true.

2. Dissolution of the Old Problem

Understandably, then, more critical thinkers have suspected that there might be something awry with the problem we are trying to solve. Come to think of it, what precisely would constitute the justification we seek? If the problem is to explain how we know that certain predictions will turn out to be correct, the sufficient answer is that we don't know any such thing. If the problem is to *find* some way of distinguishing antecedently between true and false predictions, we are asking for prevision rather than for philosophical explanation. Nor does it help matters much to say that we are merely trying to show that or why certain predictions are *probable*. Often it is said that while we cannot tell in advance whether a prediction concerning a given throw of a die is true, we can decide whether the prediction is a probable one. But if this means determining how the prediction is related to actual frequency distributions of future throws of the die, surely there is no way of knowing or proving this in advance. On the other hand, if the judgment that the prediction is probable has nothing to do with subsequent occurrences, then the question remains in what sense a probable prediction is any better justified than an improbable one.

Now obviously the genuine problem cannot be one of attaining unattainable knowledge or of accounting for knowledge that we do not in fact have. A better understanding of our problem can be gained by looking for a moment at what is involved in justifying non-inductive inferences. How do we justify a *de*duction? Plainly, by showing that it conforms to the general rules of deductive inference. An argument that so conforms is justified or valid, even if its conclusion happens to be false. An argument that violates a rule is fallacious even if its conclusion happens to be true. To justify a deductive conclusion therefore requires no knowledge of the facts it pertains to. Moreover, when a deductive argument has been shown to conform to the rules of logical inference, we usually consider it justified without going on to ask what justifies the rules. Analogously, the basic task in justifying an inductive inference is to show that it conforms to the general rules of *in*duction. Once we have recognized this, we have gone a long way towards clarifying our problem.

Yet, of course, the rules themselves must eventually be justified. The validity of a deduction depends not upon conformity to any purely arbitrary rules we may contrive, but upon conformity to valid rules. When we speak of *the* rules of inference we mean the valid rules—or better, *some* valid rules, since there may be alternative sets of equally valid rules. But how is the validity of rules to be determined? Here again we encounter philosophers who insist that these rules follow from some self-evident axiom, and others who try to show that the rules are grounded in the very nature of the human mind. I think the answer lies much nearer the surface. Principles of deductive inference are justified by their conformity with accepted deductive practice. Their validity depends upon accordance with the particular deductive inferences we actually make and sanction. If a rule yields inacceptable inferences, we drop it as invalid. Justification of general rules thus derives from judgments rejecting or accepting particular deductive inferences.

This looks flagrantly circular. I have said that deductive inferences are justified by their conformity to valid general rules, and that general rules are justified by their conformity to valid inferences. But this circle is a virtuous one. The point is that rules and particular inferences alike are justified by being brought into agreement with each other. *A rule is amended if it yields an inference we are unwilling to accept; an inference is rejected if it violates a rule we are unwilling to amend.* The process of justification is the delicate one of making mutual adjustments between rules and accepted inferences; and in the agreement achieved lies the only justification needed for either.

All this applies equally well to induction. An inductive inference, too, is justified by conformity to general rules, and a general rule by conformity to accepted inductive inferences. Predictions are justified if they conform to valid canons of induction; and the canons are valid if they accurately codify accepted inductive practice.

A result of such analysis is that we can stop plaguing ourselves with certain spurious questions about induction. We no longer demand an explanation for guarantees that we do not have, or seek keys to knowledge that we cannot obtain. It dawns upon us that the traditional smug insistence upon a hard-and-fast line between justifying induction and describing ordinary inductive practice distorts the problem. . . .

This clears the air but leaves a lot to be done. As principles of *deductive* inference, we have the familiar and highly developed laws of logic; but there are available no such precisely stated and well-recognized principles of inductive inference. . . .

3. The Constructive Task of Confirmation Theory

The task of formulating rules that define the difference between valid and invalid inductive inferences is much like the task of defining any term with an established usage. If we set out to define the term "tree," we try to compose out of already understood words an expression that will apply to the familiar objects that standard usage calls trees, and that will not apply to objects that standard usage refuses to call trees. A proposal that plainly violates either condition is rejected; while a definition that meets these tests may be adopted and used to decide cases that are not already settled by actual usage. Thus the interplay we observed between rules of induction and particular inductive inferences is simply an instance of this characteristic dual adjustment between definition and usage, whereby the usage informs the definition, which in turn guides extension of the usage.

Of course this adjustment is a more complex matter than I have indicated. Sometimes, in the interest of convenience or theoretical utility, we deliberately permit a definition to run counter to clear mandates of common usage. We accept a definition of "fish" that excludes whales. Similarly we may decide to deny the term "valid induction" to some inductive inferences that are commonly considered valid, or apply the term to others not usually so considered. A definition may modify as well as extend ordinary usage.

Some pioneer work on the problem of defining confirmation or valid induction has been done by Professor Hempel.[2] Let me remind you briefly of a few of his results. Just as deductive logic is concerned primarily with a relation between statements—namely the consequence relation—that is independent of their truth or falsity, so inductive logic as Hempel conceives it is concerned primarily with a comparable relation of confirmation between statements. Thus the problem is to define the relation that obtains between any statement S_1 and another S_2 if and only if S_1 may properly be said to confirm S_2 in any degree.

With the question so stated, the first step seems obvious. Does not induction proceed in just the opposite direction from deduction? Surely some of the evidence-statements that inductively support a general hypothesis are consequences of it. Since the consequence relation is already well defined by deductive logic, will we not be on firm ground in saying that confirmation embraces the converse relation?[3] The laws of deduction in reverse will then be among the laws of induction.

Let's see where this leads us. We naturally assume further that whatever confirms a given statement confirms also whatever follows from that statement. But if we combine this assumption with our proposed principle, we get the embarrassing result that every statement confirms every other. Surprising as it may be that such innocent beginnings lead to such an intolerable conclusion, the proof is very easy. Start with any statement S_1. It is a consequence of, and so by our present criterion confirms, the conjunction of S_1 and any statement whatsoever—call it S_2. But the confirmed conjunction, $S_1 \cdot S_2$[4] of course has S_2 as a consequence. Thus every statement confirms all statements.

The fault lies in careless formulation of our first proposal. While some statements that confirm a general hypothesis are consequences of it, not all its consequences confirm it. . . . Consider the heterogeneous conjunction:

> 8497 is a prime number and the other side of the moon is flat and Elizabeth the First was crowned on a Tuesday.

To show that any one of the three component statements is true is to support the conjunction by reducing the net undetermined claim. But support of this kind is not confirmation; for establishment of one component endows the whole statement with no credibility that is transmitted to other component statements. Confirmation of a hypothesis occurs only when an instance imparts to the hypothesis some credibility that is conveyed to other instances. . . .

Our formula thus needs tightening. This is readily accomplished, as Hempel points out, if we observe that a hypothesis is genuinely confirmed only by a statement that is an instance of it in the special sense of entailing not the hypothesis itself but its

---

2. Carl G. Hempel (1905–1997), philosopher of science. The work Goodman discusses is presented in Hempel's "Studies in the Logic of Confirmation" in his *Aspects of Scientific Explanation* (Free Press, 1965).

3. The *converse* of a **relation** R is the relation in which b stands to a if and only if a bears R to b. For example, the converse of *taller than* is *shorter than*; the converse of *loves* is *is loved by*, and so forth.

4. The dot means "and."

relativization or restriction to the class of entities mentioned by that statement. The relativization of a general hypothesis to a class results from restricting the range of its . . . quantifiers to the members of that class.[5] Less technically, what the hypothesis says of all things the evidence statement says of one thing. . . . This obviously covers the confirmation of the conductivity of all copper by the conductivity of a given piece; and it excludes confirmation of our heterogeneous conjunction by any of its components. And, when taken together with the principle that what confirms a statement confirms all its consequences, this criterion does not yield the untoward conclusion that every statement confirms every other.

New difficulties promptly appear from other directions, however. One is the infamous paradox of the ravens.[6] The statement that a given object, say this piece of paper, is neither black nor a raven confirms the hypothesis that all non-black things are non-ravens. But this hypothesis is logically equivalent to the hypothesis that all ravens are black. Hence we arrive at the unexpected conclusion that the statement that a given object is neither black nor a raven confirms the hypothesis that all ravens are black. The prospect of being able to investigate ornithological theories without going out in the rain is so attractive that we know there must be a catch in it. The trouble this time, however, lies not in faulty definition, but in tacit and illicit reference to evidence not stated in our example. Taken by itself, the statement that the given object is neither black nor a raven confirms the hypothesis that everything that is not a raven is not black as well as the hypothesis that everything that is not black is not a raven. We tend to ignore the former hypothesis because we know it to be false from abundant other evidence—from all the familiar things that are not ravens but are black. But we are required to assume that no such evidence is available. Under this circumstance, even a much stronger hypothesis is also obviously confirmed: that nothing is either

---

5. A *general hypothesis* is a statement of the form: "All *F*s are *G*s." **Quantifiers** are expressions such as "all," "every," "some," and "at least one." To *relativize* a general hypothesis to a class is to consider a restricted version of the hypothesis that applies only to members of that class. So for example, if we start with the hypothesis:

> All bats are blind.

we can relativize it to the class of North American animals by restricting the initial quantifier as follows:

> All bats *in North America* are blind.

The proposal under discussion holds that the *instances of* a general hypothesis of the form "All *F*s are *G*s" are statements of the form "The *F* that is *H* is also *G*." For example, the statement "The bat *in that cave* is blind" would count as an instance of "All bats are blind." According to Hempel, a statement *confirms* a generalization only when it is an instance of that generalization in this sense.

6. The paradox of the ravens is a problem first identified by Hempel in his "Studies in the Logic of Confirmation" (see footnote 2). Start with the intuitive idea that generalizations are confirmed by their instances, and in particular, that "All ravens are black" is confirmed (to some degree) by observations of the form "This raven is black." Now focus on the odd-sounding generalization "All non-black things are non-ravens." If all generalizations are confirmed by their instances, then this generalization is confirmed (to some degree) by observations of the form "this non-black thing is not a raven." Then note that the two generalizations are logically equivalent: to say that all ravens are black *is just to say* that all non-black things are non-ravens. This means that whatever confirms one generalization confirms the other. And *that* means that one way to confirm "All ravens are black" is to observe a bunch of non-black things—say, a bunch of bananas—and to note that each is not a raven. But that's absurd. So something has gone wrong somewhere.

black or a raven. In the light of this confirmation of the hypothesis that there are no ravens, it is no longer surprising that under the artificial restrictions of the example, the hypothesis that all ravens are black is also confirmed. And the prospects for indoor ornithology vanish when we notice that under these same conditions, the contrary hypothesis that no ravens are black is equally well confirmed. . . .[7]

No one supposes that the task of confirmation-theory has been completed. But the few steps I have reviewed—chosen partly for their bearing on what is to follow—show how things move along once the problem of definition displaces the problem of justification. Important and long-unnoticed questions are brought to light and answered; and we are encouraged to expect that the many remaining questions will in time yield to similar treatment.

But our satisfaction is shortlived. New and serious trouble begins to appear.

4. The New Riddle of Induction

Confirmation of a hypothesis by an instance depends rather heavily upon features of the hypothesis other than its syntactical form. That a given piece of copper conducts electricity increases the credibility of statements asserting that other pieces of copper conduct electricity, and thus confirms the hypothesis that all copper conducts electricity. But the fact that a given man now in this room is a third son does not increase the credibility of statements asserting that other men now in this room are third sons, and so does not confirm the hypothesis that all men now in this room are third sons. Yet in both cases our hypothesis is a generalization of the evidence statement. The difference is that in the former case the hypothesis is a *lawlike* statement; while in the latter case, the hypothesis is a merely contingent or accidental generality. Only a statement that is *lawlike*—regardless of its truth or falsity or its scientific importance—is capable of receiving confirmation from an instance of it; accidental statements are not. Plainly, then, we must look for a way of distinguishing lawlike from accidental statements.

So long as what seems to be needed is merely a way of excluding a few odd and unwanted cases that are inadvertently admitted by our definition of confirmation, the problem may not seem very hard or very pressing. We fully expect that minor defects will be found in our definition and that the necessary refinements will have to be worked out patiently one after another. But some further examples will show that our present difficulty is of a much graver kind.

---

7. Goodman's proposed solution to the paradox of the ravens is this: The observation of a non-black non-raven (e.g., a white handkerchief) does indeed confirm the hypothesis that all ravens are black. But it equally confirms contrary hypotheses like "All ravens are blue" and even "There are no ravens." To see this, suppose you start out with no evidence and then observe a white handkerchief. This gives you *some* (very weak) reason to believe that everything is a handkerchief, and hence that everything is a non-raven. Still you cannot do ornithology by examining white handkerchiefs. Why? Because the ornithologist is in the market for evidence that confirms "All ravens are black" *without simultaneously confirming contrary hypotheses* like "All ravens are blue" or "There are no ravens." The observation of a black raven satisfies this condition; the observation of a non-black non-raven does not. For discussion, see S. Morgenbesser, "Goodman on the Ravens," *Journal of Philosophy* 59:18 (1962): 493–95.

Suppose that all emeralds examined before a certain time *t* are green. At time *t*, then, our observations support the hypothesis that all emeralds are green; and this is in accord with our definition of confirmation. Our evidence statements assert that emerald *a* is green, that emerald *b* is green, and so on; and each confirms the general hypothesis that all emeralds are green. So far, so good.

Now let me introduce another predicate[8] less familiar than "green." It is the predicate "grue" and it applies to all things examined before *t* just in case they are green but to other things just in case they are blue. Then at time *t* we have, for each evidence statement asserting that a given emerald is green, a parallel evidence statement asserting that that emerald is grue. And the statements that emerald *a* is grue, that emerald *b* is grue, and so on, will each confirm the general hypothesis that all emeralds are grue. Thus according to our definition, the prediction that all emeralds subsequently examined will be green and the prediction that all will be grue are alike confirmed by evidence statements describing the same observations. But if an emerald subsequently examined is grue, it is blue and hence not green. Thus although we are well aware which of the two incompatible predictions is genuinely confirmed, they are equally well confirmed according to our present definition. Moreover, it is clear that if we simply choose an appropriate predicate, then on the basis of these same observations we shall have equal confirmation, by our definition, for any prediction whatever about other emeralds—or indeed about anything else. As in our earlier example, only the predictions subsumed under lawlike hypotheses are genuinely confirmed; but we have no criterion as yet for determining lawlikeness. And now we see that without some such criterion, our definition not merely includes a few unwanted cases, but is so completely ineffectual that it virtually excludes nothing. . . .

Nevertheless, the difficulty is often slighted because on the surface there seem to be easy ways of dealing with it. Sometimes, for example, the problem is thought to be much like the paradox of the ravens. We are here again, it is pointed out, making tacit and illegitimate use of information outside the stated evidence: the information, for example, that different samples of one material are usually alike in conductivity, and the information that different men in a lecture audience are usually not alike in the number of their older brothers. But while it is true that such information is being smuggled in, this does not by itself settle the matter as it settles the matter of the ravens. There the point was that when the smuggled information is forthrightly declared, its effect upon the confirmation of the hypothesis in question is immediately and properly registered by the definition we are using. On the other hand, if to our initial evidence we add statements concerning the conductivity of pieces of other materials or concerning the number of older brothers of members of other lecture audiences, this will not in the least affect the confirmation, according to our definition, of the hypothesis concerning copper or of that concerning this lecture audience. Since our

---

8. A **predicate** is a linguistic expression that combines with a proper name (or a sequence of proper names) to yield a complete sentence. So, for example, ". . . is tall" and ". . . loves . . ." are predicates, since they yield complete sentences when the blanks are filled in by names. Sometimes we omit the copula (the linking verb) and say that "tall" by itself qualifies as a predicate.

definition is insensitive to the bearing upon hypotheses of evidence so related to them, even when the evidence is fully declared, the difficulty about accidental hypotheses cannot be explained away on the ground that such evidence is being surreptitiously taken into account. . . .

The most popular way of attacking the problem takes its cue from the fact that accidental hypotheses seem typically to involve some spatial or temporal restriction, or reference to some particular individual. They seem to concern the people in some particular room, or the objects on some particular person's desk; while lawlike hypotheses characteristically concern all ravens or all pieces of copper whatsoever. Complete generality is thus very often supposed to be a sufficient condition of lawlikeness; but to define this complete generality is by no means easy. Merely to require that the hypothesis contain no term naming, describing, or indicating a particular thing or location will obviously not be enough. The troublesome hypothesis that all emeralds are grue contains no such term; and where such a term does occur, as in hypotheses about men in *this room*, it can be suppressed in favor of some predicate (short or long, new or old) that contains no such term but applies only to exactly the same things. One might think, then, of excluding not only hypotheses that actually contain terms for specific individuals but also all hypotheses that are equivalent to others that do contain such terms. But, as we have just seen, to exclude only hypotheses of which *all* equivalents contain such terms is to exclude nothing. On the other hand, to exclude all hypotheses that have *some* equivalent containing such a term is to exclude everything; for even the hypothesis

All grass is green.

has as an equivalent:

All grass in London or elsewhere is green.

The next step, therefore, has been to consider ruling out predicates of certain kinds. A syntactically universal hypothesis is lawlike, the proposal runs, if its predicates are "purely qualitative" or "non-positional." This will obviously accomplish nothing if a purely qualitative predicate is then conceived either as one that is equivalent to some expression free of terms for specific individuals, or as one that is equivalent to no expression that contains such a term; for this only raises again the difficulties just pointed out. The claim appears to be rather that at least in the case of a simple enough predicate we can readily determine by direct inspection of its meaning whether or not it is purely qualitative. But even aside from obscurities in the notion of "the meaning" of a predicate, this claim seems to me wrong. I simply do not know how to tell whether a predicate is qualitative or positional, except perhaps by completely begging the question at issue and asking whether the predicate is "well-behaved"—that is whether simple syntactically universal hypotheses applying it are lawlike.

This statement will not go unprotested. "Consider," it will be argued, "the predicates 'blue' and 'green' and the predicate 'grue' introduced earlier, and also the predicate 'bleen' that applies to emeralds examined before time *t* just in case they are blue and to other emeralds just in case they are green. Surely it is clear," the argument runs, "that the first two are purely qualitative and the second two are not; for the meaning of each of the latter two plainly involves reference to a specific temporal position." To this I reply that indeed I do recognize the first two as well-behaved predicates admissible in lawlike hypotheses, and the second two as ill-behaved predicates. But the argument that the former but not the latter are purely qualitative seems to me quite unsound. True enough, if we start with "blue" and "green," then "grue" and "bleen" will be explained in terms of "blue" and "green" and a temporal term. But equally truly, if we start with "grue" and "bleen," then "blue" and "green" will be explained in terms of "grue" and "bleen" and a temporal term; "green," for example, applies to emeralds examined before time *t* just in case they are grue, and to other emeralds just in case they are bleen. Thus qualitativeness is an entirely relative matter and does not by itself establish any dichotomy of predicates. . . .

We have so far neither any answer nor any promising clue to an answer to the question what distinguishes lawlike or confirmable hypotheses from accidental or non-confirmable ones; and what may at first have seemed a minor technical difficulty has taken on the stature of a major obstacle to the development of a satisfactory theory of confirmation. It is this problem that I call the new riddle of induction.

5. The Pervasive Problem of Projection

At the beginning of this lecture, I expressed the opinion that the problem of induction is still unsolved, but that the difficulties that face us today are not the old ones; and I have tried to outline the changes that have taken place. The problem of justifying induction has been displaced by the problem of defining confirmation, and our work upon this has left us with the residual problem of distinguishing between confirmable and non-confirmable hypotheses. . . .

The vast amount of effort expended on the problem of induction in modern times has thus altered our afflictions but hardly relieved them. The original difficulty about induction arose from the recognition that anything may follow upon anything. Then, in attempting to define confirmation in terms of the converse of the consequence relation, we found ourselves with the distressingly similar difficulty that our definition would make any statement confirm any other. And now, after modifying our definition drastically, we still get the old devastating result that any statement will confirm any statement. Until we find a way of exercising some control over the hypotheses to be admitted, our definition makes no distinction whatsoever between valid and invalid inductive inferences.

The real inadequacy of Hume's account lay not in his descriptive approach but in the imprecision of his description. Regularities in experience, according to him, give rise to habits of expectation; and thus it is predictions conforming to past regularities that are normal or valid. But Hume overlooks the fact that some regularities do and some do not establish such habits; that predictions based on some regularities are valid while predictions based on other regularities are not. Every word you have heard me say has occurred prior to the final sentence of this lecture; but that does not, I hope, create any expectation that every word you will hear me say will be prior to that sentence. Again, consider our case of emeralds. All those examined before time *t* are green; and this leads us to expect, and confirms the prediction, that the next one will be green. But also, all those examined are grue; and this does not lead us to expect, and does not confirm the prediction, that the next one will be grue. Regularity in greenness confirms the prediction of further cases; regularity in grueness does not. To say that valid predictions are those based on past regularities, without being able to say *which* regularities, is thus quite pointless. Regularities are where you find them, and you can find them anywhere. As we have seen, Hume's failure to recognize and deal with this problem has been shared even by his most recent successors.

TEST YOUR UNDERSTANDING

1. Explain Goodman's claim that principles of inductive reasoning are justified when they "accurately codify accepted inductive practice."

2. Restate Goodman's definition of "grue" and illustrate it with examples.

3. Say what Goodman means by a "lawlike or projectable hypothesis."

4. True or false: According to Goodman, there is no formal test for distinguishing good inductive arguments from bad ones.

READER'S GUIDE

Goodman's New Riddle of Induction

Goodman's Thesis

"Good reasoning follows rules." This can seem obvious if you think about it. Even if we cannot *state* the rules that distinguish good reasoning from bad reasoning, surely there must *be* rules of this sort—rules we somehow tacitly apply when we distinguish good arguments from bad ones, and which philosophers aim to make explicit.

This idea is encouraged by the success of formal logic. When it comes to *deductive* reasoning, philosophers have discovered an elaborate body of formal rules that distinguish the valid arguments from the rest. (See the "Brief Guide to Logic and Argumentation" in the front of the book for examples.) You can program a computer to check a mathematical proof by applying these formal rules. This is hard to do in practice; but in theory it's always possible.

Can we do the same for inductive reasoning? Can we lay down formal rules that distinguish the good inductive arguments from the bad ones?[9] Can we program a computer with formal rules to say how well a given body of evidence (say, astronomical data) supports a given prediction or a general theory? This will obviously be hard to do in practice. But surely it must be possible in principle. Right?

At the heart of Goodman's paper is a proof that this cannot be done. More specifically, Goodman shows that

> For every good inductive argument there is a bad inductive argument with exactly the same form.

Before we ask why this matters, let's see why Goodman thinks it's true.

Grue and Bleen

We've examined millions of emeralds from around the world, and every single one of them has been green. From this we conclude that rare oddities aside,[10] *all* emeralds are green, and in particular, that the emeralds we dig up in 2026 will all be green. This is obviously good reasoning. So here's a toy example of a good inductive argument:

(1) In our (abundant) experience, all emeralds are green.

(2) So all emeralds are green.

We now present an argument of exactly the same form that is clearly bad. In order to do this, we have to learn some new words.

> An object is *grue* if and only if it is green and first examined before 2025 or blue and unexamined before 2025.
> An object is *bleen* if and only if it is blue and first examined before 2025 or green and unexamined before 2025.

Take a minute to practice with these odd words. The grass in Central Park in 1965 was green. It was also *grue*. The grass in Central Park in 2026 will be green (we think!). If so, it will be *bleen*. The sky on a summer day in 1965 was blue. It was also *bleen*. The summer skies of 2026 will be blue (we hope!). If so, they will be *grue*. Got it? Good.

Now consider the following argument:

(3) In our experience, all emeralds are grue.

(4) So all emeralds are grue.

This argument has exactly the same form as the good argument from (1) to (2). The only difference is the substitution of "grue" for "green." Moreover, premise (3) is true. (If you doubt this, review the definition of "grue.") And yet the inference from (3) to (4) is clearly *lousy*. It would be silly to conclude, given our evidence, that all emeralds are grue. To see this, consider the emeralds that will be extracted from the world's emerald mines in 2026. To conclude

---

9. An inductive argument is *good* in the intended sense when anyone who knows the premise is thereby justified in accepting the conclusion; an argument is bad when this is not so.

10. We should not be distracted by the possibility of rare oddities. What we actually conclude from this evidence is that *almost* all emeralds are green. We omit this qualification to keep things simple; this will not affect the main point.

that these emeralds are grue is to make the prediction that when we look at them, they will be *blue*. (Everything that is grue and first examined after 2025 is *blue*.) But no reasonable person would make that prediction. We know that the emeralds of 2026 will be green.

Goodman's Moral

The inference from (1) to (2) is good; the inference from (3) to (4) is bad. But they have exactly the same form. So good inductive reasoning is not a matter of following formal rules.

You may think that it begs the question to assume (with common sense!) that the ordinary inference from (1) to (2) is good. But that's not really essential to the argument. Given any good inductive argument, we can produce a "gruesome" argument for a preposterous conclusion with the same form. So if there are any good inductive arguments, they are not distinguished by their form alone. A computer armed only with purely formal rules could not possibly distinguish the good inductive arguments from the bad ones.

The New Riddle

And yet *we* draw this distinction thousands of times a day whenever we generalize from experience and make predictions. *We* know that the inference from (1) to (2) is good and that the inference from (3) to (4) is bad. How do we draw the line? Evidently, the particular words that figure in the inference matter. Somehow we know that "green" is a good word for induction but "grue" is not. In Goodman's terminology, we somehow know that "green" is **projectable** while "grue" is not. The problem of characterizing the good inductive arguments comes down to saying how *this* line is to be drawn. That is the "new riddle" of induction.

Why is it a riddle? Because it's harder than it looks. One natural thought is that the main difference between "green" and "grue" is that the green things are similar, whereas the grue things are motley, some green and others blue. Goodman argues that that won't do. We might just as well say that the grue things are similar—they're all grue, after all!—whereas the green things are a motley: some are grue and others bleen. The trick is to find something to say about "green" that cannot be said with equal justice about "grue."

Goodman ultimately concludes that the only relevant difference is that "green" is *entrenched* in our scientific community. We have used it many times in past inductions, and it has proved its mettle. If we had somehow hit upon "grue" a thousand years ago and started using it to make predictions about the grass on the lawn or the emeralds in the mines, then "grue" would be entrenched and the inference from (3) to (4) would be a good one. But that is just to say that if our linguistic history had been different in this trivial way, it would have been reasonable for us to predict, given our evidence, that the grass in Central Park in 2026 will be *blue*. That is hard to believe. A better solution to the new riddle will point to an *objective* distinction between the projectable predicates and the rest. At the time of this writing that remains an unsolved problem.

NOTES AND QUESTIONS

1. *Goodman's coherentism.* Philosophers often suppose that when a particular case of reasoning is justified, it is justified because it conforms to a general rule that is independently justified. This is analogous to a similar claim in ethics; namely, that when an action is morally right, that is because it is permitted by moral rules that can be established prior to any examination of particular cases. One of Goodman's most

radical proposals is that this conception of justification must be rejected. At any given stage, we have a large stock of examples of good inferences, or morally good actions, and any number of provisional rules that we accept. When we are challenged to justify some particular inference or action, we may reply by showing that it conforms to previously accepted rules. But when we face a question about the status of a *rule*, we can assess it by asking how well it coheres with concrete examples of good reasoning or good conduct. This conception of justification has been influential. For its application in ethics, see John Rawls, "Outline of a Decision Procedure for Ethics," *Philosophical Review* 60, 2 (1951).

2. *Goodman's "theorem."* Goodman's paper contains the materials for a proof of the following proposition:

> All purely formal inductive rules are inconsistent, in the sense that they yield incompatible predictions when applied to any body of evidence.

Consider a simple inductive rule:

> All observed Fs are G.
> Therefore, the next F we examine will be G.

Now suppose that as of December 31, 2018, we have examined a million emeralds from all over the world and found them all to be green. (Suppose that emeralds are identified by a chemical test, and not by their color.) Tomorrow morning a new emerald—call it Bob—will be brought to light and examined. Our question is: What color will Bob be?

We have the following instance of the simple rule:

> All observed emeralds are green.
> Therefore, Bob will be green.

So the simple rule tells us to predict that Bob will be green.

Now we follow Goodman's lead and define a new word:

> x is *gred* if and only if x has been examined before 2019 and x is green or x has not been examined before 2019 and x is red.

(Stop here and practice using the word. Give yourself examples of green things that are gred, green things that are not gred, and so on.) That gives us another instance of the simple rule:

> All observed emeralds have been gred.
> Therefore, Bob will be gred.

The premise here is true. (If that's not obvious, check the definition of "gred" and confirm it.) So the simple rule tells us that Bob will be gred. But we know that Bob will not be examined before 2019. So when we describe the evidence in this way, the simple rule tells us to predict that Bob will be *red*! (If that's not obvious, check the definition one more time.)

So we have two instances of the simple rule. They have exactly the same form. They both have true premises. But they yield *incompatible* conclusions. And any rule that does that is no good.

Exercise: Show that whenever the simple rule applies, it can be made to yield any prediction you like about Bob given a suitable choice of vocabulary.

Exercise: Goodman asserts that his argument will apply to any purely formal rule of induction. Consider the following more sophisticated rule and show that it falls to Goodman's argument as well:

> *If the ratio of Fs to Gs in a large random sample is r, then in the population as a whole, the ratio of Fs to Gs is (roughly) r.*

3. *Solving the "new riddle."* A solution to the "new riddle" will take the form of a restriction on vocabulary suitable for inductive reasoning. "Green" is clearly projectable—suitable for induction—since we are familiar with many good inductive arguments about the colors of objects. Goodman's invented word *grue* is not projectable. The challenge is to provide a principled way of drawing the distinction. Goodman considers some possibilities in his essay, but there are many others. For a sampling of proposals, see D. Stalker, Ed., *Grue! The New Riddle of Induction* (Open Court, 1994).

Exercise: Invent a test for projectability—a rule of the form:

> *A predicate "F" is suitable for inductive reasoning if and only if . . .*

Then assess your test using Goodman's methodology. Does your rule exclude any of the good inductive inferences we already accept? Does it ratify bad inductive inferences we would ordinarily reject?

Gilbert Harman (b. 1938)

Harman is the James S. McDonnell Distinguished University Professor of Philosophy at Princeton University. His books include major studies in the philosophy of mind (*Thought*, 1973), epistemology (*Change in View*, 1986), moral philosophy (*The Nature of Morality*, 1978), and statistical learning theory (*Reliable Reasoning*, 2007, with Sanjeev Kulkarni).

THE INFERENCE TO THE BEST EXPLANATION

I wish to argue that enumerative induction should not be considered a warranted form of nondeductive inference in its own right.[1] I claim that, in cases where it appears that a warranted inference is an instance of enumerative induction, the inference

---

1. Enumerative induction infers from observed regularity to universal regularity or at least to regularity in the next instance. [Harman's note.]

should be described as a special case of another sort of inference, which I shall call "the inference to the best explanation."

The form of my argument in the first part of this paper is as follows: I argue that even if one accepts enumerative induction as one form of nondeductive inference, one will have to allow for the existence of "the inference to the best explanation." Then I argue that all warranted inferences which may be described as instances of enumerative induction must also be described as instances of the inference to the best explanation.

So, on my view, either (a) enumerative induction is not always warranted or (b) enumerative induction is always warranted but is an uninteresting special case of the more general inference to the best explanation. Whether my view should be expressed as (a) or (b) will depend upon a particular interpretation of "enumerative induction."

In the second part of this paper, I attempt to show how taking the inference to the best explanation (rather than enumerative induction) to be the basic form of nondeductive inference enables one to account for an interesting feature of our use of the word "know." This provides an additional reason for describing our inferences as instances of the inference to the best explanation rather than as instances of enumerative induction.

|

"The inference to the best explanation" corresponds approximately to what others have called "abduction," "the method of hypothesis," "hypothetic inference," "the method of elimination," "eliminative induction," and "theoretical inference." I prefer my own terminology because I believe that it avoids most of the misleading suggestions of the alternative terminologies.

In making this inference one infers, from the fact that a certain hypothesis would explain the evidence, to the truth of that hypothesis. In general, there will be several hypotheses which might explain the evidence, so one must be able to reject all such alternative hypotheses before one is warranted in making the inference. Thus one infers, from the premise that a given hypothesis would provide a "better" explanation for the evidence than would any other hypothesis, to the conclusion that the given hypothesis is true.

There is, of course, a problem about how one is to judge that one hypothesis is sufficiently better than another hypothesis. Presumably such a judgment will be based on considerations such as which hypothesis is simpler, which is more plausible, which explains more, which is less *ad hoc*, and so forth. I do not wish to deny that there is a problem about explaining the exact nature of these considerations; I will not, however, say anything more about this problem.

Uses of the inference to the best explanation are manifold. When a detective puts the evidence together and decides that it *must* have been the butler, he is reasoning that no other explanation which accounts for all the facts is plausible enough or simple enough to be accepted. When a scientist infers the existence of atoms and subatomic particles, he is inferring the truth of an explanation for various data which he wishes to account for. These seem the obvious cases; but there are many others. When we infer that a witness is telling the truth, our inference goes as follows: (i) we infer that he says what he does because he believes it; (ii) we infer that he believes what he does because he actually did witness the situation which he describes. That is, our confidence in his testimony is based on our conclusion about the most plausible explanation for that testimony. Our confidence fails if we come to think there is some other possible explanation for his testimony (if, for example, he stands to gain a great deal from our believing him). Or, to take a different sort of example, when we infer from a person's behavior to some fact about his mental experience, we are inferring that the latter fact explains better than some other explanation what he does.

It seems to me that these examples of inference (and, of course, many other similar examples) are easily described as instances of the inference to the best explanation. I do not see, however, how such examples may be described as instances of enumerative induction. It may seem plausible (at least prima facie) that the inference from scattered evidence to the proposition that the butler did it may be described as a complicated use of enumerative induction; but it is difficult to see just how one would go about filling in the details of such an inference. Similar remarks hold for the inference from testimony to the truth of that testimony. But whatever one thinks about these two cases, the inference from experimental data to the theory of subatomic particles certainly does not seem to be describable as an instance of enumerative induction. The same seems to be true for most inferences about other people's mental experiences.

I do not pretend to have a conclusive proof that such inferences cannot be made out to be complicated uses of enumerative induction. But I do think that the burden of proof here shifts to the shoulders of those who would defend induction in this matter, and I am confident that any attempt to account for these inferences as inductions will fail. Therefore, I assert that even if one permits himself the use of enumerative induction, he will still need to avail himself of at least one other form of nondeductive inference.

As I shall now try to show, however, the opposite does not hold. If one permits himself the use of the inference to the best explanation, one will not still need to use enumerative induction (as a separate form of inference). Enumerative induction, as a separate form of nondeductive inference, is superfluous. All cases in which one appears to be using it may also be seen as cases in which one is making an inference to the best explanation.

Enumerative induction is supposed to be a kind of inference that exemplifies the following form. From the fact that all observed A's are B's we may infer that all A's are B's (or we may infer that at least the next A will probably be a B). Now, in practice we always know more about a situation than that all observed A's are B's, and before we make the inference, it is good inductive practice for us to consider the total evidence. Sometimes, in the light of the total evidence, we are warranted in making our induction, at other times not. So we must ask ourselves the following question: under what conditions is one permitted to make an inductive inference?

I think it is fair to say that, if we turn to inductive logic and its logicians for an answer to this question, we shall be disappointed. If, however, we think of the inference as an inference to the best explanation, we can explain when a person is and when he is not warranted in making the inference from "All observed *A*'s are *B*'s" to "All *A*'s are *B*'s." The answer is that one is warranted in making this inference whenever the hypothesis that all *A*'s are *B*'s is (in the light of all the evidence) a better, simpler, more plausible (and so forth) hypothesis than is the hypothesis, say, that someone is biasing the observed sample in order to make us think that all *A*'s are *B*'s. On the other hand, as soon as the total evidence makes some other, competing hypothesis plausible, one may not infer from the past correlation in the observed sample to a complete correlation in the total population.

The inference from "All observed *A*'s are *B*'s" to "The next observed *A* will be *B*" may be handled in the same way. Here, one must compare the hypothesis that the next *A* will be different from the preceding *A*'s with the hypothesis that the next *A* will be similar to preceding *A*'s. As long as the hypothesis that the next *A* will be similar is a better hypothesis in the light of all the evidence, the supposed induction is warranted. But if there is no reason to rule out a change, then the induction is unwarranted.

I conclude that inferences which appear to be applications of enumerative induction are better described as instances of the inference to the best explanation. My argument has been (1) that there are many inferences which cannot be made out to be applications of enumerative induction but (2) that we can account for when it is proper to make inferences which appear to be applications of enumerative induction, if we describe these inferences as instances of the inference to the best explanation.

II

I now wish to give a further reason for describing our inferences as instances of the inference to the best explanation rather than enumerative inductions. Describing our inference as enumerative induction disguises the fact that our inference makes use of certain lemmas, whereas, as I show below, describing the inference as one to the best explanation exposes these lemmas. These intermediate lemmas play a part in the analysis of knowledge based on inference. Therefore, if we are to understand such knowledge, we must describe our inference as inference to the best explanation.

Let me begin by mentioning a fact about the analysis of "know" which is often overlooked.[2] It is now generally acknowledged by epistemologists that, if a person is to know, his belief must be both true and warranted. We shall assume that we are now speaking of a belief which is based on a (warranted) inference.[3] In this case, it is

2 . But see Edmund L. Gettier, "Is Justified True Belief Knowledge?" *Analysis* 23 (1963): 121–23; and Clark, "Knowledge and Grounds: A Comment on Mr. Gettier's Paper," *Analysis* 24 (1963); 46–48. [Harman's note.] (See Chapter 3 of this anthology.)

3 . Cf. "How Belief Is Based on Inference," *Journal of Philosophy* 61 (1964): 353–60. [Harman's note.]

not sufficient for knowledge that the person's final belief be true. If these intermediate propositions are warranted but false, then the person cannot be correctly described as *knowing* the conclusion. I will refer to this necessary condition of knowledge as "the condition that the lemmas be true."

To illustrate this condition, suppose I read on the philosophy department bulletin board that Stuart Hampshire is to read a paper at Princeton tonight. Suppose further that this warrants my believing that Hampshire will read a paper at Princeton tonight. From this belief, we may suppose I infer that Hampshire will read a paper (somewhere) tonight. This belief is also warranted. Now suppose that, unknown to me, tonight's meeting was called off several weeks ago, although no one has thought to remove the announcement from the bulletin board. My belief that Hampshire will read a paper at Princeton tonight is false. It follows that I do not know whether or not Hampshire will read a paper (somewhere) tonight, even if I am right in believing that he will. Even if I am accidentally right (because Hampshire has accepted an invitation to read a paper at N.Y.U.), I do not know that Hampshire will read a paper tonight. The condition that the lemmas be true has not been met in this case.

I will now make use of the condition that the lemmas be true in order to give a new reason for describing the inferences on which belief is based as instances of the inference to the best explanation rather than of enumerative induction. I will take two different sorts of knowledge (knowledge from authority and knowledge of mental experiences of other people) and show how our ordinary judgment of when there is and when there is not knowledge is to be accounted for in terms of our belief that the inference involved must make use of certain lemmas. Then I will argue that the use of these lemmas can be understood only if the inference is in each case described as the inference to the best explanation.

First, consider what lemmas are used in obtaining knowledge from an authority. Let us imagine that the authority in question either is a person who is an expert in his field or is an authoritative reference book. It is obvious that much of our knowledge is based on authority in this sense. When an expert tells us something about a certain subject, or when we read about the subject, we are often warranted in believing that what we are told or what we read is correct. Now one condition that must be satisfied if our belief is to count as knowledge is that our belief must be true. A second condition is this: what we are told or what we read cannot be there by mistake. That is, the speaker must not have made a slip of the tongue which affects the sense. Our belief must not be based on reading a misprint. Even if the slip of the tongue or the misprint has changed a falsehood into truth, by accident, we still cannot get knowledge from it. This indicates that the inference which we make from testimony to truth must contain as a lemma the proposition that the utterance is there because it is believed and not because of a slip of the tongue or typewriter. Thus our account of this inference must show the role played by such a lemma.

My other example involves knowledge of mental experience gained from observing behavior. Suppose we come to know that another person's hand hurts by seeing how he jerks it away from a hot stove which he has accidentally touched. It is easy to see that our inference here (from behavior to pain) involves as lemma the proposition that the pain is responsible for the sudden withdrawal of the hand. (We do not know the hand hurts, even if we are right about the pain being there, if in fact there is some alternative explanation for the withdrawal.) Therefore, in accounting for the inference here, we will want to explain the role of this lemma in the inference.

My claim is this: if we describe the inferences in the examples as instances of the inference to the best explanation, then we easily see how lemmas such as those described above are an essential part of the inference. On the other hand, if we describe the inferences as instances of enumerative induction, then we obscure the role of such lemmas. When the inferences are described as basically inductive, we are led to think that the lemmas are, in principle, eliminable. They are not so eliminable. If we are to account properly for our use of the word "know," we must remember that these inferences are instances of the inference to the best explanation.

In both examples, the role of the lemmas in our inference is explained only if we remember that we must infer an explanation of the data. In the first example we infer that the best explanation for our reading or hearing what we do is given by the hypothesis that the testimony is the result of expert belief expressed without slip of tongue or typewriter. From this intermediate lemma we infer the truth of the testimony. Again, in making the inference from behavior to pain, we infer the intermediate lemma that the best explanation for the observed behavior is given by the hypothesis that this behavior results from the agent's suddenly being in pain.

If in the first example we think of ourselves as using enumerative induction, then it seems in principle possible to state all the relevant evidence in statements about the correlation between (on the one hand) testimony of a certain type of person about a certain subject matter, where this testimony is given in a certain manner, and (on the other hand) the truth of that testimony. Our inference appears to be completely described by saying that we infer from the correlation between testimony and truth in the past to the correlation in the present case. But, as we have seen, this is not a satisfactory account of the inference which actually does back up our knowledge, since this account cannot explain the essential relevance of whether or not there is a slip of the tongue or a misprint. Similarly, if the inference used in going from behavior to pain is thought of as enumerative induction, it would again seem that getting evidence is in principle just a matter of finding correlations between behavior and pain. But this description leaves out the essential part played by the lemma whereby the inferred mental experience must figure in the explanation for the observed behavior.

If we think of the inferences which back up our knowledge as inferences to the best explanation, then we shall easily understand the role of lemmas in these inferences. If we think of our knowledge as based on enumerative induction (and we forget that induction is a special case of the inference to the best explanation), then we will think that inference is solely a matter of finding correlations which we may project into the future, and we will be at a loss to explain the relevance of the intermediate lemmas. If we are adequately to describe the inferences on which our knowledge rests, we must think of them as instances of the inference to the best explanation.

I have argued that enumerative induction should not be considered a warranted form of inference in its own right. I have used two arguments: (a) we can best account for when it is proper to make inferences which appear to be applications of enumerative induction by describing these inferences as instances of the inference to the best explanation; and (b) we can best account for certain necessary conditions of one's having knowledge (for example, which is knowledge from authority or which is knowledge of another's mental experience gained through observing his behavior) if we explain these conditions in terms of the condition that the lemmas be true and if we think of the inference on which knowledge is based as the inference to the best explanation rather than as enumerative induction.

TEST YOUR UNDERSTANDING

1. What is inference to the best explanation (IBE)?

2. Is IBE a deductively **valid** form of inference?

3. Give an example of enumerative induction and recast it as an example of IBE.

4. Give an instance of IBE that cannot be recast as a case of enumerative induction.

NOTES AND QUESTIONS

1. *What makes one explanation "better" than another?* Harman notes that a complete characterization of IBE will need an account of what makes one explanation "better" than another, but he does not pursue the issue. Consider a simple example. You hear scratching noises in the kitchen late at night. You notice that your cheese is starting to disappear. You conclude that you have a mouse in your kitchen. Of course, there are other hypotheses consistent with your evidence. Maybe your roommates are playing a trick on you; maybe you have a cheese-loving iguana in your kitchen. But in an ordinary case, it would be unreasonable to accept any of these hypotheses.

   Exercise: Say why the "mouse hypothesis" is a better explanation of the evidence than these alternatives. Try to develop a general account of what makes one explanation better than another. Then assess your account.

2. *Formulating IBE.* The simplest formulation of IBE would be this:

   Certain facts $F_1, F_2 \ldots$ have been established.
   The best explanation for these facts is H.
   Therefore, H is (probably) true.

   But this is clearly much too crude. Consider:

   a. We know that life emerged on Earth about 4.5 billion years ago. Scientists have a hypothesis about how this happened—the so-called *RNA world* hypothesis—that explains the known facts better than its rivals. But the explanation is still quite weak by scientific standards, and no one thinks that it would be reasonable to accept it given the evidence we now possess. It's the best explanation we've got, but it's not nearly good enough to merit acceptance in its present form.

b. Detectives are investigating a crime, and they have two suspects. The hypothesis that Mustard is the culprit explains the evidence brilliantly, but so does the hypothesis that Plum did it. Suppose the Mustard hypothesis is slightly better: a smudged fingerprint left at the scene is a slightly better fit to Mustard but could easily have come from Plum. It would be unreasonable to conclude on this basis that Mustard did it; and yet this is the best explanation of the evidence.

Exercise: Give a better formulation of IBE that accommodates these cases. Then assess the proposed rule.

ANALYZING THE ARGUMENTS

1. *Bootstrapping and the "inductive" justification of induction.* Consider the following argument:

> Hume argued that no inductive argument could show that the future will resemble the past, since every inductive argument includes this assumption (or something like it) as a premise. But Hume was wrong about the last point: As Goodman and Strawson note, inductive arguments of the form
>
>> All observed *F*s have been *G*.
>> Therefore, in the future, *F*s will be *G*.
>
> can be cogent as they stand, without a further premise connecting the premise to the conclusion. They are not **formally valid**, but they are good arguments all the same.
>
> But if this is right, then we can justify the assumption that Hume regarded as unjustifiable. After all, we have engaged in a great many inductive inferences in the past, and almost all of them have been successful. (We tend to remember the spectacular failures, but they are relatively rare.) So we know this:
>
>> In (almost) all observed cases, the future has resembled the past.
>
> And from this we may conclude, *by induction*, that
>
>> In the future, the future will resemble the past.
>
> But this is just to say that we can provide an inductive argument for the conclusion that in the future, induction will be reliable.

This argument does not literally beg the question; it does not include its conclusion as a premise. And yet one is tempted to say, "This argument shows nothing, since it *presupposes* what it seeks to prove."

Exercise: Assess the argument in light of this challenge.

2. *The counterinductivists.* You encounter a tribe who do not reason as we do. Their senses and their memories are every bit as good as ours, but when they notice that all observed emeralds have been green, they conclude that the next emerald they encounter will *not* be green. In general, they follow a rule of *counterinduction.*

> All observed *F*s have been *G*.
> Therefore, the next *F* we examine will not be *G*.

You are deep in conversation with a counterinductivist when you are told that a new emerald has just come to light. The two of you are asked to predict its color. You say it will be green; the counterinductivist says the opposite. You point out that the examined emeralds have all been green. The counterinductivist says, "I know. That gives us reason to think this one will be different." You say, "But induction has almost always worked in the past." The counterinductivist says, "Precisely. That gives us reason to think that it will fail in this case." You say, "But your track record is terrible; almost all of your predictions have been wrong!" And the counterinductivist replies, "Exactly. That gives us reason to believe that this time we'll be right!"

Exercise: Is the counterinductivist irrational (despite his maddening consistency)? If so, say why. If not, say why not.

3. *Evolutionary epistemology.* Hume is surely right that we have an innate tendency to form expectations about the future on the basis of regularities in our experience. This tendency can be shaped by education and training, but there can be no doubt that it has a biological basis. Hume declined to speculate about the origin of this tendency, but after Darwin a plausible hypothesis suggests itself. As W. V. O. Quine put it, "Creatures inveterately wrong in their inductions have a pathetic but praiseworthy tendency to die before reproducing their kind."[1] The plausible speculation is that the biological basis for inductive reasoning is the result of evolution by natural selection.

Exercise: Suppose this is right. Does it provide the basis for a justification of induction?

4. *Inference to the best explanation.* By the middle of the nineteenth century, scientists had accumulated abundant evidence to suggest that the earth is much older than a literal reading of the Bible would suggest. In 1857, in an effort to reconcile biblical literalism with this body of evidence, the British naturalist Philip Henry Gosse proposed the *Omphalos hypothesis.* According to his proposal, the earth is in fact quite young—as the Bible suggests—but was created by God with all of the traces of a (fictional) distant past in place. Gosse gave what he thought were good theological reasons for this elaborate ruse on God's part.[2]

Gosse's theory fits the observed facts perfectly. It also explains them. (Why are the apparently ancient fossils in place? Because God put them there!) So why isn't Gosse's theory a *good* explanation of the facts? Consider Stephen Jay Gould's answer:

> [W]hat is so desperately wrong with Omphalos? Only this really (and perhaps paradoxically): that we can devise no way to find out whether it is wrong—or for that matter, right. Omphalos is the classic example of an utterly untestable notion, for the world will look exactly the same in all its intricate detail whether fossils and strata are prochronic [signs of a fictitious past] or products of an extended history. . . .
>
> Science is a procedure for testing and rejecting hypotheses, not a compendium of certain knowledge. Claims that can be proved incorrect lie within its domain. . . . But theories that cannot be tested in principle are not part of science. . . . [W]e reject Omphalos as useless, not wrong.[3]

Is this persuasive?

Exercise: Assess the following response to Gould's argument:

> Gould says that good scientific theories are testable, and that Omphalos is not. But compare a standard scientific account of the distant past, *T*, with its Omphalos version, *T**: the claim God made the world 6,000 years ago so as to give the appearance that *T* is true. These theories make exactly the same predictions about future excavations and experiments. So any test that would refute *T* would also refute *T**. So if *T* is testable, as Gould claims, then *T** must be testable as well.

---

1. W. V. O. Quine, "Natural Kinds," in *Ontological Relativity and Other Essays* (Columbia University Press, 1969).

2. For an account of Gosse's theory, see Stephen Jay Gould, "Adam's Navel," in *The Flamingo's Smile: Reflections in Natural History* (W. W. Norton, 1985).

3. Gould, "Adam's Navel," pp. 110–11.

How Can You Know Your Own Mind or the Mind of Another Person?

Does your mother love you? Does your friend believe that you're the one who drank the last of the milk and didn't replace it? Does the well-built man who is waving his fist in your face want your iPhone or does he just want directions to the nearest nail salon? Imagine what life would be like if you couldn't answer these sorts of questions. If people in general didn't have huge swaths of knowledge about the mental lives of others, human society would not exist.

What about knowledge of your own mind, or *self-knowledge*, as philosophers often call it: Is that important, too, or is it like knowledge of baseball batting averages—trivial knowledge that isn't of much use in daily life? Suppose your instructor has announced that a philosophy quiz will be held tomorrow. Failing the quiz will mean a poor final grade, at best. There's still time to drop the class. Should you drop it or take the exam? Your career prospects may hang on the correct answer to this question. To give it your best shot, you need some knowledge of your own mind—specifically, you need to know what you know and don't know about philosophy.

Here's another example to illustrate the importance of knowledge of your own mind. Suppose you meet some strangers while backpacking. If they believe you want food, then they'll give you some. Similarly for water. If they believe you want water, then they'll give you some. But what will make them believe these things? Merely seeing you won't do it, because you don't look obviously undernourished or dehydrated, and a typical backpacker on this trail carries enough food and water. In practice, the only way to get them to believe that you want food or water is to say "I want food!" or "I want water!" (Ideally you should be a little more polite.) Suppose, in fact, you have run out of supplies, are hungry, and want food; you have had plenty to drink and don't want water. You know that if you want food, you should say so.

You also know that if you want water, you should say so. What should you do? Say you want food? Say you want water? Say nothing? If you *don't know* that you want food, you don't know what to do.

Knowledge of others' minds and of our own minds could hardly be more fundamental to our lives. But how do we obtain such knowledge? What is the relation between knowledge of one's own mind and knowledge of others' minds? These are the topics of the readings in this chapter.

The Traditional "Problem of Other Minds"

Here is a line of thought that can seem very plausible:

> How do I know that you have a mind? Well, I can't observe your mind directly as I can the movement of your legs or the color of your hair. What I can observe directly is the behavior of your body in a variety of circumstances—your arm waving, your eyes widening, and so forth. Somehow, I have to get from this behavioral evidence to a conclusion about your inner mental life—that you feel pain, want pizza, and so on. How can I connect your behavior with your mental life? Well, I have *myself* as an example. I know that certain things cause me to feel pain and that my feeling pain causes me to behave in a certain way; similarly with wanting pizza and other mental states. That is, I have amassed a large amount of evidence of the form: circumstances C cause *me* to be in mental state M, and this in turn causes *me* to behave in manner B. I now see that *you* are in circumstances C, and *you* are behaving in manner B. That's pretty good evidence that you are in mental state M.

According to the argument, you and I are similar in relevant respects; that's why this is called the "argument by analogy" for other minds.[1] A classic expression of the argument by analogy is this passage by the nineteenth-century British philosopher John Stuart Mill:

> I conclude that other human beings have feelings like me, because, first, they have bodies like me, which I know, in my own case, to be the antecedent condition of feelings; and because, secondly, they exhibit the acts, and other outward signs, which in my own case I know by experience to be caused by feelings. I am conscious in myself of a series of facts connected by a uniform sequence, of which the beginning is modifications of my body, the middle is feelings, the end is outward demeanor. In the case of other human beings I have the evidence of my senses for the first and last links of the series, but not for the intermediate link. I find, however, that the sequence between the

---

1. William Paley's argument for the existence of God is sometimes taken to be an argument by analogy. See page 20 of this anthology.

first and last is as regular and constant in those other cases as it is in mine. In my own case I know that the first link produces the last through the intermediate link, and could not produce it without. Experience, therefore, obliges me to conclude that there must be an intermediate link; which must either be the same in others as in myself, or a different one: I must either believe them to be alive, or to be automatons: and by believing them to be alive, that is, by supposing the link to be of the same nature as in the case of which I have experience, and which is in all other respects similar, I bring other human beings, as phenomena, under the same generalizations which I know by experience to be the true theory of my own existence.[2]

In "The Argument from Analogy," Bertrand Russell develops this argument and suggests a "postulate" (or assumption) that justifies our beliefs in the mental lives of others.

There are two frequently made objections to the argument by analogy. First, the argument is on shaky ground because the evidence about the links between bodily "modifications" (e.g., the stubbing of a toe), "feelings" (e.g., pain), and "outward demeanor" (e.g., hopping up and down) all concern *one case*—my own. The sample size $N = 1$, so isn't the argument at best very speculative?

We can illustrate this with—appropriately—an analogy. Suppose I have a closed box. When a button is pushed on one side, a light on the other side flashes on. I open up my box and find that the mechanism involves a strange beetle who, when it hears the click of the pushed button, runs to an electrical circuit inside the box and flips a switch, causing the outside light to flash. I now see that you also have a closed box. Superficially, it looks the same as mine on the outside and exhibits the same response to button-pushing—a light briefly turns on. I cannot see inside your box. Should I conclude "by analogy" that your box has a beetle inside it, too? That sounds no better than an educated guess: even if there is a beetle in your box, I cannot *know* that there is on the basis of such weak evidence. Maybe there's no beetle in your box, and the button is connected directly to the circuit. Or maybe there's a team of ants who get the job done—how can I rule out these rival possibilities?

The second objection points to a *disanalogy* between the argument by analogy and the beetle in the box example. In principle, I could open up your box and observe what's inside, and thus independently check my conclusion. But (one might think) I *cannot* observe your own mental life—if I could, there would be no need for the argument by analogy. And this is a limitation that holds of *necessity*—it makes no sense to say that I can perceive your thoughts, feel your pains, or peek at your intentions. And how can the argument by analogy be any good if it's absolutely impossible for me to check that the conclusion is correct?

There is another, much more subtle objection to the argument by analogy, or more precisely to the motivation for taking it to be important. The conclusion of the argument is about your unobservable mind. The premises include *facts about minds*,

2. J. S. Mill, *An Examination of Sir William Hamilton's Philosophy* (1889), quoted in Norman Malcolm, "Knowledge of Other Minds," in his *Knowledge and Certainty* (Prentice Hall, 1963), 130–31. Selections from Mill's other writings are in Chapters 16 and 21 of this anthology.

specifically about *my* mind. Why is this? Often, we can know about unobservable *X*s on the basis of premises that are not themselves about *X*s. For example, physicists discovered in the nineteenth century that matter was composed of atoms without ever observing a single atom. The atomic hypothesis provided an elegant explanation of a range of phenomena, including the ratios in which elements combine to form compounds, and that's why the physicists accepted it. Why can't I know about your mind in a similar fashion, by reasoning that the hypothesis that you are in such-and-such mental states provides the best explanation of your behavior? (This would be an "inference to the best explanation"; see Harman, "The Inference to the Best Explanation," in Chapter 4 of this anthology.) Presumably, a proponent of the argument by analogy thinks that premises about my mind are essential if I am to know about your mind, but why? Why do I need to know about my own mental life in order to know about yours? Why is *self*-knowledge needed for *other*-knowledge?

A tempting answer is that it is needed because we only *understand* what mental states are from our own case. Bodily sensations are the most persuasive example. To know what pain is, for example, arguably I need to know that *this* (clutching my painful knee) is pain. If I didn't have that special first-person knowledge of my own pain, I wouldn't really understand the word "pain" and couldn't even entertain the hypothesis that *you* are in pain. And if I cannot so much as entertain that hypothesis, there is no question of my knowing it.

Ludwig Wittgenstein was one of the most important philosophers of the past century, and in his posthumously published *Philosophical Investigations* (Blackwell, 1953), he suggests that this is mistaken:

> If one has to imagine someone else's pain on the model of one's own, this is none too easy a thing to do: for I have to imagine pain which I do not feel on the model of the pain which I do feel. That is, what I have to do is not simply to make a transition in imagination from one place of pain to another. As, from pain in the hand to pain in the arm. For I am not to imagine that I feel pain in some region of his body. (Which would also be possible.) (§302)

Why, exactly, does Wittgenstein think that there is a difficulty in imagining "someone else's pain on the model of one's own"? The selection by Saul Kripke offers an interpretation and defense of Wittgenstein's complaint. If Wittgenstein (as interpreted by Kripke) is right, then the traditional problem of other minds is relatively superficial—the profound problem is explaining how *my* pain could help me understand what the hypothesis that *you* are in pain could possibly amount to.

Knowledge of Other Minds without Self-Knowledge

At the very least, the idea that you need to know about your own mind to know about others' minds should not be assumed uncritically. And if that assumption is given up, then other options come into view. We have already seen one: you know about others' minds on the basis of an "inference to the best explanation" of their behavior. A closely related idea, widely discussed in the psychological literature, is that we implicitly possess a theory of psychology and its relation to behavior (often called a *theory of mind*), and we apply that theory to gain knowledge of others' minds.[3]

The traditional problem of other minds makes another assumption that should not be taken for granted; namely, that the minds of others are "unobservable." Supposedly, all I can strictly and literally perceive is the condition of your body, your head nodding, your face flushing, and so on. But is that right? Suppose that two people are having a heated conversation right in front of you. If asked to describe what you observed, you would naturally use psychological vocabulary: she *insulted* him, he got *upset*, she *felt embarrassed*, he *walked off in a huff*, and so on. It would be quite contrived to describe what you observed using some austere vocabulary of "bodily movements," purged of all traces of psychology. So what's wrong with saying the natural thing? As Maurice Merleau-Ponty puts it in "Man Seen from the Outside," "I could not imagine the malice and cruelty which I discern in my opponent's looks separated from his gestures, speech, and body. None of this takes place in some other-worldly realm, in some shrine located beyond the body of the angry man." (The English Philosopher Gilbert Ryle defends a similar view in his 1949 book *The Concept of Mind*, a selection from which is in Chapter 7 of this anthology.)

Self-Knowledge

So far we have discussed the view that we have knowledge of other minds by (a) an analogical inference, and we briefly touched on the alternative suggestions that such knowledge involves (b) an inference to the best explanation, (c) the use of an implicit theory of mind, and (d) perception. (Some versions of these last three views may well be compatible.) What about knowledge of our *own* minds?

Knowledge of one's own mind seems as immediate and direct as knowledge of objects in one's environment. And of course we get knowledge of our environment

---

3. This view is called the "theory-theory." It is not easy to explain the sense in which we are said to "implicitly possess" a theory of mind: the principles of that theory are not generally supposed to be ones that ordinary people would recognize as correct. Similarly, the principles posited by linguists to explain our ability to produce grammatical sentences of English and other natural languages are taken to be equally unfamiliar. Sometimes this is put by saying that these psychological or linguistic principles are "tacitly known." If so-called tacit knowledge really is a kind of *knowledge*, then the theory-theory does take my knowledge of *your* mind to depend on my knowledge of *minds*. Unlike the knowledge at work in the argument by analogy, however, this knowledge is not knowledge of *my* mind.

The theory-theory is usually opposed to a view called the "simulation theory." The basic idea of the simulation theory is something like this: I know about your mental life by imagining how *I* would think or feel in *your* circumstances. As with the theory-theory, it is a complicated matter to state the theory in a relatively precise and clear way. For an introduction to this debate and an argument for the theory-theory over the simulation theory, see Shaun Nichols and Stephen Stich, *Mindreading* (Oxford University Press, 2003).

by perception—we know that this tomato is red by seeing it. So one very natural (and popular) idea is that self-knowledge is a variety of *perceptual* knowledge, in many respects like our perceptual knowledge of our environment. "The *Perception of the Operations of our own Minds* within us," according to the seventeenth-century English philosopher John Locke, "is very like [the perception of "External Material things"], and might properly enough be call'd internal Sense" (*Essay Concerning Human Understanding*, II.1.iv).[4] D. M. Armstrong defends such an *inner-sense theory*. As he sums it up in his 1968 book, *A Materialist Theory of the Mind* (from which the selection is taken):

> Kant suggested the correct way of thinking about introspection when he spoke of the awareness of our own mental states as the operation of "inner sense."[5] He took sense-perception as the model of introspection. By sense-perception we become aware of current physical happenings in our environment and our body. By inner sense we become aware of current happenings in our own mind. (p. 95)

In her essay, Sarah Paul attacks this idea. In its place she proposes the simplest possible replacement. No special faculty is needed, because our knowledge of our own minds is achieved simply by applying our ability to know the minds of others to ourselves. Here she follows Gilbert Ryle, who argued in *The Concept of Mind* that "[t]he sorts of things that I can find out about myself are the same as the sorts of things that I can find out about other people, and *the methods of finding them out are much the same*" (emphasis added).

Finally, there is yet another assumption behind the traditional problem of other minds that can be questioned. The traditional problem takes knowledge of one's own mind for granted—that the argument by analogy appeals to my knowledge of *my* mind is not taken to be problematic. Why is knowledge of *other* minds taken to be problematic? Because there are (it is said) powerful considerations in favor of **skepticism** *about other minds*, the view that we cannot have knowledge of another's mind. Similarly, perceptual knowledge of one's environment is typically taken to be problematic because there are (it is said) powerful considerations in favor of *skepticism about the external world*, the view that we cannot have knowledge of our environment (see Chapter 6 of this anthology). In his essay, Alex Byrne argues that the really troubling sort of skepticism is not skepticism about the external world (or, he would presumably add, other minds), but rather *skepticism about the internal world*, the view that we cannot have knowledge of our own minds. On Byrne's view, the case for skepticism about the internal world is *stronger* than the case for skepticism about the external world, so, far from being unproblematic, self-knowledge turns out to be the most problematic of all.

---

4. A selection from Locke's *Essay* is in Chapter 11 of this anthology, and a selection from another of Locke's works is in Chapter 21.

5. Armstrong is referring to Kant's *Critique of Pure Reason* (1781). Selections from Kant's *Groundwork of the Metaphysics of Morals* are in Chapters 16 and 18 of this anthology.

Bertrand Russell (1872–1970)

The 3rd Earl Russell, a British philosopher, logician, and writer, was a central figure in analytic philosophy, a philosophical tradition that dominated academic philosophy in Britain, the United States, and Australia in the twentieth century. His numerous books include *Principia Mathematica* (with A. N. Whitehead, 3 volumes, 1910–13), on the foundations of mathematics. A prominent political activist, Russell's opposition to the First World War led to his dismissal from the University of Cambridge in 1916; his position was reinstated in 1920. Russell was awarded the Nobel Prize in Literature in 1950.

THE ARGUMENT FROM ANALOGY
from *Human Knowledge: Its Scope and Limits*

The postulates hitherto considered have been such as are required for knowledge of the physical world. Broadly speaking, they have led us to admit a certain degree of knowledge as to the space-time structure of the physical world, while leaving us completely agnostic as regards its qualitative character. But where other human beings are concerned, we feel that we know more than this; we are convinced that other people have thoughts and feelings that are qualitatively fairly similar to our own. We are not content to think that we know only the space-time structure of our friends' minds, or their capacity for initiating causal chains that end in sensations of our own. A philosopher might pretend to think that he knew only this, but let him get cross with his wife and you will see that he does not regard her as a mere spatio-temporal edifice of which he knows the logical properties but not a glimmer of the intrinsic character. We are therefore justified in inferring that his scepticism is professional rather than sincere.

The problem with which we are concerned is the following. We observe in ourselves such occurrences as remembering, reasoning, feeling pleasure and feeling pain. We think that stocks and stones do not have these experiences, but that other people do. Most of us have no doubt that the higher animals feel pleasure and pain, though I was once assured by a fisherman that "fishes have no sense nor feeling." I failed to find out how he had acquired this knowledge. Most people would disagree with him, but would be doubtful about oysters and starfish. However this may be, common sense admits an increasing doubtfulness as we descend in the animal kingdom, but as regards human beings it admits no doubt.

It is clear that belief in the minds of others requires some postulate that is not required in physics, since physics can be content with a knowledge of structure. My present purpose is to suggest what this further postulate may be.

It is clear that we must appeal to something that may be vaguely called "analogy." The behaviour of other people is in many ways analogous to our own, and we suppose that it must have analogous causes. What people say is what we should say if we had certain thoughts, and so we infer that they probably have these thoughts. They give us information which we can sometimes subsequently verify. They behave in ways in which we behave when we are pleased (or displeased) in circumstances in which we should be pleased (or displeased). We may talk over with a friend some incident which we have both experienced, and find that his reminiscences dovetail with our own; this is particularly convincing when he remembers something that we have forgotten but that he recalls to our thoughts. Or again: you set your boy a problem in arithmetic, and with luck he gets the right answer; this persuades you that he is capable of arithmetical reasoning. There are, in short, very many ways in which my responses to stimuli differ from those of "dead" matter, and in all these ways other people resemble me. As it is clear to me that the causal laws governing my behaviour have to do with "thoughts," it is natural to infer that the same is true of the analogous behaviour of my friends.

The inference with which we are at present concerned is not merely that which takes us beyond solipsism,[1] by maintaining that sensations have causes about which *something* can be known. This kind of inference, which suffices for physics, has already been considered. We are concerned now with a much more specific kind of inference, the kind that is involved in our knowledge of the thoughts and feelings of others— assuming that we have such knowledge. It is of course obvious that such knowledge is more or less doubtful. There is not only the general argument that we may be dreaming; there is also the possibility of ingenious automata. There are calculating machines that do sums much better than our schoolboy sons; there are gramophone records that remember impeccably what So-and-so said on such-and-such an occasion; there are people in the cinema who, though copies of real people, are not themselves alive. There is no theoretical limit to what ingenuity could achieve in the way of producing the illusion of life where in fact life is absent.

But, you will say, in all such cases it was the thoughts of human beings that produced the ingenious mechanism. Yes, but how do you know this? And how do you know that the gramophone does *not* "think"?

There is, in the first place, a difference in the causal laws of observable behaviour. If I say to a student "write me a paper on Descartes's reasons for believing in the existence of matter," I shall, if he is industrious, cause a certain response. A gramophone record might be so constructed as to respond to this stimulus, perhaps better than the student, but if so it would be incapable of telling me anything about any other philosopher, even if I threatened to refuse to give it a degree. One of the most notable peculiarities of human behaviour is change of response to a given stimulus. An ingenious person could construct an automaton which would always laugh at his jokes, however often it heard them; but a human being, after laughing a few times, will yawn, and end by saying "how I laughed the first time I heard that joke."

But the differences in observable behaviour between living and dead matter do not suffice to prove that there are "thoughts" connected with living bodies other than my own. It is probably possible theoretically to account for the behaviour of living bodies by purely physical causal laws, and it is probably impossible to refute materialism by

---

1. **Solipsism** is the view that only oneself exists.

external observation alone. If we are to believe that there are thoughts and feelings other than our own, that must be in virtue of some inference in which our own thoughts and feelings are relevant, and such an inference must go beyond what is needed in physics.

I am of course not discussing the history of how we come to believe in other minds. We find ourselves believing in them when we first begin to reflect; the thought that Mother may be angry or pleased is one which arises in early infancy. What I am discussing is the possibility of a postulate which shall establish a rational connection between this belief and data, e.g. between the belief "Mother is angry" and the hearing of a loud voice.

The abstract schema seems to be as follows. We know, from observation of our-selves, a causal law of the form "A causes B," where A is a "thought" and B a physical occurrence. We sometimes observe a B when we cannot observe any A; we then infer an unobserved A. For example: I know that when I say "I'm thirsty," I say so, usually, because I am thirsty, and therefore, when I hear the sentence "I'm thirsty" at a time when I am not thirsty, I assume that someone else is thirsty. I assume this the more readily if I see before me a hot drooping body which goes on to say "I have walked twenty desert miles in this heat with never a drop to drink." It is evident that my con-fidence in the "inference" is increased by increased complexity in the datum and also by increased certainty of the causal law derived from subjective observation, provided the causal law is such as to account for the complexities of the datum.

It is clear that, in so far as plurality of causes is to be suspected, the kind of inference we have been considering is not valid. We are supposed to know "A causes B," and also to know that B has occurred; if this is to justify us in inferring A, we must know that *only* A causes B. Or, if we are content to infer that A is probable, it will suffice if we can know that in most cases it is A that causes B. If you hear thunder without having seen lightning, you confidently infer that there was lightning, because you are convinced that the sort of noise you heard is seldom caused by anything except lightning. As this example shows, our principle is not only employed to establish the existence of other minds, but is habitually assumed, though in a less concrete form, in physics. I say "a less concrete form" because unseen lightning is only abstractly similar to seen lightning, whereas we suppose the similarity of other minds to our own to be by no means purely abstract.

Complexity in the observed behaviour of another person, when this can all be ac-counted for by a simple cause such as thirst, increases the probability of the inference by diminishing the probability of some other cause. I think that in ideally favourable circumstances the argument would be formally as follows:

From subjective observation I know that A, which is a thought or feeling, causes B, which is a bodily act, e.g. a statement. I know also that, whenever B is an act of my own body, A is its cause. I now observe an act of the kind B in a body not my own, and I am having no thought or feeling of the kind A. But I still believe, on the basis of self-observation, that only A can cause B; I therefore infer that there was an A which caused B, though it was not an A that I could observe. On this ground I infer that other people's bodies are associated with minds, which resemble mine in proportion as their bodily behaviour resembles my own.

In practice, the exactness and certainty of the above statement must be soft-ened. We cannot be sure that, in our subjective experience, A is the only cause of B. And even if A is the only cause of B in our experience, how can we know that this holds outside our experience? It is not necessary that we should know this with any certainty; it is enough if it is highly probable. It is the assumption of probability in such cases that is our postulate. The postulate may therefore be stated as follows:

> If, whenever we can observe whether A and B are present or absent, we find that every case of B has an A as a causal antecedent, then it is probable that most B's have A's as causal antecedents, even in cases where observation does not enable us to know whether A is present or not.

This postulate, if accepted, justifies the inference to other minds, as well as many other inferences that are made unreflectingly by common sense.

TEST YOUR UNDERSTANDING

1. According to Russell, what does physics tell us?

   a. Minds are simply space-time structures.

   b. Minds are physical things.

   c. The world has such-and-such space-time structure.

2. According to Russell, what does physics *not* tell us?

   a. Solipsism is false.

   b. Other minds exist.

   c. There are causal laws.

3. If you are to discover that I have thoughts and feelings, Russell thinks a crucial piece of your evidence is that

   a. you have thoughts and feelings.

   b. my body is not dead matter.

   c. my body is living matter.

4. Suppose you observe many Bs and find that they are all caused by As. You now observe another B. On Russell's view, given this evidence, what is likely to be true?

   a. You will observe another A.

   b. The B you observe was caused by an A.

   c. Some As are unobservable.

NOTES AND QUESTIONS

1. One (relatively) modest project is to find evidence establishing that other people are in various mental states, like feeling pain, believing that it's raining, wanting pizza, and so forth. A more ambitious project is to find out how *ordinary people* know that others feel pain, believe that it's raining, want pizza, and so forth. Explain, using examples, why the success of the modest project doesn't guarantee the success of the ambitious project. Which project do you think Russell is engaged in? Suppose that one can establish the existence of other minds by an analogical inference, and thus that the modest project succeeds. Are there any reasons for doubting that ordinary people know about others' minds by an analogical inference?

2. For surveys of the problem of other minds, see Alec Hyslop, "Other Minds," in *Stanford Encyclopedia of Philosophy,* ed. Edward Zalta (https://plato.stanford.edu/archives /spr2016/entries/other-minds), and Anita Avramides, *Other Minds* (Routledge, 2001).

Saul Kripke (b. 1940)

Kripke is Distinguished Professor of Philosophy at the City University of New York. He previously taught at Princeton University, where he gave a series of lectures that became *Naming and Necessity* (1980), one of the most influential books in philosophy in the twentieth century.

WITTGENSTEIN[1] AND OTHER MINDS
from *Wittgenstein on Rules and Private Language*

Traditional philosophy of mind had argued, in its "problem of other minds," that given that I know what it means for *me* to feel a tickle, I can raise the sceptical question whether others ever feel the same as I do, or even whether there are conscious minds behind their bodies at all. The problem is one of the epistemic *justification* of our "belief" that other minds exist "behind the bodies" and that their sensations are similar to our own. For that matter, we might equally well ask whether stones, chairs, tables, and the like think and feel; it is assumed that the hypothesis that they do think and feel makes perfect sense. A few philosophers—solipsists—doubt or positively deny that any body other than one ("my body") has a mind "back of" it. Some others— panpsychists—ascribe minds to all material objects. Yet others—Cartesians[2]—believe

---

1. The Austrian philosopher Ludwig Wittgenstein (1889–1951) was one of the major figures in twentieth-century philosophy.

2. Those holding similar views to the French philosopher René Descartes (1596–1650).

that there are minds behind human bodies, but not those of animals, let alone inanimate bodies. Perhaps the most common position ascribes minds to both human and animal bodies, but not to inanimate bodies. All presuppose without argument that we begin with an antecedently understood general concept of a given material object's "having," or not having, a mind; there is a problem as to which objects in fact have minds and why they should be thought to have (or lack) them. In contrast, Wittgenstein seems to believe that the very *meaningfulness* of the ascription of sensations to others is questionable if, following the traditional model, we attempt to extrapolate it from our own case. On the traditional model in question, Wittgenstein seems to be saying, it is doubtful that we could *have* any "belief" in other minds, and their sensations, that ought to be justified. . . .

Let me attempt to give the reader a feeling for the difficulty, and for its historical roots. According to Descartes, the one entity of whose existence I may be certain, even in the midst of doubts of the existence of the external world, is myself.[3] I may doubt the existence of bodies (including my own), or, even assuming that there are bodies, that there ever are minds "behind" them; but I cannot doubt the existence of my own mind. Hume's[4] reaction to this is notorious: "There are some philosophers, who imagine we are intimately conscious of what we call our *self*; that we feel its existence and its continuance in existence; and are certain, beyond the evidence of a demonstration, both of its perfect identity and simplicity. The strongest sensation, the most violent passion, say they, instead of distracting us from this view, only fix it the more intensely, and make us consider their influence on *self* either by their pain or pleasure. To attempt a further proof of this were to weaken its evidence; since no proof can be derived from any fact of which we are so intimately conscious; nor is there any thing, of which we can be certain, if we doubt of this. Unluckily all these positive assertions are contrary to that very experience, which is pleaded for them, nor have we any idea of *self*, after the manner it is here explain'd. . . . For my part, when I enter most intimately into what I call *myself*, I always stumble on some particular impression or other, of heat or cold, light or shade, love or hatred, pain or pleasure. I never can catch *myself* at any time without a perception, and never can observe any thing but the perception. . . . If any one, upon serious and unprejudic'd reflection, thinks he has a different notion of *himself*, I must confess I can reason no longer with him. All I can allow him is, that he may be in the right as well as I, and that we are essentially different in this particular. He may, perhaps, perceive something simple and continu'd, which he calls *himself*; tho' I am certain there is no such principle in me."

So: where Descartes would have said that I am certain that "I have a tickle," the only thing Hume is aware of is the tickle itself. The self—the Cartesian ego—is an entity which is wholly mysterious. We are aware of no such entity that "has" the tickle, "has" the headache, the visual perception, and the rest; we are aware only of the tickle, the headache, the visual perception, itself. Any direct influences from Hume to Wittgenstein are difficult to substantiate; but the Humean thoughts here sketched continued

3. See Descartes, Meditation II, in Chapter 7 of this anthology.

4. Scottish philosopher David Hume (1711–1776); the quotation following is from Hume's most famous work, *A Treatise of Human Nature* (1739). Selections from the *Treatise* are in Chapters 6 and 18 of this anthology.

through much of the philosophical tradition, and it is very easy to find the idea in the *Tractatus*.[5] In 5.631 of that work, Wittgenstein says, "There is no such thing as the subject that thinks or entertains ideas. If I wrote a book called *The World as I found it . . .* it alone could *not* be mentioned in that book." Continuing in 5.632–5.633, he explains: "The subject does not belong to the world: rather, it is a limit of the world. Where *in* the world is a metaphysical subject to be found? You will say that this is exactly like the case of the eye and the visual field. But really you do *not* see the eye. And nothing *in the visual field* allows you to infer that it is seen by an eye."

Wittgenstein returned to this theme in several of his writings, lectures, and discussions of the late 1920s and early 1930s, during the period usually regarded as transitional between the "early" philosophy of the *Tractatus* and the "late" philosophy of the *Investigations*.[6] In his account of Wittgenstein's Cambridge lectures in 1930–3, Moore reports that Wittgenstein "said that 'just as no (physical) eye is involved in seeing, so no Ego is involved in thinking or in having toothache'; and he quotes, with apparent approval, Lichtenberg's saying 'Instead of "I think" we ought to say "It thinks"' ('it' being used, as he said, as 'Es' is used in 'Es blitzet'); and by saying this he meant, I think, something similar to what he said of the 'eye of the visual field' when he said that it is not anything which is *in* the visual field."[7] In *Philosophical Remarks*,[8] §58, Wittgenstein imagines a language in which "I have a toothache" is replaced by "There is toothache," and, following Lichtenberg; "I am thinking" becomes "It is thinking."

Now the basic problem in extending talk of sensations from to "myself" to "others" ought to be manifest. Supposedly, if I concentrate on a particular toothache or tickle, note its qualitative character, and abstract from particular features of time and place, I can form a concept that will determine when a toothache or tickle comes again. . . . How am I supposed to extend this notion to the sensations of "others"? What is this supposed to mean? If I see ducks in Central Park, I can imagine things which are "like these"—here, still *ducks*—except that they are *not* in Central Park. I can similarly "abstract" even from *essential* properties[9] of these particular ducks to entities like these but lacking the properties in question—ducks of different parentage and biological origin, ducks born in a different century, and so on. . . . But what can be meant by something "just like this toothache, only it is not I, but someone else, who has it"? In what ways is this supposed to be similar to the paradigmatic toothache on which I concentrate my attention, and in what ways dissimilar? We are supposed to imagine another entity, similar to "me"—another "soul," "mind" or "self"—that "has" a toothache *just like* this toothache, except that it (he? she?) "has" it, just as "I have" this one. All this makes little sense, given the Humean critique of the notion of the self that Wittgenstein accepts.

---

5. Wittgenstein's *Tractatus Logico-Philosophicus* was published in 1921.

6. *Philosophical Investigations*, published posthumously in 1953.

7. "Moore": British philosopher George Edward Moore (1873–1958). "Lichtenberg": German physicist and satirist Georg Christoph Lichtenberg (1742–1799). "Es blitzet": literally, it flashes (German, i.e., there is lightning).

8. Published in 1964.

9. An essential **property** of an object is a property that the object could not have lacked; an object's nonessential properties are its *accidental* properties, those properties that it could have lacked.

I have no idea of a "self" in my own case, let alone a generic concept of a "self" that in addition to "me" includes "others." Nor do I have any idea of "having" as a relation between such a "self" and the toothache. Supposedly, by concentrating my attention on one or more particular toothaches, I can form the concept of toothache, enabling me thereby to recognize at later times when "there is a toothache" or "it toothaches" (as in, "it is raining") on the basis of the "phenomenological quality" of toothaches. Although we have expressed this in the Lichtenbergian terminology Wittgenstein commends, "it toothaches" means what we naively would have expressed by "I have a toothache." The concept is supposed to be formed by concentrating on a particular toothache: when something just like this recurs, then "it toothaches" again. What are we supposed to abstract from this situation to form the concept of an event which is like the given paradigm case of "it toothaches," except that the toothache is not "mine," but "someone else's"? I have no concept of a "self" nor of "having" to enable me to make the appropriate abstraction from the original paradigm. The formulation "it toothaches" makes this quite clear: consider the total situation, and ask what I am to abstract if I wish to remove "myself."

I think that it is at least in part because of this kind of consideration that Wittgenstein was so much concerned with the appeal of solipsism, and of the behavioristic idea that to say of someone else that he has a toothache is simply to make a statement about his behavior. When he considers the adoption of Lichtenberg's subjectless sensation language, attributions of sensations to others give way to expressions like "The body A is behaving similarly to the way X behaves when it pains," where "X" is a name for what I would ordinarily call "my body." This is a crude behaviorist ersatz for imagining the sensations of others on the model of my own: attributing a sensation to A in no way says that something is happening that resembles what happens when I am in pain (or, rather, when it pains). The attraction, for Wittgenstein, of this combination of solipsism and behaviorism, was never free of a certain discontent with it. Nevertheless, during the most verificationist[10] phase of his transitional period, Wittgenstein felt that it is hard to avoid the conclusion that since behavior is our sole method of verifying attributions of sensations to others, the behaviorist formulation is all that I can mean when I make such an attribution (see *Philosophical Remarks*, §§64–5).

The point comes into sharp relief when we consider many customary formulations of the problem of other minds. How do I know, it is said, that other bodies "have" "minds" like my own? It is assumed that I know from my own case *what* a "mind" is, and what it is for a "body" to "have" it. But the immediate point of the Hume–Lichtenberg criticism of the notion of the self is that I have no such idea in my own case that can be generalized to other bodies. I *do* have an idea, from my own case, of what it is like for there "to be pain," but I have no idea what it would be like for there to be a pain "just like this, except that it belongs to a mind other than my own." . . .

---

10. Verificationism is the view that the meaning of a sentence consists in its method of verification—the ways in which one could find out that the sentence is true. Verificationism was a core commitment of the early-twentieth-century movement known as *logical positivism,* which drew inspiration from Wittgenstein's *Tractatus Logico-Philosophicus.*

§350[11] questions whether we know what it means to say that "someone else has pain" on the basis of my own case. At the end, the example given is that of a *stove*: do we know what it means to say of a stove that it is in pain? As we said above, the traditional view assumes, without supposing the need of any further justification, that we have a general concept of an arbitrary material object "having" sensations, or, rather, "having" a "mind" that in turn is the "bearer" of the sensations. (The physical object "has" sensations in a derivative sense, if it "has" a "mind" that "has" the sensations.) Now: are we so sure that we understand all this? As we have emphasized, we have no idea what a "mind" is. And do we know what relation is to hold between a "mind" and a physical object that constitutes "having"? Suppose a given chair "has" a "mind." Then there are many "minds" in the universe, only one of which a given chair "has." What relationship is that "mind" supposed to have to the chair, that another "mind" does not? Why is this "mind," rather than that one, the one the chair "has"? (Of course I don't mean: what is the (causal) *explanation* why in fact the chair "has" this "mind" rather than that? I mean: what relation is supposed to hold between the chair and one mind, rather than another, that *constitutes* its having this mind, rather than that?) For that matter, why is it the chair as a whole, rather than just its back, or its legs, that is related to the given mind? (Why not another physical object altogether?) Under what circumstances would it be the back of the chair, rather than the whole chair, that "has" a given "mind" and hence thinks and feels? (This is not the question: how would we *verify* that the relation holds, but rather, under what circumstances would it hold?) Often discussions of the problem of other minds, of panpsychism, and so on, simply ignore these questions, supposing, without further ado, that the notion of a given body "having" a given "mind" is self-evident. Wittgenstein simply wishes to question whether we really have such a clear idea what this means: he is raising intuitive questions. See, e.g., §361 ("The chair is thinking to itself: ... WHERE? In one of its parts? Or outside its body; in the air around it? Or not *anywhere* at all? But then what is the difference between the chair's saying anything to itself and another one's doing so, next to it?") or §283 ("Can we say of the stone that it has a soul [or: a mind] and *that* is what has the pain? What has a soul [or: mind], or pain, to do with a stone?").

It is possible to make various attempts to understand the idea of an object—even an inanimate one—"having" a "mind" or a sensation without invoking the notions of "minds" and "having" themselves. I might, for example, imagine that the physical object I call "my body" turns to stone while my thoughts, or my pains, go on (see §283). This could be expressed in Lichtenberg's jargon: There is thinking, or pain, even while such-and-such an object turns to stone. But: "if that has happened, in what sense will the *stone* have the thoughts or the pains? In what sense will they be ascribable to the stone?" Suppose I were thinking, for example, of the proof that π is irrational, and my body turned to stone while I was still thinking of this proof. Well: what relation would my thoughts of this proof have to the stone? In what sense is the stone still "my body," not just "formerly my body"? What difference is there between this case and the case where after "my body" turned to stone, "my mind switched bodies"—perhaps to

---

11. Of the *Investigations*. All subsequent section-number references are to this book.

another stone? Suppose for the moment that after I turn to stone I think only about mathematics. In general, what could connect a thought about mathematics with one physical object rather than another? In the case where my body turns to stone, the only connection is that the stone *is* what my body *has become*. In abstraction from such a prior history, the connection between the thought and the physical object is even harder to spell out: yet if there is a connection, it must be a connection that exists *now*, independently of an imagined prior history.

Actually, in §283 Wittgenstein is concerned with the connection of a pain, a sensation, with the stone. Now if we forget for a moment that sensations are ascribed to a "mind" that a physical object "has," and if we think simply of the connection between the sensation and the physical object without worrying about the intermediate links, then in some cases we may still be able to make sense of the connection between a given sensation and a given physical object, even an inert one such as a stone. Pains, for example, are *located*. They are located in the causal sense that damage or injury to a certain area produces the pain. In another causal sense, relief applied to a certain area may alleviate or eliminate the pain. They are also located in the more primitive, non-causal sense in which I *feel* a pain as "in my foot," "in my arm," and the like. Very often these senses coincide, but not always—certainly there is no conceptual reason why they must coincide. But: what if they all coincide, and, by all three tests, a certain pain is "located" in a certain position in a stone? As I understand Wittgenstein, he deals with this particular question in §302 where someone else's body, not a stone, is in question. Assuming that I can imagine that a pain is "located" in another body, does that give a sense to the idea that "someone else" might be in pain? Recall the Lichtenbergian terminology: if "there is pain," perhaps "there is pain in the stone," or "there is pain in that arm," where the arm in question is not my arm. Why isn't this just to imagine that *I* feel pain, only "in" the arm of another body, or even in a stone? Remember that "there is pain" means "I have pain," with the mysterious subject suppressed: so it would seem that to imagine "pain in that arm" is to imagine that *I* have pain in the arm of another body (in the way a person who has lost his arm can feel a pain in the area where his arm once was). There is no concept here of *another* "self" who feels the pain in the stone, or in the other body. It is for this reason that the experiment of ignoring the other "mind," and trying to imagine a direct connection between the sensation and the body, fails. To repeat some of what was quoted in §302: "If one has to imagine someone else's pain on the model of one's own, this is none too easy a thing to do . . . what I have to do is not simply to make a transition in imagination from one place of pain to another. As, from . . . the hand to . . . the arm. For I am not to imagine that I feel pain in some region of his body. (Which would also be possible.)" In the Lichtenbergian jargon, "there is pain" *always* means that *I* feel pain.

Even if we ignore the Lichtenbergian terminology, the problem can be restated: What is the difference between the case where *I* have a pain in another body, and where that pain in the other body is "someone else's" pain and not mine? It would seem that this difference can be expressed only by a direct attack on the problems we have just now been trying to evade: what is a mind, what is it for it to "have" a sensation, what is it for a body to "have" a mind? The attempt to bypass these intermediaries and deal directly with the connection of the sensation and the physical object fails, precisely because I cannot then define what it means for "another mind" to have the sensation in a given physical object, as opposed to "my" having it there. Wittgenstein insists that the possibility that one person might have a sensation in the body of another is perfectly intelligible, even if it never occurs: "Pain behavior can point to a painful place—but the subject of pain is the person who gives it expression" (§302). . . .

In sum, any attempt to imagine a direct connection between a sensation and a physical object without mentioning a "self" or "mind" leads me simply to imagine that *I* have a sensation located elsewhere. So we are compelled to contemplate the original mystery: What is a "mind," what is it for a "mind" to "have" a sensation, what is it for a body to "have" a "mind"? Here the argument of Hume and Lichtenberg, and the other considerations we have mentioned, say that we have no such notions. As Wittgenstein puts the question in §283, speaking of the ascription of sensations to other bodies: "One has to say it of a body, or, if you like, of a soul [mind] which some body *has*. And how can a body *have* a soul [mind]?"

TEST YOUR UNDERSTANDING

1. What does Wittgenstein (as interpreted by Kripke) think of the traditional problem of other minds?

    a. The problem rests on a mistaken assumption.

    b. It is hard to decide which of the proposed solutions to the problem is correct.

    c. Solipsism is the correct solution.

2. Whose views on the self are supposed to be quite different from Wittgenstein's?

    a. Descartes

    b. Hume

    c. Lichtenberg

3. Descartes was confident that he was thinking. What, according to Wittgenstein (as interpreted by Kripke), should he have been confident of instead?

4. According to Wittgenstein (as interpreted by Kripke), if I imagine turning to stone while the pain in my toe continues to throb, have I thereby understood the hypothesis that a stone is in pain?

NOTES AND QUESTIONS

1. If it makes no sense to attribute *a sensation like this* (here I attend to my aching tooth) to "another mind," perhaps statements like "Griffin has a toothache" and "Sabine has a toothache" *don't* characterize Griffin and Sabine as having sensations *like this*, because then they would be nonsense, and surely statements like this are not nonsense.

Indeed, they are sometimes true. Here is an alternative: while first-person statements like "I have a toothache" report the existence of a sensation *like this*, these third-person statements say nothing about sensations, and instead just characterize Griffin's and Sabine's outward behavior. On this view (which Kripke mentions), there is a radical difference in meaning between "I have a toothache" and "Griffin has a toothache": the first statement concerns a sensation; the second statement concerns Griffin's behavior.

Exercise: First motivate this view, drawing on the considerations raised by Kripke. Then criticize it.

2.   The selection is taken from Kripke's book *Wittgenstein on Rules and Private Language*, which is mostly concerned with Wittgenstein's views on linguistic meaning, as they appear in his *Philosophical Investigations* (Blackwell, 1953). The interpretation of Wittgenstein that Kripke advances in the book is controversial, but the arguments that Kripke attributes to Wittgenstein are of great interest in their own right, and for this reason the book is regarded as a contemporary classic. It is quite accessible and relatively short. For an introduction to the *Philosophical Investigations*, see Marie McGinn, *The Routledge Guidebook to Wittgenstein's Philosophical Investigations* (Routledge, 2013).

Maurice Merleau-Ponty (1908–1961)

Merleau-Ponty was Chair of Philosophy at the Collège de France in Paris from 1952 until his death. Influenced by the German philosopher Edmund Husserl (1859–1938), Merleau-Ponty's major work is *The Phenomenology of Perception* (1945), which criticizes Cartesian dualism and emphasizes the importance of embodiment to our experience of the world.

MAN SEEN FROM THE OUTSIDE
from *The World of Perception*

[In previous lectures] we have tried to look at space and the things which inhabit it, both animate and inanimate, through the eyes of perception and to forget what we find "entirely natural" about them simply because they have been familiar to us for too long; we have endeavoured to consider them as they are experienced naïvely. We must now try to do the same with respect to human beings themselves. Over the last thirty or more centuries, many things have undoubtedly been said about human beings. Yet these were often the products of reflection. What I mean by this is that Descartes,[1]

---

1. René Descartes (1596–1650), French philosopher, scientist, and mathematician; a central figure in Western philosophy.

when he wanted to know what man is, set about subjecting the ideas which occurred to him to critical examination. One example would be the idea of mind and body. He purified these ideas; he rid them of all trace of obscurity and confusion. Whereas most people understand spirit to be something like very subtle matter, or smoke, or breath (consistent, in this regard, with primitive peoples), Descartes showed admirably that spirit is something altogether different. He demonstrated that its nature is quite other, for smoke and breath are, in their way, things—even if very subtle ones—whereas spirit is not a thing at all, does not occupy space, is not spread over a certain extension as all things are, but on the contrary is entirely compact and indivisible—a being—the essence of which is none other than to commune with, collect and know itself. This gave rise to the concepts of pure spirit and pure matter, or things. Yet it is clear that I can only find and, so to speak, touch this absolutely pure spirit in myself. Other human beings are never pure spirit for me: I only know them through their glances, their gestures, their speech—in other words, through their bodies. Of course *another human being* is certainly more than simply a body to me: rather, this other is a body animated by all manner of intentions, the origin of numerous actions and words. These I remember and they go to make up my sketch of their moral character. Yet I cannot detach someone from their silhouette, the tone of their voice and its accent. If I see them for even a moment, I can reconnect with them instantaneously and far more thoroughly than if I were to go through a list of everything I know about them from experience or hearsay. Another person, for us, is a spirit which haunts a body and we seem to see a whole host of possibilities contained within this body when it appears before us; the body is the very presence of these possibilities. So the process of looking at human beings from the outside—that is, at other people—leads us to reassess a number of distinctions which once seemed to hold good such as that between mind and body.

Let us see what becomes of this distinction by examining a particular case. Imagine that I am in the presence of someone who, for one reason or another, is extremely annoyed with me. My interlocutor gets angry and I notice that he is expressing his anger by speaking aggressively, by gesticulating and shouting. But where is this anger? People will say that it is in the mind of my interlocutor. What this means is not entirely clear. For I could not imagine the malice and cruelty which I discern in my opponent's looks separated from his gestures, speech and body. None of this takes place in some other-worldly realm, in some shrine located beyond the body of the angry man. It really is here, in this room and in this part of the room, that the anger breaks forth. It is in the space between him and me that it unfolds. I would accept that the sense in which the place of my opponent's anger is on his face is not the same as that in which, in a moment, tears may come streaming from his eyes or a grimace may harden on his mouth. Yet anger inhabits him and it blossoms on the surface of his pale or purple cheeks, his blood-shot eyes and wheezing voice. . . . And if, for one moment, I step out of my own viewpoint as an external observer of this anger and try to remember what it is like for me when I am angry, I am forced to admit that it is no different. When I reflect on my own anger, I do not come across any element that might be separated or, so to speak, unstuck, from my own body. When I recall being angry at Paul, it does not strike me that this anger was in my mind or among my thoughts but rather, that it lay entirely between me who was doing the shouting and that odious Paul who just sat there calmly and listened with an ironic air. My anger is nothing less than an attempt to destroy Paul, one which will remain verbal if I am a pacifist and even courteous, if I am polite. The location of my anger, however, is in the space we both share—in which we exchange arguments instead of blows—and not in me. It is only afterwards, when I reflect on what anger is and remark that it involves a certain (negative) evaluation of another person, that I come to the following conclusion. Anger is, after all, a thought; to be angry is to think that the other person is odious and this thought, like all others, cannot—as Descartes has shown—reside in any piece of matter and therefore must belong to the mind. I may very well think in such terms but as soon as I turn back to the real experience of anger, which was the spur to my reflections, I am forced to acknowledge that this anger does not lie beyond my body, directing it from without, but rather that in some inexplicable sense it is bound up with my body.

There is something of everything in Descartes, as in the work of all great philosophers. And so it is that he who draws an absolute distinction between mind and body also manages to say that the soul is not simply like the pilot of a ship, the commander-in-chief of the body, but rather that it is very closely united to the body, so much so that it suffers with it, as is clear to me when I say that I have toothache.[2]

Yet this union of mind and body can barely be spoken of, according to Descartes; it can only be experienced in everyday life. As far as Descartes is concerned, whatever the facts of the matter may be—and even if we live what he himself calls a true *mélange*[3] of mind and body—this does not take away my right to distinguish absolutely between parts that are united in my experience. I can still posit, by rights, an absolute distinction between mind and body which is denied by the fact of their union. I can still define man without reference to the immediate structure of his being and as he appears to himself in reflection: as thought which is somehow strangely joined to a bodily apparatus without either the mechanics of the body or the transparency of thought being compromised by their being mixed together in this way. It could be said that even Descartes's most faithful disciples have always asked themselves exactly how it is that our reflection, which concerns the human being as given, can free itself from the conditions to which it appears to have been subject at the outset.

When they address this issue, today's psychologists emphasise the fact that we do not start out in life immersed in our own self-consciousness (or even in that of things) but rather from the experience of other people. I never become aware of my own existence until I have already made contact with others; my reflection always brings me back to myself, yet for all that it owes much to my contacts with other people. An infant of a few months is already very good at differentiating between goodwill, anger and fear on the face of another person, at a stage when he could not have learned the physical signs of these emotions by examining his own body. This is because the body of the other and its various movements appear to the infant to have been invested from

2. See Descartes, Meditation VI, on page 317 of this anthology.
3. Mixture or blend (French).

the outset with an emotional significance; this is because the infant learns to know mind as visible behaviour just as much as in familiarity with its own mind. The adult himself will discover in his own life what his culture, education, books and tradition have taught him to find there. The contact I make with myself is always mediated by a particular culture, or at least by a language that we have received from without and which guides us in our self-knowledge. So while ultimately the notion of a pure self, the mind, devoid of instruments and history, may well be useful as a critical ideal to set in opposition to the notion of a mere influx of ideas from the surrounding environment, such a self only develops into a free agent by way of the instrument of language and by taking part in the life of the world.

This leaves us with a very different view of the human being and humanity from the one with which we began. Humanity is not an aggregate of individuals, a community of thinkers, each of whom is guaranteed from the outset to be able to reach agreement with the others because all participate in the same thinking essence. Nor, of course, is it a single Being in which the multiplicity of individuals are dissolved and into which these individuals are destined to be reabsorbed. As a matter of principle, humanity is precarious: each person can only believe what he recognises to be true internally and, at the same time, nobody thinks or makes up his mind without already being caught up in certain relationships with others, which leads him to opt for a particular set of opinions. Everyone is alone and yet nobody can do without other people, not just because they are useful (which is not in dispute here) but also when it comes to happiness. There is no way of living with others which takes away the burden of being myself, which allows me to not have an opinion; there is no "inner" life that is not a first attempt to relate to another person. In this ambiguous position, which has been forced on us because we have a body and a history (both personally and collectively), we can never know complete rest. We are continually obliged to work on our differences, to explain things we have said that have not been properly understood, to reveal what is hidden within us and to perceive other people. Reason does not lie behind us, nor is that where the meeting of minds takes place: rather, both stand before us waiting to be inherited. Yet we are no more able to reach them definitively than we are to give up on them.

It is understandable that our species, charged as it is with a task that will never and can never be completed, and at which it has not necessarily been called to succeed, even in relative terms, should find this situation both cause for anxiety and a spur to courage. In fact, these are one and the same thing. For anxiety is vigilance, it is the will to judge, to know what one is doing and what there is on offer. If there is no such thing as benign fate, then neither is there such a thing as its malign opposite. Courage consists in being reliant on oneself and others to the extent that, irrespective of differences in physical and social circumstance, all manifest in their behaviour and their relationships that very same spark which makes us recognise them, which makes us crave their assent or their criticism, the spark which means we share a common fate. It is simply that this modern form of humanism has lost the dogmatic tone of earlier centuries. We should no longer pride ourselves in being a community of pure spirits; let us look instead at the real relationships between people in our societies.

For the most part, these are master–slave relationships. We should not find excuses for ourselves in our good intentions; let us see what becomes of these once they have escaped from inside us. There is something healthy about this unfamiliar gaze we are suggesting should be brought to bear on our species. Voltaire[4] once imagined, in *Micromégas*, that a giant from another planet was confronted with our customs. These could only seem derisory to an intelligence higher than our own. Our era is destined to judge itself not from on high, which is mean and bitter, but in a certain sense from below. Kafka[5] imagines a man who has metamorphosed into a strange insect and who looks at his family through the eyes of such an insect. Kafka also imagines a dog that investigates the human world which it rubs up against. He describes societies trapped in the carapace of customs which they themselves have adopted. In our day, Maurice Blanchot[6] describes a city held fast in the grip of its laws: everyone is so compliant that all lose the sense of their difference and that of others. To look at human beings from the outside is what makes the mind self-critical and keeps it sane. But the aim should not be to suggest that all is absurd, as Voltaire did. It is much more a question of implying, as Kafka does, that human life is always under threat and of using humour to prepare the ground for those rare and precious moments at which human beings come to recognise, to find, one another.

TEST YOUR UNDERSTANDING

1. On Descartes's view (as recounted by Merleau-Ponty), mind (or spirit) should not be thought of as a kind of ghostly smoke because

    a. spirit is located at a tiny point in space, unlike smoke, which is spread out.

    b. smoke cannot think.

    c. smoke is located in space, unlike spirit.

2. Does Merleau-Ponty think that while I cannot separate the anger of *another* person from his behavior, *my* anger is a condition of an indivisible pure spirit?

3. Does Merleau-Ponty disagree with the view that "The mind is the commander-in-chief of the body"? Does Descartes?

4. Does Merleau-Ponty think that we first acquire knowledge of our own minds, and only later acquire knowledge of the minds of others?

---

4. The pen name of François-Marie Arouet (1694–1778), a French writer and philosopher; "Micromégas" is one of his short stories.

5. Franz Kafka (1883–1924), Austro-Hungarian novelist and short story writer. He was born in Prague, Bohemia, then part of the Austro-Hungarian Empire, to a German-speaking Jewish family. He wrote in German. The two works mentioned are his novella *The Metamorphosis* and short story "Investigations of a Dog."

6. Maurice Blanchot (1907–2003), French novelist and literary critic; the work mentioned is his novel *The Most High*.

NOTES AND QUESTIONS

1. Toward the end of the selection, Merleau-Ponty writes that "[t]his leaves us with a very different view of the human being and humanity from the one with which we began." What are these two views? Explain and evaluate Merleau-Ponty's argument for the superiority of the "very different view."

2. For a defense of the idea that we can perceive that others are in mental states (e.g., that Sabine is angry) without inference from their behavior, see chapter 5 of Quassim Cassam, *The Possibility of Knowledge* (Oxford University Press, 2007).

D. M. Armstrong (1926–2014)

Armstrong was Challis Professor of Philosophy at the University of Sydney, retiring in 1991. He is known for his many contributions to philosophy of mind and metaphysics, including *A Materialist Theory of the Mind* (1968), *Universals and Scientific Realism* (1978), *What Is a Law of Nature?* (1983), and *Sketch for a Systematic Metaphysics* (2010).

INTROSPECTION
from *A Materialist Theory of the Mind*

I. Recapitulation[1]

In sense-perception we become aware of current happenings in the physical world. . . . In introspection, on the contrary, we become aware of current happenings in our own mind. . . . Nevertheless, introspection may properly be compared to sense-perception, and Kant's description of introspection as "inner sense"[2] is perfectly justified.

The possession of language may alter, and make more sophisticated, our perceptions. But perception is not logically dependent on language for its existence, as is shown by the fact that animals and young children can perceive although they cannot speak. In the same way, there seems no reason to think that introspection is logically dependent on language. That is to say, introspection does not logically demand the making of introspective reports, or having the power of making introspective reports. It seems plausible to say that animals and young children do not merely have pains,

1. This section summarizes Armstrong's views on perception, defended in earlier chapters of *A Materialist Theory of the Mind*.

2. In his *Critique of Pure Reason*, the German philosopher Immanuel Kant (1724–1804) writes that "inner sense . . . [is] the intuition of ourselves and of our inner state" (A33/B49).

but are aware of having pains. It seems perfectly possible that they not merely have desires, perceptions and mental images, but that they are aware of having such things. If so, they have the power of introspection, although they lack the power to make introspective reports. Incidentally, this is compatible with the view that there is a close empirical[3] connection between the possession of any extensive introspective ability, and the power to use language.

In the case of perception, we must distinguish between the perceiving, which is a mental event, and the thing perceived, which is something physical. In the case of introspection we must similarly distinguish between the introspecting and the thing introspected. Confusion is all the more easy in the latter case because *both* are mental states of the same mind. Nevertheless, although they are both mental states, it is impossible that the introspecting and the thing introspected should be one and the same mental state. A mental state cannot be aware of itself, any more than a man can eat himself up. The introspection may itself be the object of a further introspective awareness, and so on, but, since the capacity of the mind is finite, the chain of introspective awareness of introspections must terminate in an introspection that is not an object of introspective awareness.

If we make the materialist[4] identification of mental states with material states of the brain, we can say that introspection is a self-scanning process in the brain. The scanning operation may itself be scanned, and so on, but we must in the end reach an unscanned scanner. However, the unscanned scanner is not a logically unscannable scanner, for it is always possible to imagine a further scanning operation. Although the series logically must end somewhere, it need not have ended at the particular place it did end.

The distinction between the introspecting and the introspected state casts light on the much-lamented "systematic elusiveness of the subject."[5] The "elusiveness" of that mental state which is an awareness of some other state of affairs, physical or mental, is a mere logical elusiveness, the consequence of the fact that the awareness of something logically cannot also be an awareness of that awareness.

In the case of most forms of sense-perception we say that we perceive *with* certain parts of the body. These parts of the body we call sense-organs. The full concept of a sense-organ involves both (i) that perceptions of a certain characteristic range arise as a causal result of the stimulation of these parts of the body; (ii) that certain alterations in these parts of the body are under the direct control of the will, alterations which enable us to perceive different features of the environment. . . . The so-called proprioceptors, stimulation of which gives rise to bodily perception, are not *organs* in the fullest sense because their operation is not under the direct control of the will. In bodily perception there is nothing we perceive *with*.

---

3. Here: contingent; that is, could have been otherwise. N.B. there are other uses of **"empirical."**

4. **Materialism** (or **physicalism**) is the view that the mind—and the world in general—is wholly physical.

5. Famously noticed by the Scottish philosopher David Hume (1711–1776); see Kripke's quotation from Hume in the reading earlier in this chapter (p. 222).

Bodily perception has the further peculiarity that its object—our own body—is private to each perceiver. If each of us were confined to bodily sense, there would be no overlap between our sense-fields, in the way that there is overlap in the case of the other senses. This privacy is purely empirical, and we can imagine having the same direct perceptual access to states of other people's bodies that we now have to our own.

These two features of bodily perception make it an appropriate model for introspection conceived of as "inner sense." In the first place, when we are aware of happenings in our own minds, there is nothing that we are aware *with*. (If there were an organ involved it would be something whose operation was under the direct control of our will. This, in turn, would demand a power of gaining direct awareness of the different states of this "introspective organ." At some point there would have to be a direct awareness that did not involve the use of an organ.) In the second place, our introspective awareness is confined to our own minds. It was argued elsewhere that it is only an empirical fact that our direct awareness of mental states is confined to our own mind. We could conceive of a power of acquiring non-verbal non-inferential knowledge of current states of the minds of others. This would be a direct awareness, or perception, of the minds of others. Indeed, when people speak of "telepathy" it often seems to be this they have in mind.

When we perceive, there are many (indeed innumerable) features of our environment that we do not perceive. In the same way, when we are aware of our own current mental states, there are mental states and features of mental states of which we are unaware. These are mental states or features of mental states of which we are unconscious. Unconscious mental states stand to conscious mental states, in the realm of our own mind, as unperceived states of affairs stand to perceived states of affairs in the physical realm. In between the unperceived and the perceived there are those things which are just perceived, or are marginally perceived. In the case of introspective awareness there is a similar twilight zone.

Perception may be erroneous. Contrary to what might be called the Cartesian tradition, it is equally possible for introspection to be erroneous.[6] This does not mean that introspective awareness may not *in fact* regularly satisfy the conditions for *knowledge*.

Eccentric cases apart, perception, considered as a mental event, is the acquiring of information or misinformation about our environment. It is not an "acquaintance" with objects, or a "searchlight" that makes contact with them, but is simply the getting of beliefs. Exactly the same must be said of introspection. It is the getting of information or misinformation about the current state of our mind.

It is the burden of this book that a mental state is a state of the person apt for the bringing about of certain bodily behaviour. So when I acquire by introspection the information that, for example, I am sad now or that I have a certain sort of perception now, this information is information about certain of my behaviour-producing or potentially behaviour-producing states. Now if introspection is conceived of as "acquaintance" with mental states, or a searchlight that makes contact with them, it is

---

6. "Cartesian": relating to the French philosopher René Descartes (1596–1650). Armstrong argues for this claim in an earlier chapter of *A Materialist Theory of the Mind.*

difficult to see how all it can yield is information of such highly abstract nature about inner causes or potential inner causes. But if introspection as well as perception is conceived of as a mere flow of information or beliefs, then there is no difficulty.

We can even find an analogy for the sort of information acquired in introspection in the tactual perception of pressure upon our body. In such tactual perception we may be aware of no more than that something we know not what is pressing, with greater or lesser force, upon us. "Pressing with greater or lesser force" here seems to mean no more than a greater or lesser aptness for producing a certain sort of effect: either the distortion or motion of our flesh.

The only further topic to be recapitulated is that concerning the biological value of introspection. We argued that without introspection there could be no purposive mental activity. As we have seen, purposive physical behaviour logically demands perception. For unless we can become apprised of the situation as it develops, so that this awareness can react back upon the cause that initiates and sustains purposive behaviour, there will be no possibility of the adjustment of behaviour to circumstances that is an essential part of such behaviour. And it is by perception that we become apprised of the situation as it develops.

If there are to be purposive trains of mental activity, then there must equally be some means by which we become apprised of our current mental state. Only so can we adjust mental behaviour to mental circumstances. For instance, if we are doing a calculation "in our head" we will need to become aware of the current stage in the mental calculation that we have reached. Only if we do become so aware will we know what to do next. So there must be a way of becoming aware of our current mental state, which means that there must be introspection. The biological value of purposive mental activity is, of course, obvious. It permits of a far more sophisticated response to stimuli if we can "think before we act." But such thinking must be purposive thinking to be of real value.

This does not imply that purposive mental activity demands a highly self-conscious introspective scrutiny. Something far less may be, and normally is, all that is required. But without information of some sort about the current state of our mind, purposive trains of mental activity would be impossible. . . .

III. Introspection and Behaviour

We have argued that introspection is the acquiring of information (or misinformation) about our own current mental states. These mental states will be, *qua*[7] mental states, states of the person apt in their various ways for the production of certain sorts of physical behaviour. So introspection will be the acquiring of information about current states of ourselves apt for the production of certain behaviour. But, of course, introspective awareness of mental states is itself a (distinct) mental state (more precisely, it

---

7. As (Latin).

is a mental event). So it, too, must be an aptness for certain behaviour: a certain sort of selection-behaviour towards ourselves. Now since the concept of a mental state is such a complex one, as compared to simpler concepts like "red" or "round," it will be advisable to spell out in more detail the sort of behaviour a person would have to exhibit to convince us that he had the capacity for introspective discriminations. This is the business of this section.

It may be helpful to consider an imaginary model first. What behaviour would convince us that a person could acquire a *non-inferential* knowledge[8] that certain substances, such as untoughened glass, were brittle simply by putting their fingers in contact with the substance?

It will not be enough that the person was able to discriminate in a systematic way between material that is brittle, and material that is not brittle. Such behaviour will show that the perceiver can make a distinction between two sorts of material, a distinction that is in fact the distinction between being brittle and not being brittle. But does the perceiver perceive the distinction *as* the distinction between being brittle and not being brittle? The successful sorting does not demonstrate this.

What must be added? In the first place, the perceiver must be able to discriminate between those occurrences which constitute the manifestation of the disposition of brittleness and those which do not. For instance, a number of samples of material are struck sharply. Some break up, shatter or fly apart. Some do not. The perceiver must demonstrate that he can discriminate between the first sort of performance and the second sort.

This addition, although necessary, is clearly insufficient. The perceiver has still got to demonstrate that he understands the link between the first sort of discrimination (where nothing actually happens to the samples of material) and the occurrence or non-occurrence on other occasions of breaking, shattering or flying apart as a result of being struck. What sort of behaviour will demonstrate understanding of this link?

The answer is that the behaviour must have as its *objective* the actualization of the disposition or the prevention of the actualization of the disposition. Suppose the perceiver is rewarded when samples of material do not break, but punished when they do break. Suppose, after touching samples of material, the perceiver sorts them into two groups which are in fact the group of the brittle and the group of the non-brittle materials. Suppose furthermore that he treats objects in the two groups differently. The first group are handled very carefully, that is to say they are handled in a way that is, as an objective matter of physical fact, not conducive to their breaking. The other group are handled in a quite normal way, that is to say, a way that would as an objective matter of physical fact be conducive to their breaking if, contrary to the facts, they had been brittle. Does not such behaviour show that the perceiver perceives the connection between the original tactual discrimination and the brittleness or lack of brittleness of

---

8. *Inferential* knowledge is the result of **reasoning**, as when one comes to know that Smith killed Jones by reasoning from the fact that Jones's blood was found on Smith's hand. Knowledge that is not inferential is *non-inferential*.

the samples? The perceiver has shown a capacity to link the original discrimination with later easy breaking and absence of easy breaking.

Let us now use this case as a model (over-simple and over-schematic perhaps) to unfold the behaviour that will betoken the making of non-inferential introspective discriminations. Let us take as our example the non-inferential awareness that we are angry.

We must in the first place exhibit a capacity to behave towards ourselves in a systematically different way when we are angry and when we are not angry. (Such behaviour, of course, must be something more than the behaviour the anger itself expresses itself in, if it does express itself. For this would allow no distinction between a mere angry state, and *being aware* that one was in an angry state.) To take a quite artificial example, we might exhibit the behaviour of pressing a button that lighted up a red light, when, and only when, we are angry.

(It is clear, incidentally, that the teaching and learning of such discriminations will be a rather tricky business in the case of anger that is not expressed in angry behaviour. Nevertheless, even if there are [empirical] difficulties in *checking* on whether discrimination has been successful, we can still have the possibility that it *is* successful and that in fact we light up the red light when and only when we are angry.)

This behaviour so far only shows that we can discriminate between the cases where we are in fact angry, and the cases where we are not. It does not show that we are aware of the distinction *as* a distinction between being angry and not being angry. What further capacities for behaviour must we exhibit?

In the next place, we must have the capacity to discriminate systematically between angry behaviour and non-angry behaviour in ourselves and others. When I say "angry behaviour" here I do not mean behaviour that actually springs from anger, I mean angry *behaviour*. There can be angry behaviour that has not sprung from anger, and some behaviour brought about by anger is not what we would call *angry* behaviour. But there are certain typical sets of behaviours which occur when we are angry. (The relation of anger to its expression is more complicated than the relation of brittleness to its manifestations.) We must have the capacity to discriminate this sort of behaviour from other behaviour.

Finally, we must exhibit the capacity to link the original discrimination with angry behaviour. We must show ourselves capable of behaviour having as its *objective* the aiding or the inhibiting of the expression of anger. Suppose, for instance, we exhibit the following behaviour. After picking out those cases which are in fact cases where we are angry, we take action that has an inhibiting effect on anger but no similar effect on other mental states. We put our heads in cold water, or address soothing words to ourselves. We take no such action in the other cases. Have we not shown that the original introspective awareness was an awareness *of anger*?

No doubt what I have said here is oversimplified. But I think it has shown that there is no difficulty in principle in giving an account of the introspective acquiring of information about our own mental states as an acquiring of a capacity for certain sorts of discriminative behaviour. The parallel between perception and introspection is therefore maintained.

IV. Mental States and the Mind

One final topic remains to be discussed. The account given in the last section would seem to be adequate for no more than an awareness of a current happening apt for the production of a certain sort of behaviour in a certain body. (If it is asked "What body?," the answer is that the awareness is itself an acquiring of a capacity for discriminative behaviour by a certain body, and that the discriminative behaviour is directed towards that selfsame body.)

Now if we consider a statement such as "I am angry now" (taken as a purely descriptive remark), it seems to say more than is involved in the introspective awareness. For does not the use of the word "I" here imply (among other things) that the current happening apt for the production of a certain sort of behaviour belongs to an organised set of happenings—a mind—all of which are happenings apt for the production of behaviour in the same body? The analysis of the last section does not do justice to this implication.

One might try to brush aside this difficulty by arguing that what is *meant* by "a mind" is simply that group of happenings which are apt for the production of certain sorts of behaviour in a particular body. Unfortunately, however, this does not seem to be correct. For we can perfectly well understand the suggestion that something which is not *our* mind should have a capacity to bring about certain behaviour by our body of the sort that betokens mind. The notion of such "possession" of our body seems a perfectly intelligible one, even if we think that in fact it never occurs.

What, then, does constitute the unity of the group of happenings that constitute a single mind? We are back at the problem that proved Hume's downfall.[9] . . .

I do not see any way to solve the problem except to say that the group of happenings constitute a single mind because they are all states of, processes in or events in, a single *substance*.[10] Resemblance, causal relationship and memory are all of them important. Unless there were extensive relations of this sort between the different mental states that qualify the one substance we should not talk of the substance as "a mind." But the concept of a mind is the concept of a substance.

In taking the mind to be a substance, then, the Cartesian Dualists[11] show a true understanding of the formal features of the concept of mind. Their view that the mind is a *spiritual* substance is, however, a further theory about the nature of this substance, and, while it is an intelligible theory, it is a singularly empty one. For it seems that we can only characterize the spiritual (except for its *temporal* characteristics) as "that which is not spatial." Modern materialism is able to put forward a much more plausible (and much more easily falsified) theory: the view that the mind is the brain. Mental

---

9. In his *Treatise of Human Nature*, Hume argues that "what we call a *mind*, . . . is nothing but a heap or collection of different perceptions, united together by certain relations" (book 1, part 4, section 2). When discussing this view later in the Appendix to the *Treatise*, he writes that "I find myself involv'd in such a labyrinth, that, I must confess, I neither know how to correct my former opinions, nor how to render them consistent." See also footnote 5 earlier.

10. Philosophical term dating back to the ancient Greek philosopher Aristotle (384–322 BCE). In the use of the term here, a **substance** is a particular object or individual (a rock, a horse, an atom, a banana, etc.); **properties** (hardness, yellowness, etc.) are not substances.

11. Those who follow Descartes in taking mind and body to be distinct (nonidentical) things (i.e., substances).

states, processes and events are physical states of the brain, physical processes in the brain or physical events in the brain. . . .

But we must however grant Hume that the existence of the mind is not something that is given to unaided introspection. All that "inner sense" reveals is the occurrence of individual mental happenings. This is the difficulty from which this section started. I suggest that the solution is that the notion of "a mind" is a *theoretical* concept: something that is *postulated* to link together all the individual happenings of which introspection makes us aware. In speaking of minds, perhaps even in using the word "I" in the course of introspective reports, we go beyond what is introspectively observed. Ordinary language here embodies a certain theory. The particular *nature* of this substance is a *further* theoretical question, but when ordinary language speaks of "minds" it postulates *some* sort of substance.

The position, then, is this. Introspection makes us aware of a series of happenings apt for the production of certain sorts of behaviour in the one body. In a being without language, it may be presumed that introspection goes no further than this. Beings with language go on to form the notion that all these states are states of a single substance. This postulated substance is called "the mind." Once the notion of "the mind" is introduced, there can be further speculation about its particular nature. (Just as, once the notion of the gene is introduced, there can be further speculation about *its* particular nature.) There is no absolute necessity for such a postulation of a single substance in the observed facts: it is simply a natural postulate to make. And sometimes, particularly in the case of primitive persons, a mental state, of which we become introspectively aware may seem so alien to the other members of the "bundle" that we may form the hypothesis that it is not a state of the same substance of which the other members are states. "It is not I, but something alien." Such an hypothesis is perfectly intelligible, even if it is not true, and even if it is a mark of maturity to recognize that everything we become aware of by introspection is part of the *one* mind: our own.

A *person* is something that has both body and mind. It will be seen, then, that when in the past we have spoken of a mental state as a state of a *person* apt for the production of certain sorts of behaviour we already presuppose the existence of *minds*. To that extent, this account of a mental state goes beyond the bare deliverances of introspection, and puts forward a *theory* about the objects of introspective awareness. But provided it is clear that we are doing so, there seems to be no objection to this procedure.

TEST YOUR UNDERSTANDING

1. In what two respects are introspection and proprioception similar, according to Armstrong?

2. Does Armstrong think that introspection is immune to error?

3. According to Armstrong, a mental state is

    a. a state of a person that tends to cause certain behavior.

    b. a state of a person that actually brings about certain behavior.

    c. a state of a person that can be detected by the person's faculty of inner sense.

4. Armstrong is not a **dualist** like Descartes; rather, he is a **physicalist** or **materialist** like J. J. C. Smart (see Chapter 7 of this anthology for Descartes and Smart). Nonetheless, he agrees with the Cartesian dualist on one important point. What is it?

NOTES AND QUESTIONS

1. For a defense of an Armstrong-style account of self-knowledge, see chapter 4 of Shaun Nichols and Stephen Stich, *Mindreading* (Oxford University Press, 2003). For a critical discussion of the inner-sense theory, see chapter 5 of Brie Gertler, *Self-Knowledge* (Routledge, 2011), and section 3.2 of Gertler, "Self-Knowledge," in *Stanford Encyclopedia of Philosophy*, ed. Edward Zalta (https://plato.stanford.edu/archives/sum2015/entries/self-knowledge).

Sarah K. Paul (b. 1980)

Paul is Associate Professor of Philosophy at the University of Wisconsin, Madison. She specializes in the philosophy of action, philosophy of mind, self-knowledge, and the theory of practical reason and is the author of *The Philosophy of Action* (Routledge, forthcoming).

JOHN DOE AND RICHARD ROE

To discover what is going on in someone else's mind, it can seem obvious that complex theorizing is required. As Whitney Houston once asked, "How will I know if he really loves me?" According to Aretha Franklin, you cannot find out from the way he acts, the look in his eyes, or even what he says (since he may aim to deceive you); the answer is in his kiss. Others may disagree, taking the evidence provided by his verbal behavior to be more significant than his kisses. Either way, the presumption is that the attribution of mental states to others such as *being in love, believing* that change is gonna come, *wanting* the revolution to begin, or *intending* to wait a lonely lifetime is based on observational evidence and mediated by a theory of the symptoms people exhibit when they are in those states.

It can seem just as obvious that this is not how it works in one's own case. To know about my own mental goings-on, I do not appear to need evidence about how I have been behaving. Surely I can know whether I love him without observing my own kisses! I need not check my agenda to know that I intend to travel to Abu Dhabi or my pulse to know that I am excited about it. It would be inappropriate to ask me how I know that I believe that Topeka is the capital of Kansas or what my evidence is that I desire to eat a burrito for lunch. And whereas I could easily be wrong about whether someone else likes my new haircut, the presumption is that I cannot be mistaken about whether I like theirs.

Let us make these claims about self-knowledge more precise. According to common wisdom, our knowledge of our own minds is *nonevidential, infallible,* and *distinctively first-personal*:

> [No Evidence]: When a subject ascribes a mental state M to herself, it is not on the basis of evidence or grounds for thinking that she is in M.
>
> [Infallible]: If a subject sincerely believes herself to be in some mental state M, then she is in M.
>
> [First-Personal]: The method a subject normally uses to ascribe mental states to herself cannot be used in the same way to ascribe mental states to other people.

These three theses express a deep asymmetry between access to one's own mind and knowledge of other minds, the latter of which is evidence based and highly fallible. They arise from a classic view about the nature of the mind and what we mean when we use mental terms such as "pain," "belief," "desire," and "love." On this view, [Infallible] and [No Evidence] are true because a person's mind is transparent to her. There is nothing she needs to go by in order to know what is going on within it; she knows directly and immediately, in a way that leaves no room for error. It is like an inner theater that she can see perfectly, and that only she can see.

Because this inner theater is essentially private, it is consistent with everything we can observe about other people that they have no minds at all. We might hypothesize that their behavior is caused by mental events similar to our own, in something like the way we posit the existence of subatomic particles that we cannot observe. But we can in principle never confirm this hypothesis. Ludwig Wittgenstein[1] compared this situation to a scenario in which everyone has a box, and each person uses the word "beetle" to refer to the contents of his own box, but in which no one can ever look inside another person's box. Since it is perfectly possible that each person has something different in his box—or nothing at all—no one will be in a position to know whether anyone else has what they themselves call "beetle," even if everyone uses the same word. And similarly for terms such as "pain" and "belief": it might be that the inner states others refer to with these mental terms are wholly unlike what you call "pain" and "belief" in yourself. Genuine knowledge of others' minds turns out to be impossible.

I submit that though we began with what seemed like common wisdom, we have been led to a consequence that is absurd. We *can* have knowledge of other people's mental states, often effortlessly so. One can know at a single glance that a complete stranger sees a poisonous snake in his path, is afraid of it, and desires not to get bitten. And when it comes to those we have spent a great deal of time with, we sometimes know their mental condition better than they do. Think of a relative who sincerely denies she is angry when you can easily tell that she is, or a friend who genuinely believes he wants the salad when you know he really wanted the fries. Indeed, part of what we mean by

---

1. Ludwig Wittgenstein (1889–1951), Austrian philosopher. See the selection from Saul Kripke in this chapter.

"angry" is a condition that normally involves a flushed face, furrowed brow, and raised voice, or the often visible effort to refrain from exhibiting these symptoms. When a loved one's anger is written across her face in this way, to insist that we can still only guess at a fundamentally unknowable inner life is to embrace a dubious form of solipsism.[2]

We should conclude instead that at least one of our theses is mistaken. In fact, I will argue that they are all mistaken, and that the common wisdom should be completely uprooted. First, the cases of the raging relative and the gluttonous friend show that [Infallible] is false. [Infallible] can seem undeniable when we use sensations such as "pain" as our guiding example, as we tend to do out of a desire for simplicity. Pain is a state that wears its essence on its sleeve, so to speak, in that *being in pain* and *seeming to be in pain* do not generally come apart. But if we shift our focus to more complicated states, it is easier to see how we could be wrong about ourselves. When it comes to the motives behind the things that we do or what it is in life we truly want, we often need to pay therapists a great deal of money to help us know our own minds. Similarly with our beliefs—a person can think that she believes in God but realize in a sudden epiphany that she has been an atheist for a long time.

Might we replace [Infallible] with a more modest principle that allows for error but preserves the intuition that access to one's own mind is *privileged* over knowledge of other minds?

[Privileged]: Beliefs about one's own mental states are more likely to be true and amount to knowledge than beliefs about others' mental states.

This principle is much more plausible than [Infallible]. But now we must ask what the source of the gaps and errors in self-knowledge might be. If we retain our allegiance to [No Evidence], self-ignorance cannot be the result of misinterpreting or reasoning badly about the data. Nor can it be that we make mistakes because we are merely guessing, since guessing would not satisfy [First-Personal] or be reliable enough to vindicate [Privileged]. Rather, it would have to be that we have a way of subconsciously "sensing" our mental states that is reliable but imperfect, somewhat like the way in which we can sense external objects by using vision.

Let us flesh out what this "inner-sense" hypothesis would mean. Assuming that physicalism[3] is true, this introspective mechanism would have to be realized physically—presumably in the brain. If it delivers results that are sometimes mistaken, this must be because the mental states it is dedicated to detecting (also physically realized) exist independently of being introspected. These mental states and the introspective mechanism would need to stand in a causal relation with one another, akin to the way in which the visual system stands in a causal relation with trees and tables via the reflection of light. The mechanism would causally detect the mental states one is in and deliver that information to conscious awareness, in a way that is generally accurate but that is also subject to breakdowns and mix-ups.[4]

2. **Solipsism** is the view that only oneself exists.

3. **Physicalism** is the view that the mind—and the world in general—is wholly physical.

4. See D. M. Armstrong, "Introspection," this chapter.

Note that the inner-sense view as I have characterized it is an empirical hypothesis, which means that it can be assessed partly on empirical grounds. To date, however, there is no direct empirical evidence of the existence of a mechanism that is dedicated to detecting mental states. This need not prevent us from hypothesizing that it must be there, but this would be an "extravagant" hypothesis, in that it posits a mechanism not needed to explain any data other than our capacity for self-knowledge. In contrast, an "economical" hypothesis would appeal only to capacities that we have good independent reason to believe that we have, and that have more general explanatory power. By this measure, the inner-sense view fares poorly.

Further doubt about the idea of an inner sense emerges when we try to imagine the possibility of a creature who lacks it. After all, just as some creatures who are otherwise intact have a defective capacity for visual perception, it should be possible to have a defective or missing inner-sense mechanism. Such a creature would possess mental concepts such as "belief" and "desire" and would be able to attribute those states to others in the normal way, but would have no special introspective access to her own mind—she would be "self-blind." But in fact, we do not seem to encounter people who are self-blind; indeed, many philosophers have thought that self-blindness is impossible in an otherwise rational creature. This would be difficult to explain if the capacity for self-knowledge depended on a sense mechanism that could well be missing or damaged without impairing any other rational capacities. The impossibility of rational self-blindness is another strike against the inner-sense hypothesis.

[No Evidence] and [First-Personal] are the culprits that led us to consider the inner-sense model, so let us now try giving them up. This frees us to entertain a hypothesis that is extremely economical and easily explains the impossibility of rational self-blindness: the capacity for self-knowledge just is the same capacity for theorizing that we use to know of other minds. As Gilbert Ryle memorably put it, "John Doe's ways of finding out about John Doe are the same as John Doe's ways of finding out about Richard Roe."[5] This hypothesis is economical because it appeals only to capacities that we independently know that we have—competence with mental concepts and the capacity to theorize on the basis of evidence. There is no need to posit a special mechanism dedicated to acquiring self-knowledge. It easily explains the impossibility of self-blindness in a creature who is otherwise rational and conceptually competent because this is all that is required for self-knowledge. We can call this view the "theory-theory" to emphasize the claim that self-knowledge is not based on nothing—it is obtained by theorizing about ourselves in light of evidence.

All parties to the debate should concede that we sometimes achieve self-knowledge by theorizing about ourselves, as the example of visiting a therapist shows. But could all substantive knowledge of our own minds be achieved in this way? Some have interpreted Ryle's remark to mean that we can only find out about our own minds by observing how our bodies are moving around and interacting with the environment (hence the old joke about two Ryleans who meet on the street. The one looks the other up and down and says "You're fine. How am I?"). This version of the view, in

---

5. Gilbert Ryle (1900–1976), English philosopher. The quotation is from Ryle's *The Concept of Mind* (Hutchinson, 1949), 156. A selection from Ryle's book appears in Chapter 7 of this anthology.

which theorizing about the mind is entirely based on behavioral evidence, is woefully inadequate to explain the extent of the self-knowledge we possess. Surely I need not wait to see what my arm is reaching toward to know that I want an apple and intend to eat one. And we can clearly come to know facts about our own minds even when sitting quietly, with no behavior to observe.

What this shows, I think, is that any plausible version of the theory-theory must allow some inputs to theorizing that are not themselves the product of theorizing or sense perception. We must have something to go on other than our circumstances and behavior. This concession may appear to undermine whatever economical advantage the theory-theory initially had, since now some further explanation is needed of our access to these additional data. However, some inputs are cheaper than others. For instance, in addition to speaking out loud, we often engage in "inner speech"—we talk silently to ourselves. We conjure up mental pictures, such as the image of a burrito or one's childhood home, and walk around with songs running through our heads. To allow that these various forms of mental imagery can be inputs into theorizing about ourselves is not especially extravagant, since there is good evidence that inner speech and imagery are produced by the same neural machinery responsible for audible speech and sensory experience. If seeing my arm move toward the apple or hearing myself say "I'm so hungry!" are permissible inputs, it is no big leap to include mental images of apples and silent utterances of "Mmm, lunchtime."

Further, we can draw on somatosensory cues such as pains, nausea, and arousal. The key claim for the theory-theory is that conscious awareness of inner speech, imagery, and certain bodily conditions does not in itself amount to the kind of self-knowledge that is substantive and perplexing, such as knowledge of our attitudes and complex emotions. To know that my stomach is constricted and my heart is pounding is not yet to know whether I am fearful, enraged, or attracted to my neighbor, and to experience a mental image of a burrito is not yet to know that I desire a burrito for lunch. However, these "internal promptings" are good evidence of my attitudes and emotions, just as it would be good evidence that my neighbor desires to eat a burrito if I observed him doodling one. This extra source of information about our own minds that only we (normally) have access to helps explain the truth of [Privileged], as well as the initial appeal of [First-Personal]. We are generally more knowledgeable about our own minds than others are because we have far more evidence, including evidence that others cannot possess.

To be clear, the claim is not that self-knowledge derives entirely from these internal cues. A general theory of mind, autobiographical information, and information about one's current and future circumstances also play important roles. Do I believe there is a table in front of me? A visual experience of a table is generally a sufficient basis for concluding that I do. Do I intend to have breakfast tomorrow morning? I need only consult my normal habits to know that the answer is a resounding "yes." Thinking about what we have most *reason* to do and believe is also enormously helpful, assuming one does not have strong evidence of being an unreasonable person. If I have excellent reason to show up at an important job interview, I can know on that basis that I intend to be there (unless I also know that I tend to sabotage myself in important situations). If I know my evidence overwhelmingly supports the conclusion that climate change is real, I can know on that basis that I believe it is real (unless my behavior of buying coastal real estate strongly suggests otherwise). Finally, social scripts and customs help greatly to narrow down the possibilities that I need to consider. To sum up:

> [Theory-Theory]: All knowledge of our own attitudes and emotions is the product of theorizing about ourselves, usually on the basis of evidence.

Return now to the question of why we would sometimes make mistakes about our own attitudes and emotions, and why someone else might be in a better position to get it right. Unlike views that accept [No Evidence], the theory-theory offers a clear explanation. Erroneous self-attributions will generally be the result of misinterpreting one's evidence, often in ways that are perfectly intelligible. For instance, we would expect people to be prone to misattributing mental states to themselves when their flattering self-conception conflicts with a reality they are reluctant to face. We would also expect that people can be induced to self-attribute states erroneously by providing them with misleading evidence, and this is indeed what we find. In one such study, Western subjects who were prompted to nod their heads while listening to a speech were more likely to report agreement with the speech than those who were prompted to shake their heads. Plausibly, the nodding behavior inclined the subjects to interpret themselves as agreeing with the content of what they heard.

Why have so many taken [No Evidence] to be true, if in reality our access to our own minds is evidence based? To account for this datum, the theory-theory must hold that mental theorizing is normally swift and unconscious (although it can happen at the conscious level). It is akin in this respect to the process by which we understand speech, which often involves complex interpretation. To understand my utterance of the sentence "He saw her duck," you must work out that "he" refers to Gilbert and "she" refers to Aretha, that "duck" is a verb in this sentence and not a noun, and that I meant that she ducked the subway turnstile even though I never said those words. Yet it will normally feel effortless; we are usually unaware of having considered any other possibilities aside from the interpretation we arrived at. It may seem conveniently ad hoc to insist that all this complicated theorizing is going on under the surface of conscious awareness. But as independent support for this claim, we can appeal to experiments like "nodding versus shaking," in which the conditions strongly suggest that the subjects' self-reports are being influenced by what they take to be evidence. Such subjects appear to be completely unaware of this influence; it feels just as spontaneous as any other mental report.

Further, the proposed symmetry between John Doe and Richard Roe is not just a claim about *self*-knowledge. We were led to reject [First-Personal] in part by noticing that knowledge of other minds is often not so difficult to get. Attributions of mental states to others are clearly theory driven, mediated by a general model of human psychology, background knowledge of the person, one's own experience, and observational evidence. And yet it normally feels quite effortless; we need not think long and hard to finish our best friend's sentences or rack our brains to conclude that this person would like a freshly baked chocolate chip cookie. It is thus even less surprising that theorizing about one's own mind feels effortless, since the open possibilities are dramatically narrowed down by the vast amounts of evidence we have in our own case.

Finally, we may have mistakenly taken [No Evidence] to be true because it is presumed by our social customs. From the fact that it is generally *inappropriate* to ask "How do you know?" it does not follow that there is no answer. It might simply be that we have a practice of deferring to a person's claims about her own mind unless there is strong reason to think that something is amiss. None of these considerations conclusively shows that [No Evidence] must be false, but they cast enough doubt on that constraint to render the theory-theory a legitimate contender.

The theory-theory is not without challenges of its own. A potential worry is that it depicts us as being *alienated* from our own attitudes and emotions. If I must theorize about what they are, am I not a mere spectator of my own mind rather than the subject of it? This kind of alienation is certainly exhibited in cases where the evidence reveals us to have a belief, desire, intention, or emotion that we see no good reason to have or that conflicts with our self-conception. It is displayed, for instance, when people are shown experimental data indicating the presence of implicit attitudes that are racist and sexist. At the conscious level, most such people genuinely do not see any good reason to value people differently on the basis of race and sex, and do not think of themselves as bigoted. They are legitimately alienated from the attitudes they attribute to themselves on the basis of theorizing.

However, normal cases will not involve this kind of divergence between your attitudes and your assessment of the reasons to have those attitudes. We will ordinarily take ourselves to have good reason to intend and believe the things we do (even if this is far from true), and will thus have no cause to feel alienated from them in this respect. And as I see it, acceptance of the theory-theory offers relief from a different kind of social alienation. Giving up the idea that our minds are necessarily transparent to us while opaque to others frees us from the loneliness of solipsism, and allows us to reconcile with the fact that we are sometimes opaque to ourselves.

TEST YOUR UNDERSTANDING

1. Which of the following does Paul think are false? (You may select more than one.)

   a. [Theory-Theory]

   b. [No Evidence]

   c. [Infallible]

   d. [First-Personal]

2. What does Paul think about "common wisdom" concerning knowledge of our own minds?

   a. It is probably true.

   b. It implies an absurd conclusion.

   c. It is endorsed by Aretha Franklin.

   d. It implies the inner-sense hypothesis.

3. Does Paul hold that our knowledge of our own minds is exclusively supported by behavioral evidence?

4. Which of the following does Paul appeal to in arguing against the inner-sense hypothesis? (You may select more than one.)

   a. There could be a rational person who was self-blind.

   b. There could not be a rational person who was self-blind.

   c. If there is a mechanism of inner sense, it is in the brain.

   d. If there is a mechanism of inner sense, it only explains our capacity for self-knowledge.

NOTES AND QUESTIONS

1. According to Paul, we often use "internal promptings" as evidence for our beliefs and other attitudes. What are these internal promptings? Is Paul's claim plausible? Even if it is, how do we know about these internal promptings? Isn't our knowledge of them just as puzzling and in need of explanation as our knowledge of our beliefs and other attitudes?

2. Paul tries to explain why we are attracted to [No Evidence], even though, in her view, it is false. Evaluate her explanation.

3. Contemporary accounts of self-knowledge similar to Paul's include Peter Carruthers, *The Opacity of Mind* (Oxford University Press, 2011), and Alison Gopnik, "How We Know Our Own Minds: The Illusion of First-Person Knowledge of Intentionality," *Behavioral and Brain Sciences* 16 (1993): 29–113. See also section 3.3 of Brie Gertler, "Self-Knowledge," in *Stanford Encyclopedia of Philosophy*, ed. Edward Zalta (https://plato.stanford.edu/archives/sum2015/entries/self-knowledge/).

Alex Byrne (b. 1960)

Byrne is Professor of Philosophy at the Massachusetts Institute of Technology. He works mainly in philosophy of mind and epistemology.

SKEPTICISM ABOUT THE INTERNAL WORLD[1]

1. Introduction

You know much about your own mental or psychological life. Perhaps there is some of it that you can only know after years of therapy, but it's easy to know,

---

1. This essay is dedicated to the memory of Fred Dretske. [Byrne's note.]

for example, that you have a headache, that you want water, that you believe that it's raining, and that you see a cat.

Epistemologists (philosophers who study knowledge) have generally concentrated on knowledge of another sort, namely knowledge about your environment that you gain through perception—knowledge that there is water in the glass, that it's raining, that the cat is on the mat, and so on. The chief reason for this focus on "external world" knowledge is the threat of skepticism. There is, it is often said, an apparently compelling argument for "skepticism about the external world," the alarming claim that we do not know anything about our environment. According to the skeptic about the external world, we may know many things about our mental lives, but as to whether there is beer in the fridge or whether the fridge exists at all, we are irremediably ignorant. Because many philosophers think the skeptic's case is hard to answer, they conclude that there is something deeply puzzling about our knowledge of our environment.

I shall argue that this is all back to front. The real puzzle is not how we know about our environment, but how we know about our own minds. The argument for skepticism about the external world has an obvious weak point, but the argument for skepticism about our own minds—skepticism about the "internal world"—is much more difficult to dismiss.

Let us start by discussing a standard argument for skepticism about the external world. Once we have seen how this is not very convincing, we will be in a position to mount a parallel and potentially more powerful argument for skepticism about the internal world.

2. Skepticism about the External World

In his *Meditations*,[2] Descartes considers the possibility that he is not, as he seems to be, sitting by a fire and holding a piece of paper, but instead is in bed enjoying an especially vivid dream. He "sees plainly," he says, "that there are never any sure signs by means of which being awake can be distinguished from being asleep." Accordingly, he (provisionally) concludes that he does not know that he is awake and sitting by the fire.

What goes for Descartes goes for the rest of us, of course. If he is right, I do not know that I am sitting in a chair, balancing a laptop on my knees. And—it is easy to think—he *is* right. After all, if I were vividly dreaming that I am sitting in a chair, things would *seem just the same* as they do when I really am sitting in a chair.

2.1   THE EXTERNAL WORLD SKEPTICAL ARGUMENT EXAMINED

Descartes is not very explicit about why there are no "sure signs" that indicate that he is awake and sitting by the fire, rather than in bed fast asleep. For some assistance, let us turn to a passage from Barry Stroud's classic book *The Significance of Philosophical Scepticism*,[3] in which Stroud draws some lessons from the *Meditations*:

2. See page 264 of this anthology.

3. B. Stroud, *The Significance of Philosophical Scepticism* (Oxford University Press, 1984). [Byrne's note.]

If we are in the predicament Descartes finds himself in at the end of his *First Meditation* we cannot tell by means of the senses whether we are dreaming or not; all the sensory experiences we are having are *compatible with* our merely dreaming. . . . Our knowledge is in that way *confined to our sensory experiences. . . .* There seems to be *no way of going beyond them* to know that the world around us really is this way rather than that. (p. 31, my italics)

To see the significance of the italicized phrases, imagine a detective investigating a murder. Mr. Boddy has been found stabbed in the library with a chef's knife, and Colonel Mustard and Professor Plum are the two suspects. Both men wanted Boddy dead, and both lack alibis for the night of the crime. A witness says he saw a tall man with a mustache enter the library, clutching a large knife. And that's it—the witness cannot be more helpful, there are no fingerprints or incriminating blood stains, nothing. The detective's problem is that *both* Mustard and Plum are tall and mustached. She might sum up her predicament as follows: "The witness's testimony and my other evidence are *compatible with* the hypothesis that Mustard is the murderer, and the rival hypothesis that Plum is the murderer. There *seems to be no way of going beyond this evidence* to know that one hypothesis is correct; my evidence, in other words, does not favor one hypothesis over the other. My knowledge is therefore *confined to my evidence*: I know that the murderer is tall and mustached, and used a chef's knife, but that is all."

So the extract from Stroud suggests the following argument for skepticism about the external world. In general—the argument begins—our evidence for claims or hypotheses about the external world consists in facts about our sensory experiences. For example, your evidence for the hypothesis that you are sitting in a chair is that you seem to see the arms of the chair, seem to feel the pressure of the chair against your back, and so on. This evidence is compatible with other hypotheses; for instance, the hypothesis that you are lying in bed vividly dreaming that you are sitting in a chair. And there seems to be no way of going beyond this evidence to know that one hypothesis is correct. Your evidence, in other words, does not favor the *sitting hypothesis* over the *dreaming hypothesis*, and so you do not know that the sitting hypothesis is true.

It will be useful to set out the argument with numbered premises and a conclusion:

P1.   If you know that the sitting hypothesis is true, you know this solely on the basis of your evidence about your sensory experiences.

P2.   This evidence does not favor the sitting hypothesis over the dreaming hypothesis, and so does not allow you to know that the sitting hypothesis is true.

Hence:

C.   You do not know that the sitting hypothesis is true; that is, you do not know that you are sitting in a chair.

Obviously, this argument generalizes from you to others, and from claims about sitting in a chair to other sorts of external world claims. If it is sound, then everyone is completely ignorant about their environment. Setting aside the issue of whether this is faithful to Descartes's intentions, it is certainly one of the standard arguments for skepticism about the external world.

Since the argument is valid, the only way to avoid the conclusion is to deny one of the premises. And in fact, one premise looks highly suspicious on closer examination, namely P1.[4]

According to P1, if you know that you are sitting in a chair, that knowledge is based on your evidence about your sensory experiences. Now if someone knows a hypothesis *H* on the basis of her evidence *E*, this implies that she has concluded or inferred *H* from *E*, which in turn implies that she knew *E*. For example, if part of the detective's evidence is that no fingerprints were found at the scene, and she knows that the murderer wore gloves on that basis, then the detective must have known that no fingerprints were found at the scene. If the scene was fingerprint free, but for some reason the detective was ignorant of this piece of evidence, then she couldn't have used it as a basis on which to extend her knowledge. As we might put it, if the detective didn't know that no fingerprints were found, this piece of evidence was not part of *her* evidence.[5]

Now consider certain nonhuman animals; for instance, dogs. They have sensory experiences (or so we may suppose), but there is not much reason to think that they *know* that they have sensory experiences. Knowledge of one's own mind requires a sophistication that dogs appear to lack. So if a dog knows that there is a rabbit behind a tree by using its eyes, it is not on the basis of evidence about its sensory experiences. And if evidence about sensory experiences is not needed for a *dog* to have environmental knowledge, it isn't needed for *us* to have environmental knowledge either. You could know that you are sitting in a chair without appealing to evidence about your sensory experiences, and presumably you do. Hence P1 is false.

Not surprisingly, proponents of the argument will have replies to this objection, which we cannot examine here. But whether or not those replies succeed in rescuing P1, at the very least that premise should not strike us as initially plausible. Let us see if the parallel argument for internal world skepticism is any better.

3. Skepticism about the Internal World[6]

Let us start with an example. Suppose you are facing a cat asleep on a mat, the light is good, your visual system is working perfectly, and so on. Then, by using your eyes, you can come to know that the cat is asleep on the mat (or so we think). *What* you know—that the cat is asleep on the mat—has nothing to do with you or your perceptual state. The cat would have been peacefully sleeping whether or not you had been around to notice that fact.

---

4. P2 might also be called into question: see Vogel, "Skepticism and Inference to the Best Explanation." [Byrne's note.] (See page 284 of this anthology.)

5. For a difficult but rewarding discussion of evidence and its relation to knowledge, see T. Williamson, *Knowledge and Its Limits* (Oxford University Press, 2000), chapter 9. [Byrne's note.]

6. The classic presentation of internal world skepticism is in F. Dretske, "How Do You Know You Are Not a Zombie?" in *Privileged Access: Philosophical Accounts of Self-Knowledge*, ed. B. Gertler (Ashgate, 2003), to which this section is much indebted. [Byrne's note.]

Here is a second fact: that *you see* the cat. It is important to realize that this is a very different sort of fact than the first. This fact, unlike the first, *is* about you and your perceptual state. You know the first fact, that the cat is asleep on a mat, by using your eyes. How do you know the second fact, that you *see* the cat? That is not an easy question to answer.

But here is a clue. Suppose I ask you a question that is *not* about you or your perceptual state: "Is a cat here?" You may answer by attending to the scene before your eyes: "Yes, there's a cat, asleep on the mat." Now suppose I ask you a question that *is* about you and your perceptual state: "Do you see a cat?" Is your way of answering that second question much different from the way you answered the first question? That is, don't you answer the second question *also* by *looking*? And looking is, apparently, *all* you need to do. If there's a cat right there, then you don't need any further information to answer confidently "Yes, I do see a cat."

Since this point is absolutely crucial for what follows, we should dwell on it for a moment. Consider the following example. You are reading a newspaper story about last night's baseball game, in which the Red Sox came back in the bottom of the ninth to squeak out a victory over the Yankees. If the story is sufficiently interesting, the newspaper itself will fade into the background: you will be preoccupied with the message, not the medium. If I ask you "Were the bases loaded?" you will not be thinking about the newspaper font or the color of the page. But of course you can always shift your attention back from the message (the details of the game) to the medium (the newspaper). And indeed you must, if I ask you "Is the story printed in two columns?" or "Are you reading about the game in a newspaper?" To answer those questions, you have to turn your attention from the home run with the bases loaded to something quite different—paper and ink, held in your hands. In other words, you can't know *that you are reading about the game* just by attending to *the game*.

The point is that the newspaper example is *not* a good model for how you know you see something. That is, if I ask you "Do you see a cat?" you do *not* have to attend to something that is analogous to the newspaper (perhaps a "sensory experience" or a "visual sensation"). When you read about the Red Sox, you don't just find facts about baseball, you also find the newspaper. But when you open your eyes, your seeing is in a way invisible. What you initially find is the *world*, not your *seeing* of the world.[7]

This suggests that in order to know *that* you see, you must somehow reach that conclusion from *what* you see. In other words, the evidence you use to find out that you see something is simply evidence about *your visual environment*, your environment as revealed to you by your sense of sight. That evidence includes facts about the cat (e.g., that it is black and furry) and the cat's spatial relation to you (e.g., that you are facing it).

Now if someone claims to know hypothesis H on the basis of evidence E, one can challenge whether E really is good enough evidence for H by formulating a rival hypothesis H^* that seems to be equally well supported by E. This happens all the time

---

7. For a much earlier version of the newspaper example, used to argue for (something close to) the *opposite* conclusion, see C. D. Broad, *Scientific Thought* (Kegan Paul, Trench Trubner & Co., 1927), 247. [Byrne's note.]

in science and everyday life and was the basic idea of the external world skeptical argument, using the dreaming hypothesis as the alternative. But what hypothesis should we oppose to the *seeing hypothesis*, that you see a cat?

For maximum vividness and generality, we can make the alternative hypothesis as radical as can be. Consider the hypothesis that you do not have a mind at all. Outwardly, you look and behave just as a minded person does, but really all is dark within: you do not see anything, think or believe or want or feel anything, and so on. So, in particular, you do not see the cat, despite its being (say) a few feet away in front of you in broad daylight. Call this the *mindless hypothesis*.

Now your evidence about your visual environment—that the cat is black and furry, that you are facing it a few feet away in broad daylight, and other similar pieces of evidence—are compatible with both the seeing hypothesis and the rival mindless hypothesis. Offhand, it is not clear at all why this evidence favors the seeing hypothesis over the mindless hypothesis. Compare our earlier discussion of external world skepticism: if you agree that your evidence about your sensory experiences doesn't favor the sitting hypothesis over the dreaming hypothesis, then the parallel move for internal world skepticism should seem hard to resist. And if the evidence you have for the seeing hypothesis doesn't favor it over the mindless hypothesis, you don't know that the seeing hypothesis is true—you don't know that you see a cat.

We can now set out our parallel argument with numbered premises and a conclusion:

P1*.   If you know that the seeing hypothesis is true, you know this solely on the basis of your evidence about your environment.

P2*.   This evidence does not favor the seeing hypothesis over the mindless hypothesis, and so does not allow you to know that the seeing hypothesis is true.

Hence:

C*.   You do not know that the seeing hypothesis is true; that is, you do not know that you see a cat.

Notice that P1* seems more secure than P1. P1* was defended by reflection on how we actually go about discovering that we see things like cats and is immune to the dog objection at the end of the previous section. If P1 is defensible at all, its defense is less straightforward.

So far, so good, but how is the argument supposed to generalize to *all* mental states? It is fairly easy to see how the argument of the previous section generalizes—that's why it amounts to an argument for skepticism about *the external world*, rather than merely for skepticism about *sitting*. P1 seems no less plausible if we replace "the sitting hypothesis" by "the hypothesis that it's raining," or "the hypothesis that the earth is round," and so on. But now consider various other hypotheses about your mental life, say:

The *believing* hypothesis: that you believe that the cat is asleep on the mat
The *liking* hypothesis: that you like chocolate
The *feeling* hypothesis: that you feel a twinge in your elbow

Are the corresponding versions of P1* at all plausible? Perhaps surprisingly, a case can be made that they are. Take the believing hypothesis first. On the face of it, your way of answering the question "Do you *believe* that the cat is asleep on the mat?" (a question about your own mind) is not much different from your way of answering the very different question "Is the cat asleep on the mat?" In both cases you consider the cat, its state of wakefulness, and its relation to the mat, not your own mind. Once you have good evidence that the cat *is* asleep on the mat, then that is *all* you need to conclude that you *believe* that the cat is asleep on the mat.[8]

Now take the liking hypothesis. Why do you think you like chocolate? Isn't the answer something about *the chocolate*? You like chocolate because it *tastes good*. That is a fact about the chocolate, not about you. When you savor a piece of chocolate on your tongue, your sensory systems are detecting features of the chocolate, in particular its agreeable sweet taste. On the basis of this evidence *about the chocolate*, you conclude that *you like* it.

Finally, the feeling hypothesis. Surely here the corresponding version of P1* is obviously wrong! Well, that's right, if the "environment" is taken to be the environment *external* to your body, but there is no reason to adopt such a narrow construal. Your body is as much a part of your physical environment as the cat and the piece of chocolate. So consider the question "Do you feel a twinge in your elbow?" How do you go about answering it? By examining your own mind, wherever that is? No, by examining *the elbow*, of course. If there is the sort of disturbance in the elbow that has the character of a twinge (rather than a dull ache, for example), then you will answer "Yes, I do feel a twinge in my elbow."[9]

Of course, this is only a sketch of an argument for a fully general skepticism about the internal world. But let's assume that the details can be filled out. Does the argument face any obvious objections?

4. Two Objections

It is easy enough to feel the pull of the skeptic's claim that you can't rule out the hypothesis that you are dreaming. Many books and movies trade on this idea. It is considerably harder to see the force of skepticism about the *internal* world—the claim that you don't know that you have a mind might understandably strike you as too absurd to be worth discussing. Still, philosophy does not progress by dismissing arguments for absurd conclusions, but by carefully explaining where they go awry.

---

8. For an in-depth examination of this idea, see R. Moran, *Authority and Estrangement* (Princeton University Press, 2001). [Byrne's note.]

9. It is clear that the corresponding version of P2* is plausible for the *believing* hypothesis: How could the evidence that the cat is on the mat favor the believing hypothesis over the mindless hypothesis? The cat would be on the mat whether you believed it or not. (*Exercise:* Are the corresponding versions of P2* as plausible for the liking and feeling hypotheses?) (See also pp. 4–6 of the paper by Dretske cited in footnote 6.) [Byrne's note.]

Let's consider two objections. Seeing why neither works will help clarify the skeptical argument and indicate that diagnosing its flaws is no easy matter.

The first objection is that something must have gone badly wrong with the argument because the mindless hypothesis is incoherent. According to the mindless hypothesis, the objection runs, it *seems* to you that you have a mental life. It seems to you that you see, believe, desire, and so forth—even though you do not. But if it seems to you that such-and-such, then you are *not* mindless, because seemings *are* mental states. If it seems to you that you see a cat, then you might not be seeing a cat, but you certainly have a mind.

This objection rests on a simple confusion. If you find it tempting, then you have failed to grasp just how outlandish the mindless hypothesis really is. According to the mindless hypothesis, it does *not* seem to you that you see a cat, for exactly the reason given in the objection. If the mindless hypothesis is right, you do not perceive, believe, or desire, and *neither does it seem to you that you see, believe, or desire.* The mindless hypothesis is not incoherent—at least, not in the way the first objection claims. So it is not misleadingly named: in the mindless scenario you are facing the cat with your eyes open, yet you seem to see nothing.

The second objection also rests on a confusion, but this time it is more subtle. Return to the argument for external world skepticism and the skeptic's claim that your knowledge is confined to evidence about your sensory experiences: there is no way of "going beyond" this evidence to know what the external world is like. If the argument for internal world skepticism is parallel, the internal world skeptic should presumably say something similar; namely, your knowledge is confined to *evidence about your environment*—there is no way of going beyond this evidence to know what the *internal* world is like. But wait: if the skeptic concedes that you *know* something, then the mindless hypothesis is false! (You can't know something if you don't have a mind.)

All that is quite correct, but it does not affect the argument. The skeptic is *not* arguing that the mindless hypothesis is *true*, but rather that *you do not know that it is false.* If it is false, then you do have a mind, and in particular you know various things about your environment. But, according to the skeptic, that is *all* you know—you can't "go beyond" this evidence to know what your mental life is like.

The second objection does highlight one difference between external and internal world skepticism. The external world skeptic will allow that you have knowledge of some evidence (namely, evidence about your sensory experiences) if the dreaming hypothesis is true. In contrast, the internal world skeptic will *not* allow that you have *any* knowledge if the mindless hypothesis is true. That difference does not spoil the parallel between the two arguments, however.

The point of this article is not to convince you that you don't know anything about your own mind. Rather, the point is to highlight the problem of self-knowledge. We surely know a lot about our own minds—yet it is obscure how this is possible. Our knowledge of *cats* is quite well understood; our knowledge that we *see* cats, in contrast, remains a mystery.

TEST YOUR UNDERSTANDING

1. Does Byrne think that external world skepticism is a profoundly difficult philosophical problem?

2. Does Byrne think that in order to answer the question "What do you see?" there is no need to turn your attention to your sensory experience?

3. Byrne thinks that P1 faces an objection that P1* does not. What is it?

4. Does the skeptic about the external world argue that you don't have a hand? Does the skeptic about the internal world argue that you don't see a hand? If they aren't arguing for these conclusions, what conclusions are they arguing for instead?

NOTES AND QUESTIONS

1. If we say that a zombie is a creature who looks and behaves like a normal human being but who has no mind at all, then Byrne's "mindless hypothesis" can be put as follows: you are a zombie. Consider the following suggestion:

   > It is true that besides seeing objects in the world, you see these objects from a point of view. There is a perspective we have on the world, a "boundary," if you will, between things we see and things we don't see. And of the things we see, there are parts (surfaces) we see and parts (surfaces) we don't see. This partition determines a point of view that changes as we move around. Since zombies don't have points of view, it may be thought that this is our way of knowing we are not zombies. Although everything we see exists in the world of a zombie, what does not exist in the world of a zombie is this egocentric partition, this boundary, between things (and surfaces) we see and things (and surfaces) we don't see, and the fact that there is, for us, this point of view, this perspective, is what tells us we are not zombies.[10]

   Is this a way in which one could come to know that Byrne's "seeing hypothesis" is true, and so that the mindless hypothesis is false?

2. Some philosophers have attempted to explain how one can know of one's mental states (or at least some of them) by attending to one's environment; for instance, how one can know that one *sees* a cat by attending to *the cat*. This is called the *transparency* view. The transparency view comes in many different varieties; a recent defense of one version is Jordi Fernández, *Transparent Minds: A Study of Self-Knowledge* (Oxford University Press, 2013). For criticisms of this approach, see chapter 6 of Brie Gertler, *Self-Knowledge* (Routledge, 2011), and section 3.5 of Gertler, "Self-Knowledge," in *Stanford Encyclopedia of Philosophy*, ed. Edward Zalta (https://plato.stanford.edu /archives/sum2015/entries/self-knowledge).

10. Fred Dretske, "How Do You Know You Are Not a Zombie?" in *Privileged Access: Philosophical Accounts of Self-Knowledge*, ed. B. Gertler (Ashgate, 2003), 2.

ANALYZING THE ARGUMENTS

1. Here is one version of an analogical argument for the existence of other minds:

    P1. I have a mind and a body.

    P2. Others have bodies.

    C.   Others have minds.

    This argument is not very persuasive. Why not? How should the analogical argument for the existence of other minds be set out so that it is as persuasive as possible?

2. Suppose you are wondering whether I have a mind, and if so what my mental life is like. Is the fact that I am biologically similar to you an important piece of evidence? Is the fact that I appear to speak a language you can understand an important piece of evidence? Is the fact that I move around and interact with my environment in a similar way to you an important piece of evidence? In addressing these questions, use a variety of examples in which some of these features are absent: languageless chimpanzees, talking space aliens, immobile computers, and so forth.

3. Search on the Internet for "Heider and Simmel video." You should find a short (1:40) video showing two triangles and a circle moving in and around a box with a door. (This video was used in a series of famous experiments reported in Fritz Heider and Marianne Simmel, "An Experimental Study of Apparent Behavior," *American Journal of Psychology* 57 [1944]: 243–59.)

    Watch the video and write a paragraph describing what you saw. If you are like most of the subjects studied by Heider and Simmel, you will have described what you saw using psychological vocabulary. Does this support the view that we can directly observe what others are thinking, feeling, and intentionally doing, so that no "argument by analogy" is needed?

4. How well do we know our own minds? Is it significantly easier to know our own minds than it is to know the minds of others? Are there cases where it is easier to know someone else's mind than one's own? In answering these questions, consider a wide range of examples: perception (vision, audition), sensation (pain, dizziness), emotion (anger, disgust, pride), mood (depression, anxiety), imagining, believing, wanting, hoping, and so on.

5. Consider the following four principles. For all subjects S:

    i-b.   If S is in pain, S believes she is in pain.

    i-k.   If S is in pain, S knows she is in pain.

    ii-b. If S believes she is in pain, S is in pain.

    ii-k. If S knows she is in pain, S is in pain.

    Assume that knowing p **entails** believing p. Does i-b entail i-k? Does i-b entail ii-b? Does i-b entail ii-k? Answer similar questions for the other possibilities. Three of these principles are controversial; one is uncontroversial. Which is the uncontroversial one? Formulate similar principles for the mental state of *believing that it is raining*. Are they as plausible? A creature (say, a dog) might have beliefs but not have the conceptual capacity to think about its mental life. If that's right, some of the four principles are false. Which ones? Can you amend the false principles to avoid this problem?

6. In his *Essay Concerning Human Understanding* (1689), John Locke describes a case in which "by the different Structure of our Organs, it were so ordered, That *the same Object should produce in several Men's Minds different* Ideas at the same time; [for example] if the *Idea*, that a *Violet* produced in one Man's Mind by his Eyes, were the same that a *Marigold* produces in another Man's, and *vice versâ*" (book 2, chapter 32, section 15).

   Locke is imagining a situation like this: ripe tomatoes, strawberries, and Elmo look to me the way grass, guacamole, and Kermit the Frog do to you, and vice versa. This is a so-called *inverted spectrum scenario*. Do you know that I am not spectrum inverted with respect to you? Suppose you ask me how tomatoes look to me, and I reply "They look red." You might think that helps, because presumably I know how tomatoes look to me and am perfectly capable of communicating that piece of knowledge to you. And if you know that tomatoes look red to me, since you know that tomatoes look red to you, you know that they look red to both of us. However, you might think that this linguistic evidence shows nothing, because if we *were* spectrum inverted, I would have replied in the same way. This is because if we were spectrum inverted, you would have come to associate the word "red" with the "reddish" sensations tomatoes produce in you, and I would have come to associate the word "red" with the "greenish" sensations tomatoes produce in me, with the result that we use the word similarly. Does linguistic evidence help? Could there be behavioral evidence of any other kind that would count against the spectrum inversion hypothesis? Could neuroscience somehow settle the question?

How Can We Know about the External World?

You know that the earth is round, that penguins inhabit Antarctica, that trees shed their leaves in the fall, that you have a heart, and so on and so on. In other words, you know a lot about the "external world," including your own body.[1] That much is obvious.

Or is it? Consider the hypothesis that your entire life has been a remarkably vivid dream. Not only have you been dreaming the whole time, but the earth never existed. No penguins, trees, nothing like that. In fact, you don't even have a heart. You are a heartless android, lying comatose in a robot junkyard on a planet orbiting the star Kepler-11. "From the inside," things seem exactly the same to you: you seem to see this page, you seem to remember that penguins inhabit Antarctica, and so on, even though there is no page, and no Antarctica. So how can you know that this "android hypothesis" is false? That question can seem very difficult to answer, which suggests that you *can't* know that the android hypothesis is false.

This claim of ignorance might not seem so bad by itself, but once it is conceded, it is difficult to stop ignorance from spreading much more widely. Take, for example, one thing that you apparently know; namely, that penguins inhabit Antarctica. Now the claim that penguins inhabit Antarctica straightforwardly **entails** that the android hypothesis is false. If penguins inhabit Antarctica, you are *not* a dreaming android who lives in a penguin-free world. So, *if* you know that penguins inhabit Antarctica, you can perform an elementary logical inference and come to know that the android hypothesis is false. So, if you *can't* know that the android hypothesis is false, you don't know that penguins inhabit Antarctica. By the same **argument**,

---

1. This kind of knowledge is called **propositional knowledge**, or *factual knowledge*. See the introduction to Chapter 3, "What Is Knowledge?"

neither do you know that the earth is round, that trees shed their leaves in the fall, and so on. In short, if you can't know that the android hypothesis is false, you are completely ignorant about the external world; that is, *external world* **skepticism** is true. (A *skeptic* about some subject matter *M* is someone who denies that we have knowledge about *M*.)

Still, you might wonder whether even external world skepticism is worth worrying about. Suppose you're offered a choice between going on a roller coaster ride and entering the roller coaster simulator. The simulator is perfect: as far as excitement goes, it's just as good as the real thing, although you aren't really rattling down a narrow track at 100 mph. The choice doesn't seem to matter much (actually, you might even prefer the simulator on the grounds that it's much safer). Here, virtual reality is no worse than reality itself. Isn't that true in general? Why care whether you're a dreaming android? The thrills and spills of life would be the same in any case.

But this reaction is overly complacent. The dreaming android has no friends, has no mother who loves it, and has never accomplished anything—vividly dreaming that you are acing your final exams is not a way of doing well in school. Having friends, to say nothing of a mother who loves you, is a valuable thing. (Imagine discovering that someone whom you thought a faithful friend was just pretending.) So if you are a dreaming android, you are in a very unfortunate predicament—friendless, unloved, and unaccomplished. You should want to be reassured that you are *not* in this predicament. That is, you should want to *know* that you have friends, are loved, and so forth. If external world skepticism is true, reassurance that your life is not an empty sham is forever beyond your reach.

The readings in this chapter respond to the threat of skepticism about the external world. (One exception, as we will see below, is the essay by Rae Langton.) Before getting to the many different responses, it will help to set out the argument for the skeptical conclusion more precisely. And in the course of doing that, we will see how the argument is a particular instance of a general form of skeptical argument.

A General Skeptical Argument

Let a *skeptical hypothesis* be a hypothesis according to which the world is different from how you take it to be. We have already seen one skeptical hypothesis, according to which you're a dreaming android and the earth never existed. There are other similar skeptical hypotheses, the most famous of which is René Descartes's *demon hypothesis*: "some malicious demon of the utmost power and cunning has employed all his energies in order to deceive me." The contemporary version of the demon hypothesis is the *brain in a vat hypothesis*: you are a brain kept alive in a vat by some evil scientist and stimulated so that "from the inside" things seem exactly as if you see this page, and so on.

These hypotheses are *global* skeptical hypotheses; that is, if they are true, almost *nothing* you take yourself to know about the external world is true. But skeptical hypotheses can be more modest. Indeed, in an everyday situation in which you wonder whether you really are right to think that you left your laptop at home, you are entertaining a very modest skeptical hypothesis—that the world is very similar to the way you take it to be, except that your laptop is not at home. Philosophers have devised many other skeptical hypotheses that are intermediate in strength between global skeptical hypotheses and very modest skeptical hypotheses like the one just mentioned.

For instance, there is the *no other minds hypothesis*, according to which you are the only creature with a mind—everyone else behaves just *as if* they believe, feel, and perceive but are actually entirely mindless (see Saul Kripke's "Wittgenstein and Other Minds" in Chapter 5). And there is the *unexpected future hypothesis*, according to which the future is radically different from the past—if this hypothesis is true, bread will not nourish tomorrow, the sun will not rise tomorrow, and so on (see the introduction to Chapter 4, "How Can We Know about What We Have Not Observed?").

Now take a skeptical hypothesis SH, and any claim *p* that entails that SH is false. We can argue that you don't know *p* as follows:

1. If you know *p*, you can know that SH is false.

2. You can't know that SH is false.

So:

3. You don't know *p*.

For example, suppose you think (*p*) that your bike is where you left it, padlocked to a bike rack. Let SH be the modest skeptical hypothesis that your bike has been stolen. The claim *p* (your bike is where you left it) entails that SH (your bike has been stolen) is false, in other words that your bike has not been stolen. So we can argue that you don't know that your bike is where you left it as follows:

1†. If you know that your bike is where you left it, you can know that your bike has not been stolen.

2†. You can't know that your bike has not been stolen.

So:

3†. You don't know that your bike is where you left it.

This form of argument—If *P* then *Q*, it is not the case that *Q*, so it is not the case that *P*—is called **modus tollens**.

Let us look more carefully at **premise** 1. Suppose you know that all fish have gills and that Wanda is a fish. Now the statement that all fish have gills and Wanda is a fish entails that Wanda has gills. So you are now in a position to draw the conclusion that Wanda has gills from what you already know. And if you go ahead and do that, it seems very plausible that you will end up *knowing* that Wanda has gills. In general, one way to extend our knowledge is to trace out the **logical consequences** of what we already know: this happens whenever someone proves a theorem in mathematics, for example. Put more precisely: if *p* entails (or logically implies) *q*, and you know *p*, then you are in a position to know *q*. This is (one version of) a principle called **closure**.

Given closure, premise 1 of the skeptical argument is true. Closure is difficult to deny and the argument is **valid**, so when faced with a skeptical argument of this form you have two options: deny premise 2 or accept the conclusion.[2]

We can generate an argument for external world skepticism by letting SH be a global skeptical hypothesis, say, Descartes's demon hypothesis, and letting *p* be any claim about the external world that entails that the demon hypothesis is false, say, that the earth is round:

1*. If you know that the earth is round, you can know that the demon hypothesis is false.

2*. You can't know that the demon hypothesis is false.

So:

3*. You don't know that the earth is round.

Again, assuming closure, there are two options: deny premise 2* or accept 3*, the skeptical conclusion.

Responses to External World Skepticism

The readings from David Hume, G. E. Moore, and Jonathan Vogel offer contrasting responses to external world skepticism.[3]

According to Hume, our senses provide scant evidence for hypotheses about the external world. In a paragraph omitted from the selection he writes: "'Tis impossible . . . that from the existence or any of the qualities of [perceptions], we can ever form any conclusion concerning the existence of [objects]." So Hume is a (rare) example of a real-life skeptic: he accepts the conclusion of the skeptical argument. His main concern is not so much to defend skepticism (which he thinks is pretty much unassailable) but rather to give a psychological explanation for why we think that there is an external world of familiar tables, chairs, penguins, and so on, even though we have no good reason for doing so.

---

2. In fact, despite the plausibility of closure, some philosophers deny it. A notable example is Robert Nozick: see his *Philosophical Explanations* (Harvard University Press, 1981), chapter 3. But none of the contributors to this chapter deny it. See "Analyzing the Arguments" at the end of this chapter.

3. You can find another response by Stewart Cohen at http://digital.wwnorton.com/introphilosophy2.

Vogel, in effect, directly replies to Hume. While Hume thinks that our senses cannot show us that we are not brains in vats or deceived by an evil demon, Vogel thinks otherwise, and so denies the second premise. Vogel argues that the "real world hypothesis"—that the earth is round, you have a head, are reading this book, and so on—provides a much better explanation of your "sensory experiences" (or, in Hume's terminology, "perceptions") than any global skeptical hypothesis. So you have a good reason to believe the real world hypothesis by an "inference to the best explanation."[4]

Moore is principally concerned to deny the conclusion of the skeptical argument, rather than to explain which premise is false. He tries to turn the tables on the skeptic by offering what he claims is a *proof* of the existence of things like tables and books. For example: here is a book (Moore holds up a copy of this book), here is another book (Moore holds up a copy of his own famous book on ethics, *Principia Ethica*), therefore books exist. Of course, the skeptic will not grant that this is a proof, on the grounds that Moore does not know the premises. But, as Moore points out, in ordinary life we take arguments of this sort "as absolutely conclusive proofs of certain conclusions." For instance, we allow that someone can prove that there are at least three misprints on a page from the premises "There's one misprint here, another there, and another here." And if we really can prove such things, we must have knowledge about the external world. Why isn't the skeptic just being unreasonable in rejecting Moore's proof?

Kantian Skepticism

Rae Langton's essay defends a limited but nonetheless fascinating form of skepticism, which she finds suggested by the work of the German philosopher Immanuel Kant (1724–1804). This Kantian skepticism (or "Kantian humility," as Langton calls it) is not external world skepticism. As both Moore and Langton note, Kant thought we had plenty of knowledge about the external world.

However, in his *Critique of Pure Reason*, Kant argues for another kind of skepticism: as he put it, we have no knowledge of "things in themselves." What did he mean by that? Langton offers an answer, and a defense of a kind of skepticism that she thinks is at least in the spirit of Kant's actual view. According to Langton, the physical sciences can only penetrate so far into reality: there is a layer further down that is in principle beyond their reach. If that is right, then although we can know that there are books, and that we have friends, ignorance of the fundamental nature of the world is part of the human condition.

---

4. For more on this kind of inference, see Gilbert Harman, "The Inference to the Best Explanation," in Chapter 4 of this anthology.

René Descartes (1596–1650)

Descartes was a French philosopher, mathematician, and scientist. He made important early contributions to mathematical physics, invented the Cartesian coordinate system familiar from high school geometry, and is widely regarded as "the founder of modern philosophy." The *Meditations on First Philosophy* (1641) is his most famous book; his other major works include *Principles of Philosophy* (1644) and *The Passions of the Soul* (1649).

MEDITATION I: WHAT CAN BE CALLED INTO DOUBT
from *Meditations on First Philosophy*

Some years ago I was struck by the large number of falsehoods that I had accepted as true in my childhood, and by the highly doubtful nature of the whole edifice that I had subsequently based on them. I realized that it was necessary, once in the course of my life, to demolish everything completely and start again right from the foundations if I wanted to establish anything at all in the sciences that was stable and likely to last. But the task looked an enormous one, and I began to wait until I should reach a mature enough age to ensure that no subsequent time of life would be more suitable for tackling such inquiries. This led me to put the project off for so long that I would now be to blame if by pondering over it any further I wasted the time still left for carrying it out. So today I have expressly rid my mind of all worries and arranged for myself a clear stretch of free time. I am here quite alone, and at last I will devote myself sincerely and without reservation to the general demolition of my opinions.

But to accomplish this, it will not be necessary for me to show that all my opinions are false, which is something I could perhaps never manage. Reason now leads me to think that I should hold back my assent from opinions which are not completely certain and indubitable just as carefully as I do from those which are patently false. So, for the purpose of rejecting all my opinions, it will be enough if I find in each of them at least some reason for doubt. And to do this I will not need to run through them all individually, which would be an endless task. Once the foundations of a building are undermined, anything built on them collapses of its own accord; so I will go straight for the basic principles on which all my former beliefs rested.

Whatever I have up till now accepted as most true I have acquired either from the senses or through the senses. But from time to time I have found that the senses deceive, and it is prudent never to trust completely those who have deceived us even once.

Yet although the senses occasionally deceive us with respect to objects which are very small or in the distance, there are many other beliefs about which doubt is quite impossible, even though they are derived from the senses—for example, that I am here, sitting by the fire, wearing a winter dressing-gown, holding this piece of paper in my hands, and so on. Again, how could it be denied that these hands or this whole body are mine? Unless perhaps I were to liken myself to madmen, whose brains are so damaged by the persistent vapours of melancholia that they firmly maintain they are kings when they are paupers, or say they are dressed in purple when they are naked, or that their heads are made of earthenware, or that they are pumpkins, or made of glass. But such people are insane, and I would be thought equally mad if I took anything from them as a model for myself.

A brilliant piece of reasoning! As if I were not a man who sleeps at night, and regularly has all the same experiences while asleep as madmen do when awake—indeed sometimes even more improbable ones. How often, asleep at night, am I convinced of just such familiar events—that I am here in my dressing-gown, sitting by the fire—when in fact I am lying undressed in bed! Yet at the moment my eyes are certainly wide awake when I look at this piece of paper; I shake my head and it is not asleep; as I stretch out and feel my hand I do so deliberately, and I know what I am doing. All this would not happen with such distinctness to someone asleep. Indeed! As if I did not remember other occasions when I have been tricked by exactly similar thoughts while asleep! As I think about this more carefully, I see plainly that there are never any sure signs by means of which being awake can be distinguished from being asleep. The result is that I begin to feel dazed, and this very feeling only reinforces the notion that I may be asleep.

Suppose then that I am dreaming, and that these particulars—that my eyes are open, that I am moving my head and stretching out my hands—are not true. Perhaps, indeed, I do not even have such hands or such a body at all. Nonetheless, it must surely be admitted that the visions which come in sleep are like paintings, which must have been fashioned in the likeness of things that are real, and hence that at least these general kinds of things—eyes, head, hands and the body as a whole—are things which are not imaginary but are real and exist. For even when painters try to create sirens and satyrs with the most extraordinary bodies, they cannot give them natures which are new in all respects; they simply jumble up the limbs of different animals. Or if perhaps they manage to think up something so new that nothing remotely similar has ever been seen before—something which is therefore completely fictitious and unreal—at least the colours used in the composition must be real. By similar reasoning, although these general kinds of things—eyes, head, hands and so on—could be imaginary, it must at least be admitted that certain other even simpler and more universal things are real. These are as it were the real colours from which we form all the images of things, whether true or false, that occur in our thought.

This class appears to include corporeal nature in general, and its extension; the shape of extended things; the quantity, or size and number of these things; the place in which they may exist, the time through which they may endure, and so on.

So a reasonable conclusion from this might be that physics, astronomy, medicine, and all other disciplines which depend on the study of composite things, are doubtful; while arithmetic, geometry and other subjects of this kind, which deal only with the simplest and most general things, regardless of whether they really exist in nature or not, contain something certain and indubitable. For whether I am awake or asleep, two and three added together are five, and a square has no more than four sides. It seems impossible that such transparent truths should incur any suspicion of being false.

And yet firmly rooted in my mind is the long-standing opinion that there is an omnipotent God who made me the kind of creature that I am. How do I know that he has not brought it about that there is no earth, no sky, no extended thing, no shape, no size, no place, while at the same time ensuring that all these things appear to me to exist just as they do now? What is more, since I sometimes believe that others go astray in cases where they think they have the most perfect knowledge, may I not similarly go wrong every time I add two and three or count the sides of a square, or in some even simpler matter, if that is imaginable? But perhaps God would not have allowed me to be deceived in this way, since he is said to be supremely good. But if it were inconsistent with his goodness to have created me such that I am deceived all the time, it would seem equally foreign to his goodness to allow me to be deceived even occasionally; yet this last assertion cannot be made.

Perhaps there may be some who would prefer to deny the existence of so powerful a God rather than believe that everything else is uncertain. Let us not argue with them, but grant them that everything said about God is a fiction. According to their supposition, then, I have arrived at my present state by fate or chance or a continuous chain of events, or by some other means; yet since deception and error seem to be imperfections, the less powerful they make my original cause, the more likely it is that I am so imperfect as to be deceived all the time. I have no answer to these arguments, but am finally compelled to admit that there is not one of my former beliefs about which a doubt may not properly be raised; and this is not a flippant or ill-considered conclusion, but is based on powerful and well thought-out reasons. So in future I must withhold my assent from these former beliefs just as carefully as I would from obvious falsehoods, if I want to discover any certainty.

But it is not enough merely to have noticed this; I must make an effort to remember it. My habitual opinions keep coming back, and, despite my wishes, they capture my belief, which is as it were bound over to them as a result of long occupation and the law of custom. I shall never get out of the habit of confidently assenting to these opinions, so long as I suppose them to be what in fact they are, namely highly probable opinions—opinions which, despite the fact that they are in a sense doubtful, as has just been shown, it is still much more reasonable to believe than to deny. In view of this, I think it will be a good plan to turn my will in completely the opposite direction and deceive myself, by pretending for a time that these former opinions are utterly false and imaginary. I shall do this until the weight of preconceived opinion is counter-balanced and the distorting influence of habit no longer prevents my judgement from perceiving things correctly. In the meantime, I know that no danger or error will result from my plan, and that I cannot possibly go too far in my distrustful attitude. This is because the task now in hand does not involve action but merely the acquisition of knowledge.

I will suppose therefore that not God, who is supremely good and the source of truth, but rather some malicious demon of the utmost power and cunning has employed all his energies in order to deceive me. I shall think that the sky, the air, the earth, colours, shapes, sounds and all external things are merely the delusions of dreams which he has devised to ensnare my judgement. I shall consider myself as not having hands or eyes, or flesh, or blood or senses, but as falsely believing that I have all these things. I shall stubbornly and firmly persist in this meditation; and, even if it is not in my power to know any truth, I shall at least do what is in my power, that is, resolutely guard against assenting to any falsehoods, so that the deceiver, however powerful and cunning he may be, will be unable to impose on me in the slightest degree. But this is an arduous undertaking, and a kind of laziness brings me back to normal life. I am like a prisoner who is enjoying an imaginary freedom while asleep; as he begins to suspect that he is asleep, he dreads being woken up, and goes along with the pleasant illusion as long as he can. In the same way, I happily slide back into my old opinions and dread being shaken out of them, for fear that my peaceful sleep may be followed by hard labour when I wake, and that I shall have to toil not in the light, but amid the inextricable darkness of the problems I have now raised.

TEST YOUR UNDERSTANDING

1. Does Descartes think he cannot doubt that he is "here, sitting by the fire, wearing a winter dressing-gown"?

2. Why does Descartes switch from considering the hypothesis that he might be dreaming to considering the hypothesis that God, or a malicious demon, is deceiving him?

3. Does Descartes think he cannot doubt that $2 + 3 = 5$?

4. Do the (provisional) conclusions of Meditation I include the following?

    a. A demon has deceived Descartes into believing that he has hands.

    b. Descartes doesn't know that he has hands.

READER'S GUIDE

Descartes's Meditations

The *Meditations* has this ambitious subtitle: "Wherein are demonstrated the Existence of God and the Distinction of Soul from Body." It has six chapters ("meditations"), and this anthology contains Meditation I, Meditation II, and part of Meditation VI. To put these selections in context, here is an outline of the book.

Meditation I

Descartes investigates which of his opinions can be "called into doubt," principally by considering the possibility that he is dreaming and the possibility that an evil demon is deceiving him. Alarmingly, he ends up concluding that pretty much all of them can be.

Meditation II

Descartes finds something that he cannot doubt: that he exists. But what kind of thing is he? He argues that he is "a thing that thinks." Using the example of a piece of wax, he argues that perception only gives us a confused understanding of physical objects and that he knows his mind much better than he knows his body.

Meditation III

Descartes examines whether "there is a God, and, if there is, whether he can be a deceiver." He argues that the only cause of his idea of God could be God Himself: "I recognize that it would be impossible for me to exist with the kind of nature I have—that is, having within me the idea of God—were it not the case that God really existed." Further, God is no deceiver, since he is perfect, and "it is manifest by the natural light that all fraud and deception depend on some defect." (This is often classified as a **cosmological argument**.)

Meditation IV

Since God is supremely perfect and powerful, presumably he would not create something with a defect. So why did he create Descartes, who is apparently defective because he makes mistakes? This is actually no defect in God's creation, Descartes argues, because his mistakes are due to his voluntary actions, an exercise of his capacity for **free will**. And God has endowed Descartes with a perfect (limitless) capacity for free will.

Meditation V

Before turning to the question of whether physical objects ("material things") exist, Descartes examines his ideas of them. He finds that he has ideas of shapes (like triangles) and can prove various things about them (e.g., that the interior angles of a triangle add up to two right angles). This leads him to another proof or demonstration of the existence of God, a version of Anselm's **ontological argument** (see Chapter 1 of this anthology). In Descartes's version, the argument purports to derive the existence of God from the premise that the "clear and distinct" idea of God is that of a "supremely perfect being" whose existence is part of its nature.

Meditation VI

Finally, Descartes examines whether physical objects exist. They exist, Descartes concludes, because he has a natural tendency to believe this, and God is no deceiver. He also argues for the "real distinction" between mind and body: he is "a thinking non-extended thing"; his body is "an extended, non-thinking thing." The two things are, however, intimately joined together. Descartes ends with a discussion of the ways in which his senses can lead to error, but he has regained most of his former opinions that he questioned in Meditation I: "The exaggerated doubts of the last few days should be dismissed as laughable."

NOTES AND QUESTIONS

1. Descartes claims he "regularly has all the same experiences while asleep as madmen do when awake." Suppose your dreams aren't quite as vivid as Descartes's: you only dream in faint shades of gray, and you only dream about dragons. Does that mean that you should not be worried by the thought that you don't know you are not dreaming?

2. For Descartes's attempt to demonstrate the distinction between soul and body, see the selections from Meditations II and VI in Chapter 7 of this anthology.

3. Skepticism deriving from the considerations of Meditation I is called *Cartesian skepticism*. Skeptical ideas were also prevalent in antiquity, associated with philosophers such as Pyrrho (c. 365–275 BCE) and Arcesilaus (c. 316–241 BCE). The relationship

between ancient skepticism and the later Cartesian kind is controversial. For more on ancient skepticism, see Katja Vogt, "Ancient Skepticism," in *Stanford Encyclopedia of Philosophy*, ed. Edward Zalta (https://plato.stanford.edu/archives/win2016/entries /skepticism-ancient/).

David Hume (1711–1776)

Hume was a Scottish philosopher, essayist, and historian, as well as a central figure in Western philosophy. His *Treatise of Human Nature* (1739), *An Enquiry Concerning Human Understanding* (1748), and *An Enquiry Concerning the Principles of Morals* (1751) have been very influential. (The two *Enquiries* revise material in the *Treatise*.) Many contemporary philosophical discussions in epistemology, metaphysics, and ethics are reactions to Hume's theories and arguments. Hume's *Dialogues Concerning Natural Religion* (published posthumously in 1779) is a classic attack on "design arguments" for the existence of God.

OF SCEPTICISM WITH REGARD TO THE SENSES
from *A Treatise of Human Nature*

Thus the sceptic still continues to reason and believe, even tho' he asserts, that he cannot defend his reason by reason; and by the same rule he must assent to the principle concerning the existence of body, tho' he cannot pretend by any arguments of philosophy to maintain its veracity. Nature has not left this to his choice, and has doubtless esteem'd it an affair of too great importance to be trusted to our uncertain reasonings and speculations. We may well ask, *What causes induce us to believe in the existence of body?* but 'tis in vain to ask, *Whether there be body or not?* That is a point, which we must take for granted in all our reasonings.

The subject, then, of our present enquiry is concerning the *causes* which induce us to believe in the existence of body: And my reasonings on this head I shall begin with a distinction, which at first sight may seem superfluous, but which will contribute very much to the perfect understanding of what follows. We ought to examine apart those two questions, which are commonly confounded together, *viz.* Why we attribute a continu'd existence to objects, even when they are not present to the senses; and why we suppose them to have an existence distinct from the mind and perception. . . . These two questions concerning the continu'd and distinct existence of body are intimately connected together. For if the objects of our senses continue to exist, even when they are not perceiv'd, their existence is of course independent of and distinct from the perception; and *vice versa*, if their existence be independent of the perception and distinct from it, they must continue to exist, even tho' they be not perceiv'd. But tho' the decision of the one question decides the other; yet that we may the more easily discover the principles of human nature, from whence the decision arises, we shall carry along with us this distinction, and shall consider, whether it be the *senses, reason,* or the *imagination,* that produces the opinion of a *continu'd* or of a *distinct* existence. These are the only questions, that are intelligible on the present subject. . . .

To begin with the senses, 'tis evident these faculties are incapable of giving rise to the notion of the *continu'd* existence of their objects, after they no longer appear to the senses. For that is a contradiction in terms, and supposes that the senses continue to operate, even after they have ceas'd all manner of operation. These faculties, therefore, if they have any influence in the present case, must produce the opinion of a distinct, not of a continu'd existence; and in order to that, must present their impressions either as images and representations, or as these very distinct and external existences.

That our senses offer not their impressions as the images of something *distinct,* or *independent,* and *external,* is evident; because they convey to us nothing but a single perception, and never give us the least intimation of any thing beyond. A single perception can never produce the idea of a double existence, but by some inference either of the reason or imagination. . . .

If our senses, therefore, suggest any idea of distinct existences, they must convey the impressions as those very existences, by a kind of fallacy and illusion. Upon this head we may observe, that all sensations are felt by the mind, such as they really are, and that when we doubt, whether they present themselves as distinct objects, or as mere impressions, the difficulty is not concerning their nature, but concerning their relations and situation. Now if the senses presented our impressions as external to, and independent of ourselves, both the objects and ourselves must be obvious to our senses, otherwise they cou'd not be compar'd by these faculties. The difficulty, then, is how far we are *ourselves* the objects of our senses.

'Tis certain there is no question in philosophy more abstruse than that concerning identity, and the nature of the uniting principle, which constitutes a person. So far from being able by our senses merely to determine this question, we must have recourse to the most profound metaphysics to give a satisfactory answer to it; and in common life 'tis evident these ideas of self and person are never very fix'd nor determinate. 'Tis absurd, therefore, to imagine the senses can ever distinguish betwixt[1] ourselves and external objects. . . .

The senses give us no notion of continu'd existence, because they cannot operate beyond the extent, in which they really operate. They as little produce the opinion of a distinct existence, because they neither can offer it to the mind as represented, nor as original. To offer it as represented, they must present both an object and an image. To make it appear as original, they must convey a falsehood . . . and even in that case they do not, nor is it possible they shou'd, deceive us. We may, therefore, conclude with certainty, that the opinion of a continu'd and of a distinct existence never arises from the senses.

To confirm this we may observe, that there are three different kinds of impressions convey'd by the senses. The first are those of the figure,[2] bulk,[3] motion and solidity of bodies. The second those of colours, tastes, smells, sounds, heat and cold. The third

---

1. Between.
2. Shape.
3. Size.

are the pains and pleasures, that arise from the application of objects to our bodies, as by the cutting of our flesh with steel, and such like. Both philosophers and the vulgar[4] suppose the first of these to have a distinct continu'd existence. The vulgar only regard the second as on the same footing. Both philosophers and the vulgar, again, esteem the third to be merely perceptions; and consequently interrupted and dependent beings.

Now 'tis evident, that, whatever may be our philosophical opinion, colours, sounds, heat and cold, as far as appears to the senses, exist after the same manner with motion and solidity, and that the difference we make betwixt them in this respect, arises not from the mere perception. So strong is the prejudice for the distinct continu'd existence of the former qualities, that when the contrary opinion is advanc'd by modern philosophers, people imagine they can almost refute it from their feeling and experience, and that their very senses contradict this philosophy. 'Tis also evident, that colours, sounds, etc. are originally on the same footing with the pain that arises from steel, and pleasure that proceeds from a fire; and that the difference betwixt them is founded neither on perception nor reason, but on the imagination. For as they are confest to be, both of them, nothing but perceptions arising from the particular configurations and motions of the parts of body, wherein possibly can their difference consist? Upon the whole, then, we may conclude, that as far as the senses are judges, all perceptions are the same in the manner of their existence.

We may also observe in this instance of sounds and colours, that we can attribute a distinct continu'd existence to objects without ever consulting reason, or weighing our opinions by any philosophical principles. And indeed, whatever convincing arguments philosophers may fancy they can produce to establish the belief of objects independent of the mind, 'tis obvious these arguments are known but to very few, and that 'tis not by them, that children, peasants, and the greatest part of mankind are induc'd to attribute objects to some impressions, and deny them to others. Accordingly we find, that all the conclusions, which the vulgar form on this head, are directly contrary to those, which are confirm'd by philosophy. For philosophy informs us, that every thing, which appears to the mind, is nothing but a perception, and is interrupted, and dependent on the mind; whereas the vulgar confound perceptions and objects, and attribute a distinct continu'd existence to the very things they feel or see. This sentiment, then, as it is entirely unreasonable, must proceed from some other faculty than the understanding.... So that upon the whole our reason neither does, nor is it possible it ever shou'd, upon any supposition, give us an assurance of the continu'd and distinct existence of body. That opinion must be entirely owing to the imagination: which must now be the subject of our enquiry.

Since all impressions are internal and perishing existences, and appear as such, the notion of their distinct and continu'd existence must arise from a concurrence of some of their qualities with the qualities of the imagination; and since this notion does not extend to all of them, it must arise from certain qualities peculiar to some impressions. 'Twill therefore be easy for us to discover these qualities by a comparison of the impressions, to which we attribute a distinct and continu'd existence, with those, which we regard as internal and perishing.

We may observe, then, that 'tis neither upon account of the involuntariness of certain impressions, as is commonly suppos'd, nor of their superior force and violence,

4. Ordinary people, nonphilosophers.

that we attribute to them a reality, and continu'd existence, which we refuse to others, that are voluntary or feeble. For 'tis evident our pains and pleasures, our passions and affections, which we never suppose to have any existence beyond our perception, operate with greater violence, and are equally involuntary, as the impressions of figure and extension, colour and sound, which we suppose to be permanent beings. The heat of a fire, when moderate, is suppos'd to exist in the fire; but the pain, which it causes upon a near approach, is not taken to have any being except in the perception.

These vulgar opinions, then, being rejected, we must search for some other hypothesis, by which we may discover those peculiar qualities in our impressions, which makes us attribute to them a distinct and continu'd existence.

After a little examination, we shall find, that all those objects, to which we attribute a continu'd existence, have a peculiar *constancy*, which distinguishes them from the impressions, whose existence depends upon our perception. Those mountains, and houses, and trees, which lie at present under my eye, have always appear'd to me in the same order; and when I lose sight of them by shutting my eyes or turning my head, I soon after find them return upon me without the least alteration. My bed and table, my books and papers, present themselves in the same uniform manner, and change not upon account of any interruption in my seeing or perceiving them. This is the case with all the impressions, whose objects are suppos'd to have an external existence; and is the case with no other impressions, whether gentle or violent, voluntary or involuntary.

This constancy, however, is not so perfect as not to admit of very considerable exceptions. Bodies often change their position and qualities, and after a little absence or interruption may become hardly knowable. But here 'tis observable, that even in these changes they preserve a *coherence*, and have a regular dependence on each other; which is the foundation of a kind of reasoning from causation, and produces the opinion of their continu'd existence. When I return to my chamber[5] after an hour's absence, I find not my fire in the same situation, in which I left it: But then I am accustom'd in other instances to see a like alteration produc'd in a like time, whether I am present or absent, near or remote. This coherence, therefore, in their changes is one of the characteristics of external objects, as well as their constancy.

Having found that the opinion of the continu'd existence of body depends on the coherence and constancy of certain impressions, I now proceed to examine after what manner these qualities give rise to so extraordinary an opinion. To begin with the coherence; we may observe, that tho' those internal impressions, which we regard as fleeting and perishing, have also a certain coherence or regularity in their appearances, yet 'tis of somewhat a different nature, from that which we discover in bodies. Our passions[6] are found by experience to have a mutual connexion with and dependence on each other; but on no occasion is it necessary to suppose, that they have existed and operated, when they were not perceiv'd, in order to preserve the same dependence and connexion, of which we have had experience. The case is not the same with relation to external objects. Those require a continu'd existence, or otherwise lose, in a great measure, the regularity of their operation. I am here seated in my chamber with my

5. Private room.

6. Desires, emotions, and feelings.

face to the fire; and all the objects, that strike my senses, are contain'd in a few yards around me. My memory, indeed, informs me of the existence of many objects; but then this information extends not beyond their past existence, nor do either my senses or memory give any testimony to the continuance of their being. When therefore I am thus seated, and revolve over these thoughts, I hear on a sudden a noise as of a door turning upon its hinges; and a little after see a porter, who advances towards me. This gives occasion to many new reflexions and reasonings. First, I never have observ'd, that this noise cou'd proceed from any thing but the motion of a door; and therefore conclude, that the present phenomenon is a contradiction to all past experience, unless the door, which I remember on t'other side the chamber, be still in being. Again, I have always found, that a human body was possest of a quality, which I call gravity, and which hinders it from mounting in the air, as this porter must have done to arrive at my chamber, unless the stairs I remember be not annihilated by my absence. But this is not all. I receive a letter, which upon opening it I perceive by the hand-writing and subscription to have come from a friend, who says he is two hundred leagues[7] distant. 'Tis evident I can never account for this phenomenon, conformable to my experience in other instances, without spreading out in my mind the whole sea and continent between us, and supposing the effects and continu'd existence of posts[8] and ferries, according to my memory and observation. To consider these phaenomena of the porter and letter in a certain light, they are contradictions to common experience, and may be regarded as objections to those maxims, which we form concerning the connexions of causes and effects. I am accustom'd to hear such a sound, and see such an object in motion at the same time. I have not receiv'd in this particular instance both these perceptions. These observations are contrary, unless I suppose that the door still remains, and that it was open'd without my perceiving it: And this supposition, which was at first entirely arbitrary and hypothetical, acquires a force and evidence by its being the only one, upon which I can reconcile these contradictions. There is scarce a moment of my life, wherein there is not a similar instance presented to me, and I have not occasion to suppose the continu'd existence of objects, in order to connect their past and present appearances, and give them such an union with each other, as I have found by experience to be suitable to their particular natures and circumstances. Here then I am naturally led to regard the world, as something real and durable, and as preserving its existence, even when it is no longer present to my perception. . . .

Objects have a certain coherence even as they appear to our senses; but this coherence is much greater and more uniform, if we suppose the objects to have a continu'd existence; and as the mind is once in the train of observing an uniformity among objects, it naturally continues, till it renders the uniformity as compleat as possible. The simple supposition of their continu'd existence suffices for this purpose, and gives us a notion of a much greater regularity among objects, than what they have when we look no farther than our senses.

But whatever force we may ascribe to this principle, I am afraid 'tis too weak to support alone so vast an edifice, as is that of the continu'd existence of all external

---

7. One league is approximately 3 miles.

8. Vehicles used to carry mail.

bodies; and that we must join the *constancy* of their appearance to the *coherence*, in order to give a satisfactory account of that opinion. . . .

'Tis indeed evident, that as the vulgar *suppose* their perceptions to be their only objects, and at the same time *believe* the continu'd existence of matter, we must account for the origin of the belief upon that supposition. Now upon that supposition, 'tis a false opinion that any of our objects, or perceptions, are identically the same after an interruption; and consequently the opinion of their identity can never arise from reason, but must arise from the imagination. The imagination is seduc'd into such an opinion only by means of the resemblance of certain perceptions; since we find they are only our resembling perceptions, which we have a propension[9] to suppose the same. This propension to bestow an identity on our resembling perceptions, produces the fiction of a continu'd existence; since that fiction, as well as the identity, is really false, as is acknowledg'd by all philosophers, and has no other effect than to remedy the interruption of our perceptions, which is the only circumstance that is contrary to their identity. In the last place this propension causes belief by means of the present impressions of the memory; since without the remembrance of former sensations, 'tis plain we never shou'd have any belief of the continu'd existence of body. . . .

But tho' we are led after this manner, by the natural propensity of the imagination, to ascribe a continu'd existence to those sensible objects or perceptions, which we find to resemble each other in their interrupted appearance; yet a very little reflection and philosophy is sufficient to make us perceive the fallacy of that opinion. I have already observ'd, that there is an intimate connexion betwixt those two principles, of a *continu'd* and of a *distinct* or *independent* existence, and that we no sooner establish the one than the other follows, as a necessary consequence. 'Tis the opinion of a continu'd existence, which first takes place, and without much study or reflection draws the other along with it, wherever the mind follows its first and most natural tendency. But when we compare experiments, and reason a little upon them, we quickly perceive, that the doctrine of the independent existence of our sensible perceptions is contrary to the plainest experience. This leads us backward upon our footsteps to perceive our error in attributing a continu'd existence to our perceptions, and is the origin of many very curious opinions, which we shall here endeavour to account for.

'Twill first be proper to observe a few of those experiments, which convince us, that our perceptions are not possest of any independent existence. When we press one eye with a finger, we immediately perceive all the objects to become double, and one half of them to be remov'd from their common and natural position. But as we do not attribute a continu'd existence to both these perceptions, and as they are both of the same nature, we clearly perceive, that all our perceptions are dependent on our organs, and the disposition of our nerves and animal spirits. This opinion is confirm'd by the seeming increase and diminution of objects, according to their distance; by the apparent alterations in their figure; by the changes in their colour and other qualities from our sickness and distempers[10]; and by an infinite number of other experiments of

9. Propensity.

10. Illnesses.

the same kind; from all which we learn, that our sensible perceptions are not possest of any distinct or independent existence.

The natural consequence of this reasoning shou'd be, that our perceptions have no more a continu'd than an independent existence; and indeed philosophers have so far run into this opinion, that they change their system, and distinguish, (as we shall do for the future) betwixt perceptions and objects, of which the former are suppos'd to be interrupted, and perishing, and different at every different return; the latter to be uninterrupted, and to preserve a continu'd existence and identity. But however philosophical this new system may be esteem'd, I assert that 'tis only a palliative remedy, and that it contains all the difficulties of the vulgar system, with some others, that are peculiar to itself. There are no principles either of the understanding or fancy, which lead us directly to embrace this opinion of the double existence of perceptions and objects, nor can we arrive at it but by passing thro' the common hypothesis of the identity and continuance of our interrupted perceptions. Were we not first persuaded, that our perceptions are our only objects, and continue to exist even when they no longer make their appearance to the senses, we shou'd never be led to think, that our perceptions and objects are different, and that our objects alone preserve a continu'd existence. . . .

There is a great difference betwixt such opinions as we form after a calm and profound reflection, and such as we embrace by a kind of instinct or natural impulse, on account of their suitableness and conformity to the mind. If these opinions become contrary, 'tis not difficult to foresee which of them will have the advantage. As long as our attention is bent upon the subject, the philosophical and study'd principle may prevail; but the moment we relax our thoughts, nature will display herself, and draw us back to our former opinion. Nay she has sometimes such an influence, that she can stop our progress, even in the midst of our most profound reflections, and keep us from running on with all the consequences of any philosophical opinion. Thus tho' we clearly perceive the dependence and interruption of our perceptions, we stop short in our career, and never upon that account reject the notion of an independent and continu'd existence. That opinion has taken such deep root in the imagination, that 'tis impossible ever to eradicate it, nor will any strain'd metaphysical conviction of the dependence of our perceptions be sufficient for that purpose.

But tho' our natural and obvious principles here prevail above our study'd reflections, 'tis certain there must be some struggle and opposition in the case; at least so long as these reflections retain any force or vivacity. In order to set ourselves at ease in this particular, we contrive a new hypothesis, which seems to comprehend both these principles of reason and imagination. This hypothesis is the philosophical one of the double existence of perceptions and objects; which pleases our reason, in allowing, that our dependent perceptions are interrupted and different; and at the same time is agreeable to the imagination, in attributing a continu'd existence to something else, which we call *objects*. This philosophical system, therefore, is the monstrous offspring of two principles, which are contrary to each other, which are both at once embrac'd by the mind, and which are unable mutually to destroy each other. The imagination tells us, that our resembling perceptions have a continu'd and uninterrupted existence, and are not annihilated by their absence. Reflection tells us, that even our resembling perceptions are interrupted in their existence, and different from each other. The contradiction betwixt these opinions we elude by a new fiction, which is conformable to the hypotheses both of reflection and fancy, by ascribing these contrary qualities to different existences; the *interruption* to perceptions, and the *continuance* to objects. Nature is obstinate, and will not quit the field, however strongly attack'd by reason; and at the same time reason is so clear in the point, that there is no possibility of disguising her. Not being able to reconcile these two enemies, we endeavour to set ourselves at ease as much as possible, by successively granting to each whatever it demands, and by feigning a double existence, where each may find something, that has all the conditions it desires. Were we fully convinc'd, that our resembling perceptions are continu'd, and identical, and independent, we shou'd never run into this opinion of a double existence; since we shou'd find satisfaction in our first supposition, and wou'd not look beyond. Again, were we fully convinc'd, that our perceptions are dependent, and interrupted, and different, we shou'd be as little inclin'd to embrace the opinion of a double existence; since in that case we shou'd clearly perceive the error of our first supposition of a continu'd existence, and wou'd never regard it any farther. 'Tis therefore from the intermediate situation of the mind, that this opinion arises, and from such an adherence to these two contrary principles, as makes us seek some pretext to justify our receiving both; which happily at last is found in the system of a double existence.

Another advantage of this philosophical system is its similarity to the vulgar one; by which means we can humour our reason for a moment, when it becomes trouble-some and solicitous,[11] and yet upon its least negligence or inattention, can easily return to our vulgar and natural notions. Accordingly we find, that philosophers neglect not this advantage; but immediately upon leaving their closets, mingle with the rest of mankind in those exploded opinions, that our perceptions are our only objects, and continue identically and uninterruptedly the same in all their interrupted appearances.

TEST YOUR UNDERSTANDING

1. This book exists when you are not seeing it. Given this, does Hume think that you sometimes see this book?

2. Why does Hume think "reason" does not explain why we believe in the continued and distinct existence of the objects that are present to our senses?

3. According to Hume, when "the vulgar" (i.e., ordinary people) see a thing *X*, they typically make a mistake about *X*. What is that mistake?

4. "This philosophical system, therefore, is the monstrous offspring of two principles, which are contrary to each other, which are both at once embrac'd by the mind, and which are unable mutually to destroy each other." What is "this philosophical system"? What are the "two principles"?

11. Anxious.

READER'S GUIDE

Hume on Skepticism

At the end of Meditation I, Descartes finds himself "amid the inextricable darkness" of the problem of skepticism: How can he know anything about the "external world"? For instance, that he is awake and sitting by the fire in his dressing-gown? It turns out that "inextricable" is an exaggeration—at the end of the *Meditations*, Descartes has argued his way back into the light. Thanks to a non-deceiving God, he knows he is sitting by the fire after all.

You can think of Hume as continuing Meditation I in a different way. The problem of skepticism is indeed inextricable. Ordinary people ("the vulgar") believe in the familiar world of physical objects, but they have no reason to do so. Why do they have these un-justified beliefs, then? That is the question that Hume sets out to answer.

1. Look at a physical object, say your copy of this book. We think that the book continues to exist even when you turn away and look at something else. In Hume's terminology, we think it has *continued existence*. We also think that the book is something nonmental—it is not an "idea," "sensation," or anything like that. In Hume's terminology, we think it has *distinct existence*. Even though, according to Hume, continued and distinct existence always go together, he finds it useful to distinguish them. Accordingly, he considers two questions: Why do we think that the book has continued existence? Why do we think the book has distinct existence?

2. He starts by examining which faculty of the mind is responsible for our "entirely unrea-sonable" beliefs about continued and distinct existence. Is it the faculty of perception (the "senses"), reason (the "understanding"), or imagination? Hume argues that it is the faculty of imagination.

3. According to Hume, when the vulgar think they see a book, they are really only aware of something mental (which he calls an "impression" or a "perception"). Some im-pressions, for instance those we are aware of when our hand gets burned by the fire, don't produce the unreasonable opinion of continued and distinct existence: we don't think that the pain exists when we are not aware of it. Somehow, the imagination must produce the unreasonable opinion only when we have impressions of a distinctive kind. Hume argues that the distinctive kind of impressions comprises those that have what he calls "*constancy*" and "*coherence*."

4. In the rest of the selection (from the paragraph beginning "But tho' we are led . . ."), Hume turns from the opinions of the vulgar to the opinions of philosophers. He reviews some "experiments" that have convinced philosophers that we are only ever aware of impressions or perceptions "that are not possest of any independent existence." The vulgar mistakenly take these "fleeting and perishing" items to be *the very same things as* physical objects such as books, having a continued and distinct existence. The philosophers, however, have distinguished the two: they hold that our ("interrupted") perceptions are produced by ("uninterrupted") physical objects such as books. Hume argues that this philosophical view—that there are *two* kinds of things, perceptions *and* physical objects—is just as confused as the vulgar one.

NOTES AND QUESTIONS

1. Hume argues that the phenomenon of double vision shows that "our perceptions are not possest of any independent existence." What does Hume mean by "perception"? What does it mean to say that something has no "independent existence"? Set out Hume's argument in the form of premises and conclusion. Is the argument convincing?

2. What does Hume mean by "coherence" and "constancy"? What is his explanation of how the coherence and constancy of "certain impressions" give rise to our belief in the continued existence of tomatoes, trees, tables, and so on? Is his proposed explanation correct?

3. Hume talks a lot about the vulgar, and the psychological mechanisms that might explain their opinions. But how can he do this, since apparently by his own lights he has no good reason to believe that other people exist? How do you think Hume might reply? (See also question 2 in "Analyzing the Arguments" at the end of this chapter.)

4. The selection omits parts of Hume's complicated psychological explanation of "what causes induce us to believe in the existence of body." For discussion of this, see Barry Stroud, *Hume* (Routledge, 1981), chapter 5; and Harold Noonan, *Hume* (Oneworld, 2007), chapter 4.

G. E. Moore (1873–1958)

Moore was an English philosopher who taught at the University of Cambridge for most of his career. He was a central figure in analytic philosophy, a philosophical tradition that dominated academic philosophy in Britain, the United States, and Australia in the twentieth century. Moore wrote a seminal book on ethics, *Principia Ethica* (1903), and a number of classic articles on philosophy of mind and epistemology.

PROOF OF AN EXTERNAL WORLD

In the Preface to the second edition of Kant's *Critique of Pure Reason*[1] some words occur, which, in Professor Kemp Smith's translation, are rendered as follows:

> It still remains a scandal to philosophy . . . that the existence of things outside of us . . . must be accepted merely on *faith*, and that, if anyone thinks good to doubt their existence, we are unable to counter his doubts by any satisfactory proof.

---

1. The most famous of the German philosopher Immanuel Kant's (1724–1804) three "Critiques": the other two are the *Critique of Practical Reason* (about ethics) and the *Critique of Judgment* (about aesthetics).

It seems clear from these words that Kant thought it a matter of some importance to give a proof of "the existence of things outside of us" or perhaps rather (for it seems to me possible that the force of the German words is better rendered in this way) of "the existence of *the* things outside of us"; for had he not thought it important that a proof should be given, he would scarcely have called it a "scandal" that no proof had been given. And it seems clear also that he thought that the giving of such a proof was a task which fell properly within the province of philosophy; for, if it did not, the fact that no proof had been given could not possibly be a scandal to *philosophy*.

Now, even if Kant was mistaken in both of these two opinions, there seems to me to be no doubt whatever that it is a matter of some importance and also a matter which falls properly within the province of philosophy, to discuss the question what sort of proof, if any, can be given of "the existence of things outside of us." And to discuss this question was my object when I began to write the present lecture. But I may say at once that, as you will find, I have only, at most, succeeded in saying a very small part of what ought to be said about it.

The words "it . . . remains a scandal to philosophy . . . that we are unable . . ." would, taken strictly, imply that, at the moment at which he wrote them, Kant himself was unable to produce a satisfactory proof of the point in question. But I think it is unquestionable that Kant himself did not think that he personally was at the time unable to produce such a proof. On the contrary, in the immediately preceding sentence, he has declared that he has, in the second edition of his *Critique*, to which he is now writing the Preface, given a "rigorous proof" of this very thing; and has added that he believes this proof of his to be the only possible proof. . . .

If, therefore, it were certain that the proof of the point in question given by Kant in the second edition is a satisfactory proof, it would be certain that at least one satisfactory proof can be given; and all that would remain of the question which I said I proposed to discuss would be, firstly, the question as to what *sort* of a proof this of Kant's is, and secondly the question whether (contrary to Kant's own opinion) there may not perhaps be other proofs, of the same or of a different sort, which are also satisfactory. But I think it is by no means certain that Kant's proof is satisfactory. I think it is by no means certain that he did succeed in removing once for all the state of affairs which he considered to be a scandal to philosophy. And I think, therefore, that the question whether it is possible to give *any* satisfactory proof of the point in question still deserves discussion.

But what is the point in question? I think it must be owned that the expression "things outside of us" is rather an odd expression, and an expression the meaning of which is certainly not perfectly clear. It would have sounded less odd if, instead of "things outside of us" I had said "external things," and perhaps also the meaning of this expression would have seemed to be clearer; and I think we make the meaning of "external things" clearer still if we explain that this phrase has been regularly used by philosophers as short for "things external to *our minds*." The fact is that there has been a long philosophical tradition, in accordance with which the three expressions "external things," "things external to *us*," and "things external to *our minds*" have been used as equivalent to one another, and have, each of them, been used as if they needed no explanation. The origin of this usage I do not know. It occurs already in Descartes; and since he uses the expressions as if they needed no explanation, they had presumably been used with the same meaning before. Of the three, it seems to me that the expression "external to *our minds*" is the clearest, since it at least makes clear that what is meant is not "external to *our bodies*"; whereas both the other expressions might be taken to mean this: and indeed there has been a good deal of confusion, even among philosophers, as to the relation of the two conceptions "external things" and "things external to *our bodies*." But even the expression "things external to our minds" seems to me to be far from perfectly clear.[2] . . .

It seems to me that, so far from its being true, as Kant declares to be his opinion, that there is only one possible proof of the existence of things outside of us, namely the one which he has given, I can now give a large number of different proofs, each of which is a perfectly rigorous proof; and that at many other times I have been in a position to give many others. I can prove now, for instance, that two human hands exist. How? By holding up my two hands, and saying, as I make a certain gesture with the right hand, "Here is one hand," and adding, as I make a certain gesture with the left, "and here is another." And if, by doing this, I have proved *ipso facto*[3] the existence of external things, you will all see that I can also do it now in numbers of other ways: there is no need to multiply examples.

But did I prove just now that two human hands were then in existence? I do want to insist that I did; that the proof which I gave was a perfectly rigorous one; and that it is perhaps impossible to give a better or more rigorous proof of anything whatever. Of course, it would not have been a proof unless three conditions were satisfied; namely (1) unless the premiss which I adduced as proof of the conclusion was different from the conclusion I adduced it to prove; (2) unless the premiss which I adduced was something which I *knew* to be the case, and not merely something which I believed but which was by no means certain, or something which, though in fact true, I did not know to be so; and (3) unless the conclusion did really follow from the premiss. But all these three conditions were in fact satisfied by my proof. (1) The premiss which I adduced in proof was quite certainly different from the conclusion, for the conclusion was merely "Two human hands exist at this moment"; but the premiss was something far more specific than this—something which I expressed by showing you my hands, making certain gestures, and saying the words "Here is one hand, and here is another." It is quite obvious that the two were different, because it is quite obvious that the conclusion might have been true, even if the premiss had been false. In asserting the premiss I was asserting much more than I was asserting in asserting the conclusion. (2) I certainly did at the moment *know* that which I expressed by the combination of certain gestures with saying the words "There is one hand and here is another." I *knew* that there was one hand in the place indicated by combining a certain gesture with my first utterance of "here" and that there was another in the different place indicated by combining a certain gesture with

---

2. Moore then spends many pages investigating what this expression might mean. He finally concludes that to say that some thing is "external to our minds" is to say that "there is no contradiction in supposing [it] to exist at a time when [we] are having no experiences."

3. By that very fact (Latin).

my second utterance of "here." How absurd it would be to suggest that I did not know it, but only believed it, and that perhaps it was not the case! You might as well suggest that I do not know that I am now standing up and talking—that perhaps after all I'm not, and that it's not quite certain that I am! And finally (3) it is quite certain that the conclusion did follow from the premiss. This is as certain as it is that if there is one hand here and another here *now*, then it follows that there are two hands in existence *now*.

My proof, then, of the existence of things outside of us did satisfy three of the conditions necessary for a rigorous proof. Are there any other conditions necessary for a rigorous proof, such that perhaps it did not satisfy one of them? Perhaps there may be; I do not know; but I do want to emphasize that, so far as I can see, we all of us do constantly take proofs of this sort as absolutely conclusive proofs of certain conclusions—as finally settling certain questions, as to which we were previously in doubt. Suppose, for instance, it were a question whether there were as many as three misprints on a certain page in a certain book. A says there are, B is inclined to doubt it. How could A prove that he is right? Surely he *could* prove it by taking the book, turning to the page, and pointing to three separate places on it, saying "There's one misprint here, another here, and another here": surely that is a method by which it *might* be proved! Of course, A would not have proved, by doing this, that there were at least three misprints on the page in question, unless it was certain that there was a misprint in each of the places to which he pointed. But to say that he *might* prove it in this way, is to say that it *might* be certain that there was. And if such a thing as that could ever be certain, then assuredly it was certain just now that there was one hand in one of the two places I indicated and another in the other.

I did, then, just now, give a proof that there were *then* external objects; and obviously, if I did, I could then have given many other proofs of the same sort that there were external objects *then*, and could now give many proofs of the same sort that there are external objects *now*.

But, if what I am asked to do is to prove that external objects have existed *in the past*, then I can give many different proofs of this also, but proofs which are in important respects of a different *sort* from those just given. And I want to emphasize that, when Kant says it is a scandal not to be able to give a proof of the existence of external objects, a proof of their existence in the past would certainly *help* to remove the scandal of which he is speaking. He says that, if it occurs to anyone to question their existence, we ought to be able to confront him with a satisfactory proof. But by a person who questions their existence, he certainly means not merely a person who questions whether any exist at the moment of speaking, but a person who questions whether any have *ever* existed; and a proof that some have existed in the past would certainly therefore be relevant to *part* of what such a person is questioning. How then can I prove that there have been external objects in the past? Here is one proof. I can say: "I held up two hands above this desk not very long ago; therefore two hands existed not very long ago; therefore at least two external objects have existed at some time in the past, Q.E.D."[4] This is a perfectly good proof, provided I *know* what is asserted in the

---

4. *Quod erat demonstrandum*, Latin for "which was to be demonstrated."

premiss. But I *do* know that I held up two hands above this desk not very long ago. As a matter of fact, in this case you all know it too. There's no doubt whatever that I did. Therefore I have given a perfectly conclusive proof that external objects have existed in the past; and you will all see at once that, if this is a conclusive proof, I could have given many others of the same sort, and could now give many others. But it is also quite obvious that this sort of proof differs in important respects from the sort of proof I gave just now that there were two hands existing *then*.

I have, then, given two conclusive proofs of the existence of external objects. The first was a proof that two human hands existed at the time when I gave the proof; the second was a proof that two human hands had existed at a time previous to that at which I gave the proof. These proofs were of a different sort in important respects. And I pointed out that I could have given, then, many other conclusive proofs of both sorts. It is also obvious that I could give many others of both sorts now. So that, if these are the sort of proof that is wanted, nothing is easier than to prove the existence of external objects.

But now I am perfectly well aware that, in spite of all that I have said, many philosophers will still feel that I have not given any satisfactory proof of the point in question. And I want briefly, in conclusion, to say something as to why this dissatisfaction with my proofs should be felt.

One reason why, is, I think, this. Some people understand "proof of an external world" as including a proof of things which I haven't attempted to prove and haven't proved. It is not quite easy to say *what* it is that they want proved—what it is that is such that unless they got a proof of it, they would not say that they had a proof of the existence of external things; but I can make an approach to explaining what they want by saying that if I had proved the propositions which I used as *premisses* in my two proofs, then they would perhaps admit that I had proved the existence of external things, but, in the absence of such a proof (which, of course, I have neither given nor attempted to give), they will say that I have not given what they mean by a proof of the existence of external things. In other words, they want a proof of what I assert *now* when I hold up my hands and say "Here's one hand and here's another"; and, in the other case, they want a proof of what I assert *now* when I say "I did hold up two hands above this desk just now." Of course, what they really want is not merely a proof of these two propositions, but something like a general statement as to how *any* propositions of this sort may be proved. This, of course, I haven't given; and I do not believe it can be given: if this is what is meant by proof of the existence of external things, I do not believe that any proof of the existence of external things is possible. Of course, in some cases what might be called a proof of propositions which seem like these can be got. If one of you suspected that one of my hands was artificial he might be said to get a proof of my proposition "Here's one hand, and here's another," by coming up and examining the suspected hand close up, perhaps touching and pressing it, and so establishing that it really was a human hand. But I do not believe that any proof is possible in nearly all cases. How am I to prove now that "Here's one hand, and here's another"? I do not believe I can do it. In order to do it, I should need to prove for one thing, as Descartes pointed out, that I am not now dreaming.[5] But how can I prove that I am not? I have, no doubt, conclusive reasons for asserting that I am not now dreaming; I have conclusive evidence that I am awake: but that is a very different thing from being able to prove it. I could not tell you what all my evidence is; and I should require to do this at least, in order to give you a proof.

But another reason why some people would feel dissatisfied with my proofs is, I think, not merely that they want a proof of something which I haven't proved, but that they think that, if I cannot give such extra proofs, then the proofs that I have given are not conclusive proofs at all. And this, I think, is a definite mistake. They would say: "If you cannot prove your premiss that here is one hand and here is another, then you do not know it. But you yourself have admitted that, if you did not know it, then your proof was not conclusive. Therefore your proof was not, as you say it was, a conclusive proof." This view that, if I cannot prove such things as these, I do not know them, is, I think, the view that Kant was expressing in the sentence which I quoted at the beginning of this lecture, when he implies that so long as we have no proof of the existence of external things, their existence must be accepted merely on *faith*. He means to say, I think, that if I cannot prove that there is a hand here, I must accept it merely as a matter of faith—I cannot know it. Such a view, though it has been very common among philosophers, can, I think, be shown to be wrong—though shown only by the use of premisses which are not known to be true, unless we do know of the existence of external things. I can know things, which I cannot prove; and among things which I certainly did know, even if (as I think) I could not prove them, were the premisses of my two proofs. I should say, therefore, that those, if any, who are dissatisfied with these proofs merely on the ground that I did not know their premisses, have no good reason for their dissatisfaction.

TEST YOUR UNDERSTANDING

1. Does Moore think that one has proved a conclusion from some premises only if one knows the premises?

2. Does Moore think that one has proved a conclusion from some premises only if one is able to prove the premises?

3. Why does Moore think that the premises of his proofs are different from their conclusions?

4. "It is snowing, therefore it is snowing" is a valid **argument** (see the "Brief Guide to Logic and Argumentation" in the front of this anthology). Suppose I know that it is snowing, and argue from the premise that it is snowing to the conclusion that it is snowing. Does Moore think I have proved that it is snowing?

---

5. See Descartes's Meditation I earlier in this chapter.

NOTES AND QUESTIONS

1. Consider the following argument:

    P1. I am wide awake.

    P2. If I am wide awake, then I am not dreaming.

    C.   I am not dreaming.

    Can you use this argument to prove that you are not dreaming? If not, why not? Moore says he cannot prove that he is "not now dreaming." Are his reasons persuasive?

Jonathan Vogel (b. 1954)

Vogel is Professor of Philosophy at Amherst College and has made many contributions to skepticism and related topics in epistemology.

SKEPTICISM AND INFERENCE TO THE BEST EXPLANATION

More than two thousand years ago, the philosopher Zhuangzi posed the question: How can a man know that he is a man, rather than a butterfly dreaming that he is a man? Later, René Descartes asked how he could be sure that his sensory experience wasn't caused by an evil demon, who was bent on deceiving him.[1] And, today, you might consider the possibility that, instead of you really seeing this book, your brain is being stimulated by a computer to make it appear to you, falsely, that you're seeing this book. What reason do you have for thinking that this isn't happening to you now?

Thoughts like these raise one of the oldest and deepest problems in philosophy, the problem of skepticism about the external world. Skepticism is the sweeping and unsettling doctrine that we have no knowledge of the world around us. It presents a philosophical problem because it is supported by a simple, formidable line of thought, known as the *deceiver argument*:

1. Your sensory experiences could come about through ordinary perception, so that most of what you believe about the world is true. But your sensory experiences could also be caused deceptively, so that what you believe about the world is entirely false.

---

1. According to tradition, Zhuangzi (Chinese, fourth century BCE) is the author of the influential treatise that bears his name. René Descartes (French, 1596–1650) is often viewed as the founder of modern philosophy in the West. His best known work is *Meditations on First Philosophy* (1641), where Descartes raises the possibility that an evil demon is deceiving him (see the selection from the *Meditations* earlier in this chapter). Other selections from the *Meditations* are in Chapter 7 of this anthology.

2. You have no reason at all to believe that your sensory experiences arise in one way rather than the other.

3. Therefore, you have no knowledge of the world around you.[2]

But, of course you do have knowledge of the world. There must be something wrong with the deceiver argument. What, though? Premise 1 seems extremely plausible.[3] So, if the deceiver argument fails, either premise 2 must be false or else the conclusion 3 doesn't really follow from premise 2.

I think the conclusion does follow from premise 2, by way of a general principle about knowledge called the underdetermination principle. This principle says that if you are faced with two (or more) mutually exclusive hypotheses, and the information available to you gives you no reason to believe one rather than the other, then you don't know that either hypothesis is the case. For example, consider the claim that there is water on Mars. It might be that water formed there long ago and remains to this day. However, Mars is smaller than Earth and has a very different surface and atmosphere. Maybe the martian water, if any, was lost over the ages. In the absence of any information one way or the other—say, evidence provided by telescopes or by probes sent to Mars—a scientist who maintained or denied the presence of water on Mars would just be guessing. She wouldn't know that her hypothesis is true, precisely because she has no information favoring that hypothesis over its competitor. This is an illustration of how the underdetermination principle governs what counts as knowledge.[4]

---

2. There are subtle but significant questions about exactly how the argument ought to proceed, but I'm setting those aside. See Jonathan Vogel, "Skeptical Arguments," *Philosophical Issues* 14 (2004): 426–55. [Vogel's note.]

3. Some philosophers have rejected premise 1. J. L. Austin, *Sense and Sensibilia* (Oxford University Press, 1962), may have held such a view, and nowadays John McDowell, "Criteria, Defeasibility, and Knowledge," *Proceedings of the British Academy* 68 (1982): 455–79, and Timothy Williamson, *Knowledge and Its Limits* (Oxford University Press, 2000), might be read as denying premise 1, too. Another response regards the whole argument as somehow misconceived, perhaps because it involves hidden presuppositions about knowledge we need not accept or ought to reject. See the classic writings of Ludwig Wittgenstein, *On Certainty*, ed. G. E. M. Anscombe and G. H. Von Wright (Blackwell, 1975), and J. L. Austin, "Other Minds," *Proceedings of the Aristotelian Society*, supplementary vol. 20 (1946): 148–87, and more recently Michael Williams, *Unnatural Doubts: Epistemological Realism and the Basis of Scepticism* (Blackwell, 1992), and Alex Byrne, "How Hard Are the Skeptical Paradoxes?" *Noûs* 38 (2004): 299–325. [Vogel's note.]

4. In my opinion, the underdetermination principle is perfectly correct. However, some philosophers have developed sophisticated views about knowledge that are inconsistent with it. *Relevant alternatives theorists* hold that, to know a proposition, a person may need to have reasons to reject some competitors to it, but she doesn't need to have reasons to reject *all* the competitors, in every case. Thus, the underdetermination principle doesn't hold in full generality, and the conclusion of the deceiver argument doesn't follow from premise 2 after all. Certain *reliabilist* theories of knowledge go further than the relevant alternatives theory. They deny that there is any fundamental connection between knowing a proposition and having reasons to believe that proposition (and to reject its competitors). In particular, advocates of these accounts hold that we can know propositions about the world, whether we have reasons to reject skeptical hypotheses or not. Thus they, too, will deny that the conclusion of the deceiver argument is supported by premise 2. I've offered various criticisms of the relevant alternatives and reliabilist approaches. See Jonathan Vogel, "The New Relevant Alternatives Theory," *Philosophical Perspectives* 13 (1999): 155–80; Jonathan Vogel, "Reliabilism Leveled," *Journal of Philosophy* 97 (2000): 602–23; Jonathan Vogel, "Externalism Resisted," *Philosophical Studies* 131 (2006): 729–42; and Jonathan Vogel, "Subjunctivitis," *Philosophical Studies* 134 (2006): 73–88. [Vogel's note.]

This principle matters for our purposes as follows. The deceiver argument confronts you with two competing hypotheses. One is that the world is the way it appears to be, the other is that you are the victim of massive sensory deception. If premise 2 is true, you have no reason to favor the first over the second or vice versa. It then follows by the underdetermination principle that you don't know that either hypothesis is true. In particular, you may believe that the world is the way it appears to be, but you don't know that it is. So, premise 2 leads to the conclusion, given the underdetermination principle.

Since premise 2 does support the conclusion, the only way to escape the deceiver argument is to deny premise 2. If premise 2 is false, then skepticism is incorrect because we really do possess some reason for believing that we aren't victims of sensory deception after all. Contemporary philosophers have advanced three principal proposals as to what such a reason might be. One is the *Moorean* view.[5] The Moorean maintains that a sensory experience has a distinctive character or content, and, other things being equal, your having such an experience justifies you in holding a corresponding belief. For instance, suppose you seem to see a tree. The experience you have makes you justified in believing that there is a tree before you. But if there really is a tree before you, it can't be that you're deceived by a nefarious computer when you seem to see a tree.[6] So, according to the Moorean, your sensory experience gives you reason to believe that there is a tree before you, which in turn gives you a reason to believe that you're not deceived by a computer when you seem to see a tree before you. The same goes for any other sensory experience you may have. In general, your sensory experience gives you a reason to believe that you're not deceived by a computer, and premise 2 of the skeptical argument is false.

The Moorean approach is simple and decisive, but it strikes many as unsatisfactory. The trouble can be brought out by an analogy. Suppose you use the gas gauge in your car to tell you how much gas is in the fuel tank. You take a look and determine that the tank is half full. But surely, you can't then infer that, because the gauge says that the tank is half full, the gauge must be reading correctly! The Moorean seems to be up to something just as dubious. You can't use a particular sensory experience to establish that the experience itself isn't deceptive, any more than you can use a gauge to establish that the gauge itself isn't deceptive (i.e., to establish that it is reading correctly).

One reaction to this situation is to think that experience can't give you *any* reason for believing that you're not deceived by a computer. If you do have some basis for this belief, the basis can't be experience; your belief must be justified nonexperientially, or *a priori*. This is a second strategy for denying premise 2 of the deceiver argument. However, what is being suggested is somewhat hard to fathom. If you have nonexperiential grounds for thinking that your sensory experience isn't deceptive, it seems that

---

5. Named for the British philosopher G. E. Moore. A classic statement of Moore's view is his "Proof of an External World," *Proceedings of the British Academy* 25 (1939): 273–300 [see earlier in this chapter]. For a more recent version, see James Pryor, "The Skeptic and the Dogmatist," *Noûs* 34 (2000): 517–49. [Vogel's note.]

6. To be more explicit: If the computer is deceiving you, then there is no tree before you. But, then, if there is a tree before you, the computer isn't deceiving you. [Vogel's note.]

the source of those grounds would have to be reason. But how could reasoning—just thinking about things—establish whether your sensory experience is caused by a computer or not? In the face of such worries, some philosophers maintain that believing that one's sensory experience isn't generally deceptive is simply part of what it is to *be rational*.[7] But what would make that so? And how is this different from just coming up with something nice to say ("it's rational") about an assumption that we make blindly and without any reason whatsoever?

These remarks about the Moorean and a priori replies to the deceiver argument leave a great deal unsaid. But let's move on and consider a third sort of reply, which I'll call *explanationism*.[8] The idea behind this approach is that very often we are justified in adopting hypotheses because they do a good job of explaining the data we have. Here is an illustration. Suppose that a patient, Roger, goes to see Dr. G, his physician. Roger is sneezing, he has moist eyes, and his condition recurs at a certain time of the year. Roger's having an allergy explains these symptoms. There are other possible explanations. It could be that Roger has had a series of colds over the years or that he has a chronic respiratory infection that lies dormant for much of the time. But if Roger's having an allergy explains his symptoms extremely well, and his having any of these other conditions would explain his symptoms much less well, then Dr. G has good reason to reject those other diagnoses. Dr. G would be in a position to conclude that Roger's symptoms are due to an allergy. Dr. G's arriving at a diagnosis in this way is an example of what is known as *inference to the best explanation*. In general, if one hypothesis provides a significantly better explanation of the available evidence than its competitors do, that is a reason to accept the explanation and to reject the competitors.

This point carries over to the deceiver argument as follows. One explanation for the occurrence of your sensory experiences is that the world is actually the way you think it is and you're perceiving it properly. For example, we normally suppose that you have a visual experience of the ocean, because you are seeing the ocean. Similarly, you have a visual experience of sand dunes, because you are really seeing sand dunes, and so on. Call the collection of your ordinary beliefs about the world the "real world hypothesis." Skepticism emerges as a problem because there are alternative explanations of how your sensory experiences as a body come about. Call these "skeptical hypotheses." If the real world hypothesis explains the occurrence of your sensory experiences as a body better than skeptical hypotheses do, then, by inference to the best explanation, you have good reason to accept the real world hypothesis and to reject the skeptical alternatives. This outcome contradicts premise 2 of the deceiver argument, which says that you have no reason to believe one thing rather than the other. We see that premise 2 is false, and that the deceiver argument as a whole is no good.

7. Wittgenstein (1975) wrote (see footnote 3): "The reasonable man does not have certain doubts" (Remark 220, p. 29e). [Vogel's note.]

8. Other philosophers have offered explanationist approaches to skepticism that differ from the one presented here. See, for example, Laurence BonJour, *The Structure of Empirical Knowledge* (Harvard University Press, 1985), and Christopher Peacocke, *The Realm of Reason* (Oxford University Press, 2006). [Vogel's note.]

In my view, inference to the best explanation provides a refutation of the deceiver argument along the lines just set out. But to make this response to skepticism work, a proponent has to show why and how the real world hypothesis offers better explanations than the skeptical hypotheses do. There are some significant obstacles in the way. For one thing, there is no philosophical consensus about what an explanation is or about the details of what makes one explanation superior to another. Another difficulty is that skeptical hypotheses can be formulated in importantly different ways. These issues can't be fully resolved here, but it's possible nonetheless to take some significant steps toward formulating an explanationist response to skepticism. I'll proceed by examining two diametrically different kinds of skeptical hypothesis. One is reticent and minimal, and we'll find that it is too impoverished to be acceptable. The other is more explicit and elaborate. It turns out that this fully developed version also fails to match the real world hypothesis in explanatory merit.

At bottom, the concern raised by skepticism is that our sensory experiences are caused *unveridically*; that is, in such a way that they don't correctly reflect the way the world really is. Consider some particular experience you have, such as your seeing this page now (hereafter, *P*). On the one hand, the real world hypothesis furnishes what seems like a perfectly adequate explanation of how *P* comes about (there is a page in front of you, your eyes are open, there is light shining on the page, and so you see it). Now, suppose that the skeptic offers, as an alternative, the following *minimal skeptical hypothesis*: Your experiences are caused unveridically (i.e., caused deceptively by something other than what you think). That's it. The minimal skeptical hypothesis is incompatible with the real world hypothesis. In particular, the minimal skeptical hypothesis and the real world hypothesis differ as to what the cause of your experience *P* is. But the minimal skeptical hypothesis says little or nothing about why you have *P* or how *P* comes about. In fact, it hardly explains the occurrence of *P* at all. Explanations that are defective in this way are called *ad hoc* explanations.

To get a feel for what's wrong with ad hoc explanations, you may recall the example of Dr. G diagnosing Roger's symptoms. Dr. G considers various hypotheses about the cause of Roger's symptoms (it's an allergy, a series of colds, or an ongoing respiratory infection). Roger's having an allergy explains his symptoms better than the other possibilities do, so Dr. G concludes that Roger does, indeed, have an allergy. Now imagine that someone else, Mr. S, comes along and says to Dr. G: "You don't really have a reason to think Roger suffers from an allergy. There's a competing explanation that's just as good, which you have no reason to reject. That competing explanation is: Something other than an allergy (don't ask me what) is causing Roger's symptoms." Taken verbatim, Mr. S's suggestion does little or nothing to explain why or how Roger's symptoms have come about. Dr. G would be foolish to set aside her diagnosis that Roger has an allergy, if all that Mr. S can offer as an alternative is the bare suggestion that Roger's symptoms are due to something other than an allergy. Similarly, you have no reason to set aside your belief that you are seeing the page of a book if the competing hypothesis is just the bare claim that your experience of the page is caused by something else.

The upshot is that our ordinary beliefs about the world provide a rich and comprehensive explanation of why we have the experiences we do, and the minimal skeptical hypothesis falls short by comparison. If a skeptical hypothesis is going to keep up with the real world hypothesis, it will have to go into more detail than the minimal skeptical hypothesis does as to how our experiences arise. But it's possible to overshoot in this direction, too. As a general matter, we want hypotheses that say enough to get the explanatory job done, and no more. Some hypotheses are defective because they say too little, but others are defective because they say too much.

Here is an example of this second failing. You believe that the earth is round. The fact that the earth is round explains why someone traveling in the same direction eventually gets back to the same spot, why the earth appears as a disk from the surface of the moon, and so on. However, there are people who belong to an organization called the "Flat Earth Society," and they believe that the earth isn't really round at all. To explain why travelers can get back to the same spot by apparently going in the same direction, Flat Earthers have to claim that compasses and other navigational devices systematically mislead us. We think we're going in the same direction, but we're really not. To explain why pictures from the moon show the earth as a disk, Flat Earthers say that there was a conspiracy to preserve the conviction that the earth is round, and the moon landings and pictures were all faked. The Flat Earth story is just too complicated to be believable. A much simpler and better explanation of everything is that the earth really is round. This point generalizes. Other things being equal, a simpler, more economical explanatory hypothesis is better than a less simple, unnecessarily complicated one.

Now, we've seen that some hypotheses of massive sensory deception, like the minimal skeptical hypothesis, don't serve the skeptic's purposes. The skeptic needs to advance a hypothesis of massive sensory deception that will match exactly the explanatory success of the real world hypothesis. Could there be such a skeptical hypothesis, and if so, what would it look like? Consider what I'll call the *isomorphic skeptical hypothesis*.[9] Imagine a computer that simulates the world item by item, feature by feature. For example, suppose you have the experience of seeing a cat eating. The computer has a file for a cat and an entry in the file that says the cat is eating. This file, rather than a real cat, causes you to have a visual experience like that of a real cat eating. Next, suppose you have the experience of the cat stopping eating and then grooming itself. The ordinary explanation of why you have this experience is, of course, that you are seeing a real cat that has stopped eating and is now grooming itself. But, according to the isomorphic skeptical hypothesis, what's going on instead is that the computer's cat file has been updated. The entry for eating has been deleted and replaced by an entry for grooming, which causes the corresponding experience in you. Overall, the isomorphic skeptical hypothesis denies that your experience is caused by everyday objects with familiar properties. Your experience is caused instead by computer files with electronic properties, such that the files exactly mimic everyday objects with

---

9. *Isomorphic* means "similar in structure."

familiar properties. The isomorphic skeptical hypothesis is supposed to match the real world hypothesis explanation for explanation. If it does, then the real world hypothesis is no better than the isomorphic skeptical hypothesis from an explanatory point of view, and explanatory considerations give us no basis for accepting the real world hypothesis rather than the skeptical alternative.

However, it is doubtful that the isomorphic skeptical hypothesis is truly the equal of the real world hypothesis in explanatory terms. Here is the basic thought, setting aside some important points: The real world hypothesis ascribes various familiar properties to ordinary objects. For example, if you have an experience of seeing a round peg, you ascribe the property of being round to an object, namely a peg. According to the real world hypothesis, the round peg behaves like something that is round (it looks round to you, it fits into a round hole, and so forth). Moreover, it appears that very little needs to be said to explain why a round thing like the peg behaves as it does. The peg behaves like a round thing *because it is round.* By contrast, on the side of the isomorphic skeptical hypothesis, something that *isn't* round is supposed to behave as though it were round. The isomorphic skeptical hypothesis can't explain such behavior the way the real world hypothesis does; the computer file doesn't behave like a round thing because it is round. Some *further, more complicated* explanation needs to be given as to why the computer file behaves systematically as though it were a round thing.[10] In this way, the explanatory apparatus of the isomorphic skeptical hypothesis turns out to be more complicated than that of the real world hypothesis after all.

The claim here is that the difference between the real world hypothesis and the isomorphic skeptical hypothesis is comparable to the difference between the "round earth hypothesis" and the "flat earth hypothesis." On the round earth hypothesis, the earth's really being round explains why it behaves as though it's round (e.g., why you're able to get back to the same spot by going in what is apparently one direction). On the flat earth hypothesis, the earth behaves in various respects as though it were round (e.g., you're able to get back to the same spot by going in what is apparently one direction), but the flat earth hypothesis doesn't explain this behavior by ascribing roundness to the earth. Instead, that hypothesis needs to be loaded up with some additional rigamarole to account for why the earth behaves as though round when it's not (e.g., why compasses and other navigational devices systematically mislead us, etc.). Ultimately, just as you are entitled to reject the flat earth hypothesis because of its explanatory deficiencies, so, too, you are entitled to reject the isomorphic skeptical hypothesis in light of its similar explanatory shortcomings.

Let's sum up. The deceiver argument is philosophically a stroke of brilliance, which seems to make skepticism about the external world inevitable. However, there are in principle two ways out of trouble. We may deny that the argument's conclusion follows

---

10. The same point applies to other properties besides roundness, of course. There is more to say about exactly why the isomorphic skeptical hypothesis turns out to be more complicated than the real world hypothesis. See Jonathan Vogel, "Cartesian Skepticism and Inference to the Best Explanation," *Journal of Philosophy* 87 (1990): 658–66, and Jonathan Vogel, "The Refutation of Skepticism," in *Contemporary Debates in Epistemology,* ed. Matthias Steup and Ernest Sosa (Blackwell, 2005). [Vogel's note.]

from premise 2 or we may deny the truth of premise 2. The first maneuver doesn't work. The conclusion does follow from premise 2, by way of the underdetermination principle. However, the second path lies open. The real world hypothesis provides better explanations than skeptical hypotheses do. The explanatory superiority of the real world hypothesis gives you reason to believe it and to reject its skeptical competitors. Thus, premise 2 of the deceiver argument is wrong, and the argument as a whole fails. Explanationism gives us the answer to the problem of skepticism about the external world.

TEST YOUR UNDERSTANDING

1. Does Vogel think that the problem with the deceiver argument is that the underdetermination principle needs to be assumed in order to derive the conclusion?

2. What is the example of the gas gauge supposed to show?

   a. That gauges can sometimes give incorrect readings.

   b. That seeming to see a tree does not make you justified in believing that there is a tree before you.

   c. That premise 2 is true.

3. Vogel discusses two failings an explanatory hypothesis may have. What are they?

4. Which of the two failings is supposed to afflict the isomorphic skeptical hypothesis?

NOTES AND QUESTIONS

1. There is arguably a disanalogy between Vogel's example of Dr. G and ordinary cases of knowledge by perception, say, knowing that there is a book on the table by vision. Suppose Dr. G knows that Roger has an allergy because this hypothesis best explains Roger's symptoms. Then this involves fairly sophisticated reasoning by Dr. G from her evidence that Roger is sneezing, that Roger has moist eyes, and so forth. If knowing by vision that there is a book on the table is similar, presumably it also involves sophisticated reasoning. Is this plausible? How do you think Vogel would respond to this worry?

2. For another example of this kind of response to the skeptic, see Laurence BonJour, "A Version of Internalist Foundationalism," in *Epistemic Justification: Internalism vs. Externalism, Foundations vs. Virtues*, ed. L. BonJour and E. Sosa (Blackwell, 2003), 3–96.

   A general discussion of "inference to the best explanation" is in Gilbert Harman, "The Inference to the Best Explanation," in Chapter 4 of this anthology. See also the "Notes and Questions" to William Paley, "The Argument from Design," in Chapter 1 of this anthology.

Rae Langton (b. 1961)

Langton is Professor of Philosophy at the University of Cambridge and has made influential contributions to the history of philosophy, ethics, metaphysics, and feminist philosophy. She is the author of *Kantian Humility* (2001) and *Sexual Solipsism* (2009).

IGNORANCE OF THINGS IN THEMSELVES

1. Skepticism and Humility

Many philosophers have wanted to tell us that things may not be quite as they seem: many have wanted to divide appearance from reality. Democritus wrote in the fifth century BCE:

> by convention sweet and by convention bitter, by convention hot, by convention cold, by convention color; but in reality atoms and void.[1]

Plato argued for a different division: the imperfect, changeable things we see around us are mere appearance, and reality is an independent realm of perfect, invisible, eternal forms. Much later, Descartes wondered whether the familiar world of stoves and dressing gowns, streets and people, might turn out to be mere appearance—not because it is less real than the realm of atoms, or Forms, but because, for all we know, the stoves and dressing gowns, streets and people, don't exist at all.[2] Perhaps I am dreaming or deceived by an evil demon who interferes with my mind (like that evil neuroscientist of science fiction!) so that what appears to me is nothing like what's really there.

That demon still haunts the halls of philosophy, despite Descartes's own efforts to banish him. The mere possibility of his deceptive machinations persuades some philosophers that even if there is actually no demon, and appearance captures reality very nicely, we nevertheless can't be quite *sure* that it does. This means we don't know what we thought we knew. We confront skepticism. We don't have knowledge of "the external world." We are ignorant of "things in themselves," in some sense of that phrase: we lack knowledge of things independent of our minds.

---

1. Trans. C. C. W. Taylor, *The Atomists: Leucippus and Democritus. Fragments, A Text and Translation with a Commentary* (University of Toronto Press, 1999), cited by Sylvia Berryman, "Democritus," in *Stanford Encyclopedia of Philosophy*, ed. Edward Zalta (https://plato.stanford.edu/archives/win2016/entries/democritus/). [Langton's note.]

2. René Descartes, *Meditations on First Philosophy* (1641), trans. John Cottingham (Cambridge University Press, 1986). [Langton's note.] See the selection from the *Meditations* earlier in this chapter. Other selections from the *Meditations* are in Chapter 7 of this anthology.

Kant described skepticism as a scandal, and in 1781 he published his *Critique of Pure Reason* to set the scandal to rest.[3] The *Critique* is a brilliant but formidably difficult work. In it, Kant aims to show that skepticism is wrong because, roughly, we could not have thoughts at all unless we had thoughts about things. Perhaps he was trying to say that appearance just *is* reality: for provided we are thinking at all, we can't be wholly ignorant of things.

Whether Kant set skepticism to rest is one question. Whether he was really trying to, is another. For Kant said something else as well, famously and often. Although we have knowledge of things, these things are only "phenomena," and "we have no knowledge of things in themselves." Are those the words of someone offering a cure for skepticism? The skeptic says we have knowledge only of appearances: Kant says we have knowledge only of phenomena. The skeptic says we have no knowledge of things independent of our minds: Kant says we have no knowledge of things "in themselves." Appearance is not reality after all. It looks like Kant is saying just what the skeptic says—doesn't it?

Evidently, it depends what Kant means by "things in themselves." If "things in themselves" means things independent of our minds, then being ignorant of them is a way of being a skeptic. Instead of having a cure for skepticism, Kant has the disease. To be sure, Kant's proposal relieves the symptoms: he offers a wealth of arguments about the very special knowledge we have of objects—but they are *phenomenal* objects, mere appearances. What a disappointment, if we were hoping for knowledge of reality, of things independent of our minds. What consolation is it to learn that we have special knowledge if it's knowledge of mere appearance? Kant's subtle arguments about the conditions of our thought look irrelevant if they deny knowledge of reality, and again land us in skepticism.

What, though, if Kant means something quite different by "things in themselves"? Then ignorance of "things in themselves" needn't be skepticism. Knowledge of phenomena needn't restrict us to knowledge of mind-dependent appearance. That is exactly the idea we're going to pursue here. We won't go into Kant's famous arguments against skepticism—about how we can't think unless we think about objects. We're going to look instead at what "ignorance of things in themselves" amounts to. We'll take seriously the possibility that you and I, right now, are ignorant of things in themselves, just as Kant said—and that we can welcome this conclusion without thereby welcoming skepticism.

The key idea is this. The phrase "things in themselves" does not mean "things independent of our minds." It means "the way things are independently"; that is, independently of their relations not just to our minds but to *anything else* at all.

We are often interested in the relations one thing bears to another. Sometimes the relevant relations are spatial: the tennis ball flew over the net and over the white line. Sometimes the relevant relations are biological: Jane is Jim's cousin and Joan's granddaughter. But when we talk about the relations a thing has to other things, we tend to assume there is something *more* to the thing than those relations. There is more

---

3. Immanuel Kant, *Critique of Pure Reason*, trans. Norman Kemp Smith (Macmillan, 1929). [Langton's note.]

to Jane than being Jim's cousin and Joan's granddaughter. There is more to the tennis ball than its passage over the net and the white line. Now, Kant sometimes uses the word "phenomenon" to mean, quite generally, an object "in a relation" to some other object. And he sometimes talks about this assumption that there must be something more to an object than its relations to other things:

> The understanding, when it entitles an object in a relation mere phenomenon, at the same time forms, apart from that relation, a representation of an *object in itself*. (*Critique*, B306, emphasis added)

He also says:

> Concepts of relation presuppose things which are absolutely [i.e., independently] given, and without these are impossible. (A284/B340)

This absolute or independent thing, which isn't exhausted by its relations to other things, is something to which we can give the name "substance," which just means an independent thing that has an independent, or intrinsic, nature:

> Substances in general must have some intrinsic nature, which is therefore free from all external relations. (A274/B330)

Putting this all together, the idea that there is a thing "in itself" turns out to be the idea that there is something to an object over and above its relations to other things: something more to you than being the son or daughter of *A*, the cousin of *B*, the grandchild of *C*; something more to the tennis ball than its spatial relations to nets and lines on a tennis court. A thing that has relations to something else must have something more to it than that: it must have some intrinsic nature, independent of those relations. It is this something else, this something more, that is the thing "in itself."

If we take this idea at face value, it promises to solve the difficulty we face. Ignorance of things "in themselves" is not skepticism. It doesn't rule out knowledge of things independent of our minds. It rules out knowledge only of a thing's non-relational, intrinsic properties.

We can know a lot! Appearance *is* reality: things as they appear to us are things as they really are. But something is still ruled out; namely, knowledge of how things are independent of their relations to other things. Appearance is reality, but it's not *all* of reality. We can know a lot about the world, but we can't know everything about it: we can't know its independent, *intrinsic* nature.

To say we can know a lot about something, but not everything, is not skepticism but a kind of epistemic modesty—so let's call it "humility." And since it is at the center of Kant's philosophy (or so I'm arguing), let's call it "Kantian humility."[4] In what follows, I'm going to say why Kant believed it. And then I'll say why you, too, should believe it.

---

4. Rae Langton, *Kantian Humility: Our Ignorance of Things in Themselves* (Oxford University Press, 1998, 2001). [Langton's note.]

2. Humility in Kant

I've suggested that Kant's distinction between "phenomena" and "things in themselves" is a contrast not between "appearance" and "reality," but between extrinsic and intrinsic aspects of something. On this usage, if we say a tennis ball fell over the white line, we ascribe to it a relational, hence "phenomenal," property, whereas if we say it is spherical, we ascribe to it an intrinsic property, which concerns the tennis ball as it is "in itself." Let's summarize the distinction this way:

> *Distinction:* "Things in themselves" are things that have intrinsic properties; "phenomena" are their extrinsic, or relational, properties.

Against this backdrop, ignorance of things in themselves is not skepticism but ignorance of certain properties—intrinsic properties:

> *Humility:* We have no knowledge of the intrinsic properties of things.

This could be construed as the idea that we have no knowledge of *any* of the intrinsic properties of things, and that (I think) is the idea we should ascribe to Kant. Admittedly, it sounds odd. If an intrinsic property is a property something has, independent of its relations to other things, then many of those seem perfectly accessible to us; for example, the sphericality of the tennis ball. But Kant himself seemed to think we lack knowledge of any intrinsic properties: we do have knowledge of certain physical properties of things, such as their shape and their powers of attraction and impenetrability, but he thinks these are not intrinsic, as the following passages illustrate.

> The *Intrinsic* and *Extrinsic*. In an object of pure understanding the intrinsic is only that which has no relation whatsoever (so far as its existence is concerned) to anything different from itself. It is quite otherwise with a *substantia phaenomenon* [phenomenal substance] in space; its intrinsic properties are nothing but relations, and it itself is entirely made up of mere relations. We are acquainted with substance in space only through forces which are active in this and that space, either drawing other objects (attraction) or preventing their penetration (repulsion and impenetrability). We are not acquainted with any other properties constituting the concept of the substance which appears in space and which we call matter. As object of pure understanding, on the other hand, every substance must have intrinsic properties and powers which concern its inner reality. (A265/B321)
>
> Substances in general must have some intrinsic nature, which is therefore free from all external relations. . . . But what is intrinsic to the state of a substance cannot consist in place, shape, contact, or motion (these determinations being all external relations). (A274/B330)
>
> All that we know in matter is merely relations (what we call its intrinsic properties are intrinsic only in a comparative sense), but among these relations some are . . . enduring, and through these we are given a determinate object. . . . It is certainly

startling to hear that a thing is to be taken as consisting wholly of relations. Such a thing is, however, mere appearance. (A285/B341)

Kant thinks the physical world is made up of matter, "phenomenal substance," but that matter somehow "consists wholly of relations." He is drawing on a dynamical account of matter (further developed in his works on physical theory) according to which matter is constituted by forces. He has a proto–*field theory*, which had an important historical role to play, influencing scientists who went on to develop field theory proper in the nineteenth century.[5] And familiar physical properties—shape, impenetrability, attractive power—count, for him, as extrinsic or relational properties.

Whether that is the right way to classify them depends on how we understand the intrinsic/relational distinction. We have said, loosely, that an intrinsic property is one that doesn't depend on relations to anything else. Some philosophers have tried to make this more precise by saying a property is intrinsic just in case it is compatible with *isolation*; that is, it does not imply the existence of another wholly distinct object.[6] On this way of thinking, a tennis ball's sphericality will be intrinsic: a tennis ball can be spherical and be the only thing in the universe. And the tennis ball's bounciness will also be intrinsic. After all, a tennis ball can be *bouncy* and be the only thing in the universe, although, to be sure, it will not bounce unless there is something else for it to bounce off! On the face of things, shape properties like sphericality and dispositional properties like bounciness are intrinsic: something could have them and exist all on its own.

If Kant nonetheless describes them as relational, perhaps he has a different conception of intrinsicness in mind. Perhaps he thinks a thing's shape properties are relational because they depend on a relation to the *parts* of the thing. For example, the sphericality of the tennis ball depends on how the parts making up its surface are equidistant from its center. Perhaps he thinks dispositional properties are relational because they depend on how something *would* relate to other things if they were there. For example, whether something is bouncy depends on what it *would* do in relation to something else—if, say, it were dropped on the ground or thwacked against a tennis racket.

Some metaphysicians like to ponder the distinction between intrinsic and relational properties, but we needn't settle it here. All we need is that Kant denies us knowledge of any intrinsic properties, in some defensible sense of "intrinsic," and that this is what he means by denying us knowledge of "things in themselves."

Why does Kant deny us knowledge of intrinsic properties? The answer, I suggest, has two parts. First, he thinks, as many philosophers do, that our knowledge is "receptive": our minds need to be causally affected by something if we are to have knowledge of it.

> The receptivity of our mind, its power of receiving representations in so far as it is affected in any way, is called "sensibility." . . . Our nature is such that our intuition

---

5. According to Faraday's biographer: see L. P. Williams, *Michael Faraday: A Biography* (Chapman & Hall, 1965). [Langton's note.]

6. For some efforts to define "intrinsic" see, for example, Rae Langton and David Lewis, "Defining Intrinsic," *Philosophy and Phenomenological Research* 58 (1998): 333–45; I. L. Humberstone, "Intrinsic/Extrinsic," *Synthèse* 108 (1996): 205–67. The "isolation" test has many difficulties, which I won't go into here. [Langton's note.]

can never be other than sensible, that is, it contains only the way in which we are affected by objects. (A51/B75)

Our knowledge of things is receptive, "sensible": we gain knowledge only through being affected by objects.

> *Receptivity:* Human knowledge depends on sensibility, and sensibility is receptive: we can have knowledge of an object only insofar as it affects us.

This simple fact about our knowledge, he seems to think, dooms us to ignorance of things in themselves.

> Properties that belong to things as they are in themselves can never be given to us through the senses. (A36/B52)
>   It is not that through sensibility we are acquainted in a merely confused way with the nature of things as they are in themselves; we are not acquainted with that nature in any way at all. (A44/B62)

Why should the "receptivity" of knowledge imply ignorance of things in themselves? Many philosophers have wondered about this on Kant's behalf, and some have criticized him roundly on the topic. P. F. Strawson wrote:

> Knowledge through perception of things . . . as they are in themselves is impossible. For the only perceptions which could yield us any knowledge at all of such things must be the outcome of our being affected by those things; and for this reason such knowledge can be knowledge only of those things as they appear . . . and not of those things as they . . . are in themselves. The above is a fundamental and unargued complex premise of the *Critique*.[7]

Is Kant really taking this for granted, as a "fundamental and unargued complex premise"? Perhaps not. Perhaps he has good reason to connect receptivity to ignorance—but a reason that has gone unnoticed.

Here is a simple suggestion. According to receptivity, we have knowledge only of what affects us. But things "as they are in themselves" *do not affect us*: the intrinsic properties of things do not affect us. If Kant believed this, then that, together with his commitment to receptivity about knowledge, would certainly explain why we are ignorant of things in themselves.

A case can be made that this is just what Kant believes. I confess that, as a matter of interpretation, it is controversial. Here is not the place to do it justice. It involves detailed investigative work of a kind we historians of philosophy find strangely thrilling, although we're aware not everyone shares our enthusiasm. But here at least are two small gestures in this direction. In an early philosophical treatise, Kant argues:

---

7. P. F. Strawson, *The Bounds of Sense* (Methuen, 1966), 250. [Langton's note.]

> A substance never has the power through its own intrinsic properties to determine others different from itself, as has been proven.[8]

According to Kant, the causal powers of a substance are something over and above its intrinsic properties. At this stage of his thinking, he believes that they require an additional act of creation on God's part—an act that is "obviously arbitrary on God's part." He took this idea about the insufficiency of intrinsic properties for causal power to imply not only the contingency of causal power, but also the inertia of intrinsic properties. The idea returns in the *Critique of Pure Reason*:

> When everything is merely intrinsic . . . the state of one substance cannot stand in any active connection whatsoever with the state of another. (A274/B330)[9]

Receptivity requires that if we are to have knowledge of something, we have to be in active causal connection with it: but we're not in active causal connection with a thing's intrinsic properties. Receptivity means we can be acquainted with the causal powers of things, the ways they relate to each other and to ourselves: but however deeply we explore this causal nexus, we cannot reach the things in themselves.

3. Why We Are Ignorant of Things in Themselves

Kant said we are ignorant of things in themselves: ignorant of the intrinsic properties of things. The picture I have painted on his behalf is, I hope, appealing, in certain respects: Kantian humility does not, at least, condemn us to skepticism. But the picture will not appeal to everyone. Kant's conclusion seems too strong: we have no knowledge of *any* of the intrinsic properties of things. His reasons invoke a seemingly idiosyncratic conception of intrinsicness: a tennis ball's sphericality and bounce are not among its intrinsic properties. And they invoke a seemingly implausible causal thesis: intrinsic properties are causally inert. So however this interpretation succeeds as a way to understand Kant, it is unlikely to succeed in reaching a wider audience.

But wait. There is a conclusion very similar to Kant's that is significantly closer to home. Kant says we are ignorant of the intrinsic properties of things, and he is *right*, though not for quite the reasons we have been looking at. And if he is right, of course, then *you* too should believe we are ignorant of things in themselves.

Imagine that a detective is investigating a murder case. She puts together the clues. The murderer had a key, since no windows were broken. He was known to the dog, since

---

8. Kant, *Principiorum primorum cognitionis metaphysicae nova dilucidatio* (1755), Royal Prussian Academy of Sciences, vol. 1, 415. English translation (here amended) from "A New Exposition of the First Principles of Metaphysical Knowledge," in *Kant's Latin Writings: Translations, Commentaries and Notes*, ed. L.W. Beck et al. (P. Lang, 1986). [Langton's note.]

9. The context is a discussion of Kant's predecessor, Gottfried Leibniz, who denied causal interaction between substances. [Langton's note.]

there was no barking. He had size 10 shoes—there are his footprints. More and more of the picture begins to be filled out. He wore gloves, since there were no fingerprints. He had a tame parakeet—there are green feathers on the rug. The detective learns a lot about the murderer. Does she know who he is? She knows who the murderer is in relation to other things—houses, shoes, parakeets, and so on. She knows that the murderer is *whoever fits this role*. But does she, so to speak, know the murderer *in himself*? Is there something more to the murderer than being a possessor of keys, parakeets, and shoes? Of course. There must, in the end, be more to something or someone than their merely relational properties, as Kant pointed out. And ultimately, let us hope, the detective finds herself in a position to identify the person who exists independently of these relations to other things: "Aha! There is one person who fits this role. There is one person who is known to the dog, wears size 10 shoes, has a tame parakeet, could have a key, and that person is . . . Pirate Pete!" Then she knows who the murderer is. Then she knows who fits the role: she knows, so to speak, the murderer "in himself."

Some philosophers have suggested we are in a situation rather like that of the detective. An important recent attempt to show this is that of David Lewis, whose "Ramseyan Humility" explicitly claims inspiration from "Kantian" humility.[10] We are trying to find out, not about a murderer, but about the fundamental features of the world. We put our best theorists on the job, and they tell us a lot. Suppose we want to find out about our tennis ball. They tell us that a tennis ball is whatever fits this sort of profile: it's something that can be hit across a net with a tennis racket, something that has a specific degree of resistance and elasticity, something that is readily visible to human eyes in normal conditions, something that will roll smoothly downward when placed on a slope. These relational descriptions, suitably filled out, give us a story about the role something must fit if it's to be a tennis ball. They capture the relational or (if you like) "phenomenal" aspect of the tennis ball. Is there something more to the tennis ball than this relational role? Of course there must be, just as there is something more to Pirate Pete than his relations to keys and parakeets.

And our theorists can tell us about this "something more." They tell us not only that the tennis ball can land over the white line, not only that it is spherical and bouncy, but that it is made of rubber and felt, which in turn are made of very tiny parts called molecules, which in turn are made up of tinier parts, called atoms, which in turn are made up of still tinier parts, called protons, neutrons, and electrons—and more, with names too peculiar to recount here. Our experts give detailed descriptions of the tiny parts something must have, and their particular arrangements, if that something is to fit the "tennis ball" role. They are giving us a splendid account of what the tennis ball is, "in itself." What more could there be to know about what the tennis ball is, "in itself"?

We certainly know a lot about the tennis ball. In Kant's terms, we know a lot about the tennis ball as "phenomenon"—how it relates to tennis rackets, nets, and players.

---

10. David Lewis, "Ramseyan Humility," in *Conceptual Analysis and Philosophical Naturalism*, ed. Robert Nola and David Braddon-Mitchell (MIT Press, 2009), 203–22. This section is in turn inspired by Lewis's argument, though it is very far from doing him justice. There have been many attempts to respond, but see, for example, Jonathan Schaffer, "Quiddistic Knowledge," *Philosophical Studies* 123 (2005): 1–32; Anne Whittle, "On an Argument for Humility," *Philosophical Studies* 130 (2006): 461–97. [Langton's note.]

And yes: we also know a lot about the tennis ball "as it is in itself," what its parts are made of and how they are arranged. But now shift the question: What exactly do we know about those tiny parts of the tennis ball?

Take the electron, for example. Our story about the electron has something in common with the detective's story about the murderer. It captures a complicated relational profile. An electron is whatever it is that fits a distinctive role, whatever it is that fits the "electron" pattern of relating to other things. An electron is the thing that repels other things we call "electrons" and attracts other things we call "protons." It's the thing that, in company with lots of other electrons, makes the lightbulb go on, makes your hair stand on end on a cold, dry day, and so on. The physicist will have a more detailed story, but it will nevertheless be a story that has this relational form. "Electron" refers to whatever fits the physicist's relational "electron" role, just as "the murderer" refers to whoever fits the detective's relational "murderer" role.

The detective discovers who the murderer is, "in himself" as we put it, when she discovers who fits the relational "murderer" role; namely, Pirate Pete. The physicist discovers what the electron is when she discovers what fits the relational "electron" role; namely, . . . what? Here the analogy with the detective breaks down. The detective is able to find out who the murderer is, apart from the story about how the murderer relates to keys, shoes, parakeets. But the physicist is unable to find out what the electron is, apart from the story about how the electron relates to protons, hair, and lightbulbs. For the detective, there is something more to say. For the physicist, there is nothing more to say. The electron is, to borrow a phrase from Kant, merely a "something = x" about which we can say nothing, or rather nothing *more* than what's given in our relational description. The upshot: we know the electron as "phenomenon," so to speak, but we don't know the electron "as it is in itself."

Here is another way to bring out the point. Suppose, inconveniently, more than one person fits the role given by the detective's list of clues: suppose Pirate Pete, Pirate Percy, and Pirate Peggy all have keys, parakeets, large shoes, and so on. Then although the detective knows a lot, she still doesn't know who the murderer is. That, or something like it, is the situation we face with the electron. Consider the thing, whatever it is, that fits the electron role. We are supposing its intrinsic properties are not inert (we are leaving that part of Kant behind) but are the causal grounds of its power to repel other electrons, attract protons, and so on. We are, indirectly, in causal contact with those intrinsic properties—but, receptivity notwithstanding, that is still not enough for us to know what those intrinsic properties are. Why not? Suppose we give a name to the intrinsic property responsible for this complex causal profile: let's call it "negative charge," or "NC" for short. Now let's draw on Kant's insight about the contingency of causal power, which is shared, in some form, by many philosophers today (including Lewis). This contingency means that NC *could have been* associated with a completely different relational, causal profile, and a different intrinsic property—call it NC*—*could have been* associated with the electron's relational, causal profile. But now ask: Is the electron's intrinsic property NC or NC*? We don't know, any more than the detective knows whether the murderer is Pirate Pete or Pirate Percy. So we are faced with humility again.

Humility: We have no knowledge of the most fundamental intrinsic properties of things.

This is admittedly a modified version of humility: the conclusion is less drastic than Kant's. We are not denied knowledge of all intrinsic properties: the tennis ball is spherical and is made of rubber and felt, which in turn are constituted by molecules, elements, and subatomic particles. We know a lot about the intrinsic nature of the tennis ball.

But we do lack knowledge of things in themselves. Kant was right to say it, and we need to accept it. It's not so bad. It's not skepticism. It is what it is. We face the sad fact that we know less than we thought: there are some intrinsic properties of which we shall forever be ignorant. And, sadly, they are the most fundamental properties of all.

TEST YOUR UNDERSTANDING

1. Does Kant (as interpreted by Langton) think we can only have knowledge of mind-dependent appearances?

2. Kant said we are ignorant of "things in themselves." On Langton's interpretation, Kant meant that we are ignorant of the "intrinsic properties" of things. As she notes, the property of being spherical is often counted as an "intrinsic property." Does this mean that, according to Kant, we don't know whether tennis balls are spherical?

3. The argument for Kant's version of humility appeals to the premise that the intrinsic properties of things do not affect us. Does the argument for Langton's version of humility appeal to this premise, too?

4. According to Langton, will physicists eventually discover all the fundamental properties of elementary particles such as electrons and neutrinos?

NOTES AND QUESTIONS

1. Set out the **argument** for the version of humility endorsed by Langton in the form of premises and conclusion. Is the argument **valid**? If not, what premises need to be added so that the argument is valid?

2. Now that you have a valid argument for humility, is it also **sound**?

3. In footnote 10, Langton mentions David Lewis's defense of "Ramseyan humility" and defends it herself in the last section of her article. For a more detailed comparison of Ramseyan and Kantian humility, see Rae Langton, "Elusive Knowledge of Things in Themselves," *Australasian Journal of Philosophy* 82 (2004): 129–36.

ANALYZING THE ARGUMENTS

1. Hume, Moore, and Vogel offer very different responses to the skeptic about the external world. Compare and contrast their views.

2. Even though Hume finds the case for skepticism compelling, he admits that it is difficult or impossible to be a skeptic once one stops thinking about philosophy and turns to finding a good place for lunch or paying one's library fines. At the end of "Of Scepticism with Regard to the Senses" he writes (in a paragraph omitted from the selection):

> This sceptical doubt, both with respect to reason and the senses, is a malady, which can never be radically cur'd, but must return upon us every moment, however we may chase it away, and sometimes may seem entirely free from it. 'Tis impossible upon any system to defend either our understanding or senses; and we but expose them farther when we endeavour to justify them in that manner. As the sceptical doubt arises naturally from a profound and intense reflection on those subjects, it always increases, the farther we carry our reflections, whether in opposition or conformity to it. Carelessness and inattention alone can afford us any remedy. For this reason I rely entirely upon them; and take it for granted, whatever may be the reader's opinion at this present moment, that an hour hence he will be persuaded there is both an external and internal world.

Indeed, if Hume were able to fully live his skepticism, why did he bother writing a book? If you don't know that there are any books, and readers to read them, the ambition to write a book is as pointless as the ambition to meet Bigfoot.

Does this show that there is something badly wrong with skepticism? The fact that skepticism can seem plausible in the classroom and absurd outside might be thought to support **contextualism,** a response to skepticism defended in Stewart Cohen's "Contextualism" (go to digital.wwnorton.com/introphilosophy2). Explain why. Does it really support Cohen's position? How do you think Moore and Vogel would explain the appeal of skepticism?

3. *Defining the principle of closure.* Consider this statement of closure:

Closure$_1$: If p entails q, and you know p, then you know q.

There is a simple objection to closure$_1$ that motivates the following revised version of closure (the one used in the introduction to this section):

Closure$_2$: If p entails q, and you know p, then you are in a position to know q.

What is that objection? *Hint*: Sometimes someone can *come to know* a truth q of which she was previously ignorant by proving or deducing q from some premises.

4. *Counterexamples to closure.* Suppose you are at the zoo, looking at a black-and-white-striped animal in a cage marked "Common Zebra, *Equus quagga*." The animal is indeed a zebra. Explain why one might think the following argument provides a **counterexample** to closure:

   1-z. This is a zebra.

   2-z. If this is a zebra, it is not a mule cleverly disguised by the zoo authorities to look exactly like a zebra.

   3-z. This is not a mule cleverly disguised by the zoo authorities to look exactly like a zebra.[1]

   Now do the same for the following argument:

   1-h. I have a hand.

   2-h. If I have a hand, I am not a handless brain-in-a-vat.

   3-h. I am not a handless brain-in-a-vat.

   Does either one of these arguments provide a genuine counterexample to closure? Assuming that closure is true, can you explain why someone might be tempted by either one of these arguments into thinking that it is false?

   For discussion of the case for and against closure, see Fred Dretske and John Hawthorne, "Is Knowledge Closed under Known Entailment?" in *Contemporary Debates in Epistemology*, ed. M. Steup, J. Turri, and E. Sosa (Wiley-Blackwell, 2013), 27–59.

5. Consider the following account of knowledge (simplified from Robert Nozick, *Philosophical Explanations* [Harvard University Press, 1981], chapter 3):

   S knows *p* **iff** (i) *p* is true, (ii) *S* believes *p*, and (iii) if *p* had been false, *S* would not have believed *p*.

   Nozick thought that it was an advantage of his account that it had the following two features:

   (1) You can know that you have a hand.

   (2) You cannot know that you are not a handless brain-in-a-vat.

   Because of (1), the account agrees with common sense. Because of (2), the account also concedes something to the skeptic. Explain why Nozick's account has these two features, and why Nozick must deny closure.

---

1. This example is from Fred Dretske, "Epistemic Operators," *Journal of Philosophy* 67 (1970): 1007–23.

Part III

METAPHYSICS AND THE PHILOSOPHY OF MIND

Is Mind Material?

A chunk of ice is transparent and slippery. Physics and chemistry can explain why it has these properties. The chunk of ice is composed of H_2O molecules arranged in a repeating hexagonal pattern. It is transparent because H_2O molecules do not absorb (much) light in the visible spectrum. It is slippery because friction on the ice breaks the chemical bonds that hold the H_2O molecules together, creating a thin lubricating layer of H_2O in its liquid state—water, in other words.

Admittedly, the explanation for its transparency is incomplete. Snowballs are composed of small chunks of ice, so why aren't they transparent? And the explanation of why ice is slippery is actually controversial—other explanations have been proposed. Still, no one doubts that the slipperiness of ice, and indeed *all* of the characteristic properties of ice, can in principle be completely explained in terms of its chemical or physical makeup. In this sense, a chunk of ice is a wholly material or physical thing: it is "nothing but" H_2O molecules bound together in a certain crystalline form.

As far as objects in our environment go, a chunk of ice is pretty simple. A rock is considerably more complex. Still, there's every reason to think that rocks are wholly physical things, in the sense that our ice cube is. A lump of granite is hard, dense, and radioactive. No geologist would dispute that these and other characteristic properties of granite can be completely explained in terms of its physical or chemical makeup.

What about living things? Let's start with something relatively simple: a virus. A virus basically consists of some genetic material inside a protective structure made from protein. The genetic material and the proteins themselves are incredibly complex molecules. But again, virology proceeds (extremely successfully) on the assumption that a virus is a wholly material thing, "nothing but" a complex molecular structure.

Viruses are not cellular organisms, and for that reason are sometimes not counted as living things. So consider a clear case of a simple living thing, a single-celled organism, for instance, a bacterium. Is this where the explanatory limits of biochemistry are apparent? Not according to modern bacteriology, which, just like virology, supposes that its objects of study are wholly material. The theory known as *vitalism*, according to which a special "vital spirit" is needed to explain life, is no longer regarded as credible.

How could it make a difference if we multiply the number of cells? If single-celled organisms are wholly material, aren't multicellular organisms wholly material too? And if they are, *we* are wholly material things.

We certainly have many properties that can be explained in terms of our physical or chemical makeup. Suppose, for example, that Adam has a body temperature of 98°F and that Eve is digesting a bagel. Although the regulation of body temperature and the regulation of digestion are far from easy to explain, it seems a very safe bet that complete explanations of these phenomena need not appeal to anything more than the physical and chemical makeup of organisms.

What about our *psychological* or **mental states**, though? Tom thinks it's time for lunch, Dick has a headache, and Harriet hears her phone ring. Are thinking, feeling, and perceiving "nothing but" physical states of organisms? To take a particularly vivid example, imagine having a throbbing headache. Could this be "nothing but" having a certain pattern of neural activity in your brain?

There is an intuitive difficulty here, which the German philosopher and mathematician Gottfried Wilhelm Leibniz captured in 1714 with the following thought experiment:

> Suppose that there be a machine, the structure of which produces thinking, feeling, and perceiving; imagine this machine enlarged but preserving the same proportions, so that you could enter it as if it were a mill. This being supposed, you might visit its inside; but what would you observe there? Nothing but parts which push and move each other, and never anything that could explain perception.[1]

It doesn't affect the force of the example if we imagine, not a machine with parts that push and move each other, but a brain with parts that interact by sending and receiving chemical and electrical signals. Imagine the brain enlarged so you can walk through it, each neuron and glial cell (the two sorts of cells in the brain) being clearly visible, as they might be in a model seen in a science museum. Admittedly, walking around the brain might take some time (the number of neurons is in the order of 100 billion, and the number of glial cells is even greater). But could you find anything among this tangle of biological wiring that could explain the occurrence of a headache?

Contrast digestion. Imagine the stomach and intestines enlarged so you can see the chemical processes at work. Taking a submarine trip through the body, as in the 1966 movie *Fantastic Voyage*, you see particles of chewed bagel being broken down by enzymes and gastric acid, and so on. There doesn't seem to be much of a problem in supposing that what you are seeing *just is* digestion.

1. Leibniz, *Monadology*, trans. P. Schrecher and A. M. Schrecher (Bobbs-Merrill, 1965), section 17.

There appears to be a deep puzzle, then, about how to fit the mind into the material world. This is called the **mind-body problem**, and is the topic of the selections that follow. You will find them easier to understand if you have a basic grasp of the four main theories of mind, which are explained in the remainder of this introduction.

Behaviorism

Lieutenant Commander Data, a character in *Star Trek: The Next Generation*, is an android—a robot who looks and behaves like a human being. Even though Data's innards are quite different from ours, the other *Star Trek* characters simply assume without argument that he has a mental life. They are quite sure that Data thinks that his home planet is Omicron Theta, wants to understand humans better, and can see objects that are before his eyes. Could they be completely and utterly wrong? Might Data actually be as mindless as a robotic vacuum cleaner?

If you think that Data's behavior *guarantees* that he has a mental life, then you are some sort of *behaviorist*. According to **behaviorism**, to have a mind, or to be in such-and-such mental states, *just is* to behave in certain ways or, more precisely, to be *disposed* or *inclined* to behave in certain ways.

Our bodily movements can presumably be explained in terms of our physical and chemical makeup. Your hand goes up because muscle fibers contract; muscle fibers contract because signals reach them via nerves; the signals themselves are produced by activity in your motor cortex; and so on. At no point in this chain of explanations do we need to assume that you are more than a purely physical thing. Accordingly, if our mental life is just a matter of our behavior, then there is no puzzle about how a purely material object can have a mind.

But is behaviorism correct? Suppose Data's behavior is controlled remotely via wireless links by the alien Romulans. These diabolical puppeteers ensure that Data behaves exactly *as if* he had a mind. No one on the starship *Enterprise* knows that this is going on. As before, they are all convinced that Data has beliefs, desires, intentions, perceptions, and so forth. If behaviorism is true, they are right. Are they?

Consider another example, this time drawn from real life. In 1995, the French journalist Jean-Dominique Bauby suffered a stroke that left him almost completely paralyzed—he could move his left eyelid, but little else. Despite his almost total paralysis, he was able to communicate by blinking. Using this method, he managed to write a memoir, *The Diving Bell and the Butterfly*, later made into a movie of the same name. If Bauby had lost the use of his left eyelid, becoming completely paralyzed, that would not have made his rich mental life vanish. We may further imagine that Bauby becomes completely resigned to his behavior-free condition and begins to enjoy being alone with his own thoughts. He has now lost even any disposition or inclination to behave: if his paralysis were cured, he wouldn't speak or move at all. Yet surely his mental life continues on.

These examples suggest that complex behavior, although it may be excellent *evidence* of a mental life, is not *what it is* to have a mind. And isn't this just common sense? Mental states are inner states of a creature that *cause and explain* behavior or tendencies to behave. Bauby has the mental causes, but without their typical behavioral effects. And Data, when he is controlled by the Romulan puppet masters, has the typical behavioral effects without the mental causes.

The Identity Theory

If thinking, perceiving, and feeling are inner states that cause behavior, then we might expect that science (in particular neuroscience) will tell us what they are. Suppose the desire for water causes you to turn on the faucet on Monday and go to the store for a bottle of spring water on Tuesday. Suppose that neuroscience tells us that neural firing pattern W caused you to turn on the faucet on Monday and go to the store on Tuesday. Enough evidence of this sort might support the view that desiring water *just is* having a brain in neural firing pattern W. We can put this in terms of *property identity*. Here is one **property** (feature, attribute) you had on Monday and Tuesday: the property of desiring water. Here is another property you had on Monday and Tuesday: the property of having a brain in neural firing pattern W. And here is a hypothesis: the first property and the second property are *the very same property*. If that's right, the property of having a brain in neural firing pattern W is not really "another" property: it is *identical to* the property of desiring water. This is an illustration of the **identity theory**, or (as in the selection by J. J. C. Smart) the *brain process thesis*. Science discovers property identities all the time; for instance, the property of being table salt has turned out to be identical to the property of being sodium chloride.

The selection by Smart, published in 1959, is one of the earliest defenses of the identity theory. Smart concentrates on what might be thought to be the hardest case for a materialist theory of the mind: bodily sensations (such as a headache).[2] To have a sensation, Smart argues, is simply to have a certain physical process occurring in one's brain, nothing more.

One worry about the identity theory is that it is too narrow in scope. Let's go back to Data. As portrayed on *Star Trek*, Data has a "positronic brain," not a biological brain. He has no neurons, thus he cannot have a brain in neural firing pattern W. So if desiring water just is to have a brain in neural firing pattern W, Data cannot desire water. In general, if the identity theory is correct, Data cannot have a mental life at all, simply because he doesn't have a biological brain. Is that plausible?

---

2. Conscious states like *being in pain* or *seeing green* are often supposed to be especially resistant to physical explanation. For more on this, see the introduction to Chapter 8, "What Is Consciousness?"

Functionalism

Data himself supplies our final materialist theory of mind, **functionalism**. Data's positronic brain is some kind of computer, programmed with software that (in the *Star Trek* fiction) results in a mind. Computer hardware can be made out of almost anything. The first programmable computer, as designed by the English mathematician Charles Babbage in the 1830s but never built, was entirely mechanical. Computers could be made from water pipes and valves, or (as they actually are made now) out of minute electronic circuits printed on silicon chips. The problem with the identity theory, one might think, is that it ties mental states too tightly to *hardware*—in particular, our biological hardware.

But perhaps mental states are more a matter of *software*: what matters is that the right program is running, not whether it is running on a Mac, or a clockwork computer, or a biological brain. Put more generally: mental states are identical to *functional states*. Functional states are those that perform a certain *function*; for instance, the function of causing a certain piece of information to be stored for subsequent use in a long calculation. And functions in general (whether or not they can involve computation) can be implemented in a variety of "hardware." For example, a bottle opener is something that performs the function of opening bottles. Bottle openers can be made from different materials and can work in different ways: they can be made of steel or aluminum, and they can magnetically lift up the bottle cap or lever it off.

Functionalism—specifically the version holding that the brain is some kind of computer—is probably the dominant theory of mind in philosophy and cognitive science today. Yet it is not without objectors, and the philosopher John Searle is prominent among them. His famous "Chinese room argument" is supposed to show that running a computer program, no matter how complicated, is not a **sufficient condition** for having a mind.

Dualism

If behaviorism, the identity theory, and functionalism all face serious problems, this suggests the mind is not material after all, a position known as **dualism**. Dualism has a long history, going back to Plato, and the selection by René Descartes is a classic defense of it. Descartes argues that he is "simply a thinking, non-extended thing," somehow connected to his physical body. But the connection could be broken: Descartes is "really distinct" from his body, and he could "exist without it." The selection by Gilbert Ryle gives a series of objections to dualism or, as he disparagingly calls it, "the dogma of the ghost in the machine." The selection is from Ryle's influential book *The Concept of Mind*, published in 1949, which sets out his own sophisticated behaviorist theory.

René Descartes (1596–1650)

Descartes was a French philosopher, mathematician, and scientist. He made important early contributions to mathematical physics, invented the Cartesian coordinate system familiar from high school geometry, and is widely regarded as "the founder of modern philosophy." The *Meditations on First Philosophy* (1641) is his most famous book; his other major works include *Principles of Philosophy* (1644) and *The Passions of the Soul* (1649).

MEDITATION II: THE NATURE OF THE HUMAN MIND, AND HOW IT IS BETTER KNOWN THAN THE BODY
from *Meditations on First Philosophy*

So serious are the doubts into which I have been thrown as a result of yesterday's meditation[1] that I can neither put them out of my mind nor see any way of resolving them. It feels as if I have fallen unexpectedly into a deep whirlpool which tumbles me around so that I can neither stand on the bottom nor swim up to the top. Nevertheless I will make an effort and once more attempt the same path which I started on yesterday. Anything which admits of the slightest doubt I will set aside just as if I had found it to be wholly false; and I will proceed in this way until I recognize something certain, or, if nothing else, until I at least recognize for certain that there is no certainty. Archimedes[2] used to demand just one firm and immovable point in order to shift the entire earth; so I too can hope for great things if I manage to find just one thing, however slight, that is certain and unshakeable.

I will suppose then, that everything I see is spurious. I will believe that my memory tells me lies, and that none of the things that it reports ever happened. I have no senses. Body, shape, extension, movement and place are chimeras. So what remains true? Perhaps just the one fact that nothing is certain.

Yet apart from everything I have just listed, how do I know that there is not something else which does not allow even the slightest occasion for doubt? Is there not a God, or whatever I may call him, who puts into me the thoughts I am now having? But why do I think this, since I myself may perhaps be the author of these thoughts? In that case am not I, at least, something? But I have just said that I have no senses and no body. This is the sticking point: what follows from this? Am I not so bound up with a body and with senses that I cannot exist without them? But I have convinced myself that there is absolutely nothing in the world, no sky, no earth, no minds, no bodies. Does it now follow that I too do not exist? No: if I convinced myself of something then I certainly existed. But there is a deceiver of supreme power and cunning who is deliberately

---

1. Meditation I; see Chapter 6 of this anthology.
2. Ancient Greek scientist and mathematician (c. 287–c. 212 BCE).

and constantly deceiving me. In that case I too undoubtedly exist, if he is deceiving me; and let him deceive me as much as he can, he will never bring it about that I am nothing so long as I think that I am something. So after considering everything very thoroughly, I must finally conclude that this proposition, *I am, I exist,* is necessarily true whenever it is put forward by me or conceived in my mind.

But I do not yet have a sufficient understanding of what this "I" is, that now necessarily exists. So I must be on my guard against carelessly taking something else to be this "I," and so making a mistake in the very item of knowledge that I maintain is the most certain and evident of all. I will therefore go back and meditate on what I originally believed myself to be, before I embarked on this present train of thought. I will then subtract anything capable of being weakened, even minimally, by the arguments now introduced, so that what is left at the end may be exactly and only what is certain and unshakeable.

What then did I formerly think I was? A man. But what is a man? Shall I say "a rational animal"? No; for then I should have to inquire what an animal is, what rationality is, and in this way one question would lead me down the slope to other harder ones, and I do not now have the time to waste on subtleties of this kind. Instead I propose to concentrate on what came into my thoughts spontaneously and quite naturally whenever I used to consider what I was. Well, the first thought to come to mind was that I had a face, hands, arms and the whole mechanical structure of limbs which can be seen in a corpse, and which I called the body. The next thought was that I was nourished, that I moved about, and that I engaged in sense-perception and thinking; and these actions I attributed to the soul. But as to the nature of this soul, either I did not think about this or else I imagined it to be something tenuous, like a wind or fire or ether, which permeated my more solid parts. As to the body, however, I had no doubts about it, but thought I knew its nature distinctly. If I had tried to describe the mental conception I had of it, I would have expressed it as follows: by a body I understand whatever has a determinable shape and a definable location and can occupy a space in such a way as to exclude any other body; it can be perceived by touch, sight, hearing, taste or smell, and can be moved in various ways, not by itself but by whatever else comes into contact with it. For, according to my judgement, the power of self-movement, like the power of sensation or of thought, was quite foreign to the nature of a body; indeed, it was a source of wonder to me that certain bodies were found to contain faculties of this kind.

But what shall I now say that I am, when I am supposing that there is some supremely powerful and, if it is permissible to say so, malicious deceiver, who is deliberately trying to trick me in every way he can? Can I now assert that I possess even the most insignificant of all the attributes which I have just said belong to the nature of a body? I scrutinize them, think about them, go over them again, but nothing suggests itself; it is tiresome and pointless to go through the list once more. But what about the attributes I assigned to the soul? Nutrition or movement? Since now I do not have a body, these are mere fabrications. Sense-perception? This surely does not occur without a body, and besides, when asleep I have appeared to perceive through the senses many things which I afterwards realized I did not perceive through the senses at all. Thinking? At last I have discovered it—thought; this alone is inseparable from me. I am, I exist—that is certain. But for how long? For as long as I am thinking. For it could be that were I totally to cease from thinking, I should totally cease to exist. At present I am not admitting anything except what is necessarily true. I am, then, in the strict sense only a thing that thinks; that is, I am a mind, or intelligence, or intellect, or reason—words whose meaning I have been ignorant of until now. But for all that I am a thing which is real and which truly exists. But what kind of a thing? As I have just said—a thinking thing.

What else am I? I will use my imagination. I am not that structure of limbs which is called a human body. I am not even some thin vapour which permeates the limbs—a wind, fire, air, breath, or whatever I depict in my imagination; for these are things which I have supposed to be nothing. Let this supposition stand; for all that I am still something. And yet may it not perhaps be the case that these very things which I am supposing to be nothing, because they are unknown to me, are in reality identical with the "I" of which I am aware? I do not know, and for the moment I shall not argue the point, since I can make judgements only about things which are known to me. I know that I exist; the question is, what is this "I" that I know? If the "I" is understood strictly as we have been taking it, then it is quite certain that knowledge of it does not depend on things of whose existence I am as yet unaware; so it cannot depend on any of the things which I invent in my imagination. And this very word "invent" shows me my mistake. It would indeed be a case of fictitious invention if I used my imagination to establish that I was something or other; for imagining is simply contemplating the shape or image of a corporeal thing. Yet now I know for certain both that I exist and at the same time that all such images and, in general, everything relating to the nature of body, could be mere dreams. . . . Once this point has been grasped, to say "I will use my imagination to get to know more distinctly what I am" would seem to be as silly as saying "I am now awake, and see some truth; but since my vision is not yet clear enough, I will deliberately fall asleep so that my dreams may provide a truer and clearer representation." I thus realize that none of the things that the imagination enables me to grasp is at all relevant to this knowledge of myself which I possess, and that the mind must therefore be most carefully diverted from such things if it is to perceive its own nature as distinctly as possible.

But what then am I? A thing that thinks. What is that? A thing that doubts, understands, affirms, denies, is willing, is unwilling, and also imagines and has sensory perceptions.

This is a considerable list, if everything on it belongs to me. But does it? Is it not one and the same "I" who is now doubting almost everything, who nonetheless understands some things, who affirms that this one thing is true, denies everything else, desires to know more, is unwilling to be deceived, imagines many things even involuntarily, and is aware of many things which apparently come from the senses? Are not all these things just as true as the fact that I exist, even if I am asleep all the time, and even if he who created me is doing all he can to deceive me? Which of all these activities is distinct from my thinking? Which of them can be said to be separate from myself? The fact that it is I who am doubting and understanding and willing is so evident that I see no way of making it any clearer. But it is also the case that the "I" who imagines is the same "I." For even if, as I have supposed, none of the objects of imagination are real, the power of imagination is something which really exists and is part of my thinking. Lastly, it is also the same "I" who has sensory perceptions, or is aware of bodily things as it were through the senses. For example, I am now seeing light, hearing a noise, feeling heat. But I am asleep, so all this is false. Yet I certainly *seem* to see, to hear, and to be warmed. This cannot be false; what is called "having a sensory perception" is strictly just this, and in this restricted sense of the term it is simply thinking.

From all this I am beginning to have a rather better understanding of what I am. But it still appears—and I cannot stop thinking this—that the corporeal things of which images are formed in my thought, and which the senses investigate, are known with much more distinctness than this puzzling "I" which cannot be pictured in the imagination. And yet it is surely surprising that I should have a more distinct grasp of things which I realize are doubtful, unknown and foreign to me, than I have of that which is true and known—my own self. But I see what it is: my mind enjoys wandering off and will not yet submit to being restrained within the bounds of truth. Very well then; just this once let us give it a completely free rein, so that after a while, when it is time to tighten the reins, it may more readily submit to being curbed.

Let us consider the things which people commonly think they understand most distinctly of all; that is, the bodies which we touch and see. I do not mean bodies in general—for general perceptions are apt to be somewhat more confused—but one particular body. Let us take, for example, this piece of wax. It has just been taken from the honeycomb; it has not yet quite lost the taste of the honey; it retains some of the scent of the flowers from which it was gathered; its colour, shape and size are plain to see; it is hard, cold and can be handled without difficulty; if you rap it with your knuckle it makes a sound. In short, it has everything which appears necessary to enable a body to be known as distinctly as possible. But even as I speak, I put the wax by the fire, and look: the residual taste is eliminated, the smell goes away, the colour changes, the shape is lost, the size increases; it becomes liquid and hot; you can hardly touch it, and if you strike it, it no longer makes a sound. But does the same wax remain? It must be admitted that it does; no one denies it, no one thinks otherwise. So what was it in the wax that I understood with such distinctness? Evidently none of the features which I arrived at by means of the senses; for whatever came under taste, smell, sight, touch or hearing has now altered—yet the wax remains.

Perhaps the answer lies in the thought which now comes to my mind; namely, the wax was not after all the sweetness of the honey, or the fragrance of the flowers, or the whiteness, or the shape, or the sound, but was rather a body which presented itself to me in these various forms a little while ago, but which now exhibits different ones. But what exactly is it that I am now imagining? Let us concentrate, take away everything which does not belong to the wax, and see what is left: merely something extended, flexible and changeable. But what is meant here by "flexible" and "changeable"? Is it what I picture in my imagination: that this piece of wax is capable of changing from a round shape to a square shape, or from a square shape to a triangular shape? Not at all; for I can grasp that the wax is capable of countless changes of this kind, yet I am unable to run through this immeasurable number of changes in my imagination, from which it follows that it is not the faculty of imagination that gives me my grasp of the wax as flexible and changeable. And what is meant by "extended"? Is the extension of the wax also unknown? For it increases if the wax melts, increases again if it boils, and is greater still if the heat is increased. I would not be making a correct judgement about the nature of wax unless I believed it capable of being extended in many more different ways than I will ever encompass in my imagination. I must therefore admit that the nature of this piece of wax is in no way revealed by my imagination, but is perceived by the mind alone. (I am speaking of this particular piece of wax; the point is even clearer with regard to wax in general.) But what is this wax which is perceived by the mind alone? It is of course the same wax which I see, which I touch, which I picture in my imagination, in short the same wax which I thought it to be from the start. And yet, and here is the point, the perception I have of it is a case not of vision or touch or imagination—nor has it ever been, despite previous appearances—but of purely mental scrutiny; and this can be imperfect and confused, as it was before, or clear and distinct as it is now, depending on how carefully I concentrate on what the wax consists in.

But as I reach this conclusion I am amazed at how . . . prone to error my mind is. For although I am thinking about these matters within myself, silently and without speaking, nonetheless the actual words bring me up short, and I am almost tricked by ordinary ways of talking. We say that we see the wax itself, if it is there before us, not that we judge it to be there from its colour or shape; and this might lead me to conclude without more ado that knowledge of the wax comes from what the eye sees, and not from the scrutiny of the mind alone. But then if I look out of the window and see men crossing the square, as I just happen to have done, I normally say that I see the men themselves, just as I say that I see the wax. Yet do I see any more than hats and coats which could conceal automatons? I *judge* that they are men. And so something which I thought I was seeing with my eyes is in fact grasped solely by the faculty of judgement which is in my mind.

However, one who wants to achieve knowledge above the ordinary level should feel ashamed at having taken ordinary ways of talking as a basis for doubt. So let us proceed, and consider on which occasion my perception of the nature of the wax was more perfect and evident. Was it when I first looked at it, and believed I knew it by my external senses, or at least by what they call the "common" sense[3]—that is, the power of imagination? Or is my knowledge more perfect now, after a more careful investigation of the nature of the wax and of the means by which it is known? Any doubt on this issue would clearly be foolish; for what distinctness was there in my earlier perception? Was there anything in it which an animal could not possess? But when I distinguish the wax from its outward forms—take the clothes off, as it were, and consider it naked—then although my judgement may still contain errors, at least my perception now requires a human mind.

---

3. The supposed faculty which integrates the data from the five specialized senses (the notion goes back ultimately to Aristotle). [Translator's note.]

But what am I to say about this mind, or about myself? (So far, remember, I am not admitting that there is anything else in me except a mind.) What, I ask, is this "I" which seems to perceive the wax so distinctly? Surely my awareness of my own self is not merely much truer and more certain than my awareness of the wax, but also much more distinct and evident. For if I judge that the wax exists from the fact that I see it, clearly this same fact entails much more evidently that I myself also exist. It is possible that what I see is not really the wax; it is possible that I do not even have eyes with which to see anything. But when I see, or think I see (I am not here distinguishing the two), it is simply not possible that I who am now thinking am not something. By the same token, if I judge that the wax exists from the fact that I touch it, the same result follows, namely that I exist. If I judge that it exists from the fact that I imagine it, or for any other reason, exactly the same thing follows. And the result that I have grasped in the case of the wax may be applied to everything else located outside me. Moreover, if my perception of the wax seemed more distinct after it was established not just by sight or touch but by many other considerations, it must be admitted that I now know myself even more distinctly. This is because every consideration what-soever which contributes to my perception of the wax, or of any other body, cannot but establish even more effectively the nature of my own mind. But besides this, there is so much else in the mind itself which can serve to make my knowledge of it more distinct, that it scarcely seems worth going through the contributions made by considering bodily things.

I see that without any effort I have now finally got back to where I wanted. I now know that even bodies are not strictly perceived by the senses or the faculty of imagination but by the intellect alone, and that this perception derives not from their being touched or seen but from their being understood; and in view of this I know plainly that I can achieve an easier and more evident perception of my own mind than of anything else. But since the habit of holding on to old opinions cannot be set aside so quickly, I should like to stop here and meditate for some time on this new knowledge I have gained, so as to fix it more deeply in my memory.

MEDITATION VI: . . . THE REAL DISTINCTION BETWEEN MIND AND BODY

from *Meditations on First Philosophy*

But now,[4] when I am beginning to achieve a better knowledge of myself and the author of my being, although I do not think I should heedlessly accept everything I seem to have acquired from the senses, neither do I think that everything should be called into doubt.

---

4. Descartes has just reviewed the reasons he earlier gave for doubting his "confident belief in the truth of the things perceived by the senses."

First, I know that everything which I clearly and distinctly understand is capable of being created by God so as to correspond exactly with my understanding of it. Hence the fact that I can clearly and distinctly understand one thing apart from another is enough to make me certain that the two things are distinct, since they are capable of being separated, at least by God. The question of what kind of power is required to bring about such a separation does not affect the judgement that the two things are distinct. Thus, simply by knowing that I exist and seeing at the same time that absolutely nothing else belongs to my nature or essence except that I am a thinking thing, I can infer correctly that my essence consists solely in the fact that I am a thinking thing. It is true that I may have (or, to anticipate, that I certainly have) a body that is very closely joined to me. But nevertheless, on the one hand I have a clear and distinct idea of myself, in so far as I am simply a thinking, non-extended thing; and on the other hand I have a distinct idea of body, in so far as this is simply an extended, non-thinking thing. And accordingly, it is certain that I am really distinct from my body, and can exist without it. . . .

There is nothing that my own nature teaches me more vividly than that I have a body, and that when I feel pain there is something wrong with the body, and that when I am hungry or thirsty the body needs food and drink, and so on. So I should not doubt that there is some truth in this.

Nature also teaches me, by these sensations of pain, hunger, thirst and so on, that I am not merely present in my body as a sailor is present in a ship, but that I am very closely joined and, as it were, intermingled with it, so that I and the body form a unit. If this were not so, I, who am nothing but a thinking thing, would not feel pain when the body was hurt, but would perceive the damage purely by the intellect, just as a sailor perceives by sight if anything in his ship is broken. Similarly, when the body needed food or drink, I should have an explicit understanding of the fact, instead of having confused sensations of hunger and thirst. For these sensations of hunger, thirst, pain and so on are nothing but confused modes of thinking which arise from the union and, as it were, intermingling of the mind with the body. . . .

There is a great difference between the mind and the body, inasmuch as the body is by its very nature always divisible, while the mind is utterly indivisible. For when I consider the mind, or myself in so far as I am merely a thinking thing, I am unable to distinguish any parts within myself; I understand myself to be something quite single and complete. Although the whole mind seems to be united to the whole body, I recognize that if a foot or arm or any other part of the body is cut off, nothing has thereby been taken away from the mind. As for the faculties of willing, of understanding, of sensory perception and so on, these cannot be termed parts of the mind, since it is one and the same mind that wills, and understands and has sensory perceptions. By contrast, there is no corporeal or extended thing that I can think of which in my thought I cannot easily divide into parts; and this very fact makes me understand that it is divisible. This one argument would be enough to show me that the mind is completely different from the body, even if I did not already know as much from other considerations.

My next observation is that the mind is not immediately affected by all parts of the body, but only by the brain, or perhaps just by one small part of the brain, namely the part which is said to contain the "common" sense.[5] Every time this part of the brain is in a given state, it presents the same signals to the mind, even though the other parts of the body may be in a different condition at the time. This is established by countless observations, which there is no need to review here.

TEST YOUR UNDERSTANDING

1. Is Descartes using the expression "thinking" as it is used in ordinary life?

2. Does Descartes think that it is easier to know what bodies (like pieces of wax) are than it is to know what his mind is?

3. According to Descartes, are he and his body

    a. joined as a sailor is to a ship?

    b. related as a fog is to a ship when the fog permeates every part of the ship?

    c. related so they form a third thing, a unit composed of Descartes and his body?

4. According to Richard Watson's *Cogito, Ergo Sum: The Life of René Descartes* (Godine, 2007, p. 173), Descartes was short in height, perhaps a little over 5 feet. Speaking strictly, would Descartes have agreed? Explain your answer.

NOTES AND QUESTIONS

1. The example of the piece of wax is supposed to show that "bodies are not strictly perceived by the senses or the faculty of imagination but by the intellect alone" (Meditation II). Set out Descartes's **argument** for this in the form of premises and conclusion, and evaluate it.[6]

2. You may have noticed that Descartes's famous phrase "I think, therefore I am" (in Latin "Cogito, ergo sum") does not occur in the selection. (It is in Descartes's *Discourse on Method* [1637] and *Principles of Philosophy* [1644]; the *Meditations* was published in 1641.) Instead, Descartes writes in Meditation II that "this proposition, *I am, I exist*, is necessarily true whenever it is put forward by me or conceived in my mind." That raises the question whether the difference in formulation in the *Meditations* is significant.[7]

---

5. The pineal gland, according to Descartes. This small gland is near the center of the brain and produces the hormone melatonin.

6. For a discussion of the wax example, see chapter 2 of Margaret Wilson, *Descartes* (Routledge, 1993).

7. For discussion, see Wilson, *Descartes*, chapter 2.

Elisabeth of Bohemia (1618–1680)

Princess Elisabeth was the daughter of Frederick V, briefly King of Bohemia, a region in the present-day Czech Republic, and Elizabeth Stuart, daughter of James I of England. She had an extended correspondence with Descartes, famously pressing him to explain how an immaterial mind can affect a material body.

CORRESPONDENCE WITH DESCARTES
[The Hague] May 16, 1643

M. Descartes,

I learned, with much joy and regret, of the plan you had to see me a few days ago; I was touched equally by your charity in your willingness to share yourself with an ignorant and intractable person and by the bad luck which robbed me of such a profitable conversation. . . .

. . . I ask you please to tell me how the soul of a human being, (it being only a thinking substance), can determine the bodily spirits,[1] in order to bring about voluntary actions. For it seems that all determination of movement is made by the impulsion[2] of the thing moved, by the manner in which it is pushed by that which moves it, or else by the particular qualities and shape of the surface of the latter. Physical contact is required for the first two conditions, extension for the third. You entirely exclude the one [extension] from the notion that you have of the soul, and the other [physical contact] appears to me incompatible with an immaterial thing. This is why I ask you for a more precise definition of the soul than that you give in your *Metaphysics*,[3] that is to say, of its substance separate from its action, that is, from thought. For even if we were to suppose them inseparable, (which is all the same difficult to prove in the mother's womb and in great fainting spells), as are the attributes of God, we could, in considering them apart, acquire a more perfect idea of them.

Knowing that you are the best doctor for my soul, I expose to you quite freely the weaknesses of its speculations, and hope that in observing the Hippocratic oath,[4] you will supply me with remedies without making them public; such I beg of you to do, as to suffer the badgerings of

> Your affectionate friend at your service,
> Elisabeth.

---

1. Gaseous substances thought to control movement by flowing through nerves from the brain to the muscles.
2. Pushing.
3. The *Meditations*.
4. Pledge taken by physicians, named for the Greek physician Hippocrates (c. 460–c. 370 BCE).

TEST YOUR UNDERSTANDING

1. If an object X causes motion (e.g., causes your arm to rise), what features must X have, according to Elisabeth?

2. If an object X is an immaterial soul or mind, what features must X lack, according to Elisabeth?

3. Set out Elisabeth's objection in the form of a **valid argument**.

NOTES AND QUESTIONS

1. For more about Elisabeth, including her own philosophical views, see Lisa Shapiro, "Elisabeth, Princess of Bohemia," in *Stanford Encyclopedia of Philosophy*, ed. Edward Zalta (https://plato.stanford.edu/archives/win2014/entries/elisabeth-bohemia/).

2. Elisabeth and Descartes exchanged 58 letters between 1643 and 1649. You can find them all in Princess Elisabeth of Bohemia and René Descartes, *The Correspondence Between Princess Elisabeth of Bohemia and René Descartes*, ed. and trans. Lisa Shapiro (University of Chicago Press, 2007). The more philosophically relevant correspondence, put in stylistically modern English, is available at www.earlymoderntexts.com/authors/descartes. Elisabeth was not satisfied with Descartes's complicated reply to her letter.

3. Someone might think that the problem Elisabeth identifies depends crucially on an old-fashioned view of the causation of motion, which has been overturned by contemporary physics. Is that right? For discussion, see David Robb and John Heil, "Mental Causation," in *Stanford Encyclopedia of Philosophy*, ed. Edward Zalta (https://plato.stanford.edu/archives/spr2014/entries/mental-causation/), section 2.1.

Antoine Arnauld (1612–1694)

Arnauld was a French theologian and philosopher and was influential in Europe during the seventeenth century. The first edition of the *Meditations* contained six sets of objections from a variety of theologians and philosophers (including the English philosopher Thomas Hobbes[1]), together with Descartes's replies. Arnauld, who was sympathetic to many of Descartes's ideas, wrote the fourth set.

---

1. See Chapter 20 of this anthology.

FOURTH SET OF OBJECTIONS

. . . The first thing that I find remarkable is that our distinguished author has laid down as the basis for his entire philosophy exactly the same principle as that laid down by St Augustine[2]—a man of the sharpest intellect and a remarkable thinker, not only on theological topics but also on philosophical ones. In . . . *De Libero Arbitrio*[3] [Augustine writes] the following: "First, if we are to take as our starting point what is most evident, I ask you to tell me whether you yourself exist. Or are you perhaps afraid of making a mistake in your answer, given that, if you did not exist, it would be quite impossible for you to make a mistake?" This is like what M. Descartes says: "But there is a deceiver of supreme power and cunning who is deliberately and constantly deceiving me. In that case I too undoubtedly exist, if he is deceiving me."[4] But let us go on from here and, more to the point, see how this principle can be used to derive the result that our mind is separate from our body.

I can doubt whether I have a body, and even whether there are any bodies at all in the world. Yet for all that, I may not doubt that I am or exist, so long as I am doubting or thinking.

Therefore I who am doubting and thinking am not a body. For, in that case, in having doubts about my body I should be having doubts about myself.

Indeed, even if I obstinately maintain that there are no bodies whatsoever, the proposition still stands, namely that I am something, and hence I am not a body.

This is certainly very acute. But someone is going to bring up the objection which the author raises against himself: the fact that I have doubts about the body, or deny that it exists, does not bring it about that no body exists. "Yet may it not perhaps be the case that these very things which I am supposing to be nothing, because they are unknown to me, are in reality identical with the 'I' of which I am aware? I do not know," he says "and for the moment I shall not argue the point. I know that I exist; the question is, what is this 'I' that I know? If the 'I' is understood strictly as we have been taking it, then it is quite certain that knowledge of it does not depend on things of whose existence I am as yet unaware."

But the author admits that . . . the sense of the passage was that he was aware of nothing at all which he knew belonged to his essence[5] except that he was a thinking thing. From this answer it is clear that the objection still stands in precisely the same form as it did before, and that the question he promised to answer still remains outstanding: How does it follow, from the fact that he is aware of nothing else belonging to his essence, that nothing else does in fact belong to it? I must confess that I am somewhat slow, but I have been unable to find anywhere in the Second Meditation

---

2. Christian theologian and philosopher (354–430), born in present-day Algeria (then part of the Roman Empire).

3. On free choice (Latin).

4. See pages 312–13 of this anthology.

5. Descartes's "essence" is his nature, the fundamental kind of thing he is. See **essence and accident**.

an answer to this question. As far as I can gather, however, the author does attempt a proof of this claim in the Sixth Meditation, since he takes it to depend on his having clear knowledge of God, which he had not yet arrived at in the Second Meditation. This is how the proof goes:

> I know that everything which I clearly and distinctly understand is capable of being created by God so as to correspond exactly with my understanding of it. Hence the fact that I can clearly and distinctly understand one thing apart from another is enough to make me certain that the two things are distinct, since they are capable of being separated, at least by God. The question of what kind of power is required to bring about such a separation does not affect the judgement that the two things are distinct. . . . Now on the one hand I have a clear and distinct idea of myself, in so far as I am simply a thinking, non-extended thing; and on the other hand I have a distinct idea of body, in so far as this is simply an extended, non-thinking thing. And accordingly, it is certain that I am really distinct from my body, and can exist without it.[6]

We must pause a little here, for it seems to me that in these few words lies the crux of the whole difficulty. . . .

I cannot see anywhere in the entire work an argument which could serve to prove [that the mind can be completely and adequately understood apart from the body], apart from what is suggested at the beginning: "I can deny that any body exists, or that there is any extended thing at all, yet it remains certain to me that I exist, so long as I am making this denial or thinking it. Hence I am a thinking thing, not a body, and the body does not belong to the knowledge I have of myself."[7]

But so far as I can see, the only result that follows from this is that I can obtain some knowledge of myself without knowledge of the body. But it is not yet transparently clear to me that this knowledge is complete and adequate, so as to enable me to be certain that I am not mistaken in excluding body from my essence. I shall explain the point by means of an example.

Suppose someone knows for certain that [a] triangle . . . is right-angled. In spite of this, he may doubt, or not yet have grasped for certain, that the square on the hypotenuse is equal to the squares on the other two sides; indeed he may even deny this if he is misled by some fallacy. But now, if he uses the same argument as that proposed by our illustrious author, he may appear to have confirmation of his false belief, as follows: "I clearly and distinctly perceive," he may say, "that the triangle is right-angled; but I doubt that the square on the hypotenuse is equal to the squares on the other two sides; therefore it does not belong to the essence of the triangle that the square on its hypotenuse is equal to the squares on the other sides."

Again, even if I deny that the square on the hypotenuse is equal to the square on the other two sides, I still remain sure that the triangle is right-angled, and my mind

---

6. See page 318 of this anthology.

7. Not an exact quotation. See pages 313–14 of this anthology.

retains the clear and distinct knowledge that one of its angles is a right angle. And given that this is so, not even God could bring it about that the triangle is not right-angled.

I might argue from this that the property which I doubt, or which can be removed while leaving my idea intact, does not belong to the essence of the triangle.

Moreover, "I know," says M. Descartes, "that everything which I clearly and distinctly understand is capable of being created by God so as to correspond exactly with my understanding of it. And hence the fact that I can clearly and distinctly understand one thing apart from another is enough to make me certain that the two things are distinct, since they are capable of being separated . . . by God."[8] Yet I clearly and distinctly understand that this triangle is right-angled, without understanding that the square on the hypotenuse is equal to the squares on the other sides. It follows on this reasoning that God, at least, could create a right-angled triangle with the square on its hypotenuse not equal to the squares on the other sides.

I do not see any possible reply here, except that the person in this example does not clearly and distinctly perceive that the triangle is right-angled. But how is my perception of the nature of my mind any clearer than his perception of the nature of the triangle? He is just as certain that the triangle . . . has one right angle (which is the criterion of a right-angled triangle) as I am certain that I exist because I am thinking.

Now although the man in the example clearly and distinctly knows that the triangle is right-angled, he is wrong in thinking that the aforesaid relationship between the squares on the sides does not belong to the nature of the triangle. Similarly, although I clearly and distinctly know my nature to be something that thinks, may I, too, not perhaps be wrong in thinking that nothing else belongs to my nature apart from the fact that I am a thinking thing? Perhaps the fact that I am an extended thing may also belong to my nature.

TEST YOUR UNDERSTANDING

1. Is Arnauld arguing that the mind is not separate from the body?

2. According to Descartes, "everything which I clearly and distinctly understand is capable of being created by God so as to correspond exactly with my understanding of it." Is Arnauld denying this?

3. In the example of the triangle, what is supposed to be analogous to the **property** of being spatially extended?

   a. being a right-angled triangle

   b. being a triangle with hypotenuse h and other sides a, b, such that $h^2 = a^2 + b^2$.

   c. being a right-angled triangle with hypotenuse h and other sides a, b, such that $h^2 = a^2 + b^2$

8. See page 318 of this anthology.

NOTES AND QUESTIONS

1. For more about Arnauld, see Elmar Kremer, "Antoine Arnauld," in *Stanford Encyclopedia of Philosophy*, ed. Edward Zalta (https://plato.stanford.edu/archives/fall2012/entries/arnauld/).

2. The complete set of objections, together with Descartes's replies, all put in stylistically modern English, is available at www.earlymoderntexts.com/authors/descartes.

3. Suppose that a particular ball is painted pink. *Being pink* is surely an *accidental* property of the ball, one that it could have lacked—God could have created this ball and colored it green. As Descartes and Arnauld would put it, being pink does not "belong to the essence" of the ball. But don't we think this precisely because we can "clearly and distinctly understand one thing apart from another"; that is, clearly and distinctly imagine this ball being, not pink, but some *other* color? Yet this method is exactly what Arnauld is objecting to! If his objection to Descartes works, we don't know the obvious and mundane fact that this pink ball could have been green. So his objection doesn't work. How should Arnauld respond?

Gilbert Ryle (1900–1976)

Ryle was an English philosopher who spent his entire career at the University of Oxford, where he was elected Waynflete Professor of Metaphysical Philosophy in 1945. His most influential work is *The Concept of Mind* (1949), a sustained attack on Cartesian dualism and a defense of a more behaviorist approach.

DESCARTES' MYTH
from *The Concept of Mind*

1. The Official Doctrine

There is a doctrine about the nature and place of minds which is so prevalent among theorists and even among laymen that it deserves to be described as the official theory. Most philosophers, psychologists and religious teachers subscribe, with minor reservations, to its main articles and, although they admit certain theoretical difficulties in it, they tend to assume that these can be overcome without serious modifications being made to the architecture of the theory. It will be argued here that the central principles of the doctrine are unsound and conflict with the whole body of what we know about minds when we are not speculating about them.

The official doctrine, which hails chiefly from Descartes,[1] is something like this. With the doubtful exceptions of idiots and infants in arms every human being has both a body and a mind. Some would prefer to say that every human being is both a body and a mind. His body and his mind are ordinarily harnessed together, but after the death of the body his mind may continue to exist and function.

Human bodies are in space and are subject to the mechanical laws which govern all other bodies in space. Bodily processes and states can be inspected by external observers. So a man's bodily life is as much a public affair as are the lives of animals and reptiles and even as the careers of trees, crystals and planets.

But minds are not in space, nor are their operations subject to mechanical laws. The workings of one mind are not witnessable by other observers; its career is private. Only I can take direct cognisance of the states and processes of my own mind. A person therefore lives through two collateral histories, one consisting of what happens in and to his body, the other consisting of what happens in and to his mind. The first is public, the second private. The events in the first history are events in the physical world, those in the second are events in the mental world.

It has been disputed whether a person does or can directly monitor all or only some of the episodes of his own private history; but, according to the official doctrine, of at least some of these episodes he has direct and unchallengeable cognisance. In consciousness, self-consciousness and introspection he is directly and authentically apprised of the present states and operations of his mind. He may have great or small uncertainties about concurrent and adjacent episodes in the physical world, but he can have none about at least part of what is momentarily occupying his mind.

It is customary to express this bifurcation of his two lives and of his two worlds by saying that the things and events which belong to the physical world, including his own body, are external, while the workings of his own mind are internal. This antithesis of outer and inner is of course meant to be construed as a metaphor, since minds, not being in space, could not be described as being spatially inside anything else, or as having things going on spatially inside themselves. But relapses from this good intention are common and theorists are found speculating how stimuli, the physical sources of which are yards or miles outside a person's skin, can generate mental responses inside his skull, or how decisions framed inside his cranium can set going movements of his extremities.

Even when "inner" and "outer" are construed as metaphors, the problem how a person's mind and body influence one another is notoriously charged with theoretical difficulties. What the mind wills, the legs, arms and the tongue execute; what affects the ear and the eye has something to do with what the mind perceives; grimaces and smiles betray the mind's moods and bodily castigations lead, it is hoped, to moral improvement. But the actual transactions between the episodes of the private history and those of the public history remain mysterious, since by definition they can belong

---

1. René Descartes (1596–1650). See Meditations II and VI in this chapter.

to neither series. They could not be reported among the happenings described in a person's autobiography of his inner life, but nor could they be reported among those described in some one else's biography of that person's overt career. They can be inspected neither by introspection nor by laboratory experiment. They are theoretical shuttlecocks which are forever being bandied from the physiologist back to the psychologist and from the psychologist back to the physiologist.

Underlying this partly metaphorical representation of the bifurcation of a person's two lives there is a seemingly more profound and philosophical assumption. It is assumed that there are two different kinds of existence or status. What exists or happens may have the status of physical existence, or it may have the status of mental existence. Somewhat as the faces of coins are either heads or tails, or somewhat as living creatures are either male or female, so, it is supposed, some existing is physical existing, other existing is mental existing. It is a necessary feature of what has physical existence that it is in space and time; it is a necessary feature of what has mental existence that it is in time but not in space. What has physical existence is composed of matter, or else is a function of matter; what has mental existence consists of consciousness, or else is a function of consciousness.

There is thus a polar opposition between mind and matter, an opposition which is often brought out as follows. Material objects are situated in a common field, known as "space," and what happens to one body in one part of space is mechanically connected with what happens to other bodies in other parts of space. But mental happenings occur in insulated fields, known as "minds," and there is, apart maybe from telepathy, no direct causal connection between what happens in one mind and what happens in another. Only through the medium of the public physical world can the mind of one person make a difference to the mind of another. The mind is its own place and in his inner life each of us lives the life of a ghostly Robinson Crusoe.[2] People can see, hear and jolt one another's bodies, but they are irremediably blind and deaf to the workings of one another's minds and inoperative upon them.

What sort of knowledge can be secured of the workings of a mind? On the one side, according to the official theory, a person has direct knowledge of the best imaginable kind of the workings of his own mind. Mental states and processes are (or are normally) conscious states and processes, and the consciousness which irradiates them can engender no illusions and leaves the door open for no doubts. A person's present thinkings, feelings and willings, his perceivings, rememberings and imaginings are intrinsically "phosphorescent"; their existence and their nature are inevitably betrayed to their owner. The inner life is a stream of consciousness of such a sort that it would be absurd to suggest that the mind whose life is that stream might be unaware of what is passing down it.

True, the evidence adduced recently by Freud[3] seems to show that there exist channels tributary to this stream, which run hidden from their owner. People are actuated by impulses the existence of which they vigorously disavow; some of their thoughts

2. The title character of Daniel Defoe's novel *Robinson Crusoe* (1719), in which Crusoe is stranded on an island for 28 years.

3. Sigmund Freud (1856–1939), Austrian neurologist and founder of psychoanalysis.

differ from the thoughts which they acknowledge; and some of the actions which they think they will to perform they do not really will. They are thoroughly gulled by some of their own hypocrisies and they successfully ignore facts about their mental lives which on the official theory ought to be patent to them. Holders of the official theory tend, however, to maintain that anyhow in normal circumstances a person must be directly and authentically seized of the present state and workings of his own mind.

Besides being currently supplied with these alleged immediate data of consciousness, a person is also generally supposed to be able to exercise from time to time a special kind of perception, namely inner perception, or introspection. He can take a (non-optical) "look" at what is passing in his mind. Not only can he view and scrutinize a flower through his sense of sight and listen to and discriminate the notes of a bell through his sense of hearing; he can also reflectively or introspectively watch, without any bodily organ of sense, the current episodes of his inner life. This self-observation is also commonly supposed to be immune from illusion, confusion or doubt. A mind's reports of its own affairs have a certainty superior to the best that is possessed by its reports of matters in the physical world. Sense-perceptions can, but consciousness and introspection cannot, be mistaken or confused.

On the other side, one person has no direct access of any sort to the events of the inner life of another. He cannot do better than make problematic inferences from the observed behaviour of the other person's body to the states of mind which, by analogy from his own conduct, he supposes to be signalised by that behaviour. Direct access to the workings of a mind is the privilege of that mind itself; in default of such privileged access, the workings of one mind are inevitably occult[4] to everyone else. For the supposed arguments from bodily movements similar to their own to mental workings similar to their own would lack any possibility of observational corroboration. Not unnaturally, therefore, an adherent of the official theory finds it difficult to resist this consequence of his premises, that he has no good reason to believe that there do exist minds other than his own. Even if he prefers to believe that to other human bodies there are harnessed minds not unlike his own, he cannot claim to be able to discover their individual characteristics, or the particular things that they undergo and do. Absolute solitude is on this showing the ineluctable destiny of the soul. Only our bodies can meet. . . .

2. The Absurdity of the Official Doctrine

Such in outline is the official theory. I shall often speak of it, with deliberate abusiveness, as "the dogma of the Ghost in the Machine." I hope to prove that it is entirely false, and false not in detail but in principle. It is not merely an assemblage of particular mistakes. It is one big mistake and a mistake of a special kind. It is, namely, a category-mistake. It represents the facts of mental life as if they belonged to one logical type or category

4. Hidden.

(or range of types or categories), when they actually belong to another. The dogma is therefore a philosopher's myth. In attempting to explode the myth I shall probably be taken to be denying well-known facts about the mental life of human beings, and my plea that I aim at doing nothing more than rectify the logic of mental-conduct concepts will probably be disallowed as mere subterfuge.

I must first indicate what is meant by the phrase "category-mistake." This I do in a series of illustrations.

A foreigner visiting Oxford or Cambridge for the first time is shown a number of colleges, libraries, playing fields, museums, scientific departments and administrative offices. He then asks "But where is the University? I have seen where the members of the Colleges live, where the Registrar works, where the scientists experiment and the rest. But I have not yet seen the University in which reside and work the members of your University." It has then to be explained to him that the University is not another collateral institution, some ulterior counterpart to the colleges, laboratories and offices which he has seen. The University is just the way in which all that he has already seen is organized. When they are seen and when their co-ordination is understood, the University has been seen. His mistake lay in his innocent assumption that it was correct to speak of Christ Church, the Bodleian Library, the Ashmolean Museum *and* the University,[5] to speak, that is, as if "the University" stood for an extra member of the class of which these other units are members. He was mistakenly allocating the University to the same category as that to which the other institutions belong. . . .

The theoretically interesting category-mistakes are those made by people who are perfectly competent to apply concepts, at least in the situations with which they are familiar, but are still liable in their abstract thinking to allocate those concepts to logical types to which they do not belong. An instance of a mistake of this sort would be the following story. A student of politics has learned the main differences between the British, the French and the American Constitutions, and has learned also the differences and connections between the Cabinet, Parliament, the various Ministries, the Judicature and the Church of England. But he still becomes embarrassed when asked questions about the connections between the Church of England, the Home Office[6] and the British Constitution. For while the Church and the Home Office are institutions, the British Constitution is not another institution in the same sense of that noun. So inter-institutional relations which can be asserted or denied to hold between the Church and the Home Office cannot be asserted or denied to hold between either of them and the British Constitution. "The British Constitution" is not a term of the same logical type as "the Home Office" and "the Church of England." In a partially similar way, John Doe may be a relative, a friend, an enemy or a stranger to Richard Roe; but he cannot be any of these things to the Average Taxpayer. He knows how to talk sense in certain sorts of discussions about the Average Taxpayer, but he is baffled to say why he could not come across him in the street as he can come across Richard Roe.

5. Christ Church is a college of the University of Oxford; the Bodleian Library and the Ashmolean Museum are also part of the university.

6. Government department of the United Kingdom, similar to the U.S. Department of State but also responsible for domestic security and immigration.

It is pertinent to our main subject to notice that, so long as the student of politics continues to think of the British Constitution as a counterpart to the other institutions, he will tend to describe it as a mysteriously occult institution; and so long as John Doe continues to think of the Average Taxpayer as a fellow-citizen, he will tend to think of him as an elusive insubstantial man, a ghost who is everywhere yet nowhere.

My destructive purpose is to show that a family of radical category-mistakes is the source of the double-life theory. The representation of a person as a ghost mysteriously ensconced in a machine derives from this argument. Because, as is true, a person's thinking, feeling and purposive doing cannot be described solely in the idioms of physics, chemistry and physiology, therefore they must be described in counterpart idioms. As the human body is a complex organised unit, so the human mind must be another complex organised unit, though one made of a different sort of stuff and with a different sort of structure. Or, again, as the human body, like any other parcel of matter, is a field of causes and effects, so the mind must be another field of causes and effects, though not (Heaven be praised) mechanical causes and effects.

3. The Origin of the Category-Mistake

One of the chief intellectual origins of what I have yet to prove to be the Cartesian category-mistake seems to be this. When Galileo[7] showed that his methods of scientific discovery were competent to provide a mechanical theory which should cover every occupant of space, Descartes found in himself two conflicting motives. As a man of scientific genius he could not but endorse the claims of mechanics, yet as a religious and moral man he could not accept, as Hobbes[8] accepted, the discouraging rider to those claims, namely that human nature differs only in degree of complexity from clockwork. The mental could not be just a variety of the mechanical.

He and subsequent philosophers naturally but erroneously availed themselves of the following escape-route. Since mental-conduct words are not to be construed as signifying the occurrence of mechanical processes, they must be construed as signifying the occurrence of non-mechanical processes; since mechanical laws explain movements in space as the effects of other movements in space, other laws must explain some of the non-spatial workings of minds as the effects of other non-spatial workings of minds. The difference between the human behaviours which we describe as intelligent and those which we describe as unintelligent must be a difference in their causation; so, while some movements of human tongues and limbs are the effects of mechanical causes, others must be the effects of non-mechanical causes, i.e. some issue from movements of particles of matter, others from workings of the mind.

The differences between the physical and the mental were thus represented as differences inside the common framework of the categories of "thing," "stuff," "attribute,"

7. Galileo Galilei (1564–1642), Italian physicist and astronomer.
8. Thomas Hobbes (1588–1679), English philosopher.

"state," "process," "change," "cause" and "effect." Minds are things, but different sorts of things from bodies; mental processes are causes and effects, but different sorts of causes and effects from bodily movements. And so on. Somewhat as the foreigner expected the University to be an extra edifice, rather like a college but also considerably different, so the repudiators of mechanism represented minds as extra centres of causal processes, rather like machines but also considerably different from them. Their theory was a para-mechanical hypothesis.

That this assumption was at the heart of the doctrine is shown by the fact that there was from the beginning felt to be a major theoretical difficulty in explaining how minds can influence and be influenced by bodies. How can a mental process, such as willing, cause spatial movements like the movements of the tongue? How can a physical change in the optic nerve have among its effects a mind's perception of a flash of light? This notorious crux by itself shows the logical mould into which Descartes pressed his theory of the mind. It was the self-same mould into which he and Galileo set their mechanics. Still unwittingly adhering to the grammar of mechanics, he tried to avert disaster by describing minds in what was merely an obverse vocabulary. The workings of minds had to be described by the mere negatives of the specific descriptions given to bodies; they are not in space, they are not motions, they are not modifications of matter, they are not accessible to public observation. Minds are not bits of clockwork, they are just bits of not-clockwork.

As thus represented, minds are not merely ghosts harnessed to machines, they are themselves just spectral machines. Though the human body is an engine, it is not quite an ordinary engine, since some of its workings are governed by another engine inside it—this interior governor-engine being one of a very special sort. It is invisible, inaudible and it has no size or weight. It cannot be taken to bits and the laws it obeys are not those known to ordinary engineers. Nothing is known of how it governs the bodily engine. . . .

It is an historical curiosity that it was not noticed that the entire argument was broken-backed. Theorists correctly assumed that any sane man could already recognise the differences between, say, rational and non-rational utterances or between purposive and automatic behaviour. Else there would have been nothing requiring to be salved from mechanism. Yet the explanation given presupposed that one person could in principle never recognise the difference between the rational and the irrational utterances issuing from other human bodies, since he could never get access to the postulated immaterial causes of some of their utterances. Save for the doubtful exception of himself, he could never tell the difference between a man and a Robot. It would have to be conceded, for example, that, for all that we can tell, the inner lives of persons who are classed as idiots or lunatics are as rational as those of anyone else. Perhaps only their overt behaviour is disappointing; that is to say, perhaps "idiots" are not really idiotic, or "lunatics" lunatic. Perhaps, too, some of those who are classed as sane are really idiots. According to the theory, external observers could never know how the overt behaviour of others is correlated with their mental powers and processes and so they could never know or even plausibly conjecture whether their applications of mental-conduct concepts to these other people were correct or incorrect. It would then be hazardous or impossible for a man to claim sanity or logical consistency even for himself, since he would be debarred from comparing his own performances with those of others. In short, our characterisations of persons and their performances as intelligent, prudent and virtuous or as stupid, hypocritical and cowardly could never have been made, so the problem of providing a special causal hypothesis to serve as the basis of such diagnoses would never have arisen. The question, "How do persons differ from machines?" arose just because everyone already knew how to apply mental-conduct concepts before the new causal hypothesis was introduced. This causal hypothesis could not therefore be the source of the criteria used in those applications. Nor, of course, has the causal hypothesis in any degree improved our handling of those criteria. We still distinguish good from bad arithmetic, politic from impolitic conduct and fertile from infertile imaginations in the ways in which Descartes himself distinguished them before and after he speculated how the applicability of these criteria was compatible with the principle of mechanical causation.

He had mistaken the logic of his problem. Instead of asking by what criteria intelligent behaviour is actually distinguished from non-intelligent behaviour, he asked "Given that the principle of mechanical causation does not tell us the difference, what other causal principle will tell it us?" He realised that the problem was not one of mechanics and assumed that it must therefore be one of some counterpart to mechanics. Not unnaturally psychology is often cast for just this role. . . .

4. Historical Note

It would not be true to say that the official theory derives solely from Descartes' theories, or even from a more widespread anxiety about the implications of seventeenth century mechanics. . . . Descartes was reformulating already prevalent theological doctrines of the soul in the new syntax of Galileo. . . .

It would also not be true to say that the two-worlds myth did no theoretical good. Myths often do a lot of theoretical good, while they are still new. One benefit bestowed by the para-mechanical myth was that it partly superannuated the then prevalent para-political myth. Minds and their Faculties had previously been described by analogies with political superiors and political subordinates. The idioms used were those of ruling, obeying, collaborating and rebelling. They survived and still survive in many ethical and some epistemological discussions. As, in physics, the new myth of occult Forces was a scientific improvement on the old myth of Final Causes,[9] so, in anthropological and psychological theory, the new myth of hidden operations, impulses and agencies was an improvement on the old myth of dictations, deferences and disobediences.

---

9. Ends or purposes: the final cause of studying is knowledge (or good grades, or admission to medical school, etc.). One of the four types of cause distinguished by the Greek philosopher Aristotle (384–322 BCE), supposed to be central to scientific explanations.

TEST YOUR UNDERSTANDING

1. According to Ryle, why did the Cartesian category-mistake arise?

    a. Because theorists assumed that the mind was a complicated physical machine whose workings were not predictable by Galileo's mechanics.

    b. Because theorists took the mind to be like the Average Taxpayer.

    c. Because it reconciled the view that the mind is not physical with the view that the mind is a sort of machine.

    d. Because it was a consequence of Galileo's theory of spectral machines.

2. Is it a category-mistake to think that you have never met the Average Taxpayer?

3. Does Ryle think the human mind is a complicated physical machine?

4. Does Ryle think you can never know for sure what the inner lives of other people are like?

NOTES AND QUESTIONS

1. There are many mistakes that aren't category-mistakes. So it is possible to hold that Cartesian dualism is a mistake without thinking that it is "a mistake of a special kind . . . namely, a category-mistake." Does Ryle give good reasons for thinking that Cartesian dualism is a mistake of this "special kind"?

2. Ryle is usually taken to be some kind of behaviorist, although this interpretation is not straightforward. See Julia Tanney, "Gilbert Ryle," in *Stanford Encyclopedia of Philosophy*, ed. Edward Zalta (https://plato.stanford.edu/archives/spr2015/entries/ryle/).

J. J. C. Smart (1920–2012)

Smart was an Australian philosopher known for his contributions to the philosophy of mind, metaphysics, and ethics. His books include *Philosophy and Scientific Realism* (1963), *Utilitarianism: For and Against* (with Bernard Williams; 1973), and *Essays Metaphysical and Moral* (1987).

SENSATIONS AND BRAIN PROCESSES

Suppose that I report that I have at this moment a roundish, blurry-edged after-image which is yellowish towards its edge and is orange towards its centre. What is it that I am reporting? One answer to this question might be that I am not reporting anything, that when I say that it looks to me as though there is a roundish yellowy orange patch of light on the wall I am expressing some sort of *temptation*, the temptation to say that there *is* a roundish yellowy orange patch on the wall (though I may know that there is not such a patch on the wall). . . . Similarly, when I "report" a pain, I am not really reporting anything (or, if you like, I am reporting in a queer sense of "reporting"), but am doing a sophisticated sort of wince. . . . I prefer most of the time to discuss an after-image rather than a pain, because the word "pain" brings in something which is irrelevant to my purpose: the notion of "distress." I think that "he is in pain" entails "he is in distress," that is, that he is in a certain agitation-condition. Similarly, to say "I am in pain" may be to do more than "replace pain behavior": it may be partly to report something, though this something is quite nonmysterious, being an agitation-condition, and so susceptible of behavioristic analysis.[1] The suggestion I wish if possible to avoid is a different one, namely that "I am in pain" is a genuine report, and that what it reports is an irreducibly psychical something. And similarly the suggestion I wish to resist is also that to say "I have a yellowish orange after-image" is to report something irreducibly psychical.

Why do I wish to resist this suggestion? Mainly because of Occam's razor.[2] It seems to me that science is increasingly giving us a viewpoint whereby organisms are able to be seen as physico-chemical mechanisms: it seems that even the behavior of man himself will one day be explicable in mechanistic terms. There does seem to be, so far as science is concerned, nothing in the world but increasingly complex arrangements of physical constituents. All except for one place: in consciousness. That is, for a full description of what is going on in a man you would have to mention not only the physical processes in his tissue, glands, nervous system, and so forth, but also his states of consciousness: his visual, auditory, and tactual sensations, his aches and pains. That these should be *correlated* with brain processes does not help, for to say that they are *correlated* is to say that they are something "over and above." You cannot correlate something with itself. You correlate footprints with burglars, but not Bill Sikes the burglar with Bill Sikes the burglar. So sensations, states of consciousness, do seem to be the one sort of thing left outside the physicalist picture, and for various reasons I just cannot believe that this can be so. That everything should be explicable in terms of physics (together of course with descriptions of the ways in which the parts are put together—roughly, biology is to physics as radio-engineering is to electro-magnetism) except the occurrence of sensations seems to me to be frankly unbelievable. Such sensations would be "nomological danglers," to use Feigl's expression.[3] It is not often realized how odd would be the laws whereby these nomological danglers would dangle. It is sometimes asked, "Why can't there be psycho-physical laws which are of a novel sort, just as the laws of electricity and magnetism were novelties from the standpoint of Newtonian mechanics?" Certainly we are pretty sure in the future to come across

1. Behaviorism is the view that to have a mind is simply to behave (or to be disposed or inclined to behave) in various ways.

2. A methodological principle of parsimony in theorizing, often rendered as "Do not multiply entities beyond necessity." Named after the English philosopher William of Occam (or Ockham) (c. 1287–1347).

3. "Nomological": relating to laws of nature. Herbert Feigl (1902–1988) was an Austrian philosopher of science.

new ultimate laws of a novel type, but I expect them to relate simple constituents: for example, whatever ultimate particles are then in vogue. I cannot believe that ultimate laws of nature could relate simple constituents to configurations consisting of perhaps billions of neurons (and goodness knows how many billion billions of ultimate particles) all put together for all the world as though their main purpose in life was to be a negative feedback mechanism of a complicated sort. Such ultimate laws would be like nothing so far known in science. They have a queer "smell" to them. I am just unable to believe in the nomological danglers themselves, or in the laws whereby they would dangle. If any philosophical arguments seemed to compel us to believe in such things, I would suspect a catch in the argument. In any case it is the object of this paper to show that there are no philosophical arguments which compel us to be dualists.[4] . . .

Why should not sensations just be brain processes of a certain sort? There are, of course, well-known (as well as lesser-known) philosophical objections to the view that reports of sensations are reports of brain processes, but I shall try to argue that these arguments are by no means as cogent as is commonly thought to be the case.

Let me first try to state more accurately the thesis that sensations are brain processes. It is not the thesis that, for example; "after-image" or "ache" means the same as "brain process of sort *X*" (where "*X*" is replaced by a description of a certain sort of brain process). It is that, in so far as "after-image" or "ache" is a report of a process, it is a report of a process that *happens to be* a brain process. It follows that the thesis does not claim that sensation statements can be *translated* into statements about brain processes. Nor does it claim that the logic of a sensation statement is the same as that of a brain-process statement. All it claims is that in so far as a sensation statement is a report of something, that something is in fact a brain process. Sensations are nothing over and above brain processes. Nations are nothing "over and above" citizens, but this does not prevent the logic of nation statements being very different from the logic of citizen statements, nor does it insure the translatability of nation statements into citizen statements. (I do not, however, wish to assert that the relation of sensation statements to brain-process statements is very like that of nation statements to citizen statements. Nations do not just *happen to be* nothing over and above citizens, for example. I bring in the "nations" example merely to make a negative point: that the fact that the logic of A-statements is different from that of B-statements does not insure that A's are anything over and above B's.)

Remarks on identity. When I say that a sensation is a brain process or that lightning is an electric discharge, I am using "is" in the sense of strict identity. (Just as in the—in this case necessary—proposition "7 is identical with the smallest prime number greater than 5.") When I say that a sensation is a brain process or that lightning is an electric discharge I do not mean just that the sensation is somehow spatially or temporally continuous with the brain process or that the lightning is just spatially or temporally continuous with the discharge. . . . I wish to make it clear that the brain-process doctrine asserts identity in the *strict* sense.

I shall now discuss various possible objections to the view that the processes reported in sensation statements are in fact processes in the brain. Most of us have met some

---

4. Those who believe, following the French philosopher René Descartes (1596–1650), that the mind and the body are distinct things.

of these objections in our first year as philosophy students. All the more reason to take a good look at them. Others of the objections will be more recondite and subtle.

Objection 1.[5] Any illiterate peasant can talk perfectly well about his after-images, or how things look or feel to him, or about his aches and pains, and yet he may know nothing whatever about neurophysiology. A man may, like Aristotle, believe that the brain is an organ for cooling the body without any impairment of his ability to make true statements about his sensations. Hence the things we are talking about when we describe our sensations cannot be processes in the brain.

Reply. You might as well say that a nation of slug-abeds, who never saw the morning star or knew of its existence, or who had never thought of the expression "the Morning Star," but who used the expression "the Evening Star" perfectly well, could not use this expression to refer to the same entity as we refer to (and describe as) "the Morning Star."[6]

You may object that the Morning Star is in a sense not the very same thing as the Evening Star, but only something spatiotemporally continuous with it. That is, you may say that the Morning Star is not the Evening Star in the strict sense of "identity" that I distinguished earlier. I can perhaps forestall this objection by considering the slug-abeds to be New Zealanders and the early risers to be Englishmen. Then the thing the New Zealanders describe as "the Morning Star" could be the very same thing (in the strict sense) as the Englishmen describe as "the Evening Star." And yet they could be ignorant of this fact.

There is, however, a more plausible example. Consider lightning. Modern physical science tells us that lightning is a certain kind of electrical discharge due to ionization of clouds of water-vapor in the atmosphere. This, it is now believed, is what the true nature of lightning is. Note that there are not two things: a flash of lightning and an electrical discharge. There is one thing, a flash of lightning, which is described scientifically as an electrical discharge to the earth from a cloud of ionized water-molecules. The case is not at all like that of explaining a footprint by reference to a burglar. We say that what lightning really is, what its true nature as revealed by science is, is an electric discharge. (It is not the true nature of a footprint to be a burglar.)

To forestall irrelevant objections, I should like to make it clear that by "lightning" I mean the publicly observable physical object, lightning, not a visual sense-datum[7] of lightning. I say that the publicly observable physical object lightning is in fact the electric discharge, not just a correlate of it. The sense-datum, or at least the having of the sense-datum, the "look" of lightning, may well in my view be a correlate of the electric discharge. For in my view it is a brain state *caused* by the lightning. But we should no more confuse sensations of lightning with lightning than we confuse sensations of a table with the table.

In short, the reply to Objection 1 is that there can be contingent statements of the form "A is identical with B," and a person may well know that something is an A without knowing that it is a B. An illiterate peasant might well be able to talk about his sensations without knowing about his brain processes, just as he can talk about lightning though he knows nothing of electricity.

5. Smart discusses eight objections, two of which are omitted from this selection.

6. The Morning Star and the Evening Star are both the planet Venus.

7. A sense datum (plural *data*) is an object that (according to some philosophers) one is aware of when one sees a physical object and that (unlike the physical object) always is as it appears to be.

Objection 2. It is only a contingent fact (if it is a fact) that when we have a certain kind of sensation there is a certain kind of process in our brain. Indeed it is possible, though perhaps in the highest degree unlikely, that our present physiological theories will be as out of date as the ancient theory connecting mental processes with goings on in the heart. It follows that when we report a sensation we are not reporting a brain-process.

Reply. The objection certainly proves that when we say "I have an after-image" we cannot *mean* something of the form "I have such and such a brain process." But this does not show that what we report (having an after-image) is not *in fact* a brain process. "I see lightning" does not *mean* "I see an electric discharge." Indeed, it is logically possible (though highly unlikely) that the electrical discharge account of lightning might one day be given up. Again, "I see the Evening Star" does not *mean* the same as "I see the Morning Star," and yet "the Evening Star and the Morning Star are one and the same thing" is a contingent proposition. Possibly Objection 2 derives some of its apparent strength from a "Fido"-Fido theory of meaning.[8] If the meaning of an expression were what the expression named, then of course it *would* follow from the fact that "sensation" and "brain process" have different meanings that they cannot name one and the same thing.

Objection 3. Even if Objections 1 and 2 do not prove that sensations are something over and above brain processes, they do prove that the qualities of sensations are something over and above the qualities of brain processes. That is, it may be possible to get out of asserting the existence of irreducibly psychic processes, but not out of asserting the existence of irreducibly psychic *properties.* For suppose we identify the Morning Star with the Evening Star. Then there must be some properties which logically imply that of being the Morning Star, and quite distinct properties which entail that of being the Evening Star. Again, there must be some properties (for example, that of being a yellow flash) which are logically distinct from those in the physicalist story. . . .

Now how do I get over [this] objection that a sensation can be identified with a brain process only if it has some [irreducibly psychic] property . . . whereby one-half of the identification may be, so to speak, pinned down?[9]

My suggestion is as follows. When a person says, "I see a yellowish-orange after-image," he is saying something like this: "*There is something going on which is like what is going on when* I have my eyes open, am awake, and there is an orange illuminated in good light in front of me, that is, when I really see an orange." . . . Notice that the italicized words, namely "there is something going on which is like what is going on when," are all quasi-logical or topic-neutral words. This explains why the ancient Greek peasant's reports about his sensations can be neutral between dualistic metaphysics or my materialistic metaphysics. It explains how sensations can be brain processes and yet how those who

---

8. The theory (given this derogatory label by the English philosopher Gilbert Ryle [1900–1976]) that the meaning of an expression is the thing it refers to. Thus the meaning of the name "Fido" is the dog, Fido.

9. In a true identity statement like "The Morning Star = the Evening Star," the object in question, namely Venus, has two properties corresponding to the different ways Venus is identified or picked out by the two expressions "the Morning Star" and "the Evening Star." These two properties of Venus are *being the brightest object in the morning sky* and *being the brightest object in the evening sky.* Objection 3 is that if an identity statement like "This pain sensation = such-and-such brain process" is true, then the property corresponding to the way the noun phrase "this pain sensation" identifies or picks out the thing it refers to cannot be a neurophysiological property, and must instead be an irreducibly mental one.

report them need know nothing about brain processes. For he reports them only very abstractly as "something going on which is like what is going on when . . ." Similarly, a person may say "someone is in the room," thus reporting truly that the doctor is in the room, even though he has never heard of doctors. (There are not two people in the room: "someone" *and* the doctor.) This account of sensation statements also explains the singular elusiveness of "raw feels"[10]—why no one seems to be able to pin any properties on them. Raw feels, in my view, are colorless for the very same reason that *something* is colorless. This does not mean that sensations do not have properties, for if they are brain processes they certainly have properties. It only means that in speaking of them as being like or unlike one another we need not know or mention these properties.

This, then, is how I would reply to Objection 3. The strength of my reply depends on the possibility of our being able to report that one thing is like another without being able to state the respect in which it is like. I am not sure whether this is so or not, and that is why I regard Objection 3 as the strongest with which I have to deal.

Objection 4. The after-image is not in physical space. The brain process is. So the after-image is not a brain process.

Reply. This is an *ignoratio elenchi.*[11] I am not arguing that the after-image is a brain process, but that the experience of having an after-image is a brain process. It is the *experience* which is reported in the introspective report. Similarly, if it is objected that the after-image is yellowy-orange but that a surgeon looking into your brain would see nothing yellowy-orange, my reply is that it is the experience of seeing yellowy-orange that is being described, and this experience is not a yellow-orange something. So to say that a brain-process cannot be yellowy-orange is not to say that a brain-process cannot in fact be the experience of having a yellowy-orange after-image. There is, in a sense, no such thing as an after-image or a sense-datum, though there is such a thing as the experience of having an image, and this experience is described indirectly in material object language, not in phenomenal language, for there is no such thing. We describe the experience by saying, in effect, that it is like the experience we have when, for example, we really see a yellowy-orange patch on the wall. Trees and wallpaper can be green, but not the experience of seeing or imagining a tree or wallpaper. (Or if they are described as green or yellow this can only be in a derived sense.)

Objection 5. It would make sense to say of a molecular movement in the brain that it is swift or slow, straight or circular, but it makes no sense to say this of the experience of seeing something yellow.

Reply. So far we have not given sense to talk of experiences as swift or slow, straight or circular. But I am not claiming that "experience" and "brain process" mean the same or even that they have the same logic. "Somebody" and "the doctor" do not have the same logic, but this does not lead us to suppose that talking about somebody telephoning is talking about someone over and above, say, the doctor. The ordinary man when he reports an experience is reporting that something is going on, but he leaves it open as

---

10. Sensations.

11. Literally, "ignorance of refutation" (Latin). Used to label reasoning to an irrelevant conclusion.

to what sort of thing is going on, whether in a material solid medium, or perhaps in some sort of gaseous medium, or even perhaps in some sort of nonspatial medium (if this makes sense). All that I am saying is that "experience" and "brain process" may in fact refer to the same thing, and if so we may easily adopt a convention (which is not a change in our present rules for the use of experience words but an addition to them) whereby it would make sense to talk of an experience in terms appropriate to physical processes. . . .

Objection 7. I can imagine myself turned to stone and yet having images, aches, pains, and so on.

Reply. I can imagine that the electrical theory of lightning is false, that lightning is some sort of purely optical phenomenon. I can imagine that lightning is not an electrical discharge. I can imagine that the Evening Star is not the Morning Star. But it is. All the objection shows is that "experience" and "brain process" do not have the same meaning. It does not show that an experience is not in fact a brain process.

This objection is perhaps much the same as one which can be summed up by the slogan: "What can be composed of nothing cannot be composed of anything." The argument goes as follows: on the brain process thesis the identity between the brain process and the experience is a contingent one. So it is logically possible that there should be no brain process, and no process of any other sort, either (no heart process, no kidney process, no liver process). There would be the experience but no "corresponding" physiological process with which we might be able to identify it empirically.

I suspect that the objector is thinking of the experience as a ghostly entity. So it is composed of something, not of nothing, after all. On his view it is composed of ghost stuff, and on mine it is composed of brain stuff. Perhaps the counter-reply will be that the experience is simple and uncompounded, and so it is not composed of anything after all. This seems to be a quibble, for, if it were taken seriously, the remark "What can be composed of nothing cannot be composed of anything" could be recast as an a priori argument against Democritus and atomism and for Descartes and infinite divisibility.[12] And it seems odd that a question of this sort could be settled a priori. We must therefore construe the word "composed" in a very weak sense, which would allow us to say that even an indivisible atom is composed of something (namely, itself). The dualist cannot really say that an experience can be composed of nothing. For he holds that experiences are something over and above material processes, that is, that they are a sort of ghost stuff. (Or perhaps ripples in an underlying ghost stuff.) I say that the dualist's hypothesis is a perfectly intelligible one. But I say that experiences are not to be identified with ghost stuff but with brain stuff. This is another hypothesis, and in my view a very plausible one. The present argument cannot knock it down a priori. . . .

---

12. "A priori argument": an argument proceeding from premises that are knowable independently of experience. "Democritus and atomism . . .": according to the ancient Greek philosopher Democritus (c. 460–370 BCE), physical objects are composed of tiny indivisible particles ("atoms"); Descartes held the opposing position, that physical objects are infinitely divisible.

I have now considered a number of objections to the brain-process thesis. I wish now to conclude by some remarks on the logical status of the thesis itself. U. T. Place[13] seems to hold that it is a straight-out scientific hypothesis. If so, he is partly right and partly wrong. If the issue is between (say) a brain-process thesis and a heart thesis, or a liver thesis, or a kidney thesis, then the issue is a purely empirical one, and the verdict is overwhelmingly in favor of the brain. The right sorts of things don't go on in the heart, liver, or kidney, nor do these organs possess the right sort of complexity of structure. On the other hand, if the issue is between a brain-or-heart-or-liver-or-kidney thesis (that is, some form of materialism) on the one hand and epiphenomenalism[14] on the other hand, then the issue is not an empirical one. For there is no conceivable experiment which could decide between materialism and epiphenomenalism. This latter issue is not like the average straight-out empirical issue in science, but like the issue between the nineteenth-century English naturalist Philip Gosse and the orthodox geologists and paleontologists of his day. According to Gosse, the earth was created about 4000 B.C. exactly as described in *Genesis,* with twisted rock strata, "evidence" of erosion, and so forth, and all sorts of fossils, all in their appropriate strata, just as if the usual evolutionist story had been true. Clearly this theory is in a sense irrefutable: no evidence can possibly tell against it. Let us ignore the theological setting in which Philip Gosse's hypothesis had been placed, thus ruling out objections of a theological kind, such as "what a queer God who would go to such elaborate lengths to deceive us." Let us suppose that it is held that the universe just began in 4004 B.C. with the initial conditions just everywhere as they were in 4004 B.C., and in particular that our own planet began with sediment in the rivers, eroded cliffs, fossils in the rocks, and so on. No scientist would ever entertain this as a serious hypothesis, consistent though it is with all possible evidence. The hypothesis offends against the principles of parsimony and simplicity. There would be far too many brute and inexplicable facts. Why are pterodactyl bones just as they are? No explanation in terms of the evolution of pterodactyls from earlier forms of life would any longer be possible. We would have millions of facts about the world as it was in 4004 B.C. that just have to be *accepted.*

The issue between the brain-process theory and epiphenomenalism seems to be of the above sort. (Assuming that a behavioristic reduction of introspective reports is not possible.) If it be agreed that there are no cogent philosophical arguments which force us into accepting dualism, and if the brain-process theory and dualism are equally consistent with the facts, then the principles of parsimony and simplicity seem to me to decide overwhelmingly in favor of the brain-process theory. As I pointed out earlier, dualism involves a large number of irreducible psychophysical laws (whereby the "nomological danglers" dangle) of a queer sort, that just have to be taken on trust, and are just as difficult to swallow as the irreducible facts about the paleontology of the earth with which we are faced on Philip Gosse's theory.

---

13. U. T. Place (1924–2000), British philosopher and psychologist who published a famous paper defending the brain-process thesis in 1956.

14. "Epiphenomenalism": the view that the mental does not causally affect anything physical.

TEST YOUR UNDERSTANDING

1. According to Smart, is a statement such as "I am in pain" not a genuine report of an irreducibly psychical fact but instead a sophisticated sort of wince?

2. Is Smart arguing that after-images are brain processes?

3. Does Smart think that experiments have shown epiphenomenalism to be false?

4. Are "identical twins" strictly identical? If not, in what sense are identical twins identical?

NOTES AND QUESTIONS

1. Explain—using examples that are not about the mind or the brain—the difference between saying that sensations are (identical to) brain processes and saying that sensations are (merely) correlated with brain processes. Explain and assess Smart's main motivation for the thesis that sensations are brain processes.

2. For a lengthy defense of the identity theory, see Christopher Hill, *Sensations: A Defense of Type Materialism* (Cambridge University Press, 1991).

John Searle (b. 1932)

Searle is Slusser Professor Emeritus of Philosophy at the University of California, Berkeley, where he has taught since 1959. He has made many important contributions to the philosophy of language, philosophy of mind, and philosophy of social science. His books include *Speech Acts* (1969), *Intentionality* (1983), *The Rediscovery of the Mind* (1992), and *The Construction of Social Reality* (1995).

CAN COMPUTERS THINK?
from *Minds, Brains, and Science*

In the previous chapter, I provided at least the outlines of a solution to the so-called "mind-body problem." Though we do not know in detail how the brain functions, we do know enough to have an idea of the general relationships between brain processes and mental processes. Mental processes are caused by the behaviour of elements of the brain. At the same time, they are realised in the structure that is made up of those elements. I think this answer is consistent with the standard biological approaches to biological phenomena. Indeed, it is a kind of commonsense answer to the question, given what we know about how the world works. However, it is very much a minority point of view. The prevailing view in philosophy, psychology, and artificial intelligence is one which emphasises the analogies between the functioning of the human brain and the functioning of digital computers. According to the most extreme version of this view, the brain is just a digital computer and the mind is just a computer program. One could summarise this view—I call it "strong artificial intelligence," or "strong AI"—by saying that the mind is to the brain, as the program is to the computer hardware.

This view has the consequence that there is nothing essentially biological about the human mind. The brain just happens to be one of an indefinitely large number of different kinds of hardware computers that could sustain the programs which make up human intelligence. On this view, any physical system whatever that had the right program with the right inputs and outputs would have a mind in exactly the same sense that you and I have minds. So, for example, if you made a computer out of old beer cans powered by windmills; if it had the right program, it would have to have a mind. And the point is not that for all we know it might have thoughts and feelings, but rather that it must have thoughts and feelings, because that is all there is to having thoughts and feelings: implementing the right program.

Most people who hold this view think we have not yet designed programs which are minds. But there is pretty much general agreement among them that it's only a matter of time until computer scientists and workers in artificial intelligence design the appropriate hardware and programs which will be the equivalent of human brains and minds. These will be artificial brains and minds which are in every way the equivalent of human brains and minds. . . .

Unlike most philosophical theses, [this view is] reasonably clear, and it admits of a simple and decisive refutation. It is this refutation that I am going to undertake in this chapter.

The nature of the refutation has nothing whatever to do with any particular stage of computer technology. It is important to emphasise this point because the temptation is always to think that the solution to our problems must wait on some as yet uncreated technological wonder. But in fact, the nature of the refutation is completely independent of any state of technology. It has to do with the very definition of a digital computer, with what a digital computer is.

It is essential to our conception of a digital computer that its operations can be specified purely formally; that is, we specify the steps in the operation of the computer in terms of abstract symbols—sequences of zeroes and ones printed on a tape, for example. A typical computer "rule" will determine that when a machine is in a certain state and it has a certain symbol on its tape, then it will perform a certain operation such as erasing the symbol or printing another symbol and then enter another state such as moving the tape one square to the left. But the symbols have no meaning; they have no semantic content; they are not about anything. They have to be specified purely in terms of their formal or syntactical structure. The zeroes and ones, for example, are just numerals; they don't even stand for numbers. Indeed, it is this feature of digital computers that makes them so powerful. One and the same type of hardware, if it is appropriately designed, can be used to run an indefinite range of different programs. And one and the same program can be run on an indefinite range of different types of hardwares.

But this feature of programs, that they are defined purely formally or syntactically, is fatal to the view that mental processes and program processes are identical. And the reason can be stated quite simply. There is more to having a mind than having formal or syntactical processes. Our internal mental states, by definition, have certain sorts of contents. If I am thinking about Kansas City or wishing that I had a cold beer to drink or wondering if there will be a fall in interest rates, in each case my mental state has a certain mental content in addition to whatever formal features it might have. That is, even if my thoughts occur to me in strings of symbols, there must be more to the thought than the abstract strings, because strings by themselves can't have any meaning. If my thoughts are to be *about* anything, then the strings must have a *meaning* which makes the thoughts about those things. In a word, the mind has more than a syntax, it has a semantics. The reason that no computer program can ever be a mind is simply that a computer program is only syntactical, and minds are more than syntactical. Minds are semantical, in the sense that they have more than a formal structure, they have a content.

To illustrate this point I have designed a certain thought-experiment. Imagine that a bunch of computer programmers have written a program that will enable a computer to simulate the understanding of Chinese. So, for example, if the computer is given a question in Chinese, it will match the question against its memory, or data base, and produce appropriate answers to the questions in Chinese. Suppose for the sake of argument that the computer's answers are as good as those of a native Chinese speaker. Now then, does the computer, on the basis of this, understand Chinese, does it literally understand Chinese, in the way that Chinese speakers understand Chinese? Well, imagine that you are locked in a room, and in this room are several baskets full of Chinese symbols. Imagine that you (like me) do not understand a word of Chinese, but that you are given a rule book in English for manipulating these Chinese symbols. The rules specify the manipulations of the symbols purely formally, in terms of their syntax, not their semantics. So the rule might say: "Take a squiggle-squiggle sign out of basket number one and put it next to a squoggle-squoggle sign from basket number two." Now suppose that some other Chinese symbols are passed into the room, and that you are given further rules for passing back Chinese symbols out of the room. Suppose that unknown to you the symbols passed into the room are called "questions" by the people outside the room, and the symbols you pass back out of the room are called "answers to the questions." Suppose, furthermore, that the programmers are so good at designing the programs and that you are so good at manipulating the symbols, that very soon your answers are indistinguishable from those of a native Chinese speaker. There you are locked in your room shuffling your Chinese symbols and passing out Chinese symbols in response to incoming Chinese symbols. On the basis of the situation as I have described it, there is no way you could learn any Chinese simply by manipulating these formal symbols.

Now the point of the story is simply this: by virtue of implementing a formal computer program from the point of view of an outside observer, you behave exactly as if you understood Chinese, but all the same you don't understand a word of Chinese. But if going through the appropriate computer program for understanding Chinese is not enough to give *you* an understanding of Chinese, then it is not enough to give *any other digital computer* an understanding of Chinese. And again, the reason for this can be stated quite simply. If you don't understand Chinese, then no other computer could understand Chinese because no digital computer, just by virtue of running a program, has anything that you don't have. All that the computer has, as you have, is a formal program for manipulating uninterpreted Chinese symbols. To repeat, a computer has a syntax, but no semantics. The whole point of the parable of the Chinese room is to remind us of a fact that we knew all along. Understanding a language, or indeed, having mental states at all, involves more than just having a bunch of formal symbols. It involves having an interpretation, or a meaning attached to those symbols. And a digital computer, as defined, cannot have more than just formal symbols because the operation of the computer, as I said earlier, is defined in terms of its ability to implement programs. And these programs are purely formally specifiable—that is, they have no semantic content.

We can see the force of this argument if we contrast what it is like to be asked and to answer questions in English, and to be asked and to answer questions in some language where we have no knowledge of any of the meanings of the words. Imagine that in the Chinese room you are also given questions in English about such things as your age or your life history, and that you answer these questions. What is the difference between the Chinese case and the English case? Well again, if like me you understand no Chinese and you do understand English, then the difference is obvious. You understand the questions in English because they are expressed in symbols whose meanings are known to you. Similarly, when you give the answers in English you are producing symbols which are meaningful to you. But in the case of the Chinese, you have none of that. In the case of the Chinese, you simply manipulate formal symbols according to a computer program, and you attach no meaning to any of the elements.

Various replies have been suggested to this argument by workers in artificial intelligence and in psychology, as well as philosophy. They all have something in common; they are all inadequate. And there is an obvious reason why they have to be inadequate, since the argument rests on a very simple logical truth, namely, syntax alone is not sufficient for semantics, and digital computers insofar as they are computers have, by definition, a syntax alone.

I want to make this clear by considering a couple of the arguments that are often presented against me.

Some people attempt to answer the Chinese room example by saying that the whole system understands Chinese. The idea here is that though I, the person in the room manipulating the symbols, do not understand Chinese, I am just the central processing unit of the computer system. They argue that it is the whole system, including the room, the baskets full of symbols and the ledgers containing the programs and perhaps other items as well, taken as a totality, that understands Chinese. But this is subject to exactly the same objection I made before. There is no way that the system can get from the syntax to the semantics. I, as the central processing unit, have no way of figuring out what any of these symbols means; but then neither does the whole system.

Another common response is to imagine that we put the Chinese understanding program inside a robot. If the robot moved around and interacted causally with the world, wouldn't that be enough to guarantee that it understood Chinese? Once again the inexorability of the semantics-syntax distinction overcomes this manoeuvre. As long as we suppose that the robot has only a computer for a brain then, even though it might behave exactly as if it understood Chinese, it would still have no way of getting from the syntax to the semantics of Chinese. You can see this if you imagine that I am the computer. Inside a room in the robot's skull I shuffle symbols without knowing that some of them come in to me from television cameras attached to the robot's head and others go out to move the robot's arms and legs. As long as all I have is a formal computer program, I have no way of attaching any meaning to any of the symbols. And the fact that the robot is engaged in causal interactions with the outside world won't help me to attach any meaning to the symbols unless I have some way of finding out about that fact. Suppose the robot picks up a hamburger and this triggers the symbol for hamburger to come into the room. As long as all I have is the symbol with no knowledge of its causes or how it got there, I have no way of knowing what it means. The causal interactions between the robot and the rest of the world are irrelevant unless those causal interactions are represented in some mind or other. But there is no way they can be if all that the so-called mind consists of is a set of purely formal, syntactical operations.

It is important to see exactly what is claimed and what is not claimed by my argument. Suppose we ask the question that I mentioned at the beginning: "Could a machine think?" Well, in one sense, of course, we are all machines. We can construe the stuff inside our heads as a meat machine. And of course, we can all think. So, in one sense of "machine," namely that sense in which a machine is just a physical system which is capable of performing certain kinds of operations, in that sense, we are all machines, and we can think. So, trivially, there are machines that can think. But that wasn't the question that bothered us. So let's try a different formulation of it. Could an artefact think? Could a man-made machine think? Well, once again, it depends on the kind of artefact. Suppose we designed a machine that was molecule-for-molecule indistinguishable from a human being. Well then, if you can duplicate the causes, you can presumably duplicate the effects. So once again, the answer to that question is, in principle at least, trivially yes. If you could build a machine that had the same structure as a human being, then presumably that machine would be able to think. Indeed, it would be a surrogate human being. Well, let's try again.

The question isn't: "Can a machine think?" or: "Can an artefact think?" The question is: "Can a digital computer think?" But once again we have to be very careful in how we interpret the question. From a mathematical point of view, anything whatever can be described as if it were a digital computer. And that's because it can be described as instantiating or implementing a computer program. In an utterly trivial sense, the pen that is on the desk in front of me can be described as a digital computer. It just happens to have a very boring computer program. The program says: "Stay there." Now since in this sense, anything whatever is a digital computer, because anything whatever can be described as implementing a computer program, then once again, our question gets a trivial answer. Of course our brains are digital computers, since they implement any number of computer programs. And of course our brains can think. So once again, there is a trivial answer to the question. But that wasn't really the question we were trying to ask. The question we wanted to ask is this: "Can a digital computer, as defined, think?" That is to say: "Is instantiating or implementing the right computer program with the right inputs and outputs, sufficient for, or constitutive of, thinking?" And to this question, unlike its predecessors, the answer is clearly "no." And it is "no" for the reason that we have spelled out, namely, the computer program is defined purely syntactically. But thinking is more than just a matter of manipulating meaningless symbols, it involves meaningful semantic contents. These semantic contents are what we mean by "meaning."

It is important to emphasise again that we are not talking about a particular stage of computer technology. The argument has nothing to do with the forthcoming, amazing advances in computer science. It has nothing to do with the distinction between serial and parallel processes, or with the size of programs, or the speed of computer operations, or with computers that can interact causally with their environment, or even with the invention of robots. Technological progress is always grossly exaggerated, but even subtracting the exaggeration, the development of computers has been quite remarkable, and we can reasonably expect that even more remarkable progress will be made in the future. No doubt we will be much better able to simulate human behaviour on computers than we can at present, and certainly much better than we have been able to in the past. The point I am making is that if we are talking about having mental states, having a mind, all of these simulations are simply irrelevant. It doesn't matter how good the technology is, or how rapid the calculations made by the computer are. If it really is a computer, its operations have to be defined syntactically, whereas consciousness, thoughts, feelings, emotions, and all the rest of it involve more than a syntax. Those features, by definition, the computer is unable to *duplicate* however powerful may be its ability to *simulate*. The key distinction here is between duplication and simulation. And no simulation by itself ever constitutes duplication.

... There is a puzzling question in this discussion though, and that is: "Why would anybody ever have thought that computers could think or have feelings and emotions and all the rest of it?" After all, we can do computer simulations of any process whatever that can be given a formal description. So, we can do a computer simulation of the flow of money in the British economy, or the pattern of power distribution in the Labour party.[1] We can do computer simulation of rain storms in the home counties,[2] or warehouse fires in East London. Now, in each of these cases, nobody supposes that the computer simulation is actually the real thing; no one supposes that a computer simulation of a storm will leave us all wet, or a computer simulation of a fire is likely to burn the house down. Why on earth would anyone in his right mind suppose a computer simulation of mental processes actually had mental processes? I don't really know the answer to that, since the idea seems to me, to put it frankly, quite crazy from the start. But I can make a couple of speculations.

First of all, where the mind is concerned, a lot of people are still tempted to some sort of behaviourism.[3] They think if a system behaves as if it understood Chinese, then it really must understand Chinese. But we have already refuted this form of behaviourism with the Chinese room argument. Another assumption made by many people is that the mind is not a part of the biological world, it is not a part of the world of nature. The strong artificial intelligence view relies on that in its conception that the mind is

---

1. One of the main political parties in the United Kingdom.

2. Counties in England surrounding London.

3. The view that to have a mind is simply to behave (or to be disposed or inclined to behave) in various ways.

purely formal; that somehow or other, it cannot be treated as a concrete product of biological processes like any other biological product. There is in these discussions, in short, a kind of residual dualism.[4] AI partisans believe that the mind is more than a part of the natural biological world; they believe that the mind is purely formally specifiable. The paradox of this is that the AI literature is filled with fulminations against some view called "dualism." But in fact, the whole thesis of strong AI rests on a kind of dualism. It rests on a rejection of the idea that the mind is just a natural biological phenomenon in the world like any other.

TEST YOUR UNDERSTANDING

1. Does Searle think that there is some sense in which we are machines?

2. Does Searle think our brains don't run computer programs?

3. Does Searle think of himself as a dualist?

4. Does Searle think that the proponents of strong AI assume that the mind is a part of the natural biological world?

NOTES AND QUESTIONS

1. Let us grant that when you are manipulating the symbols in the Chinese room you do not understand Chinese. One reply Searle considers (sometimes called the "Systems Reply") is that "the whole system understands Chinese." One might argue that the whole system does not understand Chinese because you are a part of the system and you don't understand Chinese, but this would be a fallacy. Things can be true of a whole that are not true of its parts: you are a philosophy student, and your liver is part of you, but that doesn't imply that your liver is a philosophy student. What is Searle's response to the Systems Reply? Does he avoid the fallacy just mentioned?

2. Some of the standard objections to the Chinese room argument are in Ned Block, "The Mind as the Software of the Brain," section 4 (www.nyu.edu/gsas/dept/philo/faculty/block/papers/msb.html). The original article in which the Chinese room argument appeared is in Searle's article "Minds, Brains, and Program," *Behavioral and Brain Sciences* 3 (1980): 417–57 (http://cogprints.org/7150/1/10.1.1.83.5248.pdf). Searle talks about the Chinese room argument in a 1987 clip from the BBC television program *Horizon*: search on the Internet for "Searle Chinese room BBC Horizon."

3. A short explanation of functionalism together with a discussion of some standard objections is in Ned Block, "Functionalism" (www.nyu.edu/gsas/dept/philo/faculty/block/papers/functionalism.html).

4. The view, associated with the French philosopher René Descartes (1596–1650), that the mind and the body are distinct things.

ANALYZING THE ARGUMENTS

1. Consider this passage, excerpted from Raymond M. Smullyan's "An Unfortunate Dualist," in his *This Book Needs No Title* (Prentice Hall, 1980):

> Once upon a time there was a dualist. He believed that mind and matter are separate substances. Just how they interacted he did not pretend to know—this was one of the "mysteries" of life. But he was sure they were quite separate substances.
>
> This dualist, unfortunately, led an unbearably painful life—not because of his philosophical beliefs, but for quite different reasons. . . . He longed for nothing more than to die. But he was deterred from suicide by such reasons as . . . he did not want to hurt other people by his death. . . . So our poor dualist was quite desperate.
>
> Then came the discovery of the miracle drug! Its effect on the taker was to annihilate the soul or mind entirely but to leave the body functioning exactly as before. Absolutely no observable change came over the taker; the body continued to act just as if it still had a soul. Not the closest friend or observer could possibly know that the taker had taken the drug, unless the taker informed him. . . . [O]ur dualist was, of course, delighted! Now he could annihilate himself (his soul, that is) in a way not subject to any of the foregoing objections. And so, for the first time in years, he went to bed with a light heart, saying: "Tomorrow morning I will go down to the drugstore and get the drug. My days of suffering are over at last!" With these thoughts, he fell peacefully asleep.
>
> Now at this point a curious thing happened. A friend of the dualist who knew about this drug, and who knew of the sufferings of the dualist, decided to put him out of his misery. So in the middle of the night, while the dualist was fast asleep, the friend quietly stole into the house and injected the drug into his veins. The next morning the body of the dualist awoke—without any soul indeed—and the first thing it did was to go to the drugstore to get the drug. He took it home and, before taking it, said, "Now I shall be released." So he took it and then waited the time interval in which it was supposed to work. At the end of the interval he angrily exclaimed: "Damn it, this stuff hasn't helped at all! I still obviously have a soul and am suffering as much as ever!"
>
> Doesn't all this suggest that perhaps there might be something just a little wrong with dualism?

   Does it? What is Smullyan's argument against dualism? How might a dualist respond?

2. Here is one very simple behaviorist theory of belief:

   S believes that *p* **iff** *S* would answer "Yes" if *S* were asked "Is it true that *p*?"

   (To get a specific consequence of this theory, replace the letter *S* by the name of any person and replace the letter *p* by any declarative sentence of English.)

   a. Why does the theory have the consequence that a monolingual Spanish speaker does not believe that snow is white?

b. Why does the theory have the consequence that some ordinary cases of lying are impossible?

c. Can you repair the theory so that it at least avoids these two problems? It is certain that your repaired theory has *other* problems—what are some of them?

3. In "Troubles with Functionalism" (*Minnesota Studies in the Philosophy of Science* 9 [1978]: 261–325), Ned Block presents the following "prima facie **counterexample**" to functionalism:

> Suppose we convert the government of China to functionalism, and we convince its officials to realize a human mind for an hour. We provide each of the billion people in China (I chose China because it has a billion inhabitants) with a specially designed two-way radio that connects them in the appropriate way to other persons and to [an] artificial body....
>
> The system of a billion people communicating with one another plus satellites plays the role of an external "brain" connected to the artificial body by radio. There is nothing absurd about a person being connected to his brain by radio. Perhaps the day will come when our brains will be periodically removed for cleaning and repairs. Imagine that this is done initially by treating neurons attaching the brain to the body with a chemical that allows them to stretch like rubber bands, thereby assuring that no brain-body connections are disrupted. Soon clever businessmen discover that they can attract more customers by replacing the stretched neurons with radio links so that brains can be cleaned without inconveniencing the customer by immobilizing his body.
>
> It is not at all obvious that the China-body system is physically impossible. It could be functionally equivalent to you for a short time, say an hour....
>
> Of course, there are signals the system would respond to what you would not respond to—for example, massive radio interference or a flood of the Yangtze River. Such events might cause a malfunction, scotching the simulation, just as a bomb in a computer can make it fail to realize the machine table it was built to realize. But just as the computer *without* the bomb *can* realize the machine table, the system consisting of the people and artificial body can realize the machine table so long as there are no catastrophic interferences, e.g., floods, etc....
>
> Objection: The Chinese system would work too slowly. The kind of events and processes with which we normally have contact would pass by far too quickly for the system to detect them. Thus, we would be unable to converse with it, play bridge with it, etc.
>
> Reply: It is hard to see why the system's time scale should matter. Is it really contradictory or nonsensical to suppose we could meet a race of intelligent beings with whom we could communicate only by devices such as time-lapse photography? When we observe these creatures, they seem almost inanimate. But when we view the time-lapse movies, we see them conversing with one another. Indeed, we find they are saying that the only way they can make any sense of us is by viewing movies greatly slowed down. To take time scale as all important seems crudely behavioristic.

What makes the homunculi-headed system . . . just described a prima facie counterexample to (machine) functionalism is that there is prima facie doubt whether it has any mental states at all—especially whether it has what philosophers have variously called "qualitative states," "raw feels," or "immediate phenomenological qualities." (You ask: What is it that philosophers have called qualitative states? I answer, only half in jest: As Louis Armstrong said when asked what jazz is, "If you got to ask, you ain't never gonna get to know.") In Nagel's terms [see "What Is It Like to Be a Bat?" in Chapter 8 of this anthology], there is a prima facie doubt whether there is anything which it is like to be the homunculi-headed system.

Is this a counterexample to functionalism? Block thinks that it is a more credible counterexample to a functionalist theory of "qualitative states," like *being in pain* or *seeing blue,* than it is to a functionalist theory of other mental states, like *believing that Mars has two moons* or *intending to apply to law school.* Is he right about that? If he is, then that suggests a better theory of mind would be some *combination* of the theories discussed in this chapter. What theories, and in what combination?

What Is Consciousness?

Pinch the skin on the back of your hand—the harder the better. As a result, an electrical signal will travel through nerve fibers in your hand to your spinal cord; the signal is then relayed to your brain, where more electrical activity takes place. So far, all we have is something of interest to neuroscientists or physicians—your nervous system is activated in a complicated way. But of course there's something else going on that is of very great interest to you—you are *in pain*. Surely there could hardly be a better example of *two very different things*! And yet, are they *really* two things? Isn't the sensible scientific view that—somehow—being in pain is *nothing more than* having a complicated pattern of physical events occur in your brain?

The experience of pain is a paradigm example of *consciousness*. Why is consciousness supposed to present an acute difficulty for **materialism**, the view that everything is wholly material or physical? More generally: What is special about consciousness compared to other mental phenomena? The readings in this chapter grapple with these questions.

Varieties of Consciousness

Philosophers have distinguished a number of different (although related) kinds of consciousness. A review of some of these will help us to home in on the kind of consciousness that—as Thomas Nagel claims in "What Is It Like to Be a Bat?"—"makes the mind-body problem really intractable."

The first kind of consciousness is illustrated by statements of the following sort: Sam is conscious of the burning toast, Shannon is conscious of being watched. Here, "conscious of" means "aware of": Sam is aware of the burning toast, Shannon is aware of being watched. So this first kind of consciousness is *awareness*.

The second kind of consciousness is *self*-consciousness. This kind of consciousness is related to, but is not quite the same as, the ordinary sense of "self-conscious": if Sam feels self-conscious about his odd socks, then he feels embarrassed about his odd socks. To feel embarrassed about his socks he must be aware of the socks, and moreover know or believe that the socks are *his*. Embarrassment is a self-regarding emotion. So self-consciousness in the ordinary sense requires Sam to be aware of himself, and *awareness of oneself* is self-consciousness as philosophers understand it. To put it another way, Sam is self-conscious in the philosophical sense if he can think thoughts *about himself*, thoughts that he would report using "I," the first-person pronoun.[1]

The third kind of consciousness is the opposite of "unconsciousness" in the ordinary sense. Shannon falls off her bike and becomes unconscious, entirely unresponsive to her surroundings. Later she opens her eyes and "regains consciousness." To say that someone is conscious in this sense simply means that she is awake and alert. This kind of consciousness is sometimes called *creature* consciousness or *agent* consciousness.

We haven't yet gotten to the really puzzling kind of consciousness. To introduce it, first find something colored—something blue, say—and place it before you. Now pinch the back of your hand again. You are now in two **mental states**:

(i)   seeing blue;

(ii)   feeling pain.

At the same time, no preparation was needed to ensure that you are also in these two mental states:

(iii)   believing that Norton has published an introduction to philosophy;

(iv)   hoping to do well in your classes.

Probably you have believed for at least a few weeks that Norton has published an introduction to philosophy and have hoped to do well in your classes for much longer. In any case, the important point is that you have believed that Norton has published an introduction to philosophy and have hoped to do well in your classes during times when you were not thinking about philosophy books or school at all. In fact, when you were asleep last night, you believed that Norton has published an introduction to philosophy and hoped to do well in school. And you are not unusual in this respect. Your classmate Sidney, say, is in a deep, dreamless sleep. Standing by her bedside, we can point to her and truly say: "She believes that Norton has published an introduction to philosophy and hopes to do well in school."

Bearing all that in mind, isn't there a striking difference between (i) and (ii), on the one hand, and (iii) and (iv), on the other? Seeing blue and feeling pain make a difference to your *conscious experience*, while believing that Norton has published an introduction to philosophy and hoping to do well in your classes do not. Put another way, just after you followed the instruction for (i) and (ii), there was a change in *how things seemed or felt*. Put yet another way, there was *something it was like* for you to see blue, and there was *something it was like* for you to feel pain.

1. Interestingly, some cases of awareness of oneself are not cases of self-consciousness. Suppose you see yourself on the security monitor in a store, but you don't recognize the person *as* yourself. You are aware *of* yourself, but this is not a case of self-consciousness.

But although you also believed that Norton was the publisher and hoped to do well in school, this did *not* make a difference to your conscious experience. What was it like for you to believe that Norton has published an introduction to philosophy or to hope to do well in school? It wasn't like *anything*, presumably.

In this sense, seeing blue and feeling pain are *conscious* mental states: there is something it's like to see blue and something it's like to feel pain.[2] Believing and hoping, by contrast, are arguably never conscious in the same sense. Believing that the earth is round is a perfectly good mental state, but there's nothing it's like to be in it.

This kind of consciousness, which in the first instance is a **property** of mental states, has a number of names in philosophy of mind. Thomas Nagel simply calls it *consciousness*. David Chalmers calls it *experience*. We will use the term introduced by the philosopher Ned Block: **phenomenal consciousness**.

Seeing blue and feeling pain are (at least typically) phenomenally conscious states. But they differ in phenomenally conscious respects. What it's like to see blue and what it's like to feel pain are different. Similarly, what it's like to see blue is different from what it's like to see red. When philosophers talk about how these states differ with respect to what it's like to be in them, they often use the term **qualia** (as in the title of Frank Jackson's essay; the singular is *quale*) or *phenomenal character* (Michael Tye) or the *subjective character of experience* (Nagel).

The Explanatory Gap

Consider the bodily process of digestion. Very plausibly, it can be fully explained in terms of physical and chemical processes. We can be confident that digestion can be fully explained even if we don't know all the complicated details. Mental phenomena, however, present an apparent contrast, as the German philosopher Gottfried Wilhelm Leibniz argued with a famous thought experiment (mentioned in the introduction to Chapter 7). Supposing the brain, in Leibniz's words, "enlarged but preserving the same proportions, so that you could enter it as if it were a mill," you would not observe anything there, he says, that could explain thinking, feeling, and perceiving.

But perhaps Leibniz's pessimism is too hasty. Consider your belief that the earth is round. At a first pass, to believe that the earth is round is to store the information that the earth is round in a way that makes it available to control action in certain ways. So, for example, if you tick the "earth is round" box on the astronomy multiple-choice exam or form a lump of clay into a ball when making a model of the earth, the information that the earth is round—presumably stored in your brain—is making a contribution to bringing those actions about. And it doesn't seem so

---

2. This should really be put more cautiously: *typically* they are conscious mental states. In typical cases, there is something it's like to see blue and something it's like to feel pain.

mysterious that a physical thing could store information and use it to govern its behavior. After all, aren't computers actual examples? Moreover, perhaps the brain *is* some kind of computer, running mental software (see the introduction to Chapter 7). Admittedly, some philosophers think that this idea is flat wrong: John Searle (see "Can Computers Think?" in Chapter 7) is a notable example. But many think it's at least along the right lines, in which case there seems to be a very real prospect of explaining our mental lives in computational terms. And since computers can certainly be built out of biochemical materials, a computational explanation of the mind is in effect a materialist explanation of the mind.

Leibniz's thought experiment, on this view, is misleading. To understand how a computer works, you need to zoom *out* and see how everything is wired together, not zoom *in* to a few transistors on a chip. Similarly, zooming in to small groups of neurons (as in Leibniz's thought experiment) is not going to reveal how the brain can generate thought, but that's because it's at the wrong scale.

This sort of strategy might deal with the *cognitive* aspects of mind—roughly, the storage, manipulation, and use of information. But what about the *phenomenal* aspects of mind; that is, *phenomenal consciousness*? The mind-as-computer idea might find a place for believing and hoping in a purely material universe, but what about seeing blue and feeling pain? Here many philosophers (and cognitive scientists) think that pessimism is warranted. Why do certain physical states give rise to phenomenal consciousness? We don't know, and according to the pessimists we have no idea how to find out the answer. Physical phenomena are very well suited to explaining digestion, and perhaps also can explain believing and hoping. But they seem quite ill suited to explain phenomenal consciousness. As the philosopher Joseph Levine puts it, there is an *explanatory gap* between the physical world and phenomenal consciousness.[3] This is what David Chalmers calls the **hard problem**.

Dualism

There might be an explanation of consciousness in entirely physical terms even though we don't know what it is. The science of the mind has only made really serious progress in the past 50 years or so, and perhaps another millennium of neuroscience combined with new ways of thinking about both the mind and the physical world will bring us complete enlightenment? Nagel expresses some sympathy with this position. Some other philosophers are less sanguine. Although a satisfactory physical explanation of phenomenal consciousness is out there to be found, they think, human beings are just not smart enough to find it.[4]

3. See Levine's "Materialism and Qualia: The Explanatory Gap," *Pacific Philosophical Quarterly* 64 (1983): 354–61.

4. For an argument for this conclusion, see Colin McGinn, "Can We Solve the Mind-Body Problem?" *Mind* 98 (1989): 349–66. For related views, see "Analyzing the Arguments" at the end of this chapter.

Alternatively, one might argue that the explanatory gap is a sign that phenomenal consciousness *cannot* be given a complete explanation in physical terms, and so **physicalism** or **materialism** is false. On this view, consciousness is an *additional* ingredient in nature, over and above the ingredients recognized by physics and chemistry. This is a version of **dualism** (see the introduction to Chapter 7). In their essays, David Chalmers and Frank Jackson both argue for dualism.

Chalmers's argument turns on the claim that there could have been **zombies**: creatures physically exactly the same as ourselves, living in the same sort of physical world, but who lack phenomenal consciousness. Zombies, being physically the same as ourselves, give every impression of having mental lives that are also the same as ours. Perhaps zombies have beliefs, hopes, and intentions, like us. Perhaps they also see things. But, by stipulation, there is nothing it's like to be a zombie. When a zombie looks at a ripe cranberry in good light and says (as we might) "That's red," all is dark within. If zombies see cranberries, there is nothing it's like for them to do so. If physicalists are right in thinking that the mind (including phenomenal consciousness) is wholly physical, then once a physical system has reached a certain level of complexity, phenomenal consciousness is inevitable. But if zombies could have existed, phenomenal consciousness is *not* inevitable, and so physicalism is false.

Jackson's essay "Epiphenomenal Qualia" sets out his **knowledge argument** against physicalism. His most vivid and famous thought experiment in that essay concerns Mary, a brilliant scientist who knows every physical fact about colors and color vision, but who has been locked in a black-and-white room since birth. She has never seen anything chromatically colored. According to Jackson, if physicalism is true, then Mary knows everything about color experiences when she is imprisoned. But, he thinks, she clearly does not know everything: when she is released and sees something red for the first time, she will learn something; in particular, she will come to know a fact about qualia. (Jackson later changed his mind: see "Notes and Questions" on page 376.)

Patricia Smith Churchland argues that Jackson's argument, and also Nagel's, fail for multiple reasons. If you read Churchland's essay, you may well suspect that she is similarly unimpressed by Chalmers's argument—which indeed she is.[5]

The Transparency of Consciousness

Once the notion of phenomenal consciousness has been explained, you might think that it is the most obvious and striking thing in the world. Michael Tye argues that, on the contrary, phenomenal consciousness is extremely elusive. Look at something

---

5. See Patricia Smith Churchland, "The Hornswoggle Problem," reprinted in *Explaining Consciousness: The Hard Problem*, ed. Jonathan Shear (MIT Press, 1999).

blue again and put yourself into the phenomenally conscious state of seeing blue. There is something it's like to see blue; in other words, the state of seeing blue has a distinctive quale, or phenomenal character. Try and attend to that phenomenal character, a property of a mental state, not a property of anything in the scene before your eyes. According to Tye, you can't do it. You just end up attending to blue, which is a property of objects like sapphires and the petals of forget-me-nots, not a property of a mental state.

Here's another way of putting the point. Imagine Frank Jackson's Mary seeing a red apple for the first time. Will she be struck by the novel phenomenal character or qualia of her mental state or by the redness of the apple? The redness of the apple! Her eyes will widen with astonishment, she will pick up the apple and examine it more closely, and so on. What has grabbed her attention is something remarkable *in her environment,* not in her mind.

As Tye sums up the problem:

> The conclusion to which we seem driven is that the phenomenal character of your visual experience, as you view the apple, is *hidden* from you, as is your visual experience. You are *blind* to these things. For you, it is as if they aren't there. They are, as it were, transparent to you. You "see" right through them when you try to attend to them and you end up focusing on things outside you. But surely this cannot be right. Your visual experience is an inherently conscious thing. . . . Something has gone terribly wrong.

What has gone wrong? Tye's essay attempts to answer that question.

Thomas Nagel (b. 1937)

Nagel is Emeritus University Professor of Philosophy and Law at New York University. He has made influential contributions to ethics, political philosophy, epistemology, and philosophy of mind. His books include *The Possibility of Altruism* (1970), *The View from Nowhere* (1986), *Equality and Partiality* (1991), and *Mind and Cosmos* (2012).

WHAT IS IT LIKE TO BE A BAT?

Consciousness is what makes the mind-body problem really intractable. Perhaps that is why current discussions of the problem give it little attention or get it obviously wrong. The recent wave of reductionist euphoria has produced several analyses of mental phenomena and mental concepts designed to explain the possibility of some variety of materialism, psychophysical identification, or reduction.[1] But the problems dealt with are those common to this type of reduction and other types, and what makes the mind-body problem unique, and unlike the water-H_2O problem or the Turing machine[2]–IBM machine problem or the lightning–electrical discharge problem or the gene-DNA problem or the oak tree–hydrocarbon problem, is ignored.

Every reductionist has his favorite analogy from modern science. It is most unlikely that any of these unrelated examples of successful reduction will shed light on the relation of mind to brain. But philosophers share the general human weakness for explanations of what is incomprehensible in terms suited for what is familiar and well understood, though entirely different. This has led to the acceptance of implausible accounts of the mental largely because they would permit familiar kinds of reduction. I shall try to explain why the usual examples do not help us to understand the relation between mind and body—why, indeed, we have at present no conception of what an explanation of the physical nature of a mental phenomenon would be. Without consciousness the mind-body problem would be much less interesting. With consciousness it seems hopeless. The most important and characteristic feature of conscious mental phenomena is very poorly understood. Most reductionist theories do not even try to explain it. And careful examination will show that no currently available concept of reduction is applicable to it. Perhaps a new theoretical form can be devised for the purpose, but such a solution, if it exists, lies in the distant intellectual future.

Conscious experience is a widespread phenomenon. It occurs at many levels of animal life, though we cannot be sure of its presence in the simpler organisms, and it is very difficult to say in general what provides evidence of it. (Some extremists have been prepared to deny it even of mammals other than man.) No doubt it occurs in countless forms totally unimaginable to us, on other planets in other solar systems throughout the universe. But no matter how the form may vary, the fact that an organism has conscious experience *at all* means, basically, that there is something it is like to *be* that organism. There may be further implications about the form of the experience; there may even (though I doubt it) be implications about the behavior of the organism. But fundamentally an organism has conscious mental states if and only if there is something that it is to *be* that organism—something it is like *for* the organism.

We may call this the subjective character of experience. It is not captured by any of the familiar, recently devised reductive analyses of the mental, for all of them are logically compatible with its absence. It is not analyzable in terms of any explanatory

---

1. "The recent wave . . .": recent in 1974, as exemplified by J. J. C. Smart's 1959 paper "Sensations and Brain Processes" (in Chapter 7 of this anthology). "Materialism": the view that the mind—and the world in general—is wholly physical; also known as *physicalism*. "Psychophysical identification": the materialist identification of mental states with physical states (in particular brain states: see again Smart, "Sensations and Brain Processes"). "Reduction": Nagel cites some examples of scientific reduction in the next sentence: the reduction of water to H_2O, the reduction of genes to certain regions of DNA, and so on. Roughly put, to say that *A* can be reduced to *B* is to say that *A* is nothing over and above *B*.

2. A simple form of hypothetical computer, devised by the English mathematician Alan Turing (1912–1954).

system of functional states, or intentional states,[3] since these could be ascribed to robots or automata that behaved like people though they experienced nothing. It is not analyzable in terms of the causal role of experiences in relation to typical human behavior—for similar reasons. I do not deny that conscious mental states and events cause behavior, nor that they may be given functional characterizations. I deny only that this kind of thing exhausts their analysis. Any reductionist program has to be based on an analysis of what is to be reduced. If the analysis leaves something out, the problem will be falsely posed. It is useless to base the defense of materialism on any analysis of mental phenomena that fails to deal explicitly with their subjective character. For there is no reason to suppose that a reduction which seems plausible when no attempt is made to account for consciousness can be extended to include consciousness. Without some idea, therefore, of what the subjective character of experience is, we cannot know what is required of physicalist theory.

While an account of the physical basis of mind must explain many things, this appears to be the most difficult. It is impossible to exclude the phenomenological features of experience from a reduction in the same way that one excludes the phenomenal features of an ordinary substance from a physical or chemical reduction of it—namely, by explaining them as effects on the minds of human observers. If physicalism is to be defended, the phenomenological features must themselves be given a physical account. But when we examine their subjective character it seems that such a result is impossible. The reason is that every subjective phenomenon is essentially connected with a single point of view, and it seems inevitable that an objective, physical theory will abandon that point of view.

Let me first try to state the issue somewhat more fully than by referring to the relation between the subjective and the objective, or between the *pour-soi* and the *en-soi*.[4] This is far from easy. Facts about what it is like to be an *X* are very peculiar, so peculiar that some may be inclined to doubt their reality, or the significance of claims about them. To illustrate the connection between subjectivity and a point of view, and to make evident the importance of subjective features, it will help to explore the matter in relation to an example that brings out clearly the divergence between the two types of conception, subjective and objective.

I assume we all believe that bats have experience. After all, they are mammals, and there is no more doubt that they have experience than that mice or pigeons or whales have experience. I have chosen bats instead of wasps or flounders because if one travels too far down the phylogenetic tree, people gradually shed their faith that there is experience there at all. Bats, although more closely related to us than those other species, nevertheless present a range of activity and a sensory apparatus so different from ours that the problem I want to pose is exceptionally vivid (though it

3. "Functional states": states of a system definable in terms of causal relations between the system's inputs, outputs, and other states (computers and washing machines, for example, have many complex functional states). "Intentional states": mental states that are about or directed on something else; the state of *believing that Nagel is a philosopher* is about or directed on Nagel, and is thus an intentional state.

4. *Pour-soi*: "for-itself"; *en-soi*: "in-itself" (French). This terminology is from the French philosopher Jean-Paul Sartre's *Being and Nothingness* (1943).

certainly could be raised with other species). Even without the benefit of philosophical reflection, anyone who has spent some time in an enclosed space with an excited bat knows what it is to encounter a fundamentally *alien* form of life.

I have said that the essence of the belief that bats have experience is that there is something that it is like to be a bat. Now we know that most bats (the microchiroptera, to be precise) perceive the external world primarily by sonar, or echolocation, detecting the reflections, from objects within range, of their own rapid, subtly modulated, high-frequency shrieks. Their brains are designed to correlate the outgoing impulses with the subsequent echoes, and the information thus acquired enables bats to make precise discriminations of distance, size, shape, motion, and texture comparable to those we make by vision. But bat sonar, though clearly a form of perception, is not similar in its operation to any sense that we possess, and there is no reason to suppose that it is subjectively like anything we can experience or imagine. This appears to create difficulties for the notion of what it is like to be a bat. We must consider whether any method will permit us to extrapolate to the inner life of the bat from our own case, and if not, what alternative methods there may be for understanding the notion.

Our own experience provides the basic material for our imagination, whose range is therefore limited. It will not help to try to imagine that one has webbing on one's arms, which enables one to fly around at dusk and dawn catching insects in one's mouth; that one has very poor vision, and perceives the surrounding world by a system of reflected high-frequency sound signals; and that one spends the day hanging upside down by one's feet in an attic. In so far as I can imagine this (which is not very far), it tells me only what it would be like for *me* to behave as a bat behaves. But that is not the question. I want to know what it is like for a *bat* to be a bat. Yet if I try to imagine this, I am restricted to the resources of my own mind, and those resources are inadequate to the task. I cannot perform it either by imagining additions to my present experience, or by imagining segments gradually subtracted from it, or by imagining some combination of additions, subtractions, and modifications.

To the extent that I could look and behave like a wasp or a bat without changing my fundamental structure, my experiences would not be anything like the experiences of those animals. On the other hand, it is doubtful that any meaning can be attached to the supposition that I should possess the internal neurophysiological constitution of a bat. Even if I could by gradual degrees be transformed into a bat, nothing in my present constitution enables me to imagine what the experiences of such a future stage of myself thus metamorphosed would be like. The best evidence would come from the experiences of bats, if we only knew what they were like.

So if extrapolation from our own case is involved in the idea of what it is like to be a bat, the extrapolation must be incompletable. We cannot form more than a schematic conception of what it *is* like. For example, we may ascribe general *types* of experience on the basis of the animal's structure and behavior. Thus we describe bat sonar as a form of three-dimensional forward perception; we believe that bats feel some versions of pain, fear, hunger, and lust, and that they have other, more familiar types of perception besides sonar. But we believe that these experiences also have in each case a specific subjective character, which it is beyond our ability to conceive. And if there's conscious life elsewhere in the universe, it is likely that some of it will not be describable even in the most general experiential terms available to us. (The problem is not confined to exotic cases, however, for it exists between one person and another. The subjective character of the experience of a person deaf and blind from birth is not accessible to me, for example, nor presumably is mine to him. This does not prevent us each from believing that the other's experience has such a subjective character.)

If anyone is inclined to deny that we can believe in the existence of facts like this whose exact nature we cannot possibly conceive, he should reflect that in contemplating the bats we are in much the same position that intelligent bats or Martians would occupy if they tried to form a conception of what it was like to be us. The structure of their own minds might make it impossible for them to succeed, but we know they would be wrong to conclude that there is not anything precise that it is like to be us: that only certain general types of mental state could be ascribed to us (perhaps perception and appetite would be concepts common to us both; perhaps not). We know they would be wrong to draw such a skeptical conclusion because we know what it is like to be us. And we know that while it includes an enormous amount of variation and complexity, and while we do not possess the vocabulary to describe it adequately, its subjective character is highly specific, and in some respects describable in terms that can be understood only by creatures like us. The fact that we cannot expect ever to accommodate in our language a detailed description of Martian or bat phenomenology should not lead us to dismiss as meaningless the claim that bats and Martians have experiences fully comparable in richness of detail to our own. It would be fine if someone were to develop concepts and a theory that enabled us to think about those things; but such an understanding may be permanently denied to us by the limits of our nature. And to deny the reality or logical significance of what we can never describe or understand is the crudest form of cognitive dissonance. . . .

Reflection on what it is like to be a bat seems to lead us, therefore, to the conclusion that there are facts that do not consist in the truth of propositions expressible in a human language. We can be compelled to recognize the existence of such facts without being able to state or comprehend them.

I shall not pursue this subject, however. Its bearing on the topic before us (namely, the mind-body problem) is that it enables us to make a general observation about the subjective character of experience. Whatever may be the status of facts about what it is like to be a human being, or a bat, or a Martian, these appear to be facts that embody a particular point of view.

I am not adverting here to the alleged privacy of experience to its possessor. The point of view in question is not one accessible only to a single individual. Rather it is a *type*. It is often possible to take up a point of view other than one's own, so the comprehension of such facts is not limited to one's own case. There is a sense in which phenomenological facts are perfectly objective: one person can know or say of another what the quality of the other's experience is. They are subjective, however, in the sense that even this objective ascription of experience is possible only for someone sufficiently similar to the object of ascription to be able to adopt his point of view—to understand the ascription in the first person as well as in the third, so to speak. The more different from oneself the other experiencer is, the less success one can expect with this enterprise. In our own case we occupy the relevant point of view, but we will have as much difficulty understanding our own experience properly if we approach it from another point of view as we would if we tried to understand the experience of another species without taking up *its* point of view.

This bears directly on the mind-body problem. For if the facts of experience—facts about what it is like *for* the experiencing organism—are accessible only from one point of view, then it is a mystery how the true character of experiences could be revealed in the physical operation of that organism. The latter is a domain of objective facts *par excellence*—the kind that can be observed and understood from many points of view and by individuals with differing perceptual systems. There are no comparable imaginative obstacles to the acquisition of knowledge about bat neurophysiology by human scientists, and intelligent bats or Martians might learn more about the human brain than we ever will.

This is not by itself an argument against reduction. A Martian scientist with no understanding of visual perception could understand the rainbow, or lightning, or clouds as physical phenomena, though he would never be able to understand the human concepts of rainbow, lightning, or cloud, or the place these things occupy in our phenomenal world. The objective nature of the things picked out by these concepts could be apprehended by him because, although the concepts themselves are connected with a particular point of view and a particular visual phenomenology, the things apprehended from that point of view are not: they are observable from the point of view but external to it; hence they can be comprehended from other points of view also, either by the same organisms or by others. Lightning has an objective character that is not exhausted by its visual appearance, and this can be investigated by a Martian without vision. To be precise, it has a *more* objective character than is revealed in its visual appearance. In speaking of the move from subjective to objective characterization, I wish to remain noncommittal about the existence of an end point, the completely objective intrinsic nature of the thing, which one might or might not be able to reach. It may be more accurate to think of objectivity as a direction in which the understanding can travel. And in understanding a phenomenon like lightning, it is legitimate to go as far away as one can from a strictly human viewpoint.

In the case of experience, on the other hand, the connection with a particular point of view seems much closer. It is difficult to understand what could be meant by the *objective* character of an experience, apart from the particular point of view from which its subject apprehends it. After all, what would be left of what it was like to be a bat if one removed the viewpoint of the bat? But if experience does not have, in addition to its subjective character, an objective nature that can be apprehended from many different points of view, then how can it be supposed that a Martian investigating my brain might be observing physical processes which were my mental processes (as he might observe physical processes which were bolts of lightning), only from a different point of view? How, for that matter, could a human physiologist observe them from another point of view?

We appear to be faced with a general difficulty about psychophysical reduction. In other areas the process of reduction is a move in the direction of greater objectivity, toward a more accurate view of the real nature of things. This is accomplished by reducing our dependence on individual or species-specific points of view toward the object of investigation. We describe it not in terms of the impressions it makes on our senses, but in terms of its more general effects and of properties detectable by means other than the human senses. The less it depends on a specifically human viewpoint, the more objective is our description. It is possible to follow this path because although the concepts and ideas we employ in thinking about the external world are initially applied from a point of view that involves our perceptual apparatus, they are used by us to refer to things beyond themselves—toward which we *have* the phenomenal point of view. Therefore we can abandon it in favor of another, and still be thinking about the same things.

Experience itself however, does not seem to fit the pattern. The idea of moving from appearance to reality seems to make no sense here. What is the analogue in this case to pursuing a more objective understanding of the same phenomena by abandoning the initial subjective viewpoint toward them in favour of another that is more objective but concerns the same thing? Certainly it *appears* unlikely that we will get closer to the real nature of human experience by leaving behind the particularity of our human point of view and striving for a description in terms accessible to beings that could not imagine what it was like to be us. If the subjective character of experience is fully comprehensible only from one point of view, then any shift to greater objectivity—that is, less attachment to a specific viewpoint—does not take us nearer to the real nature of the phenomenon: it takes us farther away from it.

In a sense, the seeds of this objection to the reducibility of experience are already detectable in successful cases of reduction; for in discovering sound to be, in reality, a wave phenomenon in air or other media, we leave behind one viewpoint to take up another, and the auditory, human or animal viewpoint that we leave behind remains unreduced. Members of radically different species may both understand the same physical events in objective terms, and this does not require that they understand the phenomenal forms in which those events appear to the senses of members of the other species. Thus it is a condition of their referring to a common reality that their more particular viewpoints are not part of the common reality that they both apprehend. The reduction can succeed only if the species-specific viewpoint is omitted from what is to be reduced.

But while we are right to leave this point of view aside in seeking a fuller understanding of the external world, we cannot ignore it permanently, since it is the essence of the internal world, and not merely a point of view on it. Most of the neo-behaviorism of recent philosophical psychology results from the effort to substitute an objective concept of mind for the real thing, in order to have nothing left over which cannot be reduced.[5] If we acknowledge that a physical theory of mind must account for the subjective character of experience, we must admit that no presently

---

5. *Behaviorism* identifies mental states with dispositions to behave. The main successor to behaviorism was *functionalism*, which identifies mental states with functional states (see footnote 3 earlier). The relevant functional states are often partly specified in terms of the organism's behavior, and this is why Nagel labels recent theories as "neobehaviorism."

available conception gives us a clue how this could be done. The problem is unique. If mental processes are indeed physical processes, then there is something it is like, intrinsically, to undergo certain physical processes. What it is for such a thing to be the case remains a mystery.

What moral should be drawn from these reflections, and what should be done next? It would be a mistake to conclude that physicalism must be false. Nothing is proved by the inadequacy of physicalist hypotheses that assume a faulty objective analysis of mind. It would be truer to say that physicalism is a position we cannot understand because we do not at present have any conception of how it might be true. Perhaps it will be thought unreasonable to require such a conception as a condition of understanding. After all, it might be said, the meaning of physicalism is clear enough: mental states are states of the body; mental events are physical events. We do not know *which* physical states and events they are, but that should not prevent us from understanding the hypothesis. What could be clearer than the words "is" and "are"?

But I believe it is precisely this apparent clarity of the word "is" that is deceptive. Usually, when we are told that X is Y we know *how* it is supposed to be true, but that depends on a conceptual or theoretical background and is not conveyed by the "is" alone. We know how both "X" and "Y" refer, and the kinds of things to which they refer, and we have a rough idea how the two referential paths might converge on a single thing, be it an object, a person, a process, an event, or whatever. But when the two terms of the identification are very disparate it may not be so clear how it could be true. We may not have even a rough idea of how the two referential paths could converge, or what kind of things they might converge on, and a theoretical framework may have to be supplied to enable us to understand this. Without the framework, an air of mysticism surrounds the identification.

This explains the magical flavor of popular presentations of fundamental scientific discoveries, given out as propositions to which one must subscribe without really understanding them. For example, people are now told at an early age that all matter is really energy. But despite the fact that they know what "is" means, most of them never form a conception of what makes this claim true, because they lack the theoretical background.

At the present time the status of physicalism is similar to that which the hypothesis that matter is energy would have had if uttered by a pre-Socratic philosopher. We do not have the beginnings of a conception of how it might be true. In order to understand the hypothesis that a mental event is a physical event, we require more than an understanding of the word "is." The idea of how a mental and a physical term might refer to the same thing is lacking, and the usual analogies with theoretical identification in other fields fail to supply it. They fail because if we construe the reference of mental terms to physical events on the usual model, we either get a reappearance of separate subjective events as the effects through which mental reference to physical events is secured, or else we get a false account of how mental terms refer (for example, a causal behaviorist one).

Strangely enough, we may have evidence for the truth of something we cannot really understand. Suppose a caterpillar is locked in a sterile safe by someone unfamiliar with insect metamorphosis, and weeks later the safe is reopened, revealing a butterfly. If the person knows that the safe has been shut the whole time, he has reason to believe that the butterfly is or was once the caterpillar, without having any idea in what sense this might be so. (One possibility is that the caterpillar contained a tiny winged parasite that devoured it and grew into the butterfly.)

It is conceivable that we are in such a position with regard to physicalism. . . .

I should like to close with a speculative proposal. It may be possible to approach the gap between subjective and objective from another direction. Setting aside temporarily the relation between the mind and the brain, we can pursue a more objective understanding of the mental in its own right. At present we are completely unequipped to think about the subjective character of experience without relying on the imagination—without taking up the point of view of the experiential subject. This should be regarded as a challenge to form new concepts and devise a new method—an objective phenomenology not dependent on empathy or the imagination. Though presumably it would not capture everything, its goal would be to describe, at least in part, the subjective character of experiences in a form comprehensible to beings incapable of having those experiences.

We would have to develop such a phenomenology to describe the sonar experiences of bats; but it would also be possible to begin with humans. One might try, for example, to develop concepts that could be used to explain to a person blind from birth what it was like to see. One would reach a blank wall eventually, but it should be possible to devise a method of expressing in objective terms much more than we can at present, and with much greater precision. The loose intermodal analogies—for example, "Red is like the sound of a trumpet"—which crop up in discussions of this subject are of little use. That should be clear to anyone who has both heard a trumpet and seen red. But structural features of perception might be more accessible to objective description, even though something would be left out. And concepts alternative to those we learn in the first person may enable us to arrive at a kind of understanding even of our own experience which is denied us by the very ease of description and lack of distance that subjective concepts afford.

Apart from its own interest, a phenomenology that is in this sense objective may permit questions about the physical[6] basis of experience to assume a more intelligible form. Aspects of subjective experience that admitted this kind of objective description might be better candidates for objective explanations of a more familiar sort. But whether or not this guess is correct, it seems unlikely that any physical theory of mind can be contemplated until more thought has been given to the general problem of subjective and objective. Otherwise we cannot even pose the mind-body problem without sidestepping it.

6. I have not defined the term "physical." Obviously it does not apply just to what can be described by the concepts of contemporary physics, since we expect further developments. Some may think there is nothing to prevent mental phenomena from eventually being recognized as physical in their own right. But whatever else may be said of the physical, it has to be objective. So if our idea of the physical ever expands to include mental phenomena, it will have to assign them an objective character—whether or not this is done by analyzing them in terms of other phenomena already regarded as physical. It seems to me more likely, however, that mental-physical relations will eventually be expressed in a theory whose fundamental terms cannot be placed clearly in either category. [Nagel's note.]

TEST YOUR UNDERSTANDING

1. Does Nagel think that we completely understand the hypothesis that mental events are physical events?

2. Does Nagel think that acting like a bat would enable you to know what it's like to be one?

3. Does Nagel argue that physicalism is false?

4. Does Nagel think there may be facts we could never know?

5. According to Nagel, "we appear to be faced with a general difficulty about psychophysical reduction." What is that difficulty?

NOTES AND QUESTIONS

1. Nagel contrasts the scientific study of lightning with the scientific study of consciousness. "Lightning has an objective character that is not exhausted by its visual appearance, and this can be investigated by a Martian without vision." He argues that consciousness ("experience") is quite unlike lightning in this respect: "Experience itself . . . does not fit the pattern. The idea of moving from appearance to reality seems to make no sense here." Reconstruct Nagel's **argument** in the form of premises and conclusion. Assess the argument. Is it **valid**? Is it **sound**?

2. Can we know what it's like to be a bat? For some reasons for optimism (together with a detailed discussion of the complexities of bat echolocation), see Kathleen Akins, "What Is It Like to Be Boring and Myopic?" in *Dennett and His Critics*, ed. B. Dahlbom (Blackwell, 1993).

3. Nagel summarizes his current view of the mind-body problem in chapter 3 of his *Mind and Cosmos* (Oxford University Press, 2012).

Frank Jackson (b. 1943)

Jackson is an Australian philosopher who has made many contributions to philosophy of mind and language, metaphysics, and ethics. His books include *Perception: A Representative Theory* (1977), *Conditionals* (1987), and *From Metaphysics to Ethics: A Defense of Conceptual Analysis* (1997). He is Distinguished Professor at the Australian National University and a former Visiting Professor of Philosophy at Princeton University.

EPIPHENOMENAL QUALIA[1]

I t is undeniable that the physical, chemical and biological sciences have provided a great deal of information about the world we live in and about ourselves. I will use the label "physical information" for this kind of information, and also for information that automatically comes along with it. For example, if a medical scientist tells me enough about the processes that go on in my nervous system, and about how they relate to happenings in the world around me, to what has happened in the past and is likely to happen in the future, to what happens to other similar and dissimilar organisms, and the like, he or she tells me—if I am clever enough to fit it together appropriately—about what is often called the functional role of those states in me (and in organisms in general in similar cases). This information, and its kin, I also label "physical."

I do not mean these sketchy remarks to constitute a definition of "physical information," and of the correlative notions of physical property, process, and so on, but to indicate what I have in mind here. It is well known that there are problems with giving a precise definition of these notions, and so of the thesis of Physicalism that all (correct) information is physical information. But—unlike some—I take the question of definition to cut across the central problems I want to discuss in this paper.

I am what is sometimes known as a "qualia freak." I think that there are certain features of the bodily sensations especially, but also of certain perceptual experiences, which no amount of purely physical information includes. Tell me everything physical there is to tell about what is going on in a living brain, the kind of states, their functional role, their relation to what goes on at other times and in other brains, and so on and so forth, and be I as clever as can be in fitting it all together, you won't have told me about the hurtfulness of pains, the itchiness of itches, pangs of jealousy, or about the characteristic experience of tasting a lemon, smelling a rose, hearing a loud noise or seeing the sky.

There are many qualia freaks, and some of them say that their rejection of Physicalism is an unargued intuition. I think that they are being unfair to themselves. They have the following argument. Nothing you could tell of a physical sort captures the smell of a rose, for instance. Therefore, Physicalism is false. By our lights this is a perfectly good argument. It is obviously not to the point to question its validity, and the premise is intuitively obviously true both to them and to me.

I must, however, admit that it is weak from a polemical point of view. There are, unfortunately for us, many who do not find the premise intuitively obvious. The task then is to present an argument whose premises are obvious to all, or at least to as many as possible. This I try to do in §1 with what I will call "the Knowledge argument." In §2 I contrast the Knowledge argument with the Modal argument and in §3 with the "What is it like to be" argument. In §4 I tackle the question of the causal role of qualia. The major factor in stopping people from admitting qualia is the belief that they would

---

1. "Epiphenomenal": lacking causal power (here: the power to causally affect anything physical). "Qualia": qualities of mental states that specify their subjective character, or phenomenology. See the third paragraph of the reading for some examples.

have to be given a causal role with respect to the physical world and especially the brain; and it is hard to do this without sounding like someone who believes in fairies. I seek in §4 to turn this objection by arguing that the view that qualia are epiphenomenal is a perfectly possible one.

1. The Knowledge Argument for Qualia

People vary considerably in their ability to discriminate colours. Suppose that in an experiment to catalogue this variation Fred is discovered. Fred has better colour vision than anyone else on record; he makes every discrimination that anyone has ever made, and moreover he makes one that we cannot even begin to make. Show him a batch of ripe tomatoes and he sorts them into two roughly equal groups and does so with complete consistency. That is, if you blindfold him, shuffle the tomatoes up, and then remove the blindfold and ask him to sort them out again, he sorts them into exactly the same two groups.

We ask Fred how he does it. He explains that all ripe tomatoes do not look the same colour to him, and in fact that this is true of a great many objects that we classify together as red. He sees two colours where we see one, and he has in consequence developed for his own use two words "red_1" and "red_2" to mark the difference. Perhaps he tells us that he has often tried to teach the difference between red_1 and red_2 to his friends but has got nowhere and has concluded that the rest of the world is red_1-red_2 colour-blind—or perhaps he has had partial success with his children, it doesn't matter. In any case he explains to us that it would be quite wrong to think that because "red" appears in both "red_1" and "red_2" that the two colours are shades of the one colour. He only uses the common term "red" to fit more easily into our restricted usage. To him red_1 and red_2 are as different from each other and all the other colours as yellow is from blue. And his discriminatory behaviour bears this out: he sorts red_1 from red_2 tomatoes with the greatest of ease in a wide variety of viewing circumstances. Moreover, an investigation of the physiological basis of Fred's exceptional ability reveals that Fred's optical system is able to separate out two groups of wave-lengths in the red spectrum as sharply as we are able to sort out yellow from blue.

I think that we should admit that Fred can see, really see, at least one more colour than we can; red_1 is a different colour from red_2. We are to Fred as a totally red-green colour-blind person is to us. H. G. Wells' story "The Country of the Blind" is about a sighted person in a totally blind community. This person never manages to convince them that he can see, that he has an extra sense. They ridicule this sense as quite inconceivable, and treat his capacity to avoid falling into ditches, to win fights and so on as precisely that capacity and nothing more. We would be making their mistake if we refused to allow that Fred can see one more colour than we can.

What kind of experience does Fred have when he sees red_1 and red_2? What is the new colour or colours like? We would dearly like to know but do not; and it seems that no amount of physical information about Fred's brain and optical system tells us.

We find out perhaps that Fred's cones respond differentially to certain light waves in the red section of the spectrum that make no difference to ours (or perhaps he has an extra cone) and that this leads in Fred to a wider range of those brain states responsible for visual discriminatory behaviour. But none of this tells us what we really want to know about his colour experience. There is something about it we don't know. But we know, we may suppose, everything about Fred's body, his behaviour and dispositions to behaviour and about his internal physiology, and everything about his history and relation to others that can be given in physical accounts of persons. We have all the physical information. Therefore, knowing all this is *not* knowing everything about Fred. It follows that Physicalism leaves something out.

To reinforce this conclusion, imagine that as a result of our investigations into the internal workings of Fred we find out how to make everyone's physiology like Fred's in the relevant respects; or perhaps Fred donates his body to science and on his death we are able to transplant his optical system into someone else—again the fine detail doesn't matter. The important point is that such a happening would create enormous interest. People would say, "At last we will know what it is like to see the extra colour, at last we will know how Fred has differed from us in the way he has struggled to tell us about for so long." Then it cannot be that we knew all along all about Fred. But *ex hypothesi*[2] we did know all along everything about Fred that features in the physicalist scheme; hence the physicalist scheme leaves something out.

Put it this way. *After* the operation, we will know *more* about Fred and especially about his colour experiences. But beforehand we had all the physical information we could desire about his body and brain, and indeed everything that has ever featured in physicalist accounts of mind and consciousness. Hence there is more to know than all that. Hence Physicalism is incomplete.

Fred and the new colour(s) are of course essentially rhetorical devices. The same point can be made with normal people and familiar colours. Mary is a brilliant scientist who is, for whatever reason, forced to investigate the world from a black-and-white room *via* a black and white television monitor. She specialises in the neurophysiology of vision and acquires, let us suppose, all the physical information there is to obtain about what goes on when we see ripe tomatoes, or the sky, and use terms like "red," "blue," and so on. She discovers, for example, just which wave-length combinations from the sky stimulate the retina, and exactly how this produces *via* the central nervous system the contraction of the vocal chords and expulsion of air from the lungs that results in the uttering of the sentence "The sky is blue." (It can hardly be denied that it is in principle possible to obtain all this physical information from black-and-white television, otherwise the Open University[3] would *of necessity* need to use colour television.)

What will happen when Mary is released from her black-and-white room or is given a colour television monitor? Will she *learn* anything or not? It seems just obvious that she will learn something about the world and our visual experience of it. But then it is

---

2. By hypothesis (Latin).

3. A distance-learning university in the United Kingdom.

inescapable that her previous knowledge was incomplete. But she had *all* the physical information. *Ergo*[4] there is more to have than that, and Physicalism is false.

Clearly the same style of Knowledge argument could be deployed for taste, hearing, the bodily sensations and generally speaking for the various mental states which are said to have (as it is variously put) raw feels, phenomenal features or qualia. The conclusion in each case is that the qualia are left out of the physicalist story. And the polemical strength of the Knowledge argument is that it is so hard to deny the central claim that one can have all the physical information without having all the information there is to have.

2. The Modal Argument

By the Modal argument I mean an argument of the following style. Sceptics about other minds are not making a mistake in deductive logic, whatever else may be wrong with their position. No amount of physical information about another *logically entails* that he or she is conscious or feels anything at all. Consequently there is a possible world with organisms exactly like us in every physical respect (and remember that includes functional states, physical history, *et al.*) but which differ from us profoundly in that they have no conscious mental life at all. But then what is it that we have and they lack? Not anything physical *ex hypothesi*. In all physical regards we and they are exactly alike. Consequently there is more to us than the purely physical. Thus Physicalism is false. . . .

The trouble . . . with the Modal argument is that it rests on a disputable modal intuition. Disputable because it is disputed. Some sincerely deny that there can be physical replicas of us in other possible worlds which nevertheless lack consciousness. Moreover, at least one person who once had the intuition now has doubts.

Head-counting may seem a poor approach to a discussion of the Modal argument. But frequently we can do no better when modal intuitions are in question, and remember our initial goal was to find the argument with the greatest polemical utility.

Of course, *qua*[5] protagonists of the Knowledge argument we may well accept the modal intuition in question; but this will be a *consequence* of our already having an argument to the conclusion that qualia are left out of the physicalist story, not our ground for that conclusion. Moreover, the matter is complicated by the possibility that the connection between matters physical and qualia is like that sometimes held to obtain between aesthetic qualities and natural ones. Two possible worlds which agree in all "natural" respects (including the experiences of sentient creatures) must agree in all aesthetic qualities also, but it is plausibly held that the aesthetic qualities cannot be reduced to the natural.

4. Therefore (Latin).

5. As (Latin).

3. The "What Is It Like to Be" Argument

In "What is it like to be a bat?" Thomas Nagel argues that no amount of physical information can tell us what it is like to be a bat, and indeed that we, human beings, cannot imagine what it is like to be a bat.[6] His reason is that what this is like can only be understood from a bat's point of view, which is not our point of view and is not something capturable in physical terms which are essentially terms understandable equally from many points of view.

It is important to distinguish this argument from the Knowledge argument. When I complained that all the physical knowledge about Fred was not enough to tell us what his special colour experience was like, I was not complaining that we weren't finding out what it is like to *be* Fred. I was complaining that there is something *about* his experience, a property of it, of which we were left ignorant. And if and when we come to know what this property is we still will not know what it is like *to be* Fred, but we will know more *about* him. No amount of knowledge about Fred, be it physical or not, amounts to knowledge "from the inside" concerning Fred. We are not Fred. There is thus a whole set of items of knowledge expressed by forms of words like "that it is *I myself* who is . . ." which Fred has and we simply cannot have because we are not him.

When Fred sees the colour he alone can see, one thing he knows is the way his experience of it differs from his experience of seeing red and so on, *another* is that he himself is seeing it. Physicalist and qualia freaks alike should acknowledge that no amount of information of whatever kind that *others* have *about* Fred amounts to knowledge of the second. My complaint though concerned the first and was that the special quality of his experience is certainly a fact about it, and one which Physicalism leaves out because no amount of physical information told us what it is.

Nagel speaks as if the problem he is raising is one of extrapolating from knowledge of one experience to another, of imagining what an unfamiliar experience would be like on the basis of familiar ones. In terms of Hume's example, from knowledge of some shades of blue we can work out what it would be like to see other shades of blue.[7] Nagel argues that the trouble with bats *et al.* is that they are too unlike us. It is hard to see an objection to Physicalism here. Physicalism makes no special claims about the imaginative or extrapolative powers of human beings, and it is hard to see why it need do so.

Anyway, our Knowledge argument makes no assumptions on this point. If Physicalism were true, enough physical information about Fred would obviate any need to extrapolate or to perform special feats of imagination or understanding in order to know all about his special colour experience. *The information would already be in our possession.* But it clearly isn't. That was the nub of the argument.

---

6. See Nagel's "What Is It Like to Be a Bat" earlier in this chapter.

7. The Scottish philosopher David Hume (1711–1776) considered the example of a person "who enjoyed his sight for thirty years" and who became "perfectly well acquainted with colours of all kinds, excepting one particular shade of blue" (*Treatise of Human Nature*, I.1.i).

4. The Bogey of Epiphenomenalism

Is there any really *good* reason for refusing to countenance the idea that qualia are causally impotent with respect to the physical world? I will argue for the answer no, but in doing this I will say nothing about two views associated with the classical epiphenomenalist position. The first is that mental *states* are inefficacious with respect to the physical world. All I will be concerned to defend is that it is possible to hold that certain *properties* of certain mental states, namely those I've called qualia, are such that their possession or absence makes no difference to the physical world. The second is that the mental is *totally* causally inefficacious. For all I will say it may be that you have to hold that the instantiation of *qualia* makes a difference to *other mental states* though not to anything physical. Indeed general considerations to do with how you could come to be aware of the instantiation of qualia suggest such a position.

Three reasons are standardly given for holding that a quale like the hurtfulness of a pain must be causally efficacious in the physical world, and so, for instance, that its instantiation must sometimes make a difference to what happens in the brain. None, I will argue, has any real force. (I am much indebted to Alec Hyslop[8] and John Lucas[9] for convincing me of this.)

(i) It is supposed to be just obvious that the hurtfulness of pain is partly responsible for the subject seeking to avoid pain, saying "It hurts" and so on. But, to reverse Hume, anything can fail to cause anything.[10] No matter how often *B* follows *A*, and no matter how initially obvious the causality of the connection seems, the hypothesis that *A* causes *B* can be overturned by an over-arching theory which shows the two as distinct effects of a common underlying causal process.

To the untutored the image on the screen of Lee Marvin's fist moving[11] from left to right immediately followed by the image of John Wayne's head moving in the same general direction looks as causal as anything. And of course throughout countless Westerns images similar to the first are followed by images similar to the second. All this counts for precisely nothing when we know the over-arching theory concerning how the relevant images are both effects of an underlying causal process involving the projector and the film. The epiphenomenalist can say exactly the same about the connection between, for example, hurtfulness and behaviour. It is simply a consequence of the fact that certain happenings in the brain cause both.

(ii) The second objection relates to Darwin's Theory of Evolution. According to natural selection the traits that evolve over time are those conducive to physical survival. We may assume that qualia evolved over time—we have them, the earliest forms of

---

8. Alec Hyslop (1938–), Australian philosopher.

9. John Lucas (1929–), British philosopher.

10. According to David Hume, "there are no objects, which by the mere survey, without consulting experience, we can determine to be the causes of any other. . . . Any thing may produce anything" (*Treatise of Human Nature*, I.3.xv).

11. The American actors Lee Marvin (1924–1987) and John Wayne (1907–1979) appeared in three movies together in the early 1960s.

life do not—and so we should expect qualia to be conducive to survival. The objection is that they could hardly help us to survive if they do nothing to the physical world.

The appeal of this argument is undeniable, but there is a good reply to it. Polar bears have particularly thick, warm coats. The Theory of Evolution explains this (we suppose) by pointing out that having a thick, warm coat is conducive to survival in the Arctic. But having a thick coat goes along with having a heavy coat, and having a heavy coat is *not* conducive to survival. It slows the animal down.

Does this mean that we have refuted Darwin because we have found an evolved trait—having a heavy coat—which is not conducive to survival? Clearly not. Having a heavy coat is an unavoidable concomitant of having a warm coat (in the context, modern insulation was not available), and the advantages for survival of having a warm coat outweighed the disadvantages of having a heavy one. The point is that all we can extract from Darwin's theory is that we should expect any evolved characteristic to be *either* conducive to survival *or* a by-product of one that is so conducive. The epiphenomenalist holds that qualia fall into the latter category. They are a by-product of certain brain processes that are highly conducive to survival.

(iii) The third objection is based on a point about how we come to know about other minds. We know about other minds by knowing about other behaviour, at least in part. The nature of the inference is a matter of some controversy, but it is not a matter of controversy that it proceeds from behaviour. That is why we think that stones do not feel and dogs do feel. But, runs the objection, how can a person's behaviour provide any reason for believing he has qualia like mine, or indeed any qualia at all, unless this behaviour can be regarded as the *outcome* of the qualia. Man Friday's[12] footprint was evidence of Man Friday because footprints are causal outcomes of feet attached to people. And an epiphenomenalist cannot regard behaviour, or indeed anything physical, as an outcome of qualia.

But consider my reading in *The Times* that Spurs[13] won. This provides excellent evidence that *The Telegraph* has also reported that Spurs won, despite the fact that (I trust) *The Telegraph* does not get the results from *The Times*. They each send their own reporters to the game. *The Telegraph*'s report is in no sense an outcome of *The Times*', but the latter provides good evidence for the former nevertheless.

The reasoning involved can be reconstructed thus. I read in *The Times* that Spurs won. This gives me reason to think that Spurs won because I know that Spurs' winning is the most likely candidate to be what caused the report in *The Times*. But I also know that Spurs' winning would have had many effects, including almost certainly a report in *The Telegraph*.

I am arguing from one effect back to its cause and out again to another effect. The fact that neither effect causes the other is irrelevant. Now the epiphenomenalist allows that qualia are effects of what goes on in the brain. Qualia cause nothing physical but are caused by something physical. Hence the epiphenomenalist can argue from the

---

12. A character in the novel *Robinson Crusoe* (1719) by the English writer Daniel Defoe (1659–1731).

13. Tottenham Hotspur, London football (soccer) team.

behaviour of others to the qualia of others by arguing from the behaviour of others back to its causes in the brains of others and out again to their qualia.

You may well feel for one reason or another that this is a more dubious chain of reasoning than its model in the case of newspaper reports. You are right. The problem of other minds is a major philosophical problem, the problem of other newspaper reports is not. But there is no special problem of Epiphenomenalism as opposed to, say, Interactionism[14] here.

There is a very understandable response to the three replies I have just made. "All right, there is no knockdown refutation of the existence of epiphenomenal qualia. But the fact remains that they are an excrescence. They *do* nothing, they *explain* nothing, they serve merely to soothe the intuitions of dualists,[15] and it is left a total mystery how they fit into the world view of science. In short we do not and cannot understand the how and why of them."

This is perfectly true; but is no objection to qualia, for it rests on an overly optimistic view of the human animal, and its powers. We are the products of Evolution. We understand and sense what we need to understand and sense in order to survive. Epiphenomenal qualia are totally irrelevant to survival. At no stage of our evolution did natural selection favour those who could make sense of how they are caused and the laws governing them, or in fact why they exist at all. And that is why we can't.

It is not sufficiently appreciated that Physicalism is an extremely optimistic view of our powers. If it is true, we have, in very broad outline admittedly, a grasp of our place in the scheme of things. Certain matters of sheer complexity defeat us—there are an awful lot of neurons—but in principle we have it all. But consider the antecedent probability that everything in the Universe be of a kind that is relevant in some way or other to the survival of *homo sapiens*. It is very low surely. But then one must admit that it is very likely that there is a part of the whole scheme of things, maybe a big part, which no amount of evolution will ever bring us near to knowledge about or understanding. For the simple reason that such knowledge and understanding is irrelevant to survival.

Physicalists typically emphasise that we are a part of nature on their view, which is fair enough. But if we are a part of nature, we are as nature has left us after however many years of evolution it is, and each step in that evolutionary progression has been a matter of chance constrained just by the need to preserve or increase survival value. The wonder is that we understand as much as we do, and there is no wonder that there should be matters which fall quite outside our comprehension. Perhaps exactly how epiphenomenal qualia fit into the scheme of things is one such.

This may seem an unduly pessimistic view of our capacity to articulate a truly comprehensive picture of our world and our place in it. But suppose we discovered living on the bottom of the deepest oceans a sort of sea slug which manifested intelligence. Perhaps survival in the conditions required rational powers. Despite their intelligence, these sea slugs have only a very restricted conception of the world by comparison

14. The view that the mental has physical effects and vice versa.

15. Those who hold that the mind and body are distinct things, or that mental properties are distinct from physical properties.

with ours, the explanation for this being the nature of their immediate environment. Nevertheless they have developed sciences which work surprisingly well in these restricted terms. They also have philosophers, called slugists. Some call themselves tough-minded slugists, others confess to being soft-minded slugists.

The tough-minded slugists hold that the restricted terms (or ones pretty like them which may be introduced as their sciences progress) suffice in principle to describe everything without remainder. These tough-minded slugists admit in moments of weakness to a feeling that their theory leaves something out. They resist this feeling and their opponents, the soft-minded slugists, by pointing out—absolutely correctly— that no slugist has ever succeeded in spelling out how this mysterious residue fits into the highly successful view that their sciences have and are developing of how their world works.

Our sea slugs don't exist, but they might. And there might also exist super beings which stand to us as we stand to the sea slugs. We cannot adopt the perspective of these super beings, because we are not them, but the possibility of such a perspective is, I think, an antidote to excessive optimism.

TEST YOUR UNDERSTANDING

1. Does Jackson think the heavy coat of the polar bear is epiphenomenal?

2. Does Jackson think it is a mystery how epiphenomenal qualia fit into the world as described by science?

3. If we set out the knowledge argument using Fred instead of Mary, do we need to assume that Fred knows everything about himself that can be given in physical accounts of persons?

4. Does Jackson think that Nagel's argument in "What Is It Like to Be a Bat?" shows that physicalism is false?

READER'S GUIDE

Jackson's Knowledge Argument

The meaning of "Epiphenomenal Qualia" is likely to be unclear to you, and anyway the point of the title only emerges at the end. So let's ignore the title for the moment and focus on Jackson's main conclusion and his argument for it. His main conclusion is that **physicalism** is false, and he calls his argument for this conclusion, the **knowledge argument**.

What is physicalism? Put loosely but intuitively, it is supposed to be the view that the world—everything there is—is "entirely physical." But what does that mean? Jackson explains it in terms of *physical information*, the sort of information provided by "the physical, chemical and biological sciences." For example, the fact that protons are positively charged, that table salt contains chlorine, and that bacteria have evolved antibiotic resistance are three bits of physical information. Put in terms of physical information, the thesis of physicalism is that "all (correct) information is physical information" (p. 366). (The parenthetical "correct" signals that Jackson is not taking information to include *mis*information—that protons are negatively charged is not a bit of information in Jackson's sense, because it's not true.)

However, Jackson's explanation of physicalism has a drawback—it makes it hard to see why physicalism is a thesis worth defending. Why think that *all* information is physical information? You might think economics, literature, psychology, and history are worth studying precisely because they provide a lot of information that *isn't* provided by physics, chemistry, and biology. So here is another way of explaining what physicalism is, which at least doesn't have this drawback. (As Jackson says, there are problems with giving a "precise definition" of physicalism, but for the purposes of understanding Jackson's essay, you don't need to worry about them.)

Some things are made out of *purely physical ingredients, combined in purely physical ways*; that is, made only out of ingredients and combined only in ways recognized by the physical, chemical, and biological sciences. For example, a proton is made from quarks combined by the strong nuclear force, table salt is made from sodium and chlorine combined by the electromagnetic force, and the story for simple organisms like bacteria is basically the same, although vastly more complicated. If something is made out of purely physical ingredients, combined in purely physical ways, then we can say, for short, that it is *purely physical*—there's nothing about a purely physical thing that can't be accounted for in terms of the physical sciences. Then physicalism can be put like this: *everything* is purely physical. And if physicalism is put this way, then it can seem very plausible. Just like bacteria, the cells in your body are purely physical. But you are made out of cells, combined in purely physical ways. So you are purely physical too. Similarly with Mount Everest, the planet Jupiter, New York City, and anything else you like. If the knowledge argument shows that physicalism is false, then that is a significant result.

We know what the conclusion of the knowledge argument is, but what are its premises? Jackson presents the argument twice, first using Fred, who can see more colors than we can, and then using Mary, a brilliant scientist trapped in a black-and-white room. In fact, Mary grabbed the philosophical imagination more than Fred, and she played the starring role in all the subsequent commentaries on the knowledge argument. Using Mary as the example, a simple way of setting out the knowledge argument is this:

P1.   When she is released from her black-and-white room and first sees a red tomato, Mary will *learn* something—she will come to know something she didn't know before.

P2.   If physicalism is true, Mary will not learn *anything* when she is released.

C.   Physicalism is false.

This argument is **valid**, and so if you want to reject the conclusion you must reject at least one of the premises. Some philosophers reject the first one, some the second, and some—like Jackson when he wrote his essay—accept the conclusion.

Now back to the title. Supposing Mary does learn something, *what* does she learn about, exactly? Jackson's answer is this: Mary learns about **qualia**, which are features of "bodily sensations" and "certain perceptual experiences." This answer indicates *which part of reality is not purely physical*, if physicalism is indeed false—it's *consciousness*.

What about "epiphenomenal"? Jackson holds that the physical sciences give *complete* causal explanations of the phenomena they study—they don't leave any causes out. Since the physical sciences cannot account for qualia, qualia don't cause anything physical—in the jargon, they are **epiphenomenal**. The *quale* distinctive of painful sensations, for instance, doesn't cause you to jump around when someone drops a hammer on your toe. The title, then, expresses the overall conclusion of Jackson's essay: *there are epiphenomenal qualia.* This is *stronger* than his main conclusion, that physicalism is false; Jackson thinks that once his main conclusion is accepted, it is hard to avoid the stronger one.

This stronger conclusion is stated at the beginning of the last section: "qualia are causally impotent with respect to the physical world" (p. 371). Notably, Jackson later came to think that this could not be right, and joined the ranks of those who reject the premises of the knowledge argument—specifically, premise P1.

NOTES AND QUESTIONS

1. According to Jackson, what are "qualia"? What does it mean to say that qualia are "epiphenomenal"? Evaluate the three objections to the claim that qualia are epiphenomenal, discussed by Jackson in section 4 of his essay. Does Jackson succeed in rebutting them? Are qualia epiphenomenal?

2. Set out the "modal argument" (p. 369) in the form of premises and conclusion so that the **argument** is **valid**. How would Jackson object to the argument as you have set it out? Is the objection convincing?

3. Different authors use the term "qualia" differently. For a short explanation of the various senses of the term, see Michael Tye, "Qualia," in *Stanford Encyclopedia of Philosophy*, ed. Edward Zalta (http:// plato.stanford.edu/archives/win2016/entries/qualia/), section 1.

4. Jackson's knowledge argument is still hotly debated. For some interesting essays and a helpful editorial introduction, see Peter Ludlow, Yujin Nagasawa, and Daniel Stoljar (Eds.), *There's Something about Mary* (MIT Press, 2004). Jackson himself famously changed his mind: he now thinks that Mary would *not* learn anything when released from her black-and-white room, and so the knowledge argument fails. He explains why in "Mind and Illusion," reprinted in *There's Something about Mary*.

Patricia Smith Churchland (b. 1943)

Churchland is Emeritus Professor of Philosophy at the University of California, San Diego. She is known for her work connecting neuroscience and traditional philosophical topics such as consciousness, the self, free will, and ethics. Among other books, she is the author of *Brain-Wise: Studies in Neurophilosophy* (2002) and *Touching a Nerve: The Self as Brain* (2013).

ARE MENTAL STATES IRREDUCIBLE TO NEUROBIOLOGICAL STATES?

from *Neurophilosophy: A Unified Science of the Mind/Brain*

Knowing from the Inside/Having a Point of View

For Nagel (1974),[1] there is something special about having an introspective capacity—a capacity to know one's thoughts, feelings, and sensations from the inside, as it were. One's experiences have a certain unmistakable phenomenological character, such as the felt quality of pain or the perceived character of red. One therefore has a subjective point of view. It is the *qualia* or qualitative character of experiences, sensations, feelings, and so forth, to which we have introspective access, and it is this that, in Nagel's view, is not reducible to neural states. These mental states resist reduction because introspective access to them has an essentially different character, yielding essentially different information, than does external access via neuroscience. The argument does exert a powerful attraction, but as stated it is still teasingly vague. In order to see exactly how it works, it is necessary to set out a more precise version.

(A)

(1)   The qualia of my sensations are knowable to me by introspection.

(2)   The properties of my brain states are *not* knowable to me by introspection.

Therefore:

(3)   The qualia of my sensations ≠ the properties of my brain states.

A second argument, complementary to the first, seems also in play:

(B)

(1)   The properties of my brain states are knowable by the various external senses.

(2)   The qualia of my sensations are *not* knowable by the various external senses.

Therefore:

(3)   The qualia of my sensations ≠ the properties of my brain states.

The general form of the argument seems to be this:

(1) a is F

(2) b is not F

Therefore:

(3) $a \neq b$

---

1. See "What Is It Like to Be a Bat?" earlier in this chapter.

Leibniz's law says that $a = b$ if and only if a and b have every property in common. So if a = b, then if a is red, b is red, if a weighs ten pounds, then b weighs ten pounds, and so forth. If a is red and b is not, then $a \neq b$. Assuming their premises are true, arguments (A) and (B) appear to establish the nonidentity of brain states and mental states. But are their premises true?

Let us begin with argument (A). There is no quarrel with the first premise (the qualia of my sensations are known-to-me-by-introspection), especially since qualia are defined as those sensory qualities known by introspection, and in any case I have no wish to deny introspective awareness of sensations. In contrast, the second premise (the properties of my brain states are *not* known-to-me-by-introspection) looks decidedly troublesome. Its first problem is that it begs the very question at issue—that is, the question of whether or not mental states are identical to brain states. This is easy to see when we ask what the justification is for thinking that premise true.

The point is this: *if in fact* mental states are identical to brain states, then when I introspect a mental state, I do introspect the brain state with which it is identical. Needless to say, I may not *describe* my mental state as a brain state, but whether I do depends on what information I have about the brain, not upon whether the mental state really is identical to some brain state. The identity can be a fact about the world independently of my knowledge that it is a fact about the world. Similarly, when Jones swallows an aspirin, he thereby swallows acetylsalicylic acid, whether or not he thinks of himself thus; when Oedipus kissed Jocasta, he kissed his mother, whether or not he thought of himself thus. In short, identities may obtain even when we have not discovered that they do. The problem with the second premise is that the only justification for denying that introspective awareness of sensations *could be* introspective awareness of brain states derives from the assumption that mental states are not identical with brain states. And that is precisely what the argument is supposed to prove. Hence the charge of begging the question. (Although I have used (A) as an illustration, the same kind of criticism applies equally to (B).)

Other problems with these arguments are more subtle. One difficulty is best brought out by constructing an argument analogous to (A) or (B) with respect to the character of the properties under discussion and comparing the arguments for adequacy. Consider the following arguments:

(c)

(1)   Smith believes Hitler to be a mass murderer.

(2)   Smith does not believe Adolf Schicklgruber to be a mass murderer.

Therefore:

(3)   Adolf Schicklgruber $\neq$ Adolf Hitler.

As it happens, however, Adolf Schicklgruber = Adolf Hitler, so the argument cannot be right.

Or consider another instance of the general argument form where the property taking the place of F is a complex property concerning what John believes or knows:

(D)

(1) Aspirin is *known by John to be a pain reliever.*

(2) Acetylsalicylic acid is *not* known by John to be a pain reliever.

Therefore:

(3) Aspirin ≠ acetylsalicylic acid.

And one final example more closely analogous to the arguments at issue:

(E)

(1) Temperature is *directly apprehendable by me as a feature of material objects.*

(2) Mean molecular kinetic energy is *not* directly apprehendable by me as a feature of material objects.

Therefore:

(3) Temperature ≠ mean molecular kinetic energy.

These arguments fail because being-recognized-as-a-something or being-believed-to-be-a-something is not a genuine feature of the object itself, but rather is a feature of the object *as apprehended under some description or other* or *as thought about in some manner.* Having a certain mass is a property of the object, but being-thought-by-Smith-to-have-a-certain-mass is not a genuine property of the object. Such queer properties are sometimes called "intentional properties" to reflect their thought-mediated dependency. Notice that in (B) the property is being-knowable-by-the-various-external-senses, and in (A) the property is being-known-by-me-by-introspection. Both are sterling examples of thought-dependent properties.

Now the arguments (C) through (E) are fallacious because they treat intentional properties as though they were genuine properties of the objects, and a mistake of this type is called the *intentional fallacy.* It is evident that the arguments designed to demonstrate the nonidentity of qualia and brain states are analogous to arguments (C) through (E). Consequently, they are equally fallacious, and the nonidentity of mental states and brain states cannot be considered established by arguments such as (A) and (B).

The last difficulty with the arguments is better seen in a slightly different and more compelling version of the argument for the nonidentity of mental states and brain states, which I present and discuss below.

Knowing Our Sensations: Jackson's Argument

The strategy of this second argument once again involves showing that differences between knowing our states via introspection and knowing via nonintrospective means are of such a nature as to constitute grounds for denying the reducibility of psychology to neuroscience. In order to clarify those differences, Frank Jackson (1982)[2] has constructed the following thought-experiment. Suppose that Mary is a neuroscientist who has lived her entire life in a room carefully controlled to display no colors, but only shades of white, gray, and black. Her information about the outside world is transmitted to her by means of a black-and-white television. Suppose further that one way or another she comes to know everything there is to know about the brain and how it works. That is, she comes to understand a completed neuroscience that, among other things, explains the nature of thinking, feeling, and perception, including the perception of colors. (This is all wildly unlikely, of course, but just suppose.)

Now for the argument: despite her knowing everything there is to know about the brain and about the visual system, there would still be something Mary would not know that her cohorts with a more regular childhood would, namely, the nature of the experience of seeing a red tomato. Granted, she knows all about the neural states at work when someone sees a red tomato—after all, she has the utopian neuroscience at hand. What she would not know is *what it is like to see red*—what it is like to have that specific experience. Conclusion: her utopian neuroscience leaves something out. This omission implies that there is something in psychology that is not captured by neuroscience, which in turn implies that psychology cannot be reduced to neuroscience.

More formally and with some simplifications, the argument is this:

(F)

(1)   Mary knows everything there is to know about brain states and their properties.

(2)   It is not the case that Mary knows everything there is to know about sensations and their properties.

Therefore:

(3)   Sensations and their properties ≠ brain states and their properties.

The argument is very interesting, and it gives an unusually clean line to the intuition that mental states are essentially private and have an irreducibly phenomenological character. Nonetheless I am not convinced, and I shall try to explain why.

First, I suspect that the intentional fallacy, which caused problems for arguments (A) and (B), likewise haunts the premises of argument (F). That aside, there are perhaps more revealing criticisms to be made. Paul M. Churchland (1985) and David Lewis (1983) have independently argued that "knows about" is used in different senses in the two premises. As they see it, one sense involves the manipulation of concepts, as when one knows about electromagnetic radiation and can use the concept "electromagnetic radiation" by having been tutored in the theory. The other sense involves a prelinguistic apprehension, as when one knows about electromagnetic radiation by having had one's retina stimulated in the light of day, though one cannot use the expression "electromagnetic radiation." The latter sense may involve innate dispositions to make certain discriminations, for example. If the first premise uses "knows about" in the

2. See "Epiphenomenal Qualia" earlier in this chapter.

first sense and the second uses it in the second sense, then the argument founders on the fallacy of equivocation.

The important point is this: if there are two (at least) modes of knowing about the world, then it is entirely possible that what one knows about via one method is identical to what one knows about via a different method. Pregnancy is something one can know about by acquiring the relevant theory from a medical text or by being pregnant. What a childless obstetrician knows about is the very same process as the process known by a pregnant but untutored woman. They both know about pregnancy. By parity of reasoning, the object of Mary's knowledge when she knows the neurophysiology of seeing red might well be the very same state as the state known by her tomato-picking cohort. Just as the obstetrician does not become pregnant by knowing all about pregnancy, so Mary does not have the sensation of redness by knowing all about the neurophysiology of perceiving and experiencing red. Clearly it is no argument in support of nonidentity to say that Mary's knowledge fails to cause the sensation of redness. Whyever suppose that it should?

There is a further reservation about this argument. With the first premise I take no issue, since we are asked to adopt it simply for the sake of argument. The second premise, in contrast, is supposed to be accepted because it is highly credible or perhaps dead obvious. Now although it does have a first blush plausibility, it is the premise on which the argument stands or falls, and closer scrutiny is required.

On a second look, its obviousness dissolves into contentiousness, because the premise asks me to be confident about something that is too far beyond the limits of what I know and understand. How can I assess what Mary will know and understand if she knows *everything* there is to know about the brain? Everything is a lot, and it means, in all likelihood, that Mary has a radically different and deeper understanding of the brain than anything barely conceivable in our wildest flights of fancy.

One might say well, if Mary knew everything about *existing* neuroscience, she would not know what it was like to experience red, and knowing *absolutely* everything will just be more of the same. That is an assumption to which the property dualist is not entitled to help himself. For to know everything about the brain might well be qualitatively different, and it might be to possess a theory that would permit exactly what the premise says it will not. First, utopian neuroscience will probably look as much like existing neuroscience as modern physics looks like Aristotelian physics. So it will not be just more of the same. Second, all one need imagine is that Mary internalizes the theory in the way an engineer has internalized Newtonian physics, and she routinely makes introspective judgments about her own states using its concepts and principles. Like the engineer who does not have to make an effort but "sees" the world in a Newtonian manner, we may consider that Mary "sees" her internal world via the utopian neuroscience. Such a neuroscience might even tell her how to be very efficient at internalizing theories. It is, after all, the premise tells us, a *complete* neuroscience.

Intuitions and imaginability are, notoriously, a function of what we believe, and when we are very ignorant, our intuitions will be correspondingly naive. Gedanken-experiments[3]

---

3. Thought experiments (*Gedanke* is German for "thought").

are the stuff of theoretical science, but when their venue is so surpassing distant from established science that the pivotal intuition is not uncontroversially better than its opposite, then their utility in deciding issues is questionable.

Moreover, intuitions opposite to those funding premise (2) are not only readily available, they can even be fleshed out a bit. How can I be reasonably sure that Mary would not know what a red tomato looks like? Here is a test. Present her with her first red object, and see whether she can recognize it as a red object. Given that she is supposed to know absolutely *everything* there is to know about the nervous system, perhaps she could, by introspective use of her utopian neuroscience, tell that she has, say, a gamma state in her O patterns, which she knows from her utopian neuroscience is identical to having a red sensation. Thus, she might recognize redness on that basis.

The telling point is this: whether or not she can recognize redness is clearly an empirical question, and I do not see how in our ignorance we can confidently insist that she must fail. Short of begging the question, there is no a priori reason why this is impossible. For all I know, she might even be able to produce red in her imagination if she knows what brain states are relevant. One cannot be confident that such an exercise of the imagination must be empirically impossible. To insist that our make-believe Mary could not make introspective judgments using her neuroscience *because* mental qualia are not identical to brain states would, obviously, route the argument round in a circle.

How could an alchemist assess what he could and could not know if he knew everything about substances? How could a monk living in the Middle Ages assess what he could and could not know if he knew everything there was to know about biology? He might insist, for example, that even if you knew everything there was to know about biology, you still would not know the nature of the vital spirit. Well, we still do not have a complete biology, but even so we know more than this hypothetical monk thought we could. We know (a) that there is no such thing as vital spirit, and (b) that DNA is the "secret" of life—it is what all living things on the planet share.

The central point of this reply to Jackson has been that he needs independent evidence for premise (2), since it is palpably not self-evident. It cannot be defended on a priori grounds, since its truth is an empirical question, and it cannot be defended on empirical grounds, since given the data so far, as good a case can be made for the negation of premise (2) as for premise (2) itself. I do not see, therefore, how it can be defended.

REFERENCES

Churchland, Paul M. (1985). "Reduction, Qualia, and the Direct Introspection of Brain States." *Journal of Philosophy* 82: 8–28.

Jackson, Frank (1982). "Epiphenomenal Qualia." *Philosophical Quarterly* 32: 127–36.

Lewis, David (1983). Postscript to "Mad Pain and Martian Pain." In *Philosophical Papers*, vol. I, 122–30. Oxford University Press.

Nagel, Thomas (1974). "What Is It Like to Be a Bat?" *Philosophical Review* 83: 435–50.

TEST YOUR UNDERSTANDING

1. Suppose Churchland agrees that the "general form" of **arguments** (A) and (B) is

    (1) a is F

    (2) b is not F

    Therefore:

    (3) $a \neq b$,

    where *F-ness is "a genuine property of the object."* Given this assumption, would Churchland think (A) and (B) are **valid**?

2. Here is an argument with a missing premise:

    (1) Lois knows that Clark Kent works for the *Daily Planet.*

    (2) _____.

    Therefore:

    (3) Clark Kent ≠ Superman.

    Fill in the second premise so the argument commits the "intentional fallacy."

3. Consider this argument:

    (1) The pig is in the pen.

    (2) The pen is in my pocket.

    Therefore:

    (3) The pig is in my pocket.

    With the premises interpreted in the most natural way, this argument commits a fallacy. Churchland mentions this fallacy and suggests that one of her labeled arguments commits it. What is the fallacy, and what is the argument?

4. Jackson asks: "What will happen when Mary is released from her black-and-white room?" What is Churchland's reply?

NOTES AND QUESTIONS

1. Evaluate Churchland's criticisms of Nagel's argument, as she interprets it. Is her interpretation correct or is Nagel's argument different?

2. Evaluate Churchland's criticisms of Jackson's argument, as she interprets it. Is her interpretation correct or is Jackson's argument different?

3. For Jackson's reply to similar criticisms (offered by Paul Churchland in "Reduction, Qualia, and the Direct Introspection of Brain States," *Journal of Philosophy* 82 [1985]: 8–28), see his "What Mary Didn't Know," *Journal of Philosophy* 83 (1986): 291–95.

4. The selection by Churchland is entirely critical; for an introduction to her positive views about the mind and the brain, see her *Touching a Nerve: The Self as Brain* (Norton, 2013).

David Chalmers (b. 1966)

Chalmers is an Australian philosopher specializing in philosophy of mind and is known in particular for his influential book *The Conscious Mind* (1996), which set out more rigorous forms of traditional arguments for the view that the mind is not wholly material. He is Professor of Philosophy at New York University and Distinguished Professor of Philosophy at the Australian National University. He is also the author of *The Character of Consciousness* (2010) and *Constructing the World* (2012).

THE HARD PROBLEM OF CONSCIOUSNESS[1]

1. Introduction

Why does physical processing in the brain give rise to a conscious inner life: consciousness of shapes, colors, sounds, emotions, and a stream of conscious thought, all experienced from the first-person point of view? This is perhaps the most baffling problem in the science of the mind. All sorts of mental phenomena have yielded to scientific investigation in recent years, but consciousness has stubbornly resisted. Many have tried to explain it, but the explanations always seem to fall short of the target. Some have been led to suppose that the problem is intractable, and that no good explanation can be given.

In this paper, I first isolate the truly hard part of the problem, separating it from more tractable parts and giving an account of why it is so difficult to explain. In the second half of the paper, I argue that if we move to a new kind of explanation that does not try to reduce consciousness to something it is not, a naturalistic account of consciousness can be given.

2. The Easy Problems and the Hard Problem

There is not just one problem of consciousness. "Consciousness" is an ambiguous term, referring to many different phenomena. Each of these phenomena needs to be explained, but some are easier to explain than others. At the start, it is useful to divide the associated problems of consciousness into "hard" and "easy" problems. The easy problems

---

1. The arguments in this paper are presented in greater depth in David Chalmers, *The Conscious Mind* (Oxford University Press, 1996). [Chalmers's note.]

of consciousness are those that seem directly susceptible to the standard methods of cognitive science, whereby a phenomenon is explained in terms of computational or neural mechanisms. The hard problems are those that seem to resist those methods.

The easy problems of consciousness include those of explaining the following phenomena:

the ability to discriminate, categorize, and react to environmental stimuli;
the integration of information by a cognitive system;
the reportability of mental states;
the ability of a system to access its own internal states;
the focus of attention;
the deliberate control of behavior;
the difference between wakefulness and sleep.

All of these phenomena are associated with the notion of consciousness. For example, one sometimes says that a mental state is conscious when it is verbally reportable or when it is internally accessible. Sometimes a system is said to be conscious of some information when it has the ability to react on the basis of that information, or, more strongly, when it attends to that information, or when it can integrate that information and exploit it in the sophisticated control of behavior. We sometimes say that an action is conscious precisely when it is deliberate. Often, we say that an organism is conscious as another way of saying that it is awake.

There is no real issue about whether *these* phenomena can be explained scientifically. All of them are straightforwardly vulnerable to explanation in terms of computational or neural mechanisms. To explain access and reportability, for example, we need only specify the mechanism by which information about internal states is retrieved and made available for verbal report. To explain the integration of information, we need only exhibit mechanisms by which information is brought together and exploited by later processes. For an account of sleep and wakefulness, an appropriate neurophysiologic account of the processes responsible for organisms' contrasting behavior in those states will suffice. In each case, an appropriate cognitive or neurophysiologic model can clearly do the explanatory work.

If these phenomena were all there was to consciousness, then consciousness would not be much of a problem. Although we do not yet have anything close to a complete explanation of these phenomena, we have a clear idea of how we might go about explaining them. This is why I call these problems the easy problems. Of course, "easy" is a relative term. Getting the details right will probably take a century or two of difficult empirical work. Still, there is every reason to believe that the methods of cognitive science and neuroscience will succeed.

The really hard problem of consciousness is the problem of *experience*. When we think and perceive, there is a whir of information processing, but there is also a subjective aspect. As Nagel[2] has put it, there is *something it is like* to be a conscious

---

2. Thomas Nagel, "What Is It Like to Be a Bat?" *Philosophical Review* 83 (1974): 435–50, excerpted earlier in this chapter.

organism. This subjective aspect is experience. When we see, for example, we *experience* visual sensations: the felt quality of redness, the experience of dark and light, the quality of depth in a visual field. Other experiences go along with perception in different modalities: the sound of a clarinet, the smell of mothballs. Then there are bodily sensations, from pains to orgasms; mental images that are conjured up internally; the felt quality of emotion, and the experience of a stream of conscious thought. What unites all of these states is that there is something it is like to be in them. All of them are states of experience.

It is undeniable that some organisms are subjects of experience. But the question of how it is that these systems are subjects of experience is perplexing. Why is it that when our cognitive systems engage in visual and auditory information processing, we have visual or auditory experience: the quality of deep blue, the sensation of middle C? How can we explain why there is something it is like to entertain a mental image or to experience an emotion? It is widely agreed that experience arises from a physical basis, but we have no good explanation of why and how it so arises. Why should physical processing give rise to a rich inner life at all? It seems objectively unreasonable that it should, and yet it does.

If any problem qualifies as *the* problem of consciousness, it is this one. In this central sense of "consciousness," an organism is conscious if there is something it is like to be that organism, and a mental state is conscious if there is something it is like to be in that state. Sometimes terms such as "phenomenal consciousness" and "qualia" are also used here, but I find it more natural to speak of "conscious experience" or simply "experience."

3. Functional Explanation

Why are the easy problems easy, and why is the hard problem hard? The easy problems are easy precisely because they concern the explanation of cognitive *abilities* and *functions*. To explain a cognitive function, we need only specify a mechanism that can perform the function. The methods of cognitive science are well suited for this sort of explanation, and so are well suited to the easy problems of consciousness. By contrast, the hard problem is hard precisely because it is not a problem about the performance of functions. The problem persists even when the performance of all the relevant functions is explained. (Here, "function" is not used in the narrow sense of something that a system is designed to do, but in the broader sense of any causal role in the production of behavior that a system might perform.)

To explain reportability, for instance, is just to explain how a system could perform the function of producing reports on internal states. To explain internal access, we need to explain how a system could be appropriately affected by its internal states and use information about those states in directing later processes. To explain integration and control, we need to explain how a system's central processes can bring information contents together and use them in the facilitation of various behaviors. These are all problems about the explanation of functions.

How do we explain the performance of a function? By specifying a *mechanism* that performs the function. Here, neurophysiologic and cognitive modeling are perfect for the task. If we want a detailed low-level explanation, we can specify the neural mechanism that is responsible for the function. If we want a more abstract explanation, we can specify a mechanism in computational terms. Either way, a full and satisfying explanation will result. Once we have specified the neural or computational mechanism that performs the function of verbal report, for example, the bulk of our work in explaining reportability is over.

Throughout the higher-level sciences, reductive explanation—explanation that explains a high-level phenomenon wholly in terms of lower-level phenomena—works in just this way. To explain the gene, for instance, we needed to specify the mechanism that stores and transmits hereditary information from one generation to the next. It turns out that DNA performs this function; once we explain how the function is performed, we have explained the gene. To explain life, we ultimately need to explain how a system can reproduce, adapt to its environment, metabolize, and so on. All of these are questions about the performance of functions, and so are well suited to reductive explanation.

The same holds for most problems in cognitive science. To explain learning, we need to explain the way in which a system's behavioral capacities are modified in light of environmental information, and the way in which new information can be brought to bear in adapting a system's actions to its environment. If we show how a neural or computational mechanism does the job, we have explained learning. We can say the same for other cognitive phenomena, such as perception, memory, and language. Sometimes the relevant functions need to be characterized quite subtly, but it is clear that insofar as cognitive science explains these phenomena at all, it does so by explaining the performance of functions.

When it comes to conscious experience, this sort of explanation fails. What makes the hard problem hard and almost unique is that it goes *beyond* problems about the performance of functions. To see this, note that even when we have explained the performance of all the cognitive and behavioral functions in the vicinity of experience—perceptual discrimination, categorization, internal access, verbal report—there may still remain a further unanswered question: *Why is the performance of these functions accompanied by experience?* A simple explanation of the functions leaves this question open.

There is no analogous further question in the explanation of genes, or of life, or of learning. If someone says "I can see that you have explained how DNA stores and transmits hereditary information from one generation to the next, but you have not explained how it is a *gene*," then they are making a conceptual mistake. All it means to be a gene is to be an entity that performs the relevant storage and transmission function. But if someone says "I can see that you have explained how information is discriminated, integrated, and reported, but you have not explained how it is *experienced*," they are not making a conceptual mistake. This is a nontrivial further question.

This further question is the key question in the problem of consciousness. Why doesn't all this information processing go on "in the dark," free of any inner feel? Why is it that when electromagnetic waveforms impinge on a retina and are discriminated and categorized by a visual system, this discrimination and categorization is experienced as a sensation of vivid red? We know that conscious experience *does* arise when these functions are performed, but the very fact that it arises is the central mystery. There is an *explanatory gap* (a term due to Levine[3]) between the functions and experience, and we need an explanatory bridge to cross it. A mere account of the functions stays on one side of the gap, so the materials for the bridge must be found elsewhere.

This is not to say that experience *has* no function. Perhaps it will turn out to play an important cognitive role. But for any role it might play, there will be more to the explanation of experience than a simple explanation of the function. Perhaps it will even turn out that in the course of explaining a function, we will be led to the key insight that allows an explanation of experience. If this happens, though, the discovery will be an *extra* explanatory reward. There is no cognitive function such that we can say in advance that explanation of that function will *automatically* explain experience.

To explain experience, we need a new approach. The usual explanatory methods of cognitive science and neuroscience do not suffice. These methods have been developed precisely to explain the performance of cognitive functions, and they do a good job of it. But as these methods stand, they are *only* equipped to explain the performance of functions. When it comes to the hard problem, the standard approach has nothing to say.

4. Zombies and the Explanatory Gap

The hard problem of consciousness arises for any physical explanation of consciousness. For any physical process we specify, there will be an unanswered question: Why should this process give rise to experience?

One way to see this point is via a philosophical thought-experiment: that of a philosophical zombie. A philosophical zombie is a being that is atom-for-atom identical to a conscious being such as you and me, but it is not conscious. Unlike the zombies found in Hollywood movies, philosophical zombies look just like normal humans from the outside, and their behavior is indistinguishable from that of a conscious being. But on the inside, all is dark. There is nothing it is like to be a zombie.

There is little reason to think that philosophical zombies really exist. But what matters for our purposes is simply that the idea is coherent. There is no internal contradiction in the idea of a zombie, the way that there is an internal contradiction in the idea of a round square. I may believe that you are not a zombie, but I cannot rule out the hypothesis that you are a zombie by a priori reasoning alone.

---

3. Joseph Levine, "Materialism and Qualia: The Explanatory Gap," *Pacific Philosophical Quarterly* 64 (1983): 354–61.

The hard problem of consciousness might then be put as the problem: Why are we not zombies? In our world, in fact, there is consciousness. But everything in physics and in neuroscience seems to be compatible with the hypothesis that we are zombies. If that is right, then physics and neuroscience alone cannot explain why we are not zombies. More generally, it appears that no purely physical explanation can explain why we are not zombies. If so, no purely physical explanation can solve the hard problem of consciousness.

We can even use this sort of reasoning to generate an argument against materialism, the thesis that our world is wholly physical. To explain materialism, we can use the metaphor of God creating the world. If materialism is true, then God simply needed to create microphysical entities such as atoms and fields and arrange them in the right way: then everything else, such as cells and organisms and tables, followed automatically.

But zombies suggest that materialism must be false. To see this, note that because there is no contradiction in the idea of a zombie, it seems that it would be within God's powers to create a zombie world: a world that is physically identical to ours, but without consciousness. If this is right, then even after God ensured that all the physical truths about our world obtained, the truths about consciousness did not automatically follow. After creating everything in physics, God had to do more work to put consciousness into the world. This suggests that consciousness is something over and above the physical, and that materialism is false.

Of course God here is a metaphor, but the idea can also be put in terms of the philosophers' idea of a possible world. For example, there may be no antigravity machines in the actual world, but there is no contradiction in the idea (one can tell coherent science fiction about antigravity), so there is at least a possible world in which there is antigravity. Likewise, even if there are no zombies in the actual world, there is at least a possible world in which there are zombies. And if there is a possible world in which there are physical processes just like those in our world but no consciousness, then consciousness does not follow from those processes with absolute necessity. It follows that materialism is false.

We might put the underlying problem as follows. Physical explanation is ultimately cast entirely in terms of microphysical structure and dynamics. This sort of explanation is well suited to explaining macroscopic structure and dynamics. For problems such as the problem of learning or the problem of life, this is good enough, as in these cases macroscopic structure and dynamics were all that needed explaining. But we have seen that in the case of consciousness, structure and dynamics is not all that needs explaining: we also need to explain why macroscopic structure and dynamics is accompanied by consciousness. And here, physical explanation has nothing to say: structure and dynamics adds up only to more structure and dynamics. So consciousness cannot be wholly explained in physical terms.

If all this is right, then although consciousness may be associated with physical processing in systems such as brains, it is not reducible to that processing. Any *reductive* explanation of consciousness, in purely physical terms, must fail. No matter what sort of physical processes we might invoke, we find an explanatory gap between those processes and consciousness.

5. Nonreductive Explanation

At this point, some are tempted to give up, holding that we will never have a theory of conscious experience. I think this pessimism is premature. This is not the place to give up; it is the place where things get interesting. When simple methods of explanation are ruled out, we need to investigate the alternatives. Given that reductive explanation fails, *nonreductive* explanation is the natural choice.

Although a remarkable number of phenomena have turned out to be explicable wholly in terms of entities simpler than themselves, this is not universal. In physics, it occasionally happens that an entity has to be taken as *fundamental*. Fundamental entities are not explained in terms of anything simpler. Instead, one takes them as basic and gives a theory of how they relate to everything else in the world. For example, in the nineteenth century it turned out that electromagnetic processes could not be explained in terms of the wholly mechanical processes that previous physical theories appealed to, so Maxwell[4] and others introduced electromagnetic charge and electromagnetic forces as new fundamental components of a physical theory. To explain electromagnetism, the ontology of physics had to be expanded. New basic properties and basic laws were needed to give a satisfactory account of the phenomena.

Other features that physical theory takes as fundamental include mass and space-time. No attempt is made to explain these features in terms of anything simpler. But this does not rule out the possibility of a theory of mass or of space-time. There is an intricate theory of how these features interrelate, and of the basic laws they enter into. These basic principles are used to explain many familiar phenomena concerning mass, space, and time at a higher level.

I suggest that a theory of consciousness should take experience as fundamental. We know that a theory of consciousness requires the addition of *something* fundamental to our ontology, as everything in physical theory is compatible with the absence of consciousness. We might add some entirely new nonphysical feature, from which experience can be derived, but it is hard to see what such a feature would be like. More likely, we will take experience itself as a fundamental feature of the world, alongside mass, charge, and space-time. If we take experience as fundamental, then we can go about the business of constructing a theory of experience.

Where there is a fundamental property, there are fundamental laws. A nonreductive theory of experience will add new principles to the furniture of the basic laws of nature. These basic principles will ultimately carry the explanatory burden in a theory of consciousness. Just as we explain familiar high-level phenomena involving mass in terms of more basic principles involving mass and other entities, we might explain familiar phenomena involving experience in terms of more basic principles involving experience and other entities.

In particular, a nonreductive theory of experience will specify basic principles telling us how experience depends on physical features of the world. These *psychophysical* principles will not interfere with physical laws, as it seems that physical laws already

---

4. James Clerk Maxwell (1831–1879), Scottish physicist.

form a closed system. Rather, they will be a supplement to a physical theory. A physical theory gives a theory of physical processes, and a psychophysical theory tells us how those processes give rise to experience. We know that experience depends on physical processes, but we also know that this dependence cannot be derived from physical laws alone. The new basic principles postulated by a nonreductive theory give us the extra ingredient that we need to build an explanatory bridge.

Of course, by taking experience as fundamental, there is a sense in which this approach does not tell us why there is experience in the first place. But this is the same for any fundamental theory. Nothing in physics tells us why there is matter in the first place, but we do not count this against theories of matter. Certain features of the world need to be taken as fundamental by any scientific theory. A theory of matter can still explain all sorts of facts about matter by showing how they are consequences of the basic laws. The same goes for a theory of experience.

This position qualifies as a variety of dualism, the view that the mind is not wholly physical, as it postulates basic mental properties over and above the properties invoked by physics. But it is a version of dualism that is entirely compatible with the scientific view of the world. Nothing in this approach contradicts anything in physical theory; we simply need to add further *bridging* principles to explain how experience arises from physical processes. There is nothing particularly spiritual or mystical about this theory—its overall shape is like that of a physical theory, with a few fundamental properties connected by fundamental laws. It expands the class of primitive properties, to be sure, but Maxwell did the same thing. Indeed, the overall structure of this position is entirely naturalistic, allowing that ultimately the universe comes down to a network of basic entities obeying simple laws, and allowing that there may ultimately be a theory of consciousness cast in terms of such laws. If the position is to have a name, a good choice might be *naturalistic dualism*.

6. Conclusion

Most existing theories of consciousness either deny the phenomenon, explain something else, or elevate the problem to an eternal mystery. I hope to have shown that it is possible to make progress on the problem even while taking it seriously. To make further progress, we will need further investigation, more refined theories, and more careful analysis. The hard problem is a hard problem, but there is no reason to believe that it will remain permanently unsolved.

TEST YOUR UNDERSTANDING

1. Does Chalmers think that explaining the performance of all cognitive and behavioral functions leaves consciousness unexplained?

2. Does Chalmers think that consciousness has no function?

3. According to Chalmers, electromagnetic charge is analogous to consciousness in what respect?

   a. It cannot be seen.

   b. It is fundamental.

   c. It cannot be explained in terms of wholly mechanical processes.

   d. The brain cannot be understood without it.

4. Does Chalmers think that we will never be able to explain how consciousness arises from physical processes?

NOTES AND QUESTIONS

1. According to Chalmers, "zombies suggest that materialism must be false." What are "zombies"? What does Chalmers mean by "materialism"? Reconstruct Chalmers's zombie **argument** for the falsity of materialism in the form of premises and conclusion. Assess the argument. Is it **valid**? Is it **sound**?

2. Chalmers defends naturalistic dualism at greater length in *The Conscious Mind* (Oxford University Press, 1996), much of which is accessible to the general reader. Chalmers surveys the main positions on the mind-body problem in "Consciousness and Its Place in Nature," reprinted in his book *The Character of Consciousness* (Oxford University Press, 2010). A collection of critical work on Chalmers is Jonathan Shear (Ed.), *Explaining Consciousness: The Hard Problem* (MIT Press, 1999).

3. For more on zombies, see Robert Kirk, "Zombies," in *Stanford Encyclopedia of Philosophy*, ed. Edward Zalta (https://plato.stanford.edu/archives/sum2015/entries/zombies/).

Michael Tye (b. 1950)

Tye is Professor of Philosophy at the University of Texas at Austin and specializes in the philosophy of mind. He is the author of many influential books and articles, including *Ten Problems of Consciousness* (1995), *Consciousness Revisited: Materialism without Phenomenal Concepts* (2009), and (with Mark Sainsbury) *Seven Puzzles of Thought (and How to Solve Them): An Originalist Theory of Concepts* (2012).

THE PUZZLE OF TRANSPARENCY

Sit, facing a red apple in good light. In front of you is a particular thing—an apple. You see the apple. In doing so, you have a visual experience caused by the apple—an experience as of a red, round, bulgy shape before you. That visual experience is also a particular thing, but unlike the apple it is mental. There is, then, or so it is standardly assumed, the external thing (the apple), an internal thing (the experience), and a causal relationship between the two.

Your experience, being an experience, has a *phenomenology*. There is something it is *like* for you subjectively in seeing the apple. What it is like for you is different from what it is like for you to see a banana or an orange in good light. What it is like for you, as you see the apple, is *radically* different from what it is like for you to undergo certain other experiences. Think, for example, of the experience of sharp pain caused by accidentally stepping on a thumbtack. What it is like to undergo an experience is sometimes called the "phenomenal character" of that experience. One natural way to think of the phenomenal character of an experience is as a quality of the experience.

Since what it is like to see a red, round shape has something in common subjectively with what it is like to see a red, square shape, it is also natural to suppose that in many cases, the overall phenomenal character of an experience is made up of a number of different subjective qualities. The subjective qualities of which the overall phenomenal character of the experience is composed are often called "qualia." There is, then, the external thing (the apple) and its qualities, and there is also the internal thing (the experience) and its phenomenal character (or qualia). Whether the experience has further qualities not connected to its phenomenal character, as the apple has further qualities not accessible to your eyes (e.g., its weight or cost), is something on which we need take no stand for present purposes.

Now I want you to attend carefully to the apple you are viewing. As you do so, you will likely notice some variations of color that had not stood out before, or you may notice an irregularity in the shape. Next, place a banana to the left of the apple, some distance away but still visible to you from your viewing position, and look again. You can choose to attend to the apple or to the banana or to both. You can switch your attention from one to the other. When you do this, you can attend to the color of the apple or the shape of the banana, for example.

Now I want you to switch your attention from the apple to your visual experience of it. Are you able to do so easily? As easily as you can switch your attention from the apple to the banana? If you think you can, do you notice any new quality of the experience? If these questions puzzle you, well and good. For reasons that will become clear shortly, they *should* puzzle you.

I am not asking you here to fixate your eyes upon your experience in the way that you can fixate your eyes on the apple and then on the banana. Obviously, an experience, being a mental entity, is not the sort of thing upon which you can train your eyes.[1]

I am not asking you to do these things because even in the visual case I take it that attention is not the same as eye fixation. To appreciate what I am getting at here, fixate your eyes on the plus sign in the center of Figure 1. As you continue to fixate your eyes on the plus sign and also to focus mentally on it, you can tell which rectangles are gray and which are black. However, you cannot tell which rectangles have longer

---

1. Of course, if experiences are brain states, then they can be viewed through cerebroscopes while the experiences are occurring. But this is not relevant to the points being made here. [Tye's note.]

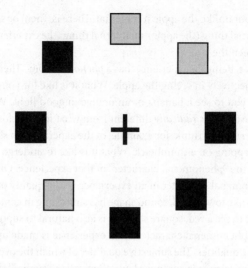

Figure 1

vertical sides. To find that out, you need to switch your attention; that is, your mental focus. As you vary your mental focus, you can attend to the rectangles, one by one, while still fixating on the plus sign, and as you do so, you can determine which have longer vertical sides. Attending to something typically (perhaps always) reveals new qualities of the thing or at least qualities you experience the thing as having, qualities of which you were not aware before.

Returning to the apple and your experience of it, I can only say that in my own case I find that I cannot switch my attention from the apple to my visual experience. Indeed, I find that I cannot attend to my visual experience at all. Moreover, I cannot attend to any of its qualities.[2] When I try to follow the instructions given above in my own case, my very strong belief is that *nothing at all* changes except perhaps that, in trying to do what is asked, I come to notice new qualities of the *apple* of which I was not aware before.

What does this show? Well, if you accept the claims of the previous paragraph in your own case (and I think that they are very hard to deny, though not everyone agrees[3]), at a minimum they should make you extremely puzzled. If you cannot attend to your visual experience, then there is an inherently conscious thing—namely, your experience—that is not accessible to your attention. Further, if you cannot attend to any

2. The first philosopher to comment upon this phenomenon was G. E. Moore, "The Refutation of Idealism," *Philosophical Studies* (Routledge and Kegan Paul, 1922). He remarked, "When we try to introspect the sensation of blue, all we can see is the blue. The other element is as if it were diaphanous." See also Gilbert Harman, "The Intrinsic Quality of Experience," *Philosophical Perspectives* 4 (1990): 31–52. [Tye's note.]

3. See Ned Block, "Inverted Earth," *Philosophical Perspectives* 4 (1990): 53–79; and Ned Block, "Mental Paint," in *Reflections and Replies: Essays on the Philosophy of Tyler Burge*, ed. M. Hahn and B. Ramberg (MIT Press, 2003). [Tye's note.]

Figure 2

of your visual experience's qualities, then the phenomenal character of your experience is something to which you cannot attend either. How can that be?

To appreciate why this should be puzzling, look at Figure 2 and fixate your eyes on the man resting on an elbow at the bottom in the middle. I predict that, as you do so, you will be unable to mentally focus on the writing implement or the notebook or the beard of the man leaning in on the far left. For you, it will be as if these items are not there, and likewise for their qualities, for example, their shapes. Because you are unable to attend to these things as you fixate on the man in the middle, they are hidden from you. You are blind to them.

Here is another example. Fixate on the plus sign in Figure 3. As you do so, you won't be able to focus on or attend to the fifth vertical bar away from the plus sign. If you

Figure 3

think otherwise, tell me how many bars there are on the right without moving your fixation point. I predict that you won't be able to do so. The reason is straightforward: it is not the case that each and every bar on the right is clearly and individually marked out in the phenomenology of your experience. The fifth bar is one of the bars not so marked out. It is effectively hidden from you, given your fixation point. That's why you can't count the bars. This is not to say that *the bars* (plural) are hidden from you. Obviously, they aren't. You are certainly conscious of the bars. But there are individual bars of which you are not conscious. (Compare: You can weigh a bunch of marbles without weighing each marble. Having weighed the marbles, you may still have no precise idea of how much the fifth marble in the bunch weighs.)

The conclusion to which we seem driven is that the phenomenal character of your visual experience, as you view the apple, is *hidden* from you, as is your visual experience. You are *blind* to these things. For you, it is as if they aren't there. They are, as it were, transparent to you. You "see" right through them when you try to attend to them, and you end up focusing on things outside you. But surely this cannot be right. Your visual experience is an inherently conscious thing. Its phenomenal character—what it is like for you subjectively—is inherently conscious. How can these things be hidden from you? If you cannot attend to the phenomenal character of your visual experience, then it no more contributes to your subjective, conscious life than do the shapes of some of the figures on the left of the picture in Figure 2 as you fixate on the pensive man in the middle. In that case, its presence (or absence) is simply irrelevant to your consciousness.

Something has gone terribly wrong. But what exactly? One reaction is to say that the above considerations show that the phenomenal character of a visual experience isn't a quality at all. Instead it is something else, something that isn't hidden. Well, what is it then?

One proposal is that it is a *representational content* that the experience has. This jargon needs a little explanation. If I have an experience as of a red, round thing before me, my experience is accurate if there is a red, round thing before me and inaccurate otherwise. So we may say that my experience has *accuracy conditions*: it is accurate in the condition in which there is a red, round thing before me, and inaccurate in all other conditions. And in having accuracy conditions, it has representational content—for present purposes, the jargon of "representational content" is just another way of talking about "accuracy conditions." My experience represents the world as being a certain way; namely, as containing a red, round thing in front of me. Philosophers have often supposed that the phenomenology of an experience is something entirely distinct from its representational content. But in recent work a number of philosophers have argued that the phenomenology cannot be pulled apart from the content.[4]

Here is an illustration of this view. Consider a visual experience as of a red, round thing in front of you and a second visual experience as of a yellow, square thing in front of you. Obviously, what it is like for you subjectively to undergo the first experience is different from what it is like for you subjectively to undergo the second. Correspondingly, there is a difference in accuracy conditions: the first experience is

---

4. See, for example, Alex Byrne, "Intentionalism Defended," *Philosophical Review* 110 (2001): 49–90; Fred Dretske, *Naturalizing the Mind* (Bradford Books: MIT Press, 1995); and Michael Tye, *Ten Problems of Consciousness* (MIT Press, 1995). [Tye's note.]

accurate under different circumstances than the second. Now consider a third, later visual experience having exactly the same accuracy conditions as the first. Could there be any difference in what it is like for you to undergo that experience and what it is like for you to undergo the first? Many philosophers hold that it is clear that there could be no such difference: the phenomenal character of the one experience would *have* to be the same as the phenomenal character of the other. Why should this be?

A simple explanation is that the phenomenal character of an experience just *is* its representational content. This proposal, which is usually labeled "strong representationalism," is problematic in a number of respects. To mention one: some experiences do not seem to have any representational content (e.g., an undirected feeling of anger).

Let us put this worry to one side. Does strong representationalism solve the puzzle of transparency? I have come to think that it does not.[5] If the phenomenal character of your experience, as you view the apple, is the same as the representational content of your experience, and thus not a quality of your experience, it is still something different from any of the apple's perceived qualities. So, you ought to be able to switch your attention from the redness of the apple to the phenomenal character of your experience just as you can switch your attention from the color of the apple to its shape. You ought to be able to focus your attention upon this additional thing. But you can't. Once again, then, the phenomenal character of your experience is hidden from you. That's absurd.

It might be replied that the situation here is like that which obtains when I hear you utter certain words—"Snow is white," say. I hear the words and I have an auditory experience of certain auditory qualities (e.g., pitch and loudness). I can focus my attention on the sounds and their auditory qualities or I can focus my attention on the meaning of the sentence, on its representational content. Why not suppose that things are like that in the case of your seeing an apple?

The answer is that in the visual case (a) the bearer of the representational content is the experience itself and (b) the qualities experienced are not qualities of that bearer but rather qualities of the thing experienced; namely, the apple. The experience isn't red and round; the apple is. Furthermore, even though the representational content is something the experience possesses, it is not separable from the qualities experienced (redness, roundness, etc.) in the way that the meaning of the sentence "Snow is white" is separable from the auditory qualities of loudness and pitch. In the case of your visual experience, the qualities experienced are involved in or, at any rate, play a role in specifying the representational content. Not so in the auditory example. "Snow is white" is true if and only if snow is white. The accuracy conditions for this sentence, and thus its representational content, have nothing to do with the auditory qualities belonging to a particular utterance of that sentence.

It might now be said that the very fact that the perceived qualities of the apple enter into or are involved in the representational content of the visual experience is what makes it so difficult to pry apart the content and the qualities when it comes to focusing attention. When you focus your attention on the phenomenal character of

---

5. See Michael Tye, *Consciousness Revisited* (MIT Press, 2009). [Tye's note.]

your experience, inevitably you also focus your attention on the redness and roundness of the apple (since they are involved in the content, which just is the phenomenal
character on the view I am considering). That is why it seems to you that you can't
focus on the phenomenal character of your experience alone. This proposal also might
be held to explain why you can't switch your attention from the redness of the apple
to the phenomenal character of your experience in the same way that you can switch
your attention from the redness of the apple to the yellowness of the banana. The redness of the apple does not involve the yellowness of the banana, but the phenomenal
character of your experience does involve redness.

Again I am unpersuaded. Even if the representational content of your experience
has redness as a component, why can't you focus on the former without focusing on
the latter? Consider the two crowds of balls in Figure 4.[6] You can certainly focus your
attention on the upper crowd rather than the lower one. But in doing so, you need not
be focusing your attention on each particular ball in that crowd as well. Indeed, it seems
impossible to focus your attention simultaneously on each ball. This is one reason why
if the crowds are presented one after the other rather than simultaneously, it is very
likely that you will fail to notice any difference in them (though they do differ in a ball).
To change examples, just as you can weigh a bunch of marbles without weighing any
particular marble or think of a department at your university without thinking of any
member of that department in particular, so you can attend to a complex thing without
attending to any particular component part of that thing. We're still in deep trouble.

So what is the way out? At one level, the answer seems obvious. We must hold that
the phenomenal character of your experience, as you view the apple, is one and the
same as the complex of qualities you experience the apple as having. That is why you
cannot switch your attention from the apple's qualities to the phenomenal character of
your experience. That is why you cannot focus on the phenomenal character apart from
those qualities. The trouble is that the phenomenal character of your experience, what
it is like for you subjectively, is now out there in the world beyond your head where the
qualities of the apple are! You *confront* it when you see the apple. Since phenomenal
character is mental if anything is, that means that mental items are out there in the world.[7]

That may seem totally crazy. The apple has the relevant complex of qualities even
when no one is viewing it. But it surely does not then have the phenomenal character
of a visual experience.

This is true. But the natural reply, it seems to me, is to say that the complex of qualities
is the phenomenal character of your visual experience only if it meets certain further
conditions, where these conditions rule out the apple's having a visual phenomenal
character when no one is seeing it. Still, what are these conditions?

That, in my view, is a really tough question. One part of the answer, I believe, is
that the relevant complex of qualities must be *represented* by an internal state meeting

6. The example is from Fred Dretske, "What We See: The Texture of Conscious Experience," in *Perceiving the World: New Essays on Perception*, ed. B. Nanay (Oxford University Press, 2010). [Tye's note.]

7. What if you are hallucinating? I would say that you are still confronted by a certain complex of qualities, a complex you *take* to belong to something before you when in reality nothing before you has the relevant qualities. [Tye's note.]

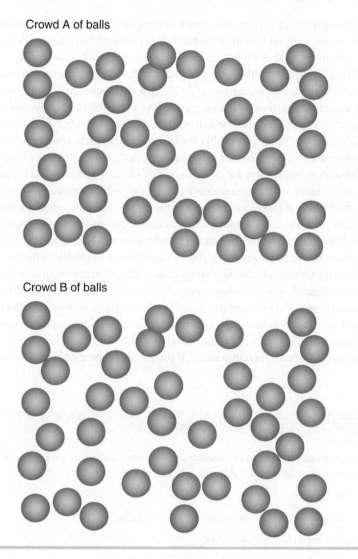

Figure 4

certain further conditions. However, we had better not say that these further conditions involve the internal state's having a phenomenal character, or circularity threatens (that is to say, our account of phenomenal character will itself appeal to phenomenal character and so no progress will have been made).

On this proposal, the complex of qualities you confront in seeing the apple would not be a phenomenal character if it did not bear an appropriate relation to a mind. Thus in a world without minds there is no phenomenology, just as in a world without bifocals there is no inventor of bifocals.

Philosophers often suppose that there is nothing incoherent in the idea that there are creatures who are just like normal human beings physically but who lack experiences. Such creatures are often called "zombies" in philosophy, but philosophical zombies should not be confused with Hollywood zombies. Philosophical zombies are supposed to behave just as normal human beings do (being just the same physically). Thus, unlike Hollywood zombies, they do not keep going if you chop off their heads. Nor do they come out only at night and eat the flesh of others. Philosophers often claim that the idea of a (philosophical) zombie is not like the idea of a square circle. Unlike the latter idea, there is no internal inconsistency in the former idea. According to these philosophers, even though in reality there are no zombies, we can easily make sense of the *idea* that there are zombies. We simply imagine or conceive of there being creatures who are like us in their physical makeup right down to the last detail but for whom on the inside all is dark, as it were. If zombies really are conceivable, an interesting question now arises. What is the difference between you and your zombie duplicate, as he views the apple from the same viewpoint as you? It cannot be in the qualities the two of you confront: for both of you, the same complex of qualities is represented as belonging to the apple. The difference, it seems to me, is that your zombie twin *mistakenly* believes that *that* (pointing at the complex of qualities he confronts) is what it is like for him to *experience* the apple. In reality, for your zombie replica, there is no experience: the complex of qualities is not a phenomenal character.[8]

So, that is the puzzle of transparency. If you are not yet puzzled by it, you should be!

TEST YOUR UNDERSTANDING

1. Suppose you are looking at a banana. In Tye's terminology, you are having a "visual experience of the banana." According to Tye, can you attend to

   a. the banana?

   b. the qualities of the banana (e.g., its color and shape)?

   c. your experience of the banana?

   d. the qualities of your experience of the banana?

2. According to Tye, does the view that the phenomenal character of an experience is identical to its representational content solve the puzzle of transparency?

3. Does Tye think that you can attend to the phenomenal character of your experience?

4. Suppose you see something that looks green and cubical. According to Tye, the phenomenal character of your experience is a "complex of qualities" (or **properties**) that "meets certain further conditions." What are the qualities?

---

8. One further issue that now arises is how it is you know that you are not yourself a zombie. See here Fred Dretske, "How Do You Know You Are Not a Zombie?" in *Privileged Access: Philosophical Accounts of Self-Knowledge*, ed. B. Gertler (Ashgate, 2003); and Michael Tye, *Consciousness Revisited*. [Tye's note.]

NOTES AND QUESTIONS

1. What is "strong representationalism," and why does Tye think it fails to solve the puzzle of transparency? What is Tye's solution? The solution, he says, "may seem totally crazy." Does Tye succeed in explaining why it isn't?

2. In footnote 2, Tye refers to Gilbert Harman's paper, "The Intrinsic Quality of Experience" (*Philosophical Perspectives* 4 [1990]: 31–52), which is frequently cited as the main contemporary source for the idea that experience is "transparent." Here is the relevant passage from that paper:

   > When Eloise sees a tree before her, the colors she experiences are all experienced as features of the tree and its surroundings. None of them are experienced as intrinsic features of her experience. Nor does she experience any features of anything as intrinsic features of her experiences. And that is true of you too. There is nothing special about Eloise's visual experience. When you see a tree, you do not experience any features as intrinsic features of your experience. Look at a tree and try to turn your attention to intrinsic features of your visual experience. I predict you will find that the only features there to turn your attention to will be features of the presented tree. (p. 39)

   Not everyone agrees with Tye and Harman that experience is transparent. For the dissenting view, see Amy Kind, "What's So Transparent about Transparency?" *Philosophical Studies* 115 (2003): 225–44.

3. The "transparency of experience" can be used to motivate the "transparency view" of self-knowledge (see "Notes and Questions" to Alex Byrne, "Skepticism about the Internal World," in Chapter 5 of this anthology).

ANALYZING THE ARGUMENTS

1. Jackson (in "Epiphenomenal Qualia") and Chalmers both argue against physicalism. (You may take the thesis Jackson calls "physicalism" to be the same as the one Chalmers calls "materialism.") Do either of their arguments succeed? How should the committed physicalist best object to the knowledge argument and the zombie argument?

2. Jackson distinguishes the knowledge argument from Nagel's argument in "What Is It Like to Be a Bat?" What is Nagel's argument according to Jackson? Evaluate his criticism of the argument. Sometimes philosopher A will (unintentionally) slightly distort philosopher B's argument and so end up criticizing a different argument, not the one B intended. Is this what is going on here or is Jackson's interpretation of Nagel's argument correct? If it isn't, explain how Nagel's argument differs from the knowledge argument.

3. According to Tye, "The conclusion to which we seem driven is that the phenomenal character of your visual experience, as you view the apple, is *hidden* from you, as is your visual experience. You are *blind* to these things. For you, it is as if they aren't there. They are, as it were, transparent to you." (He later takes it back about phenomenal character, but the point about the experience remains.)

   It seems that Nagel would dispute this passage and deny that your experience is transparent. In "What Is It Like to Be a Bat?" he writes that you "apprehend" your experience, and in a paragraph omitted from this selection he wonders if it "make[s] sense . . . to ask what my experiences are really like, as opposed to how they appear to me." If you "apprehend" your experience or if experiences "appear" to you, then presumably they are not transparent. Tye would say, rather, that it is only the *apple* that one apprehends, and that appears, say, red and round.

   Are there passages from Jackson ("Epiphenomenal Qualia") and Chalmers that suggest they too would deny that your visual experience of an apple is transparent? Is Tye right in supposing that experiences are transparent? Assuming he is, does this affect the arguments of Nagel, Jackson, and Chalmers?

4. One of Churchland's objections to Jackson's knowledge argument is this:

   > How can I assess what Mary will know and understand if she knows *everything* there is to know about the brain? Everything is a lot and it means, in all likelihood, that Mary has a radically different and deeper understanding of the brain than anything barely conceivable in our wildest flights of fancy.

   Here are three versions of this objection:

   a. We have no idea whether someone who knew *everything* that *current neuroscience* tells us about the brain would know what it's like to see red.

   b. Granted, someone whose knowledge was limited by *current* neuroscience wouldn't know what it's like to see red, but we have no idea whether someone who knew everything that *complete neuroscience* (neuroscience that human scientists could not improve any further) tells us about the brain would know what it's like to see red.

c. Granted, someone whose knowledge was limited by *complete neuroscience* would not know what it's like to see red, but *this is no reason for denying that consciousness is entirely physical.* Why should our physical theories, even the ones that we cannot improve any further, tell the *whole physical story* about the universe? Maybe there are physical aspects of the universe (and, in particular, of our brains) that our best physical theories are going to leave out. And we have no idea whether someone who knew about these hidden physical aspects of our brains would know what it's like to see red.

Which version of the objection is the one (or is closest to the one) Churchland is endorsing? Are any of these three versions plausible?

In support of (c), one might appeal to a conclusion argued for in Rae Langton's "Ignorance of Things in Themselves" (see Chapter 6 of this anthology):

Humility: We have no knowledge of the most fundamental intrinsic properties of things.

If humility is right, then science—even our best science—will never tell us about the fundamental properties of physical things. In particular, it will never tell us about the fundamental properties of brains, neurons, and so on. And if those fundamental properties are physical, then perhaps (c) is the right response to the knowledge argument. Imprisoned Mary is ignorant of crucial facts—knowledge of which would enable her to know what it's like to see red—but these crucial facts concern fundamental *physical* properties, which are out of reach of our best science.

For more on this sort of view, see the discussion of "Type F Monism" in David Chalmers, "Consciousness and Its Place in Nature," reprinted in *The Character of Consciousness* (Oxford University Press, 2010), and Galen Strawson, "Real Materialism," in *Real Materialism* (Oxford University Press, 2008). For a lengthy defense of the weaker claim that either (b) or (c) is right, see Daniel Stoljar, *Ignorance and Imagination* (Oxford University Press, 2006).

5. What is physicalism (or materialism)? "Physicalism" is a piece of technical jargon, and so its meaning needs to be carefully explained. Physicalism should be a thesis that

a. is a clear expression of the vague and intuitive thought that the world is "wholly physical";

b. is not obviously false;

c. is not obviously true.

Exercise: Why are (b) and (c) needed?

According to René Descartes, in addition to spatially extended things like tables and rocks, the world also contains unextended minds or souls (see Meditations

II and VI in Chapter 7 of this anthology). And Descartes's theory, *Cartesian dualism*, is certainly not a physicalist theory. That suggests that we could define physicalism simply as follows:

Physicalism$_1$: Cartesian dualism is false.

Exercise: Explain why this definition won't work.

Suppose we define a "physical **property**" as follows: *P* is a physical property **iff** current physics says that some things have *P*. So: *Having mass* is a physical property because current physics says that protons have mass; *being negatively charged* is a physical property because current physics says that electrons are negatively charged. (Combinations of physical properties can themselves be counted as physical properties, so *having mass or being negatively charged* and *having mass and being negatively charged* both count as physical properties.) Consider:

Physicalism$_2$: Everything has physical properties.

Exercise: Explain why this definition won't work. (More than one reason could be given.)

Let a *nonphysical* property be a property that is not a physical property in the sense explained above. Consider:

Physicalism$_3$: Nothing has nonphysical properties.

Exercise: Explain why this definition won't work either. (Again, more than one reason could be given.)

Defining physicalism properly is not an easy matter. For an introduction to the way physicalism is usually defined in the contemporary literature, see Daniel Stoljar, "Physicalism," in *Stanford Encyclopedia of Philosophy*, ed. Edward Zalta (http:// plato .stanford.edu/archives/win2016/entries/physicalism/), sections 1–3.

Are Things as They Appear?

Start with what seems to be an obvious fact: perception tells us a lot about objects in our environment—rocks, smart phones, cats, lemons, and so forth. By seeing lemons, you can discover that they are yellow, egg-shaped, and have a dimpled texture. Similarly, by tasting a slice of lemon, you can discover that lemons are sour.

That is not to say that perception always gets things right, that appearances always match reality. Take, for example, Figure 1. The figure in the circles looks to have curved sides, but you can easily check that they are straight. (This is called the *Ehrenstein illusion*, named after its discoverer, the German psychologist Walter Ehrenstein.) Here, the appearance of a squashed-in square does not match reality.

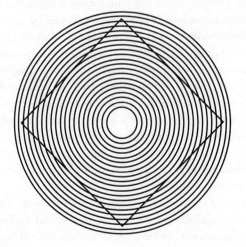

Figure 1

It would be overly hasty to conclude from the fact that *sometimes* ordinary perception leads us to error that it *always* leads us to error or anyway is not to be trusted. *The New York Times* sometimes gets the facts wrong, but this is not a good reason for thinking that it always gets the facts wrong or that it is not a credible source of news. Still, the phenomenon of perceptual illusions at least raises the question of whether illusions might be much more widespread than we commonly think.

Consider a lemon again, and in particular its apparent color. Why does the lemon look yellow? Presumably because it affects light in a certain way—the lemon absorbs light of some frequencies and reflects the rest. But wait—this seems to be an explanation of why the lemon *looks yellow* that doesn't appeal to the fact that it *is* yellow. And if we don't need to appeal to the fact that the lemon is yellow in order to explain why it looks yellow, why suppose that there is any such fact in the first place? A simpler hypothesis is that the lemon has *no color at all*.

There's nothing special about lemons, of course, and this line of thought quickly leads to the conclusion that color perception is *always* illusory. Physical objects are entirely colorless: blood spots look red, but they aren't red (or any other color); sapphires look blue, but they aren't blue (or any other color); snowballs look white, but they aren't white (or any other color); and so on.

The view that no physical objects are colored, that the appearance of a colored world does not match reality, is sometimes called color **eliminativism**. (It is so called because according to the color eliminativist, the colors should be "eliminated" from an accurate description of physical objects.) We can distinguish similar theses for other perceptual qualities: *taste* eliminativism, *shape* eliminativism, *odor* eliminativism, and so on.

In fact, color eliminativism—as well as other kinds of eliminativism, like taste and odor eliminativism—has proved remarkably popular among both scientists and philosophers. The ancient Greek philosopher Democritus (c. 460–370 BCE) is famously reported as saying: "By convention, sweet; by convention, bitter; by convention, hot; by convention, cold; by convention, color; but in reality, atoms and void" (Democritus, frag. 9). "By convention, sweet," "by convention, color," and so on, are usually interpreted to imply that sugar cubes are *not* sweet, and lemons are *not* yellow—we merely have a conventional practice of calling them "sweet" and "yellow." The Italian physicist Galileo Galilei (1564–1642) wrote that "tastes, odors, colors, and so on are no more than mere names so far as the object in which we place them is concerned, and that they reside only in the consciousness."[1] Galileo was tried and convicted by the Catholic Church for proclaiming that the earth went around the sun; his equally heretical view that cardinals' robes are not red apparently went unpunished.

Many contemporary scientists and philosophers join Democritus and Galileo in their subscription to color eliminativism. Open a textbook on perception and you may well read that colors are not "in objects" but are instead "constructed by the

---

1. "The Assayer," in *Discoveries and Opinions of Galileo*, trans. Stilman Drake (Doubleday, 1957), 274.

brain." The philosopher C. L. Hardin flatly denies in his book *Color for Philosophers* "that anything is colored."[2]

The Argument from Science Extended

We have seen one reason for the extraordinary claim that no physical object is colored; namely, that the apparent colors of things can be explained in terms of the way they reflect light, which seems to make the hypothesis that they really are colored unnecessary. This is a compressed version of a historically influential argument called the *argument from science*. If the argument from science is any good, then it works equally well for tastes and odors, as Democritus and Galileo seem to have recognized. For example, the chemical composition of Stilton cheese explains why it has certain effects on sensory receptors in the mouth and nose, and so explains why it appears to have that distinctive taste and odor. According to the argument from science, there is no need to suppose, in addition, that the taste and odor are really "in" the cheese—that hypothesis is not needed to explain the data.

One might hope that the argument from science would not eliminate *all* perceptible properties. Granted, the lemon is not yellow, does not have that distinctive sharp and fresh smell, and is not sour, but surely it is at least egg-shaped and dimpled!

Galileo and many of his contemporaries agreed with this reassuring assessment, which they expressed by drawing a distinction between "primary" and "secondary" qualities. Here is how George Berkeley (writing almost a century after Galileo) explains the distinction in the selection from his *Three Dialogues*:

> [S]ensible qualities [i.e., qualities or **properties** that we can perceive] are by philosophers divided into *primary* and *secondary*. The former are extension, figure [i.e., shape], solidity, gravity, motion, and rest. And these they hold exist really in bodies. The latter are those above enumerated; or briefly, all sensible qualities beside the primary, which they assert are only so many sensations or ideas existing nowhere but in the mind.[3]

According to Galileo and others, the lemon does not have any *secondary* qualities (like color), but it does have *primary* qualities (like shape). The lemon does not have any color because science has no need of colors—fundamental physics can explain why the lemon looks yellow without supposing that it is. But the situation is quite different with respect to shape, because fundamental physics *does* need shapes—in particular, it supposes that physical objects like lemons are made up of tiny particles (atoms or "corpuscles") that themselves have shapes.

However, that was at the start of the scientific revolution, and physics has progressed far from its beginnings. If you open a textbook on quantum mechanics,

---

2. Hardin, *Color for Philosophers* (Hackett, 1988), xxiv.

3. See page 422 of this anthology.

you will discover that electrons and other "particles" are not miniature versions of marbles or golf balls. Electrons, we are told, are mysterious things that behave a bit like particles and a bit like waves, and do not even have "definite" positions in space (at least, not before something called a "measurement" is made). The shapes we encounter in ordinary life don't appear in the mathematical formulations of modern fundamental physics any more than colors do. And if fundamental physics has no need of "egg-shaped" any more than it has need of "yellow," then we can presumably explain why the lemon looks egg-shaped without supposing that it really is egg-shaped. From the perspective of modern science, Galileo's optimism is unjustified: the argument from science threatens to "eliminate" *all* properties that we apparently perceive.

The Argument from Variation

Let's leave the argument from science for the moment and turn to another historically influential argument for the same conclusion, that no physical object is as it appears; namely, the *argument from variation*. Here is the argument as formulated by the Scottish philosopher David Hume (a contemporary of Berkeley)[4]:

> The fundamental principle of that philosophy is the opinion concerning colours, sounds, tastes, smells, heat and cold; which it asserts to be nothing but impressions in the mind, derived from the operation of external objects, and without any resemblance to the qualities of the objects. Upon examination, I find only one of the reasons commonly produced for this opinion to be satisfactory, viz. that derived from the variations of those impressions, even while the external object, to all appearance, continues the same. These variations depend upon several circumstances. Upon the different situations of our health: A man in a malady feels a disagreeable taste in meats, which before pleased him the most. Upon the different complexions and constitutions of men: That seems bitter to one, which is sweet to another. Upon the difference of their external situation and position: Colours reflected from the clouds change according to the distance of the clouds, and according to the angle they make with the eye and luminous body.[5]

If a cloud looks purple from here but gray from over there, which is the "real color" of the cloud? According to the argument from variation, there is no reason for choosing one answer over the other. As Bertrand Russell puts it, in the selection from his 1912 classic *The Problems of Philosophy*, "to avoid favouritism, we are compelled to deny that, in itself, the [cloud] has any one particular color."

4. Selections from Hume are in Chapters 4, 6, and 18 of this anthology.
5. *A Treatise of Human Nature*, Book I, section iv.

Like the argument from science, the argument from variation generalizes from color to taste and odor, as the quotation from Hume shows. And—even more clearly than the argument from science—the argument from variation generalizes from the secondary qualities to the primary qualities. As Figure 1 demonstrates, we can vary the apparent shape of an object by merely placing it against a different background. Similarly, apparent shape depends on "the different situations of our health" (the condition of the lens in the eye, for instance), and on our "external situation and position." The selections from Berkeley and Russell both emphasize the wide scope of the argument from variation.

The Lemon Lost—and Regained

So we have seen two arguments for the conclusion that the appearances of colors, odors, tastes, sounds, shapes, textures, and so on, do not match physical reality. A physical object, our lemon, appears yellow, sour, dimpled, and egg-shaped, but in fact it has none of these properties. The physical lemon is a strange object indeed! So strange that you might wonder whether there really is such a thing. How could subtracting color, taste, texture, and shape from a lemon leave a *lemon*, rather than *nothing*? Surely the physical lemon, if it exists, is something you can *see*. But how can you see something that has no shape, or color, or any other perceptible property? Instead of maintaining that there are colorless shapeless lemons, the more straightforward conclusion is that lemons don't exist. *Perhaps* there are some (mysterious) physical objects "out there" that cause us to seem to see lemons, but lemons themselves are not among them.

As noted, lemons are nothing special. The sweeping conclusion is that *we never perceive physical objects* (or "corporeal substances" in Berkeley's terminology). And if we never perceive them, why suppose there are any? At this point **idealism** looks like a distinct possibility. According to the idealist, *there are no physical objects*: reality is immaterial or mental. As Berkeley puts it, reality consists of "minds or spirits" and their "ideas." Idealism is defended both by Berkeley and, in the selection from the *Twenty Verses*, by the fourth-century Buddhist philosopher Vasubandhu. Idealism might well sound crazy, but the agreement between these two philosophers, despite their separation by vast temporal and cultural distances, suggests that it should be taken seriously.

Berkeley and Vasubandhu deny that the lemon is a physical object capable of existing without the mind. Put that way, you can see that the idealist does not have to deny that the lemon exists—all that follows from idealism is that *if* the lemon exists, then it is *mind-dependent*, not capable of existing unperceived. And Berkeley, at least, was at pains to insist that lemons exist. Moreover, Berkeley thinks that *lemons are yellow, sour, dimpled, and egg-shaped*. Thus we have come full-circle, "back to common sense," as Berkeley puts it (p. 428). We started with the common-sense view that lemons are yellow, examined arguments that appearances never match reality, and ended up where we began: lemons are yellow, after all. But we have learned, according to Berkeley, some astonishing news along the way: lemons are mere "collections of ideas."[6] What's more—for reasons you will discover when reading the *Three Dialogues*—lemons are collections of ideas *in the mind of God*.[7]

Are You a Sim?

Although Berkeley thinks lemons, clouds, and tables are collections of ideas, he does not think that *we* are collections of ideas. Rather, on Berkeley's view, we are finite minds (or "spirits") who perceive ideas. (Berkeley's God is the single "infinite mind.") Vasubandhu, however, holds the Buddhist view that minds simply *are* collections of ideas: *we* are just as much "appearance" as lemons.[8] Vasubandhu's view about ourselves could be combined with Berkeley's view about God; on that combined view, we are collections of ideas in God's mind.

A collection of lemon-ideas in a mind is analogous to a simulation of a lemon in a computer (say, a simulation of a lemon in a video game): the simulated lemon has no existence outside the computer, just as the lemon-ideas have no existence outside the mind. Now computers can simulate just about anything; in particular, they can simulate *people*, as in the life simulation game *The Sims*. So the modern secular counterpart to the combined Vasubandhu-Berkeley view is this: *we are simulated people*, virtual creatures created by a computer program.

Are you living in a computer simulation devised by some technologically advanced civilization? That might seem to be an excellent example of an unanswerable and thus pointless question. However, in the selection by Nick Bostrom, he argues that it is *not* unanswerable. He stops short of concluding that we definitely are living in a simulation, but he thinks that this hypothesis has a decent chance of being true.

6. See George Berkeley, *A Treatise Concerning the Principles of Human Knowledge* (Hackett, 1982), 23.

7. At any rate, that is what Berkeley says in the *Dialogues*. His view is different in the *Principles of Human Knowledge*.

8. A view close to David Hume's: see the quotation from Hume in Saul Kripke, "Wittgenstein and Other Minds," in Chapter 5, page 221, of this anthology.

Bertrand Russell (1872–1970)

The 3rd Earl Russell, a British philosopher, logician, and writer, was a central figure in analytic philosophy, a philosophical tradition that dominated academic philosophy in Britain, the United States, and Australia in the twentieth century. His numerous books include *Principia Mathematica* (with A. N. Whitehead, 3 volumes, 1910–13), concerning the foundations of mathematics. A prominent political activist, Russell's opposition to the First World War led to his dismissal from the University of Cambridge in 1916; his position was reinstated in 1920. Russell was awarded the Nobel Prize in Literature in 1950.

APPEARANCE AND REALITY
from *The Problems of Philosophy*

I s there any knowledge in the world which is so certain that no reasonable man could doubt it? This question, which at first sight might not seem difficult, is really one of the most difficult that can be asked. When we have realized the obstacles in the way of a straightforward and confident answer, we shall be well launched on the study of philosophy—for philosophy is merely the attempt to answer such ultimate questions, not carelessly and dogmatically, as we do in ordinary life and even in the sciences, but critically after exploring all that makes such questions puzzling, and after realizing all the vagueness and confusion that underlie our ordinary ideas.

In daily life, we assume as certain many things which, on a closer scrutiny, are found to be so full of apparent contradictions that only a great amount of thought enables us to know what it is that we really may believe. In the search for certainty, it is natural to begin with our present experiences, and in some sense, no doubt, knowledge is to be derived from them. But any statement as to what it is that our immediate experiences make us know is very likely to be wrong. It seems to me that I am now sitting in a chair, at a table of a certain shape, on which I see sheets of paper with writing or print. By turning my head I see out of the window buildings and clouds and the sun. I believe that the sun is about ninety-three million miles from the earth; that it is a hot globe many times bigger than the earth; that, owing to the earth's rotation, it rises every morning, and will continue to do so for an indefinite time in the future. I believe that, if any other normal person comes into my room, he will see the same chairs and tables and books and papers as I see, and that the table which I see is the same as the table which I feel pressing against my arm. All this seems to be so evident as to be hardly worth stating, except in answer to a man who doubts whether I know anything. Yet all this may be reasonably doubted, and all of it requires much careful discussion before we can be sure that we have stated it in a form that is wholly true.

To make our difficulties plain, let us concentrate attention on the table. To the eye it is oblong, brown and shiny, to the touch it is smooth and cool and hard; when I tap it, it gives out a wooden sound. Any one else who sees and feels and hears the table will agree with this description, so that it might seem as if no difficulty would arise; but as soon as we try to be more precise our troubles begin. Although I believe that the table is "really" of the same colour all over, the parts that reflect the light look much brighter than the other parts, and some parts look white because of reflected light. I know that, if I move, the parts that reflect the light will be different, so that the apparent distribution of colours on the table will change. It follows that if several people are looking at the table at the same moment, no two of them will see exactly the same distribution of colours, because no two can see it from exactly the same point of view, and any change in the point of view makes some change in the way the light is reflected.

For most practical purposes these differences are unimportant, but to the painter they are all-important: the painter has to unlearn the habit of thinking that things seem to have the colour which common sense says they "really" have, and to learn the habit of seeing things as they appear. Here we have already the beginning of one of the distinctions that cause most trouble in philosophy—the distinction between "appearance" and "reality," between what things seem to be and what they are. The painter wants to know what things seem to be, the practical man and the philosopher want to know what they are; but the philosopher's wish to know this is stronger than the practical man's, and is more troubled by knowledge as to the difficulties of answering the question.

To return to the table. It is evident from what we have found, that there is no colour which preeminently appears to be *the* colour of the table, or even of any one particular part of the table—it appears to be of different colours from different points of view, and there is no reason for regarding some of these as more really its colour than others. And we know that even from a given point of view the colour will seem different by artificial light, or to a colour-blind man, or to a man wearing blue spectacles, while in the dark there will be no colour at all, though to touch and hearing the table will be unchanged. This colour is not something which is inherent in the table, but something depending upon the table and the spectator and the way the light falls on the table. When, in ordinary life, we speak of *the* colour of the table, we only mean the sort of colour which it will seem to have to a normal spectator from an ordinary point of view under usual conditions of light. But the other colours which appear under other conditions have just as good a right to be considered real; and therefore, to avoid favouritism, we are compelled to deny that, in itself, the table has any one particular colour.

The same thing applies to the texture. With the naked eye one can see the grain, but otherwise the table looks smooth and even. If we looked at it through a microscope, we should see roughnesses and hills and valleys, and all sorts of differences that are imperceptible to the naked eye. Which of these is the "real" table? We are naturally tempted to say that what we see through the microscope is more real, but that in turn would be changed by a still more powerful microscope. If, then, we cannot trust what we see with the naked eye, why should we trust what we see through a microscope? Thus, again, the confidence in our senses with which we began deserts us.

The *shape* of the table is no better. We are all in the habit of judging as to the "real" shapes of things, and we do this so unreflectingly that we come to think we actually see the real shapes. But, in fact, as we all have to learn if we try to draw, a given thing looks different in shape from every different point of view. If our table is "really" rectangular, it will look, from almost all points of view, as if it had two acute angles and two obtuse angles. If opposite sides are parallel, they will look as if they converged to a point away from the spectator; if they are of equal length, they will look as if the nearer side were longer. All these things are not commonly noticed in looking at a table, because experience has taught us to construct the "real" shape from the apparent shape, and the "real" shape is what interests us as practical men. But the "real" shape is not what we see; it is something inferred from what we see. And what we see is constantly changing in shape as we move about the room; so that here again the senses seem not to give us the truth about the table itself, but only about the appearance of the table.

Similar difficulties arise when we consider the sense of touch. It is true that the table always gives us a sensation of hardness, and we feel that it resists pressure. But the sensation we obtain depends upon how hard we press the table and also upon what part of the body we press with; thus the various sensations due to various pressures or various parts of the body cannot be supposed to reveal *directly* any definite property of the table, but at most to be signs of some property which perhaps *causes* all the sensations, but is not actually apparent in any of them. And the same applies still more obviously to the sounds which can be elicited by rapping the table.

Thus it becomes evident that the real table, if there is one, is not the same as what we immediately experience by sight or touch or hearing. The real table, if there is one, is not *immediately* known to us at all, but must be an inference from what is immediately known. Hence, two very difficult questions at once arise; namely, (1) Is there a real table at all? (2) If so, what sort of object can it be?

It will help us in considering these questions to have a few simple terms of which the meaning is definite and clear. Let us give the name of "sense-data" to the things that are immediately known in sensation: such things as colours, sounds, smells, hardnesses, roughnesses, and so on. We shall give the name "sensation" to the experience of being immediately aware of these things. Thus, whenever we see a colour, we have a sensation *of* the colour, but the colour itself is a sense-datum, not a sensation. The colour is that *of* which we are immediately aware, and the awareness itself is the sensation. It is plain that if we are to know anything about the table, it must be by means of the sense-data—brown colour, oblong shape, smoothness, etc.—which we associate with the table; but, for the reasons which have been given, we cannot say that the table is the sense-data, or even that the sense-data are directly properties of the table. Thus a problem arises as to the relation of the sense-data to the real table, supposing there is such a thing.

The real table, if it exists, we will call a "physical object." Thus we have to consider the relation of sense-data to physical objects. The collection of all physical objects is called "matter." Thus our two questions may be re-stated as follows: (1) Is there any such thing as matter? (2) If so, what is its nature?

The philosopher who first brought prominently forward the reasons for regarding the immediate objects of our senses as not existing independently of us was Bishop Berkeley. His *Three Dialogues between Hylas and Philonous, in Opposition to Sceptics and Atheists*, undertake to prove that there is no such thing as matter at all, and that the world consists of nothing but minds and their ideas.[1] Hylas has hitherto believed in matter, but he is no match for Philonous, who mercilessly drives him into contradictions and paradoxes, and makes his own denial of matter seem, in the end, as if it were almost common sense. The arguments employed are of very different value: some are important and sound, others are confused or quibbling. But Berkeley retains the

---

1. See the following selection by George Berkeley.

merit of having shown that the existence of matter is capable of being denied without absurdity, and that if there are any things that exist independently of us they cannot be the immediate objects of our sensations.

There are two different questions involved when we ask whether matter exists, and it is important to keep them clear. We commonly mean by "matter" something which is opposed to "mind," something which we think of as occupying space and as radically incapable of any sort of thought or consciousness. It is chiefly in this sense that Berkeley denies matter; that is to say, he does not deny that the sense-data which we commonly take as signs of the existence of the table are really signs of the existence of *something* independent of us, but he does deny that this something is nonmental, that it is neither mind nor ideas entertained by some mind. He admits that there must be something which continues to exist when we go out of the room or shut our eyes, and that what we call seeing the table does really give us reason for believing in something which persists even when we are not seeing it. But he thinks that this something cannot be radically different in nature from what we see, and cannot be independent of seeing altogether, though it must be independent of *our* seeing. He is thus led to regard the "real" table as an idea in the mind of God. Such an idea has the required permanence and independence of ourselves, without being—as matter would otherwise be—something quite unknowable, in the sense that we can only infer it, and can never be directly and immediately aware of it.

Other philosophers since Berkeley have also held that, although the table does not depend for its existence upon being seen by me, it does depend upon being seen (or otherwise apprehended in sensation) by *some* mind—not necessarily the mind of God, but more often the whole collective mind of the universe. This they hold, as Berkeley does, chiefly because they think there can be nothing real—or at any rate nothing known to be real except minds and their thoughts and feelings. We might state the argument by which they support their view in some such way as this: "Whatever can be thought of is an idea in the mind of the person thinking of it; therefore nothing can be thought of except ideas in minds; therefore anything else is inconceivable, and what is inconceivable cannot exist."

Such an argument, in my opinion, is fallacious; and of course those who advance it do not put it so shortly or so crudely. But whether valid or not, the argument has been very widely advanced in one form or another; and very many philosophers, perhaps a majority, have held that there is nothing real except minds and their ideas. Such philosophers are called "idealists." When they come to explaining matter, they either say, like Berkeley, that matter is really nothing but a collection of ideas, or they say, like Leibniz,[2] that what appears as matter is really a collection of more or less rudimentary minds.

But these philosophers, though they deny matter as opposed to mind, nevertheless, in another sense, admit matter. It will be remembered that we asked two questions; namely, (1) Is there a real table at all? (2) If so, what sort of object can it be? Now both Berkeley and Leibniz admit that there is a real table, but Berkeley says it is certain

---

2. Gottfried Wilhelm Leibniz (1646–1716), German philosopher and mathematician.

ideas in the mind of God, and Leibniz says it is a colony of souls. Thus both of them answer our first question in the affirmative, and only diverge from the views of ordinary mortals in their answer to our second question. In fact, almost all philosophers seem to be agreed that there is a real table, they almost all agree that, however much our sense-data—colour, shape, smoothness, etc.—may depend upon us, yet their occurrence is a sign of something existing independently of us, something differing, perhaps, completely from our sense-data whenever we are in a suitable relation to the real table . . . .

Before we go farther it will be well to consider for a moment what it is that we have discovered so far. It has appeared that, if we take any common object of the sort that is supposed to be known by the senses, what the senses *immediately* tell us is not the truth about the object as it is apart from us, but only the truth about certain sense-data which, so far as we can see, depend upon the relations between us and the object. Thus what we directly see and feel is merely "appearance," which we believe to be a sign of some "reality" behind. But if the reality is not what appears, have we any means of knowing whether there is any reality at all? And if so, have we any means of finding out what it is like?

Such questions are bewildering, and it is difficult to know that even the strangest hypotheses may not be true. Thus our familiar table, which has roused but the slightest thoughts in us hitherto, has become a problem full of surprising possibilities. The one thing we know about it is that it is not what it seems. Beyond this modest result, so far, we have the most complete liberty of conjecture. Leibniz tells us it is a community of souls: Berkeley tells us it is an idea in the mind of God; sober science, scarcely less wonderful, tells us it is a vast collection of electric charges in violent motion.

Among these surprising possibilities, doubt suggests that perhaps there is no table at all. Philosophy, if it cannot answer so many questions as we could wish, has at least the power of asking questions which increase the interest of the world, and show the strangeness and wonder lying just below the surface even in the commonest things of daily life.

TEST YOUR UNDERSTANDING

1. Is Russell arguing that there are no tables?

2. Suppose you see a red spot. Is a "sense-datum," in Russell's terminology, (a) the red spot, (b) the color red, or (c) your awareness of the red spot?

3. Does Russell think we "immediately know" (a) sensations, (b) sense-data, or (c) communities of souls?

4. Russell agrees with one of the following claims made by Berkeley. Which one?

   a. Matter does not exist.

   b. Tables are ideas in the mind of God.

   c. The things we are immediately aware of cannot exist unperceived.

NOTES AND QUESTIONS

1. In the second chapter of *The Problems of Philosophy*, Russell argues for the existence of physical objects by an **inference to the best explanation**:

    > In one sense it must be admitted that we can never *prove* the existence of things other than ourselves and our experiences. No logical absurdity results from the hypothesis that the world consists of myself and my thoughts and feelings and sensations, and that everything else is mere fancy. In dreams a very complicated world may seem to be present, and yet on waking we find it was a delusion; that is to say, we find that the sense-data in the dream do not appear to have corresponded with such physical objects as we should naturally infer from our sense-data. (It is true that, when the physical world is assumed, it is possible to find physical causes for the sense-data in dreams: a door banging, for instance, may cause us to dream of a naval engagement. But although, in this case, there is a physical *cause* for the sense-data, there is not a physical object *corresponding* to the sense-data in the way in which an actual naval battle would correspond.) There is no logical impossibility in the supposition that the whole of life is a dream, in which we ourselves create all the objects that come before us. But although this is not logically impossible, there is no reason whatever to suppose that it is true; and it is, in fact, a less simple hypothesis, viewed as a means of accounting for the facts of our own life, than the common-sense hypothesis that there really are objects independent of us, whose action on us causes our sensations.

    Is this a convincing argument for the existence of physical objects such as tables and other physical objects that "cause our sensations"? (See also Jonathan Vogel, "Skepticism and Inference to the Best Explanation," in Chapter 6 of this anthology.)

2. If you look at a table while walking around it, the table does not seem to change shape or color: it *looks* rectangular and brown throughout, even though the quality and arrangement of light striking your retinas is changing as you move. (Contrast seeing the table with seeing an inflating balloon or pH paper dipped in lemon juice—the balloon does seem to change shape, and the paper does seem to change color.) This phenomenon, of constant perceptual appearance despite varying perceptual stimulation, is called *perceptual constancy*. Russell, however, suggests that the table "looks different in shape from every different point of view," and likewise for color. Does perceptual constancy show that Russell is wrong? How do you think he would respond?

George Berkeley (1685–1753)

Bishop Berkeley was an Irish philosopher and a major proponent of idealism, as expounded in his *Treatise Concerning the Principles of Human Knowledge* (1710) and later in the *Three Dialogues* (1713). He subsequently lived in America for several years, and the city of Berkeley in California is named—with a change of pronunciation, *bark* to *burk*—after him. Berkeley became Bishop of Cloyne in Ireland in 1734.

THREE DIALOGUES BETWEEN HYLAS AND PHILONOUS

The First Dialogue

Philonous[1]: In reading a book, what I immediately perceive are the letters; but mediately, or by means of these, are suggested to my mind the notions of God, virtue, truth, &c. Now, that the letters are truly sensible things, or perceived by sense, there is no doubt: but I would know whether you take the things suggested by them to be so too.

Hylas[2]: No, certainly: it were absurd to think *God* or *virtue* sensible things; though they may be signified and suggested to the mind by sensible marks, with which they have an arbitrary connection.

P: It seems then, that by *sensible things* you mean those only which can be perceived immediately by sense?

H: Right.

P: Doth[3] it not follow from this, that though I see one part of the sky red, and another blue, and that my reason doth thence evidently conclude there must be some cause of that diversity of colors, yet that cause cannot be said to be a sensible thing, or perceived by the sense of seeing?

H: It doth.

P: In like manner, though I hear variety of sounds, yet I cannot be said to hear the causes of those sounds?

H: You cannot.

P: And when by my touch I perceive a thing to be hot and heavy, I cannot say, with any truth or propriety, that I feel the cause of its heat or weight?

H: To prevent any more questions of this kind, I tell you once for all, that by *sensible things* I mean those only which are perceived by sense, and that in truth the senses perceive nothing which they do not perceive immediately: for they make no inferences. The deducing therefore of causes or occasions from effects and appearances, which alone are perceived by sense, entirely relates to reason.

P: This point then is agreed between us, that *sensible things are those only which are immediately perceived by sense.* You will farther inform me, whether we immediately perceive by sight anything beside light, and colors, and figures[4]: or by hearing,

---

1. "Lover of mind" in ancient Greek.

2. From *hyle*, meaning "matter" in ancient Greek.

3. Does.

4. Shapes.

anything but sounds: by the palate, anything beside tastes: by the smell, beside odors: or by the touch, more than tangible qualities.

H: We do not.

P: It seems, therefore, that if you take away all sensible qualities, there remains nothing sensible?

H: I grant it.

P: Sensible things therefore are nothing else but so many sensible qualities, or combinations of sensible qualities?

H: Nothing else.

P: Heat then is a sensible thing?

H: Certainly.

P: Doth the reality of sensible things consist in being perceived? or, is it something distinct from their being perceived, and that bears no relation to the mind?

H: To *exist* is one thing, and to be *perceived* is another.

P: I speak with regard to sensible things only. And of these I ask, whether by their real existence you mean a subsistence exterior to the mind, and distinct from their being perceived?

H: I mean a real absolute being, distinct from, and without any relation to, their being perceived.

P: Heat therefore, if it be allowed a real being, must exist without the mind?

H: It must.

P: Tell me, Hylas, is this real existence equally compatible to all degrees of heat, which we perceive, or is there any reason why we should attribute it to some, and deny it to others? And if there be, pray let me know that reason.

H: Whatever degree of heat we perceive by sense, we may be sure the same exists in the object that occasions it.

P: What, the greatest as well as the least?

H: I tell you, the reason is plainly the same in respect of both. They are both perceived by sense; nay, the greater degree of heat is more sensibly perceived; and consequently, if there is any difference, we are more certain of its real existence than we can be of the reality of a lesser degree.

P: But is not the most vehement and intense degree of heat a very great pain?

H: No one can deny it.

P: And is any unperceiving thing capable of pain or pleasure?

H: No certainly.

P: Is your material substance a senseless being, or a being endowed with sense and perception?

H: It is senseless, without doubt.

P: It cannot therefore be the subject of pain?

H: By no means.

P: Nor consequently of the greatest heat perceived by sense, since you acknowledge this to be no small pain?

H: I grant it.

P: What shall we say then of your external object; is it a material substance, or no?

H: It is a material substance with the sensible qualities inhering in it.

P: How then can a great heat exist in it, since you own it cannot in a material substance? I desire you would clear this point.

H: Hold, Philonous, I fear I was out in yielding intense heat to be a pain. It should seem rather, that pain is something distinct from heat, and the consequence or effect of it.

P: Upon putting your hand near the fire, do you perceive one simple uniform sensation, or two distinct sensations?

H: But one simple sensation.

P: Is not the heat immediately perceived?

H: It is.

P: And the pain?

H: True.

P: Seeing therefore they are both immediately perceived at the same time, and the fire affects you only with one simple or uncompounded idea, it follows that this same simple idea is both the intense heat immediately perceived, and the pain; and, consequently, that the intense heat immediately perceived is nothing distinct from a particular sort of pain.

H: It seems so.

P: Again, try in your thoughts, Hylas, if you can conceive a vehement sensation to be without pain, or pleasure.

H: I cannot.

P: Or can you frame to yourself an idea of sensible pain or pleasure in general, abstracted from every particular idea of heat, cold, tastes, smells? &c.

H: I do not find that I can.

P: Doth it not therefore follow, that sensible pain is nothing distinct from those sensations or ideas, in an intense degree?

H: It is undeniable; and, to speak the truth, I begin to suspect a very great heat cannot exist but in a mind perceiving it.

P: What! Are you then in that skeptical state of suspense, between affirming and denying?

H: I think I may be positive in the point. A very violent and painful heat cannot exist without the mind.

P: It hath[5] not therefore, according to you, any real being.

H: I own it.

P: Is it therefore certain, that there is no body in nature really hot?

H: I have not denied there is any real heat in bodies. I only say, there is no such thing as an intense real heat.

P: But, did you not say before that all degrees of heat were equally real: or, if there was any difference, that the greater were more undoubtedly real than the lesser?

H: True: but it was because I did not then consider the ground there is for distinguishing between them, which I now plainly see. And it is this: because intense

5. Has.

heat is nothing else but a particular kind of painful sensation; and pain cannot exist but in a perceiving being; it follows that no intense heat can really exist in an unperceiving corporeal substance. But this is no reason why we should deny heat in an inferior degree to exist in such a substance.

P: But how shall we be able to discern those degrees of heat which exist only in the mind from those which exist without it?

H: That is no difficult matter. You know the least pain cannot exist unperceived; whatever, therefore, degree of heat is a pain exists only in the mind. But as for all other degrees of heat, nothing obliges us to think the same of them.

P: I think you granted before that no unperceiving being was capable of pleasure, any more than of pain.

H: I did.

P: And is not warmth, or a more gentle degree of heat than what causes uneasiness, a pleasure?

H: What then?

P: Consequently, it cannot exist without the mind in an unperceiving substance, or body.

H: So it seems.

. . .

H: . . . I am content to yield this point, and acknowledge that heat and cold are only sensations existing in our minds. But there still remain qualities enough to secure the reality of external things.

P: But what will you say, Hylas, if it shall appear that the case is the same with regard to all other sensible qualities, and that they can no more be supposed to exist without the mind, than heat and cold?

H: Then indeed you will have done something to the purpose; but that is what I despair of seeing proved. . . .

P: And I hope you will make no difficulty to acknowledge [that colors "have no real being without the mind"].

H: Pardon me: the case of colors is very different. Can anything be plainer than that we see them on the objects? . . .

P: . . . Only be pleased to let me know, whether the same colors which we see exist in external bodies, or some other.

H: The very same.

P: What! Are then the beautiful red and purple we see on yonder clouds really in them? Or do you imagine they have in themselves any other form, than that of a dark mist or vapor?

H: I must own, Philonous, those colors are not really in the clouds as they seem to be at this distance. They are only apparent colors.

P: *Apparent* call you them? how shall we distinguish these apparent colors from real?

H: Very easily. Those are to be thought apparent, which appearing only at a distance, vanish upon a nearer approach.

P: And those I suppose are to be thought real, which are discovered by the most near and exact survey.

H: Right.

P: Is the nearest and exactest survey made by the help of a microscope, or by the naked eye?

H: By a microscope, doubtless.

P: But a microscope often discovers colors in an object different from those perceived by the unassisted sight. And in case we had microscopes magnifying to any assigned degree; it is certain that no object whatsoever viewed through them, would appear in the same color which it exhibits to the naked eye.

H: And what will you conclude from all this? You cannot argue that there are really and naturally no colors on objects: because by artificial managements they may be altered, or made to vanish.

P: I think it may evidently be concluded from your own concessions, that all the colors we see with our naked eyes, are only apparent as those on the clouds, since they vanish upon a more close and accurate inspection which is afforded us by a microscope. Then as to what you say by way of prevention: I ask you whether the real and natural state of an object is better discovered by a very sharp and piercing sight, or by one which is less sharp?

H: By the former without doubt.

P: Is it not plain from *dioptrics*[6] that microscopes make the sight more penetrating, and represent objects as they would appear to the eye, in case it were naturally endowed with a most exquisite sharpness?

H: It is.

P: Consequently the microscopical representation is to be thought that which best sets forth the real nature of the thing, or what it is in itself. The colors therefore by it perceived, are more genuine and real than those perceived otherwise.

H: I confess there is something in what you say.

P: Besides, it is not only possible but manifest, that there actually are animals, whose eyes are by nature framed to perceive those things, which by reason of their minuteness escape our sight. What think you of those inconceivably small animals perceived by glasses? Must we suppose they are all stark blind? Or, in case they see, can it be imagined their sight hath not the same use in preserving their bodies from injuries, which appears in that of all other animals? And if it hath, is it not evident, they must see particles less than their own bodies, which will present them with a far different view in each object from that which strikes our senses? Even our own eyes do not always represent objects to us after the same manner. In the jaundice, everyone knows that all things seem yellow.[7] Is it not therefore highly probable, those animals in whose eyes we discern a very different texture from that of ours, and whose bodies abound with different humors,[8] do not see the same colors in every object that we do? From all which, should it not seem

---

6. The optics of lenses.

7. Severe cases of jaundice (an excess of bilirubin in the blood) can cause yellow-tinged vision (xanthopsia).

8. Bodily fluids.

to follow, that all colors are equally apparent, and that none of those which we perceive are really inherent in any outward object?

H: It should.

P: The point will be past all doubt, if you consider, that in case colors were real properties or affections inherent in external bodies, they could admit of no alteration, without some change wrought in the very bodies themselves: but is it not evident from what hath been said, that upon the use of microscopes, upon a change happening in the humors of the eye, or a variation of distance, without any manner of real alteration in the thing itself, the colors of any object are either changed, or totally disappear? Nay, all other circumstances remaining the same, change but the situation of some objects, and they shall present different colors to the eye. The same thing happens upon viewing an object in various degrees of light. And what is more known than that the same bodies appear differently colored by candle-light, from what they do in the open day? Add to these the experiment of a prism, which separating the heterogeneous rays of light, alters the color of any object, and will cause the whitest to appear of a deep blue or red to the naked eye. And now tell me whether you are still of opinion, that every body hath its true real color inhering in it; and, if you think it hath, I would fain[9] know farther from you, what certain distance and position of the object, what peculiar texture and formation of the eye, what degree or kind of light is necessary for ascertaining that true color, and distinguishing it from apparent ones. . . .

H: I frankly own, Philonous, that it is in vain to stand out any longer. Colors, sounds, tastes, in a word, all those termed *secondary qualities*, have certainly no existence without the mind. But by this acknowledgment I must not be supposed to derogate anything from the reality of matter, or external objects; seeing it is no more than several philosophers maintain, who nevertheless are the farthest imaginable from denying matter. For the clearer understanding of this, you must know sensible qualities are by philosophers divided into *primary* and *secondary*. The former are extension, figure, solidity, gravity, motion, and rest. And these they hold exist really in bodies. The latter are those above enumerated; or briefly, all sensible qualities beside the primary, which they assert are only so many sensations or ideas existing nowhere but in the mind. But all this, I doubt not, you are apprised of. For my part, I have been a long time sensible there was such an opinion current among philosophers, but was never thoroughly convinced of its truth until now.

P: You are still then of the opinion, that extension and figures are inherent in external unthinking substances?

H: I am.

P: But what if the same arguments which are brought against secondary qualities, will hold good against these also?

H: Why then I shall be obliged to think, they too exist only in the mind.

P: Is it your opinion the very figure and extension which you perceive by sense exist in the outward object or material substance?

9. Gladly.

H: It is.

P: Have all other animals as good grounds to think the same of the figure and extension which they see and feel?

H: Without doubt, if they have any thought at all.

P: Answer me, Hylas. Think you the senses were bestowed upon all animals for their preservation and well-being in life? Or were they given to men alone for this end?

H: I make no question but they have the same use in all other animals.

P: If so, is it not necessary they should be enabled by them to perceive their own limbs, and those bodies which are capable of harming them?

H: Certainly.

P: A mite therefore must be supposed to see his own foot, and things equal or even less than it, as bodies of some considerable dimension; though at the same time they appear to you scarce discernible, or at best as so many visible points?

H: I cannot deny it.

P: And to creatures less than the mite they will seem yet larger?

H: They will.

P: Insomuch that what you can hardly discern, will to another extremely minute animal appear as some huge mountain?

H: All this I grant.

P: Can one and the same thing be at the same time in itself of different dimensions?

H: That were absurd to imagine.

P: But from what you have laid down it follows, that both the extension by you perceived, and that perceived by the mite itself, as likewise all those perceived by lesser animals, are each of them the true extension of the mite's foot; that is to say, by your own principles you are led into an absurdity.

H: There seems to be some difficulty in the point.

P: Again, have you not acknowledged that no real inherent property of any object can be changed without some change in the thing itself?

H: I have.

P: But, as we approach to or recede from an object, the visible extension varies, being at one distance ten or a hundred times greater than at another. Doth it not therefore follow from hence likewise, that it is not really inherent in the object?

H: I own that I am at a loss what to think.

P: Your judgment will soon be determined, if you will venture to think as freely concerning this quality, as you have done concerning the rest. Was it not admitted as a good argument, that neither heat nor cold was in the water, because it seemed warm to one hand and cold to the other?[10]

H: It was.

P: Is it not the very same reasoning to conclude, there is no extension or figure in an object, because to one eye it shall seem little, smooth, and round, when at the same time it appears to the other, great, uneven, and angular?

---

10. Philonous gives this argument earlier in "The First Dialogue." See question 5 in the "Analyzing the Arguments" at the end of this chapter.

H: The very same. But doth this latter fact ever happen?

P: You may at any time make the experiment, by looking with one eye bare, and with the other through a microscope. . . .

H: . . . But still I fear there is some fallacy or other. Pray what think you of this? It is just come into my head that the ground of all our mistake lies in your treating of each quality by itself. Now, I grant that each quality cannot singly subsist without the mind. Color cannot without extension, neither can figure without some other sensible quality. But, as the several qualities united or blended together form entire sensible things, nothing hinders why such things may not be supposed to exist without the mind.

P: Either, Hylas, you are jesting, or have a very bad memory. Though indeed we went through all the qualities by name one after another, yet my arguments, or rather your concessions, nowhere tended to prove that the secondary qualities did not subsist each alone by itself; but, that they were not at all without the mind. Indeed, in treating of figure and motion we concluded they could not exist without the mind, because it was impossible even in thought to separate them from all secondary qualities, so as to conceive them existing by themselves. But then this was not the only argument made use of upon that occasion. But (to pass by all that hath been hitherto said, and reckon it for nothing, if you will have it so) I am content to put the whole upon this issue. If you can conceive it possible for any mixture or combination of qualities, or any sensible object whatever, to exist without the mind, then I will grant it actually to be so.

H: If it comes to that the point will soon be decided. What more easy than to conceive a tree or house existing by itself, independent of, and unperceived by, any mind whatsoever? I do at this present time conceive them existing after that manner.

P: How say you, Hylas, can you see a thing which is at the same time unseen?

H: No, that were a contradiction.

P: Is it not as great a contradiction to talk of conceiving a thing which is unconceived?

H: It is.

P: The tree or house therefore which you think of is conceived by you?

H: How should it be otherwise?

P: And what is conceived is surely in the mind?

H: Without question, that which is conceived is in the mind.

P: How then came you to say, you conceived a house or tree existing independent and out of all minds whatsoever?

H: That was I own an oversight; but stay, let me consider what led me into it. —It is a pleasant mistake enough. As I was thinking of a tree in a solitary place, where no one was present to see it, methought that was to conceive a tree as existing unperceived or unthought of; not considering that I myself conceived it all the while. But now I plainly see that all I can do is to frame ideas in my own mind. I may indeed conceive in my own thoughts the idea of a tree, or a house, or a mountain, but that is all. And this is far from proving that I can conceive them existing out of the minds of all Spirits.

P: You acknowledge then that you cannot possibly conceive how any one corporeal sensible thing should exist otherwise than in a mind?

H: I do. . . .

The Second Dialogue

Hylas: Other men may think as they please, but for your part you have nothing to reproach me with. My comfort is, you are as much a *skeptic* as I am.

Philonous: There, Hylas, I must beg leave to differ from you.

H: What! Have you all along agreed to the premises, and do you now deny the conclusion, and leave me to maintain those paradoxes by myself which you led me into? This surely is not fair.

P: I deny that I agreed with you in those notions that led to skepticism. You indeed said, the *reality* of sensible things consisted in an *absolute existence out of the minds of spirits,* or distinct from their being perceived. And pursuant to this notion of reality, *you* are obliged to deny sensible things any real existence: that is, according to your own definition, you profess yourself a *skeptic.* But I neither said nor thought the reality of sensible things was to be defined after that manner. To me it is evident, for the reasons you allow of, that sensible things cannot exist otherwise than in a mind or spirit. Whence I conclude, not that they have no real existence, but that seeing they depend not on my thought, and have an existence distinct from being perceived by me, *there must be some other mind wherein they exist.* As sure, therefore, as the sensible world really exists, so sure is there an infinite omnipresent spirit who contains and supports it.

H: What! This is no more than I and all Christians hold; nay, and all others too who believe there is a God, and that he knows and comprehends all things.

P: Aye, but here lies the difference. Men commonly believe that all things are known or perceived by God, because they believe the being of a God; whereas I on the other side, immediately and necessarily conclude the being of a God, because all sensible things must be perceived by him.

H: But so long as we all believe the same thing, what matter is it how we come by that belief?

P: But neither do we agree in the same opinion. For philosophers, though they acknowledge all corporeal beings to be perceived by God, yet they attribute to them an absolute subsistence distinct from their being perceived by any mind whatever, which I do not. Besides, is there no difference between saying, *There is a God, therefore he perceives all things:* and saying, *Sensible things do really exist: and, if they really exist, they are necessarily perceived by an infinite mind: therefore there is an infinite mind, or God.* This furnishes you with a direct and immediate demonstration, from a most evident principle, of the *being of a God.* Divines and philosophers had proved beyond all controversy, from the beauty and usefulness of the several parts of the creation, that it was the workmanship of God. But that setting aside all help of astronomy and natural philosophy, all contemplation of the contrivance, order, and adjustment of things, an infinite mind should be necessarily inferred from the bare existence of the sensible world, is an advantage to them only who have made this easy reflection: that the sensible world is that which we perceive by our several senses; and that nothing is perceived by the senses beside ideas; and that no idea or archetype of an idea can exist otherwise than in a mind. You may now, without any laborious search into the sciences, without any subtlety of reason, or tedious length of discourse, oppose and baffle the most strenuous advocate for atheism. Those miserable refuges, whether in an eternal succession of unthinking causes and effects, or in a fortuitous concourse of atoms; those wild imaginations of Vanini, Hobbes, and Spinoza[11]: in a word the whole system of atheism, is it not entirely overthrown, by this single reflection on the repugnancy included in supposing the whole, or any part, even the most rude and shapeless of the visible world, to exist without a mind? Let any one of those abettors of impiety but look into his own thoughts, and then try if he can conceive how so much as a rock, a desert, a chaos, or confused jumble of atoms; how anything at all, either sensible or imaginable, can exist independent of a mind, and he need go no farther to be convinced of his folly. Can anything be fairer than to put a dispute on such an issue, and leave it to a man himself to see if he can conceive, even in thought, what he holds to be true in fact, and from a notional to allow it a real existence?

The Third Dialogue

Hylas: . . . do you in earnest think, the real existence of sensible things consists in their being actually perceived? If so; how comes it that all mankind distinguish between them? Ask the first man you meet, and he shall tell you, *to be perceived* is one thing, and *to exist* is another.

Philonous: I am content, Hylas, to appeal to the common sense of the world for the truth of my notion. Ask the gardener, why he thinks yonder cherry tree exists in the garden, and he shall tell you, because he sees and feels it; in a word, because he perceives it by his senses. Ask him why he thinks an orange tree not to be there, and he shall tell you, because he doth not perceive it. What he perceives by sense, that he terms a real being, and saith[12] it *is*, or *exists;* but that which is not perceivable, the same, he saith, hath no being.

H: Yes, Philonous, I grant the existence of a sensible thing consists in being perceivable, but not in being actually perceived.

11. Lucilio Vanini (1585–1619), Italian philosopher and physician; Thomas Hobbes (1588–1679), English philosopher; Baruch Spinoza (1632–1677), Dutch philosopher. All three were known for their heterodox religious views. (Selections from Hobbes are in Chapter 20 of this anthology.)

12. Says.

P: And what is perceivable but an idea? And can an idea exist without being actually perceived? These are points long since agreed between us.

H: But be your opinion never so true, yet surely you will not deny it is shocking, and contrary to the common sense of men. Ask the fellow, whether yonder tree hath an existence out of his mind: what answer think you he would make?

P: The same that I should myself, to wit, that it doth exist out of his mind. But then to a Christian it cannot surely be shocking to say, the real tree existing without his mind is truly known and comprehended by (that is, *exists in*) the infinite mind of God. Probably he may not at first glance be aware of the direct and immediate proof there is of this, inasmuch as the very being of a tree, or any other sensible thing, implies a mind wherein it is. But the point itself he cannot deny. The question between the materialists and me is not, whether things have a real existence out of the mind of this or that person, but whether they have an absolute existence, distinct from being perceived by God, and exterior to all minds. This indeed some heathens and philosophers have affirmed, but whoever entertains notions of the Deity suitable to the Holy Scriptures, will be of another opinion.

H: But according to your notions, what difference is there between real things, and chimeras[13] formed by the imagination, or the visions of a dream, since they are all equally in the mind?

P: The ideas formed by the imagination are faint and indistinct; they have, besides, an entire dependence on the will. But the ideas perceived by sense, that is, real things, are more vivid and clear, and being imprinted on the mind by a spirit distinct from us, have not a like dependence on our will. There is therefore no danger of confounding these with the foregoing: and there is as little of confounding them with the visions of a dream, which are dim, irregular, and confused. And though they should happen to be never so lively and natural, yet by their not being connected, and of a piece with the preceding and subsequent transactions of our lives, they might easily be distinguished from realities. In short, by whatever method you distinguish *things* from *chimeras* on your own scheme, the same, it is evident, will hold also upon mine. For it must be, I presume, by some perceived difference, and I am not for depriving you of any one thing that you perceive.

. . .

P: I do not pretend to be a setter-up of *new notions*. My endeavors tend only to unite, and place in a clearer light, that truth which was before shared between the vulgar[14] and the philosophers—the former being of opinion, that *those things they immediately perceive are the real things;* and the latter, that *the things immediately perceived, are ideas which exist only in the mind.* Which two notions put together, do in effect constitute the substance of what I advance.

H: I have been a long time distrusting my sense; methought I saw things by a dim light, and through false glasses. Now the glasses are removed, and a new light breaks in upon my understanding. I am clearly convinced that I see things in their

13. Illusions.

14. Ordinary people, nonphilosophers.

native forms; and am no longer in pain about their unknown natures or absolute existence. This is the state I find myself in at present: though indeed the course that brought me to it, I do not yet thoroughly comprehend. You set out upon the same principles that Academics, Cartesians, and the like sects, usually do[15]; and for a long time it looked as if you were advancing their philosophical *skepticism;* but in the end your conclusions are directly opposite to theirs.

P: You see, Hylas, the water of yonder fountain, how it is forced upwards, in a round column, to a certain height; at which it breaks and falls back into the basin from whence it rose: its ascent as well as descent, proceeding from the same uniform law or principle of *gravitation.* Just so, the same principles which at first view lead to *skepticism,* pursued to a certain point, bring men back to common sense.

TEST YOUR UNDERSTANDING

1. Suppose you hear a car passing in the street. Does Philonous (i.e., Berkeley) think you immediately perceive the car?

2. Philonous persuades Hylas to change his mind about heat, and to accept some new claims. Put the following claims in the order in which Hylas holds them.

   a. Gentle warmth is a kind of pleasure.

   b. Intense heat is a kind of pain.

   c. All degrees of heat can exist unperceived.

   d. No degree of heat can exist unperceived.

   e. Intense heat cannot exist unperceived.

3. Does Philonous think that microscopes reveal the true colors of things?

4. Does Philonous think that the **design argument** establishes the existence of God?

5. Assume you are one of the vulgar, standing in front of a tree. According to Philonous, do you think that the tree you see continues to exist when you close your eyes?

NOTES AND QUESTIONS

1. As the *Dialogues* make very clear, Berkeley's idealism is not supposed to be a form of skepticism, and God plays an essential role in his system. This is also emphasized in the subtitle:

   > The design of which is plainly to demonstrate the reality and perfection of human knowledge, the incorporeal nature of the soul, and the immediate

---

15. "Academics": a school of skeptics in ancient Greece; "Cartesians": followers of the French philosopher René Descartes (1596–1650). Selections from Descartes are in Chapters 6 and 7 of this anthology.

providence of a Deity: in opposition to Sceptics and Atheists. Also to open a method for rendering the Sciences more easy, useful, and compendious.

2. This famous limerick expresses a misconception about Berkeley's idealism:

> There once was a man who said, "God
>
> Must think it exceedingly odd
>
> If he finds that this tree
>
> Continues to be
>
> When there's no one about in the Quad."

The misconception was answered by another limerick[16]:

> Dear Sir: Your astonishment's odd;
>
> I am always about in the Quad.
>
> And that's why the tree
>
> Will continue to be
>
> Since observed by, Yours faithfully, God.

What is the misconception? What is the reply Berkeley gives in the *Dialogues*?[17]

3. At the end of the First Dialogue, Philonous argues that it is *impossible* "to conceive a tree or house existing by itself, independent of, and unperceived by, any mind whatsoever." This is known as Berkeley's *master argument*. Bertrand Russell gives a version of the master argument in "Appearance and Reality" (p. 414), pronouncing it "fallacious," but without explaining why. Try setting out the master argument in the form of **premises** and conclusion. Is it **valid**? Is it **sound**?

4. For more on Berkeley's idealism, including the master argument, see Lisa Downing, "George Berkeley," in *Stanford Encyclopedia of Philosophy*, ed. Edward Zalta (https://plato.stanford.edu/archives/spr2013/entries/berkeley/). Also helpful is the "Introduction" to the edition of the *Dialogues* edited by David Hilbert and John Perry (Arete Press, 1994).

---

16. Both are by the English theologian and priest Ronald Knox (1888–1957).

17. As mentioned in the introduction to this chapter (see footnote 7 on page 410), he gives another answer in the *Principles of Human Knowledge*: see section 3.2.4 of Lisa Downing's article cited above in number 4.

Vasubandhu (Fourth to Fifth Century CE)

Vasubandhu was a Buddhist monk and philosopher who was born in Peshawar (in present-day Pakistan) and then lived in the Kingdom of Gāndhāra, which included part of present-day Afghanistan. Vasubandhu is one of the founders of the Yogācāra school of Buddhism, and his many philosophical and religious works have been highly influential in Buddhist thought.

TWENTY VERSES WITH AUTO-COMMENTARY[1]

Translated by Nilanjan Das

I. A Statement of the View

[Proponent:] In the Mahāyāna system, it has been established that everything in the three realms is nothing but appearance.[2] This is obvious from the canonical utterance [of the Buddha himself], "O sons of victorious ones! Everything in the three realms is nothing but mind." The expressions "mind," "mental faculty," "awareness," and "appearance" are synonyms. Here, the term "mind" is meant to include associated mental factors [such as feelings, perception, etc.]. The expression "nothing but" is meant to rule out the existence of external objects.

> *Verse 1.* This is all appearance only; for even non-existent objects are presented to us, as, for instance, a person with faulty vision sees unreal hair, etc.

II. Objections and Responses

II.1   OBJECTIONS

[Opponent:]

> *Verse 2.* If appearances do not arise from external objects, then there is no reason why appearances should arise at particular times and places, or why they should be produced across different minds, or why objects of such appearances should have causal efficacy.

What is being said?

If color-appearances are produced, not by the colors themselves, but in their absence, then why are such appearances produced at some places, and not everywhere?

Even then, they are produced only sometimes, and not always.

Such appearances are [also] produced in the minds of all thinkers located at the relevant places and times, and not just in that of a particular thinker. The latter is the case with the appearances of unreal hair, etc., which are produced only in the minds of people with faulty vision, but not in those of others.

---

1. From Sylvain Lévi (Ed.), *Vijñaptimātratāsiddhi: Deux Traités de Vasubandhu: Viṃśatikā (La Vingtaine), Accompagnée d'une explication en prose, et Triṃśikā (La Trentaine), avec le Commentaire de Sthiramati* (Paris: Libraire Ancienne Honoré Champion, 1925), 1–11. With corrections from Sylvain Lévi, *Un système de philosophie bouddhique: Matériaux Pour L'etude du Système Vijñāptimātra* (Paris: Honoré Champion, 1932), 175.

2. "Mahāyāna system": major tradition of Buddhism; "three realms": three worlds into which one may be reborn.

Why do the hair, flies, etc., perceived by people with faulty vision fail to be causally efficacious in the way hair, flies, etc., should be? But others [i.e., the hair, flies, etc., seen by people with normal vision] are causally efficacious in that way. The food, drink, clothes, poison, weapons, etc., that we encounter in dreams aren't causally efficacious in a manner that food, etc., ought to be. But others [i.e., the food, etc., seen outside of dreams] are causally efficacious in that way. An illusory city in the sky, in virtue of being non-existent, isn't causally efficacious in the way a city should be.[3] But others [i.e., real cities] are causally efficacious in that way.

Therefore, without external objects, one cannot make sense of the production of appearances at particular times and places, or the production of appearances across different minds, or the causal efficacy of their objects.

II.2   RESPONSES

[Proponent:] It is not the case that these constraints on appearances are unexplained, because

> Verse 3. The production of appearances at particular times and places is established, just as in the case of dreams.

. . . In dreams, even without the presence of any external object, certain objects like flies, gardens, women, men, etc., are seen, only at certain places [within those dreams] and not everywhere. Even when a particular place is fixed, they are only seen only at certain times [in the course of those dreams], and not always. Hence, even without the presence of any external object, appearances may arise only at particular places and times.

> Verse 3 (continued). The production of appearances across different minds is established, just as in the case of hungry ghosts.[4]

. . . How is the analogy with hungry ghosts established?

> Verse 3 (continued). Because all of them [i.e., all hungry ghosts] experience a pus-river, and so on.

. . . When placed in the same predicament with respect to the ripened fruit of their previous acts, all hungry ghosts—and not just one of them—see a river full of pus. They also see a river full of urine and excrement, governed by men armed with swords

---

3. Vasubandhu is alluding here to a *fata morgana*, a kind of mirage involving multiple images, for example of buildings, which appears just above the horizon and which thus could get mistaken for a city in the sky.

4. In Buddhist cosmology, hungry ghosts are beings who in previous lives had committed acts of lust and greed, and, as a result, find themselves in a state of unquenched thirst and unsated hunger. They linger at the margins of the human world, and where ordinary humans see streams of clear water, they undergo shared visions of rivers of pus.

and clubs, etc.[5] This is captured by the expression "and so on." Thus, the production of appearances across different minds is established even in the absence of external objects.

> *Verse 4.* The causal efficacy of objects of appearances is established just as in the case of nocturnal emissions.

. . . The analogy is that even though there is no sexual intercourse in a dream, the dreamer still discharges semen.

In the same manner, the four constraints on appearances, namely the production of appearances at particular places and their production at particular times, etc., are established by other examples too.

> *Verse 4 (continued).* All four constraints on appearances are established as in the case of hell.

How is the analogy with hell established?

> *Verse 4 (continued).* Through the perception of the wardens of hell, etc., and through torture at their hands.

The inhabitants of hell undergo visions of hell-wardens. These visions arise at particular places and particular times. The expression "etc." refers to the visions of dogs, crows, and iron-mountains, of comings and goings, etc. Such visions arise in everyone, and not just in one person. And even though hell-wardens don't exist, the suffering that the hell-wardens cause to the inhabitants of hell is still established [as real]; for the ripened fruit of their past morally equivalent acts holds sway [over their present experiences]. It is to be known that in this manner, in other cases too, all these four constraints on appearances are established. . . .

III. The Argument for Idealism

[Opponent:] Then, why is it to be understood that the Buddha spoke about the existence of the external bases of sensory cognition like color, intending to convey that there is no external object which is presented by each appearance, for example, by the appearance of color?

[Proponent:] Because

> *Verse 11.* This object [presented by appearances] cannot be simple, nor can it be a plurality of atoms. It cannot be the latter even if the atoms are conjoined to each other; for atoms themselves cannot be established.

---

5. According to the classical Indian doctrine of *karma*, agents who perform morally equivalent acts are subjected to the same experiences in the afterlife or when reborn.

What is being said?

[Option 1:] The external basis of sensory cognition, such as colour, etc., which appears as an object of our awareness can be simple, for example, the *part-possessing form* accepted by the Vaiśeṣikas.[6]

[Option 2:] Or, it can be a plurality of atoms.

[Option 3:] Or, it can be a unified collection of atoms [which are conjoined to each other].

[Response to option 1:] The object of awareness cannot be simple, because we are never aware of an object without also being aware of its parts.

[Response to option 2:] Neither can a plurality of atoms be the object of awareness, because we are never aware of an individual atom.

[Response to option 3:] Nor can a unified collection of atoms be the object of awareness, because the status of an atom as a simple substance[7] isn't established.

[Opponent:] Why not?

III.1 THE ARGUMENT AGAINST OPTION 3: THE STATUS OF ATOMS AS SIMPLE SUBSTANCES CANNOT BE ESTABLISHED

[Proponent:] Because

Verse 12. If an atom could be simultaneously conjoined to six other atoms on its six sides, then it would have six parts.

If an atom could simultaneously be conjoined to six other atoms on its six sides [so as to produce a composite object], then each atom would have six parts; for the region which is in contact with one atom cannot be occupied by another.

Verse 12 (continued). Moreover, if the six atoms were to occupy the same location, the composite object consisting of the atoms would also be an atom.

Suppose each atom is located at the same place where all six are. In that case, since all the atoms are at the same place, all composite objects would just be an atom; for the atoms which constitute such objects now wouldn't be distinct from each other. Thus, no unified collection of atoms would now be visible.

The Kashmiri Vaibhāṣikas[8] say, "Atoms are not conjoined to each other, because they don't have parts. So, this unacceptable consequence doesn't follow [on our view]. Rather, unified collections of atoms are in contact with each other."

They are to be asked this: "A unified collection of atoms isn't something distinct from the atoms themselves. So,

---

6. A school of classical Indian philosophy.

7. An independently existing thing or entity; see **substance**.

8. An early Buddhist subschool from Kashmir, a region that overlaps both present-day India and Pakistan.

> *Verse 13.* If atoms cannot be conjoined, whose conjoining do we see in unified collections of atoms?" . . . So, unified collections of atoms cannot be established by appeal to the conjoining of atoms, because atoms have no parts.

Well, even unified collections of atoms are not conjoined to each other! Therefore, it cannot be said that the reason why the conjoining of atoms cannot be established is that they don't have parts; for even the conjoining of unified collections of atoms—which are objects with parts—cannot be accepted. Thus, the status of atoms as simple substances cannot be established.

Whether or not you accept the conjoining of atoms,

> *Verse 14.* Anything which is spatially extended cannot be simple.

If atoms were spatially extended, having a region facing east or a lower region, why would such atoms be simple?

> *Verse 14 (continued).* [If atoms weren't spatially extended,] how then could they have shadows or be concealed?

If no individual atom were spatially extended, how could shadows be cast at dawn at one place and sunlight at another? For [without spatial extension] the atom would have no region which was untouched by sunlight. How could one atom be concealed by another atom if atoms were not spatially extended? For, in that case, there wouldn't be any front region of an atom such that when another atom arrives at that region, it blocks the original one. If one atom didn't block another, all unified collections of atoms would be reduced to a single atom. This has been said.

III.2   AGAINST COMPOSITE WHOLES

[Opponent:] Why don't you accept that only composite wholes are subject to shadows and concealment?

[Proponent:] Do you think that there is a composite whole over and above the atoms themselves, which is subject to shadows and concealment? That cannot be. It is said:

> *Verse 14 (continued).* If the composite whole isn't distinct from its constituent atoms, then they [i.e., the shadows and the concealment] are not its properties [i.e., properties of the composite whole].

If you don't accept the view that the composite whole is distinct from its constituent atoms, then the shadows and the concealment are not properties of the composite object. The composite object is just a constructed idea.

[Opponent:] As long as the defining characteristics [of various objects of awareness] such as color, etc., remain uncontradicted, why even bother speculating whether the object of awareness is an atom or a unified collection of atoms?

[Proponent:] What, then, is the defining characteristic of the object of awareness?

[Opponent:] "Being an object detected by the eye, etc.," and "being blue," etc.

[Proponent:] This is being considered: Is the thing which is blue, yellow, etc., and which is also taken to be the object of visual perception, etc., a simple substance, or a plurality?

[Opponent:] What is the point of this question?

III.3   BACK TO OPTION 1

[Proponent:] The problem with its being a plurality has already been stated [in response to options 2 and 3].

> *Verse 15.* If it were simple, gradual traversal wouldn't be possible; nor would simultaneous perception and non-perception [of the same object with respect to different parts] be possible; nor could separate objects reside at different places; nor would very small objects be imperceptible.

If one imagines that the object of visual perception is just one unbroken substance—not many—then gradual traversal across the earth would be impossible, where "traversal" means *motion*; for, in a single step, the whole earth would be traversed.

Neither could the near part of an object be perceived at the same time as the distant part isn't perceived; for perception and non-perception of the same thing at the same time isn't possible.

Nor could elephants, horses, etc., which are separate and distinct, be located at different places; for, wherever one was, there would be the other. Then, how could they be separated by distance? Or [if you deny that they are separated by distance], how could the places that they occupy and do not occupy be one, given that empty space is apprehended between them?

[Furthermore] if the difference between distinct substances is only to be explained in terms of their defining characteristics, and not otherwise [i.e., not in terms of their parts], then very small aquatic creatures which have the same characteristics as large ones wouldn't remain unperceived. Thus [in order to distinguish such creatures from one another], we have to accept that different substances can differ with respect to their atomic compositions.

III.4   CONCLUSION

Therefore, the object of awareness cannot be established as a simple entity. If the object of awareness cannot be established as a simple entity, then the status of color, etc., as external objects of vision, etc., is also disproved [since options 2 and 3 have already been rejected]. Hence, these are nothing but appearances.

IV. Further Objections

IV.1 PERCEPTUAL THOUGHT, MEMORY AND DREAMS

[Opponent:] Existence and non-existence are determined by various means of knowing. Amongst all the means of knowing, perception is the best. If there is no external object, then how does the thought, "[This is] perceived [by me]" arise?
   [Proponent:]

> *Verse 16.* The perceptual thought arises as in the case of dreams.

That is, without any external object. This has already been made clear.

> *Verse 16 (continued).* When the perceptual thought arises, the object isn't seen; why then is that object treated [by the opponent] as perceptible?

When the perceptual thought arises in the form, "This object is perceived by me," then the external object isn't seen; for it is by mental awareness that the object is then discerned, since visual awareness by then has ceased. Why, then, is that object to be treated as *perceptible*? More specifically, if the object of visual awareness is momentary, then [its properties such as] color, etc., are indeed gone [when the perceptual thought arises].[9]
   [Opponent:] That which hasn't been directly apprehended cannot be recalled by mental awareness. So, the mental awareness must indeed be generated by a direct apprehension of an object. Such direct apprehension just is perception. Therefore, the objects of such apprehension, such as color, etc., are to be treated as perceptible.
   [Proponent:] This principle, namely that only directly apprehended objects can be recalled, cannot be established, because

> *Verse 17.* It has already been said that appearances present objects as if they were real.

It has been said that even without the presence of an object, appearances constituted by visual awareness arise, presenting things as if they were real.

> *Verse 17 (continued).* The same goes for recollection.

From such an appearance, a mental awareness which makes manifest the previous appearance, but is infused with constructions like color, etc., arises due to recollection. Therefore, the direct apprehension of an object cannot be established by appealing to recollection.

---

9. Here, Vasubandhu is appealing to the Buddhist theory of momentariness, according to which there are no objects that persist over time. So when you think, "*This object* is perceived by me," the object no longer exists at the time you have the thought, and so "isn't seen."

[Opponent:] If appearances that arise when one is awake were about unreal objects just like appearances produced in dreams, then one would oneself recognize the non-existence of such objects. This doesn't happen. Therefore, it cannot be the case that all awareness is objectless like dreams.

[Proponent:] This isn't helpful, because

Verse 17 (continued). The absence of objects in dreams isn't recognized unless one is awake.

The ordinary person—enwrapped in the sleep of traces left by her habits of false imaginative construction—sees as in dreams unreal objects. Thus, she fails to recognize the absence of such objects in that unawakened state. But suppose she wakes up, having gained the transcendent awareness which is free from imaginative construction and thus is opposed to that earlier state of sleep. Then, faced with the purified worldly awareness that arises as a result of that transcendent awareness, she recognizes the absence of external objects. Therefore, appearances that arise while one is dreaming are no different from the appearances that arise while one is awake.

IV.2   CAUSATION AND MORAL RESPONSIBILITY

[Opponent:] If appearances are produced in sentient beings not by external objects, but rather by events within their own minds, then how can we establish that particular appearances arise in particular sentient beings from the company of good or bad friends, or from hearing good or bad teaching? For such good or bad company, and good or bad teaching don't exist at all!

[Proponent:]

Verse 18. Appearances are mutually constrained, in virtue of their dominance over one another.

In all sentient beings, the appearances that belong to those beings are mutually constrained in virtue of their dominance over each other, as the case may be. Here, the expression "mutually" means "by one another." Therefore, it is a specific appearance in one mind—not any specific external object—which produces a specific appearance in another mind.

[Opponent:] If the appearances produced in a wakeful state have no object just like appearances produced in a dream, then why do good and bad acts performed in wakeful states and dreams not have the same desirable and undesirable consequences in the future?

[Proponent:] Because

Verse 18 (continued). In dreams, the mind languishes in a state of torpor; that is why the fruits of acts are different [in the two states].

That is the cause here, not the absence of objects.

438 CHAPTER 9: ARE THINGS AS THEY APPEAR?

[Opponent:] If all this is just appearance, then no one has a body or speech. Then, how do butchers kill approaching sheep? If they do not kill the sheep, why are the butchers subject to the sin of killing?

[Proponent:]

Verse 19. Death is a change brought about by a mental event that arises in another being, just as certain mental powers of demons bring about the loss of memory, etc., in others.

The mental powers of demons can induce loss of memory, dreams, and possession by spirits in others. Similarly, the mental powers of those with supernatural abilities give rise to such effects: for example, Sāraṇa saw a dream due to the influence of Ārya Mahakātyāyana, while the mental sins of the forest-dwelling sages led to the conquest of Vemacitra.[10] Analogously, it is to be understood that due to the influence of one being's mental events, a change opposed to the life of another being arises. This interruption of the homogeneous continuum [that constitutes the mind of the latter being] is called *death*.

Verse 20. How else could the Daṇḍaka Forest have been emptied owing to the anger of the sages,

if one doesn't accept that mental events of one being can bring about the death of another?

The householder Upāli was asked by the Buddha, who wanted to establish the sinfulness of mental torture, "O householder, have you heard that the Daṇḍaka Forest, the Forest of Mātaṅga, and the Forest of Kaliṅga, were emptied and turned into grounds fit for sacrificial rites?" And he said, "I have heard, o Gautama! It was through the mental sins of the sages."

Verse 20 (continued). How else would the sinfulness of mental torture be established by that [action]?

If one imagines that the beings living in those forests were destroyed by demonic creatures who were pleased with the sages, and not killed by the mental sins of the sages, then how can that action establish that mental torture is the greatest sin? It can only be established if the death of those beings came about solely due to the mental sins of the sages.

IV.3   OUR KNOWLEDGE OF OTHER MINDS

[Opponent:] If all this is just appearance, do knowers of other minds become aware of other minds, or not?

[Proponent:] Why is this relevant?

---

10. Sāraṇa, a monk, asked the permission of his teacher, Ārya Mahakātyāyana, to leave monastic life and wage war against King Pradyota; Ārya Mahakātyāyana, in turn, made Sāraṇa undergo a nightmare by means of his mental powers. The King of Asuras, Vemacitra, who experienced nightmares after receiving the curses of the sages he once scorned, subsequently became fearful and angst-ridden.

[Opponent:] If they are not aware of other minds, how are they knowers of other minds?

[Proponent:] Well, then, they are aware of other minds. [But]

Verse 21. Awareness of other minds is illusory. How? Just like one's awareness of one's own mind.

[Opponent:] Why is the latter illusory?
[Proponent:]

Verse 21 (continued). Because one's own mind is unknown to one in the manner in which it is known to the Buddhas.[11]

Since one isn't acquainted with the ineffable manner in which the mind [both another's and one's own] is known to the Buddhas, one's awareness of both another's and one's own minds turns out to be illusory; for [in such awareness] the misleading appearance of a distinction between the graspable object and the grasping awareness isn't dispelled.[12]

Even though the doctrine of appearance-only is composed of innumerable theories and distinctions, and is unfathomably profound,

Verse 22. I have established the doctrine of appearance-only according to my capacities; but it is in fact not thinkable in its entirety.

This doctrine cannot be reflected upon under all its aspects, because it outruns the limits of inquiry. How then can it be fully grasped? It is said:

Verse 22 (continued). It is grasped by the Buddhas.

This doctrine, under all its aspects, is grasped by the supreme Buddhas; for nothing stands in the way of their grasping graspable things of all forms.

TEST YOUR UNDERSTANDING

1. A forest is made up of trees. Taking the forest to be analogous to an object that we seem to see and the trees to be analogous to the atoms that supposedly make it up, what is Vasubandhu's objection to option 2 (p. 433)?

   a. You can see the trees without seeing the forest.

   b. You can't see the trees without seeing the forest.

11. The Buddhas are those who have achieved perfect spiritual enlightenment.

12. Vasubandhu is alluding here to a central teaching of the Yogācāra school of Buddhism that there is no distinction between awareness and its object.

    c. You can see the forest without seeing the trees.

    d. You can't see the forest without seeing the trees.

2. Does Vasubandhu think there are mind-independent atoms?

3. Does Vasubandhu think that when we dream, we recognize that the objects of our dreams are unreal?

4. If we have no bodies, how can we die? What is Vasubandhu's answer?

    a. Bodies are appearances only.

    b. It is grasped by the Buddhas.

    c. Death is an illusion.

    d. Death is a mental disruption.

READER'S GUIDE

Vasubandhu on Idealism

Vasubandhu supplemented his *Twenty Verses* with a commentary on them. The verses and commentary in effect form a dialogue between a proponent of idealism (representing Vasubandhu) and an opponent (as in Berkeley's *Three Dialogues*). The complete *Twenty Verses* contains lengthy examinations of the teachings of Gautama Buddha, the founder of Buddhism, who lived in India in the fifth century BCE. This selection concentrates on Vasubandhu's defense of idealism.

Suppose you see a fly or, more cautiously, *seem* to see a fly. On Vasubandhu's view, there is no *mind-independent* fly that you see—no fly that is capable of existing unperceived. He starts by considering three objections:

1. At some times, and at some places, we seem to see flies; at other times and places we don't. Why is this? The natural explanation is that at some times and some places there are (mind-independent) flies buzzing around for us to see, and at other times and places there aren't.

2. You and I might both seem to see a fly at the same time and place. Why is this? The natural explanation is that there is a single fly that we both see.

3. When we seem to see flies, there are often effects that are naturally explained by the hypothesis that there are flies around us: we become sick, and so forth.

So, by an **inference to the best explanation**, Vasubandhu's opponent could argue that when we seem to see flies, there are (usually) flies that we see.

Vasubandhu responds by giving three sorts of examples that, he thinks, together show that explanations involving real flies are not needed. The first example is dreaming. Sometimes we dream of flies and sometimes we don't. Whatever the explanation of this, it doesn't involve real flies. So there's no need to invoke real flies to explain why we sometimes seem to see flies and sometimes don't. (The dreaming example supplies a reply to the first and third objections, but not the second.) The second example is of hungry ghosts who undergo shared visions of rivers of pus because of their past deeds. This is supposed to deal with the second objection: in order to explain the shared visions that the hungry ghosts undergo, we don't need to posit any real rivers of pus. The third example is suffering in hell, where one may go after a life of evil actions, spending a long period there before being reborn in more pleasant circumstances. Like the second example, this is not persuasive unless you accept Buddhist cosmology, but in any case, how is it supposed to help? Vasubandhu thinks that hell is a kind of shared dream: the torturers in hell, the "hell-wardens," do not exist outside the sufferers' minds. (In part of the *Twenty Verses* not included in this selection, Vasubandhu argues that hell-wardens do not exist in hell, because they do not suffer, and hell contains only suffering beings.) Hell has all the features mentioned in the three objections. Whatever the explanation of why hell has these features, it does not invoke mind-independent hell-wardens or other mind-independent objects. So there's no need to invoke mind-independent flies to explain the phenomena in the three objections.

Vasubandhu now moves on to his positive argument for idealism. Imagine you seem to see a fly. If there really is a fly that you see, it seems to have parts—wings, legs, a head, and so forth. Those parts themselves have parts—the eyes are parts of the head (and so of the fly), and so forth. The eyes also have parts. Assuming that this process of decomposition into parts cannot go on forever, we must eventually reach things that are parts of the fly but which themselves have *no* parts. Vasubandhu calls these partless parts *atoms*.

Vasubandhu then considers three possibilities, set out in verse 11. The third possibility is probably the one you would think of first, and the first possibility is the one you would think of last, so let's put them in the reverse order. The fly you see is:

Option 3. An object consisting of atoms joined together in a certain way.

Option 2: An object consisting of atoms, which don't have to be joined to constitute the object.

Option 1: A simple spatially extended object with no parts.[13]

Options 3 and 2 assume that physical objects have atoms as parts; option 1 does not. Here is an analogy to illustrate the difference between options 3 and 2. On option 3, the fly is like a *finished* jigsaw puzzle, consisting of "atoms" (the puzzle pieces) joined together in a certain way. The finished puzzle did not exist when the pieces were jumbled together in the box. On option 2, the fly is like a jigsaw puzzle (finished or not). The pieces do not have to be joined together for the puzzle to exist—it exists when the pieces are in the box or tipped out onto a table.

Vasubandhu then offers a battery of arguments against each of these three options. For instance, he argues (against option 3) that atoms can't be joined to each other, because only things with parts can be joined. Since the three options are supposed to be exhaustive, he concludes that there is no fly that you see, merely the appearance of one. When you seem to see a fly, or anything else, you are not aware of anything that can exist outside your mind.

After giving this positive argument for idealism, Vasubandhu concludes by examining more objections against his view. For example: we can vividly remember a fly buzzing around the kitchen yesterday; how can we do that, if we never saw a fly in the first place? And, if the flies we seem to see are unreal figments of our minds, why is it wrong to kill them? He ends by discussing the objection that idealism makes it hard to see how we could have knowledge of others' minds.[14] Vasubandhu replies, in effect, by agreeing with the

---

13. Alternatively, an object that is (in some sense) a thing "over and above" its parts, or that cannot be *reduced* to its parts (see **reductionism**). See M. Kapstein, "Mereological Considerations in Vasubandhu's 'Proof of Idealism,'" *Idealistic Studies* 18 (1988): 32–54, in particular 37–38. But for an introductory reading of the *Twenty Verses*, it is better to concentrate on option 1 as stated in the text.

14. See Chapter 5 of this anthology.

objector, but by disputing that this result is problematic. Knowledge of one's own mind, he thinks, is *also* very hard to attain. (And it is presumably *no easier* to get knowledge of others' minds than knowledge of one's own.) Knowledge of minds is not impossible, though. Although you don't have that knowledge now, you will when you achieve the highest state of spiritual enlightenment.

NOTES AND QUESTIONS

1. For more on Vasubandhu's philosophical writings, see Jonathan C. Gold, "Vasubandhu," in *Stanford Encyclopedia of Philosophy*, ed. Edward Zalta (https://plato.stanford.edu/archives/sum2015/entries/vasubandhu/). The Buddhist tradition in general is a rich source of philosophy, having many points of contact with contemporary issues. A useful introduction is Mark Siderits, *Buddhism As Philosophy* (Hackett, 2007).

2. Vasubandhu discusses how some objects could form or compose another object, which is a standard topic in metaphysics today. Consider the following three objects: the planet Mars, the Statue of Liberty, and your copy of this book. They are not very much alike, and neither are they touching each other (unless you are reading this on Liberty Island, they are quite far apart). Is there a *fourth* object, composed or made up of these three? The "commonsense" answer is no: there is no object composed of the planet Mars, the Statue of Liberty, and your copy of this book. But many metaphysicians would answer yes (and this answer fits nicely with option 2). If you think the answer is no, then you face this question: Under what conditions *do* some objects compose another object? This is sometimes called the *special composition question*—see Peter van Inwagen, *Material Beings* (Cornell University Press, 1990), chapter 2.

3. A sample answer to the special composition question is this: some objects compose another object if (and only if) they touch. The sample answer above to the special composition question does not seem satisfactory. For example, if you touch this book, we do not ordinarily suppose that a new thing has been created, composed of you and this book, which goes out of existence when you leave the book on the shelf. (Another relevant example is in the preceding "Reader's Guide.") Consider this alternative answer: some objects compose another object if (and only if) they are stuck together. Is that correct? If not, is there a better answer to the special composition question?

Nick Bostrom (b. 1973)

Bostrom is Professor of Philosophy at Oxford University and Director of the Future of Humanity Institute. His many publications include *Anthropic Bias* (Routledge, 2002), *Human Enhancement* (edited, Oxford University Press, 2009), and *Superintelligence: Paths, Dangers, Strategies* (Oxford University Press, 2014).

ARE WE LIVING IN A COMPUTER SIMULATION?

I. Introduction

Many works of science fiction as well as some forecasts by serious technologists and futurologists predict that enormous amounts of computing power will be available in the future. Let us suppose for a moment that these predictions are correct. One thing that later generations might do with their super-powerful computers is run detailed simulations of their forebears or of people like their forebears. Because their computers would be so powerful, they could run a great many such simulations. Suppose that these simulated people are conscious (as they would be if the simulations were sufficiently fine-grained and if a certain quite widely accepted position in the philosophy of mind is correct). Then it could be the case that the vast majority of minds like ours do not belong to the original race but rather to people simulated by the advanced descendants of an original race. It is then possible to argue that, if this were the case, we would be rational to think that we are likely among the simulated minds rather than among the original biological ones. Therefore, if we don't think that we are currently living in a computer simulation, we are not entitled to believe that we will have descendants who will run lots of such simulations of their forebears. That is the basic idea. The rest of this paper will spell it out more carefully.

Apart from the interest this thesis may hold for those who are engaged in futuristic speculation, there are also more purely theoretical rewards. The argument provides a stimulus for formulating some methodological and metaphysical questions, and it suggests naturalistic analogies to certain traditional religious conceptions, which some may find amusing or thought-provoking.

The structure of the paper is as follows. First, we formulate an assumption that we need to import from the philosophy of mind in order to get the argument started. Second, we consider some empirical reasons for thinking that running vastly many simulations of human minds would be within the capability of a future civilization that has developed many of those technologies that can already be shown to be compatible with known physical laws and engineering constraints. This part is not philosophically necessary but it provides an incentive for paying attention to the rest. Then follows the core of the argument, which makes use of some simple probability theory, and a section providing support for a weak indifference principle that the argument employs. Lastly, we discuss some interpretations of . . . the conclusion of the simulation argument.

II. The Assumption of Substrate-Independence

A common assumption in the philosophy of mind is that of *substrate-independence*. The idea is that mental states can supervene[1] on any of a broad class of physical substrates.

---

1. Depend. See **supervenience**.

Provided a system implements the right sort of computational structures and processes, it can be associated with conscious experiences. It is not an essential property of consciousness that it is implemented on carbon-based biological neural networks inside a cranium: silicon-based processors inside a computer could in principle do the trick as well.

Arguments for this thesis have been given in the literature, and although it is not entirely uncontroversial, we shall here take it as a given.

The argument we shall present does not, however, depend on any very strong version of functionalism or computationalism.[2] For example, we need not assume that the thesis of substrate-independence is *necessarily* true ... —just that, in fact, a computer running a suitable program would be conscious. Moreover, we need not assume that in order to create a mind on a computer it would be sufficient to program it in such a way that it behaves like a human in all situations, including passing the Turing test, etc.[3] We need only the weaker assumption that it would suffice for the generation of subjective experiences that the computational processes of a human brain are structurally replicated in suitably fine-grained detail, such as on the level of individual synapses. This attenuated version of substrate-independence is quite widely accepted.

Neurotransmitters, nerve growth factors, and other chemicals that are smaller than a synapse clearly play a role in human cognition and learning. The substrate-independence thesis is not that the effects of these chemicals are small or irrelevant, but rather that they affect subjective experience only *via* their direct or indirect influence on computational activities. For example, if there can be no difference in subjective experience without there also being a difference in synaptic discharges, then the requisite detail of simulation is at the synaptic level (or higher).

III. The Technological Limits of Computation

At our current stage of technological development, we have neither sufficiently powerful hardware nor the requisite software to create conscious minds in computers. But persuasive arguments have been given to the effect that *if* technological progress continues unabated *then* these shortcomings will eventually be overcome. Some authors argue that this stage may be only a few decades away.[4] Yet present purposes require no assumptions about the time-scale. The simulation argument works equally well for those who think that it will take hundreds of thousands of years to reach a "posthuman" stage of civilization, where

2. **Functionalism** is the view that mental states are defined by their causes and effects; *computationalism* is (roughly) the view that the mind is a kind of computer, which is usually taken to be a specific version of functionalism.

3. The Turing test, proposed by the English mathematician Alan Turing (1912–1954), is a test for intelligence that is based on a conversation with a judge. If the judge cannot tell that the tested subject is not a human, then the tested subject "passes" the Turing test.

4. See, for example, ... R. Kurzweil, *The Age of Spiritual Machines: When Computers Exceed Human Intelligence* (Viking Press, 1999). [Bostrom's note.]

humankind has acquired most of the technological capabilities that one can currently show to be consistent with physical laws and with material and energy constraints.

Such a mature stage of technological development will make it possible to convert planets and other astronomical resources into enormously powerful computers. It is currently hard to be confident in any upper bound on the computing power that may be available to posthuman civilizations. As we are still lacking a "theory of everything," we cannot rule out the possibility that novel physical phenomena, not allowed for in current physical theories, may be utilized to transcend those constraints that in our current understanding impose theoretical limits on the information processing attainable in a given lump of matter. We can with much greater confidence establish *lower* bounds on posthuman computation, by assuming only mechanisms that are already understood. For example ... [Robert Bradbury] gives a rough estimate of 10^{42} operations per second for a computer with a mass on order of a large planet.[5]

The amount of computing power needed to emulate a human mind can likewise be roughly estimated. One estimate, based on how computationally expensive it is to replicate the functionality of a piece of nervous tissue that we have already understood and whose functionality has been replicated *in silico*,[6] namely, contrast enhancement in the retina, yields a figure of $\sim 10^{14}$ operations per second for the entire human brain. An alternative estimate, based on the number of synapses in the brain and their firing frequency, gives a figure of $\sim 10^{16}$ to 10^{17} operations per second ....

Memory seems to be a no more stringent constraint than processing power. Moreover, since the maximum human sensory bandwidth is $\sim 10^8$ bits per second,[7] simulating all sensory events incurs a negligible cost compared to simulating the cortical activity. We can therefore use the processing power required to simulate the central nervous system as an estimate of the total computational cost of simulating a human mind.

If the environment is included in the simulation, this will require additional computing power—how much depends on the scope and granularity of the simulation. Simulating the entire universe down to the quantum level is obviously infeasible, unless radically new physics is discovered. But in order to get a realistic simulation of human experience, much less is needed—only whatever is required to ensure that the simulated humans, interacting in normal human ways with their simulated environment, don't notice any irregularities. ...

Moreover, a posthuman simulator would have enough computing power to keep track of the detailed belief-states in all human brains at all times. Therefore, when it saw that a human was about to make an observation of the microscopic world, it could fill in sufficient detail in the simulation in the appropriate domain on an as-needed basis. Should any error occur, the director could easily edit the states of any brains that have become aware of an anomaly before it spoils the simulation. Alternatively, the director could skip back a few seconds and rerun the simulation in a way that avoids the problem.

---

5. See https://en.wikipedia.org/wiki/Matrioshka_brain.

6. *In silico*: in silicon (Latin).

7. "Bandwidth": rate of information transfer. "Bit" (a contraction of "binary digit"): smallest unit of information. A system that can be in one of two states (say, a flipped coin that can either be heads or tails) can store 1 bit of information. Measured in information, the text of this book is $\sim 10^7$ bits.

It thus seems plausible that the main computational cost in creating simulations that are indistinguishable from physical reality for human minds in the simulation resides in simulating organic brains down to the neuronal or sub-neuronal level. While it is not possible to get a very exact estimate of the cost of a realistic simulation of human history, we can use $\sim 10^{33}$ to 10^{36} operations as a rough estimate.[8] As we gain more experience with virtual reality, we will get a better grasp of the computational requirements for making such worlds appear realistic to their visitors. But in any case, even if our estimate is off by several orders of magnitude, this does not matter much for our argument. We noted that a rough approximation of the computational power of a planetary-mass computer is 10^{42} operations per second, and that assumes only already known nanotechnological designs, which are probably far from optimal. A single such computer could simulate the entire mental history of humankind (call this an *ancestor-simulation*) by using less than one millionth of its processing power for one second. A posthuman civilization may eventually build an astronomical number of such computers. We can conclude that the computing power available to a posthuman civilization is sufficient to run a huge number of ancestor-simulations even it allocates only a minute fraction of its resources to that purpose. We can draw this conclusion even while leaving a substantial margin of error in all our estimates.

Posthuman civilizations would have enough computing power to run hugely many ancestor-simulations even while using only a tiny fraction of their resources for that purpose.

IV. The Core of the Simulation Argument

The basic idea of this paper can be expressed roughly as follows: If there were a substantial chance that our civilization will ever get to the posthuman stage and run many ancestor-simulations, then how come you are not living in such a simulation?

We shall develop this idea into a rigorous argument. Let us introduce the following notation:

p: Fraction of all human-level technological civilizations that survive to reach a posthuman stage
N: Average number of ancestor-simulations run by a posthuman civilization
H: Average number of individuals that have lived in a civilization before it reaches a posthuman stage

The actual fraction of all observers with human-type experiences that live in simulations is then

$$f_{\text{sim}} = \frac{pNH}{pNH + H}$$

8. 100 billion humans × 50 years/human × 30 million seconds/year [10^{14}, 10^{17}] operations in each human brain per second ≈ [10^{33}, 10^{36}] operations. [Bostrom's note.]

Writing *i* for the fraction of posthuman civilizations that are interested in running ancestor-simulations (or that contain at least some individuals who are interested in that and have sufficient resources to run a significant number of such simulations), and N_i for the average number of ancestor-simulations run by such interested civilizations, we have

$$N = iN_i$$

and thus:

$$(F) \qquad f_{\text{sim}} = \frac{piN_i}{piN_i + 1}$$

Because of the immense computing power of posthuman civilizations, N_i is extremely large, as we saw in the previous section. By inspecting (F) we can then see that *at least one* of the following three propositions must be true:

1. $p \approx 0$

2. $i \approx 0$

3. $f_{\text{sim}} \approx 1$

V. A Bland Indifference Principle

We can take a further step and conclude that conditional on the truth of (3), one's credence in the hypothesis that one is in a simulation should be close to unity.[9] More generally, if we knew that a fraction *x* of all observers with human-type experiences live in simulations, and we don't have any information that indicates that our own particular experiences are any more or less likely than other human-type experiences to have been implemented *in vivo* rather than *in machina*, then our credence that we are in a simulation should equal *x*. . . .[10]

This step is sanctioned by a very weak indifference principle.[11] Let us distinguish two cases. The first case, which is the easiest, is where all the minds in question are like your own in the sense that they are exactly qualitatively identical to yours: they have exactly the same information and the same experiences that you have. The second case is where the minds are "like" each other only in the loose sense of being the sort of minds that are typical of human creatures, but they are qualitatively distinct from

---

9. That is: assuming that the fraction of all observers with human-type experiences that live in simulations is close to 1, the probability that you live in a simulation is also close to 1.

10. *In vivo*: in a living organism (Latin). *In machina*: in a machine (Latin).

11. "Indifference principle": a principle saying that certain outcomes should be given the same probability. For example, when a die is thrown, there are six outcomes: it lands ⋅ , it lands ∶ , . . . it lands ⁙ . The principle of indifference we usually adopt in this case is that each of the six outcomes is equally likely, with a probability of 1/6.

one another and each has a distinct set of experiences. I maintain that even in the latter case, where the minds are qualitatively different, the simulation argument still works, provided that you have no information that bears on the question of which of the various minds are simulated and which are implemented biologically. . . .

VI. Interpretation

The possibility represented by proposition (1) is fairly straightforward. If (1) is true, then humankind will almost certainly fail to reach a posthuman level; for virtually no species at our level of development become posthuman, and it is hard to see any justification for thinking that our own species will be especially privileged or protected from future disasters. Conditional on (1), therefore, we must give a high credence to *DOOM*, the hypothesis that humankind will go extinct before reaching a posthuman level. . . .

One can imagine hypothetical situations where we have such evidence as would trump knowledge of *p*. For example, if we discovered that we were about to be hit by a giant meteor, this might suggest that we had been exceptionally unlucky. We could then assign a credence to *DOOM* larger than our expectation of the fraction of human-level civilizations that fail to reach posthumanity. In the actual case, however, we seem to lack evidence for thinking that we are special in this regard, for better or worse.

Proposition (1) doesn't by itself imply that we are likely to go extinct soon, only that we are unlikely to reach a posthuman stage. This possibility is compatible with us remaining at, or somewhat above, our current level of technological development for a long time before going extinct. Another way for (1) to be true is if it is likely that technological civilization will collapse. Primitive human societies might then remain on Earth indefinitely.

There are many ways in which humanity could become extinct before reaching posthumanity. Perhaps the most natural interpretation of (1) is that we are likely to go extinct as a result of the development of some powerful but dangerous technology. One candidate is molecular nanotechnology, which in its mature stage would enable the construction of self-replicating nanobots capable of feeding on dirt and organic matter—a kind of mechanical bacteria. Such nanobots, designed for malicious ends, could cause the extinction of all life on our planet.

The second alternative in the simulation argument's conclusion is that the fraction of posthuman civilizations that are interested in running ancestor-simulation is negligibly small. In order for (2) to be true, there must be a strong *convergence* among the courses of advanced civilizations. If the number of ancestor-simulations created by the interested civilizations is extremely large, the rarity of such civilizations must be correspondingly extreme. Virtually no posthuman civilizations decide to use their resources to run large numbers of ancestor-simulations. Furthermore, virtually all posthuman civilizations lack individuals who have sufficient resources and interest to run ancestor-simulations; or else they have reliably enforced laws that prevent such individuals from acting on their desires.

What force could bring about such convergence? One can speculate that advanced civilizations all develop along a trajectory that leads to the recognition of an ethical prohibition against running ancestor-simulations because of the suffering that is inflicted on the inhabitants of the simulation. However, from our present point of view, it is not clear that creating a human race is immoral. On the contrary, we tend to view the existence of our race as constituting a great ethical value. Moreover, convergence on an ethical view of the immorality of running ancestor-simulations is not enough: it must be combined with convergence on a civilization-wide social structure that enables activities considered immoral to be effectively banned.

Another possible convergence point is that almost all individual posthumans in virtually all posthuman civilizations develop in a direction where they lose their desires to run ancestor-simulations. This would require significant changes to the motivations driving their human predecessors, for there are certainly many humans who would like to run ancestor-simulations if they could afford to do so. But perhaps many of our human desires will be regarded as silly by anyone who becomes a posthuman. Maybe the scientific value of ancestor-simulations to a posthuman civilization is negligible (which is not too implausible given its unfathomable intellectual superiority), and maybe posthumans regard recreational activities as merely a very inefficient way of getting pleasure—which can be obtained much more cheaply by direct stimulation of the brain's reward centers. One conclusion that follows from (2) is that posthuman societies will be very different from human societies: they will not contain relatively wealthy independent agents who have the full gamut of human-like desires and are free to act on them.

The possibility expressed by alternative (3) is the conceptually most intriguing one. If we are living in a simulation, then the cosmos that we are observing is just a tiny piece of the totality of physical existence. The physics in the universe where the computer is situated that is running the simulation may or may not resemble the physics of the world that we observe. While the world we see is in some sense "real," it is not located at the fundamental level of reality.

It may be possible for simulated civilizations to become posthuman. They may then run their own ancestor-simulations on powerful computers they build in their simulated universe. Such computers would be "virtual machines," a familiar concept in computer science. (Java script web-applets, for instance, run on a virtual machine—a simulated computer—inside your desktop.) Virtual machines can be stacked: it's possible to simulate a machine simulating another machine, and so on, in arbitrarily many steps of iteration. If we do go on to create our own ancestor-simulations, this would be strong evidence against (1) and (2), and we would therefore have to conclude that we live in a simulation. Moreover, we would have to suspect that the posthumans running our simulation are themselves simulated beings; and their creators, in turn, may also be simulated beings.

Reality may thus contain many levels. Even if it is necessary for the hierarchy to bottom out at some stage—the metaphysical status of this claim is somewhat obscure—there may be room for a large number of levels of reality, and the number could be increasing over time. (One consideration that counts against the multi-level hypothesis is that the computational cost for the basement-level simulators would be very great. Simulating even a single posthuman civilization might be prohibitively expensive. If so, then we should expect our simulation to be terminated when we are about to become posthuman.)

Although all the elements of such a system can be naturalistic, even physical, it is possible to draw some loose analogies with religious conceptions of the world. In some ways, the posthumans running a simulation are like gods in relation to the people inhabiting the simulation: the posthumans created the world we see; they are of superior intelligence; they are "omnipotent" in the sense that they can interfere in the workings of our world even in ways that violate its physical laws; and they are "omniscient" in the sense that they can monitor everything that happens. However, all the demigods except those at the fundamental level of reality are subject to sanctions by the more powerful gods living at lower levels.

Further rumination on these themes could climax in a *naturalistic theogony*[12] that would study the structure of this hierarchy, and the constraints imposed on its inhabitants by the possibility that their actions on their own level may affect the treatment they receive from dwellers of deeper levels. For example, if nobody can be sure that they are at the basement-level, then everybody would have to consider the possibility that their actions will be rewarded or punished, based perhaps on moral criteria, by their simulators. An afterlife would be a real possibility. Because of this fundamental uncertainty, even the basement civilization may have a reason to behave ethically. The fact that it has such a reason for moral behavior would of course add to everybody else's reason for behaving morally, and so on, in truly virtuous circle. One might get a kind of universal ethical imperative, which it would be in everybody's self-interest to obey, as it were "from nowhere."

In addition to ancestor-simulations, one may also consider the possibility of more selective simulations that include only a small group of humans or a single individual. The rest of humanity would then be zombies or "shadow-people"—humans simulated only at a level sufficient for the fully simulated people not to notice anything suspicious. It is not clear how much cheaper shadow-people would be to simulate than real people. It is not even obvious that it is possible for an entity to behave indistinguishably from a real human and yet lack conscious experience. Even if there are such selective simulations, you should not think that you are in one of them unless you think they are much more numerous than complete simulations. There would have to be about 100 billion times as many "me-simulations" (simulations of the life of only a single mind) as there are ancestor-simulations in order for most simulated persons to be in me-simulations.

There is also the possibility of simulators abridging certain parts of the mental lives of simulated beings and giving them false memories of the sort of experiences that they would typically have had during the omitted interval. If so, one can consider the following (far-fetched) solution to the problem of evil: that there is no suffering in the world and all memories of suffering are illusions. Of course, this hypothesis can be seriously entertained only at those times when you are not currently suffering.

---

12. A *theogony* is an account of the origin of the gods. A "naturalistic" theogony is a scientific or **empirical** account of their origin, as opposed to one based on faith or sacred writings.

Supposing we live in a simulation, what are the implications for us humans? The foregoing remarks notwithstanding, the implications are not all that radical. Our best guide to how our posthuman creators have chosen to set up our world is the standard empirical study of the universe we see. The revisions to most parts of our belief networks would be rather slight and subtle—in proportion to our lack of confidence in our ability to understand the ways of posthumans. Properly understood, therefore, the truth of (3) should have no tendency to make us "go crazy" or to prevent us from going about our business and making plans and predictions for tomorrow. The chief empirical importance of (3) at the current time seems to lie in its role in the tripartite conclusion established above. We may hope that (3) is true since that would decrease the probability of (1), although if computational constraints make it likely that simulators would terminate a simulation before it reaches a posthuman level, then out best hope would be that (2) is true.

If we learn more about posthuman motivations and resource constraints, maybe as a result of developing towards becoming posthumans ourselves, then the hypothesis that we are simulated will come to have a much richer set of empirical implications.

VII. Conclusion

A technologically mature "posthuman" civilization would have enormous computing power. Based on this empirical fact, the simulation argument shows that *at least one* of the following propositions is true: (1) The fraction of human-level civilizations that reach a posthuman stage is very close to zero; (2) The fraction of posthuman civilizations that are interested in running ancestor-simulations is very close to zero; (3) The fraction of all people with our kind of experiences that are living in a simulation is very close to one.

If (1) is true, then we will almost certainly go extinct before reaching posthumanity. If (2) is true, then there must be a strong convergence among the courses of advanced civilizations so that virtually none contains any relatively wealthy individuals who desire to run ancestor-simulations and are free to do so. If (3) is true, then we almost certainly live in a simulation. In the dark forest of our current ignorance, it seems sensible to apportion one's credence roughly evenly between (1), (2), and (3).

Unless we are now living in a simulation, our descendants will almost certainly never run an ancestor-simulation.

TEST YOUR UNDERSTANDING

1. Suppose that, in the entire universe, 1 percent of all civilizations at roughly the level of our current development go on to invent technologies that allow computers to simulate human-type minds. Suppose that 1 percent of those "posthuman" civilizations

are interested in running simulations of their entire ancestral history (an "ancestor-simulation"), and suppose that the average number of ancestor-simulations run by such posthuman civilizations is 100. What, according to equation (F), is the fraction of all observers with human-type experiences that live in simulations?

2. Bostrom thinks that one of the suppositions in (1) above is unreasonable. Which is it?

3. Suppose p and i are each approximately 1/10. What follows, according to Bostrom?

   a. It is fairly likely that you are not living in a simulation.

   b. It is fairly likely that you are living in a simulation.

   c. You are almost certainly living in a simulation.

   d. The probability that you are living in a simulation is about 1 in 100.

4. Bostrom thinks that "reality may contain many levels." This is because

   a. simulators may reward simulated beings in an afterlife.

   b. civilizations go through many levels as they develop.

   c. simulated beings may run their own simulations.

   d. the physics we observe may not be the true physics of the universe.

NOTES AND QUESTIONS

1. For more about the simulation argument, see Bostrom's website, www.simulation-argument.com. The CEO of Tesla Inc. and SpaceX, Elon Musk, goes further than Bostrom and thinks that we are *almost certainly* living in a simulation. See https://youtu.be/J0KHiiTtt4w.

2. If it's not obvious to you how equation (F) follows from Bostrom's assumptions, you are on to something—it doesn't. This glitch doesn't seriously affect his overall argument, however. Bostrom explains why (F) doesn't follow, and how the argument can be repaired, in Nick Bostrom and Marcin Kulczycki, "A Patch for the Simulation Argument," *Analysis* 71 (2011): 54–61, available on Bostrom's website.

ANALYZING THE ARGUMENTS

1. *The conditional analysis of colors.* Bertrand Russell claims that "in ordinary life," when "we speak of *the* colour of the table, we only mean the sort of colour which it will seem to have to a normal spectator from an ordinary point of view under usual conditions of light" (p. 412).

   This suggests the following *conditional analysis of colors* (taking the color green as an example):

   > (CA$_{GREEN}$) *x* is green if and only if a normal observer were to see *x* in normal conditions, *x* would look green.

   Exercise: Explain why this has the (desirable) results that (a) a cucumber under red light, which looks black, is actually green, and (b) a cucumber lying in a deserted field is green.

   Exercise: Explain why the conditional analysis seems to contradict what Russell says immediately following the above quotation.

   Now consider the following example:

   > There might have been a shy but powerfully intuitive chameleon which . . . was green but also would intuit when it was about to be put in a viewing condition and would instantaneously blush bright red as a result. So although . . . the chameleon is green it is not true . . . that were it to be viewed it would look green. It would look bright red. (Mark Johnston, "How to Speak of the Colors," reprinted in *Readings on Color*, Vol. 1: *The Philosophy of Color*, ed. A. Byrne and D. R. Hilbert [MIT Press, 1997], 145.)

   That is, the chameleon is green, but if a normal perceiver were to see it in normal conditions it would look red.

   Exercise: Explain why Johnston's example makes trouble for the conditional analysis.

   (Compare the "conditional analysis" of what a person could have done; see question 6 in the Chapter 13 "Analyzing the Arguments" of this anthology.)

2. *Microscopes.* Berkeley (p. 421) and Russell (p. 412) both appeal to the following fact:

   > M: Objects often look quite different under a microscope than they do viewed with the naked eye.

   Set out Berkeley's and Russell's arguments that each use M (or something close to M) as a **premise**. Do the arguments have the same conclusion? Are they **sound**?

3. *Computer displays (and pointillist paintings).* Here is an ordinary illustration of M. Suppose that your computer display appears to be a uniform shade of bright yellow all over. If you look at a part of the display with a strong magnifying glass, you will see a

pattern of green and red pixels, and no yellow ones at all. Supply the missing premise so that the following argument is valid:

P1.   Parts of the display are green.

P2.   _____.

C.   The display is not yellow all over.

The "best answer" will be a general principle, not a specific claim about computer displays in particular.

Is the missing premise that you have supplied true?

4. *Honey, I Shrunk the Kids.* In this 1989 movie, four children are accidentally shrunk by a homemade ray gun. (Since they are all able to ride on an ant, they seem to be about the size of mites, although the movie is not consistent on this point.) As the movie shows, and in Berkeley's words, to the "extremely minute" children, ordinary small objects "appear as some huge mountain" (p. 423). According to Berkeley, this fact about the perception of size shows that "visible extension . . . is not really inherent in the object." Explain what Berkeley means by this. Set out his argument. Is it **valid**? Is it **sound**?

5. *Heat and pain.* The English philosopher John Locke (1632–1704)—who, together with Berkeley and David Hume, is one of the three "British Empiricists"—writes in his *An Essay Concerning Human Understanding* (1689):

> *Flame* is denominated *Hot* . . . from the *Ideas* they produce in us. Which Qualities are commonly thought to be the same in those Bodies, that those *Ideas* are in us, the one the perfect resemblance of the other, as they are in a Mirror; and it would by most Men be judged very extravagant, if one should say otherwise. And yet he, that will consider, that *the same Fire,* that at one distance *produces* in us the Sensation of *Warmth,* does at a nearer approach, produce in us the far different Sensation of *Pain,* ought to bethink himself, what Reason he has to say, That his *Idea* of *Warmth,* which was produced in him by the Fire, is actually *in the Fire*; and his *Idea* of *Pain,* which the same Fire produced in him the same way, is *not in the Fire.*[1]

Contrast this passage with Philonous's similar comparison of heat and pain on pages 418–20. How are Berkeley and Locke's arguments different? Can the connection between heat and pain somehow show, as Philonous says, that "no body in nature [is] really hot"?

6. *Other minds.* Presumably we know what others are thinking and feeling from their behavior—from how their *physical bodies* move, contort into facial expressions, and so forth. But the idealist thinks that there are no physical bodies. (For Berkeley, your body is a mere collection of ideas; for Vasubandhu, apparently, you don't have a body at all—see the Opponent's objection before *verse 19* in the selection.) So how does the idealist explain how we can know what others are thinking and feeling, and even whether there are other minds at all? Vasubandhu's answer is at the end of the *Twenty Verses,* and Berkeley gave this answer in the *Principles of Human Knowledge*:

1. *An Essay Concerning Human Understanding,* ed. P. Nidditch (Oxford University Press, 1975), 137.

From what has been said, it is plain that we cannot know the existence of other spirits otherwise than by their operations, or the ideas by them excited in us. I perceive several motions, changes, and combinations of ideas, that inform me there are certain particular agents, like myself, which accompany them and concur in their production. Hence, the knowledge I have of other spirits is not immediate, as is the knowledge of my ideas; but depending on the intervention of ideas, by me referred to agents or spirits distinct from myself, as effects or concomitant signs.[2]

Exercise: Assess both Vasubandhu's and Berkeley's answers. (You may find the introduction to Chapter 5 helpful.)

7. *Vasubandhu against option 1.* Assume that option 1 (p. 433) is this: ordinary objects of perception, like lemons and flies, have no parts. (Sometimes philosophers use a more inclusive sense of "part" in which every object is a part of itself; the parts of an object that are not itself are called its *proper* parts. In this terminology, option 1 is that ordinary objects have no proper parts.) This view might seem bizarre and unmotivated, but some contemporary philosophers actually hold something close to it. (Peter van Inwagen, mentioned in the "Notes and Questions" to the *Twenty Verses*, is a prominent example.) On option 1, flies do not have heads, or eyes, or legs, or atoms as parts. Presumably, if fly heads (for example) exist, they are parts of flies, so on option 1 there are no heads, eyes, legs, or atoms.

Vasubandhu gives a brief objection to option 1 after first introducing it, and then some other objections in section III.3.

Exercise: Explain and evaluate Vasubandhu's objections.

8. *Simulations.* Suppose we release an apple from a great height and let it fall freely under gravity. Ignoring air resistance and other complications, the relation between the distance d the apple has fallen and the time t after its release is expressed by this equation:

$$d = \tfrac{1}{2}gt^2$$

(g is the acceleration due to gravity.) This equation is a simple *mathematical model* of the falling apple. If we program a computer to compute d for a succession of times (say, every second for a minute), then we are running a *computer simulation* of the falling apple. To create a slightly more impressive simulation, we could also program the computer to display the result as a red spot moving down the screen.

There are no apples in this computer simulation, and nothing is really falling under gravity. As John Searle puts it in "Can Computers Think?": "We can do a computer simulation of rain storms . . . nobody supposes that the computer simulation is actually the real thing; no one supposes that a computer simulation of a storm will leave us all wet" (p. 346). Generally, a simulation of an X is not an X.

Bostrom, however, thinks that minds are an exception to this general rule—an appropriately complex simulation of a mind would *be* a mind. Is that plausible? Here you will find Chapter 7 of this anthology helpful.

---

2. George Berkeley, *A Treatise Concerning the Principles of Human Knowledge* (Hackett, 1982), 81.

9. *The Truman Show.* In the 1998 movie *The Truman Show*, Jim Carrey plays Truman Burbank, who has been unwittingly starring from birth in a reality television show. Burbank is not a computer simulation—he is a flesh and blood human being trapped on a giant movie set in Hollywood, and his "wife" and "friends" are all actors. A "posthuman" civilization might amuse itself by raising people in Truman-style shows. Imagine a paper very much like Bostrom's, but with the title "Are We Living in a Truman Show?" The conclusion is put exactly as in Bostrom's paper: "In the dark forest of our ignorance, it seems sensible to apportion one's credence roughly evenly between (1), (2), and (3)." But in this imagined paper, (3) is different: the fraction of all people with our kind of experiences that are living in a Truman Show is very close to one. What are (1) and (2)? Would the argument of that paper be as plausible as Bostrom's actual argument? Can you think of other futuristic speculations that could be treated like Bostrom treats the simulation hypothesis?

What Is There?

Every field of study aims to provide an illuminating taxonomy of its objects. Biology seeks a comprehensive inventory of living things; mineralogy catalogues the rocks; physics supplies an elegant taxonomy of the elementary particles; and so on. Of course in all of these cases, the aim is not to list all of the *individual* objects of study. Biology, for example, does not aim to catalogue the individual bugs and birds. The aim is rather to identify the most important *categories* into which those individuals may be grouped, and to explain what distinguishes one category from another.

Metaphysics has taxonomical aspirations as well. But since the subject matter of metaphysics is *absolutely everything*, the taxonomy is pitched at a rather lofty level of abstraction. Metaphysics does not care about the distinction between the giant panda and the lesser panda, or about the distinction between stars and planets. From the standpoint of the metaphysician, these things are all of a piece: they are all **physical objects**. To get a feel for the sort of contrast that might matter to the metaphysician, consider the difference between Mount Everest (a physical object) and iTunes (a computer application). Mount Everest takes up space; it has a certain weight and chemical composition. In these respects it is no different from a dog or a star. By contrast, it makes no good sense at all to ask how much iTunes weighs, or how much space it occupies, or what it's made of. An app and a physical object are *radically* different in kind. That is the sort of difference with which metaphysics is concerned.

Having noted this, we should also note that despite their differences, there is a sense in which iTunes and Mount Everest are rather similar: they are both **objects**. To be sure, iTunes is not a *physical* object. But it is still an object in the following sense: it has **properties**—properties such as *being a computer program that is more than 100 lines long*—but it is not itself a property or anything of the sort. Suppose you have three green books on your desk. They may differ in size and shape and literary merit. But they have something in common, or so we might well say. What exactly is this "thing" they have in common? It is not a physical object. (The books do not have any *molecules* in common.) Nor is it some sort of ghostly nonphysical object. When a book is green, it possesses a *property*, the property of being green, and *that* (among other things) is something your three green books have in common. This is controversial, but if it is right, reality must contain, in addition to objects such as Mount Everest and iTunes, the various properties that these objects possess. And if we go this far, we must go further. Suppose that Fred is Sarah's brother and Al is Margaret's brother. There is then a **relation**—namely, *brotherhood*—in which Fred stands to Sarah and Al stands to Margaret. This relation is not an object, nor is it a property. So in addition to objects (both physical and nonphysical) and properties, we must apparently recognize a new category of relations.

A Preliminary Metaphysical Taxonomy

Let's pause to reflect on what just happened. We began with the sciences, which divide the world up rather finely, distinguishing dogs from cats and protons from neutrons. We then moved easily to a level of abstraction at which these things belong to a single category—the category of physical objects—as distinct from apparently nonphysical objects such as computer programs. We then moved (perhaps somewhat less easily) to an even loftier level of abstraction at which physical and nonphysical objects belong to a single category—the category of objects—which we distinguished from other equally abstract categories: properties and relations (sometimes collectively called **universals**). The result is a preliminary taxonomical scheme (Figure 1).

Is this taxonomy complete? Does absolutely everything find a place in it? Consider the Battle of Waterloo. This battle is obviously not a property, and it would be odd to call it an object (physical or otherwise). It is an **event**. How might we incorporate events into our taxonomy? In one crucial respect, events are more like objects than they are like properties. Like Mount Everest and iTunes, the Battle of Waterloo has various properties, but nothing *has* it. And yet events are also different from objects: they are spread out in time; they don't *exist*; they *occur*. So we might posit a basic contrast between universals and what we might call **particulars**—things that have properties but are not themselves *had*—treating objects and events as two distinct species of particular (Figure 2).

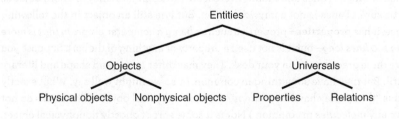

Figure 1

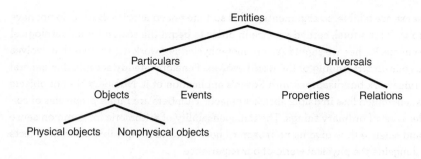

Figure 2

Is *this* taxonomy complete? Not obviously. Consider *milk*—not some particular glass of milk, but *milk itself.* (When you say "Milk is delicious" you're not talking about some particular glass of milk, but you are talking about *something*.) It has properties, but it is not a property, so it must be a particular. But is it an object? Is it an event? Or consider *the fact that philosophy is difficult.* Again, this fact would appear to be a particular. But it is neither an object nor an event nor a **stuff** (like milk). So we're not done yet.

Ontology: The Study of Being

This part of metaphysics is called **ontology**: the study of being. Ontology aims to provide a comprehensive taxonomy in which absolutely everything finds a place and which discloses order by ranging things into a relatively small number of categories. It is not obvious that this is possible, but even our very cursory reflections should be encouraging. Try this as an exercise: Start with the proposals we have been discussing. Ask yourself what we have left out. Try to range the excluded items into categories at roughly the same level of abstraction as those we have been discussing. Spend an hour at this. You *may* come away with the sense that the task is hopeless, that ontological categories are like species of beetle: whenever you think you've found them all, you find another. But you may also come away with the sense that even if your homemade scheme is not perfectly adequate as it stands, something like this should be possible: it's only a matter of finding the right categories and drawing the lines in the right places.

The selections that follow touch on questions that arise in this part of philosophy. Gideon Rosen's paper argues that any ontological scheme must recognize a category of nonphysical **abstract objects**, taking as its main example the numbers of basic arithmetic. Since both science and common sense take arithmetic for granted, any adequate ontological scheme must leave room for numbers. But numbers are not physical objects. So we must reject the otherwise attractive hypothesis that physical objects are the only objects that exist. Of course science and common sense are fallible, so arguments of this sort are not conclusive. But we do not have to wait for a final, settled science in order to begin the search for an ontological scheme. Rather, we should see our metaphysics as a work in progress that evolves as our understanding of the world evolves. Penelope Maddy accepts this general framework but disagrees with Rosen's application of it. Numbers are not objects at all—much less invisible abstract objects. Numbers are rather *properties* of collections of ordinary things. The indispensability of arithmetic for common sense and science thus give us no reason to posit a world of invisible abstract objects alongside the physical world of our experience.

Stephen Yablo's essay takes up the metaphysics of ordinary physical objects. As we normally think, physical objects exist in space in a distinctive way: there cannot be two physical objects in the same place at the same time. Ordinary experience seems to confirm this. (You can't park two cars in a single parking space, after all. Each car excludes the other from the space it occupies.) But a clever argument seems to show the opposite. Take a lump of clay (call it CLAY) and make a statue (call it STATUE). When you're done, you have a statue occupying a certain region of space. But of course the clay did not disappear when you made your statue. So you also have some clay that occupies the very same region of space. "Big deal," you say. "This is not a case of *two* objects occupying the same place at the same time. The clay and the statue are the same thing. CLAY = STATUE." But not so fast. Suppose you made your statue today with clay that had been sitting around for weeks. We can then argue as follows:

(1)   CLAY existed yesterday.

(2)   STATUE did not exist yesterday.

(3)   Therefore, CLAY ≠ STATUE.

The premises of this argument are extremely plausible. Is the argument valid? The principle that underlies it can be put as follows:

(*)   If X differs from Y in some respect, then $X \neq Y$.

And again, this seems obvious. How can a thing differ from itself? But if (*) is true, the argument is sound and we have refuted the commonsensical idea that two physical objects cannot occupy the same place at the same time. (The principle (*) is sometimes called the **indiscernibility of identicals**.)

This is an odd result, and so you may find yourself hoping that it can be resisted. Peter Unger suggests a way— though his conclusion is even odder. Yablo's argument assumes that ordinary things exist and that our commonsense beliefs about them are mostly right. Unger argues, from premises that seem quite hard to deny, that ordinary things such as statues and tables *simply do not exist*. If he's right about that, then Yablo's problem does not arise; but this is not because common sense was in good order to begin with; it is rather because common sense is radically misguided about what the world is like.

These debates are important for the light they shed on particular questions in metaphysics. But they also bear on a larger question. Metaphysics is supposed to be a *philosophical* inquiry into the structure of reality. But you might well wonder: How can there be such a thing? Scientists test hypotheses about the structure of reality by conducting experiments. But philosophers don't conduct experiments. Nor do they have a special faculty of extrasensory intuition that allows them to perceive the structure of reality directly. So how is metaphysical inquiry possible? One response is that metaphysics should proceed by interpreting the experimental results produced by scientists. But the debates discussed in this chapter suggest that this cannot be the whole story. For note: *there is hardly any science in these debates.* Yablo's argument, for example, begins with a *hypothetical* case and appeals to general **a priori** principles such as (*). At no point did we rely on observations of real statues. And yet the argument appears to tell us something about real physical objects; namely, that it is *possible* for two of them to occupy the same place at the same time. How is a priori metaphysical knowledge of this sort possible? Good question. But let's not get ahead of ourselves. Before we ask how metaphysicians can possibly do what they claim to do, we should take a proper look at what they in fact do. The selections that follow are designed to get you started.

Stephen Yablo (b. 1957)

Yablo is Professor of Philosophy at the Massachusetts Institute of Technology. Some of his papers are collected in *Thoughts* (Oxford University Press, 2009) and *Things* (Oxford University Press, 2010).

A THING AND ITS MATTER

Here is a small wooden box. I want you to guess its contents based on the following clues. Clue 1: There is a piece of copper in the box. Clue 2: Everything in the box is the exact same size, shape, weight, and appearance. Clue 3: Everything in the box is in the exact same place. Clue 4: If you were to open the box and inspect its contents, you would say it had one thing in it.

The first clue tells you that the box contains at least a piece of copper, call it Cop. The second suggests that the box contains nothing but pieces of copper, all very similar to Cop. The possibility of several pieces of copper is eliminated by the third clue. Probably, then, the box has just Cop in it. This hypothesis is confirmed by the fourth clue. It looks like the box contains just the one piece of copper.

Now consider another box. The clues this time are different. Clue 1*: The box contains something rare and valuable, and it contains something common and inexpensive. Clue 2*: The box contains something very old along with something relatively new. Clue 3*: The box contains things made in different ways out of different materials. Clue 4*: Experts who have inspected the box's contents tend to agree that it contains more than one thing.

This box has *things* in it—more than one. You might suspect, copper being common, inexpensive, and old, that one of them is our old friend Cop. But Cop has company. There is an unidentified further item *X*, about which we know mainly that it is rare, valuable, and a relative youngster compared to Cop.

Now I'm going to tell you something that may strike you as ridiculous. The first box, which seemed to contain just the one thing, and the second box, which seemed to contain two or more things, are in actual fact the same. You have given then incompatible answers to a single question; namely, *what is in the box?* Not a very promising start to your career in metaphysics.

Why should this seem ridiculous? Well, clues 1–4 don't sit very well with clues 1*–4*, and that's putting it mildly. The box supposedly contains a thing *X*, which is the same size, shape, weight, and appearance as a certain piece of copper and is sitting in the exact same place as that piece of copper but is nevertheless distinct from the piece of copper. How is that possible? What is this mysterious *X* that's invisible to ordinary mortals (by 4) but reveals itself (by 4*) to the "experts"? Who are these experts, anyway? Since when does expertise give you supervision?

I hate to brag, but the "experts" here are metaphysicians like me. They're the ones who have thought the hardest about material objects and how to count them. Thinking doesn't improve your eyes, exactly, but it does enable you to see more by teaching you how to interpret the scene already before you. (Compare the way that musical training lets you hear more, without improving your score on a hearing test.)

The question is, what is this additional item *X* that, although outwardly indistinguishable from Cop, is seen by (most) metaphysicians as distinct from Cop? You're going to kick yourself when I tell you, because it's something very familiar. The extra thing is a U.S. penny. Call it Pen. Pen is the penny that came into being when, one fine day in 1909, Cop was pressed at the U.S. Mint into a certain familiar shape.

Now everything falls into place. Pen is the same size, shape, weight, and appearance as Cop simply because it is (and always has been, since that day in 1909) *made* of Cop. They are differently constituted because Pen was and is made of Cop, while Cop is *not* made of Cop; a thing is not made of itself. They are differently made because Pen was made in 1909 according to a design by a Lithuanian sculptor named Victor David Brenner. Cop was made billions of years earlier, according to a design by God. Pen is rare owing to the appearance on it of Brenner's initials (VDB). Cop is common because it is a regular old piece of copper. It may perhaps be in a rare condition, the condition of composing a 1909-S VDB penny. But that doesn't make Cop itself rare, any more than being the one piece of copper on Mount Everest would. Pen is valuable because it is rare. A good 1909-S VDB penny is worth several thousand dollars. The amount of copper in Cop can be had for a few cents.

Metaphysicians (not all, but most) think the box contains two (or more) items, I suggested. I should have said that lots of metaphysicians think this. Some deny it: "one-thingers" they're called, or "monists." Monists do not deny that the box contains

Pen or that it contains Cop. It is just that Pen and Cop are the very same item. "They" are like water and H_2O or Ludacris and Chris Bridges.

There are lots of phenomena monists can point to as supporting their view. It is not just that Pen and Cop are so exceedingly similar. If they are really distinct, why would any ordinary person say there's just one thing in the box? If they are really distinct, shouldn't it be possible to pull them apart and send them to their separate corners? Why can't we take Pen to Venice while leaving Cop at home in Colorado? Or, given that this is not possible—Pen and Cop are inseparable—shouldn't the collector who purchases Pen be asked to pay again for Cop? And yet this never occurs. If we put Pen and Cop on the scale together, we find that they weigh 3.11 grams. Shouldn't it be 6.22 grams if there are really two of them?

Of course, there are lots of phenomena that pluralists can point to as well, as we just saw. Pen is more valuable than Cop, Cop is much older than Pen, they are differently made, and so on. Another seeming difference between them is this. Imagine that someone is interested in purchasing Cop; they want, let's say, to melt it down and reshape it into a copper hatpin. Cop would still exist in the hatpin scenario. It would merely have taken on a different shape. The same cannot be said of Pen, however. A penny cannot assume the shape of a hat pin. To be melted down and thoroughly reconfigured would mean the end of Pen's life.

It's a real conundrum, then. The data are genuinely equivocal; they point in two directions at once. Whatever we ultimately decide about Pen and Cop, we will have some explaining to do; we will have to explain away the data appealed to by the other side. This may sound discouraging, but it in fact suggests a way forward. Our decision ought to be guided by who can best explain away the other side's data. Which is more puzzling: Why we would have guessed "two" when the answer was really "one" or why we would have guessed "one" when the true answer was "two"?

To come finally to what I think, I think it is easier to explain why we would *undercount* than why we would overcount. There is no huge mystery about how someone could fail to pick up on a supersubtle distinction between otherwise indiscernible objects (and the distinction between Pen and Cop is nothing if not supersubtle). This is so unremarkable a failure that we even have a name for it: one falls into an "understandable confusion."

If there's a similarly familiar term for the opposite mistake, of construing one thing as two, I don't know what it is. And normally when this happens, there's a perfectly simple explanation for it: Superman and Clark Kent present such different appearances, and we seem to encounter them on different occasions. Nothing like that is happening with Pen and Cop. They are encountered on the *same* occasions and are virtually indiscernible on those occasions. If the pluralist nevertheless sees a difference, that suggests she is looking past the appearances rather than just acquiescing in them.

The pluralist's error would be an error of *commission*; those are harder to explain away. But maybe not impossible. Sometimes a thing can present different appearances on the *same* occasion, depending on the perspective we take.

Imagine we are watching a unicyclist from opposite sides of the street. You name the wheel you see "Lefty," because you are looking from the rider's left; I name the wheel I see "Righty." If you ask me which way Righty is turning, I will say it is turning clockwise; if I ask you which way Lefty is turning, you will say it is turning counterclockwise. What's more, both of these answers are correct! I wouldn't dream of correcting you, nor you me. And yet, Righty and Lefty are one and the same wheel.

How can that be, you ask, when they are spinning in different directions? The one unbreakable law of metaphysics is "the indiscernibility of identicals," also known as Leibniz's law (LL):

(LL) x is identical to y only if x and y have the same properties.

This seems to imply that Righty cannot be Lefty, after all; for only one of the two is turning clockwise. At this point, in fact, we might begin to wonder how anything can be identical to anything. I am not the Little Steve who used to live in my parents' house in Toronto, for he attended Sheppard Avenue West Public School, while I teach at MIT. Clark Kent is distinct from Superman, because Clark is a mild-mannered reporter, while Superman is the Caped Crusader.

Now, clearly something has gone wrong here. Lefty really is the same wheel as Righty, Clark Kent really is Superman, and I really am Little Steve. Does this mean there is something wrong with Leibniz's law?

Not at all; it's just that we were misapplying it. We were assuming that the only reason things would be described differently is that they differ in their properties. But sometimes the different descriptions reflect just a difference in the perspective taken. Righty is turning clockwise *from my vantage point*; but then so is Lefty. Little Steve went to public school *in 1967*, but then so did the author of this article. Clark Kent is in fact a caped superhero; that's just not how we think of him when we think of him as Clark Kent. If these claims sound funny, it's because the two names conjure up alternative lines of sight, ones that it is difficult to maintain at the same time.

This gives the monist a possible comeback. Pen and Cop *seem* different; there is no denying that. But so they would if the two names conjured up distinct perspectives on one and the same object. Let that putative object be *Pop*. Pop strikes us as rare, the monist says, when we think of it as a 1909-S VDB penny, but common when we think of it as a piece of copper. She might add that it's difficult to think of it both ways at once, just as it's difficult to watch a wheel from both sides of the street. But it's the same item either way. Pluralists have been taken in by a trick of perspective.

The monist is not taking issue with Leibniz's law; she agrees Pen and Cop are distinct *if* they differ in their properties. She simply thinks that their properties are exactly the same. This idea could work in principle, but it has to be handled with care. Otherwise, what is to prevent us from saying, of any two things, that they only *seem* different because of our changing perspective on them? Suppose with the monist that Cop = Pen (= Pop). Still, these are *clearly* not identical to the box they (it?) came in.

Ah, but we can imagine a supermonist who holds (ridiculously) that Cop = Box. The monist protests that that can't be right, since Cop is *in* Box, while Box is not in Cop. But this might seem hypocritical. After all, the monist's claim that Cop = Pen was questioned on a similar basis: *that can't be right, since Cop constitutes Pen and not the other way around*. And the monist turned a deaf ear to that objection. To defend herself against the charge of hypocrisy, the monist needs to tell us how it's determined which apparent differences are to be explained away as mere tricks of perspective.

The paradigm here is Righty and Lefty. Offered the choice between "Righty turns clockwise, period" and "Righty turns clockwise when viewed from the right side of the street," the second sounds *better*, in the sense of closer to what we meant all along. Let's say, then, that

> we've got a merely apparent difference when "*x* is *F* from perspective *P*, and *y* is not *F* from perspective *Q*" sounds better—closer to what we meant all along—than "*x* is *F*, period, and *y* is not *F*, period."

(In the case of relational differences, substitute "*x* bears *R* to *y*" for "*x* is *F*" and "*y* does not bear *R* to *x*" for "*y* is not *F*.") This helps the monist in her battle with the supermonist, because when we compare

(i) "Pen is in Box from this perspective; however, Box is in Pen from that other one."

to

(ii) "Pen is in Box, period, and Box is not in Pen, period."

the first sounds absolutely ridiculous, while the second sounds absolutely fine. The question is, does it help the monist in her battle with the pluralist? That depends on which we prefer:

(i) "Cop constitutes Pen, judged from this perspective, while Pen does not constitute Cop, judged from that other perspective."

(ii) "Cop constitutes Pen, period, while Pen does not constitute Cop, period."

It appears that (i), far from clarifying the meaning of (ii), is in fact an obscure and unnecessary twist. To that extent, the monist loses her battle with the pluralist over whether Pen and Cop are "really" different or only apparently so.

We have shown, at most, that pluralism is the "intuitive" view—the one that best respects our intuitive judgments on these matters. This is the beginning of the debate, though, not the end. Some monists will insist that they *can* explain away pluralist intuitions. They think they possess a strategy superior to the one set out above. One can't reject this out of hand; every explaining-away strategy has to be considered on its own merits. I don't know, however, of a strategy that does markedly better than the one we have looked at.

A better monistic objection is this. Intuitions are not a good basis for theory building, anyway. They are commonsensical, to be sure. But that doesn't mean they're reliable. Common sense is the distillate of ancient superstitions and prejudices. Everyday intuitions embody, in Bertrand Russell's phrase, "the metaphysics of the Stone Age." Is this really where we want to turn for guidance about the real, underlying nature of things?

No one has ever won a Nobel Prize for investigations into the commonsense view of pennies and pieces of copper, or missed out on one by making claims that did not fit well with ordinary ways of thinking. (Imagine complaining to Einstein that relativity theory conflicts with "what we all know" about simultaneity.) Nobel Prizes are won by people who pull the curtain aside to reveal truths we had no idea of—truths that, in the popular metaphor, reflect the way things are in themselves.

Let it be that physicists have no use for the distinctions postulated by pluralists. The question is what conclusion to draw from this. It would be one thing if the distinctions were physically untenable. You might indeed have worries on this score. Wouldn't Pen-and-Cop weigh 6.22 grams, rather than 3.11, if they were distinct items? "Distinct" can mean nonidentical or it can mean disjoint (non-overlapping). Pen and Cop would have to be distinct in the second, stronger sense for the prediction to be in order. (It would be "double-counting" to add in the weight of overlapping items twice.) The pluralist maintains only that they are weakly distinct; that is, there are two of them rather than one.

The question is, how much should it bother us if physicists do not postulate a distinction between Pen and Cop? I don't see why it should bother us at all. Neglecting to postulate a thing is not the same as postulating its *non-existence*! Consider an analogy. Wars, fingernails, and cupcakes do not loom large on the physicist's research agenda. This is not taken, even by them, to decide the issue of their reality. Take again Einstein. He was a pacifist. "Nothing will end war," he said, "unless the people themselves refuse to go to war." Why worry yourself about this, if wars are not, in your view, there in the first place? Philosophers can hitch their wagon to science, if they like. But they should not pretend that they are only following the scientist's lead here. Distinctions do not have to be physically fundamental to be fully real.

TEST YOUR UNDERSTANDING

1. True or false: Yablo thinks that PEN and COP are exactly alike in every respect.

2. Explain and illustrate Leibniz's law.

3. Give a fresh example to illustrate the debate over "monism" that Yablo discusses. Construct an explicit argument, based on your example, for the conclusion that two physical objects can be in the same place at the same time.

4. True or false: Yablo argues that since physicists have no use for the distinction between PEN and COP, we should revise common sense so as to identify these objects.

NOTES AND QUESTIONS

1. Yablo argues that when we have a rare 1909 penny (PEN) made of a certain piece of copper (COP), then PEN and COP are not literally the same object, even though they exist in exactly the same location. The main arguments are applications of Leibniz's law:

PEN is rare/valuable/less than 200 years old.
COP is *not* rare/valuable/less than 200 years old.
Therefore, PEN ≠ COP.

But consider the following argument of the same form:

Clark Kent wears glasses.
Superman does not wear glasses.
Therefore, Clark Kent ≠ Superman.

It is not hard to say where the second argument goes wrong. The argument is **valid**, but one of the premises is false. Superman *does* wear glasses sometimes—when he's dressed up as Clark Kent. The premise is superficially plausible, but as we think about it we can see that it is not strictly true.

Now consider a similar response to Yablo's arguments. Are we sure that COP isn't rare? For an object to be *rare* is for it to be an instance of a kind of which there are relatively few examples. And COP *is* an instance of such a kind: there are very few pieces of copper in the shape of a 1909-S VDB penny. Are we sure that COP is not *valuable*? The value of a thing depends how much people are willing to pay for it given its condition, and people are willing to pay thousands of dollars for COP so long as it is in the shape of a 1909-S VDB penny. (It would be less valuable if it were melted down; but that doesn't mean that it isn't valuable as it is.)

Exercise: Review the arguments Yablo gives for distinguishing PEN from COP and ask whether they can all be resisted in this way. What is the best argument of this form? Can it be resisted? If so, what does this imply for Yablo's position?

For a sampling of responses to the problem raised in Yablo's paper, see M. Rea (Ed.), *Material Constitution* (Rowman & Littlefield, 1997).

Peter Unger (b. 1942)

Unger is Professor of Philosophy at New York University. He has made important contributions to epistemology (*Ignorance: A Case for Skepticism* [Oxford University Press, 1975]), philosophy of language (*Philosophical Relativity* [Oxford University Press, 1984]), and moral philosophy (*Living High and Letting Die: Our Illusion of Innocence* [Oxford University, Press, 1996]).

THERE ARE NO ORDINARY THINGS

Human experience, it may be said, naturally leads us to have a certain view of reality, which I call *the view of common sense*. This view is tempered by cultural advance, but in basic form it is similar for all cultures on this planet, even the most primitive and isolated. According to this prevalent view, there are various sorts of *ordinary things* in the world. Some of these are made by man, such as tables and chairs and spears, and in some "advanced" cultures also swizzle sticks and sousaphones. Some are found in nature such as stones and rocks and twigs, and also tumbleweeds and fingernails. I believe that none of these things exist, and so that the view of common sense is badly in error. In this paper, I shall argue for this negative belief of mine. . . .

1. Ordinary Things and the Sorites of Decomposition

. . .

To jolt our minds away from common sense thinking, and toward the denial of desks and stones, a bit of "general science" may be of more help than any celebrated philosophy. Even from the early grades, we are given some simple scientific learning which in broad outline, and with fatal incoherence, is this: our ordinary things, like stones, which most certainly exist, comprise or consist of many atoms, and even many more sub-atomic particles. The point here . . . may be put this way: in any situation where there are no atoms, or no particles, there are in fact none of our ordinary things. This should move us to deny, with proper reasoning, the existence of all alleged ordinary things.

The reasoning for this denial does not require atoms or particles. But for jolting the mind, I have found it helpful to cast it in such terms. I will do so here, choosing stones as my ordinary things and atoms as removable constituents. Accordingly, we may express these three propositions, which reasoning informs us form an inconsistent set:

(1) There is at least one stone.

(2) For anything there may be, if it is a stone, then it consists of many atoms but a finite number.

(3) For anything there may be, if it is a stone (which consists of many atoms but a finite number), then the net removal of one atom, or only a few, in a way which is most innocuous and favorable, will not mean the difference as to whether there is a stone in the situation.

The reasoning here is simple. Consider a stone, consisting of a certain finite number of atoms. If we or some physical process should remove one atom, without replacement, then there is left that number minus one, presumably constituting a stone still. . . . Now, after another atom is removed, there is that original number minus two; so far, so good. But after that certain number has been removed, in similar stepwise fashion, there are no atoms at all in the situation, while we must still be supposing that there is a stone there. But as we have already agreed, in (2), if there is a stone present, then there must be some atoms.

There is, then, a rather blatant inconsistency in our thought. However discomforting it may be, I suggest that any adequate response to this contradiction must include a denial of the first proposition, that is, the denial of the existence of even a single stone. . . .

I call this argument, *the sorites of decomposition*.[1] . . . It is an indirect argument for the conclusion that there are no stones and, by generalization, no other ordinary things. I believe this indirect argument to be not only compelling but sound. Let us consider a number of points of commentary which may help us to assess this belief of mine. . . .

[The first] point worth noting is that the central idea of this argument does not depend on atoms, or on anything else so very minute. For example, we may remove "a speck of dust's worth" at a time to the detriment of any putative stone. . . .

. . . Further, our argument implies no particular, not to say particulate, theory of matter. For all we care, the only physical reality may be a single plenum,[2] modifications of which are perhaps poorly labeled as atoms or as particles. . . .

As a [second] point, we should allow that our third premise, and even our second, has not been stated in a manner which is very clear or explicit. But the statement of a premise may be refined, while no substantial change in the argument will result from any relevant alteration. . . . For example, one may squabble over the word "many" or over the word "few." I chose these vague words because they rather faithfully express, I supposed, the unreflective beliefs on these matters which most people have, so few of us being scientists. But we may of course replace them by more definite expressions which, upon reflection, must be admitted to yield acceptable propositions. Thus, we may say, by way of illustration, that any stone consists of *at least one billion* atoms, and that removing *no more than ten thousand* leaves a stone. . . .

As a [third] point, we may reply to the Mooreian gambit[3] of clutching onto common sense at the expense of anything else, most especially any philosophical reasoning. According to this way of thinking it is *always* most appropriate to reply to philosophical challenges as follows. We are *more certain* that there are tables than of *anything* in the contrary philosophic reasoning. Hence, while we may never be able to tell *what* is wrong with the reasoning, at least one thing *must* be wrong with it. But while such a generalization may prove a useful guide in addressing many philosophical challenges, is it to have *no exceptions at all*? I think that an unquestioning affirmative answer here is not only likely to be untrue, or incorrect, but is extremely dogmatic. What of the *present* case, then, *might not that* be just such an *exception*? The merits of the case must be judged in terms of the particulars. . . .

We have an inconsistency to which to respond. If we persist with our belief in ordinary things what rational responses are available? As a [fourth] point, we may

1. The so-called *sorites* [*sor-EYE-tees*] *paradox* is an ancient puzzle:

    A single grain of sand is not a *heap* of sand.
    Adding a single grain to something that is not a heap of sand cannot make it a heap.
    So there are no heaps of sand.

The premises seem true; the argument seems valid. And yet the conclusion seems clearly false. Puzzles of this sort arise whenever we use vague words and concepts. See "A Brief Guide to Logic and Argumentation" in the front of the book for discussion.

2. An allusion to ancient theories according to which matter is not composed of atoms, but is rather continuous even at the smallest scales.

3. A reference to G. E. Moore's 1925 paper "A Defense of Common Sense," which argues that whenever a philosophical argument clashes with firm common sense, the rational response is to suppose that there must be a mistake in the argument.

note that any response other than our suggested one involves us in the acceptance of a *miracle*, in a fair employment of that term. The miracle expected will be of one of these following two kinds. . . . First, tables and stones might be preserved by natural breaks in the world order, so to say, by disjoint happenings whose occurrence prevents nature from being relevantly gradual. For example, after a few atoms were successively removed, or a few minute chips, it might be physically impossible to remove another. Or, for another example, after the sixth atom or chip was removed, the removal of the seventh might occasion a drastic result: the remainder might "go out of existence," or turn into a frog, or whatever. Such happenings as this go against our daily experience, as with sanding a piece of wood or smoothing stones. They also conflict with our scientific perspective which, taking things down to deeper levels, fits nicely with this everyday experience. To expect tables and stones to be saved by such cooperative breaks in nature is, I say, to expect a *miracle of metaphysical illusion*. Thinking nature relevantly gradual, this response has little appeal for me.

Now, given that the world is in fact relevantly gradual, and apparently quite uncooperative, the only hope for ordinary things will lie with the human mind. We must suppose, contrary to what our intuitions seem to be telling us now, . . . that we are all the time employing ideas that have precise limits. We must suppose that with, say, a trillion trillion atoms there, in a certain case, there really is a stone, whether anyone can ever tell or not. But, with one or a few, say fifty, gingerly removed from the outside, the situation suddenly changes, even if no one can ever tell. And this means that with *any* one, or *any* fifty, of the atoms gone, there is no stone there. That's the sensitivity of our word "stone" for you! To believe in this is, I say, to believe in a *miracle of conceptual comprehension*. Thinking of our everyday thought as relevantly imprecise and unrefined, this alternative response also has little appeal for me. Accordingly, I must abandon my belief in stones. . . .

2. The Sorites of Cutting and Separating

There is another variation of our sorites which I should like to present and consider, *the sorites of cutting and separating*. My introduction of it will be a bit roundabout; I hope instructively so.

When focusing on our sorites of decomposition . . . which proceeds atom by atom, or at least tiny chip by tiny chip, we may easily get the idea that *fairly sizable physical objects* are more stable, or better able to endure changes, than are ordinary things.[4] As the atoms come off one by one, or a few at a time, we get to a situation where, even according to common sense judgements, there is no table, stone or sousaphone. It seems, however, that there is still a physical object before us, one consisting of many

---

4. Unger here distinguishes between *ordinary* objects and *physical* objects. Ordinary objects are things such as stones and tables. *Physical* objects include atoms and sharply delineated collections of atoms—things we rarely talk about in ordinary life.

atoms, perhaps even many millions of them. Moreover, though I have foresworn serious inquiry here into matters of identity, we do have the thought that this remaining physical object might well be the same one as the bigger item with which we started, and which we wrongly called a table, a stone or a sousaphone. One who thinks along these lines, then, may well get the idea that "table" names a state or phase which a given physical object may occupy, whether during a certain portion of its career or throughout its entire history. The term "table" may thus be thought to bear much the same relation to "physical object" as "infant" or "philosopher" may bear to "man" or to "human being." Finally, it may be thought that terms for ordinary things, like "table," really do apply after all, and that our conclusion to the contrary was based on a confusion as to what sort of logical role the terms have in our conceptual scheme for things. . . .

Whatever we may think of the previous thoughts which may thus lead to it, however, this last idea is a *non sequitur,* and is in any case badly in error. For whatever the category or categories in which one may place a term, whether one identifies it as a term for an object, a process, a quality or whatever, if that term is incoherent, so it will remain. If "table" is best thought of as a term for a state or a phase, it will be an *incoherent* term of *that* sort, and so it will apply to no real state or phase, just as it will apply to no real object, quality, or whatever. In any case, then, as our sorites arguments have already shown, terms for ordinary things will apply to no reality at all.

Placing this most important point to the side now, it is still a mistake to suppose that any of these terms, "table" for example, has much to do with putative phases, or with anything of the kind. . . . Rather than looking to denote any transitory phase, terms for many sorts of ordinary things, "table" for example, appear to transcend particular physical objects. . . . For example, let us consider a putative table which is, we shall suppose, initially made of a single piece of metal, say, of iron. Let us cut off a substantial piece of the metal from the rest, say, a piece somewhere between two-fifths and one-half of the whole, perhaps measured by volume, and let us send it miles away. Now, we may well think that we have two rather substantial physical objects, whereas before we had but one. But the same table may be thought to exist throughout, first consisting in the one physical object, and then in the two created by the cutting, which we may call its separated "parts." If the parts are brought back together, and joined by solder, we may think of the result as the original table, now again consisting in one substantial material object. It is, then, not only very natural and ordinary, but in a wider respect sustained by common sense, to think of the table as existing in the interim, part here and part miles away, perhaps in California. And the same thought will occur, of course, for such putative tables as are thus cut apart but are never made whole again.

According to our common view of the matter, then, it is not very easy to get rid of tables by such a procedure of cutting and separating. Such putative ordinary things, even if they don't really exist at all, appear at least to be rather stable, and hardly like the potentially fleeting phases we extracted from our original sorites of decomposition. This newly encountered appearance of stability, however, is also an illusion. To make this plain, we may construct an additional piece of reasoning, *the sorites of cutting and separating.* This applies, first, to those ordinary things whose identity seems to transcend any particular material object, as recently indicated, like tables and sousaphones, and such rocks and stones as are "important or well known," like Plymouth Rock and the Rosetta Stone. It applies equally, reflection will reveal, to those ordinary things whose identity appears more ephemeral, like a rock or stone of little importance or familiarity. Let us take these two cases in turn beginning with those things whose identity appears rather more stable.

We begin by assuming that if we cut a table into two roughly equal parts, and do so most innocuously and favorably, then there is still a table left in the case, no matter how widely the parts are separated. Common sense has us make this assumption. Further, even where we always choose a "largest available part," as we always shall, no single operation of cutting and separating will be enough to take us from a situation involving a table to one involving none. By a series of such operations, however, we shall eventually have upon us a situation where there are only resultant specks of dust, or even atoms, scattered all over the solar system or even into regions far more remote. In such a situation as this last, however, we quite clearly have no table at all. To suppose that we still have one is to be committed to all sorts of absurdities, even according to the view of common sense. For one will, presumably, then suppose as well that every table that ever was still does exist and also, presumably, every mountain and every lake, every star and every planet. Hence, we have again uncovered a contradiction in our ordinary thinking. The only adequate response to it is, I suggest, to conclude that we have reduced to absurdity yet again the idea that there are, or ever were, any such things as tables. . . .

This sorites of cutting and separating adapts easily to application with things whose identity does not appear to transcend one sizable physical object, for example, to unfamiliar, unimportant stones and rocks. Now, I do not mean to suggest that there is a rigid distinction here between, say, such stones and typical tables. Rather, I wish only to remark a certain tendency in our thinking, and to show that it makes no difference to the matters under discussion. For the important point is that, according to our ordinary thinking, an operation of cutting and separating leaves us with *at least one* stone. No such operation performed upon any stone, including any stone which results from such an operation, is enough to mean the difference between a situation with at least one stone involved and a situation where there isn't any stone at all. Accordingly, when choosing largest resultants, we shall still have at least one stone present, we must conclude, even where all we have is specks of dust, or even atoms, widely scattered throughout the solar system and even far beyond. But, on the contrary, in such a case as that, there will truly be no stone. Thus we disclose again a contradiction in our thought, the only rational response to which is, I suggest, to abandon our supposition of existence for stones. . . .

3. Accumulation Arguments and the Place of Paradox

. . . Our original sorites of decomposition by minute removals proceeded by the stepwise removal of very small items, tiny chips or even atoms, from the putative ordinary thing in question. The sorites of accumulation which we shall here examine involves the reverse of that procedure: A series of very small items will be accumulated, in some putatively relevant manner, upon some small beginning item, or in some chosen region. . . .

Our relevant sorites of accumulation will be a *direct* argument for the idea that ordinary things do not exist. We shall derive this result from acceptable beginnings. . . .

. . . I shall again begin by focusing on stones as my example of putative ordinary things. And I shall again use the atom as my unit, now of increment rather than decrement. We may begin with an empty region, and say that there is *no stone in it,* or we may begin with a single atom somewhere, and say that it is *something which is not a stone*; the upshot will be the same. I will choose the latter beginning. Now, if we add a single atom to something which is not a stone, it seems that such a minute addition, however carefully and cleverly executed, will never in fact leave us with a stone. For a single atom, I suggest, will never mean the difference between there being no stone before us and, then, there being one there. . . .

Now, there is an asymmetry, which may be worth noting, between the proper way of formulating a premise of addition here and that of stating our third premise, of removal, with our sorites of decomposition. Before we said that if we removed an atom in a way *most favorable to there continuing to be a stone,* there would still be a stone. And this allowed us to derive our absurd result. But if we *add* an atom in a way *most favorable* to there continuing to be only something which is *not* a stone, no absurdity will ever be felt by anyone. For we shall never thus construct anything which, even according to quick common sense judgements, will be even remotely like a stone. We might well thus construct, for example, what quick common sense would call a wooden table, or a planet, or perhaps even a duck. . . . Accordingly, our new premise will say, rather, that if there is, in a certain situation, only something which is not a stone, . . . the addition of *any* single atom, *no matter in what way,* will not mean the difference. Presumably, the ways now most relevant will be those *least* favorable to there continuing to be no stone there. But this asymmetry scarcely affects our argument, for even according to common sense, our new premise is as hard to deny as was our older one.

In any event, then, by repeated application of this new principle, we must conclude that there is no stone before us no matter how many atoms we add to our original one, and no matter how they are arranged. Even when we have before us something which "looks for all the world like a stone," and which would prompt people to think that there is a stone there, we must conclude that there really is no stone. We have again, this time by accumulation, exposed a contradiction in our ordinary beliefs. This raises again for us the question of how to respond to such a contradiction. I submit that the proper response, as before, is to deny the supposition that stones exist. . . .

TEST YOUR UNDERSTANDING

1. What does Unger mean by an "ordinary thing"?

2. Unger claims that our commonsense views about ordinary objects are self-contradictory. Give an example to illustrate Unger's claim.

3. Give an example of the "sorites of accumulation." It should take the form of a short argument for the conclusion that there are no tables.

4. True or false: Unger takes his argument to show that there are no medium-sized objects, and that only atoms (or other very small things) exist.

NOTES AND QUESTIONS

1. *Sorites arguments.* As Unger notes, his arguments are instances of a puzzling style of argument called the *sorites* (from the Greek word for "heap"). Consider two examples:

EVERYONE IS RICH!

(1) Someone with a million dollars is rich.

(2) If someone with n dollars is rich, so is someone with $n - 1$ dollars.

(3) So someone with $999,999 is rich.

From (2) and (3) it follows that

(4) Someone with $999,998 is rich.

Repeat this argument roughly a million times and it follows that

(5) Someone with $0 is rich.

EVERYONE IS POOR!

(A) Someone with $0 is poor.

(B) If someone with n dollars is poor, then so is someone with $n + 1$ dollars.

(C) So someone with only $1 is poor.

From (B) and (C) it follows that

(D) Someone with only $2 is poor.

Repeat the argument roughly a million times and it follows that

(E) Someone with a million dollars is poor.

These arguments have exactly the same form, but they contradict one another. (The conclusion of each contradicts the first premise of the other.) So we know they can't both be **sound**. But we knew that anyway: the conclusions are absurd. So either the arguments are **invalid** or they have false premises. And that's the problem. The premises *seem* true, and each step seems clearly valid. A solution to the **sorites paradox** is an account of where these arguments go wrong. *This is an unsolved problem.* For discussion of some of the possibilities, see Rosanna Keefe, *Theories of Vagueness* (Cambridge University Press, 2000).

Exercise: Consider the following response to Unger's argument and imagine how Unger might respond:

> *We know in advance that sorites arguments with plausible-looking premises are often unsound. Your arguments are sorites arguments with plausible-looking premises. So why should we regard them as sound? Why isn't the right response to say, "These arguments must go wrong somewhere even if we can't say exactly where"?*

2. *Animals and people.* Unger officially excludes living things from his discussion, but one might well think that his arguments can be used to show that there are no dogs and cats, and even that there are no people.

> Suppose Felix is a cat made of n atoms.
> The result of removing a single atom from a cat is still a cat.
> So if we were to remove a single atom from Felix, the result would be a cat made of $n - 1$ atoms.
> Repeat the process $n - 2$ times and the result will be a cat made of a single atom.
> But it is impossible for there to be a cat made of a single atom.
> So there are no cats.

Exercise: Say how this argument might be resisted, and then ask whether your response applies to Unger's arguments for the non-existence of stones and tables.

3. *Making liars of us all.* If Unger is right, then almost everything we say is false. If I tell you that John is at his desk, then strictly speaking, I'm mistaken, since an Unger-style argument can be used to show that there are no desks. Now we usually try to avoid saying things that might be false. That's what honest people do. Does this mean that if we can't refute Unger, we should stop talking about ordinary things?

Exercise: Complete a dialogue with Unger that starts like this:

> You: Hey, Professor Unger. Where's John?
> Unger: He's at his desk.
> You: What are you talking about? I read your paper and I'm convinced: *There are no desks.* So what you just said is false and you know it. You wouldn't lie to me, would you, Professor Unger?
> Unger: Of course not. What I just said is literally false, for the reasons I gave in my paper. Still it's okay for me to say it because . . .

What comes next should be an account of what we're doing when we talk about ordinary things that is consistent with Unger's view that ordinary things do not exist.

Gideon Rosen (b. 1963)

Rosen is Stuart Professor of Philosophy at Princeton University and works in the philosophy of mathematics, metaphysics, and moral philosophy. The argument in the essay that follows is developed in his book with John P. Burgess, *A Subject with No Object* (Oxford University Press, 1997).

NUMBERS AND OTHER IMMATERIAL OBJECTS

1

The book in front of you is a physical object. It is located in space—it is there on your desk and not on Mars. It exists in time—it exists now but not a million years ago. It has physical attributes: a certain shape, a certain mass. Most important, the book is ultimately composed of smaller objects—quarks, electrons, and other subatomic particles—that can be completely and exhaustively described in the language of basic physics.

Everyday objects are presumably physical objects in this sense: animals and plants, rocks and clouds, cars and computers. So are the exotic objects of the sciences such as viruses and black holes. Our knowledge of these things is of course profoundly limited. We may never be in a position to give a complete description of any of them. Still we know (or think we know) that these things are wholly physical, in the sense that they admit, in principle, of a complete description in the language of an ideal physics.

Physicalism is the thesis that every object is a physical object in this sense. It is the thesis that absolutely everything in the universe (or out of it!) is, in fundamental metaphysical respects, rather like the book you are now holding, or the tree outside your window, or an atom, or a black hole: a thing whose nature might be captured by a description in the language of a perfect physics. This definition of physicalism is not entirely satisfactory.[1] A better account would say what it means for a thing to admit of a complete description in such a language.[2] But let us not pause over these subtle matters. We have a fair intuitive idea of what it means for a thing to be a physical object through and through. The question is whether everything is a physical object in this sense.

---

1. For doubts about this definition, see T. Crane and D. Mellor, "There Is No Question of Physicalism," *Mind* 99 (1990): 185–206. For general discussion, see D. Stoljar, "Physicalism," in *Stanford Encyclopedia of Philosophy*, ed. Edward Zalta (http://plato.stanford.edu/archives/fall2008/entries/physicalism/). [Rosen's note.]

2. Here is the rough idea. This book has many properties: it weighs 2 pounds; it's made mostly of paper; it's about philosophy, and so forth. Some of these properties are *intrinsic*: they concern the book considered in isolation, without regard for its relations to other things. The intrinsic properties of a thing are the properties it would share with any *perfect duplicate* of it. (Your book *belongs to you*. That's a property it has, but it's not an intrinsic property, since a perfect duplicate of your book might not belong to you.) A thing admits of a complete description in the language of physics if and only if its intrinsic properties are *fully determined by* the physical properties of its parts and their relations to one another. Of course, this definition takes the notion of a *physical property* for granted. A complete account would have to explain this idea. [Rosen's note.]

The first thing to say about physicalism is that it is not obviously true. God is supposed to be a spirit without a body. He may be "everywhere" in some sense, and if so, he exists in space. But God is certainly not composed of matter, and it makes no sense to ask how much God weighs or whether he is negatively charged. So if God exists, physicalism is false. Similarly, many philosophers believe that even the most exhaustive physical description of a human being would inevitably leave something out. Consider Jones, who has just stepped on a tack and is now in pain. A complete physical account of his brain and body would be terrifically informative. But according to these philosophers, it would inevitably fail to specify, even implicitly, how it *feels* to be Jones right now. For it seems that there could have been a creature who was like Jones in every physical respect down to the last atom, but who had no conscious mental life at all. If this is possible, then a physical description of Jones would omit a crucial fact. And if that is so, physicalism is false.[3]

These examples may suggest that any serious discussion of physicalism must immediately confront the deepest mysteries in philosophy—the existence of God, the nature of consciousness, and so forth. But this is not so. Physicalism is false, I claim, and the case against it is straightforward. To see what I have in mind, let's review some elementary facts about . . . arithmetic.

2

There are two odd numbers between 6 and 10. You probably knew this already, but even if the question never crossed your mind, you can easily verify the claim right now. (Let's see: 7 is an odd number between 6 and 10; so is 9. Any others? No. Therefore. . . .) So let's take this as our starting point and consider the following argument:

1. There are two odd numbers between 6 and 10.

2. Therefore, there are at least two odd numbers.

3. Therefore, there are at least two numbers.

4. Therefore, there are numbers.

The argument has one premise. This was established by informal reflection, though a rigorous proof could easily be given. Each subsequent claim follows logically from the claim above it. The argument thus shows conclusively that anyone who accepts a trivial bit of grade school arithmetic cannot deny that there are numbers.

Now notice: It may be silly to ask how much God weighs, but it's even sillier to ask how much the number 7 weighs, or how fast it's moving, or whether it is round or square or made of carbon. No one ever bothers to ask these questions, but if we

---

3. See D. Chalmers, "The Hard Problem of Consciousness," and F. Jackson, "Epiphenomenal Qualia," *Philosophical Quarterly* 32 (1982); 127–36 (both in Chapter 8 of this anthology). [Rosen's note.]

take them seriously for a moment, the answers are obvious in every case: the number 7 does not have a mass; it is not in motion or at rest; it is not made of carbon, and so forth. But this is just to say that numbers are not physical objects. We thus have a simple refutation of physicalism:

5. There are numbers.

6. Numbers are not physical objects.

7. Therefore, physicalism is false.

3

Are you tempted to deny the second premise? If so, you may be confused in an instructive way. The book in front of you contains certain marks shaped like this: 7. If you are reading the Latin translation, it may instead contain marks shaped like this: VII. These marks are physical objects. They are made of ink; they contain carbon. But these marks are not numbers. Suppose I write the numeral "7" on the blackboard and then erase what I have written. I have destroyed the mark I made. Have I destroyed the number 7? Is there now only one odd number between 6 and 10? Surely not. So this particular inscription was not the number 7. But we can run the same argument for every inscription, and this shows that these agglomerations of ink and chalk must be distinguished from the numbers.

We must also distinguish these concrete inscriptions—called *numeral tokens*—from the *numerals* themselves. Suppose I write a list on the board:

6, 7, 125, VII, 7

The list contains five numeral tokens representing three different numbers.[4] But there is also a sense in which the list contains four different numerals: the Arabic numerals "6," "7," and "125" and the Roman numeral "VII." The two instances of the numeral "7" are tokens of the same *numeral type*, just as the two "t"s in the word "letter" are tokens of the same *letter* type. The type/token distinction is one of the most important in metaphysics, and it applies in a variety of domains. Jane Austen wrote six novels, but there are millions of copies of those novels. The novels are types; the copies are tokens. Goya's etching *The Sleep of Reason Produces Monsters* is a type; its many physical impressions (the paper and ink copies that hang in museums) are tokens of that type; and so on.[5]

We have said that numeral tokens (at least those of the ink-on-paper variety) are physical objects, and the same goes for the token words and letters on this page, my

---

4. We count "125" as a single numeral, ignoring the smaller numerals that make it up. [Rosen's note.]

5. For an account of the **type/token** distinction and its significance, see Linda Wetzel, *Types and Tokens: An Essay on Universals* (MIT Press, 2008). [Rosen's note.]

personal copy of *Northanger Abbey*, and so forth. But now focus on the types: the Arabic numeral "7," Jane Austen's novel *Northanger Abbey*. Are *they* physical objects? Where exactly is the numeral "7"? How much does it weigh? What is it made of? Once again, the only sensible answers to these silly questions are wholly negative: the numeral type is not really anywhere; it does not have a weight; it is not made of anything. The idea that one might describe a numeral or a novel by means of physical properties such as mass or charge is just confused. And so we have another simple argument against physicalism:

8. Types of various sorts exist.

9. These types are not physical objects.

10. Therefore, physicalism is false.

4

These counterexamples to physicalism have something in common. Numbers, numerals, and other types are *abstract objects*. It is sometimes said that abstract objects do not exist in space or time. But this is not strictly correct. *Northanger Abbey* was written in 1798. Before that it did not exist, so there is a sense in which the novel does exist "in time." To choose a rather different example, the *game of chess* is presumably an abstract object. (It is certainly not a physical object.) But the game originated in Persia in the sixth century, later spreading to India and then to Europe, so there is a sense in which the game exists "in space" (which is not to say that it *takes up* space). We get a better characterization if we say that abstract objects are distinguished by their *causal inefficacy*. You can't *interact* with numbers or with types like the letter "t." Abstract objects do not exert forces on other things, and this means that you can't bump into them or bounce photons off of them. In an intuitive and yet elusive sense, abstract objects are incapable of inducing changes in other things. Another argument against physicalism then goes like this:

11. Abstract objects of various sorts exist. (We have seen many examples.)

12. Abstract objects are not physical objects.

13. Therefore, physicalism is false.

5

We have three arguments against physicalism. Each is clearly valid, so the only way to resist them is to reject the premises. Let us focus on the argument from numbers:

5. There are numbers.

6. Numbers are not physical objects.

7. Therefore, physicalism is false.

In our discussion, we derived (5) from basic arithmetic by means of an impeccable deductive argument. This means that anyone who wishes to resist the argument must reject basic arithmetic.

Imagine a philosopher who says:

> My attitude towards arithmetic is like the atheist's attitude towards theology. I know what the theory *says*; I just don't believe it. In this case, the theory says that there are infinitely many abstract things called "numbers," 1, 2, 3, and so on, which stand in various relations to one another. I reject the theory because in my view these alleged objects do not exist. (I've never seen one. Have you?) Your premise that there are two odd numbers between 6 and 10 is false. It is false because there are no numbers of any sort.

This position is not absurd. There is no contradiction in the claim that there are no numbers. But it is not enough for this philosopher to show that her view is consistent. She must show that we have reason to believe it. The question before us, then, is whether we, given all we know, have reason to reject the arithmetic we learned in school.

This way of framing the issue makes it clear that in this dispute about whether to accept basic arithmetic, the burden lies with the rejectionist. This is a consequence of a general principle. In philosophy as in every intellectual endeavor, we must begin where we are. Whenever we approach a novel question, we bring to bear a vast body of commonsensical and scientific opinion that we do not doubt and which we have seen no reason to doubt. Philosophy and the other intellectual disciplines are in the business of giving us reasons to modify this starting point. The Cartesian idea that we should begin *afresh* in philosophy by setting our received opinions to one side is not just impractical: it is a mistake about the nature of rational inquiry.[6]

Arithmetic is part of our shared starting point in these metaphysical investigations. Before you started reading this essay, you accepted the arithmetic you learned in school without the slightest reservation. And of course you're not the only one. The physicists, engineers, actuaries, and accountants who rely on mathematics in their work may have doubts about certain controversial principles in their fields. But they have no doubt whatsoever that there are two odd numbers between 6 and 10. Perhaps most importantly, the mathematicians who have been studying this topic for millennia have turned up nothing to call our basic mathematical opinions into question.

Needless to say, this is not a conclusive defense of our starting point. Common sense is fallible. So is physics. So is mathematics on rare occasions. The point is rather to insist that any argument against basic arithmetic must be a *skeptical* argument—one that seeks to undermine by philosophical means a body of settled opinion that is fully acceptable both by ordinary standards and by the most exacting scientific standards.[7] How might such an argument proceed?

---

6. G. Harman, *Change in View* (MIT Press, 1986). [Rosen's note.]

7. Cf. Descartes's argument for skepticism about the senses in Meditation I, reprinted in Chapter 6 of this anthology.

6

One approach begins by noting that physicalism is a wonderfully *simple* theory. It provides an elegant picture of reality according to which absolutely everything falls into a single category. Now other things being equal, a simple theory is likely to be correct. We thus have reason to believe that physicalism is correct. As we have seen, however, physicalism is incompatible with arithmetic. And so, the argument concludes, we should reject basic arithmetic.

Such appeals to simplicity are common in metaphysics, and we need not deny their force. Given two theories that do equal justice to all pertinent evidence and argument, the simpler theory *is* normally to be preferred. (We might ask why this should be. Do we know a priori that the world is a simple place?) In the present context, however, the argument is unpersuasive. After all, we have just argued that physicalism is incompatible with both common sense and settled science, both of which endorse arithmetic. Until we have some positive reason for revising this starting point, we should think: physicalism is indeed a simple theory. So is the view that there is nothing at all! The trouble with both of these views is that given our starting point, they are *too* simple. We know in advance that there are two odd numbers between 6 and 10. Any theory that says otherwise (without giving us some reason to change our minds) is therefore incompatible with "the facts." We may use simplicity as a tiebreaker when choosing among theories that are consistent with our background knowledge. But when a theory fails to fit the facts, considerations of simplicity are quite irrelevant. (As Einstein is supposed to have said, "Everything should be made as simple as possible, but no simpler.")

7

A more compelling challenge runs as follows.[8] When we asserted our premise that there are two odd numbers between 6 and 10, we implicitly claimed to *know* that there are two odd numbers between 6 and 10. This follows from the general fact that anyone who asserts that *p* implicitly claims to know that *p*. (That's why it sounds paradoxical to say: "It's snowing, but I don't know that it's snowing.") In arguing as we have, we have taken it for granted that mathematical knowledge of a certain sort is possible.

But we have also said that mathematics is concerned with abstract entities, and that abstract entities are causally inert. This means that we cannot see them or touch them, since seeing and touching are causal processes. But it also means that we cannot detect them with special instruments, since "detection" is also invariably a causal process. And yet our scientific knowledge of unobservable objects such as atoms and black holes always depends on the fact that these objects affect the environment, and

---

8. See Paul Benacerraf, "Mathematical Truth," *Journal of Philosophy* 70 (1973): 661–79. [Rosen's note.]

ultimately our brains and bodies, in characteristic ways. And this suggests a general principle, according to which knowledge *always* requires some causal link between the knower and the objects of his knowledge. This is the core of the so-called *causal theory of knowledge*.[9]

It is easy to see why this might seem plausible. Suppose you're at a conference on extraterrestrial civilizations when Professor Zipstein stands up and asserts that there is an underground city on the dark side of the moon. You ask him how he knows this. Has he been there? Has he seen photographs? Has he spoken to someone with firsthand knowledge of the place? In response, he admits that he has never interacted with the city in any way. You ask again how he knows what he claims to know, and he replies: "Look, I just find these claims intuitively obvious. They strike me as commonsensical, and I've never encountered any positive grounds for doubt."

I think we can agree that even if Zipstein's theory turns out to be correct, as things stand he does not *know* that there is a city on the moon. Moreover, it is natural to support this verdict by saying that Zipstein cannot possibly know what he claims to know because, by his own admission, he has never interacted with the object of his alleged knowledge.

Armed with this principle, the physicalist may go on the offensive:

> You're no better than Zipstein! Your argument begins with a mathematical claim, but by your own admission you've never interacted with the alleged objects of this alleged knowledge. You can't possibly *know* that there are two odd numbers between 6 and 10. And if you don't know this, you have no business asserting it in the context of a serious philosophical discussion.

This is an ingenious challenge. Our case against physicalism turns on examples.[10] The idea was that some claims about numbers and other abstract objects are so well established by scientific standards that it would be unreasonable for a philosopher to deny them without good reasons. The objection we have been discussing, if sound, would show that we are not entitled to our examples. We are entitled to assert a proposition only if we know that it is true. But if the causal theory of knowledge is correct, we don't know anything about abstract objects.

The best response is to reject the causal theory of knowledge. We need not deny that knowledge *sometimes* requires causal interaction. Zipstein really is an ignoramus: he does not know what he claims to know. And perhaps the best way to explain this is to suppose that knowledge of *this sort*—knowledge of contingent features of the physical environment—always requires a causal link. But the causal theory of knowledge is supposed to be a *general* theory, one that applies to mathematical knowledge as well. And yet there is no reason to suppose that mathematical knowledge requires causal interaction with the numbers. This is no part of ordinary mathematical methodology.

9. Alvin Goldman, "A Causal Theory of Knowing," *Journal of Philosophy* 64 (1967): 357–72. [Rosen's note.]

10. Compare G. E. Moore, "Proof of an External World," *Proceedings of the British Academy* 25 (1939): 273–300. [Rosen's note.] (This essay is excerpted in Chapter 6 of this anthology.)

Mathematicians don't pretend to observe the numbers or to detect them by means of instruments. Just as arithmetic itself is part of our commonsense starting point, so is the epistemological principle that the usual ways of doing arithmetic (calculation, proof, etc.) are perfectly good ways of arriving at mathematical knowledge. Given this, the causal theory of knowledge looks like a crude overgeneralization—a claim about knowledge in general that seems plausible only when we focus on *empirical* knowledge and ignore the mathematical knowledge that we know we have.[11]

This is another application of our master principle. When an ambitious philosophical claim is incompatible with our firm prephilosophical commitments, the reasonable response is to reject the philosophical claim until it can be supported by independent arguments. The causal theory of knowledge is incompatible with the prephilosophical claim that we know quite a bit about arithmetic. There are no compelling independent arguments for the theory. So we should reject it, and with it the indirect defense of physicalism that we have been discussing.

8

The case against physicalism may be summarized as follows:

a. Arithmetic assures us that there are two odd numbers between 6 and 10.

b. Arithmetic is part of our shared starting point. We accept it without reservation, as do the experts who are professionally concerned with such matters.

c. It is rational to affirm our starting point unless there are positive grounds for doubt.

d. There are no good scientific or mathematical reasons for doubting basic arithmetic.

e. Moreover, there are no good *philosophical* grounds for doubt. In particular, the arguments from simplicity and the causal theory of knowledge are unsuccessful.

f. Therefore, it is reasonable to accept the claims of arithmetic, including the claim that there are two odd numbers between 6 and 10.

g. Numbers are not physical objects. Unlike the concrete numeral tokens by means of which we refer to them, they do not possess physical properties such as mass and velocity.

h. Therefore, physicalism is false.

Physicalism is a seductive thesis. When first encountered, it can seem like the nat-ural expression in metaphysics of a hardheaded scientific worldview, one that rejects ghosts and gods and vital spirits and the like. But when we realize that physicalism

11. J. Burgess and G. Rosen, *A Subject with No Object* (Oxford University Press, 1997), 23–41. [Rosen's note.]

entails much more than this—that it entails the rejection of the claim that there are two odd numbers between 6 and 10—it becomes clear that physicalism is an unwarranted extrapolation from the sensible core of this hardheaded view. In its place, we might consider the weaker claim that every *concrete, causally efficacious* entity is a physical entity wholly composed of objects that admit of a complete description in the language of an ideal physics. Nothing in this essay refutes this view. If there is a version of physicalism worth defending, this is it.

TEST YOUR UNDERSTANDING

1. Rosen distinguishes numbers and numerals. Explain the distinction.

2. Rosen claims that the existence of numbers is incompatible with **physicalism**. Explain the basis for this claim.

3. Give fresh examples to illustrate the distinction between types and tokens.

4. True or false: Rosen rejects the causal theory of knowledge.

NOTES AND QUESTIONS

1. Rosen argues that we are **justified** in believing that numbers exist simply because (a) we already believe basic arithmetic, which **entails** the existence of numbers, and (b) science and (other areas of) mathematics have turned up no reason to doubt these basic claims. But is this enough to show that our arithmetical beliefs are *justified*? Suppose you meet a stranger from a distant land who says:

    > We have the same arithmetic that you have, and we use it exactly as you do. But it never occurred to us to <u>believe</u> in numbers. Arithmetic is just a useful tool. We sometimes <u>pretend</u> that in addition to the real physical objects we find around us, there are infinitely many nonphysical objects—1, 2, 3, . . . — just as you sometimes pretend that the surface of the earth is marked by lines of longitude and latitude. But you don't think the lines of longitude and latitude are real, and we don't think that these numbers are real. So why should we believe that arithmetic is more than just a useful fiction?

    How might Rosen respond? Suppose there is no good response. If you cannot provide these strangers with a reason to believe basic arithmetic, are your arithmetical beliefs then unjustified?

2. *Types and tokens.* Rosen's examples of nonphysical abstract entities include *types*, such as the numeral "2" (not the *tokens* of this numeral, of which there are many scattered around the world, but the type itself, of which there is only one). We certainly do take the existence of such things for granted in many contexts, but they are puzzling.

The numeral "2," for example, is rounded at the top and flat on the bottom, so it has a shape. But if we ask how big it is, the question obviously has no answer. According to our ordinary ways of thinking, then, the numeral is a thing with a shape but no size! Worse, when we consider the many ways in which tokens of the numeral can differ in shape—2, 2, 2, 2—we must conclude that even if the numeral has some sort of shape, it has no *particular* shape.

Exercise: Using these materials (or others), construct an argument for the claim that types do not exist. Then imagine how Rosen might respond.

Penelope Maddy (b. 1950)

Maddy is UCI Distinguished Professor of Logic and Philosophy of Science at the University of California, Irvine. She is the author of many important studies in the philosophy of mathematics, with a special focus on the search for new axioms in set theory.

DO NUMBERS EXIST?

We deal with ordinary counting numbers from our earliest years, but even mathematicians find it difficult to say what they are or even whether they exist. Given that simple arithmetic tells us, for example, that there's a number between 3 and 5, it's tempting to conclude that numbers do exist, that they are objects—much as stones and cats and planets are objects—on the straightforward grounds that arithmetic is true. We then note that numbers don't appear to be located anywhere in space, that they don't begin or end in time, that we don't pet them or trip over them or observe them in the night sky, which makes them different from cats and stones and planets. Unlike "concrete" or "physical" objects like these, numbers are "abstract."[1]

I don't exactly disbelieve this nice story, but I do think it misses some of what's most interesting and intriguing about numbers and arithmetic. Let me explain.

We first encounter numbers in perfectly ordinary circumstances of everyday life: we find three apples on the table, five fingers on each hand, nine players on the baseball diamond. It's natural to describe these experiences as encounters with numbers, but perhaps more accurately, what we encounter are apples, fingers, and baseball players—not numbers exactly, but numbering. In the baseball case, for someone sadly unfamiliar with the game, this numbering might involve explicit counting; in other cases, the result will be obvious at a glance. But what is it that's obvious here or detected by a counting routine?

---

1. For a defense of this view, see G. Rosen, "Numbers and Other Immaterial Objects" earlier in this chapter.

Now you might want to say that this ordinary visual experience or counting procedure has brought us into contact with the abstract object 3 or 5 or 9. This raises a question of what kind of contact this could be, given the lack of petting or tripping or observing,[2] but what troubles me more is that these ordinary situations don't seem on their face to involve anything other than the apples, fingers, and baseball players; what we've detected in each case appears to be simply a feature of that portion of the world. To get pedantic about it, there are, on the table, molecules held together in certain arrangements; some of these conglomerations of molecules are apples (a certain phase in a life cycle from seed, to tree, to fruit, to seed again); there is such a conglomeration here (pointing), another here (pointing again), yet another here (pointing yet again), and after these, there are no more such conglomerations on the table.[3] This is a simple fact about the stuff on the table, a fact that's truly described by saying three apples are there. Likewise for the fingers and the baseball players. Much as some of the apples are red, others green, some of the fingers longer than others; one of the baseball players is a pitcher, another a center fielder; the stuff on the table is three apples. In each case, some portion of the world is made of objects, and those objects have various properties and stand in various relations.

Understood in this way, "number" is a straightforward feature of a worldly situation, as real as any other property.[4] But concrete objects like apples aren't the only things we number: if you're lucky, a genie might grant you three wishes. I'll leave it to others to decide whether wishes are objects and if so of what kind; all I want to claim is this: in whatever sense we speak of a wish, another wish, and yet another wish, in that sense, it seems to me, we're entitled to speak of three wishes. What matters is that our subject, real or imagined, comes separated into distinct items with properties and relations: as long as that structure is present, the items, real or not, can be numbered. For simplicity, let's stick to the concrete.

So far, the number talk we've considered has involved the detection of number properties: the apples on the table have *the property of being three,* much as the individual apples have *the property of being red.* But claims like "there are three apples on the table" are only the entering wedge of our engagement with numbers. The argument for the existence of numbers sketched at the beginning is built on arithmetic, on claims like "$2 + 2 = 4$" or "there are three odd numbers between 2 and 8." As it happens, the understanding in terms of number properties can be extended to cases such as these: to say there are three odd numbers between 2 and 8 is to say that there are three

---

2. Professor Rosen explores this challenge in §7 of his essay earlier in this chapter, suggesting that our confidence that we do know about 3 and 5 and 9 shows that nothing like tripping or bumping is required. That may be right, but it leaves a lingering curiosity about how that knowledge *is* obtained, if not by this kind of contact.

3. Notice that the stuff on the table also consists of many more than three molecules of various sorts. That structure is equally real and that larger number property equally present. But the fact that various worldly structures can overlap or cross-cut each other doesn't show that any structure at all can be attributed willy-nilly or that the structures that are there aren't real.

4. The status of properties is part of the general problem of universals (see number 2 in the "Analyzing the Arguments" at the end of this chapter).

odd-number-properties between the-number-property-2 and the-number-property-8.[5] To say that $2 + 2 = 4$ is to say that if you have a batch of stuff with twoness and another (non-overlapping) batch of stuff with twoness, then you have a big batch of stuff with fourness. We can understand all this talk about numbers as talk about properties of ordinary things without appeal to any special abstract objects.

Of course, there's far more to arithmetic than simple existence claims like "there's a number between 3 and 5" and simple identities like "$2 + 2 = 4$." Our more sophisticated arithmetical beliefs include, for example, generalities like the commutativity of addition: adding n to m gives the same answer as adding m to n, no matter what numbers n and m might be. This too can be understood as a claim about the behavior of number properties: the number property of the result of combining a batch of stuff with the number property n and a non-overlapping batch with property m is the same as it would be if they were combined in the reverse order. More ambitiously, we believe that for any number, there's a next biggest number. We picture the numbers marching off into the distance without end, describing this with the suggestive notation of the dot-dot-dot: 1, 2, 3, 4. . . . Can this too be understood in terms of our down-to-earth number properties?

Let me sneak up on this question by asking another first: How do we come to believe that the numbers go on forever? As a matter of fact, this conviction comes rather late in childhood: youngsters of kindergarten age, despite a full grasp of counting and of elementary arithmetic, are often stumped by questions like "Is there a biggest of all numbers?" or "Is there a last number?" and even by leading questions like "If we count and count and count, will we ever get to the end of the numbers?" and "Can we always add one more or is there a number so big we'd have to stop?"[6] Asked to explain their answers, they suggest that we have to stop counting "because you need to eat breakfast and dinner" or "because we need sleep" and we couldn't start up again where we left off because "you forget where you stopped" or that an attempt to add one more after counting to a very big number might fail because "I guess you'll be old, very old."

The psychologists who conducted these experiments naturally classified responses like these as "unacceptable," but if we look at the question without preconceptions, there's a real sense in which these young children are right: there *are* limits to how far any of us is willing to count, and more to the point, there are physical limits on how high any of us—or even the human race, assuming it dies out eventually—*can* count. For that matter, as far as physicists have been able to determine, there may well be a limit on the number of particles in the universe, a limit on the number properties realized anywhere in the world. What makes the young children's answers "unacceptable" is that this isn't what we're thinking of when we ask if there's a largest number; we aren't thinking of the amount of breath we have or the fate of the human race or

---

5. Can you characterize "odd-number-property" and "between" for number properties?

6. See Penelope Maddy, "Psychology and the A Priori Sciences," to appear in S. Bangu (Ed.), *Naturalizing Logico-Mathematical Knowledge* (Routledge, forthcoming), for discussion and references. "A Second Philosophy of Arithmetic," *Review of Symbolic Logic* 7 (2014): 222–49, gives a more detailed version of the overall view presented in this essay.

the size of the physical universe. Where the young children have gone wrong is that they've failed to enter into the spirit of the question.

So what *are* we thinking of when we so confidently declare that there's no largest number? Why are we so dismissive of the child's concern that we might drop dead before we get around to counting the next number or the physicist's possibility that the universe might be finite? My suggestion is that the underlying line of thought here goes something like this: even if there are only finitely many number properties actually present in our world, this is just happenstance—*in principle,* there could be arbitrarily large arrangements of things. Even if I can only count finitely far in my lifetime, this is just an accidental impediment—*in principle,* I could always generate a new number by adding one. What the kindergarteners are missing is that the question isn't about what can actually be done or what actually exists, but about what holds *in principle.*

It turns out that second-graders do understand the question this way: they answer without hesitation that there is no largest number, end of story. So, what's changed between kindergarten and second grade that turned this into the utterly obvious answer? The relevant difference, the researchers found, was the older children's fluency with the various ways of generating numerical words and phrases, what philosophers call numerical "expressions." After the single digits (0–9), the teen words (eleven, twelve, thirteen, . . .), and the decade terms (twenty, thirty, forty, . . .) have all been memorized, the older children come to recognize the immensely useful shortcut that the digits repeat (twenty-one, twenty-two, . . . , thirty-one, thirty-two, . . .), and that, after 100, the decade terms too begin to repeat (one-hundred-and-ten, one-hundred-and-twenty, . . .). While the younger children are still at an early stage in this process, still memorizing the teen and decade terms, the older children have reached the point of seeing how these linguistic building blocks can be repeated, and from there, it's apparently an easy step to the conviction that they can be repeated *indefinitely.* So the puzzle becomes: What makes this step so easy?

Now even younger children know that if you've counted out three things and you add one more thing, then when you count them all again, you'll get four, the next number word in the counting sequence—they know, in other words, that the sequence of number properties marches in lockstep with the sequence of numerical expressions—but they apparently regard neither sequence in the *in principle* sense. The slightly older children, after more experience with the sequence of numerical expressions, see both in the *in principle* sense. Psychologists hypothesize that it's the conviction that the sequence of numerical expressions continues indefinitely (regardless of limitations of breath) that produces the conviction that arbitrarily large numerical properties are possible—*in principle.* We think there's no largest number property because we think there's no largest numerical expression.

This train of thought leaves us with one last question: When we become fluent in generating larger and larger numerical expressions, why is it so natural to move to the *in principle* understanding, to think that the sequence can be continued indefinitely? Why does any worry about the limits of breath or lifetime spontaneously fall away? I want to suggest that the answer traces to a simple fact about human language—a fact that separates it from the communication systems of even the most intelligent non-human animals—namely, that it's generative: at its core, there are a few basic elements and a set of rules that produce new expressions from old (think of "your father's friend, your father's father's friend, your father's father's father's friend . . . " or "the cat who saw the rat who ate the cheese that fell from the shelf . . . "). The current theory is that humans come equipped at birth with a generative learning mechanism that enables the young of our species to learn the full range of their native language from a small array of samples.[7] The encoded rules of this system are apparently fully general, with no special proviso for accidental limitations, despite the perfectly ordinary limitations we obviously encounter in practice. The suggestion, then, is that the unlimited generative rules of this inborn mechanism, on vivid display in the recurring patterns of ever-larger numerical expressions, is the unconscious source that makes it so natural to think the sequence continues indefinitely.

Assuming this is right—a big if, subject to empirical test—then the dot-dot-dot of arithmetic, our intuitive picture of the endless series of numbers, is grounded in an innate cognitive mechanism that's part of our genetic endowment as humans. Claims like "every number has a successor" are descriptions, not of the physical world, not of some independent realm of abstract objects, but of this shared human picture implicit in the psychological mechanisms that underlie our capacity for language. This means that arithmetic as a whole in fact serves two masters: on the one hand, it answers to ordinary number properties of ordinary things, properties we often simply see or discover by counting; on the other, it involves the dot-dot-dot, our idealized picture of the numbers going on forever, a picture entirely independent of how many ordinary physical things there actually are in nature. Nothing guarantees that the two will mesh successfully, that the sophisticated mathematical treatment of the shared picture might not imply, for example, false elementary identities like "3 = 5" or "2 + 2 = 5." Still, the apparent coherence of the picture and our long practical and mathematical experience with arithmetic provide some evidence that we aren't in for any such rude surprises down the road.

Which brings us back, at last, to the question addressed by the argument we opened with: Do numbers exist? On the view I've been sketching, simple claims like "there's a number between 3 and 5" and "2 + 2 = 4" are straightforward truths about the number properties exemplified in the world. If we take "numbers" to be these number properties, then they're on a par with other properties—like color or flexibility or being an infielder— and the question of their existence is subsumed under the larger question of the existence of properties, much discussed by metaphysicians.[8] I leave that debate to the experts. For our purposes, what matters is that when we take the apples on the table to have the number property three, the only objects involved are the apples, not some abstract object three.

Looking back at the argument itself, then, notice that it's simple claims like these that figure there as premises: the reader is expected to agree without hesitation that of course there's a number between 3 and 5, which is supposed to imply the existence of the abstract object 4. The trouble with this, we now see, is that the truth of "there's a number between 3 and 5" only guarantees the existence of a number property, not an abstract object. To reach beyond this, we have to call on idealized arithmetic—the full

---

7. For a readable account of this view of language, see S. Pinker, *The Language Instinct* (Harper Perennial, 1994).

8. See footnote 4.

force of the dot-dot-dot—for claims like "every number has a successor" or "there is no largest number." If these more sophisticated claims are true, what makes them true isn't garden-variety properties like the number of fingers on my right hand; instead, they're true in our intuitive picture of the numbers as objects marching off endlessly into the distance, objects just like stones and cats and planets except that they aren't spatial or temporal, can't be petted, tripped over, or observed. Our opening argument was intended to show that there are abstract objects, but it only works if it's based on sophisticated claims of idealized arithmetic, because it's only the truth of claims like this that actually require such things.[9] Would the argument be so compelling if the premise were "the numbers go on forever"?

Perhaps not, but what really matters is this: Are these stronger premises true? Does the argument establish the existence of abstract objects? Some philosophers would say that it does, that idealized arithmetic is true and thus that there are numbers, which are abstract objects. Other philosophers would say that it doesn't, that idealized arithmetic is an extremely useful theory, but that—like other idealizations—it's not literally true. Though it might jeopardize my membership in the philosophers' union, I'm not convinced that there's a fact of the matter about the existence or not of abstract "numbers" in this sense. I take the simple-minded position that ordinary science is where our inquiry into what's true and what exists begins. It tells us about those stones and cats and planets, and many other things detected by tests far finer and theorizing far more subtle. Along the way, we uncover simple number properties and the truths about them. Eventually, we take the step to the sophisticated arithmetic of the dot-dot-dot, a step guided not by the world but by our shared intuitive picture of numbers marching off endlessly into the distance. Up to that point, our understanding of "true" and "exist" has involved only concrete situations, known by ordinary scientific means, so the question before us now is whether the new mathematical enterprise of idealized arithmetic is just more of the same (where "true" and "exist" apply as before) or something else entirely (where truth and existence perhaps aren't the point).

In many ways, our pursuit of mathematical arithmetic *is* like our previous scientific investigations: it speaks of objects with properties, standing in relations; it uses the same logic; it values more general claims over less general ones (e.g., "for all numbers n and m, $n + m = m + n$" over "$2 + 3 = 3 + 2$"); and so on. However, its objects are abstract rather than concrete, and its methods too are quite different: one uses observation, experimentation, theory formation, and testing; the other uses axioms, definitions, and proofs. If you weigh the similarities more heavily than the differences, you're inclined to think that idealized arithmetic is well confirmed, most likely true, and as a result, that our argument shows there probably are abstract objects in addition to concrete ones. If, in contrast, you weigh the differences more heavily, you might think truth and existence aren't really what's at issue here; you might think we're using our shared intuitive picture of the endless number sequence to guide the development of

---

9. There might be metaphysical reasons to regard these "numbers" as properties rather than objects, but if so, those properties would still be detached from worldly exemplars in the same way, still quite different from ordinary number properties. So I ignore this nicety.

a mathematical theory that serves to organize and systematize the many simple truths about number properties—a mathematical theory that's been wonderfully effective in that role, as well as a source of the fascinating, purely mathematical elaborations of advanced number theory. On this second view, the only truths are the elementary ones; the rest is a theoretical apparatus, a story, in which those elementary truths have been embedded. The question, then, is which considerations are in fact more weighty, which of these understandings of arithmetic is correct. Is idealized arithmetic a well-confirmed theory of an abstract subject matter or a wonderfully effective perspective on ordinary number properties that's not really in the business of describing a domain of objects?

Most philosophers would insist that there's a right and a wrong answer here—though they differ sharply over which is which—but this is where my union membership comes under suspicion: I'm not so sure. Suppose we agree that the elementary claims like "2 + 2 = 4" are straightforward truths about the world and that the mathematical theory of the dot-dot-dot is guided by our intuition of the number sequence and serves to systematize the elementary claims. One side is inclined to conclude from this that the theory is true and numbers exist, the other that the theory is a wonderful thing, but not one where truth and existence are relevant. It seems to me that they're just describing the same facts, the facts they agree on, in different ways.

Consider for comparison a case from physical chemistry. When water is cooled very quickly, it forms a solid without the usual crystalline structure of ordinary ice, but with an amorphous structure more like that of glass. Some chemists speak of this as a kind of ice; they call it "amorphous ice." Others describe it as a distinct way that water can solidify; they call it an "ice-like solid." So who's right? It seems to me that there's no fact of the matter here; once we agree on the underlying facts about how water solidifies, those facts can be described either way. What I'm proposing is the analogous stance on numbers: once we agree on the underlying facts—about ordinary number properties, about the cognitive basis of our picture of the dot-dot-dot, about the role of mathematical arithmetic in organizing and systematizing the elementary truths about number properties—once we agree to all that, we can describe the situation either way, with "true" and "exist" or without.

But even if you disagree with this last potentially heretical move, I commend to your attention those underlying facts!

TEST YOUR UNDERSTANDING

1. Maddy claims that ordinary counting numbers are not **abstract objects** but rather **properties**. Give an example of a number property.

2. According to Maddy, what are we saying when we say that 2 + 3 = 5?

3. Maddy distinguishes ordinary arithmetic from idealized arithmetic. Explain the distinction.

4. Maddy gives a speculative psychological account of why we believe that the numbers go on forever. Briefly restate that account.

NOTES AND QUESTIONS

1. *Numbers as properties.* Maddy's paper is a response to Rosen's "Numbers and Other Immaterial Objects," which appeared earlier in this chapter. Rosen argues that ordinary counting numbers are immaterial abstract objects, and hence that there is more to reality than the physical world. Maddy maintains that this is a confusion. We can say that "the number of apples on the table is three," and that may look like a claim about the apples and another object: the number three. But in reality we have the apples, and they are *three.* The italicized phrase is not a name. It is a **predicate**, like "happy" in "Alicia is happy." Predicates don't stand for objects; they stand for properties. In the case of number properties, we can often see these properties just by looking or detect them by counting. (Think how easy it is to determine that there are three apples on the table.) So it's a mistake to think of numbers as invisible objects. They are ordinary properties that are often simply there for us to see.

   This raises a number of questions:

   a. What are number properties properties *of*? Suppose you have a Lego house made of 100 blocks. If numbers are properties of things like houses, then we can ask: Which number properties does this house have? It's one house; but it's also 100 blocks, a billion molecules, and so on. So does this single thing have *many* number properties: the property of being one, the property of being 100, and so forth?

   One answer is yes. A single object can't have many shapes or many colors (at a single time), but maybe a single object can have many number properties. Still it sounds odd to say that the house *is a billion.* That sounds like bad English.

   Another response abandons the claim numbers are properties of ordinary objects in favor of the view that numbers are properties of *sets* or *collections.* The set containing the 100 blocks

$$\{block_1, block_2, \ldots, block_{100}\}$$

   is not the same as the set containing the 1 billion molecules

$$\{molecule_1, molecule_2, \ldots, molecule_{1,000,000,000}\}$$

   Sets are distinct when they have different members. And these sets have different members, so they're distinct. The view that numbers are properties of sets avoids the odd conclusion that a single thing can have many number properties. The set of blocks will have the property of *having 100 members*; the set of molecules will have the property of *having a billion members.* But since these sets are distinct, no single thing will have both properties.

   Question: Would anything in Maddy's discussion require modification if she took the view that numbers are properties of sets?

   b. Where are the numbers? Maddy's aim is to take the metaphysical mystery out of mathematics: no spooky invisible objects, just ordinary properties that are often there for all to see. But as Maddy notes, properties are not entirely unmysterious. Suppose we have three apples on one table and three oranges on another. Each collection has the property three, according to Maddy. But where is this property? If we can see it, it must be there in front of us when we look at the apples, and also when we look at the oranges. Does that mean the property can be present in two places at once?

This points to an ancient debate about the nature of properties. Some philosophers hold that properties don't exist in space at all. Others hold that properties exist in the things that have them, and that unlike ordinary objects, properties can indeed be in several places at once. For discussion, see D. M. Armstrong, *Universals: An Opinionated Introduction* (Westview Press, 1989).

Question: Does Maddy's view require the assumption that properties exist in the things that have them? If Maddy adopted the alternative view (that properties don't exist in space at all), what would be the difference between her account and Rosen's?

2. *Do the numbers go on forever?* Standard arithmetic assumes that every number has a successor. Maddy regards this as an idealization that reflects certain deep aspects of our psychology, not as a discovery about what exists in reality. Her main argument for this is that for all we know, the physical universe is finite. Suppose there are in fact N things in the physical universe—where N is some enormous but finite number. There will then be no collection with $N + 1$ members in the physical world, and hence, for all we know, no such thing as the number $N + 1$.

But note: We can count apples and stars, but we can also count numbers (i.e., number properties). There are two odd numbers between 6 and 10, for example. But given this, we can *prove* that the numbers go on forever. Start with zero, as mathematicians normally do. Then argue as follows.

A collection whose only member is zero—$\{0\}$—exists. This collection has one member. So the property of having one member exists. This property is the number 1.
A collection whose only members are 0 and 1—$\{0, 1\}$—exists and has two members. So the property of having two members exists. This property is the number 2.
. . .
A collection whose only members are 0, . . . N exists and has $N + 1$ members. So the property of having $N + 1$ members exists. This property is the number $N + 1$.

The idea is that given *any* number M, the collection $\{0, \ldots M\}$ will have $M + 1$ members, and so the number $M + 1$ will exist. And from this it follows that the numbers *must* go on forever, even if there are only finitely many *physical* things.

If this is a sound argument, then Maddy need not regard "idealized arithmetic" as a speculative extrapolation. Even if there are only finitely many physical objects, there must be infinitely many number *properties*, hence infinitely many numbers. (This is a loosely adapted version of an argument due to Gottlob Frege in the founding text of modern philosophy of mathematics: *The Foundations of Arithmetic* [1884].)

Exercise: Make this argument fully explicit, spelling out every key assumption. Are any of these assumptions questionable?

ANALYZING THE ARGUMENTS

1. *Leibniz's law.* Many arguments in metaphysics rely on principles that are meant to apply, as a matter of absolute necessity, to absolutely everything. One of the most important examples is Leibniz's law (LL):

   LL: For any entities X and Y, $X = Y$ iff X and Y share all of their properties at any given time.

   This principle has two components:

   The indiscernibility of identicals: If $X = Y$, then X and Y share all of their properties at any given time.
   The identity of indiscernibles: If X and Y share all of their properties at any given time, then $X = Y$.

   Yablo's arguments rely only on the first of these principles. (*Exercise: Check this yourself.*) This principle is almost entirely uncontroversial, but consider the following apparent counterexample:

   Mark Twain = Samuel Clemens.
   Mark Twain is famous.
   Samuel Clemens is not famous.

   Exercise: Say how the defender of the indiscernibility of identicals should respond.

   The identity of indiscernibles has been much more controversial. Consider the following apparent counterexample due to Max Black ("The Identity of Indiscernibles," *Mind* 61 [1952]).

   Imagine a universe that consists only two iron spheres, A and B, each 1 meter in diameter, orbiting one another endlessly at a distance of 100 kilometers. Suppose the spheres are qualitatively indiscernible: the same shape, size, color, composition, and so forth. These spheres are not numerically identical: $A \neq B$. (There are two of them, after all.) But they have all of their properties in common. Each is round and made of iron; each is 100 kilometers from an iron sphere, floating in otherwise empty space, and so on.

   Exercise: Say how the defender of the identity of indiscernibles might respond.

2. *Objects and properties.* All the essays in this chapter speak freely both of objects and their properties. Any ontological theory that takes this way of speaking seriously must tell us what sort of thing a property is, and how properties are related to the objects that bear them. Consider, for example, *the property of weighing exactly 1 kilogram.* The instances of this property are physical objects (e.g., certain rocks). But what is the property itself like? It used to be common to say that properties exist only *in the mind.* But this implies that nothing had the property of *weighing 1 kilogram* before minds existed, and yet we know full well that there were rocks that weighed 1 kilogram before human beings were around to think about them. This suggests that properties, if they exist at all, must be *mind-independent* things.

According to one view—sometimes called *transcendent realism*—properties are abstract entities that do not exist in space. According to another view—sometimes called *immanent realism*—properties literally exist *in* their concrete instances. Both views are strange, and this has led some philosophers to suggest that properties do not exist at all: the rock may indeed weigh 1 kilogram; but there is no such thing as the *property of weighing 1 kilogram*. On this view—sometimes called *nominalism*—linguistic expressions such as "... weighs 1 kilogram," though obviously meaningful, do not stand for entities of any kind. According to the nominalist, treating these expressions as names of entities leads us on a wild-goose chase, positing entities that do not exist and asking unanswerable questions about what they are like. For a discussion of this ancient debate, see D. M. Armstrong, *Universals: An Opinionated Introduction* (Westview Press, 1989).

3. *Non-existent objects.* Consider the following argument.

   a. Ponce de León was searching for the Fountain of Youth.

   b. So Ponce de León was searching for *something*.

   c. But the Fountain of Youth does not exist.

   d. So there are things that do not exist.

The conclusion of this argument can sound harmless. Surely there are lots of things that don't exist: dragons, witches, the Greek gods,... But look more closely. The conclusion says that there *are* things that don't exist. But "There are..." and "There exist..." are basically synonyms in English. And to say that there *exist* things that don't exist is a contradiction. And anyway it sounds bizarre to suppose that there are non-existent things like the Fountain of Youth. If there are such things, where are they? Why can't we see them? Clearly something has gone wrong.

We might respond to the puzzle in several ways:

(1) We might deny (c). Of course, it would be ridiculous to maintain that the Fountain of Youth exists *as a real fountain*. But we might say: "There is indeed such a thing as the Fountain of Youth. But it is not a physical object, hence not a fountain. It is an abstract object, like a number."

(2) We might reject the transition from (a) to (b). Grammar is slippery; it sounds fine to say that Ponce de León was searching for *something*. But when we see where this leads, we should balk. We should say instead that while he was indeed searching, there is no thing that he was searching *for*. The phrase "Fountain of Youth," as it occurs in (a), does not stand for a thing of any kind.

(3) We might accept (d) and insist on a distinction between *being* and *existence*. On this view, everything we can think of has some sort of being, but only some things have real *existence*. (For an early version of this view, see Anselm's "Ontological Argument" in Chapter 1 of this anthology.)

Exercise: Explain and explore a solution to the problem posed by "non-existent objects."

For an important discussion of this topic, see W. V. O. Quine, "On What There Is," reprinted in his *From a Logical Point of View* (MIT Press, 1953).

4. When a philosopher presents an ontological theory that posits a certain category (type, token, property, event), she aims to provide a clear and explicit account of what it takes for a thing to belong to that category. Sometimes the category cannot be explained in more fundamental terms, so we must explain it by means of examples and informal hints. But this is always second best. One should always aim to provide explicit necessary and sufficient conditions for membership in a category.

Exercise: Consider the categories mentioned in the selections:

physical object, abstract entity, type, property . . .

In each case, attempt to produce an explicit account:

X is a physical object (etc.) if and only if X is . . .

Note: The philosophical terms you are analyzing may be vague, in which case any precise account will revise our understanding to some degree. That is to be expected. The aim of the exercise is not to conform exactly to ordinary usage or the usage of any particular philosopher. It is to provide a clear and useful account of the category—one that carves reality "at its joints," in Plato's phrase.

Part IV

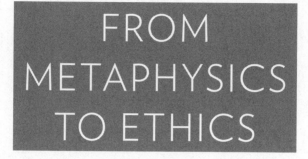

FROM
METAPHYSICS
TO ETHICS

What Is Personal Identity?

When you die, do you cease to exist? Is death The End? According to many religious traditions, no: bodily death is a mere transition to life in heaven or some other celestial realm, or perhaps to reincarnated life in another body on Earth. And even if death is the end at present, some think that future technology might defeat it. The futurist Ray Kurzweil, for instance, has predicted that by mid-century we will be able to "upload our knowledge, memories and insights into a computer," allowing us to enjoy a kind of "virtual life" inside a computer-generated virtual reality, somewhat as depicted in the movie *The Matrix*.[1]

Keeping our eyes on the future, suppose that the *Star Trek* fiction of "teletransportation" (or "teleportation") becomes fact. If you step into the transporter, your brain and body are instantly scanned, and the resulting information is beamed to your chosen destination, say Mars. On Mars, the receiving station instantly reconstructs your brain and body from new matter, exactly as it was on Earth.[2] The process of scanning vaporizes the original brain and body, but why should you care? Here you are on Mars, stepping out of the receiving station with a new brain and body that are just as good as the original. If you're afraid of teletransportation, that's like being afraid of flying—you should just try and get over it.

Now consider another scenario. Imagine a perfect three-dimensional (3D) photocopier, which can duplicate not just physical objects such as stones and tables, but also animals. Would you like another dog, exactly like your beloved Fido, to keep him company? No problem: place Fido on top of the photocopier, press "copy," and a perfect replica of Fido comes out of a chute on the side, barking and wagging his tail. You could even photocopy yourself, getting a perfect "identical twin."

Photocopying yourself would lead to all sorts of practical problems, of course, but being photocopied doesn't harm you in any way. Suppose, though, that the 3D

---

1. See www.kurzweilai.net/live-forever-uploading-the-human-braincloser-than-you-think. Kurzweil's view in this essay is somewhat similar to Derek Parfit's (see his essay in this chapter).

2. This is not quite how teletransportation works in *Star Trek,* but for our philosophical purposes it's better to think of teletransportation this way.

photocopier develops a fault: it produces a copy just as before, but now destroys the original in the process of scanning it. Would you photocopy yourself now? Surely not—that would be suicide! Perhaps having a replica around after your death to write your term papers and fool your family into thinking you are still alive is some compensation, but nowhere near enough.

Hold on a moment: What's the difference between teletransportation and the malfunctioning 3D photocopier? The product of teletransportation emerges at a great distance from the transporter, unlike the product of 3D photocopying, which emerges right next to the photocopier, but there doesn't seem to be any other significant difference. If so, "teletransportation" is not a means of *transportation* at all. Instead, the misleadingly named "transporter" is a device that destroys the person who steps into it and creates a replica at the receiving station. Instead of saying "Beam me up, Scotty," it would be more accurate to say "Kill me, Scotty." The person called "James T. Kirk" in this week's episode has not had an eventful life as a Starfleet captain after all! If he stepped out of the transporter chamber on the starship *Enterprise* yesterday, he is only one day old.

The issues raised above all concern our *survival*: What sorts of changes can we undergo and survive? Can we survive the destruction of our bodies? And does it matter if we don't? These questions are discussed in philosophy under the heading of "personal identity," the topic of the selections that follow.

Survival and Identity

Personal identity is a special case of a more general topic, the survival (or, as philosophers often say, the **persistence**) of objects over time. It is useful to have a little background in this more general topic when discussing the specific issue of our survival over time.

Commonsense opinion holds that inorganic things (e.g., rocks, laptops, and planets) and plants and animals typically come into existence at some time and cease to exist at a later time. For example, a certain cottage might come into existence when enough beams and bricks are assembled, and cease to exist a century later when it is demolished to make room for a McMansion. A mighty oak tree began life as a tiny green shoot, or perhaps an acorn, and will end its existence when it is sawn into planks.

The cottage and the oak survive a variety of events throughout their careers. The house survives a flood, say. That is, the house existed before the flood and also existed after the flood. We can put this in terms of "identity": the house existed before the flood, and something existed after the flood that was *identical* to the house.

Explaining what survival amounts to in terms of **identity** helps to clarify the notion, but it is potentially confusing. Suppose your house burns down and you build "an identical house" in its place. That is not a situation in which your house *survives*—it is a situation in which your house is destroyed and a replica is built in its place. Although your original house and the replica are "identical" in the sense that they are very *similar*, there is another sense in which they are *not* identical. There are *two* houses in the story, and in the "numerical" (or "strict") sense of "identity" *two* things are *never* identical. We have the strict or numerical sense in mind when we say that Lady Gaga and Stefani Germanotta are identical: we don't just mean that Gaga and Germanotta are *similar*, like your smart phone and your friend's smart phone. Gaga and Germanotta are not *two* at all. "They" are one and the same person, with two different names ("Lady Gaga" and "Stefani Germanotta"). Similarly, when we say "$3^2 = 9$," we are not saying that 3^2 and 9 are *two* numbers. We are instead speaking about *one* number with *two* names ("3^2" and "9"). Survival, then, should be defined in terms of strict or numerical identity. When we ask whether you will survive some event, our question is best understood as follows: Will there be someone around after the event who is numerically identical to *you*?

Houses can survive repainting and the addition of a porch; they cannot survive being reduced to ashes or having their parts scattered all at once. But what if the parts of your house are scattered and replaced over a long period of time? Imagine that your ancient family home has been lovingly repaired over the years so that now not a single brick or beam from the original construction remains—the crumbling bricks and rotted beams have been slowly replaced with period bricks and beams from architectural salvage. Has the original house survived? Not an easy question, but it's unlikely to keep you up at night. Sentiment or pure theoretical curiosity aside, it doesn't much matter whether this is (numerically) identical to the house your grandfather lived in, as opposed to one just like it that is built on the same spot. But from your point of view, there is at least one thing whose genuine survival seems to matter a great deal, namely *you*. Suppose you are told that your body will undergo some ordeal—brain surgery or teletransportation or physical death and resurrection—and that there will be someone around afterward who is like you in many ways. You might reasonably say: "That's all very well, but will that person be *me*?" A theory of personal identity is designed to shed light on this question.

A "Criterion of Personal Identity"

The philosophical literature on personal identity is often structured around a search for a **"criterion of personal identity."** This is an idea that can be difficult to understand, so it is worth spending some effort getting clear about it.

Suppose someone—call him or her "Casey"—exists at a certain time, say on Monday. Consider someone who exists the following Friday—call him or her "Drew." What would *absolutely guarantee* that Casey and Drew are numerically identical? In other words: What are **sufficient conditions** for Casey and Drew to be numerically identical? For example, suppose that Casey looks a lot like Drew: same hair color, same eyes, and so forth. Does that guarantee that Casey = Drew?

Now let's ask a different question: What *must be the case*, given that Casey and Drew are numerically identical? In other words: What are **necessary conditions** for Casey and Drew to be numerically identical? For example, given that Casey = Drew, must it be the case that Casey and Drew look alike?

We can write out these two suggestions for, respectively, a necessary condition and a sufficient condition a little more formally. First, the sufficient condition:

> It must be the case that: *if* Casey on Monday looks like Drew on Friday, then Casey, who exists on Monday = Drew, who exists on Friday.

Second, the necessary condition:

> It must be the case that: Casey, who exists on Monday = Drew, who exists on Friday, *only if* Casey on Monday looks like Drew on Friday.

If we generalize these two theses to all people and all times and combine them together, we get a thesis stating necessary *and* sufficient conditions for personal identity, which we can express as follows:

> *The Physical Appearance Criterion*: It must be the case that: A, who exists at t_1 = B, who exists at t_2, *if and only if* A at t_1 physically resembles B at t_2.

This is a *criterion of personal identity*. In general, a criterion of personal identity is a statement of the following form (leaving the "It must be the case that" implicit, and abbreviating "if and only if" as **"iff"**):

> A, who exists at t_1 = B, who exists at time t_2, iff _____.

The Physical Appearance Criterion has the right form, but it is obviously wrong. Sameness of appearance is not *sufficient* for numerical identity: "identical twins" may look alike, but they are not literally one and the same person. Nor is sameness of appearance *necessary* for numerical identity. Drew on Friday may look very different from Casey on Monday; but if Casey underwent cosmetic surgery on Tuesday, they may be the same person nonetheless.

The challenge is to fill in the blank so as to render the resulting statement *true*. Of course, there's an easy way to do that. Just replace the blank with "$A = B$"! Although the resulting statement is undeniably true, it is of absolutely no help in answering questions about our survival—whether we can survive bodily death, for instance. What we want is an *informative* replacement for the blank—one that does not presuppose the notion of identity that we are trying to understand. We should not assume that there *is* such a replacement, but that has certainly not stopped philosophers from trying.

One suggestion that might occur to you on reading Descartes's Meditation II (see Chapter 7 of this anthology) is this:

The Soul Criterion: A, who exists at t_1 = B, who exists at t_2, iff A's immaterial soul at t_1 = B's immaterial soul at t_2.

The Soul Criterion highlights something important about a criterion of personal identity. A criterion of personal identity is supposed to state *how things must be* if (and only if) A = B. It need not be an account of *how we tell* that A (say, someone we met last week) is identical to B (someone before us right now). We can often tell that A = B because A's physical appearance is the same as B's. But the corresponding criterion of identity, based on "same physical appearance," is mistaken. Conversely, it is no strike against the Soul Criterion that we do not find out that A = B by discovering that A has the same immaterial soul as B.

The Soul Criterion is defended in the selection by Richard Swinburne (who also emphasizes the point started in the previous paragraph). An obvious objection to the Soul Criterion is that the existence of immaterial souls is extremely controversial: if there are such things, you won't be learning about them in Psychology 101. In the selection by John Locke, you can find a subtler objection.

While the existence of our souls is debatable, the existence of our bodies seems plain enough. So a natural replacement for the Soul Criterion is this:

The Bodily Criterion: A, who exists at t_1 = B, who exists at t_2, iff A's body at t_1 = B's body at t_2.

Is this right? Imagine that you swap brains with someone else—call him or her "Emerson." (The selection by Swinburne discusses an example of this sort.) Emerson's brain is transplanted into your body, and your brain is transplanted into Emerson's. Suppose that medical technology is sufficiently well advanced so that after the operation there are two people, alive and well: one with Emerson's old body, and one with yours. Where are *you*? Where your original body is, or where Emerson's body is?

Many people think that in cases of this sort, you follow your brain and not your body. So perhaps a better suggestion is:

The Brain Criterion: A, who exists at t_1 = B, who exists at t_2, iff A's brain at t_1 = B's brain at t_2.

But again, there are objections. Imagine that you have some brain disease that will eventually destroy all your brain cells if left unchecked. Suppose that medical technology has advanced to the point where we can gradually replace each brain cell with a prosthetic artificial cell (a tiny device containing a silicon chip). At the end of the process, your brain has completely vanished, replaced by a prosthetic brain. If the artificial cells are sufficiently good, won't you still be around, thankful that the new technology has saved your life? But if you can survive the loss of your original brain, then the Brain Criterion is incorrect.

A quite different idea, proposed by Locke, is that our survival does not consist in the survival of a *thing*, like a soul, body, or brain, but rather in *psychological connections* across time. And Locke had a specific suggestion for what sorts of psychological connections are important; namely, those provided by memory. "[A]s far as this consciousness can be extended backwards to any past action or thought," he writes in his *Essay Concerning Human Understanding*, "so far reaches the identity of that person" (see section 9 of Locke's essay on page 507). This suggests the following:

> *The Memory Criterion: A*, who exists at t_1 = *B*, who exists at t_2, iff *B* can remember at t_2 (some of) the experiences of *A* at t_1.

The Memory Criterion implies that amnesia—perfect and total amnesia—amounts to death, and this may seem implausible. Faced with a grim choice between death and amnesia, a self-interested person might well choose amnesia as the lesser of two evils. "At least I'll still be around to start again," he might think. His friends and family might have a similar thought. And if this is right, then the Memory Criterion is unacceptable.

Many philosophers have tried to develop Locke's basic idea in a way that avoids this objection, among others. The most famous neo-Lockean theory of personal identity comes from Derek Parfit in his 1984 book *Reasons and Persons*. In the selection from that book given in this chapter, Parfit argues for a "psychological criterion" of personal identity—one that emphasizes various forms of psychological continuity over time, not just memory. But he also argues, astonishingly, that "personal identity is not what matters." According to Parfit, granted that the Psychological Criterion is correct, in some circumstances your survival should be of *no* concern to you! Compare the case in which the teletransporter functions properly and the case in which it malfunctions, creating *two* duplicates of the original body instead of one. In the latter case, Parfit argues, the original person does not survive. But from the point of view of the person himself, this case is not relevantly different from the case in which the machine works properly. In both cases, there is someone around after the event who is psychologically (though not physically) continuous with the original. The only difference is the *number* of such people. Parfit argues that no one should care very much about this numerical fact, and hence that no one should care very much about whether *he* will exist in the future. All that matters is that people will exist in the future who are psychologically continuous with us as we now are. Since genuine identity and psychological continuity normally go together in our experience, we confuse them and mistakenly think that personal identity is what matters when we worry about our own survival. According to Parfit, a correct account of the nature of personal identity can disabuse us of this error.

As the reader will have noticed, philosophical discussions of personal identity often invoke wild science-fiction thought experiments. We are asked to imagine a bizarre scenario involving brain swapping or teletransportation and to consult our "intuitions" about survival and identity. It is not hard to see why this method should be necessary. A philosophical theory of personal identity is meant to apply to every *possible* case. So we must consider far-out cases in order to assess our theories. And yet the method has its pitfalls. The problem is not that our judgments about far-out cases are uncertain, though that may be so. As Bernard Williams argues in his essay in this chapter, the problem is that a single case may elicit different intuitions when presented in different ways. In particular, cases that appear to refute the "bodily" criterion of personal identity can be reformulated so as to confirm it. If this is right, then the method of cases must be deployed with care. It is not useless, but it is fallible. As all of the authors in this chapter stress, the method must be supplemented by reflection on the deepest question in the area: "Why exactly does it *matter* whether I survive, and what could personal identity be that it should matter in this way?"

John Locke (1632–1704)

Locke was an English philosopher and medical doctor. His greatest work is *An Essay Concerning Human Understanding* (1689), which is about the limits of human knowledge. His *Two Treatises of Government* (1689) and *Letter Concerning Toleration* (1689), both published anonymously, made important contributions to political philosophy. The second *Treatise* gives a theory of legitimate government in terms of natural rights and the social contract. Locke's political views influenced the Founders of the United States, in particular Thomas Jefferson.

OF IDENTITY AND DIVERSITY
from *An Essay Concerning Human Understanding*

3. Let us suppose an atom . . . existing in a determined time and place; it is evident, that, considered in any instant of its existence, it is in that instant the same with itself. For, being at that instant what it is, and nothing else, it is the same, and so must continue as long as its existence is continued. In like manner, if two or more atoms be joined together into the same mass, every one of those atoms will be the same, by the foregoing rule: and whilst they exist united together, the mass, consisting of the same atoms, must be the same mass, or the same body, let the parts be ever so differently jumbled. But if one of these atoms be taken away, or one new one added, it is no longer the same mass or the same body. In the state of living creatures, their identity depends not on a mass of the same particles, but on something else. For in them the variation

of great parcels of matter alters not the identity: an oak growing from a plant to a great tree, and then lopped, is still the same oak; and a colt grown up to a horse, sometimes fat, sometimes lean, is all the while the same horse: though, in both these cases, there may be a manifest change of the parts; so that truly they are not either of them the same masses of matter, though they be truly one of them the same oak, and the other the same horse. The reason whereof is, that, in these two cases—a mass of matter and a living body—identity is not applied to the same thing.

4. We must therefore consider wherein an oak differs from a mass of matter, and that seems to me to be in this, that the one is only the cohesion of particles of matter any how united, the other such a disposition of them as constitutes the parts of an oak; and such an organization of those parts as is fit to receive and distribute nourishment, so as to continue and frame the wood, bark, and leaves, &c., of an oak, in which consists the vegetable life. That being then one plant which has such an organization of parts in one coherent body, partaking of one common life, it continues to be the same plant as long as it partakes of the same life, though that life be communicated to new particles of matter vitally united to the living plant, in a like continued organization conformable to that sort of plants.

5. The case is not so much different in *brutes*.[1] . . . Something we have like this in machines, and may serve to illustrate it. For example, what is a watch? It is plain it is nothing but a fit organization or construction of parts to a certain end, which, when a sufficient force is added to it, it is capable to attain. If we would suppose this machine one continued body, all whose organized parts were repaired, increased, or diminished by a constant addition or separation of insensible parts, with one common life, we should have something very much like the body of an animal; with this difference, That, in an animal the fitness of the organization, and the motion wherein life consists, begin together, the motion coming from within; but in machines the force coming sensibly from without, is often away when the organ is in order, and well fitted to receive it.

6. This also shows wherein the identity of the same *man*[2] consists; viz. in nothing but a participation of the same continued life, by constantly fleeting particles of matter, in succession vitally united to the same organized body. He that shall place the identity of man in anything else . . . will find it hard to make an embryo, one of years, mad and sober, the same man, by any supposition, that will not make it possible for Seth, Ismael, Socrates, Pilate, St. Austin, and Caesar Borgia, to be the same man.[3] For if the identity of soul alone makes the same man; and there be nothing in the nature of matter why the same individual spirit may not be united to different bodies, it will be possible that those men, living in distant ages, and of different tempers, may have been the same man: which way of speaking must be from a very strange use of the word

---

1. Non-human animals.

2. Locke distinguishes the claim that *A* and *B* are the same *man*—that is, the same human animal—from the claim that *A* and *B* are the same *person*. The point of this paragraph is to insist that even if we possess immaterial souls, the fact that *A* and *B* share the same soul is not enough to make them one and the same man.

3. Seth and Ismael (Ishmael): characters in the biblical book of Genesis. Socrates: Greek philosopher (c. 469–399 BCE). (Pontius) Pilate: judge at the trial of Jesus. St. Austin (Augustine of Hippo): Christian theologian (354–430). Cesare Borgia: Italian politician and cardinal (1475/6–1507).

man, applied to an idea out of which body and shape are excluded. And that way of speaking would agree yet worse with the notions of those philosophers who allow of transmigration, and are of opinion that the souls of men may, for their miscarriages, be detruded[4] into the bodies of beasts, as fit habitations, with organs suited to the satisfaction of their brutal inclinations. But yet I think nobody, could he be sure that the soul of Heliogabalus[5] were in one of his hogs, would yet say that hog were a man or Heliogabalus. . . .

8. An animal is a living organized body; and consequently the same animal, as we have observed, is the same continued life communicated to different particles of matter, as they happen successively to be united to that organized living body. And whatever is talked of other definitions, ingenuous observation puts it past doubt, that the idea in our minds, of which the sound *man* in our mouths is the sign, is nothing else but of an animal of such a certain form. Since I think I may be confident, that, whoever should see a creature of his own shape or make, though it had no more reason all its life than a cat or a parrot, would call him still a man; or whoever should hear a cat or a parrot discourse, reason, and philosophize, would call or think it nothing but a cat or a parrot; and say, the one was a dull irrational man, and the other a very intelligent rational parrot.

9. This being premised, to find wherein *personal identity* consists, we must consider what *person* stands for; which, I think, is a thinking intelligent being, that has reason and reflection, and can consider itself as itself, the same thinking thing, in different times and places; which it does only by that consciousness which is inseparable from thinking: it being impossible for any one to perceive without perceiving that he does perceive. When we see, hear, smell, taste, feel, meditate, or will anything, we know that we do so. Thus it is always as to our present sensations and perceptions: and by this every one is to himself that which he calls *self*: it not being considered, in this case, whether the same self be continued in the same or divers substances. For, since consciousness always accompanies thinking, and it is that which makes every one to be what he calls *self*, and thereby distinguishes himself from all other thinking things, in this alone consists personal identity, i.e. the sameness of a rational being: and as far as this consciousness can be extended backwards to any past action or thought, so far reaches the identity of that *person*; it is the same *self* now it was then; and it is by the same *self* with this present one that now reflects on it, that that action was done.

10. But it is further inquired, whether it be the same identical substance.[6] This few would think they had reason to doubt of, if these perceptions, with their consciousness, always remained present in the mind. . . . But that which seems to make the difficulty is this, that this consciousness being interrupted always by forgetfulness, there being no moment of our lives wherein we have the whole train of all our past actions before

---

4. Pushed.

5. Roman emperor for the period 218–222.

6. An animal persists through time even though the matter that composes it may change completely. The cub that exists in 1985 may be the same animal as the mature lion that exists in 1995 even though they have no material parts in common. In Locke's terminology, this is a case in which we have a persisting *animal* but no persisting **substance**. The point of this paragraph is to insist that a *person* may similarly persist even though no substance persists in it.

our eyes in one view, but even the best memories losing the sight of one part whilst they are viewing another; and we sometimes, and that the greatest part of our lives, not reflecting on our past selves, being intent on our present thoughts, and in sound sleep having no thoughts at all, or at least none with that consciousness which remarks our waking thoughts; I say, in all these cases, our consciousness being interrupted, and we losing the sight of our past selves, doubts are raised whether we are the same thinking thing, i.e. the same substance or no. Which, however reasonable or unreasonable, concerns not *personal identity* at all. The question being what makes the same *person*; and not whether it be the same identical substance, which always thinks in the same person: different substances, by the same consciousness (where they do partake in it) being united into one person, as well as different bodies by the same life are united into one animal, whose identity is preserved in that change of substances by the unity of one continued life. For, it being the same consciousness that makes a man be himself to himself, personal identity depends on that only, whether it be annexed solely to one individual substance, or can be continued in a succession of several substances. For as far as any intelligent being can repeat the idea of any past action with the same consciousness it had of it at first, and with the same consciousness it has of any present action; so far it is the same personal self. For it is by the consciousness it has of its present thoughts and actions, that it is self to itself now, and so will be the same self, as far as the same consciousness can extend to actions past or to come, and would be by distance of time, or change of substance, no more two persons, than a man be two men by wearing other clothes to-day than he did yesterday, with a long or a short sleep between: the same consciousness uniting those distant actions into the same person, whatever substances contributed to their production.

11. That this is so, we have some kind of evidence in our very bodies, all whose particles, whilst vitally united to this same thinking conscious self, so that we feel when they are touched, and are affected by, and conscious of good or harm that happens to them, as a part of ourselves; i.e. of our thinking conscious self. Thus, the limbs of his body are to every one a part of Himself; he sympathizes and is concerned for them. Cut off a hand, and thereby separate it from that consciousness he had of its heat, cold, and other affections, and it is then no longer a part of that which is himself, any more than the remotest part of matter. Thus, we see the substance whereof personal self consisted at one time may be varied at another, without the change of personal identity; there being no question about the same person, though the limbs which but now were a part of it, be cut off.

12. But the question is, Whether if the same substance which thinks be changed, it can be the same person; or, remaining the same, it can be different persons? And to this I answer: First, This can be no question at all to those who place thought in a purely material animal constitution, void of an immaterial substance.[7] For, whether their supposition be true or no, it is plain they conceive personal identity preserved in something

---

7. Locke alludes to a dispute over whether the thing that thinks in us is material or immaterial. Locke takes the latter view to be "more probable" *(Essay* II, xxvii.25) but insists that no matter how this dispute is resolved, A and B may be the same person even though the substance that thinks in A is distinct from the substance that thinks in B.

else than identity of substance; as animal identity is preserved in identity of life, and not of substance. And therefore those who place thinking in an immaterial substance only, before they can come to deal with these men, must show why personal identity cannot be preserved in the change of immaterial substances, or variety of particular immaterial substances, as well as animal identity is preserved in the change of material substances.

13. As to the first part of the question, Whether, if the same thinking substance (supposing immaterial substances only to think) be changed, it can be the same person? I answer, that cannot be resolved but by those who know what kind of substances they are that do think; and whether the consciousness of past actions can be transferred from one thinking substance to another. . . . But yet, . . . , it must be allowed, that, if the same consciousness can be transferred from one thinking substance to another, it will be possible that two thinking substances may make but one person. For the same consciousness being preserved, whether in the same or different substances, the personal identity is preserved.

14. As to the second part of the question, Whether the same immaterial substance remaining, there may be two distinct persons; which question seems to me to be built on this, Whether the same immaterial being, being conscious of the action of its past duration, may be wholly stripped of all the consciousness of its past existence, and lose it beyond the power of ever retrieving it again: and so as it were beginning a new account from a new period, have a consciousness that cannot reach beyond this new state. . . . Suppose a Christian Platonist or a Pythagorean[8] should, upon God's having ended all his works of creation the seventh day, think his soul hath existed ever since; and should imagine it has revolved in several human bodies; as I once met with one, who was persuaded his had been the soul of Socrates (how reasonably I will not dispute); . . . would any one say, that he, being not conscious of any of Socrates's actions or thoughts, could be the same person with Socrates? Let any one reflect upon himself, and conclude that he has in himself an immaterial spirit, which is that which thinks in him, and, in the constant change of his body keeps him the same: and is that which he calls himself: let him also suppose it to be the same soul that was in Nestor or Thersites,[9] at the siege of Troy, (for souls being, as far as we know anything of them, in their nature indifferent to any parcel of matter, the supposition has no apparent absurdity in it . . .): but he now having no consciousness of any of the actions either of Nestor or Thersites, does or can he conceive himself the same person with either of them? Can he be concerned in either of their actions? Attribute them to himself, or think them his own, more than the actions of any other men that ever existed? So that this consciousness, not reaching to any of the actions of either of those men, he is no more one self with either of them than if the soul or immaterial spirit that now informs him had been created, and began to exist, when it began to inform his present body; though it were never so true, that the same

---

8. The followers of Pythagoras (sixth century BCE) were said to believe in the transmigration of souls, according to which a single thinking soul can, at death, move from one body to another. Many Christian theologians follow Plato in endorsing the immortality and immateriality of the soul; however, the Church has consistently rejected the Pythagorean doctrine of transmigration.

9. Greek mythological figures, both said by Homer to have participated in the siege of Troy.

spirit that informed Nestor's or Thersites' body were numerically the same that now informs his. For this would no more make him the same person with Nestor, than if some of the particles of matter that were once a part of Nestor were now a part of this man; the same immaterial substance, without the same consciousness, no more making the same person, by being united to any body, than the same particle of matter, without consciousness, united to any body, makes the same person. But let him once find himself conscious of any of the actions of Nestor, he then finds himself the same person with Nestor. . . .

16. [Thus] it is plain, consciousness, as far as ever it can be extended, should it be to ages past, unites existences and actions very remote in time into the same person, as well as it does the existences and actions of the immediately preceding moment: so that whatever has the consciousness of present and past actions, is the same person to whom they both belong. Had I the same consciousness that I saw the ark and Noah's flood, as that I saw an overflowing of the Thames[10] last winter, or as that I write now, I could no more doubt that I who write this now, that saw the Thames overflowed last winter, and that viewed the flood at the general deluge, was the same self, place that self in what substance you please, than that I who write this am the same myself now whilst I write (whether I consist of all the same substance, material or immaterial, or no) that I was yesterday. For as to this point of being the same self, it matters not whether this present self be made up of the same or other substances, I being as much concerned, and as justly accountable for any action that was done a thousand years since, appropriated to me now by this self-consciousness, as I am for what I did the last moment. . . .

19. This may show us wherein personal identity consists: not in the identity of substance, but, as I have said, in the identity of consciousness, wherein if Socrates and the present mayor of Quinborough agree, they are the same person: if the same Socrates waking and sleeping do not partake of the same consciousness, Socrates waking and sleeping is not the same person. And to punish Socrates waking for what sleeping Socrates thought, and waking Socrates was never conscious of, would be no more of right, than to punish one twin for what his brother-twin did, whereof he knew nothing, because their outsides were so like, that they could not be distinguished; for such twins have been seen.

20. But yet possibly it will still be objected, suppose I wholly lose the memory of some parts of my life, beyond a possibility of retrieving them, so that perhaps I shall never be conscious of them again; yet am I not the same person that did those actions, had those thoughts that I once was conscious of, though I have now forgot them? To which I answer, that we must here take notice what the word *I* is applied to; which, in this case, is the man only. And the same man being presumed to be the same person, *I* is easily here supposed to stand also for the same person. But if it be possible for the same man to have distinct incommunicable consciousness at different times, it is past doubt the same man would at different times make different persons; which, we see, is the sense of mankind in the solemnest declaration of their opinions, human laws not punishing the mad man for the sober man's actions, nor the sober man for what

---

10. River running through London.

the mad man did, thereby making them two persons: which is somewhat explained by our way of speaking in English when we say such an one is "not himself," or is "beside himself"; in which phrases it is insinuated, as if those who now, or at least first used them, thought that self was changed; the selfsame person was no longer in that man. . . .

22. But is not a man drunk and sober the same person? why else is he punished for the fact he commits when drunk, though he be never afterwards conscious of it? Just as much the same person as a man that walks, and does other things in his sleep, is the same person, and is answerable for any mischief he shall do in it. Human laws punish both, with a justice suitable to their way of knowledge; because, in these cases, they cannot distinguish certainly what is real, what counterfeit: and so the ignorance in drunkenness or sleep is not admitted as a plea. For, though punishment be annexed to personality, and personality to consciousness, and the drunkard perhaps be not conscious of what he did, yet human judicatures justly punish him; because the fact is proved against him, but want of consciousness cannot be proved for him. But in the Great Day,[11] wherein the secrets of all hearts shall be laid open, it may be reasonable to think, no one shall be made to answer for what he knows nothing of, but shall receive his doom,[12] his conscience accusing or excusing him. . . .

26. *Person*, as I take it, is the name for this self. Wherever a man finds what he calls himself, there, I think, another may say is the same person. It is a forensic[13] term, appropriating actions and their merit; and so belongs only to intelligent agents, capable of a law, and happiness, and misery. This personality extends itself beyond present existence to what is past, only by consciousness, whereby it becomes concerned and accountable; owns and imputes to itself past actions, just upon the same ground and for the same reason as it does the present. All which is founded in a concern for happiness, the unavoidable concomitant of consciousness; that which is conscious of pleasure and pain, desiring that that self that is conscious should be happy. And therefore whatever past actions it cannot reconcile or appropriate to that present self by consciousness, it can be no more concerned in than if they had never been done: and to receive pleasure or pain, i.e. reward or punishment, on the account of any such action, is all one as to be made happy or miserable in its first being, without any demerit at all. For, supposing a man punished now for what he had done in another life, whereof he could be made to have no consciousness at all, what difference is there between that punishment and being created miserable? And therefore, conformable to this, the Apostle[14] tells us, that, at the Great Day, when every one shall "receive according to his doings, the secrets of all hearts shall be laid open." The sentence shall be justified by the consciousness all persons shall have, that they themselves, in what bodies soever they appear, or what substances soever that consciousness adheres to, are the same that committed those actions, and deserve that punishment for them.

---

11. The biblical day of judgment.

12. Judgment.

13. Pertaining to the law.

14. Paul the Apostle (c. 5–c. 67).

TEST YOUR UNDERSTANDING

1. Secretariat starts off as a foal in 1970, eats and drinks and grows larger, and then 3 years later wins the Kentucky Derby. According to Locke, cases of this sort show that a horse is not a "mass of matter." Explain why.

2. Locke distinguishes the claim that X and Y are the same *man* from the claim that X and Y are the same *person*. Explain the distinction.

3. State Locke's criterion of personal identity by completing the sentence:

   According to Locke, a later person Y is identical to an earlier person X if and only if . . .

4. In every state in the United States, a person who commits a crime when drunk can be punished when he sobers up, even if he can't remember anything about the crime. Is Locke's view consistent with this practice?

NOTES AND QUESTIONS

1. *Locke against the Soul Theory.* Locke argues that even if you have an immaterial soul, the persistence of your soul is neither necessary nor sufficient for personal survival. A soul in the relevant sense is an immaterial thinking substance whose thoughts can in principle be "erased" or transferred to another soul. (A soul is like an immaterial computer hard drive.) Given this view of what a soul would be, Locke argues as follows.

   a. The soul in you now could be the soul that was in Heliogabalus (a famously debauched Roman emperor), but if the soul has been completely erased, so that you have no memory whatsoever of his crimes, you are not responsible for his crimes, and are therefore not the same person. This shows that "sameness of soul" is not sufficient for sameness of person.

   b. For all we know, the soul associated with your body is replaced every night while you're sleeping with a new soul into which the old memories have been transferred. So if the soul theory were true, it would be an open question whether ordinary people survive a good night's sleep. But this is *not* an open question. This shows that "sameness of soul" is not necessary for sameness of person.

   Exercise: Make these arguments fully explicit and then imagine how a proponent of the Soul Theory might respond.

   For a modern presentation of Locke's arguments, see John Perry, *A Dialogue on Personal Identity and Immortality* (Hackett, 1978).

2. In section 9, Locke defines a person as "a thinking, intelligent being, that has reason and reflection, and can consider itself as itself, the same thing, in different times and places." Many writers have noted that if this is what a person is, then it is quite

unclear whether human infants and certain cognitively disabled human beings count as persons.

Exercise: Develop an objection to Locke's theory of personal identity on this basis and imagine how Locke might respond.

3. Locke holds that a later person is the same as some earlier person when the later person *partakes in the same consciousness* as the earlier person. But what does this mean? Locke clearly thinks that ordinary memory is sufficient. If the later person can remember some experience of the earlier person, then they both partake in the consciousness of that event and are thus the same person. But consider the following odd possibilities:

   a. Marvin is obsessed with Bill Clinton; he has studied his life and has come to have what he takes to be vivid memories of Clinton's experiences as president. In fact, Marvin's memories are completely accurate.

   b. A mad scientist has scanned Clinton's brain and implanted accurate versions of some of Clinton's memories into Marvin.

   c. Marvin is hit on the head and by shear coincidence has acquired accurate apparent "memories" of Clinton's time in office.

   Does Locke's theory entail that Marvin is Bill Clinton in these cases? That would be absurd, so it better not.

   Exercise: Set out a version of Locke's theory that does not have this result and assess its merits.

4. Alice is hit on the head and suffers complete and irreversible amnesia. She can't remember her name and has no memories of her former life. Still, she retains her personality, her quirky sense of humor, her love of jazz, and other aspects of her psychology.

   Question: Does Locke's theory imply that Alice has not survived her injury? Is that a plausible result? If not, how might Locke's theory be modified so as to avoid this implication.

5. All modern discussions of personal identity are reactions to Locke's views in this chapter from his *Essay Concerning Human Understanding* (1689). (The chapter does not appear in the first edition of the *Essay*, but was added to the second edition.) As you will have discovered from reading the selection, Locke's views on personal identity are not especially clear. For discussion, see chapter 2 of Harold Noonan, *Personal Identity* (Routledge, 2003), and Galen Strawson, *Locke on Personal Identity: Consciousness and Concernment*, revised edition (Princeton University Press, 2014).

Richard Swinburne (b. 1934)

Swinburne is Nolloth Professor Emeritus of the Philosophy of the Christian Religion at the University of Oxford. His books include *The Coherence of Theism*, revised edition (1993), *Providence and the Problem of Evil* (1998), and, most recently, *Mind, Brain, and Free Will* (2013).

THE DUALIST THEORY
from *Personal Identity*

There seems no contradiction in the supposition that a person might acquire a totally new body (including a completely new brain)—as many religious accounts of life after death claim that men do. To say that this body, sitting at the desk in my room, is my body is to say two things. First it is to say that I can move parts of this body (arms, legs, etc.), just like that, without having to do any other intentional action and that I can make a difference to other physical objects only by moving parts of this body. By holding the door handle and turning my hand, I open the door. By bending my leg and stretching it I kick the ball and make it move into the goal. But I do not turn my hand or bend my leg by doing some other intentional action; I just do these things. Secondly, it is to say that my knowledge of states of the world outside this body is derived from their effects on this body—I learn about the positions of physical objects by seeing them, and seeing them involves light rays reflected by them impinging on my eyes and setting up nervous impulses in my optic nerve. My body is the vehicle of my agency in the world and my knowledge of the world. But then is it not coherent to suppose that I might suddenly find that my present body no longer served this function, that I could no longer acquire information through these eyes or move these limbs, but might discover that another body served the same function? I might find myself moving other limbs and acquiring information through other eyes. Then I would have a totally new body. If that body, like my last body, was an occupant of Earth, then we would have a case of reincarnation, as Eastern religions have understood that. If that body was an occupant of some distant planet or an environment which did not belong to the same space as our world, then we would have a case of resurrection as on the whole Western religions (Christianity, Judaism and Islam) have understood that.

This suggestion of a man acquiring a new body (with brain) may be more plausible, to someone who has difficulty in grasping it, by supposing the event to occur gradually. Suppose that one morning a man wakes up to find himself unable to control the right side of his body, including his right arm and leg. When he tries to move the right-side parts of his body, he finds that the corresponding left-side parts of his body move; and when he tries to move the left-side parts, the corresponding right-side parts of his wife's body move. His knowledge of the world comes to depend on stimuli to his left side and to his wife's right side (e.g., light rays stimulating his left eye and his wife's right eye). The bodies fuse to some extent physiologically as with Siamese twins, while the man's wife loses control of her right side. The focus of the man's control of and knowledge of the world is shifting. One may suppose the process completed as the man's control is shifted to the wife's body, while the wife loses control of it.

Equally coherent, I suggest, is the supposition that a person might become disembodied. A person has a body if there is one particular chunk of matter through which he has to operate on and learn about the world. But suppose that he finds himself able to operate on and learn about the world within some small finite region, without having to use one particular chunk of matter for this purpose. He might find himself with knowledge of the position of objects in a room (perhaps by having visual sensations, perhaps not), and able to move such objects just like that, in the ways in which we know about the positions of our limbs and can move them. But the room would not be, as it were, the person's body; for we may suppose that simply by choosing to do so he can gradually shift the focus of his knowledge and control, e.g., to the next room. The person would be in no way limited to operating and learning through one particular chunk of matter. Hence we may term him disembodied. The supposition that a person might become disembodied also seems coherent.

I have been arguing so far that it is coherent to suppose that a person could continue to exist with an entirely new body or with no body at all. . . . Could a person continue to exist without any apparent memory of his previous doings? Quite clearly, we do allow not merely the logical possibility, but the frequent actuality of amnesia—a person forgetting all or certain stretches of his past life. Despite Locke, many a person does forget much of what he has done. But, of course, we normally only suppose this to happen in cases where there is the normal bodily and brain continuity. Our grounds for supposing that a person forgets what he has done are that the evidence of bodily and brain continuity suggests that he was the previous person who did certain things, which he now cannot remember having done. And in the absence of both of the main kinds of evidence for personal identity, we would not be justified in supposing that personal identity held. . . . For that reason I cannot describe a case where we would have good reason to suppose that P_2 was identical with P_1, even though there was neither brain continuity nor memory continuity between them. However, only given verificationist dogma[1] is there any reason to suppose that the only things which are true are those of whose truth we can have evidence. . . . We can make sense of states of affairs being true, of which we can have no evidence that they are true. And among them surely is the supposition that the person who acquires another body loses not merely control of the old one, but memories of what he did with its aid. . . .

Those who hope to survive their death, despite the destruction of their body, will not necessarily be disturbed if they come to believe that they will then have no memory of their past life on Earth; they may just want to survive and have no interest in continuing to recall life on Earth. Again, apparently, there seems to be no contradiction involved in their belief. . . .

Not merely is it not logically necessary that a person have a body made of certain matter, or have certain apparent memories, if he is to be the person which he is; it is not even necessitated by laws of nature. For let us assume that natural laws dictated the course of evolution and the emergence of consciousness. In 4000 million BC the Earth was a cooling globe of inanimate atoms. Natural laws then, we assume, dictated how this globe would evolve, and so which arrangements of matter will be the bodies of conscious men, and just how apparent memories of conscious men depend on their brain states. My point now is that what natural laws in no way determine is which animate body is yours and which is mine. Just the same arrangement of matter and

1. Verificationism is the view that a statement is meaningful—and therefore capable of being true—only if it can in principle be supported by evidence. Swinburne argues against verificationism in Sydney Shoemaker and Richard Swinburne, *Personal Identity* (Blackwell, 1984), chapter 3.

just the same laws could have given to me the body (and so the apparent memories) which are now yours, and to you the body (and so, the apparent memories) which are now mine. It needs either God or chance to allocate bodies to persons; the most that natural laws determine is that bodies of a certain construction are the bodies of some person or other, who in consequence of this construction have certain apparent memories. Since the body which is presently yours (together with the associated apparent memories) could have been mine (logic and even natural laws allow), that shows that none of the matter of which my body is presently made (nor the apparent memories) is essential to my being the person I am. That must be determined by something else. . . .

I could just leave my positive theory at that—that personal identity is unanalyzable.[2] But it will, I hope, be useful to express it in another way, to bring out more clearly what it involves and to connect it with another whole tradition of philosophical thought.

[According to] Aristotle's account of the identity of substances: . . . a substance at one time is the same substance as a substance at an earlier time if and only if the later substance has the same form as, and continuity of matter . . . with, the earlier substance.[3] On this view a person is the same person as an earlier person if he has the same form as the earlier person (i.e., both are persons) and has continuity of matter with him (i.e., has the same body).

Certainly, to be the same person as an earlier person, a later person has to have the same form—i.e., has to be a person. If my arguments for the logical possibility of there being disembodied persons are correct, then the essential characteristics of a person constitute a narrower set than those which Aristotle would have included. My arguments suggest that all that a person needs to be a person are certain mental capacities—for having conscious experiences (e.g., thoughts or sensations) and performing intentional actions. Thought-experiments of the kind described earlier allow that a person might lose his body, but they describe his continuing to have conscious experiences and his performing or being able to perform intentional actions, i.e., to do actions which he means to do, bring about effects for some purpose.

Yet if my arguments are correct, showing that two persons can be the same, even if there is no continuity between their bodily matter, we must say that in the form stated the Aristotelian account of identity applies only to inanimate objects and plants and has no application to personal identity. We are then faced with a choice either of saying that the criteria of personal identity are different from those for other substances, or of trying to give a more general account than Aristotle's of the identity of substances which would cover both persons and other substances. It is possible to widen the Aristotelian account so that we can do the latter. We have only to say that two substances are the same if and only if they have the same form and there is continuity of the stuff of which they are made, and allow that there may be kinds of stuff

2. To **"analyze"** personal identity would be to provide a general account of the following form:

P_1 is the same person as P_2 if and only if P_1 stands in relation R to P_2,

where the relation R is specified without using the word "person" or any synonym thereof. Swinburne maintains that no such account is possible.

3. According to Aristotle's theory as Swinburne understands it, each thing belongs to a specific kind—person, dog, oak—and the form of a thing is the set of properties and capacities that make it a thing of that kind.

other than matter. I will call this account of substance identity the wider Aristotelian account. We may say that there is a stuff of another kind, immaterial stuff, and that persons are made of both normal bodily matter and this immaterial stuff but that it is the continuity of the latter which provides that continuity of stuff which is necessary for the identity of the person over time.

This is in essence the way of expressing the simple theory which is adopted by those who say that a person living on Earth consists of two parts—a material part, the body; and an immaterial part, the soul. The soul is the essential part of a person, and it is its continuing which constitutes the continuing of the person. While on Earth, the soul is linked to a body (by the body being the vehicle of the person's knowledge of and action upon the physical world). But, it is logically possible, the soul can be separated from the body and exist in a disembodied state (in the way described earlier) or linked to a new body. This way of expressing things has been used in many religious traditions down the centuries, for it is a very natural way of expressing what is involved in being a person once you allow that a person can survive the death of his body. Classical philosophical statements of it are to be found in Plato and, above all, in Descartes. I shall call this view classical dualism. . . .

The arguments which Descartes gave in support of his account of persons are among the arguments which I have given in favour of the simple theory and since they take for granted the wider Aristotelian framework, they yield classical dualism as a consequence. Thus Descartes argues:

> Just because I know certainly that I exist, and that meanwhile I do not remark that any other thing necessarily pertains to my nature or essence, excepting that I am a thinking thing, I rightly conclude that my essence consists solely in the fact that I am a thinking thing. And although possibly . . . I possess a body with which I am very intimately conjoined, yet because, on the one side, I have a clear and distinct idea of myself inasmuch as I am only a thinking and unextended thing, and as, on the other, I possess a distinct idea of body, inasmuch as it is only an extended and unthinking thing, it is certain that this I [that is to say, my soul by which I am what I am], is entirely and absolutely distinct from my body, and can exist without it. [Descartes, Sixth Meditation]

Descartes is here saying that he can describe a thought-experiment in which he continues to exist although his body does not. I have also described such a thought-experiment and have argued, as Descartes in effect does, that it follows that his body is not logically necessary for his existence, that it is not an essential part of himself. Descartes can go on "thinking" (i.e., being conscious) and so existing without it. Now if we take the wider Aristotelian framework for granted that the continuing of a substance involves the continuing of some of the stuff of which it is made, and since the continuing existence of Descartes does not involve the continuing of bodily matter, it follows that there must now be as part of Descartes some other stuff, which he calls his soul, which forms the essential part of Descartes. . . .

So Descartes argues, and his argument seems to me correct—given the wider Aristotelian framework. If we are prepared to say that substances can be the same, even though none of the stuff (in a wide sense) of which they are made is the same, the conclusion does not follow. The wider Aristotelian framework provides a partial definition of "stuff" rather than a factual truth.

To say that a person has an immaterial soul is not to say that if you examine him closely enough under an acute enough microscope you will find some very rarefied constituent which has eluded the power of ordinary microscopes. It is just a way of expressing the point within a traditional framework of thought that persons can—it is logically possible—continue, when their bodies do not. It does, however, seem a very natural way of expressing the point—especially once we allow that persons can become disembodied. . . .

It does not follow from all this that a person's body is no part of him. Given that what we are trying to do is to elucidate the nature of those entities which we normally call "persons," we must say that arms and legs and all other parts of the living body are parts of the person. My arms and legs are parts of me. The crucial point that Descartes was making is that the body is only, contingently and possibly temporarily, part of the person; it is not an essential part. . . .

The other arguments which I have given for the "simple theory," e.g., that two embodied persons can be the same despite their being no bodily continuity between them, can also, like the argument of Descartes just discussed, if we assume the wider Aristotelian framework, be cast into the form of arguments for classical dualism. . . .

There is, however, one argument often put forward by classical dualists—their argument from the indivisibility of the soul to its natural immortality—from which I must dissociate myself. Before looking at this argument, it is necessary to face the problem of what it means to say that the soul continues to exist. Clearly the soul continues to exist if a person exercises his capacities for experience and action, by having experiences and performing actions. But can the soul continue to exist when the person does not exercise those capacities? Presumably it can. For we say that an unconscious person (who is neither having experiences or acting) is still a person. We say this on the grounds that natural processes (i.e., processes according with the laws of nature) will, or at any rate may, lead to his exercising his capacities again—e.g., through the end of normal sleep or through some medical or surgical intervention. Hence a person, and so his soul, if we talk thus, certainly exists while natural processes may lead to his exercising those capacities again. But what when the person is not exercising his capacities, and no natural processes (whether those operative in our present material universe or those operative in some new world to which the person has moved) will lead to his exercising his capacities? We could say that the person and so his soul still exists on the grounds that there is the logical possibility of his coming to life again. To my mind, the more natural alternative is to say that when ordinary natural processes cannot lead to his exercising his capacities again, a person and so his soul has ceased to exist; but there remains the logical possibility that he may come into existence again (perhaps through God causing him to exist again). One argument against taking the latter alternative is the argument that no substance can have two beginnings of existence. If a person really ceases to exist, then there is not even the logical possibility of his coming into existence again. It would follow that the mere logical possibility of the person coming into existence again has the consequence that a person once existent, is always existent (even when he has no capacity for experience and action). But this principle—that no substance can have two beginnings of existence—is one which I see no good reason for adopting; and if we do not adopt it, then we must say that souls cease to exist when there is no natural possibility of their exercising their capacities. But that does not prevent souls which have ceased to exist coming into existence again. This way of talking does give substantial content to claims that souls do or do not exist, when they are not exercising their capacities.

Now classical dualists assumed (in my view, on balance, correctly) that souls cannot be divided. But they often argued from this, that souls were indestructible, and hence immortal, or at any rate naturally immortal (i.e., immortal as a result of the operation of natural processes, and so immortal barring an act of God to stop those processes operating). That does not follow. Material bodies may lose essential properties without being divided—an oak tree may die and become fossilized without losing its shape. It does not follow from a soul's being indivisible that it cannot lose its capacity for experience and action—and so cease to be a soul. Although there is (I have been arguing) no logical necessity that a soul be linked to a body, it may be physically necessary that a soul be linked to one body if it is to have its essential properties (of capacity for experience and action) and so continue to exist.

TEST YOUR UNDERSTANDING

1. A criterion of personal identity is a statement of the form "Later person Y is identical to an earlier person X if and only if X and Y are related thus and so," where "thus and so" is specified without using the word "person" or anything like it. Does Swinburne propose a criterion of personal identity in this sense?

2. Does Swinburne think that a person is an immaterial soul with no material parts?

3. Swinburne argues that it is possible for a person to exist without her body (and that a person is therefore not identical to her body). Give a quick statement of the argument.

4. True or false: Swinburne thinks that it is possible for a person to survive complete amnesia (and that Locke's theory of personal identity is therefore mistaken).

NOTES AND QUESTIONS

1. What is "classical dualism"? Set out Swinburne's **argument** for it in the form of premises and conclusion. Is the argument **valid**? Is it **sound**?

2. *Identity as analyzable.* Every other theory of personal identity considered in this chapter holds that when a later person Y is identical with an earlier person X, there is also something to say about what *makes* Y identical to X: sameness of body, continuity of memory, and so forth. Swinburne holds that there is no criterion of personal identity in this sense. For him, the facts of personal identity over time are not grounded in more basic facts. This raises a question.

Suppose we have a situation we would ordinarily describe as follows: Serena and Venus are having lunch together. Each sits in her own chair for an hour, then they get up and leave. Now entertain the following possibility: Although the Serena-body and the Venus-body remained in their chairs, and although each retained a single coherent set of thoughts and memories while they were lunching, nonetheless, Serena *the person* and Venus *the person* were switching places—and bodies and memories—every 5 minutes.

Question: Is this a real possibility on Swinburne's view? Is there anything absurd or self-contradictory in this story? If not, how can we be sure that this sort of thing is not happening all the time? Swinburne does not address this epistemological question in this selection. Imagine how he might respond.

3. The selection is from *Personal Identity* (Blackwell, 1984) in which Swinburne engages in a debate with Sydney Shoemaker, who holds a theory of personal identity similar to Derek Parfit's (see the next reading). If you want to explore Swinburne's view further, Shoemaker's objections to Swinburne's theory in that book would be a good place to start.

Derek Parfit (1942–2017)

At the time of his death, Parfit was Fellow Emeritus in Philosophy at All Souls College, University of Oxford. In addition to *Reasons and Persons* (1984), from which the selections below are drawn, he is the author of the two-volume work *On What Matters* (2011) and numerous essays in moral philosophy.

PERSONAL IDENTITY
from *Reasons and Persons*

I enter the Teletransporter. I have been to Mars before, but only by the old method, a spaceship journey taking several weeks. This machine will send me at the speed of light. I merely have to press the green button. Like others, I am nervous. Will it work? I remind myself what I have been told to expect. When I press the button, I shall lose consciousness, and then wake up at what seems a moment later. In fact I shall have been unconscious for about an hour. The Scanner here on Earth will destroy my brain and body, while recording the exact states of all of my cells. It will then transmit this information by radio. Traveling at the speed of light, the message will take three minutes to reach the Replicator on Mars. This will then create, out of new matter, a brain and body exactly like mine. It will be in this body that I shall wake up.

Though I believe that this is what will happen, I still hesitate. But then I remember seeing my wife grin when, at breakfast today, I revealed my nervousness. As she reminded me, she has often been teletransported, and there is nothing wrong with *her*. I press the button. As predicted, I lose and seem at once to regain consciousness, but in a different cubicle. Examining my new body, I find no change at all. Even the cut on my upper lip, from this morning's shave, is still there.

Several years pass, during which I am often Teletransported. I am now back in the cubicle, ready for another trip to Mars. But this time, when I press the green button, I do not lose consciousness. There is a whirring sound, then silence. I leave the cubicle, and say to the attendant: "It's not working. What did I do wrong?"

"It's working," he replies, handing me a printed card. This reads: "The New Scanner records your blueprint without destroying your brain and body. We hope that you will welcome the opportunities which this technical advance offers."

The attendant tells me that I am one of the first people to use the New Scanner. He adds that, if I stay for an hour, I can use the Intercom to see and talk to myself on Mars.

"Wait a minute," I reply, "If I'm here I can't *also* be on Mars." Someone politely coughs, a white-coated man who asks to speak to me in private. We go to his office, where he tells me to sit down, and pauses. Then he says, "I'm afraid that we're having problems with the New Scanner. It records your blueprint just as accurately, as you will see when you talk to yourself on Mars. But it seems to be damaging the cardiac systems which it scans. Judging from the results so far, though you will be quite healthy on Mars, here on Earth you must expect cardiac failure within the next few days.". . .

Simple Teletransportation and the Branch-Line Case

Simple Teletransportation, as just described, is a common feature in science fiction. And it is believed by some readers of this fiction merely to be the fastest way of traveling. They believe that my Replica *would* be *me*. Other science fiction readers, and some of the characters in this fiction, take a different view. They believe that when I press the green button, I die. My Replica is *someone else,* who has been made to be exactly like me.

This second view seems to be supported by the end of my story. The New Scanner does not destroy my brain and body. Besides gathering the information, it merely damages my heart. While I am in the cubicle, with the green button pressed, nothing seems to happen. I walk out, and learn that in a few days I shall die. I later talk, by two-way television, to my Replica on Mars. Let us continue the story. Since my Replica knows that I am about to die, he tries to console me with the same thoughts with which I recently tried to console a dying friend. It is sad to learn, on the receiving end, how unconsoling these thoughts are. My Replica then assures me that he will take up my life where I leave off. He loves my wife, and together they will care for my children. And he will finish the book that I am writing. Besides having all of my drafts, he has all of my intentions. I must admit that he can finish my book as well as I could. All these facts console me a little. Dying when I know that I shall have a Replica is not quite as bad as, simply, dying. Even so, I shall soon lose consciousness, forever.

In Simple Teletransportation, I do not co-exist with my Replica. This makes it easier to believe that this is a way of traveling, that my Replica *is* me. At the end of my story, my life and that of my Replica overlap. Call this the *Branch-Line Case*. In this case, I cannot hope to travel on the *Main Line,* waking up on Mars with forty years of life ahead. I shall remain on the Branch-Line, on Earth, which ends a few days later. Since I can talk to my Replica, it seems clear that he is *not* me. Though he is exactly like me, he is one person, and I am another. When I pinch myself, he feels nothing. When I have my heart attack, he will again feel nothing. And when I am dead he will live for another forty years.

If we believe that my Replica is not me, it is natural to assume that my prospect, on the Branch Line, is almost as bad as ordinary death. I shall deny this assumption. As I shall argue later, I ought to regard having a Replica as being about as good as ordinary survival. . . .

Qualitative and Numerical Identity

There are two kinds of sameness, or identity. I and my Replica are *qualitatively identical,* or exactly alike. But we may not be *numerically identical,* or one and the same person. Similarly, two white billiard balls are not numerically but may be qualitatively identical. If I paint one of these balls red, it will not now be qualitatively identical to itself yesterday. But the red ball that I see now and the white ball that I painted red are numerically identical. They are one and the same ball.

We might say, of someone, "After his accident, he is no longer the same person." This is a claim about both kinds of identity. We claim that *he,* the same person, is *not* now the same person. This is not a contradiction. We merely mean that this person's character has changed. This numerically identical person is now qualitatively different.

When we are concerned about our future, it is our numerical identity that we are concerned about. I may believe that after my marriage, I shall not be the same person. But this does not make marriage death. However much I change, I shall still be alive if there will be some person living who is numerically identical with me.

The philosophical debate is about the nature both of persons and of personal identity over time. It will help to distinguish these questions:

(1) What is the nature of a person?

(2) What is it that makes a person at two different times one and the same person?

(3) What is necessarily involved in the continued existence of each person over time?

The answer to (2) can take this form: "X today is one and the same person as Y at some past time *if and only if. . . .*" This answer states the *necessary and sufficient conditions* for personal identity over time. And the answer to (2) provides the answer to (3). Each person's continued existence has the *same* necessary and sufficient conditions.

In answering (2) and (3) we shall also partly answer (1). The necessary features of our continued existence depend upon our nature. And the simplest answer to (1) is that, to be a person, a being must be self-conscious, aware of its identity and its continued existence over time. . . .

The Physical Criterion of Personal Identity

On one view, what makes me the same person over time is that I have the same brain and body. . . . I shall continue to exist if and only if this particular brain and body continue both to exist and to be the brain and body of a living person.

This is the simplest version of this view. There is a better version.

> *The Physical Criterion:* (1) What is necessary is not the continued existence of the whole body, but the continued existence of *enough* of the brain to be the brain of a living person. X today is one and the same person as Y at some past time if and only if (2) enough of Y's brain continued to exist, and is now X's brain, and (3) there does not exist a different person who also has enough of Y's brain. (4) Personal identity over time just consists in the holding of facts like (2) and (3).

(1) is clearly needed in certain actual cases. Some people continue to exist even though they lose much of their bodies, perhaps including their hearts and lungs if they are on heart-lung machines. The need for (3) will be clear later.

Those who believe in the Physical Criterion would reject Teletransportation. They would believe this to be a way not of traveling, but of dying. They would also reject, as inconceivable, reincarnation. They believe that someone cannot have a life after death, unless he lives this life in a resurrection of the very same, physically continuous body. . . .

The Psychological Criterion

Some people believe in a kind of psychological continuity that resembles physical continuity. This involves the continued existence of a purely mental *entity* or thing, a soul, or spiritual substance. I shall return to this view. But I shall first explain another kind of psychological continuity. This is less like physical continuity, since it does not consist in the continued existence of some entity. But this other kind of psychological continuity involves only facts with which we are familiar.

What has been most discussed is the continuity of memory. This is because it is memory that makes most of us aware of our own continued existence over time. The exceptions are the people who are suffering from amnesia. Most amnesiacs lose only two sets of memories. They lose all of their memories of having particular past experiences—or, for short, their *experience memories*. They also lose some of their memories about facts, those that are about their own past lives. But they remember other facts, and they remember how to do different things, such as how to speak, or swim.

Locke suggested that experience memory provides the criterion of personal identity.[1] Though this is not, on its own, a plausible view, I believe that it can be part of such a view. I shall therefore try to answer Locke's critics.

---

1. See section 9 of Locke's "Of Identity and Diversity" earlier in this chapter.

Locke claimed that someone cannot have committed some crime unless he now remembers doing so. We can understand a reluctance to punish people for crimes that they cannot remember. But, taken as a view about what is involved in a person's continued existence, Locke's claim is clearly false. If it was true, it would not be possible for someone to forget any of the things that he once did, or any of the experiences that he once had. But this *is* possible. I cannot now remember putting on my shirt this morning.

There are several ways to extend the experience-memory criterion so as to cover such cases. I shall appeal to the concept of an overlapping chain of experience-memories. Let us say that, between X today and Y twenty years ago, there are *direct memory connections* if X can now remember having some of the experiences that Y had twenty years ago. On Locke's view, this makes X and Y one and the same person. Even if there are *no* such direct memory connections, there may be *continuity of memory* between X now and Y twenty years ago. This would be so if between X now and Y at that time there has been an overlapping chain of direct memories. In the case of most people who are over twenty-three, there would be such an overlapping chain. In each day within the last twenty years, most of these people remembered some of their experiences on the previous day. On the revised version of Locke's view, some present person X is the same as some past person Y if there is between them continuity of memory.

This revision meets one objection to Locke's view. We should also revise the view so that it appeals to other facts. Besides direct memories, there are several other kinds of direct psychological connection. One such connection is that which holds between an intention and the later act in which this intention is carried out. Other such direct connections are those which hold when a belief, or a desire, or any other psychological feature, continues to be had.

I can now define two general relations:

> *Psychological connectedness* is the holding of particular direct psychological connections.
> *Psychological continuity* is the holding of overlapping chains of *strong* connectedness.

Of these two general relations, connectedness is more important both in theory and in practice. Connectedness can hold to any degree. Between X today and Y yesterday there might be several thousand direct psychological connections, or only a single connection. If there was only a single connection, X and Y would not be, on the revised Lockean view, the same person. For X and Y to be the same person, there must be over every day *enough* direct psychological connections. Since connectedness is a matter of degree, we cannot plausibly define precisely what counts as enough. But we can claim that there is enough connectedness if the number of connections, over any day, is *at least half* the number of direct connections that hold, over every day, in the lives of nearly every actual person. When there are enough direct connections, there is what I call *strong* connectedness.

This relation cannot be the criterion of personal identity. A relation F is *transitive* if it is true that, if X is F-related to Y, and Y is F-related to Z, X and Z *must* be F-related. Personal identity is a transitive relation. If Bertie was one and the same person as the philosopher Russell,[2] and Russell was one and the same person as the author of *Why I Am Not a Christian*, this author and Bertie must be one and the same person.

Strong connectedness is *not* a transitive relation. I am now strongly connected to myself yesterday, when I was strongly connected to myself two days ago, when I was strongly connected to myself three days ago, and so on. It does not follow that I am now strongly connected to myself twenty years ago. And this is not true. Between me now and myself twenty years ago there are many fewer than the number of direct psychological connections that hold over any day in the lives of nearly all adults. For example, while these adults have many memories of experiences that they had in the previous day, I have few memories of experiences that I had twenty years ago.

By "the criterion of personal identity over time" I mean what this identity *necessarily involves or consists in*. Because identity is a transitive relation, the criterion of identity must be a transitive relation. Since strong connectedness is not transitive, it cannot be the criterion of identity. And I have just described a case in which this is shown. I am the same person as myself twenty years ago, though I am not now strongly connected to myself then.

Though a defender of Locke's view cannot appeal to psychological connectedness, he can appeal to psychological continuity, which *is* transitive. He can appeal to . . .

> *The Psychological Criterion:* (1) There is *psychological continuity* if and only if there are overlapping chains of strong connectedness. X today is one and the same person as Y at some past time if and only if (2) X is psychologically continuous with Y, (3) this continuity has the right kind of cause, and (4) there does not exist a different person who is also psychologically continuous with Y. (5) Personal identity over time just consists in the holding of facts like (2) to (4).

As with the Physical Criterion, the need for (4) will be clear later. . . .

What Happens When I Divide?

Suppose first that I am one of a pair of identical twins, and that both my body and my twin's brain have been fatally injured. Because of advances in neurosurgery, it is not inevitable that these injuries will cause us both to die. We have between us one healthy brain and one healthy body. Surgeons can put these together.

This could be done even with existing techniques. Just as my brain could be extracted, and kept alive by a connection with a heart-lung machine, it could be kept alive by a connection with the heart and lungs in my twin's body. The drawback, today, is that the nerves from my brain could not be connected with the nerves in my twin's body. My brain could survive if transplanted into his body, but the resulting person would be paralysed. . . .

---

2. British philosopher Bertrand Russell (1872–1970).

Let us suppose, however, that surgeons are able to connect my brain to the nerves in my twin's body. The resulting person would have no paralysis, and would be completely healthy. Who would this person be?

This is not a difficult question. . . .

On all versions of the Psychological Criterion, the resulting person would be me. And most believers in the Physical Criterion could be persuaded that, in this case, this is true. As I have claimed, the Physical Criterion should require only the continued existence of *enough* of my brain to be the brain of a living person, provided that no one else has enough of this brain. This would make it me who would wake up, after the operation. And if my twin's body was just like mine, I might even fail to notice that I had a new body.

It is in fact true that one hemisphere is enough. There are many people who have survived, when a stroke or injury puts out of action one of their hemispheres. With his remaining hemisphere, such a person may need to re-learn certain things, such as adult speech, or how to control both hands. But this is possible. In my example I am assuming that, as may be true of certain actual people, both of my hemispheres have the full range of abilities. I could thus survive with either hemisphere, without any need for re-learning.

I shall now combine these last two claims. I would survive if my brain was successfully transplanted into my twin's body. And I could survive with only half my brain, the other half having been destroyed. Given these two facts, it seems clear that I would survive if half my brain was successfully transplanted into my twin's body, and the other half was destroyed.

What if the other half was *not* destroyed? This is [a case] in which a person, like an amoeba, divides. To simplify the case, I assume that I am one of three identical triplets. Consider

> *My Division.* My body is fatally injured, as are the brains of my two brothers. My brain is divided, and each half is successfully transplanted into the body of one of my brothers. Each of the resulting people believes that he is me, seems to remember living my life, has my character, and is in every other way psychologically continuous with me. And he has a body that is very like mine. . . .

It may help to state, in advance, what I believe this case to show. . . . The main conclusion to be drawn is that *personal identity is not what matters.*

It is natural to believe that our identity is what matters. Reconsider the Branch-Line Case, where I have talked to my Replica on Mars, and am about to die. Suppose we believe that I and my Replica are different people. It is then natural to assume that my prospect is almost as bad as ordinary death. In a few days, there will be no one living who will be me. It is natural to assume that *this* is what matters. In discussing My Division, I shall start by making this assumption.

In this case, each half of my brain will be successfully transplanted into the very similar body of one of my two brothers. Both of the resulting people will be fully psychologically continuous with me, as I am now. What happens to me?

There are only four possibilities: (1) I do not survive; (2) I survive as one of the two people; (3) I survive as the other; (4) I survive as both.

The objection to (1) is this. I would survive if my brain was successfully transplanted. And people have in fact survived with half their brains destroyed. Given these facts, it seems clear that I would survive if half my brain was successfully transplanted, and the other half was destroyed. So how could I fail to survive if the other half was also successfully transplanted? How could a double success be a failure?

Consider the next two possibilities. Perhaps one success is the maximum score. Perhaps I shall be one of the two resulting people. The objection here is that, in this case, each half of my brain is exactly similar, and so, to start with, is each resulting person. Given these facts, how can I survive as only one of the two people? What can make me one of them rather than the other?

These first three possibilities cannot be dismissed as incoherent. We can understand them. But, while we assume that identity is what matters, (1) is not plausible. It is not plausible that My Division is equivalent to death. Nor are (2) and (3) plausible. There remains the fourth possibility: that I survive as both of the resulting people. . . .

After I have had this operation, the two "products" each have all the features of a person. They could live at opposite ends of the Earth. Suppose that they have poor memories, and that their appearance changes in different ways. After many years, they might meet again, and fail even to recognise each other. We might have to claim of such a pair, innocently playing tennis: "What you see out there is a single person, playing tennis with himself. In each half of his mind he mistakenly believes that he is playing tennis with someone else." If we are not yet Reductionists,[3] we believe that there is one true answer to the question whether these two tennis-players are a single person. Given what we mean by "person," the answer must be No. . . .

On the Reductionist View, the problem disappears. On this view, the claims that I have discussed do not describe different possibilities, any of which might be true, and one of which must be true. These claims are merely different descriptions of the same outcome. We know what this outcome is. There will be two future people, each of whom will have the body of one of my brothers, and will be fully psychologically continuous with me, because he has half of my brain. Knowing this, we know everything. I may ask, "But shall I be one of these two people, or the other, or neither?" But I should regard this as an empty question. Here is a similar question. In 1881 the French Socialist Party split. What happened? Did the French Socialist Party cease to exist, or did it continue to exist as one or other of the two new Parties? Given certain further details, this would be an empty question. Even if we have no answer to this question, we could know just what happened.

I must now distinguish two ways in which a question may be empty. About some questions we should claim both that they are empty, and that they have no answers. We could decide to *give* these questions answers. But . . . any possible answer would be arbitrary. . . .

There is another kind of case in which a question may be empty. In such a case, this question has an answer. The question is empty because it does not describe different

---

3. "Reductionism" is Parfit's name for the view that the facts of personal identity are wholly determined by more basic facts about bodily continuity, psychological continuity, and the like, and that when these facts fail to settle whether a future person Y is the same person as some present person X, then there is *simply no answer to the question* whether X and Y are the same person.

possibilities, any one of which might be true, and one of which must be true. The question merely gives us different descriptions of the same outcome. We could know the full truth about this outcome without choosing one of these descriptions. But, if we do decide to give an answer to this empty question, one of these descriptions is better than the others. Since this is so, we can claim that this description is the answer to this question. And I claim that there is a best description of the case where I divide. The best description is that neither of the resulting people will be me. . . .

What Matters When I Divide?

Some people would regard division as being as bad, or nearly as bad, as ordinary death. This reaction is irrational. We ought to regard division as being about as good as ordinary survival. As I have argued, the two "products" of this operation would be two different people. Consider my relation to each of these people. Does this relation fail to contain some vital element that is contained in ordinary survival? It seems clear that it does not. I would survive if I stood in this very same relation to only one of the resulting people. It is a fact that someone can survive even if half his brain is destroyed. And on reflection it was clear that I would survive if my whole brain was successfully transplanted into my brother's body. It was therefore clear that I would survive if half my brain was destroyed, and the other half was successfully transplanted into my brother's body. In the case that we are now considering, my relation to each of the resulting people thus contains everything that would be needed for me to survive as that person. It cannot be the *nature* of my relation to each of the resulting people that, in this case, causes it to fail to be survival. Nothing is *missing*. What is wrong can only be the duplication.

Suppose that I accept this, but still regard division as being nearly as bad as death. My reaction is now indefensible. I would be like someone who, when told of a drug that could double his years of life, regarded the taking of this drug as death. The only difference in the case of division is that the extra years are to run concurrently. This is an interesting difference. But it cannot mean that there are *no* years to run. We might say: "You will lose your identity. But there are at least two ways of doing this. Dying is one, dividing is another. To regard these as the same is to confuse two with zero. Double survival is not the same as ordinary survival. But this does not make it death. It is further away from death than ordinary survival."

The problem with double survival is that it does not fit the logic of identity. Like certain other Reductionists, I claim

> *Relation R* is what matters. R is psychological connectedness and/or psychological continuity, with the right kind of cause. . . .

In the imagined case where I divide, R takes a "branching" form. But personal identity cannot take a branching form. I and the two resulting people cannot be one and the same person. Since I cannot be identical with two different people, and it would be arbitrary to call one of these people me, we can best describe the case by saying neither of these people will be me.

Which is the relation that is important? Is what matters personal identity, or relation R? In ordinary cases we need not decide which of these is what matters, since these relations coincide. In the case of My Division these relations do not coincide. We must therefore decide which of the two is what matters.

If we believe that we are separately existing entities,[4] we could plausibly claim that identity is what matters. On this view, personal identity is a deep further fact. But we have sufficient evidence to reject this view. If we are Reductionists, we *cannot* plausibly claim that, of these two relations, it is identity that matters. On our view, the fact of personal identity just consists in the holding of relation R, when it takes a non-branching form. If personal identity just consists in this other relation, this other relation must be what matters.

It may be objected: "You are wrong to claim that there is nothing more to identity than relation R. As you have said, personal identity has one extra feature, not contained in relation R. Personal identity consists in R holding *uniquely*—holding between one present person and *only one* future person. Since there is something more to personal identity than to relation R, we can rationally claim that, of the two, it is identity which is what matters."

In answering this objection, it will help to use some abbreviations. Call personal identity PI. When some relation holds uniquely, or in a one-one form, call this fact U. The view that I accept can be stated with this formula:

$$PI = R + U$$

Most of us are convinced that PI matters, or has value. Assume that R may also have value. There are then four possibilities:

(1) R without U has no value.

(2) U enhances the value of R, but R has value even without U.

(3) U makes no difference to the value of R.

(4) U reduces the value of R (but not enough to eliminate this value, since R + U = PI, which has value).

Can the presence or absence of U make a great difference to the value of R? As I shall argue, this is not plausible. If I will be R-related to some future person, the presence or absence of U makes no difference to the intrinsic nature of my relation to this person. And what matters most must be the intrinsic nature of this relation.

Since this is so, R without U would still have most of its value. Adding U makes R = PI. If adding U does not greatly increase the value of R, R must be what fundamentally matters, and PI mostly matters just because of the presence of R. If U makes no difference to the value of R, PI matters only because of the presence of R. Since U can be plausibly claimed to make a small difference, PI may, compared with R, have

---

4. That is, entities whose persistence through time is not determined by the underlying facts of physical and psychological continuity.

some extra value. But this value would be much less than the intrinsic value of R. The extra value of PI is much less than the value that R would have in the absence of PI, when U fails to hold.

If it were put forward on its own, it would be difficult to accept the view that personal identity is not what matters. But I believe that, when we consider the case of division, this difficulty disappears. When we see *why* neither resulting person will be me, I believe that, on reflection, we can also see that this does not matter, or matters only a little. . . .

In the case where I divide, though my relation to each of the resulting people cannot be called identity, it contains what fundamentally matters. When we deny identity here, we are not denying an important judgement. Since my relation to each of the resulting people is about as good as if it were identity, it carries most of the ordinary implications of identity. Even when the person in Jack's body cannot be called me, because the other transplant succeeds, he can just as much deserve punishment or reward for what I have done. So can the person in Bill's body. As Wiggins writes: "a malefactor could scarcely evade responsibility by contriving his own fission."[5] . . .

Is the True View Believable?

I have now reviewed the main arguments for the Reductionist View. Do I find it impossible to believe this view?

What I find is this. I can believe this view at the intellectual or reflective level. I am convinced by the arguments in favour of this view. But I think it likely that, at some other level, I shall always have doubts.

My belief is firmest when I am considering some of these imagined cases. I am convinced that if I divided, it would be an empty question whether I would then be one, or the other, or neither of the resulting people. I believe that there is nothing that could make these different possibilities, any of which might be what would really happen. . . .

When I consider certain other cases, my conviction is less firm. One example is Teletransportation. I imagine that I am in the cubicle, about to press the green button. I might suddenly have doubts. I might be tempted to change my mind, and pay the larger fare of a spaceship journey.

I suspect that reviewing my arguments would never wholly remove my doubts. At the reflective or intellectual level, I would remain convinced that the Reductionist View is true. But at some lower level I would still be inclined to believe that there must always be a real difference between some future person's being me, and his being someone else. Something similar is true when I look through a window at the top of a sky-scraper. I know that I am in no danger. But looking down from this dizzying height, I am afraid. I would have a similar irrational fear if I was about to press the green button.

It may help to add these remarks. On the Reductionist View, my continued existence just involves physical and psychological continuity. On the Non-Reductionist View, it

---

5. David Wiggins, "Locke, Butler and the Stream of Consciousness," in *The Identities of Persons*, ed. Amelie Rorty (University of California Press, 1976), 146. [Parfit's note.]

involves a further fact. It is natural to believe in this further fact, and to believe that, compared with the continuities, it is a *deep* fact, and is the fact that really matters. When I fear that, in Teletransportation, I shall not get to Mars, my fear is that the abnormal cause may fail to produce this further fact. As I have argued, there is no such fact. What I fear will not happen, *never* happens. I want the person on Mars to be me in a specially intimate way in which no future person will ever be me. My continued existence never involves this deep further fact. What I fear will be missing is *always* missing. Even a spaceship journey would not produce the further fact in which I am inclined to believe.

When I come to see that my continued existence does not involve this further fact, I lose my reason for preferring a spaceship journey. But, judged from the standpoint of my earlier belief, this is not because Teletransportation is *about as good as* ordinary survival. It is because ordinary survival is *about as bad as*, or little better than, Teletransportation. *Ordinary survival is about as bad as being destroyed and having a Replica.*

By rehearsing arguments like these, I might do enough to reduce my fear. I might be able to bring myself to press the green button. But I expect that I would never completely lose my intuitive belief in the Non-Reductionist View. It is hard to be serenely confident in my Reductionist conclusions. It is hard to believe that personal identity is not what matters. If tomorrow someone will be in agony, it is hard to believe that it could be an empty question whether this agony will be felt by *me*. And it is hard to believe that, if I am about to lose consciousness, there may be no answer to the question "Am I about to die?"

Nagel[6] once claimed that it is psychologically impossible to believe the Reductionist View. Buddha claimed that though this is very hard, it is possible.[7] I find Buddha's claim to be true. After reviewing my arguments, I find that, at the reflective or intellectual level, though it is very hard to believe the Reductionist View, this is possible. My remaining doubts or fears seem to me irrational. Since I can believe this view, I assume that others can do so too. We can believe the truth about ourselves.

TEST YOUR UNDERSTANDING

1. Which of the following pairs are (a) **numerically identical**, (b) not numerically identical but only **qualitatively identical**?

   a. the author of the *Essay Concerning Human Understanding*; John Locke

   b. your copy of this book; your classmate's copy of this book

   c. 2 + 3; 5

   d. the teenager who played Harry Potter in the movies; the adult British actor Daniel Radcliffe

   e. the can of Acme soup on the left of the supermarket shelf; the can of Acme soup on the right of the shelf

---

6. American philosopher Thomas Nagel (1937–), author of selections in Chapters 8, 17, and 19 of this anthology.

7. In an appendix to *Reasons and Persons,* Parfit gives some quotations from Buddhist texts to support his claim that the Buddha was a reductionist.

2. Which of the following **relations** are transitive?

   a. Person *x is exactly the same height as* person *y*.

   b. Number *x is greater than* number *y*.

   c. Person *x loves* person *y*.

   d. Person *x is almost the same height as* person *y*.

   e. Object *x* is *qualitatively* identical to object *y*.

   f. Object *x* is *indiscriminable by the naked eye* from object *y*.

3. Parfit accepts a certain "criterion of personal identity." Which one?

4. According to Parfit, "relation R" does not fit the "logic of identity." Explain what he means.

5. Does Parfit think that teletransportation is a method of *transportation*, a way of getting you to Mars?

NOTES AND QUESTIONS

1. Parfit takes the case of My Division to show that "personal identity is not what matters." What does he mean by this, and how is My Division supposed to show that it is true? Set out Parfit's argument in the form of premises and conclusion. Is the argument valid? Is it sound?

2. Assuming that the conclusion of the argument is true, should we be less concerned about our own deaths, as Parfit suggests?

3. Suppose you have a favorite restaurant. First it moves to a new location. Then it's name is changed. Then it changes ownership. Then they change the menu. We can ask whether your old favorite restaurant still exists at each stage in this process. But intuitively, once you know these stipulated facts, you know everything there is to know about what happened. If you find yourself uncertain about what to say about your old favorite restaurant, that will not be because you lack hidden information. It will be because there simply is no answer to your question, "Is this restaurant the same as the old one?" Parfit argues that *people* are like restaurants in this respect, but he concedes that many will find this impossible to believe.

   Exercise: Give an example of a case in which all of the underlying facts are stipulated, and yet there remains no clear answer to the question, "Will I survive such and such an ordeal?" The reductionist says that in such a case, there is simply no fact as to whether you will survive. Explain why this is hard to believe. Then assess Parfit's claim that it is nevertheless the right thing to believe.

4. Parfit's views have been the subject of much discussion. For an introduction, see chapter 9 of Harold Noonan, *Personal Identity* (Routledge, 2003).

Bernard Williams (1929–2003)

Bernard Williams was, at the time of his death, Monroe Deutsch Professor of Philosophy at the University of California, Berkeley. His books include *Descartes: The Project of Pure Inquiry* (1978), *Ethics and the Limits of Philosophy* (1985), and *Shame and Necessity* (1993). His early essays on personal identity and the nature of the self are collected in *Problems of the Self* (1973).

THE SELF AND THE FUTURE

Suppose that there were some process to which two persons, A and B, could be subjected as a result of which they might be said—question-beggingly—to have *exchanged bodies*. That is to say—less question-beggingly—there is a certain human body which is such that when previously we were confronted with it, we were confronted with person A, certain utterances coming from it were expressive of memories of the past experiences of A, certain movements of it partly constituted the actions of A and were taken as expressive of the character of A, and so forth; but now, after the process is completed, utterances coming from this body are expressive of what seem to be just those memories which previously we identified as memories of the past experiences of B, its movements partly constitute actions expressive of the character of B, and so forth; and conversely with the other body. . . .

One radical way of securing that condition in the imagined exchange case is to suppose that the brains of A and of B are transposed. We may not need so radical a condition. Thus suppose it were possible to extract information from a man's brain and store it in a device while his brain was repaired, or even renewed, the information then being replaced: it would seem exaggerated to insist that the resultant man could not possibly have the memories he had before the operation. With regard to our knowledge of our own past, we draw distinctions between merely recalling, being reminded, and learning again, and those distinctions correspond (roughly) to distinctions between no new input, partial new input, and total new input with regard to the information in question; and it seems clear that the information-parking case just imagined would not count as new input in the sense necessary and sufficient for "learning again." Hence we can imagine the case we are concerned with in terms of information extracted into such devices from A's and B's brains and replaced in the other brain; this is the sort of model which, I think not unfairly for the present argument, I shall have in mind.

We imagine the following. The process considered above exists; two persons can enter some machine, let us say, and emerge changed in the appropriate ways. If A and B are the persons who enter, let us call the persons who emerge the *A-body-person* and the *B-body-person*: the A-body-person is that person (whoever it is) with whom I am confronted when, after the experiment, I am confronted with that body which previously was A's body—that is to say, that person who would naturally be taken for

A by someone who just saw this person, was familiar with *A*'s appearance before the experiment, and did not know about the happening of the experiment. A non-question-begging description of the experiment will leave it open which (if either) of the persons *A* and *B* the *A*-body-person is; the description of the experiment as "persons changing bodies" of course implies that the *A*-body-person is actually *B*.

We take two persons *A* and *B* who are going to have the process carried out on them. . . . We further announce that one of the two resultant persons, the *A*-body-person and the *B*-body-person, is going after the experiment to be given $100,000, while the other is going to be tortured. We then ask each of *A* and *B* to choose which treatment should be dealt out to which of the persons who will emerge from the experiment, the choice to be made (if it can be) on selfish grounds.

Suppose that *A* chooses that the *B*-body-person should get the pleasant treatment and the *A*-body-person the unpleasant treatment; and *B* chooses conversely (this might indicate that they thought that "changing bodies" was indeed a good description of the outcome). The experimenter cannot act in accordance with both these sets of preferences, those expressed by *A* and those expressed by *B*. Hence there is one clear sense in which *A* and *B* cannot both get what they want: namely, that if the experimenter, before the experiment, announces to *A* and *B* that he intends to carry out the alternative (for example), of treating the *B*-body-person unpleasantly and the *A*-body-person pleasantly—then *A* can say rightly, "That's not the outcome I chose to happen," and *B* can say rightly, "That's just the outcome I chose to happen." So, evidently, *A* and *B* before the experiment can each come to know either that the outcome he chose will be that which will happen, or that the one he chose will not happen, and in that sense they can get or fail to get what they wanted. But is it also true that when the experimenter proceeds *after* the experiment to act in accordance with one of the preferences and not the other, then one of *A* and *B* will have got what he wanted, and the other not?

There seems very good ground for saying so. For suppose the experimenter, having elicited *A*'s and *B*'s preference, says nothing to *A* and *B* about what he will do; conducts the experiment; and then, for example, gives the unpleasant treatment to the *B*-body-person and the pleasant treatment to the *A*-body-person. Then the *B*-body-person will not only complain of the unpleasant treatment as such, but will complain (since he has *A*'s memories) that that was not the outcome he chose, since he chose that the *B*-body-person should be well treated; and since *A* made his choice in selfish spirit, he may add that he precisely chose in that way because he did not want the unpleasant things to happen to *him*. The *A*-body-person meanwhile will express satisfaction both at the receipt of the $100,000, and also at the fact that the experimenter has chosen to act in the way that he, *B*, so wisely chose. These facts make a strong case for saying that the experimenter has brought it about that *B* did in the outcome get what he wanted and *A* did not. It is therefore a strong case for saying that the *B*-body-person really is *A*, and the *A*-body-person really is *B*; and therefore for saying that the process of the experiment really is that of changing bodies. . . . This seems to show that to care about what happens to me in the future is not necessarily to care about what happens to *this* body (the one I now have); and this in turn might be taken to show that in some sense of Descartes's obscure phrase, I and my body are "really distinct"[1] (though, of course, nothing in these considerations could support the idea that I could exist without a body at all). . . .

Let us now consider something apparently different. Someone in whose power I am tells me that I am going to be tortured tomorrow. I am frightened, and look forward to tomorrow in great apprehension. He adds that when the time comes, I shall not remember being told that this was going to happen to me, since shortly before the torture something else will be done to me which will make me forget the announcement. This certainly will not cheer me up, since I know perfectly well that I can forget things, and that there is such a thing as indeed being tortured unexpectedly because I had forgotten or been made to forget a prediction of the torture: that will still be a torture which, so long as I do know about the prediction, I look forward to in fear. He then adds that my forgetting the announcement will be only part of a larger process: when the moment of torture comes, I shall not remember any of the things I am now in a position to remember. This does not cheer me up, either, since I can readily conceive of being involved in an accident, for instance, as a result of which I wake up in a completely amnesiac state and also in great pain; that could certainly happen to me, I should not like it to happen to me, nor to know that it was going to happen to me. He now further adds that at the moment of torture I shall not only not remember the things I am now in a position to remember, but will have a different set of impressions of my past, quite different from the memories I now have. I do not think that this would cheer me up, either. For I can at least conceive the possibility, if not the concrete reality, of going completely mad, and thinking perhaps that I am George IV or somebody; and being told that something like that was going to happen to me would have no tendency to reduce the terror of being told authoritatively that I was going to be tortured, but would merely compound the horror. Nor do I see why I should be put into any better frame of mind by the person in charge adding lastly that the impressions of my past with which I shall be equipped on the eve of torture will exactly fit the past of another person now living, and that indeed I shall acquire these impressions by (for instance) information now in his brain being copied into mine. Fear, surely, would still be the proper reaction: and not because one did not know what was going to happen, but because in one vital respect at least one did know what was going to happen—torture, which one can indeed expect to happen to oneself, and to be preceded by certain mental derangements as well.

If this is right, the whole question seems now to be totally mysterious. For what we have just been through is of course merely one side, differently represented, of the transaction which we considered before; and it represents it as a perfectly hateful prospect, while the previous considerations represented it as something one should rationally, perhaps even cheerfully, choose out of the options there presented. It is differently presented, of course, and in two notable respects; but when we look at these two differences of presentation, can we really convince ourselves that the second presentation is wrong or misleading, thus leaving the road open to the first version which at the time seemed so convincing? Surely not.

---

1. Descartes's Meditation VI (see page 317 of this anthology) argues that mind and body are not merely "formally distinct"—distinguishable in thought—but also "really distinct," in the sense that each can exist without the other. Williams borrows Descartes's phrase but explicitly rejects this understanding of it.

The first difference is that in the second version the torture is throughout represented as going to happen to *me*: "you," the man in charge persistently says. Thus he is not very neutral. But should he have been neutral? Or, to put it another way, does his use of the second person have a merely emotional and rhetorical effect on me, making me afraid when further reflection would have shown that I had no reason to be? It is certainly not obviously so. The problem just is that through every step of his predictions I seem to be able to follow him successfully. And if I reflect on whether what he has said gives me grounds for fearing that I shall be tortured, I could consider that behind my fears lies some principle such as this: that my undergoing physical pain in the future is not excluded by any psychological state I may be in at the time, with the platitudinous exception of those psychological states which in themselves exclude experiencing pain, notably (if it is a psychological state) unconsciousness. In particular, what impressions I have about the past will not have any effect on whether I undergo the pain or not. This principle seems sound enough. . . .

I said that there were two notable differences between the second presentation of our situation and the first. The first difference, which we have just said something about, was that the man predicted the torture for *me*, a psychologically very changed "me." We have yet to find a reason for saying that he should not have done this, or that I really should be unable to follow him if he does; I seem to be able to follow him only too well. The second difference is that in this presentation he does not mention the other man, except in the somewhat incidental role of being the provenance of the impressions of the past I end up with. He does not mention him at all as someone who will end up with impressions of the past derived from me (and, incidentally, with $100,000 as well—a consideration which, in the frame of mind appropriate to this version, will merely make me jealous).

But why *should* he mention this man and what is going to happen to him? My selfish concern is to be told what is going to happen to me, and now I know: torture, preceded by changes of character, brain operations, changes in impressions of the past. The knowledge that one other person, or none, or many will be similarly mistreated may affect me in other ways, of sympathy, greater horror at the power of this tyrant, and so forth; but surely it cannot affect my expectations of torture? But—someone will say—this is to leave out exactly the feature which, as the first presentation of the case showed, makes all the difference: for it is to leave out the person who, as the first presentation showed, will be you. It is to leave out not merely a feature which should fundamentally affect your fears, it is to leave out the very person for whom you are fearful. So of course, the objector will say, this makes all the difference.

But can it? Consider the following series of cases. In each case we are to suppose that after what is described, A is, as before, to be tortured; we are also to suppose the person A is informed beforehand that just these things followed by the torture will happen to him:

(i)   A is subjected to an operation which produces total amnesia;

(ii) amnesia is produced in A, and other interference leads to certain changes in his character;

(iii) changes in his character are produced, and at the same time certain illusory "memory" beliefs are induced in him; these are of a quite fictitious kind and do not fit the life of any actual person;

(iv) the same as (*iii*), except that both the character traits and the "memory" impressions are designed to be appropriate to another actual person, *B*;

(v) the same as (*iv*), except that the result is produced by putting the information into *A* from the brain of *B*, by a method which leaves *B* the same as he was before;

(vi) the same happens to *A* as in (*v*), but *B* is not left the same, since a similar operation is conducted in the reverse direction.

I take it that no one is going to dispute that *A* has reasons, and fairly straightforward reasons, for fear of pain when the prospect is that of situation (*i*); there seems no conceivable reason why this should not extend to situation (*ii*), and the situation (*iii*) can surely introduce no difference of principle—it just seems a situation which for more than one reason we should have grounds for fearing, as suggested above. Situation (*iv*) at least introduces the person *B*, who was the focus of the objection we are now discussing. But it does not seem to introduce him in any way which makes a material difference; if I can expect pain through a transformation which involves new "memory"-impressions, it would seem a purely external fact, relative to that, that the "memory"-impressions had a model. . . .

But two things are to be noticed about this situation. First, if we concentrate on *A* and the *A*-body-person, we do not seem to have added anything which from the point of view of his fears makes any material difference; just as, in the move from (*iii*) to (*iv*), it made no relevant difference that the new "memory"-impressions which precede the pain had, as it happened, a model, so in the move from (*iv*) to (*v*) all we have added is that they have a model which is also their cause: and it is still difficult to see why that, to him looking forward, could possibly make the difference between expecting pain and not expecting pain. To illustrate that point from the case of character: if *A* is capable of expecting pain, he is capable of expecting pain preceded by a change in his dispositions—and to that expectation it can make no difference, whether that change in his dispositions is modeled on, or indeed indirectly caused by, the dispositions of some other person. If his fears can, as it were, reach through the change, it seems a mere trimming how the change is in fact induced. The second point about situation (*v*) is that if the crucial question for *A*'s fears with regard to what befalls the *A*-body-person is whether the *A*-body-person is or is not the person *B*, then that condition has not yet been satisfied in situation (*v*): for there we have an undisputed *B* in addition to the *A*-body-person, and certainly those two are not the same person.

But in situation (*vi*), we seemed to think, that is finally what he is. But if *A*'s original fears could reach through the expected changes in (*v*), as they did in (*iv*) and (*iii*), then certainly they can reach through in (*vi*). Indeed, from the point of view of *A*'s expectations and fears, there is less difference between (*vi*) and (*v*) than there is between (*v*) and (*iv*) or between (*iv*) and (*iii*). In those transitions, there were at least differences—though we could not see that they were really relevant differences—in the content and cause of what happened to him; in the present case there is absolutely no difference at all in what happens to him, the only difference being in what happens to someone else. If he can fear pain when (*v*) is predicted, why should he cease to when (*vi*) is?

I can see only one way of relevantly laying great weight on the transition from (*v*) to (*vi*); and this involves a considerable difficulty. This is to deny that, as I put it, the transition from (*v*) to (*vi*) involves merely the addition of something happening to *somebody else*; what rather it does, it will be said, is to involve the reintroduction of *A* himself, as the *B*-body-person; since he has reappeared in this form, it is for this person, and not for the unfortunate *A*-body-person, that *A* will have his expectations. This is to reassert, in effect, the viewpoint emphasized in our first presentation of the experiment. But this surely has the consequence that *A* should not have fears for the *A*-body-person who appeared in situation (*v*). For by the present argument, the *A*-body-person in (*vi*) is not *A*; the *B*-body-person is. But the *A*-body-person in (*v*) is, in character, history, everything, exactly the same as the *A*-body-person in (*vi*); so if the latter is not *A*, then neither is the former. . . . But no one else in (*v*) has any better claim to be *A*. So in (*v*), it seems, *A* just does not exist. This would certainly explain why *A* should have no fears for the state of things in (*v*)—though he might well have fears for the path to it. But it rather looked earlier as though he could well have fears for the state of things in (*v*). Let us grant, however, that that was an illusion, and that *A* really does not exist in (*v*); then does he exist in (*iv*), (*iii*), (*ii*), or (*i*)? It seems very difficult to deny it for (*i*) and (*ii*); are we perhaps to draw the line between (*iii*) and (*iv*)? . . .

Thus, to sum up, it looks as though there are two presentations of the imagined experiment and the choice associated with it, each of which carries conviction, and which lead to contrary conclusions. . . . Following from all that, I am not in the least clear which option it would be wise to take if one were presented with them before the experiment. I find that rather disturbing. . . .

I will end by suggesting one rather shaky way in which one might approach a resolution of the problem, using only the limited materials already available.

The apparently decisive arguments of the first presentation, which suggested that *A* should identify himself with the *B*-body-person, turned on the extreme neatness of the situation in satisfying, if any could, the description of "changing bodies." But this neatness is basically artificial; it is the product of the will of the experimenter to produce a situation which would naturally elicit, with minimum hesitation, that description. By the sorts of methods he employed, he could easily have left off earlier or gone on further. He could have stopped at situation (*v*), leaving *B* as he was; or he could have gone on and produced two persons each with *A*-like character and memories, as well as one or two with *B*-like characteristics. If he had done either of those, we should have been in yet greater difficulty about what to say; he just chose to make it as easy as possible for us to find something to say. Now if we had some model of ghostly persons in bodies, which were in some sense actually moved around by certain procedures, we could regard the neat experiment just as the *effective* experiment: the one method that really did result in the ghostly persons' changing places without being destroyed, dispersed, or whatever. But we cannot seriously use such a model. The experimenter has not in the sense of that model *induced* a change of bodies; he has rather produced the one situation out of a range of equally possible situations which we should be most disposed to call a change of bodies. As against this, the principle that one's fears can extend to future pain whatever psychological changes precede it seems positively straightforward. Perhaps, indeed, it is not; but we need to be shown what is wrong with it. Until we are shown what is wrong with it, we should perhaps decide that if we were the person *A* then, if we were to decide selfishly, we should pass the pain to the *B*-body-person. It would be risky: that there is room for the notion of a *risk* here is itself a major feature of the problem.

TEST YOUR UNDERSTANDING

1. Explain what Williams means by saying that a certain description of "the experiment" is "question-begging."

2. Williams describes a second case, in which someone "tells me that I am going to be tortured tomorrow." How are the previous experiment and the second case related?

3. Williams describes a "series of cases," (i)–(vi), in response to an objection. What is that objection?

4. True or false: Williams concludes that the "bodily" criterion is correct, and that we were simply wrong to describe the first experiment as a case in which *A* and *B* switch bodies.

NOTES AND QUESTIONS

1. Suppose you are *A* in the experiment. Would you choose torture for the *A*-body-person or the *B*-body-person? Give reasons for your answer.

2. Williams's essay is sometimes read as a criticism of the "method of cases" in the philosophy of personal identity. The method proceeds by presenting wild science-fiction scenarios and then asking questions like: If that scenario were actual, would *A* survive as the *A*-body person or as the *B*-body person? We often find ourselves with confident judgments—"intuitions"—about such cases. The method of cases treats these intuitions as constraints on any adequate general theory of personal identity. Williams's article shows, however, that our judgments about cases are sometimes highly sensitive to the manner in which the case is presented to us. Present the case in one way, and we have the confident intuition that *A* switches bodies; present *the very same case* in another way, and we have the intuition that *A* remains with his original body.

   Exercise: Use the examples from Williams's paper or others of your own to mount a full-throated critique of the method of cases. Then imagine how a defender of the method might respond.

3. Williams's classic papers on personal identity and related topics are collected in his *Problems of the Self* (Cambridge University Press, 1973).

ANALYZING THE ARGUMENTS

1. Locke's theory of personal identity is often taken to be something like this:

    The Memory Criterion of personal identity: a person Y existing at a later time is identical to a person X at an earlier time if and only if Y can remember some of X's experiences.

    The Scottish philosopher Thomas Reid (1710–1796) gave the following famous counterexample to the Memory Criterion:

    An old general recalls taking a flag from the enemy as a young officer. When he was a young officer, he could remember being flogged as a boy. But now, when an old general, he can't remember this.

    Explain why this is a counterexample to the Memory Criterion. (You may need to fill out some details of the case.) Parfit's Psychological Criterion is designed to evade Reid's objection. Say how it does so.

2. Preliminary definitions:

    A person P *survives* some event or happening E just in case P exists before E occurs, and when E is over, there exists some person who is (numerically) identical to P.

    Teletransportation is the process described by Parfit (see "Personal Identity" in this chapter).

    The Cartesian Criterion of personal identity: A person Y at a later time is identical to a person X at an earlier time if and only if X and Y have the same soul.

    The Bodily Criterion of personal identity: A person Y at a later time is identical to a person X at an earlier time if and only if X and Y have the same body.

    The Brain Criterion of personal identity: A person Y at a later time is identical to a person X at an earlier time if and only if X and Y have the same brain.

    Exercise: Consider the question:

    Does a person survive teletransportation?

    and say how proponents of the Cartesian, Body, Brain, and Parfit's Psychological criteria would answer. Try to imagine a real case in which you desperately need to get to Mars and are offered a choice between teletransportation and a much more expensive and time-consuming journey by spaceship. Say which option you would choose and why. (Assume that teletransportation will certainly work as advertised, and in particular that there is no chance of inadvertent duplication.)

3. Were you once a 4-week-old fetus in your mother's womb? Say how Locke, Swinburne, Parfit, and Williams might answer. Then defend your own answer in light of the arguments given by these authors.

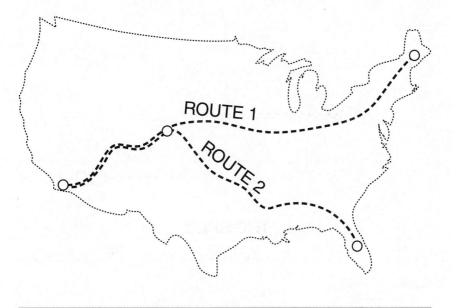

Figure 1

4. Parfit argues that in the case of My Division, I cease to exist, since the person who exists before the split is not identical to either of the people who exist afterward. This has been disputed by the American philosopher David Lewis (1941–2001). We are all familiar with cases in which two roads coincide in certain places while diverging elsewhere. So consider two transcontinental highways, Route 1 and Route 2. The roads begin together in Los Angeles and coincide until Denver, at which point Route 1 heads off to Maine, while Route 2 heads off to Florida (Figure 1).

Someone who is crossing the road near Los Angeles may well think that he is only crossing one road, but in fact he's crossing two. The false impression is due to the fact that these two roads, while clearly *different*, nonetheless share an "initial segment." According to Lewis, just as roads are spread out in space, so people and other persisting objects are spread out in time. There is a part of you that stretches from your birth until your fifth birthday, and another (larger) part that stretches from your birth until your twelfth birthday. This is a controversial view, but suppose it is right. The case of My Division then looks like Figure 2.

There are definitely two people at the end of the process, here called "*B*" and "*C*." But how many people were there at the start? Parfit assumes that there was only one—call him or her "*A*"—and argues that $A \neq B$ and $A \neq C$, from which it follows that fission is a sort of death. Lewis denies this assumption. Just as there were two roads between California and Denver that share an initial (spatial) segment, so there were two people prior to the division who share an initial (temporal) segment. If this is right, then it is a mistake to ask whether *the* person prior to the division survived as *B* or as *C*, just as it is a mistake to ask whether *the* road from Los Angeles to Denver continues on to Maine.

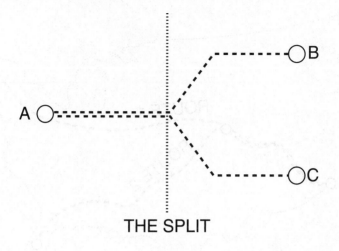

THE SPLIT

Figure 2

This view allows us to say that division is sometimes a matter of genuine survival, in the sense that *everyone* who is present before the split is also present afterward.

The view raises fascinating questions. For discussion, see Lewis's difficult but rewarding paper, "Survival and Identity," in his *Philosophical Papers*, Vol. 1 (Cambridge University Press, 1983).

5. *The paradox of increase.* The selections focus on *personal* identity, but some puzzles about identity over time arise even in the case of inanimate material things. Consider the *paradox of increase*:

> We have a tower T made out of five wooden blocks. You might think that we could make T taller by adding another block on the top. But we can't. After all, T and the five-block stack are identical. But when we add a new block on top, the five-block stack does not grow. It's still there, and it still contains five blocks. Adding a sixth block may bring a new object into existence: a six-block stack, which contains the original five-block stack as a part. But nothing has *grown* in this story. An old object has stayed the same, and a new object has come to be. But of course there is nothing special about towers made of wooden blocks. The case shows that *material objects cannot grow by acquiring new parts.* Every case that we might be tempted to describe in this way is really a matter of an old object remaining as it was, and a new object coming to be.

Exercise: Consider a response to this bizarre argument and say whether or not it succeeds. For discussion, see Eric Olson, "The Paradox of Increase," Monist 89 (2006): 390–417.

12

What Is Race?
What Is Gender?

What do the U.S. Census, college application forms, and online dating websites have in common? They are all very keen to find out your *sex, race,* and *age.* The social and personal significance of these three categories can hardly be overestimated. Of these three, age is clear-cut and not open to debate. Once we know your date of birth, your age is settled. Whether you "feel like a 20-year-old" or whether people treat you as a teenager is irrelevant. But sex and race are much more complicated. The Common Application for U.S. colleges recently replaced "sex" with "sex assigned at birth" and added a field on gender identity. The first U.S. Census—the census of 1790—had three non-overlapping socio-racial categories: "Free whites," "All other free persons," and "Slaves." Starting in 2000, the census allowed people to identify with more than one race. The past decennial census, in 2010, had six single-race categories (including "Some other race"), with 3 percent of Americans choosing from more than one category.

You are, say, an Asian woman. Like it or not, your race and sex have significantly affected how people relate to you and how you think of yourself. But what is it to be Asian? Or a woman? The readings in this chapter grapple with these questions.

Out of Africa

Your ancestors lived in Africa. Maybe your parents live there today, if you are an immigrant from Nigeria. But even if your great great . . . great great grandparents came to America on the *Mayflower* and your family lives in Ohio, your ancestry eventually reaches back to Africa. That is where modern humans—*Homo sapiens*—evolved, about 200,000 years ago.

According to the currently favored theory, the most significant wave of human migration out of Africa occurred between 80,000 and 40,000 years ago. The migrants spread into Europe, Asia, and Australia around 50,000 years ago and reached the

Americas relatively recently, around 15,000 years ago. When groups of the same species become isolated from each other, for instance by oceans and mountains, they begin to genetically diverge. Some of this divergence will be due to random factors that have limited effects on reproductive success, but natural selection will also play a role, especially if the environments of the separated groups are significantly different. In the case of modern humans, increased genetic diversity arose via interbreeding with at least two extinct kinds of human: Neanderthals in Europe and Asia, and Denisovans in Asia. The visible marks of these events are the anatomical differences between individuals that, taken together, correlate (imperfectly) with their geographic ancestry. There are invisible marks too, the extent of them only recently revealed by modern genomics. Your DNA contains complex patterns of genetic variants (alleles) that indicate whether your distant ancestors stayed in (sub-Saharan) Africa or settled in Eurasia (here stipulated to be North Africa/Europe/Asia east and south of the Himalayas[1]), East Asia, Oceania (which includes Australia and the Pacific Islands), or the Americas.[2] You may well have significant ancestry from more than one of these groups; for instance, according to one estimate, the ancestry of the average African American is 73 percent African, 24 percent Eurasian (specifically, European), and 1 percent Native American.[3] If you want to find this sort of thing out about yourself, you can pay a modest fee and mail a saliva sample to a personal genomics company.

For brevity, let's say that if your ancestry is predominantly African (Eurasian, American, . . .), then you *are* African (Eurasian, American, . . .). Although Africans, Eurasians, Americans, East Asians, and Oceanians carry a signature of their origins in their DNA, there are no genes shared by all and only those people who belong to one of these five groups. So there are no "East Asian" genes, although (to take just one example) East Asians are especially unlikely to have alleles that allow the digestion of milk beyond childhood.

People living in the nineteenth century would have been Oceanian, East Asian, and so on, even if humanity had blown itself up in the twentieth century and never developed the Out of Africa theory or DNA sequencing techniques. In that sense, the five categories are perfectly "objective." But biology provides no basis for thinking that these categories "carve nature at the joints"[4]: the distinction between Africans and Eurasians is more like the distinction between water from different

---

1. Strictly speaking, Eurasia is composed of Europe and Asia.

2. Studies typically use genetic variants (alleles) in regions of DNA that do not code for proteins (which is the main function of genes), so-called *non-coding* regions. Coding regions are only about 2 percent of human DNA (also known as the *human genome*). "Allele" is often used more narrowly to mean "variant of a gene" (as in some of the selections in this chapter).

3. See K. Bryc et al., "The Genetic Ancestry of African Americans, Latinos, and European Americans across the United States," *American Journal of Human Genetics* 96: 37–53 (2015).

4. This metaphor is from the ancient Greek philosopher Plato (excerpts from Plato's works are in Chapters 3 and 18 of this anthology). A "joint" in nature is supposed to be a "natural" or "nonarbitrary" division, like the division between gold and silver, or plants and animals. The division between things you like and things you don't like, or things that happen on Tuesdays and things that happen on Wednesdays, are "unnatural" divisions. Some divisions—arguably those between the five categories (African, Eurasian, . . .)—are in between.

ocean regions than that between the elements nickel and iron. Someone (like former U.S. President Barack Obama) whose ancestry is evenly split between African and Eurasian is in no interesting biological sense a "mixture" of purer ingredients. Obama is not like bronze, a mixture or alloy of pure nickel and iron; he is more like a blend of samples from different parts of the Pacific. Chemically, the ocean waters that are blended are just as "mixed" as the resulting blend.

A different but equally important point is that the *fivefold* division is just one of many that can be extracted from the genetic data and the facts about human migrations. We could divide humanity more coarsely (say, between the Africans and the rest) or much more finely, dividing the Africans or Eurasians into numerous geographically based subgroups. Using the same basic genetic techniques, we might even be able to tell that your ancestors lived in a remote village in northeastern Italy.

As with science in general, researchers don't all agree on the fine details of genetics and human history. But the real controversy starts when we ask how our everyday racial categories fit into the broad-brush scientific picture just sketched. One possibility is that the five "continental" categories simply *are* (some of) the racial categories recognized in everyday life, although ordinary people use different names: "black" instead of "African," "white/Caucasian" instead of "Eurasian," "Asian" instead of "East Asian," "Native American" instead of "American," "Pacific Islander" instead of "Oceanian."[5] However, Barack Obama is black, despite the fact that his mother is white. And the notorious "one drop rule" prevalent in the southern United States in the nineteenth and early twentieth centuries labeled a person with any African ancestry as black (a "Negro," in the language of the time). Focusing on the immense social significance that has been attached to race, racial terms can look more like ways of classifying people as subordinate or privileged, like "serf" or "aristocrat," than as belonging to (relatively superficial) human ancestral groups.

At least a serf can hope for upward mobility, but historically human races were supposed to correspond to levels in some natural (or perhaps divine) immutable hierarchy of basic human types, with whites at the top. For example, the eighteenth-century Swedish naturalist Carl Linnaeus (who founded modern biological classification), characterized what he called "*Homo sapiens asiaticus*" as "yellow, melancholy, greedy. Hair black. Eyes dark. Severe, haughty, desirous. Covered by loose garments. Ruled by opinion."[6] If something like that is built in to the meaning of "Asian" and other ordinary words for races, then a better comparison is with terms such as "angel" and "demon." There really were serfs and aristocrats, but there never were any angels or demons (despite the fact that some people claimed to have seen them).

5. What about South Asians (e.g., Indians)? Their racial classification has varied. The 1970 U.S. Census included them as white; in the 2010 census, "Asian Indian" is an option, which is a subcategory of "Asian."

What about Aboriginal Australians? For simplicity we can set them aside, because the most widely cited paper that identified these five "continental" categories—N. A. Rosenberg et al., "Genetic Structure of Human Populations," *Science* 298: 2381–85 (2002)—did not include genetic data from this group. (For a recent genetic study, see A.-S. Malaspinas et al., "A Genomic History of Aboriginal Australia," *Nature* 538: 207–14 [2016].)

6. Quoted in L. E. Lassiter, *Invitation to Anthropology* (AltaMira Press, 2009), 25.

This gives us (at least) three positions: races are populations with a common ancient ancestry, social categories of some kind, or nothing at all. The first two are forms of **realism** about race; the latter is **eliminativism** about race, so called because races have been "eliminated" from the categories that really apply to things. According to the racial eliminativist, no one is white or Asian, just as no one is an angel or a demon. All three positions are represented in the selections: Quayshawn Spencer uses the genetic results just discussed to defend the first,[7] and Anthony Appiah defends the third. The second position is represented by Sally Haslanger—but with a twist.

Suppose that Appiah is right, and that no one belongs to any race. Then what? Should we continue to classify people as white, Asian, and so on, even though no one really is white or Asian? Suppose, alternatively, that Spencer is right, and our racial classifications are often correct, because people belong to the appropriate ancestral/biological category. Given the pernicious influence that biological theories of race have had in the past, is it really a good idea to think of our fellow humans as members of different biological kinds? (Similar questions could be raised if we suppose that races are like the social categories of *serf* and *aristocrat*.) Whatever races turn out to be, there is the further question of how we should continue to talk.

And this is where Haslanger joins the debate. She is not primarily concerned to find out *what races are*, but how we *should* use terms like "white race" and "Asian race" in a way that will "contribute to empowering critical social agents" (see page 569 of this anthology). And, as we will shortly see, Haslanger takes a similar approach to the terms "man" and "woman."

Sex and Gender

Eliminativism about race is endorsed by a number of eminent biologists. But biologists do not seriously entertain eliminativism about sex (the categories of male and female). Any textbook will tell you that humans come in two main varieties, males and females. (This is compatible with the occasional case of neither or both.[8]) Male and female humans differ not just in sexual organs but also in many other respects; for example, size, the presence of breasts, and distribution of body hair. In biological terminology, our species (like many others) is *sexually dimorphic*.

With few exceptions, humans have 23 pairs of chromosomes in their cells, essentially packages of DNA.[9] The two *sex chromosomes* form one of these pairs, with one chromosome inherited from the father and the other from the mother. A typical

---

7. However, Spencer defines the five continental groups a bit differently, so that every person (no matter how diverse his or her ancestry) belongs to at least one group.

8. Biology provides many non-human examples of both (e.g., slugs) or neither (e.g., bacteria). Some species possess the ability to change from one sex to another (e.g., clownfish).

9. More exactly, 23 pairs in all cells other than the *gametes*, or *sex cells* (sperm and eggs), which have 23 unpaired chromosomes.

human female has two X chromosomes (and so is *genetically female*); a typical male has one X and one Y chromosome.[10] A typical human female is *externally female*, having a distinctive cluster of external bodily features: breasts (in the adult), vagina, a smaller forehead, . . . ; a typical male is *externally male*. A typical human female is *gonadally female*, with ovaries (female gonads) that produce eggs; a typical male is *gonadally male*, with testes that produce sperm. A typical human female is sexually attracted to males, and vice versa for typical males—this is their *sexual orientation*. Finally, a typical human female thinks of herself as female, or "identifies as" female, and vice versa for typical males—this is their *sexual identity*. The following mostly go together: XX, external female, gonadal female, sexual orientation to males, female sexual identity, with a similar clustering for typical males. Do they *always* go together? The common phenomenon of homosexuality shows that they don't. But this is just the tip of the iceberg: almost every other combination can occur.[11] Someone with a condition called *complete androgen insensitivity syndrome (CAIS)* is XY and gonadally male (with undescended testes) but externally female, and will likely have an attraction to males and a female sexual identity. Someone with *XX male syndrome* is XX but gonadally male and usually externally male with a male sexual identity. And there are plenty more examples.

Scientists do not usually waste time debating whether someone with CAIS is *really* female—the necessary distinctions can be made using the appropriate technical terms ("XY," "externally female," and so on). Still, although "female" (like most other terms) cannot be precisely defined, it's still very useful for theorizing about the biological world.

Unlike "XY," "externally female," and so forth, "male" and "female" are not special bits of scientific jargon but words of ordinary English. "Female" and "male," as they appear in biology and psychology journals, seem to mean whatever they mean on birth certificates or college application forms. However, outside the sciences (and the police force), people are rarely called "female" or "male": instead they are called "women," "girls," "men," or "boys." So what's the relation between, say, being a woman and being female?

One obvious answer, found in dictionaries, is that a woman is an *adult human female*. Suppose that is right. It makes perfect sense to suppose that there are adult human females who live isolated from any kind of society: presumably there have been some real examples over the course of 200,000 years of human history. Being an adult human female, then, is not something that requires the presence of social organizations, cultural expectations and standards, power relations, or anything like that. So being a woman doesn't require that either: "woman" does not pick out a *social category* (or social **property**). In that respect, "woman" is quite

---

10. There is nothing especially "male" about having two kinds of sex chromosome: in birds, the female is the one with two kinds.

11. In addition to the various combinations of these features, there are also cases where *neither* of each feature pair is present. For instance, someone may be *asexual*, not having a sexual orientation either to males or females. Or someone might be genetically XO (just one X) or XYY, among other possibilities.

unlike "queen," "policewoman," or "wife"—without society, there are no queens, policewomen, or wives.

An obvious answer might not be the *right* answer. And, in this case, the obvious answer has been disputed. As the philosopher Mari Mikkola puts it:

> Most people ordinarily seem to think that sex and gender are coextensive: women are human females, men are human males. Many feminists have historically disagreed and have endorsed the sex/gender distinction.[12]

What is the "sex/gender distinction"? Roughly, it is the distinction between *sex* (male, female, and related biological categories such as XY, externally female, etc.) and (as Sally Haslanger says in her essay) the "social meaning of sex" (p. 563). So, for example, if, in society A, adult human females are expected to look after the children and work in the fields, and adult human males are expected to wear pants and take all the political decisions, then these are *facts about gender* (in society A)— facts about the social meaning or significance attaching to biological categories.[13]

If the sex/gender distinction is explained this way, it is compatible with the obvious answer above, that someone is a woman if and only if she is an adult human female. If the obvious answer is right, then the category picked out by "woman" lies on the sex side of the sex/gender distinction: the fact that Eve is a woman is simply a biological fact, not a fact about gender. But of course that is not to *deny* that there are facts about gender, that there is something on the gender side of the sex/gender distinction—perhaps Eve is expected to help Adam and to obey him.

However, as the quotation from Mikkola shows, some writers who attach a lot of importance to the sex/gender distinction have done so *because* they disagree with the obvious answer. According to them, the category of women is *not* the same as the category of adult human females or any other biological category. What is it, then? Perhaps some sort of *social* category, something on the gender side of the sex/gender distinction, but there are other options. In her essay, Elizabeth Barnes addresses this issue. She first argues that *being a woman* is not a biological category and then examines some leading proposals for what it might be instead. She argues that they are all problematic. According to Barnes, we need an answer to the question "What is a woman?" but no existing answers are satisfactory.

In her essay, Haslanger is concerned with the same issues but (as with race) from a more prescriptive angle. Rather than investigating what it is to *be* a woman (or to *be* white), she asks what the *word* "woman" (or "white") *should* pick out, given that we have "the goal of understanding racial and sexual oppression, and of

---

12. "Feminist Perspectives on Sex and Gender," in *Stanford Encyclopedia of Philosophy*, ed. Edward Zalta, (https://plato.stanford.edu/archives/spr2016/entries/feminism-gender/), section 1.1.

13. Terminological warning! Scientists often use "gender" more-or-less equivalently with "sex/sexual," thus using "gender identity" to mean *sexual identity*, "gender differences" to mean *sex differences*, and so on. A scientific paper on the "effects of gender" in the rat is unlikely to be about the meaning of sex in rat society. And in ordinary life, "gender" is usually just a way to talk about males and females, as in "gender pay gap."

achieving sexual and racial equality" (p. 568). She recommends a "terminological shift," so that "woman" picks out a kind of *subordinated* social category. With the shift made, "part of the project of feminism [is] to bring about a day when there are no more women (though, of course, we should not aim to do away with females!)" (pp. 567–68).

Some of the chapters in this anthology concern issues that have preoccupied philosophers since ancient Greece. But philosophy is a living subject and, as this chapter shows, new questions and topics can come to seem just as important and puzzling as the old ones.

Anthony Appiah (b. 1954)

Kwame Anthony Appiah is Professor of Philosophy and Law at New York University and works principally in ethics, political philosophy, philosophy of mind, and philosophy of race. His many books include *In My Father's House: Africa in the Philosophy of Culture* (Oxford University Press, 1992) and *As If: Idealization and Ideals* (Harvard University Press, 2017). He is also the ethicist columnist for the *New York Times Magazine*.

THE UNCOMPLETED ARGUMENT: DU BOIS AND THE ILLUSION OF RACE

Introduction

Contemporary biologists are not agreed on the question of whether there are any human races, despite the widespread scientific consensus on the underlying genetics. For most purposes, however, we can reasonably treat this issue as terminological. What most people in most cultures ordinarily believe about the significance of "racial" difference is quite remote, I think, from what the biologists are agreed on. Every reputable biologist will agree that human genetic variability between the populations of Africa or Europe or Asia is not much greater than that within those populations; though how much greater depends, in part, on the measure of genetic variability the biologist chooses. If biologists want to make interracial difference seem relatively large, they can say that "the proportion of genic variation attributable to racial differences is . . . 9–11%."[1] If they want to make it seem small, they can say that, for two people who are both Caucasoid, the chances of difference in genetic constitution at one site on a given chromosome are currently estimated at about 14.3 percent, while for any

---

1. Masatoshi Nei and Arun K. Roychoudhury, "Genetic Relationship and Evolution of Human Races," *Evolutionary Biology* 14 (1983): 11; all further references to this work, abbreviated "GR," will be included in the text. [Appiah's note.]

two people taken at random from the human population, they are estimated at about 14.8 percent. (I will discuss why this is considered a measure of genetic difference in section 2.) The statistical facts about the distribution of variant characteristics in human populations and subpopulations are the same, whichever way the matter is expressed. Apart from the visible morphological characteristics of skin, hair, and bone, by which we are inclined to assign people to the broadest racial categories—black, white, yellow—there are few genetic characteristics to be found in the population of England that are not found in similar proportions in Zaire or in China; and few too (though more) which are found in Zaire but not in similar proportions in China or in England. All this, I repeat, is part of the consensus (see "GR," pp. 1–59). A more familiar part of the consensus is that the differences between peoples in language, moral affections, aesthetic attitudes, or political ideology—those differences which most deeply affect us in our dealings with each other—are not biologically determined to any significant degree.

These claims will, no doubt, seem outrageous to those who confuse the question of whether biological difference accounts for our differences with the question of whether biological similarity accounts for our similarities. Some of our similarities as human beings in these broadly cultural respects—the capacity to acquire human languages, for example, or, more specifically, the ability to smile—*are* to a significant degree biologically determined. We can study the biological basis of these cultural capacities and give biological explanations of our exercise of them. But if biological difference between human beings is unimportant in these explanations—and it is—then racial difference, as a species of biological difference, will not matter either.

In this essay, I want to discuss the way in which W. E. B. Du Bois[2]—who called his life story the "autobiography of a race concept"—came gradually, though never completely, to assimilate the unbiological nature of races. . . .

1. "The Conservation of Races"

Du Bois' first extended discussion of the concept of race is in "The Conservation of Races" (1897), a paper he delivered to the American Negro Academy in the year it was founded. The "American Negro," he declares, has "been led to . . . minimize race distinctions" because "back of most of the discussions of race with which he is familiar, have lurked certain assumptions as to his natural abilities, as to his political, intellectual and moral status, which he felt were wrong." Du Bois continues: "Nevertheless, in our calmer moments we must acknowledge that human beings are divided into races," even if when we "come to inquire into the essential difference of races we find it hard to come at once to any definite conclusion." For what it is worth, however, the "final

---

2. William Edward Burghardt Du Bois (1868–1963), American sociologist and cofounder of the National Association for the Advancement of Colored People (NAACP). In 1895, Du Bois became the first African American to receive a PhD from Harvard University.

word of science, so far, is that we have at least two, perhaps three, great families of human beings—the whites and Negroes, possibly the yellow race."[3]

Du Bois is not, however, satisfied with the final word of nineteenth-century science. For, as he thinks, what matter are not the "grosser physical differences of color, hair and bone" but the "differences—subtle, delicate and elusive, though they may be—which have silently but definitely separated men into groups" ("CR," p. 75).

> While these subtle forces have generally followed the natural cleavage of common blood, descent and physical peculiarities, they have at other times swept across and ignored these. At all times, however, they have divided human beings into races, which, while they perhaps transcend scientific definition, nevertheless, are clearly defined to the eye of the historian and sociologist.
>
> If this be true, then the history of the world is the history, not of individuals, but of groups, not of nations, but of races. . . . What, then, is a race? It is a vast family of human beings, generally of common blood and language, always of common history, traditions and impulses, who are both voluntarily and involuntarily striving together for the accomplishment of certain more or less vividly conceived ideals of life. ["CR," pp. 75–76]

We have moved, then, away from the "scientific"—that is, biological and anthropological—conception of race to a sociohistorical notion. Using this sociohistorical criterion—the sweep of which certainly encourages the thought that no biological or anthropological definition is possible—Du Bois considers that there are not three but eight "distinctly differentiated races, in the sense in which history tells us the word must be used" ("CR," p. 76). The list is an odd one: Slavs, Teutons, English (both in Great Britain and America), Negroes (of Africa and, likewise, America), the Romance race, Semites, Hindus and Mongolians.

. . . For Du Bois . . . the problem for the Negro is the discovery and expression of the message of his or her race.

> The full, complete Negro message of the whole Negro race has not as yet been given to the world.
>
> The question is, then: how shall this message be delivered; how shall these various ideals be realized? The answer is plain: by the development of these race groups, not as individuals, but as races. . . . For the development of Negro genius, of Negro literature and art, of Negro spirit, only Negroes bound and welded together, Negroes inspired by one vast ideal, can work out in its fullness the great message we have for humanity.
>
> For this reason, the advance guard of the Negro people—the eight million people of Negro blood in the United States of America—must soon come to realize that if they are to take their just place in the van of Pan-Negroism, then their destiny is not absorption by the white Americans. ["CR," pp. 78, 79]

---

3. W. E. B. Du Bois, "The Conservation of Races," in *W. E. B. Du Bois Speaks: Speeches and Addresses, 1890–1919,* ed. Philip S. Foner (1897; New York, 1970), pp. 73, 74, 75; all further references to this work, abbreviated "CR," will be included in the text. [Appiah's note.]

Du Bois ends by proposing his Academy Creed, which begins with words that echo down almost a century of American race relations:

1. We believe that the Negro people, as a race, have a contribution to make to civilization and humanity, which no other race can make.

2. We believe it the duty of the Americans of Negro descent, as a body, to maintain their race identity until this mission of the Negro people is accomplished, and the ideal of human brotherhood has become a practical possibility. ["CR," p. 84]

What can we make of this analysis and prescription?

On the face of it, Du Bois' argument in "The Conservation of Races" is that "race" is not a scientific—that is, biological—concept. It is a sociohistorical concept. Sociohistorical races each have a "message" for humanity—a message which derives, in some way, from God's purpose in creating races. The Negro race has still to deliver its full message, and so it is the duty of Negroes to work together—through race organizations—so that this message can be delivered.

We do not need the theological underpinnings of this argument. What is essential is the thought that through common action Negroes can achieve, by virtue of their sociohistorical community, worthwhile ends which will not otherwise be achieved. On the face of it, then, Du Bois' strategy here is the antithesis in the classic dialectic[4] of reaction to prejudice.

The thesis in this dialectic—which Du Bois reports as the American Negro's attempt to "minimize race distinctions"—is the denial of difference. Du Bois' antithesis is the acceptance of difference, along with a claim that each group has its part to play; that the white race and its racial Other are related not as superior to inferior but as complementaries; that the Negro message is, with the white one, part of the message of humankind.

I call this pattern the classic dialectic for a simple reason: we find it in feminism also—on the one hand, a simple claim to equality, a denial of substantial difference; on the other, a claim to a special message, revaluing the feminine Other not as the helpmeet of sexism, but as the New Woman.

... At the center of Du Bois' conception ... is the claim that a race is "a vast family of human beings, ... always of common history [and] traditions." So, if we want to understand Du Bois, our question must be: What is a family of common history? ...

The criterion Du Bois actually uses amounts to this: people are members of the same race if they share features in virtue of being descended largely from people of the same region. Those features may be physical—hence Afro-Americans are Negroes—or cultural—hence Anglo-Americans are English. Focusing on one sort of feature—"grosser ... differences of color, hair and bone"—defines "whites and

---

4. "Classic dialectic": process beginning with a *thesis* and an (apparently) incompatible **proposition**, the *antithesis*, with the (apparent) incompatibility being resolved by the *synthesis*.

Negroes, possibly the yellow race" as the "final word of science, so far." Focusing on a different feature—language or shared customs—defines instead Teutons, Slavs, and Romance peoples. The tension in Du Bois' definition of race reflects the fact that, for the purposes of European historiography . . . , it was the latter that mattered; but for the purposes of American social and political life, it was the former.

The real difference in Du Bois' conception, therefore, is not that his definition of race is at odds with the scientific one. It is, rather, as the classic dialectic requires, that he assigns to race a moral and metaphysical significance different from that of his contemporaries. The distinctive claim is that the Negro race has a positive message, a message not only of difference but of value. . . .

2. "Crisis": August 1911

We have seen that, for the purpose that concerned him most—understanding the status of the Negro—Du Bois was thrown back on the scientific definition of race, which he officially rejected. But the scientific definition (Du Bois' uneasiness with which is reflected in his remark that races "perhaps transcend scientific definition") was itself threatened as he spoke at the first meeting of the Negro Academy. In the later nineteenth century most thinking people (like too many even today) believed that what Du Bois called the "grosser differences" were a sign of an inherited racial essence which accounted for the intellectual and moral deficiency of the "lower" races. In "The Conservation of Races" Du Bois elected, in effect, to admit that color was a sign of a racial essence but to deny that the cultural capacities of the black-skinned, curly-haired members of humankind were inferior to those of the white-skinned, straighter-haired ones. But the collapse of the sciences of racial inferiority led Du Bois to deny the connection between cultural capacity and gross morphology—the familiar impulses and strivings of his earlier definition.

We can find evidence of his change of mind in an article in the August 1911 issue of the *Crisis*.

> The leading scientists of the world have come forward . . . and laid down in categorical terms a series of propositions which may be summarized as follows:
>
> 1. It is not legitimate to argue from differences in physical characteristics to differences in mental characteristics. . . .
>
> 2. The civilization of a . . . race at any particular moment of time offers no index to its innate or inherited capacities.[5]

---

5. Du Bois, "Races," *Crisis*, August 1911, pp. 157–58. [Appiah's note.]

These results have been amply confirmed since then. And we do well, I think, to remind ourselves of the current picture.

Human characteristics are genetically determined, to the extent that they are determined, by sequences of DNA in the chromosome—in other words, by genes. The region of a chromosome occupied by a gene is called a locus. Some loci are occupied in different members of a population by different genes, each of which is called an allele; and a locus is said to be polymorphic in a population if there is at least one pair of alleles for it. Perhaps as many as half the loci in the human population are polymorphic; the rest, naturally enough, are monomorphic.

. . . The chances . . . that two people taken at random from the human population will have the same characteristic at a locus, are about 85.2 percent, while the chances for two (white) people taken from the population of England are about 85.7 percent. And since 85.2 is 100 minus 14.8 and 85.7 is 100 minus 14.3, this is equivalent to what I said in the introduction: the chances of two people who are both Caucasoid differing in genetic constitution at one site on a given chromosome are about 14.3 percent, while, for any two people taken at random from the human population, they are about 14.8 percent. The conclusion is obvious: given only a person's race, it is hard to say what his or her biological characteristics will be, except in respect of the "grosser" features of color, hair, and bone (the genetics of which are, in any case, rather poorly understood)—features of "morphological differentiation," as the evolutionary biologist would say. As Nei and Roychoudhury express themselves, somewhat coyly, "The extent of genic differentiation between human races is not always correlated with the degree of morphological differentiation" ("GR," p. 44).

To establish that race is relatively unimportant in explaining biological differences between people, where biological difference is measured in the proportion of differences in loci on the chromosome, is not yet to show that race is unimportant in explaining cultural difference. It could be that large differences in intellectual or moral capacity are caused by differences at very few loci and that, at these loci, all (or most) black-skinned people differ from all (or most) white-skinned or yellow-skinned ones. As it happens, there is little evidence for any such proposition and much against it. But suppose we had reason to believe it. In the biological conception of the human organism, in which characteristics are determined by the pattern of genes in interaction with environments, it is the presence of the alleles (which give rise to these moral and intellectual capacities) that accounts for the observed differences in those capacities in people in similar environments. So the characteristic racial morphology—skin and hair and bone—could only be a sign of those differences if it were (highly) correlated with those alleles. Furthermore, even if it were so correlated, the causal explanation of the differences would be that they differed in those alleles, not that they differed in race. Since there are no such strong correlations, even those who think that intellectual and moral character are strongly genetically determined must accept that race is at best a poor indicator of capacity.

But it was earlier evidence, pointing similarly to the conclusion that "the interracial genic variation is small compared with the intraracial variation" ("GR," p. 40) and that differences in morphology were not correlated strongly with intellectual and moral capacity, which led Du Bois in the *Crisis* to an explicit rejection of the claim that biological race mattered for understanding the status of the Negro:

> So far at least as intellectual and moral aptitudes are concerned, we ought to speak of civilizations where we now speak of races. . . . Indeed, even the physical characteristics, excluding the skin color of a people, are to no small extent the direct result of the physical and social environment under which it is living. . . . These physical characteristics are furthermore too indefinite and elusive to serve as a basis for any rigid classification or division of human groups.[6]

This is straightforward enough. Yet it would be too swift a conclusion to suppose that Du Bois here expresses his deepest convictions. After 1911, he went on to advocate Pan-Africanism, as he had advocated Pan-Negroism in 1897, and whatever Afro-Americans and Africans, from Ashanti to Zulu, share, it is not a single civilization.

Du Bois managed to maintain Pan-Africanism while officially rejecting talk of race as anything other than a synonym for color. We can see how he did this by turning to his second autobiography, *Dusk of Dawn*, published in 1940.

3. "Dusk of Dawn"

In *Dusk of Dawn*—the "essay toward an autobiography of a race concept"—Du Bois explicitly allies himself with the claim that race is not a scientific concept.

> It is easy to see that scientific definition of race is impossible; it is easy to prove that physical characteristics are not so inherited as to make it possible to divide the world into races; that ability is the monopoly of no known aristocracy; that the possibilities of human development cannot be circumscribed by color, nationality, or any conceivable definition of race.[7]

But we need no scientific definition, for

> all this has nothing to do with the plain fact that throughout the world today organized groups of men by monopoly of economic and physical power, legal enactment and intellectual training are limiting with determination and unflagging zeal the development of other groups; and that the concentration particularly of economic power today puts the majority of mankind into a slavery to the rest. [*D*, pp. 137–38]

Or, as he puts it pithily a little later,

> the black man is a person who must ride "Jim Crow"[8] in Georgia. [*D*, p. 153]

---

6. Du Bois, "Races," p. 158. [Appiah's note.]

7. Du Bois, *Dusk of Dawn: An Essay toward an Autobiography of a Race Concept* (1940; New York, 1975), p. 137. All further references to this work, abbreviated *D*, will be included in the text. [Appiah's note.]

8. "Ride 'Jim Crow'": be confined to legally and socially enforced black-only spaces.

Yet, just a few pages earlier, he has explained why he remains a Pan-Africanist, committed to a political program which binds all this indefinable black race together. The passage is worth citing extensively.

Du Bois begins with Countee Cullen's question, "What is Africa to me?"[9] and answers,

> Once I should have answered the question simply: I should have said "fatherland" or perhaps better "motherland" because I was born in the century when the walls of race were clear and straight; when the world consisted of mut[u]ally exclusive races; and even though the edges might be blurred, there was no question of exact definition and understanding of the meaning of the word. . . .
>
> Since then [the writing of "The Conservation of Races"] the concept of race has so changed and presented so much of contradiction that as I face Africa I ask myself: what is it between us that constitutes a tie which I can feel better than I can explain? Africa is, of course, my fatherland. Yet neither my father nor my father's father ever saw Africa or knew its meaning or cared overmuch for it. My mother's folk were closer and yet their direct connection, in culture and race, became tenuous; still, my tie to Africa is strong. On this vast continent were born and lived a large portion of my direct ancestors going back a thousand years or more. The mark of their heritage is upon me in color and hair. These are obvious things, but of little meaning in themselves; only important as they stand for real and more subtle differences from other men. Whether they do or not, I do not know nor does science know today.
>
> But one thing is sure and that is the fact that since the fifteenth century these ancestors of mine and their other descendants have had a common history; have suffered a common disaster and have one long memory. The actual ties of heritage between the individuals of this group, vary with the ancestors that they have in common [with] many others: Europeans and Semites, perhaps Mongolians, certainly American Indians. But the physical bond is least and the badge of color relatively unimportant save as a badge; the real essence of this kinship is its social heritage of slavery; the discrimination and insult; and this heritage binds together not simply the children of Africa, but extends through yellow Asia and into the South Seas. It is this unity that draws me to Africa. [D, pp. 116–17]

This passage is affecting, powerfully expressed. We might like to be able to follow it in its conclusions. But we should not; since the passage seduces us into error, we should begin distancing ourselves from the appeal of its argument by noticing how it echoes an earlier text. Color and hair are unimportant save "as they stand for real and more subtle differences," Du Bois says here, and we recall the "subtle forces" that "generally followed the natural cleavage of common blood, descent and physical peculiarities" of

---

9. Countee Cullen (1903–1946) was an American poet; "What is Africa to me?" is from Cullen's poem "Heritage."

"The Conservation of Races." There it was an essential part of the argument that these subtle forces—"impulses" and "strivings"—were the common property of those who shared a "common blood"; here, Du Bois does "not know nor does science" whether this is so. But if it is not so, then, on Du Bois' own admission, these "obvious things" are "of little meaning." If they are of little meaning, then his mention of them marks, on the surface of his argument, the extent to which he cannot quite escape the appeal of the earlier conception of race.

Du Bois' yearning for the earlier conception which he prohibited himself from using accounts for the pathos of the gap between the unconfident certainty that Africa is "of course" his fatherland and the concession that it is not the land of his father or his father's father. What use is such a fatherland? What use is a motherland with which your own mother's connection is "tenuous"? What does it matter that a large portion of his ancestors have lived on that vast continent, if there is no subtler bond with them than brute—that is, culturally unmediated-biological descent and its entailed "badge" of hair and color?

Even in the passage that follows Du Bois' explicit disavowal of the scientific conception of race, the references to "common history"—the "one long memory," the "social heritage of slavery"—only lead us back into the now familiar move of substituting a sociohistorical conception of race for the biological one; but that is simply to bury the biological conception below the surface, not to transcend. Because he never truly "speaks of civilization," Du Bois cannot ask if there is not in American culture—which undoubtedly is his—an African residue to take hold of and rejoice in, a subtle connection mediated not by genetics but by intentions, by meaning. Du Bois has no more conceptual resources here for explicating the unity of the Negro race—the Pan-African identity—than he had in "The Conservation of Races" half a century earlier. A glorious non sequitur must be submerged in the depths of the argument. It is easily brought to the surface.

If what Du Bois has in common with Africa is a history of "discrimination and insult," then this binds him, by his own account, to "yellow Asia and . . . the South Seas" also. How can something he shares with the whole non-white world bind him to only a part of it? Once we interrogate the argument here, a further suspicion arises that the claim to this bond may be based on a hyperbolic reading of the facts. Du Bois' experience of "discrimination and insult" in his American childhood and as an adult citizen of the industrialized world was different in character from that experienced by, say, Kwame Nkrumah[10] in colonized West Africa; it is absent altogether in large parts of "yellow Asia." What Du Bois shares with the non-white world is not insult but the badge of insult; and the badge, without the insult, is the very skin and hair and bone which it is impossible to connect with a scientific definition of race.

10. Kwame Nkrumah (1909–1972), politician who led Ghana to independence from the United Kingdom in 1957.

4. Concluding Unscientific Postscript[11]

Du Bois died in Nkrumah's Ghana, led there by the dream of Pan-Africanism and the reality of American racism. If he escaped that racism, he never completed the escape from race. The logic of his argument leads naturally to the final repudiation of race as a term of difference and to speaking instead "of civilizations where we now speak of races." The logic is the same logic that has brought us to speak of genders where we spoke of sexes, and a rational assessment of the evidence requires that we should endorse not only the logic but the premises of each argument. I have only sketched the evidence for these premises in the case of race, but it is all there in the scientific journals. Discussing Du Bois has been largely a pretext for adumbrating the argument he never quite managed to complete.

I think the argument worth making because I believe that we—scholars in the academy—have not done enough to share it with our fellow citizens. One barrier facing those of us in the humanities has been methodological. Under Saussurian hegemony, we have too easily become accustomed to thinking of meaning as constituted by systems of differences purely internal to our endlessly structured *langues*.[12] Race, we all assume, is, like all other concepts, constructed by metaphor and metonymy; it stands in, metonymically, for the Other; it bears the weight, metaphorically, of other kinds of difference.

Yet, in our social lives away from the text-world of the academy, we take reference for granted too easily. Even if the concept of race is a structure of oppositions—white opposed to black (but also to yellow), Jew opposed to Gentile (but also to Arab)—it is a structure whose realization is, at best, problematic and, at worst, impossible. If we can now hope to understand the concept embodied in this system of oppositions, we are nowhere near finding referents for it. The truth is that there are no races: there is nothing in the world that can do all we ask "race" to do for us. The evil that is done is done by the concept and by easy—yet impossible—assumptions as to its application. What we miss through our obsession with the structure of relations of concepts is, simply, reality.

. . . In his early work, Du Bois took race for granted and sought to revalue one pole of the opposition of white to black. The received concept is a hierarchy, a vertical structure, and Du Bois wished to rotate the axis, to give race a "horizontal" reading. Challenge the assumption that there can be an axis, however oriented in the space of values, and the project fails for loss of presuppositions. In his later work, Du Bois—whose life's work was, in a sense, an attempt at just this impossible project—was unable to escape the notion of race he had explicitly rejected. We may borrow his own metaphor: though he saw the dawn coming, he never faced the sun. And we must surely admit that he is followed in this by many in our culture today; we too live in the dusk of that dawn.

11. An allusion to a work of the same title by the Danish philosopher Søren Kierkegaard (1813–1855).

12. "Saussurian": characterizing the theories of the Swiss linguist Ferdinand de Saussure (1857–1913), who thought of the meaning of a word as dependent on its relations to other words; "*langues*": languages (French, Saussure's term).

TEST YOUR UNDERSTANDING

1. Is Du Bois an **eliminativist** about race?

2. On Du Bois's "sociohistorical" notion of race, what do members of the same race have in common?

   a. blood

   b. civilization

   c. language

   d. history

3. Appiah argues that "race is relatively unimportant in explaining biological differences between people" (p. 554). What premise(s) does he appeal to?

   a. Half the loci in the human population are polymorphic.

   b. Genetic variation within races is much greater than genetic variation between races.

   c. Genetic variation between races is much greater than genetic variation within races.

   d. The propositions endorsed by "leading scientists" as listed by Du Bois in the August 11 issue of *Crisis*.

4. Appiah says that the Du Bois passage quoted on page 556 "seduces us into error." What does Appiah think Du Bois fails to establish?

   a. The Negro race is unified.

   b. There are sharp boundaries between races.

   c. A large portion of his ancestors lived in Africa.

   d. He has had the experience of "discrimination and insult."

NOTES AND QUESTIONS

1. Appiah argues that Du Bois's attempt in *Dusk of Dawn* to forge a nonbiological sociohistorical conception of race fails. What is Appiah's argument? Can you offer a response on Du Bois's behalf to Appiah's objection? Are there other more promising sociohistorical accounts of race? (Another kind of nonbiological conception of race is proposed in the selection by Sally Haslanger in this chapter.)

2. In "The Conservation of Races," Du Bois writes of the "message of the whole Negro race." Suppose we disagree with Du Bois's claim that any racial "message" derives from God's purpose. Suppose, further, that we agree with Du Bois (and disagree with Appiah) on the issue of whether people belong to races. (We can remain neutral on the issue of what races are, exactly.) People of different races have experienced various forms of systematic discrimination, oppression, advantage, and disadvantage. These experiences may provide special knowledge and insight. Is this a way of seeing some truth in DuBois's view that, as Appiah puts it, "races have a 'message' for humanity"?

3. In the final section, Appiah writes that "[T]he logic of [Du Bois's] argument leads naturally to the final repudiation of race as a term of difference." Set out the argument in the form of **premises** and conclusion, so that it is **valid**. (Add premises, if necessary.) Is it **sound**?

4. Appiah himself has an interesting background, counting among his relatives a former king of the Ashanti and the British politician and wartime ambassador to the USSR, Sir Stafford Cripps. His father was a lawyer and politician from Ghana and his mother was an English writer of children's books. Their interracial society wedding in 1953 caused quite a stir, with the justice minister of apartheid-era South Africa condemning it as "disgusting." Appiah's background informs his book *Cosmopolitanism: Ethics in a World of Strangers* (Norton, 2007).

Sally Haslanger (b. 1955)

Haslanger is the Ford Professor of Philosophy at the Massachusetts Institute of Technology and a member of the American Academy of Arts and Sciences. She has worked in metaphysics, epistemology, ancient philosophy, social and political philosophy, feminist philosophy, and critical race theory. Her papers on gender and race are collected in *Resisting Reality* (Oxford University Press, 2012).

GENDER AND RACE: (WHAT) ARE THEY? (WHAT) DO WE WANT THEM TO BE?

If her functioning as a female is not enough to define woman, if we decline also to explain her through "the eternal feminine," and if nevertheless we admit, provisionally, that women do exist, then we must face the question: what is a woman?

—Simone de Beauvoir, *The Second Sex*

I guess you could chuckle and say that I'm just a woman trapped in a woman's body.

—Ellen DeGeneres, *My Point . . . and I Do Have One*

The truth is that there are no races: there is nothing in the world that can do all we ask race to do for us.

—Kwame Anthony Appiah, *In My Father's House*

It is always awkward when someone asks me informally what I'm working on and I answer that I'm trying to figure out what gender is. For outside a rather narrow segment of the academic world, the term "gender" has come to function as the polite way to talk about the sexes. And one thing people feel pretty confident about is their knowledge of the difference between males and females. Males are those human beings with a range of familiar primary and secondary sex characteristics, most important being the penis; females are those with a different set, most important being the vagina or, perhaps, the uterus. Enough said. Against this background, it isn't clear what could be the point of an inquiry, especially a philosophical inquiry, into "what gender is."

But within that rather narrow segment of the academic world concerned with gender issues, not only is there no simple equation of sex and gender, but the seemingly straightforward anatomical distinction between the sexes has been challenged as well. What began as an effort to note that men and women differ socially as well as anatomically has prompted an explosion of different uses of the term "gender." Within these debates, not only is it unclear what gender is and how we should go about understanding it, but whether it is anything at all.

The situation is similar, if not worse, with respect to race. The self-evidence of racial distinctions in everyday American life is at striking odds with the uncertainty about the category of race in law and the academy. Work in the biological sciences has informed us that our practices of racial categorization don't map neatly onto any useful biological classification; but that doesn't settle much, if anything. For what should we make of our tendency to classify individuals according to race, apparently on the basis of physical appearance? And what are we to make of the social and economic consequences of such classifications? Is race real or is it not?

I. The Question(s)

It is useful to begin by reflecting on the questions: "What is gender?" "What is race?" and related questions such as: "What is it to be a man or a woman?"[1] "What is it to be White? Latino? Asian?" There are several different ways to understand, and so respond to, questions of the form, "What is X?" or "What is it to be an X?" For example, the question "What is knowledge?" might be construed in several ways. One might be asking: What is *our* concept of knowledge (looking to a priori methods for an answer)? On a more naturalistic reading one might be asking: What (natural) kind (if any) does our epistemic vocabulary track? Or one might be undertaking a more revisionary project: What is the point of having a concept of knowledge? What concept (if any) would do that work best? These different sorts of projects cannot be kept entirely distinct, but draw upon different methodological strategies. Returning to the questions, "What is race?" or "What is gender?" we can distinguish, then, three projects with importantly different priorities: *conceptual*, *descriptive*, and *analytical*. . . .

[O]n an analytical approach, the questions "What is gender?" or "What is race?" require us to consider what work we want these concepts to do for us; why do we need

---

1. I use the terms "man" and "woman" to distinguish individuals on the basis of gender, the terms "male" and "female" to distinguish individuals on the basis of sex. [Haslanger's note.]

them at all? The responsibility is ours to define them for our purposes. In doing so we will want to be responsive to some aspects of ordinary usage. . . . However, neither ordinary usage nor empirical investigation is overriding, for there is a stipulative element to the project: *this* is the phenomenon we need to be thinking about. Let the term in question refer to it. On this approach, the world by itself can't tell us what gender is, or what race is; it is up to us to decide what in the world, if anything, they are.

This essay pursues an analytical approach to defining race and gender. . . . Although the analyses I offer will point to existing social kinds (and this is no accident), I am not prepared to defend the claim that these social kinds are what our race and gender talk is "really" about. My priority in this inquiry is not to capture what we do mean, but how we might usefully revise what we mean for certain theoretical and political purposes. . . .

II. Critical (Feminist, Antiracist) Theory

. . . [T]he goal of the project is to consider what work the concepts of gender and race might do for us in a critical—specifically feminist and antiracist—social theory, and to suggest concepts that can accomplish at least important elements of that work. So to start: why might feminist antiracists want or need the concepts of gender and race? What work can they do for us?

At the most general level, the task is to develop accounts of gender and race that will be effective tools in the fight against injustice. The broad project is guided by four concerns:

(i) The need to identify and explain persistent inequalities between females and males, and between people of different "colors"[2]; this includes the concern to identify how social forces, often under the guise of biological forces, work to perpetuate such inequalities.

(ii) The need for a framework that will be sensitive to both the similarities and differences among males and females, and the similarities and differences among individuals in groups demarcated by "color"; this includes the concern to identify the effects of interlocking oppressions, e.g., the intersectionality of race, class, and gender.[3]

2. We need here a term for those physical features of individuals that mark them as members of a race. One might refer to them as "racial" features, but to avoid any suggestion of racial essences I will use the term "color" to refer to the (contextually variable) physical "markers" of race, just as I use the term "sex" to refer to the (contextually variable) physical "markers" of gender. I mean to include in "color" more than just skin tone: common markers also include eye, nose, and lip shape, hair texture, physique, etc. [Haslanger's note.]

3. That is, how race, class, and gender interact. See **intersectionality**.

(iii) The need for an account that will track how gender and race are implicated in a broad range of social phenomena extending beyond those that obviously concern sexual or racial difference, e.g., whether art, religion, philosophy, science, or law might be "gendered" and/or "racialized."

(iv) The need for accounts of gender and race that take seriously the agency of women and people of color of both genders, and within which we can develop an understanding of agency that will aid feminist and antiracist efforts to empower critical social agents.

III. What Is Gender?

Even a quick survey of the literature reveals that a range of things have counted as "gender" within feminist theorizing. The guiding idea is sometimes expressed with the slogan: "gender is the social meaning of sex." But like any slogan, this one allows for different interpretations. Some theorists use the term "gender" to refer to the subjective experience of sexed embodiment, or a broad psychological orientation to the world ("gender identity"); others to a set of attributes or ideals that function as norms for males and females ("masculinity" and "femininity"); others to a system of sexual symbolism; and still others to the traditional social roles of men and women. My strategy is to offer a focal analysis that defines gender, in the primary sense, as a social class. A focal analysis undertakes to explain a variety of connected phenomena in terms of their relations to one that is theorized as the central or core phenomenon. As I see it, the core phenomenon to be addressed is the pattern of social relations that constitute the social classes of men as dominant and women as subordinate; norms, symbols, and identities are gendered in relation to the social relations that constitute gender. . . .

Among feminist theorists there are two problems that have generated pessimism about providing any unified account of women; I'll call them the *commonality problem* and the *normativity problem*. Very briefly, the commonality problem questions whether there is anything social that females have in common that could count as their "gender." If we consider *all* females—females of different times, places, and cultures—there are reasons to doubt that there is anything beyond body type (if even that) that they all share. The normativity problem raises the concern that any definition of "what woman is" is value-laden, and will marginalize certain females, privilege others, and reinforce current gender norms.

Given the priority I place on concerns with justice and sexual inequality, I take the primary motivation for distinguishing sex from gender to arise in the recognition that males and females do not only differ physically, but also systematically differ in their social positions. What is of concern, to put it simply, is that societies, on the whole, privilege individuals with male bodies. Although the particular forms and mechanisms of oppression vary from culture to culture, societies have found many ways—some ingenious, some crude—to control and exploit the sexual and reproductive capacities of females.

The main strategy of materialist feminist accounts of gender has been to define gender in terms of women's subordinate position in systems of male dominance ... the materialist strategy offers three basic principles to guide us in understanding gender:

(i) Gender categories are defined in terms of how one is socially positioned, where this is a function of, e.g., how one is viewed, how one is treated, and how one's life is structured socially, legally, and economically; gender is not defined in terms of an individual's intrinsic physical or psychological features.

(This allows that there may be other categories—such as sex—that are defined in terms of intrinsic physical features. Note, however, that once we focus our attention on gender as social position, we must allow that one can be a woman without ever (in the ordinary sense) "acting like a woman," "feeling like a woman," or even having a female body.)

(ii) Gender categories are defined hierarchically within a broader complex of oppressive relations; one group (viz., women) is socially positioned as subordinate to the other (viz., men), typically within the context of other forms of economic and social oppression.

(iii) Sexual difference functions as the physical marker to distinguish the two groups, and is used in the justification of viewing and treating the members of each group differently.

(Tentatively) we can capture these main points in the following analyses:

S *is a woman* iff$_{df}$: S is systematically subordinated along some dimension (economic, political, legal, social, etc.), and S is "marked" as a target for this treatment by observed or imagined bodily features presumed to be evidence of a female's biological role in reproduction.

S *is a man* iff$_{df}$: S is systematically privileged along some dimension (economic, political, legal, social, etc.), and S is "marked" as a target for this treatment by observed or imagined bodily features presumed to be evidence of a male's biological role in reproduction.

It is a virtue, I believe, of these accounts, that depending on context, one's sex may have a very different meaning and it may position one in very different kinds of hierarchies. The variation will clearly occur from culture to culture (and sub-culture to sub-culture); so e.g., to be a Chinese woman of the 1790s, a Brazilian woman of the 1890s, or an American woman of the 1990s may involve very different social relations, and very different kinds of oppression. Yet on the analysis suggested, these groups count as women insofar as their subordinate positions are marked and justified by reference to (female) sex. Similarly, this account allows that the substantive import of gender varies even from individual to individual within a culture depending on how the meaning of sex interacts with other socially salient characteristics (e.g., race, class, sexuality, etc.). For example, a privileged White woman and a Black woman of the underclass will both be women insofar as their social positions are affected by the social meanings of being female; and yet the social implications of being female vary for each because sexism is intertwined with race and class oppression. There are points in the proposed analysis that require clarification, however. . . . What does it mean to say that women are oppressed, and what does the qualification "as women" add?

. . . It is clear that women are oppressed in the sense that women are members of groups that suffer exploitation, marginalization, etc. But how should we understand the claim that women are oppressed *as women*? Frye[4] explains this as follows:

> One is marked for application of oppressive pressures by one's membership in some group or category. . . . In the case at hand, it is the category, *woman*. . . . If a woman has little or no economic or political power, or achieves little of what she wants to achieve, a major causal factor in this is that she is a woman. For any woman of any race or economic class, being a woman is significantly attached to whatever disadvantages and deprivations she suffers, be they great or small. . . . [In contrast,] being male is something [a man] has going *for* him, even if race or class or age or disability is going against him.

. . . Although I agree with Frye that in sexist societies social institutions are structured in ways that on the whole disadvantage females and advantage males, we must keep in mind that societies are not monolithic and that sexism is not the only source of oppression. For example, in the contemporary US, there are contexts in which being Black *and male* marks one as a target for certain forms of systematic violence (e.g., by the police). In those contexts, contrary to Frye's suggestion, *being male* is not something that a man "has going *for* him"; though there are other contexts (also in the contemporary US) in which Black males benefit from being male.

. . . Although an adequate account of gender must be highly sensitive to contextual variation, if we focus entirely on the narrowly defined contexts in which one's gender is negotiated, we could easily lose sight of the fact that for most of us there is a relatively fixed interpretation of our bodies as sexed either male or female, an interpretation that marks us within the dominant ideology as eligible for only certain positions or opportunities in a system of sexist oppression. Given our priority in theorizing systems of inequality, it is important first to locate the social classes men and women in a broad structure of subordination and privilege:

S *is a woman* iff

(i) S is regularly and for the most part observed or imagined to have certain bodily features presumed to be evidence of a female's biological role in reproduction;

(ii) that S has these features marks S within the dominant ideology of S's society as someone who ought to occupy certain kinds of social position that are in fact subordinate (and so motivates and justifies S's occupying such a position); and

---

4. Marilyn Frye (1941–), American philosopher. The following quotation is from Frye's *The Politics of Reality* (Crossing Press, 1983), 15–16.

(iii) the fact that S satisfies (i) and (ii) plays a role in S's systematic subordination, i.e., *along some dimension*, S's social position is oppressive, and S's satisfying (i) and (ii) plays a role in that dimension of subordination.[5]

. . . These accounts are, however, compatible with the idea that (at least for some of us) one's gender may not be entirely stable, and that other systems of oppression may disrupt gender in particular contexts: a woman may not always function socially as a woman; a man may not always function socially as a man. To return to a previous example, when systems of White supremacy and male dominance collide, a Black man's male privilege may be seen as so threatening that it must be violently wrested from him.

. . . It is important to note that the definitions don't require that the background ideology in question must use (assumed) reproductive function as itself the justification for treating men or women in the way deemed "appropriate"; (assumed) reproductive features may instead simply be "markers" of supposedly "deeper" (and morally relevant?) characteristics that the ideology supposes justifies the treatment in question.

IV. What Is Race?

One advantage of this account of gender is the parallel it offers for race. To begin, let me review a couple of points that I take to be matters of established fact: First, there are no racial genes responsible for the complex morphologies and cultural patterns we associate with different races. Second, in different contexts racial distinctions are drawn on the basis of different characteristics, e.g., the Brazilian and US classification schemes for who counts as "Black" differ. For these reasons and others, it appears that race, like gender, could be fruitfully understood as a position within a broad social network.

Although suggestive, this idea is not easy to develop. It is one thing to acknowledge that race is *socially* real, even if a biological fiction; but it is another thing to capture in general terms "the social meaning of color." There seem to be too many different forms race takes. Note, however, that we encountered a similar problem with gender: is there any prospect for a unified analysis of "the social meaning of sex"? The materialist feminist approach offered a helpful strategy: don't look for an analysis that assumes that the meaning is always and everywhere the same; rather, consider how members of the group are *socially positioned*, and what *physical markers* serve as a supposed basis for such treatment. How might we extend this strategy to race? Transposing the slogan, we might say that race is the social meaning of the geographically marked body, familiar markers being skin color, hair type, eye shape, physique. To develop this, I propose the following account. . . .

A group is *racialized* iff$_{df}$ its members are socially positioned as subordinate or privileged along some dimension (economic, political, legal, social, etc.), and the group

---

5. Haslanger then defines "S *is a man*" similarly, with "male" replacing "female," "privileged" replacing "subordinate" and "oppressive," and "privilege" replacing "subordination."

is "marked" as a target for this treatment by observed or imagined bodily features presumed to be evidence of ancestral links to a certain geographical region.

... In other words, races are those groups demarcated by the geographical associations accompanying perceived body type, when those associations take on evaluative significance concerning how members of the group should be viewed and treated. As in the case of gender, the ideology need not use physical morphology or geography as the entire basis for "appropriate" treatment; these features may instead simply be "markers" of other characteristics that the ideology uses to justify the treatment in question.

Given this definition, we can say that S is of the White (Black, Asian . . .) race . . . iff Whites (Blacks, Asians . . .) are a racialized group . . . , and S is a member. On this view, whether a group is racialized, and so how and whether an individual is raced, is not an absolute fact, but will depend on context. For example, Blacks, Whites, Asians, Native Americans, are currently racialized in the US insofar as these are all groups defined in terms of physical features associated with places of origin, and insofar as membership in the group functions socially as a basis for evaluation. However, some groups are not currently racialized in the US, but have been so in the past and possibly could be again (and in other contexts are), e.g., the Italians, the Germans, the Irish. . . .

V. Normativity and Commonality

So what, if anything, is achieved by adopting the above analyses? Are they the tools we need? Let's first consider the problems of commonality and normativity, and begin with gender.

Remember, the problem of commonality questions whether there is anything social that all females can plausibly be said to have in common. If we ask whether females share any intrinsic (non-anatomical!) features such as psychological makeup, character traits, beliefs, values, experiences or, alternatively, whether there is a particular social role that all females have occupied across culture and history, the answer seems to be "no."

On my analysis women are those who occupy a particular *kind* of social position, viz., one of sexually-marked subordinate. So women have in common that their (assumed) sex has socially disadvantaged them; but this is compatible with the kinds of cultural variation that feminist inquiry has revealed, for the substantive content of women's position and the ways of justifying it can vary enormously. Admittedly, the account accommodates such variation by being very abstract; nonetheless, it provides a schematic account that highlights the interdependence between the material forces that subordinate women, *and* the ideological frameworks that sustain them.

One might complain, however, that there must be *some* women (or rather, females) who aren't oppressed, and in particular, aren't oppressed *as women*. Perhaps there are; e.g., some may "pass" as men, others may be recognizably female but not be subordinated in any way linked to that recognition. I'm not convinced that there are many cases (if any) of the latter, but I'll certainly grant that there *could be* females who did not satisfy the definition that I've offered. In fact, I believe it is part of the project of feminism to bring about a day when there are no more women (though, of course, we should not aim to do away with females!). I'm happy to admit that there could be females who aren't women in the sense I've defined, but these individuals (or possible individuals) are not counterexamples to the analysis. The analysis is intended to capture a meaningful political category for critical feminist efforts, and non-oppressed females do not fall within that category (though they may be interesting for other reasons).

But this leads us directly from the commonality problem to the normativity problem. The normativity problem raises the challenge that any effort to define *women* will problematically privilege some women and (theoretically) marginalize others, and will itself become normative. One worry is that bias inevitably occurs in deciding which experiences or social roles are definitive; a second worry is that if someone wants to be a "real" woman, she should conform to the definition of women provided, and this will reinforce rather than challenge male dominance.

On the account I've offered, it is true that certain females don't count as "real" women; and it is true that I've privileged certain facts of women's lives as definitive. But given the epistemological framework outlined above, it is both inevitable and important for us to choose what facts are significant on the basis of explicit and considered values. For the purposes of a critical feminist inquiry, oppression is a significant fact around which we should organize our theoretical categories; it may be that non-oppressed females are marginalized within my account, but that is because for the broader purposes at hand—relative to the feminist and antiracist values guiding our project—they are not the ones who matter. The important issue is not whether a particular account "marginalizes" some individuals, but whether its doing so is in conflict with the feminist values that motivate the inquiry. And as far as I can tell, *not* focusing our theoretical efforts on understanding the position of oppressed females would pose just such a conflict.

The question remains whether my definition of woman helps sustain gender hierarchy by implicitly offering a normative ideal of woman. Given that women on my definition are an oppressed group, I certainly hope not! Instead, the definition is more likely to offer a negative ideal that challenges male dominance.

I won't defend here my account of racialized groups against an extension of the normativity and commonality complaints, for I would simply repeat the strategy just employed. Although there are interesting nuances in adapting the arguments to apply to racialized groups, I don't see anything peculiar to race that would present an obstacle to developing the same sort of response.

VI. Negotiating Terms

. . . Does it serve both the goal of understanding racial and sexual oppression, and of achieving sexual and racial equality to think of ourselves as men or women, or raced in the ways proposed? . . . Given the normative force and political potential of identifying someone (or self-identifying) in racial or gendered terms, how do we evaluate a terminological appropriation of the kind I'm proposing? For example, isn't there something disingenuous about appropriating race and gender terminology *because* it is used to frame how we think of ourselves and each other, in order to use them for new concepts that are *not* part of our self-understandings?

This latter question is especially pressing because the appropriation under consideration intentionally invokes what many find to be positive self-understandings—being Latina, being a White man—and offers analyses of them which emphasize the broader context of injustice. Thus there is an invitation not only to revise one's understanding of these categories (given their instability, this happens often enough), but to revise one's relationship to their prescriptive force. By offering these analyses of our ordinary terms, I call upon us to reject what seemed to be positive social identities. I'm suggesting that we should work to undermine those forces that make being a man, a woman, or a member of a racialized group possible; we should refuse to be gendered man or woman, refuse to be raced. This goes beyond denying essentialist claims about one's embodiment and involves an active political commitment to live one's life differently. In one sense this appropriation is "just semantics": I'm asking us to use an old term in a new way. But it is also politics: I'm asking us to understand ourselves and those around us as deeply molded by injustice and to draw the appropriate prescriptive inference. This, I hope, will contribute to empowering critical social agents. However, whether the terminological shift I'm suggesting is politically useful will depend on the contexts in which it is employed and the individuals employing it. The point is not to legislate what terms to use in all contexts, but to offer resources that should be used judiciously. . . .

VIII. Conclusion[6]

On the accounts I've offered, there are striking parallels between race and gender. Both gender and race are real, and both are social categories. Neither gender nor race is chosen, but the forms they take can be resisted or mutated. Both race and gender (as we know it) are hierarchical, but the systems that sustain the hierarchy are contingent. And although the ideologies of race and gender and the hierarchical structures they sustain are substantively very different, they are intertwined.

There are many different types of human bodies; it is not the case that there is a unique "right" way of classifying them, though certain classifications will be more useful for some purposes than others. How we classify bodies can and does matter politically, for our laws, social institutions, and personal identities are profoundly linked to understandings of the body and its possibilities. This is compatible with the idea that what possibilities a human body has is not wholly a function of our understandings of it. Our bodies often outdo us, and undo us, in spite of the meanings we give them.

. . . In short, (speaking of my analyses) I'm less committed to saying that *this* is what gender is and what race is, than to saying that *these* are important categories that a

6. Section VII is omitted from this selection.

feminist antiracist theory needs. As I've explained above, I think there are rhetorical advantages to using the terms "gender," "man" and "woman," and "race" for the concepts I've defined, but if someone else is determined to have those terms, I'll use different ones. To return to the point made much earlier in characterizing analytic projects: it is our responsibility to define gender and race for our theoretical purposes. The world itself can't tell us what gender is. The same is true for race. It may be as Appiah claims that "there is nothing in the world that can do all we ask race to do for us,"[7] if our project inevitably inherits the concept's complex history; but we might instead ask "race" to do different things than have been asked before. Of course, in defining our terms, we must keep clearly in mind our political aims both in analyzing the past and present, and in envisioning alternative futures. But rather than worrying, "what is gender, really?" or "what is race, really?" I think we should begin by asking (both in the theoretical and political sense) what, if anything, we want them to be.

TEST YOUR UNDERSTANDING

1. Human females (often) have certain bodily features (call them "F_c") that are signs or evidence of the ability to bear children (at least for some period in the female's life). Suppose S is a woman. Which of these follow, on Haslanger's view? (You may select more than one.)

   a. S has F_c.

   b. S might, for all we know, have F_c.

   c. S is for the most part observed to have F_c.

   d. S is for the most part believed to have F_c.

2. Does Haslanger think that racial categories correspond to biological differences between people?

3. Oprah Winfrey is one of the richest African Americans, is a recipient of the Presidential Medal of Freedom, and is sometimes said to be the most influential woman in the world. Would Haslanger deny that she is a woman, or black? If not, why not?

4. What does Haslanger mean when she says that part of the project of feminism is to bring about a day when there are no more women?

NOTES AND QUESTIONS

1. *Revision versus description.* The introduction to this chapter stressed the revisionary nature of Haslanger's project: her "appropriation" of "race and gender terminology" (p. 569). Her analysis does not purport to reveal *what women are*, for example, but should be taken instead as a *recommendation*: this is how we should use the word "woman"

7. See Appiah's essay in this chapter, page 558.

"for certain theoretical and political purposes" (p. 562). Given that, attempting to find **counterexamples** to the view would seem to be beside the point (see Haslanger, p. 568).

However, in later work, Haslanger suggests that her analyses *do* capture the meanings of race and gender terminology. But how can they do that, since they are (as Haslanger admits) "at odds . . . with common sense"?[8] Here Haslanger argues (along with many other philosophers) that we can be seriously mistaken about what our words in fact mean, so "common sense" doesn't count for much.

So counterexamples *are* objections to Haslanger's analyses, provided that they are understood in the later way, as offering a *descriptive* account of what it is to be a woman or of the white race. Apparent counterexamples to Haslanger's analysis of "S is a woman" are suggested in the next question and in Elizabeth Barnes's essay in this chapter. Whether any of these are genuine counterexamples, and hence refute the analysis, is for you to decide.

2. Consider two MTF (male-to-female) transgender people. Alice and Betty were both assigned the sex "male" at birth and both have typical male anatomy. Alice considers herself a woman and lives as one. Most people who interact with Alice do not know that Alice has typical male anatomy; rather, they assume that Alice has typical female anatomy. Betty also considers herself a woman and lives as one. However, Betty is open about being transgender and about the fact that she has not had sex-reassignment surgery or hormone replacement therapy. People who interact with Betty do not believe that she has typical female anatomy; rather, they believe that Betty has typical male anatomy.

    What does Haslanger's analysis imply about whether Alice or Betty is a woman? Does this implication raise a problem for her view?

3. Suppose that we make the "terminological shift" and use "woman" in the way Haslanger suggests. Assuming that we have the goal of ending oppression, subordination, injustice, and so on, how would that terminological shift help? Would it help?

8. See Haslanger, *Resisting Reality* (Oxford University Press, 2012), 12.

Quayshawn Spencer (b. 1979)

Spencer is Assistant Professor of Philosophy at the University of Pennsylvania, specializing in philosophy of science, philosophy of biology, and philosophy of race. He is the editor of *The Race Debates from Metaphysics to Medicine* (Oxford University Press, forthcoming).

ARE FOLK RACES LIKE DINGOES, DIMES, OR DODOS?

1. Introduction

Almost all metaphysicians of race believe that the races we talk about in ordinary language (what I will call *folk races*) either don't exist or are not biological entities.

Here are a few representative quotes, from Anthony Appiah, Lawrence Blum, and Sally Haslanger:

> The truth is that there are no races: there is nothing in the world that can do all we ask "race" to do for us.[1]
>
> Races are not socially constructed; they simply do not exist.[2]
>
> I am happy to say that "race" can have several meanings, depending on context. But in public discourse, it is wrong to say that race is biological, or to say that races don't exist.[3]

Many metaphysicians of race, like Appiah and Blum, think that folk races are like the species dodo (*Raphus cucullatus*). Just as there are no dodos, there are no Asians, blacks, whites, and so forth. Many other metaphysicians of race, like Haslanger, think that folk races are like dimes. Folk races clearly exist, but what makes a group of people a folk race is a complex array of social properties. However, the goal of this essay is to show that *some* folk races are more like the species dingo (*Canis dingo*) than like dimes or dodos. In other words, I aim to show that some folk races are real biological entities.

I will defend my thesis by showing that some real biological populations in the human species turn out to be folk races. My official argument is the following. First, human continental populations are real biological entities. Second, human continental populations are folk races. So, some folk races are real biological entities. This argument is deductively valid, which means that its conclusion is true if all of its premises are true. So, the only remaining question is whether all of these premises *are* true. In the rest of this essay, I will show that all of the premises of this argument are indeed true. However, first, I should clarify the jargon I use in my premises.

2. Some Clarifications

2.1   FOLK RACES

Remember that by a "folk race" I mean a race that's talked about in ordinary language. But what do I mean by a race? Since I think it's a good idea to use definitions that are as least biased as possible when starting an investigation, I will say that a *race* is a group of people called a "race" in some language. For instance, if you read a newspaper in the United States today, you will see that *whites* are a race in American English. However, who *whites* are varies with context. The U.S. Census Bureau includes Jews and Arabs

---

1. K. A. Appiah, *In My Father's House* (Oxford University Press, 1992), 45. [Spencer's note.] See also page 558 of this anthology.

2. L. Blum, *I'm Not A Racist But . . . : The Moral Quandary of Race* (Cornell University Press, 2002), 163. [Spencer's note.]

3. S. Haslanger, "Race, Intersectionality, and Method: A Reply to Critics," *Philosophical Studies* 171 (2014): 113. [Spencer's note.]

as white people, but the Ku Klux Klan excludes Jews and Arabs as white people. In any event, whites (in either use) are a folk race since both groups of people are called a "race" in the American English dialect of English.

You may be wondering why I am being so careful here. For one, why don't I just talk about races without any qualification? But also, why qualify that the focus is on folk races? Well, first, to talk about races without any qualification is a recipe for confusion. Here's an analogy. You may think that the question "When did humans evolve?" is utterly clear. However, I was at a talk given by a paleoanthropologist not too long ago whose talk was on exactly that question, and his answer generated a heated debate. The date he gave was 2.5 million years ago, which I immediately thought was wrong. I love studying human evolution, and the oldest date I've ever heard was 250,000 years ago. So we argued back and forth until it became clear that we were not arguing at all, we were simply using the word "human" in two different ways! It turns out that in paleoanthropology, the word "human" is colloquial for "*Homo*," which stands for the genus that our species is in. However, I was using "human" as colloquial for "*Homo sapiens*," which, of course, stands for our species. This sort of equivocation on words happens frequently in academia, so it's important to emphasize that I'm focused on folk races as opposed to races as understood in some other way. For instance, for many systematic zoologists, "race" is a synonym for "subspecies," but the metaphysicians that I'm engaging with are not interested in whether human subspecies exist. They're interested in whether folk races exist and whether they're biological.

2.2   REAL BIOLOGICAL ENTITIES

My first premise states that human continental populations are real biological entities, but what do I mean by a biological entity? Since Aristotle,[4] metaphysicians have been fascinated with *essences*. Also since Aristotle, metaphysicians have considered an essence to be that which makes something what it is. In other words, an essence is the minimal set of qualities that a thing has that the thing cannot exist without. For instance, bipedalism and opposable thumbs are not essential to humans (in the *Homo sapiens* sense) because humans can be born without thumbs or legs. This brings me to biological entities.

By a *biological entity*, I mean a thing whose essence consists of biological qualities in whole or in part. For instance, in genetics, a *homozygote* is, essentially, an organism that possesses identical *alleles* (variants) for a particular gene. Since possessing alleles is a biological quality, the homozygote is a biological entity. Also, I will say that a biological entity is *real* if careful biology has determined that the entity actually exists.

2.3   HUMAN CONTINENTAL POPULATIONS

Finally, both of my premises mention the term "human continental populations." That's a technical term in population genetics. Population genetics is the study of genetics at the population level as well as the study of how evolutionary forces change species over time. One major project in population genetics is studying how different species

---

4. Aristotle (384–322 BCE), ancient Greek philosopher and scientist. Selections from Aristotle's works are in Chapters 16 and 20 of this anthology.

naturally subdivide into *biological populations*. Biological populations come in two types: *breeding populations* and *genealogical populations*. Breeding populations are groups of organisms that reproduce much more with one another than with organisms outside the group, such as polar bears (*Ursus maritimus*). Genealogical populations are groups of organisms that share much more ancestry with one another than with organisms outside the group, such as haplogroup M in humans.[5]

The study of population subdivision is important in population genetics because the low interbreeding rates that cause a species to subdivide into biological populations can be a major driver of evolution in a species and can, eventually, lead to speciation. For instance, the evolution of *Homo sapiens* is thought to have occurred from the population subdivision of our immediate ancestor *Homo ergaster*. In any case, population geneticists have been studying human population subdivision for decades, but a breakthrough happened in 2000 when a new method of identifying population subdivision arose that allowed population membership to be graded. In other words, instead of identifying an organism as either a member of a population or not, this new method allowed an organism to be, say, 60 percent in one population and 40 percent in another. The new method used a computer program called *structure*. Subsequently, other similar programs were developed: I will call all of these *structure-like* computer programs for ease of reference.

The genius of *structure-like* computer programs lies in how multiple population membership is conceived. An organism with unmixed population membership has, by definition, inherited all of her alleles from ancestors in a single population. An organism with mixed population membership has, by definition, inherited all of her alleles from ancestors in multiple populations. The proportion of one's genome inherited from ancestors in a specific population is known as one's *genomic ancestry* from that population. Given how these programs assign population membership, it's clear that they're identifying genealogical populations.

As for how *structure-like* computer programs work, it's complicated. But, basically, *structure-like* computer programs guess the populations at a specific level of possible population subdivision, guess the degree of membership for each population member at that level, and keep doing these two things until they find a population subdivision at that level that best fits the data, which is just a set of alleles at the same *locus* (location in the genome) for multiple loci from each organism in the sample. If no single, best population assignment is found, the computer program declares that the species has no population subdivision at that level. If a single, best population assignment is found, the computer program declares the population subdivision that yields the best assignment as the species' population subdivision at that level. The computer program user can search for population subdivisions from 2 on up.[6] Also, of course, these programs output results that are only as reliable as the data put into them. So,

5. A *haplogroup* is a group of organisms consisting of the first organism to possess a specific DNA sequence and all of the descendants of that organism that possess the same sequence. M is a *mitochondrial DNA* haplogroup in humans. (Mitochondrial DNA is a tiny fraction—0.000535 percent—of your total DNA and is found in cell structures called *mitochondria*.) [Spencer's note.]

6. The maximum number of subdivisions will be the number of *local populations*—randomly mating groups—in the species. [Spencer's note.]

the data should be from a representative sample of the species if what one wants to find is all of the species' *actual* population subdivisions.

In 2002, the geneticist Noah Rosenberg and his colleagues used *structure* on a worldwide sample of human ethnic groups and discovered that humans have multiple levels of population subdivision.[7] However, the result that caught everyone's attention was that humans can be divided into five continent-level biological populations that are called "human continental populations" in the literature. The five human continental populations are Africans, East Asians, Eurasians, Native Americans, and Oceanians.

Specifically, the African population mostly includes the indigenous people of sub-Saharan Africa (e.g., Maasai Kenyans, Mbuti Congolese, San Namibians, Yoruba Nigerians, etc.); the East Asian population mostly includes the indigenous people of Eurasia east of the Himalayas (e.g., Han Chinese, Khmer Cambodians, Yakut Siberians, etc.); the Eurasian population mostly includes the indigenous people of Eurasia west of the Himalayas and the indigenous people of North Africa (e.g., Ashkenazi Jews, Kalash Pakistanis, Mozabite Algerians, Norwegians, etc.); the Native American population mostly includes the indigenous people of the Americas (e.g., Greenlandic Inuit, Maya Mexicans, Suruí Brazilians, etc.); and, finally, the Oceanian population mostly includes the indigenous people of Melanesia, Polynesia, Micronesia, and Australia (e.g., Chamorro Mariana Islanders, Nasioi Bougainville Islanders, Native Hawaiians, Tiwi Australians, etc.).

3. Why Human Continental Populations Are Real Biological Entities

Remember that the sole membership condition for being in a human continental population is having genomic ancestry from that population. Since a human continental population's membership conditions are part of its essence, having genomic ancestry is a biological quality, and, as already mentioned, having genomic ancestry from a human continental population is a membership condition for being in that population, it follows from my definition of "biological entity" that human continental populations are biological entities. So much for that. Now, why are these biological populations real?

Notably, some philosophers and biologists have objected that Rosenberg's sample of human ethnic groups was too small and skewed to represent the human species, so that conclusions about the existence of human continental populations are premature.[8] To be clear, Rosenberg's sample consisted of 52 ethnic groups, most of which were isolated indigenous people with little or no genomic mixture, such as Mbuti Congolese and Kalash Pakistanis.

7. See N. Rosenberg et al., "Genetic Structure of Human Populations," *Science* 298: 2381–85 (2002). [Spencer's note.]

8. See, for example, D. Serre and S. Pääbo, "Evidence for Gradients of Human Genetic Diversity within and among Continents," *Genome Research* 14: 1679–85 (2004). [Spencer's note.]

While Rosenberg's sample of human ethnic groups was not random, so far it appears to be representative. This is for two reasons. First, the largest study on human population subdivision to date has confirmed Rosenberg's result. In a landmark study by the geneticist Trevor Pemberton and his colleagues, a worldwide sample of 267 human ethnic groups was subdivided into the human continental populations using 645 loci.[9] Furthermore, this was despite the fact that hundreds of heavily mixed people were in the sample, such as African Americans, Mestizo Mexicans, Indians, Polynesians, and colored South Africans. Second, if we look at a representative sample of the human population subdivision studies conducted since 2002 that are in a position to test Rosenberg's result, we will find that ~70 percent of them confirm it, and this is so even though they use different genomic data, different ethnic group samples, and different *structure-like* computer programs. So, doubts about the existence of human continental populations can be answered.

4. Why Human Continental Populations Are Folk Races

Believe it or not, the U.S. government has official races. They were introduced by the Office of Management and Budget (OMB) in 1997. The *OMB races* (as I will call them) are American Indians, Asians, blacks, Pacific Islanders, and whites. Hispanic (or Latino) is not a race in the OMB's racial scheme but rather an ethnicity composed of people from multiple races. Furthermore, people can belong to more than one OMB race at a time. Also, the OMB says it has attempted to define its race terms in a way that is "nonduplicative" and "comprehensive in coverage." In other words, no OMB race is supposed to be redundant, and any immigrant to the United States and any child born from an interracial mating should belong to at least one OMB race. To meet these aims, the OMB has attempted to define its race terms primarily using ancestral links to the original people of certain continental regions. For instance, the OMB says that its "definition" for a *white* person is "A person having origins in any of the original peoples of Europe, the Middle East, or North Africa."[10]

Because of the influence the U.S. government has on ordinary language, the OMB's racial scheme has become a scheme of *folk races* in the United States. The OMB's racial scheme is used widely on college applications, job applications, mortgage loan applications, new patient forms from health providers, birth certificate applications, and on many other official forms.

Soon after the human continental populations were discovered, some medical scientists claimed that these groups are folk races; namely, the OMB races. The primary evidence that they offered was that geneticists can predict U.S. adults' self-reported OMB

9. See T. Pemberton et al., "Population Structure in a Comprehensive Genomic Data Set on Human Microsatellite Variation," *G3: Genes, Genomes, Genetics* 3: 891–907 (2013). [Spencer's note.]

10. See document 97-28653 in the *Federal Register* at www.federalregister.gov. [Spencer's note.]

race with very high accuracy using only their primary genomic ancestry in a human continental population. For instance, one study was able to predict the self-reported OMB race (Asian, black, or white) of 3,224 U.S. residents with 99.9 percent accuracy.[11]

While these predictions are impressive, this argument faced criticisms from many race scholars. For instance, the philosopher Joshua Glasgow has argued that folk races in the United States are, by definition, distinguishable from one another by visible physical features of the relevant kind—namely, skin color, hair texture, and facial features—that are disproportionately prevalent in one race but not the others.[12] So, even if there is high overlap among, say, black people and African people, that is orthogonal to whether blacks *are* Africans. The only way blacks could *be* Africans is if they shared the same essence; or, said another way, if "black" and "African" shared the same meaning. However, according to Glasgow, "black" and "African" do not share the same meaning. The former is defined by visible physical features, while the latter is defined by genomic ancestry.

I completely agree with Glasgow that high overlap among the members of OMB races and the members of human continental populations is insufficient evidence for the claim that OMB races are human continental populations. It's good evidence, but not enough. However, I disagree with Glasgow that OMB race terms are defined by a set of superficial properties as opposed to the referents of those terms. This assumption is made a lot in race theory. However, the problem here is that philosophers have come up with two different possibilities for identifying a name's meaning.

One possibility is providing a list of superficial properties, and the other is providing the referent of the name. The former is known as *descriptivism*, and the latter is known as *referentialism*. Furthermore, whether a name has a descriptive or referential meaning depends entirely on how the name is intended to be used. So, in order to see whether Glasgow is right about what OMB race terms mean, we need to turn to how the OMB intends to use these terms.

First of all, given who the OMB intends to pick out with "black" and "Pacific Islander," it's pretty easy to see that OMB races are not intended to be visibly distinguishable, at least not by definition. To be specific, the OMB is quite clear that "black" is supposed to pick out, among other groups, sub-Saharan Africans, and that "Pacific Islander" is supposed to pick out, among other groups, Melanesians. However, given the widely known fact among biological anthropologists that Melanesians are, on average, not visibly distinguishable from sub-Saharan Africans with respect to skin color, facial features, and hair texture, and given the demographic fact that ~75 percent of Pacific Islanders are Melanesian, it follows that Pacific Islanders currently don't possess any visible physical features of the relevant kind that are disproportionately prevalent among them and not blacks.[13] But this is not all.

---

11. See H. Tang et al., "Genetic Structure, Self-Identified Race/Ethnicity, and Confounding in Case-Control Association Studies," *American Journal of Human Genetics* 76: 268–75 (2005). [Spencer's note.]

12. See page 33 in J. Glasgow, *A Theory of Race* (Routledge, 2009). [Spencer's note.]

13. For this demographic fact, see Q. Spencer, "Philosophy of Race Meets Population Genetics," *Studies in History and Philosophy of Biological and Biomedical Sciences* 52: 46–55 (2015). [Spencer's note.]

Not only do Glasgow's superficial properties fail to capture the meanings of OMB race terms, so do the OMB's so-called definitions! There are several problems with the OMB's so-called definitions for its race terms with respect to what the OMB itself wants to pick out with its race terms. For instance, remember I said that the OMB intends its racial scheme to be "nonduplicative." Well, it turns out that given its so-called definition for "white," the Asian, Pacific Islander, and American Indian races are redundant.

While OMB demographers might not know this, it turns out that any human with any non-African human ancestor has ancestral links to the original people of the Middle East.[14] Hence, everyone except unmixed Africans have origins in the original people of the Middle East (and, specifically, the Arabian Peninsula or the Levant), and thus satisfies the OMB's so-called definition for "White." Thus, the only nonredundant OMB races are whites and blacks if we consider the OMB's so-called definitions the actual definitions for these terms.

Fortunately, there is another option. We can view the meanings of OMB race terms as their referents as opposed to some set of superficial properties. Furthermore, if we consider the meaning of each OMB race term to be a unique human continental population (e.g., "black" means African, "white" means Eurasian, etc.), we will get a predictively powerful and simple theory for what these terms mean. For instance, each human continental population is not redundant because genomic ancestry is different from mere ancestry. The set of human continental populations is also "comprehensive in coverage" because every living human belongs to at least one human continental population. It's also possible to have multiple human continental population memberships at once, just like the OMB intends to be the case for its racial memberships. Last, but not least, we shouldn't forget that there is ~99 percent overlap among the members of OMB races and human continental populations. That seems like plenty of evidence to reliably say that human continental populations are folk races.

5. Concluding Remarks

In this essay, I have argued that some folk races are real biological entities. I used the following argument to defend my thesis. First, human continental populations are real biological entities. Second, human continental populations are folk races. Thus, the majority of metaphysicians of race may be right that *some* folk races are not real biological entities, but that's not true for OMB races.

---

14. For the fascinating evidence, see L. Cavalli-Sforza and M. Feldman, "The Application of Molecular Genetic Approaches to the Study of Human Evolution," *Nature Genetics* 33: 266–75 (2003). [Spencer's note.]

TEST YOUR UNDERSTANDING

1. Which of the following, if true, pose a problem for Spencer's account of race? (You may select more than one.)

   a. Barack Obama is white.

   b. Barack Obama is black and not white.

   c. Barack Obama is neither black nor white.

   d. Barack Obama is both black and white.

2. Which of these are true, according to Spencer? (You may select more than one.)

   a. Human continental populations are breeding populations.

   b. Some folk races are human continental populations.

   c. Human continental populations can be distinguished by their different genes.

   d. All human continental populations are folk races.

3. What are human continental populations?

   a. Populations of humans living on separate continents.

   b. Populations of humans who were geographically separated by roughly continental divisions after humans migrated out of Africa and spread around the world.

   c. Populations of humans with genomic ancestry from the original geographically separated humans resulting from migration out of Africa.

   d. The indigenous peoples of Africa, Oceania, the Americas, and so forth.

4. The "color/race" terms used in Brazil include "pardo" (brown) (feminine: "parda"), "branco" (white), and "negro" (black). It turns out that the connection between self-ascribed "color/race" and genomic ancestry is very loose among Brazilians—one can't read off someone's color/race by looking at his or her genome.[15] So the Brazilian folk races don't appear to be (in Spencer's phrase) "real biological entities."

   Is this a decisive objection to Spencer's view? If not, why not?

NOTES AND QUESTIONS

1. Crucial to Spencer's argument is the distinction between *descriptivism* and *referentialism,* two accounts of the meanings of words (in particular, names). Descriptivism and referentialism have been developed as part of the *philosophy of language,* an area of philosophy not covered in this anthology. There are many exciting issues in the philosophy of language, which you may encounter if you take further philosophy classes.

15. For one study conducted in Rio de Janeiro, see R. Santos et al., "Color, Race, and Genomic Ancestry in Brazil," *Current Anthropology* 50: 787–819 (2009).

Consider a name, say "Quayshawn Spencer," which refers to a certain philosopher who teaches at the University of Pennsylvania. Suppose you come across the name in something that you're reading and wonder who it names. Someone might explain: "He's the guy who teaches philosophy at U. Penn. and who wrote an essay in the *Norton Introduction to Philosophy*." That description of Spencer *uniquely identifies* him—there are no other U. Penn. philosophers who have essays in this book. Given that, you might think that this description gives the *meaning* of the name "Quayshawn Spencer." In other words, when that name is used to refer to the U. Penn. philosopher, it is simply a *two-word abbreviation* of the description "The man who teaches philosophy at U. Penn. and who wrote an essay in the *Norton Introduction to Philosophy*." This is an example of a *descriptivist* account of the meaning of a name.

One problem (among many) with descriptivism is that sometimes the descriptions we associate with names are *wrong*. Do you know who Betsy Ross is? If you're like many people, you will say that she's the person who sewed the first American flag. Although that was a story that Betsy's family was fond of telling, it is very likely a myth. Who did sew the flag? No one knows, but suppose it was Martha Dandridge, George Washington's wife. If "Betsy Ross" is a two-word abbreviation of "The person who sewed the first American flag," then, given our supposition, the following sentence is *true*: "Betsy Ross sewed the first American flag and was married to George Washington." That is clearly the wrong result. The truth is that Betsy did *not* sew the flag, so "Betsy Ross" does not mean *the person who sewed the first American flag*.

Because of these and other problems, many philosophers have adopted *referentialism*. According to that view, the meanings of names such as "Quayshawn Spencer" and "Betsy Ross" are not the same as the meanings of any descriptions—rather, the meaning of "Quayshawn Spencer" is simply *the thing it refers to*, its *referent*, the man Spencer himself.

Exercise: Explain why, if descriptivism is the right account of the meanings of OMB race terms, Spencer's overall argument is in trouble. How does Spencer argue that referentialism is a better account?

2. Consider the category of *redheads*, which includes Lindsay Lohan and Conan O'Brien. The redheads can be subdivided into the *natural* redheads and the *artificial* redheads (those who dye their hair). Natural redheads have red hair because they have certain alleles of the MC1R gene, located on chromosome 16. (Other genes may also be involved, and anyway different redheads can have different alleles.) The category *natural redhead* appears to be a biological category. It's not very important, biologically speaking, but it's not entirely unimportant either: redheads tend to have pale skin and are more susceptible to sunburn than others; they also have different sensitivities to pain, needing greater quantities of some anesthetics.

> *Objection 1.* If race is biologically real in any interesting sense, it has got to be a biological category of more explanatory significance than categories such as *natural redhead*. Races are supposed to correspond to major subdivisions within the species *Homo sapiens*. For all Spencer has said, the human continental populations are as biologically superficial as the category *natural redhead*. Surely that's not enough to show that those populations *are* races. If it is, shouldn't we announce the amazing discovery of a *new* race, the natural redheads?

Objection 2. The ordinary word "redhead" does not appear to refer to a biological category, because it applies not just to *natural* redheads—an *artificial* redhead is also rightly called "a redhead." This would be true even if there were only a handful of artificial redheads, perhaps living (unbeknownst to us) on a remote desert island. In this hypothetical scenario, everyone we actually (and rightly) call "a redhead" is a natural redhead. But our word "redhead" still applies to the isolated artificial redheads, even though we never have the chance to actually call them "redheads." Thus the fact *all* the things that we *actually* (and rightly) call "X" are members of a biological category B does *not* show that "X" refers to B. Okay, let's grant that everyone we actually (and rightly) call "white" is a member of the Eurasian continental population. By the argument just given, that does not show that "white" refers to the category *Eurasian continental population.* In other words, even granted all the fancy stuff about genetics, Spencer has not shown that (some) terms for folk races refer to biological categories.

Exercise: How might Spencer respond to these two objections? Are they damaging to his theory or not?

Elizabeth Barnes (b. 1983)

Barnes is Associate Professor of Philosophy at the University of Virginia and works in metaphysics, social philosophy, and feminist philosophy. She is the author of *The Minority Body: A Theory of Disability* (Oxford University Press, 2016).

THE METAPHYSICS OF GENDER

Ama is genderqueer. She is female, but identifies as neither a man nor a woman. People often say they are confused about whether Ama is a man or a woman. Ama uses the women's bathroom because it's easiest both in terms of not getting harassed and of menstruation needs.

Ben is a trans man. He has some characteristically female anatomy, but he's taken regular testosterone supplements for several years, and most people think he's male when they meet him. He uses the women's bathroom because his state recently passed a law requiring him to. When he does, people yell at him and tell him he's in the wrong place.

Chi-ah is a gender-nonconforming woman. She identifies as a butch lesbian and typically wears mens' clothing. People often mistake Chi-ah for a man, especially when she's with her wife. She uses the women's bathroom because she's always identified as a woman.

Deena is a feminine woman. She uses the women's bathroom because it has never occurred to her that she would use anything else. However, unbeknownst to her, she has XY sex chromosomes instead of XX sex chromosomes.

What does it mean to really be a woman (or a man, or a genderqueer person, etc.)? Is it a matter of how you think about yourself? Of how others treat you? Of your personality? Of what your body is like? People disagree about which of Ama, Ben, Chi-ah, and Deena are really women. And they disagree about which of them belong in women-only spaces like a woman's bathroom. But there's a lot of confusion about what we even mean when we ask whether someone is really a woman.

1. Sex and Gender

People often assume that the issue is pretty simple: you're a woman if you have XX chromosomes, and you're a man if you have XY chromosomes. But it turns out not to be that simple at all.

To start off, let's talk about sex. Your biological sex is determined by a special set of anatomical features—although the relationship between sex characteristics and sex classification is complicated, and not all human bodies can easily be classified into a particular sex category. Biological features that determine sex include chromosomes (XX or XY in typical cases, but there are also rare combinations like XXY), hormones (overall balance of testosterone, estrogen, progesterone, etc.), reproductive organs (ovaries, testes, uterus, vagina, penis), and more diffuse anatomical characteristics that often correlate with sex (e.g., prominent Adam's apple, body hair patterns, facial shape, etc.). A typical male has XY chromosomes, testes, and higher levels of testosterone; a typical female has XX chromosomes, a uterus and ovaries, and higher levels of estrogen and progesterone. But it's important to note that these characteristics can be combined in various different ways, which is part of why human bodies don't sort neatly into a sex binary of male and female—there's a lot of intersex variation between those two categories. Still, sexed characteristics are an important biological aspect of human bodies, especially because of the role they play in human reproduction.

So our anatomical sex characteristics are an important part of our bodies—but do they explain or determine our gender? Once we look closely, it seems pretty clear that they don't.

To begin with, someone can be a woman without clearly being female. Some women, like Deena for example, have a condition known as androgen insensitivity syndrome (AIS). AIS is one of many conditions that can result in bodies that don't easily fit our classifications of male or female. In some cases of AIS, for example, a person with XY chromosomes can develop all the external sex characteristics we associate with female bodies, but lack a uterus and have undescended testes (often in a location similar to that of the ovaries in most females.) This type of body is a classic example of the kinds of bodies we often call "intersex." But someone who has all the external physical characteristics we associate with being female will be treated as a woman and experience all the social norms and expectations we apply to people with female bodies. And many people with AIS identify strongly as women, regardless of the biological complexity of their sex. Contra the proponents of various exclusionary "bathroom laws," who often say that you're a woman only if you have XX chromosomes, you can clearly be a woman in the ways that matter to us socially even if you're not classifiable as female.

But perhaps more important, there's a lot that we pack in to our idea of what it is to be a woman—of what it is to be a real woman—or of what it is to be a man, a genderqueer person, and so forth, that goes beyond basic anatomy. There are lots of ways that your body can be. You can have brown eyes or green eyes, you can be 5′5″ or 6′, you can have straight hair or curly hair, and so on. But some ways your body can be are more socially significant than others. If people perceive you as a person with brown eyes, they don't typically make immediate assumptions about your personality, your interests, or your skills. We don't think brown-eyed people are all the same or that brown-eyed people share deeply meaningful traits that green-eyed people lack. But if you're perceived as someone who is female, people will often make significant assumptions about what you're like based on this perception. And even more important, they'll often make significant assumptions about what you should be like. Maybe people will think that you're likely to be nurturing, or likely to talk a lot, or likely to be emotional, or likely to be particularly good at organizing but not that great at abstract reasoning and innovation, and so forth. The particular assumptions can vary a lot from place to place and time to time. The main point is just that people's perceptions of your sex characteristics are deeply socially significant, in a way that people's perceptions of your eye color or shoe size aren't. If you're perceived as someone with breasts and a vagina, people will tend to think this is something that matters a very great deal to what kind of person you are. They'll think you probably have some significant things in common with other people perceived to have breasts and vaginas, and they'll perhaps think there are some things you should do and some ways you should behave because you're perceived as being female.

This kind of deep social significance doesn't look like it can be explained just by the biological differences between males and females. Our cultural stereotypes tell us things like "men are from Mars, women are from Venus"—they tell us that men and women are radically different, perhaps so different that they can never understand each other. Our current scientific evidence, though, seems to suggest that while there are biological differences between sexes that might influence personality and behavior, these differences typically aren't very dramatic, and there's a lot of commonality as well. Height is a good example of this—on average, males are taller than females, but the differences often aren't very substantial (it's not like the height difference between adults and children), and plenty of individual females are taller than individual males. Similar things hold true for a lot of the biological sex characteristics that might influence some of our behavior or personality—yes, there are differences that might influence behavior to some degree, but probably not the kind of vast differences that could explain "men are from Mars, women are from Venus" understanding of gender.

We often do try to give biological explanations for our gender stereotypes, though, so it's important to realize that what's considered stereotypical or normal for men and women can change fairly drastically from place to place and time to time. So many of the things we currently consider feminine—shopping, the color pink, makeup, fashion—have in other times and places been considered masculine. Consider the difference between our current gender stereotypes and those prevalent in eighteenth and early nineteenth-century England. At that time and place, the greatest heights of emotionality were thought to be the preserve of men—women, it was thought, weren't capable of the same depths of feeling as men, to the extent that the declaration that "women feel just as much as men feel" in the novel Jane Eyre was considered genuinely shocking. Jobs we now think of as characteristically feminine, such as secretary, were typically thought of as men's work. Much factory work, in contrast, was thought of as work primarily for women and children. What a culture associates as stereotypically masculine or feminine can and does vary greatly, even though differences between anatomical sex characteristics remain fairly stable.

There's a specific way in which gender and sexed anatomy can come apart that has recently come under the political spotlight: trans gender. The term "trans" refers to people who identify as a gender other than the one they were assigned at birth (and typically other than the one people assume they ought to identify as based on their anatomy). Some people, like Ama, identify strongly as genderqueer, or nonbinary; that is, they think of themselves as neither a man nor a woman, regardless of their sex anatomy. Likewise, some people who are assigned a particular gender at birth based on their sex characteristics—woman, for example, if they have a vulva and vagina—might later decide that this gender assignment isn't right for them and that a different gender category is correct. A trans man like Ben, for example, is a man who was assigned a different gender category (typically woman) when he was young.

Some people argue that trans and nonbinary people are not really the gender they identify as. When people say this, it typically implies a strong connection between gender and sex—so you are not really a man unless you have the right kind of anatomical characteristics, and if you have those anatomical characteristics you are really a man even if you say you're some other gender. But as we've seen, it isn't true that you have to have a specific set of biological characteristics (such as the correct chromosomes) to be a particular gender. People also sometimes seem to mean that that you can't really be a man unless you were raised with the "right" kind of social experiences and social expectations—but as we've seen, the social expectations and experiences we associate with men can vary pretty drastically from place to place and time to time. So when people say that trans men like Ben aren't really men, the claim is confusing and possibly inconsistent with other things they think. It's not even clear what it means to really be a man (or a woman, or a genderqueer person), especially if being a man doesn't neatly correlate to being male, and if the social significance of being a man isn't fully explained by male sex characteristics.

2. Social Construction

So if gender isn't biology, what it is it? As it turns out, that's a really tough question. It's tempting to say that gender is just a matter of our current social norms. We currently have norms for lots of things—what's cool, what's fashionable, what's polite, and so forth.

And you can make conscious choices about how to interact with those norms—you can be nice or rude, stylish or intentionally counterculture, and so on. Maybe gender is just another set of norms—whatever we currently think of as masculine and feminine. You can then express your own gender by making conscious choices about how gender conforming or nonconforming you want to be, and in what way.

The trouble with this picture of gender, though, is that it has difficulty accounting for the ways in which gendered social systems—and gender oppression—have been systematic across strikingly different cultures and times. Although specific norms about gender can vary a lot, it appears to be a very stable feature of human society that we divide people into genders. Indeed, the way in which societies sort people into gender categories is strikingly more stable than the way in which societies sort people into other social categories. While plenty of cultures haven't had social categories that play the role of racial categories, and plenty haven't had social categories that play the role of sexual orientation categories, our current knowledge suggests that nearly all (possibly all) cultures divide people into categories that play the role of gender; that is, which assign significant social meaning to (real or perceived) anatomical sex characteristics. And while not all cultures have understood gender as an exhaustive man/woman binary, nearly all ways of understanding gender have included categories that roughly correspond to our understanding of the binary categories man and woman. What norms and behaviors we associate as masculine or feminine varies dramatically. But it is virtually universal that we associate some significant norms and behaviors as being the kinds of things that apply to those with bodies we perceive as female, and some significant norms and behaviors as being the kinds of things that apply to those with bodies we perceive as male. Moreover, very often our social justification for why these norms and behaviors are appropriate is rooted in our understanding of differing roles in reproduction (and especially, the characteristic female role in reproduction). And very often, this type of systematic gender categorization leads to the systematic oppression of women.

Given how systematic gender is across so many different cultural contexts, it makes sense to think that gender is something more than just how we think and speak and behave in particular contexts. Gender appears to be a very real part of the social world—something that isn't just explained by the particular beliefs that particular people have, but which explains why sometimes those beliefs are so entrenched and hard to change (in a way that beliefs about what is cool or what is fashionable are not.)

But if we think that gender is a real part of the world—not just a projection of our collective beliefs—we're faced with the question of what in the world gender could be. Here we can divide philosophers into two main camps: those who say that your gender is determined primarily by how other people react to you, and those who say that your gender is determined primarily by your own internal sense of yourself. Let's call the former externalists (since they think you gender is primarily determined by things external to you) about gender and the latter internalists about gender (since they think your gender is determined primarily by things internal to you).

Gender externalists want to understand gender—and what the members of a particular gender have in common with each other—in terms of commonalities of social experience. Most especially, gender externalists have often argued that what women have in common with each other is their social experience of sex-based oppression. What unifies all the individual women into a social kind is the disadvantage they experience because of the expectations and norms we have about how people with female bodies should behave and what they should do.

Gender realists have to tread carefully here, though, because in attempting to talk about what social experiences women have in common with each other, it is very easy to overlook the dramatic differences between different women's social experience of gender. Intersectionality, very simply, is the idea that no one ever has a social feature like gender in isolation from other social features: different social categories intersect with each other, and that affects what it's like to experience each of them. You're never just a woman—you're a woman with a particular race, class, sexual orientation, disability status, nationality, and so on. Your experience of gender will be different if, for example, you're an upper-middle-class Latina woman than it would be if you were a working-class Asian woman. Gender externalists thus tend to focus more on the structural features that our treatment of different genders have in common.

Sally Haslanger's theory of gender is a paradigm example of this kind of view. According to Haslanger, a person, S, is a woman iff:

(i) S is regularly and for the most part observed or imagined to have certain bodily features presumed to be evidence of a female's biological role in reproduction;

(ii) That S has these features marks S within the dominant ideology of S's society as someone who ought to occupy certain kinds of social position that are in fact subordinate (and so motivates and justifies S's occupying such a position); and

(iii) The fact that S satisfies (i) and (ii) plays a role in S's systematic subordination; i.e., *along some dimension*, S's social position is oppressive, and S's satisfying (i) and (ii) plays a role in that dimension of subordination.[1]

Let's unpack this a little. On this view, whether you are a woman is a matter of both how other people perceive your sexed anatomy and of the social position you are expected to occupy based on that perception. In almost every culture, there are strong norms about women's work, women's behavior, women's roles—the kinds of things it is appropriate for you to do or which you ought to do because of your (perceived) sex characteristics. What we think of as women's work or women's roles or women's behavior can and does vary dramatically. What stays strikingly constant across so many different cultures and times, however, is that whatever we in fact consider to be women's work or women's roles or women's behavior is something we then think of as less valuable. When men were thought of as more emotional than women, that was taken to be a mark of their superiority—a sign that they were capable of more depth and more insight than women. When women are thought of as more emotional

---

1. See pages 565–66 of this anthology.

than men, it is often taken as a subtle mark of their inferiority—a sign that they are somewhat less rational or less reliable or less sensible than men.

What all the women have in common with each other, in Haslanger's view, is that they are expected to occupy social roles that are, within the context they are expected to occupy them, considered less valuable than the roles that men are expected to occupy. And the justification for why they are expected to occupy these roles is rooted in beliefs about their sex characteristics. Of course, it doesn't follow that all women are disadvantaged relative to all men. Middle-class women are typically economically disadvantaged compared to middle-class men, for example, but they aren't economically disadvantaged compared to working-class men. We still have to keep our eye on intersectionality. But Haslanger's idea is that all women will experience disadvantage along some dimension based on the roles they are expected to occupy because of their perceived sex characteristics. And for Haslanger, gender is just this system (or "social structure") that disadvantages people based on perceptions of female sex and a female's role in reproduction.

A worry for Haslanger's theory of gender, though, is that it doesn't give an adequate account of what it is to be a woman because it misclassifies some women as men (and some not-women as women). For example, a woman like Chi-ah wouldn't reliably meet condition (i) of Haslanger's definition—she isn't regularly and for the most part perceived as having the anatomical features associated with a female's role in reproduction. But it seems wrong to say that Chi-ah is not a woman just because people are confused by masculine-appearing women. If we explain what it is to be a woman simply in terms of how people respond to you, then we risk saying that if people are confused enough by your gender, that's enough to make you not really a woman. And that seems wrong.

The view also has some interesting hypothetical consequences. We typically think of myths about Amazons as myths about a race of powerful women.[2] But Haslanger's view has the curious result that these stories aren't really stories about women, since in the stories Amazons are not oppressed and do not occupy disadvantaged social roles.

Gender internalists often use these kinds of worries to argue for their favored view of gender. An internalist view of gender will be more adequate and inclusive, the thought goes, because it will respect people's gender self-identification, and thus avoid misgendering. If we say that gender is determined (at least in part) by gender identity, then we can say that you are a woman if you identify as a woman, you are a man if you identify as a man, you are genderqueer if you identify as genderqueer, and so on.

But what is gender identity, in this sense? Importantly, it's not quite the same thing that psychologists mean when they talk about gender identity. That sense of gender identity typically develops in very early childhood, whereas if you're genderqueer you might not think of yourself in those terms until you're older. For the most part, when philosophers talk about gender identity, they mean your internally felt sense of your relationship to the gender norms and categories that are common within our

---

2. In Greek mythology, the Amazons were a race of female warriors.

society. So if you identify as a woman, this typically means that the norms we have about women are appropriately applied to you. Importantly, this does not mean that you think those norms are themselves correct or appropriate. You may think that most of our norms and stereotypes about what women are like are wrong—you just think that people aren't making a categorical mistake when they classify you with other women and apply those norms to you as a result. If you identify as a woman, you can think it's completely obnoxious that people expect you to behave in stereotypically feminine ways because you're a woman. You can agree that you're a woman but reject the assumptions that people make about you because you're a woman. But that's a very different thing from thinking that people are making a mistake when they label you as a woman, which is how many genderqueer people who are often misgendered as women describe their experience.

But things get tricky once we delve into to the details of what, exactly, this sense of gender identity is, and how it determines gender categories. For example, there are many—increasingly many—terms used to describe gender identities. Is there a unique gender identity—a unique internally felt sense of one's relationship to dominant gender norms—that corresponds to each gender term? If gender identities are the substantial social facts that determine gender, we're left with the perplexing question of what, if anything, the difference is between identifying as genderqueer, nonbinary, gender fluid, pan-gender, agender, androgyne, and so on.[3]

And these questions bring up a larger skeptical worry for internalist accounts. What gender you are, on such views, is inherently private—it is a matter of how you feel about yourself and how you relate to society's sex-based norms and expectations. It's also crucially separable from any public behavior. You can identify as a man even if this is something you keep secret and even if you present publicly in ways we think of as stereotypically feminine. (That is, you can identify as a man but socially "pass" as a woman.) So whether you are really a woman (or a man, or genderqueer, etc.) on such views is a matter of whether you have a particular internally felt response to being classified as a woman (or man, etc.). But here's the problem: How do you know whether what you experience in response to gender norms is the same or similar to what other people experience? If Chi-ah says "I identify as a woman" and Deena says "I identify as a woman," do we have reason to think that this internally felt experience is the same or similar, given how different their gender expression and social experience of gender seem to be? Maybe what Chi-ah means by this is something very, very different from what Deena means by it. And this would be hard to find out, given that any of the ways we might explain what gender identity means to us are invariably personal and will probably be different for different people. Even if we both identify as women, I might explain my internally felt sense of gender by talking about how I feel about my relationship to other women, but you

3. "Genderqueer," "nonbinary": having a gender identity other than the usual two "binary" ones (although there are subtle differences between the two terms); "gender fluid": not identifying with a single gender; "pan-gender": identifying with many genders; "agender": not identifying with any gender; "androgyne": identifying, in varying degrees, with both binary genders.

might explain it by talking about how you feel about yourself. So it's not clear how we'd tell if we have some internal state in common. Again, intersectionality is very important to think about—your internally felt sense of gender might be very different from mine, or something you explain very differently if your social position is very different from mine. The worry is that we don't really know whether internally felt sense of gender can unify or explain what it is to be a woman, or what women have in common with each other.

Perhaps more significant, though, internalist accounts also face problems with misgendering—they just face different problems. For example, many cognitively disabled women plausibly don't experience anything like an internally felt sense of their relationship to sex-based social norms. So whatever it is to identify as a woman, these women probably aren't in that internal state. And yet it seems utterly wrong to say that cognitively disabled women are not women. Cognitively disabled women are often treated in specific ways and experience specific forms of oppression because of social perception and norms about their sexed bodies. We need to be able to talk about their gender to talk about this oppression. And think about what it would mean to say that cognitively disabled women are not women because they lack the right kind of self-identification: we would, in effect, be saying that because of their disabilities cognitively disabled women are not really women, they are merely female. This is similar to the way we say that non-human animals cannot be women, they can merely be female.

3. Conclusion

Let's take stock. In trying to understand what gender is, we need to distinguish between gender and anatomical sex characteristics. We also, plausibly, need an account of gender that allows us to say that gender isn't determined or fully explained by sex characteristics. That leads us to views which say that gender is "socially constructed." But granting that gender is something social, it's still extraordinarily difficult to say what kind of social thing it is. If we say it's just norms and beliefs in a particular context, it's hard to make sense of the systematicity of gender and gender oppression. If we say that gender is social role, it's hard to adequately explain the experience of people whose gender seems to come apart from their public social role. If we say that gender is gender identity, it's both hard to specify what we mean by gender identity and hard to adequately explain how people who experience self-identity differently than most people do can still have genders. What we're left with is a lot of confusion. It's both philosophically and politically important that we understand what gender is. But the project of understanding gender is very hard—we're pulled in many different directions, and there are many different, sometimes conflicting, aims for our theories. As it stands, it doesn't seem like there's any one theory of gender that explains everything we want a theory of gender to explain.

TEST YOUR UNDERSTANDING

1. Consider:

   (W) S is a woman **iff** S is an adult human female.

   According to Barnes, Deena provides a **counterexample** to which of the following? (You may select more than one.)

   a. (W)

   b. the "if" part of (W)

   c. the "only if" part of (W)

   d. someone is a woman only if they have XX chromosomes

2. Which of the following claims about biological differences between (human) males and females does Barnes agree with? (You may select more than one.)

   a. They do not completely explain personality and behavioral differences between males and females.

   b. They do not completely explain why people think that men are from Mars, women are from Venus.

   c. They completely explain why men are from Mars, women are from Venus.

   d. They do not completely explain the social significance of being a woman or a man.

3. Sally Haslanger's theory of gender (roughly stated) is that to be a woman is to be perceived as female and thereby to be subordinated. What objections does Barnes raise to this theory? (You may select more than one.)

   a. Some women are not subordinated.

   b. Some women are not perceived as female.

   c. Some stories about women who are not subordinated are not incoherent.

   d. The Amazons lived apart from men and so were not subordinated by them.

4. Gender internalists hold (roughly) that a person is a woman just in case she "identifies as" a woman. What objections does Barnes raise to gender internalism? (You may select more than one.)

   a. A man could mistakenly think he is a woman.

   b. There may be no "internally felt sense of gender" common to all women.

   c. Some women don't identify as women.

   d. Gender internalism implies that we might not able to know whether someone is a woman, which is absurd.

NOTES AND QUESTIONS

1. Barnes does not draw a positive conclusion about the metaphysics of gender. She explains three different types of views and raises problems for each of them. These views are

   a. to be a woman is to be an adult human female (or, more generally, to belong to some broadly biological category);

   b. to be a woman is a matter of being regarded in a certain way (*gender externalism*); and

   c. that to be a woman is a matter of feeling a certain way about oneself (*gender internalism*).

   Barnes raises problems for all three types of views. Which problems seem most serious? How could proponents of these views respond to the problems Barnes raises? If one of these views is correct, which one is it?

2. *The sex/gender distinction.* The introduction to this chapter explained the "sex/gender distinction" as the distinction between *sex* (male, female, and associated biological categories) and the *social meaning or significance* of sex. For Barnes, the sex/gender distinction is primarily one between sex and categories such as *man* and *woman*. This alternative—and quite different—way of explaining the sex/gender distinction derives from a common (although disputed) interpretation of a famous remark by the French philosopher Simone de Beauvoir (1908–1986) in her classic book *The Second Sex*, published in 1949. Here is an influential example of such an interpretation, from the American philosopher Judith Butler (1956–):

   > "One is not born, but rather becomes, a woman"—Simone de Beauvoir's formulation distinguishes sex from gender and suggests that gender is an aspect of identity gradually acquired. The distinction between sex and gender has been crucial to the long-standing feminist effort to debunk the claim that anatomy is destiny[4]; *sex* is understood to be the invariant, anatomically distinct, and factic aspects[5] of the female body, whereas gender is the cultural meaning and form that that body acquires, the variable modes of that body's acculturation. With the distinction intact, it is no longer possible to attribute the values or social functions of women to biological necessity, and neither can we refer meaningfully to natural or unnatural gendered behavior: all gender is, by definition, unnatural. Moreover, if the distinction is consistently applied, it becomes unclear whether being a given sex has any necessary consequence for becoming a given gender. . . . If being a woman is one cultural interpretation of being female, and if that interpretation is in no way necessitated by being female, then it appears that the female body is the arbitrary locus of the gender "woman," and there is no reason to preclude the possibility of that body becoming the

---

4. The line "anatomy is destiny" is from "The Dissolution of the Oedipus Complex" by the Austrian founder of psychoanalysis, Sigmund Freud (1856–1939).

5. Factic aspects: "natural" features such as having XX chromosomes.

locus of other constructions of gender. At its limit, then, the sex/gender distinction implies a radical heteronomy of natural bodies and constructed genders[6] with the consequence that "being female" and "being a woman" are two very different sorts of being. This last insight, I would suggest, is the distinguished contribution of Simone de Beauvoir's formulation, "one is not born, but rather becomes, a woman."[7]

3. *Sex differences.* A trait such as height is *distributed* in a certain way in a population: approximately 15 percent of American men are over 6 feet, for example. If the distribution of a trait differs between (human) males and females, then that trait shows a *sex difference* (or *gender difference*—see footnote 13 in the introduction to this chapter). Some examples of traits that show sex differences are earring wearing, life span, upper body strength, sexual orientation, physical aggression, depression, height, drug metabolism, verbal fluency, and visuospatial abilities. *Psychological* sex differences (e.g., depression, verbal fluency, visuospatial abilities) are typically significantly smaller than differences in nonpsychological traits such as height—with sexual orientation being one glaring exception. Sometimes biological explanations of sex differences (or their absence) are opposed to cultural or social explanations. But since culture and society are influenced by biology, and vice versa, these kinds of explanations need not be in competition.

For a balanced introduction to the biology of sex differences by a leading researcher, see Melissa Hines, *Brain Gender* (Oxford University Press, 2004).

6. "Heteronomy" (literally, rule by another) is a term used by (among others) the French philosopher Emmanuel Levinas (1906–1995). For the purposes of understanding the main ideas of the quotation, you can read Butler as simply saying that the sex/gender distinction implies that there is a radical difference between natural bodies and constructed genders.

7. Judith Butler, "Sex and Gender in Simone de Beauvoir's *Second Sex*," *Yale French Studies* 72 (1986): 35. In her later book *Gender Trouble* (Routledge, 2006), Butler suggests that "the distinction between sex and gender turns out to be no distinction at all" (p. 10).

ANALYZING THE ARGUMENTS

1. *No biological foundation.* Consider the following argument:

   > No biologist has ever been able to provide a satisfactory definition of "race"—that is, a definition that includes all members of a given race and excludes all others. Attempts to give the term a biological foundation lead to absurdities: parents and children of different races, or the well-known phenomenon that a white woman can give birth to a black child, but a black woman can never give birth to a white child. The only logical conclusion is that people are members of different races because they have been assigned to them.[1]

   Set out this argument so that it is **valid**. Is it **sound**? How would Spencer object to the argument?

2. *BiDil.* Why are we even having this discussion? Races are clearly biological categories. In 2005 the U.S. Food and Drug Administration approved a heart drug, BiDil, *specifically for African Americans.* How could that be reasonable if races aren't biological categories? What, if anything, is wrong with this argument?

3. *Arbitrariness.* Racial divisions between humans are *clinal* or *gradual.* If we took the time, we could line up 1,000 men according to the following specifications. (a) There is a stereotypical Ethiopian man on the far left and a stereotypical Norwegian man on the far right. (b) Everyone in the 1,000-man line is very similar to his immediate neighbors, both anatomically and ancestrally. Where does "being black" end, and where does "being white" begin? The answers to both can only be *arbitrary*. But if races are biological categories, the answers would not be arbitrary. Therefore, races are not biological categories.

   What, if anything, is wrong with this argument? (It might be helpful to look at Section 6 of "A Brief Guide to Logic and Argumentation" in the front of this anthology.)

4. *Human beings.* In *Feminism Unmodified* (Harvard University Press, 1987), legal scholar Catharine MacKinnon writes that she has learned "that feminism—in the form of a tacit belief that women are human beings in truth but not in social reality—has gone deep into women and some younger men, becoming taken for granted, becoming part of the background" (p. 216).

   Consider the accounts of gender discussed by Haslanger and Barnes. Do any of them allow that there could be women who are *not* human beings? If so, is this a problem for these views?

5. *Intersectionality.* Both Haslanger and Barnes make use of the notion of **intersectionality**. What examples do they give of it? Are these examples convincing? How does intersectionality figure in their overall arguments? If intersectionality is emphasized,

---

1. N. Ignatiev, *How the Irish Became White* (Routledge, 1995), 1.

one might wonder whether there are *any* interesting generalizations about the experiences of women in general, or black people in general, or even middle-aged black women living in Philadelphia in 2018 in general. Is this a serious worry for attempts to theorize about the experiences of *classes* of people, as opposed to just theorizing about the experiences of individuals?

6. *Gender and race.* This chapter treats two topics. But just how connected are they? Haslanger offers a unified account, and Appiah thinks that we should speak of civilizations where we now speak of races, just as we "speak of genders where we spoke of sexes" (see page 558 of this anthology). Both Appiah and Haslanger claim to find deep connections, but not the same ones. Is a unified account of gender and race plausible?

Do We Possess
Free Will?

A Question about Responsibility

In March 2007, New York newspapers reported the brutal mugging of a 101-year-old woman in the lobby of her apartment building. As surveillance tapes show, the mugger held the door open for his victim, followed her inside, then donned a ski mask and beat her mercilessly for several minutes before fleeing with her purse.

This attack was not just a tragedy, as it would have been if the woman had been injured in a fall or mauled by an animal. It was a grotesque moral wrong and we blame the man who did it, which is to say that we hold the man **morally responsible** for his act.

This is not a special case. The conviction that human beings are morally responsible for what they do is deeply rooted in common sense. We take it for granted every day when we praise people for the good they do and blame them for the harm they cause. As a society, we take it for granted when we punish people for their crimes. As we usually think, this is one of the most important differences between human beings and other animals. (It may be perfectly natural to blame your dog for tracking mud all over the house, but in a cool moment you know this makes no sense. He's just a dog, after all.) But if this is right, there must be something about us that explains it. And so we ask—not in a skeptical spirit but in a spirit of open-minded curiosity—Why are we morally responsible for what we do when animals are not? What is it about us that makes us special in this regard?

The Free Will Hypothesis

Think about the mugger in the moments just prior to the attack. There he is, holding the door open for his victim and watching her walk through. As he does this he is buffeted by biological and psychological forces of many kinds, including, we may suppose, a powerful impulse to attack. But if we think he is responsible for his act, we must think that he is capable of resisting this impulse—of "stepping back" and deciding for himself whether to act on it. This ability is sometimes called **free will**—though this phrase is used in other ways as well. An act is free, on this conception, when the agent *could have done otherwise*. Before he acts, the free agent is in a certain psychological state: he has beliefs about his circumstances; he has desires, feelings, and values; he has various habits and capacities; and so on. In other animals, this prior state *settles* what the animal will do (insofar as anything settles it). Holding all of these factors fixed, an animal has no real options. For human beings as we normally understand them, by contrast, while these factors may strongly incline a person to make one choice rather than another, it is ultimately *up to him* to choose. According to the free will hypothesis, that is why we are normally responsible for what we do while other animals are not.

Let's put this cluster of commonsensical ideas under the microscope. It has several components.

1. A person is morally responsible for an action only if she performs it freely.

2. A person acts freely only if she could have done otherwise.

3. A person could have done otherwise only if her choice was not determined by prior factors over which she had no control.

Taken together, these entail:

4. A person is morally responsible for an action only if her choice was not determined by prior factors over which she had no control.

But we've said repeatedly that as we normally think,

5. People are usually responsible for what they do.[1]

And so we have disclosed what might be called a *presupposition* of ordinary thought. If this commonsensical cluster of ideas is correct, then our practice of holding one another responsible—our practices of praise and blame, punishment and reward—take it for granted that

6. Typical human choices are not determined by factors over which the agent had no control.

And now that we have isolated this presupposition, we must examine it. We may take it for granted as we go about our business. But is there any reason to believe that it is true?

---

1. Why "usually"? Because we know that human beings are not always responsible for what they do. Someone who has been forced or hypnotized or tricked into acting badly is not responsible for what he does. Proposition 5 makes the commonsensical point that such excuses are not always available.

Doubts about Free Will

You might think that the claim is supported by introspection. Consider how it feels to make an ordinary choice. There you are, deciding whether to read the rest of this page or to take a break. Even if you're bored and really *want* to take that break, it may seem obvious that nothing literally "forces" you one way or the other. So it's tempting to think that the *experience of conscious choice* confirms that our choices are not determined in advance.

In fact, however, the experience of conscious choice shows no such thing. It may show that we are not normally *aware* of factors that determine our choices. But our choices might still be determined by factors of which we are unaware. (When you see a flash of lightning, you don't see what caused the flash, but that doesn't mean that nothing caused it!) The opponent of (6) suspects that our choices are determined by factors of which we are unaware. Introspection can do nothing to exclude this possibility.

Free Will and Divine Foreknowledge

Why might someone think that our choices are determined by factors of which we are unaware? One venerable argument comes from theology. If God is eternal and all-knowing, then God always knew—from the beginning of time—that the mugger would attack the woman. So assume there is such a God and focus again on the moment just before the mugger's choice. It may seem to him in that moment that he has two options: to attack or to walk away. But what he does not know is that before he was born, God *predicted* that he would attack. This prediction is settled; it lies in the past and the mugger cannot do anything about it. To say that he is nonetheless capable of doing otherwise is therefore to say that he is capable of falsifying God's prediction. And the trouble is that no one has that power. It is *impossible* for God to be mistaken, and so it is impossible for a person to act in a way that would cause God to have been mistaken.[2] If every human choice is foreseen by an infallible God, it follows that everything we do is settled in advance by a factor—God's prediction—that was in place before we were born. So if a free choice must be an undetermined choice, this theology entails that human freedom is an illusion. (See Nelson Pike, "Divine Omniscience and Voluntary Action," *Philosophical Review* 74, 1 [1965]: 27–46.)

Free Will and Physical Determinism

You can resist this argument by denying the existence of an eternal, all-knowing God. (You should ask whether there are other ways to resist it.) But a very different and wholly secular argument seems to lead to the same conclusion. From its origins in the

---

2. The view in question holds that it is part of God's **essence** to be infallible, just as it is part of the essence of a triangle to have three sides. No one can draw a four-sided triangle because four-sided triangles are impossible. Likewise, no one can falsify God's prediction because a mistaken God is impossible.

seventeenth century, modern science seemed to confirm the ancient speculation that the universe as a whole is a **deterministic** *system* in which the state of the cosmos at any one time is determined by its state at any prior time, together with the laws of nature. On this view, the state of the universe at any point in the past—say, exactly 1 billion years ago—and the laws of nature together fix the state of the universe at every future time. If this view is correct, then given the past and the laws, absolutely everything that happens—every supernova, every mugging—is determined to occur just as it does.

It must be stressed that physical determinism of this sort is a scientific hypothesis. The physics of Newton and his successors, including Einstein, was for the most part deterministic. However, contemporary physics leaves open the possibility that the basic laws of nature assign probabilities to future occurrences without determining what will happen. Since physics is a work in progress, *no one knows at present whether physical determinism is true*. And this means that we should not assume determinism (or its opposite) in our philosophy.

Instead, we focus on the consequences of determinism. Suppose you wake up tomorrow to this headline:

SCIENTISTS DISCOVER, BEYOND DOUBT: UNIVERSE IS A DETERMINISTIC SYSTEM

What would this mean? It would mean that the motion of every particle, including the particles in our brains and bodies, was determined by the state of the universe a billion years ago together with the laws of nature. In particular, it would mean that it was settled a billion years ago that the particles in the mugger's brain and body would do just what they did, and hence that he would do just what he did. And, of course, the same would be true of every human action. So if a free act must be an undetermined act, this sort of physics entails that human freedom is an illusion.

This argument should worry anyone who accepts determinism. But it should also worry anyone—and this should be all of us—who is genuinely uncertain about whether the laws of physics will turn out to be deterministic. For if the argument is cogent, it shows that *for all we know at present*, human freedom is an illusion. And that is an unsettling thought. Think of the mugger again—or anyone else whom you regard as obviously responsible for what he's done. If this line of thought is sound, you have no right to this confidence, since for all you know, the whole business was settled eons ago by factors over which the agent had no control.

Free Will and Indeterminism

All of this may leave you hoping for a different headline. So imagine you wake up tomorrow to find this on the front page of the *New York Times*:

SCIENTISTS DISCOVER, BEYOND DOUBT: PHYSICAL UNIVERSE IS INDETERMINISTIC

Would this really be any better? Return to the moment just before the mugger's choice. His brain and body are in a certain state. Because the universe is indeterministic, this state does not determine his choice. Rather, the laws of nature assign a certain probability to a decision to attack and a certain (presumably lower) probability to a decision to walk away. Now a moment passes and he decides to attack. Why did he make *that* decision? If the process is genuinely indeterministic, this question may have no answer. When the choice was made, it was as if a coin were flipped in the mugger's head. His decision was a chance occurrence, a random fluctuation. And just as it is hard to see how a person can be responsible for a choice determined by factors beyond his control, it is hard to see how he can be responsible for a choice that simply happens in him as a result of random chance.

The Dilemma of Determinism

Putting these pieces together, we face what is sometimes called the *dilemma of determinism*:

A. If determinism is true, we are not responsible, since our choices are determined by factors over which we have no control.

B. If indeterminism is true, we are not responsible, since our choices are chance occurrences.

C. But either determinism is true or indeterminism is true.

D. Therefore, we are not morally responsible for what we do.

This is a profound problem. Common sense assures us that we are responsible because we are free to choose. The dilemma tells us that we cannot be free, and that we are therefore not responsible. The only way to vindicate common sense is to find some flaw in the dilemma. The selections below represent a range of strategies.

A. J. Ayer, Harry Frankfurt, and P. F. Strawson all reject (A). These writers are **compatibilists** who hold in various ways that we can be responsible for a choice even though that choice was determined in advance. Roderick Chisholm rejects (B), distinguishing mere chance occurrences, which have no cause, from genuine free choices, which are caused not by prior events but by "the agent himself."

Against all of this, Galen Strawson defends a version of the dilemma, arguing that there is no credible account of human choice that would vindicate our commonsensical view of ourselves as free and responsible.

Some philosophers have suggested that even if human freedom is ultimately an illusion, the illusion is unshakable in the sense that it is psychologically impossible for us to overcome it. To see what they may be getting at, try an experiment. Next time someone steals your parking space, try to persuade yourself that even though the act was selfish and obnoxious, it wasn't really the driver's fault, since no one is ever morally responsible for what he does. Next time you read a news story about a lying politician or a vicious murderer, try to tell yourself that your immediate reaction—that these people deserve blame and punishment—assumes an incoherent view of human action. Say to yourself, "For all I know, these acts are mere regrettable occurrences for which no one is responsible." The exercise will give you a vivid sense of what is at stake in this debate.

Galen Strawson (b. 1952)

Strawson is Professor of Philosophy at the University of Reading and at the University of Texas, Austin. His work ranges widely in the history of philosophy (*The Secret Connexion,* 1989), the philosophy of mind (*Mental Reality,* 1994), and metaphysics (*Selves: An Essay in Revisionary Metaphysics,* 2009).

FREE WILL

1

You set off for a shop on the evening of a national holiday, intending to buy a cake with your last $10 bill to supplement the preparations you've already made. There's one cake left in the shop and it costs $10; everything is closing down. On the steps of the shop someone is shaking a box, collecting money for famine relief. You stop, and it seems clear to you that it is entirely up to you what you do next. It seems clear to you that you are truly, radically free to choose, in such a way that you will be ultimately morally responsible for whatever you do choose.

There is, however, an argument, which I will call the Basic Argument, that appears to show that we can never be truly or ultimately morally responsible for our actions. According to the Basic Argument, it makes no difference whether determinism is true or false.

The central idea can be quickly conveyed.

(A) Nothing can be *causa sui*—nothing can be the cause of itself.

(B) To be ultimately morally responsible for one's actions, one would have to be *causa sui*, at least in certain crucial mental respects.

(C) Therefore, no one can be ultimately morally responsible.

We can expand it as follows.

(1) Interested in free action, we're particularly interested in actions performed for a reason (as opposed to reflex actions or mindlessly habitual actions).

(2)   When one acts for a reason, what one does is a function of how one is, mentally speaking. (It's also a function of one's height, one's strength, one's place and time, and so on; but the mental factors are crucial when moral responsibility is in question.)

(3)   So if one is to be truly or ultimately responsible for how one acts, one must be truly or ultimately responsible for how one is, mentally speaking—at least in certain respects.

(4)   But to be truly or ultimately responsible for how one is, in any mental respect, one must have brought it about that one is the way one is, in that respect. And it's not merely that one must have caused oneself to be the way one is, in that respect. One must also have consciously and explicitly chosen to be the way one is, in that respect, and one must have succeeded in bringing it about that one is that way.

(5)   But one can't really be said to choose, in a conscious, reasoned fashion, to be the way one is in any respect at all, unless one already exists, mentally speaking, already equipped with some principles of choice, "P1"—preferences, values, ideals—in the light of which one chooses how to be.

(6)   But then to be truly or ultimately responsible, on account of having chosen to be the way one is, in certain mental respects, one must be truly or ultimately responsible for one's having the principles of choice P1 in the light of which one chose how to be.

(7)   But for this to be so, one must have chosen P1 in a reasoned, conscious, intentional fashion.

(8)   But for this to be so, one must already have had some principles of choice P2, in the light of which one chose P1.

(9)   And so on. Here we are setting out on a regress that we cannot stop. True or ultimate self-determination is impossible because it requires the actual completion of an infinite series of choices of principles of choice.

(10)   So true or ultimate moral responsibility is impossible, because it requires true or ultimate self-determination, as noted in (3).

This may seem contrived, but essentially the same argument can be given in a more natural form. (1) It's undeniable that one is the way one is, initially, as a result of heredity and early experience, and it's undeniable that these are things for which one can't be held to be in any way responsible (morally or otherwise). (2) One can't at any later stage of life hope to accede to true or ultimate moral responsibility for the way one is by trying to change the way one already is as a result of heredity and previous experience. For (3) both the particular way in which one is moved to try to change oneself, and the degree of one's success in one's attempt to change, will be determined by how one already is as a result of heredity and previous experience. And (4) any further changes that one can bring about only after one has brought about certain initial changes will in turn be determined, via the initial changes, by heredity and previous experience. (5) This may not be the whole story; there may be some changes in the way one is that can't be traced to heredity and experience but rather to the influence of indeterministic or random factors. It is, however, absurd to suppose that indeterministic or random factors, for which one is obviously not responsible, can contribute in any way to one's being truly or ultimately morally responsible for how one is.

2

But what is this supposed "true" or "ultimate" moral responsibility? As I understand it, it's responsibility of such a kind that, if we have it, it means that it *makes sense* to suppose that it could be just to punish some of us with (eternal) torment in hell and reward others with (eternal) bliss in heaven. The stress on the words "makes sense" is important, for one certainly doesn't have to believe in any version of the story of heaven and hell in order to understand, or indeed believe in, the kind of true or ultimate moral responsibility that I'm using the story to illustrate. A less colorful way to convey the point, perhaps, is to say that true or ultimate responsibility exists if punishment and reward can be fair without having any sort of pragmatic justification.

One certainly doesn't have to refer to religious faith in order to describe the sorts of everyday situation that give rise to our belief in such responsibility. Choices like the one with which I began (the cake or the collection box) arise all the time and constantly refresh our conviction about our responsibility. Even if one believes that determinism is true in such a situation and that one will in 5 minutes' time be able to look back and say that what one did was determined, this doesn't seem to undermine one's sense of the absoluteness and inescapability of one's freedom and of one's moral responsibility for one's choice. Even if one accepts the validity of the Basic Argument, which concludes that one cannot be in any way ultimately responsible for the way one is and decides, one's freedom and true moral responsibility seem, as one stands there, obvious and absolute.

Large and small, morally significant or morally neutral, such situations of choice occur regularly in human life. I think they lie at the heart of the experience of freedom and moral responsibility. They're the fundamental source of our inability to give up belief in true or ultimate moral responsibility. We may wonder why human beings experience these situations of choice as they do. It's an interesting question whether any cognitively sophisticated, rational, self-conscious agent must inevitably experience situations of choice in this way (MacKay 1960; Strawson 1986, 281–86). But they are the experiential rock on which the belief in ultimate moral responsibility is founded.

Most people who believe in ultimate moral responsibility take its existence for granted and don't ever entertain the thought that one needs to be ultimately responsible for the way one *is* in order to be ultimately responsible for the way one *acts*. Some, however, reveal that they see its force. E. H. Carr states that "normal adult human beings are morally responsible for their own personality" (1961, 89). Sartre holds that "man is responsible for what he is" (1989, 29) and seeks to give an account of how we "choose ourselves" (1969, 440, 468, 503). In a later interview, he judges his earlier assertions about freedom to be incautious, but still holds that "in the end one is always responsible for what is made of one" (1969). Kant puts it clearly when he claims that "man *himself* must make or have made himself into whatever, in a moral sense, whether good or evil, he is to become. Either condition must be an effect of his free choice; for otherwise he could not be held responsible for it and could therefore be *morally* neither good nor evil" (1960, 40). Since he is committed to belief in radical moral responsibility, Kant holds that such self-creation does indeed take place and writes accordingly of "man's character, which he himself creates," and of "knowledge of oneself as a person who . . . is his own originator" (1956, 101). John Patten claims that "it is . . . self-evident that as we grow up each individual chooses whether to be good or bad."[1] Robert Kane, an eloquent recent defender of this view, writes as follows: "if . . . a choice issues from, and can be sufficiently explained by, an agent's character and motives (together with background conditions) then to be ultimately responsible for the choice, the agent must be at least in part responsible by virtue of choices or actions voluntarily performed in the past for having the character and motives he or she now has" (2009, 317–18). Christine Korsgaard agrees: "judgements of responsibility don't really make sense unless people create themselves" (2009, 20).

Most of us, as remarked, never follow this line of thought. It seems, though, that we do tend, in some vague and unexamined fashion, to think of ourselves as responsible for—answerable for—how we are. The point is somewhat delicate, for we don't ordinarily suppose that we have gone through some sort of active process of self-determination at some past time. It seems nevertheless that we do unreflectively experience ourselves, in many respects, rather as we might experience ourselves if we did believe that we had engaged in some such activity of self-determination, and we may well also think of others in this way.

Sometimes a part of one's character—a desire or tendency—may strike one as foreign or alien. But it can do this only against a background of character traits that aren't experienced as foreign, but are rather "identified" with. (It's only relative to such a background that a character trait can stand out as alien.) Some feel tormented by impulses that they experience as alien, but in many a sense of general identification with their character predominates, and this identification seems to carry within itself an implicit sense that one is, generally speaking, in control of, or at least answerable for, how one is (even, perhaps, for aspects of one's character that one doesn't like). So it is arguable that we find, semi-dormant in common thought, an implicit recognition of the idea that true or ultimate moral responsibility for what one does somehow involves responsibility for how one is. It seems that ordinary thought is ready to move this way under pressure.

There are also many aspects of our ordinary sense of ourselves as morally responsible free agents that we don't feel to be threatened in any way by the fact that we can't be ultimately responsible for how we are. We readily accept that we are products of our heredity and environment without feeling that this poses any threat to our freedom and moral responsibility at the time of action. It's very natural to feel that so long as one is fully consciously aware of oneself as able to choose in a situation of choice, then this

---

1. Quoted in the *Spectator*, April 17, 1992, p. 9. [Strawson's note.]

is already entirely sufficient for one's radical freedom of choice—*whatever* else is or is not the case. It seems, then, that our ordinary conception of moral responsibility may contain mutually inconsistent elements. If this is so, it is a profoundly important fact; it would explain a great deal about the character of the philosophical debate about free will (Strawson 1986, §6.4). But these other elements in our ordinary notion of moral responsibility, important as they are, are not my present subject.

3

I want now to restate the Basic Argument in very loose—as it were conversational—terms. New forms of words allow for new forms of objection, but they may be helpful nonetheless.

(1) You do what you do, in any situation in which you find yourself, because of the way you are.

So

(2) To be truly morally responsible for what you do, you must be truly responsible for the way you are—at least in certain crucial mental respects.

Or:

(1) When you act, what you do is a function of how you are.

(What you do won't count as an action at all unless it flows appropriately from your beliefs, preferences, and so on.) Hence

(2) You have to get to have some responsibility for how you are in order to get to have some responsibility for what you intentionally do.

Once again I take the qualification about "certain mental respects" for granted. Obviously, one isn't responsible for one's sex, basic body pattern, height, and so on. But if one weren't responsible for anything about oneself, how could one be responsible for what one did, given the truth of (1)? *This is the fundamental question*, and it seems clear that if one is going to be responsible for any aspect of oneself, it had better be some aspect of one's mental nature.

I take it that (1) is incontrovertible, and that it is (2) that must be resisted. For if (1) and (2) are conceded the case seems lost, because the full argument runs as follows.

(1) You do what you do because of the way you are.

So

(2) To be truly morally responsible for what you do, you must be truly responsible for the way you are—at least in certain crucial mental respects.

But

(3) You can't be truly responsible for the way you are, so you can't be truly responsible for what you do.

Why can't you be truly responsible for the way you are? Because

(4) To be truly responsible for the way you are, you must have intentionally brought it about that you are the way you are, and this is impossible.

Why is it impossible? Well, suppose it isn't. Suppose

(5) You have somehow intentionally brought it about that you are the way you now are, and that you have brought this about in such a way that you can now be said to be truly responsible for being the way you are now.

For this to be true

(6) You must already have had a certain nature N in the light of which you intentionally brought it about that you are as you now are.

But then

(7) For it to be true that you are truly responsible for how you now are, you must be truly responsible for having had the nature N in the light of which you intentionally brought it about that you are the way you now are.

So

(8) You must have intentionally brought it about that you had that nature N, in which case you must have existed already with a prior nature in the light of which you intentionally brought it about that you had the nature N in the light of which you intentionally brought it about that you are the way you now are. . . .

Here one is setting off on the regress. Nothing can be *causa sui* in the required way. Even if this attribute is allowed to belong (unintelligibly) to God, it can't plausibly be supposed to be possessed by ordinary finite human beings. "The *causa sui* is the best self-contradiction that has been conceived so far," as Nietzsche remarked in *Beyond Good and Evil* in 1886:

> It is a sort of rape and perversion of logic. But the extravagant pride of man has managed to entangle itself profoundly and frightfully with just this nonsense. The desire for "freedom of the will" in the superlative metaphysical sense, which still holds sway, unfortunately, in the minds of the half-educated; the desire to bear the entire and ultimate responsibility for one's actions oneself, and to absolve God, the world, ancestors, chance, and society involves nothing less than to be precisely this *causa sui* and, with more than Baron Münchhausen's audacity, to pull oneself up into existence by the hair, out of the swamps of nothingness. [1966 (1866), 21]

The rephrased argument is essentially exactly the same as before, although the first two steps are now more simply stated. Can the Basic Argument simply be dismissed? Is it really of no importance in the discussion of free will and moral responsibility, as some have claimed? (No and no.) Shouldn't any serious defense of free will and moral responsibility thoroughly acknowledge the respect in which the Basic Argument is valid before going on to try to give its own positive account of the nature of free will and moral responsibility? Doesn't the argument go to the heart of things if the heart of the free will debate is a concern about whether we can be truly morally responsible in the absolute way that we ordinarily suppose? (Yes and yes.)

We are what we are, and we can't be thought to have made ourselves *in such a way* that we can be held to be free in our actions *in such a way* that we can be held to be morally responsible for our actions *in such a way* that any punishment or reward for our actions is ultimately just or fair. Punishments and rewards may seem deeply appropriate or intrinsically "fitting" to us; many of the various institutions of punishment and reward in human society appear to be practically indispensable in both their legal and nonlegal forms. But if one takes the notion of justice that is central to our intellectual and cultural tradition seriously, then the consequence of the Basic Argument is that there is a fundamental sense in which no punishment or reward is ever just. It is exactly as just to punish or reward people for their actions as it is to punish or reward them for the (natural) color of their hair or the (natural) shape of their faces.

4

I have suggested that it is step (2) of the restated Basic Argument that must be rejected, and of course it can be rejected, because the phrases "truly responsible" and "truly morally responsible" can be defined in many ways. I'll sketch three sorts of response.

(I) The first response is *compatibilist*. Compatibilists say that one can be a free and morally responsible agent even if determinism is true. They claim that one can correctly be said to be truly responsible for what one does, when one acts, just so long as one isn't caused to act by any of a certain set of constraints (kleptomaniac impulses, obsessional neuroses, desires that are experienced as alien, posthypnotic commands, threats, instances of *force majeure*, and so on). They don't impose any requirement that one should be truly responsible for how one is, so step (2) of the Basic Argument comes out as false. They think one can be fully morally responsible even if the way one is is totally determined by factors entirely outside one's control. They simply reject the Basic Argument. They know that the kind of responsibility ruled out by the Basic Argument is impossible, and conclude that it can't be the kind of responsibility that is really in question in human life, because we are indeed genuinely morally responsible agents. No theory that concludes otherwise can possibly be right, on their view.

(II) The second response is *libertarian*. *Incompatibilists* believe that freedom and moral responsibility are incompatible with determinism, and some incompatibilists are libertarians, who believe that we are free and morally responsible agents, and that determinism is therefore false. Robert Kane, for example, allows that we may act responsibly from a will already formed, but argues that the will must in this case be "'our own' free will by virtue of other past 'self-forming' choices or other actions that were undetermined and by which we made ourselves into the kinds of persons we are. . . . [T]hese undetermined self-forming actions (SFAs) occur at those difficult times of life when we are torn between competing visions of what we should do or become" (2009, 279). They paradigmatically involve a conflict between moral duty and non-moral desire, and it is essential that they involve indeterminism, on Kane's view, for this "screens off complete determination by influences of the past" (Ibid.). He proposes that we are in such cases of "moral, prudential and practical struggle . . . truly 'making ourselves' in such a way that we are ultimately responsible for the outcome," and that this "making of ourselves" means that "we can be ultimately responsible for our present motives and character by virtue of past choices which helped to form them and for which we were ultimately responsible" (1989, 252).

Kane, then, accepts step (2) of the Basic Argument and challenges step (3) instead. He accepts that we have to "make ourselves," and so be ultimately responsible for ourselves, in order to be morally responsible for what we do. But the old objection to libertarianism recurs. How can indeterminism help with moral responsibility? How can the occurrence of partly random or indeterministic events contribute to my being truly or ultimately morally responsible either for my actions or for my character? If my efforts of will shape my character in an admirable way and are in so doing partly indeterministic in nature, while also being shaped (as Kane grants) by my already existing character, why am I not merely *lucky*?

(III) The third response begins by accepting that one can't be held to be ultimately responsible for one's character or personality or motivational structure. It accepts that this is so whether determinism is true or false. It then directly challenges step (2) of the Basic Argument. It appeals to a certain picture of the *self* in order to argue that one can be truly free and morally responsible in spite of the fact that one can't be held to be ultimately responsible for one's character or personality or motivational structure.

This picture can be set out as follows. One is free and truly morally responsible because one's self is, in a crucial sense, independent of one's character or personality or motivational structure—one's CPM, for short. Suppose one is in a situation that one experiences as a difficult choice between *A*, doing one's duty, and *B*, following one's non-moral desires. Given one's CPM, one responds in a certain way. One's desires and beliefs develop and interact and constitute reasons in favor both of *A* and of *B*, and one's CPM makes one tend toward either *A* or *B*. So far the problem is the same as ever: whatever one does, one will do what one does because of the way one's CPM is, and since one neither is nor can be ultimately responsible for the way one's CPM is, one can't be ultimately responsible for what one does.

Enter one's self, *S*. *S* is imagined to be in some way independent of one's CPM. *S* (i.e., one) considers the outputs of one's CPM and decides in the light of them, but it—*S*—incorporates a power of decision that is independent of one's CPM in such a way that one can after all count as truly and ultimately morally responsible in one's decisions and actions, even though one isn't ultimately responsible for one's CPM. The idea is that step (2) of the Basic Argument is false because of the existence of *S* (Campbell 1957).

The trouble with the picture is obvious. *S* (i.e., one) decides on the basis of the deliverances of one's CPM. But whatever *S* decides, it decides as it does because of the way it is (or because of the occurrence in the decision process of indeterministic factors for which it—i.e., one—can't be responsible, and which can't plausibly be thought to contribute to one's true moral responsibility). And this brings us back to where we started. To be a source of true or ultimate responsibility, *S* must be responsible for being the way it is. But this is impossible, for the reasons given in the Basic Argument. So while the story of *S* and CPM adds another layer to the description of the human decision process, it can't change the fact that human beings cannot be ultimately self-determining in such a way as to be ultimately morally responsible for how they are, and thus for how they decide and act.

In spite of all these difficulties, many (perhaps most) of us continue to believe that we are truly morally responsible agents in the strongest possible sense. Many feel that our capacity for fully explicit self-conscious deliberation in a situation of choice suffices—all by itself—to constitute us as such. All that is needed for true or ultimate responsibility, on this view, is that one is in the moment of action *fully self-consciously aware of oneself as an agent facing choices.*

The Basic Argument, however, appears to show that this is a mistake: however self-consciously aware we are as we deliberate and reason, every act and operation of our mind happens as it does as a result of features for which we are ultimately in no way responsible. Nevertheless, the conviction that self-conscious awareness of one's situation can be a sufficient foundation of strong free will is very powerful. It runs deeper than rational argument, and it survives untouched, in the everyday conduct of life, even after the validity of the Basic Argument has been admitted.

REFERENCES

Campbell, C. A. 1957. "Has the Self Free Will?" In C. A. Campbell, *On Selfhood* and *Godhood*. Allen & Unwin, London.

Carr, E. H. 1961. *What Is History?* Macmillan, London.

Kane, R. 1989. "Two Kinds of Incompatibilism." *Philosophy and Phenomenological Research* 50: 219–54.

Kane, R. 2009. "Free Will: New Directions for an Ancient Problem." In D. Pereboom (Ed.), *Free Will*, 2nd ed. Hackett, Indianapolis, IN.

Kant, I. 1956. *Critique of Practical Reason*, trans. L. W. Beck. Bobbs-Merrill, Indianapolis, IN.

Kant, I. 1960. *Religion within the Limits of Reason Alone*, trans. T. M. Greene and H. H. Hudson. Harper & Row, New York.

Korsgaard, C. 2009. *Self-Constitution: Agency, Identity, and Integrity*. Oxford University Press, Oxford.

Mackay, D. M. 1960. "On the Logic of Free Choice." *Mind* 69: 31–40.

Nietzsche, F. 1966 [1886]. *Beyond Good and Evil*, trans. Walter Kaufmann. Random House, New York.

Sartre, J.-P. 1969. *Being and Nothingness*, trans. Hazel E. Barnes. Methuen, London.

Sartre, J.-P. 1989. *Existentialism and Humanism*, trans. Philip Mairet. Methuen, London.

Strawson, G. 1986. *Freedom and Belief*. Oxford University Press, Oxford.

TEST YOUR UNDERSTANDING

1. Galen Strawson's conclusion is that we cannot be "truly and ultimately" responsible for what we do. Say what this means.

2. Strawson says that no one can be "*causa sui*." What does that mean?

3. Explain the basis for Strawson's claim that "true or ultimate self-determination is impossible because it requires the actual completion of an infinite series of choices of principles of choice."

4. In Section 4, Strawson considers a response to the Basic Argument due to Robert Kane. Briefly explain Kane's view and say why Strawson rejects it.

NOTES AND QUESTIONS

1. Galen Strawson's argument depends crucially on what is sometimes called a *transfer principle:* a principle according to which a person is only responsible for an action if she is responsible for the attitudes and principles in light of which she chose it. In Strawson's case, the principle maintains that we are morally responsible for an action only if we are morally responsible for the beliefs, desires, and values that led us to perform it, even if these prior mental states did not causally determine the act in question.

   But is this right? Suppose Jones kills Smith because he hates Smith and wants to see him dead. At trial the prosecutor says:

   > The defendant has hated Smith for years, but he is not on trial for hating Smith. The defendant is clearly a bad man, but he is not on trial for being a bad man. So it does not matter whether he is morally responsible for being the man he is. The defendant is on trial for killing Smith, and for this he has no excuse. No one made him kill Smith. He was not determined by prior causes to kill Smith. After all, many people in the defendant's circumstances were just as bad as he, and hated Smith just as much, but they did not kill Smith. The defendant alone acted on his hatred, and we seek to punish him for this act. His attorney, Professor Strawson, will tell you that since the choice was not determined by his prior mental states, the defendant is a "victim of random chance," and that it would therefore be a travesty to blame him. Nonsense. Chance did not make him act. Chance is not a force in our lives. To say that his choice occurred by "chance" is just to say that nothing forced him to choose. That is not an excuse! He is responsible.

   How might Strawson respond?

2. In Section 4, Strawson considers the compatibilist who holds that one can be "fully morally responsible [for an action] even if the way one is is totally determined by factors outside one's control." He then goes on to suggest that these compatibilists agree that

the kind of responsibility ruled out by the basic argument is impossible, and so hold that some other kind of responsibility is the responsibility that matters in human life.

Exercise: Develop this compatibilist view more fully. Describe an alternative to "the kind of responsibility ruled out by the basic argument"—that is, the sort of responsibility that would justify eternal punishment in hell. Then assess the claim that this kind of responsibility is the sort of responsibility that matters in human life.

Galen Strawson's view is developed in detail in his *Freedom and Belief* (Oxford University Press, 1986; revised edition, 2010).

Roderick Chisholm (1916–1999)

Chisholm is the author of influential studies in metaphysics (*Person and Object*, 1976), epistemology (*The Foundations of Knowing*, 1982), and the philosophy of mind and language (*The First Person*, 1981). His collection of texts (*Realism and the Background of Phenomenology*, 1960) was an early effort to connect twentieth-century analytic philosophy with the tradition of European phenomenology.

HUMAN FREEDOM AND THE SELF

A staff moves a stone, and is moved by a hand, which is moved by a man.
—Aristotle, *Physics* (256a)

1. The metaphysical problem of human freedom might be summarized in the following way: Human beings are responsible agents: but this fact appears to conflict with a deterministic view of human action (the view that every event that is involved in an act is caused by some other event): and it *also* appears to conflict with an indeterministic view of human action (the view that the act, or some event that is essential to the act, is not caused at all). To solve the problem, I believe, we must make somewhat far-reaching assumptions about the self or the agent—about the man who performs the act. . . .

2. Let us consider some deed, or misdeed, that may be attributed to a responsible agent: one man, say, shot another. If the man *was* responsible for what he did, then, I would urge, what was to happen at the time of the shooting was something that was entirely up to the man himself. There was a moment at which it was true, both that he could have fired the shot and also that he could have refrained from firing it. And if this is so, then, even though he did fire it, he could have done something else instead. (He didn't find himself firing the shot "against his will," as we say.) I think we can say,

more generally, then, that if a man is responsible for a certain event or a certain state of affairs (in our example, the shooting of another man), then that event or state of affairs was brought about by some act of his, and the act was something that was in his power either to perform or not to perform.

But now if the act which he *did* perform was an act that was also in his power *not* to perform, then it could not have been caused or determined by any event that was not itself within his power either to bring about or not to bring about. For example, if what we say he did was really something that was brought about by a second man, one who forced his hand upon the trigger, say, or who, by means of hypnosis, compelled him to perform the act, then since the act was caused by the *second* man it was nothing that was within the power of the *first* man to prevent. And precisely the same thing is true, I think, if instead of referring to a second man who compelled the first one, we speak instead of the *desires* and *beliefs* which the first man happens to have had. For if what we say he did was really something that was brought about by his own beliefs and desires, if these beliefs and desires in the particular situation in which he happened to have found himself caused him to do just what it was that we say he did do, then, since *they* caused it, *he* was unable to do anything other than just what it was that he did do. It makes no difference whether the cause of the deed was internal or external; if the cause was some state or event for which the man himself was not responsible, then he was not responsible for what we have been mistakenly calling his act. . . . (It is true, of course, that if the man is responsible for the beliefs and desires that he happens to have, then he may also be responsible for the things they lead him to do. But the question now becomes: *is* he responsible for the beliefs and desires he happens to have? If he is, then there was a time when they were within his power either to acquire or not to acquire, and we are left, therefore, with our general point.). . .

There is one standard objection to all of this and we should consider it briefly.

3. The objection takes the form of a stratagem—one designed to show that determinism (and divine providence) is consistent with human responsibility. The stratagem is one that was used by Jonathan Edwards and by many philosophers in the present century, most notably, G. E. Moore.[1]

One proceeds as follows: The expression

(a) He could have done otherwise,

it is argued, means no more nor less than

(b) If he had chosen to do otherwise, then he would have done otherwise.

(In place of "chosen," one might say "tried," "set out," "decided," "undertaken," or "willed.") The truth of statement (b), it is then pointed out, is consistent with determinism (and with divine providence): for even if all of the man's actions were causally

1. Jonathan Edwards, *Freedom of the Will* (Yale University Press, 1957); G. E. Moore, *Ethics* (Home University Library, 1912), chapter 6. [Chisholm's note.]

determined, the man could still be such that, *if* he had chosen otherwise, then he would have done otherwise. What the murderer saw, let us suppose, along with his beliefs and desires, *caused* him to fire the shot: yet he was such that *if,* just then, he had chosen or decided *not* to fire the shot, then he would not have fired it. All of this is certainly possible. . . . And therefore, the argument proceeds, if (b) is consistent with determinism, and if (a) and (b) say the same thing, then (a) is also consistent with determinism; hence we can say that the agent *could* have done otherwise even though he was caused to do what he did do; and therefore determinism and moral responsibility are compatible.

Is the argument sound? The conclusion follows from the premises, but the catch, I think, lies in the first premise—the one saying that statement (a) tells us no more nor less than what statement (b) tells us. For (b), it would seem, could be true while (a) is false. That is to say, our man might be such that, if he had chosen to do otherwise, then he would have done otherwise, and yet *also* such that he could not have done otherwise. Suppose, after all, that our murderer could not have *chosen,* or could not have *decided,* to do otherwise. Then the fact that he happens also to be a man such that, if he had chosen not to shoot he would not have shot, would make no difference. For if he could *not* have chosen *not* to shoot, then he could not have done anything other than just what it was that he did do. In a word: from our statement (b) above ("If he had chosen to do otherwise, then he would have done otherwise"), we cannot make an inference to (a) above ("He could have done otherwise") unless we can *also* assert:

(c) He could have chosen to do otherwise.

And therefore, if we must reject this third statement (c), then, even though we may be justified in asserting (b), we are not justified in asserting (a). If the man could not have chosen to do otherwise, then he would not have done otherwise—*even if* he was such that, if he *had* chosen to do otherwise, then he would have done otherwise.

The stratagem in question, then, seems to me not to work, and I would say, therefore, that the ascription of responsibility conflicts with a deterministic view of action.

4. Perhaps there is less need to argue that the ascription of responsibility also conflicts with an indeterministic view of action—with the view that the act, or some event that is essential to the act, is not caused at all. If the act—the firing of the shot—was not caused at all, if it was fortuitous or capricious, happening so to speak out of the blue, then, presumably, no one—and nothing—was responsible for the act. Our conception of action, therefore, should be neither deterministic nor indeterministic. Is there any other possibility?

5. We must not say that every event involved in the act is caused by some other event; and we must not say that the act is something that is not caused at all. The possibility that remains, therefore, is this: We should say that at least one of the events that are involved in the act is caused, not by any other events, but by something else instead.

And this something else can only be the agent—the man. If there is an event that is caused, not by other events, but by the man, then there are some events involved in the act that are not caused by other events. But if the event in question is caused by the man then it *is* caused and we are not committed to saying that there is something involved in the act that is not caused at all.

But this, of course, is a large consequence, implying something of considerable importance about the nature of the agent or the man.

6. If we consider only inanimate natural objects, we may say that causation, if it occurs, is a relation between *events* or *states of affairs.* The dam's breaking was an event that was caused by a set of other events—the dam being weak, the flood being strong, and so on. But if a man is responsible for a particular deed, then, if what I have said is true, there is some event, or set of events, that is caused, *not* by other events or states of affairs, but by the agent, whatever he may be.

I shall borrow a pair of medieval terms, using them, perhaps, in a way that is slightly different from that for which they were originally intended. I shall say that when one event or state of affairs (or set of events or states of affairs) causes some other event or state of affairs, then we have an instance of *transeunt* causation. And I shall say that when an *agent,* as distinguished from an event, causes an event or state of affairs, then we have an instance of *immanent* causation.

The nature of what is intended by the expression "immanent causation" may be illustrated by this sentence from Aristotle's *Physics*: "Thus, a staff moves a stone, and is moved by a hand, which is moved by a man" (VII, 5, 256a, 6–8). If the man was responsible, then we have in this illustration a number of instances of causation—most of them transeunt but at least one of them immanent. What the staff did to the stone was an instance of transeunt causation, and thus we may describe it as a relation between events: "the motion of the staff caused the motion of the stone." And similarly for what the hand did to the staff: "the motion of the hand caused the motion of the staff." And, as we know from physiology, there are still other events which caused the motion of the hand. Hence we need not introduce the agent at this particular point, as Aristotle does—we *need* not, though we *may.* We *may* say that the hand was moved by the man, but we may *also* say that the motion of the hand was caused by the motion of certain muscles; and we may say that the motion of the muscles was caused by certain events that took place within the brain. But some event, and presumably one of those that took place within the brain, was caused by the agent and not by any other events. . . .

7. One may object, firstly: "If the *man* does anything, then, as Aristotle's remark suggests, what he does is to move the *hand.* But he certainly does not *do* anything to his brain—he may not even know that he *has* a brain. And if he doesn't do anything to the brain, and if the motion of the hand was caused by something that happened within the brain, then there is no point in appealing to 'immanent causation' as being something incompatible with 'transeunt causation'—for the whole thing, after all, is a matter of causal relations among events or states of affairs."

The answer to this objection, I think, is this: It is true that the agent does not *do* anything with his brain, or to his brain, in the sense in which he *does* something with his hand and does something to the staff. But from this it does not follow that the agent was not the immanent cause of something that happened within his brain.

We should note a useful distinction that has been proposed by Professor A. I. Melden—namely, the distinction between "making something A happen" and "doing A."[2] If I reach for the staff and pick it up, then one of the things that I *do* is just that— reach for the staff and pick it up. And if it is something that I do, then there is a very clear sense in which it may be said to be something that I know that I do. If you ask me, "Are you doing something, or trying to do something, with the staff?," I will have no difficulty in finding an answer. But in doing something with the staff, I also make various things happen which are not in this same sense things that I do: I will make various air-particles move; I will free a number of blades of grass from the pressure that had been upon them; and I may cause a shadow to move from one place to another. If these are merely things that I make happen, as distinguished from things that I do, then I may know nothing whatever about them; I may not have the slightest idea that, in moving the staff, I am bringing about any such thing as the motion of air-particles, shadows, and blades of grass.

We may say, in answer to the first objection, therefore, that it is true that our agent does nothing to his brain or with his brain; but from this it does not follow that the agent is not the immanent cause of some event within his brain; for the brain event may be something which, like the motion of the air-particles, he made happen in picking up the staff. . . .

The point is, in a word, that whenever a man does something A, then (by "immanent causation") he makes a certain cerebral event happen, and this cerebral event (by "transeunt causation") makes A happen.

8. The second objection is more difficult and concerns the very concept of "immanent causation," or causation by an agent, as this concept is to be interpreted here. The concept is subject to a difficulty which has long been associated with that of the prime mover unmoved. We have said that there must be some event A, presumably some cerebral event, which is caused not by any other event, but by the agent. Since A was not caused by any other event, then the agent himself cannot be said to have undergone any change or produced any other event (such as "an act of will" or the like) which brought A about. But if, when the agent made A happen, there was no event involved other than A itself, no event which could be described as *making* A happen, what did the agent's causation consist of? What, for example, is the difference between A's just happening, and the agents' *causing* A to happen? We cannot attribute the difference to any event that took place within the agent. And so far as the event A itself is concerned, there would seem to be no discernible difference. . . . Must we conclude, then, that there is no more to the man's action in causing event A than there is to the event A's happening by itself? . . .

2. A. I. Melden, *Free Action* (Routledge and Kegan Paul, 1961), especially chapter 3. Mr. Melden's own views, however, are quite the contrary of those that are proposed here. [Chisholm's note.]

The only answer, I think, can be this: that the difference between the man's causing A, on the one hand, and the event A just happening, on the other, lies in the fact that, in the first case but not the second, the event A *was* caused and was caused by the man. There was a brain event A; the agent did, in fact, cause the brain event; but there was nothing that he did to cause it.

This answer may not entirely satisfy and it will be likely to provoke the following question: "But what are you really *adding* to the assertion that A happened when you utter the words 'The agent *caused* A to happen'?" As soon as we have put the question this way, we see, I think, that whatever difficulty we may have encountered is one that may be traced to the concept of causation generally—whether "immanent" or "transeunt." . . .

For the problem, as we put it, referring just to "immanent causation," or causation by an agent, was this: "What is the difference between saying, of an event A, that A just happened and saying that someone caused A to happen?" The analogous problem, which holds for "transeunt causation," or causation by an event, is this: "What is the difference between saying, of two events A and B, that B happened and then A happened, and saying that B's happening was the *cause* of A's happening?" And the only answer that one can give is this—that in the one case the agent was the cause of A's happening and in the other case event B was the cause of A's happening. The nature of transeunt causation is no more clear than is that of immanent causation. . . .

11. If we are responsible, and if what I have been trying to say is true, then we have a prerogative which some would attribute only to God: each of us, when we act, is a prime mover unmoved. In doing what we do, we cause certain events to happen, and nothing—or no one—causes us to cause those events to happen.

12. If we are thus prime movers unmoved and if our actions, or those for which we are responsible, are not causally determined, then they are not causally determined by our *desires*. And this means that the relation between what we want or what we desire, on the one hand, and what it is that we do, on the other, is not as simple as most philosophers would have it.

We may distinguish between what we might call the "Hobbist approach" and what we might call the "Kantian approach" to this question. The Hobbist approach is the one that is generally accepted at the present time,[3] but the Kantian approach, I believe, is the one that is true. According to Hobbism, if we *know*, of some man, what his beliefs and desires happen to be and how strong they are, if we know what he feels certain of, what he desires more than anything else, and if we know the state of his body and what stimuli he is being subjected to, then we may *deduce*, logically, just what it is that he will do—or, more accurately, just what it is that he will try, set out, or undertake to do. . . . But according to the Kantian approach to our problem, and this is the one that I would take, there is no such logical connection between wanting and doing, nor need there even be a causal connection. No set of statements about a man's desires, beliefs, and stimulus situation at any time implies any statement telling us what the man will

---

3. Chisholm's essay was first published in 1964.

try, set out, or undertake to do at that time. As Reid[4] put it, though we may "reason from men's motives to their actions and, in many cases, with great probability," we can never do so "with absolute certainty."

This means that, in one very strict sense of the terms, there can be no science of man. If we think of science as a matter of finding out what laws happen to hold, and if the statement of a law tells us what kinds of events are caused by what other kinds of events, then there will be human actions which we cannot explain by subsuming them under any laws. We cannot say, "It is causally necessary that, given such and such desires and beliefs, and being subject to such and such stimuli, the agent will do so and so." For at times the agent, if he chooses, may rise above his desires and do something else instead.

But all of this is consistent with saying that, perhaps more often than not, our desires do exist under conditions such that those conditions necessitate us to act. And we may also say, with Leibniz,[5] that at other times our desires may "incline without necessitating."

13. Leibniz's phrase presents us with our final philosophical problem. What does it mean to say that a desire, or a motive, might "incline without necessitating"? There is a temptation, certainly, to say that "to incline" means to cause and that "not to necessitate" means not to cause, but obviously we cannot have it both ways. . . .

Let us consider a public official who has some moral scruples but who also, as one says, could be had. Because of the scruples that he does have, he would never take any positive steps to receive a bribe—he would not actively solicit one. But his morality has its limits and he is also such that, if we were to confront him with a *fait accompli* or to let him see what is about to happen ($10,000 in cash is being deposited behind the garage), then he would succumb and be unable to resist. The general situation is a familiar one and this is one reason that people pray to be delivered from temptation. (It also justifies Kant's remark: "And how many there are who may have led a long blameless life, who are only *fortunate* in having escaped so many temptations."[6]) Our relation to the misdeed that we contemplate may not be a matter simply of being able to bring it about or not to bring it about. As St. Anselm noted, there are at least four possibilities. We may illustrate them by reference to our public official and the event which is his receiving the bribe, in the following way: (i) he may be able to bring the event about himself (*facere esse*), in which case he would actively cause himself to receive the bribe; (ii) he may be able to refrain from bringing it about himself (*non facere esse*), in which case he would not himself do anything to insure that he receive the bribe; (iii) he may be able to do something to prevent the event from occurring (*facere non esse*), in which case he would make sure that the $10,000 was *not* left behind the garage; or (iv) he may be unable to do anything to prevent the event from

---

4. Thomas Reid (1710–1796), Scottish philosopher famous for his defense of "common sense" against the skeptical arguments of David Hume and others. The quoted passage is from his *Essays on the Active Powers of the Human Mind* (1788).

5. Gottfried Wilhelm Leibniz (1646–1716), German philosopher and mathematician.

6. In the Preface to the "Metaphysical Elements of Ethics," in *Kant's Critique of Practical Reason and Other Works on the Theory of Ethics*, ed. T. K. Abbott (Longman, 1959), 303. [Chisholm's note.]

occurring, in which case, though he may not solicit the bribe, he would allow himself to keep it. We have envisaged our official as a man who can resist the temptation to (i) but cannot resist the temptation to (iv): he can refrain from bringing the event about himself, but he cannot bring himself to do anything to prevent it.

Let us think of "inclination without necessitation," then, in such terms as these. First we may contrast the two propositions:

1. He can resist the temptation to do something in order to make A happen;

2. He can resist the temptation to allow A to happen (i.e., to do nothing to prevent A from happening).

We may suppose that the man has some desire to have A happen and thus has a motive for making A happen. His motive for making A happen, I suggest, is one that *necessitates* provided that, because of the motive, (1) is false; he cannot resist the temptation to do something in order to make A happen. His motive for making A happen is one that *inclines* provided that, because of the motive, (2) is false; like our public official, he cannot bring himself to do anything to prevent A from happening. And therefore we can say that this motive for making A happen is one that *inclines but does not necessitate* provided that, because of the motive, (1) is true and (2) is false; he can resist the temptation to make it happen but he cannot resist the temptation to allow it to happen.

TEST YOUR UNDERSTANDING

1. True or false: Chisholm holds that a free act is an uncaused act.

2. Chisholm rejects G. E. Moore's suggestion that "He could have done otherwise" simply means "If he had chosen to do otherwise, he would have done otherwise." Explain the proposal and say why Chisholm rejects it.

3. Explain the distinction between *transeunt* and *immanent causation.*

4. Pick an ordinary free action and tell its story in Chisholm's way. Indicate the various causes it might have had and say exactly where in the story immanent causation does its work.

NOTES AND QUESTIONS

1. *Puzzles about agent causation.* According to Chisholm, a free choice is an event in the brain that is not caused by prior events, but rather by the agent himself. Chisholm calls this *immanent* causation, or sometimes **agent causation**. One of the main aims of Chisholm's essay is to suggest that agent causation is not more puzzling or mysterious than ordinary causation among events, but is this right?

The epistemological problem. We can test ordinary causal claims in many ways. If we want to know whether the mixture exploded *because it contained chemical X,* we can prepare a similar mixture that lacks *X* and see what happens. If it explodes in exactly the same way, that is good evidence that *X* was not a cause of the explosion. If it does not explode, that is evidence that *X* was indeed a cause. How can we test claims of agent causation? Suppose we observe some event in Fred's brain—his choice to scratch his nose, for example. Suppose we can rule out the possibility that this event was caused by prior events. According to Chisholm, that leaves two possibilities: either the choice was caused by *Fred* or it was a chance occurrence with no determining cause at all. What evidence could possibly allow us to choose between these two hypotheses?

The metaphysical problem. Chisholm tells us that human beings can cause events in their own brains. But are there any principled limits to this sort of causation? Suppose a radioactive atom in a box in front of you suddenly decays, and that careful investigation reveals that this event was not caused by prior events. Is it possible that this atom *caused itself to decay*? Is it possible that *you* caused it to decay? Are *rabbits* the agent-causes of their choices? These possibilities sound absurd, but how can we exclude them? Until we can say *something* about the principles that govern agent causation, we cannot pretend to understand the notion.

Exercise: Say how Chisholm might respond to these objections.

2. Chisholm's theory is presented and modified in *Person and Object* (Open Court, 1976). For a sympathetic defense, see Randolph Clarke, "Toward a Credible Agent-Causal Account of Free Will," *Noûs* 27, 2 (1993): 191–203.

A. J. Ayer (1910–1989)

Ayer was one of the most distinguished representatives in the twentieth century of the British empiricist tradition of Locke, Hume, and Mill. His early manifesto, *Language, Truth and Logic* (1936), is a vigorous defense of the view that the claims of morality, religion, and metaphysics are mostly meaningless, since they are neither analytic (true simply in virtue of the meanings of words) nor empirically verifiable.

FREEDOM AND NECESSITY

When I am said to have done something of my own free will it is implied that I could have acted otherwise; and it is only when it is believed that I could have acted otherwise that I am held to be morally responsible for what I have done. For a man is not thought to be morally responsible for an action that it was not in his power to avoid. But if human behavior is entirely governed by causal laws, it is not clear how any action that is done could ever have been avoided. It may be said of the agent that he would have acted otherwise if the causes of his action had been different, but they being what they were, it seems to follow that he was bound to act as he did. Now it is commonly assumed both that men are capable of acting freely, in the sense that is required to make them morally responsible, and that human behavior is entirely governed by causal laws: and it is the apparent conflict between these two assumptions that gives rise to the philosophical problem of the freedom of the will.

Confronted with this problem, many people will be inclined to agree with Dr. Johnson: "Sir, we *know* our will is free, and *there's* an end on't."[1] But, while this does very well for those who accept Dr. Johnson's premiss, it would hardly convince anyone who denied the freedom of the will. . . . What is evident, indeed, is that people often believe themselves to be acting freely; and it is to this "feeling" of freedom that some philosophers appeal when they wish, in the supposed interests of morality, to prove that not all human action is causally determined. But if these philosophers are right in their assumption that a man cannot be acting freely if his action is causally determined, then the fact that someone feels free to do, or not to do, a certain action does not prove that he really is so. It may prove that the agent does not himself know what it is that makes him act in one way rather than another: but from the fact a man is unaware of the causes of his action, it does not follow that no such causes exist.

So much may be allowed to the determinist; but his belief that all human actions are subservient to causal laws still remains to be justified. If, indeed, it is necessary that every event should have a cause, then the rule must apply to human behavior as much as to anything else. But why should it be supposed that every event must have a cause? The contrary is not unthinkable. Nor is the law of universal causation a necessary pre-supposition of scientific thought. The scientist may try to discover causal laws, and in many cases he succeeds; but sometimes he has to be content with statistical laws, and sometimes he comes upon events which, in the present state of his knowledge, he is not able to subsume under any law at all. In the case of these events he assumes that if he knew more he would be able to discover some law, whether causal or statistical, which would enable him to account for them. And this assumption cannot be disproved. For however far he may have carried his investigation, it is always open to him to carry it further; and it is always conceivable that if he carried it further he would discover the connection which had hitherto escaped him. Nevertheless, it is also conceivable that the events with which he is concerned are not systematically connected with any others: so that the reason why he does not discover the sort of laws that he requires is simply that they do not obtain.

Now in the case of human conduct the search for explanations has not in fact been altogether fruitless. Certain scientific laws have been established; and with the help of these laws we do make a number of successful predictions about the ways in which different people will behave. But these predictions do not always cover every detail. We may be able to predict that in certain circumstances a particular man will be angry, without being able to prescribe the precise form that the expression of his anger will take. We may be reasonably sure that he will shout, but not sure how loud

---

1. Samuel Johnson (1709–1784), English author and lexicographer. The famous remark is quoted in John Boswell's *Life of Samuel Johnson.*

his shout will be, or exactly what words he will use. And it is only a small proportion of human actions that we are able to forecast even so precisely as this. But that, it may be said, is because we have not carried our investigations very far. The science of psychology is still in its infancy and, as it is developed, not only will more human actions be explained, but the explanations will go into greater detail. The ideal of complete explanation may never in fact be attained: but it is theoretically attainable. Well, this may be so: and certainly it is impossible to show *a priori* that it is not so: but equally it cannot be shown that it is. This will not, however, discourage the scientist who, in the field of human behavior, as elsewhere, will continue to formulate theories and test them by the facts. And in this he is justified. For since he has no reason *a priori* to admit that there is a limit to what he can discover, the fact that he also cannot be sure that there is no limit does not make it unreasonable for him to devise theories, nor, having devised them, to try constantly to improve them.

But now suppose it to be claimed that, so far as men's actions are concerned, there is a limit: and that this limit is set by the fact of human freedom. An obvious objection is that in many cases in which a person feels himself to be free to do, or not to do, a certain action, we are even now able to explain, in causal terms, why it is that he acts as he does. But it might be argued that even if men are sometimes mistaken in believing that they act freely, it does not follow that they are always so mistaken. For it is not always the case that when a man believes that he has acted freely we are in fact able to account for his action in causal terms. A determinist would say that we should be able to account for it if we had more knowledge of the circumstances, and had been able to discover the appropriate natural laws. But until those discoveries have been made, this remains only a pious hope. And may it not be true that, in some cases at least, the reason why we can give no causal explanation is that no causal explanation is available; and that this is because the agent's choice was literally free, as he himself felt it to be?

The answer is that this may indeed be true, inasmuch as it is open to anyone to hold that no explanation is possible until some explanation is actually found. But even so it does not give the moralist what he wants. For he is anxious to show that men are capable of acting freely in order to infer that they can be morally responsible for what they do. But if it is a matter of pure chance that a man should act in one way rather than another, he may be free but he can hardly be responsible. And indeed when a man's actions seem to us quite unpredictable, when, as we say, there is no knowing what he will do, we do not look upon him as a moral agent. We look upon him rather as a lunatic.

To this it may be objected that we are not dealing fairly with the moralist. For when he makes it a condition of my being morally responsible that I should act freely, he does not wish to imply that it is purely a matter of chance that I act as I do. What he wishes to imply is that my actions are the result of my own free choice: and it is because they are the result of my own free choice that I am held to be morally responsible for them.

But now we must ask how it is that I come to make my choice. Either it is an accident that I choose to act as I do or it is not. If it is an accident, then it is merely a matter of chance that I did not choose otherwise; and if it is merely a matter of chance that I did not choose otherwise, it is surely irrational to hold me morally responsible for choosing as I did. But if it is not an accident that I choose to do one thing rather than another, then presumably there is some causal explanation of my choice: and in that case we are led back to determinism.

Again, the objection may be raised that we are not doing justice to the moralist's case. His view is not that it is a matter of chance that I choose to act as I do, but rather that my choice depends upon my character. Nevertheless he holds that I can still be free in the sense that he requires; for it is I who am responsible for my character. But in what way am I responsible for my character? Only, surely, in the sense that there is a causal connection between what I do now and what I have done in the past. It is only this that justifies the statement that I have made myself what I am: and even so this is an over-simplification, since it takes no account of the external influences to which I have been subjected. But, ignoring the external influences, let us assume that it is in fact the case that I have made myself what I am. Then it is still legitimate to ask how it is that I have come to make myself one sort of person rather than another. And if it be answered that it is a matter of my strength of will, we can put the same question in another form by asking how it is that my will has the strength that it has and not some other degree of strength. Once more, either it is an accident or it is not. If it is an accident, then by the same argument as before, I am not morally responsible, and if it is not an accident we are led back to determinism.

Furthermore, to say that my actions proceed from my character or, more colloquially, that I act in character, is to say that my behavior is consistent and to that extent predictable: and since it is, above all, for the actions that I perform in character that I am held to be morally responsible, it looks as if the admission of moral responsibility, so far from being incompatible with determinism, tends rather to presuppose it. But how can this be so if it is a necessary condition of moral responsibility that the person who is held responsible should have acted freely? It seems that if we are to retain this idea of moral responsibility, we must either show that men can be held responsible for actions which they do not do freely, or else find some way of reconciling determinism with the freedom of the will.

Let it be granted ... [that] when we speak of reconciling freedom with determinism we are using the word "freedom" in an ordinary sense. It still remains for us to make this usage clear: and perhaps the best way to make it clear is to show what it is that freedom, in this sense, is contrasted with. Now we began with the assumption that freedom is contrasted with causality, so that a man cannot be said to be acting freely if his action is causally determined. But this assumption has led us into difficulties and I now wish to suggest that it is mistaken. For it is not, I think, causality that freedom is to be contrasted with, but constraint. And while it is true that being constrained to do an action entails being caused to do it, I shall try to show that the converse does not hold. I shall try to show that from the fact that my action is causally determined it does not necessarily follow that I am constrained to do it: and this is equivalent to saying that it does not necessarily follow that I am not free.

If I am constrained, I do not act freely. But in what circumstance can I legitimately be said to be constrained? An obvious instance is the case in which I am compelled by another person to do what he wants. In a case of this sort the compulsion need not be such as to deprive one of the power of choice. It is not required that the other person should have hypnotized me, or that he should make it physically impossible for me to go against his will. It is enough that he should induce me to do what he wants by making it clear to me that, if I do not, he will bring about some situation that I regard as even more undesirable than the consequence of the action that he wishes me to do. Thus, if the man points a pistol at my head I may still choose to disobey him: but this does not prevent its being true that if I do fall in with his wishes he can legitimately be said to have compelled me. And if the circumstances are such that no reasonable person would be expected to choose the other alternative, then the action that I am made to do is not one for which I am held to be morally responsible.

A similar but somewhat different case is that in which another person has obtained a habitual ascendancy over me. Where this is so, there may be no question of my being induced to act as the other person wishes by being confronted with a still more disagreeable alternative: for if I am sufficiently under his influence this special stimulus will not be necessary. Nevertheless I do not act freely, for the reason that I have been deprived of the power of choice. And this means that I have acquired so strong a habit of obedience that I no longer go through any process of deciding whether or not to do what the other person wants. About other matters I may still deliberate; but as regards the fulfilment of this other person's wishes, my own deliberations have ceased to be a causal factor in my behaviour. And it is in this sense that I may be said to be constrained. It is not, however, necessary that such constraint should take the form of subservience to another person. A kleptomaniac is not a free agent, in respect of his stealing, because he does not go through any process of deciding whether or not to steal. Or rather, if he does go through such a process, it is irrelevant to his behavior. Whatever he resolved to do, he would steal all the same. And it is this that distinguishes him from the ordinary thief.

But now it may be asked whether there is any essential difference between these cases and those in which the agent is commonly thought to be free. No doubt the ordinary thief does go through a process of deciding whether or not to steal, and no doubt it does affect his behavior. If he resolved to refrain from stealing, he could carry his resolution out. But if it be allowed that his making or not making this resolution is causally determined, then how can he be any more free than the kleptomaniac? It may be that unlike the kleptomaniac he could refrain from stealing if he chose: but if there is a cause, or set of causes, which necessitate his choosing as he does, how can he be said to have the power of choice? Again, it may be true that no one now compels me to get up and walk across the room: but if my doing so can be causally explained in terms of my history or my environment, or whatever it may be, then how am I any more free than if some other person had compelled me? I do not have the feeling of constraint that I have when a pistol is manifestly pointed at my head; but the chains of causation by which I am bound are no less effective for being invisible.

The answer to this is that the cases I have mentioned as examples of constraint do differ from the others: and they differ just in the ways that I have tried to bring out. If I suffered from a compulsion neurosis, so that I got up and walked across the room, whether I wanted to or not, or if I did so because somebody else compelled me, then

I should not be acting freely. But if I do it now, I shall be acting freely, just because these conditions do not obtain; and the fact that my action may nevertheless have a cause is, from this point of view, irrelevant. For it is not when my action has any cause at all, but only when it has a special sort of cause, that it is reckoned not to be free.

But here it may be objected that, even if this distinction corresponds to ordinary usage, it is still very irrational. For why should we distinguish, with regard to a person's freedom, between the operations of one sort of cause and those of another? Do not all causes equally necessitate? And is it not therefore arbitrary to say that a person is free when he is necessitated in one fashion but not when he is necessitated in another?

That all causes equally necessitate is indeed a tautology, if the word "necessitate" is taken merely as equivalent to "cause": but if, as the objection requires, it is taken as equivalent to constrain or compel, then I do not think that this proposition is true. For all that is needed for one event to be the cause of another is that, in the given circumstances, the event which is said to be the effect would not have occurred if it had not been for the occurrence of the event which is said to be the cause, or *vice versa*, according as causes are interpreted as necessary, or sufficient, conditions: and this fact is usually deducible from some causal law which states that whenever an event of the one kind occurs then, given suitable conditions, an event of the other kind will occur in a certain temporal or spatio-temporal relationship to it. In short, there is an invariable concomitance be-tween the two classes of events; but there is no compulsion, in any but a metaphorical sense. Suppose, for example, that a psycho-analyst is able to account for some aspect of my behavior by referring it to some lesion that I suffered in my childhood. In that case, it may be said that my childhood experience, together with certain other events, necessitates my behaving as I do. But all that this involves is that it is found to be true in general that when people have had certain experiences as children, they subsequently behave in certain specifiable ways; and my case is just another instance of this general law. It is in this way indeed that my behavior is explained. But from the fact that my behavior is capable of being explained, in the sense that it can be subsumed under some natural law, it does not follow that I am acting under constraint.

If this is correct, to say that I could have acted otherwise is to say, first, that I should have acted otherwise if I had so chosen; secondly, that my action was voluntary in the sense in which the actions, say, of the kleptomaniac are not; and thirdly, that nobody compelled me to choose as I did: and these three conditions may very well be fulfilled. When they are fulfilled, I may be said to have acted freely. But this is not to say that it was a matter of chance that I acted as I did, or, in other words, that my action could not be explained. And that my actions should be capable of being explained is all that is required by the postulate of determinism.

If more than this seems to be required it is, I think, because the use of the very word "determinism" is in some degree misleading. For it tends to suggest that one event is somehow in the power of another, whereas the truth is merely that they are actually correlated. And the same applies to the use, in this context, of the word "necessity" and even of the word "cause" itself. Moreover, there are various reasons for this. One is the tendency to confuse causal with logical necessitation, and so to infer mistakenly that the effect is contained in the cause. Another is the uncritical use of a concept of force which is derived from primitive experiences of pushing and striking. A third is the survival of an animistic conception of causality, in which all causal relationships are modeled on the example of one person's exercising authority over another. As a result we tend to form an imaginative picture of an unhappy effect trying vainly to escape from the clutches of an overmastering cause. But, I repeat, the fact is simply that when an event of one type occurs, an event of another type occurs also, in a certain temporal or spatio-temporal relation to the first. The rest is only metaphor. And it is because of the metaphor, and not because of the fact, that we come to think that there is an antithesis between causality and freedom.

TEST YOUR UNDERSTANDING

1. True or false: Ayer believes that an action can be free even though it was caused by prior events over which the agent had no control.

2. True or false: Ayer believes that you are responsible for an act only if you are responsible for your character and the other prior mental states that led you to act as you did.

3. Ayer distinguishes between cases in which an agent is *constrained* to act as she does and cases in which the agent is merely *caused* to act as she does. Explain the distinction and say why it matters for Ayer's argument.

4. According to Ayer, what does it mean to say, "Jones could have acted otherwise"?

NOTES AND QUESTIONS

1. *Ayer on causation.* According to Ayer, the free will problem dissolves when we realize that even if our actions are always *caused* by prior events, it does not follow that we are *compelled* to act as we do.

> That all causes equally necessitate is indeed a tautology, if the word "necessi-tate" is taken merely as equivalent to "cause": but if ... it is taken as equivalent to "constrain" or "compel," then I do not think that this proposition is true.

As Ayer's contemporary readers would have understood, this relies on a theory of causation due to David Hume.

> [W]e may define a cause to be an object, followed by another, and where all objects similar to the first are followed by objects similar to the second. [Hume, *An Enquiry Concerning Human Understanding*, VII]

On this view, causes do not literally *force* their effects to occur: they simply precede their effects and are linked to them by a general pattern or regularity. "The gunshot caused his death" simply means: "The shot preceded his death, and in general, when people are shot in this way, they tend to die shortly thereafter." For a discussion of Hume's view, see T. Beauchamp and A. Rosenberg, *Hume and the Problem of Causation* (Oxford University Press, 1981).

2. *Causation and compulsion.* This view may help us to see that an action can be caused without being "compelled." But it raises a question about whether actions are *ever* forced or compelled. Suppose Jones kills Smith only because he has been hypnotized and "programmed" to shoot when the clock strikes midnight. Suppose that hypnotism works as it does in the movies: it is a law of nature—an exceptionless regularity—that whenever someone is hypnotized in this way, he does exactly what he has been programmed to do. Jones is on trial, and his lawyer argues that his client is not responsible, since he was compelled to act, to which the prosecutor responds, "That is no defense. We can agree that Jones was caused to act as he did, and that the cause was somewhat unusual. But causes do not compel, *as Professor Ayer has taught us.* So Jones was not compelled." How should Jones's lawyer respond?

P. F. Strawson (1919–2006)

Until his retirement in 1987, Strawson was the Waynflete Professor of Metaphysical Philosophy at the University of Oxford. His writings include seminal contributions to the philosophy of language ("On Referring," 1950), metaphysics (*Individuals*, 1959), and the interpretation of Kant's philosophy (*The Bounds of Sense*, 1966).

FREEDOM AND RESENTMENT

1. Some philosophers say they do not know what the thesis of determinism is. Others say, or imply, that they do know what it is. Of these, some—the pessimists perhaps—hold that if the thesis is true, then the concepts of moral obligation and responsibility really have no application, and the practices of punishing and blaming, of expressing moral condemnation and approval, are really unjustified. Others—the optimists perhaps—hold that these concepts and practices in no way lose their *raison d'être* if the thesis of determinism is true. . . . If I am asked which of these parties I belong to, I must say it is the first of all, the party of those who do not know what the thesis of determinism is. But this does not stop me from having some sympathy with the others, and a wish to reconcile them. Should not ignorance, rationally, inhibit such sympathies? Well, of course, though darkling, one has some inkling—some notion of what sort of thing is being talked about. This lecture is intended as a move towards reconciliation; so it is likely to seem wrong-headed to everyone. . . .

2. . . . Some optimists about determinism point to the efficacy of the practices of punishment, and of moral condemnation and approval, in regulating behaviour in

socially desirable ways. In the fact of their efficacy, they suggest, is an adequate basis for these practices; and this fact certainly does not show determinism to be false. To this the pessimists reply, all in a rush, that *just* punishment and *moral* condemnation imply moral guilt and guilt implies moral responsibility and moral responsibility implies freedom and freedom implies the falsity of determinism. And to this the optimists are wont to reply in turn that it is true that these practices require freedom in a sense, and the existence of freedom in this sense is one of the facts as we know them. But what "freedom" means here is nothing but the absence of certain conditions the presence of which would make moral condemnation or punishment inappropriate. They have in mind conditions like compulsion by another, or innate incapacity, or insanity, or other less extreme forms of psychological disorder, or the existence of circumstances in which the making of any other choice would be morally inadmissible or would be too much to expect of any man. To this list they are constrained to add other factors which, without exactly being limitations of freedom, may also make moral condemnation or punishment inappropriate or mitigate their force: as some forms of ignorance, mistake, or accident. And the general reason why moral condemnation or punishment are inappropriate when these factors or conditions are present is held to be that the practices in question will be generally efficacious means of regulating behaviour in desirable ways only in cases where these factors are *not* present. Now the pessimist admits that the facts as we know them include the existence of freedom, the occurrence of cases of free action, in the negative sense which the optimist concedes; and admits, or rather insists, that the existence of freedom in this sense is compatible with the truth of determinism. Then what does the pessimist find missing? When he tries to answer this question, his language is apt to alternate between the very familiar and the very unfamiliar. Thus he may say, familiarly enough, that the man who is the subject of justified punishment, blame or moral condemnation must really *deserve* it; and then add, perhaps, that, in the case at least where he is blamed for a positive act rather than an omission, the condition of his really deserving blame is something that goes beyond the negative freedoms that the optimist concedes. It is, say, a genuinely free identification of the will with the act. And this is the condition that is incompatible with the truth of determinism.

The conventional, but conciliatory, optimist need not give up yet. He may say: Well, people often decide to do things, really intend to do what they do, know just what they're doing in doing it; the reasons they think they have for doing what they do, often really are their reasons and not their rationalizations. These facts, too, are included in the facts as we know them. If this is what you mean by freedom—by the identification of the will with the act—then freedom may again be conceded. But again the concession is compatible with the truth of the determinist thesis. For it would not follow from that thesis that nobody decides to do anything; that nobody ever does anything intentionally; that it is false that people sometimes know perfectly well what they are doing. I tried to define freedom negatively. You want to give it a more positive look. But it comes to the same thing. Nobody denies freedom in this sense, or these senses, and nobody claims that the existence of freedom in these senses shows determinism to be false.

But it is here that the lacuna in the optimistic story can be made to show. For the pessimist may be supposed to ask: But *why* does freedom in this sense justify blame, etc.? You turn towards me first the negative, and then the positive, faces of a freedom which nobody challenges. But the only reason you have given for the practices of moral condemnation and punishment in cases where this freedom is present is the efficacy of these practices in regulating behaviour in socially desirable ways. But this is not a sufficient basis, it is not even the right *sort* of basis, for these practices as we understand them.

Now my optimist, being the sort of man he is, is not likely to invoke an intuition of fittingness at this point. So he really has no more to say. And my pessimist, being the sort of man he is, has only one more thing to say; and that is that the admissibility of these practices, as we understand them, demands another kind of freedom, the kind that in turn demands the falsity of the thesis of determinism. But might we not induce the pessimist to give up saying this by giving the optimist something more to say?

3. I have mentioned punishing and moral condemnation and approval; and it is in connection with these practices or attitudes that the issue between optimists and pessimists . . . is felt to be particularly important. But it is not of these practices and attitudes that I propose, at first, to speak. These practices or attitudes permit, where they do not imply, a certain detachment from the actions or agents which are their objects. I want to speak, at least at first, of something else: of the non-detached attitudes and reactions of people directly involved in transactions with each other; of the attitudes and reactions of offended parties and beneficiaries; of such things as gratitude, resentment, forgiveness, love, and hurt feelings. . . .

What I have to say consists largely of commonplaces. So my language, like that of commonplaces generally, will be quite unscientific and imprecise. The central commonplace that I want to insist on is the very great importance that we attach to the attitudes and intentions towards us of other human beings, and the great extent to which our personal feelings and reactions depend upon, or involve, our beliefs about these attitudes and intentions. . . . If someone treads on my hand accidentally, while trying to help me, the pain may be no less acute than if he treads on it in contemptuous disregard of my existence or with a malevolent wish to injure me. But I shall generally feel in the second case a kind and degree of resentment that I shall not feel in the first. If someone's actions help me to some benefit I desire, then I am benefited in any case; but if he intended them so to benefit me because of his general goodwill towards me, I shall reasonably feel a gratitude which I should not feel at all if the benefit was an incidental consequence, unintended or even regretted by him, of some plan of action with a different aim. . . .

We should think of the many different kinds of relationship which we can have with other people—as sharers of a common interest; as members of the same family; as colleagues; as friends; as lovers; as chance parties to an enormous range of transactions and encounters. Then we should think, in each of these connections in turn, and in others, of the kind of importance we attach to the attitudes and intentions towards us of those who stand in these relationships to us, and of the kinds of *reactive* attitudes and feelings to which we ourselves are prone. In general, we demand some degree of goodwill or regard on the part of those who stand in these relationships to us, though the forms we require it to take vary widely in different connections. The range and intensity of our *reactive* attitudes towards goodwill, its absence or its opposite vary no less widely. I have mentioned, specifically, resentment and gratitude; and they are a usefully opposed pair. But, of course, there is a whole continuum of reactive attitude and feeling stretching on both sides of these and—the most comfortable area—in between them.

The object of these commonplaces is to try to keep before our minds something it is easy to forget when we are engaged in philosophy, especially in our cool, contemporary style, viz. what it is actually like to be involved in ordinary interpersonal relationships, ranging from the most intimate to the most casual.

4. It is one thing to ask about the general causes of these reactive attitudes I have alluded to; it is another to ask about the variations to which they are subject, the particular conditions in which they do or do not seem natural or reasonable or appropriate; and it is a third thing to ask what it would be like, what it is like, not to suffer them. I am not much concerned with the first question; but I am with the second; and perhaps even more with the third.

Let us consider, then, occasions for resentment: situations in which one person is offended or injured by the action of another and in which—in the absence of special considerations—the offended person might naturally or normally be expected to feel resentment. Then let us consider what sorts of special considerations might be expected to modify or mollify this feeling or remove it altogether. It needs no saying now how multifarious these considerations are. But, for my purpose, I think they can be roughly divided into two kinds. To the first group belong all those which might give occasion for the employment of such expressions as "He didn't mean to," "He hadn't realized," "He didn't know"; and also all those which might give occasion for the use of the phrase "He couldn't help it," when this is supported by such phrases as "He was pushed," "He had to do it," "It was the only way," "They left him no alternative," etc. Obviously these various pleas . . . differ from each other in striking and important ways. But for my present purpose they have something still more important in common. None of them invites us to suspend towards the agent, either at the time of his action or in general, our ordinary reactive attitudes. They do not invite us to view the *agent* as one in respect of whom these attitudes are in any way inappropriate. They invite us to view the *injury* as one in respect of which a particular one of these attitudes is inappropriate. . . .

The second group of considerations is very different. I shall take them in two subgroups of which the first is far less important than the second. In connection with the first subgroup we may think of such statements as "He wasn't himself," "He has been under very great strain recently," "He was acting under post-hypnotic suggestion"; in connection with the second, we may think of "He's only a child," "He's a hopeless schizophrenic," "His mind has been systematically perverted," "That's purely compulsive behaviour on his part." Such pleas as these do, as pleas of my first general group do not, invite us to suspend our ordinary reactive attitudes towards the agent, either at the time of his action or all the time. They do not invite us to see the agent's action in a way consistent with the full retention of ordinary inter-personal attitudes and merely inconsistent with one particular attitude. They invite us to view the agent himself in a different light from the light in which we should normally view one who has acted as he has acted.

The second and more important subgroup of cases allows that the circumstances were normal, but presents the agent as psychologically abnormal—or as morally undeveloped. The agent was himself; but he is warped or deranged, neurotic or just a child. When we see someone in such a light as this, all our reactive attitudes tend to be profoundly modified. I must deal here in crude dichotomies and ignore the ever-interesting and ever-illuminating varieties of case. What I want to contrast is the attitude (or range of attitudes) of involvement or participation in a human relationship, on the one hand, and what might be called the objective attitude (or range of attitudes) to another human being, on the other. Even in the same situation, I must add, they are not altogether *exclusive* of each other; but they are, profoundly, *opposed* to each other. To adopt the objective attitude to another human being is to see him, perhaps, as an object of social policy; as a subject for what, in a wide range of sense, might be called treatment; as something certainly to be taken account, perhaps precautionary account, of. . . . If your attitude towards someone is wholly objective, then though you may fight him, you cannot quarrel with him, and though you may talk to him, even negotiate with him, you cannot reason with him. You can at most pretend to quarrel, or to reason, with him. . . .

What I have called the participant reactive attitudes are essentially natural human reactions to the good or ill will or indifference of others towards us, as displayed in *their* attitudes and actions. The question we have to ask is: What effect would, or should, the acceptance of the truth of a general thesis of determinism have upon these reactive attitudes? More specifically, would, or should, the acceptance of the truth of the thesis lead to the decay or the repudiation of all such attitudes? Would, or should, it mean the end of gratitude, resentment, and forgiveness; of all reciprocated adult loves; of all the essentially *personal* antagonisms?

But how can I answer, or even pose, this question without knowing *exactly* what the thesis of determinism is? Well, there is one thing we do know; that if there is a coherent thesis of determinism, then there must be a sense of "determined" such that, if that thesis is true, then all behaviour whatever is determined in that sense. Remembering this, we can consider at least what possibilities lie formally open; and then perhaps we shall see that the question can be answered *without* knowing exactly what the thesis of determinism is. We can consider what possibilities lie open because we have already before us an account of the ways in which particular reactive attitudes, or reactive attitudes in general, may be, and, sometimes, we judge, should be, inhibited. Thus I considered earlier a group of considerations which tend to inhibit, and, we judge, should inhibit, resentment, in particular cases of an agent causing an injury, without inhibiting reactive attitudes in general towards that agent. Obviously this group of considerations cannot strictly bear upon our question; for that question concerns reactive attitudes in general. But resentment has a particular interest; so it is worth adding that it has never been claimed as a consequence of the truth of determinism that one or another of *these* considerations was operative in every case of an injury being caused by an agent; that it would follow from the truth of determinism that anyone who caused an injury *either* was quite simply ignorant of causing it *or* had acceptably overriding reasons for acquiescing reluctantly in causing it *or* . . . etc. The prevalence of this happy state of affairs would not be a consequence of the reign of universal determinism, but of the reign of universal goodwill. We cannot, then, find here the possibility of an affirmative answer to our question.

Next, I remarked that the participant attitude . . . tend[s] to give place, and it is judged by the civilized should give place, to objective attitudes, just in so far as the agent is seen as excluded from ordinary adult human relationships by deep-rooted psychological abnormality—or simply by being a child. But it cannot be a consequence of any thesis which is not itself self-contradictory that abnormality is the universal condition.

Now this dismissal might seem altogether too facile; and so, in a sense, it is. But . . . we can sometimes, and in part, . . . look on the normal (those we rate as "normal") in the objective way in which we have learned to look on certain classified cases of abnormality. And our question reduces to this: could, or should, the acceptance of the determinist thesis lead us always to look on everyone exclusively in this way? For this is the only condition worth considering under which the acceptance of determinism could lead to the decay or repudiation of participant reactive attitudes.

It does not seem to be self-contradictory to suppose that this might happen. So I suppose we must say that it is not absolutely inconceivable that it should happen. But I am strongly inclined to think that it is, for us as we are, practically inconceivable. The human commitment to participation in ordinary inter-personal relationships is, I think, too thoroughgoing and deeply rooted for us to take seriously the thought that a general theoretical conviction might so change our world that, in it, there were no longer any such things as inter-personal relationships as we normally understand them. . . .

5. The reactive attitudes I have so far discussed are essentially reactions to the quality of others' wills towards us, as manifested in their behaviour: to their good or ill will or indifference or lack of concern. Thus resentment, or what I have called resentment, is a reaction to injury or indifference. The reactive attitudes I have now to discuss might be described as the sympathetic or vicarious or impersonal or disinterested or generalized analogues of the reactive attitudes I have already discussed. They are reactions to the qualities of others' wills, not towards ourselves, but towards others. Because of this impersonal or vicarious character, we give them different names. Thus one who experiences the vicarious analogue of resentment is said to be indignant or disapproving, or morally indignant or disapproving.

. . . The generalized or vicarious analogues of the personal reactive attitudes rest on, and reflect . . . the demand for the manifestation of a reasonable degree of goodwill or regard, on the part of others, not simply towards oneself, but towards all those on whose behalf moral indignation may be felt, i.e., as we now think, towards all men. . . .

Now, as of the personal reactive attitudes, so of their vicarious analogues, we must ask in what ways, and by what considerations, they tend to be inhibited. Both types of attitude involve, or express, a certain sort of demand for inter-personal regard. The fact of injury constitutes a prima facie appearance of this demand's being flouted or unfulfilled. We saw, in the case of resentment, how one class of considerations may show this appearance to be mere appearance, . . . without in any way tending to make us suspend our ordinary inter-personal attitudes to the agent. Considerations of this class operate in just the same way, for just the same reasons, in connection with moral disapprobation or indignation; they inhibit indignation without in any way inhibiting the sort of demand on the agent of which indignation can be an expression, the range of attitudes towards him to which it belongs.

But suppose we see the agent in a different light: as one whose picture of the world is an insane delusion; or as one whose behaviour, or a part of whose behaviour, is unintelligible to us, perhaps even to him, in terms of conscious purposes, and intelligible only in terms of unconscious purposes; or even, perhaps, as one wholly impervious to the self-reactive attitudes I spoke of, wholly lacking, as we say, in moral sense. Seeing an agent in such a light as this tends, I said, to inhibit resentment in a wholly different way. It tends to inhibit resentment because it tends to inhibit ordinary interpersonal attitudes in general, and the kind of demand and expectation which those attitudes involve; and tends to promote instead the purely objective view of the agent as one posing problems simply of intellectual understanding, management, treatment, and control. Again the parallel holds for those generalized or moral attitudes towards the agent which we are now concerned with. The same abnormal light which shows the agent to us as one in respect of whom the personal attitudes, the personal demand, are to be suspended, shows him to us also as one in respect of whom the impersonal attitudes, the generalized demand, are to be suspended. . . .

What concerns us now is to inquire, as previously in connection with the personal reactive attitudes, what relevance any general thesis of determinism might have to their vicarious analogues. The answers once more are parallel; though I shall take them in a slightly different order. First, we must note, as before, that when the suspension of such an attitude or such attitudes occurs in a particular case, it is *never* the consequence of the belief that the piece of behaviour in question was determined in a sense such that all behaviour *might* be, and, if determinism is true, all behaviour is, determined in that sense. For it is not a consequence of any general thesis of determinism which might be true that nobody knows what he's doing or that everybody's behaviour is unintelligible in terms of conscious purposes or that everybody lives in a world of delusion or that nobody has a moral sense, i.e., is susceptible of self-reactive attitudes, etc. In fact no such sense of "determined" as would be required for a general thesis of determinism is ever relevant to our actual suspensions of moral reactive attitudes. Second, suppose it granted, as I have already argued, that we cannot take seriously the thought that theoretical conviction of such a general thesis would lead to the total decay of the personal reactive attitudes. Can we then take seriously the thought that such a conviction . . . would nevertheless lead to the total decay or repudiation of the vicarious analogues of these attitudes? I think that the change in our social world which would leave us exposed to the personal reactive attitudes but not at all to their vicarious analogues, the generalization of abnormal egocentricity which this would entail, is perhaps even harder for us to envisage as a real possibility than the decay of both kinds of attitude together. . . . Finally, to the further question whether it would not be *rational*, given a general theoretical conviction of the truth of determinism, so to change our world that in it all these attitudes were wholly suspended, I must answer that one who presses this question has wholly failed to grasp the import of the preceding answer, the nature of the human commitment that is here involved: it is *useless* to ask whether it would not be rational for us to do what it is not in our nature to (be able to) do. . . .

6. Optimist and pessimist[, then,] misconstrue the facts in very different styles. But in a profound sense there is something in common to their misunderstandings. Both seek, in different ways, to over-intellectualize the facts. Inside the general structure or web of human attitudes and feelings of which I have been speaking, there is endless room for modification, redirection, criticism, and justification. But questions of justification are internal to the structure or relate to modifications internal to it. The existence of the general framework of attitudes itself is something we are given with the fact of human society. As a whole, it neither calls for, nor permits, an external "rational" justification. Pessimist and optimist alike show themselves, in different ways, unable to accept this. . . .

TEST YOUR UNDERSTANDING

1. P. F. Strawson sees the free will debate as a clash between "optimists" and "pessimists." State these positions.

2. What is a "reactive attitude"? Give examples and attempt a general characterization.

3. Why, according to Strawson, are we not blameworthy when we cause harm *by accident*?

4. True or false: Strawson thinks that while it would be hard for us to abandon the reactive attitudes, we are capable of doing so, and indeed we should do so if determinism turns out to be true.

READER'S GUIDE

Strawson on Freedom and Resentment

Strawson's aim is to show that what appears at first to be a deep metaphysical question—Is determinism compatible with moral responsibility?—is in fact an easy question in the ethics of the emotions.

Strawson begins an account of the nature of responsibility. According to Strawson, when we ask whether Alice is morally responsible for stepping on your foot, we are asking whether certain emotional responses to this act are justified. The relevant emotions are the so-called *reactive attitudes*. These include guilt, resentment, and indignation when the act is bad; pride, gratitude, and admiration when the act is good. Given this view, our original question amounts to this: Can the reactive attitudes be justified in a deterministic world?

Now when we ask whether an emotional response is justified, we could be asking whether it's justified by ordinary standards—the standards we now accept—or by ideal standards: the standards it would be best for us to accept. Strawson's thesis is that the reactive attitudes can be justified in both senses even if determinism is true.

The heart of the essay (§§4–5) is an analysis of our ordinary practices with the reactive attitudes. In daily life we take for granted that it makes sense to resent people when they wrong us and to feel indignant when they wrong others. But we also recognize a range of *excuses*: considerations that show that resentment would be unjustified even though the agent acted badly. These excuses are of two types.

Type 1	Type 2
"She didn't mean to."	"He's just a child."
"She was forced."	"He's been hypnotized."
"She didn't know."	"He's under a great deal of stress."
"She couldn't help it."	"He suffers from severe mental illness."

According to Strawson, the Type 1 excuses work as follows. The reactive emotions are responses to the **quality of will** with which a person acts. Bad actions often manifest ill will: malice, indifference, or contempt. Resentment and the other negative reactive emotions are justified only when the act manifests ill in this sense. The Type 1 excuses cover the special cases in which a seemingly bad act does *not*, in fact, manifest ill will.

When a Type 2 excuse applies, we allow that the agent might have acted with ill will but withhold resentment because we regard the agent as unfit—perhaps only temporarily—for the sort of normal human relationship in which resentment and the other reactive emotions have a point.

According to Strawson, *every ordinary excuse falls into one of these categories.* This yields a theory that may be put as follows:

> By ordinary standards, resentment is justified whenever an agent who is fit for normal adult relationships manifests ill will.

But note: If this is right then resentment can be justified by ordinary standards in a deterministic world. Suppose Alice, a normal adult, deliberately steps on your foot because she hates you. Let the world be as deterministic as you like. Still she is competent and her action manifest ill will. So by ordinary standards she is morally responsible for her act.

It remains to show that resentment can be justified by *ideal* standards even if the world is deterministic. Since we don't know what these standards are, we can't consult them. But according to Strawson, that doesn't matter. Whatever the best standards are, they must be standards we are psychologically capable of complying with. And the fact is that we are incapable of suspending the reactive attitudes across the board. We are hard-wired to care about what people think of us and to respond emotionally when they display good or ill will, just as we are hard-wired to believe in an external world. Since it is "useless to ask whether it would not be rational for us to do what it is in our nature to do" (p. 631), we may conclude that the best standards for regulating the reactive attitudes will license them under certain circumstances, regardless of whether the universe is deterministic.

Conclusion: By *any* plausible standard, the reactive attitudes can be justified in a deterministic world. "Determinism in this case" is no excuse, not by ordinary standards or ideal standards. But that is just to say that determinism and moral responsibility are compatible.

NOTES AND QUESTIONS

1. For P. F. Strawson, the urgent question that underlies the free will debate is whether certain emotions—guilt, resentment, admiration, etc.—are ever justified. According to Strawson, we can understand this question in two ways. We might be asking whether these emotions are justified by the standards we accept in daily life. Alternatively, we might be asking whether they are justified by some ideal standard; for example, the standard that it would be *best* for us to adopt. Strawson's conclusion is that even if determinism is true, our normal reactions are often justified in both senses. Is he right?

2. Suppose a stranger cuts in front of you in line at the bank. He's not a child, he's not insane, and there is no emergency that would justify his rude behavior, so your first reaction is to blame him. You are then informed (say, by a scientist) that his action was determined by forces that were in place before he was born, and as soon as you learn this, you conclude that it would be unfair to blame him. This suggests that if determinism is true, our reactive emotions are not justified *by ordinary standards* and that we fail to notice this in daily life only because we ignore the possibility of determinism. How might Strawson respond to this suggestion?

3. Strawson claims that if we were to abandon the negative reactive attitudes like guilt and resentment, certain immensely valuable forms of friendship and love would be impossible, and hence that the negative reactive attitudes must be justified by the standards that it would be *best* for us to adopt. But is this right? Can't we imagine a world in which people love their friends and family but never resent them and never feel guilty? Try to describe a world of this sort in some detail in order to assess Strawson's claim that the negative reactive attitudes are justified even by *ideal* standards.

Harry Frankfurt (b. 1929)

Frankfurt, Professor Emeritus of Philosophy at Princeton University, is the author of a seminal study of Descartes's philosophy (*Demons, Dreamers, and Madmen*, 1970) and the surprise best seller *On Bullshit* (2005). His papers on ethics, moral psychology, and political philosophy are collected in *The Importance of What We Care About* (1988) and *Necessity, Volition, and Love* (1999).

FREEDOM OF THE WILL AND THE CONCEPT OF A PERSON

... There is a sense in which the word "person" is merely the singular form of "people" and in which both terms connote no more than membership in a certain biological species. In those senses of the word, which are of greater philosophical interest, however, the criteria for being a person do not serve primarily to distinguish the members of our own species from the members of other species. Rather, they are designed to capture those attributes which are the subject of our most humane concern with ourselves and the source of what we regard as most important and most problematical in our lives. Now these attributes would be of equal significance to us even if they were not in fact peculiar and common to the members of our own species. What interests us most in the human condition would not interest us less if it were also a feature of the condition of other creatures as well.

Our concept of ourselves as persons is not to be understood, therefore, as a concept of attributes that are necessarily species-specific. It is conceptually possible that members of novel or even of familiar nonhuman species should be persons; and it is also conceptually possible that some members of the human species are not persons. We do in fact assume, on the other hand, that no member of another species is a person. Accordingly, there is a presumption that what is essential to persons is a set of characteristics that we generally suppose—whether rightly or wrongly—to be uniquely human.

It is my view that one essential difference between persons and other creatures is to be found in the structure of a person's will. Human beings are not alone in having desires and motives, or in making choices. They share these things with the members of certain other species, some of whom even appear to engage in deliberation and to make decisions based upon prior thought. It seems to be peculiarly characteristic of humans, however, that they are able to form what I shall call "second-order desires" or "desires of the second order."

Besides wanting and choosing and being moved *to do* this or that, men may also want to have (or not to have) certain desires and motives. They are capable of wanting to be different, in their preferences and purposes, from what they are. Many animals appear to have the capacity for what I shall call "first-order desires" or "desires of the first order," which are simply desires to do or not to do one thing or another. No animal other than man, however, appears to have the capacity for reflective self-evaluation that is manifested in the formation of second-order desires.

|

... Consider first those statements of the form "*A* wants to *X*" which identify first-order desires—that is, statements in which the term "to *X*" refers to an action. A statement of this kind does not, by itself, indicate the relative strength of *A*'s desire to *X*. It does not make it clear whether this desire is at all likely to play a decisive role in what *A* actually does or tries to do. For it may correctly be said that *A* wants to *X* even when his desire to *X* is only one among his desires and when it is far from being paramount among them. Thus, it may be true that *A* wants to *X* when he strongly prefers to do something else instead; and it may be true that he wants to *X* despite the fact that, when he acts, it is not the desire to *X* that motivates him to do what he does. On the other hand, someone who states that *A* wants to *X* may mean to convey that it is this desire that is motivating or moving *A* to do what he is actually doing or that *A* will in fact be moved by this desire (unless he changes his mind) when he acts.

It is only when it is used in the second of these ways that, given the special usage of "will" that I propose to adopt, the statement identifies *A*'s will. To identify an agent's will is either to identify the desire (or desires) by which he is motivated in some action he performs or to identify the desire (or desires) by which he will or would be motivated when or if he acts. An agent's will, then, is identical with one or more of his first-order desires. But the notion of the will, as I am employing it, is not coextensive[1] with the notion of first-order desires. It is not the notion of something that merely inclines an agent in some degree to act in a certain way. Rather, it is the notion of an *effective* desire—one that moves (or will or would move) a person all the way to action. . . .

Now consider those statements of the form "*A* wants to *X*," which identify second-order desires—that is, statements in which the term "to *X*" refers to a desire of the first order. There are also two kinds of situation in which it may be true that *A* wants to want to *X*. In the first place, it might be true of *A* that he wants to have a desire to *X* despite the fact that he has a univocal desire, altogether free of conflict and ambivalence, to refrain from *X*-ing. Someone might want to have a certain desire, in other words, but univocally want that desire to be unsatisfied.

Suppose that a physician engaged in psychotherapy with narcotics addicts believes that his ability to help his patients would be enhanced if he understood better what it is like for them to desire the drug to which they are addicted. Suppose that he is led in this way to want to have a desire for the drug. If it is a genuine desire that he wants, then what he wants is not merely to feel the sensations that addicts characteristically feel when they are gripped by their desires for the drug. What the physician wants, insofar as he wants to have a desire, is to be inclined or moved to some extent to take the drug.

It is entirely possible, however, that, although he wants to be moved by a desire to take the drug, he does not want this desire to be effective. He may not want it to move him all the way to action. He need not be interested in finding out what it is like to take the drug. And insofar as he now wants only to *want* to take it, and not to *take* it, there is nothing in what he now wants that would be satisfied by the drug itself. . . .

It would thus be incorrect to infer, from the fact that the physician now wants to desire to take the drug, that he already does desire to take it. His second-order desire to be moved to take the drug does not entail that he has a first-order desire to take it. . . . While he wants to want to take the drug, he may have *no* desire to take it; it may be that *all* he wants is to taste the desire for it. That is, his desire to have a certain desire that he does not have may not be a desire that his will should be at all different than it is.

. . . There is, however, a second kind of situation that may be described by "*A* wants to want to *X*"; and when the statement is used to describe a situation of this second kind, then it does pertain to what *A* wants his will to be. In such cases the statement means that *A* wants the desire to *X* to be the desire that moves him effectively to act. It is not merely that he wants the desire to *X* to be among the desires by which, to one degree or another, he is moved or inclined to act. He wants this desire to be effective—that is,

---

1. Two concepts are **coextensive** if they apply to exactly the same things. For example, if all human beings are featherless bipeds and every featherless biped is a human being, then the two concepts *human being* and *featherless biped* are coextensive.

to provide the motive in what he actually does. Now when the statement that *A* wants to want to *X* is used in this way, it does entail that *A* already has a desire to *X*. It could not be true both that *A* wants the desire to *X* to move him into action and that he does not want to *X*. It is only if he does want to *X* that he can coherently want the desire to *X* not merely to be one of his desires but, more decisively, to be his will. . . .

II

Someone has a desire of the second order either when he wants simply to have a certain desire or when he wants a certain desire to be his will. In situations of the latter kind, I shall call his second-order desires "second-order volitions." . . . Now it is having second-order volitions, and not having second-order desires generally, that I regard as essential to being a person. It is logically possible, however unlikely, that there should be an agent with second-order desires but with no volitions of the second order. Such a creature, in my view, would not be a person. I shall use the term "wanton" to refer to agents who have first-order desires but who are not persons because, whether or not they have desires of the second order, they have no second-order volitions.

The essential characteristic of a wanton is that he does not care about his will. His desires move him to do certain things, without its being true of him either that he wants to be moved by those desires or that he prefers to be moved by other desires. The class of wantons includes all nonhuman animals that have desires and all very young children. Perhaps it also includes some adult human beings as well. In any case, adult humans may be more or less wanton; they may act wantonly, in response to first-order desires concerning which they have no volitions of the second order, more or less frequently.

The fact that a wanton has no second-order volitions does not mean that each of his first-order desires is translated heedlessly and at once into action. He may have no opportunity to act in accordance with some of this desires. Moreover, the translation of his desires into action may be delayed or precluded either by conflicting desires of the first order or by the intervention of deliberation. For a wanton may possess and employ rational faculties of a high order. Nothing in the concept of a wanton implies that he cannot reason or that he cannot deliberate concerning how to do what he wants to do. What distinguishes the rational wanton from other rational agents is that he is not concerned with the desirability of his desires themselves. He ignores the question of what his will is to be. Not only does he pursue whatever course of action he is most strongly inclined to pursue, but he does not care which of his inclinations is the strongest. . . .

The distinction between a person and a wanton may be illustrated by the difference between two narcotics addicts. Let us suppose that the physiological condition accounting for the addiction is the same in both men, and that both succumb inevitably to their periodic desires for the drug to which they are addicted. One of the addicts hates his addiction and always struggles desperately, although to no avail, against its thrust. He tries everything that he thinks might enable him to overcome his desires for the drug. But these desires are too powerful for him to withstand, and invariably, in the end, they conquer him. He is an unwilling addict, helplessly violated by his own desires.

The unwilling addict has conflicting first-order desires: he wants to take the drug, and he also wants to refrain from taking it. In addition to these first-order desires, however, he has a volition of the second order. He is not neutral with regard to the conflict between his desire to take the drug and his desire to refrain from taking it. It is the latter desire, and not the former, that he wants to constitute his will; it is the latter desire, rather than the former, that he wants to be effective and to provide the purpose that he will seek to realize in what he actually does.

The other addict is a wanton. His actions reflect the economy of his first-order desires, without his being concerned whether the desires that move him to act are desires by which he wants to be moved to act. If he encounters problems in obtaining the drug or in administering it to himself, his responses to his urges to take it may involve deliberation. But it never occurs to him to consider whether he wants the relations among his desires to result in his having the will he has. The wanton addict may be an animal, and thus incapable of being concerned about his will. In any event he is, in respect of his wanton lack of concern, no different from an animal.

The second of these addicts may suffer a first-order conflict similar to the first-order conflict suffered by the first. Whether he is human or not, the wanton may (perhaps due to conditioning) both want to take the drug and want to refrain from taking it. Unlike the unwilling addict, however, he does not prefer that one of his conflicting desires should be paramount over the other; he does not prefer that one first-order desire rather than the other should constitute his will. It would be misleading to say that he is neutral as to the conflict between his desires, since this would suggest that he regards them as equally acceptable. Since he has no identity apart from his first-order desires, it is true neither that he prefers one to the other nor that he prefers not to take sides.

It makes a difference to the unwilling addict, who is a person, which of his conflicting first-order desires wins out. Both desires are his, to be sure; and whether he finally takes the drug or finally succeeds in refraining from taking it, he acts to satisfy what is in a literal sense his own desire. In either case he does something he himself wants to do, and he does it not because of some external influence whose aim happens to coincide with his own but because of his desire to do it. The unwilling addict identifies himself, however, through the formation of a second-order volition, with one rather than with the other of his conflicting first-order desires. He makes one of them more truly his own and, in so doing, he withdraws himself from the other. It is in virtue of this identification and withdrawal, accomplished through the formation of a second-order volition, that the unwilling addict may meaningfully make the analytically puzzling statements that the force moving him to take the drug is a force other than his own, and that it is not of his own free will but rather against his will that this force moves him to take it.

The wanton addict cannot or does not care which of his conflicting first-order desires wins out. His lack of concern is not due to his inability to find a convincing basis for preference. It is due either to his lack of the capacity for reflection or to his mindless indifference to the enterprise of evaluating his own desires and motives.[2] There is only one issue in the struggle to which his first-order conflict may lead: whether the one or the other of his conflicting desires is the stronger. Since he is moved by both desires, he will not be altogether satisfied by what he does no matter which of them is effective. But it makes no difference to *him* whether his craving or his aversion gets the upper hand. He has no stake in the conflict between them and so, unlike the unwilling addict, he can neither win nor lose the struggle in which he is engaged. When a *person* acts, the desire by which he is moved is either the will he wants or a will he wants to be without. When a *wanton* acts, it is neither.

III

There is a very close relationship between the capacity for forming second-order volitions and another capacity that is essential to persons—one that has often been considered a distinguishing mark of the human condition. It is only because a person has volitions of the second order that he is capable both of enjoying and of lacking freedom of the will. The concept of a person is not only, then, the concept of a type of entity that has both first-order desires and volitions of the second order. It can also be construed as the concept of a type of entity for whom the freedom of its will may be a problem. . . .

Just what kind of freedom is the freedom of the will? . . .

According to one familiar philosophical tradition, being free is fundamentally a matter of doing what one wants to do. Now the notion of an agent who does what he wants to do is by no means an altogether clear one: both the doing and the wanting, and the appropriate relation between them as well, require elucidation. But although its focus needs to be sharpened and its formulation refined, I believe that this notion does capture at least part of what is implicit in the idea of an agent who *acts* freely. It misses entirely, however, the peculiar content of the quite different idea of an agent whose *will* is free.

We do not suppose that animals enjoy freedom of the will, although we recognize that an animal may be free to run in whatever direction it wants. Thus, having the freedom to do what one wants to do is not a sufficient condition of having a free will. It is not a necessary condition either. For to deprive someone of his freedom of action is not necessarily to undermine the freedom of his will. When an agent is aware that there are certain things he is not free to do, this doubtless affects his desires and limits

2. In speaking of the evaluation of his own desires and motives as being characteristic of a person, I do not mean to suggest that a person's second-order volitions necessarily manifest a *moral* stance on his part toward his first-order desires. It may not be from the point of view of morality that the person evaluates his first-order desires. Moreover, a person may be capricious and irresponsible in forming his second-order volitions and give no serious consideration to what is at stake. Second-order volitions express evaluations only in the sense that they are preferences. There is no essential restriction on the kind of basis, if any, upon which they are formed. [Frankfurt's note.]

the range of choices he can make. But suppose that someone, without being aware of it, has in fact lost or been deprived of his freedom of action. Even though he is no longer free to do what he wants to do, his will may remain as free as it was before. Despite the fact that he is not free to translate his desires into actions or to act according to the determinations of his will, he may still form those desires and make those determinations as freely as if his freedom of action had not been impaired.

When we ask whether a person's will is free, we are not asking whether he is in a position to translate his first-order desires into actions. That is the question of whether he is free to do as he pleases. The question of the freedom of his will does not concern the relation between what he does and what he wants to do. Rather, it concerns his desires themselves. But what question about them is it?

It seems to me both natural and useful to construe the question of whether a person's will is free in close analogy to the question of whether an agent enjoys freedom of action. Now freedom of action is (roughly, at least) the freedom to do what one wants to do. Analogously, then, the statement that a person enjoys freedom of the will means (also roughly) that he is free to want what he wants to want. More precisely, it means that he is free to will what he wants to will, or to have the will he wants. Just as the question about the freedom of an agent's action has to do with whether it is the action he wants to perform, so the question about the freedom of his will has to do with whether it is the will he wants to have.

It is in securing the conformity of his will to his second-order volitions, then, that a person exercises freedom of the will. And it is in the discrepancy between his will and his second-order volitions, or in his awareness that their coincidence is not his own doing but only a happy chance, that a person who does not have this freedom feels its lack. The unwilling addict's will is not free. This is shown by the fact that it is not the will he wants. It is also true, though in a different way, that the will of the wanton addict is not free. The wanton addict neither has the will he wants nor has a will that differs from the will he wants. Since he has no volitions of the second order, the freedom of his will cannot be a problem for him. He lacks it, so to speak, by default.

People are generally far more complicated than my sketchy account of the structure of a person's will may suggest. There is as much opportunity for ambivalence, conflict, and self-deception with regard to desires of the second order, for example, as there is with regard to first-order desires. If there is an unresolved conflict among someone's second-order desires, then he is in danger of having no second-order volition; for unless this conflict is resolved, he has no preference concerning which of his first-order desires is to be his will. This condition, if it is so severe that it prevents him from identifying himself in a sufficiently decisive way with *any* of his conflicting first-order desires, destroys him as a person. For it either tends to paralyze his will and keep him from acting at all, or it tends to remove him from his will so that his will operates without his participation. In both cases he becomes, like the unwilling addict though in a different way, a helpless bystander to the forces that move him.

Another complexity is that a person may have, especially if his second-order desires are in conflict, desires and volitions of a higher order than the second. There is no theoretical limit to the length of the series of desires of higher and higher orders;

nothing except common sense and, perhaps, a saving fatigue prevents an individual from obsessively refusing to identify himself with any of his desires until he forms a desire of the next higher order. The tendency to generate such a series of acts of forming desires, which would be a case of humanization run wild, also leads toward the destruction of a person.

It is possible, however, to terminate such a series of acts without cutting it off arbitrarily. When a person identifies himself *decisively* with one of his first-order desires, this commitment "resounds" throughout the potentially endless array of higher orders. Consider a person who, without reservation or conflict, wants to be motivated by the desire to concentrate on his work. The fact that his second-order volition to be moved by this desire is a decisive one means that there is no room for questions concerning the pertinence of desires or volitions of higher orders. Suppose the person is asked whether he wants to want to want to concentrate on his work. He can properly insist that this question concerning a third-order desire does not arise. It would be a mistake to claim that, because he has not considered whether he wants the second-order volition he has formed, he is indifferent to the question of whether it is with this volition or with some other that he wants his will to accord. The decisiveness of the commitment he has made means that he has decided that no further question about his second-order volition, at any higher order, remains to be asked. . . .

Examples such as the one concerning the unwilling addict may suggest that volitions of the second order, or of higher orders, must be formed deliberately and that a person characteristically struggles to ensure that they are satisfied. But the conformity of a person's will to his higher-order volitions may be far more thoughtless and spontaneous than this. Some people are naturally moved by kindness when they want to be kind, and by nastiness when they want to be nasty, without any explicit forethought and without any need for energetic self-control. Others are moved by nastiness when they want to be kind and by kindness when they intend to be nasty, equally without forethought and without active resistance to these violations of their higher-order desires. The enjoyment of freedom comes easily to some. Others must struggle to achieve it.

IV

My theory concerning the freedom of the will accounts easily for our disinclination to allow that this freedom is enjoyed by the members of any species inferior to our own. It also satisfies another condition that must be met by any such theory, by making it apparent why the freedom of the will should be regarded as desirable. The enjoyment of a free will means the satisfaction of certain desires—desires of the second or of higher orders—whereas its absence means their frustration. The satisfactions at stake are those which accrue to a person of whom it may be said that his will is his own. The corresponding frustrations are those suffered by a person of whom it may be said that he is estranged from himself, or that he finds himself a helpless or a passive bystander to the forces that move him.

A person who is free to do what he wants to do may yet not be in a position to have the will he wants. Suppose, however, that he enjoys both freedom of action and freedom of the will. Then he is not only free to do what he wants to do; he is also free to want what he wants to want. It seems to me that he has, in that case, all the freedom it is possible to desire or to conceive. There are other good things in life, and he may not possess some of them. But there is nothing in the way of freedom that he lacks.

It is far from clear that certain other theories of the freedom of the will meet these elementary but essential conditions: that it be understandable why we desire this freedom and why we refuse to ascribe it to animals. Consider, for example, Roderick Chisholm's quaint version of the doctrine that human freedom entails an absence of causal determination.[3] Whenever a person performs a free action, according to Chisholm, it's a miracle. The motion of a person's hand, when the person moves it, is the outcome of a series of physical causes; but some event in this series, "and presumably one of those that took place within the brain, was caused by the agent and not by any other events" (see Chisholm, p. 18). A free agent has, therefore, "a prerogative which some would attribute only to God: each of us, when we act, is a prime mover unmoved" (Chisholm, p. 23).

This account fails to provide any basis for doubting that animals of subhuman species enjoy the freedom it defines. Chisholm says nothing that makes it seem less likely that a rabbit performs a miracle when it moves its leg than that a man does so when he moves his hand. But why, in any case, should anyone *care* whether he can interrupt the natural order of causes in the way Chisholm describes? Chisholm offers no reason for believing that there is a discernible difference between the experience of a man who miraculously initiates a series of causes when he moves his hand and a man who moves his hand without any such breach of the normal causal sequence. There appears to be no concrete basis for preferring to be involved in the one state of affairs rather than in the other.

It is generally supposed that, in addition to satisfying the two conditions I have mentioned, a satisfactory theory of the freedom of the will necessarily provides an analysis of one of the conditions of moral responsibility. The most common recent approach to the problem of understanding the freedom of the will has been, indeed, to inquire what is entailed by the assumption that someone is morally responsible for what he has done. In my view, however, the relation between moral responsibility and the freedom of the will has been very widely misunderstood. It is not true that a person is morally responsible for what he has done only if his will was free when he did it. He may be morally responsible for having done it even though his will was not free at all.

A person's will is free only if he is free to have the will he wants. This means that, with regard to any of his first-order desires, he is free either to make that desire his will or to make some other first-order desire his will instead. Whatever his will, then, the will of the person whose will is free could have been otherwise; he could have done otherwise than to constitute his will as he did. It is a vexed question just how "he could have done otherwise" is to be understood in contexts such as this one.

---

3. Roderick Chisholm, "Freedom and Action," in K. Lehrer, ed., *Freedom and Determinism* (New York: Random House, 1966), 11–44. [Frankfurt's note.] Page citations in text refer to Chisholm's paper.

But although this question is important to the theory of freedom, it has no bearing on the theory of moral responsibility. For the assumption that a person is morally responsible for what he has done does not entail that the person was in a position to have whatever will he wanted.

This assumption *does* entail that the person did what he did freely, or that he did it of his own free will. It is a mistake, however, to believe that someone acts freely only when he is free to do whatever he wants or that he acts of his own free will only if his will is free. Suppose that a person has done what he wanted to do, that he did it because he wanted to do it, and that the will by which he was moved when he did it was his will because it was the will he wanted. Then he did it freely and of his own free will. Even supposing that he could have done otherwise, he would not have done otherwise; and even supposing that he could have had a different will, he would not have wanted his will to differ from what it was. Moreover, since the will that moved him when he acted was his will because he wanted it to be, he cannot claim that his will was forced upon him or that he was a passive bystander to its constitution. Under these conditions, it is quite irrelevant to the evaluation of his moral responsibility to inquire whether the alternatives that he opted against were actually available to him.[4]

In illustration, consider a third kind of addict. Suppose that his addiction has the same physiological basis and the same irresistible thrust as the addictions of the unwilling and wanton addicts, but that he is altogether delighted with his condition. He is a willing addict, who would not have things any other way. If the grip of his addiction should somehow weaken, he would do whatever he could to reinstate it; if his desire for the drug should begin to fade, he would take steps to renew its intensity.

The willing addict's will is not free, for his desire to take the drug will be effective regardless of whether or not he wants this desire to constitute his will. But when he takes the drug, he takes it freely and of his own free will. I am inclined to understand his situation as involving the overdetermination of his first-order desire to take the drug. This desire is his effective desire because he is physiologically addicted. But it is his effective desire also because he wants it to be. His will is outside his control, but, by his second-order desire that his desire for the drug should be effective, he has made this will his own. Given that it is therefore not only because of his addiction that his desire for the drug is effective, he may be morally responsible for taking the drug.

My conception of the freedom of the will appears to be neutral with regard to the problem of determinism. It seems conceivable that it should be causally determined that a person is free to want what he wants to want. If this is conceivable, then it might be causally determined that a person enjoys free will. There is no more than an innocuous appearance of paradox in the proposition that it is determined, ineluctably and by forces beyond their control, that certain people have free wills and that others do not. . . .

On the other hand, it seems conceivable that it should come about by chance that a person is free to have the will he wants. If this is conceivable, then it might be a

---

4. For another discussion of the considerations that cast doubt on the principle that a person is morally responsible for what he has done only if he could have done otherwise, see my "Alternate Possibilities and Moral Responsibility," *Journal of Philosophy* 66, 23 (December 4, 1969): 829–39. [Frankfurt's note.]

matter of chance that certain people enjoy freedom of the will and that certain others do not. Perhaps it is also conceivable, as a number of philosophers believe, for states of affairs to come about in a way other than by chance or as the outcome of a sequence of natural causes. If it is indeed conceivable for the relevant states of affairs to come about in some third way, then it is also possible that a person should in that third way come to enjoy the freedom of the will.

TEST YOUR UNDERSTANDING

1. Frankfurt distinguishes first-order desires from second-order desires. Illustrate the distinction.

2. Frankfurt uses the word "will" in a special way. Explain what he means.

3. According to Frankfurt, *X* is a person if and only if _____.

4. Frankfurt distinguishes "freedom of action" from "freedom of the will." Explain the distinction.

NOTES AND QUESTIONS

1. *Freedom and duress.* Someone puts a gun to your head and says "Your money or your life," so you hand over your wallet. Many philosophers take this to be a clear case of unfree action. (See Ayer's "Freedom and Necessity" in this chapter.) But Frankfurt classifies this action as free. When you hand over your wallet, the desire you act on is the desire you want to act on; therefore, your act is in accord with your second-order volition—so you act freely.

   Question: Is this an objection to Frankfurt's view? If not, why not? If so, how might the view be modified as to avoid it?

2. *Implanted desires.* Andrea and Brenda both cheat on their philosophy exam when they know they shouldn't. Both desire to cheat and both desire to act on this desire, but there is a difference:

   > Andrea is an ordinary cheater. She's been cheating since kindergarten and does it whenever she can get away with it.

   > Brenda has never cheated before, but this morning she participated in a psychology experiment in which, unbeknownst to her, a powerful desire to cheat and a desire to act on this desire were implanted in her by hypnosis. Brenda is surprised by her impulse to cheat, but the impulse is strong, and so she acts on it.

Question: According to Frankfurt, does Brenda exercise free will? If so, is this a problem for his view? How might the view be modified to avoid this problem?

3. *Compulsive action.* Frankfurt's account is designed to explain why certain kinds of "compulsive" actions are not free. The unwilling addict is moved by a powerful desire to take the drug, but he opposes this desire—he does not want it to move him. If it moves him anyway, his act is not free according to Frankfurt, and that seems right.

However, many compulsive actions are not like this. Consider the verbal tics associated with Tourette Syndrome. People with Tourette feel powerful impulses (first-order desires) to make strange sounds. They can suppress these impulses for a time, but exercising this self-control is painful. As the pain increases, their second-order desires may change. At the last minute, they may come to want to act on their impulse to vocalize so as to relieve the pain.

Question: Does Frankfurt classify this sort of compulsive action as free? If so, how might the account be modified to avoid this implausible consequence?

Susan Wolf (b. 1952)

Wolf, the Edna J. Koury Professor of Philosophy at the University of North Carolina, Chapel Hill, works mainly in ethics and moral psychology. Her most recent book is *Meaning in Life and Why It Matters* (2010).

SANITY AND THE METAPHYSICS OF RESPONSIBILITY

. . . In everyday contexts, when lawyers, judges, parents, and others are concerned with issues of responsibility, they know, or think they know, what in general the conditions of responsibility are. Their questions are questions of application: . . . Is this person mature enough, or informed enough, or sane enough to be responsible? Was he or she acting under posthypnotic suggestion or under the influence of a mind-impairing drug? It is assumed, in these contexts, that normal fully developed adult human beings are responsible beings. The questions have to do with whether a given individual falls within the normal range.

By contrast, philosophers tend to be uncertain about the general conditions of responsibility and they care less about dividing the responsible from the nonresponsible agents than about determining whether, and if so why, any of us are ever responsible for anything at all.

In the classroom, we might argue that the philosophical concerns grow out of the nonphilosophical ones, that they take off where the nonphilosophical questions stop. In this way we might convince our students that even if they are not plagued by the philosophical worries, they ought to be. If they worry about whether a person is mature enough, informed enough, and sane enough to be responsible, then they should worry about whether that person is metaphysically free enough, too.

The argument I make here, however, goes in the opposite direction. My aim is not to convince people who are interested in the apparently nonphilosophical conditions of responsibility that they should go on to worry about the philosophical conditions as well, but rather to urge those who already worry about the philosophical problems not to leave the more mundane, prephilosophical problems behind. In particular, I suggest that the mundane recognition that *sanity* is a condition of responsibility has more to do with the murky and apparently metaphysical problems which surround the issue of responsibility than at first meets the eye. Once the significance of the condition of sanity is fully appreciated, at least some of the apparently insuperable metaphysical aspects of the problem of responsibility will dissolve.

My strategy is to examine a recent trend in philosophical discussions of responsibility, a trend that tries, but I think ultimately fails, to give an acceptable analysis of the conditions of responsibility. It fails due to what at first appear to be deep and irresolvable metaphysical problems. It is here that I suggest that the condition of sanity comes to the rescue. What at first appears to be an impossible requirement for responsibility—the requirement that the responsible agent have created herself or himself—turns out to be the vastly more mundane and noncontroversial requirement that the responsible agent must, in a fairly standard sense, be sane.

Frankfurt [and] Watson . . .

The trend I have in mind is exemplified by the writings of Harry Frankfurt and Gary Watson. . . . I will briefly discuss . . . their separate proposals, and then offer a composite view that, while lacking the subtlety of any of the separate accounts, will highlight some important insights and some important blind spots they share.

In his seminal article "Freedom of the Will and the Concept of a Person,"[1] Harry Frankfurt notes a distinction between freedom of action and freedom of the will. A person has freedom of action, he points out, if she (or he) has the freedom to do whatever she wills to do—the freedom to walk or sit, to vote liberal or conservative, to publish a book or open a store, in accordance with her strongest desires. Even a person who has freedom of action may fail to be responsible for her actions, however, if the wants or desires she has the freedom to convert into action are themselves not subject to her control. Thus, the person who acts under posthypnotic suggestion, the victim of brainwashing, and the kleptomaniac might all possess freedom of action. In the standard contexts in which these examples are raised, it is assumed that none of the individuals is locked up or bound. Rather, these individuals are understood to act on what, at one level at least, must be called *their own desires*. Their exemption from responsibility stems from the fact that their own desires (or at least the ones governing their actions) are not up to them.

1. Harry Frankfurt, "Freedom of the Will and the Concept of a Person." *Journal of Philosophy* LXVIII (1971): 5–20. [Wolf's note.]

These cases may be described in Frankfurt's terms as cases of people who possess freedom of action, but who fail to be responsible agents because they lack freedom of the will.

Philosophical problems about the conditions of responsibility naturally focus on an analysis of this latter kind of freedom: What *is* freedom of the will, and under what conditions can we reasonably be thought to possess it? Frankfurt's proposal is to understand freedom of the will by analogy to freedom of action. As freedom of action is the freedom to do whatever one wills to do, freedom of the will is the freedom to will whatever one wants to will. To make this point clearer, Frankfurt introduces a distinction between first-order and second-order desires. First-order desires are desires to do or to have various things; second-order desires are desires about what desires to have or what desires to make effective in action. In order for an agent to have both freedom of action and freedom of the will, that agent must be capable of governing his or her actions by first-order desires *and* capable of governing his or her first-order desires by second-order desires.

Gary Watson's view of free agency[2] . . . is similar to Frankfurt's in holding that an agent is responsible for an action only if the desires expressed by that action are of a particular kind. While Frankfurt identifies the right kind of desires as desires that are supported by second-order desires, however, Watson draws a distinction between "mere" desires, so to speak, and desires that are *values*. According to Watson, the difference between free action and unfree action cannot be analyzed by reference to the logical form of the desires from which these various actions arise, but rather must relate to a difference in the quality of their source. Whereas some of my desires are just appetites or conditioned responses I find myself "stuck with," others are expressions of judgments on my part that the objects I desire are good. Insofar as my actions can be governed by the latter type of desires—governed, that is, by my values or valuational system—they are actions that I perform freely and for which I am responsible. . . .

Although there are subtle and interesting differences among the accounts of Frankfurt and Watson . . . , my concern is with features of their views that are common to them. [Both] share the idea that responsible agency involves something more than intentional agency. Both agree that if we are responsible agents, it is not just because our actions are within the control of our wills, but because, in addition, our wills are not just psychological states *in* us, but expressions of characters that come *from* us, or that at any rate are acknowledged and affirmed *by* us. For Frankfurt, this means that our wills must be ruled by our second-order desires; for Watson, that our wills must be governable by our system of values. . . . In one way or another, . . . these philosophers seem to be saying that the key to responsibility lies in the fact that responsible agents are those for whom it is not just the case that their actions are within the control of their wills, but also the case that their wills are within the control of their *selves* in some deeper sense. Because, at one level, the differences among Frankfurt [and] Watson . . . may be understood as differences in the analysis or interpretation of what it is for an action to be under the control of this deeper self, we may speak of their . . . positions as variations of one basic view about responsibility: the *deep-self view*.

---

2. Gary Watson, "Free Agency," *Journal of Philosophy* LXXII (1975): 205–20. [Wolf's note.]

The Deep-Self View

... [T]his view explains a good portion of our pretheoretical intuitions about responsibility. It explains why kleptomaniacs, victims of brainwashing, and people acting under posthypnotic suggestion may not be responsible for their actions, although most of us typically are. In the cases of people in these special categories, the connection between the agents' deep selves and their wills is dramatically severed—their wills are governed not by their deep selves, but by forces external to and independent from them. A different intuition is that we adult human beings can be responsible for our actions in a way that dumb animals, infants, and machines cannot. Here the explanation is not in terms of a split between these beings' deep selves and their wills: rather, the point is that these beings *lack* deep selves altogether. Kleptomaniacs and victims of hypnosis exemplify individuals whose selves are *alienated* from their actions: lower animals and machines, on the other hand, do not have the sorts of selves from which actions *can* be alienated. and so they do not have the sort of selves from which, in the happier cases, actions can responsibly flow.

At a more theoretical level, the deep-self view has another virtue: It responds to at least one way in which the fear of determinism presents itself.

A naive reaction to the idea that everything we do is completely determined by a causal chain that extends backward beyond the times of our births involves thinking that in that case we would have no control over our behavior whatsoever. If everything is determined, it is thought, then what happens happens, whether we want it to or not. A common, and proper, response to this concern points out that determinism does not deny the causal efficacy an agent's desires might have on his or her behavior. On the contrary, determinism in its more plausible forms tends to affirm this connection, merely adding that as one's behavior is determined by one's desires, so one's desires are determined by something else.[3]

Those who were initially worried that determinism implied fatalism,[4] however, are apt to find their fears merely transformed rather than erased. If our desires are governed by something else, they might say, they are not *really* ours after all—or, at any rate, they are ours in only a superficial sense.

The deep-self view offers an answer to this transformed fear of determinism, for it allows us to distinguish cases in which desires are determined by forces foreign to oneself from desires which are determined *by* one's self—by one's "real," or second-order desiring, or valuing, or deep self, that is. Admittedly, there are cases, like that of

---

3. See, for example, David Hume, *A Treatise of Human Nature* (Oxford University Press, 1967), 399–406, and R.E. Hobart, "Free Will as Involving Determination and Inconceivable Without It," *Mind* 43 (1943). [Wolf's note.]

4. **Fatalism** is the view that (certain important) future events will occur regardless of what we do. **Determinism** is the view that the state of the world at any given time and the laws of nature determine the state of the world at all future times. It is sometimes said that determinism entails fatalism, but it does not. Even if we inhabit a clockwork universe in which the moment of your birth was fixed by the state of the universe a billion years ago together with the laws of nature, it does not follow that you would have been born just then *no matter what anyone had done*. Even if the universe is deterministic, it can be true that if your parents had never met, you would not have been born.

the kleptomaniac or the victim of hypnosis, in which the agent acts on desires that "belong to" him or her in only a superficial sense. But the proponent of the deep-self view will point out that even if determinism is true, ordinary adult human action can be distinguished from this. Determinism implies that the desires which govern our actions are in turn governed by something else, but that something else will, in the fortunate cases, be our own deeper selves.

This account of responsibility thus offers a response to our fear of determinism: but it is a response with which many will remain unsatisfied. Even if my actions are governed by my desires and my desires are governed by my own deeper self, there remains the question: Who, or what, is responsible for this deeper self? The response above seems only to have pushed the problem further back.

Admittedly, some versions of the deep-self view, including Frankfurt's . . . , seem to anticipate this question by providing a place for the ideal that an agent's deep self may be governed by a still deeper self. Thus, for Frankfurt, second-order desires may themselves be governed by third-order desires, third-order desires by fourth-order desires, and so on.[5] . . . However, this capacity to recursively create endless levels of depth ultimately misses the criticism's point.

First of all, even if there is no *logical* limit to the number of levels of reflection or depth a person may have, there is certainly a psychological limit—it is virtually impossible imaginatively to conceive a fourth- much less an eighth-order desire. More important, no matter how many levels of self we posit, there will still, in any individual case, be a last level—a deepest self about whom the question "What governs it?" will arise, as problematic as ever. If determinism is true, it implies that even if my actions are governed by my desires, and my desires are governed by my deepest self, my deepest self will still be governed by something that must, logically, be external to myself altogether. . . .

The problem seems even worse when one sees that one fares no better if determinism is false. For if my deepest self is not determined by something, external to myself, it will still not be determined by *me*. Whether I am a product of carefully controlled forces or a result of random mutations, whether there is a complete explanation of my origin or no explanation at all, *I* am not, in any case, responsible for my existence; I am not in control of my deepest self.

Thus, though the claim that an agent is responsible for only those actions that are within the control of his or her deep self correctly identifies a necessary condition for responsibility—a condition that separates the hypnotized and the brainwashed, the immature and the lower animals from ourselves, for example—it fails to provide a sufficient condition of responsibility that puts all fears of determinism to rest. For one of the fears invoked by the thought of determinism seems to be connected to its implication that we are but intermediate links in a causal chain, rather than ultimate, self-initiating sources of movement and change. From the point of view of one who

5. A *second-order desire* is a desire to have, or to act upon, a certain ordinary first-order desire. A *third-order* desire is a desire to have a certain second-order desire. For example, your desire to read this essay is a first-order desire; your desire to act on this desire is a second-order desire; and your desire to retain this second-order desire is a third-order desire.

has this fear, the deep-self view seems merely to add loops to the chain, complicating the picture but not really improving it. . . .

At this point, however, proponents of the deep-self view may wonder whether this fear is legitimate. For although people evidently can be brought to the point where they feel that responsible agency requires them to be ultimate sources of power, to the point where it seems that nothing short of self-creation will do, a return to the internal standpoint of the agent whose responsibility is in question makes it hard to see what good this metaphysical status is supposed to provide or what evil its absence is supposed to impose.

From the external standpoint . . . , it may appear that a special metaphysical status is required to distinguish us significantly from other members of the natural world. But proponents of the deep-self view will suggest this is an illusion that a return to the internal standpoint should dispel. The possession of a deep self that is effective in governing one's actions is a sufficient distinction, they will say. For while other members of the natural world are not in control of the selves that they are, we, possessors of effective deep selves, are in control. We can reflect on what sorts of beings we are, and on what sorts of marks we make on the world. We can change what we don't like about ourselves, and keep what we do. Admittedly, we do not create ourselves from nothing. But as long as we can revise ourselves, they will suggest, it is hard to find reason to complain. Harry Frankfurt writes that a person who is free to do what he wants to do and also free to want what he wants to want has "all the freedom it is possible to desire or to conceive."[6] This suggests a rhetorical question: If you are free to control your actions by your desires, and free to control your desires by your deeper desires, and free to control those desires by still deeper desires, what further kind of freedom can you want?

The Condition of Sanity

Unfortunately, there is a further kind of freedom we can want, which it is reasonable to think necessary for responsible agency. The deep-self view fails to be convincing when it is offered as a complete account of the conditions of responsibility. To see why, it will be helpful to consider another example of an agent whose responsibility is in question.

JoJo is the favorite son of Jo the First, an evil and sadistic dictator of a small . . . country. Because of his father's special feelings for the boy, JoJo is given a special education and is allowed to accompany his father and observe his daily routine. In light of this treatment, it is not surprising that little JoJo takes his father as a role model and develops values very much like Dad's. As an adult, he does many of the same sorts of things his father did, including sending people to prison or to death or to torture chambers on the basis of whim. He is not *coerced* to do these things; he acts according to his own desires. Moreover, these are desires he wholly *wants* to have. When he steps back and

---

6. Frankfurt, p. 16. [Wolf's note.]

asks, "Do I really want to be this sort of person?" his answer is resoundingly "Yes," for this way of life expresses a crazy sort of power that forms part of his deepest ideal.

In light of JoJo's heritage and upbringing—both of which he was powerless to control—it is dubious at best that he should be regarded as responsible for what he does. It is unclear whether anyone with a childhood such as his could have developed into anything but the twisted and perverse sort of person that he has become. However, note that JoJo is someone whose actions are controlled by his desires and whose desires are the desires he wants to have: That is, his actions are governed by desires that are governed by and expressive of his deepest self.

The Frankfurt–Watson . . . strategy that allowed us to differentiate our normal selves from the victims of hypnosis and brainwashing will not allow us to differentiate ourselves from the son of Jo the First. In the case of these earlier victims, we were able to say that although the actions of these individuals were, at one level, in control of the individuals themselves, these individuals themselves . . . were not the selves they more deeply wanted to be. In this respect, these people were unlike our happily more integrated selves. However, we cannot say of JoJo that his self . . . is not the self he wants it to be. It *is* the self he wants it to be. From the inside, he feels as integrated, free, and responsible as we do.

Our judgment that JoJo is not a responsible agent is one that we can make only from the outside—from reflecting on the fact, it seems, that his deepest self is not up to him. Looked at from the outside, however, our situation seems no different from his—for in the last analysis, it is not up to any of us to have the deepest selves we do. Once more, the problem seems metaphysical—and not just metaphysical, but insuperable. For, as I mentioned before, the problem is independent of the truth of determinism. Whether we are determined or undetermined, we cannot have created our deepest selves. . . .

If JoJo is not responsible because his deepest self is not up to him, then we are not responsible either. Indeed, in that case responsibility would be impossible for anyone to achieve. But I believe the appearance that literal self-creation is required for freedom and responsibility is itself mistaken.

The deep-self view was right in pointing out that freedom and responsibility require us to have certain distinctive types of control over our behavior and our selves. Specifically, our actions need to be under the control of our selves, and our (superficial) selves need to be under the control of our deep selves. Having seen that these types of control are not enough to guarantee us the status of responsible agents, we are tempted to go on to suppose that we must have yet another kind of control to assure us that even our deepest selves are somehow up to us. But not all the things necessary for freedom and responsibility must be types of power and control. We may need simply to *be* a certain way, even though it is not within our power to determine whether we are that way or not.

Indeed, it becomes obvious that at least one condition of responsibility is of this form as soon as we remember what, in everyday contexts, we have known all along—namely, that in order to be responsible, an agent must be *sane*. It is not ordinarily in our power to determine whether we are or are not sane. Most of us, it would seem, are lucky, but some of us are not. Moreover, being sane does not necessarily mean that one has any type of power or control an insane person lacks. Some insane people, like JoJo and some actual political leaders who resemble him, may have complete control of their actions, and even complete control of their acting selves. The desire to be sane is thus not a desire for another form of control; it is rather a desire that one's self be connected to the world in a certain way—we could even say it is a desire that one's self be *controlled by* the world in certain ways and not in others.

This becomes clear if we attend to the criteria for sanity that have historically been dominant in legal questions about responsibility. According to the M'Naghten Rule,[7] a person is sane if (1) he knows what he is doing and (2) he knows that what he is doing is, as the case may be, right or wrong. Insofar as one's desire to be sane involves a desire to know what one is doing—or more generally a desire to live in the real world—it is a desire to be controlled (to have, in this case, one's *beliefs* controlled) by perceptions and sound reasoning that produce an accurate conception of the world, rather than by blind or distorted forms of response. The same goes for the second constituent of sanity—only, in this case, one's hope is that one's *values* be controlled by processes that afford an accurate conception of the world.[8] Putting these two conditions together, we may understand sanity, then, as the minimally sufficient ability cognitively and normatively to recognize and appreciate the world for what it is.[9] . . .

The Sane Deep-Self View

. . . I now wish to argue [that] . . . deep-self view, supplemented by the condition of sanity, provides a satisfying conception of responsibility. The conception of responsibility I am proposing . . . agrees with the deep-self view in requiring that a responsible agent be able to govern her (or his) actions by her desires and to govern her desires by her deep self. In addition, my conception insists that the agent's deep self be sane, and claims that this is *all* that is needed for responsible agency. By contrast to the plain deep-self view, let us call this new proposal *the sane deep-self view*.

It is worth noting, to begin with, that this new proposal deals with the case of JoJo and related cases of deprived childhood victims in ways that better match our pretheoretical intuitions. Unlike the plain deep-self view, the sane deep-self view offers a way of explaining why JoJo is not responsible for his actions without throwing our own

---

7. The so-called M'Naghten Rule is a widely adopted legal test for insanity originally propounded by the British House of Lords in 1843.

8. Wolf distinguishes *cognitive* abilities from *normative* abilities. The former include the ability to know the ordinary facts about one's circumstances: for example, that the object in one's hand is a gun, that shooting people tends to kill them, and so on. The latter include the ability to know what one has reason to do, what it would be right to do, and so on. Someone can possess the cognitive ability to know what will happen if he shoots a gun while lacking the normative ability to know that it's wrong to kill.

9. Strictly speaking, perception and sound reasoning may not be enough to ensure the ability to achieve an accurate conception of what one is doing and especially to achieve a reasonable normative assessment of one's situation. Sensitivity and exposure to certain realms of experience may also be necessary for these goals. For the purpose of this essay, I understand "sanity" to include whatever it takes to enable one to develop an adequate conception of one's world. In other contexts, however, this would be an implausibly broad construction of the term. [Wolf's note.]

responsibility into doubt. For, although like us, JoJo's actions flow from desires that flow from his deep self, unlike us, Jo Jo's deep self is itself insane. Sanity, remember, involves the ability to know the difference between right and wrong, and a person who, even on reflection, cannot see that having someone tortured because he failed to salute you is wrong plainly lacks the requisite ability.

Less obviously, but quite analogously, this new proposal explains why we give less than full responsibility to persons who, though acting badly, act in ways that are strongly encouraged by their societies—the slave owners of the 1850s, the Nazis of the 1930s, and many male chauvinists of our fathers' generation, for example. These are people, we imagine, who falsely believe that the ways in which they are acting are morally acceptable, and so, we may assume, their behavior is expressive of or at least in accordance with these agents' deep selves. But their false beliefs in the moral permissibility of their actions and the false values from which these beliefs derived may have been inevitable, given the social circumstances in which they developed. If we think that the agents could not help but be mistaken about their values, we do not blame them for the actions those values inspired.

It would unduly distort ordinary linguistic practice to call the slave owner, the Nazi, or the male chauvinist even partially or locally insane. Nonetheless, the reason for withholding blame from them is at bottom the same as the reason for withholding it from JoJo. Like JoJo, they are, at the deepest level, unable cognitively and normatively to recognize and appreciate the world for what it is. In our sense of the term, their deepest selves are not fully *sane*.

The sane deep-self view thus offers an account of why victims of deprived child-hoods as well as victims of misguided societies may not be responsible for their actions, without implying that we are not responsible for ours. The actions of these others are governed by mistaken conceptions of value that the agents in question cannot help but have. Since, as far as we know, our values are not, like theirs, unavoidably mistaken, the fact that these others are not responsible for their actions need not force us to conclude that we are not responsible for ours.

But it may not yet be clear why sanity, in this special sense, should make such a dif-ference—why, in particular, the question of whether someone's values are unavoidably *mistaken* should have any bearing on their status as responsible agents. . . .

Earlier, it seemed that the reason JoJo was not responsible for his actions was that although his actions were governed by his deep self, his deep self was not up to him. But this had nothing to do with his deep self's being mistaken or not mistaken, evil or good, insane or sane. If JoJo's values are unavoidably mistaken, our values, even if not mistaken, appear to be just as unavoidable. When it comes to freedom and responsibility, isn't it the unavoidability, rather than the mistakenness, that matters?

Before answering this question, it is useful to point out a way in which it is ambig-uous: The concepts of avoidability and mistakenness are not unequivocally distinct. One may, to be sure, construe the notion of avoidability in a purely metaphysical way. Whether an event or state of affairs is unavoidable under this construal depends, as it were, on the tightness of the causal connections that bear on the event's or state of affairs' coming about. In this sense, our deep selves do seem as unavoidable for us as JoJo's and the others' are for them, For presumably we are just as influenced by our parents, our cultures, and our schooling as they are influenced by theirs. In another sense, however our characters are not similarly unavoidable.

In particular, in the cases of JoJo and the others, there are certain features of their characters that they cannot avoid *even though these features are seriously mistaken, misguided, or bad.* This is so because, in our special sense of the term, these characters are less than fully sane. Since these characters lack the ability to know right from wrong, they are unable to revise their characters on the basis of right and wrong, and so their deep selves lack the resources and the reasons that might have served as a basis for self-correction. Since the deep selves *we* unavoidably have, however, are sane deep selves—deep selves, that is, that unavoidably *contain* the ability to know right from wrong—we unavoidably do have the resources and reasons on which to base self-correction. What this means is that though in one sense we are no more in control of our deepest selves than JoJo et al., it does not follow in our case, as it does in theirs, that we would be the way we are, even if it is a bad or wrong way to be. However, if this does not follow, it seems to me, our absence of control at the deepest level should not upset us.

Consider what the absence of control at the deepest level amounts to for us: Whereas JoJo is unable to control the fact that, at the deepest level, he is not fully sane, we are not responsible for the fact that, at the deepest level, we are. It is not up to us to *have* minimally sufficient abilities cognitively and normatively to recognize and appreciate the world for what it is. Also, presumably, it is not up to us to have lots of other properties, at least to begin with—a fondness for purple, perhaps, or an antipathy for beets. As the proponents of the plain deep-self view have been at pains to point out, however, we do, if we are lucky, have the ability to revise our selves in terms of the values that are held by or constitutive of our deep selves. If we are lucky enough both to have this ability and to have our deep selves be sane, it follows that although there is much in our characters that we did not choose to have, there is nothing irrational or objectionable in our characters that we are compelled to keep. . . .

Self-Creation, Self-Revision, and Self-Correction

At the beginning of this chapter, I claimed that recalling that sanity was a condition of responsibility would dissolve at least some of the appearance that responsibility was metaphysically impossible. To see how this is so, and to get a fuller sense of the sane deep-self view, it may be helpful to put that view into perspective by comparing it to the other views we have discussed along the way.

As Frankfurt [and] Watson . . . showed us, in order to be free and responsible we need not only to be able to control our actions in accordance with our desires, we need to be able to control our desires in accordance with our deepest selves. We need, in other words, to be able to *revise* ourselves—to get rid of some desires and traits, and perhaps replace them with others on the basis of our deeper desires or values. . . . However, consideration of the fact that the selves who are doing the revising might themselves be either brute products of external forces or arbitrary outputs of random generation made us wonder whether the capacity for self-revision was enough to assure us of responsibility—and the example of JoJo added force to the suspicion that it was it was not. . . .

Recognizing that in order to be responsible for our actions, we have to be responsible for our selves, the sane deep-self view analyzes what is necessary in order to be responsible for our selves as (1) the ability to evaluate ourselves sensibly and accurately, and (2) the ability to transform ourselves insofar as our evaluation tells us to do so. We may understand the exercise of these abilities as a process where by we *take* responsibility for the selves that we are but did not ultimately create. The condition of sanity is intrinsically connected to the first ability; the condition that we be able to control our superficial selves by our deep selves is intrinsically connected to the second.

The difference between the plain deep-self view and the sane deep-self view, then, is the difference between the requirement of the capacity for self-revision and the requirement of the capacity for self-correction. Anyone with the first capacity can *try* to take responsibility for himself or herself. However, only someone with a sane deep self—a deep self that can see and appreciate the world for what it is—can self-evaluate sensibly and accurately. Therefore, although insane selves can try to take responsibility for themselves, only sane selves will properly be accorded responsibility.

Two Objections Considered

At least two problems with sane deep-self view are so glaring as to have certainly struck many readers. . . . First, some will be wondering how, in light of my specialized use of the term "sanity," I can be so sure that "we" are any saner than the nonresponsible individuals I have discussed. What justifies my confidence that, unlike the slave owners, Nazis, and male chauvinists, not to mention JoJo himself, we are able to understand and appreciate the world for what it is? The answer to this is that nothing justifies this except widespread intersubjective agreement and the considerable success we have in getting around in the world and satisfying our needs. These are not sufficient grounds for the smug assumption that we are in a position to see the truth about *all* aspects of ethical and social life. Indeed, it seems more reasonable to expect that time will reveal blind spots in our cognitive and normative outlook, just as it has revealed errors in the outlooks of those who have lived before. But our judgments of responsibility can only be made from here, on the basis of the understandings and values that we can develop by exercising the abilities we do possess as well and as fully as possible.

If some have been worried that my view implicitly expresses an overconfidence in the assumption that we are sane and therefore right about the world, others will be worried that my view too closely connects sanity with being right about the world, and fear that my view implies that anyone who acts wrongly or has false beliefs about the world is therefore insane and so not responsible for his or her actions. This seems to me to be a more serious worry, which I am sure I cannot answer to everyone's satisfaction.

First, it must be admitted that the sane deep-self view embraces a conception of sanity that is explicitly normative. But this seems to me a strength of that view, rather than a defect. Sanity *is* a normative concept . . . and severely deviant behavior, such as that of a serial murderer or a sadistic dictator, does constitute evidence of a psychological defect in the agent. The suggestion that the most horrendous, stomach-turning crimes could be committed only by an insane person . . . must be regarded as a serious possibility, despite the practical problems that would accompany general acceptance of that conclusion.

But, it will be objected, there is no justification, in the sane deep-self view, for regarding only horrendous and stomach-turning crimes as evidence of insanity in its specialized sense. If sanity is the ability cognitively and normatively to understand and appreciate the world for what it is, then *any* wrong action or false belief will count as evidence of the absence of that ability. This point may also be granted, but we must be careful about what conclusion to draw. To be sure, when someone acts in a way that is not in accordance with acceptable standards of rationality and reasonableness, it is always appropriate to look for an explanation of why he or she acted that way. The hypothesis that the person was unable to understand and appreciate that an action fell outside acceptable bounds will always be a possible explanation. Bad performance on a math test always suggests the possibility that the testee is stupid. Typically, however, other explanations will be possible, too—for example, that the agent was too lazy to consider whether his or her action was acceptable, or too greedy to care, or, in the case of the math testee, that he or she was too occupied with other interests to attend class or study. Other facts about the agent's history will help us decide among these hypotheses.

This brings out the need to emphasize that sanity in the specialized sense is defined as the *ability* cognitively and normatively to understand and appreciate the world for what it is. According to our commonsense understandings, having this ability is one thing and exercising it is another—at least some wrong-acting, responsible agents presumably fall within the gap. The notion of "ability" is notoriously problematic, however, and there is a long history of controversy about whether the truth of determinism would show our ordinary ways of thinking to be simply confused on this matter. At this point, then, metaphysical concerns may voice themselves again—but at least they will have been pushed into a narrower, and perhaps a more manageable, corner. . . .

TEST YOUR UNDERSTANDING

1. Wolf's target is a view she calls the Deep-Self View. Briefly state that view.

2. Wolf gives a counterexample to the Deep-Self View. Explain the example and say why it is a counterexample.

3. State Wolf's alternative to the Deep-Self View.

4. What is it for a person to be "sane," according to Wolf?

NOTES AND QUESTIONS

1. *Insanity and moral ignorance.* For Wolf, the difference between JoJo and the rest of us is that JoJo's moral beliefs are "unavoidably mistaken," whereas ours are mostly accurate. As Wolf notes, however, her characterization of JoJo applies equally to people we would not normally call "insane." Consider a nineteenth-century slave owner in the American South who believes that it is morally permissible to beat one's slaves. Like JoJo, he holds his beliefs because he was raised to hold them. Does Wolf's view imply that slaveholders who beat their slaves were not morally responsible for their actions? For discussion, see G. Rosen, "Culpability and Ignorance," *Proceedings of the Aristotelian Society*, 103, 1 (2002): 61–84, and Nomy Arpaly, "Why Moral Ignorance Is No Excuse," later in this chapter.

2. *The "ability" to know.* Consider an ordinary bad action:

   > Fred is an ordinary guy with an ordinary background. He needs money, so he steals $20 from the cash register at work. As far as he's concerned, there's nothing wrong with this. He works for a big company; he needs the money more than they do. So it's okay to steal, or so Fred thinks.

   As we ordinarily think, Fred is fully responsible for his action. And on the face of it, Wolf can agree. JoJo's horrific upbringing rendered him *incapable* of knowing right from wrong. Fred had an ordinary upbringing. True, Fred *did not* know right from wrong on this occasion. But surely he *could have* known, and in Wolf's view, that is enough to make him responsible.

   But look more closely. When we say that Fred had an ordinary upbringing, we mean that there was nothing *obvious* in his background that prevented him from knowing right from wrong, as there was in JoJo's. But for all we know, we live in a deterministic world. And if that is true, it was *inevitable*, given the details of Fred's upbringing, that he would wind up mistaken about right and wrong.

   With this in mind, consider the following argument:

   (1) JoJo is not responsible for his actions because he was incapable of knowing right from wrong.

   (2) To say that JoJo was "incapable" of knowing right from wrong is to say that factors beyond his control (his upbringing) ensured that he would not know right from wrong.

   (3) If determinism is true, then whenever anyone acts badly in the belief that his act is right, there were factors beyond his control that ensured he would not know right from wrong.

   (4) So if determinism is true, everyone who *doesn't* know right from wrong on some occasion was *incapable* of knowing right from wrong on that occasion.

   (5) So if determinism is true, anyone who acts badly in the belief that his act is right is not responsible for his actions.

   If Wolf is committed to accepting this argument, then her view entails that moral ignorance is always an excuse in a deterministic world.

   Exercise: Say how Wolf might avoid this conclusion.

Nomy Arpaly (b. 1973)

Arpaly, Professor of Philosophy at Brown University, specializes in moral philosophy, moral psychology, and action theory. Her books include *Unprincipled Virtue: An Inquiry into Moral Agency* (2002) and *Merit, Meaning, and Human Bondage: An Essay on Free Will* (2006).

WHY MORAL IGNORANCE IS NO EXCUSE

Many people believe that their actions are right, or at the very least that their actions are not wrong. Even Nazi war criminals often said that when they committed their crimes, they did not know that they were doing wrong. If a person does not know that she is doing wrong, is that a good excuse? Does her ignorance exempt her from blame? On one hand, it sounds reasonable to say that it does, because ignorance is often a good excuse. On the other hand, if a Nazi war criminal is not blameworthy, who is?

Imagine an ancient Roman who works in the circus. In homage to *Asterix,* we'll call him Gluteus Maximus. Gluteus Maximus works in the circus by choice. His job is to arrange for people to be tortured or to fight each other to the death. Gluteus Maximus enjoys watching people suffer, and his favorite thing is to watch Christians attacked by lions, so he arranges for Christians to be thrown to the lions regularly. He would not have done this if he thought he was doing wrong, but Gluteus Maximus is sure what he is doing is right. The crowd, after all, likes to watch Christians being killed by lions, and Gluteus Maximus thinks that using the suffering of people to provide entertainment to the people who come to the circus is not wrong—in fact it's the right thing to do.

Gluteus Maximus sounds like a scary person to be around, but is he blameworthy for throwing Christians to the lions? He does not, after all, know that doing so is wrong.

Quite often, "I didn't know" is an excellent excuse. Suppose I give someone a spoonful of what I reasonably believe to be sugar. The person puts some of it in her tea, drinks the tea, and drops dead immediately. Upon investigation, it turns out that some villain had replaced my sugar with poison that looks like sugar. In this case, it seems that I am not blameworthy for poisoning the poor woman, because I didn't know that I was giving her poison. My *ignorance* seems to be a good excuse. Gluteus Maximus also acts out of ignorance. If he knew that throwing Christians to the lions was wrong, he would have not done it, in the same way that if I knew the "sugar" was in fact poison, I would not have given it to anyone. He did not know it was wrong as nobody was around to tell him that it was. If being ignorant can excuse me from blame for the poisoning, why can't it excuse Gluteus Maximus from blame for throwing Christians to the lions?

There is one potentially important difference between the poisoning case and the case of Gluteus Maximus. When I mistake the poison for sugar, I make a *factual* error. I know that poisoning is wrong, but I don't know what chemical is in my sugar container. Gluteus Maximus need not be ignorant of any facts. He does not think, for example, that only through torturing Christians can he save a large number of people. He does not think Christians cannot feel pain. He knows exactly what he is doing and why. The only thing he does not know is that what he is doing is wrong. He is not ignorant about ordinary factual matters but rather about morality. He is *morally ignorant*. As we saw in the poisoning case, factual ignorance is at least sometimes an excellent excuse. The question is whether *moral ignorance* can be excusing in the same way as *factual ignorance*.

I don't think so, and to see this, we need to look not only at cases of bad actions for which one might be blameworthy but also at cases of good actions for which one might be praiseworthy. Factual ignorance not only excuses from blame, but it can also "excuse" from praiseworthiness. For example, suppose I buy a trinket at a store, and it turns out that the money from the sale of the trinket goes to charity. In this case, I give to charity, a type of action that is often praiseworthy and admirable, but I do not seem to deserve credit for my action, because I was ignorant of the fact that my money will be used for charitable purposes. Just as in the poisoning case, my factual ignorance makes the poisoning look accidental, so in the trinket case, my factual ignorance makes the charitable donation look accidental. Factual ignorance "cancels out" credit just like it does blame.

If that is true, and moral ignorance is excusing in the same way as factual ignorance, then moral ignorance should not only excuse Gluteus Maximus from blame because he doesn't know he does something bad. Rather, it should also "cancel out" the praiseworthiness of anyone who doesn't know she is doing good. Let us look at such a case.

Gottfried, a young and idealistic person, belongs to a cult that holds that it is always immoral to tell a lie, even to save a life. One day a stranger threatens Gottfried with a gun and asks him about the whereabouts of his roommate, Gottlieb. It seems clear that the stranger wants to kill Gottlieb. Gottfried believes that he should tell the stranger where Gottlieb is. This is, after all, what he takes to be the right thing to do. But when the moment comes, Gottfried finds himself unable to do it. He says "I don't know," when in fact he knows where Gottlieb is: somewhere hard to find. After the stranger leaves, Gottfried asks himself why he acted wrongly. "I realize it's immoral to tell a lie," he thinks, "but I just can't bear the thought of someone killing an innocent person because of me." He feels guilty about the lie he told, but he also feels greatly relieved. "I suppose I'm just not a moral guy," he thinks to himself. "I don't want to cause the death of an innocent person regardless of what morality says."

Gottfried, like Gluteus Maximus, is morally ignorant, but instead of mistaking wrong for right, he mistakes right for wrong. If we were to assume that moral ignorance is excusing in the same way as factual ignorance, we would have to say that Gottfried cannot be praiseworthy for effectively saving Gottlieb's life by telling the lie, because he does not know what he is doing is right. He would be analogous to a person—let's call her Gretchen—who tries to give someone sugar-like poison but accidentally gives her real sugar.

This, however, is not how we treat Gottfried. Gretchen, who tries to poison someone, seems like a bad person with bad intentions. Gottfried, however, seems in some respects like a good person—a person who cares about human lives and who is deeply averse to killing the innocent. So much does he care about preventing murder that even the weird views he got from his cult do not stop him from preventing a murder. When he refuses to tell the truth about Gottlieb, he does not seem like a person with bad intentions, the way that Gretchen does. He seems like a person who has good intentions: he intends to prevent murder. His motive for lying is good: he is motivated by a desire to prevent murder. He might think his motive is bad, but we know better. He is morally ignorant, but he still gets some credit for doing something good out of good motives. After all, an ethical person and a good ethicist are not always the same person.

The case of Gottfried is a simplified case. American literature provides us with more complicated cases that tend to lead us to the same conclusions. This is the case of Huck Finn, who helps a black slave escape despite believing, as the adults told him to believe, that one should never help a slave escape but rather turn him or her in. Huck helps Jim, the slave, even though he thinks that helping him is wrong. Again, if moral ignorance were like factual ignorance, Huck would have seemed like Gretchen: a bad person who luckily, out of ignorance, does good instead of harm. But this is not how Mark Twain and the majority of his readers think of Huck. Huck is basically a good boy. He helps Jim because, despite his racist education, he can't help but see Jim as a real person and friend. This, in itself, is a good thing about Huck. Seeing all people as people and seeing a friend of a different ethnicity the same way you see a friend of your own ethnicity are good things, even though Huck does not know they are good.

Let us go back to the case of Gluteus Maximus. If moral ignorance fails to cancel out the credit that Gottfried and Huck Finn deserve, how can it cancel out the blame that Gluteus Maximus deserves? That would seem inconsistent. Gluteus Maximus does something bad (torture people by throwing them to the lions) from a bad motive (he enjoys watching people suffer). The fact that he does not know that he is doing wrong does not cancel out the evil expressed in his actions, just as the good expressed in Gottfried's action is not canceled out by the fact that he thinks he is doing wrong. Moral ignorance, then, does not excuse.

There are a lot of people like Gluteus Maximus: they have the ordinary facts right, but they have a bad set of values, as when Gluteus Maximus thinks that it is okay to torture people as long as the people are members of conquered nations and torturing them amuses the Roman public. But what about cases in which it seems that a wrongdoer thinks she is doing right *because she gets some general facts wrong*? Does she have an excuse?

We started our query with the case of Nazi war criminals, so let us think of an anti-Semite. Suppose one believed all Jews were engaged in a global conspiracy to subjugate the world—a factual error—and only because of that error acted against Jewish people. In that way he is analogous to me when I give someone what I think is sugar but turns out to be poison. He had good intentions. The only difference between the poisoning case and the anti-Semite case seems to be that as the poisoner, I get a local fact wrong (the contents of the container labeled "sugar"), whereas the anti-Semite makes a more global error (concerning Jewish people). Other people who seem to make such errors are people with other prejudices: sexists who believe that women are stupid, racists who believe that African Americans are criminal at heart, and even violent parents who believe that beating children is good because it builds their character.

Does getting a "big" fact wrong exempt from blame? To be sure, sometimes it does. Imagine an alien recently arrived on Earth. In homage to *The Hitchhiker's Guide to the Galaxy*, we will call our alien Ford Raptor. On her home planet, Ford Raptor read in a normally reliable encyclopedia that East-Asian earthlings are a lot more intelligent than other earthlings. When Ford Raptor moves to an ethnically mixed neighborhood on earth, she prefers to hire or buy from people who look Asian and takes advice more seriously if it is given by a person who looks Asian. Ford Raptor seems to be a racist, but it seems plausible to say that "it's not her fault." She is simply *mistaken*. I, after all, believe that octopuses are more intelligent than squids because I have read it in a reputable book. Ford Raptor's reputable book happened to mislead her, which is unfortunate, but doesn't imply that Ford Raptor is morally deficient. If it turned out that I am wrong about the octopuses and the squids, it wouldn't imply a moral deficiency on my part either.

But Ford Raptor is a fictional alien, and we are concerned mostly with real cases from earth. Compare Ford Raptor to Steve, a normal and healthy adult human being who lives on twentieth-century (or even twenty-first-century) earth, and who is half-decently informed and educated but who still believes that all Jewish people are engaged in a worldwide conspiracy for world domination. Because of that, he performs actions against Jewish people, thinking it the right thing to do, because after all it is good to stop a conspiracy. Unlike Ford Raptor, Steve holds his racist beliefs despite a large pile of counterevidence. He knows, for example, that there are Jewish people who are poor or otherwise disadvantaged, which would seem unlikely if there was in fact a Jewish conspiracy. He has met Jewish people who look nothing like the sort of human that is cut out to pull off sophisticated deceptions. He knows how hard it would be to hide a conspiracy that involves millions of people. He knows that the theory that all Jews are involved in a conspiracy has been dismissed by experts. He knows all that, and still he has his crackpot beliefs. Unlike Ford Raptor, Steve is *irrational*. He is also a morally despicable person.

Is he morally despicable *because* he is irrational? Here one has to be careful, because some irrational people are morally alright. Consider Bella, who suffers from a severe mental disorder. During psychotic episodes, Bella thinks, among other things, that her mathematics professor is in fact the devil. She worries about the damage that he can do, disguised as an innocent math professor. Bella is, in this respect, irrational, but there is nothing morally wrong with her.

In fact, even if, during a psychotic episode, Bella attacks her professor as an attempt to protect the world from the devil, Bella will not be regarded as blameworthy. She would have an excuse—the excuse still known widely as "the insanity defense."

What, then, is the difference between Steve and Bella? Both are irrational, but only he is bad. The difference seems to be related to the source of their respective irrationalities. Bella's irrationality is widely considered to be due to a complex physical problem having to do with neurotransmitters in her brain. We have assumed that Steve is normal and healthy. What leads a normal, healthy person of average intelligence to believe bad things about Jewish people that are regularly contradicted by the evidence around him? One possible answer is that he hates them so much that he is disposed to believe anything about them as long as it is bad. His irrationality is caused by a strong emotion, and the strong emotion is hatred. If one hates someone very much, it is often easy for one to believe all kinds of bad things that people say about the person in question, even things that one would normally find reasons to doubt. Steve, like many other racists, hates some people so much that he is capable of believing even very tall tales about them. Hating people because they are different from you is morally bad, and it's the hatred, not the beliefs, that make Steve a bad person. Another possibility is that Steve likes to believe in a Jewish conspiracy because scapegoating makes him feel better. He can tell himself, for example, that the reason he keeps getting turned down for jobs is not because he is untalented or that the world is full of bad luck, but rather because all potential employers are affected by the conspiracy. In this case, too, something seems wrong with Steve's motives. If he cared enough about his fellow human beings—all his fellow human beings—as good people do, he would not have selfishly rushed to accept, despite evidence, a view that is harmful to some of them just because that view makes him feel good. What seems so sinister about Steve is, again, not so much what he happens to believe but the motivation—in this case, his lack of concern for his fellow humans—that made his prejudice possible.

So moral ignorance, as in the case of Gluteus Maximus, does not exempt one from blame, and factual ignorance exempts one from blame if it is an honest mistake but not if it is badly motivated.

I have left until the end what I regard as the hardest question on this topic. Imagine a wrongdoer who is not only morally ignorant but who also performs her action solely *because* she thinks it would be right. Imagine Gluteus Maximus's brother, Doofus, strongly believes that it is his duty as a soldier of the Roman Empire to conquer, pillage, and rape, and he is devoted to his "duty" to the point of risking his life regularly. Does his dutifulness speak in his favor at all?

Some have sympathy for people who have a radically false view as to what the right thing to do is and who try, even at a cost to themselves, to do what they think is right. After all, "at least they believe in something." At least they have something they care about other than their own well-being. While they can be blameworthy for doing the bad things they do, at least they get the consolation of having "a conscience," misguided though it is. I disagree. If a person's idea of morality is so different from what the accurate idea of morality would be that she thinks the moral thing to do is whatever it takes to help Romans rule the world and destroy other nations, then there is nothing particularly good about the fact that she is attracted to what she thinks of as morality. She would be a better person if, instead of a life of magnificent devotion to the sinister goals of the Roman soldier, she had an ordinary human life with nothing angelic about it but nothing satanic either. I do not have the space in this essay to argue fully for this view, but to get a sense of what I mean, consider the case of Martin Heidegger.

Heidegger (1889–1976) was a German philosopher who collaborated extensively with the Nazi government. Since the end of the Nazi era, some of Heidegger's fans have deeply wished for it to be found that he was mostly just another person who collaborated with the Nazis because the Nazis gave him status and money. By now, however, it is widely known that Heidegger was a devoted ideological Nazi.[1] This is upsetting to many fans.

---

1 . That Heidegger was an enthusiastic Nazi before the Nazis came to power and refused to express remorse after the war has been acknowledged for a long time by biographers, but the dramatic extent of his life-long anti-Semitism has recently been revealed through the publication of his so-called Black Notebooks. See Ingo Farin and Jeff Malpas, *Reading Heidegger's Black Notebooks* (MIT Press, 2016).

A Heidegger who was selfish—who simply wanted, too much, the advancement of the interests of a man named Martin Heidegger—would have been easier for them to deal with than a Heidegger who honestly wanted the Nazi project to succeed. One's own well-being is something that is possible for a person to prioritize too highly over other things; on its own, there is *nothing* wrong with wanting one's own happiness. There *is* something wrong with wanting the deaths of innocent people because of their ethnicity, even a little bit, even if one categorizes killing these people as "the right thing to do."

As a teenager, I went to a bad school in which class periods nominally devoted to literature were often used to teach nonsense. As a result, my fellow students became convinced, quite reasonably, that literature was nonsense. Given that, it would make perfect sense for them to avoid anything labeled "literature" and to say "if this is what literature is, I'm just not a literature kind of person." Similarly, if a person's school teaches her that morality is about killing people who are different from you or some other awful thing, and if she is a good person, it would make sense for her to dislike anything labeled "morality." She would say, "If killing innocent people is what morality requires of me, I suppose I am just not a moral person"; a bit like the country singer who sings, "If loving you is wrong/I don't want to be right." There are some things, such as killing innocent people, to which a true moral person would be averse, and she would be averse to them even if they were offered to her with the label "right" attached.

A person has good taste in music if and only if she generally likes *good music*. Nobody gets points toward a good taste in music simply because she likes music that she *believes to be good*; some people with terrible taste like music that they *believe to be good*. Similarly, a person who is morally good is averse to bad things and wants to do good things—whether that person wants to do things that he or she *believes to be good* is no big deal. After all, even Nazi war criminals did *that*.

Moral ignorance is no excuse for immoral action. One can be blameworthy for doing something wrong even though one believes it to be right. Factual ignorance, in contrast, is often a perfectly good excuse. However, when people get the facts wrong despite good evidence in a way that makes them do bad things, it is often the case that they are not simply mistaken but rather believe what they want to believe, or what their unsavory emotions make them believe, in which case they, too, have no excuse for their bad actions.

TEST YOUR UNDERSTANDING

1. What does Arpaly mean by "moral ignorance"?

2. True or false: Arpaly holds that ignorance is never an excuse.

3. In Arpaly's example, Gottfried believes that it is always wrong to lie but lies anyway in order save his roommate's life. Briefly restate the point of this example.

4. In Arpaly's example, Steve believes that Jews are part of a conspiracy for world domination and performs an anti-Semitic act as a result. Is he morally blameworthy in Arpaly's view, and if so, why?

NOTES AND QUESTIONS

1. *Praise, blame, and character.* Roughly speaking, Arpaly holds a person is praiseworthy for an act when it shows good character, and blameworthy when it shows the opposite. She further holds that whether one's character is good or bad is not a function of what one *believes* but rather of what one *wants* or *cares about.* Huckleberry Finn shows a fairly good character when he helps his friend escape from slavery despite believing that his act is wrong. That's why Huck is praiseworthy, even though he acts from moral ignorance.

   Question: Consider Susan Wolf's character JoJo: a sadistic dictator who has been raised by his father (also a sadistic dictator) in circumstances that would have led almost anyone to become a brutal sadist (see Wolf, "Sanity and the Metaphysics of Responsibility," earlier in this chapter). Wolf argues that JoJo is not morally responsible because he lacks the capacity to tell right from wrong. Arpaly's theory seems to entail that JoJo is fully responsible (blameworthy), since he acts badly from bad character. Who is right, and why?

2. *Acting for duty's sake.* Consider the conscientious Nazi who hates his job in the concentration camp because he dislikes brutalizing human beings but does it anyway because he thinks that it is his moral duty to serve his country. According to Arpaly, this Nazi is not redeemed *at all* by the fact that he is acting, not from hatred or malice, but from a sense of duty. Is she right?

   Exercise: Construct a defense of the view that acting for the sake of duty is praiseworthy and imagine how Arpaly might respond.

   The view that it is admirable to act "from the motive of duty" is commonly ascribed to Immanuel Kant (see *Groundwork of the Metaphysics of Morals,* excerpted in Chapter 16 of this anthology). If you have read Kant, it will be instructive to ask whether Arpaly and Kant really disagree on this point.

3. *Two concepts of blame.* Arpaly argues that people who act from moral ignorance are fully blameworthy. Whether we agree with her may depend on what we mean by *blame.*

   In one sense, to blame a person is to judge that she acted badly from bad motives and to think less well of her as a result. As Arpaly writes elsewhere, to blame someone in this sense is like judging her to be "a bad business man or a lousy violinist" (N. Arpaly, *Unprincipled Virtue* [Oxford University Press, 2003], 173). Someone who acts badly from bad motives is obviously a lousy moral specimen, regardless of whether she acted from moral ignorance.

   In another sense, to blame a person for an act is to *resent* her for it, to get angry at her for it, and to think that some form of punishment would be appropriate (see P. F. Strawson, "Freedom and Resentment," earlier in this chapter). Blame in this sense is not simply a judgment about the act; it is a harsh response that involves the thought that the agent deserves to suffer (perhaps just a little bit) for what she has done.

   With this in mind, consider the case of someone who acts badly from what we may call "blameless" moral ignorance.

   > Larry is an ancient Egyptian slave owner who lives in a homogeneous society where everyone takes it for granted that slavery is morally permissible.

Larry does what slave owners do: he forces people to work; he buys and sells them; and so on. Larry knows that his slaves are miserable. But he thinks that he's allowed to do what he likes with his property so long as he's not needlessly cruel, and so he does. It would have taken a moral genius in Larry's circumstances to appreciate that his acts are wrong. But Larry is not a moral genius.

Larry is clearly blameworthy in Arpaly's sense. (Say why.) But it is less clear that his acts merit the kind of resentment that calls for punishment.

Question: Focus on the second sort of blame and ask Arpaly's question: Does the fact that Larry acted from (blameless) moral ignorance show that his acts do not merit resentment, punishment, and other similar harsh responses? Isn't it unfair to blame a person, in this sense, when he had no good way of knowing that his acts were wrong?

4. Arpaly does not discuss free will in this essay, but consider the following Arpaly-inspired argument for the view that free will and determinism are irrelevant to moral responsibility.

    (1) A person is blameworthy if and only if she acts badly from bad character (i.e., from an insufficient concern for other human beings and other important values).

    (2) People can act badly from bad character in a deterministic world.

    (3) So people can be blameworthy—hence morally responsible—in a deterministic world.

    Question: Is this is compelling argument? If not, say which premise is false and why.

ANALYZING THE ARGUMENTS

1. *Living without free will.* Suppose that freedom and responsibility are mere illusions (perhaps for the reasons Galen Strawson gives). How should we respond to this discovery? How should it affect our relationships with other people? How should it affect our social practices, including the practice of criminal punishment? For discussion, see Derk Pereboom, *Living without Free Will* (Cambridge University Press, 2001).

2. *Alternate possibilities.* Many philosophers, including Ayer and Chisholm, assume the principle of alternate possibilities (PAP):

   > PAP: A person is morally responsible for an act only if he or she could have done otherwise at the time.

   This can sound obvious: How can we legitimately blame someone for doing something if at the time it was literally *her only option*? The trouble is that PAP seems to lead almost immediately to the conclusion that responsibility and determinism are incompatible:

   (1) PAP: A person is morally responsible for an act only if he or she could have done otherwise at the time.

   (2) If determinism is true, then we are never "able to do otherwise," since our actions are always fully determined by prior factors beyond our control.

   (3) Therefore, if determinism is true, we are not morally responsible for anything we do.

   Ayer accepts PAP and denies (2), and for many years it appeared that this was the only way to reconcile moral responsibility with determinism. Then in 1969, Harry Frankfurt provided a recipe for constructing (what appear to be) counterexamples to PAP. The examples consist of pairs of cases:

   > Case 1: Jones wants Smith dead, so he plots a murder and kills Smith at noon for his own reasons in the normal way. This is meant to be a clear case in which a person is morally responsible for an act. If you think that requires indeterminism, suppose case 1 is set in an indeterministic world.
   >
   > Case 2: Jones wants Smith dead, so he plots a murder and kills Smith at noon for his own reasons. Black also wants Smith dead but would rather not dirty his hands. Black is an evil scientist who can monitor Jones's thoughts and manipulate them from a distance, and he has formed a plan. If Jones wavers in his resolve to kill Smith before noon, Black will push a button that will cause Jones to choose to kill Smith at noon; if Jones does not waver, Black will do nothing. As it happens, Jones never wavers, so Black does nothing.

   The argument then proceeds as follows. (a) Jones is responsible in case 1. (b) If Jones is responsible in case 1, then he is responsible in case 2, since the only difference is that in case 2, Black is looking on, and that cannot make a difference to Jones's responsibility. So (c) Jones is responsible in case 2. But (d) in case 2, Jones cannot do otherwise than kill Smith. No matter what happens, Jones will wind up choosing to kill Smith at noon. So (e) PAP is false.

   Question: Does the example in fact refute PAP? If not, why not? If so, does this show that moral responsibility and determinism are compatible after all?

For discussion, see H. Frankfurt, "Alternate Possibilities and Moral Responsibility," *Journal of Philosophy* 66, 23 (1969): 829–39.

3. Albert and Boris are convicted of assault and robbery in separate attacks on defenseless victims. When asked why, both say, "I wanted the money and I get a kick out of beating people up." According to prison psychiatrists, their psychological profiles are identical. Both are selfish and cruel, but neither is insane by legal standards. The only difference lies in the past. Albert is an ordinary criminal with an ordinary history. Boris, in contrast, was a decent, law-abiding philosophy professor until quite recently, when his personality suddenly changed for the worse. A medical examination reveals that this change in personality is due to a small brain tumor. The tumor is inoperable, and its effects are permanent but not life threatening. Is Boris responsible for his behavior? Say how one of the philosophers in this chapter would approach the question and assess his or her response.

4. It is widely agreed that people who suffer from serious mental illness (acute schizophrenia, advanced dementia) are not morally responsible for their behavior. Wolf discusses this claim explicitly. How would the other writers in this chapter explain this fact?

5. Seymour has three drinks at a party, gets into his car, and drives home without incident. Chester has three drinks at the same party, gets into his car, and as he is driving home, he hits a pedestrian in a crosswalk. Suppose that (a) Seymour and Chester were equally drunk and equally reckless, and (b) if Chester had not been drunk, he would not have hit the pedestrian. By ordinary standards, both are clearly blameworthy for driving drunk, a serious moral wrong. But Chester is also blameworthy for *killing a person*, and that is a *much* more serious moral wrong. So we blame Chester more intensely and punish him more severely. Is this view coherent? Consider the following argument:

> The only difference between Chester and Seymour is that Chester happened to encounter a pedestrian. But Chester had no control over whether there would be a pedestrian in the crosswalk. From his point of view, this was just a matter of bad luck. (By the same token, Seymour had the good luck to encounter no one.) But we should not blame a person for what he cannot control. So we should not blame Chester for killing the pedestrian.

For discussion, see Thomas Nagel, "Moral Luck," in his *Mortal Questions* (Cambridge University Press, 1979).

6. Many of the arguments in this chapter turn on claims about what a person *could* have done. Following G. E. Moore, some philosophers have been tempted by the below analysis of this idiom.

> *The conditional analysis: X could* have done *A* if and only if *X would have done A* if *X* had tried.

Unfortunately, the analysis is incorrect, as the following cases show:

> *Austin's golfer:* Tiger Woods misses an easy putt. As the ball skids past the hole he says to himself: "I could have made that shot!" His claim is true. And yet the conditional, "If he had tried to make the putt, he would have made it,"

is clearly false. After all, he *did* try, and he failed. (See J. L. Austin, "Ifs and Cans," in his *Philosophical Papers* [Oxford University Press, 1961].)

Paralyzed by fear: Al is hiking when a snake crosses his path. If he tried to run away, he would succeed: he is not literally paralyzed, and the path is clear. But he cannot run away. He is so terrified by snakes that he cannot bring himself to try.

Explain why these examples make trouble for the conditional analysis and consider how a proponent of the analysis might respond.

Part V

ETHICS

What Is the Right
Thing to Do?

Life sometimes confronts us with difficult choices. Sometimes you have to decide how much to go out of your way to help another person. Sometimes you have to decide whether to follow a rule imposed by a parent or a school. Sometimes you have to decide whether to speak up or step in when you see someone else doing something wrong. Sometimes it's easy to see what you should do, but sometimes it's hard to figure out what you should do.

In addition, you've probably had conversations with friends, classmates, and family members about serious moral questions such as: Is abortion morally permissible? Is it permissible to help a suffering, dying person die more quickly? Is it morally permissible to eat meat? How much aid do we owe to distant suffering people? Sometimes conversations about these questions can be wonderful—thoughtful, penetrating, and illuminating. But sometimes conversations about these questions can be frustrating. It can seem that two people are too far apart to come to any agreement or even to communicate properly with each other.

When it seems hopeless to move forward on these questions, philosophy can offer some real help. Ethicists (philosophers working on moral questions) can clarify what's at issue, offer novel arguments, and show what conclusions follow from commitments we may already have.

Let's consider three strategies that ethicists use to make progress on difficult moral questions.

Simplifying Examples

When analyzing the ethics of complex situations, ethicists often begin with examples that are simpler or about which our judgments are clearer. Such cases also allow disputants to identify common ground and articulate justifications for their positions, facilitating engagement and reasoned discussion rather than mere exchanges of difference. From there, ethicists add complicating features to the case, one by one, to see which complications make a difference and where our disagreements emerge. Further, our confident judgments about easier cases may serve as leverage to force us to think more deeply about hard cases, to understand how our judgments relate to each other, and to adjust our judgments when we uncover a tension in our network of judgments.

For example, a philosopher considering whether it is ethical to facilitate the death of a suffering, terminally ill, and consenting patient might begin with our judgments about three clearer cases:

1. *Healthy Patient:* It seems morally wrong to help a healthy person with a bright future die if she asks for our assistance, especially if her reasons for seeking death involve minor, temporary, or soluble problems.

2. *Suffering, Nonconsenting Patient:* It seems morally wrong to facilitate the death of a terminally ill, long-suffering patient who refuses consent.

3. *Pain Relief:* It seems not only permissible but morally imperative to administer pain relief to a severely suffering patient who consents, even if the pain relief induces long periods of unconsciousness and carries, as a side effect, a higher risk of death.

These three lodestars suggest that neither a patient's consent nor a patient's terminal status, by itself, is a sufficient condition for permissibly assisting another's death. Now complicate the case. Suppose a patient is both terminally ill *and* consents. Do these two factors, when combined, make a difference and render the assistance permissible? We might answer that question by asking why assisting the *Healthy Patient* seems impermissible. If assisting the *Healthy Patient*'s suicide seems impermissible because we must never contribute to a death, then one might ask whether that reason squares with our judgments in the *Pain Relief* case.

The *Pain Relief* case suggests that we may relieve the pain of a suffering person, even if that action risks death; thus, if the risk materializes, we may permissibly, if unintentionally, contribute to a death. This judgment introduces further questions: first, whether it makes a moral difference whether a death is facilitated intentionally or occurs as a mere side effect of an otherwise permissible act; and second, whether it matters if the death was certain or merely made more likely. If neither difference is significant, then we must either reject our judgment in the *Pain Relief* case or conclude that sometimes we may permissibly contribute to a person's death, in which case there must be a different justification of the *Healthy Patient* case. Perhaps the better justification of the *Healthy Patient* case is that it is wrong to assist a patient's death when a nonlethal way to alleviate her suffering is available. That justification is compatible with our judgment in the *Pain Relief* case.

Considering simple cases moves us quickly beyond our gut reactions to giving justifications and identifying what factors require further consideration. In the example just rehearsed, starting with simple cases reveals the limits and power of consent; the need to consider whether the patient's terminal status and suffering make a moral difference; the need to consider whether intent matters; and whether it matters if the death is certain or merely risked.

Analogies

A second, related strategy deploys analogies to introduce some intellectual distance from any exaggerated emotional reactions, preconceived notions, or rigid judgments. Ethicists examine cases that are different but structurally similar to the problem under consideration and assess whether those analogical cases illuminate the case at hand or meaningfully differ. Sometimes, this technique shows that ethical disagreements turn on verifiable empirical facts or that a person's judgments are in strong tension with each other.

For instance, to analyze the permissibility of cheating in an environment where cheating is rampant, one might start with analogous cases, some where the absence of reciprocity matters and others where it does not.

4. *Charades:* Suppose, in a game of charades, each team agrees the game is better when the parties do not act out individual letters to spell words. Each team pledges to *try* not to spell out words. Still, if one team resorts to the technique in a moment of desperation, then it seems permissible for the rival team to start spelling words when they wish.

5. *Vandalism:* Suppose vandalizing another person's home is a common response to an unresolved conflict or insult within one's neighborhood. It is still impermissible for you to vandalize the home of a person with whom you have a serious conflict, despite the fact that others do it.

Reciprocity or its absence matters in the *Charades* case but not in the *Vandalism* case. The next philosophical step would be to ask why the cases differ and whether cheating is more like the *Charades* case or more like the *Vandalism* case. Notably, in the *Charades* case, others' decisions not to abide by the rule change the meaning of one's own observance of the rule. Refraining from spelling would put one at a competitive disadvantage, given that the others do spell. In the *Charades* case, the expectation that one respect the rule seems conditioned on the voluntary compliance of others. In the *Vandalism* case, by contrast, the point of resolving conflict peacefully rather than aggressively is not diminished in one's own case by others' vandalism; the reason one should not vandalize has nothing to do with others' behavior.

Which case does cheating resemble? If a test is meant to develop one's capacities and assess one's knowledge, then the point of one's honest efforts is not diminished by others' dishonesty. The closer analogy may be the *Vandalism* case. On the other hand, if one's performance is evaluated on a curve, others' dishonesty may distort the results, making it more like the *Charades* case. Still, unlike the *Charades* case, cheating would not merely impact those who do not comply with the rule but would adversely affect other students; cheating would also represent a breach of trust with the professor and would deprive the cheater of a learning experience. These additional facts render salient that there are alternative measures of response to others' cheating, such as alerting the professor and seeking a different test.

Crafting Plausible Principles

A third strategy is to propose a potential, plausible principle to justify and unify a range of relevant, related cases that might shed light on the problem at hand. Then, one identifies some implications that principle would have in other cases to assess the principle's power and to uncover any flaws with the principle. Sometimes, dissatisfaction with the proposed principle is just as helpful as its endorsement. By articulating our reservations about a principle or its implications, we inch closer toward grasping what really matters and understanding the crux of our differences.

Suppose we return to the problem about assisted suicide. We might first formulate the following principle as underlying the resistance to assisted suicide:

(P) One may never intentionally facilitate another person's death.

Then, we would attempt to assess why this principle might be true and search for any clear counterexamples to it. Although respect for the value of life and the autonomy of persons might motivate endorsement of (P), there are some significant counterexamples to (P). For example, one may cause another person's death if it is necessary to defend oneself. Further, it seems that soldiers may permissibly cause enemy soldiers' deaths during declared wars, at least if the wars are just. These counterexamples might then place pressure on the position that (P) justifies the conclusion that assisted suicide is wrong. If one may facilitate others' deaths, even when they resist death and do not consent, wouldn't it seem as though it must also be permissible to facilitate the death of a person who elects death for good reasons?

The critic of assisted suicide must either:

A. Defend a plausible principle that condemns consensual assisted suicide but that allows one to kill an involuntary victim in self-defense or in combat. To defend this principle, she must articulate a morally relevant difference between the cases of assisted suicide, on the one hand, and self-defense and combat, on the other.

Or,

B. Concede that our willingness to cause deaths in self-defense and in war must also be mistaken, and then defend those judgments.

Thus, triangulating from a mid-level principle and identifying counterexamples quickly helps us map some of the broader moral terrain in which the issue of assisted suicide is situated.

All three strategies are used by ethicists to help clarify thoughts about responsibilities to address global famine, the permissibility of abortion, and the ethical treatment of animals. Each of these issues raises hard problems about when and how much we should take steps to prevent the deaths of strangers and when we may, if ever, permissibly cause death.

Famine

None of us, at least not as individuals, caused the life-threatening circumstances faced by the poor in countries where food is scarce and terrible diseases are rampant. Nevertheless, it seems difficult to deny that, if we are able to help people in danger of losing their lives at a small cost to ourselves, we should. As Peter Singer emphasizes, advancing a simplifying example, if we see a child drowning in a lake or choking on a bone, we should put aside what we are doing and save the endangered life, even when the interruption is inconvenient and our clothes get dirty.

These straightforward ideas have profound, personally challenging implications when one considers the magnitude of global poverty. The World Health Organization estimates that *nearly a billion* people are significantly undernourished. Must each of us, personally, give as much as we *possibly* can to address this problem, even if this means forgoing many of the expenditures that most of our family and peers make (e.g., expenditures on clothes, music, films, restaurants, and electronics)?

Singer contends that yes, we are obliged to give as much as possible.

Singer points out that human suffering and premature deaths from hunger are terrible and preventable. He proposes the following principle: if we can prevent significantly bad events without sacrificing something comparably important, we should. Singer defends this principle in two ways. First, the lack of proximity of suffering people diminishes neither the significance of their suffering nor our obligation. Second, the fact that others may fail to help does not justify our own failure to help, because our help on its own would still save lives. Because most of us have more resources than famine victims and giving very generously would not make us worse off than the desperately poor, we should give *a lot*. Singer's somber conclusion is that we are each obligated to do *a very great deal* to help alleviate global poverty, even if substantial giving would considerably reduce our standard of living.

Onora O'Neill concurs with Singer that we have strong obligations to contribute to famine relief but gives a different argument that has different implications. O'Neill begins by considering how **utilitarianism** would address these questions. She advances three major criticisms of the utilitarian approach. First, the utilitarian approach is predicated on contested empirical predictions that direct forms of famine relief will yield better overall, long-term consequences than the alternatives. It is unclear whether direct aid works to the long-term benefit of the poor or instead increases detrimental forms of dependence. In the face of this empirical uncertainty, the utilitarian cannot make a determinate recommendation about what to do. But, surely, O'Neill says, we ought to do something to relieve present suffering. Second, a utilitarian might recommend ignoring those presently in need if giving help might contribute to overpopulation that could engender greater forms of poverty; this objectionably ignores the humanity of currently suffering people and treats their suffering as a (tragic) means to achieve a better overall outcome. Third, the utilitarian wrongly focuses on overall consequences assessed in terms of happiness. Our true obligations are not to maximize happiness but to ensure that each person may lead an autonomous life.

O'Neill contends that we must treat each person, not as a mere means, but as an end-in-herself, by respecting what makes people morally valuable, namely, their rational capacities to lead self-determining lives. Hence, we may not use coercion to achieve our own purposes; we should protect others from coercive treatment, and we should act to ensure that each person has access to the conditions and resources necessary for living as an autonomous being. Concretely, we may not allow some to die now to ease resource pressure later; and our famine relief efforts should be focused not on maximizing happiness but on enabling recipients to become independent and self-sufficient.

Abortion

Although the morality of famine relief is a markedly different topic than the morality of abortion, the underlying philosophical issues helpfully overlap. Don Marquis asks whether the deaths occasioned by abortion should concern us as much as the deaths food shortages impose, given that the former concerns beings who lack the developed personalities and lives that victims of famine possess. Judith Jarvis Thomson's article shows that getting clear on the moral permissibility of abortion requires thinking through how much one person may be expected to give to another, a topic continuous with the philosophical questions presented by famine relief.

Marquis argues that "the overwhelming majority of deliberate abortions are seriously immoral." He diagnoses the central dispute in the abortion debate as turning on the highly contested question of whether it matters that embryos and fetuses lack full personalities and rich lives already in progress. Marquis suggests we step back to a simplifying case and consider why it is wrong to kill where we are *certain* that killing is wrong, to see if that reason applies to killing fetuses and embryos. Killing an adult, he claims, is not primarily wrong because it ends experiences that the adult actually values; for it is surely wrong to kill severely depressed adults, even if they do not currently value their lives. Killing an adult is wrong because it deprives that adult of a *future* in which to pursue the activities, projects, and relationships that make life valuable. Toddlers, fetuses, and embryos, if they are not killed, also have long futures ahead of them in which they may engage in such valuable pursuits. Even if those pursuits are not yet fully determinate, the deprivation of those opportunities represents a tremendous loss that Marquis contends it would be wrong to impose unless there are much stronger reasons to the contrary.

By sharp contrast, Thomson argues that abortion may be permissible even if an embryo or fetus is a person with a "right to life" whose death matters just as much as an adult's. She contends that a reasonable, morally decent person could be within her rights to refuse to bear the heavy burdens and risks to health of pregnancy and childbirth, even if another person needed those efforts to live. Although we may owe some sorts of assistance to one another and some women find this form of assistance extremely rewarding, we do not owe it to any particular person to make such extraordinary efforts and to take such major risks on their behalf. Further, we may extricate ourselves from shouldering these burdens if we have not voluntarily undertaken them. Thomson makes this argument through the use of powerful, creative analogies. Her justly famous examples are best encountered for the first time in the original text, so they will not be summarized here.

Animals

Animals confront us with a host of interesting moral questions. Is it permissible to kill animals and eat them? Is it permissible to keep animals as pets? Is it permissible to use animals for recreation in competitions such as dog fighting, horse racing, or equestrian competitions? If animals' suffering matters, must we try to prevent animals from hurting each other in the wild? If animal diversity is valuable, must we try to prevent animal species from going extinct? Is there a tension between seeing individual animals as valuable and seeing animal species as valuable?

Many people grow up eating meat and not considering that it might be wrong to do so. Eventually, they learn that some people are vegetarians, and that they are vegetarians for moral reasons. The idea that it is morally wrong to eat meat is now more widely accepted than it used to be. There is more pressure on restaurants to provide vegetarian options, and there is more understanding that the suffering that factory farms cause to animals may be morally unacceptable. One reaction that some people have is to continue to eat meat but to seek humanely raised meat: the meat of animals who lived in relatively pleasant conditions until they were killed for meat. Some people believe that while factory farming is morally wrong, humane farms are morally unproblematic. Why would this be so? Consider the claim that while we have strong reasons not to cause animal suffering, we have no reasons at all against painlessly killing animals; Elizabeth Harman calls this "the Surprising Claim." If the Surprising Claim is true, then it does seem that humane farms are morally unproblematic. But Harman argues that the Surprising Claim cannot be true. She argues that if we have strong reasons against causing animals to suffer, then this must be because *animals have moral status* and *we have reasons not to harm those beings that have moral status*. Harman argues that killing an animal harms it, and thus that we have reasons not to kill animals too, if we have reasons not to cause them to suffer.

Cora Diamond casts a skeptical eye on the sort of moral framework that Harman and others use to think about our moral duties regarding animals. Diamond argues that when we think about the morality of our treatment of animals, we should not focus on the suffering of animals nor on whether animals have certain rights. Rather, she says, we should ask first "why do people not eat people?" and we will see that our aversion to eating people has to do neither with suffering nor with rights. Diamond argues that it is the nature of our relationship with people that precludes our eating them, and that we must understand the nature of our relationship with animals to know whether—and why—we should not eat them. Diamond sees it as crucial that animals are our "fellow creatures." Diamond's essay is enjoyably unconventional for a philosophical essay, in that she quotes a poem in its entirety to make a crucial point about the apparent inconsistencies in our attitudes toward animals.

Peter Singer (b. 1946)

Singer is an Australian philosopher who teaches at Princeton University and the University of Melbourne. Famous for his sustained defense of utilitarianism and his application of utilitarian principles to the issues concerning global poverty, the treatment of animals, and end-of-life decision making, his books include *Animal Liberation* (1975), *Practical Ethics* (1979), *Rethinking Life and Death* (1994), and *The Life You Can Save: Acting Now to End World Poverty* (2009).

FAMINE, AFFLUENCE, AND MORALITY

As I write this, in November 1971, people are dying in East Bengal from lack of food, shelter, and medical care. The suffering and death that are occurring there now are not inevitable, not unavoidable in any fatalistic sense of the term. Constant poverty, a cyclone, and a civil war have turned at least nine million people into destitute refugees; nevertheless, it is not beyond the capacity of the richer nations to give enough assistance to reduce any further suffering to very small proportions. The decisions and actions of human beings can prevent this kind of suffering. Unfortunately, human beings have not made the necessary decisions. At the individual level, people have, with very few exceptions, not responded to the situation in any significant way. Generally speaking, people have not given large sums to relief funds; they have not written to their parliamentary representatives demanding increased government assistance; they have not demonstrated in the streets, held symbolic fasts, or done anything else directed toward providing the refugees with the means to satisfy their essential needs. At the government level, no government has given the sort of massive aid that would enable the refugees to survive for more than a few days. . . .

So far as it concerns us here, there is nothing unique about this situation except its magnitude.[1] The Bengal emergency is just the latest and most acute of a series of major emergencies in various parts of the world, arising both from natural and from man-made causes. There are also many parts of the world in which people die from malnutrition and lack of food independent of any special emergency. . . .

What are the moral implications of a situation like this? In what follows, I shall argue that the way people in relatively affluent countries react to a situation like that in Bengal cannot be justified; indeed, the whole way we look at moral issues—our moral conceptual scheme—needs to be altered, and with it, the way of life that has come to be taken for granted in our society. . . .

I begin with the assumption that suffering and death from lack of food, shelter, and medical care are bad. . . .

My next point is this: if it is in our power to prevent something bad from happening, without thereby sacrificing anything of comparable moral importance, we ought, morally, to do it. By "without sacrificing anything of comparable moral importance" I mean without causing anything else comparably bad to happen, or doing something that is wrong in itself, or failing to promote some moral good, comparable in significance to the bad thing that we can prevent. This principle seems. . . uncontroversial. . . . It requires us only to prevent what is bad, and not to promote what is good, and it requires this of us only when we can do it without sacrificing anything that is, from the moral point of view, comparably important. I could even, as far as the application of my argument to the Bengal emergency is concerned, qualify the point so as to make it: if it is in our power to prevent something very bad from happening, without thereby sacrificing anything morally significant, we ought, morally, to do it. An application of this principle would be as follows: if I am walking past a shallow pond and see a child drowning in it, I ought to wade in and pull the child out. This will mean getting my clothes muddy, but this is insignificant, while the death of the child would presumably be a very bad thing.

The uncontroversial appearance of the principle just stated is deceptive. If it were acted upon, even in its qualified form, our lives, our society, and our world would be fundamentally changed. For the principle takes, firstly, no account of proximity or distance. It makes no moral difference whether the person I can help is a neighbor's child ten yards from me or a Bengali whose name I shall never know, ten thousand miles away. Secondly, the principle makes no distinction between cases in which I am the only person who could possibly do anything and cases in which I am just one among millions in the same position.

I do not think I need to say much in defense of the refusal to take proximity and distance into account. The fact that a person is physically near to us, so that we have

---

1. As Singer later wrote in a revised version of the essay: "The crisis in Bangladesh that spurred me to write the above article is now of historical interest only, but the world food crisis is, if anything, still more serious. . . . [P]oor people are still starving in several countries, and malnutrition remains very widespread. The need for assistance is . . . just as great as when I first wrote, and we can be sure that without it there will, again, be major famines. The contrast between poverty and affluence that I wrote about is also as great as it was then. . . . So the case for aid, on both a personal and a governmental level, remains as great now as it was in 1971."

personal contact with him, may make it more likely that we *shall* assist him, but this does not show that we *ought* to help him rather than another who happens to be further away. If we accept any principle of impartiality, universalizability,[2] equality, or whatever, we cannot discriminate against someone merely because he is far away from us (or we are far away from him). Admittedly, it is possible that we are in a better position to judge what needs to be done to help a person near to us than one far away, and perhaps also to provide the assistance we judge to be necessary. If this were the case, it would be a reason for helping those near to us first. This may once have been a justification for being more concerned with the poor in one's own town than with famine victims in India. Unfortunately for those who like to keep their moral responsibilities limited, instant communication and swift transportation have changed the situation. From the moral point of view, the development of the world into a "global village" has made an important, though still unrecognized, difference to our moral situation. . . .

There may be a greater need to defend the second implication of my principle—that the fact that there are millions of other people in the same position, in respect to the Bengali refugees, as I am, does not make the situation significantly different from a situation in which I am the only person who can prevent something very bad from occurring. Again, of course, I admit that there is a psychological difference between the cases; one feels less guilty about doing nothing if one can point to others, similarly placed, who have also done nothing. Yet this can make no real difference to our moral obligations. Should I consider that I am less obliged to pull the drowning child out of the pond if on looking around I see other people, no further away than I am, who have also noticed the child but are doing nothing? One has only to ask this question to see the absurdity of the view that numbers lessen obligation. . . .

The view that numbers do make a difference can be made plausible if stated in this way: if everyone in circumstances like mine gave £5 to the Bengal Relief Fund, there would be enough to provide food, shelter, and medical care for the refugees; there is no reason why I should give more than anyone else in the same circumstances as I am; therefore I have no obligation to give more than £5. Each premise in this argument is true, and the argument looks sound.[3] It may convince us, unless we notice that it is based on a hypothetical premise, although the conclusion is not stated hypothetically. The argument would be sound if the conclusion were: if everyone in circumstances like mine were to give £5, I would have no obligation to give more than £5. If the conclusion were so stated, however, it would be obvious that the argument has no bearing on a situation in which it is not the case that everyone else gives £5. This, of course, is the actual situation. It is more or less certain that not everyone in circumstances like mine will give £5. So there will not be enough to provide the needed food, shelter, and medical care. Therefore by giving more than £5 I will prevent more suffering than I would if I gave just £5. . . .

If my argument so far has been sound, neither our distance from a preventable evil nor the number of other people who, in respect to that evil, are in the same situation

2. The principle of universalizability roughly requires that I act only in ways that I believe others, similarly situated, should act (even if our situations and roles were reversed).

3. A **sound** argument is an **argument** with true premises and that arrives at a conclusion that logically follows from the premises.

as we are, lessens our obligation to mitigate or prevent that evil. I shall therefore take as established the principle I asserted earlier. As I have already said, I need to assert it only in its qualified form: if it is in our power to prevent something very bad from happening, without thereby sacrificing anything else morally significant, we ought, morally, to do it.

The outcome of this argument is that our traditional moral categories are upset. The traditional distinction between duty and charity cannot be drawn, or at least, not in the place we normally draw it. Giving money to the Bengal Relief Fund is regarded as an act of charity in our society. The bodies which collect money are known as "charities." These organizations see themselves in this way—if you send them a check, you will be thanked for your "generosity." Because giving money is regarded as an act of charity, it is not thought that there is anything wrong with not giving. The charitable man may be praised, but the man who is not charitable is not condemned. People do not feel in any way ashamed or guilty about spending money on new clothes or a new car instead of giving it to famine relief. (Indeed, the alternative does not occur to them.) This way of looking at the matter cannot be justified. When we buy new clothes not to keep ourselves warm but to look "well-dressed" we are not providing for any important need. We would not be sacrificing anything significant if we were to continue to wear our old clothes, and give the money to famine relief. By doing so, we would be preventing another person from starving. It follows from what I have said earlier that we ought to give money away, rather than spend it on clothes which we do not need to keep us warm. To do so is not charitable, or generous. Nor is it the kind of act which philosophers and theologians have called "supererogatory"—an act which it would be good to do, but not wrong not to do. On the contrary, we ought to give the money away, and it is wrong not to do so.

I am not maintaining that there are no acts which are charitable, or that there are no acts which it would be good to do but not wrong not to do. It may be possible to redraw the distinction between duty and charity in some other place. All I am arguing here is that the present way of drawing the distinction, which makes it an act of charity for a man living at the level of affluence which most people in the "developed nations" enjoy to give money to save someone else from starvation, cannot be supported. . . .

One objection to the position I have taken might be simply that it is too drastic a revision of our moral scheme. . . . Most people reserve their moral condemnation for those who violate some moral norm, such as the norm against taking another person's property. They do not condemn those who indulge in luxury instead of giving to famine relief. But given that I did not set out to present a morally neutral description of the way people make moral judgments, the way people do in fact judge has nothing to do with the validity of my conclusion. My conclusion follows from the principle which I advanced earlier, and unless that principle is rejected, or the arguments shown to be unsound, I think the conclusion must stand, however strange it appears.

It might, nevertheless, be interesting to consider why our society, and most other societies, do judge differently from the way I have suggested they should. In a well-known article, J. O. Urmson suggests that the imperatives of duty, which tell us what we must do, as distinct from what it would be good to do but not wrong not to do, function so as to prohibit behavior that is intolerable if men are to live together in society. This may explain the origin and continued existence of the present division between acts of duty and acts of charity. Moral attitudes are shaped by the needs of society, and no doubt society needs people who will observe the rules that make social existence tolerable. From the point of view of a particular society, it is essential to prevent violations of norms against killing, stealing, and so on. It is quite inessential, however, to help people outside one's own society.

If this is an explanation of our common distinction between duty and supererogation, however, it is not a justification of it. The moral point of view requires us to look beyond the interests of our own society. Previously, as I have already mentioned, this may hardly have been feasible, but it is quite feasible now. From the moral point of view, the prevention of the starvation of millions of people outside our society must be considered at least as pressing as the upholding of property norms within our society.

It has been argued by some writers, among them Sidgwick[4] and Urmson, that we need to have a basic moral code which is not too far beyond the capacities of the ordinary man, for otherwise there will be a general breakdown of compliance with the moral code. Crudely stated, this argument suggests that if we tell people that they ought to refrain from murder and give everything they do not really need to famine relief, they will do neither, whereas if we tell them that they ought to refrain from murder and that it is good to give to famine relief but not wrong not to do so, they will at least refrain from murder. The issue here is: Where should we drawn the line between conduct that is required and conduct that is good although not required, so as to get the best possible result? This would seem to be an empirical question, although a very difficult one. One objection to the Sidgwick-Urmson line of argument is that it takes insufficient account of the effect that moral standards can have on the decisions we make. Given a society in which a wealthy man who gives five percent of his income to famine relief is regarded as most generous, it is not surprising that a proposal that we all ought to give away half our incomes will be thought to be absurdly unrealistic. In a society which held that no man should have more than enough while others have less than they need, such a proposal might seem narrow-minded. What it is possible for a man to do and what he is likely to do are both, I think, very greatly influenced by what people around him are doing and expecting him to do. In any case, the possibility that by spreading the idea that we ought to be doing very much more than we are to relieve famine we shall bring about a general breakdown of moral behavior seems remote. . . . Finally, it should be emphasized that these considerations are relevant only to the issue of what we should require from others, and not to what we ourselves ought to do. . . .

It is sometimes said that overseas aid should be a government responsibility, and that therefore one ought not to give to privately run charities. Giving privately, it is said, allows the government and the noncontributing members of society to escape their responsibilities.

This argument seems to assume that the more people there are who give to privately organized famine relief funds, the less likely it is that the government will take over full responsibility for such aid. This assumption is unsupported, and does not strike me as at all plausible. . . .

4 Henry Sidgwick (1838–1900) was a famous utilitarian.

I do not, of course, want to dispute the contention that governments of affluent nations should be giving many times the amount of genuine, no-strings-attached aid that they are giving now. I agree, too, that giving privately is not enough, and that we ought to be campaigning actively for entirely new standards for both public and private contributions to famine relief. . . .

Another, more serious reason for not giving to famine relief funds is that until there is effective population control, relieving famine merely postpones starvation. If we save the Bengal refugees now, others, perhaps the children of these refugees, will face starvation in a few years' time. . . .

I accept that the earth cannot support indefinitely a population rising at the present rate. This certainly poses a problem for anyone who thinks it important to prevent famine. Again, however, one could accept the argument without drawing the conclusion that it absolves one from any obligation to do anything to prevent famine. The conclusion that should be drawn is that the best means of preventing famine, in the long run, is population control. It would then follow from the position reached earlier that one ought to be doing all one can to promote population control (unless one held that all forms of population control were wrong in themselves, or would have significantly bad consequences). . . .

A third point raised by the conclusion reached earlier relates to the question of just how much we all ought to be giving away. One possibility is that we ought to give until we reach the level of marginal utility—that is, the level at which, by giving more, I would cause as much suffering to myself or my dependents as I would relieve by my gift. This would mean, of course, that one would reduce oneself to very near the material circumstances of a Bengali refugee. It will be recalled that earlier I put forward both a strong and a moderate version of the principle of preventing bad occurrences. The strong version, which required us to prevent bad things from happening unless in doing so we would be sacrificing something of comparable moral significance, does seem to require reducing ourselves to the level of marginal utility. I should also say that the strong version seems to me to be the correct one. I proposed the more moderate version—that we should prevent bad occurrences unless, to do so, we had to sacrifice something morally significant—only in order to show that even on this surely undeniable principle a great change in our way of life is required. On the more moderate principle, it may not follow that we ought to reduce ourselves to the level of marginal utility, for one might hold that to reduce oneself and one's family to this level is to cause something significantly bad to happen. Whether this is so I shall not discuss, since, as I have said, I can see no good reason for holding the moderate version of the principle rather than the strong version. Even if we accepted the principle only in its moderate form, however, it should be clear that we would have to give away enough to ensure that the consumer society, dependent as it is on people spending on trivia rather than giving to famine relief, would slow down and perhaps disappear entirely. There are several reasons why this would be desirable in itself. The value and necessity of economic growth are now being questioned not only by conservationists, but by economists as well. There is no doubt, too, that the consumer society has had a distorting effect on the goals and purposes of its members.

TEST YOUR UNDERSTANDING

1. Singer argues both from an initial principle and then from a qualified version of that principle. What are the two principles, and how do they differ? Does the qualified principle yield different conclusions?

2. Singer begins his essay contending that "the whole way we look at moral issues—our moral conceptual scheme—needs to be altered." How does he think our views must be altered?

3. How does Singer respond to the objection that each person should only give her fair share? The objector holds that each person need give only a small amount, because if everyone gave only a small amount, that would be enough to take care of the refugees Singer discusses.

4. How does Singer respond to the objection that international famine relief is the responsibility of governments, not private citizens?

NOTES AND QUESTIONS

1. **The personal costs of beneficence.** Would following Singer's recommendations demand that one make major changes in the nature of one's close relationships to family members and friends? If so, would this demand provide a reason to doubt his position? An extended discussion of this question can be found in Garrett Cullity, *The Moral Demands of Affluence* (Oxford University Press, 2004).

2. **Does the starting point matter?** Singer's argument begins by asking you to imagine that while on a walk, you see a child drowning in a pond. Call this the *Single Child* case. Singer's argument draws upon your reaction that you should save the child, even if it ruins your clothes and disrupts your day. Singer then applies that judgment to other, similar cases.

   Suppose instead that we began with a modified example, the *Series* case. Suppose that as soon as you save the one child and you walk on, within seconds you immediately encounter another drowning child, and thereafter another and another yet. This happens day after day. Do you have a strong sense that you should stop and help every child in the *Series* case, even though engaging in these rescue efforts means that you will never reach your destination and that the life you had planned will be utterly disrupted?

   Exercise: Discuss whether your judgment that you should help in the Series *case is as confident as your judgment that you must help in the* Single Child *case, and what, if anything, could justify any varying reactions to these examples. Would a different reaction to the cases cast any doubt on Singer's use of the* Single Child *case as a starting point?*

3. **Is the cause of famine relevant?** Singer does not specify the cause of the drowning child's predicament. These details do not seem to matter. Whether the child fell by

accident or was pushed by another child seems irrelevant to one's obligation to aid. Is the cause of famine also irrelevant to one's duty to contribute to famine relief?

Exercise: With respect to one's obligation to contribute to famine relief, discuss whether it matters if famines are caused by unpredictable weather catastrophes or by institutional failures of the victims' governments, such as corruption or failures of planning.

4. *Is reciprocity relevant?* If bystanders lingered nearby and watched the child as she was drowning, their presence would not diminish or extinguish your obligation to save the child. So, too, Singer argues that the fact that other citizens do not give to famine relief does not excuse you from giving. Do others' failures to act make *any* sort of difference?

*Exercise: Discuss whether the failure of your peers and fellow citizens to contribute to famine relief heightens or diminishes your obligation to contribute. Should you give more because it is important that someone make up the difference for their failure, as with rescuing the child, or is it unfair for you to make sacrifices if others do not also give? (Are both **disjuncts** true?)*

A longer discussion of the obligations we may incur from others' failures to help appears in Liam Murphy, *Moral Demands in Non-Ideal Theory* (Oxford University Press, 2003).

5. *What to do?* Many people feel moved but overwhelmed after reading Singer's arguments and want to know more about what sort of help would be effective. Two sites that attempt to identify charities that efficiently put donations to use include www.givingwhatwecan .org and www.givewell.org. Some difficult problems associated with identifying effective modes of assistance are canvassed in a forum in the *Boston Review*. See Abhijit Vinayak Banerjee, "Making Aid Work" (2006), and the replies by distinguished commentators: https://bostonreview.net/banerjee-making-aid-work. Worries about the effectiveness of international aid and a call for more political, institutional solutions appear in Angus Deaton, "How to Help Those Left Behind," chapter 7 in his *The Great Escape: Health, Wealth and the Origins of Inequality* (Princeton University Press, 2013).

Onora O'Neill (b. 1941)

O'Neill is a British philosopher and politician. She was born in Ireland, educated in England and the United States, taught at Barnard College and the University of Essex, was Principal of Newnham College, and is now Emeritus Professor of Newnham College, University of Cambridge. A member of the House of Lords, she chairs the Equality and Human Rights Commission in Great Britain. Well known for her defense of **Kantian** ethics and its application to issues of poverty and bioethics, her books include *Acting on Principle* (1975), *Faces of Hunger: An Essay on Poverty, Development and Justice* (1986), *Constructions of Reason: Exploration of Kant's Practical Philosophy* (1989), *Bounds of Justice* (2000), and *Autonomy and Trust in Bioethics* (2002).

THE MORAL PERPLEXITIES OF FAMINE AND WORLD HUNGER

Through history millions have died of sheer starvation and of malnutrition or from illnesses that they might have survived with better food. Whenever there were such deaths, nearby survivors may have realized that they could help prevent some deaths and may have done so, or wondered whether to do so. But nobody sought to prevent faraway deaths. Distance made an important difference; with few exceptions there was nothing to be done for the victims of faraway famines.

In a global economy things are different. Food from areas with agricultural surplus (nowadays mainly North America, Australia, and western Europe) can be distributed to the starving in Bangladesh or Somalia. Longer-term policies that affect economic development, fertility levels, and agricultural productivity may hasten or postpone far-off famines or make them more or less severe. Consequently we can now ask whether we ought to do some of these newly possible actions. Ought we (or others) to try to distribute food or aid, to control fertility, or to further economic development? Who should foot the bills and suffer the other costs? To whom (if anyone) should aid be given and to whom should it be denied? How much hardship or sacrifice, if any, is demanded of those who have the means to help?. . .

I will try in this essay to show how certain moral theories *can* help us think about some questions about famine and also to use considerations about famine to show some of the strengths and limitations of these theories. . . .

Utilitarian Approaches to Famine Questions

. . . No disagreement over famine and world hunger could be more fundamental than one between (1) those who think that either individual citizens or social groups in the developed world are morally required to take an active part in trying to reduce and end the poverty of the Third World and (2) those who think that they are morally required not to do so. Yet utilitarian arguments have been offered for both conclusions.[1] . . .

One well-known utilitarian dispute about famine has been between the basically Malthusian[2] perspective of Garrett Hardin[3] and the more optimistic, developmentalist

---

1. O'Neill refers to the moral theory of **utilitarianism**, according to which the morally right (and obligatory) action to perform is that action that will produce the most happiness, taking into account all of those affected, whether positively or negatively and whether directly or indirectly. John Stuart Mill's essay "Utilitarianism" appears in Chapter 16 of this anthology.

2. Thomas Malthus (1766–1834) was a British economist who argued that historically, famine, among other disasters, has kept population size in check.

3. Garrett Hardin (1915–2003) was an American ecologist whose research focused on the problems associated with overpopulation.

perspectives of other utilitarian writers. For the latter position I shall draw particularly on Peter Singer's influential article, "Famine, Affluence, and Morality."[4]

Hardin's argument may be summarized as follows: the citizens of developed countries are like the passengers of a lifeboat around which other, desperate people are swimming. Those in the lifeboats can rescue some of the drowning. But if the affluent rescue some of the starving, this will—unlike many lifeboat rescues—have bad consequences. It will mean that the affluent world will then have a smaller safety margin. While this might in the short run be outweighed by the added happiness and benefit of those who have been rescued, the longer-run effects are grim. The rescued will assume that they are secure; they will multiply, and next time that similar dangers arise they will be more numerous and rescue will not be possible. It is better, from a utilitarian point of view, to lose some lives now than to lose more lives later. So it would be morally wrong to rescue those who are desperate, and the starving must be left to starve.

Hardin's use of the lifeboat analogy has often been criticized. . . . Those in the boats may be entitled to their seats, and they have no options except to stay put or to give up everything. The affluent are in a different position. They may risk little in trying to help the hungry, they may lack clear title to all that they have (perhaps, for example, some of it has been acquired by unjust exploitation of parts of the Third World), and there are many ways in which they can give up something without sacrificing everything. Hardin does not take these points seriously because he thinks that the longer-term balancing of beneficial and harmful results of attempting to help the Third World point the other way. . . . He writes:

> If poor countries received no food aid from outside, the rate of their population growth would be periodically checked by crop failures and famines. But if they can always draw on a world food bank in time of need, their population can continue to grow unchecked, and so will their "need" for aid. In the short run a world food bank may diminish that need, but in the long run it actually increases the need without limit.[5]

From this perspective it follows that the prosperous ought, if they are utilitarians, to leave the starving to themselves to die or survive as best they may.

Singer's utilitarianism, by contrast, leads to interventionist conclusions. He starts from the standard utilitarian assumption that "if it is in our power to prevent something bad from happening, without thereby sacrificing anything of comparable moral importance, we ought, morally, to do it." He then points out that contributions to famine relief, even if they amount to a large proportion of our income—say 50 percent—do not sacrifice anything of moral importance comparable to that of the famine they relieve. . . . So he concludes that the prosperous, even the modestly prosperous, ought to help feed the hungry and to give up their affluence until they have so reduced their own standard of living that any further giving would sacrifice "something of comparable moral importance."

4. Excerpted earlier in this chapter.

5. Garrett Hardin, "Lifeboat Ethics: The Case against Helping the Poor," in W. Aiken and H. La Follette, *World Hunger and Moral Obligation* (Prentice-Hall, 1977), p. 17. [O'Neill's note.]

Singer's position . . . has been challenged from within the famine-relief movement itself. Tony Jackson, an Oxfam food aid consultant, has argued in *Against the Grain* that giving food doesn't always benefit the starving.[6]

Food aid commonly takes two forms. . . . [G]overnment-to-government food aid, which Third World governments obtain from food surplus countries and sell in their own countries, . . . may do more to support a government that is failing to address needs than it does to meet those needs. The second form of food aid, so-called project food aid, is mostly channeled through the World Food Programme and various voluntary agencies. This food aid represents the very sort of action to relieve the greatest suffering that Peter Singer advocates on utilitarian grounds. . . .

Jackson disagrees with Singer . . . because he thinks that providing food aid—even project food aid, which is intended to get the food where it is needed—has been shown to harm the needy. Project food aid competes with local food production, depriving vulnerable farmers of their living and driving them into the cities. Third World food production is then decreased rather than increased. Moreover, the food that is given often fails to reach those whose need is greatest and is diverted by others. . . . In some cases food-aid dependence is institutionalized and development hindered rather than helped. Apart from genuine short-term emergencies, such as the plight of refugees or results of sudden natural catastrophes, the provision of food aid often does more to benefit the prosperous farmers of the developed world, whose surplus is bought at subsidized prices, than it does to help the Third World. So the enormous international effort that goes into providing food aid preempts other and possibly more effective moves. . . .

The radically different policy conclusions reached by different utilitarian arguments about famine policy raise sharp dilemmas. . . .

It is not surprising that utilitarians disagree over famine and development policies. For utilitarians, it is *results* and not *principles* or *intentions* that count. . . .

If we are to work out the consequences of alternative available actions and policies, as utilitarianism demands, we shall repeatedly find ourselves confronted with impossible calculations. While accepting that precision is not generally possible or required in these matters, we cannot dispense with some accurate way of listing available options and the general character of the results of each. But our capacity to make accurate, if imprecise, judgments is on the whole restricted to matters that are relatively close at hand. We lack the sort of social science that provides an exhaustive list of available options or gives a generally accurate account of the long-term and overall likely results of each. Yet problems of world hunger, possible famine, and future population and resource growth cannot be considered without attending to the longer-term global results of available courses of action. If utilitarians lack a science of society and have only a limited ability to foresee results, they may have no general way to decide whether a proposed action or policy is morally required, forbidden, or neither. . . .

Utilitarianism is an appealing theory for anyone who wants to deliberate morally about famine problems. Its scope is comprehensive and it offers a pattern of reasoning which, if we could get appropriate information, would give us accurate and precise

6. Oxfam is a nonprofit organization that works around the world to relieve hunger and poverty.

resolution of moral problems. . . . [But] the ambitious character of utilitarian thinking in the abstract is not sustained in determinate contexts. Where such reasoning is silent, we may have to look in other directions. . . .

Kantian Approaches to Some Famine Problems

The second moral theory whose scope and determinacy in dealing with famine problems I shall consider was developed by the German philosopher Immanuel Kant (1724–1804).[7]. . .

Kant does not . . . try to generate a set of precise rules defining human obligations in all possible circumstances; instead, he attempts to provide a set of *principles of obligation* that can be used as the starting points for moral reasoning in actual contexts of action. The primary focus of Kantian ethics is, then, on *action* rather than *results,* as in utilitarian thinking. . . . [T]o know *what* sort of action is required (or forbidden) in which circumstances, we should not look just at the expected results of action . . . but, in the first instance, at the nature of the proposed actions themselves.

[T]he famous Categorical Imperative plays the same role in Kantian thinking that the Greatest Happiness Principle plays in utilitarian thought.

One . . . formulation . . . of the Categorical Imperative . . . is *The Formula of the End in Itself.* . . .

> Act in such a way that you always treat humanity, whether in your own person or in the person of any other, never simply as a means but always at the same time as an end.[8]

To understand this principle we need in the first place to understand what Kant means by the term *maxim.* The maxim of an act or policy or activity is the *underlying principle* of the act, policy or activity, by which other, more superficial aspects of action are guided. . . .

It is helpful to think of some examples of maxims that might be used to guide action in contexts where poverty and the risk of famine are issues. Somebody who contributes to famine-relief work or advocates development might have an underlying principle such as, "Try to help reduce the risk or severity of world hunger." This commitment might be reflected in varied surface action in varied situations. In one context a gift of money might be relevant; in another some political activity such as lobbying for or against certain types of aid and trade might express the same underlying commitment. Sometimes superficial aspects of action may seem at variance with the underlying maxim they in fact express. For example, if there is reason to think that indiscriminate food aid damages the agricultural economy of the area to which food is given, then the maxim

---

7. Some of Kant's work is excerpted in Chapters 16 and 18 of this anthology.

8. Kant, *Groundwork for the Metaphysic of Morals,* trans. H. J. Paton as *The Moral Law* (Hutcheson, 1953), p. 430 (Prussian Academy pagination). [O'Neill's note.]

of seeking to relieve famine might be expressed in action aimed at limiting the extent of food aid. More lavish use of food aid might *seem* to treat the needy more generously, but if in fact it will damage their medium- or long-term economic prospects, then it is not (contrary to superficial appearances) aimed at improving and securing their access to subsistence. On a Kantian theory, the basis for judging action should be its *fundamental* principle or policy, and superficially similar acts may be judged morally very different. Regulating food aid in order to drive up prices and profit from them is one matter; regulating food aid in order to enable local farmers to sell their crops and to stay in the business of growing food quite another.

When we want to work out whether a proposed act or policy is morally required we should not, on Kant's view, try to find out whether it would produce more happiness than other available acts. Rather we should see whether the act or policy is required by, or ruled out by, or merely compatible with maxims that avoid using others as mere means and maxims that treat others as ends in themselves. These two aspects of Kantian duty can each be spelled out and shown to have determinate implications for acts and policies that may affect the risk and course of famines.

Using Others as Mere Means

We use others as *mere means* if what we do reflects some maxim *to which they could not in principle consent*. Kant does not suggest that there is anything wrong about using someone as a means. Evidently every cooperative scheme of action does this. A government that agrees to provide free or subsidized food to famine-relief agencies both uses and is used by the agencies; a peasant who sells food in a local market both uses and is used by those who buy it. In such examples each party to the transaction can and does consent to take part in that transaction. Kant would say that the parties to such transactions use one another but do not use one another as *mere* means. Each party assumes that the other has its own maxims of action and is not just a thing or prop to be used or manipulated.

But there are other cases where one party to an arrangement or transaction not only uses the other but does so in ways that could only be done on the basis of a fundamental principle or maxim to which the other could not in principle consent. If a false promise is given, the party that accepts the promise is not just used but used as a mere means, because it is *impossible* for consent to be given to the fundamental principle or project of deception that must guide every false promise, whatever its surface character. . . . In false promising the deceived party becomes, as it were, a prop or tool—a *mere* means—in the false promisor's scheme. . . .

Another standard way of using others as mere means is by coercing them. Coercers, like deceivers, standardly don't give others the possibility of dissenting from what they propose to do. . . . Here any "consent" given is spurious because there was no option *but* to consent. If a rich or powerful landowner or nation threatens a poorer or more vulnerable person, group, or nation with some intolerable difficulty unless a concession is made, the more vulnerable party is denied a genuine choice between consent and dissent. . . . Maxims of coercion may threaten physical force, seizure of possessions, destruction of opportunities, or any other harm that the coerced party is thought to be unable to absorb without grave injury or danger. A moneylender in a Third World village who threatens not to make or renew an indispensable loan, without which survival until the next harvest would be impossible, uses the peasant as mere means. The peasant does not have the possibility of genuinely consenting to the "offer he can't refuse." . . .

To avoid unjust action it is not enough to observe the outward forms of free agreement and cooperation; it is also essential to see that the weaker party to any arrangement has a genuine option to refuse the fundamental character of the proposal.

Treating Others as Ends in Themselves

For Kant . . . justice is only one part of duty. We may fail in our duty, even when we don't use anyone as mere means (by deception or coercion), if we fail to treat others as "ends in themselves." To treat others as "Ends in Themselves" we must not only avoid using them as mere means but also treat them as rational and autonomous beings with their own maxims. If human beings were *wholly* rational and autonomous then, on a Kantian view, duty would require only that they not use one another as mere means. But, as Kant repeatedly stressed, but later Kantians have often forgotten, human beings are *finite* rational beings. They are finite in several ways.

First, human beings are not ideal rational calculators. We *standardly* have neither a complete list of the actions possible in a given situation nor more than a partial view of their likely consequences. In addition, abilities to assess and to use available information are usually quite limited.

Second, these cognitive limitations are *standardly* complemented by limited autonomy. Human action is limited not only by various sorts of physical barrier and inability but by further sorts of (mutual or asymmetrical) dependence. To treat one another as ends in themselves such beings have to base their action on principles that do not undermine but rather sustain and extend one another's capacities for autonomous action. A central requirement for doing so is to share and support one another's ends and activities at least to some extent. Since finite rational beings cannot generally achieve their aims without some help and support from others, a general refusal of help and support amounts to failure to treat others as rational and autonomous beings, that is as ends in themselves. Hence Kantian principles require us not only to act justly, that is in accordance with maxims that don't coerce or deceive others, but also to avoid manipulation and to lend some support to others' plans and activities. Since famine, great poverty and powerlessness all undercut the possibility of autonomous action, and the requirement of treating others as ends in themselves demands that Kantians standardly act to support the possibility of autonomous action where it is most vulnerable, Kantians are required to do what they can to avert, reduce, and remedy famine. On a Kantian view, beneficence is as indispensable as justice in human lives.

Justice to the Vulnerable in Kantian Thinking

For Kantians, justice requires action that conforms (at least outwardly) to what could be done in a given situation while acting on maxims neither of deception nor of coercion. Since anyone hungry or destitute is more than usually vulnerable to deception and coercion, the possibilities and temptations to injustice are then especially strong. . . .

Where shortage of food is being dealt with by a reasonably fair rationing scheme, any mode of cheating to get more than one's allocated share involves using some others and is unjust. Equally, taking advantage of others' desperation to profiteer—for example, selling food at colossal prices or making loans on the security of others' future livelihood, when these are "offers they can't refuse"—constitutes coercion and so uses others as mere means and is unjust. Transactions that have the outward form of normal commercial dealing may be coercive when one party is desperate. Equally, forms of corruption that work by deception—such as bribing officials to gain special benefits from development schemes, or deceiving others about their entitlements—use others unjustly. . . .

[O]nce we remember the limitations of human rationality and autonomy, and the particular ways in which they are limited for those living close to the margins of subsistence, we can see that mere conformity to ordinary standards of commercial honesty and political bargaining is not enough for justice toward the destitute. If international agreements themselves can constitute "offers that cannot be refused" by the government of a poor country, or if the concessions required for investment by a transnational corporation or a development project reflect the desperation of recipients rather than an appropriate contribution to the project, then (however benevolent the motives of some parties) the weaker party to such agreements is used by the stronger. . . .

Beneficence to the Vulnerable in Kantian Thinking

In Kantian moral reasoning, the basis for beneficent action is that we cannot, without it, treat others of limited rationality and autonomy as ends in themselves. This is not to say that Kantian beneficence won't make others happier, for it will do so whenever they would be happier if (more) capable of autonomous action, but that happiness secured by purely paternalistic means, or at the cost (for example) of manipulating others' desires, will not count as beneficent in the Kantian picture. Clearly the vulnerable position of those who lack the very means of life, and their severely curtailed possibilities for autonomous action, offer many different ways in which it might be possible for others to act beneficently. Where the means of life are meager, almost any material or organizational advance may help extend possibilities for autonomy. Individual or institutional action that aims to advance economic or social development can proceed on many routes. The provision of clean water, of improved agricultural techniques, of better grain storage systems, or of adequate means of local transport may all help transform material prospects. Equally, help in the development of new forms of social organization—whether peasant self-help groups, urban cooperatives, medical and contraceptive services, or improvements in education or in the position of women—may help to extend possibilities for autonomous action. . . . [W]here some activity helps secure possibilities for autonomous action for more people, or is likely to achieve a permanent improvement in the position of the most vulnerable, or is one that can be done with more reliable success, this provides reason for furthering that project rather than alternatives.

Clearly the alleviation of need must rank far ahead of the furthering of happiness in the Kantian picture. I might make my friends very happy by throwing extravagant parties: but this would probably not increase anybody's possibility for autonomous action to any great extent. But the sorts of development-oriented changes that have just been mentioned may *transform* the possibilities for action of some. Since famine and the risk of famine are always and evidently highly damaging to human autonomy, any action that helps avoid or reduce famine must have a strong claim on any Kantian who is thinking through what beneficence requires. . . .

[W]herever we find ourselves, our duties are not, on the Kantian picture, limited to those close at hand. Duties of justice arise whenever there is some involvement between parties—and in the modern world this is never lacking. Duties of beneficence arise whenever destitution puts the possibility of autonomous action in question for the more vulnerable. When famines were not only far away, but nothing could be done to relieve them, beneficence or charity may well have begun—and stayed—at home. In a global village, the moral significance of distance has shrunk, and we may be able to affect the capacities for autonomous action of those who are far away.

The Scope of Kantian Deliberations about Famine and Hunger

. . . Kantian moral reasoning . . . does not propose a process of moral reasoning that can (in principle) rank *all* possible actions or all possible institutional arrangements from the happiness-maximizing "right" action or institution downward. It aims rather to offer a pattern of reasoning by which we can identify whether *proposed action or institutional arrangements* would be just or unjust, beneficent or lacking in beneficence. While *some* knowledge of causal connections is needed for Kantian reasoning, it is far less sensitive than is utilitarian reasoning to gaps in our causal knowledge. . . .

[T]he Kantian picture of beneficence . . . judges beneficence by its overall contribution to the prospects for human autonomy and not by the quantity of happiness expected to result. . . . For utilitarians, paternalistic imposition of, for example, certain forms of aid and development assistance need not be wrong and may even be required. But for Kantians, whose beneficence should secure others' possibilities for autonomous action, the case for paternalistic imposition of aid or development projects without the recipients' involvement must always be questionable.

In terms of some categories in which development projects are discussed, utilitarian reasoning may well endorse "top-down" aid and development projects which override whatever capacities for autonomous choice and action the poor of a certain area now have in the hopes of securing a happier future. If the calculations work out in a certain way, utilitarians may even think a "generation of sacrifice"—or of forced labor or of imposed population-control policies not only permissible but mandated. In their darkest Malthusian moments some utilitarians have thought that average happiness might best be maximized not by improving the lot of the poor but by minimizing their numbers, and so have advocated policies of "benign neglect" of the poorest and most desperate. Kantian patterns of reasoning are likely to endorse less global and less autonomy-overriding aid and development projects; they are not likely to endorse neglect or abandoning of those who are most vulnerable and lacking in autonomy. If the aim of beneficence is to keep or put others in a position to act for themselves, then emphasis must be placed on "bottom-up" projects, which from the start draw on, foster, and establish indigenous capacities and practices of self-help and local action.

Utilitarian and Kantian Moral Reasoning

In the contrasting utilitarian and Kantian pictures of moral reasoning and of their implications in famine situations we can also discern two sharply contrasting pictures of the value of human life.

Utilitarians, since they value happiness above all, aim to achieve the happiest possible world. If . . . happiness is the supreme value, then anything may and ought to be sacrificed for the sake of a greater happiness. . . .

[W]e can see that on a utilitarian view lives must be sacrificed to build a happier world if this is the most efficient way to do so, whether or not those who lose their lives are willing. There is nothing wrong with using another as mere means, provided that the end in view is a happier result than could have been achieved any other way, taking account of the misery the means may have caused. In utilitarian thinking, persons are not ends in themselves. Their special moral status, such as it is, derives from their being means to the production of happiness. . . .

Kantians reach different conclusions about human life. They see it as valuable because humans have considerable (but still quite incomplete) capacities for autonomous action. . . .

The fundamental idea behind the Categorical Imperative is that the actions of a plurality of rational beings can be mutually consistent. A minimal condition for their mutual consistency is that each, in acting autonomously, not preclude others' autonomous action. This requirement can be spelled out, as in the formula of the end in itself, by insisting that each avoid action which the other could not freely join in (hence avoid deception and coercion) and that each seek to secure others' capacities for autonomous action. What this actually takes will, as we have seen, vary with circumstances. But it is clear enough that the partial autonomy of human beings is undermined by life-threatening and destroying circumstances, such as famine and destitution. Hence a fundamental Kantian commitment must be to preserve life in two senses. First, others must not be deprived of life. . . . Second, others' lives must be preserved in forms that offer them sufficient physical energy, psychological space, and social security for action. Partial autonomy is vulnerable autonomy, and in human life psychological and social as well as material needs must be met if any but the most meager possibility of autonomous action is to be preserved. Kantians are therefore committed to the preservation not only of biological but of biographical life. To act in the typical ways humans are capable of we must not only be alive, but have a life to lead.

On a Kantian view, we may justifiably—even nobly—risk or sacrifice our lives for others. When we do so, we act autonomously, and nobody uses us as a mere means. But we cannot justly use others (nor they us) as mere means in a scheme that could only be based on some deception or on coercion. Nor may we refuse others the help they need to sustain the very possibility of autonomous action. . . .

Where others' possibilities for autonomous action are eroded by poverty and malnutrition, the necessary action must clearly include moves to change the picture. But these moves will not meet Kantian requirements if they provide merely calories and basic medicine. The action must also seek to enable those who begin to be adequately fed to act autonomously. It must therefore aim at least at minimal security and subsistence. Hence the changes that Kantians argue or work for must always be oriented to development plans that create enough economic self-sufficiency and social security for independence in action to be feasible and sustainable.

TEST YOUR UNDERSTANDING

1. Why does O'Neill reject a utilitarian approach to the ethics of famine relief? (You may select more than one.)

   a. Utilitarianism requires us to calculate long-term effects in a way that is not possible.

   b. Utilitarianism thinks that all people matter equally, even if some are strangers and some are your close friends and family.

   c. Utilitarianism is focused on creating happiness and relieving suffering, rather than on fostering autonomy.

2. What two opposing viewpoints have utilitarians sometimes offered about famine relief, according to O'Neill?

3. Does O'Neill say that utilitarians care about consequences, but Kantians do not?

4. What would the Kantian view imply about famine relief, according to O'Neill? (You may select more than one.)

   a. We are not morally obligated to do anything for famine relief, but it would be nice of us to do something.

   b. We should prevent some people from eating if, in the long run, more people will thereby have autonomy.

   c. We are morally obligated to help those experiencing famine.

   d. It is not enough to provide food for victims of famine; we must also help them toward achieving the ability to take care of themselves and have the lives they want.

NOTES AND QUESTIONS

1. O'Neill says that Singer's article "Famine, Affluence, and Morality" offers a utilitarian approach to famine relief. But Singer's argument does not rely on **utilitarianism**. While his conclusion is very demanding, the principle on which he relies might be endorsed by many non-utilitarians. (Utilitarianism is committed to several counterintuitive views, including: that sometimes it is morally required to kill one person to save many, and that it can be morally permissible to violate one person's rights to benefit many others. Nothing in Singer's essay commits him to these views.) While Singer himself endorses utilitarianism in some of his other writings, his essay is intended to convince a broader group than those who agree with utilitarianism.

2. *Why end hunger?* O'Neill argues that the primary reason to promote famine relief is to enable others' **autonomy** and help them avoid coercion. Perhaps surprisingly, she does not think the main reason to promote famine relief is to relieve the physical suffering associated with hunger.

    Consider the following objection to O'Neill's account:

    > What motivates you to eat when you are hungry is not that satisfying your hunger will help you resist coercion, but rather that hunger is uncomfortable, that your body needs nutrients, and that eating is pleasurable. Doesn't that suggest that the reasons we should enable others to eat are the same reasons we aim to satisfy our own hunger?

    Explain this objection in your own words, and then consider how O'Neill should respond to it.

3. *The plural pronoun.* Most of O'Neill's essay uses the plural pronoun "we." That is, she mainly discusses what "we" should do and not what each of us should do to contribute to famine relief. One might take this as a stylistic writing choice or one might interpret it as a more conscious decision, signaling that global poverty is a problem we share and must solve together. Is there anything about O'Neill's arguments that supports the idea that collective solutions coordinated and spearheaded by institutions and governments are more appropriate than aggregating individual efforts? Are there principled reasons to aim one's efforts toward political change and political solutions in addition to, or instead of, individual efforts at direct relief or, in deciding what to do as an individual, should one just try to assess what actions will be most effective?

Judith Jarvis Thomson (b. 1929)

Thomson is Professor Emeritus at the Massachusetts Institute of Technology. She has made a number of field-defining contributions in moral philosophy, political philosophy, legal philosophy, and metaphysics. Her books include *Rights, Restitution and Risk* (1986), *The Realm of Rights* (1998), *Goodness and Advice* (2001), and *Normativity* (2006).

A DEFENSE OF ABORTION

M ost opposition to abortion relies on the premise that the fetus is a human being, a person, from the moment of conception. . . .

How, precisely, are we supposed to get from there to the conclusion that abortion is morally impermissible? . . .

Something like this, I take it. Every person has a right to life. So the fetus has a right to life. No doubt the mother has a right to decide what shall happen in and to her body; everyone would grant that. But surely a person's right to life is stronger and more stringent than the mother's right to decide what happens in and to her body, and so outweighs it. So the fetus may not be killed; an abortion may not be performed.

It sounds plausible. But now let me ask you to imagine this. You wake up in the morning and find yourself back to back in bed with an unconscious violinist. A famous unconscious violinist. He has been found to have a fatal kidney ailment, and the Society of Music Lovers has canvassed all the available medical records and found that you alone have the right blood type to help. They have therefore kidnapped you, and last night the violinist's circulatory system was plugged into yours, so that your kidneys can be used to extract poisons from his blood as well as your own. The director of the hospital now tells you, "Look, we're sorry the Society of Music Lovers did this to you—we would never have permitted it if we had known. But still, they did it, and the violinist now is plugged into you. To unplug you would be to kill him. But never mind, it's only for nine months. By then he will have recovered from his ailment, and can safely be unplugged from you." Is it morally incumbent on you to accede to this situation? No doubt it would be very nice of you if you did, a great kindness. But do you *have* to accede to it? What if it were not nine months, but nine years? Or longer still? What if the director of the hospital says, "Tough luck, I agree, but you've now got to stay in bed, with the violinist plugged into you, for the rest of your life. Because remember this. All persons have a right to life, and violinists are persons. Granted you have a right to decide what happens in and to your body, but a person's right to life outweighs your right to decide what happens in and to your body. So you cannot ever be unplugged from him." I imagine you would regard this as outrageous, which suggests that something really is wrong with that plausible-sounding argument I mentioned a moment ago.

In this case, of course, you were kidnapped; you didn't volunteer for the operation that plugged the violinist into your kidneys. Can those who oppose abortion on the ground I mentioned make an exception for a pregnancy due to rape? Certainly. They can say that persons have a right to life only if they didn't come into existence because of rape; or they can say that all persons have a right to life, but that some have less of a right to life than others, in particular, that those who came into existence because of rape have less. But these statements have a rather unpleasant sound. Surely the question of whether you have a right to life at all, or how much of it you have, shouldn't turn on the question of whether or not you are the product of a rape. And in fact the people who oppose abortion on the ground I mentioned do not make this distinction, and hence do not make an exception in case of rape.

Nor do they make an exception for a case in which the mother has to spend the nine months of her pregnancy in bed. They would agree that would be a great pity, and hard on the mother; but all the same, all persons have a right to life, the fetus is a person, and so on. . . .

Some won't even make an exception for a case in which continuation of the pregnancy is likely to shorten the mother's life; they regard abortion as impermissible even to save the mother's life. Such cases are nowadays very rare, and many opponents of abortion do not accept this extreme view. All the same, it is a good place to begin: a number of points of interest come out in respect to it.

1. Let us call the view that abortion is impermissible even to save the mother's life "the extreme view." I want to suggest first that it does not issue from the argument I mentioned earlier without the addition of some fairly powerful premises. Suppose a woman has become pregnant, and now learns that she has a cardiac condition such that she will die if she carries the baby to term. What may be done for her? The fetus, being a person, has a right to life, but as the mother is a person too, so has she a right to life. Presumably they have an equal right to life. How is it supposed to come out that an abortion may not be performed? If mother and child have an equal right to life, shouldn't we perhaps flip a coin? Or should we add to the mother's right to life her right to decide what happens in and to her body, which everybody seems to be ready to grant—the sum of her rights now outweighing the fetus' right to life?

The most familiar argument here is the following. We are told that performing the abortion would be directly killing the child, whereas doing nothing would not be killing the mother, but only letting her die. Moreover, in killing the child, one would be killing an innocent person, for the child has committed no crime, and is not aiming at his mother's death. And then there are a variety of ways in which this might be continued. (1) But as directly killing an innocent person is always and absolutely impermissible, an abortion may not be performed. Or, (2) as directly killing an innocent person is murder, and murder is always and absolutely impermissible, an abortion may not be performed. Or, (3) as one's duty to refrain from directly killing an innocent person is more stringent than one's duty to keep a person from dying, an abortion may not be performed. Or, (4) if one's only options are directly killing an innocent person or letting a person die, one must prefer letting the person die, and thus an abortion may not be performed.

Some people seem to have thought that these are not further premises which must be added if the conclusion is to be reached, but that they follow from the very fact that an innocent person has a right to life. But this seems to me to be a mistake, and perhaps the simplest way to show this is to bring out that while we must certainly grant that innocent persons have a right to life, the theses in (1) through (4) are all false. Take (2), for example. If directly killing an innocent person is murder, and thus is impermissible, then the mother's directly killing the innocent person inside her is murder, and thus is impermissible. But it cannot seriously be thought to be murder if the mother performs an abortion on herself to save her life. It cannot seriously be said that she *must* refrain, that she *must* sit passively by and wait for her death. Let us look again at the case of you and the violinist. There you are, in bed with the violinist, and the director of the hospital says to you, "It's all most distressing, and I deeply sympathize, but you see this is putting an additional strain on your kidneys, and you'll be dead within the month. But you *have* to stay where you are all the same. Because unplugging you would be directly killing an innocent violinist, and that's murder, and that's impermissible." If anything in the world is true, it is that you do not commit murder, you do not do what is impermissible, if you reach around to your back and unplug yourself from that violinist to save your life.

The main focus of attention in writings on abortion has been on what a third party may or may not do in answer to a request from a woman for an abortion. This is in a way understandable. Things being as they are, there isn't much a woman can safely do to abort herself. So the question asked is what a third party may do, and what the mother may do, if it is mentioned at all, is deduced, almost as an afterthought, from what it is concluded that third parties may do. But it seems to me that to treat the matter in this way is to refuse to grant to the mother that very status of person which is so firmly insisted on for the fetus. For we cannot simply read off what a person may do from what a third party may do. Suppose you find yourself trapped in a tiny house with a growing child. I mean a very tiny house, and a rapidly growing child—you are already up against the wall of the house and in a few minutes you'll be crushed to death. The child on the other hand won't be crushed to death; if nothing is done to stop him from growing he'll be hurt, but in the end he'll simply burst open the house and walk out a free man. Now I could well understand it if a bystander were to say, "There's nothing we can do for you. We cannot choose between your life and his, we cannot be the ones to decide who is to live, we cannot intervene." But it cannot be concluded that you too can do nothing, that you cannot attack it to save your life. However innocent the child may be, you do not have to wait passively while it crushes you to death. Perhaps a pregnant woman is vaguely felt to have the status of a house, to which we don't allow the right of self-defense. But if the woman houses the child, it should be remembered that she is a person who houses it.

I should perhaps stop to say explicitly that I am not claiming that people have a right to do anything whatever to save their lives. I think, rather, that there are drastic limits to the right of self-defense. If someone threatens you with death unless you torture someone else to death, I think you have not the right, even to save your life, to do so. But the case under consideration here is very different. In our case there are only two people involved, one whose life is threatened, and one who threatens it. Both are innocent: the one who is threatened is not threatened because of any fault, the one who threatens does not threaten because of any fault. For this reason we may feel that we bystanders cannot intervene. But the person threatened can.

In sum, a woman surely can defend her life against the threat to it posed by the un-born child, even if doing so involves its death. And this shows not merely that the theses in (1) through (4) are false; it shows also that the extreme view of abortion is false. . . .

2. The extreme view could of course be weakened to say that while abortion is permissible to save the mother's life, it may not be performed by a third party, but

only by the mother herself. But this cannot be right either. For what we have to keep in mind is that the mother and the unborn child are not like two tenants in a small house which has, by an unfortunate mistake, been rented to both: the mother *owns* the house. The fact that she does adds to the offensiveness of deducing that the mother can do nothing from the supposition that third parties can do nothing. But it does more than this. . . . Certainly it lets us see that a third party who says "I cannot choose between you" is fooling himself if he thinks this is impartiality. If Jones has found and fastened on a certain coat, which he needs to keep him from freezing, but which Smith also needs to keep him from freezing, then it is not impartiality that says "I cannot choose between you" when Smith owns the coat. Women have said again and again "This body is *my* body!" and they have reason to feel angry, reason to feel that it has been like shouting into the wind. . . .

3. Where the mother's life is not at stake, the argument I mentioned at the outset seems to have a much stronger pull. "Everyone has a right to life, so the unborn person has a right to life." And isn't the child's right to life weightier than anything other than the mother's own right to life, which she might put forward as ground for an abortion?

This argument treats the right to life as if it were unproblematic. It is not, and this seems to me to be precisely the source of the mistake.

For we should now, at long last, ask what it comes to, to have a right to life. In some views having a right to life includes having a right to be given at least the bare minimum one needs for continued life. But suppose that what in fact *is* the bare minimum a man needs for continued life is something he has no right at all to be given? If I am sick unto death, and the only thing that will save my life is the touch of Henry Fonda's cool hand on my fevered brow,[1] then all the same, I have no right to be given the touch of Henry Fonda's cool hand on my fevered brow. It would be frightfully nice of him to fly in from the West Coast to provide it. It would be less nice, though no doubt well meant, if my friends flew out to the West Coast and carried Henry Fonda back with them. But I have no right at all against anybody that he should do this for me. Or again, to return to the story I told earlier, the fact that for continued life that violinist needs the continued use of your kidneys does not establish that he has a right to be given the continued use of your kidneys. He certainly has no right against you that *you* should give him continued use of your kidneys. For nobody has any right to use your kidneys unless you give him such a right; and nobody has the right against you that you shall give him this right—if you do allow him to go on using your kidneys, this is a kindness on your part, and not something he can claim from you as his due. Nor has he any right against anybody else that *they* should give him continued use of your kidneys. Certainly he had no right against the Society of Music Lovers that they should plug him into you in the first place. And if you now start to unplug yourself, having learned that you will otherwise have to spend nine years in bed with him, there is nobody in the world who must try to prevent you, in order to see to it that he is given something he has a right to be given.

---

1. Henry Fonda (1905–1982) was a serious actor and, for some, a heartthrob. A contemporary analog might be Denzel Washington.

Some people are rather stricter about the right to life. In their view, it does not include the right to be given anything, but amounts to, and only to, the right not to be killed by anybody. But here a related difficulty arises... [D]oes he have a right against everybody that they shall refrain from unplugging you from him? To refrain from doing this is to allow him to continue to use your kidneys. . . . [T]he violinist has no right against you that *you* shall allow him to continue to use your kidneys. As I said, if you do allow him to use them, it is a kindness on your part, and not something you owe him.

. . . I am not arguing that people do not have a right to life. I am arguing only that having a right to life does not guarantee having either a right to be given the use of or a right to be allowed continued use of another person's body—even if one needs it for life itself. . . .

4. In the most ordinary sort of case, to deprive someone of what he has a right to is to treat him unjustly. Suppose a boy and his small brother are jointly given a box of chocolates for Christmas. If the older boy takes the box and refuses to give his brother any of the chocolates, he is unjust to him, for the brother has been given a right to half of them. But suppose that, having learned that otherwise it means nine years in bed with that violinist, you unplug yourself from him. You surely are not being unjust to him, for you gave him no right to use your kidneys, and no one else can have given him any such right. But we have to notice that in unplugging yourself, you are killing him; and violinists, like everybody else, have a right to life, and thus in the view we were considering just now, the right not to be killed. So here you do what he supposedly has a right you shall not do, but you do not act unjustly to him in doing it.

The emendation which may be made at this point is this: the right to life consists not in the right not to be killed, but rather in the right not to be killed unjustly. This runs a risk of circularity, but never mind: it would enable us to square the fact that the violinist has a right to life with the fact that you do not act unjustly toward him in unplugging yourself, thereby killing him. For if you do not kill him unjustly, you do not violate his right to life, and so it is no wonder you do him no injustice.

But if this emendation is accepted, the gap in the argument against abortion stares us plainly in the face: it is by no means enough to show that the fetus is a person, and to remind us that all persons have a right to life—we need to be shown also that killing the fetus violates its right to life, i.e., that abortion is unjust killing. And is it?

I suppose we may take it as a datum that in a case of pregnancy due to rape the mother has not given the unborn person a right to the use of her body for food and shelter. Indeed, in what pregnancy could it be supposed that the mother has given the unborn person such a right? It is not as if there were unborn persons drifting about the world, to whom a woman who wants a child says "I invite you in."

But it might be argued that there are other ways one can have acquired a right to the use of another person's body than by having been invited to use it by that person. Suppose a woman voluntarily indulges in intercourse, knowing of the chance it will issue in pregnancy, and then she does become pregnant; is she not in part responsible for the presence, in fact the very existence, of the unborn person inside her? No doubt she did not invite it in. But doesn't her partial responsibility for its being there itself give it a right to the use of her body? If so, then her aborting it would be more like the boy's taking away the chocolates, and less like your unplugging yourself from the violinist—doing so would be depriving it of what it does have a right to, and thus would be doing it an injustice.

And then, too, it might be asked whether or not she can kill it even to save her own life: If she voluntarily called it into existence, how can she now kill it, even in self-defense?. . .

And we should also notice that it is not at all plain that this argument really does go even as far as it purports to. For there are cases and cases, and the details make a difference. If the room is stuffy, and I therefore open a window to air it, and a burglar climbs in, it would be absurd to say "Ah, now he can stay, she's given him a right to the use of her house—for she is partially responsible for his presence there, having voluntarily done what enabled him to get in, in full knowledge that there are such things as burglars, and that burglars burgle." It would be still more absurd to say this if I had had bars installed outside my windows, precisely to prevent burglars from getting in, and a burglar got in only because of a defect in the bars. It remains equally absurd if we imagine it is not a burglar who climbs in, but an innocent person who blunders or falls in. Again, suppose it were like this: people-seeds drift about in the air like pollen, and if you open your windows, one may drift in and take root in your carpets or upholstery. You don't want children, so you fix up your windows with fine mesh screens, the very best you can buy. As can happen, however, and on very, very rare occasions does happen, one of the screens is defective; and a seed drifts in and takes root. Does the person-plant who now develops have a right to the use of your house? Surely not—despite the fact that you voluntarily opened your windows, you knowingly kept carpets and upholstered furniture, and you knew that screens were sometimes defective. Someone may argue that you are responsible for its rooting, that it does have a right to your house, because after all you *could* have lived out your life with bare floors and furniture, or with sealed windows and doors. But this won't do—for by the same token anyone can avoid a pregnancy due to rape by having a hysterectomy, or anyway by never leaving home without a (reliable!) army. . . .

5. There is room for yet another argument here, however. We surely must all grant that there may be cases in which it would be morally indecent to detach a person from your body at the cost of his life. Suppose you learn that what the violinist needs is not nine years of your life, but only one hour: all you need do to save his life is to spend one hour in that bed with him. Suppose also that letting him use your kidneys for that one hour would not affect your health in the slightest. Admittedly you were kidnapped. Admittedly you did not give anyone permission to plug him into you. Nevertheless it seems to me plain you *ought* to allow him to use your kidneys for that hour—it would be indecent to refuse.

Again, suppose pregnancy lasted only an hour, and constituted no threat to life or health. And suppose that a woman becomes pregnant as a result of rape. Admittedly she did not voluntarily do anything to bring about the existence of a child. Admittedly she did nothing at all which would give the unborn person a right to the use of her body. All the same it might well be said, as in the newly emended violinist story, that she *ought* to allow it to remain for that hour—that it would be indecent of her to refuse.

Now some people are inclined to use the term "right" in such a way that it follows from the fact that you ought to allow a person to use your body for the hour he needs, that he has a right to use your body for the hour he needs, even though he has not been given that right by any person or act. They may say that it follows also that if you refuse, you act unjustly toward him. This use of the term is perhaps so common that it cannot be called wrong; nevertheless it seems to me to be an unfortunate loosening of what we would do better to keep a tight rein on. Suppose that box of chocolates I mentioned earlier had not been given to both boys jointly, but was given only to the older boy. There he sits, stolidly eating his way through the box, his small brother watching enviously. Here we are likely to say "You ought not to be so mean. You ought to give your brother some of those chocolates." My own view is that it just does not follow from the truth of this that the brother has any right to any of the chocolates. If the boy refuses to give his brother any, he is greedy, stingy, callous—but not unjust. I suppose that the people I have in mind will say it does follow that the brother has a right to some of the chocolates, and thus that the boy does act unjustly if he refuses to give his brother any. But the effect of saying this is to obscure what we should keep distinct, namely the difference between the boy's refusal in this case and the boy's refusal in the earlier case, in which the box was given to both boys jointly, and in which the small brother thus had what was from any point of view clear title to half. . . .

So my own view is that even though you ought to let the violinist use your kidneys for the one hour he needs, we should not conclude that he has a right to do so—we should say that if you refuse, you are, like the boy who owns all the chocolates and will give none away, self-centered and callous, indecent in fact, but not unjust. And similarly, that even supposing a case in which a woman pregnant due to rape ought to allow the unborn person to use her body for the hour he needs, we should not conclude that he has a right to do so; we should conclude that she is self-centered, callous, indecent, but not unjust, if she refuses. The complaints are no less grave; they are just different. However, there is no need to insist on this point. If anyone does wish to deduce "he has a right" from "you ought," then all the same he must surely grant that there are cases in which it is not morally required of you that you allow that violinist to use your kidneys, and in which he does not have a right to use them, and in which you do not do him an injustice if you refuse. And so also for mother and unborn child. Except in such cases as the unborn person has a right to demand it—and we were leaving open the possibility that there may be such cases—nobody is morally *required* to make large sacrifices, of health, of all other interests and concerns, of all other duties and commitments, for nine years, or even for nine months, in order to keep another person alive. . . .

[W]hile I am arguing for the permissibility of abortion in some cases, I am not arguing for the right to secure the death of the unborn child. It is easy to confuse these two things in that up to a certain point in the life of the fetus it is not able to survive outside the mother's body; hence removing it from her body guarantees its death. But they are importantly different. I have argued that you are not morally required to spend nine months in bed, sustaining the life of that violinist; but to say this is by no means to say that if, when you unplug yourself, there is a miracle and he survives, you then have a right to turn round and slit his throat. You may detach yourself even if this costs him his life; you have no right to be guaranteed his death, by some other means, if unplugging yourself does not kill him. . . .

At this place, however, it should be remembered that we have only been pretending throughout that the fetus is a human being from the moment of conception. A very early abortion is surely not the killing of a person, and so is not dealt with by anything I have said here.

TEST YOUR UNDERSTANDING

1. Thomson begins by asking what argument can proceed *from* the claim that all fetuses are persons, and thus have a right to life, *to* the conclusion that abortion is morally wrong. What crucial premise does she claim this argument needs?

   a. A woman's right to decide what happens in and to her body is stronger than a person's right to life.

   b. A person's right to life is stronger and more stringent than a woman's right to decide what happens in and to her body.

   c. Fetuses have souls from the moment of conception.

   d. A person is morally responsible for anything she caused.

2. Why does Thomson offer the violinist case? (You may select more than one.)

   a. She wants to draw attention to the plight of those with kidney problems.

   b. She uses the case to show that a certain argument against abortion does not work.

   c. She uses the case to draw an *analogy* between being hooked up to the violinist and being pregnant.

3. What does Thomson say to show that the following claim is *false*: if a person has a right to life, then they have a right to the bare minimum necessary to keep them alive? (You may select more than one.)

   a. If the only thing that will keep me alive is Henry Fonda's hand on my forehead, then I nevertheless don't have a right that he fly across the country to heal me.

   b. If the only thing that will keep you alive on a cold night is my coat, and I also need it to stay alive, then you don't have a right to my coat.

   c. The violinist does not have a right to the use of your kidneys.

4. An objector might say that Thomson's argument only establishes, at most, the permissibility of abortion when a pregnancy is due to rape. How does Thomson's essay address the question of whether abortion is permissible when pregnancy resulted from consensual sex?

   a. Thomson says that if a pregnancy resulted from consensual sex, then a woman is responsible for the pregnancy and should not abort.

   b. Thomson does not address this question.

   c. Thomson argues that having consensual sex does not make a woman responsible for the pregnancy in a way that would make abortion wrong.

NOTES AND QUESTIONS

1. *Emergency assistance.* Consider the following example offered by John Martin Fischer[2]:

> Suppose you have planned for many years to take a trip to a very remote place in the Himalaya mountains. You have secured a cabin in an extremely remote and inaccessible place in the mountains. You wish to be alone; you have enough supplies for yourself, and also have some extras in case of an emergency. Unfortunately, a very evil man has kidnapped an innocent person and brought him to die in the desolate mountain country near your cabin. The innocent person wanders for hours and finally happens upon your cabin. . . . You can radio for help, but because of the remoteness and inaccessibility of your cabin and the relatively primitive technology of the country in which it is located, the rescue party will require nine months to reach your cabin. Thus, you are faced with a choice. You can let the innocent stranger into your cabin and provide food and shelter until the rescue party arrives in nine months, or you can forcibly prevent him from entering your cabin (or staying there) and thus cause his death (or perhaps allow him to die). It is evident that he will die unless you allow him to stay in the cabin.

Fischer argues that it seems that, morally, you must allow the stranger in the cabin. He then contends that this judgment casts doubt upon Thomson's claim about the violinist and, therefore, her conclusion about the moral permissibility of abortion.

Exercise: Consider how Thomson might reply to this objection. Is Fischer correct that you must allow the stranger in the cabin? If so, is the cabin case analogous to the violinist case or are there important distinctions between them?

2. *Intentional conception and consensual attachment.* Thomson's main examples all involve people who are burdened without consenting to those burdens. The violinist is attached without one's consent. The people-seeds that take root in one's home are not sought or wanted. Is this a crucial feature of her argument?

Exercise: Suppose the argument, as Thomson presented it, is successful. Now consider a modified case similar to one introduced by Frances Kamm. As in the original case, you are the only person who could help the violinist. You consider attachment, but you are concerned that the burdens may prove too great. So, on a trial basis, you permit the violinist to be attached but discover, after experiencing the burdens, that they are too constricting, painful, and taxing. In that case, would it be wrong to detach yourself? Does a lesson follow about the permissibility of abortion after a woman tries to get pregnant (assuming the fetus is a person)?

Frances Kamm's extensive analysis of the case appears in F. M. Kamm, *Creation and Abortion* (Oxford University Press, 1992).

---

2. Fischer's case and his analysis of it appear in John Martin Fischer, "Abortion and Self-Determination," *Journal of Social Philosophy* 22 (1991): 5–11.

Don Marquis (b. 1935)

Marquis is Professor Emeritus of Philosophy at the University of Kansas. He is widely known for his articles in moral philosophy on topics concerning procreation, death, and end-of-life decisions.

WHY ABORTION IS IMMORAL

This essay sets out an argument that purports to show, as well as any argument in ethics can show, that abortion is, except possibly in rare cases, seriously immoral, that it is in the same moral category as killing an innocent adult human being.

The argument is based on a major assumption. Many of the most insightful and careful writers on the ethics of abortion . . . believe that whether or not abortion is morally permissible stands or falls on whether or not a fetus is the sort of being whose life it is seriously wrong to end. The argument of this essay will assume, but not argue, that they are correct.

Also, this essay will neglect issues of great importance to a complete ethics of abortion. Some anti-abortionists will allow that certain abortions, such as abortion before implantation or abortion when the life of a woman is threatened by a pregnancy or abortion after rape, may be morally permissible. This essay will not explore the casuistry of these hard cases. The purpose of this essay is to develop a general argument for the claim that the overwhelming majority of deliberate abortions are seriously immoral.

A sketch of standard anti-abortion and pro-choice arguments exhibits how those arguments possess certain symmetries that explain why partisans of those positions are so convinced of the correctness of their own positions, why they are not successful in convincing their opponents, and why, to others, this issue seems to be unresolvable. An analysis of the nature of this standoff suggests a strategy for surmounting it.

Consider the way a typical anti-abortionist argues. She will argue or assert that life is present from the moment of conception or that fetuses look like babies or that fetuses possess a characteristic such as a genetic code that is both necessary and sufficient for being human. Anti-abortionists seem to believe that (1) the truth of all of these claims is quite obvious, and (2) establishing any of these claims is sufficient to show that abortion is morally akin to murder.

A standard pro-choice strategy exhibits similarities. The pro-choicer will argue or assert that fetuses are not persons or that fetuses are not rational agents or that fetuses are not social beings. Pro-choicers seem to believe that (1) the truth of any of these claims is quite obvious, and (2) establishing any of these claims is sufficient to show that an abortion is not a wrongful killing.

In fact, both the pro-choice and the anti-abortion claims do seem to be true, although the "it looks like a baby" claim is more difficult to establish the earlier the pregnancy. We seem to have a standoff. How can it be resolved?

As everyone who has taken a bit of logic knows, if any of these arguments concerning abortion is a good argument, it requires not only some claim characterizing fetuses, but also some general moral principle that ties a characteristic of fetuses to having or not having the right to life or to some other moral characteristic that will generate the obligation or the lack of obligation not to end the life of a fetus. Accordingly, the arguments of the anti-abortionist and the pro-choicer need a bit of filling in to be regarded as adequate.

Note what each partisan will say. The anti-abortionist will claim that her position is supported by such generally accepted moral principles as "It is always prima facie seriously wrong to take a human life" or "It is always prima facie seriously wrong to end the life of a baby." Since these are generally accepted moral principles, her position is certainly not obviously wrong. The pro-choicer will claim that her position is supported by such plausible moral principles as "Being a person is what gives an individual intrinsic moral worth" or "It is only seriously prima facie wrong to take the life of a member of the human community." Since these are generally accepted moral principles, the pro-choice position is certainly not obviously wrong. Unfortunately, we have again arrived at a standoff.

Now, how might one deal with this standoff? The standard approach is to try to show how the moral principles of one's opponent lose their plausibility under analysis. It is easy to see how this is possible. On the one hand, the anti-abortionist will defend a moral principle concerning the wrongness of killing which tends to be broad in scope in order that even fetuses at an early stage of pregnancy will fall under it. The problem with broad principles is that they often embrace too much. In this particular instance, the principle "It is always prima facie wrong to take a human life" seems to entail that it is wrong to end the existence of a living human cancer-cell culture, on the grounds that the culture is both living and human. Therefore, it seems that the anti-abortionist's favored principle is too broad.

On the other hand, the pro-choicer wants to find a moral principle concerning the wrongness of killing which tends to be narrow in scope in order that fetuses will *not* fall under it. The problem with narrow principles is that they often do not embrace enough. Hence, the needed principles such as "It is prima facie seriously wrong to kill only persons" or "It is prima facie wrong to kill only rational agents" do not explain why it is wrong to kill infants or young children or the severely retarded or even perhaps the severely mentally ill. Therefore, we seem again to have a standoff. The anti-abortionist charges, not unreasonably, that pro-choice principles concerning killing are too narrow to be acceptable; the pro-choicer charges, not unreasonably, that anti-abortionist principles concerning killing are too broad to be acceptable.

Attempts by both sides to patch up the difficulties in their positions run into further difficulties. The anti-abortionist will try to remove the problem in her position by reformulating her principle concerning killing in terms of human beings. Now we end up with: "It is always prima facie seriously wrong to end the life of a human being." This principle has the advantage of avoiding the problem of the human cancer-cell culture counterexample. But this advantage is purchased at a high price. For although it is clear that a fetus is both human and alive, it is not at all clear that a fetus is a human *being*. There is at least something to be said for the view that something becomes a human being only after a process of development, and that therefore first trimester fetuses and perhaps all fetuses are not yet human beings. . . .

The pro-choicer fares no better. She may attempt to find reasons why killing infants, young children, and the severely retarded is wrong which are independent of her major principle that is supposed to explain the wrongness of taking human life, but which will not also make abortion immoral. This is no easy task. Appeals to social utility will seem satisfactory only to those who resolve not to think of the enormous difficulties with a utilitarian account of the wrongness of killing and the significant social costs of preserving the lives of the unproductive.[1] A pro-choice strategy that extends the definition of "person" to infants or even to young children seems just as arbitrary as an anti-abortion strategy that extends the definition of "human being" to fetuses. Again, we find symmetries in the two positions and we arrive at a standoff. . . .

There is a way out of this apparent dialectical quandary. . . .

A necessary condition of resolving the abortion controversy is a more theoretical account of the wrongness of killing. After all, if we merely believe, but do not understand, why killing adult human beings such as ourselves is wrong, how could we conceivably show that abortion is either immoral or permissible?

In order to develop such an account, we can start from the following unproblematic assumption concerning our own case: it is wrong to kill *us*. Why is it wrong? Some answers can be easily eliminated. It might be said that what makes killing us wrong is that a killing brutalizes the one who kills. But the brutalization consists of being inured to the performance of an act that is hideously immoral; hence, the brutalization does not explain the immorality. It might be said that what makes killing us wrong is the great loss others would experience due to our absence. Although such hubris is understandable, such an explanation does not account for the wrongness of killing hermits, or those whose lives are relatively independent and whose friends find it easy to make new friends.

A more obvious answer is better. What primarily makes killing wrong is neither its effect on the murderer nor its effect on the victim's friends and relatives, but its effect on the victim. The loss of one's life is one of the greatest losses one can suffer. The loss of one's life deprives one of all the experiences, activities, projects, and enjoyments that would otherwise have constituted one's future. Therefore, killing someone is wrong, primarily because the killing inflicts (one of) the greatest possible losses on the victim. To describe this as the loss of life can be misleading, however. The change in my biological state does not by itself make killing me wrong. The effect of the loss of my biological life is the loss to me of all those activities, projects, experiences, and enjoyments which would

---

1. Marquis here is referring to a criticism leveled against **utilitarians**, who explain and justify moral norms by referring to what would bring about the greatest amount of human well-being overall or what would best promote people's interests overall. They tend to argue that one course of action is morally required by showing that, lumping together the effects on everyone, that course of action fulfills a greater amount of people's interests and preferences and frustrates fewer people's interests and preferences, adjusting for intensity, than any alternative course of action. Some have criticized utilitarians as being unable to explain directly, in terms of the victim's interests, why killing is wrong. After all, killing extinguishes the victim and, as a result, there is no longer a live person whose interests are frustrated, as those interests were extinguished along with the victim. This problem is thought to be particularly severe with respect to why we should save—and forbear from killing—people who will be severely disabled, given how expensive their needs are and that, if they die, they will not suffer the frustration of their interests.

otherwise have constituted my future personal life. These activities, projects, experiences, and enjoyments are either valuable for their own sakes or are means to something else that is valuable for its own sake. Some parts of my future are not valued by me now, but will come to be valued by me as I grow older and as my values and capacities change. When I am killed, I am deprived both of what I now value which would have been part of my future personal life, but also what I would come to value. Therefore, when I die, I am deprived of all of the value of my future. Inflicting this loss on me is ultimately what makes killing me wrong. This being the case, it would seem that what makes killing *any* adult human being prima facie seriously wrong is the loss of his or her future. . . .

The claim that what makes killing wrong is the loss of the victim's future is directly supported by two considerations. In the first place, this theory explains why we regard killing as one of the worst of crimes. Killing is especially wrong, because it deprives the victim of more than perhaps any other crime. In the second place, people with AIDS or cancer who know they are dying believe, of course, that dying is a very bad thing for them.[2] They believe that the loss of a future to them that they would otherwise have experienced is what makes their premature death a very bad thing for them. . . .

[T]he claim that the loss of one's future is the wrong-making feature of one's being killed does not entail, as sanctity of human life theories do, that active euthanasia is wrong. Persons who are severely and incurably ill, who face a future of pain and despair, and who wish to die will not have suffered a loss if they are killed. It is, strictly speaking, the value of a human's future which makes killing wrong in this theory. This being so, killing does not necessarily wrong some persons who are sick and dying. Of course, there may be other reasons for a prohibition of active euthanasia, but that is another matter. Sanctity-of-human-life theories seem to hold that active euthanasia is seriously wrong even in an individual case where there seems to be good reason for it independently of public policy considerations. This consequence is most implausible, and it is a plus for the claim that the loss of a future of value is what makes killing wrong that it does not share this consequence. . . .

[T]he account of the wrongness of killing defended in this essay does straightforwardly entail that it is prima facie seriously wrong to kill children and infants, for we do presume that they have futures of value. Since we do believe that it is wrong to kill defenseless little babies, it is important that a theory of the wrongness of killing easily account for this. Personhood theories of the wrongness of killing, on the other hand, cannot straightforwardly account for the wrongness of killing infants and young children. . . .

The claim that the primary wrong-making feature of a killing is the loss to the victim of the value of its future has obvious consequences for the ethics of abortion. The future of a standard fetus includes a set of experiences, projects, activities, and such which are identical with the futures of adult human beings and are identical with the futures of young children. Since the reason that is sufficient to explain why it is wrong to kill human beings after the time of birth is a reason that also applies to fetuses, it follows that abortion is prima facie seriously morally wrong. . . .

---

2. At the time Marquis wrote, there were no effective treatments for HIV infection, and infected patients in the West rapidly deteriorated (as most do now in Africa, where treatments are financially prohibitive).

Of course, this value of a future-like-ours argument, if sound, shows only that abortion is prima facie wrong, not that it is wrong in any and all circumstances. Since the loss of the future to a standard fetus, if killed, is, however, at least as great a loss as the loss of the future to a standard adult human being who is killed, abortion, like ordinary killing, could be justified only by the most compelling reasons. The loss of one's life is almost the greatest misfortune that can happen to one. Presumably abortion could be justified in some circumstances, only if the loss consequent on failing to abort would be at least as great. Accordingly, morally permissible abortions will be rare indeed unless, perhaps, they occur so early in pregnancy that a fetus is not yet definitely an individual. Hence, this argument should be taken as showing that abortion is presumptively very seriously wrong, where the presumption is very strong—as strong as the presumption that killing another adult human being is wrong. . . .

One way to overturn the value of a future-like-ours argument would be to find some account of the wrongness of killing which is at least as intelligible and which has different implications for the ethics of abortion. Two rival accounts possess at least some degree of plausibility. One account is based on the obvious fact that people value the experience of living and wish for that valuable experience to continue. Therefore, it might be said, what makes killing wrong is the discontinuation of that experience for the victim. Let us call this the *discontinuation account*. Another rival account is based upon the obvious fact that people strongly desire to continue to live. This suggests that what makes killing us so wrong is that it interferes with the fulfillment of a strong and fundamental desire, the fulfillment of which is necessary for the fulfillment of any other desires we might have. Let us call this the *desire account*. . . .

One problem with the desire account is that we do regard it as seriously wrong to kill persons who have little desire to live or who have no desire to live or, indeed, have a desire not to live. We believe it is seriously wrong to kill the unconscious, the sleeping, those who are tired of life, and those who are suicidal. The value-of-a-human-future account renders standard morality intelligible in these cases; these cases appear to be incompatible with the desire account.

The desire account is subject to a deeper difficulty. We desire life, because we value the goods of this life. The goodness of life is not secondary to our desire for it. If this were not so, the pain of one's own premature death could be done away with merely by an appropriate alteration in the configuration of one's desires. This is absurd. Hence, it would seem that it is the loss of the goods of one's future, not the interference with the fulfillment of a strong desire to live, which accounts ultimately for the wrongness of killing. . . .

The discontinuation account looks more promising as an account of the wrongness of killing. It seems just as intelligible as the value of a future-like-ours account, but it does not justify an anti-abortion position. Obviously, if it is the continuation of one's activities, experiences, and projects, the loss of which makes killing wrong, then it is not wrong to kill fetuses for that reason, for fetuses do not have experiences, activities, and projects to be continued or discontinued. Accordingly, the discontinuation account does not have the anti-abortion consequences that the value of a future-like-ours account has. Yet, it seems as intelligible as the value of a future-like-ours account, for when we think of what would be wrong with our being killed, it does seem as if it is the discontinuation of what makes our lives worthwhile which makes killing us wrong.

Is the discontinuation account just as good an account as the value of a future-like-ours account? The discontinuation account will not be adequate at all, if it does not refer to the *value* of the experience that may be discontinued. One does not want the discontinuation account to make it wrong to kill a patient who begs for death and who is in severe pain that cannot be relieved short of killing. (I leave open the question of whether it is wrong for other reasons.) Accordingly, the discontinuation account must be more than a bare discontinuation account. It must make some reference to the positive value of the patient's experiences. But, by the same token, the value of a future-like-ours account cannot be a bare future account either. Just having a future surely does not itself rule out killing the above patient. This account must make some reference to the value of the patient's future experiences and projects also. Hence, both accounts involve the value of experiences, projects, and activities. So far we still have symmetry between the accounts.

The symmetry fades, however, when we focus on the time period of the value of the experiences, etc., which has moral consequences. Although both accounts leave open the possibility that the patient in our example may be killed, this possibility is left open only in virtue of the utterly bleak future for the patient. It makes no difference whether the patient's immediate past contains intolerable pain, or consists in being in a coma (which we can imagine is a situation of indifference), or consists in a life of value. If the patient's future is a future of value, we want our account to make it wrong to kill the patient. If the patient's future is intolerable, whatever his or her immediate past, we want our account to allow killing the patient. Obviously, then, it is the value of that patient's future which is doing the work in rendering the morality of killing the patient intelligible.

This being the case, it seems clear that whether one has immediate past experiences or not does no work in the explanation of what makes killing wrong. The addition the discontinuation account makes to the value of a human future account is otiose. Its addition to the value-of-a-future account plays no role at all in rendering intelligible the wrongness of killing. Therefore, it can be discarded with the discontinuation account of which it is a part. . . .

In this essay, it has been argued that the correct ethic of the wrongness of killing can be extended to fetal life and used to show that there is a strong presumption that any abortion is morally impermissible. If the ethic of killing adopted here entails, however, that contraception is also seriously immoral, then there would appear to be a difficulty with the analysis of this essay.

But this analysis does not entail that contraception is wrong. Of course, contraception prevents the actualization of a possible future of value. Hence, it follows from the claim that futures of value should be maximized that contraception is prima facie immoral. This obligation to maximize does not exist, however; furthermore, nothing in the ethics of killing in this paper entails that it does. The ethics of killing in this essay would entail that contraception is wrong only if something were denied a human future of value by contraception. Nothing at all is denied such a future by contraception, however.

Candidates for a subject of harm by contraception fall into four categories: (1) some sperm or other, (2) some ovum or other, (3) a sperm and an ovum separately, and (4) a sperm and an ovum together. Assigning the harm to some sperm is utterly arbitrary, for no reason can be given for making a sperm the subject of harm rather than an ovum. Assigning the harm to some ovum is utterly arbitrary, for no reason can be given for making an ovum the subject of harm rather than a sperm. One might attempt to avoid these problems by insisting that contraception deprives both the sperm and the ovum separately of a valuable future like ours. On this alternative, too many futures are lost. Contraception was supposed to be wrong, because it deprived us of one future of value, not two. One might attempt to avoid this problem by holding that contraception deprives the combination of sperm and ovum of a valuable future like ours. But here the definite article misleads. At the time of contraception, there are hundreds of millions of sperm, one (released) ovum and millions of possible combinations of all of these. There is no actual combination at all. Is the subject of the loss to be a merely possible combination? Which one? This alternative does not yield an actual subject of harm either. Accordingly, the immorality of contraception is not entailed by the loss of a future-like-ours argument simply because there is no nonarbitrarily identifiable subject of the loss in the case of contraception.

The purpose of this essay has been to set out an argument for the serious presumptive wrongness of abortion subject to the assumption that the moral permissibility of abortion stands or falls on the moral status of the fetus. Since a fetus possesses a property, the possession of which in adult human beings is sufficient to make killing an adult human being wrong, abortion is wrong. This way of dealing with the problem of abortion seems superior to other approaches to the ethics of abortion, because it rests on an ethics of killing which is close to self-evident, because the crucial morally relevant property clearly applies to fetuses, and because the argument avoids the usual equivocations on "human life," "human being," or "person." The argument rests neither on religious claims nor on Papal dogma. It is not subject to the objection of "speciesism." Its soundness is compatible with the moral permissibility of euthanasia and contraception. It deals with our intuitions concerning young children.

Finally, this analysis can be viewed as resolving a standard problem—indeed, *the* standard problem—concerning the ethics of abortion. Clearly, it is wrong to kill adult human beings. Clearly, it is not wrong to end the life of some arbitrarily chosen single human cell. Fetuses seem to be like arbitrarily chosen human cells in some respects and like adult humans in other respects. The problem of the ethics of abortion is the problem of determining the fetal property that settles this moral controversy. The thesis of this essay is that the problem of the ethics of abortion, so understood, is solvable.

TEST YOUR UNDERSTANDING

1. Why does Marquis discuss why it is wrong to kill adult humans?

   a. He says that if the reasons it is wrong to kill adult humans also apply to fetuses, then it is also wrong to kill fetuses.

   b. He wants to argue that it is not always wrong to kill adult humans.

   c. He wants to argue that the murder of adult humans is morally wrong.

2. What is Marquis's account of why it is wrong to kill an adult human?

   a. Killing brutalizes the killer.

   b. Killing someone inflicts harm on their surviving relatives.

   c. Killing someone deprives them of a valuable future.

3. What does Marquis think about euthanasia, the killing of a dying person who asks to die in order to be spared further pain?

   a. The usual explanation for the wrongness of killing does not apply in this case, because the person does not have a future of value.

   b. Euthanasia is morally wrong because it is always wrong to kill a person.

4. Marquis discusses the *desire account*, which holds that it is wrong to kill a person because the person desires to continue to live. What is Marquis's objection to this view?

NOTES AND QUESTIONS

1. *Does having a personality matter?* Marquis argues that a fetus who dies and an adult who dies prematurely are harmed in the same way. Both are deprived of their future and, in particular, enjoying life's goods and opportunities.

   Consider the following objection to his argument:

> We regard the deaths of adults and children as tragedies because they have distinctive personalities, interests, desires, and characteristics that make their lives worth living. The death of an adult or a child eliminates the future of that distinctive, individual personality and the pursuit of its development and projects. The death of a fetus differs because the fetus does not yet have any distinctively individual features.

Explain this objection and consider how Marquis might respond.

2. *The significance of potential.* Marquis's argument for the "serious presumptive wrongness of abortion" appeals to the fact that "a fetus possesses a property" such that killing it would be wrong. Namely, the fetus has the potential for a valuable future if it is not killed.

   What if kittens could have valuable futures analogous to that of adults? Michael Tooley offered the following thought experiment in his essay, "Abortion and Infanticide," *Philosophy & Public Affairs* 2 (Autumn, 1972): 37–65.

> Suppose at some future time a chemical were to be discovered which when injected into the brain of a kitten would cause the kitten to develop into a cat possessing a brain of the sort possessed by humans,

and consequently into a cat having all the psychological capabilities characteristic of adult humans. Such cats would be able to think, to use language, and so on.

Exercise: Consider the objection that Marquis's argument implausibly suggests that failing to inject the kitten is "seriously morally wrong" because it would deprive the kitten of the sort of valuable future that we think it is wrong to deprive adults of. Consider the related objection that Marquis's argument suggests if such a chemical were available: killing the kitten instead of injecting it would be comparable to killing an adult human being, for both actions would deprive a being of a valuable future that she could enjoy. How might Marquis respond to these objections?

3. What is the relationship between Marquis's essay and Thomson's essay "A Defense of Abortion"? On the one hand, their conclusions disagree: Thomson argues that many abortions are morally permissible, and Marquis argues that most abortions are morally wrong. However, the conclusion Marquis devotes the essay to arguing for is this:

> Marquis's Primary Conclusion: A fetus is the sort of being whose life it is seriously wrong to end.

But this conclusion is simply *the same claim* that Thomson discusses by talking about the claim that fetuses are persons and thus have a right to life. Thomson doesn't take a stand on whether Marquis's Primary Conclusion is true; she is simply concerned to discuss what follows from it.

Marquis makes the following assumption, which he states in the second paragraph of his essay:

> The Controversial Assumption: Whether or not abortion is morally permissible stands or falls on whether or not a fetus is the sort of being whose life it is seriously wrong to end.

If we take Marquis's Primary Conclusion and his Controversial Assumption together, we get the conclusion that abortion is morally wrong.

Thomson's essay is devoted to challenging the Controversial Assumption. Thomson's essay was already famous at the time that Marquis was writing. Although he does not mention her essay, his second paragraph is written to communicate to his readers that he is assuming that Thomson's essay is wrong and that the Controversial Assumption is true.

A reader might be convinced by most of what *both* Thomson and Marquis say. A reader might be convinced by Marquis's argument for his Primary Conclusion but be convinced by Thomson that the Controversial Assumption is false, and thus conclude (with Thomson) that many abortions are permissible.

Elizabeth Harman (b. 1975)

Harman is Laurance S. Rockefeller Professor of Philosophy and Human Values at Princeton University. She has written on topics in moral philosophy, including supererogation, moral responsibility, harm, and the ethics of procreation.

THE MORAL SIGNIFICANCE OF ANIMAL PAIN AND ANIMAL DEATH

1. Animal Cruelty and Animal Killing

In this paper, I will be concerned with this question: what follows from the claim that we have a certain kind of *strong* reason against animal cruelty? In particular, what follows for the ethics of killing animals? My discussion will be focused on examination of a view that I take some people to hold, though I find it deeply puzzling. The view is that although we have strong reasons against animal cruelty, we lack strong reasons against painlessly killing animals in the prime of life; on this view, either we have no reasons against such killings, or we have only weak reasons. My attention will be focused on animals of intermediate mental sophistication, including dogs, cats, cows, and pigs, while excluding more mentally sophisticated animals such as humans and apes, and excluding less mentally sophisticated creatures such as fish and insects. Whether any of what I say also applies to the animals I am excluding is a topic for further work.

I am interested in the claim that we have a certain kind of *strong* reason against animal cruelty. As will emerge, I take our reasons against animal cruelty to be strong in several ways. One way they are strong is the following: if an action would cause significant suffering to an animal, then that action is *pro tanto* wrong; that is, the action is wrong unless justified by other considerations. Such a view of animal cruelty is part of a more general non-consequentialist view on which there is a moral asymmetry between causing *harm* and causing *positive benefit*: our reasons against harming are stronger and of a different type than our reasons in favor of benefiting (and our reasons against preventing benefits).

Here is the claim that I take to be believed by some people, and which I plan to examine:

The Surprising Claim:
(a) we have strong reasons not to cause intense pain to animals: the fact that an action would cause intense pain to an animal makes the action wrong unless it is justified by other considerations; and
(b) we do not have strong reasons not to kill animals: it is not the case that killing an animal is wrong unless it is justified by other considerations.

The Surprising Claim seems to lie behind the following common belief:

While there is something deeply morally wrong with factory farming, there is nothing morally wrong with "humane" farms on which the animals are happy until they are killed.

Some people think that factory farming is morally wrong, and that it is morally wrong to financially support factory farming, because factory farming involves subjecting animals to intense suffering. By contrast, "humane" farms do not subject animals to suffering, but they do kill animals in the prime of life. Some people who believe factory farming is morally wrong also believe that this "humane" farming is morally permissible. They appear to believe that while we have strong moral reasons not to cause animals pain, we lack strong moral reasons against killing animals in the prime of life.[1]

I find the Surprising Claim puzzling. My goal in this paper is to examine the Surprising Claim. I will ask: how could the Surprising Claim be true? In section 2, I will argue that the Surprising Claim is not true. I will then consider [three] views on which the Surprising Claim is true; each view rejects one of the claims made in my argument of section 2. I will ask what can be said in favor of each view and whether any of these views is true. I will argue that each view is false. The [third] view I will consider is Jeff McMahan's time-relative interests view; one of my conclusions will thus be that this well-known view is false. Finally, I will draw [a] lesson about the relationship between the significance of animal pain and the significance of animal death.

2. An Argument Against the Surprising Claim

In this section, I will argue that the Surprising Claim is false.

The Surprising Claim:
  (a) we have strong reasons not to cause intense pain to animals: the fact that an action would cause intense pain to an animal makes the action wrong unless it is justified by other considerations; and
  (b) we do not have strong reasons not to kill animals: it is not the case that killing an animal is wrong unless it is justified by other considerations.

Consider part (a) of the Surprising Claim. If (a) is true, what explains its truth? It seems that it must be true because animals have moral status, and because any action that significantly harms something with moral status is impermissible unless justified by other considerations.

Here is an argument that the Surprising Claim is false:

1. If it is true that we have strong moral reasons against causing intense pain to animals, such that doing so is impermissible unless justified by other considerations, then part of the explanation of this truth is that animals have moral status.

2. If it is true that we have strong moral reasons against causing intense pain to animals, such that doing so is impermissible unless justified by other considerations, then part of the explanation of this truth is that significantly harming something with moral status is impermissible unless justified by other considerations.

---

1. Someone might believe we should *support* "humane" farming because it is so much morally *better* than factory farming, without believing "humane" farming is morally unproblematic: this person need not believe the Surprising Claim. [Harman's note.]

3. If an action painlessly kills a healthy animal in the prime of life, then that action significantly harms the animal.

4. If it is true that we have strong moral reasons against causing intense pain to animals, such that doing so is impermissible unless justified by other considerations, then painlessly killing a healthy animal in the prime of life is impermissible unless justified by other considerations (1, 2, 3).

5. Therefore, the Surprising Claim is false (4).

I endorse this argument. I think it gives the right account of why the Surprising Claim is false. In the next three sections, I will discuss [three] views on which the Surprising Claim is true; those views reject this argument.

3. First View: Killing an Animal Does Not Harm It

Consider this view:

> First View: An action that painlessly kills an animal in the prime of life deprives the animal of future life, which would be a positive benefit to the animal, but does not harm the animal.

According to the First View, death is *bad* for animals, but a proponent of the First View would point out that there are two ways that events can be bad for a being: an event can be or lead to something that is in itself bad for the being, such as suffering, or an event can be a deprivation of something that would have been in itself good for the being. A being is *harmed* when it undergoes something that is in itself bad, but a being is not typically harmed when it is merely prevented from something good.

According to the First View, claim 3 is false: while death is bad for animals in that it deprives them of futures that would be good for them, it does not harm them because it does not involve anything that is in itself bad for them, such as pain. . . .

The First View is false because, while it is typically the case that when a being fails to get a benefit, the being is not harmed, nevertheless some actions that deprive a being of a benefit do thereby harm the being. If someone deafens you (causes you to become permanently deaf), she simply deprives you of the benefit of hearing, but she thereby harms you. If someone steals your money, she simply deprives you of the benefit the money would have provided, but she thereby harms you.

In particular, actively and physically interfering with a person in such a way that she is deprived of a benefit does typically harm that person. And if this is true of persons, it should also be true of animals. But killing an animal does actively, physically interfere with the animal in such a way that the animal is deprived of a benefit. So killing an animal is harming that animal.

4. Second View: Death Is Not Bad for Animals Because Animals Lack Sufficient Psychological Connection with Their Futures

In this section, I will consider [another] view on which the Surprising Claim is true. [The view is a] more specific elaboration of the following basic idea:

> When a person dies, she *loses out* on the future she would have had. She had expectations, hopes, plans, and dreams that are thwarted. Animals, however, do not *lose out* on their futures. They do not have the right kind of psychological connection to their future lives to be losing out on them.

Here is one way of making this basic idea more precise. It is an argument that would be offered by someone who endorses the Second View:

(i)   The death of a person is bad for her only because it frustrates her desires and plans for the future.

(ii) Therefore, death is bad in general only because it frustrates desires and plans.

(iii) Animals do not have desires and plans for the future.

(iv) Therefore, animals' deaths are not bad for them.

The Second View is more radical than the First View. The First View granted that death is bad for animals but denied that animals are harmed by being killed. The Second View denies that death is bad for animals at all. It follows that animals are not harmed by death, and that claim 3 is false.

The Second View is false because its claim (i) is false. It is true that *one way* death is bad for most persons is that it frustrates their desires and plans for the future. But a person might not have any desires and plans for the future, yet her death could still be bad for her. Consider someone who is depressed and wants to die; she is so depressed that she lacks any desires about the future and has no plans for the future. Suppose she in fact would recover from her depression and have a good future if she continued to live (because her family is about to intervene and get her treatment). If she dies now, then death deprives her of a good future and is bad for her. But death does not frustrate her desires and plans. In a more far-fetched example, consider someone who *truly* lives in the moment. She enjoys life but has absolutely no expectations or desires about the future, and no plans for the future. If she dies now, her death is bad for her, although it frustrates no desires or plans.

Just as a person's death may be bad for her because she is losing out on a future life that would be good for her (even if she lacks desires and plans for the future), similarly an animal's death may be bad for it because the animal loses out on a future life that would be good for it, even if the animal lacks desires and plans for the future. This is why the Second View is false. . . .

5. [Third] View: McMahan's Time-Relative Interests View

In this section, I will discuss a [third] view on which the Surprising Claim is true. Like the First View, the [Third] View grants that we have *some reasons* against killing animals; the [Third] View denies that these reasons are *strong....*

The [Third] View is a view of Jeff McMahan's. He calls it the "time-relative interests view."[2] On this view, the badness of death for a morally significant being is not a direct function of what the being loses out on in dying; the badness of death is not simply a matter of how good the lost life would have been. Rather, it also matters what the being's *psychological relationship* is with that potential future life. If a being is such that, were it to continue to live, there would be only weak psychological connections between its current stage and its future life, then the goodness of that future is *less of a loss* for it than if the being would have stronger psychological connections with its future life: the being currently has less of an interest in continuing to live than if the psychological connection he would have to a future life would be stronger. This view has the virtue that it can explain why, as is plausible, the death of a ten year old is worse for the ten year old than the death of a one month old is bad for the one month old: while the infant loses out on more life, so loses more, the ten year old would have much greater psychological connections with its future if it continued to live. According to the time-relative interests view, the one month old has a weaker interest in continuing to live than the ten year old has.

The implications of the time-relative interests view for animal death are that animal death is not very bad for animals because animals do not have very strong psychological connections to their future selves: they do not have *strong interests* in continuing to live. But the view does not hold (nor is it plausible) that animals lack any psychological connections to their future selves: so the view does not hold that animal death is not bad for animals, nor that we have no reasons against killing animals. The view grants that animals have *some interest* in continuing to live.[3] The view supports the following claim:

We have strong reasons against causing animal pain, and we have some reasons against painlessly killing animals in the prime of life, but these reasons are weakened by animals' lack of deep psychological continuity over time.

(Note that I stipulated at the beginning of the paper that I am only concerned with animals of intermediate mental sophistication, including dogs, cats, cows, and pigs, and excluding humans, apes, fish, and insects. My claims about the time-relative interests view's implications regarding animals are restricted to these animals of intermediate mental sophistication.)

2. Jeff McMahan, *The Ethics of Killing: Problems at the Margins of Life* (Oxford University Press, 2002). [Harman's note.]

3. Note that what a being "has an interest in" is a matter of what is *in the being's interests*, not a matter of what the being desires or wants. [Harman's note.]

The [Third] View can grant claims 1 and 2 of the argument of section 2. But the [Third] View denies claim 3: it holds that, while death is a harm to animals, it is a minor harm. On this view, killing an animal does not *significantly* harm the animal, and it is not the case that killing an animal is wrong unless justified by other considerations.

I will now argue that the time-relative interests view is false. . . . My argument relies on some substantive claims about the nature of the psychological connections that animals have over time, and the way the time-relative interests view would handle these connections.[4] In particular, I assume that on the time-relative interests view, an animal now has greater psychological connection to its nearer future life than to its farther future life, and that an animal now has negligible psychological connection to its future life a sufficient amount of time into the future, such as five years into the future. It follows from this that, on the time-relative interests view, while it is currently in an animal's interest to continue to live for the next several months (at least), an animal currently lacks any interest in being alive five years from now, currently lacks any interest in having particular good experiences five years from now, and currently lacks any interest in avoiding particular bad experiences five years from now—any experiences it would have five years from now are so psychologically remote that the animal currently has no interests regarding those experiences.

My objection relies on two cases.

> Billy is a cow with a serious illness. If the illness is not treated now and is allowed to run its course, then Billy will begin to suffer mildly very soon, the suffering will get steadily worse, Billy will be in agony for a few months, and then Billy will die. If the illness is treated now, Billy will undergo surgery under anesthetic tomorrow. Billy will suffer more severely over the next two weeks (from his recovery) than he would have from the illness during that time, but then he will be discomfort-free and he will never suffer agony; he will be healthy and able to live a normal life.

It is permissible to do the surgery on Billy. This is permissible because, while the surgery will cause Billy to suffer, which he now has an interest in avoiding, it will prevent worse suffering to Billy, which he also now has an interest in avoiding.

> Tommy is a horse with a serious illness. If the illness is not treated now and is allowed to run its course, Tommy will live an ordinary discomfort-free life for five years, but then Tommy will suffer horribly for several months and then die. If the illness is treated now, then Tommy will undergo surgery under anesthetic tomorrow. Tommy will suffer over the following two weeks, but not nearly as severely as he would five years from now. Tommy will be completely cured and will be able to live a healthy normal life for another fifteen years.

---

4. I am also assuming that the time-relative interests view sees the badness of the death of animals as sufficiently diminished that it does not count as the kind of significant harm that is pro tanto wrong to cause. [Harman's note.]

It is permissible to do the surgery on Tommy. This is in fact permissible because Tommy has an interest in getting to live a full life, and though he has an interest in avoiding the pain of recovery from surgery, it is overall in his interests to have the surgery.

But the time-relative interests view cannot explain why it is permissible to do the operation on Tommy. On that view, Tommy has a reasonably strong interest in avoiding pain in the immediate future; he has no interest in avoiding suffering five years from now or in avoiding death five years from now. While the time-relative interests view can easily account for the permissibility of the surgery on Billy, it cannot account for the permissibility of the surgery on Tommy.

Because the time-relative interests view cannot accommodate the truth that it is permissible to do the surgery on Tommy, and the truth that the two surgeries on Tommy and Billy are permissible for the same basic reasons, the time-relative interests view must be false.

6. Conclusion

What lesson [has] emerged from our examination of the Surprising Claim and the [three] views? The basic lesson is that if we have strong moral reasons not to cause animal pain, we must also have strong moral reasons not to kill animals, even painlessly. In section 2, I argued that this is true. I have considered [three] ways one might reject this argument and argued that each one fails. . . .

TEST YOUR UNDERSTANDING

1. Consider this claim: we have strong reasons against causing animal suffering, but we have no reasons against painlessly killing animals. Harman discusses this claim. Does she argue that it is true or that it is false?

2. Harman disagrees with the claim that the death of a person is bad for her only because it frustrates her desires and plans for the future, because Harman thinks that there is another way that death can be bad for a person. What is that way?

3. Why would Harman disagree with the following claim? "Killing a person just deprives her of a *benefit* (future life); killing a person does not *harm* her."

   a. Future life is not always beneficial, but it is still wrong to kill someone.

   b. Sometimes the deprivation of a benefit does harm a person, and if there is physical interference with a person to deprive them of a benefit, this does typically amount to harming them.

4. What is the time-relative interests view?

   a. The view that a person should spend time with her relatives (such as grandparents).

b. The view that animals have no interest in continuing to live because they cannot form elaborate life plans.

c. The view that how much of an interest a being has in enjoying particular future experiences depends on how psychologically connected those experiences would be with its present state.

NOTES AND QUESTIONS

1. Harman does not argue for the claim that there are strong reasons against causing animal suffering. But if we assume that there are strong reasons against causing animal suffering—as many people believe—then Harman's argument implies that there are also strong reasons against painlessly killing animals. What does this mean about so-called "humane" farms that raise animals in pleasant conditions and then painlessly kill them? Does it follow from Harman's argument that "humane" farms are no better than factory farms, which cause animals to suffer during their lives before the animals are killed?

2. How could we argue for the claim that there are strong reasons against causing animal suffering? Peter Singer has argued as follows:

   (i)   It is not arbitrary to draw a moral line at *sentience* (the ability to have experiences).

   (ii) It would be arbitrary to draw a moral line anywhere else, such as between animals and persons; indeed, this would be just as arbitrary as drawing a line between men and women or between people of different races.

   (iii) Morality does not draw arbitrary lines.

   Therefore:

   (iv) Morally speaking, persons and animals count equally.[5]

   If persons and animals count equally, then it seems to follow that we have strong reasons against causing animals to suffer. Is this argument convincing? Do we have strong reasons against causing animals to suffer?

3. The time-relative interests view holds that an animal's interest in having certain experiences in the future is *relative to* the degree of psychological connection the animal would have with that future.

   a. Imagine an animal that has no capacity to form memories at all but does have experiences in the moment. Would the time-relative interests view say that death is bad for this animal?

   b. McMahan developed his view partly to defend a liberal, permissive view about the ethics of abortion. How can the time-relative interests view help to support a permissive view of abortion? Do fetuses have strong or weak psychological ties to their future lives?

5. Peter Singer, "All Animals Are Equal," in ed. Tom Regan and Peter Singer, *Animal Rights and Human Obligations* (Oxford University Press, 1989), 215–26.

Cora Diamond (b. 1937)

Diamond is Kenan Professor of Philosophy Emeritus at University of Virginia. She is the author of *The Realistic Spirit* (1991) and of many essays in philosophy of language, political philosophy, and moral philosophy.

EATING MEAT AND EATING PEOPLE

This paper is a response to a certain sort of argument defending the rights of animals. Part I is a brief explanation of the background and of the sort of argument I want to reject; Part II is an attempt to characterize those arguments: they contain fundamental confusions about moral relations between people and people *and* between people and animals. And Part III is an indication of what I think can still be said on—as it were—the animals' side.

I

The background to the paper is the recent discussions of animals' rights by Peter Singer and Tom Regan and a number of other philosophers.[1] The basic type of argument in many of these discussions is encapsulated in the word "speciesism." The word I think is originally Richard Ryder's, but Peter Singer is responsible for making it popular in connection with obvious sort of argument: that in our attitude to members of other species we have prejudices which are completely analogous to the prejudices people may have with regard to members of other races, and these prejudices will be connected with the ways we are blind to our own exploitation and oppression of the other group. We are blind to the fact that what we do to them deprives them of their rights; we do not want to see this because we profit from it, and so we make use of what are really morally irrelevant differences between them and ourselves to justify the difference in treatment. Putting it fairly crudely: if we say "You cannot live here because you are black," this would be supposed to be parallel to saying "You can be used for our experiments, because you are only an animal and cannot talk." If the first is unjustifiable prejudice, so equally is the second. . . .

It is on the basis of this sort of claim, that the rights of all animals should be given equal consideration, that Singer and Regan and Ryder and others have argued that we must give up killing animals for food, and must drastically cut back—at least—the use of animals in scientific research. And so on.

1. See especially Peter Singer, *Animal Liberation* (New York Review, 1975), and Tom Regan and Peter Singer, eds, *Animal Rights and Human Obligations* (Prentice-Hall, 1976). [Diamond's note.]

That argument seems to me to be confused. I do not dispute that there are analogies between the case of our relations to animals and the case of a dominant group's relation to some other group of human beings which it exploits or treats unjustly in other ways. But the analogies are not simple and straightforward, and it is not clear how far they go. The Singer–Regan approach makes it hard to see what is important *either* in our relationship with other human beings *or* in our relationship with animals. . . .

||

[I write this as a vegetarian, but one distressed by the obtuseness of the normal arguments. . . .]

Discussions of vegetarianism and animals' rights often start with discussion of human rights. We may then be asked what it is that grounds the claims that people have such rights, and whether similar grounds may not after all be found in the case of animals.

All such discussions are beside the point. For they ask why we do not kill people (very irrational ones, let us say) for food, or why we do not treat people in ways which would cause them distress or anxiety and so on, when for the sake of meat we are willing enough to kill *animals* or treat them in ways which cause them distress. This is a totally wrong way of beginning the discussion, because it ignores certain quite central facts—facts which, if attended to, would make it clear that *rights* are not what is crucial. *We do not eat our dead*, even when they have died in automobile accidents or been struck by lightning, and their flesh might be first class. We do not eat them; or if we do, it is a matter of extreme need, or of some special ritual—and even in cases of obvious extreme need, there is very great reluctance. We also do not eat our amputated limbs. (Or if we did, it would be in the same kinds of special circumstances in which we eat our dead.) Now the fact that we do not eat our dead is not a consequence—not a direct one in any event—of our unwillingness to kill people for food or other purposes. It is not a direct consequence of our unwillingness to cause distress to people. Of course it *would* cause distress to people to think that they might be eaten when they were dead, but it causes distress because of what it is to eat a dead person. Hence we cannot elucidate what (if anything) is wrong—if that is the word—with eating people by appealing to the distress it would cause, in the way we can point to the distress caused by stamping on someone's toe as a reason why we regard it as a wrong to him. Now if we do not eat people who are already dead and also do not kill people for food, it is at least *prima facie* plausible that our reasons in the two cases might be related, and hence must be looked into by anyone who wants to claim that we have no good reasons for not eating people which are not also good reasons for not eating animals. Anyone who, in discussing this issue, focuses on our reasons for not killing people or our reasons for not causing them suffering quite evidently runs a risk of leaving altogether out of his discussion those fundamental features of our relationship to other human beings which are involved in our not eating them. . . .

. . . One could say that it would be impious to treat the dead so, but the word "impious" does not make for clarity, it only asks for explanation. We can most naturally speak of a kind of action as morally wrong when we have some firm grasp of what *kind* of beings are involved. But there are some actions, like giving people names, that are part of the way we come to understand and indicate our recognition of *what* kind it is with which we are concerned. And "morally wrong" will often not fit our refusals to act in such a way, or our acting in an opposed sort of way. . . . Again, it is not "morally wrong" to eat our pets; people who ate their pets would not have pets in the same sense of that term. (If we call an animal that we are fattening for the table a pet, we are making a crude joke of a familiar sort.) A pet is not something to eat, it is given a name, is let into our houses and may be spoken to in ways in which we do not normally speak to cows or squirrels. That is to say, it is given some part of the character of a person. (This may be more or less sentimental; it need not be sentimental at all.) Treating pets in these ways is not at all a matter of recognizing some *interest* which pets have in being so treated. . . .

. . . We learn what a human being is in—among other ways—sitting at a table where *WE* eat *THEM* [animals]. We are around the table and they are on it. The difference between human beings and animals is not to be discovered by studies of Washoe[2] or the activities of dolphins. It is not that sort of study or ethology or evolutionary theory that is going to tell us the difference between us and animals: the difference is, as I have suggested, a central concept for human life and is more an object of contemplation than observation (though that might be misunderstood; I am not suggesting it is a matter of intuition). One source of confusion here is that we fail to distinguish between "the difference between animals and people" and "the differences between animals and people"; the same sort of confusion occurs in discussions of the relationship of men and women. In both cases people appeal to scientific evidence to show that "the difference" is not as deep as we think; but all that such evidence can show, or show directly, is that the differences are less sharp then we think. In the case of the difference between animals and people, it is clear that we form the idea of this difference, create the concept of the difference, knowing perfectly well the overwhelmingly obvious similarities.

It may seem that by the sort of line I have been suggesting, I should find myself having to justify slavery. For do we not learn—if we live in a slave society—what slaves are and what masters are through the structure of a life in which we are here and do this, and they are there and do that? Do we not learn *the difference between a master and a slave* that way? In fact I do not think it works quite that way, but at this point I am not trying to justify anything, only to indicate that our starting point in thinking about the relationships among human beings is not a *moral agent* as an item on one side, and on the other *a being capable of suffering, thought, speech*, etc; and similarly (*mutatis mutandis*) in the case of our thought about the relationship between human beings and animals. . . . [A] starting point . . . must be understanding what is involved in such things as our not eating people: no more than our not eating pets does *that* rest

---

2. Washoe, a chimpanzee who lived from 1965 to 2007, was the first non-human to learn American Sign Language.

on recognition of the claims of a being simply as one capable of suffering and enjoyment. To argue otherwise, to argue as Singer and Regan do, is not to give a defence of animals; it is to attack significance in human life. The Singer–Regan arguments amount to this: knee-jerk liberals on racism and sexism ought to go knee-jerk about cows and guinea-pigs; and they certainly show how that can be done, not that it ought to be. They might reply: If you are right, then we are, or should be, willing to let animals suffer for the sake of significance in *our* life—for the sake, as it were, of the concept of the human. And what is that but speciesism again—more high-falutin perhaps than the familiar kind but no less morally disreputable for that? Significance, though, is not an end, is not something I am proposing as an alternative to the prevention of unnecessary suffering, to which the latter might be sacrificed. The ways in which we mark what human life is belong to the source of moral life, and no appeal to the prevention of suffering which is blind to this can in the end be anything but self-destructive.

III

Have I not then, by attacking such arguments, completely sawn off the branch I am sitting on? Is there any other way of showing anyone that he does have reason to treat animals better than he is treating them? . . .

. . . [T]he utilitarian vegetarians' approach: They are not, they say, especially fond of, or interested in, animals. They may point that out they do not "love them." They do not want to anthropomorphize them, and are concerned to put their position as distinct from one which they see as sentimental anthropomorphizing. Just as you do not have to prove that underneath his black skin the black man has a white man inside in order to recognize his rights, you do not have to see animals in terms of your emotional responses to people to recognize their rights. So the direction of their argument is: *we* are only one kind of *animal*; if what is fair for us is concern for our interests, that depends only on our being living animals *with* interests—and if that *is* fair, it is fair for *any* animal. They do not, that is, want to move from concern for people to concern for four-legged people or feathered people—to beings who deserve that concern only because we think of them as having a little person inside.

To make a contrast, I want to take a piece of vegetarian propaganda of a very different sort.

LEARNING TO BE A DUTIFUL CARNIVORE[3]
Dogs and cats and goats and cows,
Ducks and chickens, sheep and sows
Woven into tales for tots,
Pictured on their walls and pots.
Time for dinner! Come and eat

---

3. *The British Vegetarian*, Jan/Feb 1969, p. 59. [Diamond's note.]

All your lovely, juicy meat.
One day ham from Percy Porker
(In the comics he's a corker),
Then the breast from Mrs Cluck
Or the wing from Donald Duck.
Liver next from Clara Cow
(No, it doesn't hurt her now).
Yes, that leg's from Peter Rabbit
Chew it well; make that a habit.
Eat the creatures killed for sale,
But never pull the pussy's tail.
Eat the flesh from "filthy hogs"
But never be unkind to dogs.
Grow up into double-think—
Kiss the hamster; skin the mink.
Never think of slaughter, dear,
That's why animals are here.
They only come on earth to die,
So eat your meat, and don't ask why.

Jane Legge

What that is trying to bring out is a kind of inconsistency, or confusion mixed with hypocrisy—what it sees as that—in our ordinary ways of thinking about animals, confusions that come out, not only but strikingly, in what children are taught about them. . . .

The extension to animals of modes of thinking characteristic of our responses to human beings is extremely complex, and includes a great variety of things. The idea of an animal as company is a striking kind of case; it brings it out that the notion of a fellow creature does not involve just the extension of moral concepts like charity or justice. Those are, indeed, among the most familiar of such extensions; thus the idea of a fellow creature may go with feeding birds in winter, thought of as something akin to charity, or again with giving a hunted animal a sporting chance, where that is thought of as something akin to justice or fairness. I should say that the notion of a fellow creature is extremely *labile*, and that is partly because it is not something over and above the extensions of such concepts as justice, charity and friendship-or-companionship-or-cordiality. . . .

. . . [T]he notion of vermin makes sense against the background of the idea of animals in general as not mere things. Certain groups of animals are then singled out as *not* to be treated fully as the rest are, where the idea might be that the rest are to be hunted only fairly and not meanly poisoned. Again, the killing of dangerous animals in self-defence forms part of a pattern in which circumstances of immediate danger make a difference, assuming as a background the independent life of the lion (say), perceived in terms not limited to the way it might serve our ends. What I am suggesting here is that certain modes of response may be seen as withdrawals from *some* animals ("vermin"), or from animals in *some* circumstances (danger), of what would otherwise belong to recognizing them as animals, just as the notion of an enemy or of a slave may involve the withdrawing from the person involved of some of what would belong to recognition of him as a human being. Thus for example in the case of slaves, there may be no formal social institution of the slave's name in the same full sense as there is for others, or there may be a denial of socially significant ancestry, and so on. Or a man who is outlawed may be killed like an animal. Here then the idea would be that the notion of a slave or an enemy or an outlaw assumes a background of response to persons, and recognition that what happens in *these* cases is that we have something which we are *not* treating as what it—in a way—is. Of course, even in these cases, a great deal of the response to "human being" may remain intact, as for example what may be done with the dead body. Or again, if the enemyhood is so deep as to remove even these restraints, and men dance on the corpses of their enemies . . . the point of this can only be understood in terms of the violation of what is taken to be how you treat the corpse of a human being. It is because you know it *is* that, that you are treating it with some point as that is *not* to be treated. And no one who does it could have the slightest difficulty—whatever contempt he might feel—in understanding why someone had gone off and been sick instead.

Now suppose I am a practical-minded hardheaded slaveholder whose neighbour has, on his deathbed, freed his slaves. I might regard such a man as foolish, but not as batty, not batty in the way I should think of someone if he had, let us say, freed his cows on his deathbed. Compare the case Orwell describes, from his experience in the Spanish Civil War, of being unable to shoot at a half-dressed man who was running along the top of the trench parapet, holding up his trousers with both hands as he ran. "I had come here to shoot at 'Fascists,' but a man who is holding up his trousers is not a 'Fascist,' he is visibly a fellow-creature, similar to yourself, and you do not feel like shooting at him."[4] The notion of enemy ("Fascist") and fellow creature are there in a kind of tension, and even a man who could shoot at a man running holding his trousers up might recognize perfectly well why Orwell could not. The tension there is in such cases (between "slave" or "enemy" and "fellow human being") may be reflected not merely in recognition of the point of someone else's actions, but also in defensiveness of various sorts, as when you ask someone where he is from and the answer is "South Africa and you do not treat them very well here either."[5] And that is like telling someone I am a vegetarian and getting the response "And what are your shoes made of?". . .

I introduced the notion of a fellow creature in answer to the question: How might I go about showing someone that he had reason not to eat animals? I do not think I have answered that so much as shown the direction in which I should look for an answer. And clearly the approach I have suggested is not usable with someone in whom there is no fellow-creature response, nothing at all in that range. I am not therefore in a weaker position than those who would defend animals' rights on the basis of an abstract principle

---

4. *Collected Essays, Journalism and Letters* (Secker and Warburg, 1968), Vol. II, p. 254. [Diamond's note.]

5. Diamond is describing a South African citizen who is sensitive about South Africa's racist policy of apartheid, in which black South Africans were second-class citizens with very limited rights; this citizen defends his country by saying that blacks are treated poorly in the United States too. Diamond's essay was published in 1978, when apartheid was still the law in South Africa.

of equality. For although they purport to be providing reasons which are reasons for anyone, Martian or human being or whatnot, to respect the rights of animals, Martians and whatnot, in fact what they are providing, I should say, is images of a vastly more uncompelling sort. . . . [I]f we appeal to people to prevent suffering, and we, in our appeal, try to obliterate the distinction between human beings and animals and just get people to speak or think of "different species of animals," there is no footing left from which to tell us what we ought to do, because it is not members of one among species of animals that have moral obligations to anything. The moral expectations of other human beings demand something of me as other than an animal; and we do something like imaginatively read into animals something like such expectations when we think of vegetarianism as enabling us to meet a cow's eyes. There is nothing wrong with that; there *is* something wrong with trying to keep that response and destroy its foundation.

. . . A fuller discussion of this would involve asking what force the analogy with racism and sexism has. It is not totally mistaken by any means. What might be called the dark side of human solidarity has analogies with the dark side of sexual solidarity or the solidarity of a human group, and the pain of seeing this is I think strongly present in the writings I have been attacking. It is their arguments I have been attacking, though, and not their perceptions, not the sense that comes through their writings of the awful and unshakeable callousness and unrelentingness with which we most often confront the non-human world. The mistake is to think that the callousness cannot be condemned without reasons which are reasons for anyone, no matter how devoid of all human imagination or sympathy. Hence their emphasis on rights, on capacities, on interests, on the biologically given; hence the distortion of their perceptions by their arguments.

TEST YOUR UNDERSTANDING

1. What is "speciesism" supposed to be?

2. Diamond argues that *human rights* have little to do with the fact that people do not eat people. She points out that we do not eat people who are already dead, nor do we eat our own severed limbs. How are these considerations supposed to show that *human rights* do not provide the fundamental explanation of our not eating people?

   a. Dead human bodies and severed limbs do not have rights, so their having human rights cannot explain why we don't eat them. But if we refrain from eating people *for the same reason* that we refrain from eating dead human bodies and severed limbs, then the reason that we refrain from eating people cannot be human rights.

   b. People don't care what happens to their bodies after they die or to their limbs after they are severed, so people's rights do not inhibit us from eating these things. But if we refrain from eating people *for the same reason* that we refrain from eating dead bodies and severed limbs, then the reason that we refrain from eating people cannot be human rights.

3. Diamond clarifies that the utilitarian argument against eating meat does not particularly involve *loving* animals or seeing them as *people* in alternate form. Why does she think the utilitarians reject this way of seeing their arguments? (You may select more than one.)

    a. They do not want to be seen as simply having an emotional reaction to animals.

    b. They do not want to be seen as self-indulgent theorists who are unwilling to make hard choices.

    c. They do not want to be seen as falsely believing that animals are more like people than animals really are.

    d. They do not want to be seen as committed to the moral importance of love.

4. Diamond thinks that the utilitarian argument against eating meat is incorrect, but she is a vegetarian and she agrees with the conclusion that we should not eat meat. What claim does she offer, which she thinks will be helpful in providing an explanation of why we should not eat meat?

    a. Factory farms contribute to climate change.

    b. It is healthier to eat a vegetarian diet.

    c. It is unkind to eat animals.

    d. Animals are our fellow creatures.

NOTES AND QUESTIONS

1. Why does Diamond think that the idea that *animal suffering is bad* cannot hold the key to explaining why we should not eat animals?

2. Diamond's paper includes a poem by Jane Legge, in which Legge talks about eating "the wing from Donald Duck." The poem points out the apparent inconsistencies in our attitudes toward animals. What inconsistencies does it point out? Are our attitudes to animals really inconsistent or is there a way of consistently making sense of our attitudes without rejecting some of them?

3. Diamond says it would be a mistake to say it is "morally wrong" to eat our pets. Rather, she says, pets are not the kind of things we eat. Diamond's idea is that we have certain kinds of relationships with animals (at least, with some animals) and certain conceptual schemes for thinking of these animals and our relationships with them, and these schemes simply *rule out* or *leave no room for* eating these animals. An animal one eats would simply not be a pet. Suppose Diamond is right about this. Does this help us to see whether we have *reasons* to not eat our pets? One might respond to Diamond by saying, "Okay, that's right, if I eat my cat then my cat is no longer my pet. Or perhaps if I eat my cat, it turns out my cat was never really my pet. But that doesn't say anything about what *reasons* I have. Is there any reason to make sure my cat is indeed a pet? What's wrong with an apparent pet turning out not to be a pet after all?" How could Diamond respond? Perhaps she might talk about the reasons we have for adopting a certain kind of relationship with animals.

ANALYZING THE ARGUMENTS

1. *Three strategies of argumentation.* As the introduction to this chapter discussed, to make headway on difficult ethical problems, ethicists commonly use three strategies: they provide simplifying examples, they offer analogies, and they attempt to identify and test hypotheses about what mid-level principles might govern the situation.

   Exercise: Can you identify where these techniques are used in the assigned selections? Which did you find the most successful, and why?

2. *Proximity and obligation.* Singer and O'Neill share the conviction that our physical distance from people in need does not intrinsically diminish the strength of our duties to them. Why do they think our lack of proximity is not morally significant? Given their positions, could either of them agree with the claim that we have some obligations to our neighbors and compatriots that we do not have to others in foreign countries? What reasons could they offer to support or reject that claim?

3. *Thomson and famine relief.* Does Thomson's position that you are not required to give life-sustaining support to the violinist have implications for the question of whether you are required to give support to innocents in danger of dying from hunger and other threats occasioned by poverty? Consider whether there are morally important differences between these cases. Could Singer agree with Thomson about the violinist but still insist that we must give a great deal to famine relief?

4. *Does it matter whether abortion is a denial of support or a killing?* Thomson's argument for the permissibility of abortion conceives of abortion as fundamentally a removal of support that one is not required to give; when the support is removed, the embryo or fetus may, regrettably, die. When Marquis analyzes abortion, he describes it as a form of killing. Do these conceptions of abortion importantly differ or are they merely varying ways of saying the same thing? If Thomson's argument is right, does it matter for the morality of abortion whether the method of abortion involves removing the fetus from the woman's body (resulting in its death) or directly killing the fetus and then removing it from the pregnant woman's body?

5. *The interests of others.* Many issues in ethics involve the question of when one may pursue one's own interests and concerns and when the interests and concerns of others, as one's moral equals, make moral claims on and against one's activity. It seems clear that one need not sacrifice *all* of one's own interests to advance those of others. It also seems clear that one may not single-mindedly attend to one's own interests without considering and responding to some needs of others. Identifying a plausible moral principle that gives adequate weight to oneself as well as to the interests of others proves challenging.

   Consider this candidate principle that attempts to strike a plausible balance:

   > *Ethical Harm Principle:* One may always permissibly act to advance one's own interests if and only if so acting would not cause harm to others.

   Despite its initial attractiveness, some **counterexamples** suggest it gives both too much and too little weight to the interests of others.

   > *Competition:* It seems permissible to apply for admission to college or for employment even when one's successful application will entail another person's failure to secure a spot.

Self-Defense: It seems permissible to defend oneself against a person posing a threat to one's life, even when defending oneself will impose harm on the threat.

Drowning Child: It is not always permissible to advance one's own interests rather than to help another person in need, even when one is not the cause of the other's peril. It is wrong to continue on one's way to work rather than to rescue a drowning child, even though one's going to work is not what would cause the child harm; the child's inability to swim to safety and the slippery banks of the pond would be what causes the child to drown.

Neighbor: It seems impermissible to ignore the request of an elderly neighbor for help when he is struggling with heavy, cumbersome packages, even when helping involves interrupting one's homework and the neighbor will not suffer harm if one ignores him; he will simply have to make more trips from the car to the house.

Explain why these examples appear to pose a challenge to the *Ethical Harm Principle.* Consider how a proponent of the principle might respond. (*Note:* One response is to modify the principle to avoid the counterexamples. Another is to argue that the cases do not really pose counterexamples.)

If the *Ethical Harm Principle* (or a revised version of it) is true, how should we understand "others"? Does this just include people or does it also include animals?

6. *Eating meat and difference-making.* Harman argues that if we have strong reasons against causing animals to suffer, then we have strong reasons against killing animals, even if we could kill them painlessly. Harman's argument appears to support the claim that all farming of animals for meat is morally wrong. Diamond herself supports vegetarianism, but not for Harman's reasons.

Suppose that we do have strong reasons against causing animals to suffer and that Harman's argument is **cogent**, so it turns out that all farming of animals for meat is morally wrong. Does it follow that it is morally wrong to buy and eat meat? One might deny that this follows. After all, when you are in the supermarket, the chicken you are considering buying was killed long ago. Whether or not you buy a chicken on this occasion will almost certainly *make no difference* to how many chickens are killed in the future: the supermarket buys in bulk and does not change its order depending on whether one more or one fewer chicken is sold this week. Given that you won't make a difference to whether any chickens are killed, is there any moral reason against your buying the chicken?

Could anything Diamond says be helpful in supporting the view that you shouldn't buy the chicken, even if it won't make a difference? (Remember that Diamond points out that we don't eat dead human bodies, even though it wouldn't involve any killing or cause any suffering.)

Is it really true that there are no difference-making-related reasons against buying the chicken? Shelly Kagan has argued that there is a small chance that your purchase would make a big difference. Even if the supermarket does order in bulk, perhaps it's near the threshold point, and if one fewer chicken is purchased this week, the supermarket will order considerably fewer chickens next week (Kagan, "Do I Make a Difference?" *Philosophy and Public Affairs* 39, 2 [2011]: 105–41). Has Kagan identified a reason that would make it morally wrong to buy the chicken?

Do Your Intentions Matter?

Suppose Betsy promises her friend Alfred that she will meet him at the local café at 10 AM tomorrow morning to help him decipher a tricky philosophical text, one she studied last term. Later that night, she starts playing the new version of *World of Warcraft* and cannot tear herself away. After her all-nighter, she stumbles into the café for coffee the next morning, having forgotten all about Alfred. To her surprise and embarrassment, she encounters Alfred, who immediately peppers Betsy with questions about Thomas Aquinas.

Betsy showed up at the appointed place and time, but only by accident, and not because she meant to keep her promise. This everyday case raises some interesting philosophical questions. Betsy was morally required to keep her promise. Did she do what she was required to do? Did she *keep* her promise if she only accidentally fulfilled its terms? That is, does keeping a promise merely involve performing the *action* one agreed to perform or does it also require that one *intends* to perform the action *because* of the commitment?

Consider another example. Suppose Betsy donates to a charity for earthquake victims, but not because she cares about their plight. Betsy hopes to impress her employer, who is collecting donations, and to make her employer think they share a commitment to a cause. This case differs somewhat from her accidentally fulfilling a promise. The accidentally fulfilled coffee date might be thought to lack the full value of the deliberately fulfilled promise. After all, part of the point of a promise is that one's deliberation about one's future action is supposed to be guided by the fact of one's commitment. By contrast, in the donation case, although Betsy's purpose is only to benefit herself, her selfishly motivated donation helps others just as much as an altruistically motivated donation would. If the value of donations lies in the effective assistance others receive, perhaps it does not matter morally *why* she donates.

Yet, in another respect, the donation case and the promise case seem similar. The selfishly motivated donation case is still troubling, even if the earthquake victims are helped. Something seems awry when an otherwise good action is performed for a selfish, deceitful motive, rather than from an appreciation of the goodness of the action itself. In that respect, Betsy's behavior in the promise case may seem better than in the donation case. In the promise case, the problem is that Betsy forgot, but she did not have a poor motive such as using others' suffering as an occasion for professional advancement.

Although something seems problematic in both cases, it is tricky to identify exactly *what*. For instance, does Betsy's selfishness make the donation *itself* morally impermissible or does it make the donation *process* morally wrongful in some other way? Perhaps, one may think, these cases reveal something troubling not about her action per se but rather about her character. Maybe we should say that although she performs the right actions, *she* is selfish and morally careless. Moreover, although we may agree that selfish purposes do not provide morally exemplary reasons for donating, we may wonder, what is the exemplary reason for donating that Betsy lacks? Is it that she should care about people in need and *want* to help them or is it that helping people in need, when one can, is one's duty and that her action should be the product of her sense of duty? Similarly, we may think that even if accidentally showing up counts as a way of keeping the promise, nonetheless it is a shabby, defective way to do so. Does its defect lie in a failure to be motivated by her duty as a promisor, by her failure to care enough about Alfred's need for help, or both? Larger questions lurk right under the surface of these cases, such as whether we should admire the person who gives from compassion as much as (or even more than) the person who gives from a sense of duty. Which motive, benevolence or a sense of duty, is morally foundational?

Further questions are raised by the following case. Suppose that everyone at Betsy's workplace teases her colleague Alfred about his obvious use of a toupee (a wig), and so Betsy teases him too. Alfred always laughs and plays along, and Betsy would stand out noticeably if she didn't join in. The truth is that Alfred's feelings are hurt by the teasing. Betsy doesn't know this, though perhaps if she thought about it she would figure it out. Betsy doesn't *aim* to hurt his feelings. Indeed, she doesn't even *know* she is hurting his feelings. Thus, it seems that Betsy doesn't *intend* to hurt his feelings. Does this render Betsy blameless for hurting his feelings? When the people around us are acting like something is morally okay, how does this affect our intentions? When we only intend to do an ordinary thing that *seems* to be a morally permissible thing to do, does that mean that our intentions render our actions blameless?

Questions about the significance of good, poor, and absent intentions have been a focal point of moral philosophy for centuries. We might divide them into three categories. First, are a person's intentions relevant to the assessment of the moral character of her action? That is, when, if ever, does a person's intention in acting serve as a central component of the moral characterization of her action, helping to make that action right or wrong or permissible or impermissible? Or, should we deny that a person's intentions are a component of the moral nature of her actions and instead insist that her intentions merely figure in the assessment of her character? The second category of questions asks *which* intention the morally motivated agent should have. When one acts morally, should one be acting from duty, from benevolent care and concern, or from some other motive? Third, is having "good intentions" enough to render an agent blameless? If someone does something awful and knows what she is doing but has no idea it is morally wrong, is that enough to absolve her of blame?

Doctrine of Double Effect

G. E. M. Anscombe argues that what an agent *intends* affects what it is morally permissible for the agent to do. Her focus is not, however, on the moral motive of benevolence but rather on the difference motives make in a concrete case. She argues that the decisions by President Truman in World War II to drop atomic bombs on the cities of Hiroshima and Nagasaki were deeply morally wrong. Although Truman's motive was to end the war, his decisions were wrong because he aimed to kill innocent people as a means to ending the war more quickly. In Anscombe's view, it is always impermissible to intend to kill innocent civilians, no matter what good result might follow.

To support this judgment, Anscombe defends a specific application of the idea that one's intention in acting may determine that action's moral status, advancing what is widely considered a classic articulation of the Doctrine of Double Effect. Anscombe, Thomas Scanlon, and Barbara Herman all characterize it slightly differently, but essentially, the Doctrine of Double Effect distinguishes between intentionally harming innocents and causing foreseen but unintended harm to them. The former is impermissible and the latter is, sometimes, permissible. Specifically, the doctrine declares one may not intend to harm innocent people as an end or a means to an end; yet, sometimes, it may be morally permissible to bring equally harmful consequences to innocents as a foreseeable, unintended side effect of one's otherwise permissible activity, if the good that one intends is proportionate to or greater than any harmful side effects.

Anscombe invokes this idea to distinguish between permissible and impermissible acts in war. She contends that to *intend* to kill an innocent person as a means to accomplishing a good end is always murder and always wrong, even if one's end is to save the lives of other innocent people. The mere killing of innocents is not always wrong, for sometimes that is an unavoidable by-product of a permissible aim. What is always wrong is to *intend* to kill the innocent. That intention involves embracing evil as though it were worthwhile, just because of its consequences. It may be permissible to bomb an enemy's munitions plant to stall their weapons production, even if predictable but unwanted civilian deaths ensue as a side effect. But it would be wrong to bomb a village with the very purpose of killing the same number of innocent civilians in order to break the enemy's morale. One may never make the deaths of civilians one's animating aim of action.

Reasons, Not Intentions

Scanlon rejects Anscombe's general thesis that a person's intention matters to the permissibility of an action because that thesis entails that the exact same physical action with the exact same consequences could be permissible in one case if the actor's intention is a good one but impermissible in another case if that actor's intention is a poor one. To Scanlon, it seems that whether bombing a munitions factory in war is permissible depends on the external qualities of the action and its consequences, including whether bombing is likely to bring significant military advantage and minimal harm to noncombatants. It doesn't make sense, he thinks, to judge that such bombing would be permissible if the pilot deeply regrets the accidental civilian deaths but impermissible if the pilot privately relishes them. Scanlon contends that whether an action is morally permissible or impermissible does not hinge upon the intentions or reasons any particular person actually *has* when acting. Instead, whether an action is permissible or impermissible depends on what reasons she *should* act on, under the circumstances.

Of course, Scanlon agrees that we often do care about a person's intentions when assessing her behavior. Hence, we should distinguish whether an action is permissible from whether the agent acts in a blameworthy way. If Bob aims to kill someone by stabbing pins in a doll, that does not make using a doll as a pin cushion itself impermissible. The *action* of sticking a pin into a stuffed cotton sack is itself harmless, whatever Bob's beliefs and intentions. There is no moral reason to forbear from using a doll this way, although Bob's intentions reveal he has a wretched character and is blameworthy. On the other hand, if Juan, while looking for sugar, absentmindedly picks up a bottle of arsenic, fails to read the label, and spoons it into his friend's coffee, Juan has done something impermissible. There is every reason in the world not to feed someone arsenic and to pay attention when feeding friends. Juan did not act with a poor intention and did not mean to hurt his friend; he is certainly not blameworthy for murder or its attempt, though perhaps he is blameworthy for negligence, since he should have paid more attention. Because giving arsenic to a person can be fatal, that action is impermissible regardless of a person's intentions.

So, Scanlon agrees that a person's bad intention may matter in making the action's meaning to others disrespectful; in showing *her* (though not her action) to be blameworthy and worthy of criticism; in making bad consequences more likely; or, perhaps, by making her actions deceptive because others would naturally assume her intention to be good. Betsy not mentioning to Albert that she had forgotten the appointment might be deceptive because he assumed she had remembered; here, Scanlon would contend that her failure to fess up, not her absentmindedness, is the real reason Betsy behaves impermissibly. In short, a poor intention may be morally significant in myriad ways, but usually it cannot render an otherwise permissible action impermissible. In other words, one can do the right thing yet have bad intentions or misguided motives.

A Kantian Defense of the Relevance of Intentions

Barbara Herman disagrees with Scanlon. She defends the central importance of a person's intentions in assessing whether her action, and not merely her character, is morally right or morally wrong. Herman writes in the **Kantian** tradition. Kantians hold that the central feature of moral action is the agent's reason for performing the action. Thus, for Kantians, intentions do matter to the moral character of actions. On Kant's view, the intention that a morally right action has is the motive of duty.

It may be helpful to read Herman's piece as advancing three main points in critical response to Scanlon. First, she argues that views like Scanlon's mistakenly emphasize moral permissibility and moral impermissibility, suggesting that these concepts are the exclusive barometers of an action's moral rightness or wrongness. Consider a burglar who stakes out a house but changes her plan upon noticing a security camera. She complies with the law against theft only to avoid arrest. She does nothing impermissible, but her intention is not to treat others' property and their privacy with respect. The would-be burglar does the required thing, intentionally, but not *because* one should do the right thing, only because it is expedient. In Herman's view, she acts wrongly, albeit permissibly. The fact that one's actions happen to coincide with the actions specified by a moral principle sometimes suffices to make one's actions morally permissible. But that correspondence is insufficient to make an action morally right. Something crucial is missing. Whether an action is morally right depends on whether a person adheres to the moral principles that apply to her. Adhering to a moral principle requires being aware of the principle *and* intending to be guided by it.

Second, Herman argues that focusing on moral prohibitions, such as the prohibition against killing, may misleadingly lend support to the idea that the external qualities of an action determine its moral character. When one instead considers positive moral requirements, such as keeping a promise or telling the truth, one errs in focusing only on an action's external qualities. The value of truth-telling depends on the agent's telling the truth *because the agent believes what she says*. An agent who accidentally lets the truth slip out does not comply with the duty of truth-telling. The person who tries to deceive her interlocutor, but accidentally tells the truth, has acted impermissibly. One's intention to tell the truth (or keep one's promise) is a crucial component of fulfilling the relevant duty.

Third, Herman recommends drawing an analogy to theoretical reasoning. The student who accidentally guesses the answer to a mathematics problem but does not know how to do the proof gives the correct answer but has not solved the problem or demonstrated knowledge; a teacher would reasonably fail to give that answer credit. Why think of morality differently? In mathematics, the right answer requires proper reasoning to the correct solution; likewise, Herman claims, the morally right action requires proper reasoning to the correct action.

Does Having "Good Intentions" Render a Person Blameless?

Michele Moody-Adams and Angela Smith both address the question of how intentions affect blameworthiness when agents appear to be *ignorant* of certain features of their actions. Moody-Adams considers an agent in a society in which everyone does a certain horrible thing, such as slaveholding. Does a slaveholder in a slaveholding society get off the hook because no one knows that slavery is morally wrong? In a sense, the slaveholder has perfectly good intentions: he doesn't intend to be doing anything morally wrong. Moody-Adams points out that the collective ignorance in a society may be *affected ignorance*: it may be an ignorance that is motivated by self-interest. If people don't realize their actions are wrong because they don't want to realize it, because it would make things hard for them if they realized, then they are not off the hook, she argues. In Moody-Adams's view, being part of a morally wrong culture does not insulate a person from responsibility for his or her wrongful actions.

Smith discusses a different way in which we might be *ignorant* of the wrongness of what we are doing. Even an agent who knows that sexism and racism are morally wrong may not realize that she herself is being sexist and racist on a particular occasion. In a sense, the agent has perfectly good intentions. She certainly does not intend to be sexist or racist. Yet a person may have *implicit biases* that affect how she acts. A person has an implicit bias if she in fact judges and treats people differently on the basis of race or sex without realizing that she is doing so. Smith argues that agents are typically blameworthy for their implicit biases, even though agents are typically unaware of their implicit biases. She points out that we blame people for lots of things that are automatic or are not the results of conscious deliberation: an action done by habit may well be blameworthy, and an instance of forgetting something may be blameworthy. Smith argues that in general people are responsible for behavior that is guided by reasons, whether or not those reasons are consciously articulated by the agent. Because choices made out of bias are choices made for reasons (albeit bad reasons), these are the kind of choices for which people can be held responsible. Furthermore, she argues, one's biases are part of oneself in a way that morally matters. If one learns about oneself that one is implicitly biased in a certain way, this makes one feel bad about oneself; this reveals that one takes oneself to be blameworthy for this bias.

G. E. M. Anscombe (1919–2001)

Anscombe was a British analytical philosopher who taught at Somerville College, the University of Oxford, and also served as Professor of Philosophy at Cambridge University. She is the author of *Intention* (1957), widely considered a classic in the fields of philosophy of mind and action, and wrote many other important works in moral philosophy, the philosophy of action, the philosophy of mind, the philosophy of language, and logic. She is also considered one of the most important Catholic philosophers of the twentieth century.

MR TRUMAN'S DEGREE[1]

I

In 1939, on the outbreak of war, the President of the United States asked for assurances from the belligerent nations that civil populations would not be attacked.

In 1945, when the Japanese enemy was known by him to have made two attempts towards a negotiated peace, the President of the United States gave the order for dropping an atom bomb on a Japanese city; three days later a second bomb, of a different type, was dropped on another city. No ultimatum was delivered before the second bomb was dropped.

Set side by side, these events provide enough of a contrast to provoke enquiry. Evidently development has taken place; one would like to see its course plotted. It is not, I think, difficult to give an intelligible account:

(1) The British Government gave President Roosevelt the required assurance with a reservation which meant "If the Germans do it we shall do it too." You don't promise to abide by the Queensberry Rules[2] even if your opponent abandons them.

(2) The only condition for ending the war was announced to be unconditional surrender. Apart from the "liberation of the subject peoples," the objectives were vague in character. Now the demand for unconditional surrender was mixed up with a determination to make no peace with Hitler's government. In view of the character of Hitler's regime that attitude was very intelligible. Nevertheless some people have doubts about it now. It is suggested that defeat of itself would have resulted in the rapid discredit and downfall of that government. On this I can form no strong opinion. The important question to my mind is whether the intention of making no peace with Hitler's government necessarily entailed the objective of unconditional surrender. If, as may not be impossible, we could have formulated a pretty definite objective, a rough outline of the terms which we were willing to make with Germany, while at the same time indicating that we would not make terms with Hitler's government, then the question of the wisdom of this latter demand seems to me a minor one; but if not, then that settles it. It was the insistence on unconditional surrender that was the root of all evil. The connection between such a demand and the need to use the most ferocious methods of warfare will be obvious. And in itself the proposal of an unlimited objective in war is stupid and barbarous.

(3) The Germans did a good deal of indiscriminate bombing in this country. It is impossible for an uninformed person to know how much, in its first beginnings, was due to indifference on the part of pilots to using their loads only on military targets, and how much to actual policy on the part of those who sent them. Nor do I know what we were doing in the same line at the time. . . .

1 . © M C Gormally. Professor Anscombe published this essay in a privately printed pamphlet to explain her opposition to Oxford University's decision to confer an honorary doctorate to President Truman in 1956.

2. The Queensberry Rules are a traditional set of boxing rules that restrict boxers from "no-holds-barred" fighting.

(4) For some time before war broke out, and more intensely afterwards, there was propaganda in this country on the subject of the "indivisibility" of modern war. The civilian population, we were told, is really as much combatant as the fighting forces. The military strength of a nation includes its whole economic and social strength. Therefore the distinction between the people engaged in prosecuting the war and the population at large is unreal. There is no such thing as a non-participator; you cannot buy a postage stamp or any taxed article, or grow a potato or cook a meal, without contributing to the "war effort." War indeed is a "ghastly evil," but once it has broken out no one can "contract out" of it. "Wrong" indeed must be being done if war is waged, but you cannot help being involved in it. There was a doctrine of "collective responsibility" with a lugubriously elevated moral tone about it. The upshot was that it was senseless to draw any line between legitimate and illegitimate objects of attack. . . . I am not sure how children and the aged fitted into this story: probably they cheered the soldiers and munitions workers up.

(5) The Japanese attacked Pearl Harbour and there was war between America and Japan. Some American (Republican) historians now claim that the acknowledged fact that the American Government knew an attack was impending some hours before it occurred, but did not alert the people in local command, can only be explained by a purpose of arousing the passions of American people. However that may be, those passions were suitably aroused and the war was entered on with the same vague and hence limitless objectives; and once more unconditional surrender was the only condition on which the war was going to end.

(6) Then came the great change: we adopted the system of "area bombing" as opposed to "target bombing." This differed from even big raids on cities, such as had previously taken place in the course of the war, by being far more extensive and devastating and much less random; the whole of a city area would be systematically plotted out and dotted with bombs. "Attila was a Sissy," as the *Chicago Tribune* headed an article on this subject.

(7) In 1945, at the Potsdam conference[3] in July, Stalin informed the American and British statesmen that he had received two requests from the Japanese to act as a mediator with a view to ending the war. He had refused. The Allies agreed on the "general principle"—marvellous phrase!—of using the new type of weapon that America now possessed. The Japanese were given a chance in the form of the Potsdam Declaration, calling for unconditional surrender in face of overwhelming force soon to be arrayed against them. The historian of the Survey of International Affairs considers that this phrase was rendered meaningless by the statement of a series of terms; but of these the ones incorporating the Allies' demands were mostly of so vague and sweeping a nature as to be rather a declaration of what unconditional surrender would be like than to constitute conditions. It seems to be generally agreed that the Japanese were

---

3 . Meeting (in Potsdam, Germany) of the Soviet Union, United Kingdom, and United States after Nazi Germany's unconditional surrender on May 8, 1945, to establish the postwar order.

desperate enough to have accepted the Declaration but for their loyalty to their Emperor[4]: the "terms" would certainly have permitted the Allies to get rid of him if they chose. The Japanese refused the Declaration. In consequence, the bombs were dropped on Hiroshima and Nagasaki. The decision to use them on people was Mr Truman's.

For men to choose to kill the innocent as a means to their ends is always murder, and murder is one of the worst of human actions. So the prohibition on deliberately killing prisoners of war or the civilian population is not like the Queensberry Rules: its force does not depend on its promulgation as part of positive law, written down, agreed upon, and adhered to by the parties concerned.

When I say that to choose to kill the innocent as a means to one's ends is murder, I am saying what would generally be accepted as correct. But I shall be asked for my definition of "the innocent," I will give it, but later. Here, it is not necessary; for with Hiroshima and Nagasaki we are not confronted with a borderline case. In the bombing of these cities it was certainly decided to kill the innocent as a means to an end. And a very large number of them, all at once, without warning, without the interstices of escape or the chance to take shelter, which existed even in the "area bombings" of the German cities. . . .

I have been accused of being "high-minded." I must be saying "You may not do evil that good may come," which is a disagreeably high-minded doctrine. The action was necessary, or at any rate it was thought by competent, expert military opinion to be necessary; it probably saved more lives than it sacrificed; it had a good result, it ended the war. Come now: if you had to choose between boiling one baby and letting some frightful disaster befall a thousand people—or a million people, if a thousand is not enough—what would you do? Are you going to strike an attitude and say "You may not do evil that good may come"? (People who never hear such arguments will hardly believe they take place, and will pass this rapidly by.)

"It pretty certainly saved a huge number of lives." Given the conditions, I agree. That is to say, if those bombs had not been dropped the Allies would have had to invade Japan to achieve their aim, and they would have done so. Very many soldiers on both sides would have been killed; the Japanese, it is said—and it may well be true—would have massacred the prisoners of war; and large numbers of their civilian population would have been killed by "ordinary" bombing.

I do not dispute it. Given the conditions, that was probably what was averted by that action. But what were the conditions? The unlimited objective, the fixation on unconditional surrender. The disregard of the fact that the Japanese were desirous of negotiating peace. The character of the Potsdam Declaration—their "chance." I will not suggest, as some would like to do, that there was an exultant itch to use the new weapons, but it seems plausible to think that the consciousness of the possession of such instruments had its effect on the manner in which the Japanese were offered their "chance." . . .

4. Emperor Hirohito (1901–1989) ruled Japan from 1926 until his death.

||

Choosing to kill the innocent as a means to your ends is always murder. Naturally, killing the innocent as an end in itself is murder too; but that is no more than a possible future development for us: in our part of the globe it is a practice that has so far been confined to the Nazis. I intend my formulation to be taken strictly; each term in it is necessary. For killing the innocent, even if you know as a matter of statistical certainty that the things you do involve it, is not necessarily murder. I mean that if you attack a lot of military targets, such as munitions factories and naval dockyards, as carefully as you can, you will be certain to kill a number of innocent people; but that is not murder. On the other hand, unscrupulousness in considering the possibilities turns it into murder. I here print as a case in point a letter which I received lately from Holland:

> We read in our paper about your opposition to Truman. I do not like him either, but do you know that in the war the English bombed the dykes of our province Zeeland,[5] an island where nobody could escape anywhere to. Where the whole population was drowned, children, women, farmers working in the field, all the cattle, everything, hundreds and hundreds, and we were your allies! Nobody ever speaks about that. Perhaps it were well to know this. Or, to remember.

That was to trap some fleeing German military. I think my correspondent has something.

It may be impossible to take the thing (or people) you want to destroy as your target; it may be possible to attack it only by taking as the object of your attack what includes large numbers of innocent people. Then you cannot very well say they died by accident. Here your action is murder.

"But where will you draw the line? It is impossible to draw an exact line." This is a common and absurd argument against drawing any line; it may be very difficult, and there are obviously borderline cases. But we have fallen into the way of drawing no line, and offering as justifications what an uncaptive mind will find only a bad joke. Wherever the line is, certain things are certainly well to one side or the other of it.

Now who are "the innocent" in war? They are all those who are not fighting and not engaged in supplying those who are with the means of fighting. A farmer growing wheat which may be eaten by the troops is not "supplying them with the means of fighting." Over this, too, the line may be difficult to draw. But that does not mean that no line should be drawn, or that, even if one is in doubt just where to draw the line, one cannot be crystal clear that this or that is well over the line.

"But the people fighting are probably conscripts! In that case they are just as innocent as anyone else." "Innocent" here is not a term referring to personal responsibility at all. It means rather "not harming." But the people fighting are "harming," so they can be attacked; but if they surrender they become in this sense innocent and so may not be maltreated or killed. Nor is there ground for trying them on a criminal charge; not, indeed, because a man has no personal responsibility for fighting, but because they were not the subjects of the state whose prisoners they are.

5 . Province of the Netherlands consisting of a number of islands.

There is an argument which I know from experience it is necessary to forestall at this point, though I think it is visibly captious. It is this: on my theory, would it not follow that a soldier can only be killed when he is actually attacking? Then, for example, it would be impossible to attack a sleeping camp. The answer is that "what someone is doing" can refer either to what he is doing at the moment or to his role in a situation. A soldier under arms is "harming" in the latter sense even if he is asleep. But it is true that the enemy should not be attacked more ferociously than is necessary to put them *hors de combat.*[6]

These conceptions are distinct and intelligible ones. . . . Anyone can see that they are good, and we pay tribute to them by our moral indignation when our enemies violate them. . . .

It is characteristic of nowadays to talk with horror of killing rather than of murder, and hence, since in war you have committed yourself to killing—for example "accepted an evil"—not to mind whom you kill. This seems largely to be the work of the devil; but I also suspect that it is in part an effect of the existence of pacifism, as a doctrine which many people respect though they would not adopt it. This effect would not exist if people had a distinct notion of what makes pacifism a false doctrine.

It therefore seems to me important to show that for one human being deliberately to kill another is not inevitably wrong. I may seem to be wasting my time, as most people do reject pacifism. But it is nevertheless important to argue the point because if one does so one sees that there are pretty severe restrictions on legitimate killing. Of course, people accept this within the state, but when it comes to war they have the idea that any restrictions are something like the Queensberry Rules—instead of making the difference between being guilty and not guilty of murder.

I will not discuss the self-defence of a private person. If he kills the man who attacks him or someone else, it ought to be accidental. To aim at killing, even when one is defending oneself, is murderous. . . .

But the state actually has the authority to order deliberate killing in order to protect its people or to put frightful injustices right. (For example, the plight of the Jews under Hitler would have been a reasonable cause of war.) The reason for this is pretty simple: it stands out most clearly if we first consider the state's right to order such killing within its confines. I am not referring to the death penalty, but to what happens when there is rioting or when violent malefactors have to be caught. Rioters can sometimes only be restrained, or malefactors seized, by force. Law without force is ineffectual, and human beings without laws miserable (though we, who have too many and too changeable laws, may easily not feel this very distinctly). So much is indeed fairly obvious, though the more peaceful the society the less obvious it is that the force in the hands of the servants of the law has to be force up to the point of killing. It would become perfectly obvious any time there was rioting or gangsterism which had to be dealt with by the servants of the law fighting. . . .

Now, this is also the ground of the state's right to order people to fight external enemies who are unjustly attacking them or something of theirs. The right to order

---

6 . "Outside the fight" (French), referring to soldiers who are unable to continue in battle because they are wounded, ill, without equipment, and so on.

to fight for the sake of other people's wrongs, to put right something affecting people who are not actually under the protection of the state, is a rather more dubious thing obviously, but it exists because of the common sympathy of human beings whereby one feels for one's neighbour if he is attacked. So in an attenuated sense it can be said that something that belongs to, or concerns, one is attacked if anybody is unjustly attacked or maltreated.

Pacifism, then, is a false doctrine. Now, no doubt, it is bad just for that reason, because it is always bad to have a false conscience. In this way the doctrine that it is a bad act to lay a bet is bad: it is all right to bet what it is all right to risk or drop in the sea. But I want to maintain that pacifism is a harmful doctrine in a far stronger sense than this. Even the prevalence of the idea that it was wrong to bet would have no particularly bad consequences; a false doctrine which merely forbids what is not actually bad need not encourage people in anything bad. But with pacifism it is quite otherwise. It is a factor in that loss of the conception of murder which is my chief interest in this pamphlet.

I have very often heard people say something like this: "It is all very well to say 'Don't do evil that good may come.' But *war* is evil. We all know that. Now, of course, it is possible to be an Absolute Pacifist. I can respect that, but I can't be one myself, and most other people won't be either. So we have to accept the evil. It is not that we do not see the evil. And once you are in for it, you have to go the whole hog."

This is much as if I were defrauding someone, and when someone tried to stop me I said: "Absolute honesty! I respect that. But of course absolute honesty really means having no property at all . . ." Having offered the sacrifice of a few sighs and tears to absolute honesty, I go on as before.

The correct answer to the statement that "war is evil" is that it is bad—for example a misfortune—to be at war. And no doubt if two nations are at war at least one is unjust. But that does not show that it is wrong to fight or that if one does fight one can also commit murder.

Naturally my claim that pacifism is a very harmful doctrine is contingent on its being a false one. If it were a true doctrine, its encouragement of this nonsensical "hypocrisy of the ideal standard" would not count against it. But given that it is false, I am inclined to think it is also very bad, unusually so for an idea which seems as it were to err on the noble side.

When I consider the history of events from 1939 to 1945, I am not surprised that Mr Truman is made the recipient of honours. But when I consider his actions by themselves, I am surprised again.

Some people actually praise the bombings and commend the stockpiling of atomic weapons on the ground that they are so horrible that nations will be afraid ever again to make war. "We have made a covenant with death, and with hell we are at an agreement." There does not seem to be good ground for such a hope for any long period of time. . . .

Protests by people who have not power are a waste of time. I was not seizing an opportunity to make a "gesture of protest" at atomic bombs; I vehemently object to *our* action in offering Mr Truman honours, because one can share in the guilt of a bad action by praise and flattery, as also by defending it.

TEST YOUR UNDERSTANDING

1. What motive does Anscombe think President Truman had in deciding to bomb Hiroshima and Nagasaki? Why is his motive a reason to condemn his action?

2. Anscombe argues that it may sometimes be permissible to bomb a munitions factory, even if some civilians will be killed as a side effect. Assuming that the good to be achieved would be substantial and very few civilians would be killed, what motive would make this action acceptable, in her view? What motive would make a bombing with the same number of civilian casualties unacceptable, in her view?

3. Why does Anscombe believe that farmers are "innocents" but that involuntarily conscripted soldiers opposed to the war effort are not "innocents"?

4. In what way does Anscombe think pacifism is a harmful doctrine?

   a. It misleads people into thinking that all killing is wrong.

   b. It misleads people by providing a caricature of the view that murder is morally wrong: by offering a view on which any killing at all is equivalent to murder, it undermines the effectiveness of pointing out that some killings are murder, and are thus morally wrong.

   c. It keeps us from protecting vulnerable countries when they are the victims of unjust attacks.

   d. It keeps us from responding appropriately by punishing wrongdoers: if pacifism is the correct view, then it applies even to how we should deal with people who have committed murder themselves.

NOTES AND QUESTIONS

1. *Whose motive matters?* Anscombe's essay represents a famous defense of the **Doctrine of Double Effect**, the view that one may not intend to harm innocents as an end or means to an end, but it may be permissible to cause harm to innocents as a foreseen but unintended side effect of one's otherwise permissible activity, if the good that one intends is proportionate to or greater than these side effects. This doctrine emphasizes the moral importance of the motive that gives rise to an action. Now consider actions that involve coordination between different people with different reasons for acting. Whose motive is relevant for assessing the morality of the action?

   Suppose, for example, that a nation is fighting a just war of self-defense against a belligerent neighbor. An air force captain of the beleaguered nation instructs a pilot to drop bombs on a munitions factory when the factory is closed. The captain's aim is to destroy an important source of weapons, thereby reducing the military power of the attackers. By bombing when the factory is closed, the captain hopes not to kill anyone, although she knows a few innocents may die if they happen to be near the factory when it is bombed. Suppose the pilot thinks that the belligerent nation has an oversupply of weapons so that eliminating the factory will make no difference to the war effort, but that the killing of the few civilians who happen to be near the factory during the bombing *will* make a difference because it will help to lower morale and to feed political sentiment to end the war.

In this case, does the captain's motive satisfy Anscombe's constraints? Does the pilot's motive? As described, the pilot drops the bomb and thereby follows the captain's order, but the pilot hopes to kill innocent people. In that case, is the pilot's action murder? Whose motive matters here: the captain's motive or the pilot's motive? (*Hint*: Note that Anscombe's essay focuses on President Truman. Why do you think she discusses Truman and not Paul Tibbets and Charles Sweeney, the pilots who flew the planes that dropped the bombs at Hiroshima and Nagasaki?)

2. *What is one's motive?* Anscombe argues that President Truman's motive was to kill innocent civilians to overwhelm the Japanese and thereby to end the war. Thus, in her view, President Truman engaged in mass murder because his motive was to kill innocents as a means to his end of bringing the war to a close (on his terms of unconditional surrender). Suppose Truman read Anscombe's essay and objected that he did not seek the *deaths* of those civilians as a means to his end at all. Of course, he knew that they would die if the bombs were dropped, but their deaths as such were not what he sought. Rather, he sought the *convincing appearance* of massive civilian deaths to generate the emperor's belief that the millions had died at the hands of an irrepressible and indefatigable foe. That they actually died was not his aim at all, although it was foreseen. If the appearance of their deaths could have been generated without their actually dying, he would have preferred it. Therefore, their deaths were not intended. He might argue that his intention is not significantly different from the bomber who targets the naval shipyard to disrupt a military supply chain but who knows that the deaths of innocents walking in the neighborhood are a predictable but unwanted side effect of the bombing. Their deaths are anticipated side effects of destroying the shipyard, but the mission would be as successful if they did not die.

Evaluate Truman's potential reply. Must we accept Truman's description of his own intention as accurate? Is it plausible to say that the person who bombs a city to convince a military opponent that further resistance is hopeless merely intends to induce the appearance of massive civilian deaths but does not intend their deaths? Why or why not? Is this case analogous to or dissimilar from the case of the accidental, but foreseeable, deaths of innocents when bombing a dockyard?

Thomas M. Scanlon (b. 1940)

Scanlon is Alford Professor of Natural Religion, Moral Philosophy, and Civil Polity at Harvard University. A leading philosopher in the areas of moral, political, and legal philosophy, he is best known for his development of the moral theory of contractualism. He has published many significant articles and books, including *What We Owe to Each Other* (1998), *The Difficulty of Tolerance* (2003), and *Moral Dimensions: Permissibility, Meaning, and Blame* (2008).

WHEN DO INTENTIONS MATTER
TO PERMISSIBILITY?

Does the permissibility of an action depend on the agent's intentions in performing it? It seems obvious that an agent's intentions can make a moral difference. For example, there is a clear moral difference between injuring a person intentionally and doing so inadvertently. But in order to assess the significance of this fact, we need to consider more carefully what kind of moral significance is involved and what is meant by "intention."

"Intention" is commonly used in wider and narrower senses. When we say that a person did something intentionally, one thing we may mean is simply that it was something that he or she was aware of doing, or realized was likely to be a consequence of his or her action. This is the sense of "intentionally" that is opposed to "unintentionally." To say that you did something unintentionally is to claim that it was something you did not realize you were doing. But "intention" is also used in a narrower sense. To ask a person what her intention was in doing a certain thing is to ask her what her aim was in doing it, and what plan guided her action.

Knowing whether an agent acted intentionally also tells us something about the agent's view of the reasons bearing on his or her action. Whether an agent acted intentionally is in the first instance a matter of what the agent believed about the likely consequences of her action. It is also true that if an agent does something intentionally in this wider sense—if she is aware of a particular aspect of her situation such as that the room's acoustics are such that her action will cause a loud noise—then even if she does not take this aspect of what she is doing to provide a reason for so acting, she at least does not (insofar as she is not acting irrationally) take it to constitute a sufficient reason not to act in that way.

When I said above that it matters morally whether a person causes harm intentionally or inadvertently, what I meant was that it makes a moral difference whether the person was aware that her action was likely to cause harm. But this moral difference need not be a difference in the moral permissibility of the action. What matters to the action's moral permissibility is not what the agent was aware of or believed but what he or she should have believed, under the circumstances. It is impermissible to act in a way that one should have seen was likely to cause unjustified harm, whether one sees this or not. And when an agent believes that his action is likely to be harmful, if the action is impermissible what makes it so is not the agent's belief but, rather, the fact that there was, under the circumstances, good reason to believe that this harm was likely to occur. If someone believes, for no good reason, that his friend will die if he himself does not eat oatmeal for breakfast every morning, this does not make it impermissible for him to fail to eat his oatmeal.

Even when acting with clueless negligence and acting with full knowledge that one's action is likely to be harmful are both impermissible, there is still a moral difference between these actions. The difference is not in permissibility, but in what I call *meaning*: the significance of an action for the agent's relations with others. Failing to consider whether one's action is likely to harm others, and doing what one knows to be harmful, involve different kinds of fault—different forms of culpable failure to take the interests of others into account in the right way.

Consider now "intention" in the narrower sense. If an agent (unjustifiably) takes the fact that his action is likely to harm someone as counting in favor of that action, this indicates a third kind of faulty attitude. An agent is open to a different kind of moral criticism for doing something that is likely to harm someone because she wants to harm this person than she would be for failure to pay due attention to whether her action is likely to cause harm, or for acting in disregard of the fact that it is likely to do this. These differences in meaning and blameworthiness remain even when all three actions are impermissible.

So differences in intention, or in whether an agent is doing something intentionally or unintentionally, can "make a moral difference" without making a difference in permissibility. It does not follow, however, that the permissibility of an action never depends on the agent's intentions, or, more broadly, on what the agent saw as reasons for so acting. One reason it may not follow is that the likely consequences of an action can depend on the reasons that the agent will be governed by as he or she carries it out. For example, whether my driving a car is likely to cause harm will depend on whether, as I drive, I will be exercising due care not to cause harm; that is, whether I will be on the lookout for possible harmful consequences, and see them as things I have reason to avoid. If I would not have these attitudes, then my driving may be unacceptably risky, and therefore impermissible. Cases like this, in which an agent's intention to avoid causing harm makes it more likely that he or she will not cause harm, are instances of what I will call the *predictive* significance of intent.

The next question is whether an agent's intention in acting can make a difference to the permissibility of an action in ways other than by affecting the likely consequences of that action. For example, there seems to be an important moral difference, in war, between, on the one hand, attacking a military target in a way that can be foreseen to lead to a certain number of civilian casualties, and, on the other, killing the same number of civilians in order to demoralize the population or discourage them from aiding the enemy. Since these two lines of action—tactical bombing and terror bombing—are expected to kill the same number of people, the difference between them seems to lie in the fact that in the latter case, but not the former, those who carry out the attack intend to kill the civilians. They are not merely aware that this will probably be the effect of what they are doing; they are aiming at it, as a means to their end.

More generally, many people are inclined to accept the Principle of Double Effect, which holds that although it can be permissible to do something that one can foresee will lead to the deaths of innocent people when doing this is necessary to achieve some greater good, it is always impermissible to aim at the deaths of innocent people, either as one's ultimate end or as one's chosen means to some greater good. This principle is controversial, but it is appealing because it seems to offer the best explanation of the distinction between terror bombing and tactical bombing, and also to explain other cases such as the following:

Rescue I: As I am driving home, I receive a phone call telling me that a car is stalled along a seldom-traveled road that I could easily take. The car is delivering medicine to someone who will die unless he receives it within the next few hours. I could easily take that road and restart the stalled car.

Clearly I should do so.

Rescue II: This is the same as the previous case except that I am also told that along yet another road I could take there is a stalled car that was taking medicine to five people in equally urgent need. There is not enough time for me to go to the aid of both cars.

Clearly in this case it is at least permissible for me to aid the second car, so as to save five rather than only one.

Rescue/Transplant: This is the same as *Rescue I* except that I know that there are five people in urgent need of transplants who will be saved using the organs of the patient awaiting the medicine, if he dies very soon, as he will if I do not go to the aid of the stalled car.

If it is impermissible to refrain from aiding the car in *Rescue I*, then it is impermissible in this case as well. But it is permissible in *Rescue II*. As before, the Principle of Double Effect provides an explanation: in *Rescue/Transplant*, but not *Rescue II*, I would be intending that the one person should die, as a means to saving the five.

But the Principle of Double Effect is not needed in order to explain the difference between these cases, or the difference between the bombing cases, and the most plausible explanations of these cases do not turn on the agents' intentions.

Our thinking about the bombing cases is shaped by certain assumptions about the principles governing the conduct of war. These principles are often formulated in terms of what that agent can *intend*, but they are better understood as having something like the following form, which makes no reference to intent:

In war, one is sometimes permitted to use destructive and potentially deadly force of a kind that would normally be prohibited. But such force is permitted only when its use is very likely to bring some military advantage, such as destroying enemy combatants or war-making materials, and it is permitted only if expected harm to noncombatants is minimized, and only if this harm is "proportional" to the importance of the military advantage to be gained.

This statement of the principle is only approximate. There are difficult questions about how the idea of a "military advantage" and the distinction between combatants and noncombatants are to be understood, and how the significance of these ideas is to be defended. I do not mean to ignore or minimize these problems, but they are problems that any view of these matters must face. My point is that there is no need, in addition, to appeal to the significance of intent in order to explain cases like the ones we have considered.

The proposed bombing of the munitions plant is permissible only if the destruction of the plant constitutes a military advantage in the relevant sense, and only if the conditions just listed are fulfilled: only if harm to noncombatants is minimized and the expected harm is "proportional." If there is no munitions plant, but a bombing raid that would kill the same number of noncombatants would hasten the end of war by undermining morale, this raid (a pure case of "terror bombing") would not be permissible. It is impermissible because it can be expected to kill noncombatants, and the circumstances are not such as to provide a justification for doing this under the principle just stated. The death of noncombatants is not rendered a "military advantage" by the fact that it would shorten the war by undermining public morale. So the fact that it would do this does not bring the case under the exception, just described, to the prohibition against doing what there is good reason to believe will cause loss of life.

As I have said, there are well-known difficulties about how the idea of a military advantage and the distinction between combatants and noncombatants are to be understood and defended. But on a plausible understanding of these ideas, the principle I have stated would rule out the nuclear bombing of Hiroshima and Nagasaki at the end of World War II, as well as the fire bombing of Tokyo and, earlier, of Dresden. There is no need to appeal to the agents' intentions in order to explain these cases.

On the view I am proposing, it remains true that a person acts wrongly if she intends to kill noncombatants in order to shorten the war by undermining morale (and has no further justification for her action). Such a person has an intention that she should abandon. But this truth should not be taken to suggest that intention has a fundamental role in determining the impermissibility of this action, in the way claimed by the Principle of Double Effect. The intention is wrongful because the act intended is wrongful, and the act is wrongful because of its likely consequences, not (fundamentally) because of this intention.

In the rescue and transplant cases, it was assumed that it is impermissible simply to take a living person's organs, even if this would benefit others, but that once a person is dead his or her organs are available for use to save others. Like the distinction between combatants and noncombatants, this assumption might be questioned, but it was presupposed in the examples as I presented them. The assumption that the person's organs would be available for transplant to save the five if, but only if, he was dead, is what forces on us the question of whether the possibility of saving others in this way justifies an exception to the general principle that requires us to save the person in *Rescue I*.

Once the question is posed in this way, however, we can see clearly why this does not justify such an exception. The general form of the question is this: as long as a person is alive, we have an obligation to him not to do X. If he were to die, and we were thus freed from this obligation, we could accomplish some good by doing X. Does this good therefore justify an exception to the principle requiring us to save the person (or a principle that would forbid killing him)? It would be absurd to think that it does, that is to say, that the fact that a person's death would release us from some obligation to him can count in favor of killing him, or against saving him. This absurdity does not itself depend on the idea that an individual has a special claim to his or her organs, although that is the particular moral claim that is at issue in the case we are discussing. The same absurdity could arise with respect to any underlying moral claim.

No similar absurdity is involved in *Rescue II*. In that case, the principle in question incorporates an exception allowing us not to save a person if we could instead save a greater number and we do not have time or resources to do both. We would be permitted, and able to, save the greater number even if the other person's life were not in jeopardy. So *Rescue II* and *Rescue/Transplant* do differ in that in the latter case, but not the former, the death of the one is seen as required in order for us to save the five (morally required, in order to make this permissible, not causally required, in order to bring it about). In this respect, the explanation I have offered has some similarity with the Principle of Double Effect. But in my explanation, this difference has nothing to do with the intentions of the agents involved.

Like a terror bomber, an agent who took the possibility of saving the five in *Rescue/Transplant* as sufficient reason not to save the one would be making a moral mistake: he or she would be taking something to be a good moral reason that is not in fact such a reason, and would have an intention (a plan) that he or she ought to abandon. But this intention is not what makes the agent's action impermissible. The action is impermissible, and the intention mistaken, because, for the reasons I have outlined, the prospect of saving five by means of transplant does not justify an exception to the duty to save the one.

If the Principle of Double Effect is mistaken, why should it seem plausible to many people? The tendency to think that the agent's intention makes a fundamental difference to the permissibility of an action in these cases may result from a failure to distinguish between the deliberative use of a principle, in which it specifies the considerations that count for or against an action, and the critical use of a principle as a standard for assessing the way in which an agent went about deciding what to do. An assessment of the latter kind will always depend on what the agent *saw* as reasons for or against an action. The deliberative use of a principle identifies the considerations that *are* reasons for or against an action, such as the harm it is likely to cause, or the fact that the agent has promised to do it. These need not be facts about the agent's beliefs.

It is easy to confuse these two forms of assessment. We might say, for example, that what I did was wrong because I took the fact that it was more fun to watch a soap opera as a reason not to pick you up at the airport, as I had promised to do. But what would make this action wrong would be the fact that I promised to pick you up, and had no sufficient reason not to keep this promise. I was in error in taking the pleasure of watching television as a sufficient reason, but the fact that this was my reason is not what made my action wrong. The failure to distinguish between these two forms of assessment may lend plausibility to the Principle of Double Effect, by making it seem that an agent's particular reason for acting is what makes his action wrong when it does not in fact do so.

It is also possible that supporters of the Principle of Double Effect may not be thinking of this principle as a criterion of permissibility in the sense I am concerned with, but rather as a criterion for assessing the moral goodness of an action, which may well depend on an agent's intention, or on the reasons he or she acted from. If so, then the disagreement about the Principle of Double Effect is not about which actions fall within a certain moral category (the permissible) but about which moral category we should be concerned with (permissibility or goodness).

There certainly are cases in which the permissibility of an action depends on the agent's reasons for so acting, albeit in a less fundamental way than the Principle of

Double Effect would suggest. One class of such cases includes ones in which the meaning of an action depends on the agent's reasons for engaging in it, and it is impermissible to mislead others about this meaning, or to fail to disclose this meaning. In what I will call *expression* cases, actions involve presenting oneself as being moved by certain reasons. When I call a sick relative and inquire about her health, for example, I may present myself as being moved by affectionate concern for her welfare. Suppose, however, that I am not moved by this reason at all. I might telephone the relative and inquire about her health just to curry favor with my wealthy grandfather, or simply to get my mother to stop nagging me about it. This may not make it impermissible for me to call. Perhaps a call from me would do so much to cheer the person up that I should make the call, despite the fact that it would be hypocritical. But the fact that I would be misrepresenting the reason for which I was calling at least counts against the action, and could do so decisively in the absence of other considerations to the contrary.

Something similar is true in a wider range of what might be called *expectation* cases. These are cases in which someone enters into a certain relation with an agent—a conversation, perhaps, or some form of cooperation—only because he or she assumes (perhaps without the agent's having done anything to encourage this assumption) that the agent has certain intentions, or is moved by certain reasons and not others. In these cases, an agent's intentions, and the reasons by which he or she is moved, are relevant to the permissibility of the agent's action. But they are relevant only in a derivative way, as a consequence of a more basic moral requirement not to mislead others or take advantage of their mistaken beliefs about one's intentions. So the question remains whether there are cases in which facts about an agent's reasons for acting are relevant to permissibility in a more fundamental way.

One class of cases in which the significance of an agent's reasons for acting is not derivative in this way is what I will call *threat* cases. There are many things to be said about the morality of threats, but in the important class of cases I have in mind a threat is wrong because it would be wrong to carry out the threat—that is to say, wrong to do the thing one has threatened to do *because the victim refused to comply*. In the case of some threats, such as the familiar "Your money or your life!" example, the condition I have italicized plays no role. Killing the victim would be wrong independent of the holdup person's reasons for doing it. But in other cases these reasons matter to the permissibility of the threatened action. Suppose, for example, that a hiring officer who has only one job to fill has sufficient reason to hire any one of several candidates, so there is no candidate whom it would be wrong not to hire. Still, it would be wrong for the hiring officer to refuse to hire a candidate because he or she would not have sex with the officer (or would not pay a bribe, or agree to do household chores). And it would consequently be wrong to threaten to do this.

The explanation of this wrong is that, first, an acceptable principle governing such cases must give the hiring officer authority to decide whom to hire. (This may be justified by considerations of the efficiency of the firm or, in the case of a single proprietor, perhaps by his or her property rights.) But a principle that permitted the hiring officer to make this decision for reasons of the kind just mentioned would give him or her an unacceptable form of control over the lives of job candidates. So such decisions are impermissible. The relevance of the agent's reasons in this case is not derivative in the way that it is in expression and expectation cases. All it depends on is the victims' having sufficient grounds for objecting to the principle permitting hiring decisions to be made for such reasons. When there are grounds for rejecting such a principle, the reasons a hiring agent acted on can make his or her action impermissible.

I have argued that we should reject the Principle of Double Effect as a criterion of permissibility, and I have identified a mistake (confusing the deliberative and the critical uses of a principle) that may lead one to conclude that intention is relevant to permissibility when in fact it is not. But I have also identified a number of ways in which an agent's intentions or, more broadly, his or her reasons for acting, can be relevant to the permissibility of an action. These include cases in which these factors have predictive significance, expression and expectation cases, and threat cases. There may be other cases beyond these. But morally objectionable reasons do not always render an action impermissible. Suppose I see a person drowning, and I could easily save him. He is someone I hate, and I would like to see him dead, but I do not want him to die *now* because his estate would go to a person with whom I am locked in a bitter electoral contest, and would provide her with much more money to spend on her campaign. If I save the man for this reason, seeing no other reason to do it, I have acted badly but not, I would say, impermissibly. There is such a thing as doing the right (permissible) thing for the wrong (that is to say, morally objectionable) reasons.

TEST YOUR UNDERSTANDING

1. Scanlon discusses the case of someone who believes he must eat oatmeal every day to keep his friend alive. Suppose one day he gets mad at his friend, and chooses not to eat oatmeal out of anger, hoping that his friend will thereby die. What would Scanlon say about this?

    a. His action of failing to eat oatmeal is perfectly harmless, and so it is morally permissible. Nevertheless, he is morally criticizable for wanting to hurt his friend.

    b. He is aiming to hurt his friend, and so he is acting morally impermissibly.

2. Scanlon says that differences in intentionality can "make a moral difference" without making a difference to the moral permissibility of an action. How can they do so?

3. In the *Rescue/Transplant* case, you must decide whether to save the life of one person. If you let him die, then his organs can be used to save five people. What is Scanlon's explanation of why it is wrong to let him die? How does he think this case differs from *Rescue II*, in which you have to choose between saving one person and saving five people?

    a. In *Rescue/Transplant*, you would be intending the one person's death as a means to your end of saving the five people. In *Rescue II*, the one person's death would merely be an unintended side effect.

    b. There is a general duty to save a life if you can, and this duty is not defeated by the fact that a person's death could benefit some other people; thus, in *Rescue/Transplant*, you must save the one person. But the duty to save a life is not absolute, because it can't be: sometimes several people are in need of saving and one cannot save all of them. In such cases (like *Rescue II*), one is allowed to save the larger group, letting the smaller group die.

4. Although Scanlon rejects the Doctrine of Double Effect, he acknowledges that sometimes intention can make a difference to moral permissibility. What are two examples he offers?

NOTES AND QUESTIONS

1. *Scanlon's opposition to terror bombing.* Scanlon contends that the wrongness of terror bombing may be explained without referring to the intent of the bomber and, therefore, without invoking the **Doctrine of Double Effect**. What is his alternative explanation, and how does it differ from arguments that appeal to intention? How might Scanlon respond to someone who objects that Scanlon's account has no principled way of distinguishing between strategic bombing and terror bombing if the number of civilian casualties is the same? Does Scanlon have a good reason for thinking that a reduction in enemy morale is not a military advantage?

2. *Scanlon's criticism of the Doctrine of Double Effect.* Philosophers who criticize widespread views often try to provide charitable explanations for their opponents' views for (at least) two related reasons. First, if you can give an account of *how and why* a person made a mistake, that person may find it easier to reject the flawed reasoning if she can see exactly where the mistake occurs. Second, if you can explain how people *reasonably* came to an incorrect position and show their mistake, you may dispel the lingering and tempting sense that because lots of intelligent people have held the view, they must have had a good reason, and thus there must be something right about it.

    Scanlon offers an explanation for why his opponents have been attracted to the Doctrine of Double Effect, a principle he claims is misguided. What is his explanation, and is it persuasive? For a fuller elaboration of his critique and his positive theory, see T. M. Scanlon, *Moral Dimensions: Permissibility, Meaning, Blame* (Belknap Press, 2008).

3. *The disunity of action and character.* It seems possible on Scanlon's view that a person could have a terrible moral character, yet always do the morally permissible thing. It also seems possible, on his view, that a person could have a wonderful moral character, yet always perform the morally impermissible action. Can you see why? Do these possibilities create a problem for his view? Should a moral theory classify the permissibility of actions and the goodness of agents in such different ways that these categories operate that distinctly?

Barbara Herman (b. 1945)

Herman is Griffin Professor of Philosophy at the University of California, Los Angeles. A leading philosopher in moral and political philosophy, she is most famous for her nuanced work on moral psychology and her sophisticated interpretations and defenses of Kantian moral theory. She has published many influential articles and books, including *The Practice of Moral Judgment* (1993) and *Moral Literacy* (2007).

IMPERMISSIBILITY AND WRONGNESS

There is now widespread agreement that rightness and wrongness are about our actions and their effects, not about our motives or intentions. If one wanted to argue that Robin Hood wasn't wrong in taking from the rich to feed the poor, his good motives wouldn't be what made it so. Motives and intentions are separate from the action, part of its history, and so should figure in the appraisal of agents (the way they come to act), not of actions (what is done). I think there is reason to doubt that this view of rightness and wrongness (call it the "acts-not-motives view") can be correct.

In recent versions of the acts-not-motives view, the central norm of wrongness in action is taken to be impermissibility. If a proposed action is impermissible, it may not be done; if it is permissible, then it may be done, even if there are better things an agent could have done instead. On the acts-not-motives view, an otherwise permissible action is not made wrong by a "bad" motive or intention, and only rarely (if ever) do motive and intention even partly explain an action's impermissibility.

Impermissibility is, I believe, a thin moral notion, best taken as a mark or sign of moral wrongness, not capturing what wrongness is. There are purposes for which its thinness is an advantage: e.g., in taking some actions off the table entirely (dismembering one to save five, terrorizing civilians as a wartime strategy), in regions of moral regulation where a clear and strict rule is what is wanted. The problem with the acts-not-motives view is not with the category of impermissibility, or with the idea that wrongness *can* sometimes attach to actions without regard to intention or motive. What should be resisted is the acts-not-motives view's generalization from contexts where the exclusion of motives *is* appropriate, to a broader view about what moral wrongness of action is. If we reverse the order and investigate moral wrongness first, we will be better able to see the reasons to include motive and intention in an account of morally wrong action (and, of course, right action as well).

1. Impermissibility tends to move to the center of attention when we think the first moral question about action is "What may I do?" when faced with alternatives whose moral availability is in doubt. I could stand in line for the next 2 hours and miss seeing an old friend, or falsely claim an emergency to elicit immediate service. It is impermissible to make the false claim. Why? In these circumstances, making a false claim would violate moral principle—be it a rule about what everyone is permitted to do, or about an appropriate balance of benefits and burdens, or about fairness. When a principle of this kind introduces the feature that makes us judge an action wrong, call it the "wrong-maker," it is no surprise that the verdict about what may or may not be done is, in almost all cases, motive- and intention-independent: neither item is involved in the explanation of wrongness.

Here's the kind of example often used to support the acts-not-motives view. Suppose moral principle requires saving a threatened life. Someone does the saving, but he is motivated by desire for fame or reward or because he has nasty plans that involve the victim later. Since despite (or even because of) his selfish motives, he does what is required, he *does* nothing wrong. That we cannot reasonably say that he should not have acted as he did—not saved the life—is a sign that the fault we find in his character or goals is not transmitted to his action. The action that should have been done was done.

But now add an example from Derek Parfit.[1] Parfit asks us to imagine a coffee-ordering gangster, thuggishly motivated to do whatever it takes to make the world conform to his will. He is ready to cause all kinds of mayhem if anyone crosses him, and regards the barista as he would a potentially recalcitrant soda machine that he will lash out at if it balks at dispensing his drink. But he is not crossed; the coffee is ordered and delivered; the easiest thing to do is pay, and so he does. Both Parfit and the acts-not-motives view conclude that since that act is one that satisfies moral principle (paying for purchases, say), nothing untoward has happened. We have a nasty guy you wouldn't want to have around, but for all that, unless and until he does something forbidden, the moral problem is all a matter of potential and probabilities—of bad motives, not bad action.

I think we should hold that, to the contrary, the gangster's action is morally wrong: not wrong in that he paid for the coffee, but wrong nonetheless. He did something he should not have done.

One might challenge the conclusion that nothing bad happened. The barista was surely put at risk in ways he ought not to have been. If we imagine that the danger is evident, it would be odd to say that nothing wrong occurred if you escape harm only by avoiding eye contact or placating or doing whatever is needed to avoid setting off those around you who are primed for easy violence. Making it safely through a minefield is not a walk in the park. (Note that the issue here is not predictive: that acting with such a nasty attitude is likely to cause harm and so wrong. There is a wrong to the agent who made it through unharmed.) But let us leave this response aside. The question I want to press is whether it is true that the gangster's action *in handing over the money* conforms to, or does not violate, moral principle.

What might lead one to think that the gangster's action does conform to moral principle? Both the movement of things and the behaviors of animals and persons blindly conform to natural laws. Actions of persons can conform to (or at least not violate) positive law without their knowing or caring that it does. When, without paying attention, someone drives 39 mph in a 40 mph zone, she drives just below the speed limit and lawfully. But what about when, not remembering a promise I have made, I show up, doing what I promised, but for some other reason. Have I kept my promise? I think not. Suppose a doctor in an emergency room acts on a private rule under which he treats the patient to his left, or the white patient, or the cute patient. Perhaps he has never treated the "wrong" patient. He is surely doing something wrong nevertheless. Is he conforming or not conforming to the triage rule in an emergency room to attend first to those with greatest need who can be saved?

---

1. Derek Parfit, *On What Matters* (Oxford University Press, 2011), 87–88. [Herman's note.]

Whichever is true, it's an interesting question whether, if there were moral police around, they should stop the doctor from this action. The sickest patient is being taken care of, even if only by happenstance. As with the gangster and the selfish life-saver, why not conclude: no harm, no foul? A moral advisor would counsel reform about *the way* decisions are being made. And normally, insofar as we care about reliably getting the right thing done, we avoid such agents if we can. But here and now, no morally wrong action was done.

There are important differences in the cases. The gangster chooses to pay for his coffee; the self-serving agent intends to save a life: each intends to do the thing morality requires even if neither their intention nor their motive is a moral one. By contrast, in the triage and promise cases, the fact that the act chosen is the act that morally must be done is a pure accident. It is not clear how the acts-not-motives view can keep these cases separate. If it cannot require that the agent be motivated or intend to do the right thing as a condition of an action's rightness, it is not clear it can require the agent to intend the action under any special description (*as* a paying-for-services or *as* a promise-keeping). Whenever an agent acts intentionally, she acts under some description; conformity to or violation of moral principle is, except in special cases, about actions and effects in the external world. It is just this fact that I think we should find puzzling. How could external conformity be enough? In none of these cases is the beneficial or according-to-principle action or outcome the result of anything working right.

The paradigm case for the acts-not-motives view is a moral requirement that we *not* do something. We succeed in omitting a prohibited action if we do something else. If there are only two possible choices for action and one is prohibited, then the other must be permitted. Prohibitions give moral space the structure of a game board: so long as we do not step on the blue squares or a square that anyone has been on before, we're fine. To the agent "playing," why the square is not available makes no difference, and that it's not available need not figure in her mind for a move to be prohibited (suppose a siren goes off if there's a misstep). The picture looks even stranger for positive moral requirements: promising, truth-telling, rescue. Then the fact that it's not a blue square is not enough. The player should be on the right square for the right reason (to put someone in checkmate, for example). It should seem odd that the prohibition pattern dominates our account of moral wrongness.

In many versions of the acts-not-motives view one catches sight of something like a sleight-of-thought. Behind what appears to be an account of wrongness or impermissibility that makes no substantive moral claims, there is a hidden assumption about moral content; namely, that moral wrongness is about action as it produces effects, either singly, or as a function of what would happen if we all acted on some principle. That is, in thinking about the permissibility of an action, we are to look to the resulting distribution of burdens and benefits, asking who should bear what costs for which goods. Morality tells us which effects or pattern of effects we may and which we may not cause by our actions, given our options. If what matters to (im) permissibility is solely the effects of actions, neither motives nor intentions could be candidate wrong-makers. But this result is not then a function of a content-neutral feature of moral requirement or obligation: something that appears to be neutral is in fact a substantive view about what matters morally in action.

Tracing out the role of the Doctrine of Double Effect (DDE)[2] in arguments for the acts-not-motives view reveals just this kind of move. DDE came about as a way to distinguish two types of good-producing actions—one where producing the good had a collateral but unintended cost, the other where the good came about by morally forbidden means. DDE did this by locating the moral difference in the agent's intention.[3] As an account of the permissibility of a certain set of cases, DDE, and so an intention-dependent argument for permissibility that relies on it, fails if there is a better account of the cases. Acts-not-motives accounts get to the same results by appeal to patterns of consequences: whether some have a claim not to be harmed for the sake of the goods in question (e.g., killing civilians to lower enemy morale vs. seeing their deaths as a collateral effect of legitimate combat). Once the cases are described in this way, as a distributive issue across goods and independent moral claims, the intention to bring about one of the patterns could not be the wrong-maker—it's the pattern of consequences that matters.

It is not at all clear that such arguments accurately capture the problem DDE was aiming to account for by bringing intention in.[4] DDE is not meant to be a primary moral principle but something like a principle of exceptions. Where an action-kind is normally morally prohibited (e.g., causing deaths in the pursuit of a good end), DDE may permit an exception in some cases if the relevant actor has the right intention. This makes sense, since the exemption that comes with an exception is only available if the agent has the right intention. For similar reasons, we wouldn't call it self-defense if A kills B without knowing (or caring?) that B is launching a lethal attack against him.

2. If what is presented as a content-neutral feature of wrongness in fact depends on a specific kind of case and a substantive view about what makes an action wrong, we might not arrive at the acts-not-motives view if we began by looking at other kinds of cases and a different account of wrongness. The idea is not to eliminate impermissibility as a category of moral assessment, but to assign it a more limited place in an account of the moral wrongness of actions. As an alternative, I want to look at a Kant-inspired account of motive and of action assessment that shifts focus from the axis of avoiding impermissibility onto the more complicated requirements of getting it right about duty and obligation.

The acts-not-motives view assumes that wrongness in action is about producing a comparatively deficient configuration of interests and claims: one should have produced a better balance of effects (as some moral principle directs). By contrast, on a Kantian view, morality may require that we do and avoid more complicated things. For example, what I am to do is: "having promised, show up," and "recognizing he is in need, extend a hand." But also I must avoid: "having promised, show up only if

2. Other discussions of DDE appear in the introduction and in readings by Anscombe and Scanlon in this chapter. [Herman's note.]

3. According to DDE, an agent may perform an action that will produce both good and harmful effects if the good effects significantly outweigh the harms, and the agent merely foresees but does not intend the harm, either for itself or as a means to the good effects. [Herman's note.]

4. Warren Quinn explored this question in "Actions, Intentions, and Consequences: The Doctrine of Double Effect," reprinted in his *Morality and Action* (Cambridge University Press, 1993), chapter 8. [Herman's note.]

it's to my advantage," and "recognizing need, help on condition that I benefit." The emphasis is on an agent's subjective principle, her maxim, what we might describe as the instrumental and evaluative representation of a possible action that moves her.

On the acts-not-motives view, motives range across appetites, instincts, habits, inclinations; they reach to emotions and passions. Their objects can be primitive (food) or complex (justice). The motive itself remains somewhat murky; it is a force that inclines or disposes an agent to activity. A moral motive is a kind of attachment to morality, a disposition to do what morality requires. No such motive could contribute to the rightness of the action; its job is to orient the agent's activity to rightness.

For Kant, however, "motive" is a general term for the way an agent exercises its causality. Some motives are opaque forces. Others involve reasoning and evaluative capacities. We are capable of being moved, of coming to act, from a recognition that something is required of us. A moral requirement—that one help the needy or promise honestly—then functions as a premise of practical reasoning. Reasoning from premise to action is not a cognitive exercise that attracts a motive (or not), but is itself what moves us. A Kantian moral motive is then not a form of attachment to a principle, but the agent's principle of reasoning, her maxim, in acting. Since the same act—a bit of effect-producing causality—can come from different maxims, it can be wrong to x if x-ing comes via one maxim and not wrong to x if its source is a different maxim. So here, the wrong-maker is a difference of motive.

There is nothing in itself odd about the idea of two doings that are externally or behaviorally the same, yet not the same action. In addition to actions that merely "look" the same (homonymous actions—inspecting and spying, for example), there are "as if" actions: imitations, pretendings, theatrical performances. "I promise" in a theatrical performance does not obligate, though in the theatrical fiction one character intelligibly holds another to what he promised. Promises between thieves might be regarded by the parties as promises, but if what's promised is immoral, there is no obligation, and so no real promise. If, having spotted a highway patrol car, I slow down to 65 mph, my driving at the speed limit for the few minutes I'm under surveillance is not driving-at-the-speed-limit, though for purposes of avoiding a ticket, it is just as good.

So why not say that the coffee-buyings of the ordinary customer and the gangster are not the same doings because their reasoning, their maxims, is different? The acts-not-motives view regards the action of the morally motivated customer as the right action plus a good motive. We might instead regard the gangster's action as the right action or outcome, minus something. It reproduces the dutiful action's external form, but it's a kind of simulation, not the real thing. As a simulation it is good enough for some purposes. But even to be a simulation, there must be something that has what it lacks.

There are other regions of rationally governed activity where we hold that a right outcome is not enough, not the real thing. An unjustified true belief is of course true and a belief, but it is also *qua* belief (that is, strictly) incorrect or wrong or defective. The flaw is a fact about the belief, not about the agent (though it may imply something about the agent). The route to the belief, by evidence or testimony, or by astrology or need, determines the belief's epistemic status, whether appropriate to hold or not.

(Only, perhaps, for bare perceptual beliefs is mere correspondence to reality sufficient to make them *correct* beliefs). An accidentally true belief can do some of the work of a well-founded one, but not all (in scientific reasoning about counterfactuals, for example, but also in simpler cases: my belief that there will not be an earthquake tomorrow may be true, but if I believe it because I think earthquakes only happen when it is sunny, I may well be unprepared for the "big one" during the rainy season).

The acts-not-motives view encourages thinking about moral choice in terms of act-outcome pairs. It tends to be a complaint-centered view of morality: for an agent faced with a pair of possible actions, her question is whether someone affected would have grounds to object to her doing one rather than the other. The framework for choice on a Kantian view isn't directly about options but about the duties and obligations that bear. These duties and obligations place demands on agents' reasoning, laying out connections between moral premises and possible actions that follow. One duty will tell us that an action type, deceit, for example, is not available as a means to an agent reasoning from self-interest ("because I want it" is a powerful premise; duties and obligations in this way constrain that premise's authority). Another duty will require that certain premises figure in our choices: where needs of others are acute and we can safely help, their needs, and not our convenience, should be our first premise in reasoning to action. In like manner we understand that making a promise involves taking on a premise in future reasoning to action.

The basic moral requirement thus involves our motives—that we reason correctly in choosing. When we don't, we are in error about our action, even if we do the very deed correct reasoning would have us do. Were we talking about Humean motives, the murky pressures, dispositions, and of mind, it would be strange to talk about a requirement on motives: we lack the kind of control over these states that would permit morality's direct rule. But Kantian motives, or the ones morality cares about, are composed of the elements of reasoning. Whatever our disposition, we can be held to standards of correct reasoning. If P is the premise that obligation requires in our circumstances, and we know that it is, we are able to reason from P. This is no less true in the sphere of action than belief. That we are vulnerable to mistake and corruptions of reasoning does not imply that correctness in reasoning was out of reach: we can reason as we should, and therefore can be obligated to do so.

3. That we could be so obligated doesn't explain why morality should require correct reasoning over and above correct action. Consider the requirement to help others in need. Some persons are naturally and directly moved to promote the well-being of others: motivated by feelings of care or concern, they offer advice or a helping hand, sometimes risking a great deal to prevent harms. The Kantian view will say that such actions simulate beneficence, a duty which also aims to promote the well-being of others. The beneficent and the natural motive do not generate actions from the same premises; the maxims are different; the agents' understanding of the needs they are responding to is different, even if the thing done to help is the same. Motivated by natural sympathy, we aim to relieve pain and suffering as such. The duty of beneficence aims to alleviate pain and suffering as or because they impede our good functioning

(suppose).[5] Of course, given the nature of our vulnerabilities, it's no surprise that a sympathetic temperament can often stand in for beneficence. But the simulation can separate from the duty in cases where sympathy directs us to alleviate varieties of pain we should not ease (such as the pain of guilt, or the pain that is part of learning).

From the point of view of a victim in the moment, it makes little difference how the action is motivated or from what reasoning it issues. He gets what he needs equally well from the real thing or a simulation. No reason for regrets; no ground for complaint. But this point of view is highly selective. The agent whose helping action flows from moral premises is oriented in her acting to getting it right about help and what helping may involve. This includes both helping in the right way (e.g., in a way that does not produce dependence), and managing the aftermath: taking further steps, if needed, and negotiating the complexities of gratitude. None of this is found in the simulation, and it (partly) explains why morality requires more.

Where morality is present to us in duties and obligations, the hard question is often not a decision between options, but determining whether our circumstances warrant making an exception to a duty or obligation that applies. We know there is a duty about truth-telling that prohibits lying to promote our purposes. But in a case where the point or value of truth-telling is subverted (say, where telling the truth will enable wrongdoing), there is a question about whether the prohibition on lying might be canceled or suspended. Likewise, a duty to respect the physical space persons are in—we may not just push each other out of the way—can yield an exception in a medical emergency because in that case, it is the frantic push and not courtesy that does the work of the duty (enabling free action and choice).[6] However, unless the exception is recognized and the action taken in its light, it does no justificatory work. If we lie to protect a friend, or shove because we always regard ourselves as entitled, what we do is wrong.

Making an exception requires an exercise of deliberative authority. The agent whose reasoning is faulty—who does not have and act from a correct practical grasp of the moral terrain—is not competent to act contrary to the rule of duty that applies. Morality requires more of us than avoiding an unhappy outcome; we can act, but only if we get it right, and that is possible only when motive and intention express the authority of the agent's reasoning.

If we generalized from this result, we would conclude that the standard of correctness of an action includes the deliberative route by which the agent came to perform it. Just as weighing evidence is not an attitude one might or might not have about correct belief-formation, the work of the moral motive is not a special attitude one might or might not have toward morally required action. In acting from the correct motive, we get it right about what morality requires of action.[7]

---

5. Learning the ins and outs of the duty of beneficence is one of the ways that we come to grasp the special needs of our kind of agency. [Herman's note.]

6. Describing the duty as a "duty to respect" rather than as a "duty not to interfere" captures this. [Herman's note.]

7. A fuller account of this interpretive claim can be found in my "Reasoning to Obligation," *Inquiry* 49, 1 (2006): 44–61. [Herman's note.]

On the Kantian alternative, several features of the acts-not-motives view remain in place. We often have moral reason not to be concerned about motive or intention: we want the drowning person saved; no one should kill one to save two. Some actions cannot be taken for any reason, and many actions are simply not available for the pursuit of our interests. We shouldn't need to deliberate to avoid cheating and shoplifting, or brutality to children. However, even though, as competent agents, there are things we know without thinking about them, moral reasoning is correctly imputed to us and retrievable. Whatever we do, it is not, strictly speaking, a morally correct action unless motive and intention are correct, unless, that is, we have acted on the right maxim.

When we correct a child who does the right thing to get a reward or to avoid the disapproval of her parents, we are in effect telling her that what she's done is not enough: she's gotten only part of the way there. It's a lesson not unlike others where we nudge children past rote performances and toward thinking out their actions for themselves. We want them to take possession of the activity and its standards of correctness so that they can, with authority, do the right thing.

On the acts-not-motives view, taking morality into our system of motives is a way to become morally reliable and to have our relations with others marked by moral concern, not just rectitude. On the alternative or Kantian view, we don't grasp what morality requires unless we come to conformity with moral principle in the right way, from the inside, in the way we deliberate and reason to action.

TEST YOUR UNDERSTANDING

1. What view is Herman advocating?

   a. The acts-not-motives view, according to which acts are right or wrong regardless of their motives.

   b. The Kantian view that the proper subject of evaluation as right or wrong is an action plus a motive.

2. What diagnosis does Herman give of why people have been led astray into thinking that impermissibility and wrongness are equivalent?

   a. They have focused on cases of moral *prohibitions*. These are cases in which an action is impermissible and it is thereby morally wrong. They have overgeneralized to think that all morally wrong actions are also impermissible.

   b. They have focused on cases of lying and deception. These are cases in which an action is impermissible and it is thereby morally wrong. They have overgeneralized to think that all morally wrong actions are also impermissible.

3. How does Herman think people have misunderstood the Doctrine of Double Effect?

   a. They have taken it to be a primary moral principle, when really it is a principle about when one is permitted to make an exception to a moral principle.

   b. They have taken it to be a principle about when one is permitted to make an exception to a moral principle, when really it is a primary moral principle.

4. What does Herman think is central to morality?

   a. avoiding doing what is morally wrong

   b. understanding moral principle and engaging in correct moral deliberation

NOTES AND QUESTIONS

1. *Moral wrong versus moral impermissibility.* Herman claims that the coffee-ordering gangster behaves wrongly, if not impermissibly. What do you think the difference is between behaving wrongly and behaving impermissibly? Why do you think she insists that the gangster acts wrongly and not merely that he has a bad character? Can you think of an example of a person with a good character who behaves permissibly yet wrongly in her sense?

2. *Morality as advice.* Consider the following objection:

> The main function of moral reasoning is to give us guidance about how to behave—about what actions to perform and what actions to forgo. A moral judgment offers advice about what to do. But you can only advise someone to perform a particular action. You cannot advise someone to perform a particular action *for a particular reason.* You do not choose which reasons strike you as valid and which reasons motivate you to act. Reasons are not matters of choice. So a moral theory that insists that having a particular reason is an essential feature of a right action must be mistaken because it cannot yield useful advice.

How might Herman respond? Should she challenge the advice-centered conception of morality or the claim that reasons are not matters of choice, or both?

Michele M. Moody-Adams (b. 1956)

Moody-Adams is Joseph Straus Professor of Political Philosophy and Legal Theory at Columbia University. She is the author of *Fieldwork in Familiar Places: Morality, Culture and Philosophy* (1997) and of essays on equality and social justice, moral psychology and the virtues, and the philosophical implications of gender and race.

CULTURE, RESPONSIBILITY, AND
AFFECTED IGNORANCE

F ew theorists concerned to understand human behavior would deny that the capacity
to be influenced by the specific culture of a given social group is an important part
of what is to be human. . . .

But what might the link between culture and agency mean for the practice of
holding people responsible for action, and for moral and legal conventions of praise
and blame? A currently influential answer to this question—to be found in much recent philosophical psychology, as well as in the social sciences and in history—is that
cultural influences can, and often do, constitute serious impediments to responsible
agency, and our attitudes toward praise and—especially—blame should acknowledge
the existence of such impediments. Some of these views attempt to establish that, at
least sometimes, widespread moral ignorance can be due principally to the cultural
limitations of an entire era, rather than to individual moral defects. Michael Slote has
argued, for example, that ancient Greek slave owners were simply "unable to see what
virtue had required in regard to slavery," and that this inability "was not due to personal limitations (alone) but requires some explanation by social and historical forces,
by cultural limitations."[1] A second group of theories has developed out of somewhat
different concerns: attempts within one culture to understand the behavior of an agent
shaped by a different culture or by a subculture that seems to differ from the dominant
culture in a complex society. Relying on notions like "social incapacitation," and even
"cultural insanity," these theories attempt to establish that some behavior is evidence
that one's cultural background may radically impair one's capacity for responsible action.

Against both kinds of views, I contend that the link between culture and agency
does not undermine the standard attributions of responsibility for action and hence
cannot exempt human beings from responsibility. In Section I, I challenge the empirical
credentials of those views which attempt to exempt historical agents from responsibility
on the grounds that they suffer from some presumed culturally generated inability to
avoid wrongdoing. Further, I show in Section II that these views rest on some dangerous misconceptions about the human potential for wrongdoing. Section III discusses
the shortcomings of more radical claims—like the claim of cultural insanity—about
cultural impediments to responsibility. Such views embody serious misunderstandings
about the connection between culture and agency. . . .

I. Moral Ignorance and Cultural Limitations

One of the most influential philosophical views about cultural impediments to responsibility involves the claim that sometimes one's upbringing in a culture simply
renders one unable to know that certain actions are wrong. I call this the inability

---

1. Michael Slote, "Is Virtue Possible?" *Analysis*, 42 (1982), reprinted in *The Virtues*, ed. R. Kruschwitz and
R. Roberts (Wadsworth, 1987), 100–105, 102. [Moody-Adams's note.]

thesis about cultural impediments. Slote's discussion of slavery in ancient Greece, cited above, provides one instance of this view. Alan Donagan defends another version of the view when he contends that "a graduate of Sandhurst or West Point who does not understand his duty to noncombatants as human beings is certainly culpable for his ignorance; an officer bred up from childhood in the Hitler *Jugend*[2] might not be."[3] Susan Wolf defends a still stronger version of the thesis. In her view, the "social circumstances" of, for instance, "slaveowners of the 1850's, Nazis of the 1930's, and many male chauvinists of our fathers' generation" may have made it inevitable that these people would hold the values and beliefs embodied in the actions that we now condemn.[4] . . .

The inability thesis represents a powerful challenge to the notion—defended at least since Aristotle—that an adult agent's ignorance of what she ought to do is, in general, no excuse for wrongdoing.[5] What this notion presupposes is that ignorance of what one ought to do can generally be traced to some personal failure, whether a culpable omission or commission. Against this view, the theories under consideration posit, as a regular occurrence, a phenomenon in which a culturally induced "blindness" to alternative cultural practices renders agents unable to question the morality of their culture's practices.

A striking shortcoming of these theories, in view of their forceful assertions about the operation of culturally induced moral blindness, is the questionable status of the inability thesis as an empirical claim. Moreover, a particular weakness of the theories under consideration is their tendency to base hypotheses about what some agent(s) *could not* do solely on evidence of what the agent(s) *did not* do. . . .

We might begin this inquiry into the empirical credentials of the inability thesis by asking whether any instance of socially widespread ignorance can be correctly attributed to cultural limitations. But before we can fully consider the possibility of cultural limitations on moral knowledge and action, we must ask what a culture is. A culture may be thought of as the way of life of a given social group, that will be shaped by more or less intricate patterns of normative expectations about emotion, thought, and action. These patterned expectations will typically take the form of social rules that give a distinctive shape to the group's practices. Of course, some kinds of social rules will be articulated more formally than others. Legal rules, for instance, which regulate and protect important aspects of the public life of the group, will typically be more formal in this way. Moreover, a group's legal rules, in particular, will be supplemented by an elaborate structure of nonlegal sources of support—including religious, economic, and even artistic cultural conventions. Indeed, the persistence of legal rules over time actually depends upon the emergence of such sources of support. But the possibility of such support is rooted in the tendency, among those concerned to protect the life

---

2. The Hitler *Jugend* ("Hitler Youth") recruited and trained young people to be Nazi soldiers. Sandhurst is a military academy in England. West Point is a military academy in the United States.

3. Alan Donagan, *The Theory of Morality* (University of Chicago Press, 1977), 135. [Moody-Adams's note.]

4. Susan Wolf, "Sanity and the Metaphysics of Responsibility," in *Responsibility, Character and the Emotions*, ed. F. Schoeman (Cambridge University Press, 1987), 46–62; see 56–57. [Moody-Adams's note.]

5. Readings by Aristotle appear in Chapters 16 and 20 of this anthology.

of the group, to develop what H. L. A. Hart has called a complex "internal" perspective on important social rules.[6]

The internal perspective on social rules is central to the life of the group. For it is from this internal perspective that those subject to the rules will take demands for conformity, as well as criticism of breaches of the rules, to be justified. From time to time, taking up the internal perspective will even allow those subject to the rules to undertake self-criticism of their own lapses in conformity to the rules. It is also from the internal perspective that children, and other cultural newcomers, are initiated into the group's practices.[7] But I contend that to the extent that we can identify the elements of such an internal perspective among the relevant members of a given social group, it will be difficult, if not impossible, to make a rationally compelling case for the inability thesis. I contend, further, that a thorough account of each case offered as an instance of the inability thesis would reveal the existence of such a perspective.

A brief discussion of one such case—Slote's example of ancient Greek slavery—will help illustrate this point. To begin, we have evidence that a complex legal structure regulated and preserved the institution of slavery. We know, for instance, of the vast legal distinctions between slaves and nonslaves with regard to voting and in the matter of protection against certain kinds of physical harm. Further, the legal regulation of slavery was intricately bound up with religion and with popular moral conceptions. Even certain theatrical conventions tended to perpetuate features of the institution: consider the extent to which Greek comedy relied for humor upon the flogging, bullying, and humiliation of slaves. Still further, though Slote insists that the Greeks mounted no real moral criticism of slavery, even in the *Politics* Aristotle takes on some unnamed opponents of slavery who denied that slavery is natural. To be sure, there is no obvious evidence of who these opponents were, and it is difficult to find much antislavery material in the surviving literature of the period. But, as Finley reminds us, the literature that does survive is principally the product of those who had reason to support the institution.[8] Finally, Dover suggests of Athens in particular that even the poorest Athenian citizen—who could vote, and who could expect certain legal protection from harm—might have seen himself as a member of an elite group.[9] All these considerations suggest that the support of ancient Greeks for the institution of slavery could well have embodied their choice to perpetuate an institution that benefitted nonslaves in various ways. The belief that slavery was justified was insufficiently examined by those who held it. But there is no convincing evidence that the blame for this should be traced to anything other than the affected ignorance, in Aquinas's phrase, of those

---

6. H. L. A. Hart, *The Concept of Law* (Oxford University Press, 1961), esp. 97–120. [Moody-Adams's note.]

7. Hart contrasts two perspectives one might take on a set of rules (or laws): an external perspective or an internal perspective. One might study the rules of another group, such as the laws of nineteenth-century France, without taking oneself to be bound by them; this is taking an external perspective on the rules. If one learns some rules and takes oneself to be bound by them, then one has an internal perspective on the rules.

8. M. I. Finley, *Ancient Slavery and Modern Ideology* (Viking, 1980), 119–20. [Moody-Adams's note.]

9. K. J. Dover, *Greek Popular Morality in the Time of Plato and Aristotle* (Blackwell, 1974), see 283–88. [Moody-Adams's note.]

who wanted to perpetuate the culture of slavery. Affected ignorance—choosing not to know what one can and should know—is a complex phenomenon, but sometimes it simply involves refusing to consider whether some practice in which one participates might be wrong.[10] Sometimes—perhaps much of the time—cultures are perpetuated by human beings who are uncritically committed to the internal perspective on the way of life they hope to preserve. . . .

II. Affected Ignorance and the Banality of Wrongdoing

In the epilogue to *Eichmann in Jerusalem,* Hannah Arendt insisted that "the trouble with Eichmann was precisely that so many were like him, and that the many were neither perverted nor sadistic, that they were, and still are, terrifyingly normal."[11] Arendt wanted to convince us that ordinary citizens can do evil—even extraordinary evil; moreover, they can come to view such evil, and their participation in it, as "routine." Some of Arendt's early critics were deeply troubled by her now-famous assertion of the "banality of evil" because they thought it threatened to trivialize the horrors of nazism. But in their distress they overlooked a central point of that assertion. Arendt wanted to reject, as a barrier to understanding, the all-too-common assumption that only "sick" or "monstrously insane" people could commit the terrifying evils of Nazi concentration camps. Evil can become routine; people who kill during the day may go home to protect their families at night. Moreover, studies of recent regimes where the internal use of torture is widespread make Arendt's message seem as urgent as ever. These studies suggest that some who become involved in the torture do not begin as crazed sadists, seeking out positions from which they can inflict harm, but that they may begin as ordinary citizens who gradually become able to inflict almost unspeakable horrors on fellow citizens. Still further, trenchant criticisms of such regimes remind us of how easily ordinary citizens can become complicit in the existence of torture—often by simply refusing to admit that it takes place. Unfortunately, a powerful resistance to Arendt's message is firmly embedded in the everyday moral consciousness. It also underwrites the inability thesis, as a tendency to deny what I call the "banality of wrongdoing." . . .

Even the most skilled interpreters of human behavior, confronted with troubling indications of the banality of wrongdoing, are sometimes unwilling to draw the appropriate conclusions. An example of this unwillingness can be found in some standard

10. Aquinas, *Summa Theologiae,* I – 2.6, 8. [Moody-Adams's note.] Aquinas's cosmological argument for the existence of God appears in Chapter 1 of this anthology.

11. Hannah Arendt, *Eichmann in Jerusalem* (Viking, 1963), 253. [Moody-Adams's note.] Adolf Eichmann (1906–1962) was one of the major organizers of the Holocaust during World War II. He was tried in Jerusalem, found guilty of war crimes, and was hanged in the Israeli city of Ramla.

accounts of experiments carried out in the 1960s by the social psychologist Stanley Milgram.[12] Milgram's subjects were tested to determine the amount of electric shock they would be willing to administer to another human being—but in a controlled setting in which the "victim" was only pretending to suffer physical pain. That act of "administering" the electric shock was set in the context of a "learning experiment" which (subjects were told) was designed to study the effect of learning on memory (see Milgram, p. 59). Milgram was surprised and dismayed by the fact that a large number of subjects were willing to administer "the most extreme shocks available," even while remarking on the further fact that those whom they believed to be their "victims" vigorously objected to the treatment (Milgram, p. 72). In commenting on the results, Milgram assures his readers that his subjects were "good people," not sadists—they were "men who in everyday life are responsible and decent" (Milgram, p. 74). But where one might have expected Milgram at least to consider the possibility that even generally good people can sometimes behave badly, he offers a very different sort of observation. In particular, he attempts to explain extraordinary displays of aggression toward the experiments' "victims" by reference to an inability to resist the experimenter's demands. He claims, for instance, that his subjects "were seen to knuckle under the demands of authority" and that the experimental situation exerted "an important press on the individual" (Milgram, pp. 74, 72). Yet a close scrutiny of the results casts doubts on the merits of such claims—indeed, it calls into question Milgram's contention that the experiment was simply a study of "some conditions of obedience and disobedience to authority."

When we examine some of the verbal, as well as nonverbal, behavior that accompanied the administering of the shocks, some surprising details emerge. Several subjects "frequently averted their eyes from the person they were shocking." One such subject explained his behavior with the following words: "I didn't want to see the consequences of what I had done." Still others offered similar explanations for averting their eyes from the people they believed they were harming (Milgram, p. 61). . . . Now in Milgram's view, these comments are evidence that the subject "was unable to invent a response that would free him from [the experimenter's] authority" (Milgram, p. 67). But surely a better interpretation of this behavior . . . is that it manifests the subject's profound unwillingness to acknowledge his responsibility for continuing to cooperate with the experiment, despite the screams of the "learner." We might say that this behavior manifests a classic case of affected ignorance. . . .

A discussion of the varied settings in which affected ignorance is linked to wrong-doing will help to support my interpretation. Affected ignorance is essentially a matter of choosing not to be informed of what we can and should know. But in practice, affected ignorance takes several forms; I discuss only four important varieties. The elaborate linguistic deceptions by which torturers are known to mask the reality of their activities illustrate a particularly malevolent variety of affected ignorance. Reports from around the world reveal a striking similarity in the way in which

---

12. Stanley Milgram, "Some Conditions of Obedience and Disobedience to Authority," *Human Relations* 18 (1965): 37–76. [Moody-Adams's note.] Page citations in text refer to Milgram's paper.

those engaged in torture describe their violent methods by means of deceptively benign phrases such as "the telephone" and the "parrot's swing." Such descriptions ultimately allow the torturer to deny the connection between his wrongdoing and the suffering of his victim. To understand the second variety of affected ignorance, we can imagine the head of an investment banking firm who demands that her employees increase the firm's profits but insists on knowing nothing about the means used to accomplish this. This executive's wish to "know nothing" of the potential wrongdoing of her employees is surely—in some degree—culpable. A third variety of affected ignorance is typically manifested in the readiness of some people to "ask no questions" about some state of affairs, in spite of evidence that an inquiry may be needed in order to stop or prevent wrongdoing. Thus a mother who repeatedly accepts expensive gifts from a teenage son with a modest income is surely complicit in her son's wrongdoing—at least morally—if the gifts have been purchased with money from the sale of drugs.

Finally, perhaps the most common form of affected ignorance is the tendency to avoid acknowledging our human fallibility: as finite and fallible beings, even our most deeply held convictions may be wrong. But it is also common for human beings to avoid or deny this possibility. . . .

III. Insanity, Incapacitation, and Respect for Culture

Presumed cultural distance tends to produce very different, and potentially quite troubling, conceptions of the relation between culture and responsibility. In one tragic and dramatic example, the culture of a foreign graduate student in an American university was claimed to be relevant to the question of the student's capacity to form the intent to murder. The student had killed a woman who rejected his romantic overtures, and defense attorneys attempted to construct an unusual defense. They tried, unsuccessfully, to establish that "cultural stresses" bound up with the defendant's cultural assumptions about women somehow produced a "mental infirmity" that diminished his capacity to form the intent to murder.[13] In a very different context, the subcultures that seem to exist within complex, highly stratified societies have been claimed to produce a variety of impairments. Thus, something once described as the "ingrained psychology" of the inner-city ghettos of America has been characterized as being "like insanity"—in virtue of a supposed tendency of ghetto subculture to impair radically the ability of ghetto residents to avoid criminal wrongdoing.[14] In a different case, appealing to the influence of an unidentified subculture, a group of antiwar protesters convicted of destroying draft records unsuccessfully appealed their conviction on the grounds that they were

---

13. People v. Poddar, App., 103 Cal. Rptr. 84 (1972). [Moody-Adams's note.]

14. Owen S. Walker, "Why Should Irresponsible Offenders Be Excused?" *Journal of Philosophy* 66 (1969): 279–90. [Moody-Adams's note.] Page citations in text refer to Walker's paper.

"culturally insane." All of these claims posit severe incapacitation or impairment as the result of a particular cultural or "subcultural" upbringing. I intend to show that these efforts dangerously distort the connection between culture and agency and hinder any careful understanding of what a culture really is. . . .

A culture—independent of agents who perpetuate culture—cannot be an "agent" of anything. Moreover, there is no brute fact about persons that can plausibly be held to constitute "having a culture." Culture is created, and even transmitted, by people. . . . [T]he language of impairment and incapacitation, in the context of a discussion about the influence of culture, cannot withstand rational scrutiny. . . .

Claims about an impairment that allegedly results from life in "severe ghetto conditions" in American inner cities present an interesting variation on the unreflective appeal to culture. In one such discussion, Owen Walker argues that the "ingrained psychology" produced by "severe ghetto conditions" is "like insanity" in the way in which it seems to impair the capacity for rational action (Walker, p. 289). But then Walker goes on to describe the alleged impairment in a most surprising fashion. The person at one point said to be suffering from near-insanity is later described as someone who "may feel, and with good reason, that he has no stake in a lawful society," and who, instead, believes that "his only opportunity to get ahead is in crime" (Walker, pp. 288–89). But this later claim describes someone who is clearly not beyond the reach of rational argument—as one whose impairment is "like insanity" surely would be. The person Walker describes may be angry, his belief may be incomplete or even incorrect, and his action—even on true beliefs—can be either indefensible or defensible. But he does not suffer from an impairment; his condition is not even remotely "like insanity." It is beyond the scope of this article to assess those features of Walker's view implicitly suggesting reasons sometimes to mitigate our response to crime. But to deny that an unimpaired person has engaged in wrongdoing—even if there are compelling reasons to mitigate our response to the behavior—is to deny the humanity of the person in question. Of course, the theorist of cultural impairments may deny that this is his aim. But the dangers of the tendency to see culture everywhere at work in the behavior of individuals are most acute when historical prejudice in a culture—in this case, primarily racial prejudice against African Americans—has marked out a confined conceptual space for some group of people. In those circumstances, an unreflective insistence on seeing that group of people as radically "other"—in virtue of a debatable presumption about their culture—simply reproduces old prejudices in new terminology. . . .

I must acknowledge that sometimes in criticizing an individual we may be unable to avoid criticizing his cultural assumptions as well. . . . Yet there is no reason to resist this possibility; only a misguided cultural relativism could support the view that moral criticism of another culture is never justified. The misguided relativist assumes that a readiness to engage in moral criticism of other cultures reveals disrespect for those cultures, or even masks a malevolent readiness to dominate and destroy the cultures that we criticize. . . . But . . . [t]o view those who accept another culture as fundamentally "other," as this misguided relativism typically does, is ultimately to view them as less than fully human. . . .

A readiness to engage in moral criticism and debate with the individuals who will perpetuate a culture manifests the highest respect for culture—principally, of course, in virtue of manifesting respect for the individual agents who must decide their culture's future. . . . Finally, a willingness to engage in cross-cultural moral debate makes us better able to lead the examined life that makes possible a reflective and critical commitment to our own culture.

TEST YOUR UNDERSTANDING

1. Suppose someone does something awful, and then in his defense someone says, "He was taught to think it's just fine to do that. Everyone around him does the same thing." Suppose those claims are true. Does Moody-Adams think that those claims are enough to show he is not blameworthy for the awful thing he did?

2. Moody-Adams discusses ancient slavery. Michael Slote said that ancient slaveholders were unable to see that slavery is wrong. Why does Moody-Adams think we lack good evidence to conclude that they were *unable* to realize that slavery is wrong?

   a. The mere fact that a person *did not* do something is not good evidence that he *could not* do it.

   b. Some ancient writings discuss the idea that slavery may be unnatural.

   c. It would have been contrary to their interests for ancient slaveholders to realize that slavery was morally wrong.

   d. All of the above.

3. Moody-Adams contrasts the "inability thesis"—the idea that some people are unable to know certain moral truths—with the thesis that these people have "affected ignorance." What does it mean to say that a person's moral ignorance is affected ignorance?

   a. A person's failure to know that something is morally wrong is a case of affected ignorance if the explanation of why he doesn't know it is morally wrong involves the fact that *he doesn't want to know* it is morally wrong.

   b. A person's apparent failure to know that something is morally wrong is a case of affected ignorance if *he is merely pretending not to know* it is morally wrong, but he really does know it is morally wrong.

4. Moody-Adams criticizes the claim that inner-city life creates a psychological condition "like insanity." Why does Moody-Adams find the claim that life in the inner city produces a condition "like insanity" to be pernicious?

   a. This claim would let wrongdoers in the inner city off the hook for their morally wrong actions.

b. This claim both ignores the reality that people who grow up in poor inner cities may have justified beliefs that their wider society is not set up to help them, and also dehumanizes the people in question.

NOTES AND QUESTIONS

1. Moody-Adams discusses the infamous Milgram experiments, in which ordinary people administered severe electric shocks (or so they thought) to other ordinary people, because scientists told them to do so. Moody-Adams presents two competing accounts of what is going on: Milgram held that his subjects were *unable* to disobey the scientists and unable to realize they were acting wrongly; Moody-Adams by contrast sees the subjects as avoiding confronting evidence for the wrongness of their actions by looking away. She thinks this is a case of *affected ignorance*. Which account of what is going on in the Milgram experiments should we embrace? The subjects were not really administering painful electric shocks to other volunteers (though they thought they were); if they had been painfully shocking people, would they have been morally responsible for hurting those people?

2. Moody-Adams outlines four types of affected ignorance: linguistic deception; a demand for a result while wanting to "know nothing" about the means to the result; an acceptance of a suspicious situation while asking no questions; and an unwillingness to acknowledge one's own fallibility. Which of these types of affected ignorance is at work in the case of the ancient slaveholders? (Perhaps more than one is at work.) Will all cases of affected ignorance fall into these categories?

3. Moody-Adams also criticizes the idea that someone might be off the hook for murdering someone because of his cultural background. Here is a case that Moody-Adams does not discuss: a man is raised in a patriarchal culture which holds that an unfaithful wife must be killed for the man to preserve his honor. The couple move to the United States, and when they are here, the wife is unfaithful to the husband. He finds out and kills her. His attorney offers a cultural defense: the man acted as his culture requires him to act. (This kind of cultural defense is discussed in Susan Moller Okin's essay "Is Multiculturalism Bad for Women?" in Chapter 22 of this anthology.) Is this a good defense? Is the man blameworthy for the murder? (What would Moody-Adams say?) Should the United States hold the man responsible for murder?

Angela M. Smith (b. 1970)

Smith is Roger Mudd Professor of Ethics and Professor of Philosophy at Washington and Lee University. Her writings explore the connections among morality, moral agency, and moral responsibility. She is coeditor of *The Nature of Moral Responsibility* (Oxford University Press, 2015).

IMPLICIT BIAS, MORAL AGENCY, AND MORAL RESPONSIBILITY

In one of the 2016 presidential debates between Hillary Clinton and Donald Trump, moderator Lester Holt asked Secretary Clinton if she "believed that police are implicitly biased against black people." In response, she said "Implicit bias is a problem for everyone, not just the police." For many viewers, this was probably their first exposure to the term "implicit bias," and they may well have been surprised (and perhaps even angered) to be told that they suffer from it. "I'm not biased—I believe all people should be treated equally!" they might have thought. "How dare she accuse me of bias—I go out of my way to support the rights of blacks, women, and other minorities!" Such reactions, while understandable, involve a misunderstanding of the term "implicit bias." "Implicit bias," as the term is used in the academic literature, refers to "relatively unconscious and relatively automatic features of prejudiced judgment and social behavior."[1] Such biases typically operate without our conscious awareness or conscious control. For example, in choosing whom to interview for a job, I may be subconsciously influenced by negative racial or sexual stereotypes. Faced with equally strong résumés, I may nevertheless form the judgment that Emily's credentials are clearly stronger than Lakisha's or that Bob's credentials are clearly stronger than Ann's.[2] "From the inside," I may feel confident that I have been fair and unbiased in my assessments; yet, unbeknownst to me, I may well have been influenced by underlying negative assumptions about the competence or abilities of African Americans or women. And this might be the case even if I am consciously and explicitly committed to principles of racial and sexual equality.

Studies have shown that racial and sexual biases are still widespread in areas such as employment, health care, education, and the criminal justice system, even though few today would explicitly endorse overtly racist and sexist claims. What is less clear is whether this evidence supports the existence of *implicit* or unconscious biases in these areas or whether it simply shows that people today are less willing to explicitly avow racist and sexist beliefs.[3] In this essay, however, I am going to assume that implicit bias

---

1. See Michael Brownstein, "Implicit Bias," in *Stanford Encyclopedia of Philosophy*, ed. Edward N. Zalta (https://plato.stanford.edu/archives/spr2017/entries/implicit-bias/). This entry provides a helpful overview of the current empirical literature on the existence of implicit biases and of the numerous metaphysical, epistemological, and ethical questions such findings raise. [Smith's note.]

2. See, for example, Marianne Bertrand and Sendhil Mullainathan, "Are Emily and Greg More Employable than Lakisha and Jamal? A Field Experiment in Labor Market Discrimination," *American Economic Review* 94, 4 (2004): 991–1013. To be clear, this field study does not necessarily establish the operation of *implicit* (as distinct from explicit) biases. But the operation of such biases is one possible explanation for findings of employment discrimination. [Smith's note.]

3. For a critical overview of one of the key tests, known as the Implicit Attitude Test, purporting to establish the existence and pervasive influence of implicit biases in everyday life, see Jesse Singal, "Psychology's Favorite Tool for Measuring Racism Isn't Up to the Job," *New York Magazine*, January 11, 2017 (http://nymag.com/scienceofus/2017/01/psychologys-racism-measuring-tool-isnt-up-to-the-job.html). As the author makes clear, however, doubts about psychological research establishing the existence of *implicit* bias does not undermine the evidence of real and continuing discrimination against women and racial minorities. It just raises questions about the best explanation of this continuing discrimination. [Smith's note.]

is a real and relatively widespread phenomenon and ask what implications this might have for our thinking about questions of moral agency and moral responsibility. More specifically, I aim to answer three questions: First, can we say that implicit biases reflect our *moral agency*? That is to say, does it make sense to attribute such biases to individuals *as moral agents* or should they be regarded as features of persons that fall outside the scope of their moral agency? Second, are individuals *morally responsible* for having and acting on implicit biases of which they are not consciously aware? If a person is sincerely *trying* to be fair in her hiring assessments, for example, is she morally responsible if her actions are influenced by attitudes she does not even realize she possesses? And third, are individuals *morally blameworthy* for having and acting on implicit biases?

I believe the answer to all of these questions is "yes." My argument will be that many of the attitudes we refer to via the label "implicit biases," while not under our conscious awareness or control, still involve exercises of rational evaluative agency that we can appropriately be asked to justify. For that reason, they, and the actions motivated by them, are things for which we are morally responsible. I will argue further that because these implicit biases involve violations of moral norms to which we are legitimately subject, we are also morally blameworthy for such biases. However, given that these biases operate below the level of reflective awareness, we are generally less blameworthy for implicit biases than for explicit biases.

1. Moral Responsibility, Moral Agency, and Moral Blameworthiness

Before we can address questions about responsibility for implicit biases, we must first be clear about our terminology. What does it *mean* to say that a person is "morally responsible" for something, and under what conditions is it appropriate to attribute such responsibility to an individual? And what, exactly, is the connection between being morally responsible for something, being the moral agent of that thing, and being morally blameworthy for that thing?

Let's begin with the definition of moral responsibility. I propose that we interpret the fundamental question of moral responsibility as a question about the conditions of *moral answerability*. To say that a person is morally responsible for something is to say that it would be *intelligible* to ask her to "answer for" that thing—that is, to give her (justificatory) reasons for thinking, feeling, or acting in the way she has—and that she is *eligible for* moral responses such as resentment, gratitude, indignation, and guilt, depending upon how well or poorly she meets this justificatory request. What is in question here is the relation between a person and her actions, attitudes, omissions, etc., and the conditions under which she can be expected to answer for them morally.

This understanding of responsibility as "answerability" highlights the tight link that exists between questions of moral responsibility and questions of moral agency. In order to be "morally answerable" for something, it seems I must be the "agent" or "author" of that thing. One is not the "agent" of a foot spasm, for example, because one does not bear the right sort of authorial relation to this sort of bodily movement. This is shown by the fact that it would make no sense for someone to demand that a person rationally justify moving her foot in such a way. "Why did you do that?" can at best be understood as a request for a causal explanation of one's foot spasm, not for an account of the justificatory reasons one took to count in favor of moving one's foot in that way. One is not the "agent" of a headache, or of the workings of one's digestive system, for a similar reason. While we may be able to explain the causes of these physiological conditions, it would make no sense to ask a person to give her *rational justification* for having a headache or for digesting her food in a certain way. One of the questions we need to ask about implicit biases, then, is whether we bear the right sort of "authorial relation" to these states such that it makes sense to expect a person to rationally defend or justify them. This, in turn, will help us to answer the question of moral responsibility. For, as we have seen, to say that a person is morally responsible for something just is to say that she is "answerable" for it as its agent.

What, then, is the relation between attributions of moral responsibility and assessments of moral praiseworthiness or blameworthiness? It is worth emphasizing that attributions of moral responsibility do not yet imply *anything* about an agent's praiseworthiness or blameworthiness for those things for which she is judged to be morally responsible. To say that an agent is morally responsible for something is simply to say that she bears an agential connection to that thing such that she can intelligibly be asked to "answer for" it. Whether she is also praiseworthy or blameworthy will depend upon whether the thing in question exceeds or violates any moral norms or expectations to which she is legitimately subject. For example, I am morally responsible for drinking coffee this morning, because it would be intelligible to ask me to give my reasons for so acting. But since this action does not seem to violate or exceed any moral norms that apply to me, I am neither praiseworthy nor blameworthy for it. Moral responsibility, then, is a *precondition* for moral praiseworthiness or moral blameworthiness, but the majority of things for which we are morally responsible are things for which we are *in fact* neither praiseworthy nor blameworthy (because they are morally neutral or indifferent).

If, then, one understands moral responsibility, in the most basic sense, as a matter of answerability, then the key question at issue when we debate whether we are morally responsible for implicit biases is this: Are we connected to these biases (and/or their manifestations) in such a way that we can intelligibly be expected to "answer for" them morally? That is, are we the *moral agents* of these implicit biases? In the next section, I will defend a positive answer to this question.

2. Moral Responsibility for Implicit Bias

To many readers, the claim that we may be morally responsible for implicit biases of which we are not consciously aware and over which we do not have direct voluntary control may seem absurd on its face. Part of this sense of absurdity, I suspect, is due to the way this question is typically framed. We are asked to consider cognitive processes ("the mechanisms of implicit bias") that "operate" in a region that is not accessible to consciousness, and that produce "effects" that we can neither identify nor control. It is almost impossible not to analogize these processes to the operations of other automatic bodily functions, such as those involved in regulating our circulation, heartbeat, and digestion. Just as it sounds absurd to say that we may be morally responsible for the mechanisms of digestion, it sounds equally absurd to say that we may be morally responsible for the mechanisms of implicit bias.

But should we think of implicit biases as akin to the mechanisms of digestion? Are these biases things that simply *happen in us*, which may be welcome or unwelcome, but for which we bear no moral responsibility? Or are we the *moral agents of* these biases, and therefore morally answerable for them? In order to answer this question, we need to ask what sort of a connection a person must bear to a thing in order to count as the "agent" of it. One plausible answer to this question is that in order for a person to count as the "agent" of something, that thing must reflect her *rational activity*. For example, we generally do not take a sneeze or a hiccup to reflect a person's rational activity—we don't think these are behaviors that a person engages in "for a reason." On the other hand, we generally do take a person's intentional actions to reflect her rational activity. This is why it is intelligible to ask a person to justify, or to "answer for," her intentional actions in a way that it would not make sense to ask a person to justify, or to "answer for," her sneezes. I can only request rational justification, after all, for things that are susceptible to reason-based critique.

Are implicit biases more like sneezes or intentional actions? Philosophers disagree about this question, and their disagreement reflects two different views about what it takes for something to reflect a person's "rational activity." According to some philosophers, the thing in question must be consciously chosen or reflectively endorsed, or must itself be the causal result of something that was (previously) consciously chosen or reflectively endorsed.[4] According to other philosophers, the thing in question must simply reflect an evaluative judgment or appraisal of some sort on the part of the agent (even if it is a judgment or appraisal that the agent is unaware of, and would not endorse, upon reflection).[5] These positions, in turn, imply two very different models of moral agency. On the first view, which I will call the "Conscious Self View," "the agent" is to be identified with the perspective of conscious deliberation, and what belongs to her "as an agent" is the set of attitudes, principles, and values she consciously endorses in reflective deliberation. An agent is morally responsible, on this view, only for those things that express her "Conscious Self," so understood. On the second view, which I will call the "Complex Self View," "the agent" is to be identified with the perspective of rational evaluation, and what belongs to her "as an agent" is that set of attitudes, principles, and values that reflect a rational appraisal of some sort (whether conscious or not). An agent is morally responsible, on this view, for anything that reflects her "Complex Self," so understood.

4. See, for example, Neil Levy, "The Importance of Awareness," *Australasian Journal of Philosophy* 91, 2 (2013): 211–29, and "Expressing Who We Are: Moral Responsibility and Awareness of Our Reasons for Action," *Analytic Philosophy* 52, 4 (2011): 243–61; and Gideon Rosen, "Skepticism about Moral Responsibility," *Philosophical Perspectives* 18, 1 (2004): 295–313, and "Culpability and Ignorance," *Proceedings of the Aristotelian Society* CIII, Part 1 (2003). [Smith's note.]

5. See, for example, T. M. Scanlon, *What We Owe to Each Other* (Harvard University Press, 1998), chapter 6; and Angela M. Smith, "Responsibility for Attitudes: Activity and Passivity in Mental Life," *Ethics* 115 (2005): 236–71. [Smith's note.]

To see the difference between these two views, we might consider how each would assess a case involving implicit bias in hiring. On the Conscious Self View, an agent who is consciously committed to norms of racial equality, but who unconsciously acts in racially biased ways (say, by systematically underrating the credentials of qualified black job applicants), is not morally responsible for this behavior because it does not reflect her conscious rational commitments. She is no more responsible for her subconscious bias than she is for the functioning of her digestive system. Since neither of these unconscious happenings reflects her explicit rational commitments, neither really belong to her "as a moral agent." On the Complex Self view, by contrast, such an agent *would* be morally responsible for her behavior, because that behavior still reflects her implicit rational evaluation that black candidates are generally less competent (or less reliable) than white candidates (even if she is not aware of the fact that she is making such rational evaluations). The Complex Self view regards implicit biases as quite different from other subconscious physiological mechanisms, insofar as they still seem to involve "rational" evaluations that we can intelligibly be asked to justify.

How might we adjudicate between these two very different models of moral agency? Are we the agents of, and thus responsible for, only those things that we consciously choose or endorse? Or does our responsibility extend even to rational evaluations that we may be unaware that we are making? The Conscious Self view has much to recommend it, as it is natural to identify our "selves" most closely with the perspective of rational deliberation. Upon reflection, however, I think we have good reasons for viewing our moral selves as much more complex. I will discuss three such reasons, before turning to the issue of blameworthiness for implicit biases.

The first reason appeals to our actual moral practices, and the fact that we typically *do* regard individuals as morally responsible for much more than what they consciously endorse in reflective deliberation. For example, we sometimes ask people to justify their failures to notice, to take into consideration, or to remember certain factors at the time they acted, when such failures were clearly neither "conscious" nor the result of prior conscious activities. We say things like, "Didn't you realize how inappropriate that joke was in the context?" or "How could you have forgotten our anniversary?" When we criticize someone for insensitivity, thoughtlessness, or selfishness, we do not normally assume that the agent was *consciously aware* of what they were doing in the context. Yet we still attribute that behavior to them and consider it reasonable to ask them to justify it. Similarly, it seems appropriate to expect people to justify racially insensitive behaviors motivated by implicit biases, even if they are not aware that they are engaging in them.[6]

The second reason for endorsing the Complex Self view is that it often feels as if we learn something important about ourselves when we become aware of our unconscious motivations. If I am given evidence that I am unconsciously behaving in racially insensitive ways, this seems to reveal something meaningful and disturbing about my *moral self*. Indeed, most of us feel *guilty* or *ashamed* when we discover that we have been

---

6. Of course, if actually confronted with such a demand, most morally decent people would not in fact try to *justify* these biases, but would instead *apologize for* and morally disavow them. The point, however, is that it makes sense to address the justificatory demand to these individuals. [Smith's note.]

harboring such subconscious biases. Such discoveries are very different from coming to discover that we have cancer, or high blood pressure, or any other physical ailment or condition. These latter discoveries, while often frightening, do not seem to reveal anything about our *moral selves* in the way that I submit the discovery that we've been harboring unconscious biases does. We seem to gain a valuable sort of self-knowledge in these moments, knowledge that may in fact conflict in uncomfortable ways with our conscious self-conceptions. If the Conscious Self View is correct, however, then these impressions of self-discovery and increased self-knowledge must be illusory. For, by definition, we cannot be identified as moral agents, with subconscious attitudes that have not passed the test of conscious endorsement. Since I think most of us *do* think we learn valuable facts about who we are as moral agents through such self-discoveries, this argument seems to tell in favor of the Complex Self View.

The final reason for endorsing the Complex Self view is that it helps to explain why the targets of implicit bias so often feel moral sentiments such as resentment and indignation when confronted with implicitly biased behavior, even when they are convinced that such bias is not conscious or intentional. A business manager who never thinks of inviting his female employees to his Super Bowl party, or who regularly passes them over for promotion, may not be intending to discriminate against them, but his behavior reflects assumptions (e.g., about women's interests in sports, or in moving into management positions) that are morally problematic. The fact that people are "well intentioned" does not seem to undermine the sense of grievance one may (understandably) feel when confronted with such behavior. The grievance stems from the fact that these behaviors appear to be motivated by subconscious rational evaluations that the agent *really is making,* even if she would disavow them, upon reflection. Because it is difficult to regard these subconscious evaluations as things that merely "happen" to a person, it is difficult to treat them as akin to the mechanisms of digestion. This again supports the claim that our "moral selves" are much more complex than the Conscious Self View suggests.

For all of these reasons, I believe the Complex Self View is more plausible than the Conscious Self View. While it is true that our conscious deliberative choices and intentions reflect our rational evaluative activity, it seems clear that our subconscious implicit biases do as well. We are, in that sense, the *moral agents* of these biases, and they "belong" to us in a way that makes demands for justification intelligible. But merely establishing that we are morally responsible for our implicit biases does not yet imply that we are morally blameworthy for them. In the case of implicit biases, it may be that we have an excuse that partially or wholly excuses us from blame (without undermining moral responsibility). In the next section, I will briefly consider this question.

3. Moral Blameworthiness for Implicit Bias

If my analysis so far is correct, we are morally responsible for our implicit biases in the sense that we are *answerable* for them: it is intelligible to ask us to justify such biases, and we are eligible targets of moral responses depending upon the quality of the "answer" we are in a position to give. In order to claim that we are also *morally blameworthy* for such biases, two further conditions must be met:

1. These biases must violate moral norms or expectations to which we are legitimately subject; and

2. we must lack a sufficient excuse or justification for such violations.

I will simply assume here that implicit biases do violate moral norms or expectations to which we are legitimately subject. We have a moral obligation, I believe, not to respond in objectionable ways to others on the basis of morally problematic stereotypes.

But do we have an excuse for such violations? One might argue that the implicit biases most of us harbor are the result of growing up in a culture that is saturated with racist and sexist stereotypes, and that it is therefore "not our fault" that we are subconsciously inclined to evaluate others in morally objectionable ways. These negative stereotypes are reinforced by movies, television, music, news, and other cultural sources, so it can be difficult for individuals to resist forming objectionable implicit biases. While this raises an extremely important point about the need to confront and challenge these objectionable cultural messages, it does not, in my view, absolve individuals completely from moral blameworthiness. It will be a complex story, for each of us, how we have come to develop the particular attitudes and evaluative judgments that structure our basic moral outlook. But once we have reached rational maturity, it is reasonable to expect us to justify these attitudes and judgments. If someone were to respond to such a request by saying "I am not responsible for my attitude—I was just raised in a racist/sexist culture," I don't think we would feel compelled to withdraw our criticism. Citing the origin of one's attitude is irrelevant when what is in question is its justification.

Our understanding of the way in which implicit biases are formed may, however, be relevant to determining just *how* blameworthy we are for holding them. In particular, the fact that many of our implicit biases were formed and persist contrary to our consciously held moral commitments means that it is probably more difficult for us to *recognize* that we have a problem of bias that needs to be addressed. This may constitute a partial excuse that renders us less blameworthy for implicit biases than for explicit biases, at least until we become informed about how pervasive these implicit biases are in everyday life. Once we *do* become aware of this fact, however, we must recognize that being "well intentioned" is not sufficient for morally good action; we must also make sure that our view of the world is not distorted by subconscious biases that cannot be rationally or morally justified.

TEST YOUR UNDERSTANDING

1. What is implicit bias?

2. Does Smith think that a person can be *morally responsible* for something without being *blameworthy* for it?

3. What is Smith's view about when a person is morally responsible for something?

   a. A person is morally responsible for something if and only if she consciously chose to do it.

   b. A person is morally responsible for something if and only if it is appropriate to ask her to offer reasons that would justify it.

   c. A person is morally responsible for something if and only if she could have avoided it.

4. Does Smith think that people are blameworthy for their implicit biases?

NOTES AND QUESTIONS

1. Smith contrasts the Conscious Self view with the Complex Self view. The Conscious Self view holds that we are morally responsible only for what we consciously choose and endorse. The Complex Self view holds that we are morally responsible for a great deal more of ourselves and our actions—every aspect of oneself that involves making a rational judgment, whether explicit or implicit, is something for which one is morally responsible. Which view is correct? If the Conscious Self view is correct, then it turns out that moral responsibility is harder to come by than we typically think. As Smith points out, we often hold people responsible for a range of behaviors and features that were not consciously chosen, including acting insensitively when they should have realized or noticed something they did not. But if the Complex Self view is correct, then we are responsible even for features of ourselves of which we are unaware, and even for features of ourselves that we would disavow if we knew about them. What is the best argument for each view? Is there a possible position between the two views that acknowledges responsibility for things like insensitivity but fails to extend responsibility to implicit bias?

2. We can see Smith as offering a kind of *test* for whether a person is morally responsible for something: is it appropriate to demand that she justify that thing? If the demand is appropriate, then the agent is morally responsible. If the demand is not appropriate, then she is not morally responsible. How does this test work? Are we supposed to ask whether the demand is appropriate *given a perspective of full information* or are we supposed to ask whether the demand is appropriate *given some more limited set of information*? Consider the following case. Suppose an observer sees Sam kick Tim. The observer might ask, "Sam, why did you kick Tim? What was your reason?" Given the observer's information, this demand seems appropriate. However, in fact, Sam had stumbled and only kicked Tim in the course of stumbling; there was no intentional action that Sam performed. Given the perspective of full information, the demand for a justification is not appropriate. Because Sam is not morally responsible in this case, this case suggests that it is the perspective of *full information* that should be used in Smith's test. But now let's turn to the case of implicit bias. Betsy judges a job candidate, Chantelle, to be less qualified than another candidate, Doris; in fact, this is a result of implicit bias. Smith says that it makes sense to demand that Betsy justify her judgment. That is true, it does seem to make sense. But does it seem to make sense

to us because we are imagining a colleague of Betsy's asking her for her reasons? Presumably this colleague would not know that the judgment was the result of bias. Now imagine that *we* do know that Betsy's judgment was the result of a racist bias, and that Betsy sincerely disavows such racism in her conscious thoughts. Would it make any sense for *us*, with our full information, to demand that Betsy justify her assessment of the candidates? It does not seem that this demand would be appropriate. We know that the assessment was made in a way that Betsy would not endorse. This poses a challenge to Smith's account. If the demand test is meant to use full information, then it is not clear that agents are responsible for implicit bias. If the demand test is meant to use partial information, then agents would turn out to be morally responsible for things for which they are not really morally responsible. How could Smith respond to this challenge?

ANALYZING THE ARGUMENTS

1. Scanlon argues that an agent's poor intentions in acting do not, generally, make a difference to the permissibility of the action, but they do make a difference for the action's *meaning*. Can you offer some additional examples of what an action's meaning is in Scanlon's sense? Does this idea correspond to or differ from Herman's sense that an action may be wrong, even if permissible?

2. Herman argues that when you promise to meet a friend for lunch at a particular restaurant, forget all about the promise, but then just happen to wander into that restaurant at the right time, you have not really kept the promise at all. Keeping a promise requires both performing a certain action and performing it in light of the fact that one promised. Do you agree? Do all morally required actions have this structure or is promising special? How might this example be thought to pose a challenge to Scanlon's position? Can he convincingly answer this challenge?

3. According to the **Doctrine of Double Effect**, it matters whether one intends to harm an innocent as a means or an end or whether that harm is merely foreseen. This raises the question: What is it to intend to harm an innocent as a means or an end? One simple answer runs as follows:

> For A to intend to harm an innocent person B as a means or as an end is for A to want B to suffer harm and to decide to act in a way that will cause B harm.

But consider the following cases:

> *Orders:* A is a soldier who, privately, hates her fellow soldier B. She wants B to suffer and frequently fantasizes about B getting a painful comeuppance, but she would never act on that desire. On the basis of faulty, but credible, information, A's commander orders A to arrest B and confine B in an uncomfortable jail where B will suffer. A decides to follow the orders because they are her commander's orders.
>
> *Russian Roulette:* A is a soldier who enjoys violence and wishes to wound a civilian, B, for pleasure. A picks up her gun, knowing that there is only one round in the six-round chamber, spins the chamber so that there is only a one-in-six chance that she will wound B, and pulls the trigger.
>
> *Reluctant Warrior:* A, a reluctant soldier, has read Anscombe's article and disagrees with Anscombe. She is horrified by war and believes it is never justified. She further believes that any action that will hasten the end of a war and minimize deaths is permissible. She becomes convinced that, in a particular war, terror bombing the enemy leader's home village will eviscerate the leader's morale and result in immediate and fair peace negotiations with fewer civilian casualties than any other method. She decides to initiate and undertake the terror bombing, but does so reluctantly. She does not want anyone to die and hopes that somehow the parties will enter peace negotiations without her having to take this terrible step.

Exercise: Explain why the examples appear to pose a problem for the simple definition. Discuss whether there are convincing replies to the purported counterexamples or whether the definition should be modified, and if so, how.

4. The Doctrine of Double Effect surfaces not only in discussions about the ethics of war but also in other important contexts, such as end-of-life care. For example, some opponents of assisted suicide argue that it is permissible for a doctor to give a suffering patient medication in order to relieve his pain, even though it may increase the risk of the patient's death as a side effect. Yet they claim it is impermissible for a doctor to give a suffering patient lethal medication that will cause his death as a means of relieving the patient's pain. Can you explain how this reasoning resembles the reasoning used by proponents of the Doctrine of Double Effect? Does it make a difference in the assisted suicide case that the recipient of the medication that may cause death *requests* it from the doctor? Could one agree with Anscombe's judgments about permissible and impermissible conduct in war but disagree with this reasoning about assisted suicide?

   Some justices of the U.S. Supreme Court invoked the Doctrine of Double Effect in justifying a state's prohibition on assisted suicide; see *Vacco v. Quill*, 521 U.S. 793 (1997). Criticism of that use may be found in Judith Jarvis Thomson, "Physician-Assisted Suicide: Two Arguments," *Ethics* 109, 3 (1999): 497–518, especially pages 507–18, and in Allison McIntyre, "The Double Life of Double Effect," *Theoretical Medicine and Bioethics* 25, 1 (2004): 61–74.

5. Moody-Adams and Smith both point out that sometimes the true psychological explanation of why someone does something is different from the reasons they may think explain their actions. A slaveholder may not understand that his actions are motivated partly by his *desire* to keep getting all the benefits of slavery and his *reluctance* to face the moral truth about his actions. A person who disavows racism may not understand that her own assessments of others involve implicit biases. Anscombe and Herman both argue that a person's *intentions* are relevant to the moral assessment of her action. What should Anscombe and Herman think of the phenomena that Moody-Adams and Smith describe? Should Anscombe and Herman count these "hidden" explanations of actions as giving the *intentions* or *motives* that are relevant to the moral assessment of these actions?

6. Scanlon and Herman both agree that a person's *intentions* (or *motives*) are relevant to whether she is praiseworthy or blameworthy for acting in a particular way. (They disagree about whether intentions are also relevant to whether an action is right or wrong.) Moody-Adams discusses agents who act impermissibly but who believe that what they are doing is morally right. What should Scanlon and Herman say about these agents? Is the fact that they believe that what they are doing is morally right enough to establish that they have the right motives? If neither Scanlon nor Herman would say it is enough, why is that?

16

Which Moral Theory
Is Correct?

We know a lot about what actions are right. It is wrong to kill another person to steal his money or his job. It is wrong to cheat on tests. It is right to be kind to one's friends and to do something to help strangers who are less fortunate than oneself.

There are also many cases in which it is hard to know what the right thing to do is. Suppose a friend starts smoking. I reasonably believe that if he continues, it will begin an addiction that risks his health and may cause him to die far earlier and more painfully than he would otherwise. May I hide his cigarettes and his pocket money to obstruct this nascent addiction? Or, does treating him with respect demand that I share my concerns but respect the decision he makes about his own habits?

In both these kinds of cases—cases in which I do know what is right and in which I don't—it is worth knowing what the correct moral theory is, if there is one. In the first kind of case, the correct moral theory should be able to tell me *why* the right thing to do is the right thing to do. In the second kind of case, knowing the correct moral theory may be able to help me to figure out what the right thing to do is. (Symmetrically, knowing that certain actions are right may help us to figure out the true moral theory.)

How can we figure out what the true moral theory is? We might start by asking what morality is. One proposal is that morality consists of a body of principles that offer guidance about how one should regard and behave toward others—principles that express the *moral perspective*, rather than the prudential or aesthetic perspectives. Of course, how to characterize the moral perspective is a vexed matter, but some jumping-off points seem relatively uncontroversial.

From the moral perspective, it seems that:

A. Each of us matters, and it matters that each person's life goes well.[1]

B. No one is intrinsically more important than anyone else: everyone matters equally.

---

1. What creatures constitute "us"? Only human beings? All possible rational agents? Do animals have moral standing? Any complete moral theory must confront these issues of scope. For reasons of space, this chapter concentrates on moral relations among people.

C. We cannot act merely to satisfy our own interests, desires, and aims. We must respect others by taking into account how our actions affect them in a manner that reflects their equal importance.

These ideas about the nature of the moral perspective suggest two questions that more specific moral views will answer in different ways:

1. *What is it for a human life to go well?* Unsurprisingly, there is heated debate about this matter. For example, **hedonists** claim that a life goes well when it contains as much pleasure and as little pain as possible. **Preference-satisfaction** theorists concur with hedonists that one should maximize (or bring about as much as possible of) what matters, but they contend that life goes well when one's preferences are maximally satisfied, whether or not that satisfaction always yields pleasure. Others, call them **autonomy** theorists, contend that a life goes well if one is respected and supported by others as a free and equal person, one has and exercises the opportunity to develop one's capacities, and one lives a well-considered life structured by choices made in response to good reasons. Or, perhaps, as some **objective list** theorists argue, a good life defies a simple formulaic summary, but features an amalgam of specific components, such as being healthy over a reasonably long life; forming good relationships; having satisfying, stimulating work and projects; having access to the resources, abilities, and social freedom that facilitate a comfortable life free from coercion and vulnerability to exploitation; and having a sufficient education and knowledge to make informed, deliberate decisions and to understand and appreciate one's life, one's environment, and the other goods life offers.

2. *What does respecting the value and equal importance of others' lives involve?* Here again, there are divergent answers. **Consequentialists** contend that the morally correct action for me must reflect the implications of my actions on my own life exactly as much as but no more than their impact on others. The correct action to take is the one that yields the best consequences, impartially considered, of all the possible alternatives.

   Non-consequentialists contend there is a different way to respect the equal importance of others' lives. Respect for the equal importance of others' lives involves subjecting myself to the same rules that others should abide by. That is, I should act in ways that I also think others should (and may) act in relevantly similar circumstances. So it is permissible for me to pay more attention to myself and my loved ones in my daily transactions, as long as I do not ignore others' needs, treat others unfairly, or cause them serious harm.

Utilitarianism

Consequentialism is the view that one is morally required to act in whichever way would have the best consequences. One version of consequentialism is **utilitarianism.** Utilitarians hold that a life goes well when it contains the maximum possible amount of **utility**; that is, as much net happiness (total happiness minus total unhappiness) as possible. They also hold that everyone's happiness is equally valuable; thus, John Stuart Mill writes that "between [an agent's] own happiness and that of others, utilitarianism requires him to be as strictly impartial as a disinterested and benevolent spectator." Hence, the utilitarian principle supplies the "one fundamental principle or law, at the root of all morality"; namely, that the morally right action is the action, from among all the alternatives, that would produce the most happiness, aggregating and giving equal weight to the effects on all people.[2]

In one sense, Mill affirms the traditional utilitarian answer to the question of what makes a life go well; namely, the doctrine that all that is intrinsically valuable is pleasure and the absence of pain. His view is more nuanced, however, than simple, hedonistic interpretations of utility that treat all forms of equally intense pleasure as interchangeable and equally valuable. Mill regards the pleasures associated with the exercise of the "higher faculties" (e.g., the pleasures associated with acquiring and appreciating knowledge) as "higher" than mere sensory pleasures. Pleasures, in Mill's view, may be ranked not merely by their intensity and duration, but by whether one sort is decidedly preferred over another by those who have experienced both.

Some of the implications of Mill's utilitarianism are clear. In general, killing or injuring others from revenge is morally wrong, because the enormous costs in happiness to victims, to their associates, and to all of us who would fear that we might be victimized, would outweigh whatever gains one might achieve by acting on one's anger. The view may be able to support general prohibitions on lying, prohibitions on promise-breaking, and an imperative to help in a similar way. Whether you should hide your friend's cigarettes would depend on whether the happiness your friend would gain from a longer, healthier life and that you would gain from facilitating it would outweigh the unhappiness your intervention might cause, including the effects of the intrusion on your friend's own choices, his possible anger and estrangement from you, and the loss of revenue to the tobacco industry.

Criticism of Utilitarianism

Utilitarianism faces fierce criticism. One line of criticism says that it gives the wrong reasons for why an action is right or wrong. For example, the moral prohibition on killing does not seem to hinge upon whether killing fails to maximize happiness. Even if it would make a killer and his enormous, rabid group of followers deliriously happy, that should not alter our opinion about the wrongness of killing an innocent person. Even if those facts were true, they would supply no reason whatsoever to

---

2. Some read Mill to claim that the morally right action is the action that conforms to *that rule* the universal adoption of which would maximize utility. This formulation is called *rule utilitarianism* because it focuses on the *rule* of action that would maximize utility, rather than on the particular *act* that would maximize utility (as *act utilitarians* do). Although this difference in formulation may matter in some contexts, it is unessential to the issues discussed here.

contemplate murder. The happiness a killer derives from murder has no positive moral significance. It does not weigh against the victim's happiness but rather is morally objectionable in itself. Further, although we should help others in need, it is not evident that the reason is that we must always maximize happiness. The idea that we are obligated to maximize aggregate happiness (or good consequences otherwise construed) would, critics allege, place overwhelming demands on each of us to devote our entire lives and each of our actions to increasing the overall aggregate of global happiness, whether or not such actions ever contributed to our own lives. A maximization requirement would demand this dedication, even if it were incompatible with leading an autonomous life, pursuing important projects of personal concern, and developing meaningful personal relationships.

Critics of utilitarianism trace these concerns to fundamental differences about the basic components of a moral theory. Some focus critical attention on utilitarian answers to the first question: *What is it for a human life to go well?* They contest that all happiness, whether pleasure or preference satisfaction, is good. They argue, further, that there are more fundamental components of well-being that a person should prefer, whether she actually does or not, such as acting rationally and freely while leading a healthy life, pursuing rewarding work, and cultivating relationships with others.

Critics also contest the utilitarian answer to the second question: *What does respecting the value and equal importance of others' lives involve?* They reject the consequentialist proposition that we must always bring about the best consequences from an impartial point of view. Non-consequentialists stress the special relationship each of us has to our own lives and the need to treat ourselves and particular people as special to develop a unified and distinctively individual character, pursue projects in depth, and enjoy strong personal relationships. They contend that recognition of the equal moral importance of others from the impartial point of view is still consistent with giving special consideration to our own interests, loved ones, and projects. On one non-consequentialist view, equality instead demands that we act in ways that do not depend on making an exception of ourselves.

Non-Consequentialist Theories

Immanuel Kant offers a prominent example of a non-consequentialist moral theory. Like Mill, Kant seeks to capture the foundations of morality through a fundamental principle. Kant concurs that as moral agents, we must act from a principle of impartiality that recognizes the equal moral status of all rational beings, but his argument about what impartiality demands emphasizes what principles of action we would affirm for everyone. Like a law of nature or a piece of legislation, the fundamental principle of morality should have universal, uniform, and mandatory application, irrespective of how we feel about the action or its consequences; in Kant's terms, it binds all rational agents *categorically*.

When I aim to act for a particular purpose, to be consistent with duty, my aim must be compatible with a system of lawlike rules. I must ask whether my *maxim*, the relevant description of my action in light of my purpose in performing it, *could possibly* operate as a principle of rational agency that could apply to, and be applied by, everyone who appropriately valued our status as rational, autonomous agents. In Kant's language, I must ask if my maxim could be *universalized*. In some cases, my maxim may not be universalizable because its universal application would undermine its own purpose, or because its universal application would conflict with the realization of other mandatory aims we have in light of the inestimable value of rational, autonomous agency. When my maxim is not universalizable, it reveals that my aim conflicts with my treating myself as one rational (valuable) agent among others, living in a community of equals governed by law.

Kant expresses this idea in different ways, the most important of which are these:

1. The *universal law formulation* of the **categorical imperative**, which says that one should "act only in accordance with that maxim through which [one] can at the same time will that it become a universal law."

2. The *humanity formulation* of the categorical imperative, which says that one should "[s]o act that you use humanity, whether in your own person or in the person of any other, always at the same time as an end, never merely as a means."

Kant would direct me to interfere with my friend's smoking only if my maxim could be universalized, and only if interfering would not treat my friend as a mere means. To assess whether these conditions are satisfied would lead us to ask specific questions about what things would be like if everyone interfered in this way, and about whether such interference is compatible with respecting others' autonomous control over themselves.

Virtue Ethics

Both Mill's utilitarianism and Kant's moral theory are traditional moral theories that offer short universal statements about which actions are morally required. Virtue ethics provides a different approach. Aristotle's view is that there is no simple universal generalizations that can be stated and then applied to particular cases. Rather, Aristotle's view is that the right thing to do is *what a virtuous person would do*. A person can develop into a virtuous person, but this does not involve learning a simple moral rule.

In answer to our first question ("What makes a life go well?"), we might say that Aristotle's answer is that a good life is a life of happiness. But this is not very informative, because Aristotle's notion of *happiness* is quite different from Mill's. For Aristotle, happiness is not a matter of pleasure (not even of higher pleasures); rather, a life that contains *whatever matters* in life is a life of happiness. What does

Aristotle think matters? His view is that to know what it would be for a person's life to go well, we must ask what it would take for a person to be functioning well. According to Aristotle, a person functions well if the parts of his soul that employ reason function well. This in turn requires that a person be virtuous. So it turns out, on Aristotle's view, a person's life goes well (is a good life to have) if and only if she is virtuous.

Writing in the Aristotelian tradition, Rosalind Hursthouse emphasizes character as the key to moral reasoning. Hursthouse contends that sound moral judgment does not involve deploying an all-purpose moral principle or theory. Rather, to reason about morality well, one must develop and exercise a virtuous character and imagine what the virtuous person would do in the specific circumstances. She argues that we have insight into what the virtues involve because we have experience and a sense of how to apply specific labels of virtue and vice through our linguistic practices that, themselves, represent generations of wisdom.

It is not clear what Aristotle or Hursthouse would say about whether you may take your friend's cigarettes. What virtues are at play? It is kind to be concerned for your friend's health; does that make it a kind thing to do to take his cigarettes? In general, it is arrogant to presume that you know better than your friend what he should do or what would be best for him. Is it arrogant (or prideful? or controlling?) to take his cigarettes?

Skepticism about Morality

Friedrich Nietzsche provides a highly critical counterpoint to all these approaches. Nietzsche not only strongly tilts against the substance of most modern moral thought but also writes in a markedly different style. He used the epigrammatic form self-consciously, declaring "it is my ambition to say in ten sentences what everyone else says in a book—what everyone else does not say in a book."[3] Refreshing and stimulating to some while exasperating for others, his tone echoes the rebellious substance of his ideas.

Nietzsche contends that reasoning will not reveal morality's content because morality is a socially created set of rules designed to serve the interests of a particular group of people (of whom he is critical). Nietzsche champions the use of the **genealogical method**, a process of excavating the origins of conventional moral ideas to expose whose interests they serve and thereby discredit conventional moral principles. Among his surprising conclusions, *contra* Mill, is that pain and suffering are not morally special or particularly bad and that we do not have strong reasons to relieve others' suffering. Rather than investigating what respect for others requires, Nietzsche advocates fostering the greatest individual lives, lives akin

---

3. Friedrich Nietzsche, *Twilight of the Idols,* from *The Portable Nietzsche,* trans. Walter Kaufman (Viking Press, 1976), 556.

to great works of art. As individuals, each of us should confront with unblinking honesty the truth about ourselves and endeavor to live joyfully and exuberantly.

John Stuart Mill (1806–1873)

Mill was born in London, England. He was educated by his father, James Mill, a distinguished Scottish philosopher, political theorist, economist, and historian. A utilitarian, empiricist, and important public thinker, Mill was author of *Utilitarianism*, *Considerations on Representative Government*, *Principles of Political Economy*, *Subjection of Women*, *System of Logic*, *The Autobiography of John Stuart Mill*, and, most famously, *On Liberty*. Apart from his writings, Mill worked at the East India Company (1823–58), served as a Member of Parliament (1865–68), and was Lord Rector of the University of St. Andrews (1865–68).

UTILITARIANISM

Chapter 1: General Remarks

There ought either to be some one fundamental principle or law, at the root of all morality, or if there be several, there should be a determinate order of precedence among them; and the one principle, or the rule for deciding between the various principles when they conflict, ought to be self-evident. . . .

On the present occasion, I shall, without further discussion of other theories, attempt to contribute something towards the understanding and appreciation of the Utilitarian or Happiness theory. . . .

I shall offer some illustrations of the doctrine itself; with the view of showing more clearly what it is, distinguishing it from what it is not, and disposing of such of the practical objections to it as either originate in, or are closely connected with, mistaken interpretations of its meaning. . . .

Chapter 2: What Utilitarianism Is

. . . The creed which accepts as the foundation of morals, Utility, or the Greatest Happiness Principle, holds that actions are right in proportion as they tend to promote happiness, wrong as they tend to produce the reverse of happiness. By happiness is intended pleasure, and the absence of pain; by unhappiness, pain, and the privation of pleasure. To give a clear view of the moral standard set up by the theory, much more requires to be said; in particular, what things it includes in the ideas of pain and pleasure; and to what extent this is left an open question. But these supplementary explanations do not affect the theory of life on which this theory of morality is grounded—namely, that pleasure, and freedom from pain, are the only things desirable as ends; and that all desirable things (which are as numerous in the utilitarian as in any other scheme) are desirable either for the pleasure inherent in themselves, or as means to the promotion of pleasure and the prevention of pain.

Now, such a theory of life excites in many minds . . . inveterate dislike. To suppose that life has (as they express it) no higher end than pleasure—no better and nobler object of desire and pursuit—they designate as utterly mean and grovelling; as a doctrine worthy only of swine, to whom the followers of Epicurus[1] were, at a very early period, contemptuously likened. . . .

The Epicureans have always answered, that it is not they, but their accusers, who represent human nature in a degrading light; since the accusation supposes human beings to be capable of no pleasures except those of which swine are capable. . . . Human beings have faculties more elevated than the animal appetites, and when once made conscious of them, do not regard anything as happiness which does not include their gratification. . . . There is no known Epicurean theory of life which does not assign to the pleasures of the intellect, of the feelings and imagination, and of the moral sentiments, a much higher value as pleasures than to those of mere sensation. . . .

If I am asked, what I mean by difference of quality in pleasures, or what makes one pleasure more valuable than another, merely as a pleasure, except its being greater in amount, there is but one possible answer. Of two pleasures, if there be one to which all or almost all who have experience of both give a decided preference, irrespective of any feeling of moral obligation to prefer it, that is the more desirable pleasure. If one of the two is, by those who are competently acquainted with both, placed so far above the other that they prefer it, even though knowing it to be attended with a greater amount of discontent, and would not resign it for any quantity of the other pleasure which their nature is capable of, we are justified in ascribing to the preferred enjoyment a superiority in quality, so far outweighing quantity as to render it, in comparison, of small account.

Now it is an unquestionable fact that those who are equally acquainted with, and equally capable of appreciating and enjoying, both, do give a most marked preference to the manner of existence which employs their higher faculties. Few human creatures would consent to be changed into any of the lower animals, for a promise of the fullest allowance of a beast's pleasures; no intelligent human being would consent to be a fool, no instructed person would be an ignoramus, no person of feeling and conscience would be selfish and base, even though they should be persuaded that the fool, the dunce, or the rascal is better satisfied with his lot than they are with theirs. They would not resign what they possess more than he for the most complete satisfaction of all

1. Epicurus (341–270 BCE) was an ancient Greek philosopher whose complete works have not survived. His fragments and the works of his followers suggest that he contended that a good life involved attaining pleasure and avoiding pain.

the desires which they have in common with him. If they ever fancy they would, it is only in cases of unhappiness so extreme, that to escape from it they would exchange their lot for almost any other, however undesirable in their own eyes. A being of higher faculties requires more to make him happy, is capable probably of more acute suffering, and certainly accessible to it at more points, than one of an inferior type; but in spite of these liabilities, he can never really wish to sink into what he feels to be a lower grade of existence. . . .

Whoever supposes that this preference takes place at a sacrifice of happiness—that the superior being, in anything like equal circumstances, is not happier than the inferior—confounds the two very different ideas, of happiness, and content. It is indisputable that the being whose capacities of enjoyment are low, has the greatest chance of having them fully satisfied; and a highly endowed being will always feel that any happiness which he can look for, as the world is constituted, is imperfect. But he can learn to bear its imperfections, if they are at all bearable; and they will not make him envy the being who is indeed unconscious of the imperfections, but only because he feels not at all the good which those imperfections qualify. It is better to be a human being dissatisfied than a pig satisfied; better to be Socrates dissatisfied than a fool satisfied. And if the fool, or the pig, are a different opinion, it is because they only know their own side of the question. The other party to the comparison knows both sides. . . .

From this verdict of the only competent judges, I apprehend there can be no appeal. On a question which is the best worth having of two pleasures, . . . the judgment of those who are qualified by knowledge of both, or, if they differ, that of the majority among them, must be admitted as final. . . .

I have dwelt on this point, as being a necessary part of a perfectly just conception of Utility or Happiness, considered as the directive rule of human conduct. But it is by no means an indispensable condition to the acceptance of the utilitarian standard; for that standard is not the agent's own greatest happiness, but the greatest amount of happiness altogether; and if it may possibly be doubted whether a noble character is always the happier for its nobleness, there can be no doubt that it makes other people happier, and that the world in general is immensely a gainer by it. Utilitarianism, therefore, could only attain its end by the general cultivation of nobleness of character, even if each individual were only benefited by the nobleness of others, and his own, so far as happiness is concerned, were a sheer deduction from the benefit. . . .

According to the Greatest Happiness Principle, as above explained, the ultimate end, with reference to and for the sake of which all other things are desirable (whether we are considering our own good or that of other people), is an existence exempt as far as possible from pain, and as rich as possible in enjoyments, both in point of quantity and quality; the test of quality, and the rule for measuring it against quantity, being the preference felt by those who in their opportunities of experience, to which must be added their habits of self-consciousness and self-observation, are best furnished with the means of comparison. This, being, according to the utilitarian opinion, the end of human action, is necessarily also the standard of morality; which may accordingly be defined, the rules and precepts for human conduct, by the observance of which an existence such as has been described might be, to the greatest extent possible, secured to all mankind; and not to them only, but, so far as the nature of things admits, to the whole sentient creation.

Against this doctrine, however, arises another class of objectors, who say that happiness, in any form, cannot be the rational purpose of human life and action; because, in the first place, it is unattainable. . . .

Something might still be said for the utilitarian theory; since utility includes not solely the pursuit of happiness, but the prevention or mitigation of unhappiness; and if the former aim be chimerical, there will be all the greater scope and more imperative need for the latter. . . . If by happiness be meant a continuity of highly pleasurable excitement, it is evident enough that this is impossible. A state of exalted pleasure lasts only moments, or in some cases, and with some intermissions, hours or days, and is the occasional brilliant flash of enjoyment, not its permanent and steady flame. Of this the philosophers who have taught that happiness is the end of life were as fully aware as those who taunt them. The happiness which they meant was not a life of rapture; but moments of such, in an existence made up of few and transitory pains, many and various pleasures, with a decided predominance of the active over the passive, and having as the foundation of the whole, not to expect more from life than it is capable of bestowing. A life thus composed, to those who have been fortunate enough to obtain it, has always appeared worthy of the name of happiness. . . .

. . . The main constituents of a satisfied life appear to be two, either of which by itself is often found sufficient for the purpose: tranquillity, and excitement. With much tranquillity, many find that they can be content with very little pleasure: with much excitement, many can reconcile themselves to a considerable quantity of pain. There is assuredly no inherent impossibility in enabling even the mass of mankind to unite both; since the two are so far from being incompatible that they are in natural alliance, the prolongation of either being a preparation for, and exciting a wish for, the other. . . . When people who are tolerably fortunate in their outward lot do not find in life sufficient enjoyment to make it valuable to them, the cause generally is, caring for nobody but themselves. To those who have neither public nor private affections, the excitements of life are much curtailed, and in any case dwindle in value as the time approaches when all selfish interests must be terminated by death: while those who leave after them objects of personal affection, and especially those who have also cultivated a fellow-feeling with the collective interests of mankind, retain as lively an interest in life on the eve of death as in the vigour of youth and health. Next to selfishness, the principal cause which makes life unsatisfactory is want of mental cultivation. A cultivated mind—I do not mean that of a philosopher, but any mind to which the fountains of knowledge have been opened, and which has been taught, in any tolerable degree, to exercise its faculties—finds sources of inexhaustible interest in all that surrounds it; in the objects of nature, the achievements of art, the imaginations of poetry, the incidents of history, the ways of mankind, past and present, and their prospects in the future. . . .

Now there is absolutely no reason in the nature of things why an amount of mental culture sufficient to give an intelligent interest in these objects of contemplation, should not be the inheritance of every one born in a civilised country. As little is there an inherent necessity that any human being should be a selfish egotist, devoid of every feeling or care but those which centre in his own miserable individuality. Something far superior to this is sufficiently common even now. . . . Genuine private affections and a sincere interest in the public good, are possible, though in unequal degrees, to every rightly brought up human being. In a world in which there is so much to interest, so much to enjoy, and so much also to correct and improve, every one who has this moderate amount of moral and intellectual requisites is capable of an existence which may be called enviable; and unless such a person, through bad laws, or subjection to the will of others, is denied the liberty to use the sources of happiness within his reach, he will not fail to find this enviable existence, if he escape the positive evils of life, the great sources of physical and mental suffering—such as indigence, disease, and the unkindness, worthlessness, or premature loss of objects of affection. . . . Most of the great positive evils of the world are in themselves removable, and will, if human affairs continue to improve, be in the end reduced within narrow limits. Poverty, in any sense implying suffering, may be completely extinguished by the wisdom of society, combined with the good sense and providence of individuals. Even that most intractable of enemies, disease, may be indefinitely reduced in dimensions by good physical and moral education, and proper control of noxious influences; while the progress of science holds out a promise for the future of still more direct conquests over this detestable foe. And every advance in that direction relieves us from some, not only of the chances which cut short our own lives, but, what concerns us still more, which deprive us of those in whom our happiness is wrapt up. As for vicissitudes of fortune, and other disappointments connected with worldly circumstances, these are principally the effect either of gross imprudence, of ill-regulated desires, or of bad or imperfect social institutions. . . .

Unquestionably it is possible to do without happiness; it is done involuntarily by nineteen-twentieths of mankind, even in those parts of our present world which are least deep in barbarism; and it often has to be done voluntarily by the hero or the martyr, for the sake of something which he prizes more than his individual happiness. But this something, what is it, unless the happiness of others or some of the requisites of happiness? It is noble to be capable of resigning entirely one's own portion of happiness, or chances of it: but, after all, this self-sacrifice must be for some end; it is not its own end; and if we are told that its end is not happiness, but virtue, which is better than happiness, I ask, would the sacrifice be made if the hero or martyr did not believe that it would earn for others immunity from similar sacrifices? Would it be made if he thought that his renunciation of happiness for himself would produce no fruit for any of his fellow creatures, but to make their lot like his, and place them also in the condition of persons who have renounced happiness? . . .

The utilitarian morality does recognise in human beings the power of sacrificing their own greatest good for the good of others. It only refuses to admit that the sacrifice is itself a good. A sacrifice which does not increase, or tend to increase, the sum total of happiness, it considers as wasted. . . .

The happiness which forms the utilitarian standard of what is right in conduct, is not the agent's own happiness, but that of all concerned. As between his own happiness and that of others, utilitarianism requires him to be as strictly impartial as a disinterested and benevolent spectator. In the golden rule of Jesus of Nazareth, we read the complete spirit of the ethics of utility. To do as you would be done by, and to love your neighbour as yourself, constitute the ideal perfection of utilitarian morality. As the means of making the nearest approach to this ideal, utility would enjoin, first, that laws and social arrangements should place the happiness, or (as speaking practically it may be called) the interest, of every individual, as nearly as possible in harmony with the interest of the whole; and secondly, that education and opinion, which have so vast a power over human character, should so use that power as to establish in the mind of every individual an indissoluble association between his own happiness and the good of the whole; especially between his own happiness and the practice of such modes of conduct, negative and positive, as regard for the universal happiness prescribes; so that not only he may be unable to conceive the possibility of happiness to himself, consistently with conduct opposed to the general good, but also that a direct impulse to promote the general good may be in every individual one of the habitual motives of action, and the sentiments connected therewith may fill a large and prominent place in every human being's sentient existence. . . .

[Some] objectors to utilitarianism . . . sometimes find fault with its standard as being too high for humanity. They say it is exacting too much to require that people shall always act from the inducement of promoting the general interests of society. But this is to mistake the very meaning of a standard of morals, and confound the rule of action with the motive of it. It is the business of ethics to tell us what are our duties, or by what test we may know them; but no system of ethics requires that the sole motive of all we do shall be a feeling of duty; on the contrary, ninety-nine hundredths of all our actions are done from other motives, and rightly so done, if the rule of duty does not condemn them. . . . He who saves a fellow creature from drowning does what is morally right, whether his motive be duty, or the hope of being paid for his trouble; he who betrays the friend that trusts him, is guilty of a crime, even if his object be to serve another friend to whom he is under greater obligations.

. . . It is a misapprehension of the utilitarian mode of thought, to conceive it as implying that people should fix their minds upon so wide a generality as the world, or society at large. The great majority of good actions are intended not for the benefit of the world, but for that of individuals, of which the good of the world is made up; and the thoughts of the most virtuous man need not on these occasions travel beyond the particular persons concerned, except so far as is necessary to assure himself that in benefiting them he is not violating the rights, that is, the legitimate and authorised expectations, of any one else. The multiplication of happiness is, according to the utilitarian ethics, the object of virtue: the occasions on which any person (except one in a thousand) has it in his power to do this on an extended scale, in other words to be a public benefactor, are but exceptional; and on these occasions alone is he called on to consider public utility; in every other case, private utility, the interest or happiness of some few persons, is all he has to attend to. Those alone the influence of whose actions extends to society in general, need concern themselves habitually about so large an object. In the case of abstinences indeed—of things which people forbear to do from moral considerations, though the consequences in the particular case might be beneficial—it would be unworthy of an intelligent agent not to be consciously aware that the action is of a class which, if practised generally, would be generally injurious, and that this is the ground of the obligation to abstain from it. . . .

The same considerations dispose of another reproach against the doctrine of utility, founded on a still grosser misconception of the purpose of a standard of morality, and of the very meaning of the words right and wrong. It is often affirmed that utilitarianism renders men cold and unsympathising; that it chills their moral feelings towards individuals; that it makes them regard only the dry and hard consideration of the consequences of actions, not taking into their moral estimate the qualities from which those actions emanate. If the assertion means that they do not allow their judgment respecting the rightness or wrongness of an action to be influenced by their opinion of the qualities of the person who does it, this is a complaint not against utilitarianism, but against having any standard of morality at all; for certainly no known ethical standard decides an action to be good or bad because it is done by a good or a bad man, still less because done by an amiable, a brave, or a benevolent man, or the contrary. These considerations are relevant, not to the estimation of actions, but of persons; and there is nothing in the utilitarian theory inconsistent with the fact that there are other things which interest us in persons besides the rightness and wrongness of their actions. . . . Utilitarians are quite aware . . . that a right action does not necessarily indicate a virtuous character, and that actions which are blamable, often proceed from qualities entitled to praise. When this is apparent in any particular case, it modifies their estimation, not certainly of the act, but of the agent. I grant that they are, notwithstanding, of opinion, that in the long run the best proof of a good character is good actions; and resolutely refuse to consider any mental disposition as good, of which the predominant tendency is to produce bad conduct. . . .

Utility is often summarily stigmatised as an immoral doctrine by giving it the name of Expediency, and taking advantage of the popular use of that term to contrast it with Principle. But the Expedient, in the sense in which it is opposed to the Right, generally means that which is expedient for the particular interest of the agent himself. . . . When it means anything better than this, it means that which is expedient for some immediate object, some temporary purpose, but which violates a rule whose observance is expedient in a much higher degree. The Expedient, in this sense, instead of being the same thing with the useful, is a branch of the hurtful. Thus, it would often be expedient, for the purpose of getting over some momentary embarrassment, or attaining some object immediately useful to ourselves or others, to tell a lie. But inasmuch as the cultivation in ourselves of a sensitive feeling on the subject of veracity, is one of the most useful, and the enfeeblement of that feeling one of the most hurtful, things to which our conduct can be instrumental; and inasmuch as any, even unintentional, deviation from truth, does that much towards weakening the trustworthiness of human assertion, which is not only the principal support of all present social well-being, but the insufficiency of which does more than any one thing that can be named to keep back civilisation, virtue, everything on which human happiness on the largest scale depends; we feel that the violation, for a present advantage, of a rule of such transcendant expediency, is not expedient, and that he who, for the sake of a convenience to himself or to some other individual, does what depends on him to deprive mankind of the good, and inflict upon them the evil, involved in the greater or less reliance which they can place in each other's word, acts the part of one of their worst enemies. Yet that even this rule, sacred as it is, admits of possible exceptions, is acknowledged by all moralists; the chief of which is when the withholding of some fact (as of information from a malefactor, or of bad news from a person dangerously ill) would save an individual (especially an individual other than oneself) from great and unmerited evil, and when the withholding can only be effected by denial. But in order that the exception may not extend itself beyond the need, and may have the least possible effect in weakening reliance on veracity, it ought to be recognised, and, if possible, its limits defined; and if the principle of utility is good for anything, it must be good for weighing these conflicting utilities against one another, and marking out the region within which one or the other preponderates.

. . . [Some object] that there is not time, previous to action, for calculating and weighing the effects of any line of conduct on the general happiness. This is exactly as if any one were to say that it is impossible to guide our conduct by Christianity, because there is not time, on every occasion on which anything has to be done, to read through the Old and New Testaments. The answer to the objection is, that there has been ample time, namely, the whole past duration of the human species. During all that time, mankind have been learning by experience the tendencies of actions; on which experience all the prudence, as well as all the morality of life, are dependent. People talk as if the commencement of this course of experience had hitherto been put off, and as if, at the moment when some man feels tempted to meddle with the property or life of another, he had to begin considering for the first time whether murder and theft are injurious to human happiness. . . .

[M]ankind must by this time have acquired positive beliefs as to the effects of some actions on their happiness; and the beliefs which have thus come down are the rules of morality for the multitude, and for the philosopher until he has succeeded in finding better. . . . The corollaries from the principle of utility, like the precepts of every practical art, admit of indefinite improvement. . . .

But to consider the rules of morality as improvable, is one thing; to pass over the intermediate generalisations entirely, and endeavour to test each individual action directly by the first principle, is another. It is a strange notion that the acknowledgment of a first principle is inconsistent with the admission of secondary ones. To inform a traveller respecting the place of his ultimate destination, is not to forbid the use of landmarks and direction-posts on the way. The proposition that happiness is the end and aim of morality, does not mean that no road ought to be laid down to that goal, or that persons going thither should not be advised to take one direction rather than another. . . . Nobody argues that the art of navigation is not founded on astronomy, because sailors cannot wait to calculate the Nautical Almanack.[2] Being rational creatures,

2. To assist in navigation, a nautical almanac offers projections about the locations and distances of celestial bodies during a calendar year. The information could be calculated by sailors, *en route*, with difficulty, but Mill's point is that it is reasonable to rely on prior calculations.

they go to sea with it ready calculated; and all rational creatures go out upon the sea of life with their minds made up on the common questions of right and wrong, as well as on many of the far more difficult questions of wise and foolish. . . . Whatever we adopt as the fundamental principle of morality, we require subordinate principles to apply it by; the impossibility of doing without them, being common to all systems, can afford no argument against any one in particular. . . .

The remainder of the stock arguments against utilitarianism mostly consist in laying to its charge the common infirmities of human nature. . . . We are told that a utilitarian will be apt to make his own particular case an exception to moral rules, and, when under temptation, will see a utility in the breach of a rule, greater than he will see in its observance. But is utility the only creed which is able to furnish us with excuses for evil doing, and means of cheating our own conscience? They are afforded in abundance by all doctrines which recognise as a fact in morals the existence of conflicting considerations; which all doctrines do, that have been believed by sane persons. It is not the fault of any creed, but of the complicated nature of human affairs, that rules of conduct cannot be so framed as to require no exceptions, and that hardly any kind of action can safely be laid down as either always obligatory or always condemnable. There is no ethical creed which does not temper the rigidity of its laws, by giving a certain latitude, under the moral responsibility of the agent, for accommodation to peculiarities of circumstances; and under every creed, at the opening thus made, self-deception and dishonest casuistry[3] get in. There exists no moral system under which there do not arise unequivocal cases of conflicting obligation. . . . If utility is the ultimate source of moral obligations, utility may be invoked to decide between them when their demands are incompatible. Though the application of the standard may be difficult, it is better than none at all: while in other systems, the moral laws all claiming independent authority, there is no common umpire entitled to interfere between them; their claims to precedence one over another rest on little better than sophistry, and unless determined, as they generally are, by the unacknowledged influence of considerations of utility, afford a free scope for the action of personal desires and partialities. We must remember that only in these cases of conflict between secondary principles is it requisite that first principles should be appealed to.

TEST YOUR UNDERSTANDING

1. For Mill, is it better to be "a human being dissatisfied than a pig satisfied"? Is it better to be "Socrates dissatisfied" or a satisfied fool?

2. For a utilitarian, happiness "forms the standard of what is right in conduct." Whose happiness counts?

---

3. Casuistry is the ethical evaluation of particular cases, with a sensitivity to their distinguishing details. The term "casuistry" is sometimes used pejoratively to suggest the use of specious reasoning to make distinctions, often to serve one's own purposes.

3. Why does Mill distinguish between the "rule of action" and the "motive of action"?

    a. Like Kant, Mill thinks that motives are part of what is evaluated when we evaluate an action: he says that it is not enough to have a rule of action; one must also consider the motive of the action.

    b. Mill responds to the objection that it would be too demanding to always expect others to be motivated by the general good: he says that morally good actions can come from a variety of motives.

4. How does Mill respond to the objection that it would be too difficult to calculate which of one's options would create the highest total amount of utility in the world?

NOTES AND QUESTIONS

1. *Mill on pleasure.* Mill responds to some critics of early forms of utilitarianism by rejecting *simple hedonism.* Mill does not equate "pleasure" with sensory experiences of pleasure. Moreover, he contends that not all pleasures are alike qualitatively; pleasure need not resemble the lovely feeling one gets when basking in the sun or enjoying an ice cream. Finally, he observes that not all pleasures are equally important. His more sophisticated view of pleasure may save his version of utilitarianism from the insult that it is a "doctrine worthy only of swine." Is his account open to the objection that one might fail to enjoy and even dislike what Mill counts as an episode of "pleasure"? Does that render his account of pleasure implausible, and does it cast doubt upon his utilitarian theory?

2. *Is pleasure always good and pain always bad?* Should we agree that pleasure and the absence of pain are always good? Consider the following criticisms: (a) The pleasure a sadist receives from contemplating another's (nonconsensual) suffering does not seem good in any way. (b) Further, the emotional pain of guilt that a criminal feels upon recognizing and regretting the wrong of her past actions is a good thing. Someone who has done something wrong but does not suffer painful pangs of guilt is defective and does not lead a better life.

3. *Is pleasure the only good?* Some critics agree with Mill that actions are right because of their consequences. They and Mill are *consequentialists.* Non-utilitarian consequentialists differ from Mill about how to characterize *which* consequences are valuable. They argue that pleasure is not the only good and that other individual and social states are also ends (or intrinsically valuable things). For example, some contend that it is intrinsically desirable for individuals to have the status of equals and for societies to manifest equal social relations; further, equality is desirable independent from its bringing pleasure (although it probably does). To take a different example, some believe that preservation of art, architecture, history, and the environment is an intrinsically desirable end, independent of whether people gain pleasure from or prefer their preservation. Indeed, people *should* prefer their preservation. How might Mill respond? Would those responses persuade you?

4. *Harming innocents as a means to generating aggregate utility.* Consider the following three scenarios:

    (i) A supersized stadium full of sadists gathers to witness the nonconsensual, public flogging of an innocent child. Enough fervent sadists attend so that the aggregate utility, given their intense experiences of elation, would outweigh the disutility experienced by the victim and his sympathizers, even taking into account his absolutely awful pain, his feelings of betrayal, and subsequent trauma.

(ii)   Suppose if a child is privately tortured, that upon hearing his screams, his parent will reveal secret information that will assist the government in trade negotiations and raise the nation's standard of living a small amount, thereby generating enough positive utility for citizens that would, in the aggregate, outweigh (numerically) the terrific disutility experienced by the solitary victim, his parents, and the torturer.

(iii)   Suppose if a child is privately tortured, that his parent will reveal secret information that will prevent a terrorist bombing, save 1,000 innocent lives, and thereby generate more positive utility than the disutility experienced by the victim and his parent.

Is utilitarianism vulnerable to the objections that (a) it would require the child to be tortured in all of these cases, and (b) if the utility produced were equal in quantity, it would not regard these cases as different and would not be sensitive to the reasons why utility was produced?

5. The issues raised by these questions are crucial points of contention between consequentialists and some non-consequentialist critics who argue that, morally, we are sometimes *prohibited* from bringing about the best consequences. For instance, they claim that some courses of action are horrific in nature and must not be taken, even if they sometimes produce good consequences. Actions such as torture, killing for sport, or scapegoating the innocent involve treating human beings in ways that are inconsistent with a core feature of morality: to show respect for each person. We must not treat any person with profound disrespect even if our purposes are otherwise good. This position represents an example of **deontology**, the view that, morally, there are certain sorts of actions we have duties to perform or to refrain from, and these duties may be characterized by features other than the consequences they happen to bring about in particular circumstances. Some important discussions of the deontological criticism of utilitarianism may be found in Bernard Williams, "A Critique of Utilitarianism," in J. J. C. Smart and Bernard Williams, *Utilitarianism: For and Against* (Cambridge University Press, 1975); Thomas Nagel, "War and Massacre," *Philosophy and Public Affairs* 1, 2 (1972): 123–44; Samuel Scheffler, *The Rejection of Consequentialism*, revised edition (Oxford University Press, 1994); Frances Kamm, "Non-consequentialism, the Person as an End-in-Itself, and the Significance of Status," *Philosophy and Public Affairs* 21, 4 (1992): 354–89.

Immanuel Kant (1724–1804)

Kant was a German philosopher of the Enlightenment whose work extolled the faculty of reason, exploring its powers and limitations. He was born in Königsberg and was a professor at the University of Königsberg. His work exerted and continues to exert a profound influence on the development of modern and contemporary philosophy in ethics, political philosophy, metaphysics, epistemology, the philosophy of mind and of psychology, aesthetics, and the philosophy of religion. His most famous books include *The Critique of Pure Reason* (1781), *Prolegomena to Any Future Metaphysics* (1783), *Groundwork of the Metaphysics of Morals* (1785), *The Critique of Practical Reason* (1788), *The Critique of Judgment* (1790), and *The Metaphysics of Morals* (1797).

GROUNDWORK OF THE METAPHYSICS OF MORALS

Second Section: Transition from Popular Moral Philosophy to the Metaphysics of Morals

Unless one wants to refuse the concept of morality all truth and reference to some possible object, one cannot deny that its law is so extensive in its significance that it must hold not merely for human beings but for all *rational beings as such,* not merely under contingent conditions and with exceptions, but with *absolute necessity.* . . . [I]t is clear that no experience can give occasion to infer even just the possibility of such apodictic laws.[1] For by what right can we bring what is perhaps valid only under the contingent conditions of humanity into unlimited respect, as a universal prescription for every rational nature?

Moreover, one could not give morality worse counsel than by seeking to borrow it from examples. For every example of it that is presented to me must itself first be judged according to principles of morality, whether it is actually worthy to serve as an original example, i.e. as a model; but by no means can it furnish the concept of it at the outset. Even the Holy One of the Gospel must first be compared with our ideal of moral perfection before he is recognized as one. . . . Imitation has no place at all in moral matters; and examples serve for encouragement only, i.e. they put beyond doubt the feasibility of what the law commands, they make intuitive what the practical[2] rule expresses more generally, but they can never entitle us to set aside their true original, which lies in reason, and to go by examples.

. . . It is clear from what has been said that all moral concepts have their seat and origin completely a priori[3] in reason . . . that they cannot be abstracted from any empirical and hence merely contingent cognition; that their dignity to serve us as supreme practical principles lies just in this purity of their origin; that every time in adding anything empirical to them one takes away as much from their genuine influence and from the unlimited worth of actions; that it is not only a requirement of the greatest

---

1. That is, indisputable or certain laws.

2. When Kant uses "practical," he is referring to principles, concepts, or reasoning relevant to action (as opposed merely to thought or reasoning independent of action).

3. Here, Kant means that moral concepts, moral principles, and their application can be known through consulting reason alone, and one need not consult experience, our behavior, or our customs to know them. They apply to us and can be known merely by virtue of our being rational.

necessity for theoretical purposes, when only speculation counts, but also a matter of the greatest practical importance to draw its concepts and laws from pure reason, to set them forth pure and unmingled, indeed to determine the scope of this entire practical but pure rational cognition, i.e. the entire faculty of pure practical reason, and in so doing not . . . to make its principles dependent on the particular nature of human reason, but because moral laws are to hold for every rational being as such, already to derive them from the universal concept of a rational being as such. . . .

Every thing in nature works according to laws. Only a rational being has the capacity to act *according to the representation* of laws, i.e. according to principles, or a *will*. Since *reason* is required for deriving actions from laws, the will is nothing other than practical reason. If reason determines the will without fail, then the actions of such a being that are recognized as objectively necessary are also subjectively necessary; i.e. the will is a capacity to choose *only that* which reason, independently of inclination, recognizes as practically necessary, i.e. as good. If, however, reason all by itself does not sufficiently determine the will, if it is also subject to subjective conditions (to certain incentives) that are not always in agreement with the objective ones; in a word, if the will does not *in itself* completely conform with reason (as is actually the case with human beings), then actions objectively recognized as necessary are subjectively contingent, and the determination of such a will, in conformity with objective laws, is *necessitation*; i.e. the relation of objective laws to a will not altogether good is represented as the determination of the will of a rational being by grounds of reason, to which this will is not, however, according to its nature necessarily obedient.

The representation of an objective principle in so far as it is necessitating for a will is called a command (of reason), and the formula of the command is called imperative.

All imperatives are expressed by an *ought*, and by this indicate the relation of an objective law of reason to a will that according to its subjective constitution is not necessarily determined by it (a necessitation). They say that to do or to omit something would be good, but they say it to a will that does not always do something just because it is represented to it that it would be good to do it. Practically *good*, however, is what determines the will by means of representations of reason, hence not from subjective causes, but objectively, i.e. from grounds that are valid for every rational being, as such. It is distinguished from the *agreeable*, as that which influences the will only by means of sensation from merely subjective causes, which hold only for the senses of this or that one, and not as a principle of reason, which holds for everyone.

. . . Now, all *imperatives* command either *hypothetically*, or *categorically*. The former represent the practical necessity of a possible action as a means to achieving something else that one wants (or that at least is possible for one to want). The categorical imperative would be the one that represented an action as objectively necessary by itself, without reference to another end.

Because every practical law represents a possible action as good and hence, for a subject practically determinable by reason, as necessary, all imperatives are formulae for the determination of an action necessary according to the principle of a will that is good in some way. Now, if the action would be good merely as a means to *something else*, the imperative is *hypothetical*; if the action is represented as good *in itself*, hence as necessary in a will that in itself conforms to reason, as its principle, then it is *categorical*.

. . . Now, the skill in the choice of the means to one's own greatest well-being can be called prudence in the narrowest sense. Thus the imperative that refers to the choice of means to one's own happiness, i.e. the prescription of prudence, is still *hypothetical*; the action is not commanded per se, but just as a means to another purpose.

Finally, there is one imperative that—without presupposing as its condition any other purpose to be attained by a certain course of conduct—commands this conduct immediately. This imperative is categorical. It concerns not the matter of the action or what is to result from it, but the form and the principle from which it does itself follow; and the essential good in it consists in the disposition, let the result be what it may. This imperative may be called that of morality. . . .

Now the question arises: how are all these imperatives possible? . . . How an imperative of skill is possible probably requires no special discussion. Whoever wills the end also wills (in so far as reason has decisive influence on his actions) the indispensably necessary means to it that is in his control. As far as willing is concerned, this proposition is analytic; for in the willing of an object, as my effect, my causality is already thought, as an acting cause, i.e. the use of means, and the imperative already extracts the concept of actions necessary to this end from the concept of a willing of this end.

The imperatives of prudence would totally and entirely coincide with those of skill, and be equally analytic, if only it were so easy to provide a determinate concept of happiness. For here as well as there it would be said: whoever wills the end also wills (in conformity with reason necessarily) the only means to it that are in his control. But, unfortunately, the concept of happiness is so indeterminate a concept that, even though every human being wishes to achieve it, yet he can never say determinately and in agreement with himself what he actually wishes and wants. The cause of this is: that the elements that belong to the concept of happiness are one and all empirical, i.e. must be borrowed from experience. . . .

By contrast, the question of how the imperative of *morality* is possible is no doubt the only one in need of a solution, since it is not hypothetical at all, and thus the objectively represented necessity cannot rely on any presupposition, as in the case of the hypothetical imperatives. However, it is never to slip our attention in this matter that it cannot be made out *by any example,* and hence empirically, whether there is any such imperative at all; but to be dreaded that all imperatives that appear categorical may yet in some hidden way be hypothetical. E.g., when it is said that you ought not to make deceitful promises; and one assumes that the necessity of this omission is not merely giving counsel for avoiding some other ill, so that what is said would be: you ought not to make lying promises lest, if it comes to light, you are deprived of your credit; but that an action of this kind must be considered as by itself evil, thus that the imperative of the prohibition is categorical; one still cannot establish in any example with certainty that the will is here determined, without another incentive, merely by the law, even if it appears so; for it is always possible that fear of embarrassment, perhaps also an obscure dread of other dangers, may covertly influence the will. . . .

We shall thus have to investigate the possibility of a *categorical* imperative entirely a priori, since we do not here enjoy the advantage that its actuality is being given in experience, in which case its possibility would be necessary not for corroboration, but merely for explanation. For the time being, however, this much can be seen: that the categorical imperative alone expresses a practical law, and that the others can indeed one and all be called *principles* of the will, but not laws; since what it is necessary to do merely for attaining a discretionary purpose can be regarded as in itself contingent, and we can always be rid of the prescription if we give up the purpose, whereas the unconditional command leaves the will no free discretion with regard to the opposite, and hence alone carries with it that necessity which we demand for a law.

In the case of this categorical imperative or law of morality the ground of the difficulty (of insight into its possibility) is actually very great. It is an a priori synthetic practical proposition[4] and since gaining insight into the possibility of propositions of this kind causes so much difficulty in theoretical cognition, it can easily be inferred that in practical cognition there will be no less.

With this problem, we shall first try to see whether the mere concept of a categorical imperative may perhaps also furnish its formula, which contains the proposition that alone can be a categorical imperative . . .

When I think of a *hypothetical* imperative as such I do not know in advance what it will contain, until I am given the condition. But when I think of a *categorical* imperative I know at once what it contains. For since besides the law the imperative contains only the necessity of the maxim[5] to conform with this law, whereas the law contains no condition to which it was limited, nothing is left but the universality of a law as such, with which the maxim of the action ought to conform, and it is this conformity alone that the imperative actually represents as necessary.

There is therefore only a single categorical imperative, and it is this: *act only according to that maxim through which you can at the same time will that it become a universal law.*

. . . Since the universality of the law according to which effects happen constitutes that which is actually called *nature* in the most general sense (according to its form), i.e. the existence of things in so far as it is determined according to universal laws, the universal imperative of duty could also be expressed as follows: *so act as if the maxim of your action were to become by your will a universal law of nature.*

We shall now enumerate some duties, according to their usual division, into duties to ourselves and to other human beings, into perfect and imperfect duties.

(1) Someone who feels weary of life because of a series of ills that has grown to the point of hopelessness is still so far in possession of his reason that he can ask himself whether it is not perhaps contrary to a duty to oneself to take one's own life. Now he tries out: whether the maxim of his action could possibly become a universal law of nature. But his maxim is: from self-love I make it my principle to shorten my life if, when protracted any longer, it threatens more ill than it promises agreeableness. The

---

4. Here, Kant means that the concept of a categorical imperative is one that could be known without consulting experience but is **synthetic**, by which he means it is not a proposition true by definition.

5. A *maxim* is the subjective principle of acting, and must be distinguished from the *objective* principle, namely the practical law. The former contains the practical rule determined by reason conformably with the conditions of the subject (often his ignorance or also his inclinations), and is therefore the principle in accordance with which the subject *acts*; but the law is the objective principle valid for every rational being, and the principle in accordance with which he *ought to act*, i.e., an imperative. [Kant's note.]

only further question is whether this principle of self-love could become a universal law of nature. But then one soon sees that a nature whose law it were to destroy life itself by means of the same sensation the function of which it is to impel towards the advancement of life, would contradict itself and would thus not subsist as a nature, hence that maxim could not possibly take the place of a universal law of nature, and consequently conflicts entirely with the supreme principle of all duty.

(2) Another sees himself pressured by need to borrow money. He knows full well that he will not be able to repay, but also sees that nothing will be lent to him unless he solemnly promises to repay it at a determinate time. He feels like making such a promise; but he still has enough conscience to ask himself: is it not impermissible and contrary to duty to help oneself out of need in such a way? Suppose that he still resolved to do so, his maxim of the action would go as follows: when I believe myself to be in need of money I shall borrow money, and promise to repay it, even though I know that it will never happen. Now this principle of self-love, or of one's own benefit, is perhaps quite consistent with my whole future well-being, but the question now is: whether it is right? I therefore transform the imposition of self-love into a universal law, and arrange the question as follows: how things would stand if my maxim became a universal law. Now, I then see at once that it could never hold as a universal law of nature and harmonize with itself, but must necessarily contradict itself. For the universality of a law that everyone, once he believes himself to be in need, could promise whatever he fancies with the intention not to keep it, would make the promise and the end one may pursue with it itself impossible, as no one would believe he was being promised anything, but would laugh about any such utterance, as a vain pretense.

(3) A third finds in himself a talent that by means of some cultivation could make him a useful human being in all sorts of respects. However, he sees himself in comfortable circumstances and prefers to give himself up to gratification rather than to make the effort to expand and improve his fortunate natural predispositions. Yet he still asks himself: whether his maxim of neglecting his natural gifts, besides its agreement with his propensity to amusement, also agrees with what one calls duty. Now he sees that a nature could indeed still subsist according to such a universal law, even if human beings . . . should let their talents rust and be intent on devoting their lives merely to idleness, amusement, procreation, in a word, to enjoyment; but he cannot possibly will that this become a universal law of nature, or as such be placed in us by natural instinct. For as a rational being he necessarily wills that all capacities in him be developed, because they serve him and are given to him for all sorts of possible purposes.

Yet a *fourth*, who is prospering while he sees that others have to struggle with great hardships (whom he could just as well help), thinks: what's it to me? May everyone be as happy as heaven wills, or as he can make himself, I shall take nothing away from him, not even envy him; I just do not feel like contributing anything to his well-being, or his assistance in need! Now, certainly, if such a way of thinking were to become a universal law of nature, the human race could very well subsist, and no doubt still better than when everyone chatters about compassion and benevolence, even develops the zeal to perform such actions occasionally, but also cheats wherever he can, sells out the right of human beings, or infringes it in some other way. But even though it is possible that a universal law of nature could very well subsist according to that maxim, it is still impossible to will that such a principle hold everywhere as a law of nature. For a will that resolved upon this would conflict with itself, as many cases can yet come to pass in which one needs the love and compassion of others, and in which, by such a law of nature sprung from his own will, he would rob himself of all hope of the assistance he wishes for himself.

These, then, are some of the many actual duties, or at least of what we take to be such, whose division can clearly be seen from the one principle stated above. One must *be able to will* that a maxim of our action become a universal law: this is as such the canon of judging it morally. Some actions are such that their maxim cannot even be *thought* without contradiction as a universal law of nature; let alone that one could *will* that it *should* become such. In the case of others that inner impossibility is indeed not to be found, but it is still impossible to *will* that their maxim be elevated to the universality of a law of nature, because such a will would contradict itself. It is easy to see that the first conflicts with strict or narrower (unrelenting) duty, the second only with wider (meritorious) duty, and thus that all duties, as far as the kind of obligation (not the object of their action) is concerned, have by these examples been set out completely in their dependence on the one principle.

If we now attend to ourselves in every transgression of a duty, we find that we actually do not will that our maxim should become a universal law, since that is impossible for us, but that its opposite should rather generally remain a law; we just take the liberty of making an *exception* to it for ourselves, or (just for this once) to the advantage of our inclination. Consequently, if we considered everything from one and the same point of view, namely that of reason, we would find a contradiction in our own will, namely that a certain principle be objectively necessary as a universal law and yet subjectively should not hold universally, but allow of exceptions.

We have thus established at least this much, that if duty is a concept that is to contain significance and actual legislation for our actions it can be expressed only in categorical imperatives, but by no means in hypothetical ones; likewise we have—and this is already a lot—presented distinctly and determined for every use the content of the categorical imperative, which would have to contain the principle of all duty (if there were such a thing at all).

. . . [One] must put the thought right out of one's mind that the reality of this principle can be derived from some *particular property of human nature.* For duty is to be practical unconditional necessity of action; it must thus hold for all rational beings (to which an imperative can at all apply), and *only in virtue of this* be a law also for every human will. By contrast, whatever is derived from the special natural predisposition of humanity, from certain feelings and propensity, and indeed even, possibly, from a special tendency peculiar to human reason, and would not have to hold necessarily for the will of every rational being—that can indeed yield a maxim for us, but not a law, a subjective principle on which propensity and inclination would fain have us act, but not an objective principle on which we would be *instructed* to act even if every propensity, inclination and natural arrangement of ours were against it. . . .

The will is thought as a capacity to determine itself to action *in conformity with the representation of certain laws.* And such a capacity can be found only in rational beings. Now, what serves the will as the objective ground of its self-determination is the *end*, and this, if it is given by mere reason, must hold equally for all rational beings. By contrast, what contains merely the ground of the possibility of an action the effect of which is an end is called the *means*. The subjective ground of desiring is the *incentive*, the objective ground of willing the *motivating ground*; hence the difference between subjective ends, which rest on incentives, and objective ones, which depend on motivating grounds that hold for every rational being. Practical principles are *formal* if they abstract from all subjective ends; they are *material* if they have these, and hence certain incentives, at their foundation. The ends that a rational being intends at its discretion as *effects* of its actions (material ends) are one and all only relative; for merely their relation to a particular kind of desiderative faculty of the subject gives them their worth, which can therefore furnish no universal principles that are valid as well as necessary for all rational beings, or for all willing, i.e. practical laws. That is why all these relative ends are the ground of hypothetical imperatives only.

But suppose there were something *the existence of which in itself* has an absolute worth, that, as an *end in itself*, could be a ground of determinate laws, then the ground of a possible categorical imperative, i.e. of a practical law, would lie in it, and only in it alone.

Now I say: a human being and generally every rational being *exists* as an end in itself, *not merely as a means* for the discretionary use for this or that will, but must in all its actions, whether directed towards itself or also to other rational beings, always be considered *at the same time as an end*. All objects of inclinations have a conditional worth only; for if the inclinations, and the needs founded on them, did not exist, their object would be without worth. But the inclinations themselves, as sources of need, are so far from having an absolute worth—so as to make one wish for them as such—that to be entirely free from them must rather be the universal wish of every rational being. Therefore the worth of any object *to be acquired* by our action is always conditional. Beings whose existence rests not indeed on our will but on nature, if they are non-rational beings, still have only a relative worth, as means, and are therefore called *things*, whereas rational beings are called *persons*, because their nature already marks them out as ends in themselves, i.e. as something that may not be used merely as a means, and hence to that extent limits all choice (and is an object of respect). These are therefore not merely subjective ends, the existence of which, as the effect of our action, has a worth *for us*; but rather *objective ends*, i.e. entities whose existence in itself is an end, an end such that no other end can be put in its place, for which they would do service *merely* as means, because without it nothing whatsoever of *absolute worth* could be found; but if all worth were conditional, and hence contingent, then for reason no supreme practical principle could be found at all.

If, then, there is to be a supreme practical principle and, with regard to the human will, a categorical imperative, it must be such that, from the representation of what is necessarily an end for everyone, because it is an *end in itself*, it constitutes an *objective* principle of the will, and hence can serve as a universal practical law. The ground of this principle is: *a rational nature exists as an end in itself*. That is how a human being by necessity represents his own existence; to that extent it is thus a *subjective* principle of human actions. But every other rational being also represents its existence in this way, as a consequence of just the same rational ground that also holds for me; thus it is at the same time an *objective* principle from which, as a supreme practical ground, it must be possible to derive all laws of the will. The practical imperative will thus be the following: *So act that you use humanity, in your own person as well as in the person of any other, always at the same time as an end, never merely as a means.* Let us try to see whether this can be done.

To keep to the previous examples:

First, according to the concept of necessary duty to oneself, someone who is contemplating self-murder will ask himself whether his action can be consistent with the idea of humanity, *as an end in itself*. If to escape from a troublesome condition he destroys himself, he makes use of a person, merely as *a means*, to preserving a bearable condition up to the end of life. But a human being is not a thing, hence not something that can be used *merely* as a means, but must in all his actions always be considered as an end in itself. Thus the human being in my own person is not at my disposal, so as to maim, to corrupt, or to kill him. . . .

Secondly, as far as necessary or owed duty to others is concerned, someone who has it in mind to make a lying promise to others will see at once that he wants to make use of another human being *merely as a means*, who does not at the same time contain in himself the end. For the one I want to use for my purposes by such a promise cannot possibly agree to my way of proceeding with him and thus himself contain the end of this action. This conflict with the principle of other human beings can be seen more distinctly if one introduces examples of attacks on the freedom and property of others. For then it is clear that the transgressor of the rights of human beings is disposed to make use of the person of others merely as a means, without taking into consideration that, as rational beings, they are always to be esteemed at the same time as ends, i.e. only as beings who must, of just the same action, also be able to contain in themselves the end.

Thirdly, with regard to contingent (meritorious) duty to oneself it is not enough that the action not conflict with humanity in our person, as an end in itself, it must also *harmonize with it*. Now there are in humanity predispositions to greater perfection, which belong to the end of nature with regard to humanity in our subject; to neglect these would perhaps be consistent with the *preservation* of humanity, as an end in itself, but not with the *advancement* of this end.

Fourthly, as concerns meritorious duty to others, the natural end that all human beings have is their own happiness. Now, humanity could indeed subsist if no one contributed anything to the happiness of others while not intentionally detracting anything from it; but this is still only a negative and not positive agreement with *humanity, as an end in itself*, if everyone does not also try, as far as he can, to advance the ends of others. For if that representation is to have its *full* effect in me, the ends of a subject that is an end in itself must, as much as possible, also be *my* ends.

This principle of humanity and of every rational nature as such, *as an end in itself* (which is the supreme limiting condition of the freedom of actions of every human being) is not borrowed from experience, first, because of its universality, as it aims at all rational beings as such, and about that no experience is sufficient to determine anything; secondly, because in it humanity is represented not as an end of human beings (subjectively), i.e. as an object that by itself one actually makes one's end, but as an objective end that, whatever ends we may have, as a law is to constitute the supreme limiting condition of all subjective ends, and hence must arise from pure reason. For the ground of all practical legislation lies *objectively in the rule* and the form of universality, which (according to the first principle) makes it capable of being a law (or perhaps a law of nature), *subjectively*, however, *in the end*; the subject of all ends, however, is every rational being, as an end in itself (according to the second principle): from this now follows the third practical principle of the will, as the supreme condition of its harmony with universal practical reason, the idea *of the will of every rational being as a universally legislating will.*

According to this principle, all maxims are rejected that are not consistent with the will's own universal legislation. Thus the will is not just subject to the law, but subject in such a way that it must also be viewed *as self-legislating*, and just on account of this as subject to the law (of which it can consider itself the author) in the first place. . . .

Now, if we look back on all the efforts that have ever been undertaken to detect the principle of morality to this day, it is no wonder why one and all they had to fail. One saw the human being bound to laws by his duty, but it did not occur to anyone that he is subject *only to his own* and yet *universal legislation*, and that he is only obligated to act in conformity with his own will which is, however, universally legislating according to its natural end. For if one thought of him just as subject to a law (whichever it may be), it had to carry with it some interest as stimulation or constraint, because it did not as a law arise from *his* will, which instead was necessitated by *something else*, in conformity with a law, to act in a certain way. Because of this entirely necessary conclusion, however, all the labor of finding a supreme ground of duty was irretrievably lost. For one never got duty, but the necessity of an action from a certain interest, be it one's own interest or that of another. But then the imperative always had to be conditional, and could not be fit to be a moral command at all. I shall therefore call this principle the principle of the autonomy of the will, in opposition to every other, which I accordingly count as heteronomy.[6]

The concept of every rational being that must consider itself as universally legislating through all the maxims of its will, so as to judge itself and its actions from this point of view, leads to a very fruitful concept attached to it, namely that *of a kingdom of ends.*

By a *kingdom*, however, I understand the systematic union of several rational beings through common laws. Now, since laws determine ends according to their universal validity, it is possible—if one abstracts from the personal differences among rational beings, and likewise from all content of their private ends—to conceive a whole of all ends (of rational beings as ends in themselves, as well as the ends of its own that each of them may set for itself) in systematic connection, i.e. a kingdom of ends, which is possible according to the above principles.

---

6. By "heteronomy," Kant refers to a force or impulse external to one's rational will.

For all rational beings stand under the *law* that each of them is to treat itself and all others *never merely as a means*, but always *at the same time as an end in itself.* But by this there arises a systematic union of rational beings through common objective laws, i.e. a kingdom, which—because what these laws have as their purpose is precisely the reference of these beings to one another, as ends and means—can be called a kingdom of ends (of course only an ideal).

The above three ways of representing the principle of morality are fundamentally only so many formulae of the selfsame law, one of which of itself unites the other two within it. . . .

We can now end where we set out from at the beginning, namely with the concept of an unconditionally good will. A *will is absolutely good* that cannot be evil, hence whose maxim, if made a universal law, can never conflict with itself. This principle is therefore also its supreme law: act always on that maxim the universality of which as a law you can will at the same time; this is the only condition under which a will can never be in conflict with itself, and such an imperative is categorical. Since the validity of the will, as a universal law for possible actions, has an analogy with the universal connection of the existence of things according to universal laws, which is what is formal in nature as such, the categorical imperative can also be expressed as follows: *act according to maxims that can at the same time have as their object themselves as universal laws of nature.* Such, then, is the formula of an absolutely good will.

A rational nature is distinguished from the others by this, that it sets itself an end. . . .

TEST YOUR UNDERSTANDING

1. How does a categorical imperative differ from a hypothetical imperative? Give an example of a hypothetical imperative.

2. A maxim is a description of the morally relevant features of an action, along with one's morally relevant reasons for acting in that way. In Kant's example of the false promise, what is the would-be promisor's maxim?

    a. When I believe myself to be in need of money, I shall borrow money and promise to repay it, even though I know that this will never happen.

    b. When I believe myself to be in need of money, I shall borrow money and promise to repay it.

3. Consider these two maxims:

    I will work hard in order to gain a promotion.
    I will kill my boss in order to gain a promotion.

    For each maxim, apply Kant's test given by the universal law formulation of the categorical imperative. Does the maxim pass the test?

4. What is the humanity formulation of the categorical imperative?

READER'S GUIDE

Kant's Moral Theory

Suppose I am thinking of lying to someone so he'll do what I want. You say to me, "Don't lie." Suppose I want to join the basketball team, and tryouts are one month away. You say to me, "Practice basketball!" Both of these *imperatives* you have offered do apply to me. You're right that I should not lie. And you're right that I should practice basketball. But there is a difference between these two imperatives. The imperative "Don't lie" applies to me, regardless of what I care about. I shouldn't lie in order to manipulate another person, and not just because I care about that person or because I care about being honest. I simply shouldn't lie. By contrast, the imperative "Practice basketball" applies to me only because I want to play basketball. If I didn't want to play, the imperative wouldn't apply to me. "Don't lie" is a *categorical imperative*—it applies to me, independently of what I care about—while "Practice basketball" is a *hypothetical imperative*—it applies to me only on the hypothesis that I want something in particular, to play basketball.

Kant distinguishes categorical from hypothetical imperatives and claims that morality provides a categorical imperative, a command that applies to everyone. Kant does seem to be right that everyone should obey the rules of morality. Kant believes that there is one general moral rule, which he calls "the categorical imperative." Kant offers more than one statement of this moral rule, though he believes the statements are equivalent.

One statement of the categorical imperative is the Formula of Universal Law. The basic idea behind this formula is that no one should make an exception of herself: no one should exempt herself from rules that others need to follow.

The Formula of Universal Law holds that one should act in such a way that one can will that one's maxim be a universal law of human nature. What in the world does this mean? First of all, what is a maxim? A maxim is a statement of *what* one is doing and *why* one is doing it. Here are some examples:

> I will study in order to do well on my test.
> I will cheat in order to do well on my test.
> I will make an honest promise in order to receive a loan.
> I will make a lying promise in order to receive a loan.

Intuitively, some of these things are morally permissible and some of them are not. How do they fare on Kant's test? Well, we must ask whether one can will that one's maxim be a universal law of human nature. A universal law of human nature would be a principle that all people followed. So we must ask whether you can will—that is, wish—that it be so. Let's see whether these maxims pass the test.

Consider the maxim "I will cheat in order to do well on my test." Suppose that it were a universal law of human nature that people who are taking tests cheat on them. If it were a universal law, then it would be well known to the administrators of tests that people cheat on them. In that case, there would be no reason to give good grades to people who write correct answers on tests; there would be no point in grading tests at all. So, cheating would not be a way of doing well on a test anymore. Here we see a *contradiction* emerging. We supposed that it is a universal law of human nature that people cheat in order to do well on tests. But if that were so, it would not be so, because it would not be an effective means to do well on tests. Thus, it's not possible that this be a universal law of human nature. And we can't wish that something impossible happen. So this maxim fails the test.

For similar reasons, the maxim "I will make a lying promise in order to receive a loan" fails the test. For both of these maxims, Kant would see a *contradiction in the conception*: there is a contradiction in the idea that these are universal laws of human nature. Thus, Kant holds that because you can't wish for something impossible, you can't wish that these be universal laws of human nature.

The maxims "I will study in order to do well on my test" and "I will work hard in order to receive a promotion" do pass Kant's test. It is perfectly *possible* that these be universal laws of human nature, and indeed we can *want* them to be universal laws of human nature.

Intuitively, if you were explaining to someone why she shouldn't cheat on a test or why she shouldn't make a lying promise to get a loan, you might say, "Don't make an exception of yourself! It's only because other people do the right thing and behave honestly that you would be able to cheat or lie in this way. You'd be exploiting others' following the rules and treating yourself as special if you cheat or lie in this way." This intuitive explanation of why it's wrong to cheat or lie corresponds very closely to Kant's explanation of why it's wrong: the fact that you cannot *universalize* your maxim (that is, you cannot wish that it was a universal law of nature) shows that you'd be making an exception of yourself.

There is another way that Kant thinks a maxim can fail the universalization test. Consider the maxim, "I will refrain from helping others when it would inconvenience me to help them and I am doing fine on my own." Could this be a universal law of human nature? It could. It is *possible* that people would universally refrain from helping others who were needier than themselves. But could you *wish* that this be a universal law of human nature? Kant thinks not. Kant thinks that there is a *contradiction in the will* if you were to wish for such a thing. If you wished for such a thing, then you would be wishing that if you yourself fell on hard times, no one would help you. Kant holds that a person must wish for his own well-being, out of respect for oneself. But then a person's will would contradict itself: the desire for one's well-being would conflict with the desire that people not help others. Such a *contradiction in the will* is impossible. So, this maxim fails Kant's test.

Kant also offers another statement of the categorical imperative: one must act so that one uses humanity, whether one's own humanity or others' humanity, always as an end in itself and never as a means. This is called the Formula of Humanity. Kant believes that these two statements of the categorical imperative—the Formula of Universal Law and the Formula of Humanity—are equivalent, if properly understood.

For example, Kant holds that a lying promise violates the Formula of Humanity because in lying to someone, you use her as a means but not as an end in herself: by deceiving her, you manipulate her through her rational faculties (which are, in Kant's view, her humanity) but you do not allow them to operate freely because she does not know she is being manipulated. The idea that you should respect humanity *in every person* (as the Formula of Humanity says) does seem to be connected to the idea that you should not *make an exception of yourself* (as the Formula of Universal Law says).

NOTES AND QUESTIONS

1. Kant says that suicide would fail the universalization test by giving rise to a *contradiction in the conception*. Can you describe in your own words what the maxim is and how it fails the universalization test? Would Kant disapprove of a person who chose to end his life because his mental capacities were deteriorating and he foresaw that he would soon fail to reason and behave well?

2. Kant says that a person's choice not to develop her talents, instead indulging in pleasure and avoiding the hard work that it would take to develop her talents, is a choice that would fail the universalization test. Kant says the choice would give rise to a *contradiction in the will*. How would Kant apply the test to get the result that the choice fails the test?

3. *Differences and specialization.* Some actions are permissible to perform, although we could not survive if everyone behaved the same way. For instance, it seems permissible that some of us grow wheat but do not dig wells, and that others of us do not engage in agriculture at all, although it is essential that some people do so. Is Kant's idea that one's maxim must be universalizable consistent with these examples? Can you say how?

4. *How specific should a maxim be?* We've seen that the maxim "I will make a lying promise in order to receive a loan" fails Kant's test given by the Formula of Universal Law. But what if we understood the liar's maxim differently? What if we stated the maxim without any mention of lying? It does seem that the liar is also following this maxim: "I will make a promise in order to receive a loan." This maxim *passes* Kant's test. What does this show? It shows that we have to be careful to state a person's maxim with the correct level of specificity to yield the result that Kant wants.

   Is the upshot that we should make a maxim as specific as possible? That may not work. Consider this maxim: "I will make a lying promise in order to receive a loan, but only if very few people are making lying promises, so that my promise will be believed." This maxim might also seem to pass Kant's test. If everyone followed it, it is not true that everyone would make lying promises, because as soon as it seemed like too many people were making lying promises, the maxim would cease to instruct people to make lying promises.

5. *Market exchange and never treating humanity as a means only.* Suppose I enter a shop and I give the shopkeeper money in exchange for milk. I do not ask the shopkeeper how she is or what her interests are. I interact with her only to get the milk I need and then I leave. Do I treat her unacceptably as a mere means to my nutrition and not as an end in herself?

6. Consider the Formula of Universal Law and the Formula of Humanity. Kant thinks that, properly understood, these are equivalent and that they provide the very same rules about which actions are morally permissible. Are they really equivalent?

Aristotle (384–322 BCE)

Aristotle was born in Stagira and joined Plato's Academy when he was eighteen. A philosopher of extraordinary intellectual reach, he wrote remarkably influential treatises on all areas of philosophy and science. His writings on logic, metaphysics, rhetoric, ethics, and politics continue to have a profound impact on philosophical discussion.

NICOMACHEAN ETHICS

Book 1

Every art and every inquiry, and similarly every action and every pursuit, is thought to aim at some good; and for this reason the good has rightly been declared to be that at which all things aim. . . .

If, then, there is some end of the things we do, which we desire for its own sake (everything else being desired for the sake of this), and if we do not choose everything for the sake of something else (for at that rate the process would go on to infinity, so that our desire would be empty and vain), clearly this must be the good and the chief good. Will not the knowledge of it, then, have a great influence on life? Shall we not, like archers who have a mark to aim at, be more likely to hit upon what is right? . . .

Since there are evidently more than one end, and we choose some of these (e.g., wealth, flutes, and in general instruments) for the sake of something else, clearly not all ends are final ends; but the chief good is evidently something final. Therefore, if there is only one final end, this will be what we are seeking, and if there are more than one, the most final of these will be what we are seeking. Now we call that which is in itself worthy of pursuit more final than that which is worthy of pursuit for the sake of something else, and that which is never desirable for the sake of something else more final than the things that are desirable both in themselves and for the sake of that other thing, and therefore we call final without qualification that which is always desirable in itself and never for the sake of something else.

Now such a thing happiness, above all else, is held to be; for this we choose always for self and never for the sake of something else, but honour, pleasure, reason, and every virtue we choose indeed for themselves (for if nothing resulted from them we should still choose each of them), but we choose them also for the sake of happiness, judging that by means of them we shall be happy. Happiness, on the other hand, no one chooses for the sake of these, nor, in general, for anything other than itself.[1] . . .

Presumably, however, to say that happiness is the chief good seems a platitude, and a clearer account of what it is still desired. This might perhaps be given, if we could first ascertain the function of man. For just as for a flute-player, a sculptor, or an artist, and, in general, for all things that have a function or activity, the good and the "well" is thought to reside in the function, so would it seem to be for man, if he has a function. Have the carpenter, then, and the tanner certain functions or activities, and has man none? Is he born without a function? Or as eye, hand, foot, and in general each of the parts evidently has a function, may one lay it down that man similarly has a function

---

1. When Aristotle speaks of *happiness*, he is talking about a person's well-being, or the extent to which the person is living a good life worth having. He is not speaking narrowly of pleasure. Even if we include what Mill calls higher-order pleasures (see the Mill essay in this chapter), Aristotle is not speaking of pleasure. Rather, as Aristotle uses the concept of *happiness*, it is by living a life that includes the things that matter, whatever they are, that one has a life of happiness.

apart from all these? What then can this be? Life seems to be common even to plants, but we are seeking what is peculiar to man. Let us exclude, therefore, the life of nutrition and growth. Next there would be a life of perception, but it also seems to be common even to the horse, the ox, and every animal. There remains, then, an active life of the element that has a rational principle; of this, one part has such a principle in the sense of being obedient to one, the other in the sense of possessing one and exercising thought.[2] And, as "life of the rational element" also has two meanings, we must state that life in the sense of activity is what we mean; for this seems to be the more proper sense of the term. Now if the function of man is an activity of soul which follows or implies a rational principle, and if we say "so-and-so" and "a good so-and-so" have a function which is the same in kind, e.g. a lyre, and a good lyre-player, and so without qualification in all cases, eminence in respect of goodness being added to the name of the function (for the function of a lyre-player is to play the lyre, and that of a good lyre-player is to do so well): if this is the case, and we state the function of man to be a certain kind of life, and this to be an activity or actions of the soul implying a rational principle, and the function of a good man to be the good and noble performance of these, and if any action is well performed when it is performed in accordance with the appropriate excellence: if this is the case, human good turns out to be activity of soul in accordance with virtue, and if there are more than one virtue, in accordance with the best and most complete.

But we must add "in a complete life." For one swallow does not make a summer, nor does one day; and so too one day, or a short time, does not make a man blessed and happy.

Let this serve as an outline of the good; for we must presumably first sketch it roughly, and then later fill in the details. . . .

Since happiness is an activity of soul in accordance with perfect virtue, we must consider the nature of virtue; for perhaps we shall thus see better the nature of happiness. . . . But clearly the virtue we must study is human virtue; for the good we were seeking was human good and the happiness human happiness. By human virtue we mean not that of the body but that of the soul; and happiness also we call an activity of soul. . . .

Some things are said about it, adequately enough, even in the discussions outside our school, and we must use these; e.g. that one element in the soul is irrational and one has a rational principle. . . .

Of the irrational element one division seems to be widely distributed, and vegetative in its nature, I mean that which causes nutrition and growth; for it is this kind of power of the soul that one must assign to all nurslings and to embryos, and this same power to full-grown creatures. . . .

There seems to be also another irrational element in the soul—one which in a sense, however, shares in a rational principle. For we praise the rational principle of the continent man and of the incontinent, and the part of their soul that has such a principle, since it urges them aright and towards the best objects; but there is found

---

2. Aristotle believes the soul has two parts: a non-rational (emotional) part and a rational (thinking) part.

in them also another element naturally opposed to the rational principle, which fights against and resists that principle. . . . the impulses of continent people move in contrary directions.[3] . . .

Therefore the irrational element also appears to be twofold. For the vegetative element in no way shares in a rational principle, but the appetitive and in general the desiring element in a sense shares in it, in so far as it listens to and obeys it; this is the sense in which we speak of "taking account" of one's father or one's friends, not that in which we speak of "accounting" for a mathematical property. That the irrational element is in some sense persuaded by a rational principle is indicated also by the giving of advice and by all reproof and exhortation. And if this element also must be said to have a rational principle, that which has a rational principle (as well as that which has not) will be twofold, one subdivision having it in the strict sense and in itself, and the other having a tendency to obey as one does one's father.

Virtue too is distinguished into kinds in accordance with this difference; for we say that some of the virtues are intellectual and others moral, philosophic wisdom and understanding and practical wisdom being intellectual, liberality and temperance moral. For in speaking about a man's character we do not say that he is wise or has understanding but that he is good-tempered or temperate; yet we praise the wise man also with respect to his state of mind; and of states of mind we call those which merit praise virtues.

Book 2

. . . Next we must consider what virtue is. . . . [Aristotle explains that virtues are states of character.]

We must, however, not only describe virtue as a state of character, but also say what sort of state it is. . . .

[A] master of any art avoids excess and defect, but seeks the intermediate and chooses this—the intermediate not in the object but relatively to us.

If it is thus, then, that every art does its work well—by looking to the intermediate and judging its works by this standard (so that we often say of good works of art that it is not possible either to take away or to add anything, implying that excess and defect destroy the goodness of works of art, while the mean preserves it; and good artists, as we say, look to this in their work), and if, further, virtue is more exact and better than any art, as nature also is, then virtue must have the quality of aiming at the intermediate. I mean moral virtue; for it is this that is concerned with passions and actions, and in these there is excess, defect, and the intermediate. For instance, both fear and confidence and appetite and anger and pity and in general pleasure and pain may be felt both too much and too little, and in both cases not well; but to feel them at the right times, with reference to the right objects, towards the right people, with the right motive, and in

---

3. When the rational part of a person's soul makes the right choice about what to do, but the emotional part of the soul is in conflict with that decision, then a man is "continent" if the rational part wins out and "incontinent" if it does not. (In the virtuous person, the two parts of the soul do not conflict.)

the right way, is what is both intermediate and best, and this is characteristic of virtue. Similarly with regard to actions also there is excess, defect, and the intermediate. Now virtue is concerned with passions and actions, in which excess is a form of failure, and so is defect, while the intermediate is praised and is a form of success; and being praised and being successful are both characteristics of virtue. Therefore virtue is a kind of mean, since, as we have seen, it aims at what is intermediate.[4] . . .

Virtue, then, is a state of character concerned with choice, lying in a mean, i.e. the mean relative to us, this being determined by a rational principle, and by that principle by which the man of practical wisdom would determine it. Now it is a mean between two vices, that which depends on excess and that which depends on defect; and again it is a mean because the vices respectively fall short of or exceed what is right in both passions and actions, while virtue both finds and chooses that which is intermediate. Hence in respect of its substance and the definition which states its essence virtue is a mean, with regard to what is best and right an extreme. . . .

Book 4

CHAPTER 3

[Aristotle distinguished earlier between intellectual and moral virtues. One of the moral virtues is a sense of pride.]

Pride seems even from its name to be concerned with great things; what sort of great things, is the first question we must try to answer. It makes no difference whether we consider the state of character or the man characterized by it. Now the man is thought to be proud who thinks himself worthy of great things, being worthy of them; for he who does so beyond his deserts is a fool, but no virtuous man is foolish or silly. The proud man, then, is the man we have described. For he who is worthy of little and thinks himself worthy of little is temperate, but not proud; for pride implies greatness, as beauty implies a good-sized body, and little people may be neat and well-proportioned but cannot be beautiful. On the other hand, he who thinks himself worthy of great things, being unworthy of them, is vain; though not every one who thinks himself worthy of more than he really is worthy of in vain. The man who thinks himself worthy of less than he is really worthy of is unduly humble, whether his deserts be great or moderate, or his deserts be small but his claims yet smaller. And the man whose deserts are great would seem most unduly humble; for what would he have done if they had been less? The proud man, then, is an extreme in respect of the greatness of his claims, but a mean in respect of the rightness of them; for he claims what is in accordance with his merits, while the others go to excess or fall short.

If, then, he deserves and claims great things, and above all the great things, he will be concerned with one thing in particular. Desert is relative to external goods; and the

---

4. Aristotle's view is that each virtue is a kind of "mean," as in an *intermediate* state between two extremes on a continuum; the two extremes are each vices. The person who is kind feels exactly the right amount of sympathy called for on a particular occasion: not too much, and not too little.

greatest of these, we should say, is that which we render to the gods, and which people of position most aim at, and which is the prize appointed for the noblest deeds; and this is honour; that is surely the greatest of external goods. Honours and dishonours, therefore, are the objects with respect to which the proud man is as he should be. And even apart from argument it is with honour that proud men appear to be concerned; for it is honour that they chiefly claim, but in accordance with their deserts. The unduly humble man falls short both in comparison with his own merits and in comparison with the proud man's claims. The vain man goes to excess in comparison with his own merits, but does not exceed the proud man's claims.

Now the proud man, since he deserves most, must be good in the highest degree; for the better man always deserves more, and the best man most. Therefore the truly proud man must be good. And greatness in every virtue would seem to be character-istic of a proud man. And it would be most unbecoming for a proud man to fly from danger, swinging his arms by his sides, or to wrong another; for to what end should he do disgraceful acts, he to whom nothing is great? If we consider him point by point we shall see the utter absurdity of a proud man who is not good. Nor, again, would he be worthy of honour if he were bad; for honour is the prize of virtue, and it is to the good that it is rendered. Pride, then, seems to be a sort of crown of the virtues; for it makes them greater, and it is not found without them. Therefore it is hard to be truly proud; for it is impossible without nobility and goodness of character. It is chiefly with honours and dishonours, then, that the proud man is concerned; and at honours that are great and conferred by good men he will be moderately pleased, thinking that he is coming by his own or even less than his own; for there can be no honour that is worthy of perfect virtue, yet he will at any rate accept it since they have nothing greater to bestow on him; but honour from casual people and on trifling grounds he will utterly despise, since it is not this that he deserves, and dishonour too, since in his case it cannot be just. In the first place, then, as has been said, the proud man is concerned with honours; yet he will also bear himself with moderation towards wealth and power and all good or evil fortune, whatever may befall him, and will be neither over-joyed by good fortune nor over-pained by evil. For not even towards honour does he bear himself as if it were a very great thing. Power and wealth are desirable for the sake of honour (at least those who have them wish to get honour by means of them); and for him to whom even honour is a little thing the others must be so too. Hence proud men are thought to be disdainful. . . .

Such, then, is the proud man; the man who falls short of him is unduly humble, and the man who goes beyond him is vain. . . .

Book 9

The question is . . . debated, whether a man should love himself most, or some one else. People criticize those who love themselves most, and call them self-lovers, using this as an epithet of disgrace, and a bad man seems to do everything for his own sake, and the more so the more wicked he is—and so men reproach him, for instance, with doing nothing of his own accord—while the good man acts for honour's sake, and the more so the better he is, and acts for his friend's sake, and sacrifices his own interest.

But the facts clash with these arguments, and this is not surprising. For men say that one ought to love best one's best friend, and man's best friend is one who wishes well to the object of his wish for his sake, even if no one is to know of it; and these attributes are found most of all in a man's attitude towards himself, and so are all the other attributes by which a friend is defined; for, as we have said, it is from this relation that all the characteristics of friendship have extended to our neighbours. All the proverbs, too, agree with this, e.g. "a single soul," and "what friends have is common property," and "friendship is equality," and "charity begins at home"; for all these marks will be found most in a man's relation to himself; he is his own best friend and therefore ought to love himself best. It is therefore a reasonable question, which of the two views we should follow; for both are plausible.

Perhaps we ought to mark off such arguments from each other and determine how far and in what respects each view is right. Now if we grasp the sense in which each school uses the phrase "lover of self," the truth may become evident. Those who use the term as one of reproach ascribe self-love to people who assign to themselves the greater share of wealth, honours, and bodily pleasures; for these are what most people desire, and busy themselves about as though they were the best of all things, which is the reason, too, why they become objects of competition. So those who are grasping with regard to these things gratify their appetites and in general their feelings and the irrational element of the soul; and most men are of this nature (which is the reason why the epithet has come to be used as it is—it takes its meaning from the prevailing type of self-love, which is a bad one); it is just, therefore, that men who are lovers of self in this way are reproached for being so. That it is those who give themselves the preference in regard to objects of this sort that most people usually call lovers of self is plain; for if a man were always anxious that he himself, above all things, should act justly, temperately, or in accordance with any other of the virtues, and in general were always to try to secure for himself the honourable course, no one will call such a man a lover of self or blame him.

But such a man would seem more than the other a lover of self; at all events he assigns to himself the things that are noblest and best, and gratifies the most authoritative element in and in all things obeys this; and just as a city or any other systematic whole is most properly identified with the most authoritative element in it, so is a man; and therefore the man who loves this and gratifies it is most of all a lover of self. Besides, a man is said to have or not to have self-control according as his reason has or has not the control, on the assumption that this is the man himself; and the things men have done on a rational principle are thought most properly their own acts and voluntary acts. That this is the man himself, then, or is so more than anything else, is plain, and also that the good man loves most this part of him. Whence it follows that he is most truly a lover of self, of another type than that which is a matter of reproach, and as different from that as living according to a rational principle is from living as passion dictates, and desiring what is noble from desiring what seems advantageous. Those, then, who busy themselves in an exceptional degree with noble actions all men approve and praise; and if all were to strive towards what is noble and strain every nerve to do the noblest deeds, everything would be as it should be for the common weal, and every one would secure for himself the goods that are greatest, since virtue is the greatest of goods.

Therefore the good man should be a lover of self (for he will both himself profit by doing noble acts, and will benefit his fellows), but the wicked man should not; for he will hurt both himself and his neighbours, following as he does evil passions. For the wicked man, what he does clashes with what he ought to do, but what the good man ought to do he does; for reason in each of its possessors chooses what is best for itself, and the good man obeys his reason. It is true of the good man too that he does many acts for the sake of his friends and his country, and if necessary dies for them; for he will throw away both wealth and honours and in general the goods that are objects of competition, gaining for himself nobility; since he would prefer a short period of intense pleasure to a long one of mild enjoyment, a twelvemonth of noble life to many years of humdrum existence, and one great and noble action to many trivial ones. Now those who die for others doubtless attain this result; it is therefore a great prize that they choose for themselves. They will throw away wealth too on condition that their friends will gain more; for while a man's friend gains wealth he himself achieves nobility; he is therefore assigning the greater good to himself. The same too is true of honour and office; all these things he will sacrifice to his friend; for this is noble and laudable for himself. Rightly then is he thought to be good, since he chooses nobility before all else. But he may even give up actions to his friend; it may be nobler to become the cause of his friend's acting than to act himself. In all the actions, therefore, that men are praised for, the good man is seen to assign to himself the greater share in what is noble. In this sense, then, as has been said, a man should be a lover of self; but in the sense in which most men are so, he ought not.

Book 10

CHAPTER 7

If happiness is activity in accordance with virtue, it is reasonable that it should be in accordance with the highest virtue; and this will be that of the best thing in us. Whether it be reason or something else that is this element which is thought to be our natural ruler and guide and to take thought of things noble and divine, whether it be itself also divine or only the most divine element in us, the activity of this in accordance with its proper virtue will be perfect happiness. That this activity is contemplative we have already said.

Now this would seem to be in agreement both with what we said before and with the truth. For, firstly, this activity is the best (since not only is reason the best thing in us, but the objects of reason are the best of knowable objects); and secondly, it is the most continuous, since we can contemplate truth more continuously than we can do anything. And we think happiness has pleasure mingled with it, but the activity of philosophic wisdom is admittedly the pleasantest of virtuous activities[5]; at all events the pursuit of it is thought to offer pleasures marvelous for their purity and their enduringness, and it is to be expected that those who know will pass their time more pleasantly than those who inquire. And the self-sufficiency that is spoken of must belong most to the contemplative activity. For while a philosopher, as well as a just man or one possessing any other virtue, needs the necessaries of life, when they are sufficiently equipped with things of that sort the just man needs people towards whom and with whom he shall act justly, and the temperate man, the brave man, and each of the others is in the same case, but the philosopher, even when by himself, can contemplate truth, and the better the wiser he is; he can perhaps do so better if he has fellow-workers, but still he is the most self-sufficient. And this activity alone would seem to be loved for its own sake; for nothing arises from it apart from the contemplating, while from practical activities we gain more or less apart from the action. And happiness is thought to depend on leisure; for we are busy that we may have leisure, and make war that we may live in peace. Now the activity of the practical virtues is exhibited in political or military affairs, but the actions concerned with these seem to be unleisurely. Warlike actions are completely so (for no one chooses to be at war, or provokes war, for the sake of being at war; any one would seem absolutely murderous if he were to make enemies of his friends in order to bring about battle and slaughter); but the action of the statesman is also unleisurely, and—apart from the political action itself—aims at despotic power and honours, or at all events happiness, for him and his fellow citizens—a happiness different from political action, and evidently sought as being different. So if among virtuous actions political and military actions are distinguished by nobility and greatness, and these are unleisurely and aim at an end and are not desirable for their own sake, but the activity of reason, which is contemplative, seems both to be superior in serious worth and to aim at no end beyond itself, and to have its pleasure proper to itself (and this augments the activity), and the self-sufficiency, leisureliness, unweariedness (so far as this is possible for man), and all the other attributes ascribed to the supremely happy man are evidently those connected with this activity, it follows that this will be the complete happiness of man, if it be allowed a complete term of life (for none of the attributes of happiness is incomplete).

But such a life would be too high for man; for it is not in so far as he is man that he will live so, but in so far as something divine is present in him; and by so much as this

---

5. By "the activity of philosophic wisdom," Aristotle means *theoretical reasoning*, including thinking about biology, physics, metaphysics, and mathematics. He does not include thinking about practical questions about what to do.

is superior to our composite nature is its activity superior to that which is the exercise of the other kind of virtue. If reason is divine, then, in comparison with man, the life according to it is divine in comparison with human life. But we must not follow those who advise us, being men, to think of human things, and, being mortal, of mortal things, but must, so far as we can, make ourselves immortal, and strain every nerve to live in accordance with the best thing in us; for even if it be small in bulk, much more does it in power and worth surpass everything. This would seem, too, to be each man himself, since it is the authoritative and better part of him. It would be strange, then, if he were to choose not the life of his self but that of something else. And what we said before will apply now; that which is proper to each thing is by nature best and most pleasant for each thing; for man, therefore, the life according to reason is best and pleasantest, since reason more than anything else is man. This life therefore is also the happiest.

TEST YOUR UNDERSTANDING

1. What does Aristotle say is the only "final good," that is, the only thing that is good in itself and that people aim at for its own sake alone, not for the sake of something else?

2. What does Aristotle say is the relationship between virtue and happiness?

    a. A virtuous person tries to steer a middle course between too much happiness and not enough happiness.

    b. A virtuous person aims to create the most happiness in the world that they can.

    c. A virtuous person, because they exercise virtue, thereby possesses happiness.

    d. A virtuous person ignores their own happiness and focuses on fulfilling their duty.

3. What does Aristotle say about the relationship between virtues and vices?

    a. Each virtue is at the middle of a continuum, with two vices at either extreme end of the continuum.

    b. Each virtue is at one extreme of a continuum, with a vice at the other extreme.

4. Which of the following does Aristotle say about the relationship between pride and the other virtues? (You may select more than one.)

    a. If a person has the virtue of pride, then he does not have very many of the other virtues.

    b. If a person has the virtue of pride, it diminishes his other virtues.

    c. To have the virtue of pride, a person must possess the other virtues.

    d. If a person has the virtue of pride, it improves his other virtues.

NOTES AND QUESTIONS

1. Aristotle's view is that a person has a happy life, or a good life, if and only if they are virtuous. Someone might object that a person could be a morally bad person but still live a great life: a person could have a lot of happiness, including intellectual fulfillment, while regularly treating other people badly. Does this pose an objection to Aristotle's view? What does Aristotle say about this?

    We might respond on Aristotle's behalf by distinguishing what he means by *happiness* from *pleasure* or pleasant experience (even including Mill's *higher-order pleasures*). Aristotle is interested in what makes for a life worth having, a life that goes well for the person who has it. Aristotle's claim is that it is a bad life *for the one who lives it* if that person has been very immoral in their life, even if the life includes a lot of pleasures, and even if it includes higher-order pleasures.

    Is Aristotle right that it's bad *for the agent* if they live a life of immorality? Isn't it an important truth that sometimes morality requires us to *sacrifice* what would be best for ourselves, for the sake of others? Here are a couple of cases in which that seems to be true:

    > *Firefighter:* You are a firefighter and you arrive at a burning house. You are morally obligated to rush inside to try to save people, even though you risk your own safety.
    >
    > *Job Application:* You and your roommate have both applied for the same job. This job would significantly improve your life. You answer the phone and take a message for your roommate: she is being offered the job, and she has 24 hours to accept. Separately, you learn that you are next in line for the job. You could rip up the message for your roommate, in which case she won't accept the job in time, and you will end up getting it. Morality requires you to deliver the message, even though it's better for you if you get the job yourself.

    When Aristotle discusses cases like these, he says that a good person chooses "nobility" in such cases, making a real sacrifice but gaining something more valuable—nobility. Aristotle's distinction between two kinds of self-love is helpful here. A selfish person might choose his own immediate pleasures, which feed the irrational part of the soul (in Aristotle's view); this is one kind of self-love. But the good person has a different kind of self-love: they choose what is best for themself even if it means sacrificing some specific joys and pleasures.

2. When Aristotle says that warlike actions are "unleisurely," he means they are called for only when trouble has already occurred. More generally, his view is that any action that has great moral value requires something bad to have happened first. Thus, Aristotle has the surprising view that no one should unconditionally desire to perform acts of great moral value, because that would involve desiring that bad things have happened. Is Aristotle right? One might object that sometimes a person does something of moral value without anything bad happening first; for example, suppose you woke up one morning and decided to buy your mother some flowers. What could Aristotle say in response?

Rosalind Hursthouse (b. 1943)

Hursthouse is a New Zealand philosopher who taught for many years at the Open University in England and is now a professor at the University of Auckland. A famous exponent of virtue ethics, she is the author of *Beginning Lives* (1987), *On Virtue Ethics* (1999), and *Ethics, Humans, and Other Animals* (2013).

VIRTUE ETHICS

In Book 6 of the *Nicomachean Ethics*, Aristotle introduced a difficult concept into moral philosophy. Taking one of the many Greek terms for knowledge, *phronesis*, he gave it his own special sense. *Phronesis* is the knowledge that enables its possessor to make correct moral decisions about what to do—to reason correctly about what is right; we translate it as (moral or practical) wisdom. He writes as though some people, albeit not many, actually have it, and as if you either have it or you do not. Nowadays we tend to take it as the concept of an ideal to which we can aspire and possess to a greater or lesser degree.

Modern moral philosophy lost sight of the concept until it was enthusiastically revived by virtue ethics, in which the question "How should we reason about what is right?" becomes inseparable from the question "What is *phronesis*?" What *does* a person who possesses it know that enables her to do this reasoning so well? And since that amounts to the question "What is wisdom?" it is very hard to answer. I am just going to discuss two aspects of it and the knowledge each involves, each derived from something Aristotle says about it.

The first is that you can't have *phronesis* without being truly virtuous, that is, a morally good person. This is what makes "moral wisdom" a good translation—we do not think that the Hitlers of this world have moral wisdom, only people we think are morally good. What follows? Well, it follows that the correct decisions about what it is right to do which the person with *phronesis* reaches are the decisions of a truly virtuous person. We all know that we still have a fair way to go before we become as good as that, so we cannot reason in exactly the way this ideal person does. How can we best approximate that reasoning?

According to modern virtue ethics, we should not reason about what to do in terms of what will maximise the best consequences, and not in terms of what will be in accordance with correct moral principles such as "Do not lie" or "Keep promises," but in terms of *what a virtuous agent would do in the circumstances*. This is in some ways very straightforward, in other ways very difficult. The difficulty is inevitable whatever account we give of how to reason about what to do. We all know that life presents us with situations in which it is agonisingly difficult, if not impossible, to know what it is right to do. But we will start with what is straightforward.

Of course, thinking in terms of "what a virtuous agent would do" does not look immediately straightforward because the word "virtue" is hardly common usage nowadays. But, oddly enough, everyone still has the concept. Google "virtues" and you find 1.6 million pages, many of them with lists of the virtues and vices. Although we might disagree (I certainly do) with some of the examples, and a few of them will sound old-fashioned to most people, they are comprehensible. We can see that the virtues listed are all supposed to be character traits that we praise and admire people for having because they constitute being a morally good person. (Web material is often a bit careless: I have seen beauty and health listed as virtues, but they cannot be because they are not character traits and hence not virtues.) Note that, although "vice" still does have a common usage, it connotes something more evil than "moral fault" or "defect," but when we speak of "the virtues and vices" in this context, "vice" is shorthand for "vice *or* moral defect."

So we are to think of "the virtuous agent" as someone who has the virtues, that is, as someone who *is*, through and through, all the way down, benevolent (or "charitable" in the original sense), courageous, generous, honest, just, kind, loyal, responsible, and trustworthy, for example. And, having the virtues, the virtuous agent acts accordingly, characteristically or typically doing what *is* benevolent, courageous, generous, honest, just, kind, loyal, responsible, and trustworthy, and not what is malevolent, cowardly, mean, dishonest, unjust, unkind, disloyal, irresponsible, or untrustworthy.

Terms for the virtues and vices generate adjectives that describe both people *and* actions. Consequently, virtue ethics offers an enormous number of moral rules for action guidance. *Every* virtue generates a prescription—do what is benevolent, etc., and *every* vice a prohibition—do not do what is malevolent, etc. Let's call these the "v-rules" (for "virtue and vice rules"). So the straightforward way to think about what to do in terms of what the virtuous agent would do is, initially, to think in terms of the v-rules. And that, often, is indeed very straightforward. Is it right not to go to my friend's birthday party when I have promised to because something more enjoyable has turned up? No, because it would be untrustworthy, disloyal, inconsiderate, selfish, and (on some construals of justice) unjust. Is it right to take her a birthday present—yes, it would be mean (in the sense of "stingy" or "ungenerous") not to. Is it right to take my dog for a walk every day? Yes, it is benevolent, kind, and responsible to do so, and callous, unkind, and irresponsible not to.

Now one might say, "But these examples are so obvious that no one needs to reason about them!" True—though it is in relation to such obvious examples that we first acquire the virtue and vice vocabulary and thereby learn to identify morally relevant features of actions which ethical theories other than virtue ethics ignore at their peril. For instance, some moral philosophers say we should reason about what is right in such a way that there turns out to be nothing wrong with breaking my promise to my friend (if I can deceive him successfully later about why I didn't turn up). Other philosophers say we should reason about what is right in such a way that it turns out not to be true that I ought to give my dog regular exercise (because I do not have any moral duties to animals). And some insist that our reasoning in these examples should be impartial and make no reference to *my* friend or *my* dog.

Here is an interesting thing about the v-rules. They are not invented or discovered by moral philosophers or peculiar to religious doctrine. They are simply created by the words—the available virtue and vice words—in ordinary language, and the ordinary use of these words is extraordinarily subtle and nuanced, heavily dependent on features of the conversation in which they occur. Hence the importance of thinking about what it is right to do in terms of what the virtuous agent would do *in the circumstances.* Suppose we tweak one of the obvious examples above a bit.

Is it right to break my promise to turn up to the school play my daughter is in, because, on my way to it, I see an old woman being threatened by a mugger? Of course—it would be cowardly, irresponsible, and callous not to stop to help, and, in *these* circumstances, not disloyal or inconsiderate or selfish to break the promise.

Would it be untrustworthy? Well, if so, the example illustrates something that it is easy to forget when we are thinking about that unfamiliar concept "the virtuous agent." It is natural to assume that the virtuous person would never do what is dishonest, such as lying, or untrustworthy, such as breaking a promise, or disloyal, such as letting a friend down; that the compassionate would never intentionally cause anyone great suffering. But as soon as we think of certain examples, we realise that that's a mistake. In *some* circumstances, they *do* do such things. They do not do them typically or willingly or cheerily (as people who are dishonest, untrustworthy, disloyal, etc. do); they regret that circumstances have made it necessary; and afterwards they look around for ways to make up for what circumstances have compelled them to do, but they do *do* them—and it is no poor reflection on their virtue.

Consult your own understanding of what it means to be a trustworthy and loyal person. You have a friend you think is both, so when he fails to keep his promise to come to your birthday party you are surprised. If you really believe he is trustworthy and loyal, will you not expect that he must have had a good reason for breaking it? And when he rings up the next day to apologise and explain about the mugger, will you not find your expectation confirmed?

We understand that even the trustworthy and loyal may do such things as break promises because we understand the virtue and vice words—we grasp what is involved in having the individual virtues and thereby the sorts of reasons for which, in particular circumstances, people with those character traits do the things they do. Even quite small children can come to understand that trustworthy people do not always keep their promises. Although they begin by saying, in tearful outrage, "But you *promised!*" they learn that their parents, and others, can be good, trustworthy people despite their occasional defaulting (assuming that they are being brought up by fairly decent parents who do not default improperly and who take time to explain the defaults). So in the straightforward cases, even quite a young child can see that the circumstances in which a promise is broken can give a good person compelling reason to break it.

Similarly, small children often do not understand why their parents hush their tactless remarks. "But it's the *truth!*" they say. "He *is* fat." But, as they begin to acquire good manners, tact, considerateness, kindness, they learn that, just as trustworthy people sometimes break their word, honest people do not always volunteer the truth. Think of the sort of person who says "I speak as I find" and "I believe in calling a spade a spade" and whose word you dread when they say (as they typically do) "I hope you won't mind my saying this, BUT . . ." I would not describe such a person as having the virtue of honesty, but, instead, as being brutally frank or candid. Candour is not a true virtue, because being an honest person is not incompatible with being a discreet, tactful, considerate, kind person.

Is honesty compatible with being a con man? No. Is it compatible with being a magician? Yes, even though deception is a magician's trade. Is it compatible with being "economical with the truth"? In some circumstances yes, in others no—when, for example, parsimony with the truth involves being phoney, sneaky, manipulative, or hypocritical.

How do we know all of this? Because a great deal of our moral knowledge—our understanding of which *particular* actions, done in the very circumstances in which they are done, are what a virtuous person would do or would not do—is, unconsciously, stored in our ordinary virtue and vice words. We started to acquire the knowledge as we learnt to use the words, and, as we get older and more experienced, we learn to use them with greater nuance and subtlety. And this is the beginning of practical wisdom—an understanding, applicable in particular circumstances, of what is involved in being an honest, trustworthy, considerate, . . . virtuous person. So here is a large part of what the person with *phronesis* knows—he really knows, as we begin to know as we grow up, what is involved in having the virtues, and this knowledge is part of what enables him to reason correctly about what it is right to do.

Consider another example. When I was very small, I thought my mother was being mean and unkind when she made me go to bed early (I was a sickly child, and often convalescent); but as I grew older, I realised this was not so. If I had known the words, I would have said she was being responsible and loving, and "doing me a kindness" by sending me to bed. And later I learnt the point of the expression "being cruel to be kind."

With this expression, we begin to enter the territory of difficult cases. As we saw, following the prescriptions "Do what is honest" and "Do not do what is dishonest" does not demand one tells the rude, inconsiderate, or unkind truth. In many circumstances, you can look for a nicer truth to tell, or remain discreetly silent. But there are other circumstances in which virtuous agents have to tell the truth. Honest and responsible judges on talent shows faced with aspirants who lack talent, people breaking off relationships that are going nowhere, doctors with patients whose tests show they are in urgent need of a somewhat risky operation, professors with mature students who dream of becoming philosophers but are not capable of postgraduate study, tell the truth and cause those on the receiving end bitter grief. Have they done what is honest but unkind or cruel or callous?

I deny that characterisation. In all these cases (in most of the circumstances in which they occur), I would say one does the recipients no kindness in concealing the truth from them. It is a shattering truth they need to know, and, in those circumstances, the only way to do what is kind is to convey it in a considerate and sensitive way. Judges of talent shows who make the audience laugh at the talentless are being cruel, and doctors and professors who just state the truth baldly without easing the recipient into a dawning realisation of what it is going to be are being insensitive and inconsiderate. (Breaking off relationships is *really* tricky. I read of someone who did it cruelly with the intention of making her partner hate her, because she thought that would make it easier for him, and I can imagine circumstances in which that would be the kindest way to do it.)

You may notice that the reasoning in the paragraph above involves a judgement about "the sort of truth that one does people no kindness in concealing, because they need to know it." What sort of truth is that? Truths that are about something important, the sort of thing that really matters in life? But then, what is "important," and what "really matters" in that way? If you have no idea, and could not understand the above paragraph, then I cannot help you. I have to rely on your knowledgeable uptake. In so doing, I am relying on your having some moral wisdom.

Now we can see why Aristotle, making the first point about *phronesis* I mentioned above, says that it is impossible without virtue. Someone who isn't at all concerned about doing what is right but only in having a good time or exercising power or making a lot of money is not going to be at all interested in acquiring the virtues, and hence will not develop an understanding of them, and his ideas of what is important or really matters in life (lots of pleasure or power or money) are going to be quite different from those of someone who is (at least fairly) virtuous. Someone who is concerned but has been corrupted by a bad upbringing or an immoral culture will have a distorted idea of the virtues and some terrible ideas about what is important and thereby reason incorrectly again and again. (Think of how corrupting racism has been and still is. Racists who are conscientious about not breaking promises, or lying, to members of their own race will cheerfully do it to those against whom they are bigoted and not think that they, or their fellow members, show themselves to be dishonest or untrustworthy in doing so. They think what race someone is is a really important thing about them, and that "keeping those people in their place" really matters in life.)

So here is another large part of what people with *phronesis* know (which is inseparable from their knowledge of what is involved in the virtues); such people know what is truly important in life, what matters, what is worthwhile. That knowledge too is part of what enables the person with *phronesis* to reason correctly about what it is right to do.

The second thing Aristotle says about *phronesis* is that it comes only with age and experience. This is what makes "practical wisdom" a good translation—we do not think of the young and inexperienced as having practical wisdom, however good they are, only those who can draw on a rich experience of life. So what difference does experience make to reasoning correctly about what to do?

When we are reasoning about what to do, aiming for a correct moral decision which we will then act upon, we are always trying to find what it would be right to do *in these circumstances*, in *this* situation. But if we are to succeed, we need to get "the situation" right; if we make a mistake about it, taking it to be thus and so when it isn't, we will reach a correct decision only by happy accident. Only through age and experience, learning from our own and others' mistakes, do we become good at knowing what "the situation" is.

The inexperienced frequently make mistakes about, for example, what other people are feeling. Taking the smiling front at face value, they do not see that the other person is hurt, or uncertain, angry, frightened, or worried; or they see shiftiness or arrogance where the more experienced see embarrassment. Often, "the situation" is not something right in front of you, but you have to ask around to find out what is going on; the inexperienced are not expert at assessing the reliability of what other people say. Sometimes they are too gullible in accepting someone else's account, instead of thinking "But he *couldn't* know all that" or "That's the sort of thing people often make mistakes, or conceal the truth, about"; sometimes they are too incredulous, unable to recognise someone else's expertise or sincerity. And so they misjudge the situation. Sometimes they don't even recognise the situation for what it is. (This frequently happens when we encounter other cultures, which is why one should be circumspect as a tourist and try to gain some secondhand experience from books of what might be offensive before one travels.) When we do not get the situation right, we cannot reason correctly about what it is right to do in *it*. But the person with *phronesis* does reason correctly. So she has the sort of knowledge, born of experience, which enables her not to make these sorts of mistakes; this knowledge we call, in general terms, knowledge of people or human nature.

Getting the situation right, and reaching a correct decision about what to do in a general way, still isn't enough for the virtuous agent. Suppose I am right that a person urgently needs to understand he is in a life-threatening situation, or that this other person needs help, or that this one has been insulted, or that we are all in danger. Suppose I correctly decide that I must tell the truth, must help, must right the wrong of the insult, must risk myself getting us out of the danger. But *how?* The devil is in the details, and if I lack experience, I may well make the wrong decision about *how* to do what is right, and hence wind up not doing it at all. Again, the person with *phronesis* does reason correctly. So again, she has the sort of knowledge, born of experience, which enables her not to make these sorts of mistakes. She possesses a sort of general know-how about what works and what doesn't in life.

This practical knowledge—both of people and of what works and doesn't—is in *part* worldly knowledge which successfully cunning and wicked people have too; you can't be an effective con man or tyrant without it. But part of it is knowledge that can only be gained by the virtuous; the wicked do not, for example, know what love and trust can do for people and wouldn't know how to set about using that knowledge if they had it.

There is more to the knowledge someone with *phronesis* has than that which I have sketched above, but I will leave the topic here and conclude with the third thing Aristotle says about *phronesis*. It is that you can't have *perfect* virtue without it. And we have just seen why. Insofar as we lack *phronesis* we mess things up, notwithstanding our virtuous intentions. We intend to convey the truth but blurt it out so brutally that the other person can't take it in; we intend to help, but we harm; we intend to right a wrong, but we compound it; we intend to save the day, and we make things worse. We don't reason correctly about what to do. So we do not do what a perfectly virtuous agent would do.

Looking back, we see that you can't have *phronesis* without having virtue and you can't have virtue without having *phronesis*. "They" turn out to be the same thing viewed from different aspects, two sides of the same coin. "It" is what we need to develop and improve if we are to reason correctly about what is right. Moral philosophers' theories may help us on the way, but there is no shortcut to virtue, and hence none to *phronesis*.

TEST YOUR UNDERSTANDING

1. Which of the following is the best translation of *phronesis*?

   a. courage

   b. rightness

   c. moral wisdom

   d. happiness

2. Is virtue ethics concerned with formulating and applying abstract moral principles?

3. According to Hursthouse's conception of virtue ethics, can one be a moral expert without also being a morally good person?

4. Why does Aristotle think that young people will not possess *phronesis*?

   a. They do not respect their elders.

   b. They do not have enough lived experience to identify the morally relevant features of the situations they find themselves in.

   c. They have not had a chance to make mistakes and to learn from them.

   d. Both (b) and (c).

NOTES AND QUESTIONS

1. What is a virtue and what is a vice? Give an example of each. Why does Hursthouse deny that beauty and health are virtues?

2. According to Hursthouse, how do we come to learn what the virtues are and what the virtuous person would do?

3. *What if the virtuous person is uncertain?* Is it possible on Hursthouse's view for a virtuous person to be uncertain about what to do in difficult circumstances? Shouldn't moral philosophy be able to offer him more specific counsel than to tell him that he should act as the virtuous person would act? How do you think Hursthouse might respond to this complaint?

4. *Is virtue ethics circular?* How do you think Hursthouse would answer the following objection?

   > To know what the virtuous person would do, we need to know what the right thing to do is. We don't have any clear, independent sense of what virtuous people do other than knowing that they regularly do the right thing. So, it is not helpful when one is uncertain about what to do to direct us to consider what the virtuous person would do.

Friedrich Nietzsche (1844–1900)

Nietzsche was a German philosopher and classical philologist who taught at the University of Basel. Most famous for his works on aesthetics, moral philosophy, philosophy of religion, and philosophy of science, Nietzsche is well known for his cutting criticism of systematic philosophy and his unusual argumentative style that makes heavy use of metaphor, poetry, and aphorism. His numerous books include *The Birth of Tragedy* (1872), *The Gay Science* (1882), *Thus Spoke Zarathustra* (1885), *Beyond Good and Evil* (1887), *On the Genealogy of Morals* (1887), and *Ecce Homo* (1888).

ON THE GENEALOGY OF MORALS

6

We need a *critique* of moral values, *the value of these values themselves must first be called in question*—and for that there is needed a knowledge of the conditions and circumstances in which they grew, under which they evolved and changed (morality as consequence, as symptom, as mask, as tartufferie,[1] as illness, as misunderstanding; but also morality as cause, as remedy, as stimulant, as restraint, as poison), a knowledge of a kind that has never yet existed or even been desired. One has taken the *value* of these "values" as given, as factual, as beyond all question; one has hitherto never doubted or hesitated in the slightest degree in supposing "the good man" to be of greater value than "the evil man," of greater value in the sense of furthering the advancement and prosperity of man in general (the future of man included). But what if the reverse were true? What if a symptom of regression were inherent in the "good," likewise a danger, a seduction, a poison, a narcotic, through which the present was possibly living *at the expense of the future*? . . . So that precisely morality would be to blame if the *highest power and splendor* actually possible to the type man was never in fact attained? . . .

BEYOND GOOD AND EVIL

257

Every enhancement of the type "man" has so far been the work of an aristocratic so-ciety—and it will be so again and again—a society that believes in the long ladder of an order of rank and differences in value between man and man, and that needs slavery

---

1. By "tartufferie," Nietzsche means "hypocrisy." The term was coined for the main character in *Tartuffe* by the French playwright Molière (1622–1673): Tartuffe falsely but convincingly appears to be a religiously pious person and gains power because of that appearance.

in some sense or other. Without that *pathos of distance* which grows out of the ingrained difference between strata—when the ruling caste constantly looks afar and looks down upon subjects and instruments and just as constantly practices obedience and command, keeping down and keeping at a distance—that other, more mysterious pathos could not have grown up either—the craving for an ever new widening of distances within the soul itself the development of ever higher, rarer, more remote, further-stretching, more comprehensive states—in brief, simply the enhancement of the type "man," the continual "self-overcoming of man," to use a moral formula in a supra-moral sense.

To be sure, one should not yield to humanitarian illusions about the origins of an aristocratic society (and thus of the presupposition of this enhancement of the type "man"): truth is hard. Let us admit to ourselves, without trying to be considerate, how every higher culture on earth so far has *begun*. Human beings whose nature was still natural, barbarians in every terrible sense of the word, men of prey who were still in possession of unbroken strength of will and lust for power, hurled themselves upon weaker, more civilized, more peaceful races, perhaps traders or cattle raisers, or upon mellow old cultures whose last vitality was even then flaring up in splendid fireworks of spirit and corruption. . . .

258

Corruption as the expression of a threatening anarchy among the instincts and of the fact that the foundation of the affects, which is called "life," has been shaken: corruption is something totally different depending on the organism in which it appears. When, for example, an aristocracy, like that of France at the beginning of the Revolution,[2] throws away its privileges with a sublime disgust and sacrifices itself to an extravagance of its own moral feelings, that is corruption; it was really only the last act of that centuries-old corruption which had led them to surrender, step by step, their governmental prerogatives, demoting themselves to a mere *function* of the monarchy (finally even to a mere ornament and showpiece). The essential characteristic of a good and healthy aristocracy, however, is that it experiences itself *not* as a function (whether of the monarchy or the commonwealth) but as their *meaning* and highest justification—that it therefore accepts with a good conscience the sacrifice of untold human beings who, *for its sake*, must be reduced and lowered to incomplete human beings, to slaves, to instruments. Their fundamental faith simply has to be that society must *not* exist for society's sake but only as the foundation and scaffolding on which a choice type of being is able to raise itself to its higher task and to a higher state of *being*—comparable to those sun-seeking vines of Java . . . that so long and so often enclasp an oak tree with their tendrils until eventually, high above it but supported by it, they can unfold their crowns in the open light and display their happiness.

---

2. Nietzsche refers to the French Revolution (1789–1799) in which a popular movement inspired by egalitarian ideals overthrew an entrenched monarchy and its supportive aristocracy.

259

Refraining mutually from injury, violence, and exploitation and placing one's will on a par with that of someone else—this may become, in a certain rough sense, good manners among individuals if the appropriate conditions are present (namely, if these men are actually similar in strength and value standards and belong together in *one* body). But as soon as this principle is extended, and possibly even accepted as the *fundamental principle of society,* it immediately proves to be what it really is—a will to the *denial* of life, a principle of disintegration and decay.

Here we must beware of superficiality and get to the bottom of the matter, resisting all sentimental weakness: life itself is *essentially* appropriation, injury, overpowering of what is alien and weaker; suppression, hardness, imposition of one's own forms, incorporation and at least, at its mildest, exploitation. . . .

Even the body within which individuals treat each other as equals, as suggested before—and this happens in every healthy aristocracy—if it is a living and not a dying body, has to do to other bodies what the individuals within it refrain from doing to each other: it will have to be an incarnate will to power, it will strive to grow, spread, seize, become predominant—not from any morality or immorality but because it is living and because life simply is will to power. . . . [E]verywhere people are now raving, even under scientific disguises, about coming conditions of society in which "the exploitative aspect" will be removed—which sounds to me as if they promised to invent a way of life that would dispense with all organic functions. "Exploitation" does not belong to a corrupt or imperfect and primitive society: it belongs to the essence of what lives, as a basic organic function; it is a consequence of the will to power, which is after all the will of life. . . .

260

Wandering through the many subtler and coarser moralities which have so far been prevalent on earth, or still are prevalent, I found that certain features recurred regularly together and were closely associated—until I finally discovered two basic types and one basic difference.

There are *master morality* and *slave morality*—I add immediately that in all the higher and more mixed cultures there also appear attempts at mediation between these two moralities, and yet more often the interpenetration and mutual misunderstanding of both, and at times they occur directly alongside each other—even in the same human being, within a *single* soul. The moral discrimination of values has originated either among a ruling group whose consciousness of its difference from the ruled group was accompanied by delight—or among the ruled, the slaves and dependents of every degree.

In the first case, when the ruling group determines what is "good," the exalted, proud states of the soul are experienced as conferring distinction and determining the order of rank. The noble human being separates from himself those in whom the opposite of such exalted, proud states finds expression: he despises them. It should be noted immediately that in this first type of morality the opposition of "good" and "bad" means approximately the same as "noble" and "contemptible." (The opposition of "good" and "*evil*" has a different origin.) One feels contempt for the cowardly, the anxious, the petty, those latent on narrow utility; also for the suspicious with their unfree glances, those who humble themselves, the doglike people who allow themselves to be maltreated, the begging flatterers, above all the liars: it is part of the fundamental faith of all aristocrats that the common people lie. "We truthful ones"—thus the nobility of ancient Greece referred to itself.

It is obvious that moral designations were everywhere first applied to *human beings* and only later, derivatively, to actions. Therefore it is a gross mistake when historians of morality start from such questions as: why was the compassionate act praised? The noble type of man experiences *itself* as determining values; it does not need approval; it judges, "what is harmful to me is harmful in itself"; it knows itself to be that which first accords honor to things; it is *value-creating*. Everything it knows as part of itself it honors: such a morality is self-glorification. In the foreground there is the feeling of fullness, of power that seeks to overflow, the happiness of high tension, the consciousness of wealth that would give and bestow: the noble human being, too, helps the unfortunate, but not, or almost not, from pity, but prompted more by an urge begotten by excess of power. The noble human being honors himself as one who is powerful, also as one who has power over himself, who knows how to speak and be silent, who delights in being severe and hard with himself and respects all severity and hardness. . . . Such a type of man is actually proud of the fact that he is *not* made for pity. . . . Noble and courageous human beings who think that way are furthest removed from that morality which finds the distinction of morality precisely in pity, or in acting for others, or in *désintéressement*[3]; faith in oneself, pride in oneself, a fundamental hostility and irony against "selflessness" belong just as definitely to noble morality as does a slight disdain and caution regarding compassionate feelings and a "warm heart."

. . . A morality of the ruling group, however, is most alien and embarrassing to the present taste in the severity of its principle that one has duties only to one's peers; that against beings of a lower rank, against everything alien, one may behave as one pleases or "as the heart desires," and in any case "beyond good and evil"—here pity and like feelings may find their place. The capacity for, and the duty of, long gratitude and long revenge—both only among one's peers—refinement in repaying, the sophisticated concept of friendship, a certain necessity for having enemies (as it were, as drainage ditches for the affects of envy, quarrelsomeness, exuberance—at bottom, in order to be capable of being good friends): all these are typical characteristics of noble morality which, as suggested, is not the morality of "modern ideas" and therefore is hard to empathize with today. . . .

It is different with the second type of morality, *slave morality*. Suppose the violated, oppressed, suffering, unfree, who are uncertain of themselves and weary, moralize: what

---

3. A French word meaning "disinterestedness" or "unselfishness."

will their moral valuations have in common? Probably, a pessimistic suspicion about the whole condition of man will find expression, perhaps a condemnation of man along with his condition. The slave's eye is not favorable to the virtues of the powerful: he is skeptical and suspicious, *subtly* suspicious, of all the "good" that is honored there—he would like to persuade himself that even their happiness is not genuine. Conversely, those qualities are brought out and flooded with light which serve to ease existence for those who suffer: here pity, the complaisant and obliging hand, the warm heart, patience, industry, humility, and friendliness are honored—for here these are the most useful qualities and almost the only means for enduring the pressure of existence. Slave morality is essentially a morality of utility.

Here is the place for the origin of that famous opposition of "good" and "evil": into evil one's feelings project power and dangerousness, a certain terribleness, subtlety, and strength that does not permit contempt to develop. According to slave morality, those who are "evil" thus inspire fear; according to master morality it is precisely those who are "good" that inspire, and wish to inspire, fear, while the "bad" are felt to be contemptible.

The opposition reaches its climax when, as a logical consequence of slave morality, a touch of disdain is associated also with the "good" of this morality—this may be slight and benevolent—because the good human being has to be *undangerous* in the slaves' way of thinking: he is good-natured, easy to deceive, a little stupid perhaps. . . . Wherever slave morality becomes preponderant, language tends to bring the words "good" and "stupid" closer together.

One last fundamental difference: the longing for *freedom*, the instinct for happiness and the subtleties of the feeling of freedom belong just as necessarily to slave morality and morals as artful and enthusiastic reverence and devotion are the regular symptom of an aristocratic way of thinking and evaluating.

This makes plain why love *as passion*—which is our European specialty—simply must be of noble origin: as is well known, its invention must be credited to the Provençal knight-poets, those magnificent and inventive human beings of the *"gai saber"*[4] [Gay Science] to whom Europe owes so many things and almost owes itself.—

261

Among the things that may be hardest to understand for a noble human being is vanity: he will be tempted to deny it, where another type of human being could not find it more palpable. The problem for him is to imagine people who seek to create a good opinion of themselves which they do not have of themselves—and thus also do not "deserve"—and who nevertheless end up *believing* this good opinion themselves. This strikes him half as such bad taste and lack of self-respect, and half as so baroquely

---

4. This term refers to the art and technique of fourteenth-century troubadours, who combined music, dance, and poetry.

is continually ready for revenge, and we others will be his victims, if only by having to endure his ugly sight. . . .

301

The fancy of the contemplatives.—What distinguishes the higher human beings from the lower is that the former see and hear immeasurably more, and see and hear thoughtfully—and precisely this distinguishes human beings from animals, and the higher animals from the lower. For anyone who grows up into the heights of humanity the world becomes ever fuller; ever more fishhooks are cast in his direction to capture his interest; the number of things that stimulate him grows constantly, as does the number of different kinds of pleasure and displeasure: The higher human being always becomes at the same time happier and unhappier. But he can never shake off a *delusion*: He fancies that he is a *spectator* and *listener* who has been placed before the great visual and acoustic spectacle that is life; he calls his own nature *contemplative* and overlooks that he himself is really the poet who keeps creating this life. . . . We who think and feel at the same time are those who really continually *fashion* something that had not been there before: the whole eternally growing world of valuations, colors, accents, perspectives, scales, affirmations, and negations. This poem that we have invented is continually studied by the so-called practical human beings (our actors) who learn their roles and translate everything into flesh and actuality, into the everyday. Whatever has *value* in our world now does not have value in itself, according to its nature—nature is always value-less, but has been *given* value at some time, as a present—and it was *we* who gave and bestowed it. Only we have created the world *that concerns man!*—But precisely this knowledge we lack, and when we occasionally catch it for a fleeting moment we always forget it again immediately. . . .

304

By doing we forego.—At bottom I abhor all those moralities which say: "Do not do this! Renounce! Overcome yourself!" But I am well disposed toward those moralities which goad me to do something and do it again, from morning till evening, and then to dream of it at night, and to think of nothing except doing this *well,* as well as *I* alone can do it. When one lives like that, one thing after another that simply does not belong to such a life drops off. . . . He may not even notice that it takes its leave; for his eye is riveted to his goal—forward, not sideward, backward, downward. What we do should determine what we forego; by doing we forego. . . . But I do not wish to strive with open eyes for my own impoverishment; I do not like negative virtues—virtues whose very essence it is to negate and deny oneself something. . . .

338

The will to suffer and those who feel pity.—Is it good for you yourselves to be above all full of pity? And is it good for those who suffer? But let us leave the first question unanswered for a moment.

Our personal and profoundest suffering is incomprehensible and inaccessible to almost everyone; here we remain hidden from our neighbor, even if we eat from one pot. But whenever people *notice* that we suffer, they interpret our suffering superficially. It is the very essence of the emotion of pity that it strips away from the suffering of others whatever is distinctively personal. Our "benefactors" are, more than our enemies, people who make our worth and will smaller. When people try to benefit someone in distress, the intellectual frivolity with which those moved by pity assume the role of fate is for the most part outrageous; one simply knows nothing of the whole inner sequence and intricacies that are distress for *me* or for *you*. The whole economy of my soul and the balance effected by "distress," the way new springs and needs break open, the way in which old wounds are healing, the way whole periods of the past are shed—all such things that may be involved in distress are of no concern to our dear pitying friends; they wish to *help* and have no thought of the personal necessity of distress, although terrors, deprivations, impoverishments, midnights, adventures, risks, and blunders are as necessary for me and for you as are their opposites. It never occurs to them that, to put it mystically, the path to one's own heaven always leads through the voluptuousness of one's own hell. No, the "religion of pity" (or "the heart") commands them to help, and they believe that they have helped most when they have helped most quickly.

If you, who adhere to this religion, have the same attitude toward yourselves that you have toward your fellow men; if you refuse to let your own suffering lie upon you even for an hour and if you constantly try to prevent and forestall all possible distress way ahead of time; if you experience suffering and displeasure as evil, hateful, worthy of annihilation, and as a defect of existence, then it is clear that besides your religion of pity you also harbor another religion in your heart that is perhaps the mother of the religion of pity: the *religion of comfortableness.* How little you know of human *happiness,* you comfortable and benevolent people, for happiness and unhappiness are sisters and even twins that either grow up together or, as in your case, *remain small* together. But now back to the first question!

How is it at all possible to keep to one's own way? Constantly, some clamor or other calls us aside; rarely does our eye behold anything that does not require us to drop our own preoccupation instantly to help. I know, there are a hundred decent and praise-worthy ways of losing *my own way,* and they are truly highly "moral"! Indeed, those who now preach the morality of pity even take the view that precisely this and only this is moral—to lose one's *own* way in order to come to the assistance of a neighbor. I know just as certainly that I only need to expose myself to the sight of some genuine distress and am lost. . . . All such arousing of pity and calling for help is secretly seductive, for our "own way" is too hard and demanding and too remote from the love and gratitude of others, and we do not really mind escaping from it—and from our very own conscience—to flee into the conscience of the others and into the lovely temple of the "religion of pity."

. . . I do not want to remain silent about my morality which says to me: Live in seclusion so that you *can* live for yourself. Live in *ignorance* about what seems most important to your age. And the clamor of today, the noise of wars and revolutions should be a mere murmur for you. You will also wish to help—but only those whose distress you *understand* entirely because they share with you one suffering and one hope—your friends—and only in the manner in which you help yourself. I want to make them bolder, more persevering, simpler, gayer. I want to teach them what is understood by so few today, least of all by these preachers of pity: *to share not suffering but joy.*

TEST YOUR UNDERSTANDING

1. What are the two basic types of morality that Nietzsche distinguishes?

2. Does Nietzsche believe we should strive to reduce pain and suffering and to achieve the social conditions of equality?

3. Nietzsche says that "one thing is needful . . . to give style to one's character." What does he mean by giving style to one's character?

4. Nietzsche distinguishes the pairing good/bad and the pairing good/evil. Which pairing grows from slave morality and which grows from an aristocratic morality?

NOTES AND QUESTIONS

1. *Recasting epigrams into claims and arguments.* Nietzsche pursues a number of provocative **metaethical** and substantive claims that it may be helpful to separate and restate into more contemporary, straightforward language. Interpretation of Nietzsche is notoriously controversial. Do you agree that Nietzsche makes the claims outlined below?

   N1. To understand and evaluate our normative beliefs, we need to understand the sociological history of those beliefs. We must pursue a **genealogy of morals**. That is, to understand and evaluate normative principles and to use normative concepts (such as "good," "bad," and "evil"), we need to understand why people began to believe in those principles and to use those concepts. [GM 6]

   N2. Values are created and constructed, not discovered, by people. [GS 301]

   N3. Pursuing a genealogy of morals reveals that the values constructed by people were norms that served (a conception of) their interests.

   N4. "Bad" and "evil" are not synonymous. The paired concepts of "good" and "bad" arise from aristocratic culture, within which "good" represents a celebration of the traits of the strong. "Bad" represents their absence and a corresponding contempt for their absence. The quite contrary paired concepts of "good" and "evil" emanate from "slave morality," the values constructed by "the weak," reflecting their resentment toward their oppression. The morality of "good" and "evil" was constructed to serve the interests of the weak by representing the natural actions of the strong as wrong and by duping the strong to suppress their will to live and their natural instincts to dominate. The resentment of the weak leads them to champion selflessness and altruism not because those traits are good in themselves, but because celebrating them serves the interests of the weak, who are at risk for being the casualties of the strong. [BGE 259, 260]

N5. Most modern ethical theories presuppose some form of moral egalitarianism, the view that each person matters equally and should be treated equally. But, such egalitarianism is unnatural and stifles the life spirit. An appreciation of the differences between people and a hierarchical social system in which some dominate others are crucial conditions for particular individuals achieving the best that humanity is capable of. [BGE 257, 258, 259, 260]

N6. The values we endorse should not emanate from destructive and reactive character traits like resentment, guilt, and pity. We, especially we "higher human beings," should value the positive, joyful expression of the individual and seek to express ourselves fully. [BGE 260; GS 290, 301, 338]

N7. A moral theory that stresses meeting the needs of others and advances such prohibitions as *do not harm others* or *do not take more than your share* is constraining and self-denying. It fails because it does not articulate what, positively, each of us should pursue to achieve our fullest personal expression. [BGE 259; GS 304, 338]

N8. Ethical views that emphasize the prevention and alleviation of pain and suffering are mistaken. Suffering is often essential to achieving excellence within a human life and, therefore, real happiness. [GS 338]

2. Many of Nietzsche's claims will understandably strike modern readers as highly offensive, especially his claims about "higher" and "lower" human beings and the "need for slavery." Is it possible to reconstruct the crux of his argument while eliminating these offensive premises? Could one accept his metaethical position (e.g., claims N1 and N2 above) but reject his anti-egalitarianism? Could one argue for his substantive claims N6, N7, and N8 while rejecting his anti-egalitarianism in N4 and N5?

3. How do you think Nietzsche might respond to the following criticism of his genealogical method?

> Initially, I formed the belief not to cross the street without looking because my parents instructed me to do so and I wished to obey them. Of course, that I wished to obey my parents is not the *real* reason to look before crossing. I learned the multiplication tables first by being told they were true. I only later came to understand *why* 6 times 7 is 42. Generally, how and why I first came to believe something often differs from the best reason to believe that thing.

Explain the objection and craft a reply on behalf of Nietzsche.

ANALYZING THE ARGUMENTS

1. *The value of beneficence.* Most moral theories have, at their center, an argument about why we should help others in need. Nietzsche, however, calls into question whether we should attempt to relieve and prevent others' pain. Further, he argues that the imperatives to help others and to constrain the pursuit of our self-interest emanate from resentment by people who are frustrated with themselves and resent the success of others. Finding themselves at a disadvantage, they produce a moral code that condemns the strength and success of others.

   Exercise: Summarize, briefly, the positive arguments for helping others in need that Mill, Kant, Aristotle, and Hursthouse offer. How do their arguments differ? Do any of these arguments address Nietzsche's skepticism?

2. *When do numbers count?* Utilitarians contend that impartial respect for all requires that we aggregate the effects of our actions on everyone and select the action with the best outcome. Many criticize aggregative methods because they would be open to the implication that we should kill an innocent young person in order to harvest her organs to save six people in need of organ transplants. The case is meant to exemplify that aggregative methods entail the sacrifice of important interests of individuals when they conflict with the interests of the many. But many utilitarians criticize alternative theories as having difficulty explaining why if you could either save one drowning person or five drowning people, but not all six, you should not flip a coin or save the one. Rather, the numbers count. You should aggregate and save the five.

   Exercise: Explain how the two non-utilitarian theories you have read about (the Kantian view and the Aristotelian view) would handle the organ transplant problem and the problem of the drowning victims. Do these theories suggest we should never consider how many people we could help or is their criticism of forced organ harvesting more subtle?

3. *Outcomes versus explanation.* Often, moral theories will converge regarding what they recommend, but offer different reasons for their recommendations. For example, utilitarians may forswear violence to express anger because peaceful methods maximize utility while violence causes pain and trauma, whereas non-utilitarians may argue that violence is wrong because it shows disrespect for the autonomy and the rational capacities of the victim or because it violates rules that rational parties would not reasonably reject to govern their interactions.

   Exercise: Consider the objection that utilitarian theories fail reliably to condemn lying for personal convenience.

   a. *Formulate this objection as an objection that utilitarianism recommends the wrong action.*

   b. *Now imagine that the utilitarian can show that, as a matter of fact, because of how the facts about utility turn out, utilitarianism would condemn lying in all the same circumstances as a Kantian would. Reformulate the objection that utilitarianism does not reliably condemn lying for personal convenience as an objection that utilitarianism offers the wrong reasons for condemning lying for personal convenience.*

c. *Now formulate an objection by the utilitarian that contends that the Kantian offers the wrong reasons for condemning lying.*

d. *Finally, explain why, even when disputants concur about what to do, philosophers think it matters that an alternate moral theory offers the wrong reason for doing the right thing. What is at stake in getting the explanation right, as opposed to just producing the correct moral recommendation?*

4. Aristotle's view is that the virtuous person experiences no conflict between the rational and emotional parts of his soul. Aristotle sees the virtuous person as morally better than the "continent" person, who experiences conflict between the two parts of the soul, but makes the right choice in the end, in line with the correct judgment of the rational part of his soul. Seemingly in contrast, Kant sees actions as having great moral worth when they arise from recognition of duty alone, in the absence of any emotional desire to perform the right action.

Are these two views in conflict?

In objecting to Aristotle, we might point out that the continent man has managed to do the right thing despite having to struggle, whereas the right action of the virtuous person arises easily, without any internal struggle. Managing to do the right thing despite the struggle may seem particularly praiseworthy.

In objecting to Kant, we might point out that a person who feels no emotional pull to help her fellow creatures or to do right by them does not seem to be a morally good person, certainly not morally better than someone who does have such an emotional pull.

Does either of these objections succeed?

Is Morality Objective?

Morality in Life

Consider three hypothetical situations:

1. You clean up after your party and find your friend's wallet. It contains $100. She had told you she lost it while shopping. Because she is so confused, you are confident that you can keep it without her knowing. But you know you should not and instead return the wallet to her.

2. Someone breaks into your apartment and steals your laptop. Luckily you are insured. Still, you are annoyed at the inconvenience of getting a new one. But beyond the annoyance, you are indignant. You have not merely been inconvenienced; you have been wronged.

3. You want to buy a shirt. But you learn that the company that made it is hiring people desperate for work who will accept $5 per hour. Is it wrong to pay so little? The company did not put the people they are hiring in desperate circumstances. And the employees are better off taking the jobs than turning them down. But is the company exploiting vulnerabilities by paying so little? Are you complicit in the exploitation if you buy the shirt? You think about the issue and discuss it with friends. Maybe you decide that it is permissible to pay the low wage. Maybe you decide that they ought to pay more. In either case, you feel the force of the idea that you should not exploit vulnerability.

In each of these cases, you are concerned about what is right: about doing the right thing and about being treated rightly. That moral concern is part of our ordinary experience, woven into our thought, feeling, conversation, and action. It shows in your decision to return the wallet, your indignation at the person who has stolen your laptop, your pause about buying the shirt.

One aspect of that experience is that moral considerations, reasons, and requirements strike us as *objective*. Think about your friend's wallet. You ought to return it. That thought about what you ought to do—what anyone in your situation should do—does not strike you as an invention, or convention, or a matter of feeling and attitude. It is not like a local cultural rule against slurping your soup or eating peas with a knife. You ought to do it, whatever your feelings, beliefs, and social and cultural circumstances happen to be. At least that is how it strikes you.

Objective does not mean simple. Sometimes, as in the case of buying the shirt, moral questions are complicated. *Are* you complicit in exploiting vulnerability when you buy it? Or are you helping someone who is willing to take a job and would be better off if he took it? These considerations pull you in different directions. You need to think about the issue, not simply apply a crisp rule. But even when the questions get complicated, the considerations, reasons, and requirements do not strike you as optional.

In life, then, moral considerations present themselves as objective. But are they what they seem to be?

J. L. Mackie says "no." "There are," he says, "no objective values." Mackie agrees that we *experience* moral requirements—like the requirement to return the wallet—as objective. The objectivist understanding, he says, has "a firm basis in ordinary thought, and even in the meanings of moral terms." But this understanding is in error. The truth about morality, Mackie argues, is a "skepticism" or "subjectivism" that denies the objectivity of moral considerations, reasons, and requirements.

Philosophy and Life

Does it matter if morality is objective? The answer might seem obvious. If morality is not objective, then isn't it fine to do whatever you want? The answer is not so easy and is a subject of considerable philosophical disagreement.

To clarify the disagreement, let's distinguish *first-order* and *second-order* moral views. First-order moral views are claims about what you ought to do: you ought to return the wallet; you ought to keep your promises; you ought to do what maximizes human welfare; you ought to respect the autonomy of other people. Second-order moral views are claims about the nature of morality. The view that morality is objective is a second-order view, as is Mackie's moral skepticism. So, too, is Sharon Street's "mind-dependent" conception of value, according to which there are no truths about what is good or what is right that are independent of our attitudes.

One answer to the question about the importance of objectivity, then, is based on the claim that first-order and second-order views are completely independent from one another. Call this the *independence thesis*. According to the independence thesis, for example, moral subjectivism (a second-order view) has no implications for first-order moral views. Even if you are convinced of moral subjectivism, you should still think it is right to return the wallet and you should still return the wallet;

you just should not think that that requirement is objective. Mackie endorses the independence thesis. Philosophy, he believes, teaches us that morality is not really objective. But when we close our philosophy books, we should go about our lives just as before. We do not need to change our first-order moral views.

Critics of the independence thesis (including Thomas Nagel and Street) deny that we can neatly separate our first- and second-order views. Moral skepticism, they argue, undermines our first-order beliefs about what we ought to do.[1]

Suppose, for example, you believe that slavery is wrong—objectively wrong. Now imagine you are persuaded of the second-order view that the wrongness of slavery is not objective. You continue to think that slavery is wrong, but now you think, say, that the wrongness of slavery is a matter of attitude or social convention.

If, however, you think the wrongness is a matter of social convention, don't you also think that if social conventions approved of slavery, then slavery would be permissible? But you started out thinking that slavery would still be wrong even if people (mistakenly) thought it was right: even if social conventions endorsed slavery. So your first-order conviction that it is wrong seems to be in tension with the second-order idea that its wrongness is a matter of social convention.

If the independence thesis is true, then skepticism about moral objectivity is an interesting intellectual challenge to our second-order views about morality, though it does not have first-order, practical implications. If the independence thesis is false, then skepticism is consequential for how we should live.

So should we be skeptics or not about moral objectivity? Much of the philosophical debate about this question focuses on the merits of three arguments for skepticism—a *metaphysical argument*, a *motivational argument*, and an *argument from disagreement*.

The Metaphysical Argument

You think that returning the wallet is right. But you find yourself wondering whether it is *really* right. Not that you think *keeping* the wallet is right. Instead, you wonder whether any action is *really* right or wrong. Rightness, you think, is not something in the world.

The world includes social conventions, religious texts, parental admonitions, social pressures, traditions, and personal attitudes instructing you to return the wallet. But when you scrutinize the world, you do not detect rightness anywhere. These doubts are *metaphysical* because they arise from a concern about whether rightness is among the constituents of the world. "Permissibility, rightness, wrongness, or blameworthiness," as R. Jay Wallace says, "do not seem to correspond to any objects or properties in the natural world."

---

1. For a vigorous rejection of the independence thesis, see Ronald Dworkin, *Justice for Hedgehogs* (Harvard University Press, 2011), part 1.

The problem Wallace is pointing to is not that we have yet to locate rightness in the way that particle physicists had not located the Higgs particle until 2012. The physicists knew what they were looking for—a spin 0 particle that decays very fast into a variety of other particles—and how to look for it. The problem, according to the metaphysical argument, arises from the odd kind of property that *rightness* would need to be. It would have to be, Mackie says, a "to-be-doneness" that is present in an action, that imposes a demand on us, and that we can recognize through our powers of intuition and perception. How could there be such "intrinsic to-be-doneness"? The metaphysical argument says that the property is too bizarre to take seriously. (Mackie calls this the "argument from queerness.") Because there is no such property of moral rightness, morality is not objective.

Philip Quinn offers an account of moral objectivity that is unworried by this metaphysical concern. Quinn defends a variant of a divine command theory of morality. For the divine command theorist, the moral status of an action depends on its relationship to God's commands: moral rightness, for example, is a matter of conformity with God's commands. Quinn's divine intention theory is a little different. He thinks that moral rightness is a matter of conformity with God's intentions, even if those intentions are not expressed as commands. But his view shares with divine command theories the idea that moral rightness comes into the world with a divine act. More particularly, Quinn holds that it is necessarily true that, for example, murder is morally prohibited. That necessary truth is made true (and necessarily true) by the fact that God "strongly intends" that no one commit an act of murder.

Quinn does not, however, think that the property of being morally prohibited is identical to the property of being at odds with God's intentions. God's intentions bring about the differences in moral status between an act of murder and an act that is not murderous. But the property of being wrong is a distinct property from the property of violating God's intentions. Quinn leaves unexplained exactly what the property of wrongness is and how it can withstand Mackie's concerns about its metaphysical oddities.

Critics of the metaphysical argument think it is founded on a misconception about moral rightness. They say that what makes it right to return the wallet is not a special property possessed by the act of returning the wallet. When I think that I ought to return the wallet, I am thinking that a kind of reasoning supports my returning it. Nagel describes the reasoning as "impersonal" practical reasoning. When I reason impersonally, I stand back from my desires and circumstances and ask not just about me, but about what "*one should* do—and that means not just what *I* should do but what *this person* should do. The same answer should be given by anyone to whom the data are presented." I reflect on the rightness of the action by considering what the balance of reasons supports, given the circumstances.

This conception of moral thought as an exercise in impersonal practical reasoning arguably defuses the metaphysical argument for skepticism. It does not, however, provide any *assurance* of objectivity. We could pursue impersonal reasoning and find that it does not give any definite answers to practical questions. What it does tell us is that moral objectivity depends on where we are led by practical reasoning, not on the results of a metaphysical expedition.

Before considering the motivational argument for skepticism, notice that the availability of this conception of moral objectivity focused on impersonal practical reasoning prompts a question about what Sarah McGrath calls "the puzzle of moral deference." Deferring to the moral judgments of others is strange, McGrath observes: not the kind of thing we recommend or even approve of. But if we think that morality is objective, *why* is deference strange? That is the puzzle of moral deference: if morality is objective, why shouldn't we defer to experts, as we do in other areas where we think there is objective knowledge?

McGrath's statement of the puzzle presents the idea of moral objectivity as part of a moral realist outlook, with mind-independent moral facts. Does the puzzle of moral deference depend on the view that moral facts are entirely mind-independent? Perhaps not. Perhaps we can reformulate McGrath's puzzle of moral deference to fit with the idea that objective moral judgments are the judgments that emerge from impersonal practical reasoning. Assume, then, that some people are much better at impersonal practical reasoning than others. They are the moral experts. And now we can ask whether, if there are such experts—such great impersonal practical reasoners—what could be wrong with deferring to them? If we accept Nagel's conception of moral objectivity, is moral deference weird?

Motivational Argument

Suppose you are tempted to keep your friend's wallet. You pause, think about it, conclude that you ought to return it, and hand it over. How does this work? How does the thought that an action is right motivate you to do it? Can a thought alone have that practical effect?

The questions are prompted by the observation that thoughts alone do not typically issue in action. When you are thirsty and drink some water, you do not drink simply because you have the belief that your body needs water. There is a thirst: an *urge* or *impulse* or *desire* to drink. The belief that you need water alone does not suffice. Is that really right? Suppose your doctor tells you to drink even when you have no thirst. Even then, it is not the belief alone that results in drinking. There also needs to be a desire to be healthy.

Suppose it is the same with morality. When you decide to return the wallet, what really happens is that you have formed a desire to return the wallet: that—not the thought that it is right—explains why you return it. This line of thinking leads to the "subjectivism" about morality that Wallace explores. The subjectivist argues that when I say "I ought to give back the wallet," what I am doing is revealing my desire to return the wallet. Having the conviction that I ought to return it is really a matter of having a desire to return it. That explains how morality motivates. And the explanation deprives morality of a claim to objectivity.

Is the subjectivist right in thinking that moral thought is really a matter of feelings and desires? Suppose the wallet left at my party belongs to a stranger. I wonder if I should return it. I need $100. I did not invite the stranger. I am annoyed that he came. He was a pain. All my feelings are negative. I don't want to give the wallet back. But I think that I ought to and that all my feelings are leading me astray. Can subjectivism make sense of this thought, which stands opposed to my feelings about returning the wallet? "The challenge," as Wallace says, "is to explain how we can achieve critical distance from our motivating attitudes, within a framework that understands moral thought essentially in terms of those attitudes."

These observations about "critical distance" may create troubles for the subjectivist criticism of moral objectivity. But they do not solve the puzzle about how morality motivates. One line of response urges that moral thoughts *do* motivate without depending on prior attitudes and desires: that I can be motivated to return the wallet simply by the thought that returning it is the right thing to do. Nagel and Wallace suggest this line of argument, pointing to parallels between moral motivation and the motivation to act in ways that promote our long-term happiness.

Argument from Disagreement

In 1864, Abraham Lincoln wrote: "If slavery is not wrong, then nothing is wrong." Lincoln thought that slavery was objectively wrong. He did not simply think that he hated it or that his party or section of the country opposed it. But Lincoln knew well that this judgment was not universally embraced. Southerners in the United States did not share it. Nor did Aristotle. He was a deeply reflective person, and he did not think that slavery is wrong.[2] This diversity of moral convictions may suggest problems for moral objectivity. If morality is objective, why do we not see more convergence in judgments? Mackie suggests that the persistent diversity of moral judgments undercuts their objectivity. Diverse moral standards reflect different "ways of life," he says. They are not insights into what is morally required.

Nagel and Elizabeth Harman resist this step from moral disagreement to lack of moral objectivity. Nagel says that facts about moral disagreement do not undermine impersonal moral reasoning; instead, they provide additional materials for such reasoning to wrestle with. Similarly, Harman resists the idea that when we find someone we disagree with about a specific ethical claim, we should suspend our judgment about the claim (even if the person is our "epistemic peer," as good an ethical judge as we are). The mere fact that others disagree does not suffice to turn a justified belief into an unjustified belief. Whatever reasons you had for holding the belief remain undisturbed by the fact of disagreement. Of course, you might want to consider the reasons that others have for holding their conflicting

---

2. In the first book of his *Politics*, Aristotle says that some people are by nature slaves (*Politics*, book I, chapter 5).

moral beliefs. And perhaps their reasons will lead you to change your mind. But the discovery of disagreement by itself is an invitation to pursue moral reasoning, not a demonstration that your view is wrong or that moral reasoning is pointless or bound to end inconclusively. Lincoln knew well that some people disagreed with him about the morality of slavery. He thought they were wrong. In addition, he thought he could defend his view with forceful arguments.

So we should be cautious about jumping too quickly from observed disagreements to the relativist idea that what is right for them and what is right for us are different. Nagel and Harman converge here. We experience moral requirements as objective. But are they really objective? We will not find the answer in second-order arguments about the nature of moral thought. The only way to answer this question is to do the hard work of substantive, first-order, moral reflection—to think about what you ought to do, consider the conflicting judgments of others, and see whether your moral thinking leads to compelling conclusions. If it does, then you have a strong case for moral objectivity.

J. L. Mackie (1917–1981)

Mackie was born in Sydney, Australia. He taught in New Zealand, Australia, and England and ended his teaching career as a fellow at University College, Oxford. A skeptically minded empiricist, Mackie made important contributions to metaphysics (*The Cement of the Universe* [1980]), philosophy of religion (*The Miracle of Theism* [1983]), and metaethics.

THE SUBJECTIVITY OF VALUES
from *Ethics: Inventing Right and Wrong*

1. Moral Scepticism

There are no objective values. . . .

The claim that values are not objective, are not part of the fabric of the world, is meant to include not only moral goodness, which might be most naturally equated with moral value, but also other things that could be more loosely called moral values or disvalues—rightness and wrongness, duty, obligation, an action's being rotten and contemptible, and so on. It also includes non-moral values, notably aesthetic ones, beauty and various kinds of artistic merit. . . .

Since it is with moral values that I am primarily concerned, the view I am adopting may be called moral scepticism. But this name is likely to be misunderstood: "moral scepticism" might also be used as a name for either of two first order views, or perhaps for an incoherent mixture of the two. A moral sceptic might be the sort of person who says "All this talk of morality is tripe," who rejects morality and will take no notice of it. Such a person may be literally rejecting all moral judgements; he is more likely to be making moral judgements of his own, expressing a positive moral condemnation of all that conventionally passes for morality; or he may be confusing these two logically incompatible views, and saying that he rejects all morality, while he is in fact rejecting only a particular morality that is current in the society in which he has grown up. But I am not at present concerned with the merits or faults of such a position. These are first order moral views, positive or negative: the person who adopts either of them is taking a certain practical, normative, stand. By contrast, what I am discussing is a second order view, a view about the status of moral values and the nature of moral valuing, about where and how they fit into the world. These first and second order views are not merely distinct but completely independent: one could be a second order moral sceptic without being a first order one, or again the other way round. A man could hold strong moral views, and indeed ones whose content was thoroughly conventional, while believing that they were simply attitudes and policies with regard to conduct that he and other people held. Conversely, a man could reject all established morality while believing it to be an objective truth that it was evil or corrupt. . . .

2. Subjectivism

Another name often used, as an alternative to "moral scepticism," for the view I am discussing is "subjectivism." But this too has more than one meaning. Moral subjectivism too could be a first order, normative, view, namely that everyone really ought to do whatever he thinks he should. This plainly is a (systematic) first order view; on examination it soon ceases to be plausible, but that is beside the point, for it is quite independent of the second order thesis at present under consideration. What is more confusing is that different second order views compete for the name "subjectivism." Several of these are doctrines about the meaning of moral terms and moral statements. What is often called moral subjectivism is the doctrine that, for example, "This action is right" *means* "I approve of this action," or more generally that moral judgements are equivalent to reports of the speaker's own feelings or attitudes. But the view I am now discussing is to be distinguished in two vital respects from any such doctrine as this. First, what I have called moral scepticism is a negative doctrine, not a positive one: it says what there isn't, not what there is. It says that there do not exist entities or relations of a certain kind, objective values or requirements, which many people have believed to exist. Of course, the moral sceptic cannot leave it at that. If his position is to be at all plausible, he must give some account of how other people have fallen into what he regards as an error, and this account will have to include some positive suggestions about how values fail to be objective, about what has been mistaken for, or has led to false beliefs about, objective values. But this will be a development of his theory, not its core: its core is the negation. Secondly, what I have called moral scepticism is an ontological thesis, not a linguistic or conceptual one. It is not, like the other doctrine often called moral subjectivism, a view about the meanings of moral statements. . . .

The denial that there are objective values does not commit one to any particular view about what moral statements mean, and certainly not to the view that they are equivalent to subjective reports. . . .

4. Is Objectivity a Real Issue?

The main tradition of European moral philosophy from Plato onwards has combined the view that moral values are objective with the recognition that moral judgements are partly prescriptive or directive or action-guiding. Values themselves have been seen as at once prescriptive and objective. In Plato's theory the Forms, and in particular the Form of the Good, are eternal, extra-mental, realities.[1] They are a very central structural element in the fabric of the world. But it is held also that just knowing them or "seeing" them will not merely tell men what to do but will ensure that they do it, overruling any contrary inclinations. The philosopher-kings in the *Republic* can, Plato thinks, be trusted with unchecked power because their education will have given them knowledge of the Forms. Being acquainted with the Forms of the Good and Justice and Beauty and the rest they will, by this knowledge alone, without any further motivation, be impelled to pursue and promote these ideals. Similarly, Kant believes that pure reason can by itself be practical, though he does not pretend to be able to explain how it can be so.[2] Again, Sidgwick argues that if there is to be a science of ethics—and he assumes that there can be, indeed he defines ethics as "the science of conduct"—what ought to be "must in another sense have objective existence: it must be an object of knowledge and as such the same for all minds"; but he says that the affirmations of this science "are also precepts," and he speaks of happiness as "an end *absolutely* prescribed by reason."[3] . . . [M]any philosophers have thus held that values are objectively prescriptive. . . .

---

1. One of the central doctrines in Plato's philosophy is his "theory of forms." Consider the many things that are good or the many things that are beautiful. According to the theory of forms, goodness itself ("the form of the good") is a single thing alongside the many good things; beauty itself ("the form of beauty") is a single thing alongside the many beautiful things.

2. Immanuel Kant (1724–1804) was a German philosopher, one of the most influential thinkers of the Enlightenment, and the author of the *Critique of Pure Reason*, the *Critique of Practical Reason*, and the *Critique of Judgment*. He explores the idea that "pure reason can by itself be practical"—that our conduct can be guided by reason itself—in his *Groundwork of the Metaphysics of Morals* and *Critique of Practical Reason*.

3. Mackie is here quoting from Henry Sidgwick's *Methods of Ethics*. Sidgwick (1838–1900) was an English moral philosopher. A classical utilitarian, he held that the standard of right conduct is the principle of utility: that conduct is right if and only if it produces the greatest sum of happiness.

7. The Claim to Objectivity

As I have said, the main tradition of European moral philosophy includes the... claim, that there are objective values of just the sort I have denied. I have referred already to Plato, Kant, and Sidgwick. Kant in particular holds that the categorical imperative[4] is not only categorical and imperative but objectively so: though a rational being gives the moral law to himself, the law that he thus makes is determinate and necessary. Aristotle begins the *Nicomachean Ethics* by saying that the good is that at which all things aim, and that ethics is part of a science which he calls "politics," whose goal is not knowledge but practice; yet he does not doubt that there can be *knowledge* of what is the good for man, nor, once he has identified this as well-being or happiness, *eudaimonia,* that it can be known, rationally determined, in what happiness consists; and it is plain that he thinks that this happiness is intrinsically desirable, not good simply because it is desired. . . .

Even the sentimentalist Hutcheson defines moral goodness as "some quality apprehended in actions, which procures approbation . . . ," while saying that the moral sense by which we perceive virtue and vice has been given to us (by the Author of nature) to direct our actions.[5] Hume indeed was on the other side, but he is still a witness to the dominance of the objectivist tradition, since he claims that when we "see that the distinction of vice and virtue is not founded merely on the relations of objects, nor is perceiv'd by reason," this "wou'd subvert all the vulgar systems of morality."[6] . . .

But this objectivism about values is not only a feature of the philosophical tradition. It has also a firm basis in ordinary thought, and even in the meanings of moral terms. . . .

Someone in a state of moral perplexity, wondering whether it would be wrong for him to engage, say, in research related to bacteriological warfare, wants to arrive at some judgement about this concrete case, his doing this work at this time in these actual circumstances. . . . The question is not, for example, whether he really wants to do this work, whether it will satisfy or dissatisfy him, whether he will in the long run have a pro-attitude towards it, or even whether this is an action of a sort that he can happily and sincerely recommend in all relevantly similar cases. Nor is he even wondering just whether to recommend such action in all relevantly similar cases. He wants to know whether this course of action would be wrong in itself. . . .

I conclude, then, that ordinary moral judgements include a claim to objectivity, an assumption that there are objective values in just the sense in which I am concerned

4. According to the categorical imperative, which Kant presents in his *Groundwork of the Metaphysics of Morals*, we ought only to act on a rule that we could approve of everyone acting on.

5. Francis Hutcheson (1694–1746) was a Scottish philosopher who held that human beings use various "senses" to navigate the world, including (in addition to the five senses commonly known) a sense of beauty, a public sense, a sense of honor, a sense of the ridiculous, and, most important, the moral sense described here. Mackie here quotes from Hutcheson's 1725 essay *An Inquiry concerning Moral Good and Evil.*

6. David Hume (1711–1776) was a Scottish philosopher and a student of Hutcheson's. Mackie is quoting from *A Treatise of Human Nature* (1739/40). A selection from Hume's writings on morality appears in Chapter 18 of this anthology.

to deny this. And I do not think it is going too far to say that this assumption has been incorporated in the basic, conventional, meanings of moral terms. Any analysis of the meanings of moral terms which omits this claim to objective, intrinsic, prescriptivity[7] is to that extent incomplete. . . .

If second order ethics were confined, then, to linguistic and conceptual analysis, it ought to conclude that moral values at least are objective: that they are so is part of what our ordinary moral statements mean: the traditional moral concepts of the ordinary man as well as of the main line of western philosophers are concepts of objective value. But it is precisely for this reason that linguistic and conceptual analysis is not enough. The claim to objectivity, however ingrained in our language and thought, is not self-validating. It can and should be questioned. But the denial of objective values will have to be put forward not as the result of an analytic approach, but as an "error theory," a theory that although most people in making moral judgements implicitly claim, among other things, to be pointing to something objectively prescriptive, these claims are all false. It is this that makes the name "moral scepticism" appropriate. . . .

Traditionally [this skeptical theory] has been supported by arguments of two main kinds, which I shall call the argument from relativity and the argument from queerness. . . .

8. The Argument from Relativity

The argument from relativity has as its premiss the well-known variation in moral codes from one society to another and from one period to another, and also the differences in moral beliefs between different groups and classes within a complex community. Such variation is in itself merely a truth of descriptive morality, a fact of anthropology which entails neither first order nor second order ethical views. Yet it may indirectly support second order subjectivism: radical differences between first order moral judgements make it difficult to treat those judgements as apprehensions of objective truths. But it is not the mere occurrence of disagreements that tells against the objectivity of values. Disagreement on questions in history or biology or cosmology does not show that there are no objective issues in these fields for investigators to disagree about. But such scientific disagreement results from speculative inferences or explanatory hypotheses based on inadequate evidence, and it is hardly plausible to interpret moral disagreement in the same way. Disagreement about moral codes seems to reflect people's adherence to and participation in different ways of life. The causal connection seems to be mainly that way round: it is that people approve of monogamy because they participate in a monogamous way of life rather than that they participate in a monogamous way of life because they approve of monogamy. Of course, the standards may be an idealization of the way of life from which they arise: the monogamy in which people participate may

---

7. Moral claims are *prescriptive*: they call for certain kinds of conduct. When we say that telling the truth is the *right* thing to do, we mean not only that it is objectively right. We are prescribing truth-telling.

be less complete, less rigid, than that of which it leads them to approve. This is not to say that moral judgements are purely conventional. Of course there have been and are moral heretics and moral reformers, people who have turned against the established rules and practices of their own communities for moral reasons, and often for moral reasons that we would endorse. But this can usually be understood as the extension, in ways which, though new and unconventional, seemed to them to be required for consistency, of rules to which they already adhered as arising out of an existing way of life. In short, the argument from relativity has some force simply because the actual variations in the moral codes are more readily explained by the hypothesis that they reflect ways of life than by the hypothesis that they express perceptions, most of them seriously inadequate and badly distorted, of objective values.

But there is a well-known counter to this argument from relativity, namely to say that the items for which objective validity is in the first place to be claimed are not specific moral rules or codes but very general basic principles which are recognized at least implicitly to some extent in all society—such principles as provide the foundations of what Sidgwick has called different methods of ethics: the principle of universalizability, perhaps, or the rule that one ought to conform to the specific rules of any way of life in which one takes part, from which one profits, and on which one relies, or some utilitarian principle of doing what tends, or seems likely, to promote the general happiness. It is easy to show that such general principles, married with differing concrete circumstances, different existing social patterns or different preferences, will beget different specific moral rules; and there is some plausibility in the claim that the specific rules thus generated will vary from community to community or from group to group in close agreement with the actual variations in accepted codes.

The argument from relativity can be only partly countered in this way. To take this line the moral objectivist has to say that it is only in these principles that the objective moral character attaches immediately to its descriptively specified ground or subject: other moral judgements are objectively valid or true, but only derivatively and contingently—if things had been otherwise, quite different sorts of actions would have been right. And despite the prominence in recent philosophical ethics of universalization, utilitarian principles, and the like, these are very far from constituting the whole of what is actually affirmed as basic in ordinary moral thought. Much of this is concerned rather with what Hare calls "ideals" or, less kindly, "fanaticism."[8] That is, people judge that some things are good or right, and others are bad or wrong, not because—or at any rate not only because—they exemplify some general principle for which widespread implicit acceptance could be claimed, but because something about those things arouses certain responses immediately in them, though they would arouse radically and irresolvably different responses in others. "Moral sense" or "intuition" is an initially more plausible description of what supplies many of our basic moral judgements than "reason." With regard to all these starting points of moral thinking the argument from relativity remains in full force.

8. R. M. Hare (1919–2002) was an English moral philosopher, author of *The Language of Morals* (1952) and *Freedom and Reason* (1963).

9. The Argument from Queerness

Even more important, however, and certainly more generally applicable, is the argument from queerness. This has two parts, one metaphysical, the other epistemological. If there were objective values, then they would be entities or qualities or relations of a very strange sort, utterly different from anything else in the universe. Correspondingly, if we were aware of them, it would have to be by some special faculty of moral perception or intuition, utterly different from our ordinary ways of knowing everything else. These points were recognized by Moore[9] when he spoke of nonnatural qualities, and by the intuitionists in their talk about a "faculty of moral intuition." Intuitionism has long been out of favour, and it is indeed easy to point out its implausibilities. What is not so often stressed, but is more important, is that the central thesis of intuitionism is one to which any objectivist view of values is in the end committed: intuitionism merely makes unpalatably plain what other forms of objectivism wrap up. Of course the suggestion that moral judgements are made or moral problems solved by just sitting down and having an ethical intuition is a travesty of actual moral thinking. But, however complex the real process, it will require (if it is to yield authoritatively prescriptive conclusions) some input of this distinctive sort, either premises or forms of argument or both. When we ask the awkward question, how we can be aware of this authoritative prescriptivity, of the truth of these distinctively ethical premises or of the cogency of this distinctively ethical pattern of reasoning, none of our ordinary accounts of sensory perception or introspection or the framing and confirming of explanatory hypotheses or inference or logical construction or conceptual analysis, or any combination of these, will provide a satisfactory answer; "a special sort of intuition" is a lame answer, but it is the one to which the clear-headed objectivist is compelled to resort. . . .

Plato's Forms give a dramatic picture of what objective values would have to be. The Form of the Good is such that knowledge of it provides the knower with both a direction and an overriding motive; something's being good both tells the person who knows this to pursue it and makes him pursue it. An objective good would be sought by anyone who was acquainted with it, not because of any contingent fact that this person, or every person, is so constituted that he desires this end, but just because the end has to-be-pursuedness somehow built into it. Similarly, if there were objective principles of right and wrong, any wrong (possible) course of action would have not-to-be-doneness somehow built into it. . . .

The need for an argument of this sort can be brought out by reflection on Hume's argument that "reason"—in which at this stage he includes all sorts of knowing as well as reasoning—can never be an "influencing motive of the will." Someone might object that Hume has argued unfairly from the lack of influencing power (not contingent upon desires) in ordinary objects of knowledge and ordinary reasoning, and might maintain that values differ from natural objects precisely in their power, when known, automatically to influence the will. To this Hume could, and would need to, reply that this objection involves the postulating of value-entities or value-features of quite a

---

9. G. E. Moore (1873–1958) was an English philosopher, author of *Principia Ethica* (1903).

different order from anything else with which we are acquainted, and of a corresponding faculty with which to detect them. That is, he would have to supplement his explicit argument with what I have called the argument from queerness.

Another way of bringing out this queerness is to ask, about anything that is supposed to have some objective moral quality, how this is linked with its natural features. What is the connection between the natural fact that an action is a piece of deliberate cruelty—say, causing pain just for fun—and the moral fact that it is wrong? It cannot be an entailment, a logical or semantic necessity. Yet it is not merely that the two features occur together. The wrongness must somehow be "consequential" or "supervenient"; it is wrong because it is a piece of deliberate cruelty. But just *what in the world* is signified by this "because"? And how do we know the relation that it signifies, if this is something more than such actions being socially condemned, and condemned by us too, perhaps through our having absorbed attitudes from our social environment? It is not even sufficient to postulate a faculty which "sees" the wrongness: something must be postulated which can see at once the natural features that constitute the cruelty, and the wrongness, and the mysterious consequential link between the two. . . .

It may be thought that the argument from queerness is given an unfair start if we thus relate it to what are admittedly among the wilder products of philosophical fancy—Platonic Forms, nonnatural qualities, self-evident relations of fitness, faculties of intuition, and the like. Is it equally forceful if applied to the terms in which everyday moral judgements are more likely to be expressed—though still, as has been argued in Section 7, with a claim to objectivity—"you must do this," "you can't do that," "obligation," "unjust," "rotten," "disgraceful," "mean," or talk about good reasons for or against possible actions? Admittedly not; but that is because the objective prescriptivity, the element a claim for whose authoritativeness is embedded in ordinary moral thought and language, is not yet isolated in these forms of speech, but is presented along with relations to desires and feelings, reasoning about the means to desired ends, interpersonal demands, the injustice which consists in the violation of what are in the context the accepted standards of merit, the psychological constituents of meanness, and so on. There is nothing queer about any of these, and under cover of them the claim for moral authority may pass unnoticed. But if I am right in arguing that it is ordinarily there, and is therefore very likely to be incorporated almost automatically in philosophical accounts of ethics which systematize our ordinary thought even in such apparently innocent terms as these, it needs to be examined, and for this purpose it needs to be isolated and exposed as it is by the less cautious philosophical reconstructions. . . .

TEST YOUR UNDERSTANDING

1. Which of the following statements best captures Mackie's conception of moral subjectivism?

    a. Each of us has his or her own personal moral code.

    b. There are no objective values.

   c. We should each do whatever we wish.

   d. Moral statements are expressions of the attitudes of the person who makes the judgments.

2. What is the difference between a first-order moral view and a second-order moral view? Give two examples of each.

3. What is the connection between ordinary moral judgments and the claim to moral objectivity?

4. What are the two parts of the "argument from queerness"?

NOTES AND QUESTIONS

1. According to Mackie, the idea that values are *objectively prescriptive* is endorsed by many philosophers and by common sense. Explain what "objectively prescriptive" means. Does the claim that values are *objective* mean that values are objects that we interact with? If not that, then what does it mean? Consider two interpretations of *prescriptive*:

   a. A moral statement is *prescriptive* if and only if a person who fully understands the statement is motivated to comply with it.

   b. A moral statement is *prescriptive* if and only if a person who fully understands the statement knows what kinds of conduct it requires of those to whom it applies.

What is the difference between these interpretations? Which interpretation does Mackie rely on in his discussions of Plato, Kant, and Sidgwick?

2. Mackie's argument from relativity begins from the fact that moral beliefs vary across societies and across groups within a single society. This variation, he says, "may indirectly support second-order subjectivism."

   a. Why is the support for subjectivism only indirect? Why doesn't moral disagreement lead directly to subjectivism?

   b. How exactly does the variation in moral views within and between societies indirectly support second-order subjectivism? (*Hint:* Focus on Mackie's contrast between explaining scientific and moral disagreement.) Is Mackie convincing on this point?

Mackie considers a "well-known counter to the argument from relativity."

   a. The counter draws on the distinction between specific moral rules and general principles. Give some examples of the distinction. How does this distinction provide the basis for a reply to the argument from relativity?

   b. How does Mackie respond to the counterargument?

   c. Consider a reply to Mackie's response. To make things more concrete, consider a **utilitarian** who thinks that the principle of utility is objectively valid. The utilitarian might say:

> You need to distinguish between making moral judgments and defending those judgments. When people make moral judgments, they often respond unreflectively to a specific situation. Their responses draw on a conventional

moral code and strong feelings that have grown up around the code. They say things like "Don't break promises to your friends" and "Tell your parents the truth." But when they are called on to defend their judgments, they appeal to general principles—in particular, they try to show that the conventional moral code is the best way to promote overall happiness. So there is variation in morality across groups and societies. But the variation is explained, as the justifications suggest, by beliefs about how to apply the principle of utility in different situations.

What response is available to Mackie? For an argument along these lines, aiming to show that commonsense morality is implicitly utilitarian, see Henry Sidgwick, *Methods of Ethics (Hackett, 1980),* book 4.

3. Mackie thinks we erroneously believe that values are objectively prescriptive. He endorses an **error theory** about values, according to which people quite generally and persistently hold a mistaken belief about values. You find error theories in other areas of philosophy as well. Error theorists about causation think people generally believe that causality is a real connection between events (one event *makes* the other happen), though there is no such real connection; error theorists about color think people generally assume colors to be objectively present in objects, though colors are only a matter of how we respond to objects; error theorists about scientific unobservables (say, quarks) think people generally believe that there are unobservable objects even though talk about unobservables is simply a way of predicting observations; error theorists about aesthetics think beauty is only in the beholder's eyes, though we believe (mistakenly) that beauty is present in the world.

   Because error theorists claim to have detected a pervasive and persistent mistake, they typically offer explanations of the roots of the error, commonly called an *objectification error.* They explain how we end up projecting some feature of our thinking, feeling, talking, or interacting onto the world. In section 10 of "The Subjectivity of Values" (omitted from this reading), Mackie suggests some explanations of the objectification error he detects in moral philosophy and ordinary moral thought. One explanation begins with the fact that we sometimes want people to do something—say, keep a promise. Instead of saying "You should keep your promise because I want you to" or "You should keep your promise because we insist that you do," we just say "You ought to keep your promise" or, more simply, "You promised." Morality thus involves "suppressing any explicit reference to demands."

   a. Why would we want to suppress any explicit reference to demands?

   b. How could Mackie's explanation work if people are aware that moral claims are simply a shorthand for expressions of demands?

4. According to the (unhappily named) argument from queerness, objective values, if there were such, would need to be objects, or relations, or qualities unlike anything we are familiar with. What precisely makes objective values so unusual? Consider three answers:

   a. Values are not in space-time.

   b. Values lead people who fully understand them to act.

   c. Values instruct us about what to do.

Which answer does Mackie offer? Once you have settled on an interpretation of Mackie, consider whether he is right that commonsense morality assumes such odd things to exist.

R. Jay Wallace (b. 1957)

Wallace is a Professor of Philosophy at the University of California, Berkeley, where he holds the Judy Chandler Webb Distinguished Chair for Innovative Teaching and Research. He writes on moral philosophy, with a particular focus on moral psychology and practical reasoning.

MORAL SUBJECTIVISM

Moral thought is commonly supposed to be a matter of subjective attitude, in a way that contrasts with thought about (say) mathematics or the natural world. If you judge that $12 \times 3 = 36$ or that the cat is sleeping on the bed, nobody is likely to conclude that that is just your opinion. Your thoughts seem to be about a subject matter that is prior to and independent of them, and in that respect objective. We might say that judgments of these kinds are answerable to independent facts of the matter, insofar as their correctness or incorrectness depends on how things are independently of the judgments being made.

With moral thought, by contrast, things are often taken to be otherwise. Consider the judgments that it is wrong to make insincere promises or to exploit the weak and vulnerable. It is widely believed that judgments of this kind are not answerable to a prior and independent subject matter, but are merely a matter of subjective opinion. This thought is the animating idea behind moral subjectivism. To a first approximation, subjectivism is the position that moral judgments—such as the judgment that lying promises are wrong—are not about a set of facts that are prior to and independent of them. Instead, the subjectivist maintains, they reflect the attitudes of the person who makes those judgments.[1]

Two aspects of moral thought particularly encourage this subjectivist interpretation of it.[2] One aspect concerns its subject matter. Moral judgments typically involve evaluative or normative concepts, as applied to persons and their actions. In moral

---

1. The term "subjectivism" is sometimes used more narrowly in philosophical discussion to refer to the view that moral judgments are about an agent's subjective states; the dispositionalist position discussed below is a subjectivist view in this more narrow sense. [Wallace's note.]

2. A third aspect of moral thought that is sometimes cited in this connection is the fact of disagreement about what it is right or wrong to do. But this consideration strikes me as less significant than the other two, so I shall set it aside in what follows. [Wallace's note.]

thought we conclude that doing X would be permissible or required, right or wrong, and we judge that people are admirable or blameworthy in virtue of their character traits and the things they have done.[3] Concepts such as permissibility, rightness, wrongness, or blameworthiness, however, do not seem to correspond to any objects or properties in the natural world. Actions are not wrong, for instance, in the way the leaf of a tree might be green or oblong or bitter to the taste. We see that the eucalyptus leaf is green and oblong when we look at it, and we taste its bitterness when we put it in our mouth; these properties can affect our sense organs in ways that make them potential objects of empirical investigation and scientific study. But the properties involved in moral thought do not in the same way seem to make a causal difference to our experiences. We don't, after all, have any special organs of perception or sensation that enable us to detect the wrongness of acts of lying.[4]

Considerations of this kind make it natural to suppose that the world is devoid of the evaluative and normative properties that moral thought apparently trades in. But if there are no evaluative and normative properties in the world, it seems to follow that moral thought cannot be understood in objective terms. It does not answer to a set of independent facts about the way things are in the world, since the world as we find it has no place for evaluative and normative objects and properties.

A second aspect that encourages the subjectivist interpretation concerns the effects of moral thought on action. One of the important ways we use moral concepts is in deliberation—the kind of systematic reflection we engage in when we attempt to get clear about what we ought to do.[5] In deliberation, we take it for granted that we could choose to act in a number of different ways (keeping a promise or breaking it, say), and we reflect on those alternatives, asking, among other things, whether they are morally permissible or required. The thoughts that figure in deliberative reflection are in this way practical in their subject matter: they are about what to do. But deliberation is practical in a very different sense as well. After reaching a conclusion about what they ought to do, those who engage in deliberation often act on the verdict they have arrived at, choosing the option that deliberation has identified to be for the best.

Consider the members of a campus club who, after deliberation, decide that it is wrong to maintain their secret policy of excluding people from certain ethnic groups, even if doing so would be to their advantage. (Perhaps there are wealthy benefactors

---

3. Normative concepts are concepts that involve the ideas of a reason or a requirement, whereas evaluative concepts involve ideas of the good. Here I gloss over large issues about the relation between reasons and values. I also simply assume, throughout my discussion, that moral thought is a species of normative thought concerning a special class of reasons or requirements. [Wallace's note.]

4. Note that this argument apparently also applies to mathematical thought, which similarly does not seem to be about objects and properties that we interact with causally. And yet, mathematical thought seems to be a paradigm of objectivity. Does this undermine the argument from metaphysics? [Wallace's note.]

5. Another important context in which normative thought figures is that of advice, where we reflect on the options that other people face and try to arrive at conclusions about what they ought to do. In what follows, I shall focus primarily on contexts of deliberation in which agents reflect on their own options for action. But you should consider how the subjectivist approaches I sketch might be extended to apply to contexts of advice. [Wallace's note.]

who will stop supporting the group if it becomes more inclusive in its membership.) Having arrived at this moral conclusion, the club members might adjust their policies accordingly, opening the club to people from all ethnic and cultural backgrounds because they have come to see that that is the right thing to do. Moral thought might not have as much influence on action as we would like, but it is at least capable of moving people directly to act. It is thus practical not merely in its subject matter but also in its effects.

This practical dimension of moral thought appears difficult to make sense of if we understand such thought in objectivist terms. The judgments that seem paradigmatically about a realm of independent objects and relations do not have this kind of influence on the will. The thought that fresh beets are available for sale in the local supermarket, for instance, does not on its own seem able to move us to action one way or another. To do so, it would need to combine with some distinct attitude on our part, such as a desire to have roast beets for dinner: if you hate beets, or are simply indifferent to them, then the true belief that you can buy some at the local supermarket will have no effect on your motivations whatsoever.[6] Moral thought, by contrast, seems capable of engaging the will directly, without the addition of attitudes that are extraneous to it. The conclusion that it is wrong to discriminate against members of certain ethnic groups, as we saw earlier, is already apt to move us to action by itself. It is natural to hypothesize that such conclusions must essentially involve the subject's desires or emotions, mobilizing the kinds of subjective attitudes that move us to act.

We might refer to these two lines of thought as the arguments from metaphysics and from motivation, respectively. They were both taken very seriously by David Hume, who was led by them to the subjectivist conclusion that morality "is more properly felt than judg'd of."[7] Hume meant by this that moral deliberation trades in attitudes of emotion or desire of the kind that move us to action, rather than judgments about an independent set of normative and evaluative facts. This conclusion is an extremely tempting one when we think about moral thought, and it contains at least a grain of truth. In the end, however, I don't believe that we should accept the Humean position. In support of this claim, I shall begin by considering a simple version of moral subjectivism, and then explore three different ways of refining the position. A particularly important theme will be the role of *critical reflection* in normative and moral thought: its role, that is, as a method of scrutinizing and improving our own subjective reactions. I shall argue that this is something the subjectivist cannot give an adequate account of.

Perhaps the simplest way to develop the subjectivist idea is to interpret it as a form of *expressivism*. This is a view in what is often called metaethics, the study of the meaning of the language that is used to express moral claims. Expressivists hold that

---

6. Of course, you might have promised a friend that you would pick up some beets for him in the store. But then you will be led to act by the moral thought that you will wrong your friend if you fail to do what you promised, a thought that is also extraneous to your factual belief about the availability of the beets. [Wallace's note.]

7. David Hume, *A Treatise of Human Nature* (Oxford University Press, 1978), 470. [Wallace's note.]

moral and other normative judgments are not in the business of representing a set of independent facts or relations. Their function is instead to give expression to practical attitudes of approval or disapproval, such as desires or intentions.[8] Moral language, on this approach, might be compared to the verbalizing that goes on at a football game or a rock concert, which does not even attempt to make claims about the way things are in the world, but rather gives expression to the spectators' attitudes toward the events they are observing. To say that it is wrong to exploit and mock the vulnerable, for instance, is to give voice to your disapproval of acting in this way; it expresses a desire that people should not perform actions of this kind, much as the lusty booing that takes place at the football stadium expresses the audience's disapproval of the botched play that just took place on the field.

This expressivist position does a good job of accommodating the considerations marshaled in the arguments from metaphysics and motivation. According to expressivism, moral and other normative assertions don't really say anything at all about the world, so we can make sense of such discourse without postulating any funny properties or states of affairs. The expressivist account also offers a nice explanation of the practical dimension of moral thought. If moral discourse is in the business of expressing the agent's desires, then we can immediately understand how it is that moral judgments can directly engage the will. The practical attitudes that moral discourse expresses guarantee that such motivations will be present whenever a moral judgment is endorsed.

The problem, however, is that the simple expressivist view seems to go too far in the direction of assimilating moral thought to the formation of such practical attitudes. If people can be motivated to act directly by their normative judgments, this connection can also break down. You might for instance think that it would be wrong to keep a wallet that you have found in the university library (rather than turning it in at the lost-and-found office) but give in to the temptation to keep the wallet when you realize how much money it contains. In cases of this kind, people act against their own moral judgments,[9] and the possibility of doing this suggests that moral judgments don't simply involve the expression of effective motivating attitudes.

Normative thought has an important critical dimension. It can be brought to bear on our own emotions and desires, including the motivations that lead us to act when we go astray by our own lights. This dimension of moral thought needs to be accounted for in an adequate development of the subjectivist position. The challenge is to explain how we can achieve critical distance from our motivating attitudes, within a framework that understands moral thought essentially in terms of such attitudes.

One way of responding to this challenge would be to modify the simple version of expressivism by restricting the class of subjective attitudes that moral and normative language is taken to express. In this spirit, normative discourse might be supposed to give voice to our second-order attitudes, including above all the preferences we form

8. See, for example, Allan Gibbard, *Thinking How to Live* (Harvard University Press, 2003). [Wallace's note.]

9. The phenomenon of action against one's better judgment is often referred to as *akrasia* (from the ancient Greek), or "weakness of will." [Wallace's note.]

about our first-order desires.[10] When you act against your better judgment concerning the permissibility of keeping the wallet, for example, you have a first-order desire to hang on to the money that the wallet contains. But you also form a distinct attitude about that desire, preferring that it should not prove effective in determining what you do. The subjectivist might say that it is second-order desires of this kind that it is the distinctive function of normative language to express. On the resulting picture, practical attitudes are subject to criticism by something outside themselves, but the standards for such critical assessment are fixed by further practical attitudes of the agent.[11]

A natural question to ask about this more sophisticated expressivism, however, concerns the standing of higher-order attitudes to constitute a basis for critical assessment. Suppose you form a second-order desire that your desire for money should not prevail in determining whether you keep the wallet you have found. This higher-order desire is an attitude of the same basic type as the first-order attitude that is its object; it is just another desire or preference that you are subject to. If there is a real issue about the credentials of the first-order attitude, it is hard to see how it can be resolved simply through the formation of further attitudes of the same basic kind. Won't those attitudes be prone to further iterations of skeptical undermining? You could, after all, step back from your second-order desire regarding the original temptation to keep the wallet and call that desire into question in turn, forming a third-order desire to ignore the scruples of conscience. Nothing in the nature of your second-order preferences seems to block such critical questions from being raised about them.

The sophisticated expressivist might respond by noting that we generally don't extend the process of reflection to such extremes. We step back from our first-order attitudes to subject them to critical scrutiny, but we rarely take this process further, scrutinizing our second-order attitudes in turn. What matters, fundamentally, is that normative thought is a reflective process in which we step back from our subjective attitudes and engage in reflection on them: this reflective character is what confers on higher-order attitudes their standing in situations of critical assessment. Higher-order attitudes function as standards of normative assessment, in other words, not because of their nature as desires, but because of the reflective procedures that lead to their formation.

This approach works, however, only in cases in which agents have actually undergone a course of reflection about their first-order desires. Prior to such reflection, the approach suggests, there are no standards for the critical assessment of our motivating attitudes, and this is an awkward result. Suppose that in thinking about the question of whether to hang onto the wallet or turn it in at the lost-and-found office, you reach the conclusion that personal financial advantage is not a good reason to keep property

---

10. See, for example, Harry G. Frankfurt, "Freedom of the Will and the Concept of a Person," in his *The Importance of What We Care About* (Cambridge University Press, 1988), 11–25. [Wallace's note.]

11. Since the higher-order attitudes that are expressed in normative discourse are themselves desires, this version of expressivism can explain the capacity of moral thought to engage the will. But it can also explain why normative thought sometimes fails to give rise to corresponding motivations, since the first-order desires the agent reflects on might be stronger than the second-order desires that normative language expresses. [Wallace's note.]

that is not rightfully yours. In arriving at this conclusion, you will probably think that you are making a moral and normative discovery about something that was true all along. It is not that your arriving at this conclusion somehow makes it the case that it is wrong to keep other people's property when it falls into your hands; rather, it was wrong even before you started thinking about the question. But how can the subjectivist make sense of this aspect of moral thought?

One possibility is to appeal to the agent's dispositions. What matters to the normative standing of a given first-order attitude, we might say, is not that the agent has actually endorsed or rejected it through critical reflection, but that the agent is disposed to endorse or reject it through such reflection (i.e., that she *would* endorse or reject the desire if she were to engage in critical reflection on it). Building on this idea, some philosophers have proposed a different way of developing the subjectivist approach, which we might call *dispositionalism*. The dispositionalist holds that normative discourse functions not to express our higher-order attitudes, but to make claims *about* the higher-order attitudes we would arrive at through rational reflection. To say that a lying promise is wrong, on this approach, is to say that one would desire that one not give in to the temptation to make a false promise, if one were to reflect rationally on the matter. When we affirm a normative claim of this kind, we might be expressing our practical attitudes, but we aren't *merely* doing that; we might also be making true statements about a normative subject matter.[12]

Dispositionalism seems to be an advance on expressivism in at least one important respect. It allows us to say that there are normative facts that moral discourse makes claims about, facts that are capable of being discovered when we engage in normative reflection. Moreover, it does this without violating the naturalistic metaphysical commitments of subjectivism. Thus, the normative facts that dispositionalism posits do not involve any weird nonnatural properties, of the kind that would be difficult to locate in the world that the natural sciences describe. Instead, they are facts about the attitudes of human agents, in particular facts about the dispositions of those agents to form higher-order attitudes through critical reflection. Your act of betraying a secret is wrong, on this approach, just in case the following conditional statement is true about you: that you would want yourself not to act on the temptation to betray the secret, if you were to reflect fully on the matter. Dispositional facts of this kind define standards for the normative assessment of the agent's practical attitudes, but the standards are in the relevant sense subjective; they are a matter, fundamentally, of the dispositions of the agents whom the standards regulate.

It is an open question, however, whether dispositionalism can really dispense with normative standards that are independent of the person whose attitudes are subject to assessment. To see this, let's go back to the motivational side of moral thought. Suppose I have arrived at the conclusion that I would want myself to refrain from deception, if I were rational. The dispositionalist says: this judgment *just is* the moral judgment that it would be wrong for me to lie. As we have emphasized, however,

---

12. See, for example, Michael Smith, *The Moral Problem* (Blackwell, 1994). [Wallace's note.]

moral judgments of this kind are supposed to provide standards not merely for the criticism of our practical attitudes, but for their control; they are practical not just in their subject matter, but in their effect, giving rise to new motivations. But how are judgments about our dispositions to desire things supposed to have this practical effect? The dispositionalist puts motivation into the content of moral judgments, construing them as claims about what we would desire if we were rational. One could form a judgment with this content, however, without having the desire that the judgment is about; how can the dispositionalist bridge this gap?

The natural answer is to appeal to rationality to do this job. That is, dispositionalists often propose the following principle of rationality (or some variant of it):

> It is irrational to judge that I would want myself to do X if I were rational, but to fail to have a desire to do X.

Applying this principle to the case at hand, we get that it would be irrational to judge that it would be wrong to tell a lie for personal advantage, but to fail to desire to act accordingly. Our responsiveness to this standard of rationality, the dispositionalist might then say, is what enables normative reflection to generate new desires. This suggestion is plausible, furthermore, because cases in which we fail to have desires that accord with our normative judgments seem to be paradigm cases of irrationality. If you really believe that you shouldn't lie to your teacher to get an extension on the paper, but you end up doing so anyway, then you are going astray by your own lights; what could be more irrational than that?[13] The problem, for the dispositionalist, is to explain where this principle of rationality comes from. It looks to be a substantive normative standard, one that is prior to and independent of the attitudes that are up for assessment. The postulation of normative standards that are in this way objective, however, violates the subjectivist's most basic metaphysical commitments.

Moral thought involves the application of rational standards, standards that are normative for the agent, in the sense that they properly regulate the agent's critical reflections. The challenge for the subjectivist, as we have now seen, is to make sense of this aspect of moral thought, without recourse to standards that are completely independent of the attitudes of the agents whose reflections they govern. *Constructivism* in moral philosophy can be understood as a response to this problem. On the constructivist view, practical attitudes are subject to scrutiny by reference to critical standards. But those standards are not independent of the attitudes to which they apply; rather, they appropriately govern the subject's deliberation precisely because the subject is already committed to complying with them.[14]

Consider the instrumental principle, which tells us to choose the means that are necessary to achieve our ends. If you intend to go to medical school, for instance, and

---

13. Thus, weakness of will is generally understood to be the most flagrant form of irrationality in action. [Wallace's note.]

14. An example of this kind of constructivist view is Christine M. Korsgaard, *The Sources of Normativity* (Cambridge University Press, 1996). [Wallace's note.]

"Introduction to Organic Chemistry" is a prerequisite for admission to medical school, then the instrumental principle says that you should take the class; your intentions are subject to criticism if you fail to act in this way. But this is because your intention to go to medical school *already* involves a commitment to take the means that are necessary for the attainment of that end. Indeed, the intention to realize the end just is (in part) a commitment to take the necessary means, and hence to comply with the instrumental principle.[15] Constructivists generalize from this example, holding that all of the standards that govern our practical reflections are likewise standards that we are committed to complying with, in virtue of practical attitudes that we have already adopted.

The constructivist approach can be thought of as combining elements of expressivism and dispositionalism. It shares with the former an emphasis on the essential involvement of practical attitudes in the processes of normative and moral reflection. Such reflection takes as its starting point the intentions and desires that we already have, and it attempts to adjust and to refine them through critical thought. We go astray, on this approach, when we fail to live up to our own commitments—as the signers of the Declaration of Independence arguably did, for example, when they condoned practices of slavery while endorsing the principle that "all men are created equal."

Normative reflection can accordingly be understood as a process of figuring out what our commitments really entail, a process that can lead to normative *discoveries*, of the kind the dispositionalist was concerned to make room for. It might take some time for people to come to see that their own commitments (say, about human equality) have the consequence that some of their other attitudes and practices should be rejected or revised. The normative standards that govern the process of critical reflection are thus not restricted to standards whose consequences the agent already explicitly acknowledges. At the same time, the fact that those standards are anchored in the agent's own commitments sheds light on the practical effects of moral thought. For it is in the nature of commitments that they involve an orientation of the will, which moves us to act once we become clear about what the commitments really entail. People who are genuinely committed to the fundamental equality of all people will be moved to abandon and even to fight against practices such as slavery, once they finally face up to the fact that those practices cannot be reconciled with their own moral principles.

This approach represents a promising way of understanding the critical dimension of practical thought, if we accept the subjectivist idea that normative standards are never prior to and independent of the agents whose attitudes they regulate. But the resulting position shares with other forms of subjectivism some consequences that are difficult to accept. Most basically, the constructivist approach makes morality itself hostage to the commitments of the agents whose actions and attitudes are up for assessment. Whether or not it is wrong for me to break a promise or to keep the wallet I have found is ultimately a question of whether, like the Founding Fathers in

---

15. Thus, if you realize that "Introduction to Organic Chemistry" is necessary to get into medical school, but you have resolved never to take the course, then it seems you have effectively abandoned your original intention to become a doctor. [Wallace's note.]

the case of slavery, I am already committed to moral principles that would prohibit conduct of these kinds.

Kantians in ethics often accept this framework for thinking about moral standards, affirming a generalized constructivism about normativity. They contend that the most basic moral requirements—the moral law or the "categorical imperative" [16]—are universal principles of willing, insofar as they are ones that every agent is *necessarily* committed to complying with. If this claim could be defended, then morality would turn out to represent a set of universal normative constraints on rational agents. But the Kantian claim is exceptionally ambitious, and it has proven very difficult to give a clear and compelling account of the idea that rational agency involves an essential, built-in commitment to follow the moral law. If the Kantian is correct, then it ought to be possible to identify the concrete commitments that villains and scoundrels are betraying when they pursue their reprehensible ends. But does this seem plausible to you? (What is it in the attitudes of the fraudster or the terrorist—people like Bernie Madoff or Timothy McVeigh, say—that would commit them to the basic moral standards that they flout in their actual behavior?)

Those who wish to make sense of morality as a set of nonnegotiable critical standards may therefore need to question the subjectivist framework within which constructivism operates. Perhaps our practical attitudes are answerable to standards that are more robustly independent of the subjects of those attitudes. Before we can accept this objectivist approach, however, we will need to come up with convincing responses to the arguments from metaphysics and motivation canvassed earlier. Can we make sense of the idea that reality includes irreducibly normative facts and truths about, for instance, the wrongness of deceptive promises or the impermissibility of exploitation and fraud? How can reflection about such facts and truths reliably give rise to new motivations to action, in the way that we have seen to be characteristic of practical deliberation? These questions continue to push some philosophers back to subjectivist ways of understanding morality, despite the serious difficulties that subjectivism faces in accounting for the critical dimension of normative thought.

TEST YOUR UNDERSTANDING

1. Which of the following statements best captures what Wallace means by "moral subjectivism"?

   a. Each of us has his or her own moral code.

   b. There are no objective values.

---

16. The categorical imperative is Kant's candidate for the supreme principle of morality, the abstract principle from which our more specific moral duties can be derived. For different formulations of this principle, and Kant's argument that it represents a universal principle of rational willing, see Immanuel Kant, *Groundwork of the Metaphysics of Morals*, ed. and trans. Mary Gregor (Cambridge University Press, 1997). [Wallace's note.]

   c. We should each do whatever we wish.

   d. Moral judgments are expressions of the attitudes of the person who makes the judgments.

2. Briefly describe the two aspects of moral thought that, according to Wallace, encourage a subjectivist interpretation of morality.

3. What is the main problem with the simple form of expressivism?

4. How does a constructivist understand the relationship between an agent and critical standards that apply to the agent's actions; for example, the standard of instrumental rationality?

NOTES AND QUESTIONS

1. Sketch Wallace's simple version of expressivism and his more sophisticated version. Then answer these questions:

   a. How does the simple version address the metaphysical and motivational concerns that motivate subjectivism?

   b. What problem does Wallace raise for the simple version?

   c. How does the more sophisticated version of expressivism respond to the specific challenge Wallace raises for the simpler version? (Do not just say how the sophisticated version is different. Explain how it handles the objection.)

   d. To challenge the more sophisticated expressivist, who brings in second-order desires, Wallace says: "This higher-order desire is an attitude of the same basic type as the first-order attitude that is its object." What does he mean by "same basic type"? Suppose the sophisticated expressivist responds by saying: "No! It is a second-order desire, and that makes it a *different* type from the first-order desire." Is this response convincing?

   e. Are second-order desires a good way to understand the kind of critical reflection that Wallace says is so central to moral thought? Think of some examples of second-order desires and explain why they help or fail to help in understanding critical reflection.

2. State the dispositionalist view in your own words.

   a. How does dispositionalism respond to the troubles Wallace finds in expressivism?

   b. Wallace says that dispositionalists appeal to a principle of rationality. What role does the principle play?

   c. Suppose I hear the dispositionalist theory and then think: "Okay, I am tempted to cheat on my taxes. But I also think it is wrong to cheat on my taxes. And (as the dispositionalist says) what that means is that *if I thought rationally about the issue, I would desire not to give in to the temptation to cheat on my taxes.* And (as the dispositionalist says) I see that it is irrational for me to have that thought about what I *would* desire, but then not desire right now to resist the temptation. So I see that rationality requires that I desire now to resist the temptation to cheat. But I am unmoved because I do not care about being rational. What grip is rationality supposed to have on me?" How can the dispositionalist respond?

3. Suppose the constructivist tries to establish a tight connection between being a rational
agent and being a moral agent. He or she argues as follows:

> Acting rationally involves acting for a purpose. But acting for a purpose commits
> you to thinking that your purpose is worth achieving. And "worth achieving"
> means not simply that achieving the purpose is *important to you*. Instead,
> you are committed to its objective importance—to the idea that achieving the
> purpose has an importance that everyone should acknowledge. But if you are
> committed to the objective importance of your achieving your purposes, then you
> are committed to the objective importance of others' achieving their purposes:
> after all, what is so special about *you*? So as a rational agent, you are committed
> to acknowledging the importance of others achieving their purposes. So as a
> rational agent, you are committed to the core moral idea that the purposes of
> others are just as important as your purposes. Moreover, as Wallace says, "it
> is in the nature of commitments that they involve an orientation of the will,
> which moves us to act once we become clear about what the commitments
> really entail." So as a rational agent, you are committed to morality. And being
> committed to morality means both that you are intellectually committed to the
> importance of being a moral agent and that you are motivated by moral reasons.

Does this argument provide a compelling response to Wallace's concerns about the
ability of subjectivism to accommodate both the *normative* character of moral thought
and its *practical* nature—the motivational concern that animates subjectivism?

Thomas Nagel (b. 1937)

Nagel is University Professor Emeritus of Philosophy and Law at New York University. He has
made influential contributions to ethics, political philosophy, epistemology, and philosophy
of mind. His books include *The Possibility of Altruism* (1970), *The View from Nowhere* (1986),
Equality and Partiality (1991), and *Mind and Cosmos* (2012).

ETHICS
from *The Last Word*

I

Let me . . . turn to the question of whether moral reasoning is . . . fundamental and
inescapable.[1] Unlike logical or arithmetical reasoning, it often fails to produce certainty,

1. This discussion of the nature of moral objectivity comes from Thomas Nagel's *The Last Word*, chapter 6.
Nagel proposes a common approach to objectivity in logic, science, and ethics in which the idea of *inescapability*
plays a central role.

justified or unjustified. It is easily subject to distortion by morally irrelevant factors, social and personal, as well as outright error. It resembles empirical reason in not being reducible to a series of self-evident steps.

I take it for granted that the objectivity of moral reasoning does not depend on its having an external reference. There is no moral analogue of the external world—a universe of moral facts that impinge on us causally. Even if such a supposition made sense, it would not support the objectivity of moral reasoning. Science, which this kind of reifying realism[2] takes as its model, doesn't derive its objective validity from the fact that it starts from perception and other causal relations between us and the physical world. The real work comes after that, in the form of active scientific reasoning, without which no amount of causal impact on us by the external world would generate a belief in Newton's or Maxwell's or Einstein's theories, or the chemical theory of elements and compounds, or molecular biology.[3]

If we had rested content with the causal impact of the external world on us, we'd still be at the level of sense perception. We can regard our scientific beliefs as objectively true not because the external world causes us to have them but because we are able to *arrive at* those beliefs by methods that have a good claim to be reliable, by virtue of their success in selecting among rival hypotheses that survive the best criticisms and questions we can throw at them. Empirical confirmation plays a vital role in this process, but it cannot do so without theory.

Moral thought is concerned not with the description and explanation of what happens but with decisions and their justification. It is mainly because we have no comparably uncontroversial and well-developed methods for thinking about morality that a subjectivist position here is more credible than it is with regard to science. But just as there was no guarantee at the beginnings of cosmological and scientific speculation that we humans had the capacity to arrive at objective truth beyond the deliverances of sense-perception—that in pursuing it we were doing anything more than spinning collective fantasies—so there can be no decision in advance as to whether we are or are not talking about a real subject when we reflect and argue about morality. The answer must come from the results themselves. Only the effort to reason about morality can show us whether it is possible—whether, in thinking about what to do and how to live, we can find methods, reasons, and principles whose validity does not have to be subjectively or relativistically qualified.

Since moral reasoning is a species of practical reasoning, its conclusions are desires, intentions, and actions, or feelings and convictions that can motivate desire, intention, and action. We want to know how to live, and why, and we want the answer in general terms, if possible. Hume famously believed that because a "passion" immune to rational assessment must underlie every motive, there can be no such thing as specifically

2. To reify is to treat as a thing. In morality, "reifying realism" is the view that moral objectivity requires moral objects or moral facts in the world that we interact with causally.

3. Sir Isaac Newton (1643–1727) was an English physicist and mathematician whose law of gravity and three laws of motion dominated modern physics until the early twentieth century. James Clerk Maxwell (1831–1879) was a Scottish physicist who developed an integrated theory of electricity, magnetism, and light, expressed in Maxwell's equations. Albert Einstein (1879–1955) won the 1921 Nobel Prize in Physics and is best known for his special and general theories of relativity.

practical reason, nor specifically moral reason either.[4] That is false, because while "passions" are the source of some reasons, other passions or desires are themselves motivated and/or justified by reasons that do not depend on still more basic desires. And I would contend that either the question whether one should have a certain desire or the question whether, given that one has that desire, one should act on it, is always open to rational consideration.

The issue is whether the procedures of justification and criticism we employ in such reasoning, moral or merely practical, can be regarded finally as just something we do—a cultural or societal or even more broadly human collective practice, within which reasons come to an end. I believe that if we ask ourselves seriously how to respond to proposals for contextualization and relativistic detachment, they usually fail to convince. Although it is less clear than in some of the other areas we've discussed, attempts to get entirely outside of the object language of practical reasons, good and bad, right and wrong, and to see all such judgments as expressions of a contingent, nonobjective perspective will eventually collapse before the independent force of the first-order judgments themselves.[5]

II

Suppose someone says, for example, "You only believe in equal opportunity because you are a product of Western liberal society. If you had been brought up in a caste society or one in which the possibilities for men and women were radically unequal, you wouldn't have the moral convictions you have or accept as persuasive the moral arguments you now accept." The second, hypothetical sentence is probably true, but what about the first—specifically the "only"? In general, the fact that I wouldn't believe something if I hadn't learned it proves nothing about the status of the belief or its grounds. It may be impossible to explain the learning without invoking the content of the belief itself, and the reasons for its truth; and it may be clear that what I have learned is such that even if I hadn't learned it, it would still be true. The reason the genetic fallacy[6] is a fallacy is that the explanation of a belief can sometimes confirm it.

---

4. David Hume (1711–1776), a Scottish philosopher and empiricist, said in his *Treatise of Human Nature* that reason can never be more than a "slave of the passions." For selections from Hume, see Chapters 4, 6, and 18 of this anthology.

5. *First-order judgments* are such judgments as *Cruelty is wrong; Cecilia Bartoli sings beautifully;* and *I have a reason to show special attention to my friends.* They are judgments about the rightness of conduct, the goodness of states of affairs, and what a person has reason to do. First-order judgments are expressed in what Nagel calls an "object language" that uses the terms "reasons," "right," and "beautiful." *Second-order judgments* are judgments about those first-order judgments. Suppose, for example, I say: "When Kant says 'Cruelty is wrong,' he is simply expressing his negative feeling about cruelty." This statement of mine expresses a second-order judgment: it does not use the term "wrong" to criticize conduct, but tells us what it means to use that term. Moreover, because it talks about language, it is sometimes said to be in a metalanguage, rather than an object language.

6. The genetic fallacy is the mistake of thinking that an idea or practice can be supported or discredited by pointing to its origins.

To have any content, a subjectivist position must say more than that my moral convictions are my moral convictions. That, after all, is something we can all agree on. A meaningful subjectivism must say that they are *just* my moral convictions—or those of my moral community. It must *qualify* ordinary moral judgments in some way, must give them a self-consciously first-person (singular or plural) reading. That is the only type of antiobjectivist view that is worth arguing against or that it is even possible to disagree with.

But I believe it is impossible to come to rest with the observation that a belief in equality of opportunity, and a wish to diminish inherited inequalities, are merely expressions of our cultural tradition. True or false, those beliefs are essentially objective in intent. Perhaps they are wrong, but that too would be a nonrelative judgment. Faced with the fact that such values have gained currency only recently and not universally, one still has to try to decide whether they are right—whether one ought to continue to hold them. That question is not displaced by the information of contingency: The question remains, at the level of moral content, whether I would have been in error if I had accepted as natural, and therefore justified, the inequalities of a caste society, or a fairly rigid class system, or the orthodox subordination of women. It can take in additional facts as material for reflection, but the question of the relevance of those facts is inevitably a moral question: Do these cultural and historical variations and their causes tend to show that I and others have less reason than we had supposed to favor equality of opportunity? Presentation of an array of historically and culturally conditioned attitudes, including my own, does not disarm first-order moral judgment but simply gives it something more to work on—including information about influences on the formation of my convictions that may lead me to change them. But the relevance of such information is itself a matter for moral reasoning—about what are and are not good grounds for moral belief.

When one is faced with these real variations in practice and conviction, the requirement to put oneself in everyone's shoes when assessing social institutions—some version of universalizability[7]—does not lose any of its persuasive force just because it is not universally recognized. It dominates the historical and anthropological data: Presented with the description of a traditional caste society, I have to ask myself whether its hereditary inequalities are justified, and there is no plausible alternative to considering the interests of all in trying to answer the question. If others feel differently, they must say why they find these cultural facts relevant—why they require some qualification to the objective moral claim. On both sides, it is a moral issue, and the only way to defend universalizability or equal opportunity against subjectivist qualification is by continuing the moral argument. It is a matter of understanding exactly what the subjectivist wants us to give up, and then asking whether the grounds for those judgments disappear in light of his observations.

In my opinion, someone who abandons or qualifies his basic methods of moral reasoning on historical or anthropological grounds alone is nearly as irrational as

---

7. *Universalizability* is a matter of putting yourself in the situation of others; for example, by asking whether you could approve of everyone doing what you are considering doing or whether you could approve of your conduct if you looked at it through the eyes of others.

someone who abandons a mathematical belief on other than mathematical grounds. Even with all their uncertainties and liability to controversy and distortion, moral considerations occupy a position in the system of human thought that makes it illegitimate to subordinate them completely to anything else. Particular moral claims are constantly being discredited for all kinds of reasons, but moral considerations per se keep rising again to challenge in their own right any blanket attempt to displace, defuse, or subjectivize them.

This is an instance of the more general truth that the normative cannot be transcended by the descriptive.[8] The question "What should I do?" like the question "What should I believe?" is always in order. It is always possible to think about the question in normative terms, and the process is not rendered pointless by any fact of a different kind—any desire or emotion or feeling, any habit or practice or convention, any contingent cultural or social background. Such things may in fact guide our actions, but it is always possible to take their relation to action as an object of further normative reflection and ask, "How should I act, given that these things are true of me or of my situation?"

The type of thought that generates answers to this question is practical reason. But, further, it is always possible for the question to take a specifically moral form, since one of the successor questions to which it leads is, "What should anyone in my situation do?"—and consideration of that question leads in turn to questions about what everyone should do, not only in this situation but more generally.

Such universal questions don't always have to be raised, and there is good reason in general to develop a way of living that makes it usually unnecessary to raise them. But if they are raised, as they always can be, they require an answer of the appropriate kind—even though the answer may be that in a case like this one may do as one likes. They cannot be ruled out of order by pointing to something more fundamental—psychological, cultural, or biological—that brings the request for justification to an end. Only a justification can bring the request for justifications to an end. Normative questions in general are not undercut or rendered idle by anything, even though particular normative answers may be. (Even when some putative justification is exposed as a rationalization, that implies that something else could be said about the justifiability or nonjustifiability of what was done.)

|||

The point of view to defeat, in a defense of the reality of practical and moral reason, is in essence the Humean one. Although Hume was wrong to say that reason was fit only to serve as the slave of the passions, it is nevertheless true that there are desires and sentiments prior to reason that it is not appropriate for reason to evaluate—that

8. **Normative** statements are statements about how things ought to be. Descriptive statements are statements about how things are.

it must simply treat as part of the raw material on which its judgments operate. The question then arises how pervasive such brute motivational data are, and whether some of them cannot perhaps be identified as the true sources of those grounds of action which are usually described as reasons. . . .

If there is such a thing as practical reason, it does not simply dictate particular actions but, rather, governs the *relations* among actions, desires, and beliefs—just as theoretical reason governs the relations among beliefs and requires some specific material to work on. Prudential rationality, requiring uniformity in the weight accorded to desires and interests situated at different times in one's life, is an example—and the example about which Hume's skepticism is most implausible, when he says it is not contrary to reason "to prefer even my own acknowledged lesser good to my greater, and have a more ardent affection for the former than the latter."[9] Yet Hume's position always seems a possibility, because whenever such a consistency requirement or similar pattern has an influence on our decisions, it seems possible to represent this influence as the manifestation of a systematic second-order desire[10] or calm passion, which has such consistency as its object and without which we would not be susceptible to this type of "rational" motivation. Hume need then only claim that while such a desire (for the satisfaction of one's future interests) is quite common, to lack it is not contrary to reason, any more than to lack sexual desire is contrary to reason. The problem is to show how this misrepresents the facts.

The fundamental issue is about the order of explanation, for there is no point in denying that people have such second-order desires: the question is whether they are sources of motivation or simply the manifestation in our motives of the recognition of certain rational requirements. A parallel point could be made about theoretical reason. It is clear that the belief in modus ponens, for example, is not a rationally ungrounded *assumption* underlying our acceptance of deductive arguments that depend on modus ponens: Rather, it is simply a recognition of the validity of that form of argument.[11]

The question is whether something similar can be said of the "desire" for prudential consistency in the treatment of desires and interests located at different times, I think it can be and that if one tries instead to regard prudence as simply a desire among others, a desire one happens to have, the question of its appropriateness inevitably reappears as a normative question, and the answer can only be given in terms of the principle itself. The normative can't be displaced by the psychological.

If I think, for example, "What if I didn't care about what would happen to me in the future?" the appropriate reaction is not like what it would be to the supposition that I might not care about movies. True, I'd be missing something if I didn't care

---

9. *A Treatise of Human Nature*, book 2, part 3, section 3, ed. L. A. Selby-Bigge (Oxford University Press, 1888), 416. See page 946 of this anthology.

10. A second-order desire is a desire about my desires. My desire to drink coffee is a first-order desire; my desire not to desire to drink coffee is a second-order desire, as is my desire that my future desires be satisfied.

11. **Modus ponens** is a rule of inference. If we assume the premises (1) *If P then Q* and (2) *P*, then *modus ponens* licenses us to infer the conclusion that therefore *Q*. When Nagel says that we recognize the **validity** of this form of **argument**, he means we recognize that if the premises are true, then the conclusion must be true as well.

about movies, but there are many forms of art and entertainment, and we don't have to consume them all. Note that even this is a judgment of the *rational acceptability* of such variation—of there being no reason to regret it. The supposition that I might not care about my own future cannot be regarded with similar tolerance: It is the supposition of a real failure—the paradigm of something to be regretted—and my recognition of that failure does not reflect merely the antecedent presence in me of a contingent second-order desire. Rather, it reflects a judgment about what is and what is not relevant to the justification of action against a certain factual background.

Relevance and consistency both get a foothold when we adopt the standpoint of decision, based on the total circumstances, including our own condition. This standpoint introduces a subtle but profound gap between desire and action, into which the free exercise of reason enters. It forces us to the idea of the difference between doing the right thing and doing the wrong thing (here, without any specifically ethical meaning as yet)—given our total situation, *including* our desires. Once I see myself as the subject of certain desires, as well as the occupant of an objective situation, I still have to decide what to do, and that will include deciding what justificatory weight to give to those desires.

This step back, this opening of a slight space between inclination and decision, is the condition that permits the operation of reason with respect to belief as well as with respect to action, and that poses the demand for generalizable justification. The two kinds of reasoning are in this way parallel. It is only when, instead of simply being pushed along by impressions, memories, impulses, desires, or whatever, one stops to ask "What should I do?" or "What should I believe?" that reasoning becomes possible—and, having become possible, becomes necessary. Having stopped the direct operation of impulse by interposing the possibility of decision, one can get one's beliefs and actions into motion again only by thinking about what, in light of the circumstances, one should do.

The controversial but crucial point, here as everywhere in the discussion of this subject, is that the standpoint from which one assesses one's choices after this step back is not just first-personal. One is suddenly in the position of judging what one ought to do, against the background of all one's desires and beliefs, in a way that does not merely flow from those desires and beliefs but *operates* on them—by an assessment that should enable anyone else also to see what is the right thing for you to do against that background.

It is not enough to find some higher-order desires that one happens to have, to settle the matter: such desires would have to be placed among the background conditions of decision along with everything else. Rather, even in the case of a purely self-interested choice, one is seeking the right answer. One is trying to decide what, given the inner and outer circumstances, *one should do*—and that means not just what *I* should do but what *this person* should do. The same answer should be given to that question by anyone to whom the data are presented, whether or not he is in your circumstances and shares your desires. That is what gives practical reason its generality.

The objection that has to be answered, here as elsewhere, is that this sense of unconditioned, nonrelative judgment is an illusion—that we cannot, merely by stepping back and taking ourselves as objects of contemplation, find a secure platform from which such judgment is possible. On this view whatever we do, after engaging in such an intellectual ritual, will still inevitably be a manifestation of our individual or social nature, not the deliverance of impersonal reason—for there is no such thing.

But I do not believe that such a conclusion can be established a priori,[12] and there is little reason to believe it could be established empirically. The subjectivist would have to show that all purportedly rational judgments about what people have reason to do are really expressions of rationally unmotivated desires or dispositions of the person making the judgment—desires or dispositions to which normative assessment has no application. The motivational explanation would have to have the effect of *displacing* the normative one—showing it to be superficial and deceptive. It would be necessary to make out the case about many actual judgments of this kind and to offer reasons to believe that something similar was true in all cases. Subjectivism involves a positive claim of empirical psychology.

Is it conceivable that such an argument could succeed? In a sense, it would have to be shown that all our supposed practical reasoning is, at the limit, a form of rationalization. But the defender of practical reason has a general response to all psychological claims of this type. Even when some of his actual reasonings are convincingly analyzed away as the expression of merely parochial or personal inclinations, it will in general be reasonable for him to add this new information to the body of his beliefs about himself and then step back once more and ask, "What, in light of all this, do I have reason to do?" It is logically conceivable that the subjectivist's strategy might succeed by exhaustion; the rationalist might become so discouraged at the prospect of being once again undermined in his rational pretensions that he would give up trying to answer the recurrent normative question. But it is far more likely that the question will always be there, continuing to appear significant and to demand an answer. To give up would be nothing but moral laziness.

More important, as a matter of substance I do not think the subjectivist's project can be plausibly carried out. It is not possible to give a debunking psychological explanation of prudential rationality, at any rate. For suppose it is said, plausibly enough, that the disposition to provide for the future has survival value and that its implantation in us is the product of natural selection. As with any other instinct, we still have to decide whether acting on it is a good idea. With some biologically natural dispositions, both motivational and intellectual, there are good reasons to resist or limit their influence. That this does not seem the right reaction to prudential motives (except insofar as we limit them for moral reasons) shows that they cannot be regarded simply as desires that there is no reason to have. If they were, they wouldn't give us the kind of reasons for action that they clearly do. It will never be reasonable for the rationalist to concede that prudence is just a type of consistency in action that he happens, groundlessly, to care about, and that he would have no reason to care about if he didn't already.

---

12. **A priori** means "prior to, or independent of, experience." Mathematical knowledge is often said to be *a priori* because mathematical knowledge is based on proofs, which do not depend on experience. In contrast, **a posteriori** knowledge is knowledge that depends on experience.

The null hypothesis—that in this unconditional sense there are no reasons—is acceptable only if from the point of view of detached self-observation it is superior to the alternatives; and as elsewhere, I believe it fails that test.

TEST YOUR UNDERSTANDING

1. Why does Nagel think that a subjectivist view about morality is more plausible than a subjectivist view about science?

2. According to Nagel, how should we think about the ideal of equal opportunity, once we are aware that there are slave and caste societies that reject that ideal? Should we:

   a. recognize that our convictions about equality of opportunity are simply our current way of thinking and acting, with no objective basis?

   b. dismiss the beliefs and practices of other societies as irrelevant to how we should think and act, because we can safely assume that we have learned from their mistakes and that we are right?

   c. assume that other societies know something we do not know?

   d. consider whether the disagreements with caste or slave societies give us reasons to change our convictions about the importance of equality of opportunity?

3. What does prudential rationality require of us?

4. Nagel says that practical reason has a kind of "generality." What is the source of that generality?

NOTES AND QUESTIONS

1. Nagel says that "attempts to get entirely outside of the object language of practical reasons, good and bad, right and wrong, and to see all such judgments as expressions of a contingent, nonobjective perspective will eventually collapse before the independent force of the first-order judgments themselves."

   a. Give three examples of first-order judgments of good and bad, right and wrong. (One example: Do not stick pins in babies.)

   b. What does Nagel mean by the "independent force" of these judgments? Do you agree that your examples have "independent force"?

   c. Explain what it would mean to see these judgments "as expressions of a contingent perspective."

   d. Why is Nagel so confident about the collapse of attempts to see these judgments as expressions of a contingent perspective? (Consider his example of the belief in equal opportunity.)

2. Nagel says: "If I think, for example, 'What if I didn't care about what would happen to me in the future?' the appropriate reaction is not like what it would be to the supposition

that I might not care about movies." Explain in your own words the distinction Nagel draws between not caring about movies and not caring about your future. Suppose someone (inspired by Hume) says:

> Yes, there is a difference. Most people, the overwhelming majority, desire that things go well for themselves in the future: they desire that their future desires be satisfied. In contrast, as it happens, fewer people are enthusiastic about movies. But neither caring about movies nor caring about your own future is required by reason. It is just a brute fact about us that we care about our future: perhaps a fact about us that is explained by evolution. If you don't care about your future, you are very unusual. If you do not care about movies, you are less unusual. But that is all there is to the distinction. Rationality is not relevant to the difference.

In response, Nagel says:

a. "The fundamental issue is about the order of explanation."
b. A failure to be concerned about one's own future is a "real failure—the paradigm of something to be regretted."
c. The point of view that one takes in judging that the future matters "is not just first-personal."

Look at these passages and try to explain how these points, put together, form an argument against the Hume-inspired view stated above.

Philip L. Quinn (1940–2004)

Quinn, a philosopher of science and religion, taught at Brown University and the University of Notre Dame. He is best known for his writings on religious knowledge, religious ethics, and religion and politics, and more particularly on the divine command theory of ethics.

THE DIVINE COMMAND THEORY

Judaism, Christianity, and Islam share the view that the Hebrew Bible has authority in matters of religion. They therefore have reasons for sympathy with a divine command conception of morality. Both Exodus 20:1–17 and Deuteronomy 5:6–21, which recount the revelation of the Decalogue, portray God as instructing the Chosen People about what they are to do and not to do by commanding them. One might, of course, understand these divine commands as merely God's endorsement of a moral code whose authority is independent of the commands. But it seems natural enough to suppose that the authority of the Decalogue depends in some manner on the fact it is divinely commanded or the fact that the commands express God's will. So the major monotheisms have reasons to develop accounts of morality according to which it depends upon God. A long tradition of theological voluntarism in moral theory has evolved from this natural starting point.

During roughly the last quarter of the twentieth century, there has been a revival of interest in divine command morality within the community of analytic philosophers of religion. Attention has been paid to three important questions: How can the idea that morality depends upon God best be spelled out and given a precise theoretical formulation? How can the theory thus formulated be supported by argument? And how can that theory be defended against objections? In the three sections of this essay, I propose answers to these questions.

Formulating the Theory

Settling on a precise theoretical formulation of the idea that morality depends upon God involves addressing three issues. The following schema can be used to indicate what they are:

(S)   Moral status M stands in dependency relation D to divine act A.

The first issue is the specification of the moral statuses that the theory will claim are dependent on God. The second is specifying the nature of the dependency relation the theory will assert holds between God and those moral statuses. And the third is specifying the divine acts on which the moral statuses will be said by the theory to depend. Each of the three specifications involves a choice among options.

There is general agreement that the theory should claim that some or all the deontological moral statuses depend upon God. Those statuses are moral requirement (obligation), moral permission (rightness), and moral prohibition (wrongness). This agreement is understandable if one thinks of God's will or commands as creating moral law, for then the deontological moral statuses are analogous to the ordinary categories of legal requirement, permission, and prohibition. I once proposed a theory according to which the axiological statuses of moral goodness, moral badness, and moral indifference also depend upon God (Quinn 1978, 67–73). Other theorists, however, have restricted their attention to the deontological moral statuses. In the present discussion, I will follow their lead and formulate a theory in which only deontological moral statuses depend upon God.

Several accounts of the dependency relation have been proposed in recent years. . . .

. . . My current view is that dependence of morality on God is best formulated in terms of a relation of bringing about, though care must be taken to distinguish this relation from various causal relations familiar from science and ordinary life. In particular, the divine bringing about in question will have the following marks: totality, exclusivity, activity, immediacy, and necessity. By totality, I mean that what does the bringing about is the total cause of what is brought about. By exclusivity, I mean that what does the bringing about is the sole cause of what is brought about. By activity, I mean that what does the bringing about does so in virtue of the exercise of some active power. By immediacy, I mean that what does the bringing about causes what is brought about immediately rather than by means of secondary causes or instruments. And by necessity, I mean that what does the bringing about necessitates what is brought about.

There is controversy about which divine acts bring about moral requirements, permissions, and prohibitions. As I see it, it is at the deepest level God's will, and not divine commands—which merely express or reveal God's will—that determines the deontological status of human actions. But Adams (1996) has recently objected to replacing divine commands with God's will in formulating the theory. It is therefore incumbent on me to respond to his objections. . . . Theologians often distinguish between God's antecedent will and God's consequent will. As Adams understands the distinction, "God's antecedent will is God's preference regarding a particular issue considered rather narrowly in itself, other things being equal. God's consequent will is God's preference regarding the matter, all things considered" (Adams 1996, 60–1). It is commonly held that nothing happens contrary to God's consequent will, which is partly permissive. But since wrong actions do occur, wrongness cannot be specified in terms of contrariety to God's consequent will. Nor, according to Adams, can the ground of obligation be identified with God's antecedent will because we are some-times morally obliged to make the best of a bad situation by doing something that a good God would not antecedently have preferred, other things being equal. And if we identify the ground of obligation with God's revealed will, we are in effect identifying it with divine commands.

My response to this objection is to deny that divine antecedent preferences, other things being equal, exhaust God's antecedent will. Following a suggestion by Mark Murphy (1998), I also attribute to God's antecedent will intentions, and I think divine antecedent intentions can be used to account for obligations to make the best of bad situations. Suppose I make a promise. God surely prefers that I keep it, other things being equal. Assume God also antecedently intends that I keep my promise, which makes it obligatory for me to keep it. If I break my promise, I create a bad situation by violating an obligation. But assume that God, in addition, antecedently intends that I apologize if I break my promise, which makes it obligatory for me to apologize if I break it. If I am in the bad situation of having broken my promise, then my obligation is to apologize. If I fail to apologize, I violate a second obligation. Of course, if I both break my promise and fail to apologize, then God neither consequently intends that I keep my promise nor consequently intends that I apologize, for nothing happens contrary to God's consequent intentions. My conclusion is that a sufficiently rich account of God's antecedent will allows us to identify the ground of obligation with some of its activities. . . .

. . . I propose, [then,] that the best theoretical formulations of the idea that the deontological part of morality depends upon God consists of the following three principles:

(P1) For every human agent x, state of affairs S, and time t, (1) it is morally obligatory that x bring about S at t if and only if God antecedently intends that x bring about S at t, and (2) if it is morally obligatory that x bring about S at t, then by antecedently intending that x bring about S at t God brings it about that it is morally obligatory that x bring about S at t;

(P2)   For every human agent x, state of affairs S, and time t, (1) it is morally permissible that x bring about S at t if and only if God refrains from antecedently intending that x not bring about S at t, and (2) if it is morally permissible that x bring about S at t, then by refraining from antecedently intending that x not bring about S at t God brings it about that it is morally permissible that x bring about S at t;

(P3)   For every human agent x, state of affairs S, and time t, (1) it is morally wrong that x bring about S at t if and only if God antecedently intends that x not bring about S at t, and (2) if it is morally wrong that x bring about S at t, then by antecedently intending that x not bring about S at t God brings it about that it is morally wrong that x bring about S at t.

Of course, this theory is not, strictly speaking, a divine command theory; it is instead a divine intention theory. It is, however, a version of theological voluntarism, and it pictures divine commands as expressing or revealing God's antecedent intentions. So when we speak loosely, I suppose no harm is done if we conduct the discussion in terms of divine commands. In what follows, I will do this, occasionally reminding the reader that it is the divine intentions lying behind the divine commands that really make a moral difference.

Supporting the Theory

I know of no deductive argument that is a proof of the theory I have formulated or of any of its near neighbors. . . . I am inclined to doubt that constructing deductive arguments is the most promising way of supporting theological voluntarism. I think a more fruitful approach is to support it by a cumulative case argument. . . . My cumulative case has four parts. They support theological voluntarism in ways analogous to that in which the legs of a chair support the weight of a seated person. No one leg supports all the weight, but each leg contributes to supporting the weight. I do not claim that my cumulative case for theological voluntarism is a complete case or the strongest case that could be made. I think all parts of my cumulative case should have some attractiveness for Christians. One of its parts will appeal only to Christians; two others may appeal to both Christians and some other theists; and the final part should appeal to all monotheists. I do not expect my cumulative case to persuade any nontheists to become theological voluntarists; however, I hope it will convince some nontheists that theological voluntarism is an attractive option for theists. I begin with the part with narrowest appeal and end with the part with broadest appeal.

COMMANDED CHRISTIAN LOVE

It is a striking feature of the ethics of love set forth in the New Testament that love is commanded. In Matthew's Gospel, Jesus states the command in response to a question from a lawyer about which commandment of the law is the greatest. He says: "You shall love the Lord your God with your whole heart, with your whole soul, and with all your mind. This is the greatest and first commandment. The second is like it: You shall love your neighbor as yourself" (Matthew 22:37–9). Mark 12:29–31 tells of Jesus giving essentially the same answer to a scribe, and Luke 10:27–8 speaks of a lawyer giving this answer to a question from Jesus and being told by Jesus that it is correct. In his last discourse, recorded in John's Gospel, Jesus tells his followers that "the command I give you is this, that you love one another" (John 15:17). So the authors of these books concur that the Christian ethics of love for one another is expressed in the form of a command. If Jesus is God the Son, this command and the intention behind it are divine.

Is there a reason for love of neighbor being made a matter of obligation or duty? I think there is. It is that the love of neighbor of which Jesus speaks is extremely difficult for humans in their present condition. It does not spontaneously engage their affections, and so, if it were merely permissible, they would not love their neighbors. It is therefore no accident that the love of neighbor Jesus endorses is a commanded love.

In my view, no one has seen with greater clarity than Kierkegaard just how radical the demands of love of neighbor are. In *Works of Love*, his discourse on Matthew 22:39 draws a sharp distinction between erotic love and friendship, on the one hand, and Christian love of neighbor, on the other. Both erotic love and friendship play favorites; the love of neighbor Christians are commanded to display is completely impartial. Kierkegaard says: "The object of both erotic love and friendship has therefore also the favorite's name, *the beloved*, *the friend*, who is loved in distinction from the rest of the world. On the other hand, the Christian teaching is to love one's neighbor, to love all mankind, all men, even enemies, and not to make exceptions, neither in favoritism nor in aversion" (Kierkegaard 1847/1964, 36). His shocking idea is that the obligation to love imposed by the command places absolutely every human, including one's beloved, one's friend, and one's very self, on the same footing as one's worst enemy or millions of people with whom one has had no contact. Perhaps it is easy to imagine God loving all humans in this undiscriminating way. It is hard to see how it could be either desirable or feasible for humans to respond to one another in this fashion. But if Kierkegaard is right, this is exactly what the command to love the neighbor obliges us to do. . . .

My view is that this commanded love is foundational for Christian ethics; it is also what sets Christian ethics apart from rival secular moralities. The stringency of the obligation to love is likely to give offense. In that respect it resembles the requirements of impartial benevolence or utility maximization in secular moral theories, which are criticized for setting standards impossibly high or not leaving room for personal projects. Kierkegaard wants his readers to see just how demanding the obligation is and to accept it as binding them. "Only acknowledge it," he exhorts them, "or if it is disturbing to you to have it put in this way, I will admit that many times it has thrust me back and that I am yet very far from the illusion that I fulfill this command, which to flesh and blood is offence, and to wisdom foolishness" (Kierkegaard 1847/1964, 71). I concur with Kierkegaard about the importance of highlighting rather than downplaying the stringency of the obligation to love the neighbor even if, as a result, many people are thrust back or offended. Christians who believe that humans in their present condition are fallen should not find this response surprising. It is only to be expected that people in such a condition will feel comfortable with moral laxity and be offended by moral stringency. There is, however, no reason for Christians to believe that fallen humans have no obligations whose stringency makes them uncomfortable. Loving everyone as we love ourselves is, I think, obligatory in Christian ethics, and it has that status, as the Gospels show us, because of God. It seems to me that Christians who take the Gospels seriously are not in a position to deny that they teach us that God intends us to love the neighbor and has commanded us to do so or that these facts place us under an obligation to love the neighbor. So I find, in what is most distinctive about the Christian ethics of love in the Gospels, a reason for Christians to favor a divine command conception of moral obligation.

LEX ORANDI, LEX CREDENDI

[Second argument, omitted here.]

THE IMMORALITIES OF THE PATRIARCHS

A Christian tradition of interpreting some stories in the Hebrew Bible serves as the basis for an argument to the conclusion that the deontological status of at least some actions depends upon God. These stories recount the incidents sometimes described as the immoralities of the patriarchs. They are cases in which God commands something that appears to be immoral and, indeed, to violate a prohibition God lays down in the Decalogue. Three such cases come up over and over again in medieval discussions. The first is the divine command to Abraham, recorded in Genesis 22:1–2, to sacrifice his son Isaac. The second is the divine command reported in Exodus 11:2, which was taken to be a command that the Israelites plunder the Egyptians. And the third is the divine command to the prophet Hosea, stated first in Hosea 1:2 and then repeated in Hosea 3:1, to have sexual relations with an adulteress. According to these stories, God has apparently commanded homicide, theft and adultery (or at least fornication) in particular cases, and such actions are apparently contrary to the prohibitions of the Decalogue. What should the patriarchs do? How are we to interpret these stories?

The tradition of biblical exegesis I am going to discuss takes the stories to be literally true; it presupposes that God actually did command as the stories say God did. It also assumes that these commands were binding on those to whom they were addressed. In *The City of God*, Augustine uses the case of Abraham to make the point that the divine law prohibiting killing allows exceptions "when God authorizes killing by a general law or when He gives an explicit commission to an individual for a limited time." Abraham, he says, "was not only free from the guilt of criminal cruelty, but even commended for his piety, when he consented to sacrifice his son, not, indeed, with criminal intent but in obedience to God" (Augustine of Hippo 426/1958, bk 1, ch. 21). Augustine thinks God explicitly commissioned Abraham to kill Isaac and then revoked the commission just before the killing was to have taken place. It is clear that Augustine believes Abraham did what he should do in consenting to kill Isaac because the killing had been commanded by God. He also believes that Abraham's consent, which would have been wrong in the absence of the command, was not wrong given its presence. So Augustine holds that divine commands addressed to particular individuals (or the divine intentions they express) determine the deontological status of actions those individuals perform in obedience to them.

The connection of these cases to divine command ethics is made explicit in the work of Andrew of Neufchateau, a fourteenth-century Franciscan who is judged by Idziak to have conducted "the lengthiest and most sophisticated defense of the position" (Idziak 1989, 63). Andrew claims that there are actions which, "known per se by the law of nature and by the dictate of natural reason, appear to be prohibited, actions such as homicides, thefts, adulteries, etc. But it is possible that such actions not be sins with respect to the absolute power of God" (Andrew 1514/1997, 91). Abraham, he goes on to say, "wished to kill his son so that he would be obedient to God commanding this, and he would not have sinned in doing this if God should not have withdrawn his command" (Andrew 1514/1997, 91). For Andrew, not only did Abraham do no wrong in consenting to kill Isaac but he would have done no wrong if the command had not been withdrawn and he had killed Isaac. In his view, God's absolute power is such that acts such as homicides, thefts, and adulteries, which are seen to be prohibited and so sins when known by means of natural law and natural reason, would not be sins and so would not be wrong if they were commanded by God, as some in fact have been. He shares with Augustine the view that divine commands (or the divine intentions they express) can and do determine the deontological status of actions. . . .

It is worth noting that agreement with Augustine [and] Andrew . . . about such cases need not be restricted to Christians who share their belief that there actually were the divine commands reported in the scriptural stories. Some may choose to think of such cases as merely possible but concur with the tradition of exegesis I have been describing in believing that divine commands would make a moral difference of the sort our medieval interpreters thought they in fact did make. I think there would be enough agreement about such cases among reflective Christians to make it fair to claim that Christian moral intuitions about scriptural cases support the conclusion that God is a source of moral obligation. What is more, it appears to be only a contingent fact that there are at most a few such cases. The properties, such as absolute power or lordship over life and death, in virtue of which divine commands have their moral effects, would still be possessed by God even if such commands were more numerous. So it is hard to resist the conclusion that any act of homicide, plunder, or intercourse with a person other than one's spouse would be obligatory if it were divinely commanded.

Thus the intuitions underlying this tradition of exegesis also support the conclusion that whether any action is morally obligatory or not depends on whether it is divinely commanded (or divinely intended) or not.

I cannot speak with authority about how the exegetical traditions of Judaism and Islam treat the incidents known as the immoralities of the patriarchs. It does seem to me, however, that Jews and Muslims have available to them the strategy of interpretation made use of by Augustine [and] Andrew. . . . Those among them who adopt this strategy will be able to use scriptural cases to support the view that Yahweh or Allah is a source of moral obligation.

ABSOLUTE DIVINE SOVEREIGNTY

There are several reasons why theists of all stripes—Jews, Christians, and Muslims alike—would favor including a strong doctrine of divine sovereignty in their philosophical theology. Two of the most important pertain to creation and providence. Theists customarily wish to insist on a sharp distinction between God and creation. According to traditional accounts of creation and conservation, each contingent thing depends on God's power for its existence whenever it exists. God, by contrast, depends on nothing external for existence. So God has complete sovereignty over the realm of contingent existence. Theists also usually wish to maintain that we can trust God's eschatological promises without any reservation. Even if God does not control the finest details of history because God has chosen to create a world in which there is microphysical chance or libertarian freedom, God has the power to ensure that the created cosmos will serve God's purposes for it and all its inhabitants in the long run. So God also has extensive sovereignty over the realm of contingent events. Considerations of theoretical unity then make it attractive to extend the scope of divine sovereignty from the realm of fact into the realm of value. It is an extension of this sort that we find in the remark by Andrew of Neufchateau that, with respect to God's absolute power, it is possible for homicides, thefts, and adulteries not to be sins. More controversially, the same considerations make it tempting to extend the scope of divine sovereignty from the realm of the contingent into the realm of the necessary. . . .

. . . Suppose that divine strong antecedent intentions are antecedent intentions that God, being essentially perfectly good, could not have failed to form. According to our theory, it is the case that murder, theft, and adultery are morally wrong because God antecedently intends that no one ever bring about the state of affairs of an act of murder, theft, or adultery being performed. It is by antecedently intending that no one ever bring about the state of affairs of an act of murder, theft, or adultery being performed, according to (P3), that God brings it about that it is the case that murder, theft, and adultery are morally wrong. The extension into the realm of the necessary is straightforward. If it is necessarily the case that murder, theft, and adultery are morally wrong, this is so because God strongly antecedently intends that no one ever bring about the state of affairs of an act of murder, theft, or adultery being performed. It is by strongly antecedently intending that no one ever bring about the state of affairs of an act of murder, theft, or adultery being performed, according to the natural extension of (P3), that God brings it about that it is necessarily the case that murder, theft, and adultery are morally wrong. And (P1) and (P2) can be extended in similar ways.

Less formally but more generally, the idea is that moral facts about deontological status are as they are because God has certain antecedent intentions concerning the actions of creaturely moral agents, and necessary moral facts about deontological status, if there are any, are as they are because God has certain strong antecedent intentions concerning the actions of creaturely moral agents. This idea gets support from the doctrine of divine sovereignty because it extends God's sovereignty to cover both the contingent part and, if there is one, the necessary part of the deontological realm.

I think the strength of my cumulative case for theological voluntarism derives in part from the diversity of sources to which it appeals. The ethical demands set forth by Jesus in the Gospels, considerations drawn from religious practice, commentary on incidents portrayed in the Hebrew Bible, and considerations from philosophical theology converge in supporting the position. Further support may be available from arguments to be found in medieval and early modern discussions of divine command ethics. Idziak (1989) contains a catalogue of such arguments. Perhaps some of these arguments can be updated and made parts of a contemporary cumulative case for theological voluntarism.

Defending the Theory

Before the recent revival of interest in divine command theory began, many philosophers were convinced that objections sufficient to refute theological voluntarism were known. So, particularly during the earlier phases of the revival, a lot of energy went into defending the theory against objections. A successful defense shows that the objections fail to establish the falsity of the theory. Each objection must be considered on its own merits, and objections must be replied to one by one. . . .

THE MORAL SKEPTICISM OBJECTION

It is sometimes thought that theological voluntarism inevitably leads to moral skepticism. An argument in support of this view might go along the following lines. According to theological voluntarism, we can come to know what is morally obligatory, permissible, and wrong only by first coming to know certain facts about the divine will. But we cannot, at least in this life, come to know such facts, for God's will is inscrutable. Hence, we cannot in this life come to know what is morally obligatory, permissible, and wrong. A more modest version of this objection is the complaint that, according to theological voluntarism, only people who have religious knowledge can have moral knowledge. As Eric D'Arcy puts it, "If immoral actions are immoral merely because God so wills it, merely because God legislates against them, it would be sheer coincidence if someone who knew nothing of God or his law happened to adopt the same views about particular actions as God did" (D'Arcy 1973, 194). And, of course, mere coincidence of our views with God's views, though it would give us true beliefs, would not suffice for moral knowledge.

One reply to the objection is to deny that the divine will is inscrutable. The theological voluntarist can appeal to scripture, religious tradition, personal revelation, and even natural law as sources of knowledge concerning what God has willed. But then the skeptical worry will shift to the disagreements among religious people about what the deliverances of those sources are. Another reply gets closer to the heart of the matter. Our theory asserts that divine antecedent intentions bring it about that certain things are morally obligatory, others are permissible, and others are wrong. It makes no claims in moral epistemology, and so it makes no claims about how we might come to know what God's antecedent intentions are. It does not entail that we can come to know what is morally obligatory, permissible, and wrong only by first coming to know what God's antecedent intentions are. It is consistent with the view that we can only come to know what God's antecedent intentions are by first coming to know what is morally obligatory, permissible, and wrong. This is as it should be. The subject matter of our theory is a certain kind of metaphysical dependency of deontological status on divine intentions. The order of epistemic access may run in the opposite direction from the order of metaphysical dependency. After all, though effects are metaphysically dependent on their causes, in ordinary life we often come to know causes by first coming to know their effects. It is not a consequence of our theory that only people who have religious knowledge can have moral knowledge. Hence, the objection fails.

Whether or not agreement of the views of those who know nothing of God with God's views about the morality of actions is mere coincidence depends on the explanation of the agreement. An explanation available to theological voluntarists is that God has benevolently endowed normal human creatures with a moral faculty such as conscience that, when functioning properly in appropriate circumstances, reliably tracks, unbeknownst to those who know nothing of God, divine antecedent intentions. If that explanation is correct, the agreement is not mere coincidence, and, on reliabilist accounts of knowledge, those who know nothing of God are not precluded from having moral knowledge.

THE USELESSNESS OBJECTION

It is sometimes argued that theological voluntarism is useless as an ethical standard. Jeremy Bentham says: "We may be perfectly sure, indeed, that whatever is right is conformable to the will of God; but so far is that from answering the purpose of showing us what is right, that it is necessary to know first whether a thing is right, in order to know from thence whether it be conformable to the will of God" (Bentham 1789/1948, 22). So his view is that we can come to know what is conformable to the divine will only by first coming to know what is right. Many theological voluntarists would disagree with this view and argue that sometimes we can come to know what is conformable to the will of God from such sources as revelation. But Bentham's view is consistent with our theory. If it is correct, our theory does not provide a decision procedure for the deontological part of ethics: a way of deciding or determining what is right. However, our theory makes no claim to provide a decision procedure. Ethical theories can perform functions other than teaching us how to decide what is right. It would be of theoretical interest to find out that what is morally obligatory, permissible, and wrong depends on divine antecedent intentions, even if this knowledge were not of any practical use. So even if Bentham's view were correct, it would not constitute a successful objection to our theory. Moreover, it is worth noting, by way of an ad hominem against Bentham, that his brand of utilitarianism would be in trouble if this objection were cogent. No one is in a position to calculate the exact hedonic values of all the consequences of all the alternative actions open to an agent in many circumstances in which moral decisions must be made. Nonetheless, a utilitarian may reply, it would be of theoretical interest to find out that hedonistic act-utilitarianism is true, even if applying it to generate solutions to moral problems is often not a practical possibility.

THE DIVISIVENESS OBJECTION

Another objection is that theological voluntarism is bound to be a divisive point of view. William K. Frankena puts the point this way:

> However deep and sincere one's own religious beliefs may be, if one reviews the religious scene, contemporary and historical, one cannot help but wonder if there is any rational and objective method of establishing any religious belief against the proponents of other religions or of irreligion. But then one is impelled to wonder also if there is anything to be gained by insisting that all ethical principles are or must be logically grounded on religious beliefs. For to insist on this is to introduce into the foundation of any morality whatsoever all of the difficulties involved in the adjudication of religious controversies, and to do so is hardly to encourage hope that mankind can reach, by peaceful and rational means, some desirable kind of agreement on moral and political principles. [Frankena 1973, 313]

Though Frankena is in this passage discussing views in which the relation between religion and morality is logical, presumably he would have a similar worry about our theory in which the relation is metaphysical. And, of course, Frankena is correct in pointing out that religious disagreement has in the past given rise to moral disagreement and continues to do so.

But religious disagreement does not inevitably give rise to disagreement about moral principles. A theological voluntarist can agree with a secular Kantian deontologist on the principle that torture of the innocent is always morally wrong. They will, to be sure, disagree about why torture of the innocent is always wrong.

A theological voluntarist who adopts our theory will say that it is wrong because God antecedently intends that no one ever bring about the torture of an innocent person. A secular Kantian deontologist may say that it is wrong because it involves failing to treat the humanity in another as an end in itself. Disagreement at the level of the metaphysics of morals is consistent with overlapping consensus at the level of moral principles. So despite religious disagreement, there are grounds for hope that we can reach, by peaceful and rational means, agreement on at least some moral and political principles. . . .

It is also worth noting that not all moral disagreement is divisive. A Kierkegaardian Christian may think that Mother Teresa was only doing her duty toward her neighbor as specified by the Love Commandment and regret that he fails to live up to the standards she set. One of her secular admirers may believe that much of the good she did was supererogatory. But if they agree that she did a great deal of good and that the world would be a better place if it contained more people like her, their disagreement about whether some good things she did were obligatory or supererogatory is not apt to be especially divisive.

THE ANYTHING GOES OBJECTION

Perhaps the most troublesome objection to theological voluntarism was clearly stated by Ralph Cudworth. He said that

> divers Modern Theologers do not only seriously, but zealously contend . . . , *That there is nothing Absolutely, Intrinsically, and Naturally Good and Evil, Just and Unjust, antecedently to any positive Command of God; but that the Arbitrary Will and Pleasure of God,* (that is, an Omnipotent Being devoid of all Essential and Natural Justice) *by its Commands and Prohibitions, is the first and only Rule and Measure thereof.* Whence it follows unavoidably that nothing can be imagined so grossly wicked, or so foully unjust or dishonest, but if it were supposed to be commanded by this Omnipotent Deity, must needs upon that Hypothesis forthwith become Holy, Just and Righteous. [Cudworth 1731/1976, 9–10]

Consider some foully unjust state of affairs, say, an innocent child's being tortured to death. Translated into the idiom of our theory, Cudworth's complaint would be that theological voluntarism has as a consequence the following conditional:

(11) If God were antecedently to intend that someone at some time bring about the torture to death of an innocent child, then it would be morally obligatory for that person at that time to bring about the torture to death of an innocent child.

Cudworth is right about this point. Our theory's principle of obligation, (PI), has (11) among its consequences. But this will yield a successful refutation of our theory only if it can be shown that (11) is false. In order to show that (11) is false, one must show that its antecedent is true and its consequent is false. Can this be done?

There is a very plausible claim that entails the falsity of the consequent of (11). It is this:

(12) There is no possible world in which it is morally obligatory for anyone at any time to bring about the torture to death of an innocent child.

And the following claim entails the truth of the antecedent of (11):

(13) There is a possible world in which God antecedently intends that someone at some time bring about the torture to death of an innocent child.

But a theological voluntarist who accepts (12) can reject (13). A theological voluntarist can consistently reject the claim Cudworth makes parenthetically that God is an omnipotent being devoid of all essential and natural justice. If God is essentially just, there will be constraints on the antecedent intentions God can form. If it is unjust to bring about a certain state of affairs, it is also unjust to intend that anyone else bring it about. Hence, a theological voluntarist can maintain that there is no possible world in which God antecedently intends that someone at some time bring about the torture to death of an innocent child.

Theological voluntarists who are convinced that God is essentially just thus have a straightforward response to the objection. It is to admit that (11) is a consequence of their view but to insist that its antecedent is impossible. According to most theories of counterfactual conditionals, counterfactuals with impossible antecedents are trivially true. Thus theological voluntarists can accept (11) and hold that it is true. So the objection fails to refute theological voluntarism. In morality, it is not the case that anything goes if morality depends on the will of an essentially just God. . . .

Of course, a theological voluntarist can also consistently accept (13) and reject (12). The discussions of the immoralities of the patriarchs by Augustine [and] Andrew . . . provide a precedent for this move. A theological voluntarist who takes this tack can accept (11) and hold that it is true because both its antecedent and its consequent are true at the appropriate possible world or worlds. In my opinion, this response to the present objection is less plausible than the response previously considered. However, I think it would be a mistake to generalize to the conclusion that it is an implausible kind of response in every possible case, including all the cases of the immoralities of the patriarchs. Hence I do not think the contribution those examples make to my cumulative case for theological voluntarism is undercut by my preference for the first response to Cudworth's objection.

My strategy in responding to objections has been to rebut them one at a time. This seems to me fair because they are presented in this fashion by authors who criticize theological voluntarism. But, of course, someone might try to build a cumulative case against theological voluntarism by combining several objections. For example, I think Cudworth's objection would show promise of contributing to such a cumulative case if the second response to it I have discussed were the only response available to the theological voluntarist. However, I do not think the other objections I have considered show similar promise. So while I acknowledge that it is incumbent on defenders of theological voluntarism to give a hearing to and to try to rebut a cumulative case argument against their position if one is presented, I do not think that there is at present such a case to answer.

In sum, theological voluntarism is a view of the deontological part of morality that can be formulated with precision, supported from within a monotheistic worldview by a strong cumulative case argument, and defended against numerous objections. Thus our theory should be very attractive to ethical theorists who are monotheists. It should also command respect from ethical theorists who, while not themselves monotheists, are not hostile to monotheism.[1]

REFERENCES

Adams, R. M. (1996) "The Concept of a Divine Command," in *Religion and Morality*, ed. D. Z. Phillips. London: Macmillan, pp. 59–80.

Andrew of Neufchateau (1514/1997) *Questions on an Ethics of Divine Commands*, trans. J. M. Idziak. Notre Dame, IN: University of Notre Dame Press.

Augustine of Hippo (426/1958) *The City of God*, trans. G. G. Walsh, D. B. Zema, G. Monahan, and D. J. Honan. Garden City, NY: Image.

Bentham, J. (1789/1948) *An Introduction to the Principles of Morals and Legislation*. New York: Hafner.

Cudworth, R. (1731/1976) *A Treatise Concerning Eternal and Immutable Morality*. New York: Garland.

D'Arcy, E. (1973) "Worthy of Worship: A Catholic Contribution," in *Religion and Morality*, ed. G. Outka and J. P. Reeder Jr. Graden City NY: Anchor, pp. 173–203.

Frankena, W. K. (1973) " Is Morality Logically Dependent on Religion?" in *Religion and Morality*, ed. G. Outka and J. P. Reeder Jr. Garden City, NY: Anchor, pp 295–317.

Idziak, J. M. (1989) "In Search of 'Good Positive Reasons' for an Ethics of Divine Commands: A Catalogue of Arguments," *Faith and Philosophy* 6: 47–64.

Kierkegaard, S. (1847/1964) *Works of Love*, trans. H. V. Hong and E. H. Hong. New York: Harper.

Murphy, M. (1998) "Divine Command, Divine Will, and Moral Obligation," *Faith and Philosophy* 15: 3–27.

Quinn, P. I. (1978) *Divine Commands and Moral Requirements*. Oxford: Clarendon Press.

TEST YOUR UNDERSTANDING

1. What are the three issues that a theory about the dependence of morality on God needs to clarify?

2. What kind of argument does Quinn aim to provide in support of the divine intention theory?

3. Why does the requirement of Christian love support the divine intention theory?

4. Quinn says that the "most troublesome" objection to the divine intention theory is the "anything goes objection." What is the anything goes objection?

---

1. I am grateful to Hugh LaFollette for helpful comments. [Quinn's note.]

READER'S GUIDE

Quinn's Divine Intention Theory

Philip Quinn's **divine intention theory** is a variant of a more traditional view called the **divine command theory** of morality. For both the divine intention theory and the divine command theory, morality depends in a very profound way on the relationship of human beings to God. To understand the divine intention theory, it will help to know something about the divine command theory and how it conceives of this profound dependence of morality on God.

Consider some familiar moral beliefs. Most of us think that keeping a promise is morally required and that stealing is morally wrong. What accounts for these differences in the moral status of acts? What is it for an act to be morally obligatory or morally wrong?

A divine command theory of morality offers a distinctive answer to these questions. According to the divine command theory, keeping promises is morally required if and only if God has issued the command: "Keep your promises!" Stealing is morally wrong if and only if God has issued the command: "Do not steal." The divine command theorist thus says that the moral status of an action is fixed by the relationship of the action to God's commands.

For the divine command theorist, then, being immoral is like being illegal. An action—say, punching someone in the face—is illegal in virtue of its violating a law: legality and illegality are fixed by the relationship of an action to a legal standard. Punching someone in the face may be painful, nasty, and cruel even in the absence of law. But it is illegal in virtue of there being a law that forbids it. Similarly, for the divine command theorist, an action is morally wrong in virtue of its violating a divine command: morality and immorality are fixed by the relationship of an action to a divine standard expressed in a command. An action—say, violating a promise—may be selfish, faithless, and disrespectful even in the absence of divine commands. But it is morally wrong in virtue of God's command that we keep our promises.

Three points are important in understanding the core idea of the divine command theory.

First, the divine command theorist says that the moral standing of an action is fixed by God's commands. As a result, a divine command theorist can be a **moral nihilist**, who believes that no actions are right or wrong. That is because a divine command theorist may agree that distinctions in moral status depend on God's commands, but then believe that there is no God. Thus, an atheist can endorse the divine command theory. The atheist can agree that the best way to understand the claim that an action is morally required is to think that the action conforms to God's commands. But the atheist can add that there is no God, so no actions are morally required. Consider Ivan Karamazov in Dostoevsky's great novel *The Karamazov Brothers*. Ivan Karamazov suggests a combination of divine command theory and moral nihilism when he says, "Without God ... everything is permitted." So a divine command theorist is not someone who thinks there *are* divine commands, but someone who thinks that the best way to understand moral claims is as claims about divine commands.

Second, for the divine command theorist, God is not simply the *enforcer* of morality. God does not simply impose punishments for violating moral requirements that exist independently from God's commands or rewards for following those requirements. Instead,

God's commands are the source of the difference between morally right and wrong. Moral rightness is brought about by God's commands.

Third, a divine command theorist who thinks that God exists and has issued commands may wish to explain *why* God's commands are as they are. The theorist may wish to explain why God commands, for example, that we keep our promises. Perhaps the divine command theorist thinks that God commands that we keep our promises because promise keeping produces more happiness than simply keeping the promises that we feel like keeping. That explanation of God's command does not tell us what makes promise keeping *morally required*. According to the divine command theorist, I am morally required to keep my promises because that is what God commands, not because promise keeping produces the most happiness. Whatever God's reasons are, it is God's command and not the reasons behind the command that makes the action morally required.

While the divine command theorist may wish to explain God's commands, one kind of explanation is not available. The divine command theorist cannot say that God commanded that we keep our promises *because promise keeping is right*. That explanation—*God commanded promise keeping because it is right*—makes the rightness of promise keeping prior to God's will. But the heart of divine command theory is that rightness is a matter of conformity to God's commands and is not prior to it.

A thread that runs through these three observations is that a divine command theory of morality is about the "metaphysics of morals." It is not about how we can know what morality requires of us—the epistemology of morals. Nor is it about why we should do what morality calls for—about moral motivations. Instead, it explains how the distinction between right and wrong comes into the world. God makes the distinction between right and wrong by issuing commands about how to act: nothing more or less is required.

Quinn's divine intention theory agrees with the divine command theory on all of these points: his theory is also about moral metaphysics. And the theory also claims that rightness is fixed by God. The difference, as Quinn explains, comes in the answer to the question: What is the divine act that brings it about that some action is right or wrong? The divine command theory says that the divine act is the act of commanding. Quinn rejects this view in favor of the idea that morality is based on God's intending. Thus, if God intends that I not steal, then stealing is wrong, even if God has not expressed his intention that I not steal in a command.

NOTES AND QUESTIONS

1. Consider Quinn's response to the anything goes objection, which he attributes to Ralph Cudworth, a seventeenth-century English philosopher.

   a. When Quinn describes the response, he says "there will be constraints on the antecedent intentions God can form." What does he mean by "constraints on antecedent intentions"? Formulate Quinn's point in your own words.

   b. If there are constraints on the intentions that God can form, does that mean that God is not omnipotent? Is that a problem?

c. Suppose someone objects to Quinn as follows:

> The point of the divine intention theory is that moral requirements are dependent on what God wills. The direction of explanation is from God's will (antecedent intentions) to moral requirements, not from moral requirements to God's antecedent intentions. So the divine intention theory says that murder is wrong in virtue of God's antecedent intention that human beings not commit murder. It does not say that God antecedently intends that human beings not commit murder because murder is wrong. But the response to the anything goes objection depends on the idea that God is "essentially just." The response says: because God is essentially just, there are limits on what God can possibly antecedently intend. So God cannot antecedently intend that human beings kill innocent children, for example, because killing innocent children is unjust and God is incapable of acting unjustly. But this argument reverses the order of explanation endorsed by the divine intention theory: it explains God's intentions in terms of a prior standard of what is morally right and morally wrong.

How might Quinn reply to this objection? (*Hint:* Could Quinn say that God is essentially just and therefore unable to antecedently intend certain things, without saying that God has an *obligation* to be just? Would that help?)

d. Quinn says that his discussion of the "immoralities of the patriarchs" suggests a different line of response to the anything goes objection that the divine intention theorist might pursue. What is this alternative line of response? What does it mean to accept statement (13) in Quinn's article, while rejecting (12)? Why do you think Quinn finds this response "less plausible"? Which response do you think is most plausible? Why?

2. Review Sarah McGrath's discussion of the puzzle of moral deference later in this chapter and consider how Quinn might respond to it.

a. Does Quinn think that moral requirements are objective? Explain why.

b. Does he think that there is moral expertise: that some people are better than others at figuring out what is morally obligatory, morally permissible, and morally wrong?

c. What would he think about moral deference: about deferring to the moral judgments of moral experts? Would he find it "weird"?

d. How might Quinn respond to McGrath's concern that people who morally defer end up failing to do the right thing *for the right reasons*?

Elizabeth Harman (b. 1975)

Harman is Laurance S. Rockefeller Professor of Philosophy and Human Values at Princeton University. She has written on topics in moral philosophy, including supererogation, moral responsibility, harm, and the ethics of procreation.

IS IT REASONABLE TO "RELY ON INTUITIONS" IN ETHICS?

Some philosophers argue for ethical conclusions by relying on specific ethical claims about described cases. I will discuss and defend this practice. It is often described as "relying on intuitions," though I will argue that this description is deeply misleading.

Ethical arguments can usefully rely on specific ethical claims about described cases in at least three ways. First, a specific ethical claim can be offered as a *counterexample* to a more general ethical claim. Second, a specific ethical claim can be used to motivate or *support* a more general ethical claim; for example, an author might argue that if a specific ethical claim is true, then it must be true *because* a more general ethical claim is true, and so the more general ethical claim must be true. Third, a specific ethical claim may be used in an argument for another specific ethical claim. There are many ways such an argument might proceed. For example, it might proceed via argument for a more general ethical claim or it might proceed by claiming that there are no morally significant differences between the two cases in question that could warrant different verdicts about the cases.

It will be helpful to have in mind some examples of the type of argument I am discussing. In "Famine, Affluence, and Morality," Peter Singer argues that each of us ought to give a lot of money (much more than people typically give) to famine relief.[1] His argument relies on the claim that if a man is walking by a drowning child, and he is the only person in a position to save the child, but saving the child would involve getting his suit muddy, then he ought to save the child. This specific ethical claim is used to *support* the general claim that if one can prevent something bad from happening without sacrificing anything of comparable moral importance, then one should do so, which Singer then uses to support his conclusion about famine relief. Judith Jarvis Thomson's paper "A Defense of Abortion" argues for the claim that ordinary abortions are permissible even if early fetuses have the full moral status of persons.[2] Her argument crucially depends on the claim that if a man wakes up in a hospital, perfectly healthy himself but with his kidneys being used to keep a famous violinist alive, and if the violinist will die unless the man stays in the hospital for 9 months, then it is permissible for the man to detach himself and leave the hospital, causing the violinist's death. She uses this claim as a *counterexample* to the general claim that it is never permissible to violate a right to life merely in order to have control of one's body. Both Singer's and Thomson's papers argue *from one specific ethical claim to another*.

---

1. Peter Singer, "Famine, Affluence, and Morality," *Philosophy and Public Affairs* 1 (1972): 229–43. Excerpted in Chapter 14 of this volume. [Harman's note.]

2. Judith Jarvis Thomson, "A Defense of Abortion," *Philosophy and Public Affairs* 1 (1971): 47–66. Excerpted in Chapter 14 of this volume. [Harman's note.]

Why might it be thought to be unreasonable to rely on specific claims about described cases in ethics? It is sometimes pointed out that not everyone agrees on these specific claims. Indeed, sometimes survey data are produced to *prove* that there is disagreement about the specific claims.[3] This complaint may simply misunderstand what is going on when people rely on specific claims about described cases in ethics, and in philosophy more generally. Such arguments have as a premise *a certain claim about the case.* They do not have as a premise *a claim that everyone agrees with a certain claim about the case.*

It might be thought that philosophical arguments should not have any premises about which there is disagreement. But having such premises is in the very nature of philosophical arguments, and certainly ethical arguments. Many moral philosophy papers begin by assuming Kantianism, utilitarianism, consequentialism, or virtue ethics and proceeding from there. The arguments these papers offer are not bad arguments simply because they have deeply controversial assumptions. In ethics, and in philosophy more generally, there is quite a lot of disagreement. Arguments often have substantive premises with which some people agree and some people disagree. Two things happen when someone puts forward such an argument. Those who believe the premises are invited to follow the line of reasoning outlined and to believe the conclusion of the argument. Those who do not believe the premises are invited to follow a related line of reasoning to a weaker conclusion: they are invited to believe that *if* those premises are true, *then* the argument's conclusion is true. Thus, a paper that argues from particular premises is not interesting only to those who believe the paper's premises; it has something to say to *everyone.* And the weaker conclusion (that if the premises are true then the conclusion is true) may be interesting to someone even if he does not believe the argument's premises. For example, if one of the premises is (or is implied by) a view that he thinks is false, and that he wants to convince others is false, then the paper may help him in this project by showing further implausible commitments of the rival view. Or to return to our prior examples, Singer intends his 1972 paper to convince his readers of his conclusion. But some readers may become convinced of the weaker conditional: if it is morally obligatory to save a drowning child right in front of one, at the cost of getting one's suit muddy, then it is morally obligatory to give lots of money away regularly to prevent remote children from starving. These readers may believe this conditional and be moved to employ modus tollens rather than modus ponens: because we are not morally obligated to give lots of money away, they conclude that a man who can save a drowning child only at the cost of muddying his suit is not obligated to do so.

Similarly, someone who lacks a clear belief about whether it is permissible, in Thomson's violinist case, for the man in the hospital to unplug himself may nevertheless find himself persuaded by Thomson's argument to believe that if the man's unplugging

---

3. See Joshua D. Greene, "The Secret Joke of Kant's Soul," in *Moral Psychology*, Vol. 3: *The Neuroscience of Morality: Emotion, Disease, and Development*, ed. W. Sinnott-Armstrong (MIT Press, 2007), 35–79, which makes a more complicated argument than the one I go on to discuss; see Selim Berker, "The Normative Insignificance of Neuroscience," *Philosophy and Public Affairs* 37, 4 (2009): 293–329, for a critique of Greene. [Harman's note.]

himself is permissible, then abortion of a fetus with full moral status is permissible. This person thereby comes to believe something about the relationship between the obligations to be a good Samaritan who helps others at significant cost to himself, on the one hand, and the obligation not to abort on the other: if the first obligation does not exist, then the second does not either.

Disagreement does pose another worry, which cannot be so easily dismissed. The fact that there is disagreement over a certain premise may seem to give those who believe the premise sufficient reason to doubt their judgment, so that they should cease to believe the premise.[4] This is an *epistemological worry*, that is, a worry about whether *belief* in the premise of an argument is justified; it is not a worry about whether the premise is true. Epistemological worries pose the most serious kind of challenge to the practice I am defending. I now turn to three sorts of epistemological worries: the first arises from the fact of disagreement; the second arises from a concern that mere intuitive seemings cannot justify beliefs; and the third arises from a concern that some described cases are too far-fetched.

I will begin with the worry arising from disagreement.

Suppose that Anne believes a particular specific ethical claim about the following case. A train is heading for five innocent people caught on the tracks, all of whom will die if they are hit. A person is standing on a bridge over the tracks. She can push a large fat man, who is next to her, off the bridge onto the track. His body would stop the train, preventing it from hitting the five. (Her own smaller body would not stop the train; if she jumped, she would die along with the five.) Anne believes it would be wrong for the woman to push the fat man off the bridge to save the five. Suppose that Anne learns that there is disagreement about this case. In surveys, while many people agree with Anne, many disagree with her.[5] Furthermore, the disagreement is not just among people considering the case for the first time. Even among people who have thought long and hard about this case, there is disagreement.

Upon learning this, Anne may find herself in a situation in which apparent *epistemic peers* disagree with her. That is, Anne may expect that other ordinary people would be roughly as good as she is at discerning the moral truth about a described case if they have the same evidence she does, and she may take others to have the same evidence she has. It may seem that in this situation, Anne would be unreasonable in continuing to believe that it would be wrong to push the fat man. After all, she has no particular reason to think she is better at responding to the shared evidence than other people, but she would have to have such a reason to trust her own judgment more than others'.

The view I have just outlined holds that when one faces disagreement from an epistemic peer, one should suspend judgment about the disputed claim, because one has no independent reason to take one's own judgment to be better. This view might be supported by the claim that when Anne confronts disagreement, the only thing that grounds her belief is *the fact that she has judged the claim to be true;* the question then

---

4. Jonathan Weinberg, Shaun Nichols, and Stephen Stich, "Normativity and Epistemic Intuitions," *Philosophical Topics* 29, 1/2 (2001): 429–60. [Harman's note.]

5. Greene, "The Secret Joke of Kant's Soul." [Harman's note.]

seems to become whether she believes her judgment is better than that of those she disagrees with. This claim is not true, however. Independently of the fact of disagreement (and prior to Anne's learning of the disagreement), Anne's belief was either justified or not. If it was justified, there were some factors that made it justified. Those factors remain after Anne hears of the disagreement; what is under dispute is whether they are still sufficient to justify her belief, that is, whether they are undermined by the fact of disagreement. On the view I endorse, these factors *do* make it reasonable for Anne to continue to hold her belief: *they* furthermore justify her belief that others, in this case, are in error. She concludes they are in error because they think it is permissible to push the fat man, which is false. (The fact that she judged the claim to be true plays no justifying role in her continuing to believe the claim.) However, if Anne's belief was not initially justified, then it is still not justified after she learns of the disagreement. But the fact of disagreement does not make it unjustified; it was independently unjustified.

I have endorsed a stark view on which disagreement poses no skeptical threat at all.[6] If one's beliefs are justified, learning that some others disagree should not at all undermine one's beliefs. I might instead have endorsed a more concessive view, according to which the fact that some others disagree with one makes it reasonable to be *less certain* of a belief one holds but does not require one to suspend belief.[7] Both this more concessive view and the stark view I favor vindicate Anne in continuing to believe it is wrong to push the fat man, even in the face of disagreement.[8]

Let's turn to the second epistemological worry. This worry arises out of two claims. First, all specific ethical beliefs are formed on the basis of an intuitive seeming—on the basis of a claim's seeming to be true, but not for any other reason; that is, not on the basis of any evidence other than the claim's seeming to be true. Second, it is unreasonable to form specific ethical beliefs on the basis of intuitive seemings.

Is it true that all specific ethical beliefs are formed on the basis of intuitive seemings? No. Some specific ethical beliefs are formed on the basis of explicit reasoning *from ethical theories,* despite the believer's finding their negations intuitive. For example, a consequentialist may believe it is permissible to push the fat man off the bridge despite finding it intuitive that it is impermissible.

We might revise the worry's first claim to this: if a specific ethical belief is one that a person simply finds himself with upon reading a description of a case, then it was formed on the basis of an intuitive seeming—on the basis of the claim's seeming to be true, but not for any other reason. The worry's second claim remains the same, that it is unreasonable to form specific ethical beliefs on the basis of intuitive seemings. The worry's conclusion becomes the more limited claim that *in cases where a belief was formed in this way,* the belief is not a reasonable belief and so not a reasonable basis

---

6. Thomas Kelly, "The Epistemic Significance of Disagreement," in *Oxford Studies in Epistemology*, Vol. 1, ed. John Hawthorne and Tamar Gendler Szabo (Oxford University Press, 2005), 167–96. [Harman's note.]

7. Thomas Kelly, "Peer Disagreement and Higher Order Evidence," in *Disagreement*, ed. Richard Feldman and Ted Warfield (Oxford University Press, 2010), 183–217. [Harman's note.]

8. For a defense of the view that Anne would not be reasonable to continue to hold her belief, see Adam Elga, "Reflection and Disagreement," *Noûs* 41, 3 (2007): 478–502. [Harman's note.]

for an inference to a new belief. (The worry in this form applies to an argument as read by some readers but not as read by others.)

Is it true that if a reader simply finds himself with an ethical belief about a case upon reading a description of the case, then the belief must have been formed on the basis of an intuitive seeming—on the basis of the claim's seeming to be true, but not for any other reason? Surely not. The belief may have been implicitly inferred from other ethical commitments the person has[9]; this may have happened without the person's realizing it or he may be *unsure* whether this has happened.

No *general* account will accurately describe what happens in all instances in which people read descriptions of cases and then find themselves with beliefs about the cases. Sometimes people have preexisting beliefs about the cases. (For example, some people before reading Singer's description of the case already believe that a stranger walking by a drowning child should save the child.) Sometimes people infer particular beliefs about the cases from more general beliefs they already have. Or they make explicit a particular belief they already implicitly had.

Consider the famous example of the doctor who cuts up an innocent healthy person to save five people dying of organ failure. It regularly happens that people hear this case described for the first time. They often react by believing that what the doctor does is wrong. Though they have never heard the case described, they do not *newly believe* that what the doctor does is wrong; they either already implicitly believed it or were already implicitly committed to it.

These points show that someone may simply find herself with a particular belief, upon hearing a case described, without it being true that her belief was formed on the basis of an intuitive seeming—on the basis of the claim's seeming true to her, and nothing else. We should not assume that, most of the time, beliefs about described cases are formed on the basis of intuitive seemings.

Indeed, intuitive seemings may play *no role* in the epistemology of specific ethical beliefs, as they actually occur. But if intuitive seemings do play a role, this may not be problematic. We might have the view that intuitive seemings *can* justify beliefs. We might hold that intuitive seemings justify beliefs in the same way that perceptual seemings justify beliefs. This claim could be elaborated in several different ways. One view holds that a person's intuitive seemings justify beliefs if her intuitive seemings are reliable[10]; this is an analog of a reliabilist story about perceptual justification. Another view would hold that intuitive seemings justify beliefs simply because of their content: that it seems to you that p is true is in itself a reason to believe that p is true; this is an analog of the "dogmatic" view of perceptual justification offered by James Pryor.[11]

We are now in a position to see why the practice I am defending—the making of ethical arguments that rely on specific ethical claims about described cases—should not be described as "relying on intuitions" in doing ethics. At least two mistakes are

9. F. M. Kamm, "Introduction," in *Creation and Abortion* (Oxford University Press, 1992), 3–19. [Harman's note.]

10. George Bealer, "A Theory of the A Priori," *Philosophical Perspectives* 13 (1999): 29–55. [Harman's note.]

11. James Pryor, "The Skeptic and the Dogmatist," *Noûs* 34, 4 (2000): 517–49. [Harman's note.]

present in that description. First—as I mentioned early in this paper—there is a conflation of two very different practices: relying on certain claims that may in fact be intuitive, on the one hand, and relying on the claim *that* these claims are intuitive, on the other hand. Philosophical arguments of the type I am defending (and of the type often criticized for "relying on intuitions") do not rely on any claims about intuition; they rely on specific moral claims themselves. Second, there is an assumption that whenever we believe specific moral claims about described cases, we believe them simply because they are intuitive; as I've just argued, this is not true.

The third epistemological worry is sometimes voiced as follows: "Some described cases are too odd, too complicated, or involve too much science fiction for us to have reasonable beliefs about the cases." If this worry is meant to apply to all uses of claims about described cases, it is false. Singer's case, of the man and the drowning child, is neither odd, nor complicated, nor involving science fiction. Thomson's case involves some *fiction*: she supposes that medical records have shown that the man in the hospital, attached to the violinist, is the only person who can help; she supposes that he has been kidnapped and attached; and she supposes that one person's kidneys can be used to restore another person to health across 9 months. But none of these suppositions is very far removed from the actual world: donor databases for bone marrow transplants sometimes reveal to someone that he is the only person who can save a stranger's life, organs are sometimes stolen from healthy people, and in order to donate kidneys or parts of livers, people sometimes endure serious health risks and hospital stays to restore others to health. The case of the woman on the bridge with the fat man is not very complicated. The case of the doctor who cuts up his healthy patient to save five patients with organ failure is also quite simple. Neither of these two cases involves any science fiction.

Sometimes people complain that particular described cases are too odd, too complicated, or involve too much science fiction as a way of explaining why they themselves are unmoved by the arguments that rely on claims about these cases: they find that they *lack* beliefs about the cases, or that they lack stable, confident beliefs about the cases. This fact, that *some people* lack beliefs about the claims in question, does not show that everyone lacks such beliefs. The arguments may nevertheless be perfectly good arguments that appeal to claims believed by some people but not by everyone.

It is a *much stronger* claim that some particular described cases are so odd, so complicated, or involve so much science fiction that *no one* could reasonably have a justified belief about the cases. This claim is not true about any of the four described cases I have just mentioned. Indeed, each case is such that we could come upon a similar case in real life. Would the case be too odd for us to judge whether the agent had acted permissibly? Surely not.[12]

I will briefly mention a final concern. This concern maintains that our general ethical beliefs are better grounded, or more reliable, than our specific ethical beliefs about cases, such that we should always do ethics by proceeding *from* the general

---

12. Timothy Williamson, "Thought Experiments," chapter 6 in *The Philosophy of Philosophy* (Blackwell, 2007). [Harman's note.]

to the specific, and never vice versa.[13] Kantians and utilitarians often believe this is the correct view of the epistemology of ethics. There are many different reasons that might be offered for this view. But none of the three epistemological worries I have discussed can support this view. As for the first worry, I conjecture that if we were to conduct surveys of people's beliefs in general ethical claims, we would find substantial disagreement. Consideration of disagreement will not tell in favor of general ethical claims over specific ethical claims. As for the second worry, whether intuitive seemings can be a source of justified beliefs favors neither specific nor general ethical claims. The third worry might seem to favor general claims. Whereas some specific ethical claims are about cases that may be odd or complicated, nothing corresponding holds of general ethical claims: being general, they are not focused on anything odd or complicated. But the third worry, properly understood, simply presses the point that some specific ethical claims are such that some people will be unsure what to make of them. The same is true of general ethical claims.

Conclusion

I have defended the making of arguments for ethical conclusions on the basis of specific ethical claims about described cases. I have argued that three objections to this practice fail.[14]

Where does this leave someone who wants to pursue ethical questions by reading philosophy papers? Suppose you read a paper that argues for an ethical conclusion on the basis of specific ethical claims about described cases.

If you believe the specific ethical claims the paper relies on, then the paper is offering you an argument for its conclusion, which you might well reasonably rely on in coming to believe the conclusion.

If you do not believe a specific ethical claim the paper relies on, either because you believe it is false or because you are unsure what to make of it, then the paper is not in a position to convince you of its conclusion. You may, however, find it interesting whether the weaker conditional is true—that if its premises are true, then its conclusion is true—and the paper may reasonably convince you of this claim. You may also find it interesting that this paper may convince others; you may want to engage with the paper as an argument addressed to others, perhaps showing (to those who believe the premises) that the premises do not really imply the conclusion.

When is a philosophy paper that relies on specific ethical claims criticizable for relying on such claims? No paper is criticizable simply for being *a paper that relies on*

---

13. Peter Singer, "Ethics and Intuitions," *Journal of Ethics* 9 (2005): 331–52; R. M. Hare, "Rawls' *A Theory of Justice*: Part I," *Philosophical Quarterly* 23 (1973): 144–55. [Harman's note.]

14. For two very different defenses of reliance of specific ethical claims, see Kamm, "Introduction," and the final section of Tamar Szabo Gendler, "Philosophical Thought Experiments, Intuitions, and Cognitive Equilibrium," *Midwest Studies in Philosophy* 31 (2007): 68–89. [Harman's note.]

some specific ethical claims about described cases—some papers do so and are excellent, compelling, important philosophy papers.[15] If a paper relies on claims that are only believed by some people, it is still a contribution for being of interest to those people (and it is also of interest to everyone as offering a claim about what follows from certain other claims). But a paper might rely on specific ethical claims such that no one is in a position to form a justified belief about those claims. Such a paper is less interesting because it provides no interesting argument for its conclusion, but it may still be interesting as arguing that if its premises are true, then its conclusion is true.

TEST YOUR UNDERSTANDING

1. Harman discusses "specific ethical claims." What are her three main examples of specific ethical claims?

2. Does Harman agree or disagree with the following statement: *If an argument in ethics starts from controversial premises, then there is no value in the argument.*

3. Harman talks about *epistemic peers*. What does she mean by "epistemic peer"?

4. What is Harman's "third epistemological worry"?

NOTES AND QUESTIONS

1. Suppose you learn that someone whose judgment you respect deeply disagrees with you about an ethical issue. The mere fact of disagreement, Harman argues, does not itself give you reason to doubt your own view. If it is reasonable to continue to hold fast to your position, does the discovery of difference give you any reason to think, reason, or do *anything* differently? If so, what? Or, is the discovery of this different judgment more of a mere curiosity, like discovering that your best friend strangely does not care for chocolate?

2. Harman responds to the criticism that we should not rely too heavily on conclusions drawn from strange cases. Might we have the opposite concern and worry that our reactions to highly familiar cases (e.g., our sense that it is morally permissible to spend money on going to the movies rather than giving it to charity) reflect ingrained social biases, habitual reactions, and self-serving rationalizations? Perhaps introducing fictional elements into the cases we consider might improve our reasoning. Harman briefly

15. Thomson, "A Defense of Abortion"; Singer, "Famine, Affluence, and Morality"; Michael Tooley, "Abortion and Infanticide," *Philosophy and Public Affairs* 2 (1972): 37–65; James Rachels, "Active and Passive Euthanasia," *New England Journal of Medicine* 292 (1975): 78–80; Susan Wolf, "Asymmetrical Freedom," *Journal of Philosophy* 77, 3 (1980): 151–66; Derek Parfit, "Part Three: Personal Identity," *Reasons and Persons* (Oxford University Press, 1982); Seana Shiffrin, "Wrongful Life, Procreative Responsibility, and the Significance of Harm," *Legal Theory* 5 (1999): 117–48; and Frances Kamm, "Terrorism and Several Moral Distinctions," *Legal Theory* 12, 1 (2006): 19–69. [Harman's note.]

discusses Judith Jarvis Thomson's famous violinist example. How might consideration of the violinist's plight help to address some of the potential hazards of familiarity?

3. Harman draws two important, but subtle, distinctions. The first is the distinction between

    1a. Claiming that a particular behavior is permissible.

and

    1b. Claiming that everyone agrees that a particular behavior is permissible.

The second is the distinction between

    2a. Relying on an ethical claim that may in fact be intuitive.

and

    2b. Relying on the claim *that* an ethical claim is intuitive.

Exercise: Explain these two distinctions in your own words and offer examples. (Hint: Often, one way to see a distinction more clearly is to ask what evidence you would offer if someone asked "Why do you think that?" If you would give different evidence for different contentions, that helps you see the difference between them.)

Sharon Street (b. 1973)

Street is an Associate Professor of Philosophy at New York University. She specializes in metaethics and has a particular interest in understanding the relationship between natural science and norms.

DOES ANYTHING REALLY MATTER OR DID WE JUST EVOLVE TO THINK SO?

Life is preferable to death. Health is better than sickness. We should care for our children, not harm them. Altruists are to be admired rather than condemned. Cheaters ought to be punished, not rewarded.

These and many other evaluative beliefs assail us with great emotional force. They strike us as self-evidently correct and command a high degree of consensus across time and cultures. It is tempting to suppose that they are recognitions of independent truths about what matters.

But what if we hold such values "just" because the mindless process of evolution by natural selection shaped us that way? What if the best scientific explanation of our deepest evaluative convictions is simply that these were the ones that it "paid" to have in the struggle to survive and reproduce? Would the truth of that explanation undermine our values? Or, rather, *should* it?

1

Sometimes learning the causal origins of a belief can undermine it. Suppose a friend asks you who the twentieth president of the United States was, and an answer springs to mind. "Rutherford B. Hayes," you say, feeling pleased at your mastery of U.S. history. Your friend bursts into laughter. "You really don't remember, do you?" she says. "That's one of the beliefs the hypnotist implanted in you!" Dismayed, you recall that last night you served as a volunteer in a hypnosis demonstration. Your confidence that Hayes was the twentieth president vanishes. With no other information currently at your disposal, you realize you have no idea whether Hayes was the twentieth president or not.

Other times, learning the causal origins of a belief can strengthen it. Suppose a man approaches you on the street, asking for directions, and you think to yourself, "This guy is up to no good." As you try to put your finger on it, however, there's nothing about him that you can pinpoint. The man is polite and personable. You worry that too many years in the city have made you grumpy and paranoid. Then it hits you: This is the murder suspect you saw profiled a few weeks ago on *America's Most Wanted*! Your belief that the man is up to no good reasserts itself with great force. As you reach nervously for your cell phone, you realize that although it took some moments for your conscious thought process to catch up, at some level your mind had immediately drawn the connection with the murder suspect you'd seen on television.

These cases illustrate how learning new information about a belief's genealogy can bring about an adjustment in that belief—sometimes diminishing one's confidence in the belief, other times bolstering it. Moreover, notice: Not only do we think these adjustments in belief *would* take place; we think they *should* take place. We think, in other words, that suspending belief in the hypnosis case and increasing one's confidence in the *America's Most Wanted* case are *rationally appropriate* responses to the new information about the origins of these beliefs.

Let's explore further why these responses seem rationally appropriate. In the first case, you learn that your belief that Hayes was the twentieth president has its origins in a causal process that as far as you know has nothing to do with whether Hayes was in fact the twentieth president. As far as you know, in other words, the hypnotist last night had no interest in implanting in you a true belief on the subject. When the answer "Hayes" first sprang to mind, it was natural to assume that the belief had its causal origins in your high school history class or some other reliable source. When you learn the belief's actual origin, however, you realize that you have no reason to regard your initial hunch as any guide to the truth on the matter. Moreover, as we have stipulated, you have no other relevant information currently at your disposal. It is therefore rational for you to suspend belief pending access to further information.

In the second case, in contrast, you learn that your belief was, initially without clear conscious awareness on your part, caused by facts directly relevant to the question whether the man was up to no good. Someone's having been profiled as a murder suspect on *America's Most Wanted*, after all, is a pretty good reason to think he is up to no good, and that turns out to be exactly the fact you were responding to when you formed the initial belief, though you didn't realize it at first. Upon discovering the *cause* of your initial hunch, you simultaneously discover what you recognize to be a good *reason* for it. It is therefore rational for you to increase your confidence in the belief accordingly.

2

Can we draw any general lessons? Suppose one learns a new causal explanation of one's belief that *P*, where *P* stands for some proposition. When should that genealogical discovery diminish one's confidence in the belief, and when should it increase one's confidence? Our two cases suggest the following answer:

PRINCIPLE OF UNDERMINING VERSUS VINDICATING GENEALOGIES

Undermining genealogy: If the causal process that gave rise to one's belief that *P* is such that (as far as one knows) there is no reason to think that it would lead one to form true beliefs about the subject matter in question—and if (as far as one knows) there is no other good reason to believe that *P*—then one should suspend belief that *P*.

Vindicating genealogy: If, on the other hand, the causal process that gave rise to one's belief that *P* constitutes or otherwise reveals (what is, as far as one knows) a good reason to believe that *P*—a reason of which one was not previously aware—then (all else remaining the same) one should increase one's confidence that *P*.

Notice something important about this principle. According to it, genealogical information *by itself* implies nothing one way or another about whether we should continue to hold a given belief. Rather, in order validly to draw any conclusions about whether or how to adjust one's belief that *P*, one must assess the *rational significance* of the genealogical information, locating it in the context of a larger set of premises about *what counts as a good reason* for the belief that *P*. For example, "that I was hypnotized to think so" is not a good reason to think Hayes was the twentieth president, whereas "that my competent high school teacher said so" would be a good reason. Your belief that Hayes was the twentieth president is undermined because you learn that your initial hunch was based on no good reason, whereas your belief that the man is up to no good is vindicated because you learn that your initial hunch was based on a good reason.

3

Armed with the above principle, let's turn now to what we might call our "evaluative hunches" and their genealogy. The theory of evolution by natural selection offers profound insight into the causal origins of our species' *most basic evaluative tendencies*, where by this I mean our tendencies to value certain very general types of things rather than others.

Consider, for example, the following evaluative claims:

(1) The fact that something would promote one's survival is a reason to do it.

(2) The fact that something would promote one's health is a reason to do it.

(3) The fact that something would help one's child is a reason to do it.

(4) The fact that someone is altruistic is a reason to admire, praise, and reward him or her.

(5) The fact that someone has cheated (not holding up his or her end of a cooperative deal) is a reason to shun, condemn, and punish him or her.

The most basic evaluative impulses that are expressed by (1)–(5), while of course not universal, are overwhelmingly common among human beings across history and cultures. Versions of them are even evident in close biological relatives such as the chimpanzees. Why is that?

To sharpen the question, consider the following conceivable evaluative views:

(1′) The fact that something would promote one's survival is a reason not to do it.

(2′) The fact that something would promote one's health is a reason not to do it.

(3′) The fact that something would help one's child is reason not to do it.

(4′) The fact that someone is altruistic is a reason to dislike, condemn, and punish him or her.

(5′) The fact that someone has cheated (not holding up his or her end of a cooperative deal) is a reason to seek out that person's cooperation again and praise and reward him or her.

Consider also even more bizarre possible evaluative views such as the following:

(6) The good life is one devoted to screaming constantly.

(7) One ought to do cartwheels every 4 seconds until one dies.

Why do human beings generally tend so strongly in the direction of values of the kind expressed by (1)–(5) as opposed to other conceivable values—for example, those expressed by (1′)–(5′), (6), and (7)? An evolutionary biological perspective sheds enormous light. For the theory of evolution by natural selection explains not only the existence of certain *physical* traits such as our lungs, eyes, and ears, but also the existence of certain *psychological* traits such as our devotion to our children and our enjoyment of food and sex.

Not every observable trait (whether physical or psychological) is an adaptation that can be explained by natural selection; the importance of this point cannot be overemphasized. But when it comes to the kinds of basic evaluative tendencies expressed by (1)–(5), a powerful evolutionary explanation of their widespread presence in the human population is in the offing. That explanation, very roughly, is that ancestors with a tendency toward values such as (1) through (5) would have tended to leave more descendants than others with a tendency toward values such as, say, (1′) through (5′) or (6) or (7). It is fairly obvious, for example, why a creature who thought its survival was a good thing and that its offspring deserved protection would tend to leave more descendants than a creature who thought its survival was a bad thing and that its offspring should be eliminated. It is also fairly obvious why a tendency to reward those who helped one and punish those who cheated one would have a better evolutionary "payoff" than the reverse.

Complications abound. The causes that have shaped human values are innumerable, and the suggestion that there are innate predispositions in the direction of some values rather than others does not imply that we—either as a species or as individuals—are genetically determined to hold any one particular value. On the contrary, above all we evolved to be flexible creatures—evaluatively incredibly malleable—and we are capable of holding any given value up for reflective scrutiny and rejecting it if we think rejection warranted. The point is rather that while it's often the diversity of human values that captures our attention, on another way of looking at things it's actually the *uniformity* that is striking. If we compare the evaluative views that human beings actually tend to hold with the universe of *conceivable* evaluative views, we see that these values fall within a relatively narrow range and consistently display a particular kind of content. And there appears to be a very good Darwinian explanation for that.

4

Assume such an explanation can be borne out (and more on it below). Should this information about the genealogy of our values undermine them, as in the hypnotism case? Or might it somehow vindicate them, as in the *America's Most Wanted* case?

The Principle of Undermining versus Vindicating Genealogies tells us to focus on the following question: Is the causal process in question (here, evolution by natural selection) such that there is any reason to think that it would lead us to form true beliefs about the subject matter in question (here, evaluative truths about how to live)? If yes, then the evolutionary explanation of our most basic values may vindicate them. If no, then the evolutionary explanation of our most basic values may undermine them.

Immediately we hit complications, however. Unlike the case of "Who was the twentieth president?" where we are more or less clear on what would count as reliable means of arriving at true beliefs on the subject (allowing one's beliefs to be shaped by a hypnotist is not; listening to one's history teacher is), the nature of *this* subject matter—the subject matter of *what is valuable and how to live*—is itself a highly contested and puzzling question. Indeed, the nature of this subject matter is the focal point of the whole subfield of philosophy known as *metaethics*, which is riven with disagreement.

So how do we proceed? There are any number of competing metaethical views on the nature of value. It will be helpful to focus on one key distinction among these views; namely, the contrast between *mind-independent* versus *mind-dependent* conceptions of value.

At issue between such conceptions is the question: Are things valuable ultimately *because we value them* or are at least some things valuable in a way that is robustly *independent of our valuing them*? According to *mind-independent* conceptions, it's the latter: there are at least some things that possess their value in a way that is independent of the evaluative attitudes that we might happen to hold toward them, where by *evaluative attitudes* I mean mental states such as an agent's values, cares, desires, states of approval and disapproval, unreflective evaluative tendencies, and so on. According to *mind-dependent* conceptions, in contrast, there are *no* independent truths about what is valuable. Rather, if something is valuable, then this is ultimately in virtue of our evaluative attitudes toward the thing—such that if our evaluative attitudes were to change radically enough, so that it was no longer in any way implied by our own attitudes that the thing was valuable, it would thereby cease to *be* valuable. We all hold a mind-dependent view of *some* kinds of value. For example, we all agree that the value of chocolate ultimately depends on the fact that people like it. No one thinks that had human beings all found chocolate disgusting, we would have been missing an independent fact about chocolate's value. The question is whether *all* value is ultimately like that. The mind-dependent theorist says "yes"; the mind-independent theorist says "no."

5

Our tools refined with this distinction, let's return to our question: *Is the causal process in question (here, evolution by natural selection) such that there is any reason to think that it would lead us to form true beliefs about the subject matter in question (here, evaluative truths)?* Since the nature of the subject matter is contested, let's try "plugging in" first one conception of value and then the other, and see what undermining or vindicating "results" we get. Start with a mind-independent conception of value. If we conceive of evaluative truths as robustly independent of our evaluative attitudes, is there any reason to think that evolutionary forces would have shaped us in such a way as to be reliable at detecting those truths?

You might think yes. After all, evolutionary forces seem to have made us reliable about a lot of things. We're pretty good at detecting objects and movement in our immediate environment, for example, and a great deal else. Why not think that evolutionary forces similarly made us skilled at detecting independent evaluative truths? On this line of thought, it somehow promoted reproductive success to grasp independent evaluative truths, and so ancestors with an ability to do so were selected for.

But this proposal fails. The suggestion is that *somehow* it promoted reproductive success to grasp the independent evaluative truth, but we haven't been told yet why or how, and until we've been told this, we have no explanation at all. *Why* would it promote reproductive success to detect the independent evaluative truth? In the case of predators, trees, or fires, it is obvious why it would promote reproductive success to detect them, for these things can kill you or injure you if you fail to notice them. What happens, though, if one fails to notice an independent evaluative truth about how to live? Well, one won't live in accordance with the independent evaluative truth about how to live, but that's not an answer with any explanatory power. It just leads to a repeat of the question: *Why* would it hurt reproductive success not to live in accordance with the independent evaluative truth about how to live?

Consider evaluative views (1) through (5) again. To explain why we evolved with a tendency to accept these views, there is no reason to suppose that these evaluative views are *true* and that it promoted reproductive success to recognize such truths. The best explanation is simpler: all we need to notice is that a creature who accepts these evaluative views—valuing its survival, health, and offspring, for example—will tend to look out for itself and its offspring and so will of course leave more descendants than a creature who, say, despises its own survival, health, and offspring. Truth and falsity have nothing to do with which values would proliferate and which would die out. Thus, if we assume a mind-independent conception of value, it's not at all clear why evolutionary forces would have shaped us to value those things that were, as a matter of independent fact, valuable. It seems that evolutionary forces would just push us to value those things such that valuing them motivated us to do things that promoted survival and reproduction.

It appears that if we conceive of evaluative truths as robustly mind-independent, there is no reason to think that our species arrived at its most basic evaluative assumptions in a way that is reliable with respect to those truths. The case of evolution and value would appear to be more like the hypnosis example, where the causal process that gave rise to the belief in question is not—as far as we can see anyway—one that we have any reason to suppose is a reliable means of arriving at true beliefs about the subject matter. It would seem that we should abandon all confidence in our values and conclude that they have been shaped in a way that bears no relation to the truth.

It cannot be exaggerated what a radical move this would be—to abandon all confidence in our values. To conclude that we are unreliable about the evaluative truth would be to accept *global evaluative skepticism* in the sense of a conviction that one has no idea how to live. Is it plausible, however, to think that when you wake up in the morning, you have no idea at all how to live? That as far as you know you haven't the slightest clue as to whether you should spend your life screaming constantly, doing cartwheels, or something else?

Recall, though: We arrived at this skeptical result only on a certain assumption about the nature of evaluative truths; namely, that they are mind-independent. So maybe we're not forced to it. What happens if we plug in a mind-dependent conception of evaluative truths?

If a mind-dependent conception of value is right, then the evolutionary origins of our most basic evaluative "hunches" would seem to be no threat to the idea that we're at least somewhat reliable about the subject matter of how to live. For on a mind-dependent conception, it doesn't matter *what* the causal origins of our most basic evaluative convictions are: since what *is* valuable is ultimately just a function of whatever we start out taking to be valuable on a mind-dependent conception, we are able simply to start wherever we start with no worry that those starting points are in some deep sense off-track. It's not exactly that our initial evaluative hunches are *vindicated* on a mind-dependent view; it's rather that vindication turns out not to be an issue at the deepest level. That's because on a mind-dependent view, there is no question of missing something in the very end with one's evaluative attitudes; value is instead understood as something created or constructed by those attitudes.

6

If the arguments of the previous section are correct, then whether we get an undermining result depends on the conception of value we plug in. A mind-independent conception of value, when coupled with the evolutionary genealogy, leads to global evaluative skepticism, whereas a mind-dependent conception has no such implication. Does this mean that we have to settle the issue of whether value is mind-independent or mind-dependent before we can know whether an evolutionary explanation of valuing is undermining or not?

I would argue not. Rather, I would argue that these very results—the undermining result if we assume a mind-independent conception, and the non-undermining result if we assume a mind-dependent conception—are actually what *settles* the debate between these two views of value, with the right conclusion being that the undermining result implied by the mind-independent conception is so implausible that it's the mind-independent conception that must be thrown out.

The evolutionary theory of our origins is overwhelmingly supported by our best science. Taking that as a fixed point, I suggest that it is much more plausible to think that a *mind-independent conception of value is false* than it is to think that *we have no idea how to live*, which is the conclusion that results if we pair a mind-independent conception of value with an evolutionary genealogy of valuing. Accepting this radical skeptical conclusion would involve nothing less than suspending all evaluative judgment, and either continuing to move about but regarding oneself as acting for no reason at all or else sitting paralyzed where one is and just blinking in one's ignorance of how to go forward. Accepting the conclusion that value is mind-dependent, in contrast, preserves many of our evaluative views—allowing us to see why we are reasonably reliable about matters of value—while at the same time allowing us to see ourselves as evolved creatures.

The suggestion is that in response to *this* genealogical investigation, we should—to the extent we started out with a conception of value as mind-independent—*revise our conception of the subject matter*. That move might seem odd. It's as though upon learning that your belief about Hayes had its origin in hypnosis, you find it *so implausible that you could be wrong about whether Hayes was the twentieth president* that you opt to change your conception of the subject matter, concluding that facts about who was the twentieth president are constituted by facts about who you *think* the twentieth president was, no matter what the source of your views, hypnotism included.

Obviously in that context, such a move would be absurd. But as always in philosophy, it's a question of what's most plausible, all things considered. I claim that in the case of the evolutionary origins of valuing, the weakest link in the overall picture—the thing that must go—is a mind-independent conception of value.

We have been asking whether an evolutionary biological explanation of our values ought to undermine them. The answer I've suggested is "yes and no." The answer is "yes" to the extent *you started out thinking that there are mind-independent truths about value*. If that was your view going in, then I've suggested that you ought to abandon it and move to a mind-dependent conception. But once you adopt a *mind-dependent* conception of value—or if you already held such a view to begin with—then the answer is "no," evolutionary explanations of our values aren't undermining in the least.

Your *metaethical* view might need to change, in other words. But your most basic evaluative convictions—that life is preferable to death, that health is better than sickness, that we should care for our children, that altruism is admirable while cheating is to be condemned—all these deepest values should remain untouched by genealogical revelations. In answer to the title's question: Nothing "really" matters in the sense of mattering independently of the attitudes of living beings who *take* things to matter, but the nice fact is that living beings evolved, began taking things to matter, and thereby *made* things matter.

TEST YOUR UNDERSTANDING

1. Street says: "Sometimes learning the causal origins of a belief can undermine it. . . . Other times, learning the causal origins of a belief can strengthen it." What are Street's examples of strengthening and undermining genealogies?

2. What, according to Street, is metaethics about?

3. State the distinction between mind-dependent and mind-independent conceptions of value. Which conception does Street favor?

4. Is the following statement true or false: "If a mind-independent conception of value is correct, then the theory of evolution provides a *strengthening genealogy* of our basic evaluative tendencies."

NOTES AND QUESTIONS

1. According to Street, "The theory of evolution by natural selection offers profound insight into the causal origins of our species' *most basic evaluative tendencies.*"

   a. Pick two entries from Street's list of basic evaluative tendencies and provide a brief sketch of how the theory of evolution by natural selection explains them.

   b. Think of an alternative to the evolutionary explanation of our most basic evaluative tendencies. (The explanation need not be one that you find plausible: just another candidate.)

   c. Street thinks that the evolutionary explanation provides an undermining genealogy if we accept a mind-independent conception of value. Is your alternative explanation also undermining on the mind-independent conception of value?

2. If value is mind-dependent, then, Street argues, evolutionary explanations of our basic evaluative tendencies are not undermining (though they are not vindicating either). Why not? Suppose I say:

   Mind-Dependence: X is good for people generally if and only if people generally value *X*.

   Is Mind-Dependence a plausible account of value? (Does it accurately state Street's account of mind-dependence?) Suppose we all think salt is good for us until we learn that it is unhealthy, thus not good: so we do now value it, but it is not good for us. Cases like this may have motivated Street not to endorse Mind-Dependence. She says that mind-dependent views make value "ultimately" a matter of "our evaluative attitudes." In this spirit, we might modify Mind-Dependence to something like:

   Informed Mind-Dependence: X is good for people generally if and only if people would value *X* if they were well informed about *X* and the consequences of having (using, pursuing) *X*.

   Informed Mind-Dependence does connect value "ultimately" to our evaluative attitudes: being good is a matter of what we would value under idealized conditions in which we are well informed about consequences. But it allows for some distance between what we currently value and what is good for us. Now, though, we may ask a question about Informed Mind-Dependence like the question that Street asks about mind-independent conceptions of value: Why should we suppose that evolutionary forces made us skilled at valuing what is good; that is, what we would value if we were well informed?

   Can you find a variant of Mind-Dependence that meets two requirements: (i) it presents a plausible condition on being a good thing (more plausible than Mind-Dependence); and (ii) evolutionary forces plausibly have made us good at grasping the condition (more plausibly than with Informed Mind-Dependence)?

Sarah McGrath (b. 1972)

McGrath is an Associate Professor of Philosophy at Princeton University. She has written on moral disagreement, moral testimony, moral expertise, and also about issues at the intersection of metaphysics and ethics. She has a book forthcoming on moral knowledge.

WHAT IS WEIRD ABOUT MORAL DEFERENCE?

I

Your professor invites you to lunch. At the restaurant, he orders the vegetarian sandwich. Curious, you ask him if he is a vegetarian. He tells you that he is—that he thinks eating meat is wrong. You ask what persuaded him. He says the arguments that are typically offered against eating meat strike him as pretty unconvincing. If he were simply to make up his own mind about the issue, he might be eating a roast beef sandwich now. Nevertheless, he firmly believes that he should not eat meat and, indeed, takes himself to know that he should not. He doesn't eat meat, he explains, because his wife has told him that it's wrong, and he thinks that, in general, her moral judgment is better than his own. In fact, because he believes that her moral judgment is better than his, he generally follows a policy of adopting her moral views as his own. He does this even when—as with vegetarianism—her views directly conflict with the conclusions he has arrived at on his own.

Your professor has *outsourced* his moral convictions to his wife: he simply accepts the moral conclusions that she draws and does not think for himself about moral issues. This deference may strike you as puzzling or problematic. How can a person defer to someone else on moral matters?

Two different (although related) aspects of the professor's practice in the moral case may be the source of our concern. First, the professor believes that eating meat is wrong solely on the strength of his wife's *testimony*. He didn't arrive at this view on his own: he does not think for himself. Indeed, if he had made up his own mind, he would now believe something else.

But why should this be a source of concern? We constantly rely on other people's testimony (whether spoken or written) in arriving at our own beliefs and are utterly dependent on such testimony for much of what we take ourselves to know about the world. In fact, it's plausible that you know relatively few things entirely independently of testimony. True, the perceptual knowledge that you have of your immediate physical environment does not depend on the testimony of other people. Nor does the kind of introspective knowledge you have of your own thoughts and feelings. But plausibly, almost everything that you know about history, current events, and science ultimately depends on accepting the spoken or written testimony of other people. The same is true for countless facts about your own life and personal history—who your parents are, how you are related to any of the older members of your family, what your legal name is, and the names of your friends or your significant other. In general, our reliance on the testimony of other people for much of what we believe—including many things that we believe with near certainty—is pervasive. So if morality is like any of these other topics, we would expect that arriving at a moral view by deferring to someone else would be as natural as it is in any of these other cases.

A second possible source of concern is that the professor not only accepts his wife's testimony about one particular moral question, in the way that he might if he thought that she just happened to be in a better position to answer that particular question. Rather, he has a general policy of outsourcing his moral convictions to her. He treats his wife as a *moral expert*.

But here again, if we judge his practice by comparison with what is common in many other areas, we should find nothing odd about it. For example, suppose your professor believes that his wife's sense of direction is generally much better than his. It seems perfectly natural for him to follow a policy of consistently deferring to her about driving directions. Nothing seems puzzling or problematic about his confidently believing that (for example) *we should turn right at the next intersection* on the basis of his wife's saying so, even if it very much *seems to him* as though they should turn left. Similarly, we unhesitatingly defer to the physicist about physics, the roofer about the condition of the roof, the doctor about the condition of the patient, and the attorney about the relevant points of law.

Of course, the idea of a certain type of moral expertise is familiar. Some newspapers carry "ask the ethicist" columns, in which readers ask for advice about moral problems that they face. But such columns do not consist simply of an ethicist providing answers to the readers' questions about what they should do. Rather, the ethicist offers the *reasons why* (according to the ethicist) the answers are correct. Presumably, the idea is that the reader will understand the reasons for a given answer and come to believe and act on the basis of those reasons, as opposed to simply taking the ethicist's word for it. (Compare the way in which a geometry teacher might lead a student to understand and appreciate the proof of a theorem. Once the student grasps the proof, her reason for believing the theorem will typically not be her teacher's testimony, even if that testimony played an indispensable role in her initially recognizing the theorem as true. Contrast a case in which the student fails to grasp the proof but believes the theorem on the basis of the teacher's say-so.) There are countless areas in which holding a view in the absence of any real appreciation of the underlying reasons for thinking that the view is true seems perfectly natural. A perfectly normal, intelligent layperson has compelling reason to *defer* to a physicist about physics, adopting the physicist's views as her own, even in the absence of any real appreciation of the evidence for those views, and even if those views contradict the layperson's own intuitive sense of how the relevant parts of physical reality work. Indeed, advances in technology have greatly increased the possibilities of outsourcing our beliefs about various topics and the efficiency with which we can manage the process. A tourist unfamiliar with New York City can get around well enough by relying on Google Maps. If someday soon there is a Google Morals, what reason would there be, if any, not to use it, and in that way spare yourself the burdens of moral deliberation and reflection?[1]

So deference is very common. Why then does specifically *moral* deference seem puzzling or problematic?

Your professor's willingness to outsource his moral convictions to his wife might seem to indicate that he doesn't care enough about morality. Morality is important! Someone who can't be bothered to think carefully about his moral responsibilities might seem to be showing an inappropriately casual attitude to morality. But your professor assures you that this is not true of him. Rather, it's precisely because he takes morality seriously that he scrupulously follows a policy of deferring to his wife about it. As he puts it: given the seriousness of morality, and his view that his wife's moral judgment is more reliable than his, it would be irresponsible for him to think for himself rather than deferring to her. (Besides, he adds, his deference creates no feelings of inequality within their marriage. His own scholarly specialty is American colonial history, and because his wife never studied the subject beyond high school, *she* defers to *him* about *that*.)

These reflections on the case of the vegetarian professor suggest a general puzzle, which I will call the *puzzle of moral deference*. On the one hand, we are inclined to think that there is something weird about moral deference—something puzzling or problematic about outsourcing your moral convictions. On the other hand, the professor—like many people—regards morality as a subject matter about which there are objective answers and experts who can help to provide them. The puzzle is that it is difficult to combine two ideas (a) that moral deference is weird, and (b) that morality is *objective*. If morality is objective, then moral deference should seem unproblematic. But moral deference *does* seem problematic: it seems both hard to understand and inappropriate to do.

In what follows, I want to suggest a solution to the puzzle. I want to show how we can explain what's weird about outsourcing your moral views without giving up on moral objectivity. You can accept that moral questions have objectively correct answers and still believe it is important to think for yourself about moral issues.

II

Before getting to the solution, I want to observe that some views about the nature of morality can easily account for why your professor's deference to his wife about the morality of eating meat seems weird.

For example, *classic noncognitivists* say that moral judgments such as "Eating meat is wrong" are neither true nor false. A person who sincerely utters the sentence

1. The idea of "Google Morals" is borrowed from Robert Howell, "Google Morals, Virtue, and the Asymmetry of Deference" *Noûs* 48 (2014): 389–415. [McGrath's note.]

"Eating meat is wrong" is *expressing* her negative feelings about eating meat. (As a rough comparison, consider the way in which fans at a football game might express their disapproval of a referee's call by booing. In booing the call, the fans are not saying anything true or false, as they would be if they instead chanted "You missed that call!" or even "We the fans disapprove of the call that you just made!") Notice that this view has no difficulty in accounting for why outsourcing your moral judgments to another person would make little sense. For on this view, the purpose of moral judgment is not to state facts ("the moral facts") about which another person might be more knowledgeable. Judging that eating meat is wrong is just a matter of expressing your emotional disapproval toward eating meat, so no wonder moral deference seems odd! The mere fact that someone else feels differently about it seems to be neither here nor there.

Most philosophers believe that there are decisive objections to classic noncognitivism. Still, the view usefully illustrates how an account of morality might explain why outsourcing your moral opinions seems different from outsourcing your opinions about many other topics. But notice that the noncognitivist does not think moral judgments are objective. So the noncognitivist responds to the puzzle of moral deference by rejecting one of the ideas—the idea that moral questions have objectively correct answers—that generates the puzzle.

The same does *not* seem to be true of a picture of morality that is widely accepted by both philosophers and ordinary people: *moral realism*. Unlike the classic noncognitivist, the realist holds that (1) there are moral facts, and (2) the aim of moral judgment is to accurately describe or represent those facts (not merely to express the feelings or emotions of the person who makes the judgment). Further, the realist holds that (3) these moral facts or truths are *objective*. That is, the realist holds that whether a given action or practice is right or wrong is not determined by our opinions or feelings about it; rather, the moral facts obtain *independently* of what we think about them and would not change even if we were to change our minds. In at least these three important respects, moral facts as understood by the realist are exactly like *scientific facts*, as most of us ordinarily think of them.

Morality, then, as the realist understands it, seems to be exactly the kind of subject about which it would be natural to defer to another person. According to the realist, there are moral facts, which a particular person might either know or not know. Given this picture of moral facts, it seems perfectly coherent for one person to believe that another person is simply better informed about those moral facts. So why not defer to her? Indeed, given only what has been said so far, your professor's outsourcing his moral convictions to his wife should seem just as natural as his deferring to her about the driving directions or his arriving at his scientific beliefs by deferring to a scientist.

We might appeal to precisely this line of thought in an argument *against* the existence of objective moral facts:

(i) If there were objective moral facts, then relying on other people for your moral views would be on a par with relying on other people for your views about the scientific facts (or for your views about the correct driving directions, etc.).

(ii) Relying on other people for your moral views is *not* on a par with relying on other people for your views about the scientific facts (or for your views about the correct directions, etc.).

(iii) Therefore, there are no objective moral facts.

How should the defender of objective moral facts respond to the argument? One possibility is to deny premise (ii). According to this response, your professor's outsourcing his moral views to his wife is not significantly different from his deferring to her about the driving directions or to a physicist about physics. To the extent that we think otherwise, we're simply making a mistake.

An alternative response—and this is the one I will focus on—is to deny premise (i). According to this response, there *is* some significant difference between morality and other subject matters, but this difference is consistent with the existence of objective moral facts. What might this difference be?

III

Judgment, in the moral domain, is intimately connected with action. We are creatures that form moral judgments, but we are also *moral agents*, whose actions can either meet or fail to meet various moral standards or ideals. One important moral ideal is to *do the right thing*. Another important ideal is to *do the right thing for the right reasons*. Even if there are objective moral facts, a person who arrives at her beliefs about those facts by relying on other people will typically not be in a position to achieve this second ideal: she will not be in a position to do the right thing for the reasons that make it the right thing to do.[2] In contrast, when a person arrives at her scientific beliefs by relying on other people, there is no similar ideal that she fails to achieve.

To see this, first notice that a person can do the morally right thing even if he does not do it for the right reasons. When the owner of a store passes up an opportunity to cheat his customers, he does the morally right thing. But suppose he decides not to cheat his customers because he fears that getting caught will ruin his reputation and harm his business (imagine that he *would* cheat his customers if he were certain that he would get away with it). Then, although he does the right thing, he does not do it for the right reasons.

Notice next that if a person holds a moral view on the basis of testimony, then, even if that moral view is true, she will typically not be in a position to do the right thing for the right reasons. Consider a young child who knows that stealing is wrong because she has been told this by her parents. She does not yet grasp the reasons why it is wrong

---

2. This idea is developed in Alison Hills, "Moral Testimony and Moral Epistemology," *Ethics* 120 (2009): 94–127, and Sarah McGrath, "Skepticism about Moral Expertise as a Puzzle for Moral Realism," *Journal of Philosophy* 108 (2011): 111–37. [McGrath's note.]

to steal. She is in a position to do the right thing. But, because she does not yet grasp the reasons why stealing is wrong, she is not yet in a position to do the right thing for the right reasons. In order to do the right thing for the right reasons, it's not enough to believe or *know that* the action is right; the person also has to *understand why* it's right. But when someone arrives at a true moral view on the basis of testimony (as opposed to an appreciation of the reasons why the view is true), she will not understand why the view is true. Of course, when someone holds a true *scientific* view solely on the basis of a scientist's testimony, she will also lack understanding of why that view is true. But in the moral case, this lack of understanding prevents the person from fulfilling an important ideal associated with moral agency—that of doing the right thing for the right reasons. In the scientific case, there is no parallel ideal whose achievement is frustrated. Thus, the professor's policy of outsourcing his moral convictions to his wife has costs that do not attach to the same policy of outsourcing his views about many other subjects. His deference limits his quality as a moral agent.

Consider now a second important difference between morality and many other domains. Your professor defers to his wife's sense of direction because he believes that her sense of direction is vastly better than his. It is natural to picture the professor as having a certain kind of evidence for these beliefs; for example, a history of getting lost when he relies on his own sense of direction, and not getting lost when he relies on his wife's. In general, having an unreliable sense of direction is not a significant obstacle to knowing that you have an unreliable sense of direction. People who have an unreliable sense of direction often have access to pretty clear and compelling evidence that their sense of direction is poor: they get lost when they rely on their own sense of direction. (In this respect, having an unreliable sense of direction is similar to being near-sighted or having a bad memory.) We can easily imagine having the kind of evidence that would make it perfectly reasonable to defer to another person's sense of direction (or eyesight, or memory) even when we would judge differently if we relied on our own.

Contrast the situation when your professor says, "It seems to me that there's nothing wrong with eating meat, but I'm confident that there is. After all, I have poor moral judgment, and my wife's is excellent." Even if what the professor says is true, it's natural to wonder what evidence he has for this assessment. Although having an unreliable sense of direction or poor long-distance vision is generally not a significant obstacle to knowing this about yourself, having an unreliable sense of right and wrong *does* seem like a significant obstacle to knowing that you have an unreliable sense of right and wrong. Similarly, if you have an unreliable sense of right and wrong, it seems that it will be very hard for you to recognize superior moral judgment in others. Why is that?

First, notice that if a question arose as to whose long-distance vision was more accurate, it would be easy enough to find out. We could, for example, record our perceptual judgments about objects at a distance from us, and then check those judgments by viewing the same objects up close. Crucially, we could check our long-distance perceptual judgments in a way that would *not require us to rely on our long-distance vision,* for we have *independent access* to the relevant facts. Because of this, we have a way of *calibrating* our long-distance vision for accuracy.

But there does not seem to be any similar way of calibrating the accuracy or reliability of our sense of right and wrong—we do not have any independent access to the moral facts. That is, whatever access we have to the moral facts depends on our making moral judgments. Suppose we try to rank other people with respect to the reliability of their moral judgments by checking how often they answered difficult and controversial moral questions correctly. It seems as though we would inevitably be led to engage in moral reasoning and deliberation of our own. In practice, then, people to whom we would attribute a reliable sense of right and wrong will generally be people whose sense of right and wrong agrees extensively with our own. In contrast, we typically will *not* conclude that someone has a superior sense of right and wrong when she makes judgments that conflict with the judgments that we are disposed to make on the basis of our own sense of right and wrong.

Thus, even if there are objective moral facts, and even if some people are better judges of those moral facts than other people, we would expect deference about morality to be a more marginal phenomenon than deference about many other subjects. So the puzzle of moral deference is solved. Even if morality is objective, moral deference is weird. It is weird because it is both problematic and puzzling. It is problematic because moral deference conflicts with the moral ideal of doing the right thing for the right reasons. It is puzzling because it is difficult to see how someone could be confident that a person he disagrees with on moral questions is nevertheless an expert to whom he should defer. So even if moral questions have objectively correct answers, you should still think for yourself.

TEST YOUR UNDERSTANDING

1. What does it mean to "outsource" your moral convictions?
2. McGrath describes a *puzzle of moral deference*. What are the two claims that create the puzzle?
3. Suppose a person is morally deferential. Why, according to McGrath, will he or she fail to fulfill an important moral ideal?
4. How might you come to the conclusion that another person is a moral expert?

NOTES AND QUESTIONS

1. McGrath says that a morally deferential person—like her hypothetical professor who morally defers to his wife about eating meat—does not do the right thing *for the right reasons*. But what are the right reasons? Suppose, for example, that the professor responds to McGrath as follows: "I defer to my wife's judgment on moral matters. I do regard her as a moral expert. So when my wife said to me that eating meat is wrong, I thought that I ought to follow her judgment. Because I defer to her, I believe that eating meat

is wrong. And the reason I do not eat meat is that I believe that eating meat is wrong. So I do the right thing by not eating meat, and I do it for the right reasons—because eating meat is wrong. Why, Professor McGrath, are you criticizing me?"

To see how McGrath might reply to the professor, consider what she says about the importance of understanding the reasons why conduct is wrong. True, the professor firmly believes that eating meat is wrong. But he does not know *why* it is wrong. McGrath thinks that the moral ideal of doing the right thing for the right reasons requires understanding the reasons why an action is right, not simply having the firm belief that it is right.

This answer prompts two questions. First, do you agree with McGrath that doing the right thing for the right reasons requires knowing the reasons why an action is right? If the professor really believes that vegetarianism is right and does not eat meat for that reason, why doesn't that suffice for doing the action for the right reasons? Second, consider another hypothetical professor who also morally defers to his wife. But his wife not only tells him what is right, she also tells him why it is right, and he defers to her on the reasons as well as the conclusion. So this professor is very deferential. Before he listened to her, he had very different views about the reasons and the conclusions. But once he has listened and deferred, is he able to do the right thing for the right reasons?

2. McGrath contrasts learning that another person has a better sense of direction with learning that another person has better moral judgment. We can easily see how you come to understand that another person has a better sense of direction: you repeatedly get lost, you try the routes the other person proposes, and you see that the other person's routes get you to your destination and get you there faster. But how, McGrath wonders, could you "recognize superior moral judgment in others"? How would you know that another person was consistently getting the moral answers right and you were consistently getting them wrong? You have your answers; the other person has his or hers; and the answers disagree. Why might you think that he or she is an expert and you have a poor moral sense?

   Consider a response from McGrath's hypothetical professor. He says: "In the past, I have often drawn moral conclusions and found myself disagreeing with my wife. But in every case, I found myself eventually coming around to her view. As I thought and learned more about the issue, I would always come to the conclusion that my initial judgment was too hasty, and that I was not having a vivid enough appreciation of the impact of my conduct on others. So now, I defer to her. I found that she is able to more quickly get to a clear picture of the heart of moral issues. I defer to her now because I think she quickly gets to where I eventually get to, but only after I spend lots of time reflecting on the issue."

   Does this response by the hypothetical professor show, contrary to what McGrath says, that moral deference is not so weird after all: that there is a perfectly good way to come to the conclusion that another person is a better moral judge than you are? Or is this professor not really *deferring* to his wife. After all, he thinks that he is a good moral judge, but only with more effort than is necessary, given his wife's quick moral insight.

3. Consider a more radical objection to McGrath. Suppose the professor says: "I read the essay by Philip Quinn (this chapter, pp. 879–892) on the divine intention theory. I was convinced by him that God's antecedent intentions are the basis of morality; for example, I now believe that promise keeping is morally required because God antecedently

intends that we keep our promises. Because I am convinced of the divine intention theory, I can only know what is morally right if I know what God intends. But some people are much better at discerning God's intentions than others. The moral experts are the experts on God's intentions, and the experts on God's intentions are the people who have deeply studied religious texts, which reveal God's intentions, and commentaries on those texts, which interpret those intentions. So I defer to those people. And I defer on both the moral conclusions and the reasons for the conclusions."

This professor rejects the idea that moral deference is weird, rejects the idea that a morally deferential person is unable to do the right thing for the right reasons, and rejects the idea that it is hard to understand how someone could understand that another person has better moral judgment. How might McGrath respond?

ANALYZING THE ARGUMENTS

1. Mackie says, in effect, that the objectivity of morality does not matter to substantive morality. As he puts it, questions about objectivity are second-order questions, not first-order moral questions: the two are "completely independent." So moral subjectivism leaves morality itself untouched. Nagel says that efforts to stand outside morality and see morality as the expression of a nonobjective perspective "collapse" under the weight of substantive moral judgments: when we actually reason about what morality requires, the idea that it is not objective gives way. So Mackie seems to disagree with Nagel about the connections between first- and second-order moral judgments. Street, in contrast, agrees with Nagel. She thinks that if we hold a mind-independent view of values—a second-order view—then evolutionary theory undermines our first-order values. So a second-order view has significant effects on first-order views.

    Is Mackie right? If you think, for example, that moral requirements are social conventions, does that affect the content of your first-order moral convictions? If you think of moral requirements as based on divine intent, does that affect the content of your first-order moral convictions (consider Quinn's discussion of the "ethics of love"). Consider specific moral requirements when you answer, focusing on requirements that you endorse.

2. Nagel and Harman both resist the idea that moral disagreement should drive us to moral skepticism. Disagreement may be the beginning of moral thinking, not its unhappy end. What are some of the moral disagreements that concern them? What are some moral disagreements that concern *you*? How do they see moral thinking proceeding in the face of disagreement? Do their comments about how moral thinking can work in the face of disagreement provide guidance on the moral disagreements that concern you?

3. When the great physicist Richard Feynman introduced quantum mechanics to undergraduates, he began his lecture by saying: "Things on a very small scale [including electrons, protons, neutrons, photons] behave like nothing that you have any direct experience about. They do not behave like waves, they do not behave like particles, they do not behave like clouds, or billiard balls, or weights on springs, or like anything that you have ever seen. . . . Because atomic behavior is so unlike ordinary experience, it is very difficult to get used to, and it appears peculiar and mysterious to everyone—both to the novice and to the experienced physicist."[1]

    Would Mackie respond to Feynman by saying: "Well, then we should not think that things on a small scale exist, because they are so odd, so 'utterly different from anything else in the universe.'"? If not, why not?

    How would Wallace and Nagel respond to Feynman's point? Are they troubled about the thought that objective values are unlike anything else we are familiar with? Why, or why not?

4. Consider a view along the lines proposed by Quinn: morality is objective because God set down fundamental moral laws that distinguish right from wrong. Moreover, God created us with the power to understand those laws, thus to grasp the difference between right and wrong. Describe how Street and Harman would respond to these claims about the nature of moral objectivity.

1. Richard Feynman, *The Feynman Lectures on Physics*, Vol. 3 (Pearson, 2006), section 1-1.

18

Why Do What Is Right?

Suppose you find yourself in an uncomfortable situation. Your friend has told you that when funds are tight he regularly "borrows" money from the register at the retail store where you both work and then repays it when he gets his next paycheck. The manager noticed that some money went missing during yesterday's shift when your friend was working. The manager tells you that he suspects another worker who is an annoying, uncooperative thorn in everyone's side, but the manager says he does not want to fire anyone unfairly. He asks if you have any reason to suspect anyone else. If you lie, you could protect your friend and eliminate a minor nemesis from the workplace. If you tell the truth, you may lose your friend and your friend may lose his job. You know that morality requires you to tell the truth, or at least not to lie. But you also know that you could get away with lying and that it would benefit you and your friend if you lie.

You face a moral question: "Is telling the truth the right thing to do?" But even if you know the answer to that question—you know that the right thing is to tell the truth and not to permit an innocent person to be fired for theft—you also face a further, theoretical question: "Why *ought* I do the right thing when it would be so much better for me to lie?" On many occasions, doing the right thing comes at a personal cost, perhaps even a large one. We may be confident that telling the truth, repaying a debt, or helping those in need is what's morally right, but nevertheless wonder whether that means we must do it. Why not ignore your duty just this once and enjoy a brief holiday from morality? And, as Plato's character Glaucon asks in *The Republic,* once you've raised this question, you can raise a more general question: "Why not extend this holiday even further and ignore morality altogether?" This chapter explores this skeptical question and some answers philosophers have given in response.

Self-Interested Reasons

In the moment when you feel tempted to shirk your duty, the most compelling answer to the question "Why should I do the right thing?" may be that doing the right thing

924

is in your self-interest, narrowly considered. After all, behaving badly may court the disapproval of other people. It may even risk punishment. Conversely, acting well usually elicits the approval and cooperation of others, and the good opinion of others can be useful to you. Further, in some religious traditions, acting well is a precondition of enjoying God's grace, whether in this life or a later, postmortem existence. Finally, doing the wrong thing could produce crushing guilt that will gnaw on your conscience.

Such self-interested reasons may help you resist temptation in the moment. Yet, many philosophers doubt that they provide *basic* reasons to do the right thing as such. Those who do the right thing to serve themselves, rather than others, may seem shallow and to have missed the point of acting morally. As Glaucon observes to Socrates, these self-interested considerations are really only reasons to *appear* to act morally, rather than reasons to do the right thing as such. Yet, even if one could act secretly and behave badly with impunity, suffering no adverse consequences from others, it still strikes us that we *ought* to behave well. "But God will know!" Perhaps, but even if God does not exist, we still have good reason not to harm others for fun, convenience, or mere personal benefit.

True, even without God or the sanctions of others, if you behaved immorally, *you* would still know what you did and you might not escape suffering from a guilty conscience. But that fact does not support the theory of self-interest. Although guilt is unpleasant and something one wishes to avoid, guilt is a justified reaction to the recognition that there is a prior, distinct good reason to do the right thing: a reason to which one has been irresponsibly insensitive. To make sense of the guilt we are prone to feel when we do the wrong thing, we need to locate that other, more fundamental reason.

Care for Others

Perhaps we should do the right thing not primarily *because* it is in our self-interest, narrowly construed, but because we *care* about other people. As David Hume argues, we feel a natural sympathy for others, and we have a "passion" for their welfare. Of course, if we care about others, we will *want* to do the right thing. In that sense, we will satisfy our interests and desires when we act morally. We may even derive a pleasant feeling of satisfaction when we fulfill those desires. But, if we do the right thing because we care about others, it would be misleading to think of this motive as the motive of self-interest.

Although the sympathetic person feels good when she helps others, she does not help *in order to* feel good or reap a personal benefit. She feels good as a consequence of an *independent* desire to promote the interests of *others*. That desire cannot be reduced to a form of narrow self-interest. Acting from care for others may, *as a side-effect*, promote the sympathetic person's own interest, but only because what serves her interests extends, by virtue of her concern for others, beyond the narrow sphere of herself.

Many philosophers agree that we are capable of acting directly from concern for others and that such direct concern is not selfish or self-interested. Still, some, like Immanuel Kant, contest the claim that concern for others offers the primary reason *why* we should behave morally. After all, even if one is not feeling particularly caring or sympathetic to others on a particular occasion, one *still* has reason to behave well and to refrain from immoral conduct. One's duty not to steal does not wax and wane depending on whether one actually cares about one's potential victim; so how could one's *reason* to do one's duty depend on things that may vary, such as one's mood or temperament? Moreover, sometimes one has duties whose satisfaction may constrain one's ability to advance the interests of those one actively cares about. For instance, one has a duty not to perjure oneself in court, even if telling the truth enhances the prosecution's case against a friend. Finally, it may well be that our natural sympathy runs out at a certain point: we may not care very much, or at all, about people in distant places, or about people who will exist only in the future; yet we still have powerful reasons not to wrong these people, for example, by destroying the environment in which they will live. So if we have moral reasons of this sort, they do not derive entirely from our felt concern for others.

The Role of Reason

For these reasons, Kant concludes that neither our self-interest nor our sentiments can supply general grounds for doing what is right. His reasoning is as follows:

1. Our desires, interests, and sentiments—including our concern for others—are contingent, as are their objects: they vary from person to person and from occasion to occasion.

2. Whether morality requires an action to be performed does not generally depend on how the agent feels about that action or its effects. Two people with very different desires, interests, and sentiments can both be morally required to do the same thing, for the same reason, despite their different desires, interests, and sentiments.

3. On every occasion that morality requires us to perform an action, each of us has the same basic reason to perform that action.

4. Therefore, our basic reasons for acting morally do not derive from our contingent desires, interests, and sentiments.

On this view, self-interest and our sentiments may at most reinforce our basic reason to do what is right, which is to perform the right action primarily from what Kant calls "respect for the moral law." Respect for the moral law consists of the recognition that one always has an overriding reason to do one's duty for duty's sake and not just because doing one's duty happens, as a matter of fact, to correspond to what one happens to feel like doing. This respect for the moral law is required of us, Kant thinks, no matter how we happen to feel, and from this Kant concludes that it is required by reason itself. (Kant adds that our actions have moral worth only insofar as they are motivated by respect for the moral law. It is possible to do the right thing merely for selfish reasons or from sympathy; but if you do, your action does not merit moral admiration.) Kant then argues that this recognition of the overriding reason to perform one's duty for duty's sake alone can guide us to identify the content of the moral law. That is, this recognition may help us discern what it is we ought to do (an argument he pursues more fully in Chapter 16 of this anthology).

What Can Reason and Rationality Require?

As is emerging, the question of what reason we have to do the right thing connects closely to other profound questions about how our basic faculties of desire, sympathy, and reason relate to one another and to what we ought to do. Although Kant contends that morality binds us because we are rational agents, not because we are feeling creatures, Hume's sympathetic approach is driven by his skepticism that the faculty of reason could, by itself, motivate any action, much less moral action. His preliminary question, pursued in *A Treatise of Human Nature*, is whether reason or "passion" (by which he means feeling and sentiment) is the source of our motivation to do the right thing. He argues that reason cannot be the ultimate source of moral motivation (or the source of the contents of moral requirements either) because reason alone cannot motivate the will: it can only discover what exists, what properties things have, and how ideas and things relate to one another. To initiate and propel action, some sort of sentiment or passion is necessary. One must *care* about what one is bringing about. But reason cannot itself provoke such passions; it can only give them guidance. As Hume declares, "[R]eason is, and ought only to be the slave of the passions, and can never pretend to any other office than to serve and obey them."

Kant does not directly refute these arguments, but appeals to our moral experience as evidence that the Humean conception of the bounds of reason is overly cramped. We are familiar with the difference between conforming with the requirements of duty for self-interested reasons, conforming with duty out of sympathy, and conforming with duty for its own sake. The possibility of this last form of behavior seems essential to our understanding of moral worth. Our sense of conforming with duty for its own sake gives us grounds to believe that our faculty of reason is not just a "slave of the passions." It can supply us with "ends," and not just with information about the means to our ends, and can distinguish between permissible and impermissible means to our ends. Our faculty of reason, therefore, can supply us with grounds for acting morally.

Judith Jarvis Thomson supplies another perspective on the relation between one's concerns, rationality, and what one *ought* to do. Like Hume, she connects what it would be rational to do with what one cares about, although she denies that what it is rational to do just consists of that action that would in fact advance one's concerns. She argues that what it is *rational* for you to do is what would *appear* to advance what you care about, given the information in your possession. Thomson argues that rationality is a matter of what is in the mind and how well the mind grapples with what it is justified in believing. Consequently, she claims that what it is rational to do depends on what would be most likely to advance one's concerns, relative to what one is justified in believing, even if one is ultimately mistaken about the facts. Suppose you aim to heal your sick child but mistakenly believe that he is allergic to penicillin. If this mistaken belief is justified, then it would not be rational in Thomson's sense to administer the drug. Yet, you *ought* to do it for two reasons. First, the penicillin would work and so you ought to do it because what one ought to do in order to advance one's concerns is what would in fact advance one's concerns. Second, she agrees with Kant that what one ought morally to do binds one to act whether it advances one's concerns or not. (Unlike Kant, she declines to claim that *rationality* demands the action.) So, whether one cares to cure the child or not, one ought to give him the penicillin because it would cure him, and parents owe it to their children to give them appropriate medical treatment, whether they are motivated by love and sympathy or not. Parents owe medical treatment to their children because children are dependent on their parents and parents have assumed obligations to look after them; justice therefore demands the administration of the penicillin. When justice demands a particular action, one ought to do it for the very reasons that explain why it is just to perform that action.

In Thomson's view, it may or may not be rational to do what justice or morality demands. Further, what justice or morality demands may or may not further one's deepest concerns or cares. But, she does not embrace the skeptical position we began with. She has no doubt that one *ought* to do the right thing. She thinks we go wrong by entertaining the skeptical question in the first place. If we know what the right thing to do is, we know automatically that there is a sufficient reason to do it. The reason to repay a debt to a friend in need is just whatever reason it is that repaying a debt is in fact the right thing to do. We may not be able to articulate that reason right away: that may require philosophical reflection. But if we know the act is right, we know that something about it makes it right, and that the features that make the act right also make it something one ought to do. The questions "What is the right thing to do?" and "Why *ought* I do the right thing?" are not, in her view, two distinct and separate questions; the answer to the latter is supplied by the very considerations that answer the former.

Consider again the case of your friend who steals from work and the manager who asks you if you know anything that would exonerate your unjustly suspected coworker. As you read the selections, imagine how the author would respond to the sincere questions: "I know that it would be morally wrong to lie, but does that mean I should tell the truth? Do I really have sufficient *reason* not to lie? What is that reason?"

Plato (429–347 BCE)

Plato is one of the most important figures in Western philosophy. He founded the Academy in Athens, which was a major center of learning in classical Greece, where he taught Aristotle (384–322 BCE). Plato's works typically take the form of dialogues, and nearly all of them feature his teacher Socrates (469–399 BCE). In the following dialogue, Socrates discusses our reasons to act morally, or justly, with two of Plato's brothers, Glaucon and Adeimantus.

THE REPUBLIC

Book II

GLAUCON: Socrates, do you want to seem to have persuaded us that it is better in every way to be just than unjust, or do you want truly to convince us of this?

SOCRATES: I want truly to convince you, if I can.

G: Tell me, do you think there is a kind of good we welcome, not because we desire what comes from it, but because we welcome it for its own sake—joy, for example, and all the harmless pleasures that have no results beyond the joy of having them?

S: Certainly, I think there are such things.

G: And is there a kind of good we like for its own sake and also for the sake of what comes from it—knowing, for example, and seeing and being healthy? We welcome such things, I suppose, on both counts.

S: Yes.

G: And do you also see a third kind of good, such as physical training, medical treatment when sick, medicine itself, and the other ways of making money? We'd say that these are onerous but beneficial to us, and we wouldn't choose them for their own sakes, but for the sake of the rewards and other things that come from them.

S: There is also this third kind. But what of it?

G: Where do you put justice?

S: I myself put it among the finest goods, as something to be valued by anyone who is going to be blessed with happiness, both because of itself and because of what comes from it.

G: That isn't most people's opinion. They'd say that justice belongs to the onerous kind, and is to be practiced for the sake of the rewards and popularity that come from a reputation for justice, but is to be avoided because of itself as something burdensome.

S: I know that's the general opinion. Thrasymachus[1] faulted justice on these grounds a moment ago and praised injustice, but it seems that I'm a slow learner.

G: . . . I think that Thrasymachus gave up before he had to, charmed by you as if he were a snake. But I'm not yet satisfied by the argument on either side. I want to know

---

1. A Sophist (itinerant teacher) who appears earlier in the dialogue.

what justice and injustice are and what power each itself has when it's by itself in the soul. I want to leave out of account their rewards and what comes from each of them. So, if you agree, I'll renew the argument of Thrasymachus. First, I'll state what kind of thing people consider justice to be and what its origins are. Second, I'll argue that all who practice it do so unwillingly, as something necessary, not as something good. Third, I'll argue that they have good reason to act as they do, for the life of an unjust person is, they say, much better than that of a just one.

It isn't, Socrates, that I believe any of that myself. . . . But I've yet to hear anyone defend justice in the way I want, proving that it is better than injustice. I want to hear it praised *by itself*, and I think that I'm most likely to hear this from you. Therefore, I'm going to speak at length in praise of the unjust life, and in doing so I'll show you the way I want to hear you praising justice and denouncing injustice. . . .

[To start,] let's discuss the first subject I mentioned—what justice is and what its origins are.

They say that to do injustice is naturally good and to suffer injustice bad, but that the badness of suffering it so far exceeds the goodness of doing it that those who have done and suffered injustice and tasted both, but who lack the power to do it and avoid suffering it, decide that it is profitable to come to an agreement with each other neither to do injustice nor to suffer it. As a result, they begin to make laws and covenants, and what the law commands they call lawful and just. This, they say, is the origin and essence of justice. It is intermediate between the best and the worst. The best is to do injustice without paying the penalty; the worst is to suffer it without being able to take revenge. Justice is a mean between these two extremes. People value it not as a good but because they are too weak to do injustice with impunity. Someone who has the power to do this, however, and is a true man wouldn't make an agreement with anyone not to do injustice in order not to suffer it. For him that would be madness. This is the nature of justice, according to the argument, Socrates, and these are its natural origins.

We can see most clearly that those who practice justice do it unwillingly and because they lack the power to do injustice, if in our thoughts we grant to a just and an unjust person the freedom to do whatever they like. We can then follow both of them and see where their desires would lead. And we'll catch the just person red-handed travelling the same road as the unjust. The reason for this is the desire to outdo others and get more and more. This is what anyone's nature naturally pursues as good, but nature is forced by law into the perversion of treating fairness with respect.

The freedom I mentioned would be most easily realized if both people had the power they say the ancestor of Gyges of Lydia[2] possessed. The story goes that he was a shepherd in the service of the ruler of Lydia. There was a violent thunderstorm, and an earthquake broke open the ground and created a chasm at the place where he was tending his sheep. Seeing this, he was filled with amazement and went down into it. And there, . . . he saw a hollow bronze horse. There were windowlike openings in it, and, peeping in, he saw a corpse,

2. Lydia was an ancient kingdom located in what is now the western portion of Turkey.

which seemed to be of more than human size, wearing nothing but a gold ring on its finger. He took the ring and came out of the chasm. He wore the ring at the usual monthly meeting that reported to the king on the state of the flocks. And as he was sitting among the others, he happened to turn the setting of the ring towards himself to the inside of his hand. When he did this, he became invisible to those sitting near him, and they went on talking as if he had gone. He wondered at this, and, fingering the ring, he turned the setting outwards again and became visible. So he experimented with the ring to test whether it indeed had this power—and it did. If he turned the setting inward, he became invisible; if he turned it outward, he became visible again. When he realized this, he at once arranged to become one of the messengers sent to report to the king. And when he arrived there, he seduced the king's wife, attacked the king with her help, killed him, and took over the kingdom.

Let's suppose, then, that there were two such rings, one worn by a just and the other by an unjust person. Now, no one, it seems, would be so incorruptible that he would stay on the path of justice or stay away from other people's property, when he could take whatever he wanted from the marketplace with impunity, go into people's houses and have sex with anyone he wished, kill or release from prison anyone he wished, and do all the other things that would make him like a god among humans. Rather his actions would be in no way different from those of an unjust person, and both would follow the same path. This, some would say, is a great proof that one is never just willingly but only when compelled to be. No one believes justice to be a good when it is kept private, since, wherever either person thinks he can do injustice with impunity, he does it. Indeed, every man believes that injustice is far more profitable to himself than justice. And any exponent of this argument will say he's right, for someone who didn't want to do injustice, given this sort of opportunity, and who didn't touch other people's property would be thought wretched and stupid by everyone aware of the situation, though, of course, they'd praise him in public, deceiving each other for fear of suffering injustice. So much for my second topic.

As for the choice between the lives we're discussing, we'll be able to make a correct judgment about that only if we separate the most just and the most unjust. . . . Here's the separation I have in mind. We'll subtract nothing from the injustice of an unjust person and nothing from the justice of a just one, but we'll take each to be complete in his own way of life. First, therefore, we must suppose that an unjust person will act as clever craftsmen do: A first-rate captain or doctor, for example, knows the difference between what his craft can and can't do. He attempts the first but lets the second go by, and if he happens to slip, he can put things right. In the same way, an unjust person's successful attempts at injustice must remain undetected, if he is to be fully unjust. Anyone who is caught should be thought inept, for the extreme of injustice is to be believed to be just without being just. And our completely unjust person must be given complete injustice; nothing may be subtracted from it. We must allow that, while doing the greatest injustice, he has nonetheless provided himself with the greatest reputation for justice. If he happens to make a slip, he must be able to put it right. If any of his unjust activities should be discovered, he must be able to speak persuasively or to use force. And if force is needed, he must have the help of courage and strength and of the substantial wealth and friends with which he has provided himself.

Having hypothesized such a person, let's now in our argument put beside him a just man, who is simple and noble and who, as Aeschylus[3] says, doesn't want to be believed to be good but to be so. We must take away his reputation, for a reputation for justice would bring him honor and rewards, so that it wouldn't be clear whether he is just for the sake of justice itself or for the sake of those honors and rewards. We must strip him of everything except justice and make his situation the opposite of an unjust person's. Though he does no injustice, he must have the greatest reputation for it, so that he can be tested as regards justice unsoftened by his bad reputation and its effects. Let him stay like that unchanged until he dies—just, but all his life believed to be unjust. In this way, both will reach the extremes, the one of justice and the other of injustice, and we'll be able to judge which of them is happier.

s: Glaucon, how vigorously you've scoured each of the men for our competition, just as you would a pair of statues for an art competition.

g: ... Since the two are as I've described, in any case, it shouldn't be difficult to complete the account of the kind of life that awaits each of them. And if what I say sounds crude, Socrates, remember that it isn't I who speak but those who praise injustice at the expense of justice. They'll say that a just person in such circumstances will be whipped, stretched on a rack, chained, blinded with fire, and, at the end, when he has suffered every kind of evil, he'll be impaled, and will realize then that one shouldn't want to be just but to be believed to be just. Indeed, Aeschylus' words are far more correctly applied to unjust people than to just ones, for the supporters of injustice will say that a really unjust person, having a way of life based on the truth about things and not living in accordance with opinion, doesn't want simply to be believed to be unjust but actually to be so. . . . He rules his city because of his reputation for justice; he marries into any family he wishes; he gives his children in marriage to anyone he wishes; he has contracts and partnerships with anyone he wants; and besides benefiting himself in all these ways, he profits because he has no scruples about doing injustice. In any contest, public or private, he's the winner and outdoes his enemies. And by outdoing them, he becomes wealthy, benefiting his friends and harming his enemies. . . .

ADEIMANTUS: You surely don't think that the position has been adequately stated?

s: Why not?

a: The most important thing to say hasn't been said yet. . . .

s: If Glaucon has omitted something, you must help him. Yet what he has said is enough to throw me to the canvas and make me unable to come to the aid of justice.

a: Nonsense. . . . Hear what more I have to say, for we should also fully explore the arguments that are opposed to the ones Glaucon gave, the ones that praise justice and find fault with injustice, so that what I take to be his intention may be clearer.

---

3. Aeschylus (525–456 BCE) was a famous ancient Greek poet and playwright.

When fathers speak to their sons, they say that one must be just, as do all the others who have charge of anyone. But they don't praise justice itself, only the high reputations it leads to and the consequences of being thought to be just, such as the public offices, marriages, and other things Glaucon listed. But they elaborate even further on the consequences of reputation. By bringing in the esteem of the gods, they are able to talk about the abundant good things that they themselves and the noble Hesiod and Homer[4] say that the gods give to the pious, for Hesiod says that the gods make the oak trees

> Bear acorns at the top and bees in the middle
> And make fleecy sheep heavy laden with wool

for the just, and tells of many other good things akin to these. And Homer is similar:

> When a good king, in his piety,
> Upholds justice, the black earth bears
> Wheat and barley for him, and his trees are heavy with fruit.
> His sheep bear lambs unfailingly, and the sea yields up its fish. . . .

Consider another form of argument about justice and injustice employed both by private individuals and by poets. All go on repeating with one voice that justice and moderation are fine things, but hard and onerous, while licentiousness and injustice are sweet and easy to acquire and are shameful only in opinion and law. They add that unjust deeds are for the most part more profitable than just ones, and, whether in public or private, they willingly honor vicious people who have wealth and other types of power and declare them to be happy. But they dishonor and disregard the weak and the poor, even though they agree that they are better than the others. . . .

They say that the gods, too, assign misfortune and a bad life to many good people, and the opposite fate to their opposites. Begging priests and prophets frequent the doors of the rich and persuade them that they possess a god-given power founded on sacrifices and incantations. If the rich person or any of his ancestors has committed an injustice, they can fix it with pleasant rituals. Moreover, if he wishes to injure some enemy, then, at little expense, he'll be able to harm just and unjust alike, for by means of spells and enchantments they can persuade the gods to serve them. . . . And they persuade not only individuals but whole cities that the unjust deeds of the living or the dead can be absolved or purified through ritual sacrifices and pleasant games. These initiations, as they call them, free people from punishment hereafter, while a terrible fate awaits those who have not performed the rituals. . . .

Why, then, should we still choose justice over the greatest injustice? Many eminent authorities agree that, if we practice such injustice with a false façade,

---

4. Hesiod and Homer were the two most important epic poets of ancient Greece, both of whom lived at some point between 750 BCE and 650 BCE; the precise dates are unknown.

we'll do well at the hands of gods and humans, living and dying as we've a mind to. So, given all that has been said, Socrates, how is it possible for anyone of any power—whether of mind, wealth, body, or birth—to be willing to honor justice and not laugh aloud when he hears it praised? Indeed, if anyone can show that what we've said is false and has adequate knowledge that justice is best, he'll surely be full not of anger but of forgiveness for the unjust. He knows that, apart from someone of godlike character who is disgusted by injustice or one who has gained knowledge and avoids injustice for that reason, no one is just willingly. Through cowardice or old age or some other weakness, people do indeed object to injustice. But it's obvious that they do so only because they lack the power to do injustice, for the first of them to acquire it is the first to do as much injustice as he can. . . .

Socrates, of all of you who claim to praise justice, from the original heroes of old whose words survive, to the men of the present day, not one has ever blamed injustice or praised justice except by mentioning the reputations, honors, and rewards that are their consequences. No one has ever adequately described what each itself does of its own power by its presence in the soul of the person who possesses it, even if it remains hidden from gods and humans. No one, whether in poetry or in private conversations, has adequately argued that injustice is the worst thing a soul can have in it and that justice is the greatest good. If you had treated the subject in this way and persuaded us from youth, we wouldn't now be guarding against one another's injustices, but each would be his own best guardian, afraid that by doing injustice he'd be living with the worst thing possible. . . .

[I]t's because I want to hear the opposite from you that I speak with all the force I can muster. So don't merely give us a theoretical argument that justice is stronger than injustice, but tell us what each itself does, because of its own powers, to someone who possesses it, that makes injustice bad and justice good. Follow Glaucon's advice, and don't take reputations into account, for if you don't deprive justice and injustice of their true reputations and attach false ones to them, we'll say that you are not praising them but their reputations and that you're encouraging us to be unjust in secret. In that case, we'll say that you agree with Thrasymachus that justice is the good of another, the advantage of the stronger, while injustice is one's own advantage and profit, though not the advantage of the weaker.

You agree that justice is one of the greatest goods, the ones that are worth getting for the sake of what comes from them, but much more so for their own sake, such as seeing, hearing, knowing, being healthy, and all other goods that are fruitful by their own nature and not simply because of reputation. Therefore, praise justice as a good of that kind, explaining how—because of its very self—it benefits its possessors and how injustice harms them. Leave wages and reputations for others to praise.

Others would satisfy me if they praised justice and blamed injustice in that way, extolling the wages of one and denigrating those of the other. But you, unless you order me to be satisfied, wouldn't, for you've spent your whole life investigating this and nothing else. Don't, then, give us only a theoretical argument that justice is stronger than injustice, but show what effect each has because of itself on the person who has it—the one for good and the other for bad—whether it remains hidden from gods and human beings or not. . . .

s: That's well said in my opinion, for you must indeed be affected by the divine if you're not convinced that injustice is better than justice and yet can speak on its behalf as you have done. And I believe that you really are unconvinced by your own words. I infer this from the way you live, for if I had only your words to go on, I wouldn't trust you.

TEST YOUR UNDERSTANDING

1. Glaucon distinguishes three kinds of goods. What are the differences among the three types? Give an example of each.

2. What is the special power associated with the Ring of Gyges?

3. What are the qualities of the two people that Glaucon describes and asks us to compare?

4. Adeimantus adds a clarification to the challenge for Socrates. What is the clarification?

NOTES AND QUESTIONS

1. *Glaucon's predictions.* Suppose Glaucon's prediction is correct and that those who possess the Ring of Gyges would behave terribly. According to Glaucon, this shows that we have no foundational reason to behave well, but only a reason to *appear* to behave well. Why does he think this? Are you convinced? Can you think of an alternative explanation why others' knowledge of your behavior might affect your behavior? (*Hint:* Consider how groups such as sports teams, Weight Watchers, and Alcoholics Anonymous are thought to help their members achieve their goals.)

2. *Adeimantus's challenge.* At the end of the selection, Adeimantus challenges Socrates to show that the life of justice "because of its very self . . . benefits its possessors." That is, he asks Socrates to show that independent of any external reward, living justly has a good effect on the life of the just person. Some translations represent Adeimantus as demanding that Socrates show that the just life improves the *soul* of the just person. Suppose Socrates could show this. Would this supply a person with the right sort of reason to do the right thing?

   Consider the following objection: "Showing that leading a moral life benefits you spiritually just offers a variation on an argument from self-interest. Meeting Adeimantus's challenge would still fail to show that we have non-self-interested reasons to be moral." Do you think this objection is persuasive?

Judith Jarvis Thomson (b. 1929)

Thomson was born in New York and is Professor Emeritus at Massachusetts Institute of Technology. She has made a number of field-defining contributions in moral theory, applied ethics, political philosophy, legal philosophy, and metaphysics. Her books include *Rights, Restitution and Risk* (1986), *The Realm of Rights* (1998), *Goodness and Advice* (2001), and *Normativity* (2006).

WHY OUGHT WE DO WHAT IS RIGHT?

1

In Plato's *Republic*, two young men, Glaucon and Adeimantus, ask Socrates a question. Socrates is among those who praise justice—who, in particular, believe that if justice requires a person to φ, then the person ought to φ—and they ask him why. Thus suppose justice requires Alfred to pay Bert ten dollars. Glaucon and Adeimantus know that Socrates would say that Alfred therefore ought to pay Bert ten dollars, and they want to know why.

Notice that Glaucon and Adeimantus—from here on, "G&A"—are not asking Socrates what makes it the case that justice requires a person to do a thing. They assume that is clear enough, and let us for the time being agree. So, for example, suppose that Alfred borrowed ten dollars from Bert, and promised to repay him; suppose also that Bert relied on being paid by Alfred, and now needs the ten dollars, and that no one (not even Alfred) will suffer any hardship if Alfred repays Bert. Then we can surely assume that justice requires Alfred to repay Bert. What Socrates is to do is only to say why Alfred therefore ought to repay Bert.

2

G&A plainly think they are asking Socrates a hard question, and Socrates does too. But is it a hard question?

Suppose that justice requires a person to φ. Then the person's failing to φ would be unjust. And therefore defective. And therefore bad. And therefore wrong. But if wrong, then *a fortiori*, to be avoided. Thus the person ought not fail to φ. Therefore the person ought to φ.

Similarly for the requirements of generosity, kindness, loyalty, responsibility, and so on. Suppose it is instead generosity, kindness, loyalty, or responsibility that requires the person to φ. Then the person's failing to φ would be defective, therefore bad, therefore wrong. But if wrong, then *a fortiori*, to be avoided. Thus the person ought not fail to φ. Therefore the person ought to φ.

In short, if a virtue such as justice requires a person to φ, then the person acts rightly only if he or she φs. *A fortiori*, the person ought to φ.

That certainly looks easy! So why do G&A and Socrates think they are asking Socrates a hard question? And why would so many people agree with them?—for many people would. It is very likely that G&A and Socrates, and the many who would agree with them, would dig in their heels at those "*a fortiori*"s. Thus they would agree that if justice—or generosity, kindness, loyalty, responsibility, and so on—requires a person to ɸ, then the person will act rightly only if he or she ɸs. But they would ask why it should be thought to follow that the person *ought* to ɸ. We can expect them to say that the person might well ask "Why ought I do what is right?"

That G&A have that in mind emerges when they tell Socrates about a constraint on his answer.

They say people often praise justice to the young by pointing to the profits that (as people say) come to those who act justly, namely good reputations, honors, and rewards. But G&A say that won't do. For they say that those are the profits that come, not of acting justly, but of being thought to act justly. And they say that if that is all that their elders can say for justice, then the appropriate conclusion for the young to draw is not that they ought to act justly, but rather that they ought to seem to act justly.

However, Socrates believes that the young ought to act justly, and not merely to seem to act justly. Therefore, would he please tell G&A how justice profits its possessors "because of its very self" and not because of the public rewards it brings.

What emerges from G&A's imposing that constraint on Socrates's answer is that they assume the following:

Ought Only If Profitable Thesis: Alfred ought to ɸ only if he would profit by ɸ-ing.

They say that in the case of justice, the profit has to issue from what justice *is*. Presumably they would say that in the case of the other virtues, the profits have to have different sources—for example, what generosity *is* in the case of generosity. But for each there has to be *a* profit.

Socrates accepts their constraint on his answer to their question, so we can conclude that he too assumes the Ought Only If Profitable Thesis.

We can say about all three of them, then: they think that if a person asks "Why ought I do what is right?" there had better be an answer—an answer that explains why we would be warranted in replying "You'll profit if you do."

But what is the warrant? In what way exactly would Alfred profit by repaying Bert? We can therefore see why G&A and Socrates think that G&A's question is a hard one. For while the facts I supplied entitle us to assume that justice requires Alfred to repay Bert, it is far from obvious how they could be thought to guarantee that Alfred would profit if he repaid Bert.

3

But perhaps we should just reject G&A's question? For there is room for an objection to the Ought Only If Profitable Thesis: surely it can't be right to think that Alfred ought to repay Bert only if sheer selfishness would itself motivate him to do so!

There is room for defense of the Ought Only If Profitable Thesis against that objection to it. A defender might reply as follows.

"You bring too constrained a notion of profit to bear on it.

"People often obtain 'personal profits' by doing the things they do. Let us say that Alice obtains a personal profit by doing a thing if an outcome of her doing it is her getting something for herself, where she values her getting it for herself. Thus suppose Alice sold a short story she wrote, and thereby got some money for herself, where she valued her getting that money for herself. It follows that she obtained a personal profit by selling the short story.

"Let us say that Alice obtains an 'impersonal profit' by doing a thing if an outcome of her doing it is her getting something for others, where she values her getting it for them. Thus suppose Alice sent a check to Oxfam, and thereby got some benefits for others, where she valued her getting those benefits for them; it follows that she obtained an impersonal profit by sending the check to Oxfam.

"Three things are worth stress. First: people do not act only in order to bring about that they get something good for themselves; they often act in order to bring about that others get something good for those others.[1] We can certainly suppose that Alice got a personal profit by sending that check to Oxfam, for we can suppose that by sending that check she got something for herself that she valued her getting, namely the satisfaction that comes of helping others. But we can also suppose that it was not in order to get satisfaction for herself that she sent her check, rather that it was in order to get benefits for others.

"Second: profits of both of those two kinds really are profits. What makes it the case that you obtain a profit by doing a thing is that your doing it has among its outcomes something that you value—whether the outcome that you value is your getting something for yourself, or your getting something for others.

"Third: a person's act has many outcomes, some of which are personal or impersonal profits, and others of which are personal or impersonal losses. Suppose that another outcome of Alice's selling her story was gloom in her roommate, who also writes fiction but who has had no success with hers; and suppose also that Alice places a negative value on her roommate's feeling gloomy. Then Alice's selling her story produced at least one loss for her (an impersonal loss) as well as at least one profit for her (a personal profit). Let us say that a person profits *on balance* by φ-ing just in case the sum of the amounts of profit he or she obtains by φ-ing, minus the sum of the amounts of loss, is greater than that which he or she would have obtained by doing anything else that was open to him or her at the time. To ensure clarity, then, let us rewrite the Ought Only If Profitable Thesis as follows:

---

1. G&A say it is widely thought that people would always act unjustly if they could get away with it—as they could if, for example, they acquired the mythical Ring of Gyges, which enables its owner to become invisible whenever he wishes. But that is surely an excessively sour view of what people are like. Hume, for example, rejects it in the selection reprinted in this chapter. [Thomson's note.]

> *Ought Only If Profitable Thesis*: Alfred ought to φ only if he would profit on
>   balance by φ-ing.

"So in sum, accepting the thesis does not require you to accept that Alfred ought to repay Bert only if sheer selfishness would itself motivate him to do so. If Alfred values Bert's relief from need more than he values keeping the ten dollars that he owes Bert, then he will profit on balance from giving it to Bert. But if Alfred were selfish, he wouldn't be motivated to give the ten dollars to Bert: that is because if he were selfish, he wouldn't value Bert's relief from need more than he values keeping the ten dollars that he owes Bert."

This reply may allay some of the mistrust with which we initially regarded the thesis. But we might wonder *why* we should agree that Alfred ought to repay Bert only if he would profit on balance by doing it. What has whether Alfred would profit got to do with whether he ought to repay Bert?

4

Many people would say that the answer to that question lies in the popular idea that there are tight connections first between what a person ought to do and what it would be rational for the person to do, and second between what it would be rational for the person to do and what it would profit the person to do. For suppose that

> *Ought Only If Rational Thesis*: Alfred ought to φ only if it would be rational for
>   him to φ.

and

> *Rational Only If Profitable Thesis*: It would be rational for Alfred to φ only if he
>   would profit on balance by φ-ing.

are true. They jointly entail

> *Ought Only If Profitable Thesis*: Alfred ought to φ only if he would profit on balance
>   by φ-ing.

But those two premises seem very plausible.

Notice that if we accept the conclusion on the ground of those two premises, and someone asks us "Why ought I do what is right?" then we can say not only "You'll profit if you do" but also "Rationality requires you to."

5

But should we accept those two premises? I begin with the second, namely the Rational Only If Profitable Thesis.

Suppose that Alfred's child now has an infection that only penicillin cures. Alfred, however, justifiably believes that penicillin is poisonous. (He was told so by people he has every reason to trust.) So it would be rational for him to refuse to allow his child to be given penicillin. The thesis yields that it would therefore profit him on balance to refuse. But on the assumption that he greatly values his child's life, he would lose (rather than profit) if he refused. So the thesis won't do.

Another route to that conclusion is as follows. By hypothesis, Alfred would not profit by refusing. The thesis therefore yields that his refusing would not be rational—thus that his refusing would be irrational. But given what he justifiably believes, his refusing would not be irrational. Alfred's refusing would issue from his being ill-informed, not from his being irrational. So (again) the thesis won't do.

The explanation of the fact that the thesis won't do is the fact that rationality and irrationality are "in the head." They are not a function of what will or will not happen, or of whether a person has this or that piece of information; rather they are a function of how well or ill the person reasons from what he or she is justified in believing.

The fact that rationality is in the head lies behind a very familiar contemporary account of what rationality requires of a person.[2]

Suppose you justifiably believe that your options for action here and now are ϕ-ing, ψ-ing, and so on.

Next suppose you justifiably believe that if you ϕ, then the following outcomes may come about: $O_{\phi 1}$, $O_{\phi 2}$, and so on. Suppose further that you justifiably believe that if you ϕ, then the probability that outcome $O_{\phi 1}$ will come about is $P_{O\phi 1}$. Suppose also that you justifiably believe that the amount to which $O_{\phi 1}$ is valuable is $V_{O\phi 1}$. (Since you might justifiably believe that $O_{\phi 1}$ is of negative rather than positive value, $V_{O\phi 1}$ might be a negative number.) Then let us say that the expected value to you of $O_{\phi 1}$ is $P_{O\phi 1}$ times $V_{O\phi 1}$. Similarly, the expected value to you of $O_{\phi 2}$ is $P_{O\phi 2}$ times $V_{O\phi 2}$. And so on. Then let us say that the expected value to you of your ϕ-ing is the sum of the expected values to you of $O_{\phi 1}$, $O_{\phi 2}$, and so on.

Similarly, the expected value to you of your ψ-ing is the sum of the expected values to you of $O_{\psi 1}$, $O_{\psi 2}$, and so on. And so on for all of the options you justifiably believe you now have.

Finally, let us say that you maximize your expected value just in case you choose the act that has the greatest expected value to you.

According to the theory of rationality I referred to, that is exactly what rationality requires of you. Thus if your ϕ-ing has the greatest expected value to you, then you maximize your expected value by ϕ-ing; and what rationality requires you to do is therefore to ϕ—or anyway to try to ϕ, if, as it might turn out, you were mistaken in thinking you could ϕ.

That is a *very* plausible idea. So it is very plausible that we should reject the Rational Only If Profitable Thesis, and accept, instead:

Rational Only If Maximizes Expected Value Thesis: It would be rational for Alfred to ϕ only if he would maximize his expected value by ϕ-ing.

---

2. Kant can be interpreted as offering a different account of what rationality requires of a person: on his view, what it requires is acting in accord with the categorical imperative. See the selection from Kant in this chapter. [Thomson's note.]

This thesis yields (as an account of rationality should yield) that it would be irrational for Alfred to allow his child to be given penicillin.

6

Let us turn now to the first of the two premises of Section 4, namely the Ought Only If Rational Thesis. Given the thesis about rationality that we reached in Section 5, that first premise won't do. For the thesis about rationality yields that it would be irrational for Alfred to allow his child to be given penicillin. But he ought to. Alfred's mistakenly believing that penicillin is poisonous has no bearing on what he ought to do: what he ought to do turns on what would be best for his child—and by hypothesis, what would be best for his child is for it to be given penicillin.

Since Alfred justifiably believes that penicillin is poisonous, he will not be at fault, he will not be blameworthy, if he refuses to allow his child to be given penicillin. But he himself will agree that he ought to have allowed it to be given penicillin when he learns, after its death, that allowing this would have saved it.

So we must reject the Ought Only If Rational Thesis.

7

Having to give up the Ought Only If Rational Thesis may well seem unfortunate. But perhaps we can retain what made it seem plausible if we revise it. Let us take seriously the fact that the difficulty we looked at in the preceding section issued from Alfred's believing, falsely, that penicillin is poisonous. We might then think: the answer to the question of which act would maximize Alfred's expected value rested heavily on his having had that false belief. No wonder there was trouble for the Ought Only If Rational Thesis! Maximizing expected value is surely at the heart of rationality, but not where maximizing expected value is at the mercy of false beliefs.

So let us impose a constraint that makes false beliefs irrelevant. Imagine the following about Abigail. (i) Whenever she can do a thing, she knows she can. (ii) If she knows she can do a thing, she knows what outcomes her doing it would issue in. (iii) If an outcome that her doing a thing would issue in has value, positive or negative, then she knows that it has value, and how much. That is, she knows all the actual values of all the actual outcomes of her doing the thing. Call Abigail "Relevantly Well-Informed." *A fortiori*, she has no relevant false beliefs.

Hardly anybody is like Abigail in that respect. (Is anybody?) Alfred certainly isn't. But let us now ask what rationality would require of him if he were Relevantly Well-Informed. If he were, then he would not make the mistake about penicillin that he actually made, and rationality would require him to allow his child to be given penicillin. That, of course, is exactly what he ought to do.

More generally, we can retain a tight connection between rationality and what a person ought to do, while avoiding the difficulty that was made for that connection by mistaken beliefs, if we reject the Ought Only If Rational Thesis in favor of:

> *Revised Ought Only If Rational Thesis*: Alfred ought to φ only if it would be rational for him to φ if he were Relevantly Well-Informed.

Notice that if we accept the revised thesis, and someone asks "Why ought I do what is right?" then while we can't reply "Rationality requires you to," we can reply "Rationality requires you to if you are, or would require you to if you were, free of relevant false beliefs."

8

Here, then, is what we have replaced the two premises of Section 4 with:

> *Rational Only If Maximizes Expected Value Thesis*: It would be rational for Alfred to φ only if he would maximize his expected value by φ-ing.

and

> *Revised Ought Only If Rational Thesis*: Alfred ought to φ only if it would be rational for him to φ if he were Relevantly Well-Informed.

These theses are weaker than the two premises of Section 4, and they don't entail the Ought Only If Profitable Thesis. But they do entail something weaker, namely:

> *Revised Ought Only If Profitable Thesis*: Alfred ought to φ only if he would profit on balance by φ-ing if he were Relevantly Well-Informed.

For suppose that Alfred ought to φ. Then from the Revised Ought Only If Rational Thesis, we can conclude that it would be rational for him to φ if he were Relevantly Well-Informed. So suppose he is Relevantly Well-Informed; it follows that it would be rational for him to φ. Then from the Rational Only If Maximizes Expected Value Thesis, we can conclude that he would maximize his expected value by φ-ing. Since he is (as we are supposing) Relevantly Well-Informed, maximizing his expected value is maximizing his actual value. It follows that his φ-ing would actually issue in outcomes that he (rightly) thinks would have a higher value than those that his doing anything else would issue in. So he would profit on balance by φ-ing.

And we can suppose that the fact that Alfred ought to repay Bert makes no trouble for this thesis. For if Alfred were Relevantly Well-Informed, then we can suppose that he would (rightly) regard Bert's being relieved of his needs as having a higher value than his retaining the ten dollars that he owes Bert—higher enough for his repaying Bert to profit him on balance.

Moreover, we have yet another answer available if someone asks us "Why ought I do what is right?" We can reply, "If you were free of relevant false beliefs, then it would profit you to do what is right."

9

But should we accept the Revised Ought Only If Profitable Thesis? Not unless we are prepared to accept:

> Alfred ought to φ only if the actual outcomes of his φ-ing would be of greater actual value than the actual outcomes of his doing any of the other things it is open to him to do at the time.

And there really is no good reason to accept *that* unless we accept a familiar moral theory, namely:

> *Consequentialism*: For it to be the case that a person ought to φ is for it to be the case that his or her φ-ing would maximize actual value.

Sympathetic attention to G&A's question "Why ought I do what justice requires?" led us by plausible-looking steps along an unusual route to Consequentialism.

There is a rich literature on Consequentialism—many people have written in support of it, many in objection to it.[3] A familiar kind of objection to it issues from considerations of justice. Suppose that Alfred's failing to repay Bert would issue in outcomes that have more value than the outcomes his doing anything else would have. A Consequentialist is therefore committed to the conclusion that Alfred ought not repay Bert. But many people think that since Alfred's repaying Bert is required by justice, he ought to repay Bert, despite the gain in value that would issue from his not doing so.[4]

More generally, the considerations that bear on whether a person ought to φ differ in the way they bear on that question. Some considerations would plainly be outcomes of the person's φ-ing, and they are thought by many people to bear by having higher or lower value. (Compare Bert's needs being met if Alfred repays him what he owes him.) Others, however, are not plainly *outcomes* of the person's φ-ing. The person's φ-ing's being just—or generous, kind, loyal, or responsible—are among the ones that are not. How these bear on whether the person ought to φ is disputable. But it is a very plausible idea that they bear by straightforwardly entailing that the person ought to φ.

---

3. In Chapter 16 of this anthology, the selection from Mill provides an example of a consequentialist view, and the selection from Kant provides an example of a non-consequentialist view. In Chapter 15, the essays by Anscombe, Scanlon, and Herman all endorse a non-consequentialist principle, the Doctrine of Double Effect.

4. A deeper objection to Consequentialism, and indeed to much of what the discussion of what G&A had in mind has led us to, is that it isn't clear what property we can be thought to be ascribing to an outcome of an act in saying of it that it "has value." [Thomson's note.]

10

If we opt for that very plausible idea, then we are accepting that it is trivially true that if justice requires Alfred to repay Bert, then Alfred ought to repay Bert, and that G&A's question is not the hard question they thought it was.

They should have asked Socrates a different question: What makes it the case that justice requires Alfred to repay Bert? Alternatively put: What makes it the case that justice requires Alfred to repay Bert, given that if justice does require him to repay Bert, then it trivially follows that he ought to? For an answer to the question why justice requires Alfred to repay Bert should *itself* supply an answer to the question why Alfred ought to repay Bert.

And if a person is told that he or she ought to do a thing because doing it would be right, and therefore asks "Why ought I do what is right?" then we should reply "Because of whatever it is that makes your doing the thing *be* right." We should not be misled into thinking that anything more than that is called for.

TEST YOUR UNDERSTANDING

1. Consider the following.

    > Often, what we *ought* to do or what it will be *profitable* for us to do depends on facts outside of our heads. What it is *rational* for us to do depends on facts about things inside of our heads—such as what evidence we have, what we believe, and so on. As a result, it can sometimes be rational (given what is in our heads) to do things that are not what we ought to do or that would not be profitable for us to do (given the way the world is).

    Does Thomson agree with this? If these claims were all true, which connections might be severed?

    a. no; none of them

    b. yes; the connection between what is rational for us to do and what we ought to do

    c. yes; the connection between what is rational for us to do and what will be profitable for us to do

    d. both (b) and (c)

2. Does Thomson think that you ought to do something only if you will profit from doing it?

3. What are other kinds of reasons—aside from profit—that might make it so that you ought to φ, according to Thomson?

    a. because φ-ing is the just thing to do

    b. because φ-ing is the kind thing to do

c. because φ-ing is the generous thing to do

d. all of the above

4. Does Thomson think that there is something more that we can say about why a person ought to do what is right, beyond just pointing to the facts that make it the right thing to do (facts about justice, or kindness, or generosity, or loyalty)?

NOTES AND QUESTIONS

1. *What does Thomson mean by "rational"?* Offer your own example in which what it is rational to do to further one's goals, in Thomson's sense of "rational," may fail to coincide with what one *ought* to do to further one's goals.

2. *Ought one do what it is irrational to do?* Thomson considers a two-premise **argument** for the conclusion that Alfred ought to repay a debt owed to Bert only if Alfred would profit by repaying Bert:

   (i) Alfred ought to repay Bert only if it would be rational for Alfred to repay Bert.

   (ii) It would be rational for Alfred to repay Bert only if Alfred would profit (on balance) by repaying Bert.

   Conclusion: Therefore, Alfred ought to repay Bert only if Alfred would profit (on balance) by repaying Bert.

   Thomson rejects both premises. She rejects the first premise because she contends that sometimes one ought to do something that it would be irrational to do. How is that possible? She rejects the second premise because it could be rational for Alfred to pay Bert with the aim of profiting from repayment even though Alfred might not in fact profit. How is that possible? Do you think either premise can be defended against her challenge? Would your defense involve using the terms "ought," "rational," and "irrational" in the same way that she does?

3. *Are we mistaken to ask the question "Why do what is right?"* Thomson argues that once one grasps the considerations in favor of an action that one ought, in fact, to perform, there is no sense in asking the further question why one *should* do what one ought to do. The reasons that make that action the right thing to do are the very same reasons that one ought to do it. It is a mistake to try to answer the question "Why do the action that is right?" as though it were a further question from the question "Why is that action the right action?"

   When philosophers claim that others have made a mistake, they often try to show *how* this mistake was made. It makes an argument more convincing to show where its opposition misstepped.

   Exercise: Explain how Thomson might be correct, but yet some reasonable people might have mistakenly supposed that the question of whether an action is right and why one should perform it are separate questions. Your explanation should try to pinpoint the error in reasoning that leads Thomson's opponents astray.

David Hume (1711–1776)

Hume was a Scottish philosopher, essayist, and historian, and a central figure in Western philosophy. His *Treatise of Human Nature* (1739), *An Enquiry Concerning Human Understanding* (1748), and *An Enquiry Concerning the Principles of Morals* (1751) have been very influential. (The two *Enquiries* revise material in the *Treatise*.) Many contemporary philosophical discussions in epistemology, metaphysics, and ethics are reactions to Hume's theories and arguments. Hume's *Dialogues Concerning Natural Religion* (published posthumously in 1779) is a classic attack on "design arguments" for the existence of God.

OF THE PASSIONS
from *A Treatise of Human Nature*

Book II

SECTION III. OF THE INFLUENCING MOTIVES OF THE WILL

Nothing is more usual in philosophy, and even in common life, than to talk of the combat of passion and reason, to give the preference to reason, and to assert that men are only so far virtuous as they conform themselves to its dictates. Every rational creature, 'tis said, is oblig'd to regulate his actions by reason; and if any other motive or principle challenge the direction of his conduct, he ought to oppose it, 'till it be entirely subdu'd, or at least brought to a conformity with that superior principle. . . . In order to shew the fallacy of all this philosophy, I shall endeavour to prove *first*, that reason alone can never be a motive to any action of the will; and *secondly*, that it can never oppose passion in the direction of the will.

The understanding exerts itself after two different ways, as it judges from demonstration or probability; as it regards the abstract relations of our ideas, or those relations of objects, of which experience only gives us information.[1] I believe it scarce will be asserted, that the first species of reasoning alone is ever the cause of any action. As its proper province is the world of ideas, and as the will always places us in that of realities, demonstration and volition seem, upon that account, to be totally remov'd, from each other. Mathematics, indeed, are useful in all mechanical operations, and arithmetic in almost every art and profession: But 'tis not of themselves they have any

---

1. For Hume, "ideas" are those mental items that are images or copies of perceptions or what he calls "impressions." The category of impressions encompasses "sensations, passions, and emotions." The perception you have of black ink while reading this text is an impression; your thought about or recollection of that impression is, in Hume's terminology, an idea. "Relations of ideas" concern how different ideas relate to each other; for example, they seem similar or distinct, one seems to lead to another, one seems to exclude another, or together they number a certain amount.

influence. Mechanics are the art of regulating the motions of *bodies to some design'd end or purpose*; and the reason why we employ arithmetic in fixing the proportions of numbers, is only that we may discover the proportions of their influence and operation. A merchant is desirous of knowing the sum total of his accounts with any person: Why? but that he may learn what sum will have the same *effects* in paying his debt, and going to market, as all the particular articles taken together. Abstract or demonstrative reasoning, therefore, never influences any of our actions, but only as it directs our judgment concerning causes and effects; which leads us to the second operation of the understanding.

'Tis obvious, that when we have the prospect of pain or pleasure from any object, we feel a consequent emotion of aversion or propensity, and are carry'd to avoid or embrace what will give us this uneasiness or satisfaction. 'Tis also obvious, that this emotion rests not here, but making us cast our view on every side, comprehends whatever objects are connected with its original one by the relation of cause and effect. Here then reasoning takes place to discover this relation; and according as our reasoning varies, our actions receive a subsequent variation. But 'tis evident in this case, that the impulse arises not from reason, but is only directed by it. 'Tis from the prospect of pain or pleasure that the aversion or propensity arises towards any object: And these emotions extend themselves to the causes and effects of that object, as they are pointed out to us by reason and experience. It can never in the least concern us to know, that such objects are causes, and such others effects, if both the causes and effects be indifferent to us. Where the objects themselves do not affect us, their connexion can never give them any influence; and 'tis plain, that as reason is nothing but the discovery of this connexion, it cannot be by its means that the objects are able to affect us.

Since reason alone can never produce any action, or give rise to volition, I infer, that the same faculty is as incapable of preventing volition, or of disputing the preference with any passion or emotion. . . . Nothing can oppose or retard the impulse of passion, but a contrary impulse; and if this contrary impulse ever arises from reason, that latter faculty must have an original influence on the will, and must be able to cause, as well as hinder any act of volition. But if reason has no original influence, 'tis impossible it can withstand any principle, which has such an efficacy, or ever keep the mind in suspense a moment. Thus it appears, that the principle, which opposes our passion, cannot be the same with reason, and is only call'd so in an improper sense. We speak not strictly and philosophically when we talk of the combat of passion and of reason. Reason is, and ought only to be the slave of the passions, and can never pretend to any other office than to serve and obey them.

. . . When I am angry, I am actually possest with the passion, and in that emotion have no more a reference to any other object, than when I am thirsty, or sick, or more than five foot high. 'Tis impossible, therefore, that this passion can be oppos'd by, or be contradictory to truth and reason; since this contradiction consists in the disagreement of ideas, consider'd as copies, with those objects, which they represent.

. . . [A]s nothing can be contrary to truth or reason, except what has a reference to it, and as the judgments of our understanding only have this reference, it must follow, that passions can be contrary to reason only so far as they are *accompany'd* with some judgment or opinion. According to this principle, which is so obvious and natural, 'tis only in two senses, that any affection can be call'd unreasonable. First, When a passion, such as hope or fear, grief or joy, despair or security, is founded on the supposition of the existence of objects, which really do not exist. Secondly, When in exerting any passion in action, we chuse means insufficient for the design'd end, and deceive ourselves in our judgment of causes and effects. Where a passion is neither founded on false suppositions, nor chuses means insufficient for the end, the understanding can neither justify nor condemn it. 'Tis not contrary to reason to prefer the destruction of the whole world to the scratching of my finger. 'Tis not contrary to reason for me to chuse my total ruin, to prevent the least uneasiness of a . . . person wholly unknown to me. 'Tis as little contrary to reason to prefer even my own acknowledg'd lesser good to my greater, and have a more ardent affection for the former than the latter. A trivial good may, from certain circumstances, produce a desire superior to what arises from the greatest and most valuable enjoyment. . . . In short, a passion must be accompany'd with some false judgment, in order to its being unreasonable; and even then 'tis not the passion, properly speaking, which is unreasonable, but the judgment.

The consequences are evident. Since a passion can never, in any sense, be call'd unreasonable, but when founded on a false supposition, or when it chuses means insufficient for the design'd end, 'tis impossible, that reason and passion can ever oppose each other, or dispute for the government of the will and actions. . . .

OF MORALS
from *A Treatise of Human Nature*

Book III

SECTION I. MORAL DISTINCTIONS NOT DERIV'D FROM REASON

If morality had naturally no influence on human passions and actions, 'twere in vain to take such pains to inculcate it; and nothing wou'd be more fruitless than that multitude of rules and precepts, with which all moralists abound. . . . [Morality] 'tis supposed to influence our passions and actions, and to go beyond the calm and indolent judgments of the understanding. And this is confirm'd by common experience, which informs us, that men are often govern'd by their duties, and are deter'd from some actions by the opinion of injustice, and impell'd to others by that of obligation.

Since morals, therefore, have an influence on the actions and affections, it follows, that they cannot be deriv'd from reason; and that because reason alone, as we have already prov'd, can never have any such influence. Morals excite passions, and produce or prevent actions. Reason of itself is utterly impotent in this particular. The rules of morality, therefore, are not conclusions of our reason.

Reason is the discovery of truth or falsehood. Truth or falsehood consists in an agreement or disagreement either to the *real* relations of ideas, or to *real* existence and matter of fact. Whatever, therefore, is not susceptible of this agreement or disagreement, is incapable of being true or false, and can never be an object of our reason. Now 'tis evident our passions, volitions, and actions, are not susceptible of any such agreement or disagreement; being original facts and realities, compleat in themselves, and implying no reference to other passions, volitions, and actions. 'Tis impossible, therefore, they can be pronounced either true or false, and be either contrary or conformable to reason.

. . . Actions may be laudable or blameable; but they cannot be reasonable or unreasonable: Laudable or blameable, therefore, are not the same with reasonable or unreasonable. The merit and demerit of actions frequently contradict, and sometimes control our natural propensities. But reason has no such influence. Moral distinctions, therefore, are not the offspring of reason. Reason is wholly inactive, and can never be the source of so active a principle as conscience, or a sense of morals.

. . . [R]eason, in a strict and philosophical sense, can have an influence on our conduct only after two ways: Either when it excites a passion by informing us of the existence of something which is a proper object of it; or when it discovers the connexion of causes and effects, so as to afford us means of exerting any passion. These are the only kinds of judgment, which can accompany our actions, or can be said to produce them in any manner; and it must be allow'd, that these judgments may often be false and erroneous. A person may be affected with passion, by supposing a pain or pleasure to lie in an object, which has no tendency to produce either of these sensations, or which produces the contrary to what is imagin'd. A person may also take false measures for the attaining his end, and may retard, by his foolish conduct, instead of forwarding the execution of any project. These false judgments may be thought to affect the passions and actions, which are connected with them, and may be said to render them unreasonable, in a figurative and improper way of speaking. But tho' this be acknowledg'd, 'tis easy to observe, that these errors are so far from being the source of all immorality, that they are commonly very innocent, and draw no manner of guilt upon the person who is so unfortunate as to fall into them. . . . No one can ever regard such errors as a defect in my moral character. . . .

Thus upon the whole, 'tis impossible, that the distinction betwixt moral good and evil, can be made by reason; since that distinction has an influence upon our actions, of which reason alone is incapable. . . .

. . . Take any action allow'd to be vicious: Wilful murder, for instance. Examine it in all lights, and see if you can find that matter of fact, or real existence, which you call *vice*. In which-ever way you take it, you find only certain passions, motives, volitions and thoughts. There is no other matter of fact in the case. The vice entirely escapes you, as long as you consider the object. You never can find it, till you turn your reflexion into your own breast, and find a sentiment of disapprobation, which arises in you, towards this action. Here is a matter of fact; but 'tis the object of feeling, not of reason. It lies in yourself, not in the object. So that when you pronounce any action or character to be vicious, you mean nothing, but that from the constitution of your nature you have a feeling or sentiment of blame from the contemplation of it. Vice and virtue, therefore, may be compar'd to sounds, colours, heat and cold, which, according to modern philosophy, are not qualities in objects, but perceptions in the mind: And this discovery in morals, like that other in physics, . . . has little or no influence on practice. Nothing can be more real, or concern us more, than our own sentiments of pleasure and uneasiness; and if these be favourable to virtue, and unfavourable to vice, no more can be requisite to the regulation of our conduct and behaviour.

I cannot forbear adding . . . an observation, which may, perhaps, be found of some importance. In every system of morality, which I have hitherto met with, . . . the author proceeds for some time in the ordinary way of reasoning, and establishes the being of a God, or makes observations concerning human affairs; when of a sudden I am surpriz'd to find, that instead of the usual copulations of propositions, *is*, and *is not*, I meet with no proposition that is not connected with an *ought*, or an *ought not*. This change is imperceptible; but is, however, of the last consequence. For as this *ought*, or *ought not*, expresses some new relation or affirmation, 'tis necessary that it shou'd be observ'd and explain'd; and at the same time that a reason should be given, for what seems altogether inconceivable, how this new relation can be a deduction from others, which are entirely different from it. . . .

SECTION II: MORAL DISTINCTIONS DERIV'D FROM A MORAL SENSE

Thus the course of the argument leads us to conclude, that since vice and virtue are not discoverable merely by reason, or the comparison of ideas, it must be by means of some impression or sentiment they occasion, that we are able to mark the difference betwixt them. . . . Morality, therefore, is more properly felt than judg'd of; tho' this feeling or sentiment is commonly so soft and gentle, that we are apt to confound it with an idea, according to our common custom of taking all things for the same, which have any near resemblance to each other.

. . . An action, or sentiment, or character is virtuous or vicious; why? because its view causes a pleasure or uneasiness of a particular kind. In giving a reason, therefore, for the pleasure or uneasiness, we sufficiently explain the vice or virtue. To have the sense of virtue, is nothing but to *feel* a satisfaction of a particular kind from the contemplation of a character. The very *feeling* constitutes our praise or admiration. . . .

No[t] every sentiment of pleasure or pain, which arises from characters and actions, of that *peculiar* kind, which makes us praise or condemn. The good qualities of an enemy are hurtful to us; but may still command our esteem and respect. 'Tis only when a character is considered in general, without reference to our particular interest, that it causes such a feeling or sentiment, as denominates it morally good or evil. 'Tis true, those sentiments, from interest and morals, are apt to be confounded, and naturally run into one another. It seldom happens, that we do not think an enemy vicious, and can distinguish betwixt his opposition to our interest and real villainy or baseness. But this hinders not, but that the sentiments are, in themselves, distinct.

. . . [I]f ever there was any thing, which cou'd be call'd natural . . . the sentiments of morality certainly may; since there never was any nation of the world, nor any single person in any nation, who was utterly depriv'd of them, and who never, in any instance, shew'd the least approbation or dislike of manners. These sentiments are so rooted in our constitution and temper, that without entirely confounding the human mind by disease or madness, 'tis impossible to extirpate and destroy them.

. . . [V]irtue is distinguished by the pleasure, and vice by the pain, that any action, sentiment or character gives us by the mere view and contemplation. . . .

WHY UTILITY PLEASES
from *An Enquiry Concerning the Principles of Morals*

Part I

It seems so natural a thought to ascribe to their utility the praise, which we bestow on the social virtues, that one would expect to meet with this principle everywhere in moral writers, as the chief foundation of their reasoning and enquiry. In common life, we may observe, that the circumstance of utility is always appealed to; nor is it supposed, that a greater eulogy can be given to any man, than to display his usefulness to the public, and enumerate the services, which he has performed to mankind and society. . . .

From the apparent usefulness of the social virtues, it has readily been inferred by sceptics, both ancient and modern, that all moral distinctions arise from education, and were, at first, invented, and afterwards encouraged, by the art of politicians, in order to render men tractable, and subdue their natural ferocity and selfishness, which incapacitated them for society. This principle, indeed, of precept and education, must so far be owned to have a powerful influence, that it may frequently increase or diminish, beyond their natural standard, the sentiments of approbation or dislike; and may even, in particular instances, create, without any natural principle, a new sentiment of this kind; as is evident in all superstitious practices and observances: But that *all* moral affection or dislike arises from this origin, will never surely be allowed by any judicious enquirer. Had nature made no such distinction, founded on the original constitution of the mind, the words, *honourable* and *shameful, lovely* and *odious, noble* and *despicable*, had never had place in any language; nor could politicians, had they invented these terms, ever have been able to render them intelligible, or make them convey any idea to the audience. . . .

The social virtues must, therefore, be allowed to have a natural beauty and amiableness, which, at first, antecedent to all precept or education, recommends them to the esteem of uninstructed mankind, and engages their affections. And as the public utility of these virtues is the chief circumstance, whence they derive their merit, it follows, that the end, which they have a tendency to promote, must be some way agreeable to us, and take hold of some natural affection. It must please, either from considerations of self-interest, or from more generous motives and regards.

It has often been asserted, that, as every man has a strong connexion with society, and perceives the impossibility of his solitary subsistence, he becomes, on that account, favourable to all those habits or principles, which promote order in society, and insure to him the quiet possession of so inestimable a blessing. As much as we value our own happiness and welfare, as much must we applaud the practice of justice and humanity, by which alone the social confederacy can be maintained, and every man reap the fruits of mutual protection and assistance.

This deduction of morals from self-love, or a regard to private interest, is an obvious thought, . . . yet, the voice of nature and experience seems plainly to oppose the selfish theory.

We frequently bestow praise on virtuous actions, performed in very distant ages and remote countries; where the utmost subtlety of imagination would not discover any appearance of self-interest, or find any connexion of our present happiness and security with events so widely separated from us.

A generous, a brave, a noble deed, performed by an adversary, commands our approbation; while in its consequences it may be acknowledged prejudicial to our particular interest.

Where private advantage concurs with general affection for virtue, we readily perceive and avow the mixture of these distinct sentiments, which have a very different feeling and influence on the mind. We praise, perhaps, with more alacrity, where the generous humane action contributes to our particular interest: But the topics of praise, which we insist on, are very wide of this circumstance. And we may attempt to bring over others to our sentiments, without endeavouring to convince them, that they reap any advantage from the actions which we recommend to their approbation and applause. . . .

Usefulness is agreeable, and engages our approbation. This is a matter of fact, confirmed by daily observation. But, *useful*? For what? For somebody's interest, surely. Whose interest then? Not our own only: For our approbation frequently extends farther. It must, therefore, be the interest of those, who are served by the character or action approved of; and these we may conclude, however remote, are not totally indifferent to us. By opening up this principle, we shall discover one great source of moral distinctions.

Part II

Self-love is a principle in human nature of such extensive energy, and the interest of each individual is, in general, so closely connected with that of the community, that those philosophers were excusable, who fancied that all our concern for the public might be resolved into a concern for our own happiness and preservation. . . .

But notwithstanding this frequent confusion of interests, . . . we have found instances, in which private interest was separate from public; in which it was even contrary: And yet we observed the moral sentiment to continue, notwithstanding this disjunction of interests. And wherever these distinct interests sensibly concurred, we always found a sensible increase of the sentiment, and a more warm affection to virtue, and detestation of vice. . . . Compelled by these instances, we must renounce the theory, which accounts for every moral sentiment by the principle of self-love. We must adopt a more public affection, and allow, that the interests of society are not, even on their own account, entirely, indifferent to us. Usefulness is only a tendency to a certain end; and it is a contradiction in terms, that anything pleases as means to an end, where the end itself no wise affects us. If usefulness, therefore, be a source of moral sentiment, and if this usefulness be not always considered with a reference to self; it follows, that everything, which contributes to the happiness of society, recommends itself directly to our approbation and good-will. Here is a principle, which accounts, in great part, for the origin of morality: And what need we seek for abstruse and remote systems, when there occurs one so obvious and natural?[2]

Have we any difficulty to comprehend the force of humanity and benevolence? Or to conceive, that the very aspect of happiness, joy, prosperity, gives pleasure; that of pain, suffering, sorrow, communicates uneasiness? The human countenance, says Horace,[3] borrows smiles or tears from the human countenance. Reduce a person to solitude, and he loses all enjoyment, except either of the sensual or speculative kind; and that because the movements of his heart are not forwarded by correspondent movements in his fellow-creatures. The signs of sorrow and mourning, though arbitrary, affect us with melancholy; but the natural symptoms, tears and cries and groans, never fail to infuse compassion and uneasiness. And if the effects of misery touch us in so lively a manner; can we be supposed altogether insensible or indifferent towards its causes; when a malicious or treacherous character and behaviour are presented to us?

We enter, I shall suppose, into a convenient, warm, well-contrived apartment: We necessarily receive a pleasure from its very survey; because it presents us with the pleasing ideas of ease, satisfaction, and enjoyment. The hospitable, good-humoured, humane landlord appears. This circumstance surely must embellish the whole; nor can we easily forbear reflecting, with pleasure, on the satisfaction which results to every one from his intercourse and good-offices.

His whole family, by the freedom, ease, confidence, and calm enjoyment, diffused over their countenances, sufficiently express their happiness. I have a pleasing sympathy in the prospect of so much joy, and can never consider the source of it, without the most agreeable emotions.

---

2. It is needless to push our researches so far as to ask, why we have humanity or a fellow-feeling with others. It is sufficient, that this is experienced to be a principle in human nature. We must stop somewhere in our examination of causes; and there are, in every science, some general principles, beyond which we cannot hope to find any principle more general. No man is absolutely indifferent to the happiness and misery of others. The first has a natural tendency to give pleasure; the second, pain. This every one may find in himself. [Hume's note.]

3. Quintus Horatius Flaccus (65–8 BCE), Roman poet.

He tells me, that an oppressive and powerful neighbour had attempted to dispossess him of his inheritance, and had long disturbed all his innocent and social pleasures. I feel an immediate indignation arise in me against such violence and injury.

But it is no wonder, he adds, that a private wrong should proceed from a man, who had enslaved provinces, depopulated cities, and made the field and scaffold stream with human blood. I am struck with horror at the prospect of so much misery, and am actuated by the strongest antipathy against its author.

In general, it is certain, that, wherever we go, whatever we reflect on or converse about, everything still presents us with the view of human happiness or misery, and excites in our breast a sympathetic movement of pleasure or uneasiness. In our serious occupations, in our careless amusements, this principle still exerts its active energy. . . .

Any recent event or piece of news, by which the fate of states, provinces, or many individuals is affected, is extremely interesting even to those whose welfare is not immediately engaged. Such intelligence is propagated with celerity, heard with avidity, and enquired into with attention and concern. The interest of society appears, on this occasion, to be in some degree the interest of each individual. The imagination is sure to be affected; though the passions excited may not always be so strong and steady as to have great influence on the conduct and behaviour.

The perusal of a history seems a calm entertainment; but would be no entertainment at all, did not our hearts beat with correspondent movements to those which are described by the historian. . . .

The frivolousness of the subject too, we may observe, is not able to detach us entirely from what carries an image of human sentiment and affection.

When a person stutters, and pronounces with difficulty, we even sympathize with this trivial uneasiness, and suffer for him. . . .

If any man from a cold insensibility, or narrow selfishness of temper, is unaffected with the images of human happiness or misery, he must be equally indifferent to the images of vice and virtue: As, on the other hand, it is always found, that a warm concern for the interests of our species is attended with a delicate feeling of all moral distinctions; a strong resentment of injury done to men; a lively approbation of their welfare. In this particular, though great superiority is observable of one man above another; yet none are so entirely indifferent to the interest of their fellow-creatures, as to perceive no distinctions of moral good and evil, in consequence of the different tendencies of actions and principles. How, indeed, can we suppose it possible in any one, who wears a human heart, that if there be subjected to his censure, one character or system of conduct, which is beneficial, and another which is pernicious to his species or community, he will not so much as give a cool preference to the former, or ascribe to it the smallest merit or regard? Let us suppose such a person ever so selfish; let private interest have ingrossed ever so much his attention; yet in instances, where that is not concerned, he must unavoidably feel *some* propensity to the good of mankind, and make it an object of choice, if everything else be equal. Would any man, who is walking along, tread as willingly on another's gouty toes, whom he has no quarrel with, as on the hard flint and pavement? There is here surely a difference in the case. We surely take into consideration the happiness and misery of others, in weighing the several motives of action, and incline to the former, where no private regards draw us to seek our own promotion or advantage by the injury of our fellow-creatures. And if the principles of humanity are capable, in many instances, of influencing our actions, they must, at all times, have *some* authority over our sentiments, and give us a general approbation of what is useful to society, and blame of what is dangerous or pernicious. The degrees of these sentiments may be the subject of controversy; but the reality of their existence, one should think, must be admitted in every theory or system. . . .

Thus, in whatever light we take this subject, the merit, ascribed to the social virtues, appears still uniform, and arises chiefly from that regard, which the natural sentiment of benevolence engages us to pay to the interests of mankind and society. If we consider the principles of the human make, such as they appear to daily experience and observation, we must, *a priori*,[4] conclude it impossible for such a creature as man to be totally indifferent to the well or ill-being of his fellow-creatures, and not readily, of himself, to pronounce, where nothing gives him any particular bias, that what promotes their happiness is good, what tends to their misery is evil, without any farther regard or consideration. Here then are the faint rudiments, at least, or outlines, of a *general* distinction between actions; and in proportion as the humanity of the person is supposed to encrease, his connexion with those who are injured or benefited, and his lively conception of their misery or happiness; his consequent censure or approbation acquires proportionable vigour. There is no necessity, that a generous action, barely mentioned in an old history or remote gazette, should communicate any strong feelings of applause and admiration. Virtue, placed at such a distance, is like a fixed star, which, though to the eye of reason it may appear as luminous as the sun in his meridian, is so infinitely removed as to affect the senses, neither with light nor heat. Bring this virtue nearer, by our acquaintance or connexion with the persons, or even by an eloquent recital of the case; our hearts are immediately caught, our sympathy enlivened, and our cool approbation converted into the warmest sentiments of friendship and regard. These seem necessary and infallible consequences of the general principles of human nature, as discovered in common life and practice.

Again; reverse these views and reasonings: Consider the matter *a posteriori*[5]; and weighing the consequences, enquire if the merit of social virtue be not, in a great measure, derived from the feelings of humanity, with which it affects the spectators. It appears to be matter of fact, that the circumstance of *utility*, in all subjects, is a source of praise and approbation: That it is constantly appealed to in all moral decisions concerning the merit and demerit of actions: That it is the *sole* source of that high regard paid to justice, fidelity, honour, allegiance, and chastity: That it is inseparable from all the other social virtues, humanity, generosity, charity, affability, lenity, mercy, and moderation: And, in a word, that it is a foundation of the chief part of morals, which has a reference to mankind and our fellow-creatures.

It appears also, that, in our general approbation of characters and manners, the useful tendency of the social virtues moves us not by any regards to self-interest, but

---

4. For Hume, **a priori** means "without resort to evidence from our sensory experience but ascertainable through the operation of reason alone."

5. By **a posteriori**, Hume means "in light of the evidence presented to us by our empirical experience."

has an influence much more universal and extensive. It appears that a tendency to public good, and to the promoting of peace, harmony, and order in society, does always, by affecting the benevolent principles of our frame, engage us on the side of the social virtues. And it appears, as an additional confirmation, that these principles of humanity and sympathy enter so deeply into all our sentiments, and have so powerful an influence, as may enable them to excite the strongest censure and applause.

TEST YOUR UNDERSTANDING

1. According to Hume, could an insight of reason, on its own, propel me to quit smoking?

    a. Yes. Once you deduce that smoking is dangerous to yourself, knowing that fact will be enough to get you to quit smoking.

    b. No. Reason cannot motivate on its own; desires must also play a role in motivating action.

2. Hume argues that reason is "but the slave of the passions." What are the two ways that Hume believes that reason can influence our behavior?

3. How does Hume think we come to make moral judgments that some behavior is good and some behavior is evil?

    a. These moral judgments reflect our sentiments of approval and disapproval.

    b. These moral judgments reflect our desires about what we want to happen.

    c. These moral judgments reflect our assessment of which action would provide the greatest happiness.

    d. These moral judgments reflect our assessment of which action best respects the humanity of other persons.

4. How does Hume argue that moral judgments are different from judgments of self-interest?

READER'S GUIDE

Hume on Moral Motivation

People make moral assessments: they think it is wrong to lie, right to keep an agreement, and wrong to inflict pain for no reason. We also act on our moral assessments, as when we tell the truth because we judge that it is wrong to lie. How are we to understand the relationship between the moral assessment and the action? Perhaps a better understanding of the nature of the moral assessment will put us in a better position to answer the question.

According to Hume, moral assessments are based on *human sympathy*. Our natural human tendency to care about other people leads us to approve of some actions and to disapprove of other actions. When our sympathy leads us to approve of an action, we say that it is morally good; when we disapprove, we say that it is morally bad. For example, when a child sees a bully push another child to the ground, the first child reacts emotionally to the plight of the child pushed to the ground. The result is a feeling of disapproval for what the bully did, which is expressed by saying that the bullying is wrong.

Hume contrasts his own sympathy-based view with Egoism, the view that the fundamental basis of moral assessments is *self-interest* (which he calls "self-love"). It is true that the right thing to do is *also* often in one's self-interest. And it is also true that, in general, being in a society in which people treat each other morally—tell the truth, keep promises, provide assistance when others are in need—has a lot of benefits for each person. Hume acknowledges that the benefits of being in a relationship of *mutual assistance* with others could go some way toward explaining our moral attitudes. However, Hume points out that we make moral judgments and have moral attitudes (in particular, approval and disapproval) even regarding actions that are distant in time and space, as when someone says that ancient slavery was morally wrong. The theory that bases morality on self-love has trouble explaining these moral judgments of distant times and places.

Hume points out that a morally good action has a grip on us—we feel its pull—even when performing it would be bad for us: we may not do it in the end, but we feel some pull. And he points out that we feel horror at horrible things that were done, even when they were done long ago. In general, he claims, we feel sad when we hear of others' suffering and we feel joy when we hear of others' joy. He gives the example of entering the home of a family one did not know previously and being emotionally moved by their plight and by their good fortune. Hume claims that people simply naturally care for each other. In this view, this sympathy, rooted in our human nature, is the basis of morality.

Both Hume's view and Egoism see morality as grounded in passion—either passion for other people in general, or passion for oneself. A third view, Rationalism, sees morally good action as stemming from *reason* alone, and holds that *reason* and *passion* compete for control of a person's actions. According to Rationalism, it is good when reason wins the battle with passion. Hume rejects Rationalism, arguing that reason and passion are not in any kind of conflict or competition, and that it would be impossible for reason to determine how a person acts or to ever "win" a competition with the passions.

To see why Hume thinks this, let's consider what *reasoning* can provide us. Sometimes reasoning helps us decide what to do. Suppose that you want to go to a concert on Saturday night, which is also the day of a big football game at the nearby stadium. You know that parking will be hard to find, and that the traffic will be bad. You might decide to leave for the concert much earlier than would normally be necessary, and to take a taxi rather than driving yourself. These decisions are the results of reasoning from (a) your *desire* to go to the concert and to arrive on time, and (b) your *knowledge* of some *facts* about what the parking and traffic situations will be like. Has reasoning settled on its own what you will do? It has not. Your desire to attend the concert played a crucial role in determining what you would do. What a person wants—her desires—are among her *passions*; so we see that the passions are playing a crucial role in settling what you will do.

Hume points out that reasoning is very helpful *given* that one has certain desires. By reasoning and relying on the facts we know—and in particular our knowledge of what would cause what—we can take the *means* to the *ends* that we want to achieve (like getting to the concert on time). But this kind of means-end reasoning simply won't tell us which ends to have. Reason is no help at all in telling us what to aim at, Hume holds. It can simply tell us how to achieve the aims we have.

If reason came with its own ends, then reason and passion might be in tension. But Hume says that reason is "the slave of the passions" (p. 947) because reason simply helps us to direct our actions toward the things that we want.

Of course, reason can also show us that we did something we shouldn't have done. But, on Hume's view, this will always be because we realize that what we did was not really a good way to achieve what we wanted. Perhaps, for example, you should have realized that taxis would not be available on the day of the big football game, and so the plan you made for getting to the concert was not a good plan. But reason will not tell you whether concerts are worth going to.

Similarly, reason can help you figure out how to do what morality requires, but it will not tell you what morality requires. For that, you need passions. And when it comes to morality, the essential passion is sympathy.

NOTES AND QUESTIONS

1. *Morality and the diversity of moral judgments.* Hume argues that moral distinctions between good and evil reflect the sentiments of approbation and disapprobation (i.e., approval and disapproval) we feel in contemplating certain sorts of actions. Does this mean that he believes that moral judgments are purely a matter of *individual* emotional reactions? Suppose that two people, *X* and *Y*, contemplate the same act of willful murder: *X* disapproves, and so judges the act bad, while *Y* approves and judges it good. Does Hume's view entail that these two judgments are both correct? How might Hume resist this conclusion?

2. *Must evil action involve an error of reason?* Suppose Hitler knew all of the facts about the people he murdered and about the consequences of his actions, but he celebrated those consequences and chose to engage in his aggressive crusade of genocide and war because he approved of them. On Hume's view we cannot say that Hitler behaved unreasonably or contrary to reason. For some critics, this marks a stupefying defect in Hume's theory.

   Philippa Foot, however, follows Hume on this point, arguing that the person

   > who rejects morality because he sees no reason to obey its rules can be convicted of villainy but not of inconsistency. Nor will his action necessarily be irrational. Irrational actions are those in which a man in some way defeats his own purposes, doing what is calculated to be disadvantageous or to frustrate his ends. Immorality does not *necessarily* involve any such thing.[6]

   Note that Foot appears to endorse Hume's view that what we have reason to do depends entirely on what we happen to want or care about. To say that someone acts contrary to reason, on this view, is to say that his action fails to promote his ends. So, we cannot say an informed, wholehearted mass murderer such as Hitler

---

6. Philippa Foot, "Morality as a System of Hypothetical Imperatives," *Philosophical Review* 81, 3 (1972): 305–16, esp. 310. For another important modern article decoupling moral criticism from the criticism of irrationality, see Bernard Williams, "Internal and External Reasons," in his *Moral Luck* (Cambridge University Press, 1982). Later in her career, Philippa Foot advanced a different position than that of her 1972 article. She contended in *Natural Goodness* (Oxford University Press, 2003) that acting morally *is* an aspect of our rationality in virtue of our membership within the species of human beings who must live and cooperate with one another to thrive.

was "irrational." But, with Hume, she insists that we can say he behaved wrongly and that he was a villain, even if he did not violate any dictates of reason. She and other Humeans do not regard their position as excluding their use of tough moral adjectives and condemnations.

Exercise: Explain how Hume could claim that a fully informed Hitler was a villain who acted wrongly but did not act contrary to reason. Is this plausible? If we are able to charge Hitler, so described, with being an evil, villainous, brutal mass murderer, is there anything important missing from this condemnation? Why might it add an important dimension of criticism to be able to say, in addition, that he acted contrary to reason?

Immanuel Kant (1724–1804)

Kant was a German philosopher of the Enlightenment whose work extolled the faculty of reason, exploring its powers and limitations. He was born in Königsberg and was a professor at the University of Königsberg. His work exerted and continues to exert a profound influence on the development of modern and contemporary philosophy in ethics, political philosophy, metaphysics, epistemology, the philosophy of mind and of psychology, aesthetics, and the philosophy of religion. His most famous books include *The Critique of Pure Reason* (1781), *Prolegomena to Any Future Metaphysics* (1783), *Groundwork of the Metaphysics of Morals* (1785), *The Critique of Practical Reason* (1788), *The Critique of Judgment* (1790), and *The Metaphysics of Morals* (1797).

GROUNDWORK OF THE METAPHYSICS OF MORALS

Preface

Everyone must admit that a law, if it is to hold morally, i.e. as the ground of an obligation, must carry with it absolute necessity; that the command: thou shalt not lie, does not just hold for human beings only, as if other rational beings did not have to heed it; and so with all remaining actual moral laws; hence that the ground of the obligation here must not be sought in the nature of the human being, or in the circumstances of the world in which he is placed, but a priori solely in concepts of pure reason, and that any other prescription that is founded on principles of mere experience—and even a prescription that is in some certain respect universal, in so far as it relies in the least part on empirical grounds, perhaps just for a motivating ground—can indeed be called a practical rule, but never a moral law. . . .

A metaphysics of morals is thus indispensably necessary, not merely on the grounds of speculation, for investigating the source of the practical principles that lie a priori in our reason, but because morals themselves remain subject to all sorts of corruption as long as we lack that guideline and supreme norm by which to judge them correctly. For in the case of what is to be morally good it is not enough that it *conform* with the moral law, but it must also be done *for its sake*; if not, that conformity is only very contingent and precarious, because the immoral ground will indeed now and then produce actions that conform with the law, but in many cases actions that are contrary to it. But now the moral law in its purity and genuineness . . . is to be sought nowhere else than in a pure philosophy; it (metaphysics) must thus come first, and without it there can be no moral philosophy at all; and that which mixes these pure principles in with empirical ones does not even deserve the name of a philosophy . . . much less that of a moral philosophy, since it even infringes on the purity of morals themselves by this intermingling and proceeds contrary to its own end. . . .

The present groundwork, however, is nothing more than the identification and corroboration of the *supreme principle of morality*. . . .

First Section: Transition from Common to Philosophical Moral Rational Cognition

It is impossible to think of anything at all in the world, or indeed even beyond it, that could be taken to be good without limitation, except a good will. Understanding, wit, judgment, and whatever else the *talents* of the mind may be called, or confidence, resolve, and persistency of intent, as qualities of *temperament*, are no doubt in many respects good and desirable; but they can also be extremely evil and harmful if the will that is to make use of these gifts of nature, and whose distinctive constitution is therefore called *character*, is not good. It is just the same with *gift of fortune*. Power, riches, honor, even health, and the entire well-being and contentment with one's condition, under the name of *happiness*, inspire confidence and thereby quite often overconfidence as well, unless a good will is present to correct and make generally purposive their influence on the mind, and with it also the whole principle for acting; not to mention that a rational impartial spectator can nevermore take any delight in the sight of the uninterrupted prosperity of a being adorned with no feature of a pure and good will, and that a good will thus appears to constitute the indispensable condition even of the worthiness to be happy.

Some qualities are even conducive to this good will itself and can make its work much easier; but regardless of this they have no inner unconditional worth, but always presuppose a good will, which limits the high esteem in which they are otherwise tightly held, and makes it impermissible to take them for good per se. Moderation in affects and passions, self-control and sober deliberation are not only good in many respects, they even appear to constitute part of the *inner* worth of a person; but they are far from deserving to be declared good without limitation (however unconditionally they were praised by the ancients). For without principles of a good will they can become most evil, and the cold blood of a scoundrel makes him not only far more dangerous, but also immediately more loathsome in our eyes than he would have been taken to be without it.

A good will is good not because of what it effects, or accomplishes, not because of its fitness to attain some intended end, but good just by its willing, i.e. in itself and, considered by itself, it is to be esteemed beyond compare much higher than anything that could ever be brought about by it in favor of some inclination, and indeed, if you will, the sum of all inclinations. Even if by some particular disfavor of fate, or by the scanty endowment of a stepmotherly nature, this will should entirely lack the capacity to carry through its purpose; if despite its greatest striving it should still accomplish nothing, and only the good will were to remain (not, of course, as a mere wish, but as the summoning of all means that are within our control); then, like a jewel, it would still shine by itself, as something that has its full worth in itself. Usefulness or fruitlessness can neither add anything to this worth, nor take anything away from it. It would, as it were, be only the setting to enable us to handle it better in ordinary commerce, or to attract the attention of those who are not yet expert enough; but not to recommend it to experts, or to determine its worth.

Even so, in this idea of the absolute worth of a mere will, not taking into account any utility in its estimation, there is something so strange that, regardless of all the agreement with it even of common reason, a suspicion must yet arise that it might perhaps covertly be founded merely on some high-flown fantastication, and that we may have misunderstood Nature's purpose in assigning Reason to our will as its ruler. We shall therefore submit this idea to examination from this point of view.

In the natural predispositions of an organized being, i.e. one arranged purposively for life, we assume as a principle that no organ will be found in it for any end that is not also the most fitting for it and the most suitable. Now in a being that has reason and a will, if the actual end of Nature were its *preservation,* its *prosperity,* in a word its *happiness,* then she would have made very bad arrangements for this in appointing the creature's Reason as the accomplisher of this purpose. For all the actions that it has to perform with a view to this purpose, and the whole rule of its conduct, would be marked out for it far more accurately by instinct, and that end would thereby have been obtained much more reliably than can ever be done by reason; and if in addition reason should have been bestowed on the favored creature, it would have had to serve it only to contemplate the fortunate predisposition of its nature, to admire it, to rejoice in it, and to be grateful for it to the beneficent cause; but not to subject its desiderative faculty to that weak and deceptive guidance and meddle with Nature's purpose; in a word, Nature would have prevented Reason from striking out into *practical use,* and from having the impudence, with its feeble insights, to devise its own plan for happiness and for the means of achieving it. Nature herself would have taken over the choice not only of ends, but also of means, and as a wise precaution would have entrusted them both solely to instinct.

In actual fact, we do find that the more a cultivated reason engages with the purpose of enjoying life and with happiness, so much the further does a human being stray from true contentment; and from this there arises in many, and indeed in those who are most experienced in its use, if only they are sincere enough to admit it, a certain degree of *misology*, i.e. hatred of reason, since after calculating all the advantages they derive—I do not say from the invention of all the arts of common luxury, but even from the sciences (which in the end also appear to them to be a luxury of the understanding)—they still find that they have in fact just brought more hardship upon their shoulders than they have gained in happiness, and that because of this they eventually envy, rather than disdain, the more common run of people, who are closer to the guidance of mere natural instinct, and who do not allow their reason much influence on their behavior. And to that extent one must admit that the judgment of those who greatly moderate and even reduce below zero the vainglorious eulogies extolling the advantages that reason was supposed to obtain for us with regard to the happiness and contentment of life, is by no means sullen, or ungrateful to the kindliness of the government of the world; but that these judgments are covertly founded on the idea of another and far worthier purpose of their existence, to which, and not to happiness, reason is quite properly destined, and to which, as its supreme condition, the private purpose of a human being must therefore largely take second place.

For since reason is not sufficiently fit to guide the will reliably with regard to its objects and the satisfaction of all our needs (which in part it does itself multiply)—an end to which an implanted natural instinct would have led much more reliably—but reason as a practical faculty, i.e. as one that is meant to influence has yet been imparted to us, its true function must be to produce a *will that is good*, not for other purposes *as a means*, but good *in itself*—for which reason was absolutely necessary—since nature has everywhere else gone to work purposively in distributing its predispositions. Therefore this will need not, indeed, be the only and the entire good, but it must yet be the highest good, and the condition of everything else, even of all longing for happiness; in which case it is quite consistent with the wisdom of nature when one perceives that the cultivation of reason, which is required for the first and unconditional purpose, in many ways limits—at least in this life—the attainment of the second, namely of happiness, which is always conditional, indeed that it may reduce it to less than nothing without nature's proceeding unpurposively in this; because reason, which recognizes as its highest practical function the grounding of a good will, in attaining this purpose, is capable only of a contentment after its own kind, namely from fulfilling an end that again is determined only by reason, even if this should involve much infringement on the ends of inclination.

In order, then, to unravel the concept of a will to be highly esteemed in itself and good apart from any further purpose, as it already dwells in natural sound understanding and needs not so much to be taught as rather just to be brought to light, this concept that always comes first in estimating the entire worth of our actions and constitutes the condition of everything else: we shall inspect the concept of duty, which contains that of a good will, though under certain subjective limitations and hindrances, which, however, far from concealing it and making it unrecognizable, rather bring it out by contrast and make it shine forth all the more brightly.

I here pass over all actions already recognized as contrary to duty, even though they may be useful in this or that respect; for in their case there is no question whether they might have been done *from duty*, since they even conflict with it. I also set aside actions that actually conform with duty but to which human beings immediately have *no inclination*, but which they still perform, because they are impelled to do so by another inclination. For there it is easy to distinguish whether the action that conforms with duty was done *from duty* or from a self-serving purpose. It is much more difficult to notice this difference when an action conforms with duty and the subject has in addition an *immediate* inclination towards it. E.g. it certainly conforms with duty that a shopkeeper not overcharge his inexperienced customer, and where there is much commerce, a prudent merchant actually does not do this, but keeps a fixed general price for everyone, so that a child may buy from him just as well as everyone else. Thus one is served *honestly*; but this is not nearly enough for us to believe that the merchant proceeded in this way from duty and principles of honesty; his advantage required it; it cannot be assumed here that he had, besides, an immediate inclination towards his customers, so as from love, as it were, to give no one preference over another in the matter of price. Thus the action was done neither from duty, nor from immediate inclination, but merely for a self-interested purpose.

By contrast, to preserve one's life is one's duty and besides everyone has an immediate inclination to do so. But on account of this the often anxious care with which the greatest part of humanity attends to it has yet no inner worth, and their maxim no moral content. They preserve their lives *in conformity with duty*, but not *from duty*. By contrast, if adversities and hopeless grief have entirely taken away the taste for life; if the unfortunate man, strong of soul, more indignant about his fate than despondent or dejected, wishes for death, and yet preserves his life, without loving it, not from inclination, or fear, but from duty; then his maxim has a moral content.

To be beneficent where one can is one's duty, and besides there are many souls so attuned to compassion that, even without another motivating ground of vanity, or self-interest, they find an inner gratification in spreading joy around them, and can relish the contentment of others, in so far as it is their work. But I assert that in such a case an action of this kind—however much it conforms with duty, however amiable it may be—still has no true moral worth, but stands on the same footing as other inclinations, e.g. the inclination to honor, which if it fortunately lights upon what is in fact in the general interest and in conformity with duty, and hence honorable, deserves praise and encouragement, but not high esteem; for the maxim lacks moral content, namely to do such actions not from inclination, but *from duty*. Suppose, then, that the mind of that friend of humanity were beclouded by his own grief, which extinguishes all compassion for the fate of others; that he still had the means to benefit others in need, but the need of others did not touch him because he is sufficiently occupied with his own; and that now, as inclination no longer stimulates him to it, he were yet to tear himself out of this deadly insensibility, and to do the action without any inclination, solely from duty; not until then does it have its genuine moral worth. Still further: if nature had as such placed little sympathy in the heart of this or that man; if (otherwise honest) he were by temperament cold and indifferent to the sufferings of others, perhaps because he himself is equipped with the peculiar gift of patience and enduring strength towards his own, and presupposes, or even requires, the same in every other; if nature had not actually formed such a man (who would truly not be its worst product) to be a friend of humanity, would he not still find within himself a source from which to give himself a far higher worth than that of a good-natured temperament may be? Certainly! It is just there that the worth of character commences, which is moral and beyond all comparison the highest, namely that he be beneficent, not from inclination, but from duty.

To secure one's own happiness is one's duty (at least indirectly); for lack of contentment with one's condition, in the trouble of many worries and amidst unsatisfied needs, could easily become a great *temptation to transgress one's duties*. But, even without taking note of duty, all human beings have already of their own the most powerful and intimate inclination to happiness, as it is just in this idea that all inclinations unite in one sum. However, the prescription of happiness is predominantly such, that it greatly infringes on some inclinations and yet human beings can form no determinate and reliable concept of the sum of the satisfaction of all under the name of happiness; which is why it is not surprising that a single inclination—if determinate with regard to what it promises, and to the time its satisfaction can be obtained—can outweigh a wavering idea, and that a human being, e.g. someone suffering from gout of the foot, can choose to enjoy what he fancies and to suffer what he can since, according to his calculation, at least then he has not denied himself the enjoyment of the present moment because of perhaps groundless expectations of some good fortune that is meant to lie in health. But also in this case, if the universal inclination to happiness did not determine his will, if health, at least for him, did not enter into this calculation so necessarily, then here, as in all other cases, there still remains a law, namely to advance one's happiness, not from inclination, but from duty; and it is not until then that his conduct has its actual moral worth.

It is in this way, no doubt, that we are to understand the passages from Scripture that contain the command to love one's neighbor, even our enemy. For love as inclination cannot be commanded, but beneficence from duty itself—even if no inclination whatsoever impels us to it, indeed if natural and unconquerable aversion resists—is *practical* and not *pathological* love, which lies in the will and not in the propensity of sensation, in principles of action and not in melting compassion; and only the former can be commanded.

The second proposition is: an action from duty has its moral worth *not in the purpose* that is to be attained by it, but in the maxim according to which it is resolved upon, and thus it does not depend on the actuality of the object of the action, but merely on the *principle* of *willing* according to which—regardless of any object of the desiderative faculty—the action is done. That the purposes that we may have when we act, and their effects, as ends and incentives of the will, can bestow on actions no unconditional moral worth, is clear from what was previously said. In what, then, can this worth lie, if it is not to consist in the will with reference to their hoped-for effect? It can lie nowhere else *than in the principle of the will*, regardless of the ends that can be effected by such action; for the will stands halfway between its a priori principle, which is formal, and its a posteriori incentive, which is material, as it were at a crossroads, and since it must after all be determined by something, it will have to be determined by the formal principle of willing as such when an action is done from duty, as every material principle has been taken away from it.

The third proposition, as the conclusion from both previous ones, I would express as follows: *duty is the necessity of an action from respect for the law.* For the object as the effect of the action I have in mind I can indeed have *inclination*, but *never respect*, precisely because it is merely an effect and not activity of a will. Likewise, I cannot have respect for inclination as such, whether it is mine or that of another; I can at most in the first case approve of it, in the second at times love it myself, i.e. view it as favorable to my own advantage. Only what is connected with my will merely as ground, never as effect, what does not serve my inclination, but outweighs it, or at least excludes it entirely from calculations when we make a choice, hence the mere law by itself; can be an object of respect and thus a command. Now, an action from duty is to separate off entirely the influence of inclination, and with it every object of the will; thus nothing remains for the will that could determine it except, objectively, the *law* and, subjectively, *pure respect* for this practical law, and hence the maxim of complying with such a law, even if it infringes on all my inclinations.

Thus the moral worth of the action does not lie in the effect that is expected from it, nor therefore in any principle of action that needs to borrow its motivating ground from this expected effect. For all these effects (agreeableness of one's condition, indeed even advancement of the happiness of others) could also have been brought about by other causes, and thus there was, for this, no need of the will of a rational being; even so, in it alone can the highest and unconditional good be found. Nothing other than the *representation of the law* in itself—*which of course can take place only in a rational being*—in so far as it, not the hoped-for effect, is the determining ground of the will, can therefore constitute the pre-eminent good that we call moral, which is already present in the person himself who acts according to it, and is not first to be expected from the effect.

But what kind of law can that possibly be, the representation of which—even without regard for the effect expected from it—must determine the will for it to be called good absolutely and without limitation? Since I have robbed the will of all impulses that could arise for it from following some particular law, nothing remains but as such the universal conformity of actions with law, which alone is to serve the will as its principle, i.e. I ought never to proceed except in such a way *that I could also will that my maxim should become a universal law.* Here, then, mere conformity with law as such (not founded on any law determined with a view to certain actions) is what serves the will as its principle, and must so serve it if duty is not to be as such an empty delusion and a chimerical concept; common human reason in its practical judging is actually in perfect agreement with this, and always has the envisaged principle before its eyes.

Let the question be, e.g., may I not, when I am in trouble, make a promise with the intention not to keep it? Here I easily discern the different meanings the question can have: whether it is prudent, or whether it conforms with duty to make a false promise. The former can no doubt quite often take place. I do see very well that it is not enough to extricate myself from the present predicament by means of this subterfuge, but that it requires careful deliberation whether this lie may not later give rise to much greater inconvenience for me than those from which I am now liberating myself; and—since with all my supposed *cunning* the consequences cannot be so easily foreseen that trust once lost might not be far more disadvantageous to me than any ill that I now mean to avoid—whether one might not act *more prudently* in this matter by proceeding according to a universal maxim, and by making it one's habit to promise nothing except with the intention of keeping it. But here it soon becomes clear to me that such a maxim will still only be founded on the dreaded consequences. Now, to be truthful from duty is something quite different from being truthful from dread of adverse consequences; as in the first case, the concept of the action in itself already contains a law for me, whereas in the second I must first look around elsewhere to see what effects on me this might involve. For if I deviate from the principle of duty, this is quite certainly evil; but if I defect from my maxim of prudence, that can sometimes be very advantageous to me, though it is of course safer to adhere to it. However, to instruct myself in the very quickest and yet undeceptive way with regard to responding to this problem—whether a lying promise conforms with duty—I ask myself: would I actually be content that my maxim (to extricate myself from a predicament by means of an untruthful promise) should hold as a universal law (for myself as well as for others), and would I be able to say to myself: everyone may make an untruthful promise when he finds himself in a predicament from which he can extricate himself in no other way? Then I soon become aware that I could indeed will the lie, but by no means a universal law to lie; for according to such a law there would actually be no promise at all, since it would be futile to pretend my will to others with regard to my future actions, who would not believe this pretense; or, if they rashly did so, would pay me back in like coin, and hence my maxim, as soon as it were made a universal law, would have to destroy itself.

I do not, therefore, need any wide-ranging acuteness to see what I have to do for my willing to be morally good. Inexperienced with regard to the course of the world, incapable of bracing myself for whatever might come to pass in it, I just ask myself: can you also will that your maxim become a universal law? If not, then it must be rejected, and that not because of some disadvantage to you, or to others, that might result, but because it cannot fit as a principle into a possible universal legislation, for which reason extracts from me immediate respect; and although I do not yet *see* on what it is founded (which the philosopher may investigate), at least I do understand this much: that it is an estimation of a worth that far outweighs any worth of what is extolled by inclination, and that the necessity of my actions from *pure* respect for the practical law is that which constitutes duty, to which every other motivating ground must give way, because it is the condition of a will good *in itself* whose worth surpasses everything.

Thus, then, we have progressed in the moral cognition of common human reason to reach its principle, which admittedly it does not think of as separated in this way in a universal form, but yet always actually has before its eyes and uses as the standard of its judging. Here it would be easy to show how, with this compass in hand, it is very well informed in all uses that occur, to distinguish what is good, what is evil, what conforms with duty or is contrary to it, if—without in the least teaching it anything new—one only . . . makes it aware of its own principle; and that there is thus no need of science and philosophy to know what one has to do in order to be honest and good, indeed even to be wise and virtuous. It should actually have been possible to presume all along that acquaintance with what it is incumbent upon everyone to do, and hence also to know, would be the affair of every human being, even the commonest. Here one cannot without admiration observe the great advantage the practical capacity to judge has over the theoretical in common human understanding. In the latter, when common reason dares to depart from the laws of experience and the perceptions of the senses, it falls into nothing but sundry incomprehensibilities and internal contradictions, or at least into a chaos of uncertainty, obscurity, and instability. But in practical matters the power of judging first begins to show itself to advantage just when common understanding excludes all sensuous incentives from practical laws. Then it even becomes subtle, whether it seeks to engage in legalistic quibbles with its conscience, or with other claims referring to what is to be called right, or seeks sincerely to determine the worth of actions for its own instruction; and, what is most important, in the latter case it stands just as good a chance of hitting the mark as a philosopher can ever expect; indeed it is almost more sure in this than even the latter, because he can have no other principle, but can easily confuse his judgment with a host of alien and irrelevant considerations and deflect it from the straight course. Accordingly, would it not be more advisable, in moral things, to leave it with the judgment of common reason, and at most to bring on philosophy to present the system of morals more completely and accessibly, and likewise its rules in a form more convenient for use (and still more for disputation), but not to let it lead common human understanding away from its fortunate simplicity for practical purposes, and by means of philosophy to put it on a new route of investigation and instruction?

Innocence is a glorious thing, but then again it is very sad that it is so hard to preserve and so easily seduced. Because of this even wisdom—which probably consists more in behavior than in knowledge elsewhere—yet needs science too, not in order to learn from it, but to obtain access and durability for its prescription. The human being feels within himself a powerful counterweight to all the commands of duty—which reason represents to him as so worthy of the highest respect—in his needs and inclinations, the entire satisfaction of which he sums up under the name of happiness. Now reason issues its prescriptions unrelentingly, yet without promising anything to the inclinations, and hence, as it were, with reproach and disrespect for those claims, which are so vehement and yet seem so reasonable (and will not be eliminated by any command). But from this there arises a *natural dialectic*,[1] i.e. a propensity to rationalize against those strict laws of duty, and to cast doubt on their validity, or at least their purity and strictness and, where possible, to make them better suited to our wishes and inclinations, i.e. fundamentally to corrupt them and deprive them of their entire dignity, something that in the end even common practical reason cannot endorse.

Thus *common human reason* is impelled to leave its sphere not by some need of speculation (which never comes over it as long as it is content to be mere sound

---

1. The term *dialectic* refers to the process of reasoning by which one examines opposing ideas to ascertain which, if any, have merit and whether their apparent conflict may be resolved.

reason), but rather on practical grounds, and to take a step into the field of a *practical philosophy*, in order to receive there intelligence and distinct instruction regarding the source of this principle and its correct determination in contrast with maxims based on need and inclination, so that it may escape from the predicament caused by mutual claims, and not run the risk of being deprived of all genuine moral principles because of the ambiguity into which it easily falls. Thus also in practical common reason, when it cultivates itself, a *dialectic* inadvertently unfolds that necessitates it to seek help in philosophy, just as happens to it in its theoretical use, and the one is therefore just as unlikely as the other to find rest anywhere but in a complete critique of our reason.

TEST YOUR UNDERSTANDING

1. What is Kant's view of the value of happiness and self-control?

   a. Each is good in itself; each has its value unconditionally.

   b. Neither is good at all; neither has any value.

   c. Each is good only conditionally on a person's having a good will.

2. Kant believes that an act possesses "moral worth" when it involves doing the right thing for the right reasons. What sorts of motives and reasons for action does he eliminate as possible reasons (or "grounds") for morally worthy action?

3. Explain Kant's distinction between conforming with duty and acting from duty. Formulate an example of your own in which one conforms with duty but does not act from duty. Then, formulate an example of your own in which one acts from duty but yet fails to conform with duty.

4. Why, in Kant's view, is it morally wrong to make a lying promise when one is in trouble?

READER'S GUIDE

Kant on Moral Motivation

In this selection, Kant offers an answer to the question "Which actions have moral worth?" One way of understanding what Kant means by an action's having moral worth is that only actions with moral worth are *praiseworthy*.

Suppose your classmate goes out of his way to help you with a difficult project for a class. You were feeling grateful until you realized that his only motive was to impress the teacher; he didn't really care that he was helping you. While his action might have appeared to be praiseworthy at first, it turns out not to be praiseworthy at all. This example shows that even *morally good actions* may not be praiseworthy; they may not have moral worth.

Kant's view is that actions have moral worth only if they are done for a certain kind of reason. An action that is morally required has moral worth only if it is done *because it is morally required* and not for some other reason. In Kant's view, if your classmate had helped you because helping you was the right thing to do, then your classmate's helping would be praiseworthy.

Kant acknowledges that there can be many different reasons for performing particular morally required actions. In some cases, a morally required action may also be in the agent's own interest. He gives the example of a shopkeeper, who charges the correct amount to everyone who comes to the store, even to a child whom he could easily cheat. The shopkeeper may simply be doing this because it is good for business: if anyone knew he was charging different prices to different customers, people would be horrified and would stop coming to his shop. Thus, Kant says, we just don't know whether this action has moral worth. Kant's example is compelling: if a shopkeeper charges the same price to everyone simply because this is good for business, then the shopkeeper is not *praiseworthy* for doing this. But if the shopkeeper charges the same price to everyone because that's the right thing to do, then this would be praiseworthy.

Kant also considers cases in which people have *inclinations* to do the right thing. These are cases in which a person is simply drawn to a particular morally right thing or just feels like doing a particular morally right thing. He gives as an example someone who is full of compassion for other people and treats others well out of this compassion. This example brings to mind someone whom we might think of as a naturally good person. Consider someone who is always going out of her way to help others and who has a natural warmth and affection for everyone, whether she knows them well or has just met them. She is always thinking of some way to make someone's life better or to brighten their day. She is drawn to helping others and it makes her happy. While we might think of such a person as an obvious example of a good person, this is *not* how Kant thinks of her. Kant points out that a person's inclinations and feelings are unreliable guides to morality. Inclinations and feelings vary between people, and they may vary over time. Thus, a person who acts morally out of inclination might well act immorally later, if that inclination went away. A person might gradually find herself less inclined to help others or feeling less warmth for them. If inclination was all that led her to treat others well, she would simply stop doing so. Acting out of inclination is not a stable basis for morally praiseworthy action. Kant takes the surprising position that if someone does what is morally required—say, keeping a promise—*merely out of inclination*, her action has no moral worth: it is not at all praiseworthy. She did the right thing, but not for the right reasons.

Kant's argument for this position depends on the following two thoughts. First, an action has moral worth only if it's done for the right reasons. Second, the right reason to perform a particular action does not vary with a person's inclinations or feelings. Kant considers cases of agents who have no positive sentiments toward others and yet still do the right thing. For example, suppose someone is grief-stricken and unable to feel for others, and yet still acts to help them. This person does the right thing simply because it is right. Kant holds that this action has moral worth. But it then follows that the only way an action can have moral worth is if it is done simply because it is the right thing to do.

Kant goes on in this passage to state his own view of what morality allows and rules out. Kant's view is that a person must act only in such a way that "I could also will that my maxim could become a universal law." The basic idea is that every action is done for a reason, and it is morally permissible for you to act in a particular way only if you could want (will) that, in general, everyone did the kind of thing you're doing for the kind of reason you are relying on. For more on this part of Kant's view, see the selection from Kant's writings in Chapter 16 and the accompanying "Reader's Guide."

NOTES AND QUESTIONS

1. Kant claims that the honest shopkeeper who acts from sympathy for his inexperienced customer conforms with duty but does not perform a morally worthy action when he does not overcharge the customer. So too, it might seem that the son who visits his sick father in the hospital from filial love does not perform a morally worthy action, in Kant's sense. How should Kant respond to the objection that we admire the son who visits his father out of care and concern, but recoil at the son who does so only from a sense of duty?

    (*Hint:* Consider whether Kant's purpose in identifying the conditions of morally worthy actions is to argue that we *must* always perform morally worthy actions. Might he have another reason to draw our attention to them? Might there be middle ground between acting with indifference toward morality and acting in a morally praiseworthy way?)

    A sophisticated account of the relation between sympathetic motives and the motive of duty in Kant's work appears in Barbara Herman, "On the Value of Acting from the Motive of Duty," *Philosophical Review* 90, 3 (1981): 359–82.

2. Kant argues that the source of morality lies "**a priori** in our reason," and not in our particular interests or inclinations.

    Exercise: Explain how Kant's condemnation of the lying promise meets this standard. That is, explain how his argument for the wrongness of the lying promise does not depend on the particular interests or inclinations of the promisor. Describe an alternative theory of the wrong of false promising that does not meet this standard; that is, a theory that appeals to the particular interests or inclinations of the promisor.

ANALYZING THE ARGUMENTS

1. *The Ring of Gyges: What sort of argument must we give to its possessor?*

   a. Hume's position is that we value morally good action because we approve of the motive of sympathy in ourselves and others that gives rise to such actions. How would you fashion this into a response to Glaucon and the possessor of the Ring of Gyges? Does Hume's view about the good of moral action fit into any of the categories of goods identified in Plato's *Republic*? In particular, does Hume's argument suggest that moral action is the sort of good we value for its consequences, and particularly for the good feeling it causes in us?

   b. Kant's position is, roughly, that acting immorally is contrary to reason or irrational. If his arguments are successful, should they satisfy Glaucon? Could Kant's argument be met with the further question, "Why ought I be rational?" Or is that further question nonsensical?

2. *Rationality, the emotions, and morality.*

   a. Thomson argues that what it is rational for a person to do depends, in part, on what information that person has. As she puts it, "rationality is in the head." Other philosophers, such as Hume, seem to take a different view of rationality. One point of contrast is that Hume seems to think that it can be contrary to reason to fail to take the appropriate means to one's ends, even if one is unaware of those facts that show those are the appropriate means; further, Hume thinks that a passion may be unreasonable when it is founded on the presupposition that some object exists that in fact does not exist.

   Exercise: Give an example in which (1) the agent ought to do some act A; (2) according to Hume's theory, it would be contrary to reason for the person not to do A; but (3) according to Thomson's theory, it would be rational for the person to do A. Then consider whether it is a problem for Thomson's view that it might be irrational to do what one ought to do. Is it a problem for Hume's view that, if we accepted his view of rationality, it could be that performing a certain act would be contrary to reason even though all the evidence we possess suggests that we should perform it? That is, could it really be contrary to reason to act sensibly upon the evidence we have?

   b. Kant worries that motivations from inclination, including sympathy, are contingent and variable. The authority of morality is not contingent or variable; it does not depend on how we feel. We are *always* required to do the right thing as a matter of "absolute necessity." Hence, the correct motivation to do the right thing cannot stem from inclination.

   Consider the following reply by a Humean:

   > Kant is concerned that not all rational beings necessarily, by virtue of their rationality, have sympathy. This should not concern us. Morality is a system of principles that regulate human beings, and its demands are therefore tailored to human beings. All human beings have a natural disposition to care and feel sympathy for their fellow humans. Any human being lacking this capacity is defective. We would not revise our principles of medicine or of anatomy just

because they failed to apply to rational Martians. Why should we be troubled that our theories of moral motivation only fit human beings and not other sorts of rational creatures?

Is this reply persuasive? How should Kant respond?

3. *Self-interest.* Hume and Kant concur that morally worthy action—action that commands our moral approval—is not solely or dominantly motivated by self-interest. But what is it for an action to be "self-interested"? A simple view would say that an act is self-interested whenever the agent desires to perform it. But this would deprive the label "self-interested" of useful meaning. Someone who sacrifices his life for his friend in some sense *desires* to save his friend, but such acts are not self-interested in any useful sense.

Exercise: Provide an account of what makes an action self-interested that takes the form: An action is self-interested if and only if _____ .

A successful account should satisfy these conditions: (a) it should make sense that wholly self-interested acts do not merit moral approval, and (b) it should not follow from the fact that the agent wanted to act as he did, that his action was therefore self-interested.

4. *Moral motivation.* All the authors in this chapter agree that it is possible to do the morally right thing for the wrong reasons. A complete moral theory needs an account of what more is required for a person's action to be morally worthy.

Exercise: Provide an account of what makes an action morally worthy that takes the form: When an action merits moral admiration, it does so because _____ .

Then consider the following two questions:

a. Would any of the authors in this chapter agree with your account? Would any disagree with your account? How would you reply to the one(s) who might object to your view?

b. Is it a necessary feature of those actions that merit moral admiration that the action is in fact the morally right action? Suppose a strong swimmer walks by the shore of a lake and hears a number of bystanders cry out that they see a child drowning. The swimmer jumps in, swims out to save the child, and begins to haul the child to shore. But, in fact, the child is not drowning. The child and the bystanders are all actors practicing for an outdoor performance of a play. Rather than saving a child, the swimmer has interrupted a rehearsal. Is the swimmer's action morally worthy?

What Is the Meaning of Life?

Every human life is marked by misery, pain, and loss, and most lives end badly with decrepitude and death. Even when we are not acutely miserable, we spend much of our time on trivialities. We get up, go to work, make money, spend it, watch television, get drunk, and go to sleep—and then get up and do it all again, like hamsters on a wheel. Usually we're too wrapped up in the present moment to notice the absurdity of this dreary ritual. But when we step back and reflect, it's natural to wonder why anyone should bother.

Similar thoughts arise when we reflect on our place in the cosmos. The physical universe is vast. We are minuscule. We live out our lives in a tiny, insignificant corner and then vanish, leaving only the faintest traces that themselves soon vanish. From the point of view of the universe, all our striving could hardly matter less. And as we reflect on this it is natural to wonder, "What's the point?"

The French novelist Albert Camus famously wrote:

> There is but one truly serious philosophical problem, and that is suicide. Judging whether life is or is not worth living amounts to answering the fundamental question of philosophy. All the rest—whether or not the world has three dimensions, whether the mind has nine or twelve categories—comes afterwards.[1]

This is one celebrated formulation of the question to which the essays in this chapter are devoted: the question of what, if anything, makes a human life meaningful or, as Camus puts it, "worth living." It is important to note, however, that Camus's formulation can be misleading. When we ask whether something is "worth doing," the answer is often a matter of weighing the costs and benefits. Is that new movie worth seeing? Well, it will cost you $12 and 2 hours of your time, but you'll enjoy it and it'll be fun to talk about afterwards. After weighing these costs and benefits,

---

1. A. Camus, *The Myth of Sisyphus and Other Essays*, trans. J. O'Brien (Alfred A. Knopf, 1969), 3.

you may conclude that yes, the movie is worth seeing after all. But if the movie is worth seeing, it's presumably worth postponing suicide long enough to see it. And yet surely Camus's question can't be answered by this sort of trivial calculation. (If it could, it would not be the fundamental question of philosophy.)

Camus's question is best approached as follows. Viewed objectively, our lives are lives of futile striving capped by death and obliteration. As we go about our business, we push this indisputable fact out of our minds and concentrate instead on the good things that seem to make our lives worth living. We spend time with friends and family; we read novels and listen to music; we join with others to make the world a better place; and so on. Most of the time, we take for granted that these ordinary goods are good enough to make our lives worth living. But then we step back and recall that these goods are fleeting and that they pale in magnitude when compared with the misery and oblivion that await us, and from this new perspective it's not so obvious that these fleeting goods are good enough.

The result is a clash of perspectives. From the everyday, immersed perspective, the small goods that fill our lives appear to give them meaning. From the reflective perspective, our lives look meaningless, and the everyday experience of meaning appears illusory.

As a matter of psychological fact, people respond very differently to this clash. Some people find the depressing, reflective perspective utterly compelling:

> I have of late, (but wherefore I know not) lost all my mirth . . . this goodly frame the earth, seems to me a sterile promontory; this most excellent canopy the air, look you, this brave o'er hanging firmament, this majestical roof, fretted with golden fire: why, it appeareth no other thing to me, than a foul and pestilent congregation of vapours. What a piece of work is a man! . . . And yet to me, what is this quintessence of dust? Man delights not me; no, nor Woman neither. (*Hamlet*, act II, scene 2)

Others, like the British philosopher F. P. Ramsey, note the existence of this perspective but find their cheerful confidence unshaken.

> My picture of the world is drawn in perspective, and not like a model to scale. The foreground is occupied by human beings and the stars are all as small as threepenny bits. . . . In time the world will cool and everything will die; but that is a long time off still, and its present value at compound discount is almost nothing. Nor is the present less valuable because the future will be blank. Humanity, which fills the foreground of my picture, I find interesting and on the whole admirable. I find, just now at least, the world a pleasant and exciting place. You may find it depressing; I am sorry for you.[2]

---

2. F. P. Ramsey, "Epilogue" (1925), in his *Philosophical Papers*, ed. D. H. Mellor (Cambridge University Press, 1990), 249.

The philosophical question, however, is not "How *do* we react to these reflections?" but "How *should* we react?" The reflective perspective incorporates facts we normally ignore—the fact that we will die without leaving a lasting trace; the fact that we are specks in a vast uncaring universe—and that may seem to give it a certain authority. But stepping back can also induce illusions. Someone who views the *Mona Lisa* from a distance of 100 yards will miss the beauty in the picture, but that doesn't mean the beauty isn't there.

One way to make progress is to try to produce an explicit argument for the conclusion that life is not worth living. If we try to do that using the materials we have been discussing, we may come up with something like this:

THE ARGUMENT FROM EVANESCENCE

(1) Something is worth doing only if it will have lasting impact on the universe.

(2) Nothing we do will have a lasting impact on the universe.

(3) So nothing we do is worth doing.

When we make the argument explicit in this way it looks completely unpersuasive. Imagine telling someone who is looking forward to an afternoon in the park with her dogs that that is not worth doing because it will have no lasting impact on the universe. If she's in a philosophical mood she will reply, "Who ever said it would? Maybe some things are worth doing only if they have a lasting impact—building the pyramids, for example. But some things are worth doing simply because we enjoy doing them and that's enough."

This is an important gambit in response to Camus's problem. The problem is generated by the thought that nothing could possibly have the kind of value that would justify enduring the slings and arrows of outrageous fortune. The response is to say that some things have value simply because we take satisfaction in them. And since we clearly do take satisfaction in many things, however fleeting their impact, this would be enough to block the argument from evanescence.

But is it really true that things have value simply because we take satisfaction in them? To test the hypothesis, consider Sisyphus, condemned by the gods to push a boulder up a hill only to see it roll back down, repeating this pointless ritual for all eternity. We naturally imagine that Sisyphus hates his life; but suppose he loves it and would not trade it for any other. Is this enough to render his life worth living? Some writers—including Richard Taylor—say yes. But many others—including Susan Wolf—say no. If Sisyphus enjoys his life, it is better in one way (at least he isn't miserable) but worse in another: he is deluded into thinking that his life is meaningful when it isn't.

If this is right, it puts us in a position to raise Camus's problem in its sharpest form. Most of us find our lives worth living, but so does Sisyphus as we have just imagined him. The question then can be put as follows: How do we know that we are not like him? As Thomas Nagel points out, this is a skeptical challenge. Like skeptical challenges elsewhere in philosophy, it proceeds by pointing out that in ordinary life, we ignore certain possibilities of error. We seem to see a cat on the mat and come to believe that there is in fact a cat on the mat before us. But when we do this, we're ignoring the possibility that we might be dreaming. When we bear this possibility in mind, it's not so obvious that we're justified in trusting our senses as we do.[3] Similarly, in ordinary life it strikes us that our experiences of friendship and music and the rest have the kind of value that give us reason to carry on. But in these encounters, we are ignoring the fact that we will eventually suffer and die and that all our striving will ultimately come to nothing.[4] Camus's question is whether this grim fact undermines our grounds for thinking that our lives are meaningful and worth living, and if so, why. The essays that follow are designed to help us bring this question into focus.

3. See Chapter 6 of this anthology.

4. Formulated in this way, Camus's question does not arise for the theist who believes that we live forever in God's presence. Still, versions of the question do arise even for the theist. The theist can wonder, for example, about whether his *worldly* life has the kind of meaning we normally think it has.

Richard Taylor (1919–2003)

Taylor's contributions to philosophy include *Metaphysics* (1963), *Action and Purpose* (1966), and *Good and Evil* (1970), from which the selection below is taken. He was also an internationally renowned apiarist and author of several important books on beekeeping.

THE MEANING OF LIFE

The question whether life has any meaning is difficult to interpret, and the more one concentrates his critical faculty on it the more it seems to elude him, or to evaporate as any intelligible question. One wants to turn it aside, as a source of embarrassment, as something that, if it cannot be abolished, should at least be decently covered. And yet I think any reflective person recognizes that the question it raises is important, and that it ought to have a significant answer.

If the idea of meaningfulness is difficult to grasp in this context, so that we are unsure what sort of thing would amount to answering the question, the idea of meaninglessness is perhaps less so. If, then, we can bring before our minds a clear image of meaningless existence, then perhaps we can take a step toward coping with our original question by seeing to what extent our lives, as we actually find them, resemble that image. . . .

Meaningless Existence

A perfect image of meaninglessness, of the kind we are seeking, is found in the ancient myth of Sisyphus. Sisyphus, it will be remembered, betrayed divine secrets to mortals, and for this he was condemned by the gods to roll a stone to the top of a hill, the stone then immediately to roll back down, again to be pushed to the top by Sisyphus, to roll down once more, and so on again and again, *forever*. Now in this we have the picture of meaningless, pointless toil, of a meaningless existence that is absolutely *never* redeemed. . . . Nothing ever comes of what he is doing, except simply, more of the same. . . .

I am not concerned with rendering or defending any interpretation of this myth. . . . I have cited it only for the one element it does unmistakably contain, namely, that of a repetitious, cyclic activity that never comes to anything. We could contrive other images of this that would serve just as well, and no mythmakers are needed to supply the materials of it. Thus, we can imagine two persons transporting a stone—or even a precious gem, it does not matter—back and forth, relay style. One carries it to a near or distant point where it is received by the other; it is returned to its starting point, there to be recovered by the first, and the process is repeated over and over. Except in this relay nothing counts as winning, and nothing brings the contest to any close, each step only leads to a repetition of itself. Or we can imagine two groups of prisoners, one of them engaged in digging a prodigious hole in the ground that is no sooner finished than it is filled in again by the other group, the latter then digging a new hole that is at once filled in by the first group, and so on and on endlessly.

Now what stands out in all such pictures as oppressive and dejecting is not that the beings who enact these roles suffer any torture or pain, for it need not be assumed that they do. Nor is it that their labors are great, for they are no greater than the labors commonly undertaken by most men most of the time. According to the original myth, the stone is so large that Sisyphus never quite gets it to the top and must groan under every step, so that his enormous labor is all for nought. But this is not what appalls. It is not that his great struggle comes to nothing, but that his existence itself is without meaning. Even if we suppose, for example, that the stone is but a pebble that can be carried effortlessly, or that the holes dug by the prisoners are but small ones, not the slightest meaning is introduced into their lives. . . . That is the element of the myth that I wish to capture.

Again, it is not the fact that the labors of Sisyphus continue forever that deprives them of meaning. It is, rather, the implication of this: that they come to nothing. The image would not be changed by our supposing him to push a different stone up every time, each to roll down again. But if we supposed that these stones, instead of rolling back to their places as if they had never been moved, were assembled at the top of the hill and there incorporated, say, in a beautiful and enduring temple, then the aspect of meaninglessness would disappear. His labors would then have a point, something would come of them all, and although one could perhaps still say it was not worth it, one could not say that the life of Sisyphus was devoid of meaning altogether. Meaningfulness would at least have made an appearance, and we could see what it was.

That point will need remembering. But in the meantime, let us note another way in which the image of meaninglessness can be altered by making only a very slight change. Let us suppose that the gods, while condemning Sisyphus to the fate just described, at the same time, as an afterthought, waxed perversely merciful by implanting in him a strange and irrational impulse; namely, a compulsive impulse to roll stones. We may if we like, to make this more graphic, suppose they accomplish this by implanting in him some substance that has this effect on his character and drives. I call this perverse, because from our point of view there is clearly no reason why anyone should have a persistent and insatiable desire to do something so pointless as that. Nevertheless, suppose that is Sisyphus' condition. He has but one obsession, which is to roll stones, and it is an obsession that is only for the moment appeased by his rolling them—he no sooner gets a stone rolled to the top of the hill than he is restless to roll up another.

Now it can be seen why this little afterthought of the gods, which I called perverse, was also in fact merciful. For they have by this device managed to give Sisyphus precisely what he wants—by making him want precisely what they inflict on him. However it may appear to us, Sisyphus' fate now does not appear to him as a condemnation, but the very reverse. His one desire in life is to roll stones, and he is absolutely guaranteed its endless fulfillment. Where otherwise he might profoundly have wished surcease, and even welcomed the quiet of death to release him from endless boredom and meaninglessness, his life is now filled with mission and meaning, and he seems to himself to have been given an entry to heaven. . . .

What we need to mark most carefully at this point is that the picture with which we began has not really been changed in the least by adding this supposition. Exactly the same things happen as before. The only change is in Sisyphus' view of them. The picture before was the image of meaningless activity and existence. It was created precisely to be an image of that. It has not lost that meaninglessness, it has now gained not the least shred of meaningfulness. The stones still roll back as before. . . . The *only* thing that has happened is this: Sisyphus has been reconciled to it, and indeed more, he has been led to embrace it. Not, however, by reason or persuasion, but by nothing more rational than the potency of a new substance in his veins.

The Meaninglessness of Life

I believe the foregoing provides a fairly clear content to the idea of meaninglessness and, through it, some hint of what meaningfulness . . . might be. Meaninglessness is essentially endless pointlessness, and meaningfulness is therefore the opposite. Activity, and even long, drawn-out and repetitive activity, has a meaning if it has some significant culmination, some more or less lasting end that can be considered to have been the direction and purpose of the activity. But the descriptions so far also provide something else; namely, the suggestion of how an existence that is objectively meaningless, in this sense, can nevertheless acquire a meaning for him whose existence it is.

Now let us ask: Which of these pictures does life in fact resemble? And let us not begin with our own lives, for here both our prejudices and wishes are great, but with the life in general that we share with the rest of creation. . . .

Thus, for example, there are caves in New Zealand, deep and dark, whose floors are quiet pools and whose walls and ceilings are covered with soft light. As one gazes in wonder in the stillness of these caves it seems that the Creator has reproduced there in microcosm the heavens themselves, until one scarcely remembers the enclosing presence of the walls. As one looks more closely, however, the scene is explained. Each dot of light identifies an ugly worm, whose luminous tail is meant to attract insects from the surrounding darkness. As from time to time one of these insects draws near it becomes entangled in a sticky thread lowered by the worm, and is eaten. This goes on month after month, the blind worm lying there in the barren stillness waiting to entrap an occasional bit of nourishment that will only sustain it to another bit of nourishment until. . . . Until what? What great thing awaits all this long and repetitious effort and makes it worthwhile? Really nothing. The larva just transforms itself finally to a tiny winged adult that lacks even mouth parts to feed and lives only a day or two. These adults, as soon as they have mated and laid eggs, are themselves caught in the threads and are devoured by the cannibalist worms, often without having ventured into the day, the only point to their existence having now been fulfilled. This has been going on for millions of years, and to no end other than that the same meaningless cycle may continue for another millions of years.

All living things present essentially the same spectacle. The larva of a certain cicada burrows in the darkness of the earth for seventeen years, through season after season, to emerge finally into the daylight for a brief flight, lay its eggs, and die—this all to repeat itself during the next seventeen years, and so on to eternity. . . . Some birds span an entire side of the globe each year and then return, only to insure that others may follow the same incredibly long path again and again. One is led to wonder what the point of it all is, with what great triumph this ceaseless effort, repeating itself through millions of years, might finally culminate, and why it should go on and on for so long, accomplishing nothing, getting nowhere. But then one realizes that there is no point to it at all, that it really culminates in nothing, that each of these cycles, so filled with toil, is to be followed only by more of the same. The point of any living thing's life is, evidently, nothing but life itself.

This life of the world thus presents itself to our eyes as a vast machine, feeding on itself, running on and on forever to nothing. And we are part of that life. To be sure, we are not just the same, but the differences are not so great as we like to think; many are merely invented, and none really cancels the kind of meaninglessness that we found in Sisyphus and that we find all around, wherever anything lives. We are conscious of our activity. Our goals, whether in any significant sense we choose them or not, are things of which we are at least partly aware and can therefore in some sense appraise. More significantly, perhaps, men have a history, as other animals do not, such that each generation does not precisely resemble all those before. Still, if we can in imagination disengage our wills from our lives and disregard the deep interest each man has in his own existence, we shall find that they do not so little resemble the existence of Sisyphus. We toil after goals, most of them—indeed every single one of them—of transitory significance and, having gained one of them, we immediately set forth for the next, as if that one had never been, with this next one being essentially more of the same. Look at a busy street any day, and observe the throng going hither and thither. To what? Some office or shop, where the same things will be done today as were done yesterday, and are done now so they may be repeated tomorrow. And if we think that, unlike Sisyphus, these labors do have a point, that they culminate in something lasting and, independently of our own deep interests in them, very worthwhile, then we simply have not considered the thing closely enough. Most such effort is directed only to the establishment and perpetuation of home and family; that is, to the begetting of others who will follow in our steps to do more of the same. Each man's life thus resembles one of Sisyphus' climbs to the summit of his hill, and each day of it one of his steps; the difference is that whereas Sisyphus himself returns to push the stone up again, we leave this to our children. We at one point imagined that the labors of Sisyphus finally culminated in the creation of a temple, but for this to make any difference it had to be a temple that would at least endure, adding beauty to the world for the remainder of time. Our achievements, even though they are often beautiful, are mostly bubbles; and those that do last, like the sand-swept pyramids, soon become mere curiosities while around them the rest of mankind continues its perpetual toting of rooks, only to see them roll down. Nations are built upon the bones of their founders and pioneers, but only to decay and crumble before long, their rubble then becoming the foundation for others directed to exactly the same fate. The picture of Sisyphus is the picture of existence of the individual man, great or unknown, of nations, of the race of men, and of the very life of the world.

On a country road one sometimes comes upon the ruined hulks of a house and once extensive buildings, all in collapse and spread over with weeds. A curious eye can in imagination reconstruct from what is left a once warm and thriving life, filled with purpose. There was the hearth, where a family once talked, sang, and made plans; there were the rooms, where people loved, and babes were born to a rejoicing mother; there are the musty remains of a sofa, infested with bugs, once bought at a dear price to enhance an ever-growing comfort, beauty, and warmth. Every small piece of junk fills the mind with what once, not long ago, was utterly real, with children's voices, plans made, and enterprises embarked upon. That is how these stones of Sisyphus were rolled up, and that is how they became incorporated into a beautiful temple, and that temple is what now lies before you. Meanwhile other buildings, institutions, nations, and civilizations spring up all around, only to share the same fate before long. And if the question "What for?" is now asked, the answer is clear: so that just this may go on forever. . . .

The Meaning of Life

We noted that Sisyphus' existence would have meaning if there were some point to his labors, if his efforts ever culminated in something that was not just an occasion for fresh labors of the same kind. But that is precisely the meaning it lacks. And human existence resembles his in that respect. Men do achieve things—they scale their towers and raise their stones to their hilltops—but every such accomplishment fades, providing only an occasion for renewed labors of the same kind.

But here we need to note something else that has been mentioned, but its significance not explored, and that is the state of mind and feeling with which such labors are undertaken. We noted that if Sisyphus had a keen and unappeasable desire to be doing just what he found himself doing, then, although his life would in no way be changed, it would nevertheless have a meaning for him. It would be an irrational one, no doubt, because the desire itself would be only the product of the substance in his veins, and not any that reason could discover, but a meaning nevertheless.

And would it not, in fact, be a meaning incomparably better than the other? For let us examine again the first kind of meaning it could have. Let us suppose that, without having any interest in rolling stones, as such, and finding this, in fact, a galling toil, Sisyphus did nevertheless have a deep interest in raising a temple, one that would be beautiful and lasting. And let us suppose he succeeded in this, that after ages of dreadful toil, all directed at this final result, he did at last complete his temple, such that now he could say his work was done, and he could rest and forever enjoy the result. Now what? What picture now presents itself to our minds? It is precisely the picture of infinite boredom! Of Sisyphus doing nothing ever again, but contemplating what he has already wrought and can no longer add anything to, and contemplating it for an eternity! Now in this picture we have a meaning for Sisyphus' existence, a point for his prodigious labor, because we have put it there; yet, at the same time, that which is really worthwhile seems to have slipped away entirely. Where before we were presented with the nightmare of eternal and pointless activity, we are now confronted with the hell of its eternal absence.

Our second picture, then, wherein we imagined Sisyphus to have had inflicted on him the irrational desire to be doing just what he found himself doing, should not have been dismissed so abruptly. The meaning that picture lacked was no meaning that he or anyone could crave, and the strange meaning it had was perhaps just what we were seeking.

At this point, then, we can reintroduce what has been until now, it is hoped, resolutely pushed aside in an effort to view our lives and human existence with objectivity; namely, our own wills, our deep interest in what we find ourselves doing. If we do this we find that our lives do indeed still resemble that of Sisyphus, but that the meaningfulness they thus lack is precisely the meaningfulness of infinite boredom. At the same time, the strange meaningfulness they possess is that of the inner compulsion to be doing just what we were put here to do, and to go on doing it forever. This is the nearest we may hope to get to heaven, but the redeeming side of that fact is that we do thereby avoid a genuine hell.

If the builders of a great and flourishing ancient civilization could somehow return now to see archaeologists unearthing the trivial remnants of what they had once accomplished with such effort—see the fragments of pots and vases, a few broken statues, and such tokens of another age and greatness—they could indeed ask themselves what the point of it all was, if this is all it finally came to. Yet, it did not seem so to them then, for it was just the building, and not what was finally built, that gave their life meaning. . . .

This is surely the way to look at all of life—at one's own life, and each day and moment it contains; of the life of a nation; of the species; of the life of the world; and of everything that breathes. Even the glow worms I described, whose cycles of existence over the millions of years seem so pointless when looked at by us, will seem entirely different to us if we can somehow try to view their existence from within. Their endless activity, which gets nowhere, is just what it is their will to pursue. This is its whole justification and meaning. Nor would it be any salvation to the birds who span the globe every year, back and forth, to have a home made for them in a cage with plenty of food and protection, so that they would not have to migrate any more. It would be their condemnation, for it is the doing that counts for them, and not what they hope to win by it. Flying these prodigious distances, never ending, is what it is in their veins to do, exactly as it was in Sisyphus' veins to roll stones, without end, after the gods had waxed merciful and implanted this in him.

A human being no sooner draws his first breath than he responds to the will that is in him to live. He no more asks whether it will be worthwhile, or whether anything of significance will come of it, than the worms and the birds. The point of his living is simply to be living, in the manner that it is his nature to be living. He goes through his life building his castles, each of these beginning to fade into time as the next is begun; yet, it would be no salvation to rest from all this. It would be a condemnation, and one that would in no way be redeemed were he able to gaze upon the things he has done, even if these were beautiful and absolutely permanent, as they never are. What counts is that one should be able to begin a new task, a new castle, a new bubble. It counts only because it is there to be done and he has the will to do it. The same will be the life of his children, and of theirs; and if the philosopher is apt to see in this a pattern similar to the unending cycles of the existence of Sisyphus, and to despair, then it is indeed because the meaning and point he is seeking is not there—but mercifully so. The meaning of life is from within us, it is not bestowed from without, and it far exceeds in both its beauty and permanence any heaven of which men have ever dreamed or yearned for.

TEST YOUR UNDERSTANDING

1. Give a one-sentence version of the myth of Sisyphus.

2. According to Taylor, why is Sisyphus's existence meaningless?

3. Taylor imagines a version of Sisyphus who desires nothing more than to roll his rock up the hill, again and again, forever. True or false: According to Taylor, this version of Sisyphus leads a meaningful life.

4. Ordinary human lives achieve much more than Sisyphus ever does: we build buildings, write books, have children, and so forth. According to Taylor, do our achievements give meaning to our lives?

NOTES AND QUESTIONS

1. *Camus and the myth of Sisyphus.* The myth of Sisyphus became the starting point for philosophical discussions on the meaning of life thanks to Albert Camus's famous discussion in his 1940 book, *The Myth of Sisyphus.* Camus argues that all human life is absurd—meaningless—because all of our strivings are ultimately futile and pointless, but that *consciousness* of this fact and the *decision* to persist in our futile strivings can redeem our lives and give us reason to carry on.

> If this myth is tragic, that is because its hero is conscious. Where would his torture be, indeed, if at every step the hope of succeeding upheld him? The workman of today works every day in his life at the same tasks, and this fate is no less absurd. But it is tragic only at the rare moments when it becomes conscious. Sisyphus . . . powerful and rebellious knows the whole extent of his wretched condition. It is what he thinks of during his descent. The lucidity that was to constitute his torture at the same time crowns his victory. There is no fate that cannot be surmounted by scorn. (A. Camus, *The Myth of Sisyphus and Other Essays,* trans. J. O'Brien [Alfred A. Knopf, 1969], 121)

Subsequent philosophers have generally held, to the contrary, that our lives are not in fact meaningless. The challenge for these philosophers is to explain why we are not like Sisyphus.

2. *The meaning of "the meaning of life."* It is an odd phrase. We know that words have meaning. But what is it for a *life* to have meaning? The opposite of a meaningful life is not a miserable life, or an evil life, but an "absurd" life. But this is another odd phrase. Before we ask *whether* our lives have meaning, we must understand what it means to say that a life has meaning. (Compare: Before we ask whether God exists, or whether we have free will, we must know what "God" and "free will" mean.)

   Question: As Taylor understands the question, what does it mean to ask whether human lives have meaning? Ideally, an answer will consist in a statement of the form: "A human life has meaning if and only if . . . ," where the ". . ." is filled in with words we already understand.

3. *Taylor on the value of achievement.* An account of the meaning of life will point to some feature that distinguishes ordinary human lives from the life of Sisyphus. Taylor considers a number of possibilities:

   a. We often achieve our goals; Sisyphus never does.

   b. Our achievements often last for a while; Sisyphus makes no lasting difference.

   c. Our achievements are often excellent: we build beautiful buildings, construct powerful scientific theories, and so on; Sisyphus accomplishes nothing of value.

   Taylor argues that none of these differences explains why our lives are meaningful.

Look at the busy street any day, and observe the throng going hither and thither. To what? Some office or shop, where the same things will be done today as were done yesterday, and are done now so they may be repeated tomorrow. And if we think that unlike Sisyphus, these labors do have a point, that they culminate in something lasting and, independently of our own deep interests in them, very worthwhile, then we simply have not considered the thing closely enough. (p. 980)

Exercise: Explain and assess Taylor's argument for this claim.

Susan Wolf (b. 1952)

Wolf, the Edna J. Koury Professor of Philosophy at the University of North Carolina, Chapel Hill, works mainly in ethics and moral psychology. Her most recent book is *Meaning in Life and Why It Matters* (2010).

MEANING IN LIFE AND WHY IT MATTERS

A Conception of Meaningfulness Life

. . . People sometimes complain that their lives lack meaning; they yearn for meaning; they seek meaning. People sometimes judge others to be leading exceptionally meaningful lives, looking upon them with envy or admiration. Meaning is commonly associated with a kind of depth. Often the need for meaning is connected to the sense that one's life is empty or shallow. An interest in meaning is also frequently associated with thoughts one might have on one's deathbed, or in contemplation of one's eventual death. When the word *meaningful* is used in characterizing a life (or in characterizing what is missing from a life), it calls *something* to mind, but it is not clear what. . . .

According to the conception of meaningfulness I wish to propose, meaning arises from loving objects worthy of love and engaging with them in a positive way. The words *love* and *objects*, however, are in some ways misleadingly specific, "engaging [with objects] in a positive way" regrettably vague, and the description of some objects but not others as "*worthy* of love" may be thought to be contentious. Rather than try to clarify the view by taking up one word or phrase at a time, let me try to describe the view in other terms, bringing out what I take to be salient.

What is perhaps most distinctive about my conception of meaning, or about the category of value I have in mind, is that it involves subjective and objective elements, suitably and inextricably linked. "Love" is at least partly subjective, involving attitudes and feelings. In insisting that the requisite object must be "worthy of love," however, this conception of meaning invokes an objective standard: it is implicit in insisting that an object be worthy of love (in order to make a contribution to meaning in the lover's life) that not any object will do. Nor is it guaranteed that the subject's own assessment of worthiness is privileged. One might paraphrase this by saying that, according to my conception, meaning arises when subjective attraction meets objective attractiveness.

Essentially, the idea is that a person's life can be meaningful only if she cares fairly deeply about some thing or things, only if she is gripped, excited, interested, engaged, or, as I earlier put it, if she loves something—as opposed to being bored by or alienated from most or all that she does. Even a person who is so engaged, however, will not live a meaningful life if the objects or activities with which she is so occupied are worthless. A person who loves smoking pot all day long, or doing endless crossword puzzles, and has the luxury of being able to indulge in this without restraint does not thereby make her life meaningful. Finally, this conception of meaning specifies that the relationship between the subject and the object of her attraction must be an active one. The condition that says that meaning involves engaging with the (worthy) object of love in a positive way is meant to make clear that mere passive recognition and a positive attitude toward an object's or activity's value are not sufficient for a meaningful life. One must be able to be in some sort of relationship with the valuable object of one's attention—to create it, protect it, promote it, honor it, or, more generally, to actively affirm it in some way or other.

. . . My view might be seen as a combination, or a welding together, of two other more popular views that one often hears offered, if not as analyses of meaning in life, at least as ingredients—sometimes as the *key* ingredient—in a life well lived.

The first view tells us that it doesn't matter what you do with your life as long as it is something you love. Do not get stuck, or settle into doing something just because it is expected of you, or because it is conventionally recognized as good, or because nothing better occurs to you. Find your passion. Figure out what turns you on, and go for it.[1]

The second view says that in order to live a truly satisfying life one needs to get involved in something "larger than oneself."[2] Though I think that the reference to the size of the group or the object one wants to benefit or be involved with is misleading and unfortunate, it is not unreasonable to understand such language metaphorically, as a way of gesturing toward the aim of participating in or contributing to something whose value *is independent* of oneself. . . .

Each of these . . . popular views is sometimes couched in the vocabulary of meaning, and in each case there is a basis for that choice in our ordinary uses of the term. When

1. One of those silly books that are on sale at the cashiers' desks at Barnes and Noble advanced that view a few years ago. The book, by Bradley Trevor Greive, was called *The Meaning of Life* (Andrews McMeel Publishing, 2002). Richard Taylor offers a more serious and provocative defense of the view in *Good and Evil* (Macmillan, 1970), chap. 18. [Wolf's note.]

2. Not surprisingly it is common to hear religious leaders speak in these terms, but many others do as well. For example, Peter Singer draws on this conception of the good life in his book *How Are We to Live? Ethics in an Age of Self-Interest* (Text Publishing, 1993). [Wolf's note]

thinking about one's own life, for example, a person's worry or complaint that his life lacks meaning is apt to be an expression of dissatisfaction with the subjective quality of one's life. Some subjective good is felt to be missing. One's life feels empty. One longs for finding something to do that remedies this gap and makes one feel fulfilled.

On the other hand, when we consider the lives of others, our tendency to characterize some as especially meaningful and others as less so is apt to track differences in our assessments of the objective value of what these lives are about. When we look for paradigms of meaningful lives, who comes to mind? Gandhi, perhaps, or Mother Teresa, or Einstein, or Cézanne. Sisyphus—condemned to roll a huge stone up a hill, only to have it roll down again and to have to roll it back up in an endless cycle—is a standard exemplar of a meaningless existence. Our choice of these examples seems to be based on the value (or lack of value) we take these people s activities to have, rather than on the subjective quality of their inner lives.

Insofar as the conception of meaningfulness I propose welds these two views together, it may be seen as a partial affirmation of both these more popular views. From my perspective, both these views have something right about them, though each also leaves something crucial out. . . .

The Fulfillment View

Let us turn our attention, then, to the first of the popular views I mentioned, the one that stresses the subjective element, urging each person to find his or her passion and pursue it. It is easy to see why someone would support this advice and find plausible the claim that being able to pursue a passion adds something distinctive and deeply good to life. The advice, at least as I understand it, rests on the plausible empirical supposition that doing what one loves doing, being involved with things one really cares about, gives one a kind of joy in life that one would otherwise be without. The reason one should find one's passion and go for it, then, is because doing so will give one's life a particular type of good feeling. Moreover, the distinctiveness of the type of good feeling in question makes it possible to see how the kind of life that engenders such feelings would be associated with meaningfulness, and how therefore one might be led to identify a meaningful life as a life lived pursuing one's passions.

Let us refer to the feelings one has when one is doing what one loves, or when one is engaging in activities by which one is gripped or excited, as feelings of fulfillment. Such feelings are the opposite of the very bad feelings of boredom and alienation. Although feelings of fulfillment are unquestionably good feelings, there are many other good feelings, perhaps more comfortably classified as pleasures, that have nothing to do with fulfillment. Riding a roller coaster, meeting a movie star, eating a hot fudge sundae, finding a great dress on sale can all give one pleasure, even intense pleasure. They are unlikely to contribute to a sense of fulfillment, however, and it would not be difficult to imagine a person who has an abundance of opportunities for such pleasures still finding something (subjectively) lacking in her life.

Further, someone whose life is fulfilling has no guarantee of being happy in the conventional sense of that term. Many of the things that grip or engage us make us vulnerable to pain, disappointment, and stress. Consider, for example, writing a book, training for a triathlon, campaigning for a political candidate, caring for an ailing friend.

It may later be useful to bring to mind the fact that feelings of fulfillment are but one kind of positive feeling that potentially competes with other kinds: spending one's time, energy, money, and so forth on the projects that fulfill you necessarily reduces the resources you have for engaging in activities that are "merely" fun. Moreover, to the extent that one's sources of fulfillment are also sources of anxiety and suffering, the pleasure one gets from pursuing these things may be thought, at least from a hedonistic perspective, to be qualified or balanced by the negative feelings that accompany it. Still, the fact that most of us would willingly put up with a great deal of stress, anxiety, and vulnerability to pain in order to pursue our passions can be seen as providing support for the idea that fulfillment is indeed a great and distinctive good in life. Insofar as the view that urges us "to find our passion and go for it" expresses that idea, there is a lot to be said for it. From here on, I shall refer to that view as "the Fulfillment View."

Because feelings of fulfillment are different from and sometimes compete with other types of good feeling, types that are more paradigmatically associated with terms like *happiness* and *pleasure*, it is plausible to interpret the Fulfillment View as a proposal for what gives meaning to life. To someone who finds himself puzzled by why, despite having a good job, a loving family, and a healthy body, he feels that something is missing from his life, it provides an answer. To someone trying to decide what career to pursue, or, more generally how to structure his life, it advises against focusing too narrowly on the superficial goals of ease, prestige, and material wealth. Nonetheless, the Fulfillment View, as I have interpreted it, is a form of hedonism, in that its prescription for the best possible life (in which is included the possession of meaning) rests exclusively on the question of how a life can attain the best qualitative character.[3] Positive experience is, according to this view, the only thing that matters.[4]

For this very reason, it seems to me, the view is inadequate as it stands. If, as the Fulfillment View suggests, the only thing that matters is the subjective quality of one's life, then it shouldn't matter, in our assessments of possible lives, which activities give rise to that quality. If the point of finding one's passion and pursuing it is simply to be fulfilled—that is, to get and keep the *feelings* of fulfillment—then it shouldn't matter what activities or objects one has a passion for. Considering a variety of lives, all equally fulfilling but differing radically in the sorts of things that give rise to that fulfillment, however, may make us wonder whether we can really accept that view.

Imagine, in particular, a person whose life is dominated by activities that most of us would be tempted to call worthless but which nonetheless give fulfillment to the

---

3. The **qualitative (or subjective) character** of an experience is a matter of how it feels "from the inside" to have it. If two experiences "feel the same" they have the same qualitative character, even if their causes are different.

4. The Fulfilling View might be considered a plausible extension of John Stuart Mill's view that an enlightened hedonist must take into account the differences in quality as well as quantity of pleasure in conceiving of the best possible life. See *Utilitarianism* (1861), chapter 2. [Wolf's note.]

person whose life it is. I earlier mentioned the case of the person who simply loves smoking pot all day, and another (or maybe the same person) who is fulfilled doing crossword puzzles, or worse (as personal experience will attest), Sudokus. We might also consider more bizarre cases: a man who lives to make handwritten copies of the text of *War and Peace,* or a woman whose world revolves around her love for her pet goldfish. Do we think that, from the point of view of self-interest, these lives are as good as can be—provided, perhaps, that their affections and values are stable, and that the goldfish doesn't die?

Initially, perhaps, not everyone will answer these questions in the same way; some will not know what to think. In part, I believe this is because we are uncomfortable making negative judgments about other people's lives, even about imaginary other people who are conceived realistically enough to be stand-ins for real people. . . . To avoid this problem, let me approach these question by way of reflection on a more stylized philosophical example—namely, the case of Sisyphus Fulfilled.

Sisyphus, in the ancient myth, is condemned to an existence that is generally recognized as awful. He is condemned eternally to a task that is boring, difficult, and futile. Because of this, Sisyphus's life, or more precisely his afterlife, has been commonly treated as a paradigm of a meaningless existence.[5]

Philosopher Richard Taylor, however, in a discussion of life's absurdity, suggests a thought experiment according to which the gods take pity on Sisyphus, and so insert a substance in his veins that transforms him from someone for whom stone rolling is nothing but a painful, arduous, and unwelcome chore to someone who loves stone rolling more than anything else in the (after)world.[6] There is nothing the transformed Sisyphus would rather do than roll that stone. Stone rolling, in other words, fulfills him. Sisyphus has found his passion (or perhaps his passion has found him), and he is pursuing it to his life's content. The question is, what should *we* think of him? Has his life been transformed from horribly unfortunate to exceptionally good? Taylor thinks so, but some of us might disagree.

As I have already noted, the reason Sisyphus has traditionally been taken as a paradigm of a meaningless existence is that he is condemned to the perpetual performance of a task that is boring, difficult, and futile. In Taylor's variation, Sisyphus's task is no longer boring—no longer boring to Sisyphus, that is. But it is still futile. There is no value to his efforts; nothing ever comes of them. . . .

In light of this, many will feel that Sisyphus's situation remains far from enviable. Something desirable seems missing from his life despite his experience of fulfillment. Since what is missing is not a subjective matter—from the inside, we may assume that Sisyphus's life is as good as can be—we must look for an objective feature that characterizes what is lacking. The second popular view I brought up earlier names, or at least gestures toward, a feature that might fit the bill.

---

5. See especially Albert Camus, *The Myth of Sisyphus, and Other Essays* (Alfred A. Knopf, 1955). [Wolf's note.]
6. See Taylor, *Good and Evil.* [Wolf's note.]

The Larger-than-Oneself View
and the Bipartite View

The second view tells us that the best sort of life is one that is involved in, or contributes to, something "larger than oneself," though contemplation of the case of Sisyphus should be enough to show that this must be understood metaphorically. We may, after all, imagine the rock Sisyphus is endlessly pushing uphill to be *very* large. . . .

A more promising interpretation of the view that links meaningfulness to involvement with something larger than oneself takes the metaphor of size less seriously. Its point, on this interpretation, is not to recommend that one get involved with something larger than oneself but rather that one get involved with something *other* than oneself—that is, with something whose value is independent of and has its source *outside* of oneself. Presumably, Sisyphean stone rolling has no such value—nor, it seems, does pot smoking or Sudoku solving. But devotion to a single needy individual does satisfy this condition as much as devotion to a crowd. Philosophy and basketball appear to meet this criterion, too, since the value of these activities, whatever it is, does not depend on one's own contingent interest in them.

If we interpret the advice that one get involved with something "larger than oneself" in this way, it might be thought to represent a second and independent criterion for a fully successful and flourishing life. Combining this advice with the Fulfillment View, one might think, yields a better, bipartite, conception of meaningfulness than either view taken on its own. The Fulfillment View directs our attention to a subjective component a meaningful life must contain. But, as the case of Sisyphus Fulfilled led us to see, even a life that fully satisfies the subjective condition may be one we are hesitant to describe as meaningful, if objectively the life is unconnected to anything or anyone whose value lies outside of the person whose life it is. By conjoining the Fulfillment View with the injunction to get involved with something "larger than oneself," we get a proposal that appears to remedy the problem. According to this Bipartite View, in order for a life to be meaningful, both an objective and a subjective condition must be met: a meaningful life is a life that (1) the subject finds fulfilling and (2) contributes to or connects positively with something whose value has its source in something outside the subject himself.

If meaningfulness is understood to refer to a coherent dimension of value, . . . however, it would be puzzling if it turned out to depend on the satisfaction of two unrelated conditions. The proposal I favor, which identifies meaning with a property in which subjective and objective components are suitably linked, conceives of meaningfulness in a more unified way. On my conception of meaningfulness, one can see how the subjective and objective elements fit together to constitute a coherent feature a life might or might not possess. . . .

Consider again the suggestion that a life in which a person contributes to something larger than himself (suitably interpreted) is more meaningful than a life that serves only the needs and desires of the person whose life it is. I introduced this idea in answer to the question of what . . . might be missing from a life like that of Sisyphus Fulfilled (or the pot smoker, or Sudoku player) that prevents it from representing a life we would want for ourselves or for those we love. We could add stipulations to these examples that guaranteed that the protagonists' lives and activities did contribute to some independent value. If the characters had no interest in the external or objective or independent value with which their lives were involved, however, it is not clear that that would make their lives any better or more desirable to them. Imagine, for example, that unbeknownst to Sisyphus, his stone rolling scares away vultures who would otherwise attack a nearby community and spread terror and disease. Or imagine that the pot smoker's secondary marijuana smoke is alleviating the pain of the AIDS victim next door. If Sisyphus and the pot smoker do not care about the benefits their lives are producing, however, it is hard to see how the fact that their lives yield those benefits . . . should make us any more inclined to describe their lives as meaningful . . . than we were before we learned of these consequences. . . .

. . . It seems to me that when the recommendation to get involved with something larger than oneself is offered, it is offered in the hope, if not the expectation, that if one does get so involved, it will make one feel good. The thought is that if one tries it, one will like it, and one will like it in part because of one's recognition that one is engaged with a person or an object or an activity that is independently valuable.[7] The suggestion, then, that one gets meaning in life through involvement with something larger than oneself maybe most charitably interpreted as a suggestion that is not meant to be taken in isolation, as a criterion of meaningfulness separable from any assumptions about the attitudes the subject will have toward the project or activity in question. If one gets involved in something larger than oneself—or, as I have interpreted it, in something whose value is (in part) independent of oneself—then, if one is lucky, one will find that involvement fulfilling, and if that happens, then one's life will both be and seem meaningful. If one's involvement brings no such reward, however, it is unclear that it contributes to meaning in one's life at all. . . .

In my earlier discussion of Sisyphus Fulfilled, I expressed sympathy with those who, unlike Richard Taylor, found something desirable missing from Sisyphus's life, despite his being subjectively quite content. There is room for an even stronger disagreement with Taylor, however, that I want to consider now. Specifically, one might wonder whether the transformation that Sisyphus undergoes from being unhappy, bored, and frustrated to being blissfully fulfilled makes Sisyphus better off at all. One might think that it actually makes him worse off.

From a hedonistic perspective,[8] of course, Sisyphus's transformation *must* make his life better, for the only changes in Sisyphus are subjective, replacing negative feelings and attitudes with positive ones. From a non-hedonistic perspective, however, these changes come at a cost. When I try to understand the new Sisyphus's state of mind—when I try

---

7. This does not always work. It is a standard part of the requirements of a child who is training for a bar or bat mitzvah, as it is for many middle and high school programs, that the child put in a specified number of hours of community service. Not surprisingly, the degree to which this results in a gratifying experience, an enhanced social consciousness, or a lasting commitment varies widely. [Wolf's note.]

8. That is, a perspective according to which the quality of one's experience is all that matters.

to imagine how someone might find stone rolling fulfilling—I can conceive of only two possibilities. On the one hand, I can think of the substance in Sisyphus's veins as inducing delusions: they make Sisyphus see something in stone rolling that isn't really there. On the other hand, the drug in his veins may have reduced his intelligence and his imaginative capacity, thus eliminating the possibility of his noticing the dullness and futility of his labors or of being able to compare his task to other more challenging or worthwhile things that, had the gods not condemned him, he might have been doing instead. In either case, Sisyphus is in at least one respect worse off than he was before his transformation—he is either afflicted by mental illness or delusion or diminished in his intellectual powers. . . .

To me, the first scenario, in which the transformed Sisyphus is deluded, seems a more plausible way to understand what it would be for Sisyphus to be or to feel *fulfilled* by stone rolling, for "fulfillment" seems to me to have a cognitive component to it that requires seeing the source or object of fulfillment as being, in some independent way, good or worthwhile. Even deep and intense pleasures, like lying on the beach on a beautiful day, or eating a perfectly ripe peach, would not naturally be described as fulfilling. To find something fulfilling is rather to find it such as to be characterizable in terms that would portray it as (objectively) good.

Imagining Sisyphus in terms of either scenario, however, can explain why we might hesitate to describe the life of Sisyphus Fulfilled as meaningful—and similarly, I would argue, why we would withhold that label from the life of the fulfilled pot smoker, goldfish lover, or Tolstoy copier. Imagining these characters on the model of either scenario would, in any case, help to explain why we might regard their lives as far from ideal. Earlier I suggested that we might judge these lives to be "missing something," a phrase that suggests a feature separable from fulfillment that these lives lack, rendering them less than optimally meaningful (if meaningful at all). In light of our discussion, we can now see that even the apparent condition of meaningfulness they do satisfy—that is, the condition of being fulfilled—is in a certain way defective and less desirable than fulfillment that stems from a more fitting or appropriate source.

The Fitting Fulfillment View Defended

I earlier argued that the suggestion that a life is meaningful insofar as it contributes to something larger than itself is most charitably understood if we take it not as an isolated objective criterion but rather as a criterion that functions in tandem with an expectation about the subjective feelings and attitudes that one's contribution will engender. Analogously, the suggestion that a life is meaningful insofar as one finds one's passion and goes for it (thereby being fulfilled) is best understood as a subjective criterion meant to function not in isolation but rather in conjunction with the assumption that the objects of one's passions will fall within a certain objective range.

The conception of meaningfulness that I proposed at the beginning of this lecture brings these two criteria together. That conception, you will remember, claimed that meaningfulness in life came from loving something (or a number of things) worthy of love, and being able to engage with it (or them) in some positive way. As I have put it on other occasions, meaning in life consists in and arises from actively engaging in projects of worth.[9] According to this conception, meaning in life arises when subjective attraction meets objective attractiveness, and one is able to do something about it or with it.

. . . The question remains, however, why such a feature should be thought or felt to be desirable. What, if anything, is so good, so *distinctively* good, about loving objects worthy of love, and being able actively to engage with them in a positive way? . . .

We have already noted that being able to be actively engaged with things that one loves, being able, in other words, to indulge one's passions, affords one a particularly rewarding type of subjective experience—it is, if you will, a high-quality pleasure. Like the Fulfillment View, the Fitting Fulfillment View, for lack of a better name, identifies a feature that gives this recognizable benefit to the person whose life possesses it. According to the latter view, however, what is distinctively valuable is not the state or ongoing experience of fulfillment considered in itself. Rather, what is valuable is that one's life be actively (and lovingly) engaged in projects that give rise to this feeling, when the projects in question can be seen to have a certain objective kind of worth. It is not enough, according to this view, that one is occupied with doing things that one loves. The things one loves doing must be good in some independent way. Why should this be something that matters to us? If having this in one's life answers a human need, what human need is it?

At least part of the answer, I believe, has to do with a need to be able . . . to see one's life as valuable in a way that can be recognized from a point of view other than one's own. We can better understand this need, and perhaps quell the doubts of those who are skeptical of its existence, if we see its connection to other features of human psychology with which we are familiar from other contexts.

One such feature that has long been of interest to philosophers has been especially emphasized by Thomas Nagel—namely, the human capacity, indeed the tendency, to see (or try to see) oneself from an external point of view.[10] Humans have a tendency to aspire to see things, including themselves, without bias; they take up a detached perspective on their lives; they aspire to a kind of objectivity. Nagel has characterized this as an aspiration to take a "view from nowhere"; others have talked about this feature in terms of a God's-eye point of view.

In addition, humans have a need to think well of themselves—a need for self-esteem. Being prone to imagine oneself from an external point of view, to see oneself as if from without, the wish that from that point of view one will be able to see oneself and one's life as good, valuable, and a proper source of pride seems to follow straightforwardly.

9. See "The Meanings of Lives," in *Introduction to Philosophy: Classical and Contemporary Readings*, ed. John Perry, Michael Bratman, and John Martin Fischer (Oxford University Press, 2007), 62–73; and "Meaningful Lives in a Meaningless World," in *Quaestiones Infinitae*, Vol. 19 (Department of Philosophy, Utrecht University, 1997), 1–22. This formulation fails to emphasize the element of love, passion, and identification as much as the others. [Wolf's note.]

10. See especially Thomas Nagel, *The View from Nowhere* (Oxford University Press, 1986). [Wolf's note.]

Still, the strength of that wish, and the peculiarly poignant feelings that can accompany it, suggests that something further lies behind that wish as well. I suggest that our concern to be able to think well of ourselves from an external standpoint is related to our social natures, and to our need or wish not to be alone.

Contemplation of one's mortality or of one's cosmic insignificance can call up the sort of feelings I have in mind. The thought that one's life is like a bubble that, upon bursting, will vanish without a trace can lead some people to despair. The thought that one lives in an indifferent universe makes some people shudder. Reminding oneself of the fact, if it is a fact, that one has lived or is living in a way that is actively and . . . somewhat successfully engaged in projects of independent worth may put these feelings to rest. By living in a way that is partly occupied by and directed toward the preservation or promotion or creation of value that has its source outside of oneself, one does something that can be understood, admired, or appreciated from others' points of view, including the imaginary point of view of an impartial, indifferent observer.[11]

The fact that the feature focused on by the Fitting Fulfillment View can have bearing on our reactions to thoughts about the human condition, that it can even offer some solace to those who are distressed when they think about our insignificance, gives some support to the idea that this feature is reasonably identified with "meaningfulness," since it makes the association between meaningfulness and the age-old philosophical topic of the Meaning of Life more than a coincidence.

A longing for fulfillment, and an admiration for lives engaged in projects that are fitting for fulfillment, is not restricted to times when we are especially cognizant of the human condition, however. Even when we are not thinking about our relation to the cosmos, we may intelligibly want to do something whose value extends beyond its value *for us*. Indeed, even if we never explicitly formulate a desire for our lives to be connected to something of independent value, the unarticulated *sense* that we are so connected may affect the quality of our experience. The *feeling* of being occupied with something of independent value, the engagement in an activity that takes one out of oneself, it seems to me, can be thrilling. Why? At least part of the reason, again, seems to be related to our social natures, and our desire not to be alone. If we are engaged in projects of independent value—fighting injustice, preserving a historic building, writing a poem—then presumably others will be capable of appreciating what we are doing, too. Others may actually appreciate what we are doing, or at least appreciate the same values as the ones that motivate us. This makes us at least notionally part of a community, sharing values, to some degree, and a point of view. Even when no one knows what we are doing, or when no one appreciates it, however, the thought that it is worth doing can be important to us. The scorned artist or lonely inventor, the scientist whose research no one seems to approve, may

11. Of course, there is no guarantee that such a thought *will* put the feelings in question to rest. Many people are upset by the thought that they are mere specks in a vast universe. They are upset, that is, by their smallness, their inability to make a big and lasting splash. My remarks—aimed at reminding them of the quality, not the quantity, of their contribution to the universe—do not speak directly to this concern. Such people will just have to get over it—their desire is unsatisfiable. . . . [Wolf's note.]

be sustained by the thought that her work is good, and that the day may come when others understand and value it.[12]

Although I have suggested that the desirability of living in a positive relation with something of value from an independent source is related to our sociability, these last examples show that the relation may be indirect, perhaps even metaphorical. People who, for any number of reasons, cannot or do not wish to live around or be in intimate contact with other people may still live meaningful and fulfilling lives. Some artists, for example, may make art for an only dimly conceived posterity. Conversely, for some people, the support, approval, and admiration of their contemporaries is not enough to make them feel fulfilled by what they are doing, or to judge their own lives as meaningful.

It may be suspected that the interests I am discussing are bourgeois interests, commonly found only in those from a certain place, time, and social class. Perhaps it will be thought that these concerns are confined to an even narrower class of people who are excessively intellectual or unusually reflective. If one has to struggle to get enough to eat for oneself and one's family, to get shelter from the cold, to fight a painful disease, a concern with whether one is engaged in projects of independent worth may seem to be a luxury. The fact that an interest in a meaningful life may not surface until one's more basic needs are met is no reason to dismiss its importance, however. Nor does it seem to me that the fact that a person does not consciously articulate an interest in ensuring that some of the projects or things with which his life is bound up can be judged to have independent worth is enough to warrant the view that whether they have such worth is irrelevant to him. Bernard Williams once wrote, with respect to the question of life's being desirable, that "it gets by far its best answer in never being asked at all."[13] Similarly, I think, for a person whose life is meaningful, the need to think about it might never come up. If a person is actively engaged in valuable projects, he may be getting feedback from these projects that enhances his life even if he is unaware of it. . . .

For much of this lecture, I have stressed the subjective aspect of a meaningful life—that is, the aspect that ensures a meaningful life of being fulfilling, and to that extent feeling good. This emphasis brought out what my view of meaningfulness has in common with the simpler Fulfillment View (the view that says one should find one's passion and go for it) and allowed me to make an easy argument for a way in which a meaningful life is good for the person who lives it. When we consider what deep human interests or needs a meaningful life *distinctively* answers to, however, the objective aspect of such a life needs to be stressed. Our interest in living a meaningful

12. These remarks, I think, add to the plausibility of interpreting popular references to being involved in something "larger than oneself" in terms of the idea that one should be engaged with a value that has its source outside of oneself. The thought is that such a value exists metaphorically in a public space—it is accessible to others, and so makes one at the least a potential member of a community, larger than oneself. [Wolf's note.]

13. Bernard Williams, "The Makropulos Case: Reflections on the Tedium of Immortality," in *Problems of the Self* (Cambridge University Press, 1973), 87. [Wolf's note.]

life is not an interest in a life *feeling* a certain way; it is an interest that it *be* a certain way, specifically, that it be one that can be appropriately appreciated, admired, or valued by others, that it be a life that contributes to or realizes or connects in some positive way with independent value. We do not satisfy those interests simply by thinking or feeling that they are satisfied, any more than we can satisfy our interest in not being alone by thinking or feeling that we are not alone. To have a life that not just seems meaningful but is meaningful, the objective aspect is as important as the subjective. . . .

TEST YOUR UNDERSTANDING

1. Briefly state Wolf's account of what makes life meaningful.

2. True or false: Wolf argues that Sisyphus Fulfilled lives a meaningful life.

3. Consider, for example, Jones, who believes that we are morally required to prevent famine if we can. Hence, he spends his life working at a boring but lucrative job so he can send as much money as possible to famine relief. He takes no personal satisfaction in saving lives, but does it because he thinks he must. In the course of his career, he saves thousands of lives. Does Jones live a meaningful life in Wolf's sense?

4. In Wolf's view, must a meaningful life be a happy life?

NOTES AND QUESTIONS

1. *Wolf's evaluative realism.* In Wolf's view, a meaningful life involves taking satisfaction in genuinely valuable relationships and activities. Sisyphus Fulfilled *regards* his activity as valuable, but he's deluded: the activity is worthless. As Wolf formulates it, the view presupposes **evaluative realism**: the idea that genuinely valuable things are valuable, not because we happen to value them, but in their own right, independent of our attitudes toward them. Evaluative realism is, however, a controversial view (see the essays in Chapter 17 for discussion). It is therefore worth asking how Wolf's view looks if we reject this sort of realism.

   Wolf's view is obviously incompatible with

   Simple subjectivism: An activity is valuable (in the sense relevant to Wolf's account) if and only if the agent finds it valuable.

   For on that view, Sisyphus Fulfilled is engaged in valuable activity, and his life is meaningful. But consider the following alternatives:

   Intersubjectivism: An activity is valuable if and only if many people find it valuable.

Idealized subjectivism: An activity is valuable if and only if psychologically normal human beings *would* find it valuable if they were fully informed about it.

Evaluative relativism: An activity is valuable if and only if people in the agent's society or social group generally find it valuable.

Exercise: Consider a version of Wolf's theory that is based on one of these alternatives to evaluative realism, and say whether it yields a plausible account of meaning in life.

2. *Meaning and virtue.* Must a meaningful life be a morally good life? We all know examples of extraordinary artists, scientists, and political leaders who did genuinely valuable things and took satisfaction in them but were also awful people: selfish, dishonest, even brutal.

Question: Can a vicious person lead a fully meaningful life in Wolf's view?

3. *Meaning and religious practice.* Many people find meaning in religious practice and devotion. Some of this activity is valuable even if there is no God: religious music can be beautiful, friends made at church can be good friends, and so forth. But consider the specifically devotional activities: worship, prayer, and ritual. Can a life that finds fulfillment in this sort of activity be fully meaningful in Wolf's sense if the gods do not exist or, more generally, if the metaphysical commitments of the religion are simply false?

Note the consequence of saying "no." Since the religions of the world disagree significantly in their metaphysical commitments—some positing one God, some many; some positing an afterlife, some not—we can be confident that many people spend their lives practicing a religion in which their basic commitments are mistaken. If the meaningfulness of a religious life depends on one's being *right* in one's basic commitments, we must conclude that many religious people are leading lives that are less meaningful than they think. As Wolf notes, it always sounds harsh to say this, even if we are not pointing fingers at anyone in particular. But still, it might be true.

Question: Does Wolf's view entail that a religious life based on mistaken metaphysical assumptions is less meaningful than its adherents think? If so, how might the view be modified to avoid this conclusion? Is the modification an improvement?

Thomas Nagel (b. 1937)

Nagel is University Professor Emeritus of Philosophy and Law at New York University. He has made influential contributions to ethics, political philosophy, epistemology, and philosophy of mind. His books include *The Possibility of Altruism* (1970), *The View from Nowhere* (1986), *Equality and Partiality* (1991), and *Mind and Cosmos* (2012).

THE ABSURD

Most people feel on occasion that life is absurd, and some feel it vividly and continually. Yet the reasons usually offered in defense of this conviction are patently inadequate: they *could* not really explain why life is absurd. Why then do they provide a natural expression for the sense that it is?

I

Consider some examples. It is often remarked that nothing we do now will matter in a million years. But if that is true, then by the same token, nothing that will be the case in a million years matters now. In particular, it does not matter now that in a million years nothing we do now will matter. Moreover, even if what we did now *were* going to matter in a million years, how could that keep our present concerns from being absurd? If their mattering now is not enough to accomplish that, how would it help if they mattered a million years from now? . . .

What we say to convey the absurdity of our lives often has to do with space or time: we are tiny specks in the infinite vastness of the universe; our lives are mere instants even on a geological time scale, let alone a cosmic one; we will all be dead any minute. But of course none of these evident facts can be what *makes* life absurd, if it is absurd. For suppose we lived forever; would not a life that is absurd if it lasts seventy years be infinitely absurd if it lasted through eternity? And if our lives are absurd given our present size, why would they be any less absurd if we filled the universe (either because we were larger or because the universe was smaller)? Reflection on our minuteness and brevity appears to be intimately connected with the sense that life is meaningless; but it is not clear what the connection is.

Another inadequate argument is that because we are going to die, all chains of justification must leave off in mid-air: one studies and works to earn money to pay for clothing, housing, entertainment, food, to sustain oneself from year to year, perhaps to support a family and pursue a career—but to what final end? All of it is an elaborate journey leading nowhere. (One will also have some effect on other people's lives, but that simply reproduces the problem, for they will die too.)

There are several replies to this argument. First, life does not consist of a sequence of activities each of which has as its purpose some later member of the sequence. Chains of justification come repeatedly to an end within life, and whether the process as a whole can be justified has no bearing on the finality of these end-points. No further justification is needed to make it reasonable to take aspirin for a headache, attend an exhibit of the work of a painter one admires, or stop a child from putting his hand on a hot stove. No larger context or further purpose is needed to prevent these acts from being pointless.

Even if someone wished to supply a further justification for pursuing all the things in life that are commonly regarded as self-justifying,[1] that justification would have to end somewhere too. If *nothing* can justify unless it is justified in terms of something outside itself, which is also justified, then an infinite regress results, and no chain of justification can be complete. Moreover, if a finite chain of reasons cannot justify anything, what could be accomplished by an infinite chain, each link of which must be justified by something outside itself?

Since justifications must come to an end somewhere, nothing is gained by denying that they end where they appear to, within life—or by trying to subsume the multiple, often trivial ordinary justifications of action under a single, controlling life scheme. We can be satisfied more easily than that. In fact, through its misrepresentation of the process of justification, the argument makes a vacuous demand. It insists that the reasons available within life are incomplete, but suggests thereby that all reasons that come to an end are incomplete. This makes it impossible to supply any reasons at all.

The standard arguments for absurdity appear therefore to fail as arguments. Yet I believe they attempt to express something that is difficult to state, but fundamentally correct.

II

In ordinary life a situation is absurd when it includes a conspicuous discrepancy between pretension or aspiration and reality: someone gives a complicated speech in support of a motion that has already been passed; a notorious criminal is made president of a major philanthropic foundation; you declare your love over the telephone to a recorded announcement; as you are being knighted, your pants fall down.

When a person finds himself in an absurd situation, he will usually attempt to change it, by modifying his aspirations, or by trying to bring reality into better accord with them, or by removing himself from the situation entirely. We are not always willing or able to extricate ourselves from a position whose absurdity has become clear to us. Nevertheless, it is usually possible to imagine some change that would remove the absurdity—whether or not we can or will implement it. The sense that life as a whole is absurd arises when we perceive, perhaps dimly, an inflated pretension or aspiration which is inseparable from the continuation of human life and which makes its absurdity inescapable, short of escape from life itself.

Many people's lives are absurd, temporarily or permanently, for conventional reasons having to do with their particular ambitions, circumstances, and personal relations. If there is a philosophical sense of absurdity, however, it must arise from the perception

---

1. An action is *self-justifying* if it is justified without regard to any further purpose it might accomplish. Nagel's examples from the previous paragraph (e.g., taking aspirin for a headache) may be misleading. Taking aspirin is not literally self-justifying, since we take aspirin for the further purpose of relieving pain. If we describe the act as *relieving pain*, however, then it is (or appears to be) self-justifying in Nagel's sense.

of something universal—some respect in which pretension and reality inevitably clash for us all. This condition is supplied, I shall argue, by the collision between the seriousness with which we take our lives and the perpetual possibility of regarding everything about which we are serious as arbitrary, or open to doubt.

We cannot live human lives without energy and attention, nor without making choices which show that we take some things more seriously than others. Yet we have always available a point of view outside the particular form of our lives, from which the seriousness appears gratuitous. These two inescapable viewpoints collide in us, and that is what makes life absurd. It is absurd because we ignore the doubts that we know cannot be settled, continuing to live with nearly undiminished seriousness in spite of them.

This analysis requires defense in two respects: first as regards the unavoidability of seriousness; second as regards the inescapability of doubt.

We take ourselves seriously whether we lead serious lives or not and whether we are concerned primarily with fame, pleasure, virtue, luxury, triumph, beauty, justice, knowledge, salvation, or mere survival. If we take other people seriously and devote ourselves to them, that only multiplies the problem. Human life is full of effort, plans, calculation, success and failure: we *pursue* our lives, with varying degrees of sloth and energy.

It would be different if we could not step back and reflect on the process, but were merely led from impulse to impulse without self-consciousness. But human beings do not act solely on impulse. They are prudent, they reflect, they weigh consequences, they ask whether what they are doing is worthwhile. Not only are their lives full of particular choices that hang together in larger activities with temporal structure: they also decide in the broadest terms what to pursue and what to avoid, what the priorities among their various aims should be, and what kind of people they want to be or become. Some men are faced with such choices by the large decisions they make from time to time; some merely by reflection on the course their lives are taking as the product of countless small decisions. They decide whom to marry, what profession to follow, whether to join the Country Club, or the Resistance; or they may just wonder why they go on being salesmen or academics or taxi drivers, and then stop thinking about it after a certain period of inconclusive reflection.

Although they may be motivated from act to act by those immediate needs with which life presents them, they allow the process to continue by adhering to the general system of habits and the form of life in which such motives have their place—or perhaps only by clinging to life itself. They spend enormous quantities of energy, risk, and calculation on the details. Think of how an ordinary individual sweats over his appearance, his health, his sex life, his emotional honesty, his social utility, his self-knowledge, the quality of his ties with family, colleagues, and friends, how well he does his job, whether he understands the world and what is going on in it. Leading a human life is a full-time occupation, to which everyone devotes decades of intense concern.

This fact is so obvious that it is hard to find it extraordinary and important. Each of us lives his own life—lives with himself twenty-four hours a day. What else is he supposed to do—live someone else's life? Yet humans have the special capacity to step back and survey themselves, and the lives to which they are committed, with that detached amazement which comes from watching an ant struggle up a heap of sand. Without developing the illusion that they are able to escape from their highly specific and idiosyncratic position, they can view it *sub specie aeternitatis*[2]—and the view is at once sobering and comical.

The crucial backward step is not taken by asking for still another justification in the chain, and failing to get it. The objections to that line of attack have already been stated; justifications come to an end. But this is precisely what provides universal doubt with its object. We step back to find that the whole system of justification and criticism, which controls our choices and supports our claims to rationality, rests on responses and habits that we never question, that we should not know how to defend without circularity, and to which we shall continue to adhere even after they are called into question.

The things we do or want without reasons, and without requiring reasons—the things that define what is a reason for us and what is not—are the starting points of our skepticism. We see ourselves from outside, and all the contingency and specificity of our aims and pursuits become clear. Yet when we take this view and recognize what we do as arbitrary, it does not disengage us from life, and there lies our absurdity: not in the fact that such an external view can be taken of us, but in the fact that we ourselves can take it, without ceasing to be the persons whose ultimate concerns are so coolly regarded.

III

One may try to escape the position by seeking broader ultimate concerns, from which it is impossible to step back—the idea being that absurdity results because what we take seriously is something small and insignificant and individual. Those seeking to supply their lives with meaning usually envision a role or function in something larger than themselves. They therefore seek fulfillment in service to society, the state, the revolution, the progress of history, the advance of science, or religion and the glory of God.

But a role in some larger enterprise cannot confer significance unless that enterprise is itself significant. And its significance must come back to what we can understand, or it will not even appear to give us what we are seeking. If we learned that we were being raised to provide food for other creatures fond of human flesh, who planned to turn us into cutlets before we got too stringy—even if we learned that the human race had been developed by animal breeders precisely for this purpose—that would still not give our lives meaning, for two reasons. First, we would still be in the dark

---

2. *Sub specie aeternitatis:* from the point of view or eternity (Latin). To view the universe *sub specie aeternitatis* is to "step back" from one's particular place in the universe and one's particular commitment and attachments, taking a detached perspective that does not privilege one point of view over another.

as to the significance of the lives of those other beings; second, although we might acknowledge that this culinary role would make our lives meaningful to them, it is not clear how it would make them meaningful to us.

Admittedly, the usual form of service to a higher being is different from this. One is supposed to behold and partake of the glory of God, for example, in a way in which chickens do not share in the glory of coq au vin. The same is true of service to a state, a movement, or a revolution. People can come to feel, when they are part of something bigger, that it is part of them too. They worry less about what is peculiar to themselves, but identify enough with the larger enterprise to find their role in it fulfilling.

However, any such larger purpose can be put in doubt in the same way that the aims of an individual life can be, and for the same reasons. It is as legitimate to find ultimate justification there as to find it earlier, among the details of individual life. But this does not alter the fact that justifications come to an end when we are content to have them end—when we do not find it necessary to look any further. If we can step back from the purposes of individual life and doubt their point, we can step back also from the progress of human history, or of science, or the success of a society, or the kingdom, power, and glory of God,[3] and put all these things into question in the same way. What seems to us to confer meaning, justification, significance, does so in virtue of the fact that we need no more reasons after a certain point.

What makes doubt inescapable with regard to the limited aims of individual life also makes it inescapable with regard to any larger purpose that encourages the sense that life is meaningful. Once the fundamental doubt has begun, it cannot be laid to rest.

Camus maintains in *The Myth of Sisyphus*[4] that the absurd arises because the world fails to meet our demands for meaning. This suggests that the world might satisfy those demands if it were different. But now we can see that this is not the case. There does not appear to be any conceivable world (containing us) about which unsettlable doubts could not arise. Consequently the absurdity of our situation derives not from a collision between our expectations and the world, but from a collision within ourselves.

IV

It may be objected that the standpoint from which these doubts are supposed to be felt does not exist—that if we take the recommended backward step we will land on thin air, without any basis for judgment about the natural responses we are supposed to be surveying. If we retain our usual standards of what is important, then questions about the significance of what we are doing with our lives will be answerable in the usual way. But if we do not, then those questions can mean nothing to us, since there is no longer any content to the idea of what matters, and hence no content to the idea that nothing does.

---

3. Cf. Robert Nozick, "Teleology," *Mosaic* XII, 1 (1971): 27–28. [Nagel's note.]

4. Albert Camus (1913–1960), French writer. Camus's 1942 essay *The Myth of Sisyphus* introduces modern philosophical discussions of the absurd.

But this objection misconceives the nature of the backward step. It is not supposed to give us an understanding of what is *really* important, so that we see by contrast that our lives are insignificant. We never, in the course of these reflections, abandon the ordinary standards that guide our lives. We merely observe them in operation, and recognize that if they are called into question we can justify them only by reference to themselves, uselessly. We adhere to them because of the way we are put together; what seems to us important or serious or valuable would not seem so if we were differently constituted.[5]

In ordinary life, to be sure, we do not judge a situation absurd unless we have in mind some standards of seriousness, significance, or harmony with which the absurd can be contrasted. This contrast is not implied by the philosophical judgment of absurdity, and that might be thought to make the concept unsuitable for the expression of such judgments. This is not so, however, for the philosophical judgment depends on another contrast which makes it a natural extension from more ordinary cases. It departs from them only in contrasting the pretensions of life with a larger context in which *no* standards can be discovered, rather than with a context from which alternative, overriding standards may be applied.

V

In this respect, as in others, philosophical perception of the absurd resembles epistemological skepticism.[6] In both cases the final, philosophical doubt is not contrasted with any unchallenged certainties, though it is arrived at by extrapolation from examples of doubt within the system of evidence or justification, where a contrast with other certainties *is* implied. In both cases our limitedness joins with a capacity to transcend those limitations in thought (thus seeing them as limitations, and as inescapable).

Skepticism begins when we include ourselves in the world about which we claim knowledge. We notice that certain types of evidence convince us, that we are content to allow justifications of belief to come to an end at certain points, that we feel we know many things even without knowing or having grounds for believing the denial of others which, if true, would make what we claim to know false.

For example, I know that I am looking at a piece of paper, although I have no adequate grounds to claim I know that I am not dreaming; and if I am dreaming then I am not looking at a piece of paper. Here an ordinary conception of how appearance may diverge from reality is employed to show that we take our world largely for granted;

5. For example, we take aspirin to relive pain, and that makes sense so long as we take it for granted that our physical comfort matters. When we step back, we notice that if we were differently constituted, we might not care about avoiding pain. This does not neutralize our basic concern for avoiding pain, but, according to Nagel, it does show that concern to be "unjustifiable," in the sense that no reason can be given for it.

6. The view that our beliefs are not ultimately justified since no reason can be given for certain basic beliefs on which the rest of our beliefs depend (e.g., our belief that things are normally as they appear to be). See Chapters 3–6 for discussion.

the certainty that we are not dreaming cannot be justified except circularly, in terms of those very appearances which are being put in doubt. It is somewhat far-fetched to suggest I may be dreaming; but the possibility is only illustrative. It reveals that our claims to knowledge depend on our not feeling it necessary to exclude certain incompatible alternatives, and the dreaming possibility or the total-hallucination possibility are just representatives for limitless possibilities most of which we cannot even conceive.

Once we have taken the backward step to an abstract view of our whole system of beliefs, evidence, and justification, and seen that it works only, despite its pretensions, by taking the world largely for granted, we are *not* in a position to contrast all these appearances with an alternative reality. We cannot shed our ordinary responses, and if we could it would leave us with no means of conceiving a reality of any kind.

It is the same in the practical domain.[7] We do not step outside our lives to a new vantage point from which we see what is really, objectively significant. We continue to take life largely for granted while seeing that all our decisions and certainties are possible only because there is a great deal we do not bother to rule out.

Both epistemological skepticism and a sense of the absurd can be reached via initial doubts posed within systems of evidence and justification that we accept. . . . We can ask not only why we should believe there is a floor under us, but also why we should believe the evidence of our senses at all—and at some point the framable questions will have outlasted the answers. Similarly, we can ask not only why we should take aspirin, but why we should take trouble over own comfort at all. The fact that we shall take the aspirin without waiting for an answer to this last question does not show that it is an unreal question. We shall also continue to believe there is a floor under us without waiting for an answer to the other question. In both cases it is this unsupported natural confidence that generates skeptical doubts; so it cannot be used to settle them.

Philosophical skepticism does not cause us to abandon our ordinary beliefs, but it lends them a peculiar flavor. After acknowledging that their truth is incompatible with possibilities that we have no grounds for believing do not obtain—apart from grounds in those very beliefs which we have called into question—we return to our familiar convictions with a certain irony and resignation. Unable to abandon the natural responses on which they depend, we take them back, like a spouse who has run off with someone else and then decided to return; but we regard them differently (not that the new attitude is necessarily inferior to the old, in either case).

The same situation obtains after we have put in question the seriousness with which we take our lives and human life in general and have looked at ourselves without presuppositions. We then return to our lives, as we must, but our seriousness is laced with irony. Not that irony enables us to escape the absurd. It is useless to mutter: "Life is meaningless; life is meaningless . . ." as an accompaniment to everything we do. In continuing to live and work and strive, we take ourselves seriously in action no matter what we say.

What sustains us, in belief as in action, is not reason or justification, but something more basic than these—for we go on in the same way even after we are convinced that

---

7. That is, the domain concerned with reasons for action rather than reasons for belief.

the reasons have given out.[8] If we tried to rely entirely on reason, and pressed it hard, our lives and beliefs would collapse—a form of madness that may actually occur if the inertial force of taking the world and life for granted is somehow lost. If we lose our grip on that, reason will not give it back to us.

VI

In viewing ourselves from a perspective broader than we can occupy in the flesh, we become spectators of our own lives. We cannot do very much as pure spectators of our own lives, so we continue to lead them, and devote ourselves to what we are able at the same time to view as no more than a curiosity, like the ritual of an alien religion.

This explains why the sense of absurdity finds its natural expression in those bad arguments with which the discussion began. Reference to our small size and short life span and to the fact that all of mankind will eventually vanish without a trace are metaphors for the backward step which permits us to regard ourselves from without and to find the particular form of our lives curious and slightly surprising. By feigning a nebula's-eye view, we illustrate the capacity to see ourselves without presuppositions, as arbitrary, idiosyncratic, highly specific occupants of the world, one of countless possible forms of life. . . .

The final escape [from the absurdity of existence] is suicide; but before adopting any hasty solutions, it would be wise to consider carefully whether the absurdity of our existence truly presents us with a *problem*, to which some solution must be found—a way of dealing with prima facie disaster. That is certainly the attitude with which Camus approaches the issue, and it gains support from the fact that we are all eager to escape from absurd situations on a smaller scale.

Camus—not on uniformly good grounds—rejects suicide and the other solutions he regards as escapist. What he recommends is defiance or scorn. We can salvage our dignity, he appears to believe, by shaking a fist at the world which is deaf to our pleas, and continuing to live in spite of it. This will not make our lives un-absurd, but it will lend them a certain nobility.[9]

8. As Hume says in a famous passage of the *Treatise*: "Most fortunately it happens, that since reason is incapable of dispelling these clouds, nature herself suffices to that purpose, and cures me of this philosophical melancholy and delirium, either by relaxing this bent of mind, or by some avocation, and lively impression of my senses, which obliterate all these chimeras. I dine, I play a game of backgammon, I converse, and am merry with my friends; and when after three or four hours' amusement, I would return to these speculations, they appear so cold, and strain'd, and ridiculous, that I cannot find in my heart to enter into them any farther" (book 1; part 4, section 7). [Nagel's note.]

9. "Sisyphus, proletarian of the gods, powerless and rebellious, knows the whole extent of his wretched condition: it is what he thinks of during his descent. The lucidity that was to constitute his torture at the same time crowns his victory. There is no fate that cannot be surmounted by scorn" (*The Myth of Sisyphus*, Vintage edition, p. 90). [Nagel's note.]

This seems to me romantic and slightly self-pitying. Our absurdity warrants neither that much distress nor that much defiance. At the risk of falling into romanticism by a different route, I would argue that absurdity is one of the most human things about us: a manifestation of our most advanced and interesting characteristics. Like skepticism in epistemology, it is possible only because we possess a certain kind of insight—the capacity to transcend ourselves in thought.

If a sense of the absurd is a way of perceiving our true situation (even though the situation is not absurd until the perception arises), then what reason can we have to resent or escape it? Like the capacity for epistemological skepticism, it results from the ability to understand our human limitations. It need not be a matter for agony unless we make it so. Nor need it evoke a defiant contempt of fate that allows us to feel brave or proud. Such dramatics, even if carried on in private, betray a failure to appreciate the cosmic unimportance of the situation. If *sub specie aeternitatis* there is no reason to believe that anything matters, then that doesn't matter either, and we can approach our absurd lives with irony instead of heroism or despair.

TEST YOUR UNDERSTANDING

1. What is it for a situation to be "absurd" in Nagel's sense?

2. Nagel says that the "standard arguments" for the absurdity of life fail. Give one of the standard arguments and say why Nagel thinks it fails.

3. Briefly summarize Nagel's account of the sense in which our lives are absurd.

4. Does Nagel's account of the absurdity of human life depend on the assumption that the things that matter to us do not *really* matter?

NOTES AND QUESTIONS

1. *Glimpsing absurdity.* If you have never felt that your life is in any way absurd, you won't know what Nagel is talking about. So it's worth trying to see what he sees. Take something that matters to you—something that seems to you worth worrying about, agonizing over, devoting some large part of your life to. Now imagine stepping back and treating yourself as a curious anthropological specimen. As an anthropologist, you interrogate your former self: "I see that you care enormously about X. I find that fascinating, since many people don't care about X at all. Can you tell me why X is so important?" You might have something to say at first: "X is important because it's a means to Y, and Y is important." But eventually you'll reach a point where you start sputtering: "Look, I can't say why it's important; it just is!" At this moment, Nagel thinks, you will see your life devoted in part to X as absurd. You may still pursue X with the same effort and energy. But you will pursue it in the knowledge that you cannot justify this pursuit to an imagined interlocutor or to yourself.

Exercise: When you reach the point at which you cannot articulate a justification for pursuing something that matters to you, does your life devoted to that thing strike you as absurd? Try the exercise and describe the results.

2. *A subjectivist gambit.* According to Nagel, our sense of the absurd arises when we realize we take it for granted that certain things really matter but cannot *show*, to the satisfaction of an impartial interlocutor, that they have the kind of importance we attach to them. Nagel thinks that when this happens, our only option is to retain our commitment to the objective importance of the thing we value, but to hold it in an "ironic" spirit—that is, in the full knowledge that we cannot justify it. But consider someone who says:

> Look, I don't care whether this thing (e.g., my relationship with my family) matters objectively. I devote time and energy to it because it matters *to me. I* care about it. This is a psychological fact about which I have not the slightest doubt. And that's enough to give this relationship the only kind of importance I attach to it. Nagel thinks I should find my life "absurd" when I realize that I can't justify my basic commitments. But I find it easy to justify them. What justifies the effort I devote to maintaining my relationship with my family? The fact that I care about the relationship. End of story.

Exercise: Nagel presupposes that anyone who takes his life seriously takes it for granted that things he cares about are objectively worth caring about. But this subjectivist denies this. Develop a reply to Nagel along these lines and imagine how Nagel might respond.

For relevant discussion, see T. Nagel, *The View from Nowhere* (Oxford University Press, 1986), and Chapter 17 of this anthology.

Samuel Scheffler (b. 1951)

Scheffler is University Professor and Professor of Law and Philosophy at New York University. His many contributions to moral and political philosophy include *Human Morality* (1992), *Boundaries and Allegiances* (2003), and *Equality and Tradition* (2010).

DEATH AND THE AFTERLIFE

. . . Like many people nowadays, though unlike many others, I do not believe in the existence of an afterlife as normally understood. That is, I do not believe that individuals continue to live on as conscious beings after their biological deaths. To the contrary, I believe that biological death represents the final and irrevocable end of an individual's life. So one thing I will not be doing in these lectures is arguing for the existence of the afterlife as it is commonly understood. At the same time, however, I take it

for granted that other human beings will continue to live on after my own death. . . .
[A]nd in this rather nonstandard sense, I take it for granted that there will be an
afterlife: that others will continue to live after I have died. . . .

It is my contention that the existence of an afterlife, in my nonstandard sense of
"afterlife," matters greatly to us. It matters to us in its own right, and it matters to us
because our confidence in the existence of an afterlife is a condition of many other
things that we care about continuing to matter to us. Or so I shall try to show. . . .

. . . Suppose you knew that, although you yourself would live a normal life span, the
earth would be completely destroyed thirty days after your death in a collision with a
giant asteroid. How would this knowledge affect your attitudes during the remainder
of your life? . . .

. . . One reaction that I think few of us would be likely to have . . . is complete
indifference. For example, few of us would be likely to say, if told that the earth
would be destroyed thirty days after our deaths: "So what? Since it won't happen
until thirty days after my death, and since it won't hasten my death, it isn't of any
importance to me. I won't be around to experience it, and so it doesn't matter to me
in the slightest." The fact that we would probably not respond this way is already
suggestive. It means that, at a minimum, we are not indifferent to everything that
happens after our deaths. Something that will not happen until after our deaths can
still matter or be important to us. And this in turn implies that things other than
our own experiences matter to us. A postmortem event that matters to us would
not be one of our experiences. . . .

There is another reaction to the doomsday scenario that I think few of us would be
likely to have. Few of us, I think, would be likely to deliberate about the good and bad
consequences of the destruction of the earth in order to decide whether it would, on
balance, be a good or a bad thing. This is not, I think, because the answer is so immediately
and overwhelmingly obvious that we don't need to perform the calculations. It is true,
of course, that the destruction of the earth would have many horrible consequences. It
would, for example, mean the end of all human joy, creativity, love, friendship, virtue,
and happiness. So there are, undeniably, some weighty considerations to place in the
minus column. On the other hand, it would also mean the end of all human suffering,
cruelty, and injustice. No more genocide, no more torture, no more oppression, no
more misery, no more pain. Surely, these things all go in the plus column. And it's at
least not *instantly* obvious that the minuses outweigh the pluses. Yet few of us, I think,
would react to the scenario by trying to do the sums, by trying to figure out whether on
balance the prospect of the destruction of the earth was welcome or unwelcome. On
the face of it, at least, the fact that we would not react this way suggests that there is a
nonconsequentialist dimension to our attitudes about what we value or what matters
to us.[1] It appears that what we value, or what matters to us, is not simply or solely that
the best consequences, whatever they may be, should come to pass.

---

1. Consequentialism in this context is the view that the *value* of an action or an event is to be determined by
adding up the values and disvalues of its consequences. In other contexts, it is the view that what we *morally
ought to do* is determined by values of the consequences of our actions and those of other actions open to us.

Let us now move from negative to positive characterizations of our reactions. To begin with, I think it is safe to say that most of us would respond to the doomsday scenario with what I will generically call, with bland understatement, profound dismay. This is meant only as a superficial, placeholder characterization, which undoubtedly subsumes a range of more specific reactions. Many of these reactions have to do with the deaths of the particular people we love and the disappearance or destruction of the particular things that we care most about. . . .

The fact that we would have these reactions highlights a *conservative* dimension in our attitudes toward what we value, which sits alongside the nonexperiential and nonconsequentialist dimensions already mentioned. In general, we want the people and things we care about to flourish; we are not indifferent to the destruction of that which matters most to us. Indeed, there is something approaching a conceptual connection between valuing something and wanting it to be sustained or preserved. During our lifetimes, this translates into a similarly close connection between valuing something and seeing reasons to act so as to preserve or sustain it ourselves. Part of the poignancy of contemplating our own deaths, under ordinary rather than doomsday conditions, is the recognition that we will no longer be able to respond to these reasons; we will not ourselves be able to help preserve or sustain the things that matter to us. . . .

In addition to the generic conservatism about value just noted, something more specific is involved in our reaction to the prospective destruction of the particular *people* we love and treasure. It is a feature of the scenario that I have described that all of our loved ones who survive thirty days beyond our own death will themselves die suddenly, violently, and prematurely, and this prospect itself is sufficient to fill us with horror and dread. In other words, it would fill us with horror and dread even if it were *only* our own loved ones who would be destroyed, and everything and everyone else would survive. Indeed, this dimension of our reaction is liable to be so powerful that it may make it difficult to notice some of the others. . . .

I have so far said only that the prospect of the earth's imminent destruction would induce in us reactions of grief, sadness, and distress. But we must also consider how, if at all, it would affect our subsequent motivations and our choices about how to live. To what extent would we remain committed to our current projects and plans? To what extent would the activities in which we now engage continue to seem worth pursuing? . . .

. . . Consider . . . the project of trying to find a cure for cancer. This project would seem vulnerable for at least two reasons. First, it is a project in which it is understood that ultimate success may be a long way off. . . . The doomsday scenario, by cutting the future short, makes it much less likely that such a cure will ever be found. Second, the primary value of the project lies in the prospect of eventually being able to cure the disease and to prevent the death and suffering it causes. But the doomsday scenario means that even immediate success in finding a cure would make available such benefits only for a very short period of time. Under these conditions, scientists' motivations to engage in such research might well weaken substantially. This suggests that projects would be specially vulnerable if either (a) their ultimate success is seen as something that may not be achieved until some time well in the future or (b) the value of the project derives from the benefits that it will provide to large numbers of people over a long period of time. Cancer research is threatened because it satisfies both of these conditions. But there are many other projects and activities that satisfy at least one of them. This is true, for example, of much research in science, technology, and medicine. It is also true of much social and political activism. It is true of many efforts to build or reform or improve social institutions. It is true of many projects to build new buildings, improve the physical infrastructure of society, or protect the environment. . . .

The effect of the doomsday scenario on other types of projects is less clear. For example, many creative and scholarly projects have no obvious practical aim, such as finding a cure for cancer, but they are nevertheless undertaken with an actual or imagined audience or readership of some kind in mind. Although the doomsday scenario would not mean that audiences would disappear immediately, it would mean that they would not be around for very long. Would artistic, musical, and literary projects still seem worth undertaking? Would humanistic scholars continue to be motivated to engage in basic research? Would historians and theoretical physicists and anthropologists all carry on as before? Perhaps, but the answer is not obvious. . . .

The upshot is that many types of projects and activities would no longer seem worth pursuing, or as worth pursuing, if we were confronted with the doomsday scenario. Now it is noteworthy that the attractions of these same projects and activities are not similarly undercut by the mere prospect of our own deaths. People cheerfully engage in cancer research and similar activities despite their recognition that the primary payoff of these activities is not likely to be achieved before their own deaths. Yet, if my argument is correct, their motivation to engage in these same activities would be weakened or even completely undermined by the prospect that, in consequence of the earth's destruction, there would be no payoff *after* their deaths. In other words, there are many projects and activities whose importance to us is not diminished by the prospect of our own deaths but would be diminished by the prospect that everyone else will soon die. So if by the afterlife we mean the continuation of human life on earth after our own deaths, then it seems difficult to avoid the conclusion that, in some significant respects, the existence of the afterlife matters more to us than our own continued existence. It matters more to us because it is a condition of other things mattering to us. Without confidence in the existence of the afterlife, many of the things in our own lives that now matter to us would cease to do so, or would come to matter less. . . .

. . . I have so far been concentrating on our general reactions to the doomsday scenario and the general attitudes toward the afterlife that they reveal. However, I want now to consider our more specific reactions to one feature of that scenario, namely, that it involves the sudden, simultaneous deaths of everyone that we love or care about. . . .

Some elements of our reaction seem obvious. . . . We don't want the people we love to die prematurely, whether we are alive to witness their deaths or not. . . . Still, I think that there is more to our reaction than this. One way to approach the issue is to ask why it matters to us that at least some people we care about should live on after we die? I take it that most people do regard it as a bad thing if everyone they love or care about dies before they do. . . . Why should this be?

There are, I think, a number of answers to this question. . . . The considerations about prematurity just mentioned play a large role, though our preference to predecease at least some of the people we care about may persist even if both we and they are old enough that none of our deaths would qualify as significantly premature. A different kind of consideration is that if we predecease our loved ones, then we will be spared the pain and grief that we would experience if they died first. . . .

But I think that there is something else going on as well. If, at the time of our deaths, there are people alive whom we love or about whom we care deeply, and with whom we have valuable personal relationships, then one effect of our deaths will be to disrupt those relationships. Odd as it may sound, I think that there is something that strikes us as desirable or at any rate comforting about having one's death involve this kind of relational disruption. It is not that the disruptions per se are desirable or comforting, but rather that the prospect of having one's death involve such disruptions affects one's perceived relation to the future. If at the time of one's death one will be a participant in a larger or smaller network of valuable personal relationships, and if the effect of one's death will be to wrench one out of that network, then this can affect one's premortem understanding of the afterlife: the future that will unfold after one is gone. In a certain sense, it personalizes one's relation to that future. Rather than looming simply as a blank eternity of nonexistence, the future can be conceptualized with reference to an ongoing social world in which one retains a social identity. One can imagine oneself into that world simply by imagining the resumption of one's premortem relationships with people who will themselves continue to exist and to remember and care for one. One need not fear, as many people apparently do, that one will simply be forgotten as soon as one is gone. In fact, to a surprising extent, many people seem to feel that not being remembered is what being "gone" really consists in, and, correspondingly, those who are bereaved often feel a powerful imperative not to forget the people they have lost. Faced with the fear of being forgotten, the fact that there are other people who value their relations with you and who will continue to live after you have died makes it possible to feel that you have a place in the social world of the future even if, due to the inconvenient fact of your death, you will not actually be able to take advantage of it. The world of the future becomes, as it were, more like a party one had to leave early and less like a gathering of strangers. . . .

At this point, let me pause to summarize the arguments I have presented so far. First, I have argued that our reactions to the doomsday scenario highlight some general features of the phenomenon of human valuing, which I have referred to as its nonexperientialist, nonconsequentialist, and conservative dimensions. We do not care only about our own experiences. We do not care only that the best consequences should come to pass. And we do want the things that we value to be sustained and preserved over time. Second, I have argued that the afterlife matters to us, and in more than one way. What happens after our deaths matters to us in its own right, and, in addition, our confidence that there will be an afterlife is a condition of many other things mattering to us here and now. Third, I have argued that the doomsday scenario highlights some of our attitudes toward time, particularly our impulse to personalize our relation to the future.

Let me now try to expand on these provisional conclusions. As I have noted, death poses a problem for our conservatism about value. We want to act in ways that will help preserve and sustain the things that we value, but death marks the end of our ability to do this. As I have also noted, death poses a problem for our relationship with time. We want to personalize our relation to the future, yet for most of the future we will no longer be alive. I have already made some suggestions about how we attempt to deal with these two problems as individuals. In the first case, we take steps while we are alive to ensure that others will act so as to sustain those values after our deaths. In the second case, our participation in valued personal relationships with people whom we hope will outlive us transforms our attitudes toward the future after we are gone.

These responses are important, but they have their limits. Many people supplement them by participating in group-based responses as well. One of the most important ways in which people attempt to preserve and sustain their values, for example, is by participating in traditions that themselves support those values. Traditions are . . . human practices whose organizing purpose is to preserve what is valued beyond the life span of any single individual or generation.[2] They are collaborative, multigenerational enterprises devised by human beings precisely to satisfy the deep human impulse to preserve what is valued. . . . Although traditions are not themselves guaranteed to survive, a flourishing tradition will typically have far greater resources to devote to the preservation of values, and very different kinds of resources, than any single individual is likely to have. So by participating in traditions that embody the values to which they are committed, individuals can leverage their own personal efforts to ensure the survival of those values. . . .

Our efforts to personalize our relations to the future also take group-based forms. In addition to participating in valued personal relations with other specific individuals, at least some of whom we hope will survive us, many people also belong to, and value their membership in, communal or national groups, most of whose members they do not know personally. Often it becomes important to them that these groups should survive after they are gone. Indeed, for some people, the survival of the community or the clan or the people or the nation has an importance that is comparable to—or nearly comparable to—the importance they attach to the survival of their loved ones. Similarly, the prospect that the group will survive after they as individuals are gone serves to personalize their relation to the future in much the same way as does the prospect that their own loved ones will survive. Even if, by contrast to the latter case, the survival of the group does not mean that one will personally be remembered, it nevertheless gives one license to imagine oneself as retaining a social identity in the world of the future. In neither case does this involve the false belief that one will actually survive one's death. It merely allows one to think that if, contrary to fact, one did survive, one would remain socially at home in the world. . . .

Of course, the doomsday scenario thwarts the group-based solutions as decisively as it thwarts their more individualistic counterparts, since the traditions and groups upon

---

2. Samuel Scheffler, "The Normativity of Tradition," in *Equality and Tradition*, chapter 11 (Oxford University Press, 2010). [Scheffler's note.]

which those solutions rely will also be destroyed when the doomsday collision takes place. This raises questions about the motivational sustainability under doomsday conditions of a whole new range of projects, in addition to those surveyed earlier. For example, many people have projects that are defined in relation to a particular tradition. . . . Similarly, many people have projects that are defined in relation to a particular community or nation or people. . . .

Would projects of these kinds retain their motivational appeal under doomsday conditions? In other words, would pursuing such projects continue to seem important to individuals who had previously been committed to them if those individuals knew that the tradition or community that was the focus or the source of their project would be destroyed thirty days after their own deaths? Or would it then seem to them less important to persevere with their projects? Would they see less reason to do so? The answer, of course, may depend on the nature of the particular project in question. And there might well be some variation from individual to individual. But it seems plausible that many tradition-dependent and group-dependent projects would come to seem less important to people. This seems especially true of projects whose explicit aim either was or was dependent on the long-term survival and flourishing of a particular tradition or group, for those projects would now be known in advance to be doomed to failure. And so we have here another important range of examples of the phenomenon noted earlier, in which our confidence in the existence of an afterlife is a condition of our projects continuing to matter to us while we are alive.

However, these examples may create or reinforce the impression that, to the extent that our confidence in the existence of an afterlife has this kind of importance for us, it is really the postmortem survival of specific individuals or groups that we care about. . . .

Yet this conclusion is too hasty. . . .

. . . The imminent disappearance of human life would be sufficient for us to react with horror even if it would not involve the premature deaths of any of our loved ones. This, it seems to me, is one lesson of P. D. James's novel *Children of Men*,[3] which was published in 1992, and a considerably altered version of which was made into a film in 2006 by the Mexican filmmaker Alfonso Cuarón. The premise of James's novel, which is set in 2021, is that human beings have become infertile, with no recorded birth having occurred in more than twenty-five years. The human race thus faces the prospect of imminent extinction as the last generation to be born gradually dies out.[4]

---

3. James's novel was first published by Faber and Faber (London, 1992). Page references, given parenthetically in the text, are to the Vintage Books edition published by Random House in 2006. [Scheffler's note.]

4. On July 28, 2009, *New York Times* columnist David Brooks, citing a brief item posted by Tyler Cowen a few days earlier on the *Marginal Revolution* blog (www.marginalrevolution.com/marginalrevolution/2009/07/mass-sterilization.html#comments), wrote an article titled "The Power of Posterity," in which he considered what would happen if *half* the world's population were sterilized as a result of a "freak solar event" (www.nytimes.com/2009/07/28/opinion/28brooks.html?scp=1&sq=power%20of%2oposterity &st=csc). Although some of Brooks's speculations evoke, albeit rather stridently, some of the themes of James's novel (and of these lectures), the proviso that only half of the world's population becomes infertile leads him ultimately in a different direction. Neither Cowen nor Brooks cites *Children of Men*, although online reader comments responding to Cowen's blog post and to Brooks's column both note the connection. [Scheffler's note.]

. . . [James's] asteroid-free variant of the doomsday scenario does not require anyone to die prematurely. It is entirely compatible with every living person having a normal life span. So if we imagine ourselves inhabiting James's infertile world and we try to predict what our reactions would be to the imminent disappearance of human life on earth, it is clear that those reactions would not include any feelings about the premature deaths of our loved ones, for no such deaths would occur. . . .

Of course, the infertility scenario would mean that many groups and traditions would die out sooner than they otherwise would have done, and this would presumably be a source of particularistic distress for those with group-based or traditional allegiances. Still, because the infertility scenario suppresses the influence of any particularistic concern for individuals, it is more effective than the original doomsday scenario in highlighting something that I think is evident despite the persistence of group-based particularistic responses. What is evident is that, for all the power of the particularistic elements in our reactions to the catastrophe scenarios we have been discussing, there is also another powerful element that is at work, namely, the impact that the imminent end of humanity as such would have on us.

What exactly that impact would be is of course a matter of speculation. . . . I find it plausible to suppose that such a world would be a world characterized by widespread apathy, anomie, and despair; by the erosion of social institutions and social solidarity; by the deterioration of the physical environment; and by a pervasive loss of conviction about the value or point of many activities.

In James's version of the story, an authoritarian government in Britain has largely avoided the savage anarchy that prevails in other parts of the world, and it has achieved a measure of popular support by promising people "freedom from fear, freedom from want, freedom from boredom" (see James, p. 97), though the last of these promises proves difficult to keep in the face of mounting indifference toward most previously attractive activities. This indifference extends not only to those activities with an obvious orientation toward the future but also to those, like sex, that offer immediate gratification and might therefore have seemed likely to retain their popularity in an infertile world, but which turn out not to be exempt from the growing apathy. . . . Theo Faron, the Oxford don who serves as James's protagonist and sometimes narrator, says, describing people's reactions once they became convinced that the infertility was irreversible, that suicide increased, and that "those who lived gave way to the almost universal negativism, what the French named *ennui universel*.[5] It came upon us like an insidious disease; indeed, it was a disease, with its soon-familiar symptoms of lassitude, depression, ill-defined malaise, a readiness to give way to minor infections, a perpetual disabling headache" (James, p. 9). . . . And although Theo himself continues to fight against the *ennui* by trying to take pleasure in books, music, food, wine, and nature, he finds that pleasure "now comes so rarely and, when it does, is . . . indistinguishable from pain" (Ibid.). "Without the hope of posterity," he says, "for our race if not for ourselves, without the assurance that we being dead yet live, all pleasures of the mind and senses sometimes seem to me no more than pathetic and crumbling defences shored up against our ruins" (Ibid.).

---

5. Universal boredom.

To the extent that all of this is persuasive, it suggests a significant increase in the range of activities whose perceived value might be threatened by the recognition that life on earth was about to come to an end. I have already noted several different types of activities that would be threatened by that prospect. First, there are some projects, such as cancer research or the development of new seismic safety techniques, that would be threatened because they have a goal-oriented character, and the goals they seek to achieve would straightforwardly be thwarted if the human race were imminently to disappear. Second, there are some projects, including creative projects of various kinds, that would be threatened because they tacitly depend for their perceived success on their reception by an imagined future audience. . . . Third, there are a large number of activities, including but not limited to those associated with participation in a tradition, that would be threatened because their point is in part to sustain certain values and practices over time, and the end of human life would mark the defeat of all such efforts. Fourth, and relatedly, there are activities that would be threatened because they are aimed at promoting the survival and flourishing of particular national or communal groups, and those aims too would be doomed to frustration if human life were about to come to an end.

In addition, however, James's narrative encourages us to think that there are other, less obvious, sorts of activities whose perceived value might also be threatened in an infertile world. . . . Even such things as the enjoyment of nature, the appreciation of literature, music, and the visual arts, the achievement of knowledge and understanding, and the appetitive pleasures of food, drink, and sex might be affected. This suggestion is likely to strike some people as implausible. . . .

Still, I believe that James's speculations about the effects of the infertility scenario on people's attitudes toward these dimensions of human experience are suggestive. They give imaginative expression to the not implausible idea that the imminent disappearance of human life would exert a generally depressive effect on people's motivations and on their confidence in the value of their activities—that it would reduce their capacity for enthusiasm and for wholehearted and joyful activity across a very wide front. The same speculations also invite us to consider a slightly more specific possibility. We normally understand such things as the appreciation of literature and the arts, the acquisition of knowledge and understanding of the world around us, and the enjoyment of the appetitive pleasures to be constituents of the good life. This means that we take a certain view about the place of these goods in a human life as a whole. But James's speculations invite us to consider the possibility that our conception of "a human life as a whole" relies on an implicit understanding of such a life as itself occupying a place in an ongoing human history, in a temporally extended chain of lives and generations. If this is so, then, perhaps, we cannot simply take it for granted that the activity of, say, reading *The Catcher in the Rye* or trying to understand quantum mechanics or even eating an excellent meal would have the same significance for people, or offer them the same rewards, in a world that was known to be deprived of a human future. We cannot assume that we know what the constituents of a good life would be in such a world, nor can we even be confident that there is something that we would be prepared to count as a good life. . . .

TEST YOUR UNDERSTANDING

1. What does Scheffler mean by "the afterlife"?

2. Describe Scheffler's "doomsday scenario," and say how it differs from the scenario from P. D. James's novel *Children of Men*.

3. Scheffler speculates that if we came to doubt that the human race will continue on after we die, we would be much less motivated to do many of the things we do now. Give some examples.

4. What philosophical morals does Scheffler draw from the fact that we would be much less motivated to pursue these things if we knew that there would be no "afterlife"?

NOTES AND QUESTIONS

1. Scheffler argues that the fact that we care about what happens after our own deaths shows that "things other than our own experiences matter to us" (p. 1007). This point is often made in a rather different way.

> Suppose there were an experience machine that would give you any experience you desired. Super-duper neuropsychologists could stimulate your brain so that you would think and feel you were writing a great novel, or making a friend, or reading an interesting book. All the time you would be floating in a tank, with electrodes attached to your brain. Should you plug into this machine for life, preprogramming your life's experiences? If you are worried about missing out on desirable experiences, we can suppose that . . . you can pick and choose from [a] large library or smorgasbord of such experiences, selecting your life's experiences for, say, the next two years. After two years have past, you will have ten minutes . . . out of the tank to select the experiences of your *next* two years. Of course, while in the tank you won't know that you're there; you'll think it's all actually happening.
>
> . . . Would you plug in? *What else can matter to us, other than how our lives feel from the inside?* (Robert Nozick, *Anarchy, State and Utopia* [Basic Books, 1974], 42–43)

   Nozick thinks that most of us would not plug in, and that this shows we don't just care about *the experience* of having friends or writings books but about *having real friends* and *writing real books*. Do you agree?

   For cinematic dramatizations of Nozick's thought experiment, see *The Matrix* (1999) and *Vanilla Sky* (2001).

2. *Scheffler's methodology.* It is not a surprise to learn that we care about the continued existence of the human race. It is a surprise to learn that so many of the activities and relationships that matter to us in our everyday lives depend for their value on the existence of human civilization after our deaths. Scheffler's method for making this point is

to invite us to imagine that our generation will be the last, and then to reflect on what we would care about if we made that discovery. It is therefore worth asking whether we can use this methodology to reveal other surprising facts about what matters to us. For example:

> Suppose you discover, beyond any doubt, that no one really dies. After your bodily death, you will live on in heaven or on another planet with many of the people you have known in this life. And you will live forever. Would this discovery affect what you care about in this life? If it would, then you have discovered that some things that seem to matter for their own sake only matter to us *because our lives are finite*. That would be an interesting discovery.

3. *Unconditional value.* If Scheffler is right, then many of the things that matter to us only matter *on the condition* that human society will continue after our deaths. But Scheffler does not claim that everything we value is like this. If we knew that our generation were the last, we would still find some things worth doing. These activities have a value that is independent of the continued existence of the human race, which is in that sense *unconditional.*

Exercise: Identify some of these "unconditionally" valuable activities. Try to imagine a life built around those activities. Scheffler argues that such a life would be much less meaningful than the lives we actually lead. Is he right?

ANALYZING THE ARGUMENTS

1. *Meaning and purpose.* Some people hear the question "What is the meaning of my life?" and take it to mean "What is the purpose of my life?" or "What am I meant to do?" These questions presuppose that a human life can have a purpose, and that is so only if God (or something like God) has a purpose for us. Many people of course doubt this. The selections in this chapter take for granted either that God does not exist or that God has no special role to play in an account of meaning in human life. Still, it's worth asking whether the existence of a God with a plan could give meaning to a life that would otherwise lack it.

   With this in mind, consider the following argument:

   (1) Suppose that there exists a God-like being who made you with the intention that you do something in particular: build a temple, lead a revolution, become a teacher, etc.

   (2) Either this goal is worth achieving anyway—independent of God's will—or it is not.

   (3) If it is worth achieving anyway, then a life devoted to it would be meaningful even if it were not God's purpose for you.

   (4) If it is *not* worth achieving anyway, then the mere fact that God wants you to do it cannot make it worth achieving.

   (5) Either way, the fact that God meant you to do something cannot make that thing worth doing.

   (6) So God's purpose for you—if he has one—is irrelevant to whether your life has meaning.

   Question: How might a proponent of the view that God's purposes give life meaning respond to this argument?

2. *Meaningfulness and autonomy.* In Aldous Huxley's novel *Brave New World*, citizens in a grim future dystopia are bred in laboratories and conditioned from birth to occupy narrowly circumscribed social roles. Farmers are conditioned to farm, to love living in the country, to have no interest in books or city life; coal miners are conditioned to love working in coal mines, to detest wide open spaces; and so on. This conditioning works: the farmers and coal miners are mostly happy. We can even imagine that they take pleasure in the genuinely valuable aspects of their lives. The farmers take satisfaction in working the land, providing food for others, and so on. The theories put forward by Taylor and Wolf appear to entail that these people whose desires have been manipulated from birth by a tyrannical state for its own purposes nonetheless lead fully meaningful human lives.

   Question: Is this an objection to Taylor and/or Wolf? If so, state the objection, and say how Taylor and/or Wolf might respond.

3. *Absurdity and epistemology.* In the normal course of life, we take for granted that certain things are worth doing. However, we are capable of "stepping back" and asking for a reason to believe that these things are really worth doing. According to Nagel,

it is when we realize that we cannot supply such a justification that our lives strike us as absurd. We see that for all we know, the things that matter to us don't really matter. And when we realize how much effort and energy we devote to these things, we seem to ourselves like Sisyphus: endlessly pursuing goals as if they mattered when for all we know they simply don't. The only question, then, is how to live with this sense of absurdity.

This line of thought involves a substantive assumption about knowledge. We can put it like this:

> If you cannot justify your belief that something is worth doing, then you don't *know* that it's worth doing.

Is this right? Consider the following response to Nagel:

> You're quite right to say that when I step back from my basic assumptions about value, I cannot provide verbal justifications for them. I can't persuade the skeptic that happiness, friendship, social justice, and the like are really worth pursuing. But it's not true in general that I can only know something if I can persuade the skeptic of its truth. I can know that I'm not dreaming (Chapter 6), that the future will resemble the past (Chapter 4), that other people have minds (Chapter 5), and possibly even that God exists (Chapter 2)—even if I can't justify these beliefs to the skeptic's satisfaction. And similarly, I can know that my own happiness and the happiness of others is worth pursuing even if I can't *say* why this is so. So I don't find my life absurd at all. Even when I step back and realize that I can't justify my beliefs about value, I still find it evident that those beliefs are true. So even from the "detached" point of view, I see my life as the pursuit of things that are worth pursuing.

For the view that we can know something even if we cannot provide justification for it, see Moore's "Proof of an External World" in Chapter 6 and Plantinga's "Is Belief in God Properly Basic?" in Chapter 2.

Exercise: Reconstruct Nagel's argument for the view that our lives are "absurd" as an explicit argument, making sure to state the epistemological premises. Then examine those premises and say how the argument might be resisted.

Part VI

POLITICAL PHILOSOPHY

How Can the State Be Justified?

Justifying the State

Imagine that you live in a place with lots of other people but without a state. Perhaps the state never existed. Or perhaps it existed but has now disappeared. Don't worry about the history. Just imagine that you are now living with others in a stateless condition.

What does it mean to live without a state? We have a state when a collection of people all live under a single political authority. A political authority makes and enforces rules of conduct (laws) in a territory. So I am asking you to imagine living without a common authority making and enforcing rules. You are in what some philosophers have called a **state of nature**. Anthropologists have written about stateless societies. But don't think of a state of nature as a primitive condition. Think of it, simply, as a situation—say, in your community—with no political authority. (The exercise is *hard*, but try it before you keep reading.)

One important feature of a state of nature is that there are no laws and no enforcement of public standards of conduct. You have to decide whether to keep your agreement to compensate me for the couch I delivered to you yesterday, whether to keep your hands off my shoes and food, and which shoes and food are yours and which are mine. You have to decide whether my decision to walk close to you represents a threat and, if it is, how to respond. You have to decide, as does everyone else.

Thomas Hobbes proposes this remarkable thought experiment in his *Leviathan*. Part of what is so remarkable is that he thought he could provide a definitive statement of what life would be like in the state of nature. In a world without authority, a world without public standards and enforcers, a world in which we each must rely on our own judgment and our powers, we would face, Hobbes says, a war of all against all. Not that we might. Not that we could. But that we *would*.

In the absence of a political authority, Hobbes thinks, human beings cannot live together in peace.

How do we get from that conclusion to a justification for the state? Assume, as Hobbes does, that a justification for the state is an argument directed to each individual who is subject to the state's authority—an argument designed to show that each of us, despite our many differences in interests, values, and circumstances, has sufficient reason to accept a common political authority. Variants on this idea of justification run through the **social contract** tradition in political philosophy.

Now, each of us arguably has very strong reasons to desire peace. And not just to desire it, but to act in ways that flow from that desire. We each have a very strong reason because, whatever else we care about, we care about living a happy life. But in a state of war, our lives would be, as Hobbes famously says in *Leviathan*, "solitary, poor, nasty, brutish, and short." And even more than we care about continuing to live, we fear violent death. To be sure, we sometimes celebrate violent death in the service of a great cause. But what could be worse than a violent death that serves no cause, a violent death that results simply from a lack of basic protections?

So a state of nature would be a state of war. And war is terrible for each of us. Because war is so terrible, we each have very good reason to seek peace. But how?

Suppose that we each acknowledge a common political authority—a **sovereign**, in Hobbes's terms—as having the right to rule. That authority makes and enforces public standards for conduct. You no longer need to rely solely on your own judgment of what is acceptable or of what is yours and what is mine. You no longer need to rely solely on your own capacity to protect yourself from people who may aggress against you, if only to protect themselves from what they judge to be your suspicious intentions. For these reasons, the authority can keep the peace, from which it follows that we each have sufficient reason to accept the authority of a state.

That, in essence, is Hobbes's contractual justification of the state.

This rationale for the state may seem too quick. The state of nature may be awful, but states can be awful, too. Even at their most benign, states deploy coercive tools to enforce the laws. And they are not always at their most benign. Political authorities may repress some groups of people; they may lead the state into destructive, adventurous wars; they may invade the homes and imprison the bodies of subjects.

These concerns about abuses of political authority seem especially troubling for the kind of sovereign that Hobbes defended. He argued for an **absolute sovereign**, a political authority with unlimited rule-making and rule-enforcing power. Only such an authority would suffice to keep the peace. The resulting restrictions on individual conduct, however unattractive, are needed to avoid the worst possible situation: a state of nature with what "is worst of all, continual fear and danger of violent death."

So the state is justified, according to Hobbes, because each of us has a compelling reason to accept the state's authority in exchange for the personal safety and the possibility of happiness that come with peace.

Anarchist Arguments

Anarchists reject this line of thought. Anarchists oppose the state. Not that they favor war and human calamity. Instead, they find fault with Hobbes's argument.

One kind of anarchist accepts the contractualist idea of justification but argues that Hobbes overstates the dangers in a state of nature and underplays the dangers in a state. Drawing on a mix of theoretical argument about human cooperation and historical evidence from stateless societies, these anarchists say that, even in the absence of a political authority, people are more capable than Hobbes thought. Moreover, even if a state of nature is dangerous, power is so easily abused that a state, which monopolizes the use of force, imposes greater dangers than we would face in a state of nature. And to the extent that we *do* face dangers, we have ways to address them without creating the greater dangers of a state. We can protect ourselves individually, or band together with others for self-defense, or we can hire other people to protect us. The result of such hirings will be a market in protection services, not a monopolist who extracts payments for protective services throughout the territory.

The anarchist may acknowledge that political authority will benefit *some* people. Still, it could be a bad bet for many, perhaps for most. So this first kind of anarchist might agree with Hobbes's contractual idea: that a justification needs to show that *each* person subject to the state has sufficient reason to accept its authority. But the anarchist who thinks a state of nature need not be so bad and that the state is a source of much misery rejects Hobbes's claim that each of us individually has a strong reason to accept the authority of the state.

A variant on this first kind of anarchism says that Hobbes's story about the absence of political authority is too general. Under some conditions—say, of deep social division—states may be needed to keep the peace. But in other conditions, states are not needed. Karl Marx[1] held a view of this kind. He thought that the state was needed in much of human history to serve the interests of a dominant social class (slave owners, or feudal lords, or capitalists) against the interests of subordinate social classes (slaves, or serfs, or wage laborers). But in a future classless society, without deep conflicts between social classes, the state would wither away.

A second kind of anarchist argues against the state from **utilitarian** premises. Utilitarians think that what is right is what produces the greatest sum of happiness. So they think that the state is justified if and only if the presence of the state yields a greater sum of human happiness than its absence. For utilitarians, then, a justification of the state does not need to show that each person has sufficient reason to accept the authority of the state. Utilitarians do not accept the contractualist idea of justification, with its focus on reasons for individuals. If some people do well in a state and others do not, the state is justified if and only if the gains for some outweigh the losses to others. For the utilitarian, then, the justification of

---

1. Karl Marx (1818–1883) was a German philosopher, economist, historian, and revolutionary activist. His most notable publications are *The Communist Manifesto* (1848) and *Capital* (1867–1894).

the state is a complex empirical question. Utilitarian anarchists would argue that the benefits of the state for some are outweighed by the greater losses to others.

A third kind of anarchist goes further. These anarchists think the state is not simply a bad bet. They say that states, virtually of necessity, violate our rights. We have rights to personal security and to basic liberty, they say. Moreover, we each have a right to protect these rights, and perhaps to protect the rights of others as well. John Locke, whose doctrine of **natural rights** in his *Two Treatises of Government* inspires this third anarchist argument, based these rights to protect other rights on what he called the "executive right of the law of nature"—a right we each have to protect ourselves and others from aggression. We can exercise our executive right by hiring someone to protect us, if we wish. But we can also reserve that right and exercise it ourselves.

Because we have a basic right to enforce our own rights (and the rights of others), what matters to the justification of the state is not simply that each of us has sufficient *reason* to accept the authority of a state, nor simply that it protects our other rights (to personal security and basic liberty). Instead, what matters is that we actually *agree* to hire someone to protect us. You may have reason to hire me to paint your house: the house desperately needs a fresh coat of paint. But unless you actually hire me—unless you actually consent—I am not justified in painting your house, no matter how much you may benefit. And I am certainly not justified in painting your house without your agreement and then sending you the bill. Similarly, these rights-based anarchists say, unless we each individually consent to the state's authority, it is impermissible for a state to claim authority over us. In his discussion of rights-based justifications for the state, John Simmons observes that the Lockean approach, with its focus on individual consent, may well lead us to anarchist conclusions because most political societies are simply not consensual associations.

Limited Authority

Hobbes justifies a Leviathan state. The anarchist denies that the state is justified. A third view rejects anarchism but thinks that only a state with limited political authority can be justified. Hobbes is partly right: we do need political authorities to provide basic protections. But we also need to ensure that they do not abuse their authority. The way to provide this assurance might be with such institutions as a constitution, rule of law, separation of powers, and democratic monitoring of the exercise of power. These political institutions help ensure that the authority we establish to keep the peace also protects our basic rights and interests better than if we are left to our own devices.

Utilitarian premises are one possible source of argument for such limits. A utilitarian justification for limited political authority would say that we get a greater sum of happiness from limited authority than from the unconditional authority of Hobbes's Leviathan state.

A more familiar argument for a state with limited authority is based on the **contractualist** idea of justification. According to the contractualist argument for limited authority, we do not have good reason to submit to an unlimited authority. Even if the state of nature is dangerous, unconditional authority can be dangerous, too, so we may be violating our obligations to ourselves and to others if we accept an authority without proper limits. In his classical statement of the contractualist argument for limited authority, Locke asked: Why should we protect ourselves from wily polecats and foxes by putting ourselves in the hands of a very powerful lion—a lion "made licentious by impunity"?

A Hobbesian understands the temptation to tie the hands of authorities. But the Hobbesian argues that such limits defeat the purpose of having a state. If we tie the hands of the authorities, what will happen when domestic or foreign dangers emerge? Tying the hands of the authority threatens a return to a state of nature, with all its terrible troubles.

By Whom and For Whom?

Both the Hobbesian and limited authority versions of contractualist theory base their justification of political authority on an agreement among individuals. But which individuals are assumed to participate in the agreement? Everyone in the world? No, contract theories have always focused on groups of people in separate territories. Everyone, then, within a well-defined territory? No, contract theories have always assumed that the agreement is confined to adults. So is it all adults, then?

Critics of the historical tradition of contract theory have explored a variety of exclusions from the collection of adults that are assumed to participate. One line of criticism says that only owners of property are assumed by the contract tradition to be sufficiently rational to participate in the initial agreement. So the initial agreement is a pact among property owners. They create a property-owners state, which is intended to protect their property from the propertyless.[2] Others have argued that the agreement is between and among men, who are assumed prior to the contract to be heads of male-dominated families.[3] So the initial agreement establishes a fraternal state, which serves the interests of men, in the first instance.

In his discussion of the Racial Contract, Charles Mills argues that the contract tradition is founded on racial exclusion. The fundamental pact, Mills argues, is exclusively an agreement among white people (or white men, or white male property owners). In the agreement, the white participants distinguish themselves from non-white people, who are defined as lesser and unable to govern themselves. The participants, Mills says, "categorize the remaining subset of humans as 'non-white' and of a different and inferior moral status, subpersons, so that they have a subordinate

2. C. B. MacPherson, *The Political Theory of Possessive Individualism* (Oxford University Press, 1962).

3. Carole Pateman, *The Sexual Contract* (Polity Press, 1988).

civil standing in the white of white-ruled polities." The initial agreement, then, establishes a white-supremacist state, which serves the economic and political interests of the dominant white group and establishes standards of knowledge that justify the racial exclusions. Mills says that this "differential privileging of the whites as a group with respect to the non-whites as a group" is a "basic" fact of modern politics. He argues that this differential privileging is not an inadvertent result of the social contract, but part of its fundamental nature.

Authority and Self-Government

Contractualist justifications for unlimited or limited authority present a picture of the state as founded on an exchange (made by the individual who are parties to the social contract). Contractualists think that we have sufficient reason to accept authority because, in return, we get greater security to our person, our goods, our lives, our rights. In exchange for these protections, we give obedience to rules made by the authorities. Contractualists disagree about the kinds of protections we get and the extent of the obedience we promise. But they agree that the individual persons who participate in the agreement sacrifice something they value when they have a state: their right to govern themselves.

It is hard to see an alternative. If we need to live by common rules, then each of us must accept governance by authorities who make the rules. Restrictions on our freedom appear to be the cost of political authority. How could it be otherwise?

It could be otherwise if we could live together under an authority that makes the rules but which is not a third-party rule maker and enforcer. Suppose instead that *we* are the authority. Imagine that the authority is a body of equals. Members of the body—citizens—act as a group to make rules for everyone. They make the rules for themselves and make them in the service of their common good.

An authority of that kind would solve what Jean-Jacques Rousseau describes in *The Social Contract* as the basic political problem: to find a way of living together that protects the person and the goods of each associate, while at the same time enabling each person to "remain as free as before." We need a common authority— Rousseau is not an anarchist—because our personal safety and well-being depend on shared, public rules that are enforced. But freedom is essential to our nature: "to renounce one's freedom is to renounce one's quality as a man, the rights of humanity, and even its duties." Because freedom cannot be alienated, we need to find a way to ensure security and opportunity that does not demand submission to the judgment and will of others.

Rousseau thinks we can achieve a state of this kind if, but only if, we treat one another as equal members of the sovereign authority and share a concern with others about the common good of our society. When that shared point of view lies at the basis of the laws, we each "follow the law one has prescribed to oneself." We achieve a kind of **autonomy**, which Rousseau calls "moral freedom."

In presenting his case, Rousseau relies on a version of the contractualist idea of justification. Political authority is justified by showing that each person subject to it has sufficient reason for accepting it. But the reason for being part of a common authority directed to the common good is not to pay a price in obedience for a compensating benefit in protection. The state is not based on an exchange. The reason for accepting political authority is that an equal share in political authority is how we express our nature as free. Correspondingly, the initial agreement does not assign authority to a third party. Instead, it is an agreement by individuals to form the "we" that then makes the rules.

The Best Life

The idea of a state as a self-governing community—a collection of citizens who express their free nature by ruling themselves—takes us some distance from Hobbes's justification of the state, with its emphasis on advancing our interests in life and happiness. But does the Rousseauean rationale for the state, focused on expressing our nature as free persons, accurately represent the greatest good that comes from a self-governing community of citizens? Aristotle suggests not. He offers a different account of what is at stake and a very different justification for the state, commonly described as **perfectionist**. "Our conclusion," he says, is that "political society exists for the sake of noble actions, and not of living together."

Neither the contractualist nor utilitarian justifications of the state draw on an idea of virtuous, noble actions. Perfectionists do, because they think of political philosophy as an extension of ethics, which is centrally concerned with better and worse—more or less virtuous and noble—ways to live a human life. "The true student of politics," Aristotle says in his *Nicomachean Ethics*, "is thought to have studied virtue above all things; for he wishes to make his fellow citizens good and obedient to the laws."

The best way to live, Aristotle argues, involves the virtuous exercise of our distinctive human powers of reasoning and deliberative judgment. The state is a "body of citizens" who govern themselves by playing a role in "deliberative or judicial administration." And the great good that comes from having a state is that it provides an occasion and venue for the virtuous exercise of those human powers. Though the state may "come into existence for the sake of the bare needs of life," Aristotle says, it continues to exist not simply to sustain life but "for the sake of the good life."

Rousseau does not justify the state in terms of its contribution to human virtue. Still, the Rousseauean and Aristotelian views do converge on an important point. For them, the justification of the state does not depend on the Hobbesian idea that the state of nature would be a disaster. Suppose instead that it would be a world of relative peace and material sufficiency. Still, the state would be justified as the only condition in which we can achieve a larger human good—a free community of equals, on Rousseau's view; the virtuous exercise of human powers, on Aristotle's. For them, the state is not the price we pay to avoid calamity. Instead, it enables us to do something of great value together that we cannot possibly do on our own—though as Charles Mills forcefully reminds us, it is essential to be clear about who this "we" is and to hold off on the celebration of larger political possibilities until we have an answer.

Aristotle (384–322 BCE)

Aristotle was born in Stagira and joined Plato's Academy when he was 18. A philosopher of extraordinary intellectual reach, he wrote remarkable and remarkably influential treatises on all areas of philosophy and science. His writings on logic, metaphysics, rhetoric, ethics, and politics continue to have a profound impact on philosophical discussion.

POLITICS

Book I

1. Every state[1] is a community of some kind, and every community is established with a view to some good; for everyone always acts in order to obtain that which they think good. But, if all communities aim at some good, the state or political community, which is the highest of all, and which embraces all the rest, aims at good in a greater degree than any other, and at the highest good. . . .

2. He who considers things in their first growth and origin, whether a state or anything else, will obtain the clearest view of them. In the first place there must be a union of those who cannot exist without each other; namely, of male and female, that the race may continue (and this is a union which is formed, not of choice, but because, in common with other animals and with plants, mankind have a natural desire to leave behind them an image of themselves), and of natural ruler and subject, that both may be preserved. For that which can foresee by the exercise of mind is by nature lord and master, and that which can with its body give effect to such foresight is a subject, and by nature a slave; hence master and slave have the same interest. . . .

Out of these two relationships the first thing to arise is the family, and Hesiod[2] is right when he says,

---

1. Aristotle's term is *polis*, which is sometimes translated as "city." When he discusses "states," he is thinking of Athens, Sparta, Thebes, Corinth, and other Greek city-states, which were all relatively small political units by modern standards. For example, in the fifth century BCE, some 250,000 people, including citizens, women, and slaves, lived in Athens, which was among the largest of the Greek city-states.

2. Hesiod was a Greek poet of the eighth century BCE. This quotation is taken from his poem *Works and Days* (II.405–13), which offers practical advice about daily life. He is also the author of *Theogony*, a mythic account of the origin of the universe.

First house and wife and an ox for the plough,

for the ox is the poor man's slave. The family is the association established by nature for the supply of men's everyday wants. . . . But when several families are united, and the association aims at something more than the supply of daily needs, the first society to be formed is the village. And the most natural form of the village appears to be that of a colony from the family, composed of the children and grandchildren, who are said to be "suckled with the same milk." . . .

When several villages are united in a single complete community, large enough to be nearly or quite self-sufficing, the state comes into existence, originating in the bare needs of life, and continuing in existence for the sake of a good life. And therefore, if the earlier forms of society are natural, so is the state, for it is the end of them, and the nature of a thing is its end. For what each thing is when fully developed, we call its nature, whether we are speaking of a man, a horse, or a family. Besides, the final cause and end of a thing is the best, and to be self-sufficing is the end and the best.

Hence it is evident that the state is a creation of nature, and that man is by nature a political animal. And he who by nature and not by mere accident is without a state, is either a bad man or above humanity; he is like the

Tribeless, lawless, hearthless one,

whom Homer[3] denounces—the natural outcast is forthwith a lover of war; he may be compared to an isolated piece at draughts.

Now, that man is more of a political animal than bees or any other gregarious animals is evident. Nature, as we often say, makes nothing in vain, and man is the only animal who has the gift of speech. And whereas mere voice is but an indication of pleasure or pain, and is therefore found in other animals (for their nature attains to the perception of pleasure and pain and the intimation of them to one another, and no further), the power of speech is intended to set forth the expedient and inexpedient, and therefore likewise the just and the unjust. And it is a characteristic of man that he alone has any sense of good and evil, of just and unjust, and the like, and the association of living beings who have this sense makes a family and a state. . . .

The proof that the state is a creation of nature and prior to the individual is that the individual, when isolated, is not self-sufficing; and therefore he is like a part in relation to the whole. But he who is unable to live in society, or who has no need because he is sufficient for himself, must be either a beast or a god: he is no part of a state. A social instinct is implanted in all men by nature, and yet he who first founded the state was the greatest of benefactors. For man, when perfected, is the best of animals, but, when separated from law and justice, he is the worst of all; since armed injustice is the more dangerous, and he is equipped at birth with arms, meant to be used by intelligence and

---

3. Homer is the name conventionally used for the Greek epic poet or poets, probably of the eighth century BCE, responsible for bringing the *Iliad* and *Odyssey* into written form. This quotation is taken from *Iliad* (IX.63). The Achaeans are in danger of losing the Trojan War and Nestor, a prominent Achaean elder, advises Agamemnon, the Achaean king, to reconcile with Achilles, the leading warrior.

excellence, which he may use for the worst ends. That is why, if he has not excellence, he is the most unholy and the most savage of animals, and the most full of lust and gluttony. But justice is the bond of men in states; for the administration of justice, which is the determination of what is just, is the principle of order in political society. . . .

Book III

1. He who would inquire into the essence and attributes of various kinds of government must first of all determine what a state is. . . . [A] state is composite, like any other whole made up of many parts—these are the citizens, who compose it. It is evident, therefore, that we must begin by asking, Who is the citizen, and what is the meaning of the term? . . . The citizen whom we are seeking to define is a citizen in the strictest sense, . . . and his special characteristic is that he shares in the administration of justice, and in offices. Now of offices some are discontinuous, and the same persons are not allowed to hold them twice, or can only hold them after a fixed interval; others have no limit of time—for example, the office of juryman or member of the assembly.[4] It may, indeed, be argued that these are not magistrates at all, and that their functions give them no share in the government. But surely it is ridiculous to say that those who have the supreme power do not govern. Let us not dwell further upon this, which is a purely verbal question; what we want is a common term including both juryman and member of the assembly. Let us, for the sake of distinction, call it "indefinite office," and we will assume that those who share in such office are citizens. This is the most comprehensive definition of a citizen, and best suits all those who are generally so called.

But . . . governments differ in kind, and some of them are prior and others are posterior; those which are faulty or perverted are necessarily posterior to those which are perfect. (What we mean by perversion will be hereafter explained.) The citizen then of necessity differs under each form of government; and our definition[5] is best adapted to the citizen of a democracy; but not necessarily to other states. For in some states [unlike democracies] the people are not acknowledged, nor have they any regular assembly, but only extraordinary ones; and lawsuits are distributed by sections among the magistrates. At Lacedaemon, for instance, the Ephors determine suits about contracts, which they distribute among themselves, while the elders are judges of homicide, and other causes are decided by other magistrates. . . . We may, indeed, modify our definition of the citizen so as to include these states. In them it is the holder of a definite, not an indefinite office, who is juryman and member of the

---

4. At the height of its democratic period, Athens distributed the functions of juryman and assembly member widely to free adult men (as many as 8,000 citizens would sometimes attend the assembly). This wide distribution to free adult men, without special election or appointment or qualification, is what Aristotle has in mind by an "indefinite office."

5. Aristotle is referring to the definition he stated in the previous paragraph, where he said that citizens are those who share in an *indefinite office*, with no time limit. He is emphasizing that in nondemocratic regimes, the responsibilities of juror (judging) and lawmaker (deliberating) are magisterial positions, or "definite offices."

assembly, and to some or all such holders of definite offices is reserved the right of deliberating or judging about some things or about all things. The conception of the citizen now begins to clear up.

He who has the power to take part in the deliberative or judicial administration of any state is said by us to be a citizen of that state,[6] and, speaking generally, a state is a body of citizens sufficing for the purposes of life. . . .

4. There is a point nearly allied to the preceding [discussion of who a citizen is]: Whether the excellence of a good man and a good citizen is the same or not. But before entering on this discussion, we must certainly first obtain some general notion of the excellence of the citizen. Like the sailor, the citizen is a member of a community. Now, sailors have different functions, for one of them is a rower, another a pilot, and a third a lookout man, a fourth is described by some similar term; and while the precise definition of each individual's excellence applies exclusively to him, there is, at the same time, a common definition applicable to them all. For they have all of them a common object, which is safety in navigation. Similarly, one citizen differs from another, but the salvation of the community is the common business of them all. This community is the constitution; the excellence of the citizen must therefore be relative to the constitution of which he is a member. If, then, there are many forms of government, it is evident that there is not one single excellence of the good citizen which is perfect excellence. But we say that the good man is he who has one single excellence which is perfect excellence. Hence it is evident that the good citizen need not of necessity possess the excellence which makes a good man.

The same question may also be approached by another road, from a consideration of the best constitution. If the state cannot be entirely composed of good men, and yet each citizen is expected to do his own business well, and must therefore have excellence, still, inasmuch as all the citizens cannot be alike, the excellence of the citizen and of the good man cannot coincide. All must have the excellence of the good citizen—thus, and thus only, can the state be perfect; but they will not have the excellence of a good man, unless we assume that in the good state all the citizens must be good. . . .

But will there then be no case in which the excellence of the good citizen and the excellence of the good man coincide? To this we answer that the good *ruler* is a good and wise man, but the citizen need not be wise. . . .

If the excellence of a good ruler is the same as that of a good man, and we assume further that the subject is a citizen as well as the ruler, the excellence of the good citizen and the excellence of the good man cannot be absolutely the same, although in some cases they may; for the excellence of a ruler differs from that of a citizen. It was the sense of this difference which made Jason[7] say that "he felt hungry when he was not a tyrant," meaning that he could not endure to live in a private station. But, on the other hand, it may be argued that men are praised for knowing both how to rule and how to obey, and

---

6. Having first defined a citizen as someone with an indefinite office, a definition most suited to democracy, now Aristotle corrects the definition to cover a broader range of regimes, democratic and nondemocratic: a citizen, he says, is anyone with authority to judge or deliberate.

7. Jason of Pherae was a tyrant, a *tagos* (a special office, like "great khan," held occasionally by charismatic leaders who exercised extraordinary power and commanded large armies) who ruled Thessaly 380–370 BCE.

he is said to be a citizen of excellence who is able to do both well. Now if we suppose the excellence of a good man to be that which rules, and the excellence of the citizen to include ruling and obeying, it cannot be said that they are equally worthy of praise. Since, then, it is sometimes thought that the ruler and the ruled must learn different things and not the same, but that the citizen must know and share in them both, the inference is obvious. There is, indeed, the rule of a master, which is concerned with menial offices—the master need not know how to perform these, but may employ others in the execution of them: the other would be degrading; and by the other I mean the power actually to do menial duties, which vary much in character and are executed by various classes of slaves, such, for example, as handicraftsmen, who, as their name signifies, live by the labour of their hands—under these the mechanic is included. Hence in ancient times, and among some nations, the working classes had no share in the government—a privilege which they only acquired under extreme democracy. Certainly the good man and the statesman and the good citizen ought not to learn the crafts of inferiors except for their own occasional use; if they habitually practise them, there will cease to be a distinction between master and slave.

But there is a rule of another kind, which is exercised over freemen and equals by birth—a constitutional rule, which the ruler must learn by obeying, as he would learn the duties of a general of cavalry by being under the orders of a general of cavalry, or the duties of a general of infantry by being under the orders of a general of infantry, and by having had the command of a regiment and of a company. It has been well said that he who has never learned to obey cannot be a good commander. The excellence of the two is not the same, but the good citizen ought to be capable of both; he should know how to govern like a freeman, and how to obey like a freeman—these are the excellences of a citizen. And, although the temperance and justice of a ruler are distinct from those of a subject, the excellence of a good man will include both; for the excellence of the good man who is free and also a subject, e.g. his justice, will not be one but will comprise distinct kinds, the one qualifying him to rule, the other to obey, and differing as the temperance and courage of men and women differ. For a man would be thought a coward if he had no more courage than a courageous woman, and a woman would be thought loquacious if she imposed no more restraint on her conversation than the good man; and indeed their part in the management of the household is different, for the duty of the one is to acquire, and of the other to preserve. Practical wisdom is the only excellence peculiar to the ruler: it would seem that all other excellences must equally belong to ruler and subject. The excellence of the subject is certainly not wisdom, but only true opinion; he may be compared to the maker of the flute, while his master is like the flute-player or user of the flute.

From these considerations may be gathered the answer to the question, whether the excellence of the good man is the same as that of the good citizen, or different, and how far the same, and how far different. . . .

6. Having determined these questions, we have next to consider whether there is only one form of government or many, and if many, what they are, and how many, and what are the differences between them.

A constitution is the arrangement of magistracies in a state, especially of the highest of all. The government is everywhere sovereign in the state, and the constitution is in fact the government. For example, in democracies the people are supreme, but in oligarchies, the few; and, therefore, we say that these two constitutions also are different: and so in other cases.

First, let us consider what is the purpose of a state, and how many forms of rule there are by which human society is regulated. . . .

The rule of a master, although the slave by nature and the master by nature have in reality the same interests, is nevertheless exercised primarily with a view to the interest of the master, but accidentally considers the slave, since, if the slave perish, the rule of the master perishes with him. On the other hand, the government of a wife and children and of a household, which we have called household management, is exercised in the first instance for the good of the governed or for the common good of both parties, but essentially for the good of the governed, as we see to be the case in medicine, gymnastic, and the arts in general, which are only accidentally concerned with the good of the artists themselves. For there is no reason why the trainer may not sometimes practise gymnastics, and the helmsman is always one of the crew. The trainer or the helmsman considers the good of those committed to his care. But, when he is one of the persons taken care of, he accidentally participates in the advantage, for the helmsman is also a sailor, and the trainer becomes one of those in training. And so in politics: when the state is framed upon the principle of equality and likeness, the citizens think that they ought to hold office by turns. Formerly, as is natural, everyone would take his turn of service; and then again, somebody else would look after his interest, just as he, while in office, had looked after theirs. But nowadays, for the sake of the advantage which is to be gained from the public revenues and from office, men want to be always in office. One might imagine that the rulers, being sickly, were only kept in health while they continued in office; in that case we may be sure that they would be hunting after places. The conclusion is evident: that governments which have a regard to the common interest are constituted in accordance with strict principles of justice, and are therefore true forms; but those which regard only the interest of the rulers are all defective and perverted forms, for they are despotic, whereas a state is a community of freemen.[8]. . .

9. [To understand what justice and the true forms are, let] us begin by considering the common definitions of oligarchy and democracy, and what is oligarchical and democratic justice. For all men cling to justice of some kind, but their conceptions are imperfect and they do not express the whole idea. . . . [I]f men met and associated out of regard to wealth only, their share in the state would be proportioned to their property, and the oligarchical doctrine would then seem to carry the day. It would not be just that he who paid one mina should have the same share of a hundred minae, whether of the principal or of the profits, as he who paid the remaining ninety-nine. But a state exists for the sake of a good life, and not for the sake of life only: if life only were the object, slaves and brute animals might form a state, but they cannot, for they have no share in happiness or in a life based on choice. Nor does a state exist for the sake of alliance

---

8. A state is a community that aims at the highest good. When the government exercises power for the benefit of the rulers, not for the common good, we have a "perverted form," not a true government and constitution, because a government is supposed to guide the community to the common good.

and security from injustice, nor yet for the sake of exchange and mutual intercourse; for then the Tyrrhenians and the Carthaginians, and all who have commercial treaties with one another, would be the citizens of one state. True, they have agreements about imports, and engagements that they will do no wrong to one another, and written articles of alliance. But there are no magistracies common to the contracting parties; different states have each their own magistracies. Nor does one state take care that the citizens of the other are such as they ought to be, nor see that those who come under the terms of the treaty do no wrong or wickedness at all, but only that they do no injustice to one another. Whereas, those who care for good government take into consideration political excellence and defect. Whence it may be further inferred that excellence must be the care of a state which is truly so called, and not merely enjoys the name: for without this end the community becomes a mere alliance which differs only in place from alliances of which the members live apart; and law is only a convention, "a surety to one another of justice," as the sophist Lycophron[9] says, and has no real power to make the citizens good and just. . . .

Again, if men dwelt at a distance from one another, but not so far off as to have no intercourse, and there were laws among them that they should not wrong each other in their exchanges, neither would this be a state. Let us suppose that one man is a carpenter, another a farmer, another a shoemaker, and so on, and that their number is ten thousand: nevertheless, if they have nothing in common but exchange, alliance, and the like, that would not constitute a state. Why is this? Surely not because they are at a distance from one another; for even supposing that such a community were to meet in one place, but that each man had a house of his own, which was in a manner his state, and that they made alliance with one another, but only against evildoers; still an accurate thinker would not deem this to be a state, if their intercourse with one another was of the same character after as before their union. It is clear then that a state is not a mere society, having a common place, established for the prevention of mutual crime and for the sake of exchange. These are conditions without which a state cannot exist; but all of them together do not constitute a state, which is a community of families and aggregations of families in well-being, for the sake of a perfect and self-sufficing life. Such a community can only be established among those who live in the same place and intermarry. Hence there arise in cities family connexions, brotherhoods, common sacrifices, amusements which draw men together. But these are created by friendship, for to choose to live together is friendship. The end of the state is the good life, and these are the means towards it. And the state is the union of families and villages in a perfect and self-sufficing life, by which we mean a happy and honourable life.

Our conclusion, then, is that political society exists for the sake of noble actions, and not of living together. Hence they who contribute most to such a society have a greater share in it than those who have the same or a greater freedom or nobility of birth but are inferior to them in political excellence; or than those who exceed them in wealth but are surpassed by them in excellence. . . .

9. Lycophron was a Greek Sophist. The Sophists were itinerant teachers who claimed to be able to teach students (for a fee) the correct way to manage one's own affairs and the affairs of the state.

TEST YOUR UNDERSTANDING

1. Aristotle says that the "state is a composite, like any other whole made up of many parts." What are the parts that he is referring to?

2. What is the defining feature of a "citizen in the strictest sense"?

3. What does Aristotle mean by a "constitution"?

4. How does Aristotle understand the purpose or "end" of the state? Is the central purpose to promote life, to ensure peace, or to foster a good and noble life?

NOTES AND QUESTIONS

1. Much of the Aristotle selection comes from Book III of his *Politics*, in which Aristotle presents a general account of *constitutions*. A constitution is the way a political society is organized, how it makes decisions. It is "the arrangement of magistracies in a state, especially the highest of all" (Book III, section 6 of the selection). Aristotle's account is not focused exclusively on laws and formal institutions of decision making but on who effectively exercises the ruling power, and for what purposes (by whom and for whom the decisions are made). Thus, Aristotle classifies constitutions on two dimensions:

   (i) What are the purposes for which political rule is exercised? In particular, is the constitution "true" or "perverse"? In true constitutions, rule is exercised for the common good; in perverse (corrupt) constitutions, rule is exercised for the benefit of rulers.

   (ii) Who exercises the ruling power? In particular, is supreme authority in the hands of one, a few, or many? Typically, when a few govern, it is the few rich; when it is many, it is the poor.

   Putting the two dimensions together, then, we have a sixfold classification of constitutions. The true constitutions are kingship (one), aristocracy (few), and, simply, a constitution (many). The perverse constitutions are tyranny, oligarchy, and democracy. Here, democracy is rule by the many for the benefit of the "needy," not for the "common good of all."

   The overall structure of the *Politics*, then, is as follows: In Book I, Aristotle presents a general account of the distinction between the household and polity, as different human communities, and discusses different kinds of rule (master over slave; man over wife and children; citizens over one another). Book II discusses and criticizes previous views of the best constitution, as well as a few actual constitutions that were widely thought to be well governed. Book III presents a general account of constitutions and citizenship. In Books IV–VI, Aristotle discusses actual constitutions, with a particular focus on democracy and oligarchy, and revolutions. In the final books, he considers the ideal form of state, including discussion of size, location, social structure, and education, as well as the larger purposes that politics serves.

   Bear these points about constitutions and their differences in mind as you consider Aristotle's discussion of the relationship between the good man and the good citizen. This issue is fundamental for Aristotle because he thinks of politics as continuous with ethics, which is centrally concerned with the human good (see Aristotle, *Nicomachean*

Ethics, trans. Terence Irwin [Hackett, 1985], book X, chapter 9). In section 4 of Book III in the selection from *Politics*, he starts by raising the issue of "Whether the excellence of a good man and a good citizen is the same or not." Drawing on the sketch provided above of types of constitutions, reconstruct Aristotle's argument for the conclusion that "the good citizen need not of necessity possess the excellence which makes a good man." How does that argument differ from the arguments in the subsequent paragraphs of section 4, beginning with "The same question...." and then with "But will there then be no case..."? Aristotle ends section 4 by saying, "From these considerations may be gathered the answer to the question, whether the excellence of the good man is the same as that of the good citizen, or different, and how far the same, and how far different." What is the answer?

2. In his discussion of "oligarchical and democratic justice" (Book III, section 9 of the selection), Aristotle says that "all men cling to justice of some kind, but their conceptions are imperfect and they do not express the whole idea." This comment is very important. Aristotle is saying that people are misled in politics not simply because they do not care about justice. Some people do care about justice, but are misguided about what justice requires. Correspondingly, it is important both that people pay attention to justice, and that they have reasonable ideas about justice.

    How does Aristotle apply this point about imperfect and partial ideas of justice in his criticism of oligarchical justice in section 9, beginning with "if men met and associated out of regard to wealth only . . ."? Drawing on the example Aristotle discusses, try to formulate the view of the proponent of oligarchical justice. What is the fundamental mistake of the proponent of oligarchical justice? (The trick is to see how the fundamental mistake reflects a broad misconception of the nature of the state, of its central purpose.)

Thomas Hobbes (1588–1679)

Hobbes was born in Malmesbury, England. He wrote on a wide range of philosophical, scientific, and historical topics but is best known for his contributions to political philosophy. His *Leviathan* (1651) is perhaps the most influential work of modern political philosophy. Though most political philosophers have rejected his absolutist conclusions, Hobbes's argument for the state, his defense of sovereignty, and his contractual reasoning continue to exercise considerable influence on political thought.

LEVIATHAN

Chapter XIII: Of the Natural Condition of Mankind, as Concerning Their Felicity, and Misery

Nature hath made men so equal in the faculties of body and mind as that, though there be found one man sometimes manifestly stronger in body or of quicker mind than another, yet when all is reckoned together the difference between man and man is not so considerable as that one man can thereupon claim to himself any benefit to which another may not pretend as well as he. For as to the strength of body, the weakest has strength enough to kill the strongest, either by secret machination, or by confederacy with others that are in the same danger with himself.

And as to the faculties of the mind—setting aside the arts grounded upon words, and especially that skill of proceeding upon general and infallible rules called science (which very few have, and but in few things), as being not a native faculty (born with us), nor attained (as prudence) while we look after somewhat else—I find yet a greater equality amongst men than that of strength. For prudence is but experience, which equal time equally bestows on all men in those things they equally apply themselves unto. That which may perhaps make such equality incredible is but a vain conceit of one's own wisdom, which almost all men think they have in a greater degree than the vulgar, that is, than all men but themselves and a few others whom, by fame or for concurring with themselves, they approve. . . .

From this equality of ability ariseth equality of hope in the attaining of our ends. And therefore, if any two men desire the same thing, which nevertheless they cannot both enjoy, they become enemies; and in the way to their end, which is principally their own conservation, and sometimes their delectation only, endeavour to destroy or subdue one another. And from hence it comes to pass that, where an invader hath no more to fear than another man's single power, if one plant, sow, build, or possess a convenient seat, others may probably be expected to come prepared with forces united, to dispossess and deprive him, not only of the fruit of his labour, but also of his life or liberty. And the invader again is in the like danger of another.

And from this diffidence[1] of one another, there is no way for any man to secure himself so reasonable as anticipation, that is, by force or wiles to master the persons of all men he can, so long till he see no other power great enough to endanger him. And this is no more than his own conservation requireth, and is generally allowed. Also, because there be some that taking pleasure in contemplating their own power in the acts of conquest, which they pursue farther than their security requires, if others (that otherwise would be glad to be at ease within modest bounds) should not by invasion increase their power, they would not be able, long time, by standing only on their defence, to subsist. And by consequence, such augmentation of dominion over men being necessary to a man's conservation, it ought to be allowed him.

Again, men have no pleasure, but on the contrary a great deal of grief, in keeping company where there is no power able to over-awe them all. For every man looketh that his companion should value him at the same rate he sets upon himself, and upon all signs of contempt, or undervaluing, naturally endeavours, as far as he dares (which amongst them that have no common power to keep them in quiet, is far enough to make them destroy each other), to extort a greater value from his contemners, by damage, and from others, by the example.

So that in the nature of man we find three principal causes of quarrel: first, competition; secondly, diffidence; thirdly, glory.

---

1. "Diffidence," in its archaic usage, means "distrust."

The first maketh men invade for gain; the second, for safety; and the third, for reputation. The first use violence to make themselves masters of other men's persons, wives, children, and cattle; the second, to defend them; the third, for trifles, as a word, a smile, a different opinion, and any other sign of undervalue, either direct in their persons, or by reflection in their kindred, their friends, their nation, their profession, or their name.

Hereby it is manifest that during the time men live without a common power to keep them all in awe, they are in that condition which is called war, and such a war as is of every man against every man. For WAR consisteth not in battle only, or the act of fighting, but in a tract of time wherein the will to contend by battle is sufficiently known. And therefore, the notion of *time* is to be considered in the nature of war, as it is in the nature of weather. For as the nature of foul weather lieth not in a shower or two of rain, but in an inclination thereto of many days together, so the nature of war consisteth not in actual fighting, but in the known disposition thereto during all the time there is no assurance to the contrary. All other time is PEACE.

Whatsoever therefore is consequent to a time of war, where every man is enemy to every man, the same is consequent to the time wherein men live without other security than what their own strength and their own invention shall furnish them withal. In such condition there is no place for industry, because the fruit thereof is uncertain, and consequently, no culture of the earth, no navigation, nor use of the commodities that may be imported by sea, no commodious building, no instruments of moving and removing such things as require much force, no knowledge of the face of the earth, no account of time, no arts, no letters, no society, and which is worst of all, continual fear and danger of violent death, and the life of man, solitary, poor, nasty, brutish, and short.

It may seem strange, to some man that has not well weighed these things, that nature should thus dissociate, and render men apt to invade and destroy one another. And he may, therefore, not trusting to this inference made from the passions, desire perhaps to have the same confirmed by experience. Let him therefore consider with himself—when taking a journey, he arms himself, and seeks to go well accompanied; when going to sleep, he locks his doors; when even in his house, he locks his chests; and this when he knows there be laws, and public officers, armed, to revenge all injuries shall be done him—what opinion he has of his fellow subjects, when he rides armed; of his fellow citizens, when he locks his doors; and of his children and servants, when he locks his chests. Does he not there as much accuse mankind by his actions, as I do by my words? . . .

To this war of every man against every man, this also is consequent: that nothing can be unjust. The notions of right and wrong, justice and injustice, have there no place. Where there is no common power, there is no law; where no law, no injustice. Force and fraud are in war the two cardinal virtues. Justice and injustice are none of the faculties neither of the body, nor mind. If they were, they might be in a man that were alone in the world, as well as his senses and passions. They are qualities that relate to men in society, not in solitude. It is consequent also to the same condition that there be no propriety, no dominion, no *mine* and *thine* distinct, but only that to be every man's that he can get, and for so long as he can keep it. And thus much for the ill condition which man by mere nature is actually placed in, though with a possibility to come out of it, consisting partly in the passions, partly in his reason. . . .

Chapter XVII: Of the Causes, Generation, and Definition of a Commonwealth

The final cause, end, or design of men (who naturally love liberty and dominion over others) in the introduction of that restraint upon themselves in which we see them live in commonwealths is the foresight of their own preservation, and of a more contented life thereby; that is to say, of getting themselves out from that miserable condition of war, which is necessarily consequent (as hath been shown [chapter XIII]) to the natural passions of men, when there is no visible power to keep them in awe. . . .

[B]e there never so great a multitude, yet if their actions be directed according to their particular judgments and particular appetites, they can expect thereby no defence, nor protection, neither against a common enemy, nor against the injuries of one another. For being distracted in opinions concerning the best use and application of their strength, they do not help, but hinder one another, and reduce their strength by mutual opposition to nothing; whereby they are easily, not only subdued by a very few that agree together, but also when there is no common enemy, they make war upon each other, for their particular interests. For if we could suppose a great multitude of men to consent in the observation of justice and other laws of nature[2] without a common power to keep them all in awe, we might as well suppose all mankind to do the same; and then there neither would be, nor need to be, any civil government or commonwealth at all, because there would be peace without subjection.

The only way to erect such a common power as may be able to defend them from the invasion of foreigners and the injuries of one another, and thereby to secure them in such sort as that by their own industry, and by the fruits of the earth, they may nourish themselves and live contentedly, is to confer all their power and strength upon one man, or upon one assembly of men, that may reduce all their wills, by plurality of voices, unto one will, which is as much as to say, to appoint one man or assembly of men to bear their person, and every one to own and acknowledge himself to be author of whatsoever he that so beareth their person shall act or cause to be acted, in those things which concern the common peace and safety, and therein to submit their wills, every one to his will, and their judgments, to his judgment. This is more than consent, or concord; it is a real unity of them all, in one and the same person, made by covenant of every man with every man, in such manner as if every man should say to every man *I authorise and give up my right of governing myself to this man, or to this assembly of men, on this condition, that thou give up thy right to him, and authorize all*

2. Natural laws, for Hobbes, are rules of peaceful cooperation that can be discovered by reason. Justice—which is, Hobbes says, a matter of keeping valid agreements—is among those requirements of natural law. Hobbes discusses these issues in detail in *Leviathan*, chapters 14 and 15.

his actions in like manner. This done, the multitude so united in one person is called a COMMONWEALTH, in Latin CIVITAS. This is the generation of that great LEVIATHAN[3] or rather (to speak more reverently) of that *Mortal God* to which we owe, under the *Immortal God,* our peace and defence. For by this authority, given him by every particular man in the commonwealth, he hath the use of so much power and strength conferred on him that by terror thereof he is enabled to conform the wills of them all to peace at home and mutual aid against their enemies abroad. And in him consisteth the essence of the commonwealth, which (to define it) is *one person, of whose acts a great multitude, by mutual covenants one with another, have made themselves every one the author, to the end he may use the strength and means of them all, as he shall think expedient, for their peace and common defence.*

And he that carrieth this person is called SOVEREIGN, and said to have *Sovereign Power;* and every one besides, his SUBJECT. . . .

Chapter XVIII: Of the Rights of Sovereigns by Institution

A *commonwealth* is said to be *instituted,* when a *multitude* of men do agree and *covenant, every one with every one,* that to whatsoever *man* or *assembly of men* shall be given by the major part the *right* to *present* the person of them all (that is to say, to be their *representative*) every one, as well he that *voted for it* as he that *voted against it,* shall *authorize* all the actions and judgments of that man or assembly of men, in the same manner as if they were his own, to the end, to live peaceably amongst themselves and be protected against other men.

From this institution of a commonwealth are derived all the *rights* and *faculties* of him, or them, on whom the sovereign power is conferred by the consent of the people assembled.

First, because they covenant, it is to be understood they are not obliged by former covenant to anything repugnant hereunto. And consequently they that have already instituted a commonwealth, being thereby bound by covenant to own the actions and judgments of one, cannot lawfully make a new covenant amongst themselves to be obedient to any other, in any thing whatsoever, without his permission. And therefore, they that are subjects to a monarch cannot without his leave cast off monarchy and return to the confusion of a disunited multitude, nor transfer their person from him that beareth it to another man, or other assembly of men; for they are bound, every man to every man, to own, and be reputed author of, all that he that already is their sovereign shall do and judge fit to be done; so that, any one man dissenting, all the rest should break their covenant made to that man, which is injustice. And they have also

---

3. In the Old Testament, Book of Job (41:33–34), Leviathan is the great whale, about whom God says: "Upon earth there is not his like, who is made without fear. He beholdeth all high *things:* he *is* a king over all the children of pride."

every man given the sovereignty to him that beareth their person; and therefore if they depose him, they take from him that which is his own, and so again it is injustice. . . .

Secondly, because the right of bearing the person of them all is given to him they make sovereign by covenant only of one to another, and not of him to any of them, there can happen no breach of covenant on the part of the sovereign; and consequently none of his subjects, by any pretence of forfeiture, can be freed from his subjection.

That he which is made sovereign maketh no covenant with his subjects beforehand is manifest, because either he must make it with the whole multitude, as one party to the covenant, or he must make a several covenant with every man. With the whole, as one party, it is impossible, because as yet they are not one person; and if he make so many several covenants as there be men, those covenants after he hath the sovereignty are void, because what act soever can be pretended by any one of them for breach thereof is the act both of himself and of all the rest, because done in the person and by the right of every one of them in particular.

Besides, if any one (or more) of them pretend a breach of the covenant made by the sovereign at his institution, and others (or one other) of his subjects (or himself alone) pretend there was no such breach, there is in this case no judge to decide the controversy; it returns therefore to the sword again; and every man recovereth the right of protecting himself by his own strength, contrary to the design they had in the institution. . . .

Thirdly, because the major part hath by consenting voices declared a sovereign, he that dissented must now consent with the rest, that is, be contented to avow all the actions he shall do, or else justly be destroyed by the rest. For if he voluntarily entered into the congregation of them that were assembled, he sufficiently declared thereby his will (and therefore tacitly covenanted) to stand to what the major part should ordain; and therefore, if he refuse to stand thereto, or make protestation against any of their decrees, he does contrary to his covenant, and therefore unjustly. And whether he be of the congregation or not, and whether his consent be asked or not, he must either submit to their decrees or be left in the condition of war he was in before, wherein he might without injustice be destroyed by any man whatsoever.

Fourthly, because every subject is by this institution author of all the actions and judgments of the sovereign instituted, it follows that, whatsoever he doth, it can be no injury to any of his subjects, nor ought he to be by any of them accused of injustice. For he that doth anything by authority from another doth therein no injury to him by whose authority he acteth; but by this institution of a commonwealth every particular man is author of all the sovereign doth; and consequently he that complaineth of injury from his sovereign complaineth of that whereof he himself is author, and therefore ought not to accuse any man but himself; no nor himself of injury, because to do injury to one's self is impossible. It is true that they that have sovereign power may commit iniquity, but not injustice, or injury in the proper signification.

Fifthly, and consequently to that which was said last, no man that hath sovereign power can justly be put to death, or otherwise in any manner by his subjects punished. For seeing every subject is author of the actions of his sovereign, he punisheth another for the actions committed by himself.

And because the end of this institution is the peace and defence of them all, and whosoever has right to the end has right to the means, it belongeth of right to whatsoever man or assembly that hath the sovereignty, to be judge both of the means of peace and defence, and also of the hindrances and disturbances of the same, and to do whatsoever he shall think necessary to be done, both beforehand (for the preserving of peace and security, by prevention of discord at home and hostility from abroad) and, when peace and security are lost, for the recovery of the same. And therefore,

Sixthly, it is annexed to the sovereignty to be judge of what opinions and doctrines are averse, and what conducing, to peace; and consequently, on what occasions, how far, and what men are to be trusted withal, in speaking to multitudes of people, and who shall examine the doctrines of all books before they be published. For the actions of men proceed from their opinions, and in the well-governing of opinions consisteth the well-governing of men's actions, in order to their peace and concord. And though in matter of doctrine nothing ought to be regarded but the truth, yet this is not repugnant to regulating of the same by peace. For doctrine repugnant to peace can no more be true than peace and concord can be against the law of nature. . . .

Seventhly, is annexed to the sovereignty the whole power of prescribing the rules whereby every man may know what goods he may enjoy, and what actions he may do, without being molested by any of his fellow-subjects; and this is it men call *propriety*. For before constitution of sovereign power (as hath already been shown) all men had right to all things, which necessarily causeth war; and therefore, this propriety, being necessary to peace, and depending on sovereign power, is the act of that power, in order to the public peace. . . .

Eighthly, is annexed to the sovereignty the right of judicature, that is to say, of hearing and deciding all controversies which may arise concerning law (either civil or natural) or concerning fact. For without the decision of controversies there is no protection of one subject against the injuries of another, the laws concerning *meum* and *tuum* are in vain, and to every man remaineth, from the natural and necessary appetite of his own conservation, the right of protecting himself by his private strength, which is the condition of war, and contrary to the end for which every commonwealth is instituted.

Ninthly, is annexed to the sovereignty the right of making war and peace with other nations and commonwealths, that is to say, of judging when it is for the public good, and how great forces are to be assembled, armed, and paid for that end, and to levy money upon the subjects to defray the expenses thereof. For the power by which the people are to be defended consisteth in their armies; and the strength of an army, in the union of their strength under one command; which command the sovereign instituted therefore hath, because the command of the *militia*, without other institution, maketh him that hath it sovereign. And therefore, whosoever is made general of an army, he that hath the sovereign power is always generalissimo. . . .

These are the rights which make the essence of sovereignty, and which are the marks whereby a man may discern in what man, or assembly of men, the sovereign power is placed and resideth. For these are incommunicable and inseparable. The power to coin money, to dispose of the estate and persons of infant heirs, to have preemption in markets, and all other statute prerogatives may be transferred by the sovereign, and yet the power to protect his subjects be retained. But if he transfer the *militia,* he retains the judicature in vain, for want of execution of the laws; or if he grant away the power of raising money, the *militia* is in vain; or if he give away the government of doctrines, men will be frighted into rebellion with the fear of spirits. And so if we consider any one of the said rights, we shall presently see, that the holding of all the rest will produce no effect, in the conservation of peace and justice, the end for which all commonwealths are instituted.

But a man may here object that the condition of subjects is very miserable, as being obnoxious to the lusts and other irregular passions of him or them that have so unlimited a power in their hands. And commonly, they that live under a monarch think it the fault of monarchy, and they that live under the government of democracy or other sovereign assembly attribute all the inconvenience to that form of commonwealth (whereas the power in all forms, if they be perfect enough to protect them, is the same), not considering that the estate of man can never be without some incommodity or other, and that the greatest that in any form of government can possibly happen to the people in general is scarce sensible,[4] in respect of the miseries and horrible calamities that accompany a civil war (or that dissolute condition of masterless men, without subjection to laws and a coercive power to tie their hands from rapine and revenge), nor considering that the greatest pressure of sovereign governors proceedeth not from any delight or profit they can expect in the damage or weakening of their subjects (in whose vigour consisteth their own strength and glory), but in the restiveness of themselves that, unwillingly contributing to their own defence, make it necessary for their governors to draw from them what they can in time of peace, that they may have means on any emergent occasion, or sudden need, to resist or take advantage on their enemies. For all men are by nature provided of notable multiplying glasses (that is their passions and self-love), through which every little payment appeareth a great grievance, but are destitute of those prospective glasses (namely moral and civil science), to see afar off the miseries that hang over them, and cannot without such payments be avoided.

TEST YOUR UNDERSTANDING

1. Hobbes's discussion of the state of war explores "three principal sources of quarrel." What are these sources?

2. What do people need to do to "erect . . . a common power as may be able to defend them from the invasion of foreigners and the injuries of one another?"

3. What are some of the "rights and faculties" of the sovereign? Describe in your own words three rights that Hobbes mentions.

4. Hobbes says that people have "notable multiplying glasses" but are "destitute of prospective glasses." What does he mean?

4. "Scarce sensible" literally means "barely noticeable." In the context, Hobbes is saying that the worst things that can happen under any form of government are hardly comparable to the horrors of the state of nature.

READER'S GUIDE

Hobbes's State of Nature

What would life be like without a political authority that makes and enforces rules? Some people think it would be peaceful, humane, and free. Hobbes disagrees. He paints a grim picture of life without political authority. It would be a state of war—a war of "every man against every man," in which our lives would be "solitary, poor, nasty, brutish, and short." Let's call this claim the *natural war thesis*:

> People living together without a common political authority are in a state of war.

The only way to end the war, keep the peace, and avoid these miserable consequences is, Hobbes argues, for us all to submit to a powerful political authority.

Why is Hobbes so confident that life would be so dismal? How does he defend the natural war thesis? He calls his argument an "inference made from the passions." We draw an inference when we reason from premises to a conclusion. The natural war thesis is the conclusion of Hobbes's inference. So what are the premises and what is the reasoning?

As a first premise, Hobbes asks us to assume that we are living together in a "state of nature," with no political authority. We have no laws, no police or courts, no legislatures or city councils, no army or navy. If you take my food, I cannot sue you or call the police. If you assault me, I have only my own strength to rely on, along with the strength of others whom I may be able to recruit to my cause. If I agree with you to work together on building a house, I have no legal recourse if I do my part and you break the agreement. Faced with theft, assault, and contract breaking, I cannot call on an authority to help because the state of nature lacks any political authority.

So we are in a state of nature: Why will things work out so badly? Hobbes bases his reasoning on a few claims about human nature, in particular "three principal causes of quarrel: first, competition; secondly, diffidence; thirdly, glory." About these, he says: "The first maketh men invade for gain; the second, for safety; and the third, for reputation." So passions for gain, for safety, and for reputation are the basis of the inference.

The first premise about human nature, then, is that we human beings have a passion for gain—a desire to improve our circumstances and "equality of hope in attaining our ends." The idea is that people in the state of nature may end up in a state of war because some people will try to win benefits ("gain") by taking from or injuring others. This first concern has some force, but it does not take us all the way to war. Invading for gain may be a good way to improve my circumstances, but I also have to worry that I may risk my life. And Hobbes insists that we value life more than we value gain. Maybe, then, I should pursue the desire for gain by making instead of taking. So if we focus just on the passion for gain, the case for the natural war thesis is not so clear.

The second premise about human nature is that human beings have a passion for security and "diffidence"—or mistrust—about how others will act. This idea is trickier but very important. Suppose you and I are in the state of nature and living near one another. I think you *might* come after me and my goods and threaten my "life or liberty." Maybe I am wrong. Maybe you may have no such design. But I have no assurance against your assault (that is what Hobbes means by "diffidence"). To protect myself, then, I may decide to attack you preemptively. I move first, but my goal is purely defensive. Notice that you are in the same situation as me. You do not want to attack me but may be worried that I am going to come after you. You prepare to defend yourself or even to attack me preemptively. When I see you preparing, I think your preparations confirm my fears about an attack from you. No one is being aggressive, and no one wants to fight: our passion is for security. We are just defending ourselves against potential assaults in conditions in which no authority will prevent the assaults or punish the assaulters.

Of course, attacking—like taking from other people—carries risks. But I may judge that those risks are smaller than waiting for you to come after me. Moreover, suppose I think you are a threat and see that you are pretty powerful. Before I come after you, I need first to accumulate more resources. To accumulate resources quickly, I decide to take from other people. I use "force or wiles to master the persons" of lots of other people and plan to use them in the attack on you.

The idea, then, is that each of us is ready to fight with other people, but all for a defensive purpose—because of the passion for security. Each of us wants to ensure our own security in a world in which there is no authority whose job is provide security.

The third premise about human nature is that some human beings have a passion for glory. Suppose I think you are going to come after me in the state of nature not because you want what I have (passion for gain), and not because you are preemptively protecting yourself from what you see as my threat (passion for safety). Instead, I think you may be one of those people who takes "pleasure in contemplating their own power in the acts of conquest." I may have no taste for glory myself—I would be "glad to be at ease within modest bounds." But to protect myself from you, I need to accumulate power, perhaps "by invasion," since this "augmentation of dominion over men" may be required for my "conservation." I pursue power over others not because of my own passion for glory but for the sake of safety from others who do have a passion for glory.

When you put these three considerations together, the case for conflict in the state of nature is pretty strong. I worry that there are glory-seekers around who are going to try to get power over me. I also worry that people are going to try to control me and my resources because they think they need them in order to protect themselves from other people who are trying to protect themselves. So I think I better protect myself. But as I mass resources to protect myself, other people worry about me and prepare to fight with me. If we all had plenty of resources, maybe the problem would not be so hard to solve. But faced with limited resources, we will look for ways to get what belongs to other people, if only to have enough to protect ourselves.

So the inference in support of the natural war thesis is based on passions for gain, safety, and glory. If we assume that people are moved by those passions, and also assume that they are in a state of nature with no protection from an authority, the case for conflict seems pretty strong: if not fully compelling, it is at least worth confronting. And confronting it means thinking hard about whether Hobbes is right in his premises about what people are like.

NOTES AND QUESTIONS

1. Hobbes begins his account of the state of nature by discussing certain kinds of equality. In what ways does he think human beings are equal? Do you find what he says plausible? Why does equality of "prudence," in particular, matter to his subsequent argument?

For discussion, see Kinch Hoekstra, "Hobbesian Equality," in *Hobbes Today: Insights for the 21st Century*, ed. S. A. Lloyd (Cambridge University Press, 2012), 76–112.

2. According to Hobbes, "when men live without a common power to keep them all in awe, they are in that condition which is called war, and such a war as is of every man against every man." Hobbes is saying that *without a strong power over everyone, people will be in a state of war*. For the italicized conclusion, present a **valid argument** starting from premises that you believe Hobbes endorses in the selection from *Leviathan*. Your reconstruction will need to include definitions of "common power" and "war."

   As a helpful starting point on this issue, see Jean Hampton, *Hobbes and the Social Contract Tradition* (Cambridge University Press, 1988). Also see the "Reader's Guide" to this selection.

3. If people care a great deal about self-preservation and peace, why are they unable, in the absence of a common power, to avoid conflict? And how is a sovereign able to resolve the conflicts and keep the peace? For example, suppose people end up in a state of war because they do not trust each other. To ensure peace, does the state need to get them to trust each other? How does it manage that? Suppose they end up in a state of war because some people think they are better than others. To ensure peace, does the state need them to stop thinking that? What else can the sovereign do?

4. The only way to achieve a stable peace, Hobbes says, is by creating a "real unity . . . in one and the same person." What is this "real unity"? How is it created? (You will need to think hard about Hobbes's understanding of a sovereign, and his idea of authorizing the sovereign.) Real unity is supposed to be different from "consent and concord." How so?

5. Hobbes gives us a detailed list of the rights that belong to the sovereign. Does the sovereign need all of these rights to keep the peace? Which rights do you think are not really needed? Why?

Jean-Jacques Rousseau (1712–1778)

Rousseau was born in Geneva. He was a philosopher, composer, and novelist whose writings exercised considerable impact on the French Revolution. Rousseau's *Confessions* shaped modern conventions of autobiography; his *Emile* remains an important work on education; his two *Discourses—On the Arts and Sciences* and *On Inequality*—are foundational works for the critique of modern culture; and his *The Social Contract* is an essential contribution to modern democratic thought. Rousseau exercised a profound influence on Immanuel Kant, who once described him as the Newton of the moral world.

THE SOCIAL CONTRACT

Book I

CHAPTER ONE: SUBJECT OF THIS FIRST BOOK

Man is born free, and everywhere he is in chains. One believes himself the others' master, and yet is more a slave than they. How did this change come about? I do not know. What can make it legitimate? I believe I can solve this question. . . .

CHAPTER THREE: THE RIGHT OF THE STRONGER

The stronger is never strong enough to be forever master, unless he transforms his force into right, and obedience into duty. Hence the right of the stronger; a right which is apparently understood ironically, and in principle really established. But will no one ever explain this word to us? Force is a physical power. I fail to see what morality can result from its effects. To yield to force is an act of necessity, not of will; at most it is an act of prudence. In what sense can it become a duty?

Let us assume this alleged right for a moment. I say that it can only result in an unintelligible muddle. For once force makes right, the effect changes together with the cause; every force that overcomes the first, inherits its right. Once one can disobey with impunity, one can do so legitimately, and since the stronger is always right, one need only make sure to be the stronger. But what is a right that perishes when force ceases? If one has to obey by force, one need not obey by duty, and if one is no longer forced to obey, one is no longer obliged to do so. Clearly, then, this word "right" adds nothing to force; it means nothing at all here. . . .

Let us agree, then, that force does not make right, and that one is only obliged to obey legitimate powers. Thus my original question keeps coming back.

CHAPTER FOUR: OF SLAVERY

Since no man has a natural authority over his fellow-man, and since force produces no right, conventions remain as the basis of all legitimate authority among men.

If, says Grotius, an individual can alienate his freedom, and enslave himself to a master, why could not a whole people alienate its freedom and subject itself to a king?[1] There are quite a few ambiguous words here which call for explanation, but let us confine ourselves to the word *alienate*. To alienate is to give or to sell. Now, a man who enslaves himself to another does not give himself, he sells himself, at the very least for his subsistence: but a people, what does it sell itself for? A king, far from furnishing

---

1. Hugo Grotius (1583–1645) was a Dutch jurist and one of the founders of international law. Rousseau is here referring to Grotius's *The Rights of War and Peace*, book 1, chapter 3, section 8, paragraph 1.

his subjects' subsistence, takes his own entirely from them, and according to Rabelais[2] a king does not live modestly. Do the subjects then give their persons on condition that their goods will be taken as well? I do not see what they have left to preserve.

The despot, it will be said, guarantees civil tranquility for his subjects. All right; but what does it profit them if the wars his ambition brings on them, if his insatiable greed, the harassment by his administration cause them more distress than their own dissension would have done? What does it profit them if this very tranquility is one of their miseries? Life is also tranquil in dungeons; is that enough to feel well in them? The Greeks imprisoned in the Cyclops's cave[3] lived there tranquilly, while awaiting their turn to be devoured. . . .

To renounce one's freedom is to renounce one's quality as man, the rights of humanity, and even its duties. There can be no possible compensation for someone who renounces everything. Such a renunciation is incompatible with the nature of man, and to deprive one's will of all freedom is to deprive one's actions of all morality. Finally, a convention that stipulates absolute authority on one side, and unlimited obedience on the other, is vain and contradictory. Is it not clear that one is under no obligation toward a person from whom one has the right to demand everything, and does not this condition alone, without equivalent and without exchange, nullify the act? For what right can my slave have against me, since everything he has belongs to me, and his right being mine, this right of mine against myself is an utterly meaningless expression? . . .

CHAPTER FIVE: THAT ONE ALWAYS HAS TO GO BACK TO A FIRST CONVENTION

Even if I were to grant everything I have thus far refuted, the abettors of despotism would be no better off. There will always be a great difference between subjugating a multitude and ruling a society. When scattered men, regardless of their number, are successively enslaved to a single man, I see in this nothing but a master and slaves, I do not see in it a people and its chief; it is, if you will, an aggregation, but not an association; there is here neither public good, nor body politic. That man, even if he had enslaved half the world, still remains nothing but a private individual; his interest, separate from that of the others, still remains nothing but a private interest. When this same man dies, his empire is left behind scattered and without a bond, like an oak dissolves and collapses into a heap of ashes on being consumed by fire.

A people, says Grotius, can give itself to a king. So that according to Grotius a people is a people before giving itself to a king. That very gift is a civil act, it presupposes a public deliberation. Hence before examining the act by which a people elects a king, it would be well to examine the act by which a people is a people. For this act, being necessarily prior to the other, is the true foundation of society.

---

2. Rabelais (1494–1553) was a French humanist and the author of *Gargantua and Pantagruel*, a series of fantastical novels concerning the adventures of two giants. The book also includes extended meditations on contemporary social, political, and religious issues.

3. In Homer's *Odyssey*, book 9, Odysseus and twelve of his men are trapped in the cave of Polyphemus, a Cyclops. Polyphemus plans to eat them all, but they escape because of an ingenious plan devised by Odysseus.

Indeed, if there were no prior convention, then, unless the election were unanimous, why would the minority be obliged to submit to the choice of the majority, and why would a hundred who want a master have the right to vote on behalf of ten who do not want one? The law of majority rule is itself something established by convention, and presupposes unanimity at least once.

CHAPTER SIX: OF THE SOCIAL PACT

I assume men having reached the point where the obstacles that interfere with their preservation in the state of nature prevail by their resistance over the forces which each individual can muster to maintain himself in that state. Then that primitive state can no longer subsist, and humankind would perish if it did not change its way of being.

Now, since men cannot engender new forces, but only unite and direct those that exist, they are left with no other means of self-preservation than to form, by aggregation, a sum of forces that might prevail over those obstacles' resistance, to set them in motion by a single impetus, and make them act in concert.

This sum of forces can only arise from the cooperation of many: but since each man's force and freedom are his primary instruments of self-preservation, how can he commit them without harming himself, and without neglecting the cares he owes himself? This difficulty, in relation to my subject, can be stated in the following terms.

"To find a form of association that will defend and protect the person and goods of each associate with the full common force, and by means of which each, uniting with all, nevertheless obey only himself and remain as free as before." This is the fundamental problem to which the social contract provides the solution.

The clauses of this contract are so completely determined by the nature of the act that the slightest modification would render them null and void; so that although they may never have been formally stated, they are everywhere the same, everywhere tacitly admitted and recognized; until, the social compact having been violated, everyone is thereupon restored to his original rights and resumes his natural freedom while losing the conventional freedom for which he renounced it.

These clauses, rightly understood, all come down to just one, namely the total alienation of each associate with all of his rights to the whole community: For, in the first place, since each gives himself entirely, the condition is equal for all, and since the condition is equal for all, no one has any interest in making it burdensome to the rest.

Moreover, since the alienation is made without reservation, the union is as perfect as it can be, and no associate has anything further to claim: For if individuals were left some rights, then, since there would be no common superior who might adjudicate between them and the public, each, being judge in his own case on some issue, would soon claim to be so on all, the state of nature would subsist and the association necessarily become tyrannical or empty.

Finally, each, by giving himself to all, gives himself to no one, and since there is no associate over whom one does not acquire the same right as one grants him over oneself, one gains the equivalent of all one loses, and more force to preserve what one has.

If, then, one sets aside everything that is not of the essence of the social compact, one finds that it can be reduced to the following terms: *Each of us puts his person and his full power in common under the supreme direction of the general will; and in a body we receive each member as an indivisible part of the whole.*

At once, in place of the private person of each contracting party, this act of association produces a moral and collective body made up of as many members as the assembly has voices, and which receives by this same act its unity, its common *self*, its life and its will. The public person thus formed by the union of all the others formerly assumed the name *City* and now assumes that of *Republic* or of *body politic*, which its members call *State* when it is passive, *Sovereign* when active, *Power* when comparing it to similar bodies. As for the associates, they collectively assume the name *people* and individually call themselves *Citizens* as participants in the sovereign authority, and *Subjects* as subjected to the laws of the State. But these terms are often confused and mistaken for one another; it is enough to be able to distinguish them where they are used in their precise sense.

CHAPTER SEVEN: OF THE SOVEREIGN

This formula shows that the act of association involves a reciprocal engagement between the public and private individuals, and that each individual, by contracting, so to speak, with himself, finds himself engaged in a two-fold relation: namely, as member of the Sovereign toward private individuals, and as a member of the State toward the Sovereign. But here the maxim of civil right, that no one is bound by engagements toward himself, does not apply; for there is a great difference between assuming an obligation toward oneself, and assuming a responsibility toward a whole of which one is a part.

It should also be noted that the public deliberation which can obligate all subjects toward the Sovereign because of the two different relations in terms of which each subject is viewed cannot, for the opposite reason, obligate the Sovereign toward itself, and that it is therefore contrary to the nature of the body politic for the Sovereign to impose on itself a law which it cannot break. Since the Sovereign can consider itself only in terms of one and the same relation, it is then in the same situation as a private individual contracting with himself: which shows that there is not, nor can there be, any kind of fundamental law that is obligatory for the body of the people, not even the social contract. This does not mean that this body cannot perfectly well enter into engagements with others about anything that does not detract from this contract; for with regard to foreigners it becomes a simple being, an individual.

But the body politic or Sovereign, since it owes its being solely to the sanctity of the contract, can never obligate itself, even toward another, to anything that detracts from that original act, such as to alienate any part of itself or to subject itself to another Sovereign. To violate the act by which it exists would be to annihilate itself, and what is nothing produces nothing.

As soon as this multitude is thus united in one body, one cannot injure one of the members without attacking the body, and still less can one injure the body without the members being affected. Thus duty and interest alike obligate the contracting parties to help one another, and the same men must strive to combine in this two-fold relation all the advantages attendant on it.

Now the Sovereign, since it is formed entirely of the individuals who make it up, has not and cannot have any interests contrary to theirs; consequently the Sovereign power has no need of a guarantor toward the subjects, because it is impossible for the body to want to harm all of its members, and we shall see later that it cannot harm any one of them in particular. The Sovereign, by the mere fact that it is, is always everything it ought to be.

But this is not the case regarding the subjects' relations to the Sovereign, and notwithstanding the common interest, the Sovereign would have no guarantee of the subjects' engagements if it did not find means to ensure their fidelity.

Indeed each individual may, as a man, have a particular will contrary to or different from the general will he has as a Citizen. His particular interest may speak to him quite differently from the common interest; his absolute and naturally independent existence may lead him to look upon what he owes to the common cause as a gratuitous contribution, the loss of which will harm others less than its payment burdens him and, by considering the moral person that constitutes the State as a being of reason because it is not a man, he would enjoy the rights of a citizen without being willing to fulfill the duties of a subject; an injustice, the progress of which would cause the ruin of the body politic.

Hence for the social compact not to be an empty formula, it tacitly includes the following engagement which alone can give force to the rest, that whoever refuses to obey the general will shall be constrained to do so by the entire body: which means nothing other than that he shall be forced to be free; for this is the condition which, by giving each Citizen to the Fatherland, guarantees him against all personal dependence; the condition which is the device and makes for the operation of the political machine, and alone renders legitimate civil engagements which would otherwise be absurd, tyrannical, and liable to the most enormous abuses.

CHAPTER EIGHT: OF THE CIVIL STATE

This transition from the state of nature to the civil state produces a most remarkable change in man by substituting justice for instinct in his conduct, and endowing his actions with the morality they previously lacked. Only then, when the voice of duty succeeds physical impulsion and right succeeds appetite, does man, who until then had looked only to himself, see himself forced to act on other principles, and to consult his reason before listening to his inclinations. Although in this state he deprives himself of several advantages he has from nature, he gains such great advantages in return, his faculties are exercised and developed, his ideas enlarged, his sentiments ennobled, his entire soul is elevated to such an extent, that if the abuses of this new condition did not often degrade him to beneath the condition he has left, he should ceaselessly bless the happy moment which wrested him from it forever, and out of a stupid and bounded animal made an intelligent being and a man.

Let us reduce this entire balance to terms easy to compare. What man loses by the social contract is his natural freedom and an unlimited right to everything that tempts him and he can reach; what he gains is civil freedom and property in everything he possesses. In order not to be mistaken about these compensations, one has to distinguish clearly between natural freedom which has no other bounds than the individual's forces, and civil freedom which is limited by the general will, and between possession which is merely the effect of force or the right of the first occupant, and property which can only be founded on a positive title.

To the preceding one might add to the credit of the civil state moral freedom, which alone makes man truly the master of himself; for the impulsion of mere appetite is slavery, and obedience to the law one has prescribed to oneself is freedom. But I have already said too much on this topic, and the philosophical meaning of the word *freedom* is not my subject here.

. . . I shall close this book with a comment that should serve as the basis of the entire social system; it is that the fundamental pact, rather than destroying natural equality, on the contrary substitutes a moral and legitimate equality for whatever physical inequality nature may have placed between men, and that while they may be unequal in force or in genius, they all become equal by convention and by right.[4]

Book II

CHAPTER FOUR: OF THE LIMITS OF SOVEREIGN POWER

All the services a Citizen can render the State, he owes to it as soon as the Sovereign requires them; but the Sovereign, for its part, cannot burden the subjects with any shackles that are useless to the community; it cannot even will to do so: for under the law of reason nothing is done without cause, any more than under the law of nature.

The commitments which bind us to the social body are obligatory only because they are mutual, and their nature is such that in fulfilling them one cannot work for others without also working for oneself. Why is the general will always upright, and why do all consistently will each one's happiness, if not because there is no one who does not appropriate the word *each* to himself, and think of himself as he votes for all? Which proves that the equality of right and the notion of justice which it produces follows from each one's preference for himself and hence from the nature of man; that the general will, to be truly such, must be so in its object as well as in its essence, that it must issue from all in order to apply to all, and that it loses its natural rectitude when it tends toward some individual and determinate object; for then, judging what is foreign to us, we have no true principle of equity to guide us. . . .

---

4. Under bad governments, this equality is only apparent and illusory: it serves only to keep the pauper in his poverty and the rich man in the position he has usurped. In fact, laws are always of use to those who possess and harmful to those who have nothing: from which it follows that the social state is advantageous to men only when all have something and none too much. [Rousseau's note.]

In view of this, one has to understand that what generalizes the will is not so much the number of voices, as it is the common interest which unites them: for in this institution, everyone necessarily submits to the conditions which he imposes on others; an admirable agreement between interest and justice which confers on common deliberations a character of equity that is seen to vanish in the discussion of any particular affair, for want of a common interest which unites and identifies the rule of the judge with that of the party.

From whatever side one traces one's way back to the principle, one always reaches the same conclusion: namely, that the social pact establishes among the Citizens an equality such that all commit themselves under the same conditions and must all enjoy the same rights. Thus by the nature of the pact every act of sovereignty, that is to say every genuine act of the general will, either obligates or favors all Citizens equally, so that the Sovereign knows only the body of the nation and does not single out any one of those who make it up. What, then, is, properly, an act of sovereignty? It is not a convention of the superior with the inferior, but a convention of the body with each one of its members: A convention which is legitimate because it is based on the social contract, equitable because it is common to all, and secure because the public force and the supreme power are its guarantors. So long as subjects are subjected only to conventions such as these, they obey no one, but only their own will; and to ask how far the respective rights of Sovereign and Citizens extend is to ask how far the Citizens can commit themselves to one another, each to all, and all to each.

From this it is apparent that the Sovereign power, absolute, sacred, and inviolable though it is, does not and cannot exceed the limits of the general conventions, and that everyone may fully dispose of such of his goods and freedom as are left him by these conventions: so that it is never right for the Sovereign to burden one subject more than another, because it then turns into a particular affair, and its power is no longer competent.

These distinctions once admitted, it is so [evidently] false that the social contract involves any genuine renunciation on the part of individuals, that, . . . as a result of the contract their situation really proves to be preferable to what it had been before, and that instead of an alienation they have only made an advantageous exchange of an uncertain and precarious way of being in favor of a more secure and better one, of natural independence in favor of freedom, of the power to harm others in favor of their own security, and of their force which others could overwhelm in favor of right made invincible by the social union. Their very life which they have dedicated to the State is constantly protected by it, and when they risk it for its defense, what are they doing but returning to it what they have received from it? What are they doing that they would not have done more frequently and at greater peril in the state of nature, when, waging inevitable fights, they would be defending the means of preserving their lives by risking them? All have to fight for the fatherland if need be, it is true, but then no one ever has to fight for himself. Isn't it nevertheless a gain to risk for the sake of what gives us security just a part of what we would have to risk for our own sakes if we were deprived of this security?

TEST YOUR UNDERSTANDING

1. What does Rousseau tell us is "the fundamental problem to which the social contract provides the solution"? State the fundamental problem in your own words.

2. Rousseau distinguishes among natural freedom, civil freedom, and moral freedom. What does he mean by "moral freedom," and how is moral freedom different from natural and civil freedom?

3. In discussing the general will, Rousseau states that what "generalizes the will is not so much the number of voices as it is the common interest which unites them." Give some examples of common interests.

4. Hobbes says that Grotius misunderstands the "true foundation of society." What does Rousseau think is the true foundation?

READER'S GUIDE

Rousseau's Solution to the Fundamental Problem

Living in a society governed by laws seems like a pretty good bet. Let's assume that we have a government. And assume that the government makes and enforces laws that protect personal safety and security of possessions. Then we will probably get better protection of our persons and possessions than in a world without laws. Of course, protection is never a sure thing. But it seems more likely with laws than without laws. We may not like the legal limits on our liberty. But the benefits in personal safety and security seem greater than the cost imposed by the legal restrictions on liberty.

The previous paragraph sketches a conventional way of thinking about living together in a society with a government and laws. According to this conventional approach, living with others in a society under laws imposes costs on us and provides benefits to us. Legal limits on liberty are a cost: they keep us from doing things we might like to do. Legal protections from others provide benefits: they increase the security of person and goods. Being a member of a society governed by laws, according to the conventional view, makes rational sense because the benefits from legal protections probably outweigh the costs of abiding by legal constraints.

In *The Social Contract*, Rousseau rejects this conventional way of thinking. He says—in one of the most striking sentences in *The Social Contract*—that the "fundamental problem" is to "find a form of association that will defend and protect the person and goods of each associate with the full common force, and by means of which each, uniting with all, nevertheless *obey only himself and remain as free as before*" (emphasis added).

This is a remarkable idea: individuals unite together; each individual gets basic protections; and yet each remains as free as before because each continues to obey himself or herself alone. Compliance with law is not a limit on freedom but a way of being free.

What could this possibly mean? How can you be required to obey laws that are good for other people (as well as yourself) and at the same time be as free as before—as free as you would be when you are not required to obey any laws? Aren't the laws restrictions on your freedom?

Here is a way to think about Rousseau's picture. Each person has an interest in the protection of his or her person and goods. Being protected is in my interest: it is good for me. Being protected is in your interest: it is good for you. So if we live under a system of laws that protects each one of us, that is good for all of us. Each person under the laws is better off than he or she would be in the absence of the laws. So on one interpretation of the idea of the **common good**, the laws advance the common good.

But how could it be that when I follow these laws—when I act on laws that provide protection for each, and thus advance the common good—I remain as free as before and obey only myself? The rules may be attractive and make good sense, but aren't they restrictions on my ability to act as I think best? When I obey the laws, how am I obeying only myself? Why am I free?

Suppose I care about the common good (as well as my own individual good). I care about it because I accept that people who live together in a society should be treated as equals by the laws—that the good of each person should count for the same in settling on the laws we all live by. That is a demanding expectation, but we are trying now to understand Rousseau's solution to the "fundamental problem," and whether it even makes sense.

So let's suppose we live in a society in which each member accepts that others are equals and that the good of every member is to count equally in making the laws. In that society, each person endorses the common good as the standard in making the laws, and agrees to support and uphold laws that advance the common good. This is what Rousseau means when he talks about "each associate . . . uniting himself with all." Each person unites with all by acknowledging others as equals and embracing the good of each member as having equal importance in deciding on the laws.

So now, when I act on laws that are designed to advance the common good, I am obeying myself (following my own will) because I (like all the other members) care about the common good and endorse it as the basis for making the laws. Acting for the common good is not a cost that I accept because I get greater benefits in security and protection. Acting for the common good is something I directly endorse myself.

Rousseau summarizes the solution this way: "Each of us puts his person and all his power in common under the supreme direction of the general will, and, in our corporate capacity, we receive each member as an indivisible part of the whole." The "general will" is Rousseau's term for the kind of society that solves his fundamental problem. A group of people is under the general will when each person endorses the common good as the basis for the laws and agrees to act for the common good. The general will is, then, *general* because it is shared by all and because it focused on the good of all.

Rousseau's solution to the fundamental problem leaves lots of very large questions open.

1. Can people be motivated to act for the common good and not simply pursue their own good? What happens when some members put their own good above the common good?

2. How are we supposed to figure out what the common good requires, especially when interests conflict? If a minimum wage law is in the interest of workers and not in the interest of employers, what is the common good?

3. Suppose people disagree about what the common good requires: how do they resolve the disagreements?

In other parts of *The Social Contract*, some of which are included in the selection, Rousseau tries to answer these questions with a theory about law, government, and political culture. But understanding the rest depends on understanding Rousseau's "fundamental problem" and the solution he sketches in book I, chapter 6.

NOTES AND QUESTIONS

1. In the social compact, Rousseau says, "each of us puts his person and his full power in common under the supreme direction of the general will." We agree to follow the general will, not simply our own particular will, which may be at odds with the general will. As you read the selection, you saw that understanding the general will is essential to understanding Rousseau's conception of the state. As you also saw, it is hard to understand. Rousseau writes beautifully but also telegraphically. And he was enthusiastic about apparently paradoxical ways of putting things.

   In understanding the general will, then, it helps to bear in mind some of the claims that Rousseau makes about how the general will is justified, how it is expressed, and what its content is:

   (i)   The social compact is a mutual agreement to follow the general will.

   (ii) In making a social compact, we aim to protect our person and goods, and to remain as free as we were before.

   (iii) "What generalizes the will is not so much the number of voices, as it is the common interest which unites them" (book II, chapter 4).

   (iv) The general will is directed to the common good.

   (v)   Sovereignty is the exercise of the general will.

   (vi) Acts of sovereignty (exercises of the general will) are not directives from superior to inferior but agreements of citizens with one another.

   (vii) Law is the declaration of the general will.

   (viii) An act of the general will "obligates or favors all citizens equally."

   (ix) In complying with the general will, we are morally free, which means that we give the law to ourselves.

   The challenge is to combine these pieces in a coherent and sensible way. One line of interpretation proceeds as follows: in the social compact, we agree to live together in a society in which the general will is the highest authority. In such a society, citizens share an idea of and a commitment to acting for the common good. For example, when they conduct political discussion, they all appeal to an idea of the common good. Acting for the common good consists, more specifically, in protecting the basic, common interests of each citizen, including interests in the protection of the person and goods of each. So acting for the common good requires showing equal concern for each citizen. Citizens act for the common good by making general laws. What makes the laws general is that they benefit all and impose obligations on all. Because the citizens share an idea of their common good and make laws that express that understanding, they act freely—they are "as free as before"—when they comply with the laws. More particularly, they achieve the moral freedom that consists in giving the law to oneself. For further elaboration of this line of interpretation, see Joshua Cohen, *Rousseau: A Free Community of Equals* (Oxford University Press, 2010).

In light of these comments on the general will, consider a few of Rousseau's statements and respond to the associated questions:

a. The social compact involves no "genuine renunciation on the part of individuals" (book II, chapter 4). How does he develop that idea of "no genuine renunciation" in the rest of the sentence?

b. The sovereign "cannot burden the subjects with any shackles that are useless to the community" (book II, chapter 4). Why not? How does the idea of the general will support this conclusion?

c. "Whoever refuses to obey the general will shall be constrained to do so by the entire body: which means nothing other than that he shall be forced to be free" (book I, chapter 7). What is Rousseau saying? Does it make sense? Is the idea that punishment forces people to be free? Is the idea that punishment *treats people as free* by holding them responsible for violating laws that are aimed at advancing the common good?

2. Rousseau was remarkably odd and remarkably talented. In a wonderful biography, Leo Damrosch says:

> In a series of amazingly original books, of which *The Social Contract* is the best known, he developed a political theory that deeply influenced the American Founding Fathers and the French revolutionaries, helped to invent modern anthropology, and advanced a concept of education that remains challenging and inspiring to this day. His *Confessions* virtually created the genre of autobiography as we know it, tracing lifelong patterns of feeling to formative experiences and finding a deep unity of the self beneath apparent contradictions; modern psychology owes him an immense debt. Rousseau achieved all that without ever attending school. And there is much else: *Le devin du village*, a comic opera admired by Gluck and the very young Mozart, performed 400 times (including at Fontainebleau and the Paris Opera, the first performance after the fall of the Bastille); a less successful play, *Narcissus, or the Self-Lover*, which was performed by the Comédie-Française in 1752; and *Julie, or the New Heloïse*, one of the most popular novels of the eighteenth century.

See Leo Damrosch, *Jean-Jacques Rousseau: Restless Genius* (Houghton-Mifflin, 2005).

A. John Simmons (b. 1950)

Simmons is Commonwealth Professor of Philosophy and a professor of law at the University of Virginia. A political philosopher, Simmons has written influential books on individual rights, political obligation, and political legitimacy. He is best known for his views about the importance of consent as a basis of political obligation and his skepticism that most people have consented in ways that establish obligations.

RIGHTS-BASED JUSTIFICATIONS
FOR THE STATE

W e all live in states. Because states are so familiar to us, it is easy to take their existence for granted and not think about whether they are justified. If we pause to consider their justification, however, we will see that a successful justification is very hard. To justify the state we must be able to argue that our lives are better if we live in a state than if we do not live in a state. Now states employ massive coercion—with laws, police, courts, prisons, and armies—to control (without our consent) many areas of our lives. So the costs are pretty clear and substantial. Because of these large costs, anarchists have long argued that the state cannot be justified.

Most political philosophers have strongly disagreed with the anarchists. The most popular justifications of the state have aimed to show that state coercion limits violence between people. As a result, people are happier within states than they would be without them. People are reliably able to satisfy more of their important desires by living in states because of the protections that states provide.

Other attempted justifications of the state go further. They add that our lives in states are not just happier but *morally* better than they would be without a state. Rights-based justifications of the state provide one such argument for the moral advantage for states. According to a rights-based justification, legitimate states have two moral advantages. The first advantage is that they receive the right to coerce from the people they govern: they rule with the consent of the governed. Second, such states in turn protect the rights of the governed better than those rights could be protected outside of states.

To evaluate the rights-based justification for the state, let's first consider what rights are and why they are so important. Then we will examine three rights-based justifications for the state: Hobbesian, Lockean, and Kantian. Finally, we will focus on the Lockean argument that states may have this double moral advantage: of being justified because they have the consent of the governed and because they help to protect the rights of the governed. But while states *may* have this double advantage, the Lockean standard of justification is very hard to meet. So perhaps the anarchist position may, after all, have a great deal to be said for it.

I. Rights

Rights are a familiar feature of our lives. We demand *legal* rights to practice our religions or be free of negligent injury; we declare support for the *human* rights of the victims of totalitarian regimes; and we acquire *associational* rights by joining such voluntary associations as sororities or unions. In these and countless other cases, we make *claims* to rights.

The rights we claim fall into two broad categories. Rights in the first category—call them "conventional rights"—are defined or created by social practices (including rules and laws). Our conventional rights include legal rights, as well as the associational rights conferred on us by our positions or roles in our businesses, churches, clubs, and other organizations. Conventional rights vary widely across place and time, since practices differ so widely across social groups and change over time within them. Thus, women won the legal right to vote in the United States in 1920, and 18-year-olds won it in 1971. In both cases, we have extensions of conventional rights.

Rights in the second category—call them "moral rights"—are not conferred by our social practices. Many of our conventional rights are conceived as enforcing or securing such moral rights. Laws against murder, for example, secure a moral right not to be killed. That right is protected by the law but not created by law. Moreover, we claim such moral rights even when our existing practices violate them. Abolitionists, for example, condemned slavery for violating a moral right not to be enslaved. The languages of "natural rights" (most popular in the seventeenth to nineteenth centuries) and of "human rights" (more popular since) have typically been employed to make claims about the moral rights that persons possess independent of political and legal practices.

Rights-based justifications of the state will naturally appeal to *moral* rights: our social practices could hardly *justify* themselves simply by creating new conventional rights of the relevant sort. But how should we understand the moral rights that figure in such justifications? Rights usually provide their holders with a range of options and impose corresponding restraints on the actions of others. For example, my right to freedom of speech gives me the options to speak or not, in private or in public, and also imposes duties on others not to silence me in certain ways.

Some have found it helpful to think of persons' rights as defining a kind of "walled space" around them. The "walls" represent the restraints on others' actions, and the "space" represents the range of the rightholders' permissible options. The walls and space are obviously not physical, since people violate others' rights with alarming ease and frequency. Instead, we must imagine moral (or legal) analogs of physical space.

Thinking of rights as walled spaces helps to highlight certain of the principal functions of rights. First, our rights function not only to bar aggression against us by other individuals, but also to bar certain ways of pursuing valuable group or social ends. Good ends—including the utilitarian end of social happiness—can sometimes be most efficiently pursued by bad means, including the sacrifice or exploitation of particular individuals. Rights restrict such pursuits. The spatial picture represents these restrictions both by the walls and by the space within them. The wall is the boundary to society, and the space within represents a person's range of permissible options: she need not choose to act always in a way that best promotes good ends; her space permits her sometimes to look out for herself or for her own values.

Second, the wall in the "walled space" characterization reminds us that rights make possible certain ways of regarding the moral importance of persons that would be impossible in a world without rights. In particular, in a world without rights (walls) we could not demand certain things (including others' actions) as *owed* to us; we would have to use our power to secure them or rely on others' good will to provide (or to respect) these things. Nor would it be possible without rights to think of people as possessing real dignity and independence. Instead, people would always be, at best, valuable parts of some larger (e.g., social or religious) scheme. The "wall" of my rights pulls others up short, requiring them to respect my "space" in the world, to treat me as a being who *has* a space.

To be sure, the term "right" is commonly used (in both law and morality) to designate a number of different types of relations, not all of which can be even approximately represented by thinking of "walled spaces." Consider, for example, the contrast between "claim rights" and "liberty rights." A claim right is a right that *correlates* with another's duty to respect the right (by acting or forbearing). For example, I have a claim right to bodily security: my right correlates with your duty to respect my body. With liberty rights there are no such correlative duties on others. Instead, the assertion of a liberty right to act entails only that there is no duty on the rightholder *not* to so act: when I have a liberty right to do something, it is permissible (or "alright") for me to do it. Each of us has, for example, a liberty right to pick up (and perhaps thereby establish a *claim* right in) the unowned gold nugget in the wilderness. But each person's right is here *competitive with* the rights of others: neither of us has any correlative duty to permit the other to pick it up first. In such cases, the "walled space" metaphor for rights seems particularly inapt.

II. Rights-Based Justifications

Rights-based justifications for the state have an especially natural place in the social contract tradition in political philosophy. According to social contractarians, for a (or the) state to be justified, it must be the subject of an actual, a possible, or a hypothetical contract or agreement among the subjects of that state. In each of the three great strands of social contract thought—the political philosophies of Thomas Hobbes, John Locke, and Immanuel Kant—we can see a different way of bringing the idea of individual rights to bear on a justification for the state. Each of these philosophers believes that individuals are endowed with moral rights and that the state's justification turns on how these rights are defined and exercised.

Hobbes's *Leviathan* argues for a "sovereign"—a supreme authority with an absolute (unlimited) right to rule over the state's subjects. Hobbes begins with the idea that all persons are moral equals in their possession of the "right of nature," their "right to every thing." He argues that in a state of nature, with no political authority, life is so perilous that persons are seldom able to (safely) act peaceably. They are consequently entitled to use all the "advantages of war" against others in whatever ways they judge will enhance their personal security. (Notice that, because all possess competitively this same right of aggression, the right of nature cannot be understood as a claim right, correlating with others' duties of restraint; it must be understood instead as a mere liberty right, thus not as a wall.) Political society begins when each subject lays down this right to make war on others, either "voluntarily" (out of the desire to no longer live in a miserable state of nature) or at the point of a sword. The sovereign person (or body), however, retains the right of nature and thus remains at liberty to act as he (or she, or it) judges best. That is because the sovereign is not a party to the contract between subjects that makes him sovereign, but only the beneficiary of that agreement; so the sovereign's resulting authority is absolute. What justifies this absolute dominion (ideally, in Hobbes's view, rule by a monarch) is its sovereign's continued possession of the moral (liberty) right to use force against his subjects.

An idea of rights, then, plays a central role in Hobbes's justification of the state. Everyone starts with a right to everything, including the use of force against others. Subjects all relinquish this right in forming the state; only the sovereign retains the right. The result is the sovereign's moral "monopoly" on the use of force within the state.

Locke's *Second Treatise of Government* presents a superficially similar argument. Individuals have rights, and the state—which has a sovereign monopoly on force— arises from the exercise of those rights. But in the Lockean social contract, the rights with which persons are understood to begin are (mostly transferable) moral claim rights, which correlate with the moral duties of others to respect those rights, not the competitive liberties of the Hobbesian state of nature. The rights of authorities are not—as with Hobbes's sovereign—individual rights retained from their pre-political condition. Instead, they are *composed from* portions of all citizens' pre-political endowment of moral rights; individuals construct an authority by entrusting some of their rights to the state.

More specifically, persons naturally possess both a right to govern their own lives (within the bounds of moral duty), free from the interference of others, and a right to enforce the natural (moral) law according to their own conscientious interpretation of its requirements. This latter "executive right" to punish moral wrongdoers is wielded by private individuals in the state of nature. But the exercise of the right to punish by private individuals is a source of "inconvenience" and potential conflict. The need to centralize this executive right in the hands of a neutral judge (to adjudicate disputes between individuals) is thus the key to the justification of the Lockean state. In any legitimate political society, each person subject to the coercive powers of the state must have conveyed to the state, by contract or consent, his or her private executive right (in addition to other rights necessary for a viable polity). The state thus receives a "composite" right—composed of the separate rights of each subject—to make and enforce law on behalf of all citizens, a right that correlates with the contractually undertaken political obligations of those members. The state's legislative and executive rights, still limited by the requirements of natural law and by the peoples' purposes in entrusting them to the state, are what justifies any state activities within these prescribed limits.

Kant, like Locke, begins with the idea of natural equality and a basic right to freedom. The right to freedom is the one natural ("original") "innate" right, a right that each person possesses "in virtue of his humanity": a right to the maximum freedom from constraint by others that is consistent with every individual possessing that freedom. But Kant's right to freedom (unlike Locke's) cannot possibly be fully realized and respected except in a civil society under coercive law. Most rights in the lawless state of nature (where reasonable disagreement about their nature and extent is possible) are merely "provisional" and can only be made real or conclusive by legal enforcement. Kant's innate right to freedom requires, then, that individuals join together to leave the state of nature and create (or sustain) political institutions that are capable of fully satisfying that right. They need in particular to establish a constitution and legal system that can guarantee our natural equality and independence. Because the state is necessary for protecting the innate right to freedom, each person is obligated to accept membership in a state with such institutions.

On the Kantian view, then, the state is justified because it is necessary for realizing our one innate moral right. Where Locke argues that leaving the state of nature is advisable but morally optional for each person, Kant argues that membership in the state is morally obligatory.

Each of these three strands of social contract thought continues to have its adherents among contemporary philosophers. But contemporary Hobbesians and Kantians seldom present their justifications of the state as rights-based.

Contemporary Hobbesians draw on Hobbes's idea of the justified state as a rational choice for all. Hobbes argued that only a "fool" would reject the choice of a strong, stable state, one that was unlikely to slide back into the horrors of the state of nature. But if the state is a rational choice for all, this may seem sufficient by itself to explain why the state is justified in making and coercively enforcing law. If so, there seems little need to appeal to ideas about rights.

Similarly, contemporary Kantians do not put rights at the core of their justifications for the state. They put aside Kant's claims about innate, pre-political rights and emphasize instead a variant of Kant's test for the legitimacy of particular laws: that enacted laws are legitimate just in case they could have been consented to by the people who are subject to them. Contemporary Kantian political philosophers (most famously John Rawls) have argued that just political and legal institutions are those that would have been selected by persons choosing terms of cooperation in a fair original position of choice. State coercion, then, is legitimate or justified when it is used in accordance with rules that all reasonable citizens could be expected to endorse. No further justification, in terms of innate rights, is required.

It is thus primarily contemporary representatives of Lockean social contract thought who have continued to emphasize rights-based justifications of the state. Lockeans disagree substantially with one another, however, on the kinds of moral rights with which we are naturally endowed, and therefore on the details of their arguments about the state's legitimacy. Section III sketches the core ideas of one kind of defensible Lockean theory.

III. Lockean Political Philosophy

Persons are, as Locke argued, naturally free and equal. We are not, of course, all equals in strength or intelligence, nor do we all actually enjoy political freedom. But once our rationality and socialization progress to the point that we can appreciate basic moral demands of nonaggression and mutual assistance and are capable of conforming our actions to those demands, persons enjoy a *moral* freedom and equality. Each person is equally subject to those demands of morality, and each enjoys the correlative rights to govern his or her own life within moral bounds. Each person is, in consequence, naturally free of the authority of others to command conduct. So *political authority* must be produced in ways that are consistent with our natural freedom and equality, typically by the voluntary (i.e., self-governing) choices of persons.

These Lockean claims of natural freedom and equality are much less controversial now than when Locke asserted them. Most of us are inclined to agree that enslaving or aggressing against morally innocent persons would be a wrong to them—a violation of their rights—even in a nonpolitical, nonlegal context. Locke argued both that these basic moral rights and duties can be inferred from the relation of persons to their Creator and also that they are required simply by the nature of persons—a nature that includes the capacity and motivation to set ends and pursue life plans of their own. Persons, he argues, are not mere things, morally available to be *used* for the purposes of others. They have rights and legitimate states must respect those rights.

The more controversial step, for the Lockean, comes next. Respect for our natural moral freedom and equality requires that political societies secure from each person subjected to the coercive powers of the state his or her own free consent to that subjection. Without that consent, the state (and its employment of coercive power) is illegitimate (at least with respect to those nonconsenters). Remember that for Locke, unlike Kant, we are under no moral duty to be members of a state, not even the state in which we were born or raised. To be sure, it is typically in our interest to accept membership in states whose powers are appropriately limited, or to work to create states with such a character. But because we are endowed with a right of self-government, only our own genuine, binding consent can subject us to any state's authority.

The Kantian denies that any such consent is needed. For the Kantian, justice requires that we support the states in which we find ourselves because we have an obligation to respect everyone's basic right to freedom and can only fulfill that obligation through subjection to political authority.

The Lockean replies in two ways. First, perhaps persons can fully respect the freedom of others even in a state of nature, simply by refraining from aggression and offering morally required assistance. But second (and more important), Kantian appeals to justice cannot really convincingly explain why particular persons or groups should be placed under the authority of particular states; for example, "Turkish" Kurds under Turkish political authority. Of course, we are *treated* as subjects of particular states simply as a matter of our (good or bad) luck in our births. But no plausible moral principle supports such treatment. Political custom and international law declare persons born in a particular territory to be subjects of the state controlling that territory. But that declaration has no moral relevance, especially when we remember that the territorial boundaries (and the customs and laws) at issue were produced by bloody conquest, forceful seizure, decimation of aboriginal populations, political compromise, and collusion among the powerful. We have no good reason to accept that such declarations of subjection establish our obligations. If we would respect a person's natural freedom and equality, we surely should not simply assign him or her by birth to the obligations of membership imposed by a state that claims him as its own, any more than we should randomly select some other state and ship him off for subjection there (even if we pay for his passage). We respect a person's rights to freedom and equality only by respecting that person's own free choice of membership—or, for that matter, that person's choice of *nonmembership*. Subjection or nonsubjection according to individual consent: that is the only way to take seriously each person's basic moral nature.

In addition to this requirement of individual consent as a source of political authority, a good Lockean state also provides protection for our rights that is superior to what we could reasonably hope for with no state at all: this is the second part of the double moral advantage that states have, according to a rights-based justification. Such a state is justified in virtue of its superior protections for rights. To accomplish this superior protection, the state must place legislative and coercive rights in impartial and adequately powerful hands. But to constitute an improvement for each person over the state of nature, this centralized power must be limited by the same moral constraints that naturally govern individual conduct (along with any further limits imposed by the people in entrusting their rights to governing agencies). Otherwise, the rights of some might be sacrificed to provide superior protection for the rights of others. Even in a state with suitably limited authority, achieved perhaps through a rule of law and a separation of legislative and executive powers, the actual security of our rights requires constant vigilance and preparation for united action by the people whose rights are at stake (thus Locke defended a right of popular revolution). But no state can expect better guardianship of individual rights than one in which each has freely joined herself to the society, establishing in that society clear limits on and a clear purpose for the entrusted powers of government.

Lockean political morality thus points to the two-fold moral advantage of legitimate states—two ways that rights figure in the justification of the state. It locates the state's justification in the state's potential for superior protection of our rights; and it also argues that even a state that protects rights only has legitimate authority over those particular persons who have freely consented to its authority. This Lockean position does not necessarily morally endorse all—or any—existing states. Many existing states will fail to constitute genuine improvements (in securing our rights) over the state of nature; others will fail to be legitimated by the consent of their subjects.

Because individual consent is an essential basis of legitimate authority, the Lockean insists that we think seriously about what behavior by typical citizens in typical states might plausibly be counted as binding consent. Locke himself suggested that mere continued residence in or use of the state's territories constitutes consent. But residence alone seems a clearly inadequate indication that a person accepts authority and acknowledges an obligation to obey. Indeed, given the typical course of most persons' political lives, it is hard to see just how we could credibly portray their societies as consensual associations of the requisite sort to satisfy Lockean standards for legitimacy.

A fully developed Lockean political morality, while providing us with clear standards for justified and legitimate states, may thus still point us toward skeptical, anarchistic conclusions about the moral authority of existing states. Perhaps those states cannot legitimately claim authority over us; perhaps they cannot insist that in coercing our compliance they are simply enforcing our obligation to obey.

TEST YOUR UNDERSTANDING

1. What is the main difference between conventional rights and moral rights?

2. What are the benefits of thinking of rights as "walled spaces"?

3. What are the two moral advantages of rights-based justifications of the state?

4. The Lockean theory says that only our freely given consent can rightfully subject us to the authority of the state. The Kantian says that no such consent is required. What are the Lockean responses to this Kantian view?

NOTES AND QUESTIONS

1. Simmons distinguishes the role of rights in the Hobbesian, Lockean, and Kantian arguments for a state. Sketch the main differences in the role of rights in these three theories. What do they think a right *is*? What rights do they think people have? Why does Kant think that we have an obligation to be members of a state?

2. Locke, as Simmons describes him, thinks that the case for a legitimate state has two distinct dimensions: a state's justification requires that it be good at protecting rights *and* that the people over whom it exercises authority consent to that authority. Why is the second requirement important? Imagine a state ruled by a benevolent political party that provides strong protections of individual rights to association, speech, and fair trials but whose citizens have not consented to the state's authority. If rights are of such great importance, why isn't it enough to ensure that the rights are securely protected?

3. At the end of his article, Simmons says that a "Lockean political morality" might "point us toward skeptical, anarchistic conclusions about the moral authority of existing states." Provide a careful statement of the anarchistic conclusions that might result from the Lockean view. Is the conclusion that states ought not to exist? Why might the Lockean view have these anarchistic conclusions? Are there reasonable ways to modify the conception of individual consent to avoid these conclusions?

4. For Locke's own view, see John Locke, *Two Treatises of Government and A Letter Concerning Toleration*, ed. Ian Shapiro (Yale University Press, 2003).

Charles Mills (b. 1951)

Mills is Distinguished Professor of Philosophy at the Graduate Center, City University of New York. He is a political theorist, whose work has focused on issues of race, class, and gender. Mills is best known for his 1997 book, *The Racial Contract*, which argues that the basic social contract is an agreement among members of European populations to establish a global system of white supremacy.

THE RACIAL CONTRACT

White supremacy is the unnamed political system that has made the modern world what it is today. You will not find this term in introductory, or even advanced, texts in political theory. . . . And this omission is not accidental. Rather, it reflects the fact that standard textbooks and courses have for the most part been written and designed by whites, who take their racial privilege so much for granted that they do not even see it as *political*, as a form of domination. Ironically, the most important political system of recent global history—the system of domination by which white people have historically ruled over and, in certain important ways, continue to rule over nonwhite people—is not seen as a political system at all. It is just taken for granted; it is the background against which other systems, which we *are* to see as political, are highlighted. . . .

What is needed is a global theoretical framework for situating discussions of race and white racism, and thereby challenging the assumptions of white political philosophy, which would correspond to feminist theorists' articulation of the centrality of gender, patriarchy, and sexism to traditional moral and political theory. What is needed, in other words, is a recognition that racism (or as I will argue, global white supremacy) is *itself* a political system, a particular power structure of formal or informal rule, socioeconomic privilege, and norms for the differential distribution of material wealth and opportunities, benefits and burdens, rights and duties. The notion of the Racial Contract is, I suggest, one possible way of making this connection with mainstream theory, since it uses the vocabulary and apparatus already developed for contractarianism to map this unacknowledged system. . . .

We all understand the idea of a "contract," an agreement between two or more people to do something. The "social contract" just extends this idea. If we think of human beings as starting off in a "state of nature," it suggests that they then *decide* to establish civil society and a government. What we have, then, is a theory that founds government on the popular consent of individuals taken as equals.

But the peculiar contract to which I am referring, though based on the social contract tradition that has been central to Western political theory, is not a contract between everybody ("we the people"), but between just the people who count, the people who really are people ("we the white people"). So it is a Racial Contract.

The social contract, whether in its original or in its contemporary version, constitutes a powerful set of lenses for looking at society and the government. But in its obfuscation of the ugly realities of group power and domination, it is, if unsupplemented, a profoundly misleading account of the way the modern world actually is and came to be. The "Racial Contract" as a theory—I use quotation marks to indicate when I am talking about the theory of the Racial Contract, as against the Racial Contract itself—will explain that the Racial Contract is real and that apparent racist violations of the terms of the social contract in fact *uphold* the terms of the Racial Contract.

The "Racial Contract," then, is intended as a conceptual bridge between two areas now largely segregated from each other: on the one hand, the world of mainstream (i.e., white) ethics and political philosophy, preoccupied with discussions of justice and rights in the abstract, on the other hand, the world of Native American, African American, and Third and Fourth World[1] political thought, historically focused on issues of conquest, imperialism, colonialism, white settlement, land rights, race and racism, slavery, jim crow, reparations, apartheid, cultural authenticity, national identity, *indigenismo*, Afrocentrism, etc. These issues hardly appear in mainstream political philosophy,[2] but they have been central to the political struggles of the majority of the world's population. Their absence from what is considered serious philosophy is a reflection not of their lack of seriousness but of the color of the vast majority of Western academic philosophers (and perhaps *their* lack of seriousness). . . .

. . . The "Racial Contract" I employ is . . . in keeping with the spirit of the classic contractarians—Hobbes, Locke, Rousseau, and Kant.[3] I use it not merely normatively, to generate judgments about social justice and injustice, but descriptively, to *explain* the actual genesis of the society and the state, the way society is structured, the way the government functions, and people's moral psychology. The most famous case in which the contract is used to explain a manifestly *non*ideal society, what would be

1. Indigenous people as a global group are sometimes referred to as the "Fourth World." See Roger Moody, ed., *The Indigenous Voice: Visions and Realities*, 2d ed., rev. (1988; rpt. Utrecht: International Books, 1993). [Mills's note.]

2. For a praiseworthy exception, see Iris Marion Young, *Justice and the Politics of Difference* (Princeton: Princeton University Press, 1990). Young focuses explicitly on the implications for standard conceptions of justice of group subordination, including racial groups. [Mills's note.]

3. Thomas Hobbes, *Leviathan*, ed. Richard Tuck (Cambridge: Cambridge University Press, 1991); John Locke, *Two Treatises of Government*, ed. Peter Laslett (1960; rpt. Cambridge: Cambridge University Press, 1988); Jean-Jacques Rousseau, *Discourse on the Origins and Foundation of Inequality among Men*, trans. Maurice Cranston (London: Penguin, 1984); Rousseau, *The Social Contract*, trans. Maurice Cranston (London: Penguin, 1968); Immanuel Kant, *The Metaphysics of Morals*, trans. Mary Gregor (Cambridge: Cambridge University Press, 1991). [Mills's note.]

termed in current philosophical jargon a "naturalized" account, is Rousseau's *Discourse on Inequality* (1755). Rousseau argues that technological development in the state of nature brings into existence a nascent society of growing divisions in wealth between rich and poor, which are then consolidated and made permanent by a deceitful "social contract."[4] Whereas the ideal contract explains how a just society would be formed, ruled by a moral government, and regulated by a defensible moral code, this nonideal/naturalized contract explains how an unjust, *exploitative* society, ruled by an *oppressive* government and regulated by an *immoral* code, comes into existence. If the ideal contract is to be endorsed and emulated, this nonideal/naturalized contract is to be demystified and condemned. So the point of analyzing the nonideal contract is not to ratify it but to use it to explain and expose the inequities of the actual nonideal polity and to help us to see through the theories and moral justifications offered in defense of them. It gives us a kind of X-ray vision into the real internal logic of the sociopolitical system. Thus it does normative work for us not through its own values, which are detestable, but by enabling us to understand the polity's actual history and how these values and concepts have functioned to rationalize oppression, so as to reform them. . . .

My aim here is to adopt a nonideal contract as a rhetorical trope and theoretical method for understanding the inner logic of *racial* domination and how it structures the polities of the West and elsewhere. The ideal "social contract" has been a central concept of Western political theory for understanding and evaluating the social world. . . . I am suggesting, then, that as a central concept the notion of a Racial Contract might be more revealing of the real character of the world we are living in, and the corresponding historical deficiencies of its normative theories and practices, than the raceless notions currently dominant in political theory. Both at the primary level of an alternative conceptualization of the facts and at the secondary (reflexive) level of a critical analysis of the orthodox theories themselves, the "Racial Contract" enables us to engage with mainstream Western political theory to bring in race. Insofar as contractarianism is thought of as a useful way to do political philosophy, to theorize about how the polity was created and what values should guide our prescriptions for making it more just, it is obviously crucial to understand what the original and continuing "contract" actually was and is, so that we can correct for it in constructing the ideal "contract." The "Racial Contract" should therefore be enthusiastically welcomed by white contract theorists as well. . . .

The Racial Contract is that set of formal or informal agreements or meta-agreements (higher-level contracts *about* contracts, which set the limits of the contracts' validity) between the members of one subset of humans, henceforth designated by (shifting) "racial" (phenotypical/genealogical/cultural) criteria $C_1, C_2, C_3 \ldots$ as "white," and coextensive (making due allowance for gender differentiation) with the class of full persons, to categorize the remaining subset of humans as "nonwhite" and of a different and inferior moral status, subpersons, so that they have a subordinate civil standing in the white or white-ruled politics the whites either already inhabit or establish or in

---

4. Rousseau, *Discourse on Inequality*, pt. 2. [Mills's note.]

transactions as aliens with these polities, and the moral and juridical rules normally regulating the behavior of whites in their dealings with one another either do not apply at all in dealings with nonwhites or apply only in a qualified form (depending in part on changing historical circumstances and what particular variety of nonwhite is involved), but in any case the general purpose of the Contract is always the differential privileging of the whites as a group with respect to the nonwhites as a group, the exploitation of their bodies, land, and resources, and the denial of equal socioeconomic opportunities to them. All whites are *beneficiaries* of the Contract, though some whites are not *signatories* to it.[5]

It will be obvious, therefore, that the Racial Contract is not a contract to which the nonwhite subset of humans can be a genuinely consenting party (though, depending again on the circumstances, it may sometimes be politic to pretend that this is the case). Rather, it is a contract between those categorized as white *over* the nonwhites, who are thus the objects rather than the subjects of the agreement....

Politically, the contract to establish society and the government, thereby transforming abstract raceless "men" from denizens of the state of nature into social creatures who are politically obligated to a neutral state, becomes the founding of a *racial polity*, whether white settler states (where preexisting populations already are or can be made sparse) or what are sometimes called "sojourner colonies," the establishment of a white presence and colonial rule over existing societies (which are somewhat more populous, or whose inhabitants are more resistant to being made sparse). In addition, the colonizing mother country is also changed by its relation to these new polities, so that its own citizens are altered.

In the social contract, the crucial human metamorphosis is from "natural" man to "civil/political" man, from the resident of the state of nature to the citizen of the created society. This change can be more or less extreme, depending on the theorist involved. For Rousseau it is a dramatic transformation, by which animallike creatures of appetite and instinct become citizens bound by justice and self-prescribed laws. For Hobbes it is a somewhat more laid-back affair by which people who look out primarily for themselves learn to constrain their self-interest for their own good.[6] But in all cases the original "state of nature" supposedly indicates the condition of *all* men, and the social metamorphosis affects them all in the same way.

In the Racial Contract, by contrast, the crucial metamorphosis is the preliminary conceptual partitioning and corresponding transformation of human populations into "white" and "nonwhite" men. The role played by the "state of nature" then becomes

---

5. In speaking generally of "whites," I am not, of course, denying that there are gender relations of domination and subordination or, for that matter, class relations of domination and subordination within the white population. I am not claiming that race is the only axis of social oppression. But race is what I want to focus on; so in the absence of that chimerical entity, a unifying theory of race, class, and gender oppression, it seems to me that one has to make generalizations that it would be stylistically cumbersome to qualify at every point. So these should just be taken as read. Nevertheless, I do want to insist that my overall picture is roughly accurate, i.e., that whites *do* in general benefit from white supremacy (though gender and class differentiation mean, of course, that they do not benefit equally) and that historically white racial solidarity *has* overridden class and gender solidarity.... [Mills's note.]

6. Rousseau, *Social Contract*; Hobbes, *Leviathan*. [Mills's note.]

radically different. In the white settler state, its role is not primarily to demarcate the (temporarily) prepolitical state of "all" men (who are really white men), but rather the permanently prepolitical state or, perhaps better, *non*political state (insofar as "pre-" suggests eventual internal movement toward) of nonwhite men. The establishment of society thus implies the denial that a society already existed; the creation of society *requires* the intervention of white men, who are thereby positioned as *already* socio-political beings. White men who are (definitionally) already part of society encounter nonwhites who are not, who are "savage" residents of a state of nature characterized in terms of wilderness, jungle, wasteland. These the white men bring partially into society as subordinate citizens or exclude on reservations or deny the existence of or exterminate. In the colonial case, admittedly preexisting but (for one reason or another) deficient societies (decadent, stagnant, corrupt) are taken over and run for the "benefit" of the nonwhite natives, who are deemed childlike, incapable of self-rule and handling their own affairs, and thus appropriately wards of the state. Here the natives are usually characterized as "barbarians" rather than "savages," their state of nature being somewhat farther away (though not, of course, as remote and lost in the past—if it ever existed in the first place—as the Europeans' state of nature). But in times of crisis the conceptual distance between the two, barbarian and savage, tends to shrink or collapse, for this technical distinction within the nonwhite population is vastly less important than the *central* distinction between whites and nonwhites.

In both cases, then, though in different ways, the Racial Contract establishes a racial polity, a racial state, and a racial juridical system, where the status of whites and nonwhites is clearly demarcated, whether by law or custom. And the purpose of this state, by contrast with the neutral state of classic contractarianism, is, inter alia, specifically to maintain and reproduce this racial order, securing the privileges and advantages of the full white citizens and maintaining the subordination of nonwhites. Correspondingly, the "consent" expected of the white citizens is in part conceptualized as a consent, whether explicit or tacit, to the racial order, to white supremacy, what could be called Whiteness. To the extent that those phenotypically/genealogically/culturally categorized as white fail to live up to the civic and political responsibilities of Whiteness, they are in dereliction of their duties as citizens. From the inception, then, race is in no way an "afterthought," a "deviation" from ostensibly raceless Western ideals, but rather a central shaping constituent of those ideals. . . .

[In addition,] the Racial Contract requires its own peculiar moral and empirical epistemology, its norms and procedures for determining what counts as moral and factual knowledge of the world. In the standard accounts of contractarianism it is not usual to speak of there being an "epistemological" contract, but there *is* an epistemology associated with contractarianism, in the form of natural law. This provides us with a moral compass, whether in the traditional version of Locke—the light of reason implanted in us by God so we can discern objective right and wrong—or in the revisionist version of Hobbes—the ability to assess the objectively optimal prudential course of action and what it requires of us for self-interested cooperation with others. So through our natural faculties we come to know reality in both its factual and valuational aspects, the way things objectively are and what is objectively good or bad about them. I suggest we can think of this as an idealized consensus about cognitive norms and, in this respect, an agreement or "contract" of sorts. There is an understanding about what counts as a correct, objective interpretation of the world, and for agreeing to this view, one is ("contractually") granted full cognitive standing in the polity, the official epistemic community.[7]

But for the Racial Contract things are necessarily more complicated. The requirements of "objective" cognition, factual and moral, in a racial polity are in a sense more demanding in that officially sanctioned reality is divergent from actual reality. So here, it could be said, one has an agreement to *mis*interpret the world. One has to learn to see the world wrongly, but with the assurance that this set of mistaken perceptions will be validated by white epistemic authority, whether religious or secular.

Thus in effect, on matters related to race, the Racial Contract prescribes for its signatories an inverted epistemology, an epistemology of ignorance, a particular pattern of localized and global cognitive dysfunctions (which are psychologically and socially functional), producing the ironic outcome that whites will in general be unable to understand the world they themselves have made. . . . There will be white mythologies, invented Orients, invented Africas, invented Americas, with a correspondingly fabricated population, countries that never were, inhabited by people who never were—Calibans and Tontos, Man Fridays and Sambos—but who attain a virtual reality through their existence in travelers' tales, folk myth, popular and highbrow fiction, colonial reports, scholarly theory, Hollywood cinema, living in the white imagination and determinedly imposed on their alarmed real-life counterparts.[8] One could say then, as a general rule, that *white misunderstanding, misrepresentation, evasion, and self-deception on matters related to race* are among the most pervasive mental phenomena of the past few hundred years, a cognitive and moral economy psychically required for conquest, colonization, and enslavement. And these phenomena are in no way *accidental,* but *prescribed* by the terms of the Racial Contract, which requires a certain schedule of structured blindnesses and opacities in order to establish and maintain the white polity.

The social contract in its modern version has long since given up any pretensions to be able to explain the historical origins of society and the state. Whereas the classic contractarians were engaged in a project both descriptive and prescriptive, the modern Rawls-inspired contract is purely a prescriptive thought experiment. . . .

---

7. For the notion of "epistemological communities," see recent work in feminist theory—for example, Linda Alcoff and Elizabeth Potter, eds., *Feminist Epistemologies* (New York: Routledge, 1993). [Mills's note.]

8. Robert Young, *White Mythologies: Writing History and the West* (London: Routledge, 1990); Edward W. Said, *Orientalism* (1978; rpt. New York: Vintage Books, 1979); V. Y. Mudimbe, *The Invention of Africa: Gnosis, Philosophy, and the Order of Knowledge* (Bloomington: Indiana University Press, 1988); Enrique Dussel, *The Invention of the Americas: Eclipse of "the Other" and the Myth of Modernity,* trans. Michael D. Barber (1992; rpt. New York: Continuum, 1995); Robert Berkhofer Jr., *The White Man's Indian: Images of the American Indian from Columbus to the Present* (New York: Knopf, 1978); Gretchen M. Bataille and Charles L. P. Silet, eds., *The Pretend Indians: Images of Native Americans in the Movies* (Ames: Iowa State University Press, 1980); George M. Fredrickson, *The Black Image in the White Mind: The Debate on Afro-American Character and Destiny, 1817–1914* (1971; rpt. Hanover, N.H.: Wesleyan University Press, 1987); Roberto Fernández Retamar, *Caliban and Other Essays,* trans. Edward Baker (Minneapolis: University of Minnesota Press, 1989); Peter Hulme, *Colonial Encounters: Europe and the Native Caribbean, 1492–1797* (1986; rpt. London: Routledge, 1992). [Mills's note.]

By contrast, ironically, the Racial Contract, never so far as I know explored as such, has the best claim to being an actual historical fact. Far from being lost in the mists of the ages, it is clearly historically locatable in the series of events marking the creation of the modern world by European colonialism and the voyages of "discovery" now increasingly and more appropriately called expeditions of conquest. The Columbian quincentenary a few years ago, with its accompanying debates, polemics, controversies, counterdemonstrations, and outpourings of revisionist literature, confronted many whites with the uncomfortable fact, hardly discussed in mainstream moral and political theory, that we live in a world which has been *foundationally shaped for the past five hundred years by the realities of European domination and the gradual consolidation of global white supremacy.* Thus not only is the Racial Contract "real," but—whereas the social contract is characteristically taken to be establishing the legitimacy of the nation-state, and codifying morality and law within its boundaries—the Racial Contract is *global*, involving a tectonic shift of the ethicojuridical basis of the planet as a whole, the division of the world, as Jean-Paul Sartre put it long ago, between "men" and "natives."[9]

Europeans thereby emerge as "the lords of human kind," the "lords of all the world," with the increasing power to determine the standing of the non-Europeans who are their subjects.[10] Although no single act literally corresponds to the drawing up and signing of a contract, there is a series of acts—papal bulls and other theological pronouncements; European discussions about colonialism, "discovery," and international law; pacts, treaties, and legal decisions; academic and popular debates about the humanity of nonwhites; the establishment of formalized legal structures of differential treatment; and the routinization of informal illegal or quasi-legal practices effectively sanctioned by the complicity of silence and government failure to intervene and punish perpetrators—which collectively can be seen, not just metaphorically but close to literally, as its conceptual, juridical, and normative equivalent. . . .

. . . "Race" gradually became the formal marker of differentiated status, replacing the religious divide (whose disadvantage, after all, was that it could always be overcome through conversion). Thus a category crystallized over time in European thought to represent entities who are *humanoid* but not fully *human* ("savages," "barbarians") and who are identified as such by being members of the general set of nonwhite races. Influenced by the ancient Roman distinction between the civilized within and the barbarians outside the empire, the distinction between full and question-mark humans, Europeans set up a two-tiered moral code with one set of rules for whites and another for nonwhites.[11]

Correspondingly, various moral and legal doctrines were propounded which can be seen as specific manifestations and instantiations, appropriately adjusted to

9. Jean-Paul Sartre, Preface to Frantz Fanon, *The Wretched of the Earth*, trans. Constance Farrington (1961; rpt. New York: Grove Weidenfeld, 1991). [Mills's note.]

10. V. G. Kiernan, *The Lords of Human Kind: Black Man, Yellow Man, and White Man in an Age of Empire* (1969; rpt. New York: Columbia University Press, 1986); Anthony Pagden, *Lords of All the World: Ideologies of Empire in Spain, Britain, and France, c.1500–c.1800* (New Haven: Yale University Press, 1995). [Mills's note.]

11. Pagden, *Lords*, chapter 1. [Mills's note.]

circumstances, of the overarching Racial Contract. These were specific subsidiary contracts designed for different modes of exploiting the resources and peoples of the rest of the world for Europe: the expropriation contract, the slavery contract, the colonial contract. . . .

Indian laws, slave codes, and colonial native acts formally codified the subordinate status of nonwhites and (ostensibly) regulated their treatment, creating a juridical space for non-Europeans as a separate category of beings. So even if there was sometimes an attempt to prevent "abuses" (and these codes were honored far more often in the breach than the observance), the point is that "abuse" as a concept presupposes as a norm the *legitimacy* of the subordination. Slavery and colonialism are not conceived as wrong in their denial of autonomy to persons; what it wrong is the improper administration of these regimes.

It would be a fundamental error, then—a point to which I will return—to see racism as anomalous, a mysterious deviation from European Enlightenment humanism. Rather, it needs to be realized that, in keeping with the Roman precedent, *European humanism usually meant that only Europeans were human.* European moral and political theory, like European thought in general, developed within the framework of the Racial Contract and, as a rule, took it for granted. . . .

The modern world was thus expressly created as a *racially hierarchical* polity, globally dominated by Europeans. . . .

. . . One could say that the Racial Contract creates a transnational white polity, a virtual community of people linked by their citizenship in Europe at home and abroad (Europe proper, the colonial greater Europe, and the "fragments" of Euro-America, Euro-Australia, etc.), and constituted in opposition to their indigenous subjects. In most of Africa and Asia, where colonial rule ended only after World War II, rigid "color bars" maintained the separation between Europeans and indigenes. As European, as white, one knew oneself to be a member of the superior race, one's skin being one's passport: "Whatever a white man did must in some grotesque fashion be 'civilized.'"[12] So though there were local variations in the Racial Contract, depending on circumstances and the particular mode of exploitation—for example, a bipolar racial system in the (Anglo) United States, as against a subtler color hierarchy in (Iberian) Latin America—it remains the case that the white tribe, as the global representative of civilization and modernity, is generally on top of the social pyramid. . . .

. . . [Finally,] the Racial Contract is calculatedly aimed at economic exploitation. The whole point of establishing a moral hierarchy and juridically partitioning the polity according to race is to secure and legitimate the privileging of those individuals designated as white/persons and the exploitation of those individuals designated as nonwhite/subpersons. There are other benefits accruing from the Racial Contract—far greater political influence, cultural hegemony, the psychic payoff that comes from knowing one is a member of the *Herrenvolk* (what W. E. B. Du Bois once called "the wages of whiteness")[13]—but the bottom line is material advantage. Globally, the Racial

---

12. Kiernan, *Lords,* p. 24. [Mills's note.]

13. W. E. B. Du Bois, *Black Reconstruction in America, 1860–1880* (1935; rpt. New York: Atheneum, 1992). [Mills's note.]

Contract creates Europe as the continent that dominates the world; locally, within Europe and the continents, it designates Europeans as the privileged race. . . .

Both globally and within particular nations, then, white people, Europeans and their descendants, continue to benefit from the Racial Contract, which creates a world in their cultural image, political states differentially favoring their interests, an economy structured around the racial exploitation of others, and a moral psychology (not just in whites but sometimes in nonwhites also) skewed consciously or unconsciously toward privileging them, taking the status quo of differential racial entitlement as normatively legitimate, and not to be investigated further.

TEST YOUR UNDERSTANDING

1. Who are the parties to the Racial Contract?

2. Mills says that "the Racial Contract establishes a racial polity." What does he mean by "racial polity"?

3. What is the connection between the Racial Contract and economic exploitation?

4. Does Mills think that the Racial Contract helps people to see the world more clearly?

NOTES AND QUESTIONS

1. Mills says, "All whites are *beneficiaries* of the Contract, though some whites are not *signatories* to it." What is the difference between being a beneficiary of an agreement and being a signatory to the agreement? Why does Mills think that all whites benefit from the Racial Contract, even when they are not signatories to it? What kinds of benefits does he have in mind?

2. Mills links his concern with white supremacy to "mainstream [political] theory" by introducing the idea of a Racial Contract. The Racial Contract, he says, "uses the vocabulary and apparatus already developed for contractarianism" to illuminate the system of "global white supremacy." To understand how the Racial Contract is intended to illuminate white supremacy, sketch answers to the following questions:

   a. How does Mills define the Racial Contract?

   b. Who are the participants in the Racial Contract?

   c. What is the theoretical purpose of introducing this contract?

   d. Suppose you find the idea of a social contract attractive as a basis of political argument, and also are convinced by Mills that the traditional use of the social contract has contributed to white supremacy. How would you modify the interpretation of the social contract to avoid those traditional implications?

3. Mills says that the Racial Contract includes "its own moral and empirical epistemology." What does Mills mean by a "moral and empirical epistemology"? What role does this epistemology play in the Racial Contract? To answer these questions, recall that the Racial Contract excludes non-white persons. Similarly, a fraternal contract among male heads of households excludes women, and a property-owner's contract excludes people without property. Ask yourself what reasons might be given by someone who endorses the Racial Contract for excluding non-white persons from participating in the contract. Similarly, ask yourself what reasons might be given by someone who endorses a fraternal contract for excluding women or a property-owner's contract for excluding people without property. How are your answers to these three different issues of exclusion connected to a "moral and empirical epistemology"? Do the answers vary for the three cases?

ANALYZING THE ARGUMENTS

1. Aristotle says that "man is by nature a political animal." What does that assertion mean? What reasons does Aristotle offer in support of it? A good way to approach this question is by asking whether Hobbes and Rousseau agree that we are by nature political animals. Consider two pairs of questions:

    a. Does either Hobbes or Rousseau think it is possible to live outside the state? Does Aristotle think it is possible?

    b. Does either Hobbes or Rousseau think it is possible to live a decent or good human life outside the state? Does Aristotle think it is possible?

    Once you have an interpretation of Aristotle's idea, ask yourself whether you think that people are, by their nature, political animals.

2. This section provides you with five ideas about how to justify the existence of a state. Thus, the state is said to be justified for the purpose of:

    (i)   Keeping the peace (Hobbesian contract theory)

    (ii) Promoting the general happiness (utilitarianism)

    (iii) Protecting rights (Lockean contract theory [Simmons])

    (iv) Achieving moral **autonomy** (Rousseauean contract theory)

    (v)   Living a good and noble life by realizing our political natures (Aristotle)

    How precisely do these ideas differ? Think of circumstances in which they lead to similar conclusions, and then think of circumstances in which they give conflicting results (e.g., protecting rights thwarts peace, or encouraging good and noble lives gets in the way of the general happiness). Which view seems most promising in view of these potential conflicts?

    In his discussion of the Racial Contract, Mills focuses his critical attention on contractualist justifications of the state. Does his argument apply with equal force to all versions of contract theory? Does it apply as well to utilitarian and Aristotelian arguments?

3. Suppose an anarchist friend asks you why you are not an anarchist. How, in light of what you have read, would you answer? Be sure to start by explaining how you understand "anarchism." (If you *are* an anarchist, how would you respond to the arguments in these selections?)

What Is the Value
of Liberty?

According to its preamble, the U.S. Constitution aims, among other things, to "insure domestic tranquility, provide for the common defense, promote the general welfare, and secure the blessings of liberty to ourselves and our posterity." Domestic peace, common defense, and the general welfare are all pretty uncontroversial. But what exactly are the blessings of liberty? And why are they important?

One thing is clear: most of us value liberty. As Mary Prince—a woman born into slavery in Bermuda in 1788 and freed in England in 1832—says in her autobiography, "to be free is very sweet."[1] While we do not share Prince's experience of enslavement, most of us share her sentiment about freedom's sweetness. We do not wish to be told how (or whether) to worship, with whom to associate, or what to say or do.

At the same time, however, the value of liberty is puzzling. Why shouldn't a state—responsible for security and public safety—have the authority to restrict liberty, when restrictions help to accomplish the state's purposes? In his defense of absolute authority, Thomas Hobbes argues that it should (see the selection from Hobbes in Chapter 20 of this anthology). Individuals form a state, he says, by agreeing to submit their wills and judgments to the will and judgment of the political authority on all matters "which concern the common peace and safety." The political authority also is responsible for deciding which matters bear on peace and safety. So the political authority might decide that *any* dissenting doctrine or conduct threatens peace and safety—in other words, endangers national security. When that happens, the political authority becomes the arbiter of thought, speech, and conduct.

If you find freedom sweet, then you will find this demand for extreme deference to authority troubling. The challenge is to provide a compelling response.

---

1. Mary Prince, *A History of Mary Prince: A West Indian Slave*, in *The Classic Slave Narratives*, ed. Henry Louis Gates (Signet, 1987), 214.

Limiting Authority

Among the many kinds of liberty that we value—freedom to think, to speak, to associate—religious liberty has played a particularly prominent role in philosophical argument and political life. That prominence is understandable in part because religious beliefs are such a commanding force in many peoples' lives. Those beliefs provide a basic orientation in life—a touchstone for judgments of right and wrong and for how best to live—and give larger significance to life's ordinary activities.

Religious liberty is also a central topic because religious convictions can fuel social division and destructive political conflict: Protestants and Catholics in early modern Europe, Sunnis and Shiites in contemporary Syria and Iraq, Hindus and Muslims in India. A state, responsible for ensuring social peace and promoting the general welfare, may be tempted to respond by promoting greater religious uniformity. If we accept efforts of states to encourage, through schools and public symbols, a common national identity—as Americans, or Kenyans, or Germans, or Indians—because a sense of belonging is important for peaceful and productive social cooperation, why not a common religious identity as well?

John Locke's *Letter Concerning Toleration* presents the classical case against using the state's power to establish religious uniformity. Locke rejects the idea that the state has the authority to decide which religious view is right and to make laws founded on a religious outlook. To be sure, Locke's defense of toleration has important limits. Locke does not favor toleration for Catholics or atheists. Atheists, he thinks, cannot be trusted as cooperating members of society: "Promises, covenants, and oaths, which are the bonds of human society, can have no hold upon an atheist. The taking away of God, though but even in thought, dissolves all." Catholics are not to be tolerated, Locke says, because they owe allegiance to the pope, in effect a competing political authority. Atheists and Catholics are thus denied toleration not because their beliefs are false or religiously divisive but because their views are socially disruptive. Despite these limits, Locke's argument has been influential and controversial.

One of the chief Lockean arguments for religious toleration begins from the proposition that a person's salvation depends on his or her religious beliefs, not simply on correct outward behavior. But the distinctive instruments of the state—laws and penalties—can have no impact on beliefs. "It is only light and evidence that can work a change in men's opinions; which light can in no manner proceed from corporal sufferings, or any other outward penalties." So the state should not try to coerce beliefs because force is bound to fail: the corporal sufferings and other outward penalties would serve no good purpose. This argument does not reject using penalties to change minds, if penalties might be effective. It says only that they are not effective.

Locke also suggests a **contractualist** argument for the same conclusion. The contract tradition justifies political authority by arguing that a state could (or would) be unanimously agreed to by people subject to its authority. The same contractual agreement that justifies the existence of political authority also can set limits on the use of authority. Thus, Locke says that political authorities cannot have authority over religious beliefs in part because they *cannot get that authority from the people.* They cannot get it from the people because religion is so fundamental—so much at the core of individual convictions about what to think and how to live—that individuals cannot willingly yield control over it to any other person, much less to an authority.[2] So individuals must reject a proposed social contract that does not respect their religious liberty.

This contract strategy is neither confined to John Locke nor limited to religious liberty. John Rawls's social contract theory, for example, includes rights to religious liberty and to freedom of speech and political liberty.[3] The list of liberties is more expansive than Locke's, but the strategy of argument is broadly similar. A contract view sets limits on authority by arguing that individual interests in some areas of belief and conduct are so fundamental—so nonnegotiable—that individuals cannot entrust their beliefs and conduct in these areas to others. If people can only rationally endorse a political order that leaves certain fundamental matters in their own hands, then the contract theorist's condition of unanimous agreement requires protecting those liberties from political authority.

Utilitarianism and Liberty

Utilitarians reject the contractualist's test of unanimous agreement. They hold that the right actions, rules, and institutions are those that maximize the sum of human happiness. So even if an interest is fundamental, it can be overridden by a sufficiently large sum of benefits to others. If enough people would be happier in a world of religious uniformity, for example, then utilitarianism requires such uniformity, even at the cost of denying religious liberty to a minority. For this reason, many critics of utilitarianism have argued that the principle of utility is not a promising basis for defending liberty. But the classical utilitarians, Jeremy Bentham and John Stuart Mill, both found powerful resources within utilitarianism for defending liberty.

Consider an argument that Bentham offers against "morals legislation" in *An Introduction to the Principles of Morals and Legislation.*[4] Morals legislation punishes conduct with criminal sanctions. The conduct is punished *because it is wrong or sinful,* not because it causes harm to other people. In a 1991 Supreme Court case, Justice Antonin Scalia wrote in a concurring opinion: "Our society prohibits, and all human societies have prohibited, certain activities not because they harm others but because they are considered, in the traditional phrase,

---

2. John Rawls suggests a similar line of argument in *A Theory of Justice* (Harvard University Press, 1999), 181.

3. The right interpretation of Rousseau's view is more controversial. For discussion, see Joshua Cohen, *Rousseau: A Free Community of Equals* (Oxford University Press, 2010).

4. Jeremy Bentham, *The Principles of Morals and Legislation* (Macmillan, 1948), 315–21. Bentham (1748–1832) is widely regarded as the founder of utilitarianism.

'*contra bonos mores*,' *i.e.,* immoral." And he mentions "sadomasochism, cock-fighting, bestiality, suicide, drug use, prostitution, and sodomy" as areas in which legal regulation is justified by "traditional moral belief."[5] Historically, as Scalia's comments suggest, much of morals legislation has focused on issues of sexuality. Thus, laws against same-sex sexual activity—laws that have been the historical norm, not the exception—have traditionally been justified by moral reasons, not by reasons of harm to others.

Because he was a utilitarian, Bentham thought that criminal punishment should be decided on the basis of a calculation of costs in pain and benefits in pleasure. In particular, we should not impose criminal punishments when costs outweigh benefits. Punishments clearly impose pains. When there is not sufficient gain in pleasure, the punishments are "unprofitable." Bentham thought that morals laws belong in the unprofitable category. Because the conduct is not harmful to others, the benefits of stopping it cannot be that great. But the pains are very clear. So Bentham concluded that these are not "fit objects for the legislator to control." Unlike Locke, Bentham does not make the case for liberty depend on an especially important class of human interests. Nor does he follow the contractual approach of requiring unanimous agreement. But he does think that some liberties should be protected because the benefits of abridging them are smaller than the costs.

Mill's *On Liberty* offers a more complex utilitarian case for religious liberty, as well as for liberty of thought, expression, and association, and the liberty of choosing a way of life. He defines the rightful scope of authority with "one very simple principle," commonly called the **harm principle**, which says, "the only purpose for which power can be rightfully exercised over any member of a civilized community, against his will, is to prevent harm to others. His own good, either physical or moral, is not a sufficient warrant."[6] Harm to others is, in short, a necessary condition for justifying compulsion and control. The harm principle applies equally to democratic and aristocratic power. And it applies to power exercised through informal social sanctions, which put people under heavy pressure to conform, as well as to power exercised by the state through laws. Mill thinks that this informal pressure to conform threatens to establish a "social tyranny," which is especially dangerous because it "leaves fewer means of escape, penetrating much more deeply into the details of life, and enslaving the soul itself."[7]

Mill's defense of the harm principle is based on his utilitarianism. But his utilitarian calculus is different from Bentham's, and his case for liberty reflects a deeper exploration than Bentham's of "the greater good of human freedom" and the grave costs of limiting liberty. The most fundamental human interests, Mill thinks, are in "higher-quality pleasures" (see the introduction and the selection from Mill's *Utilitarianism* in Chapter 16 of this anthology). These pleasures involve the development and exercise of our distinctively human capacities: perception,

---

5. Barnes v. Glen Theatre, Inc., 501 US 560 (1991), 575.

6. Mill, *On Liberty*, 4th ed. (London: Longman, Roberts, and Green, 1869), chapter I, paragraph 9.

7. Mill, *On Liberty*, chapter I, paragraph 5.

judgment, reasoning, imagination, and moral and aesthetic evaluation. Following the harm principle, then, promotes the sum of human happiness because it provides favorable conditions for pursuing our fundamental interest in using our human capacities, thus for the qualitatively better human pleasures.

A first link between liberty and the higher-quality pleasures is that we exercise our capacities when we make choices about how to live. Making those choices is an important human good because it requires using our distinctively human powers: "He who chooses his plan for himself, employs all his faculties." A second link is that liberty enables us to explore alternative ways to live, observe the paths tried by others, and make informed judgments about the way that is best suited to each of us individually, rather than relying on custom and convention. A third link is that the protection of liberty fosters the vigorous challenge to received ideas that is essential for broader social and political progress.

Mill expected, then, that liberty would foster human diversity, and he understood that that would make some people uncomfortable and unsettle common convictions. But comfort is not a higher-quality pleasure. Mill's utilitarian case for liberty, then, is that the "higher-quality" human pleasures are best served by following the harm principle, and that those pleasures outweigh the costs in discomfort and inconvenience. Mill is not a contractualist, so he does not require unanimous agreement regarding the scope of authority. But as Locke assigned a special importance to the interest in salvation, Mill assigns a special importance to our interest in exercising our human powers. His case for liberty, then, turns on the idea that a society that embraces the harm principle will foster that interest.

Amartya Sen's theory of human rights shares this emphasis on a class of fundamental interests. Human rights—rights to be free of torture, slavery, extreme destitution, and religious intolerance, for example—are moral entitlements of all human beings. But what else are we all entitled to? Human rights do not arrive as a fixed list. The way to identify our human rights, Sen argues, is through ethical reasoning, not through legal argument. The reasoning aims to identify freedoms—like freedoms from torture, slavery, extreme destitution, and religious intolerance—that are important, that people share an interest in, and that can be protected and promoted through concerted action.

The Lockean and Millian arguments for liberty and Sen's account of human rights converge in identifying a class of especially important human interests that have a kind of priority over other interests. If there are such interests, and if liberty bears a close connection to the pursuit and advancement of those interests, then the case for liberty—whether contractualist or utilitarian—is well launched.

A Skeptic

Patrick Devlin rejects the views of Bentham and Mill. Devlin wrote "Morals and the Criminal Law" in response to the Wolfenden Report, a 1957 British government report that proposed to decriminalize "homosexual behaviour between consenting adults in private." Devlin rejected the conclusions of the report and defended morals laws on the basis of three central claims: (1) societies have the right to protect themselves from disintegration; (2) without a common morality—"shared ideas on politics, morals, and ethics"—a society disintegrates; and (3) enforcing a common morality through criminal law is necessary to preserving that common morality. It follows that a society has the right to enforce common morality through criminal law. Public morality speaks, for example, on issues about marriage, Devlin says, by embracing the values of monogamy and fidelity. Weaken the common sensibilities on those values and the institution would be "gravely threatened."

Devlin is not indifferent to the value of liberty but rejects hard and fast rules that define its scope and limits. We need to decide, in particular cases, whether we are faced with "a vice so abominable that its mere presence is an offence." When we are, punishment is permissible. For it may well be needed to reinforce the shared political, moral, and ethical ideas that enable us to live together. Devlin does not present his case for enforcement in utilitarian terms. But it can easily be reconstructed along those lines. He thinks that Bentham and Mill both underestimate the cost of eliminating morals laws because of their singular focus on injuries to individuals and corresponding neglect of damage to society. Devlin thinks that those laws help to forestall the erosion of shared moral ideas. If that erosion would produce social disintegration, then the decrease in pleasure and increase in pain would be very great.

A striking element of Mill's view may help to locate more precisely his disagreement with Devlin. In the opening chapter of *On Liberty*, Mill says that his principle applies only to "human beings in the maturity of their faculties," and that we may "leave out of consideration those backward states of society in which the race itself may be considered as in its nonage."[8] The harm principle "has no application to any state of things anterior to the time when mankind have become capable of being improved by free and equal discussion. Until then, there is nothing for them but implicit obedience to an Akbar or a Charlemagne, if they are so fortunate as to find one."[9] Mill's view, then, is that utilitarianism supports liberty when and only when people can be improved by "free and equal discussion." When they can, utilitarianism recommends efforts at improvement through discussion and persuasion rather than coercion.

Perhaps, then, Devlin emphasizes the enforcement of shared moral ideas for the same reason that Hobbes emphasizes the importance of authority: because he doubts our capacity to listen to reason—to be improved by free and equal discussion. Mill, in contrast, thinks that we can afford the liberty and resulting diversity that worry Hobbes and Devlin, once the distinctive human capacity for improvement through discussion is in place.

8. *Nonage*: period of immaturity.

9. Mill, *On Liberty*, chapter I, paragraph 10.

John Locke (1632–1704)

Locke was an English philosopher and medical doctor. His greatest work is *An Essay Concerning Human Understanding* (1689), which is about the limits of human knowledge. His *Two Treatises of Government* (1689) and *A Letter Concerning Toleration* (1689), both published anonymously, made important contributions to political philosophy. The second *Treatise* gives a theory of legitimate government in terms of natural rights and the social contract. Locke's political views influenced the Founding Fathers of the United States, in particular Thomas Jefferson.

A LETTER CONCERNING TOLERATION

The toleration of those that differ from others in matters of religion, is so agreeable to the Gospel of Jesus Christ, and to the genuine reason of mankind, that it seems monstrous for men to be so blind, as not to perceive the necessity and advantage of it, in so clear a light. I will not here tax the pride and ambition of some, the passion and uncharitable zeal of others. These are faults from which human affairs can perhaps scarce ever be perfectly freed; but yet such as nobody will bear the plain imputation of, without covering them with some specious colour; and so pretend to commendation, whilst they are carried away by their own irregular passions. But, however, that some may not colour their spirit of persecution and unchristian cruelty with a pretence of care of the public weal, and observation of the laws, and that others, under pretence of religion, may not seek impunity for their libertinism and licentiousness; in a word, that none may impose either upon himself or others, by the pretences of loyalty and obedience to the prince, or of tenderness and sincerity in the worship of God; I esteem it above all things necessary to distinguish exactly the business of civil government from that of religion, and to settle the just bounds that lie between the one and the other. If this be not done, there can be no end put to the controversies that will be always arising between those that have, or at least pretend to have, on the one side a concernment for the interest of men's souls, and, on the other side, a care of the commonwealth.

The commonwealth seems to me to be a society of men constituted only for the procuring, preserving, and advancing their own civil interests.

Civil interest I call life, liberty, health, and indolency of body; and the possession of outward things, such as money, lands, houses, furniture, and the like.

It is the duty of the civil magistrate, by the impartial execution of equal laws, to secure unto all the people in general, and to every one of his subjects in particular, the just possession of these things belonging to this life. If any one presume to violate the laws of public justice and equity, established for the preservation of these things, his presumption is to be checked by the fear of punishment; consisting in the deprivation or diminution of those civil interests, or goods, which otherwise he might and ought to enjoy. But seeing no man does willingly suffer himself to be punished by the deprivation of any part of his goods, and much less of his liberty or life, therefore is the magistrate armed with the force and strength of all his subjects, in order to the punishment of those that violate any other man's rights.

Now that the whole jurisdiction of the magistrate reaches only to these civil concernments; and that all civil power, right, and dominion, is bounded and confined to the only care of promoting these things; and that it neither can nor ought in any manner to be extended to the salvation of souls; these following considerations seem unto me abundantly to demonstrate.

First, Because the care of souls is not committed to the civil magistrate, any more than to other men. It is not committed unto him, I say, by God; because it appears not that God has ever given any such authority to one man over another, as to compel any one to his religion. Nor can any power be vested in the magistrate by the consent of the people; because no man can so far abandon the care of his own salvation as blindly to leave it to the choice of any other, whether prince or subject, to prescribe to him what faith or worship he shall embrace. For no man can, if he would, conform his faith to the dictates of another. All the life and power of true religion consists in the inward and full persuasion of the mind; and faith is not faith without believing. Whatever profession we make, to whatever outward worship we conform, if we are not fully satisfied in our own mind that the one is true, and the other well-pleasing unto God, such profession and such practice, far from being any furtherance, are indeed great obstacles to our salvation. For in this manner, instead of expiating other sins by the exercise of religion, I say, in offering thus unto God Almighty such a worship as we esteem to be displeasing unto him, we add unto the number of our other sins, those also of hypocrisy, and contempt of his Divine Majesty.

In the second place. The care of souls cannot belong to the civil magistrate, because his power consists only in outward force: but true and saving religion consists in the inward persuasion of the mind, without which nothing can be acceptable to God. And such is the nature of the understanding, that it cannot be compelled to the belief of any thing by outward force. Confiscation of estate, imprisonment, torments, nothing of that nature can have any such efficacy as to make men change the inward judgment that they have framed of things.

It may indeed be alleged that the magistrate may make use of arguments, and thereby draw the heterodox into the way of truth, and procure their salvation. I grant it; but this is common to him with other men. In teaching, instructing, and redressing the erroneous by reason, he may certainly do what becomes any good man to do. Magistracy does not oblige him to put off either humanity or Christianity. But it is one thing to persuade, another to command; one thing to press with arguments, another with penalties. This the civil power alone has a right to do; to the other, good-will is authority enough. Every man has commission to admonish, exhort, convince another of error, and by reasoning to draw him into truth; but to give laws, receive obedience, and compel with the sword, belongs to none but the magistrate. And upon this ground

I affirm, that the magistrate's power extends not to the establishing of any articles of faith, or forms of worship, by the force of his laws. For laws are of no force at all without penalties, and penalties in this case are absolutely impertinent; because they are not proper to convince the mind. Neither the profession of any articles of faith, nor the conformity to any outward form of worship, as has been already said, can be available to the salvation of souls, unless the truth of the one, and the acceptableness of the other unto God, be thoroughly believed by those that so profess and practise. But penalties are no ways capable to produce such belief. It is only light and evidence that can work a change in men's opinions; and that light can in no manner proceed from corporal sufferings, or any other outward penalties.

In the third place. The care of the salvation of men's souls cannot belong to the magistrate; because, though the rigour of laws and the force of penalties were capable to convince and change men's minds, yet would not that help at all to the salvation of their souls. For, there being but one truth, one way to heaven; what hopes is there that more men would be led into it, if they had no other rule to follow but the religion of the court, and were put under a necessity to quit the light of their own reason, to oppose the dictates of their own consciences, and blindly to resign up themselves to the will of their governors, and to the religion, which either ignorance, ambition, or superstition had chanced to establish in the countries where they were born? In the variety and contradiction of opinions in religion, wherein the princes of the world are as much divided as in their secular interests, the narrow way would be much straitened; one country alone would be in the right, and all the rest of the world put under an obligation of following their princes in the ways that lead to destruction: and that which heightens the absurdity, and very ill suits the notion of a Deity, men would owe their eternal happiness or misery to the places of their nativity.

These considerations, to omit many others that might have been urged to the same purpose, seem unto me sufficient to conclude, that all the power of civil government relates only to men's civil interests, is confined to the care of the things of this world, and hath nothing to do with the world to come.

TEST YOUR UNDERSTANDING

1. What topic needs to be addressed "above all," according to Locke, in order to resolve the issue of religious toleration?

2. What does Locke think is the main duty of civil government?

3. Does civil government have responsibility for the salvation of its citizens?

4. Locke presents three arguments for the thesis that the concerns of civil government cannot and should not be "extended to the salvation of souls." What is the main idea in the second argument?

NOTES AND QUESTIONS

1. Locke's defense of religious toleration turns partly on the thesis that you cannot change people's beliefs by using force against them. Call this thesis *limits of force*:

    Limits of force: A person's beliefs cannot be changed by threats or applications of force against the person.

    Assume for the sake of argument that *limits of force* is true. How strong a case for religious toleration results?

    Two considerations suggest that *limits of force* does not yield a strong case. First, even if a state that aims to establish religious uniformity cannot change religious beliefs directly, it might try to ensure uniformity by using force to prohibit religious practices—say, the Eucharist or adult baptism. Because of the prohibitions, other people do not see the practices and are therefore less likely to follow them.

    Second, the state might use force against religious dissenters not for the purpose of changing the minds of *dissenters* but for the purpose of dissuading others (perhaps children) who might otherwise be tempted to follow the dissenting group. In his history of religious toleration, Perez Zagorin discusses this second consideration, which he calls the "pedagogy of fear": *How the Idea of Religious Toleration Came to the West* (Princeton University Press, 2005).

    Suppose your commitment to toleration is based on *limits of force*. Can you think of ways to respond to these two arguments and to produce a stronger argument for toleration?

2. Consider Locke's third argument for religious toleration. Even if "the rigor of laws and the force of penalties" were able to change people's minds, still, he says, political officials should not use those instruments to promote religious uniformity. The argument turns on the idea that while the religious convictions of the "princes of the world" are diverse, there is "but one truth." Reconstruct Locke's third argument. Do you find his case compelling?

3. Locke focuses here on religious toleration. He aims "to distinguish exactly the business of civil government from that of religion and settle the just bounds that lie between the one and the other." But if you consider Locke's second argument, which draws on the *limits of force* thesis, it is not clear why it is limited to *religious* toleration. If the state should be *religiously* tolerant because minds cannot be changed by force, then should it be equally tolerant of *all beliefs*? How, if at all, do Locke's arguments bear specifically on *religious* toleration?

John Stuart Mill (1806–1873)

Mill was born in London, England. He was educated by his father, James Mill, a distinguished Scottish philosopher, political theorist, economist, and historian. A utilitarian, empiricist, and important public thinker, Mill was the author of *Utilitarianism, Considerations on Representative*

Government, Principles of Political Economy, Subjection of Women, System of Logic, The Autobiography of John Stuart Mill, and, most famously, *On Liberty.* Apart from his writings, Mill worked at the East India Company (1823–58), served as a Member of Parliament (1865–68), and was Lord Rector of the University of St. Andrews (1865–68).

ON LIBERTY

Chapter I: Introductory

The object of this essay is to assert one very simple principle, as entitled to govern absolutely the dealings of society with the individual in the way of compulsion and control, whether the means used be physical force in the form of legal penalties or the moral coercion of public opinion. That principle is that the sole end for which mankind are warranted, individually or collectively, in interfering with the liberty of action of any of their number is self-protection. That the only purpose for which power can be rightfully exercised over any member of a civilized community, against his will, is to prevent harm to others. His own good, either physical or moral, is not a sufficient warrant. He cannot rightfully be compelled to do or forbear because it will be better for him to do so, because it will make him happier, because, in the opinions of others, to do so would be wise or even right. These are good reasons for remonstrating with him, or reasoning with him, or persuading him, or entreating him, but not for compelling him or visiting him with any evil in case he do otherwise. To justify that, the conduct from which it is desired to deter him must be calculated to produce evil to someone else. The only part of the conduct of anyone for which he is amenable to society is that which concerns others. In the part which merely concerns himself, his independence is, of right, absolute. Over himself, over his own body and mind, the individual is sovereign.

It is, perhaps, hardly necessary to say that this doctrine is meant to apply only to human beings in the maturity of their faculties. We are not speaking of children or of young persons below the age which the law may fix as that of manhood or womanhood. Those who are still in a state to require being taken care of by others must be protected against their own actions as well as against external injury. For the same reason we may leave out of consideration those backward states of society in which the race itself may be considered as in its nonage.[1] . . . Liberty, as a principle, has no application to any state of things anterior to the time when mankind have become capable of being improved by free and equal discussion. Until then, there is nothing for them but

---

1. "Its nonage" means "its period of immaturity." Mill is here assuming that there is a period in human history in which people are not, in his words, "capable of being improved by free and equal discussion."

implicit obedience to an Akbar[2] or a Charlemagne[3] if they are so fortunate as to find one. But as soon as mankind have attained the capacity of being guided to their own improvement by conviction or persuasion (a period long since reached in all nations with whom we need here concern ourselves), compulsion, either in the direct form or in that of pains and penalties for noncompliance, is no longer admissible as a means to their own good, and justifiable only for the security of others.

It is proper to state that I forego any advantage which could be derived to my argument from the idea of abstract right as a thing independent of utility. I regard utility as the ultimate appeal on all ethical questions; but it must be utility in the largest sense, grounded on the permanent interests of man as a progressive being. Those interests, I contend, authorize the subjection of individual spontaneity to external control only in respect to those actions of each which concern the interest of other people. If anyone does an act *hurtful* to others, there is a *prima facie* case for punishing him by law or, where legal penalties are not safely applicable, by general disapprobation. There are also many positive acts for the benefit of others which he may rightfully be compelled to perform, such as to give evidence in a court of justice, to bear his fair share in the common defense or in any other joint work necessary to the interest of the society of which he enjoys the protection, and to perform certain acts of individual beneficence, such as saving a fellow creature's life or interposing to protect the defenseless against ill usage—things which whenever it is obviously a man's duty to do he may rightfully be made responsible to society for not doing. . . .

But there is a sphere of action in which society, as distinguished from the individual, has, if any, only an indirect interest: comprehending all that portion of a person's life and conduct which affects only himself or, if it also affects others, only with their free, voluntary, and undeceived consent and participation. When I say only himself, I mean directly and in the first instance; for whatever affects himself may affect others through himself: and the objection which may be grounded on this contingency will receive consideration in the sequel. This, then, is the appropriate region of human liberty. It comprises, first, the inward domain of consciousness, demanding liberty of conscience in the most comprehensive sense, liberty of thought and feeling, absolute freedom of opinion and sentiment on all subjects, practical or speculative, scientific, moral, or theological. The liberty of expressing and publishing opinions may seem to fall under a different principle, since it belongs to that part of the conduct of an individual which concerns other people, but, being almost of as much importance as the liberty of thought itself and resting in great part on the same reasons, is practically inseparable from it. Secondly, the principle requires liberty of tastes and pursuits, of framing the plan of our life to suit our own character, of doing as we like, subject to

2. Abū al-Fath Jalāl al-Dīn Muhammad Akbar (1542–1605) was Moghul emperor of India, 1556–1605. Apart from leading a vast expansion and administrative centralization of the empire, Akbar the Great is associated with support for the arts and religious toleration.

3. Charlemagne (742–814) was King of the Franks (768–814) and crowned Holy Roman Emperor in 800 by Pope Leo II. He is associated with the "Carolingian Renaissance," comprising economic and legal reforms as well as a revival of the arts in the eighth and ninth centuries.

such consequences as may follow, without impediment from our fellow creatures, so long as what we do does not harm them, even though they should think our conduct foolish, perverse, or wrong. Thirdly, from this liberty of each individual follows the liberty, within the same limits, of combination among individuals; freedom to unite for any purpose not involving harm to others: the persons combining being supposed to be of full age and not forced or deceived.

No society in which these liberties are not, on the whole, respected is free, whatever may be its form of government; and none is completely free in which they do not exist absolute and unqualified. The only freedom which deserves the name is that of pursuing our own good in our own way, so long as we do not attempt to deprive others of theirs or impede their efforts to obtain it. Each is the proper guardian of his own health, whether bodily *or* mental and spiritual. Mankind are greater gainers by suffering each other to live as seems good to themselves than by compelling each to live as seems good to the rest. . . .

Chapter III: Of Individuality, as One of the Elements of Well-Being

[In Chapter II, I have presented] the reasons which make it imperative that human beings should be free to form opinions and to express their opinions without reserve; and such the baneful consequences to the intellectual, and through that to the moral nature of man, unless this liberty is either conceded or asserted in spite of prohibition; let us next examine whether the same reasons do not require that men should be free to act upon their opinions—to carry these out in their lives without hindrance, either physical or moral, from their fellow men, so long as it is at their own risk and peril. This last proviso is of course indispensable. No one pretends that actions should be as free as opinions. . . . Acts, of whatever kind, which without justifiable cause do harm to others may be, and in the more important cases absolutely require to be, controlled by the unfavorable sentiments, and, when needful, by the active interference of mankind. The liberty of the individual must be thus far limited; he must not make himself a nuisance to other people. But if he refrains from molesting others in what concerns them, and merely acts according to his own inclination and judgment in things which concern himself, the same reasons which show that opinion should be free prove also that he should be allowed, without molestation, to carry his opinions into practice at his own cost. . . . As it is useful that while mankind are imperfect there should be different opinions, so it is that there should be different experiments of living; that free scope should be given to varieties of character, short of injury to others; and that the worth of different modes of life should be proved practically, when anyone thinks fit to try them. It is desirable, in short, that in things which do not primarily concern others individuality should assert itself. Where not the person's own character but the traditions or customs of other people are the rule of conduct, there is wanting one of the principal ingredients of human happiness, and quite the chief ingredient of individual and social progress.

In maintaining this principle, the greatest difficulty to be encountered does not lie in the appreciation of means toward an acknowledged end, but in the indifference of persons in general to the end itself. If it were felt that the free development of individuality is one of the leading essentials of well-being; that it is not only a co-ordinate element with all that is designated by the terms civilization, instruction, education, culture, but is itself a necessary part and condition of all those things, there would be no danger that liberty should be undervalued, and the adjustment of the boundaries between it and social control would present no extraordinary difficulty. But the evil is that individual spontaneity is hardly recognized by the common modes of thinking as having any intrinsic worth, or deserving any regard on its own account. . . . Few persons, out of Germany, even comprehend the meaning of the doctrine which Wilhelm von Humboldt,[4] so eminent both as a *savant* and as a politician, made the text of a treatise—that "the end of man, or that which is prescribed by the eternal or immutable dictates of reason, and not suggested by vague and transient desires, is the highest and most harmonious development of his powers to a complete and consistent whole"; that, therefore, the object "toward which every human being must ceaselessly direct his efforts, and on which especially those who design to influence their fellow men must ever keep their eyes, is the individuality of power and development"; that for this there are two requisites, "freedom, and variety of situations"; and that from the union of these arise "individual vigor and manifold diversity," which combine themselves in "originality."[5]

Little, however, as people are accustomed to a doctrine like that of von Humboldt, and surprising as it may be to them to find so high a value attached to individuality, the question, one must nevertheless think, can only be one of degree. No one's idea of excellence in conduct is that people should do absolutely nothing but copy one another. No one would assert that people ought not to put into their mode of life, and into the conduct of their concerns, any impress whatever of their own judgment or of their own individual character. On the other hand, it would be absurd to pretend that people ought to live as if nothing whatever had been known in the world before they came into it; as if experience had as yet done nothing toward showing that one mode of existence, or of conduct, is preferable to another. Nobody denies that people should be so taught and trained in youth as to know and benefit by the ascertained results of human experience. But it is the privilege and proper condition of a human being, arrived at the maturity of his faculties, to use and interpret experience in his own way. It is for him to find out what part of recorded experience is properly applicable to his own circumstances and character. The traditions and customs of other people are, to a certain extent, evidence of what their experience has taught *them*—presumptive

4. Baron von Humboldt (1767–1835) was a philosopher, linguist, and public official. His book *On the Limits of State Action* forcefully defended liberty on the basis of its contribution to the development of individual capacities.

5. *The Sphere and Duties of Government* [*On the Limits of State Action*], from the German of Baron Wilhelm von Humboldt, pp. 11, 13. [Mill's note.]

evidence, and as such, have a claim to his deference: but, in the first place, their experience may be too narrow, or they may have not interpreted it rightly. Secondly, their interpretation of experience may be correct, but unsuitable to him. Customs are made for customary circumstances and customary characters; and his circumstances or his character may be uncustomary. Thirdly, though the customs be both good as customs and suitable to him, yet to conform to custom merely *as* custom does not educate or develop in him any of the qualities which are the distinctive endowment of a human being. The human faculties of perception, judgment, discriminative feeling, mental activity, and even moral preference are exercised only in making a choice. He who does anything because it is the custom makes no choice. He gains no practice either in discerning or in desiring what is best. The mental and moral, like the muscular, powers are improved only by being used. The faculties are called into no exercise by doing a thing merely because others do it, no more than by believing a thing only because others believe it. If the grounds of an opinion are not conclusive to the person's own reason, his reason cannot be strengthened, but is likely to be weakened, by his adopting it: and if the inducements to an act are not such as are consentaneous to his own feelings and character (where affection, or the rights of others, are not concerned), it is so much done toward rendering his feelings and character inert and torpid instead of active and energetic.

He who lets the world, or his own portion of it, choose his plan of life for him has no need of any other faculty than the ape-like one of imitation. He who chooses his plan for himself employs all his faculties. He must use observation to see, reasoning and judgment to foresee, activity to gather materials for decision, discrimination to decide, and when he has decided, firmness and self-control to hold to his deliberate decision. And these qualities he requires and exercises exactly in proportion as the part of his conduct which he determines according to his own judgment and feelings is a large one. It is possible that he might be guided in some good path, and kept out of harm's way, without any of these things. But what will be his comparative worth as a human being? . . .

It will probably be conceded that it is desirable people should exercise their understandings, and that an intelligent following of custom, or even occasionally an intelligent deviation from custom, is better than a blind and simply mechanical adhesion to it. To a certain extent it is admitted that our understanding should be our own; but there is not the same willingness to admit that our desires and impulses should be our own likewise, or that to possess impulses of our own, and of any strength, is anything but a peril and a snare. Yet desires and impulses are as much a part of a perfect human being as beliefs and restraints; and strong impulses are only perilous when not properly balanced, when one set of aims and inclinations is developed into strength, while others, which ought to coexist with them, remain weak and inactive. It is not because men's desires are strong that they act ill; it is because their consciences are weak. There is no natural connection between strong impulses and a weak conscience. The natural connection is the other way. To say that one person's desires and feelings are stronger and more various than those of another is merely to say that he has more of the raw material of human nature and is therefore capable, perhaps of more evil, but certainly of more good. Strong impulses are but another name for energy. Energy may be turned to bad uses; but more good may always be made of an energetic nature than of an indolent and impassive one. . . . Whoever thinks that individuality of desires and impulses should not be encouraged to unfold itself must maintain that society has no need of strong natures—is not the better for containing many persons who have much character—and that a high general average of energy is not desirable. . . .

In our times, from the highest class of society down to the lowest, everyone lives as under the eye of a hostile and dreaded censorship. Not only in what concerns others, but in what concerns only themselves, the individual or the family do not ask themselves, what do I prefer? or, what would suit my character and disposition? or, what would allow the best and highest in me to have fair play and enable it to grow and thrive? They ask themselves, what is suitable to my position? what is usually done by persons of my station and pecuniary circumstances? or (worse still) what is usually done by persons of a station and circumstances superior to mine? I do not mean that they choose what is customary in preference to what suits their own inclination. It does not occur to them to have any inclination except for what is customary. Thus the mind itself is bowed to the yoke: even in what people do for pleasure, conformity is the first thing thought of; they like in crowds; they exercise choice only among things commonly done; peculiarity of taste, eccentricity of conduct are shunned equally with crimes, until by dint of not following their own nature they have no nature to follow: their human capacities are withered and starved; they become incapable of any strong wishes or native pleasures, and are generally without either opinions or feelings of home growth, or properly their own. Now is this, or is it not, the desirable condition of human nature?

It is so, on the Calvinistic theory.[6] According to that, the one great offense of man is self-will. All the good of which humanity is capable is comprised in obedience. You have no choice; thus you must do, and no otherwise: "Whatever is not a duty is a sin." Human nature being radically corrupt, there is no redemption for anyone until human nature is killed within him. To one holding this theory of life, crushing out any of the human faculties, capacities, and susceptibilities is no evil: man needs no capacity but that of surrendering himself to the will of God. . . .

Many persons, no doubt, sincerely think that human beings thus cramped and dwarfed are as their Maker designed them to be, just as many have thought that trees are a much finer thing when clipped into pollards, or cut out into figures of animals, than as nature made them. But if it be any part of religion to believe that man was made by a good Being, it is more consistent with that faith to believe that this Being gave all human faculties that they might be cultivated and unfolded, not rooted out and consumed, and that he takes delight in every nearer approach made by his creatures to the ideal conception embodied in them, every increase in any of their capabilities of comprehension, of action, or of enjoyment. There is a different type of human excellence

---

6. Calvinism is the theological system associated with John Calvin (1509–1564), a leading figure in the Protestant Reformation, and with the Reformed churches. The central ideas in Calvinism are the total depravity of human nature (that everything we do is tainted by sin) and predestination. According to predestination, God makes an unconditional choice about who will be saved (unconditional election); Christ's death atoned exclusively for the sins of those whom God had chosen; those who have been predestined to salvation cannot fail to be saved (irresistible grace); and they cannot lose their salvation (perseverance of the saints).

from the Calvinistic: a conception of humanity as having its nature bestowed on it for other purposes than merely to be abnegated. "Pagan self-assertion" is one of the elements of human worth, as well as "Christian self-denial." There is a Greek ideal of self-development, which the Platonic and Christian ideal of self-government blends with, but does not supersede. It may be better to be a John Knox[7] than an Alcibiades[8]; but it is better to be a Pericles than either; nor would a Pericles,[9] if we had one in these days, be without anything good which belonged to John Knox.

It is not by wearing down into uniformity all that is individual in themselves, but by cultivating it and calling it forth, within the limits imposed by the rights and interests of others, that human beings become a noble and beautiful object of contemplation. . . . As much compression as is necessary to prevent the stronger specimens of human nature from encroaching on the rights of others cannot be dispensed with; but for this there is ample compensation even in the point of view of human development. The means of development which the individual loses by being prevented from gratifying his inclinations to the injury of others are chiefly obtained at the expense of the development of other people. And even to himself there is a full equivalent in the better development of the social part of his nature, rendered possible by the restraint put upon the selfish part. To be held to rigid rules of justice for the sake of others develops the feelings and capacities which have the good of others for their object. But to be restrained in things not affecting their good, by their mere displeasure, develops nothing valuable except such force of character as may unfold itself in resisting the restraint. If acquiesced in, it dulls and blunts the whole nature.

Having said that the individuality is the same thing with development, and that it is only the cultivation of individuality which produces, or can produce, well-developed human beings, I might here close the argument; for what more or better can be said of any condition of human affairs than that it brings human beings themselves nearer to the best thing they can be? Or what worse can be said of any obstruction to good than that it prevents this? Doubtless, however, these considerations will not suffice to convince those who most need convincing; and it is necessary further to show that these developed human beings are of some use to the undeveloped—to point out to those who do not desire liberty, and would not avail themselves of it, that they may be in some intelligible manner rewarded for allowing other people to make use of it without hindrance.[10]. . .

---

7. John Knox (1510–1572), a Scottish clergyman, was a central figure in the Protestant Reformation and a founder of Presbyterianism. Knox was closely associated with Calvin and brought Calvinism to Scotland.

8. Alcibiades was an Athenian politician and a general in the Peloponnesian War. He is a central character in Plato's *Symposium*.

9. Pericles (495–429 BCE) was a leading political and military figure in Athens, described by Thucydides as "the first citizen of Athens," and widely credited with fostering Athenian democracy.

10. In the rest of chapter III of *On Liberty*, Mill tries to make this further case. He argues that human development, which is fostered by protecting individual liberty, is also a great benefit for those who choose not to develop their own powers and who live in more conventional ways. Individuals who do not choose to develop their own powers, Mill says, might "learn something" from those who do; moreover, we all benefit, he argues, from the economic, social, and political progress that results from the choices of "developed human beings."

TEST YOUR UNDERSTANDING

1. Mill says that his aim in *On Liberty* is to "assert one very simple principle." State the principle in your own words.

2. Does Mill say that his principle of liberty applies to all people under all circumstances? If not, what are the restrictions on its application?

3. What does Mill think is wrong with acting according to "custom as custom"?

4. What is the "Calvinistic theory," and what does Mill think is wrong with it?

READER'S GUIDE

Mill on Liberty

John Stuart Mill's *On Liberty* (1859) is about individual liberty. It explores "the nature and limits of the power which can legitimately be exercised by society over the individual." Mill presents those limits in a principle of liberty that is sometimes referred to as the *harm principle*. Mill's harm principle says, in essence:

> Coercion against a person is only justified for the purpose of preventing harm to other people.

The harm principle tells us not to use coercion—either through laws, which threaten people with punishment for disobedience, or collective opinion—to control a person's conduct unless the conduct is harmful to other people. When a person's action is not harmful to other people, it may still be harmful to the person himself or herself, or we may judge it to be undignified or sinful. If that is what we think about a person's action, we are permitted to respond with advice, persuasion, or avoidance. But when a person's action is not harmful to others, we should not use coercion.

Mill argues for the harm principle, he says, on the basis of "utility," not on the basis of abstract right. He means that we should use the harm principle because that produces the best results for overall human happiness. His argument for the harm principle, then, is that the best results for happiness come when we use coercion only to prevent people from harming others, and otherwise try to convince them (or avoid their company).

In chapter II (not included in the selection), Mill applies the harm principle to freedom of speech. He argues that we should leave wide scope for free speech because the result is more robust discussion. Robust discussion is good for three reasons: (1) it helps us in correcting errors; (2) it helps us to understand the foundations and meaning of our ideas (keeps them from becoming "dead dogma"); and (3) it encourages us to think harder, which promotes "the mental well-being of mankind." Each of these three considerations points to benefits for happiness.

In chapter III, Mill considers what he calls the liberty of "tastes and pursuits." Shifting away from free speech, Mill argues for individual autonomy in the choice and execution of a life plan, and criticizes the view that we should simply rely on custom and tradition in deciding how to live our lives. Drawing on the harm principle, Mill argues that we should only restrict personal choices to prevent harm to others, not because we think the person's life choices are unwise, or undignified, or sinful.

Mill's defense of this liberty of tastes and pursuits focuses on the idea that personal liberty is required for the full development of our human capacities—our capacities for reasoning, judgment, perceptual discrimination, creative imagination, and subtlety of feeling and desire. He emphasizes this point in his *Autobiography*. He says there that the "single truth" of *On Liberty* is "the importance, to man and society, of a large variety in types of character, and of giving full freedom to human nature to expand itself in innumerable and conflicting directions."[11]

In chapter III, he argues for a close connection between liberty and the development of human capacities. The argument proceeds in two steps:

1. The liberty of tastes and pursuits is required for individuality—for distinctive, self-directed patterns of development, for innovations in writing, music, fashion, architecture, product design, organization, pedagogy, occupational choices, and styles of intimate partnership.

2. Individuality is required for development: "Individuality is the same thing with development, and it is only the cultivation of individuality which produces or can produce well-developed human beings."

So liberty is important for individuality, and individuality for the development of human capacities. (The development of human capacities is important because it plays an essential role in promoting overall happiness.)

The first step in Mill's argument—that liberty is important for individuality—is easy to understand: when people are free from interference in their personal lives, they are able to strike out in new directions. But the second step is less obvious: Is the connection between individuality and the development of our human capacities really so close? Maybe our intellectual capacities—our ability to reason and make judgments, for example—are best employed in understanding the wisdom of long-standing social customs; maybe our inclinations, desires, passions, are best developed by aligning them with traditional roles. Maybe individuality—a departure from custom and tradition—produces depravity and sorrow, not development.

Mill is concerned with this objection. "Individual spontaneity," he says, "is hardly recognized by the common modes of thinking, as having any intrinsic worth." Maybe that is because critics of individuality think that it leads to dead ends, to a sense of loss and alienation. Maybe they think human beings develop most fully by staying within the bounds of strong customs and traditions.

In response to this defense of custom and tradition, Mill makes three points:

First, society and tradition may be wrong about the best way to live; their interpretation of experience may be too narrow. Liberty enables people to strike out in new directions, which may help to correct mistakes that are not reflected in customs and traditions.

Second, people are different from one another, and no single model of life is suited for everyone. So even if custom and tradition are good for most people, there still may be benefits to liberty.

11. John Stuart Mill, *The Autobiography of John Stuart Mill* (London: Penguin 1989), chapter VII, paragraph 20.

Third, figuring out the best way to live requires that we use our human powers: "He who chooses his plan for himself, employs all his faculties. He must use observation to see, reasoning and judgment to foresee, activity to gather materials for decision, discrimination to decide, and, when he has decided, firmness and self-control to hold to his deliberate decision." By contrast, "To conform to custom, merely as custom, does not educate or develop in him any of the qualities which are the distinctive endowment of a human being"; instead, "human capacities are withered and starved." So Mill thinks there is a kind of intrinsic value to working out a plan of life for yourself, and not simply following the conventional standards.

These three arguments against simply following customs and traditions are about the benefits of liberty to the person who uses the liberty. But the exercise of personal liberty in choosing a plan of life may also produce benefits for other people. (Mill makes these points in parts of chapter III that have been omitted here.) When people strike out in new directions, they encourage "experiments in living" and "varieties of character." And this diversity provides models for other people about how to conduct their lives, and encourages individuals to develop along their own paths rather than simply accepting custom as a guide. Moreover, diversity of choices encourages social progress—in politics, education, and morals. That is why Mill says, at the end of chapter III, that "it is good there should be differences."

NOTES AND QUESTIONS

1. Mill says that if a person is acting against his own best interests, we have reason for "remonstrating with him, or reasoning with him, or persuading him, or entreating him, but not for compelling him or visiting him with any evil in case he do otherwise." Think of an example of a person (perhaps a friend) who has acted against his or her best interests: say, the person has started drinking heavily. How would you draw the distinction between actions that Mill thinks are acceptable (remonstrating, reasoning, persuading, or entreating) and actions Mill says are unacceptable (compelling him or "visiting him with any evil")? Suppose you know that your friend is very sensitive and will sink into depression if you encourage him to stop drinking. If you nevertheless encourage him, and he sinks into depression, have you entreated him or have you visited an evil on him? Or suppose the person is very susceptible to your influence or dependent on you for a grade or a salary. When there is a relation of dependence, can you provide encouragement that does not come across as a threat? Try to state a general principle that draws a line between the compulsion Mill rejects and the persuasion he allows. Does the distinction help you decide what you should do in these cases?

2. Mill claims that he defends his principle on the basis of "utility," not on the basis of "abstract right as a thing independent of utility." Critics of **utilitarianism** have argued that the principle of utility does not provide a strong case in favor of liberties. The principle of utility says that the right acts and institutions are the ones that maximize the sum of happiness. But, the critics say, if you can make enough people happy by enslaving other people, or requiring religious conformity, or demanding compliance

with customs and conventions, then utilitarianism must endorse limits on liberty. Or they say that utilitarians are too quick to favor restrictions on freedom of speech or assembly in the name of national security. How might Mill respond to these concerns? Why does he think that the principle of utility supports the liberty principle?

3. One line of argument for liberty that Mill uses is that liberty is important for individuality and that individuality is the "same thing with development." He goes on to say that "developed human beings are of some use to the undeveloped." Is that a good case for extending liberties to all? In answering, you should think about four questions:

   a. Why is liberty important for individuality?

   b. Why is individuality so closely related to the development of human powers? (Mill gives three reasons in the paragraph that begins: "Little, however, as people are accustomed to . . .")

   c. In what ways are "developed human beings" of use "to the undeveloped"?

   d. Would the results be better, in terms of the sum of happiness, if liberties were available only to people who would use the liberties to become "well developed"?

4. For a helpful discussion of utilitarianism (including Mill's version of utilitarianism) and the troubles it may have with liberty, see John Rawls, *A Theory of Justice* (Harvard University Press, 1999), 19–24, 184–85.

Patrick Devlin (1905–1992)

Devlin was born in Kent, England. A commercial lawyer and a judge—the youngest High Court judge appointed in the twentieth century—Devlin became a member of the House of Lords in 1961. He wrote "Morals and the Criminal Law" in criticism of the Wolfenden Report (1957), which called for the abolition of British laws that criminalized homosexuality. He subsequently changed his mind and, in 1965, signed a letter that urged the implementation of the reforms recommended by the Wolfenden Report.

MORALS AND THE CRIMINAL LAW[1]

What is the connexion between crime and sin and to what extent, if at all, should the criminal law of England concern itself with the enforcement of morals and punish sin or immorality as such? . . .

---

1. Lord Devlin's essay was written in response to the *Report of the Committee on Homosexual Offences and Prostitution* (commonly known as the Wolfenden Report). The Wolfenden Report, released in Britain on September 4, 1957, recommended that "homosexual behaviour between consenting adults in private should no longer be a criminal offence."

I think it is clear that the criminal law as we know it is based upon moral principle. In a number of crimes its function is simply to enforce a moral principle and nothing else. The law, both criminal and civil, claims to be able to speak about morality and immorality generally. Where does it get its authority to do this and how does it settle the moral principles which it enforces? Undoubtedly, as a matter of history, it derived both from Christian teaching. But I think that the strict logician is right when he says that the law can no longer rely on doctrines in which citizens are entitled to disbelieve. It is necessary therefore to look for some other source. . . .

I have framed three interrogatories addressed to myself to answer:

1. Has society the right to pass judgement at all on matters of morals? Ought there, in other words, to be a public morality, or are morals always a matter for private judgement?

2. If society has the right to pass judgement, has it also the right to use the weapon of the law to enforce it?

3. If so, ought it to use that weapon in all cases or only in some; and if only in some, on what principles should it distinguish?

I shall begin with the first interrogatory and consider what is meant by the right of society to pass a moral judgement, that is, a judgement about what is good and what is evil. The fact that a majority of people may disapprove of a practice does not of itself make it a matter for society as a whole. Nine men out of ten may disapprove of what the tenth man is doing and still say that it is not their business. There is a case for a collective judgement (as distinct from a large number of individual opinions which sensible people may even refrain from pronouncing at all if it is upon somebody else's private affairs) only if society is affected. Without a collective judgement there can be no case at all for intervention. Let me take as an illustration the Englishman's attitude to religion as it is now and as it has been in the past. His attitude now is that a man's religion is his private affair; he may think of another man's religion that it is right or wrong, true or untrue, but not that it is good or bad. In earlier times that was not so; a man was denied the right to practise what was thought of as heresy, and heresy was thought of as destructive of society. . . .

This view—that there is such a thing as public morality—can . . . be justified by *a priori* argument. What makes a society of any sort is community of ideas, not only political ideas but also ideas about the way its members should behave and govern their lives; these latter ideas are its morals. Every society has a moral structure as well as a political one: or rather, since that might suggest two independent systems, I should say that the structure of every society is made up both of politics and morals. Take, for example, the institution of marriage. Whether a man should be allowed to take more than one wife is something about which every society has to make up its mind one way or the other. In England we believe in the Christian idea of marriage and therefore adopt monogamy as a moral principle. Consequently the Christian institution of marriage has become the basis of family life and so part of the structure of our society. It is there not because it is Christian. It has got there because it is Christian, but it remains there because it is built into the house in which we live and could not be removed without bringing it down. The great majority of those who live in this country accept it because it is the Christian idea of marriage and for them the only true one. But a non-Christian is bound by it, not because it is part of Christianity but because, rightly or wrongly, it has been adopted by the society in which he lives. . . .

We see this more clearly if we think of ideas or institutions that are purely political. Society cannot tolerate rebellion; it will not allow argument about the rightness of the cause. Historians a century later may say that the rebels were right and the Government was wrong and a percipient and conscientious subject of the State may think so at the time. But it is not a matter which can be left to individual judgement.

The institution of marriage is a good example for my purpose because it bridges the division, if there is one, between politics and morals. Marriage is part of the structure of our society and it is also the basis of a moral code which condemns fornication and adultery. The institution of marriage would be gravely threatened if individual judgements were permitted about the morality of adultery; on these points there must be a public morality. But public morality is not to be confined to those moral principles which support institutions such as marriage. People do not think of monogamy as something which has to be supported because our society has chosen to organize itself upon it; they think of it as something that is good in itself and offering a good way of life and that it is for that reason that our society has adopted it. I return to the statement that I have already made, that society means a community of ideas; without shared ideas on politics, morals, and ethics no society can exist. Each one of us has ideas about what is good and what is evil; they cannot be kept private from the society in which we live. If men and women try to create a society in which there is no fundamental agreement about good and evil they will fail; if, having based it on common agreement, the agreement goes, the society will disintegrate. For society is not something that is kept together physically; it is held by the invisible bonds of common thought. If the bonds were too far relaxed the members would drift apart. A common morality is part of the bondage. The bondage is part of the price of society; and mankind, which needs society, must pay its price. . . .

[T]he answer to the first question determines the way in which the second should be approached and may indeed very nearly dictate the answer to the second question. If society has no right to make judgements on morals, the law must find some special justification for entering the field of morality: if homosexuality and prostitution are not in themselves wrong, then the onus is very clearly on the lawgiver who wants to frame a law against certain aspects of them to justify the exceptional treatment. But if society has the right to make a judgement and has it on the basis that a recognized morality is as necessary to society as, say, a recognized government, then society may use the law to preserve morality in the same way as it uses it to safeguard anything else that is essential to its existence. If therefore the first proposition is securely established with all its implications, society has a prima facie right to legislate against immorality as such. . . .

. . . [Devlin presents a Wolfenden Committee objection to the view he just presented, and now he responds]: I think that it is not possible to set theoretical limits to the power of the State to legislate against immorality. It is not possible to settle in advance exceptions to the general rule or to define inflexibly areas of morality into which the law is in no circumstances to be allowed to enter. Society is entitled by means of its laws to protect itself from dangers, whether from within or without. Here again I think that the political parallel is legitimate. The law of treason is directed against aiding the king's enemies and against sedition from within. The justification for this is that established government is necessary for the existence of society and therefore its safety against violent overthrow must be secured. But an established morality is as necessary as good government to the welfare of society. Societies disintegrate from within more frequently than they are broken up by external pressures. There is disintegration when no common morality is observed and history shows that the loosening of moral bonds is often the first stage of disintegration, so that society is justified in taking the same steps to preserve its moral code as it does to preserve its government and other essential institutions. The suppression of vice is as much the law's business as the suppression of subversive activities; it is no more possible to define a sphere of private morality than it is to define one of private subversive activity.... You may argue that if a man's sins affect only himself it cannot be the concern of society. If he chooses to get drunk every night in the privacy of his own home, is any one except himself the worse for it? But suppose a quarter or a half of the population got drunk every night, what sort of society would it be? You cannot set a theoretical limit to the number of people who can get drunk before society is entitled to legislate against drunkenness. The same may be said of gambling. . . .

In what circumstances the State should exercise its power is the third of the interrogatories I have framed. But before I get to it I must raise a point which might have been brought up in any one of the three. How are the moral judgements of society to be ascertained? By leaving it until now, I can ask it in the more limited form that is now sufficient for my purpose. How is the law-maker to ascertain the moral judgements of society? It is surely not enough that they should be reached by the opinion of the majority; it would be too much to require the individual assent of every citizen. English law has evolved and regularly uses a standard which does not depend on the counting of heads. It is that of the reasonable man. He is not to be confused with the rational man. He is not expected to reason about anything and his judgement may be largely a matter of feeling. It is the viewpoint of the man in the street—or to use an archaism familiar to all lawyers—the man in the Clapham omnibus.[2] He might also be called the right-minded man. For my purpose I should like to call him the man in the jury box, for the moral judgement of society must be something about which any twelve men or women drawn at random might after discussion be expected to be unanimous. . . .

Immorality then, for the purpose of the law, is what every right-minded person is presumed to consider to be immoral. Any immorality is capable of affecting society

---

2. "Man in the Clapham omnibus" is a nineteenth-century British phrase that refers to an intelligent but unremarkable person. It was used to generate a basis of comparison in court cases—what would the man in the Clapham omnibus have done in this situation?—or to make claims about public opinion. "Clapham" is a London suburb and "omnibus" is a (now archaic) term for a public bus.

injuriously and in effect to a greater or lesser extent it usually does; this is what gives the law its *locus standi*.[3] It cannot be shut out. But—and this brings me to the third question—the individual has a *locus standi* too; he cannot be expected to surrender to the judgement of society the whole conduct of his life. It is the old and familiar question of striking a balance between the rights and interests of society and those of the individual. This is something which the law is constantly doing in matters large and small. To take a very down-to-earth example, let me consider the right of the individual whose house adjoins the highway to have access to it; that means in these days the right to have vehicles stationary in the highway, sometimes for a considerable time if there is a lot of loading or unloading. There are many cases in which the courts have had to balance the private right of access against the public right to use the highway without obstruction. It cannot be done by carving up the highway into public and private areas. It is done by recognizing that each have rights over the whole; that if each were to exercise their rights to the full, they would come into conflict; and therefore that the rights of each must be curtailed so as to ensure as far as possible that the essential needs of each are safeguarded.

I do not think that one can talk sensibly of a public and private morality any more than one can of a public or private highway. Morality is a sphere in which there is a public interest and a private interest, often in conflict, and the problem is to reconcile the two. This does not mean that it is impossible to put forward any general statements about how in our society the balance ought to be struck. Such statements cannot of their nature be rigid or precise; they would not be designed to circumscribe the operation of the law-making power but to guide those who have to apply it. . . .

I believe that most people would agree upon the chief of these elastic principles. There must be toleration of the maximum individual freedom that is consistent with the integrity of society. . . . [This toleration] is not confined to thought and speech; it extends to action, as is shown by the recognition of the right to conscientious objection in war-time; this example shows also that conscience will be respected even in times of national danger. The principle appears to me to be peculiarly appropriate to all questions of morals. Nothing should be punished by the law that does not lie beyond the limits of tolerance. It is not nearly enough to say that a majority dislike a practice; there must be a real feeling of reprobation. Those who are dissatisfied with the present law on homosexuality often say that the opponents of reform are swayed simply by disgust. If that were so it would be wrong, but I do not think one can ignore disgust if it is deeply felt and not manufactured. Its presence is a good indication that the bounds of toleration are being reached. Not everything is to be tolerated. No society can do without intolerance, indignation, and disgust, they are the forces behind the moral law, and indeed it can be argued that if they or something like them are not present, the feelings of society cannot be weighty enough to deprive the individual of

---

3. *Locus standi* is the right to bring a legal action (what is commonly called "standing"). Devlin is not using the term literally here. He means that both the individual and society have substantial interests at stake in the issue under consideration about the legal enforcement of morality, not that they have a right to bring legal action.

freedom of choice. I suppose that there is hardly anyone nowadays who would not be disgusted by the thought of deliberate cruelty to animals. No one proposes to relegate that or any other form of sadism to the realm of private morality or to allow it to be practised in public or in private. It would be possible no doubt to point out that until a comparatively short while ago nobody thought very much of cruelty to animals and also that pity and kindliness and the unwillingness to inflict pain are virtues more generally esteemed now than they have ever been in the past. But matters of this sort are not determined by rational argument. Every moral judgement, unless it claims a divine source, is simply a feeling that no right-minded man could behave in any other way without admitting that he was doing wrong. It is the power of a common sense and not the power of reason that is behind the judgements of society. But before a society can put a practice beyond the limits of tolerance there must be a deliberate judgement that the practice is injurious to society. There is, for example, a general abhorrence of homosexuality. We should ask ourselves in the first instance whether, looking at it calmly and dispassionately, we regard it as a vice so abominable that its mere presence is an offence. If that is the genuine feeling of the society in which we live, I do not see how society can be denied the right to eradicate it. Our feeling may not be so intense as that. We may feel about it that, if confined, it is tolerable, but that if it spread it might be gravely injurious; it is in this way that most societies look upon fornication, seeing it as a natural weakness which must be kept within bounds but which cannot be rooted out. It becomes then a question of balance, the danger to society in one scale and the extent of the restriction in the other. . . .

This then is how I believe my third interrogatory should be answered—not by the formulation of hard and fast rules, but by a judgement in each case taking into account the sort of factors I have been mentioning. The line that divides the criminal law from the moral is not determinable by the application of any clear-cut principle. It is like a line that divides land and sea, a coastline of irregularities and indentations. There are gaps and promontories, such as adultery and fornication, which the law has for centuries left substantially untouched. Adultery of the sort that breaks up marriage seems to me to be just as harmful to the social fabric as homosexuality or bigamy. The only ground for putting it outside the criminal law is that a law which made it a crime would be too difficult to enforce; it is too generally regarded as a human weakness not suitably punished by imprisonment. All that the law can do with fornication is to act against its worst manifestations; there is a general abhorrence of the commercialization of vice, and that sentiment gives strength to the law against brothels and immoral earnings. There is no logic to be found in this. The boundary between the criminal law and the moral law is fixed by balancing in the case of each particular crime the pros and cons of legal enforcement in accordance with the sort of considerations I have been outlining. The fact that adultery, fornication, and lesbianism are untouched by the criminal law does not prove that homosexuality ought not to be touched. The error of jurisprudence in the Wolfenden Report is caused by the search for some single principle to explain the division between crime and sin. The Report finds it in the principle that the criminal law exists for the protection of individuals; on this principle fornication in private between consenting adults is outside the law and thus it becomes logically indefensible to bring homosexuality between consenting adults in private within it. But the true principle is that the law exists for the protection of society. It does not discharge its function by protecting the individual from injury, annoyance, corruption, and exploitation; the law must protect also the institutions and the community of ideas, political and moral, without which people cannot live together. Society cannot ignore the morality of the individual any more than it can his loyalty; it flourishes on both and without either it dies. . . .

I return now to the main thread of my argument and summarize it. Society cannot live without morals. Its morals are those standards of conduct which the reasonable man approves. A rational man, who is also a good man, may have other standards. If he has no standards at all he is not a good man and need not be further considered. If he has standards, they may be very different; he may, for example, not disapprove of homosexuality or abortion. In that case he will not share in the common morality; but that should not make him deny that it is a social necessity. A rebel may be rational in thinking that he is right but he is irrational if he thinks that society can leave him free to rebel.

TEST YOUR UNDERSTANDING

1. For "the purpose of the law" (p. 1100), how does Devlin understand the idea of immorality?

2. How does Devlin think that societies are held together? Does he emphasize the importance of contracts, threats of force, self-interest, or shared ideas?

3. Does Devlin endorse the idea that there is a sphere of private morality in which the state should not legislate?

4. If a majority dislikes some pattern of conduct, is that good enough reason for using criminal law to try to stop it?

READER'S GUIDE

Devlin on Enforcing Morals

In 1954, the British government established a committee—called the Wolfenden Committee after its chair, Lord John Wolfenden—to review British laws regulating prostitution and same-sex conduct. Same-sex conduct violated the Criminal Law Amendment Act, passed by Parliament in 1885. In 1957, the Wolfenden Committee issued its final report, which argued for decriminalizing "homosexual behaviour between consenting adults in private."[4] A decade later, Parliament acted on the recommendations of the Wolfenden Report and partially decriminalized same-sex conduct.

---

4. *Report of the Committee on Homosexual Offences and Prostitution* (London: Her Majesty's Stationery Office, September 1957), 115.

The arguments in the Wolfenden Report were broadly aligned with philosophical ideas about personal liberty advanced by Jeremy Bentham[5] and John Stuart Mill.[6] Bentham and Mill both endorsed a general principle commonly referred to as the "harm principle." According to the harm principle, a society should only use criminal law to punish people for actions that harm other people. A society should not punish people simply because a majority (even a large majority) judges their conduct to be immoral or sinful (even if it *really is* immoral or sinful), though not harmful to other people. The harm principle thus says that it is permissible for a society to restrict personal liberty to prevent harm to others but impermissible to restrict personal liberty to prevent conduct judged immoral, though not harmful to others.

In the essay excerpted here, Lord Patrick Devlin, a British jurist, argues against this philosophical position and the conclusions of the Wolfenden Report. Rejecting the harm principle, Devlin says that a society may rightly turn its moral convictions into criminal law. As Devlin puts it, "society has a prima facie right to legislate against immorality as such."[7]

What does Devlin mean by "legislate against immorality as such?" "For the purpose of the law," he says, immorality "is what every right-minded person is presumed to consider to be immoral."[8] So when Devlin says that a society may legislate against "immorality as such," he means that a society may rightly punish conduct because every right-minded person judges it to be immoral, even if the conduct would not be harmful to other people.[9] Devlin thus defends what is often called "the legal enforcement of morality," and rejects the conclusions of the Wolfenden Report about regulating sexual conduct. In a sweeping statement near the end of his essay, he says that the law "does not discharge its function by protecting the individual from injury, annoyance, corruption, and exploitation; the law must protect also the institutions and the community of ideas, political and moral, without which people cannot live together."[10]

Devlin's defense of the legal enforcement of morality provoked a response from the distinguished British legal theorist H. L. A. Hart. The resulting Hart-Devlin debate was an important episode in modern debate about liberty, morality, and law.[11]

To evaluate Devlin's argument, an explicit reconstruction will help. What follows is a reconstruction, which we call the "disintegration argument." It rests on three **premises**[12]:

P1.   A society has the right to protect itself from disintegration.

P2.   If a society is to protect itself from disintegration, it has the right to ensure the presence of a shared moral code.

P3.   A society has the right to ensure the presence of a shared moral code only if it has the right to ensure its moral code through criminal law.

5. Jeremy Bentham (1748–1832) is widely regarded as the founder of utilitarianism.

6. John Stuart Mill (1806–1873) was the leading British utilitarian thinker in nineteenth-century England.

7. See page 1099 of this anthology.

8. See page 1100 of this anthology.

9. Devlin's argument thus defends the legal enforcement of the community's moral sense. Others argue that it is permissible for the community to enforce what is really morally right, not simply what the consensus of the community deems to be right.

10. See page 1103 of this anthology.

11. H. L. A. Hart, *Law, Liberty, and Morality* (Stanford University Press, 1963).

12. The three premises are suggested by the paragraph on page 1099 of this anthology, which begins: "... [Devlin presents ...].

When you put these three premises together, you get the following:

A society has the right to enforce its shared moral code through criminal law.

In short, you get a defense of the legal enforcement of morality, at least as the community consensus now understands morality. Summarizing the thrust of the disintegration argument, Devlin says: "Society cannot ignore the morality of the individual any more than it can his loyalty; it flourishes on both and without either it dies."[13]

What should we make of the disintegration argument? To evaluate it, you will need to consider the three premises in turn. A few comments on each may help to guide your reflections.

P1 is obviously not right. Consider a hideously evil society: say, Nazi Germany. Perhaps Nazi Germany did not have the right to prevent itself from disintegrating. But while P1 is controversial, Devlin could have modified it to say:

P1*   A society that is not hideously evil has the right to protect itself from disintegration.

Evaluating P1* requires an interpretation of "disintegration." So lets assume that "disintegration" means the end of organized society—a collapse into a state of disorder, in which life is—as Hobbes said—"solitary, poor, nasty, brutish, and short." On that interpretation, disintegration is really bad, and it may seem at least plausible that a society that is not hideously evil has the right to protect itself from disintegration.

Consider P2: a shared moral code is required to avoid disintegration. What is a "shared moral code"? Devlin says "the moral judgment of society must be something about which any twelve men or women drawn at random might after discussion be expected to be unanimous." Devlin thus seems to take it as more or less obvious that a society must have broad agreement on a range of moral issues, including, but limited to, killing, assaulting, lying, cheating, stealing, and mental cruelty. Thus he says: "If men and women try to create a society in which there is no fundamental agreement about good and evil they will fail; if, having based it on common agreement, the agreement goes, the society will disintegrate. For society . . . is held by the invisible bonds of common thought."[14]

What about P3? Suppose a society—say, England in the 1950s—has a shared moral code that includes moral judgments condemning conduct that is harmful to others and moral judgments condemning conduct that is not harmful to others. Why do we need to use criminal law to enforce all elements of that code to prevent the disappearance of shared morality and social disintegration? A society might be able to fare perfectly well—maybe even better—if some elements of its current moral code were to change.

You might worry about change, however, if you think that social morality is very tightly integrated, so that a change in any part threatens to undermine the whole. If so, then you may be worried about any element changing. Perhaps Devlin believed in such tight integration and worried that the failure to enforce and uphold the existing sexual morality would lead to a general collapse of morality, with people embracing promise-breaking, lying, and wanton cruelty. Thus he says "history shows that the loosening of moral bonds is often the first stage of disintegration, so that society is justified in taking the same steps to preserve its moral code as it does to preserve its government and other essential institutions."[15]

13. See page 1103 of this anthology.
14. See page 1099 of this anthology.
15. Patrick Devlin, *The Enforcement of Morals* (Oxford University Press, 1965), 13.

NOTES AND QUESTIONS

1. Devlin thinks both that a society has the right to pass judgment on moral issues and that it has the right to use the law to enforce its moral judgments. He argues for the latter right on the basis of the former. In fact, he says that the right to pass judgment "very nearly dictate[s]" the right to use the law to enforce the judgments. Reconstruct Devlin's argument for the right to use the law to enforce moral judgments.

    Before beginning your reconstruction, it will help to address two prior questions:

    a. How does society "pass judgment" on a moral issue? (How would you know what a society's judgment is?)

    b. Why does a society have a right to pass judgment on a moral issue?

2. Consider three proposed **sufficient conditions** for a right to enforcement, all of which are suggested by Devlin's essay:

    (1) Society has a right to enforce moral judgments when there is a realistic concern about social "disintegration."

    (2) Society has a right to enforce moral judgments when enforcement is required by the "integrity of society."

    (3) Society has a right to enforce moral judgments when a practice provokes a "real feeling of reprobation."

    Do these three conditions come to the same thing? For example, in the United States in the 1950s, there appears to have been, in many parts of the country, a real feeling of reprobation about interracial marriage. (In 1958, 72 percent of Southern whites—and more than 40 percent of Northern whites—supported a *legal ban* on interracial marriage.) That feeling of reprobation, assuming it existed, would have provided good reason for a legal ban based on condition (3). What about conditions (1) and (2)?

    Does Devlin think that a society ought to enforce all the moral judgments it has a right to enforce? (Review his discussion of his "third question" [p. 1101].) Which of its moral judgments should a society enforce?

3. For discussion of Devlin's views, see H. L. A. Hart, *Law, Liberty, and Morality* (Stanford University Press, 1963); Ronald Dworkin, "Lord Devlin and the Enforcement of Morals," *Yale Law Journal* 75, 6 (1966): 986–1005; and Gerald Dworkin, "Devlin Was Right: Law and the Enforcement of Morality," *William and Mary Law Review* 40 (1999): 927–46.

Amartya Sen (b. 1933)

Sen was born in Santiniketan, West Bengal, India. An economist and philosopher, he is currently Thomas W. Lamont University Professor at Harvard University. He has written on a vast range of subjects, including social choice theory, welfare economics, economic development, justice, famines, democracy, rationality, poverty, inequality, and human capabilities. His books include *Poverty and Famines* (1981), *Collective Choice and Social Welfare* (1990), *Inequality Reexamined* (1995), *Development as Freedom* (1999), *Identity and Violence* (2007), and *The Idea of Justice* (2010). Sen was awarded the Nobel Memorial Prize in Economic Sciences in 1998.

ELEMENTS OF A THEORY OF HUMAN RIGHTS

I. The Need for a Theory

Few concepts are as frequently invoked in contemporary political discussions as human rights. There is something deeply attractive in the idea that every person anywhere in the world, irrespective of citizenship or territorial legislation, has some basic rights, which others should respect. The moral appeal of human rights has been used for a variety of purposes, from resisting torture and arbitrary incarceration to demanding the end of hunger and of medical neglect.

At the same time, the central idea of human rights as something that people have, and have even without any specific legislation, is seen by many as foundationally dubious and lacking in cogency. A recurrent question is, Where do these rights come from? It is not usually disputed that the invoking of human rights can be politically powerful. Rather, the worries relate to what is taken to be the "softness" (some would say "mushiness") of the conceptual grounding of human rights. . . .

Human rights activists are often quite impatient with such critiques. The invoking of human rights tends to come mostly from those who are concerned with changing the world rather than interpreting it (to use a classic distinction made famous, oddly enough, by that overarching theorist, Karl Marx). It is not hard to understand their unwillingness to spend time trying to provide conceptual justification, given the great urgency to respond to terrible deprivations around the world. This proactive stance has had its practical rewards, since it has allowed immediate use of the colossal appeal of the idea of human rights to confront intense oppression or great misery, without having to wait for the theoretical air to clear. However, the conceptual doubts must also be satisfactorily addressed, if the idea of human rights is to command reasoned loyalty and to establish a secure intellectual standing. It is critically important to see the relationship between the force and appeal of human rights, on the one hand, and their reasoned justification and scrutinized use, on the other.

There is, thus, need for some theory and also for some defense of any proposed theory. The object of this article is to do just that, and to consider, in that context, the justification of the general idea of human rights and also of the includability of economic and social rights within the broad class of human rights. For such a theory to be viable it is necessary to clarify what kind of a claim is made by a declaration of human rights, and how such a claim can be defended, and furthermore how the diverse criticisms of the coherence, cogency and legitimacy of human rights (including economic and social rights) can be adequately addressed. . . .

III. Human Rights: Ethics and Law

What kind of an assertion does a declaration of human rights make? I would submit that proclamations of human rights are to be seen as articulations of ethical demands. They are, in this respect, comparable with pronouncements in utilitarian ethics, even though their respective substantive contents are, obviously, very different. . . .

A pronouncement of human rights includes an assertion of the importance of the corresponding freedoms—the freedoms that are identified and privileged in the formulation of the rights in question—and is indeed motivated by that importance. For example, the human right of not being tortured springs from the importance of freedom from torture for all. But it includes, furthermore, an affirmation of the need for others to consider what they can reasonably do to secure the freedom from torture for any person. For a would-be torturer, the demand is obviously quite straightforward, to wit, to refrain and desist. The demand takes the clear form of what Immanuel Kant called a perfect obligation.[1] However, for others too (that is, those other than the would-be torturers) there are responsibilities, even though they are less specific and come in the general form of "imperfect obligations" (to invoke another Kantian concept). The perfectly specified demand not to torture anyone is supplemented by the more general, and less exactly specified, requirement to consider the ways and means through which torture can be prevented and then to decide what one should, thus, reasonably do. . . .

An ethical understanding of human rights goes . . . against seeing them as legal demands (and against taking them to be, as in Bentham's view, legal *pretensions*[2]), but also differs from a law-centered approach to human rights that sees them as if they are basically *grounds* for law, almost "laws in waiting." Ethical and legal rights do, of

---

1. Kant distinguishes perfect from imperfect duties. Intuitively, a perfect duty requires a specific action of an agent, whereas an imperfect duty leaves an agent with more discretion. For example, if I promise to be in my office at 3:00 PM, I have a duty to be there then: the duties associated with promising are perfect. In contrast, the duty of beneficence, a duty to help others in need, leaves me more discretion about when to help, whom to help, and precisely how much help to provide: the duty of beneficence is thus imperfect. See, for example, Kant, *Groundwork of the Metaphysics of Morals*, in Immanuel Kant, *Practical Philosophy*, trans. and ed. Mary J. Gregor (Cambridge University Press, 1996), 73n. [Sen's note.]

2. The English legal and political theorist Jeremy Bentham (1748–1832) was a leading utilitarian and a sharp critic of the idea of natural rights. Bentham said that "natural rights are nonsense," and that "imprescriptible natural rights" are "nonsense on stilts." All rights, he argued, are creatures of law, and all laws are commands of a sovereign authority: to say that a person has a right to free speech, for example, is to say that the law protects the person's speaking. If a natural right is a right that is, in some way, prior to law, a right that people have even without a legal system, then there are no such rights: indeed, the very idea, Bentham thought, makes no sense. See Jeremy Bentham, *Anarchical Fallacies*, in *The Works of Jeremy Bentham*, Vol. 2 (Edinburgh, 1838–1843), 491–534.

course, have motivational connections. In a rightly celebrated article "Are There Any Natural Rights?" Herbert Hart has argued that people "speak of their moral rights mainly when advocating their incorporation in a legal system." He added that the concept of a right "belongs to that branch of morality which is specifically concerned to determine when one person's freedom may be limited by another's and so to determine what actions may appropriately be made the subject of coercive legal rules.[3] Whereas Bentham saw rights as a "child of law," Hart's view takes the form, in effect, of seeing some natural rights as *parents* of law: they motivate and inspire specific legislations. Although Hart does not make any reference whatever to human rights in his article, the reasoning about the role of natural rights as inspiration for legislation can be seen to apply to the concept of human rights as well.

There can, in fact, be little doubt that the idea of moral rights can serve, and has often served in practice, as the basis of new legislation. . . .

However, to acknowledge that such a connection exists is not the same as taking the relevance of human rights to lie *exclusively* in determining what should "appropriately be made the subject of coercive legal rules." It is important to see that the idea of human rights can be, and is, actually used in several other ways as well. . . . For example, monitoring and other activist support, provided by such organizations as Human Rights Watch or Amnesty International or Oxfam or Médecins Sans Frontières, can themselves help to advance the effective reach of acknowledged human rights. In many contexts, legislation may not, in fact, be involved.

IV. Rights, Freedoms and Social Influence

Why are human rights important? Since declarations of human rights are ethical affirmations of the need to pay appropriate attention to the significance of freedoms incorporated in the formulation of human rights (as was discussed in the last section), an appropriate starting point must be the importance of freedoms of human beings to be so recognized. . . .

Freedoms can vary in importance and also in terms of the extent to which they can be influenced by social help. For a freedom to count as a part of the evaluative system of human rights, it clearly must be important enough to justify requiring that others should be ready to pay substantial attention to decide what they can reasonably do to advance it. It also has to satisfy a condition of plausibility that others could make a material difference through taking such an interest.

There have to be some "threshold conditions" of (i) importance and (ii) social influenceability for a freedom to figure within the interpersonal and interactive spectrum of human rights. . . .

---

3. H. L. A. Hart, "Are There Any Natural Rights?" *Philosophical Review* 64 (1955), reprinted in *Theories of Rights*, ed. Jeremy Waldron (Oxford University Press, 1984), 79. [Sen's note.]

The threshold conditions may prevent, for a variety of reasons, particular freedoms from being an appropriate subject matter of human rights. To illustrate, it is not hard to argue that some importance should be attached to all four of the following freedoms:

1. a person's freedom not to be assaulted;

2. her freedom to receive medical care for a serious health problem;

3. her freedom not to be called up regularly by her neighbors whom she detests;

4. her freedom to achieve tranquillity.

However, even though all four may be important in one way or another, it is not altogether implausible to argue that the first (freedom not to be assaulted) is a good subject matter for a human right, and so is the second (freedom to receive necessary medical care), but the third (freedom not to be called up by detested neighbors) is not, in general, important enough to cross the threshold of social significance to qualify as a human right. Also, the fourth, while quite possibly extremely important for the person, is too inward-looking—and too hard to be influenced by others—to be a good subject matter for human rights. The exclusion of a "right to tranquillity" relates not to any skepticism about the possible importance of tranquillity and the significance of a person's being free to achieve it, but to the difficulty of guaranteeing it through social help. . . .

V. Processes, Opportunities and Capabilities

I turn now to a closer scrutiny of the contents of freedom and its multiple features. I have argued elsewhere that "opportunity" and "process" are two aspects of freedom that require distinction, with the importance of each deserving specific acknowledgment. An example can help to bring out the *separate* (though not necessarily independent) relevance of both *substantive opportunities* and *freedom of processes*.

Consider an adult person, let us call her Rima, who decides that she would like to go out in the evening. To take care of some considerations that are not central to the issues involved here (but which could make the discussion more complex), it is assumed that there are no particular safety risks involved in her going out, and that she has critically reflected on this decision and judged that going out would be the sensible, indeed the ideal, thing to do. Now consider the threat of a violation of this freedom if some authoritarian guardians of society decide that she must not go out in the evening ("it is most unseemly"), and if they force her, in one way or another, to stay indoors. To see that there are two distinct issues involved in this one viola-tion, consider an alternative case in which the authoritarian bosses decide that she must—absolutely *must*—go out ("you are expelled for the evening: just obey"). There is clearly a violation of freedom here even though Rima is being forced to do exactly what she would have chosen to do anyway, and this is readily seen when we compare the two alternatives "choosing freely to go out" and "being forced to go out." The latter involves an immediate violation of the *process aspect* of Rima's freedom, since an action is being forced on her (even though it is an action she would have freely chosen also).

The opportunity aspect may also be affected, since a plausible accounting of opportunities can include having options and it can inter alia include valuing free choice. However, the violation of the opportunity aspect would be more substantial and manifest if she were not only forced to do something chosen by another, but in fact, forced to do something she herself would not otherwise choose to do. The comparison between "being forced to go out" (when she would have gone out anyway, if free) and, say, "being forced to polish the shoes of others at home" (not her favorite activity) brings out this contrast, which is primarily one of the opportunity aspect, rather than the process aspect. In being forced to stay home and polish the shoes of others, Rima loses freedom in two different ways, related respectively to (1) being forced with no freedom of choice, and (2) being obliged in particular to do something she would not choose to do.

Both processes and opportunities can figure in human rights. A denial of "due process" in being, say, imprisoned without a proper trial can be the subject matter of human rights (no matter what the outcome of the fair trial might be), and so can be the denial of the opportunity of medical treatment, or the opportunity of living without the danger of being assaulted (going beyond the exact process through which these opportunities are made real). . . .

VIII. Economic and Social Rights

I turn now to criticisms that have been particularly aimed against extending the idea of human rights to include economic and social rights, such as the right not to be hungry, or the right to basic education or to medical attention. Even though these rights did not figure in the classic presentations of rights of human beings in, say, the U.S. Declaration of Independence, or French "rights of man," they are very much a part of the contemporary domain of what Cass Sunstein calls the "rights revolution."[4] The legitimacy of including these claims within the general class of human rights has been challenged through two specific lines of reproach, which I shall call, respectively, the *institutionalization critique* and the *feasibility critique*.

The institutionalization critique, which is aimed particularly at economic and social rights, relates to the general issue of the exact correspondence between authentic rights and precisely formulated correlate duties. Such a correspondence, it is argued, would

---

4. Cass Sunstein, *After the Rights Revolution: Reconceiving the Regulatory State* (Harvard University Press, 1990). [Sen's note.]

exist only when a right is institutionalized. Onora O'Neill has presented this line of criticism with force:

> Unfortunately much writing and rhetoric on rights heedlessly proclaims universal rights to goods and services, and in particular "welfare rights," as well as to other social, economic and cultural rights that are prominent in international Charters and Declarations, without showing what connects each presumed right-holder to some specific obligation-bearer(s), which leaves the content of these supposed rights wholly obscure. . . . Some advocates of universal economic, social and cultural rights go no further than to emphasize that they *can* be institutionalized, which is true. But the point of difference is that they *must* be institutionalized: if they are not there is no right.[5]

In responding to this significant criticism, we have to invoke the understanding, already discussed, that obligations can be both perfect and imperfect. Even the classical "first generational" rights, like freedom from assault, can be seen as yielding imperfect obligations on others. . . . Depending on institutional possibilities, economic and social rights may similarly call for both perfect and imperfect obligations. There is a large area of fruitful public discussion and possibly effective pressure, concerning what the society and the state, even an impoverished one, can do to prevent violations of certain basic economic or social rights (associated with, say, the prevalence of famines, or chronic undernourishment, or absence of medical care).

Indeed, the supportive activities of social organizations are often aimed precisely at institutional change, and these activities can be seen as part of imperfect obligations that individuals and groups have in a society where basic human rights are violated. Onora O'Neill is right to emphasize the importance of institutions for the realization of "welfare rights" (and even for economic and social rights in general), but the ethical significance of these rights provide good grounds for seeking realization through institutional expansion and reform. This can be helped through a variety of approaches, including demanding and agitating for appropriate legislation, and the supplementation of legal demands by political recognition and social monitoring. To deny the ethical status of these claims would be to ignore the reasoning that motivates these constructive activities.

The *feasibility critique* proceeds from the argument that even with the best of efforts, it may not be feasible to arrange the realization of many of the alleged economic and social rights for all. This would have been only an empirical observation (of some interest of its own), but it is made into an allegedly powerful criticism of the acceptance of these claimed rights on the basis of the presumption, largely undefended, that recognized human rights must, of necessity, be wholly accomplishable. If this presumption were accepted that would have the effect of immediately putting many so-called economic and social rights outside the domain of possible human rights, especially in the poorer societies.

---

5. Onora O'Neill, *Towards Justice and Virtue* (Cambridge University Press, 1996), 131–32. See also her *Bounds of Justice* (Cambridge University Press, 2000). [Sen's note.]

Maurice Cranston puts the argument thus:

> The traditional political and civil rights are not difficult to institute. For the most part, they require governments, and other people generally, to leave a man alone. . . . The problems posed by claims to economic and social rights, however, are of another order altogether. How can governments of those parts of Asia, Africa, and South America, where industrialization has hardly begun, be reasonably called upon to provide social security and holidays with pay for millions of people who inhabit those places and multiply so swiftly?[6]

In assessing this line of rejection, we have to ask: why should complete feasibility be a condition of cogency of human rights when the objective is to work towards enhancing their actual realization, if necessary through expanding their feasibility? The understanding that some rights are not fully realized, and may not even be fully *realizable* under present circumstances, does not, in itself, entail anything like the conclusion that these are, therefore, not rights at all. Rather, that understanding suggests the need to work towards changing the prevailing circumstances to make the unrealized rights realizable, and ultimately, realized.

It is also worth noting in this context that the question of feasibility is not confined to economic and social rights only; it is a much more widespread problem. Even for liberties and autonomies, to guarantee that a person is "left alone," which Cranston seems to think is simple to guarantee, has never been particularly easy. . . .

IX. The Reach of Public Reasoning

How can we judge the acceptability of claims to human rights and assess the challenges they may face? How would such a disputation—or a defense—proceed? I would argue that like the assessment of other ethical claims, there must be some test of open and informed scrutiny, and it is to such a scrutiny that we have to look in order to proceed to a disavowal or an affirmation. The status of these ethical claims must be dependent ultimately on their survivability in unobstructed discussion. In this sense, the viability of human rights is linked with what John Rawls has called "public reasoning" and its role in "ethical objectivity."[7]

Indeed, the connection between public reasoning and the formulation and use of human rights is extremely important to understand. Any general plausibility that these ethical claims, or their denials, have is dependent, on this theory, on their survival and flourishing when they encounter unobstructed discussion and scrutiny, along with adequately wide informational availability. The force of a claim for a human right

---

6. Maurice Cranston, "Are There Any Human Rights?" *Daedalus* (1983): 13. [Sen's note.]

7. John Rawls, *A Theory of Justice* (Harvard University Press, 1971), and *Political Liberalism* (Columbia University Press, 1993), esp. 110–13. [Sen's note.]

would be seriously undermined if it were possible to show that they are unlikely to survive open public scrutiny. . . .

However, it is important not to confine the domain of public reasoning to a given society only, especially in the case of human rights, in view of the inescapably non-parochial nature of these rights, which are meant to apply to all human beings. . . .

There does, of course, exist considerable variation in the balance of manifest opinions and observed preconceptions in different countries and different societies. These opinions and beliefs often reflect, as Adam Smith noted in a powerfully illuminating analysis, strong influence of existing *practices* in different parts of the world, along with a lack of broader intellectual engagement. The need for open scrutiny, with unrestrained access to information (including that about practices elsewhere in the world and the experiences there), is particularly great because of these connections. Which is precisely why Adam Smith's insistence on the necessity of viewing actions and practices from a "certain distance" is so important for substantive ethics in general and the understanding of human rights in particular.

In a chapter entitled "On the Influence of Custom and Fashion upon the Sentiments of Moral Approbation and Disapprobation," Smith illustrated his contention:

> . . . the murder of new-born infants was a practice allowed of in almost all the states of Greece, even among the polite and civilized Athenians; and whenever the circumstances of the parent rendered it inconvenient to bring up the child, to abandon it to hunger, or to wild beasts, was regarded without blame or censure. . . . Uninterrupted custom had by this time so thoroughly authorized the practice, that not only the loose maxims of the world tolerated this barbarous prerogative, but even the doctrine of philosophers, which ought to have been more just and accurate, was led away by the established custom, and upon this, as upon many other occasions, instead of censuring, supported the horrible abuse, by far-fetched considerations of public utility. Aristotle talks of it as of what the magistrates ought upon many occasions to encourage. Plato is of the same opinion, and, with all that love of mankind which seems to animate all his writings, no where marks this practice with disapprobation.[8]

What are taken to be perfectly "normal" and "sensible" in an insulated society may not be able to survive a broad-based and less limited examination once the parochial gut reactions are replaced by critical scrutiny, including an awareness of variations of practices and norms across the world.

Scrutiny from a distance may have something to offer in the assessment of practices as different from each other as the stoning of adulterous women in Taliban's Afghanistan and the abounding use of capital punishment (sometimes with mass jubilation)

---

8. Adam Smith, *The Theory of Moral Sentiments* (revised edition, 1790, V.2.15; republished, Clarendon Press, 1976), 210. [Sen's note.]

in parts of the United States. This is the kind of issue that made Smith insist that "the eyes of the rest of mankind" must be invoked to understand whether "a punishment appears equitable." Ultimately, the discipline of critical moral scrutiny requires, among other things, "endeavouring to view [our sentiments and beliefs] with the eyes of other people, or as other people are likely to view them."

The need for interactions across the borders can be as important in rich societies as they are in poorer ones. The point to note here is not so much whether we are *permitted* to make cross-boundary scrutiny, but that the discipline of critical assessment of moral sentiments, no matter how locally established they are, *demands* that such scrutiny be undertaken.

TEST YOUR UNDERSTANDING

1. Sen distinguishes his own view about the relationship of human rights and law from the views of Bentham and Hart. What are the main differences?

2. Sen distinguishes freedom not to be assaulted, to receive medical care, not to be called up by neighbors you detest, and to achieve tranquillity. What point are these examples used to illustrate?

3. Sen mentions two criticisms of the idea that there are social and economic rights on the list of human rights. What is the "feasibility critique"?

4. Sen says that claims about human rights must be defended in what he calls "unobstructed discussion." Does he have in mind discussion within a society or a broader discussion across different societies?

NOTES AND QUESTIONS

1. According to Sen, freedoms must meet "some 'threshold conditions' of (i) importance and (ii) social influenceability . . . to figure within the interpersonal and interactive spectrum of human rights." What does he mean by "importance"? By "social influenceability"? How does Sen apply these two threshold conditions to the four freedoms listed in section 4?

2. In his discussion of social and economic rights, Sen discusses the "institutionalization critique" and the "feasibility critique." Both critiques aim to raise troubles for the idea that there are social and economic rights. While they accept that there are political and civil rights, they oppose "extending the idea of human rights to include economic and

social rights." State the distinction between economic and social rights and civil and political rights, and give some examples to illustrate the distinction. Then formulate each of the two critiques as an argument that leads to the conclusion that there are no social or economic rights. (Be sure that the arguments do not lead to the conclusion that there are no human rights at all. Remember, the proponents of the institutionalization and feasibility critiques are trying to distinguish civil and political rights, which are genuine human rights, from economic and social rights, which are not.) Does Sen provide an effective reply to these critiques? Which premises in the arguments you have reconstructed would Sen reject?

As background, you should review the Universal Declaration of Human Rights (www.un.org/en/documents/udhr/), the International Covenant on Civil and Political Rights (www.ohchr.org/en/professionalinterest/pages/ccpr.aspx), and the International Covenant on Social, Economic, and Cultural Rights (www.ohchr.org/EN/ProfessionalInterest /Pages/CESCR.aspx).

ANALYZING THE ARGUMENTS

1. Mill says that his principle of liberty

    > has no application to any state of things anterior to the time when mankind
    > have become capable of being improved by free and equal discussion. . . .
    > But as soon as mankind have attained the capacity of being guided to their
    > own improvement by conviction or persuasion (a period long since reached
    > in all nations with whom we need here concern ourselves), compulsion,
    > either in the direct form or in that of pains and penalties for noncompliance,
    > is no longer admissible as a means to their own good, and justifiable only
    > for the security of others.

    What role does this assumption—that the people Mill is thinking about can be "guided
    to their own improvement by conviction or persuasion"—play in Mill's defense of the
    liberty principle? Do you think that people are capable of being improved by free and
    equal discussion? Does Devlin think that people can be improved through free and
    equal discussion? Locke? Sen?

2. Sen says that *public reasoning* is the way to evaluate human rights claims. Beginning
    from that idea, get together with three other students from your course. Focus on
    Sen's four examples of freedom (from section 4), and discuss his application of the
    importance and *social influenceability* conditions to those examples. Be sure that
    you have a common understanding of the conditions. Then have each student in the
    group come up with two additional examples of freedoms; for example, freedom from
    illiteracy, freedom from traffic, freedom from dust, freedom from annoying questions.
    Take the pool of examples—Sen's four examples plus two examples developed from
    each of the four students in the group—and discuss whether each example meets Sen's
    conditions of importance and social influenceability. How much agreement do you find
    in the group? If you do not all agree on the examples, does that raise troubles for Sen's
    theory of human rights?

    As a final step in the exercise, consider whether your discussion has met the standards
    of unobstructed critical scrutiny that Sen describes in the last part of his paper. Have
    you achieved "an awareness of variations of practices and norms across the world"?
    If not, how might you do that?

3. In chapter IV of *On Liberty* (not included in the selection), Mill discusses some examples
    that are designed to show that his liberty principle is not directed against "imaginary
    evils," but against "serious and practical" problems. In one example, he describes a
    majority Muslim country in which people find the consumption of pork "really revolt-
    ing." Nevertheless, he thinks that it is wrong to prohibit the consumption of pork. In
    a second example, he says that the "sincere feelings" of Spanish Catholics condemn
    married clergy "as not only irreligious, but unchaste, indecent, gross, disgusting." Still,
    he thinks it is wrong to prohibit those marriages. Both prohibitions are wrong because,
    Mill says, neither the Muslim majority nor the Spanish Catholics are *harmed* by the
    conduct. Neither the consumption of pork nor married clergy "concern the interests
    of others."

Suppose a critic says that Mill is wrong in both cases. According to the critic:

The Muslims are *harmed* by the pork consumption and the Spanish Catholics are *harmed* by the married clergy. It is not simply that they think the conduct is impious or wrong. The Muslims are *revolted* and the Spanish Catholics are *disgusted*. In both cases, the negative feelings are sincerely and strongly felt. Why are these not cases of harm? Why are the interests of others not at stake? Because revulsion and disgust are mental, not physical? That response will not do, for two reasons. First, think what happens when you find something *really revolting*: the impact *is* partly physical. When you find something really revolting, you might wretch or feel queasy or nauseated. Second, even if the reaction is mental, you may still have been harmed. If you tell parents, falsely, that their child has died, and they are grief-stricken and despondent, you have harmed them. The harms are no less real because they are mental.

Consider the following Millian response:

Person *A* does not harm person *B* when *B* has undesirable feelings—say, strong revulsion—because *A* has done something that offends *B*'s religious or moral convictions. After all, *A* does not harm *B* simply because *A* violates *B*'s religious or moral standards: that is the core of Mill's liberty principle. By extension, then, *A* does not harm *B* when *A*'s conduct results in *B*'s undesirable feelings, *if* the undesirable feelings exist because of *B*'s religious or moral convictions: if, that is, the feelings would not exist if the convictions were different.

Is the Millian response compelling? If not, can you find a more forceful reply?

To explore these issues further, see Joel Feinberg, *The Moral Limits of the Criminal Law: Offence to Others* (Oxford University Press, 1988).

4. Consider a world in which most countries establish religious or moral uniformity by actively restricting liberty internally, but in which national borders are pretty easy to cross. As a result, people are able to choose the restrictions on liberty that apply to them. Is there anything wrong with this world? How might Locke, or Mill, or Sen object? Are the objections convincing?

Does Justice Require Equality?

The Problem

In the United States today, economic inequality is large and growing. The top 1 percent, which earned 11 percent of pre-tax national income in the late 1960s, now earns slightly over 20 percent; the bottom 50 percent, which earned slightly over 20 percent of pre-tax national income in the late 1960s, now earns 12 percent.[1] The distribution of wealth—housing, stocks, and other assets—is even more unequal than the income distribution.[2]

To be sure, economic inequality can be defined in many ways. Suppose John, Jean, and June have $100, $52, and $1, respectively. Now Jean loses $51, so they have $100, $1, and $1. If inequality is measured by the ratio of top income to bottom income, it remains the same, 100:1. But if inequality is measured by how far people in general are from the average income, it grows when Jean loses her money.[3] These different understandings are of considerable interest. But on any understanding, economic inequality has been growing in the United States. That much is largely undisputed. Judgments about the *justness* of economic inequalities are, in contrast, matters of intense and long-standing disagreement.

According to one familiar outlook, economic inequality is an inevitable consequence of protecting liberty. Proponents say that individual differences (e.g., in family background and culture, native abilities and acquired skills, personal aspirations and sheer good luck) mean that some people in a free society are bound to do better—perhaps much better—in income and wealth than others. Preventing or

1. Thomas Piketty, Emmanuel Saez, and Gabriel Zucman, "Distributional National Accounts: Methods and Assessments for the United States" (NBER Working Paper No. 22945, December 2016). Available at www.nber.org/papers/w22945.

2. See Thomas Piketty, *Capital in the Twenty-First Century*, trans. Arthur Goldhammer (Harvard University Press, 2014).

3. See Amartya Sen, *On Economic Inequality* (Oxford University Press, 1997).

mitigating those inequalities, they say, would require overriding individual choices. That, they say, would deprive people of what they are entitled to—for their efforts or contributions or for the simple fact of having been chosen by someone else as the recipient of a benefit. And that, they say, is wrong, an unjust deprivation of liberty.

An alternative outlook, also familiar, says that current inequalities reward people who had the undeserved good fortune to have been born rich, or endowed with some scarce, high-priced skill, or located in the right place (say, Silicon Valley) at the right time (say, 1994). An economic system, proponents say, is not a talent contest to reward the gifted or a race that goes to the swift or to the well-bred. It should be designed as a fair system that ensures reasonable conditions for all. Mitigating inequalities, they say, is required by justice, ultimately by the equal importance of each human life.

These disagreements about the justness of economic equalities mix philosophical with empirical judgments. Economists, sociologists, and political scientists debate the empirical issues about the effects of taxes and transfers on incentives to work and invest or about the consequences of increased inequality to democracy. Philosophical discussions about justice and economic inequality need to be attentive to these empirical arguments. But the distinctive contribution of philosophy lies elsewhere, in articulating the values that are at stake.

Philosophical Egalitarianism

Utilitarian thinkers in the nineteenth century offered a reason for being concerned about economic inequality. **Utilitarianism** is the view that the right action (or policy or institution) is one that produces the greatest sum of happiness. Assume first that each individual gets some additional happiness from each additional dollar that comes his or her way. Assume also that the increase in happiness declines as the person gets richer. So your 101st dollar gives you more added happiness than does your 201st, which adds more than your 1,001st. This is called "declining marginal utility." If marginal utility declines, then, all else equal, a greater sum of utility would be generated by shifting resources from someone with more (say, Warren Buffett) to someone with fewer (say, a bus driver or nurse). Buffett will lose a little happiness when he loses a dollar; but that loss will be more than compensated by the greater increase in happiness for the bus driver or nurse.[4]

But all else is not equal. The utilitarian case for equality needs to take incentives into account. Suppose Warren Buffett will not invest as much if his last dollar is taxed at a high rate. Then, to prevent damaging effects on longer-term growth and standards of living, we will need to be careful not to set the tax rate too high.

Some philosophical egalitarians think that the case for mitigating economic inequalities on grounds of justice is not as dependent as the utilitarian supposes

---

4. Harry Frankfurt sketches and criticizes the utilitarian argument in his contribution in this chapter.

on the facts about declining marginal utility and responsiveness to incentives. According to one important line of philosophical-egalitarian argument, certain kinds of inequalities are unjust because they are *unfair*. They are unfair because they are based on treating equal persons in indefensibly different ways.

That is the core idea in John Rawls's theory of "justice as fairness." Rawls presents an account of what justice requires by developing a theory about fair terms of social cooperation. Part of that theory—its most strikingly egalitarian part—is the **difference principle**. According to this principle, inequalities in income and wealth are just only if they are needed to maximize the income and wealth of people in the least advantaged social group. Fair inequalities cover training costs for developing socially valuable skills and provide incentives to encourage people to use their resources and talents for the benefit of all. According to the difference principle, then, the reason for accepting inequalities is not to ensure that people receive what they deserve or to reward contributions or efforts, but to improve the circumstances of the least advantaged group (say, people in the bottom 20 percent of the income distribution).

The rationale for the difference principle lies in the idea of fairness. To see how, it will help to take a step back and consider the idea of **equality of opportunity**. Some kind of equality of opportunity is widely agreed to be a requirement of justice. Consider a society with a caste structure or a system of racial apartheid. In those societies, the laws restrict social mobility. The laws are unjust because, as Martha Nussbaum observes, human lives are of equal importance. Given that equal importance, laws are unfair—they treat equal persons in indefensibly different ways—if they prevent some people from pursuing socially valued opportunities that are available to others.

Justice as fairness includes this principle that laws should not establish unequal chances for different groups. But it adds a more demanding requirement of equal opportunity, which says that people from different social backgrounds should have equal chances to attain desirable social positions. More specifically, *equality of fair opportunity* says that equally talented and equally motivated people should have equal chances to attain socially desirable positions. It is unfair when Albert has greater chances than Alice simply because he comes from a wealthier family with the resources to support his aspirations. Thus, as Rawls puts it, "Chances to acquire cultural knowledge and skills should not depend upon one's class position, and so the school system, whether public or private, should be designed to even out class barriers." Nussbaum suggests that an equal opportunity requirement of this kind lies at the heart of justice.

It is unfair for Albert to do better than Alice as a result of his class background, because Albert's advantage means that the society permits the accidents of social background to play a large role in shaping the course of our lives. But—returning now to the difference principle—suppose that Albert does better than Alice because of a natural talent: he has the steady hand needed to be a surgeon or the mathematical aptitude required of a financial analyst. Albert is not advantaged by social background but by something comparably accidental: the talents he happens to be born with, for which he is not responsible, and which he did nothing to deserve. But "there is no more reason to permit the distribution of income and wealth to be settled by the distribution of natural assets than by historical and social fortune." The difference principle, with its requirement that inequalities work to the benefit of the least advantaged, is Rawls's proposal about how to address this unfair dependence of a person's opportunities to gain resources on the contingencies of native endowments.

According to justice as fairness, considerations of fairness provide a rationale for both the equality of fair opportunity principle and the difference principle. It is unfair for Albert to have greater opportunities than Alice because of the contingencies of their social backgrounds, and it is unfair, too, when the resources at his command are greater simply because of the talents he happens to possess. When the two principles are joined, the result is that many familiar inequalities turn out to be unjust. They reflect a society that treats equal persons in indefensibly different ways.

You may be puzzled by the description of *justice as fairness* as a kind of egalitarianism. After all, neither the opportunity principle nor the difference principle condemns all inequalities of income and wealth as unjust. To the contrary: if a very large incentive is needed to motivate a talented person to do something that contributes a small bit to the benefit of the least advantaged, that large incentive is justified. If you are looking for an egalitarianism that condemns all inequalities as unjust, you are unlikely to find it. Egalitarians have ideas about *which* inequalities are unjust, but typically do not condemn all inequalities as unjust. "We can grant that all human beings have fundamentally equal worth," Nussbaum says, "without granting that one person should always get the same reward as another." Justice as fairness is egalitarian, then, because it claims that inequalities require a special justification—focused on the least advantaged—if they are to be consistent with fair treatment for equal persons.

To be sure, some views are more egalitarian than Rawls's. The difference principle, as he understands it, permits *incentive inequalities*. Suppose now that Albert could become a doctor and do a great deal for people's health. But Albert is willing to be a doctor only if he makes 10 times the average income. If he makes less than that, he would prefer to write indifferent literary fiction. You might think it is clear that he should get the high salary. As a practical matter, that seems right. But is it just? Albert could perfectly well be a doctor for a smaller reward. He is simply unwilling to. Is he taking unfair advantage of scarce medical talent?

Reactions differ. Some people think that justice is a matter of laws and policies: it is about the rules of social cooperation. Getting Albert to act differently, they say, is not a matter for law and policy: the challenge comes from his preferences and values, which we need to accept as given when we are thinking about justice. Others think that Albert is making an unjust demand. To be sure, the problem does not lie in laws and policies but in his preferences and values. Nevertheless, they say, he is extracting unfair advantages that offend against justice.[5]

5. See G. A. Cohen, *Rescuing Justice and Equality* (Harvard University Press, 2008).

Against Equality

Concerns about distributive fairness—for example, the idea that we need some special justification for departures from equality—focus typically on how some people are doing *relative* to how others are doing. Is that focus reasonable?

Suppose you have decided to open a small restaurant. The restaurant's success matters a great deal to you. Not that you care if it grows—you're not hoping to start a chain—but you want it to last. You think good food is important, enjoy the company of people who come to your restaurant, have an intense aversion to working for other people, and would like to support your family through income from the business. You know that some people make lots more money than you, and also know that some make less. But these differences do not matter to you. What matters is that you are doing something you value; you have sufficient resources to sustain the business, ensure that your kids have decent clothes, decent food, and a good education; and you spend time with people whose company you enjoy.

If that is what matters to you, then you may regard a concern with equality in the surrounding society as a bad thing. A concern with equality is a concern with how you are faring relative to others. And that concern may strike you as a tempting distraction from what really matters, which is that you have what you need to pursue your aspirations with some prospect of success.

Harry Frankfurt criticizes a concern with equality along these lines: "With respect to the distribution of economic assets, what *is* important from the point of view of morality is not that everyone should have *the same* but that each should have *enough*. If everyone had enough, it would be of no moral consequence whether some had more than others. I shall refer to this alternative to egalitarianism—namely, that what is morally important with respect to money is for everyone to have enough—as 'the doctrine of sufficiency.'" According to the doctrine of sufficiency, justice requires that each person have enough; relative positions, in contrast, make no inherent difference to justice. The qualification "inherent" is essential. Economic inequalities may have bad consequences for social relationships, social mobility, or political equality. Still, the inequalities in and of themselves are not an appropriate focus of political morality.

Frankfurt's focus on sufficiency resonates with popular ideas about the importance of a social safety net that ensures that each person has enough. A focus on a safety net, however, is usually associated with the idea that demanding more than that from others is demanding too much: that one is not entitled, as a matter of justice, to more than a safety net. Frankfurt's focus is different. Worrying about inequality as such is ethically misguided, he argues, because inequality is a matter of relative positions, of who is doing better than others and who is doing worse. Concerns about relative positions, he thinks, reveal a distorted view of what matters in life. What matters—as in the case of the small-restaurant owner—is having a view about what is worth doing and enough resources to do it. Nothing of genuine interest in a good human life turns directly on where one stands relative to others in the distribution of income and wealth. The focus on equality, Frankfurt says, "contributes to the moral disorientation and shallowness of our time."

Libertarianism

Robert Nozick's libertarian criticisms of egalitarianism are fundamentally different from Frankfurt's. Libertarians do not agree that justice requires sufficiency. The sufficiency theory is an example of what Nozick calls a "patterned theory" of justice. According to a patterned theory, one can tell whether a distribution is just simply by looking at it. In the case of the sufficiency doctrine, one asks whether each person has "enough." It is not necessary to know anything about how the distribution came about.

Nozick's historical-entitlement approach to justice condemns any effort to require that the distribution fit a pattern—whether of equality, sufficiency, merit or contribution, or maximizing happiness. The problem with patterns is that they are at odds with liberty. "Liberty," Nozick says, "upsets patterns." Establish any pattern, and free choices will upend it.

What matters for distributive justice is exclusively the history of initial acquisition of unowned resources and the subsequent history of transactions. If we examine acquisitions and transactions one by one, and find that each step is acceptable—in each transaction, for example, people exchange something they own for something owned by others—then the outcome is just, whatever it turns out to be. The results may be more equal or less equal, but whatever they are, they are just because they emerge from a history of individually just acquisitions and transactions, in which individuals choose, for example, who they will transact with and what the terms of the transaction will be. Distributive justice is nothing more (and nothing less) than the historical product of individually just acts of acquisition and transfer.

For justice as fairness, the result of implementing this view is a pervasively unfair society, riddled with morally arbitrary inequalities, calling for remedy through law and public policy. The libertarian will see the implications of individual freedom and reject efforts to correct inequalities as an unjust abridgement of human liberty.

Equality, Culture, and Gender

Economic inequality is an important topic. But as Nussbaum indicates, philosophical thought about justice and equality is not confined to economic inequality. Justice requires that individuals be treated as equal persons—as having equal importance, entitled to equal regard from others. Nussbaum emphasizes that the requirement of being treated as an equal applies to individuals regardless of their race, gender, and ethnicity, and whatever cultural or religious convictions they may have. Thus understood, the requirement of treating people as equals has very wide scope, and its broad practical implications are matters of large interest and considerable disagreement. Susan Moller Okin's argument about multiculturalism and women's equality explores one important area of disagreement.

Suppose, for example, that a society sets aside Sunday as a day when people cannot be required to work. Employers may require employees to work any other day and dismiss them if they refuse to work. People who keep a Saturday Sabbath—including Jews and Seventh Day Adventists—may argue that this rule is unfair. If members of these faiths can be required by their employers to work on Saturdays, and are subject to dismissal if they do not, the faiths may decline. So the groups may argue for a special exemption, for a right to be exempt from Saturday work because of the special burdens they would face if they were subject to the same requirements as everyone else. They claim a special *group right*. The argument for the special right—for differential treatment—is that they otherwise would not be respected as equals: because of their religious views, they would be subject to an especially severe burden that others are not subject to.

Okin explores this idea of group rights and possible tensions with the requirement of equal treatment for women. She identifies *multiculturalism*, for the purposes of her discussion, as the view that minority cultures are sometimes owed special group rights because the rights are needed to sustain the group, and thus the sense of self-worth and freedom of members who identify with the group. But she argues that some minority cultures fail internally to treat women as equals, and fail more than the surrounding majority culture. And she asks whether those groups have a legitimate claim to special rights. How, she asks, can they demand special rights in the name of equal treatment when they deny such equality internally? "Those who make liberal arguments for the rights of groups, then, must take special care to look at inequalities within those groups. It is especially important to consider inequalities between the sexes, since they are likely to be less public, and thus less easily discernible."

John Rawls (1921–2002)

Rawls was born in Baltimore, Maryland. After receiving his PhD from Princeton University in 1950, he taught at Princeton, Cornell University, and the Massachusetts Institute of Technology before joining the Harvard University faculty in 1962. At his retirement from Harvard in 1991, he was James Conant Bryant University Professor. Rawls wrote three powerful and influential books of political philosophy: *A Theory of Justice* (1971), *Political Liberalism* (1993), and *The Law of Peoples* (1999).

TWO PRINCIPLES OF JUSTICE

from *A Theory of Justice*

I shall now state in a provisional form the two principles of justice that I believe would be agreed to in the original position.[1] The first formulation of these principles is tentative. As we go on I shall consider several formulations and approximate step by step the final statement to be given much later. I believe that doing this allows the exposition to proceed in a natural way.

The first statement of the two principles reads as follows.

> First: each person is to have an equal right to the most extensive scheme of equal basic liberties compatible with a similar scheme of liberties for others.
>
> Second: social and economic inequalities are to be arranged so that they are both (a) reasonably expected to be to everyone's advantage, and (b) attached to positions and offices open to all.

There are two ambiguous phrases in the second principle, namely "everyone's advantage" and "open to all." Determining their sense more exactly will lead to a second formulation of the principle in § 13.[2] . . .

These principles primarily apply . . . to the basic structure of society and govern the assignment of rights and duties and regulate the distribution of social and economic advantages. . . . [I]t is essential to observe that the basic liberties are given by a list of such liberties. Important among these are political liberty (the right to vote and to hold public office) and freedom of speech and assembly; liberty of conscience and freedom of thought; freedom of the person, which includes freedom from psychological oppression and physical assault and dismemberment (integrity of the person); the right to hold personal property and freedom from arbitrary arrest and seizure as defined by the concept of the rule of law. These liberties are to be equal by the first principle.

The second principle applies, in the first approximation, to the distribution of income and wealth and to the design of organizations that make use of differences in authority and responsibility. While the distribution of wealth and income need not be equal, it must be to everyone's advantage, and at the same time, positions of authority and responsibility must be accessible to all. . . .

---

1. The *original position* is a hypothetical situation in which individuals choose the standards of justice for their society. Rawls proposes that we make this choice behind a "veil of ignorance," which keeps us from knowing our class, race, gender, religion, or any other features that distinguish us from other persons. In chapter 3 of *A Theory of Justice* (which comprises sections 20–30), Rawls argues that the two principles of justice he will state would be selected in the original position.

2. Rawls is here referring us to section 13 of *A Theory of Justice*.

12. Interpretations of the Second Principle

I have already mentioned that since the phrases "everyone's advantage" and "equally open to all" are ambiguous, both parts of the second principle have two natural senses. Because these senses are independent of one another, the principle has four possible meanings. Assuming that the first principle of equal liberty has the same sense throughout, we then have four interpretations of the two principles. These are indicated in the table below.

| | "Everyone's advantage" | |
"Equally open"	Principle of efficiency	Difference principle
Equality as careers open to talents	System of Natural Liberty	Natural Aristocracy
Equality as equality of fair opportunity	Liberal Equality	Democratic Equality

. . . In working out justice as fairness, we must decide which interpretation is to be preferred. I shall adopt that of democratic equality, explaining in the next section what this notion means. . . .

The first interpretation . . . I shall refer to as the system of natural liberty. In this rendering the first part of the second principle is understood as the principle of efficiency adjusted so as to apply to institutions or, in this case, to the basic structure of society,[3] and the second part is understood as an open social system in which, to use the traditional phrase, careers are open to talents. I assume in all interpretations that the first principle of equal liberty is satisfied and that the economy is roughly a free market system, although the means of production may or may not be privately owned. The system of natural liberty asserts, then, that a basic structure satisfying the principle of efficiency and in which positions are open to those able and willing to strive for them will lead to a just distribution. Assigning rights and duties in this way is thought to give a scheme which allocates wealth and income authority and responsibility, in a fair way whatever this allocation turns out to be. . . .

The system of natural liberty selects an efficient distribution roughly as follows. Let us suppose that we know from economic theory that under the standard assumptions defining a competitive market economy, income and wealth will be distributed in an efficient way, and that the particular efficient distribution which results in any period of time is determined by the initial distribution of assets, that is, by the initial distribution of income and wealth, and of natural talents and abilities. With each initial

---

3. According to the *principle of efficiency*, a basic structure is efficient when, roughly speaking, any change of rules that benefits some people makes other people less well off.

distribution, a definite efficient outcome is arrived at. Thus it turns out that if we are to accept the outcome as just, and not merely as efficient, we must accept the basis upon which over time the initial distribution of assets is determined.

In the system of natural liberty the initial distribution is regulated by the arrangements implicit in the conception of careers open to talents (as earlier defined). These arrangements presuppose a background of equal liberty (as specified by the first principle) and a free market economy. They require a formal equality of opportunity in that all have at least the same legal rights of access to all advantaged social positions. But since there is no effort to preserve an equality, or similarity, of social conditions, except insofar as this is necessary to preserve the requisite background institutions, the initial distribution of assets for any period of time is strongly influenced by natural and social contingencies. The existing distribution of income and wealth, say, is the cumulative effect of prior distributions of natural assets—that is, natural talents and abilities—as these have been developed or left unrealized, and their use favored or disfavored over time by social circumstances and such chance contingencies as accident and good fortune. Intuitively, the most obvious injustice of the system of natural liberty is that it permits distributive shares to be improperly influenced by these factors so arbitrary from a moral point of view.

The liberal interpretation, as I shall refer to it, tries to correct for this by adding to the requirement of careers open to talents the further condition of the principle of fair equality of opportunity. The thought here is that positions are to be not only open in a formal sense, but that all should have a fair chance to attain them. Offhand it is not clear what is meant, but we might say that those with similar abilities and skills should have similar life chances. More specifically, assuming that there is a distribution of natural assets, those who are at the same level of talent and ability, and have the same willingness to use them, should have the same prospects of success regardless of their initial place in the social system. In all sectors of society there should be roughly equal prospects of culture and achievement for everyone similarly motivated and endowed. The expectations of those with the same abilities and aspirations should not be affected by their social class.

The liberal interpretation of the two principles seeks, then, to mitigate the influence of social contingencies and natural fortune on distributive shares. To accomplish this end it is necessary to impose further basic structural conditions on the social system. Free market arrangements must be set within a framework of political and legal institutions which regulates the overall trends of economic events and preserves the social conditions necessary for fair equality of opportunity. The elements of this framework are familiar enough, though it may be worthwhile to recall the importance of preventing excessive accumulations of property and wealth and of maintaining equal opportunities of education for all. Chances to acquire cultural knowledge and skills should not depend upon one's class position, and so the school system, whether public or private, should be designed to even out class barriers.

While the liberal conception seems clearly preferable to the system of natural liberty, intuitively it still appears defective. For one thing, even if it works to perfection in eliminating the influence of social contingencies, it still permits the distribution of wealth and income to be determined by the natural distribution of abilities and talents. Within the limits allowed by the background arrangements, distributive shares are decided by the outcome of the natural lottery; and this outcome is arbitrary from a moral perspective. There is no more reason to permit the distribution of income and wealth to be settled by the distribution of natural assets than by historical and social fortune. Furthermore, the principle of fair opportunity can be only imperfectly carried out, at least as long as some form of the family exists. The extent to which natural capacities develop and reach fruition is affected by all kinds of social conditions and class attitudes. Even the willingness to make an effort, to try, and so to be deserving in the ordinary sense is itself dependent upon happy family and social circumstances. It is impossible in practice to secure equal chances of achievement and culture for those similarly endowed, and therefore we may want to adopt a principle which recognizes this fact and also mitigates the arbitrary effects of the natural lottery itself. That the liberal conception fails to do this encourages one to look for another interpretation of the two principles of justice. . . .

13. Democratic Equality and the Difference Principle

The democratic interpretation, as the table suggests, is arrived at by combining the principle of fair equality of opportunity with the difference principle. This principle removes the indeterminateness of the principle of efficiency by singling out a particular position from which the social and economic inequalities of the basic structure are to be judged. Assuming the framework of institutions required by equal liberty and fair equality of opportunity, the higher expectations of those better situated are just if and only if they work as part of a scheme which improves the expectations of the least advantaged members of society. The intuitive idea is that the social order is not to establish and secure the more attractive prospects of those better off unless doing so is to the advantage of those less fortunate. . . .

To illustrate the difference principle, consider the distribution of income among social classes. Let us suppose that the various income groups correlate with representative individuals by reference to whose expectations we can judge the distribution. Now those starting out as members of the entrepreneurial class in property-owning democracy, say, have a better prospect than those who begin in the class of unskilled laborers. It seems likely that this will be true even when the social injustices which now exist are removed. What, then, can possibly justify this kind of initial inequality in life prospects? According to the difference principle, it is justifiable only if the difference in expectation is to the advantage of the representative man who is worse off, in this case the representative unskilled worker. The inequality in expectation is permissible only if lowering it would make the working class even more worse off. Supposedly, given the rider in the second principle concerning open positions, and the principle of liberty generally, the greater expectations allowed to entrepreneurs encourages them to do things which raise the prospects of laboring class. Their better prospects act as incentives so that the economic process is more efficient, innovation proceeds at a faster pace, and so on. I shall not consider how far these things are true. The point is that something of this kind must be argued if these inequalities are to satisfy by the difference principle. . . .

Thus . . . the outcome of the last several sections is that the second principle reads as follows:

> Social and economic inequalities are to be arranged so that they are both (a) to the greatest expected benefit of the least advantaged and (b) attached to offices and positions open to all under conditions of fair equality of opportunity. . . .

17. The Tendency to Equality

I wish to conclude this discussion of the two principles by explaining the sense in which they express an egalitarian conception of justice. . . .

First we may observe that the difference principle gives some weight to the considerations singled out by the principle of redress. This is the principle that undeserved inequalities call for redress; and since inequalities of birth and natural endowment are undeserved, these inequalities are to be somehow compensated for. Thus the principle holds that in order to treat all persons equally, to provide genuine equality of opportunity, society must give more attention to those with fewer native assets and to those born into the less favorable social positions. The idea is to redress the bias of contingencies in the direction of equality. In pursuit of this principle greater resources might be spent on the education of the less rather than the more intelligent, at least over a certain time of life, say the earlier years of school. . . .

[A]lthough the difference principle is not the same as that of redress, it does achieve some of the intent of the latter principle. It transforms the aims of the basic structure so that the total scheme of institutions no longer emphasizes social efficiency and technocratic values. The difference principle represents, in effect, an agreement to regard the distribution of natural talents as in some respects a common asset and to share in the greater social and economic benefits made possible by the complementarities of this distribution. Those who have been favored by nature, whoever they are, may gain from their good fortune only on terms that improve the situation of those who have lost out. The naturally advantaged are not to gain merely because they are more gifted, but only to cover the costs of training and education and for using their endowments in ways that help the less fortunate as well. No one deserves his greater natural capacity nor merits a more favorable starting place in society. But, of course, this is no reason to ignore, much less to eliminate these distinctions. Instead, the basic structure can be arranged so that these contingencies work for the good of the least fortunate. Thus we are led to the difference principle if we wish to set up the social system so that no one gains or loses from his arbitrary place in the distribution of natural assets or his initial position in society without giving or receiving compensating advantages in return.

In view of these remarks we may reject the contention that the ordering of institutions is always defective because the distribution of natural talents and the contingencies of social circumstance are unjust, and this injustice must inevitably carry over to human arrangements. Occasionally this reflection is offered as an excuse for ignoring injustice, as if the refusal to acquiesce in injustice is on a par with being unable to accept death. The natural distribution is neither just nor unjust; nor is it unjust that persons are born into society at some particular position. These are simply natural facts. What is just and unjust is the way that institutions deal with these facts. Aristocratic and caste societies are unjust because they make these contingencies the ascriptive basis for belonging to more or less enclosed and privileged social classes. The basic structure of these societies incorporates the arbitrariness found in nature. But there is no necessity for men to resign themselves to these contingencies. The social system is not an unchangeable order beyond human control but a pattern of human action. In justice as fairness men agree to avail themselves of the accidents of nature and social circumstance only when doing so is for the common benefit. The two principles are a fair way of meeting the arbitrariness of fortune; and while no doubt imperfect in other ways, the institutions which satisfy these principles are just.

A further point is that the difference principle expresses a conception of reciprocity. It is a principle of mutual benefit. At first sight, however, it may appear unfairly biased towards the least favored. . . .

One may object that those better situated deserve the greater advantages they could acquire for themselves under other schemes of cooperation whether or not these advantages are gained in ways that benefit others. Now it is true that given a just system of cooperation as a framework of public rules, and the expectations set up by it, those who, with the prospect of improving their condition, have done what the system announces it will reward are entitled to have their expectations met. In this sense the more fortunate have title to their better situation; their claims are legitimate expectations established by social institutions and the community is obligated to fulfill them. But this sense of desert is that of entitlement. It presupposes the existence of an ongoing cooperative scheme and is irrelevant to the question whether this scheme itself is to be designed in accordance with the difference principle or some other criterion.

Thus it is incorrect that individuals with greater natural endowments and the superior character that has made their development possible have a right to a cooperative scheme that enables them to obtain even further benefits in ways that do not contribute to the advantages of others. We do not deserve our place in the distribution of native endowments, any more than we deserve our initial starting place in society. That we deserve the superior character that enables us to make the effort to cultivate our abilities is also problematic; for such character depends in good part upon fortunate family and social circumstances in early life for which we can claim no credit. The notion of desert does not apply here. To be sure, the more advantaged have a right to their natural assets, as does everyone else; this right is covered by the first principle under the basic liberty protecting the integrity of the person. And so the more advantaged are entitled to whatever they can acquire in accordance with the rules of a fair system of social cooperation. Our problem is how this scheme, the basic structure of society, is to be designed. From a suitably general standpoint, the difference principle appears acceptable to both the more advantaged and the less advantaged individual. Of course, none of this is strictly speaking an argument for the principle. . . . But these intuitive considerations help to clarify the principle and the sense in which it is egalitarian. . . .

A further merit of the difference principle is that it provides an interpretation of the principle of fraternity. In comparison with liberty and equality, the idea of fraternity has had a lesser place in democratic theory. It is thought to be less specifically a polit-ical concept, not in itself defining any of the democratic rights but conveying instead certain attitudes of mind and forms of conduct without which we would lose sight of the values expressed by these rights. Or closely related to this, fraternity is held to represent a certain equality of social esteem manifest in various public conventions and in the absence of manners of deference and servility. No doubt fraternity does imply these things, as well as a sense of civic friendship and social solidarity, but so understood it expresses no definite requirement. We have yet to find a principle of justice that matches the underlying idea. The difference principle, however, does seem to correspond to a natural meaning of fraternity: namely, to the idea of not wanting to have greater advantages unless this is to the benefit of others who are less well off. The family, in its ideal conception and often in practice, is one place where the principle of maximizing the sum of advantages is rejected. Members of a family commonly do not wish to gain unless they can do so in ways that further the interests of the rest. Now wanting to act on the difference principle has precisely this consequence. Those better circumstanced are willing to have their greater advantages only under a scheme in which this works out for the benefit of the less fortunate. . . .

[Thus] we can associate the traditional ideas of liberty, equality, and fraternity with the democratic interpretation of the two principles of justice as follows: liberty corresponds to the first principle, equality to the idea of equality in the first principle together with equality of fair opportunity, and fraternity to the difference principle. . . .

77. The Basis of Equality

I now turn to the basis of equality, the features of human beings in virtue of which they are to be treated in accordance with the principles of justice. Our conduct toward animals is not regulated by these principles, or so it is generally believed. On what grounds then do we distinguish between mankind and other living things and regard the constraints of justice as holding only in our relations to human persons? . . .

The natural answer seems to be that it is precisely the moral persons who are en-titled to equal justice. Moral persons are distinguished by two features: first they are capable of having (and are assumed to have) a conception of their good (as expressed by a rational plan of life); and second they are capable of having (and are assumed to acquire) a sense of justice, a normally effective desire to apply and to act upon the principles of justice, at least to a certain minimum degree. We use the characterization of the persons in the original position to single out the kind of beings to whom the principles chosen apply. After all, the parties are thought of as adopting these criteria to regulate their common institutions and their conduct toward one another; and the description of their nature enters into the reasoning by which these principles are selected. Thus equal justice is owed to those who have the capacity to take part in and to act in accordance with the public understanding of the initial situation. One should observe that moral personality is here defined as a potentiality that is ordinarily realized in due course. It is this potentiality which brings the claims of justice into play. I shall return to this point below.

We see, then, that the capacity for moral personality is a sufficient condition for being entitled to equal justice. Nothing beyond the essential minimum is required. Whether moral personality is also a necessary condition I shall leave aside. I assume that the capacity for a sense of justice is possessed by the overwhelming majority of mankind, and therefore this question does not raise a serious practical problem. That moral personality suffices to make one a subject of claims is the essential thing. We cannot go far wrong in supposing that the sufficient condition is always satisfied. Even if the capacity were necessary, it would be unwise in practice to withhold justice on this ground. The risk to just institutions would be too great.

It should be stressed that the sufficient condition for equal justice, the capacity for moral personality, is not at all stringent. When someone lacks the requisite potentiality either from birth or accident, this is regarded as a defect or deprivation. There is no race or recognized group of human beings that lacks this attribute. Only scattered individuals are without this capacity, or its realization to the minimum degree, and the failure to realize it is the consequence of unjust and impoverished social circumstances, or fortuitous contingencies. Furthermore, while individuals presumably have varying capacities for a sense of justice, this fact is not a reason for depriving those with a lesser capacity of the full protection of justice. Once a certain minimum is met, a person is entitled to equal liberty on a par with everyone else. . . .

TEST YOUR UNDERSTANDING

1. Explain what Rawls means by "fair equality of opportunity."

2. What does Rawls mean by "democratic equality?"

3. Suppose that some people are born with greater talents than other people. Does Rawls think this is unjust?

4. What are the two features that define moral persons?

NOTES AND QUESTIONS

1. "The social system," Rawls says, "is not an unchangeable order beyond human control but a pattern of human action." What does this mean? Why is it important to his theory of justice as fairness?

2. Rawls's case for *democratic equality* proceeds in two steps: he provides reasons for preferring liberal equality to natural liberty, and then for preferring democratic equality to liberal equality. The argument is complicated, influential, and important. It needs to be read closely.

   In motivating the move from natural liberty to liberal equality, Rawls says: "the most obvious injustice of the system of natural liberty is that it permits distributive shares to be improperly influenced by these factors so arbitrary from a moral point of view." To understand this criticism of natural liberty, you will need to answer these questions:

   a. What is the system of natural liberty?

   b. What "factors" is Rawls referring to?

   c. How, in the system of natural liberty, do the factors he has in mind influence distributive shares? (In answering this question, put aside whether or not the influence is "improper.")

   d. What makes these factors "so arbitrary from a moral point of view"?

   e. Why (if at all) is it objectionable for factors that are arbitrary from a moral point of view to influence distributive shares?

   In motivating the move from liberal equality to democratic equality, Rawls says that in a system of liberal equality, "distributive shares are decided by the outcome of the natural lottery; and this outcome is arbitrary from a moral perspective. There is no more reason to permit the distribution of income and wealth to be settled by the distribution of natural assets than by historical and social fortune." To understand the criticism of liberal equality, you will need to answer these questions:

   a. What is the system of liberal equality?

   b. What "natural assets" is Rawls referring to?

   c. How, in the system of liberal equality, does the distribution of natural assets influence distributive shares?

   d. Why is the distribution of natural assets "arbitrary from a moral perspective"?

   e. Is there "no more reason to permit the distribution of income and wealth to be settled by the distribution of natural assets than by historical and social fortune"?

3. Adam Smith uses the phrase "system of natural liberty" in *An Inquiry into the Nature and Causes of the Wealth of Nations* (ed. Edwin Cannan [London, 1904], book 4, chapter 9). He says:

   > All systems either of preference or of restraint, therefore, being thus completely taken away, the obvious and simple system of natural liberty

establishes itself of its own accord. Every man, as long as he does not violate the laws of justice, is left perfectly free to pursue his own interest his own way, and to bring both his industry and capital into competition with those of any other man, or order of men. . . . According to the system of natural liberty, the sovereign has only three duties to attend to . . . first, the duty of protecting the society from violence and invasion of other independent societies; secondly, the duty of protecting, as far as possible, every member of the society from the injustice or oppression of every other member of it, or the duty of establishing an exact administration of justice; and, thirdly, the duty of erecting and maintaining certain public works and certain public institutions which it can never be for the interest of any individual, or small number of individuals, to erect and maintain; because the profit could never repay the expence to any individual or small number of individuals, though it may frequently do much more than repay it to a great society.

In his discussion of the "system of natural liberty," Rawls does not refer to Smith's use of the phrase, but their uses closely overlap, especially in the characterization of the responsibilities of government (of "the sovereign," in Smith's terms). See James Buchanan, "The Justice of Natural Liberty," *Journal of Legal Studies* 5, 1 (January 1976): 1–16.

4. According to Rawls's difference principle, social and economic inequalities are fully just (part of a perfectly just scheme) only if they work to the greatest expected advantage of the least advantaged. How can an inequality make the least advantaged better off? (To answer, you will need to bear in mind that Rawls is assuming that the size of the economic pie is not fixed: it can be increased in ways that make everyone better off.) Provide an example of an inequality that contributes maximally to the expected advantage of the least advantaged. Provide an example of an inequality that does not contribute to the expected advantage of the least advantaged.

Rawls's own examples of inequalities that can work to the advantage of the least advantaged focus on *incentives*. For criticism of incentive inequalities, see G. A. Cohen, *If You Are an Egalitarian, How Come You Are So Rich?* (Harvard University Press, 2001), 117–47.

5. The selection from Rawls in this anthology does not include the most famous argument in *A Theory of Justice* for his two principles of justice. That argument uses the device of a **social contract**. Rawls argues that people would unanimously agree to his two principles in a hypothetical situation—he calls it the *original position*—in which people come together to choose principles of justice for their own society. The most striking feature of the original position is that the parties make their choice of principles under a *veil of ignorance*. In particular, they do not know their social class, race, gender, religion, moral convictions, talents, or goals in life. The idea is that these characteristics are not relevant to the choice of principles of justice. So we are to put them behind the veil of ignorance to keep them from shaping our decision. The parties in the original position do know, however, that they represent the interests of a free and equal moral person who has a conception of the good (without knowing what that conception is), an interest in being able to choose and revise that conception, and an interest in forming and acting on a sense of justice.

The intuitive reasoning, then, proceeds as follows: You are asked to choose, under conditions of ignorance, principles of justice for your society. You do not know which person you will be, but you have to live with the principles you choose—you have no recourse for a bad decision. So you want to be sure, if you can, that your situation is (roughly) acceptable whatever it turns out to be. Because of the veil of ignorance, you want to be sure that the society is acceptable from the point of view of each person, *because you may be that person.* In particular, you want to be sure that it will be acceptable even if you land in the lowest social position, where it is least likely to be acceptable. So you try to make sure that the minimum position is as good as it can be. Rawls argues, this is the assurance—the strong protection against great risks—that the two principles provide: they ensure that social arrangements are acceptable to each member of society. If you choose the two principles in the original position, in effect you provide protection against luck or inheritance or talent not working out well, since you ensure that the minimum is as high as possible.

See John Rawls, *A Theory of Justice,* chapter 3, especially sections 26 and 29. For a particularly illuminating criticism of Rawls's argument, see John Harsanyi, "Can the Maximin Principle Serve as the Basis for Morality? A Critique of John Rawls's Theory," in *Essays on Ethics, Social Behavior, and Scientific Explanation* (Reidel, 1976), chapter 4.

Harry Frankfurt (b. 1929)

Frankfurt is Professor Emeritus of Philosophy at Princeton University. After receiving his PhD from Johns Hopkins University (1954), he taught at Rockefeller University and Yale University before moving to Princeton. He has written on Descartes, freedom of the will, and the nature and importance of love and care. Frankfurt is best known for his 2005 book, *On Bullshit* (originally published as a paper in 1986), which explains what bullshit is and deplores its cultural proliferation.

EQUALITY AS A MORAL IDEAL

> First man: "How are your children?"
> Second man: "Compared to what?"

I

Economic egalitarianism is, as I shall construe it, the doctrine that it is desirable for everyone to have the same amounts of income and of wealth (for short, "money"). Hardly anyone would deny that there are situations in which it makes sense to tolerate deviations from this standard. It goes without saying, after all, that preventing or correcting such deviations may involve costs which—whether measured in economic terms or in terms of noneconomic considerations—are by any reasonable measure unacceptable. Nonetheless, many people believe that economic equality has considerable moral value in itself. For this reason they often urge that efforts to approach the egalitarian ideal should be accorded—with all due consideration for the possible effects of such efforts in obstructing or in conducing to the achievement of other goods—a significant priority.

In my opinion, this is a mistake. Economic equality is not, as such, of particular moral importance. With respect to the distribution of economic assets, what *is* important from the point of view of morality is not that everyone should have *the same* but that each should have *enough*. If everyone had enough, it would be of no moral consequence whether some had more than others. I shall refer to this alternative to egalitarianism—namely, that what is morally important with respect to money is for everyone to have enough—as "the doctrine of sufficiency."

The fact that economic equality is not in its own right a morally compelling social ideal is in no way, of course, a reason for regarding it as undesirable. My claim that equality in itself lacks moral importance does not entail that equality is to be avoided. . . .

But despite the fact that an egalitarian distribution would not necessarily be objectionable, the error of believing that there are powerful moral reasons for caring about equality is far from innocuous. In fact, this belief tends to do significant harm. . . .

To the extent that people are preoccupied with equality for its own sake, their readiness to be satisfied with any particular level of income or wealth is guided not by their own interests and needs but just by the magnitude of the economic benefits that are at the disposal of others. In this way egalitarianism distracts people from measuring the requirements to which their individual natures and their personal circumstances give rise. It encourages them instead to insist upon a level of economic support that is determined by a calculation in which the particular features of their own lives are irrelevant. How sizable the economic assets of others are has nothing much to do, after all, with what kind of person someone is. A concern for economic equality, construed as desirable in itself, tends to divert a person's attention away from endeavoring to discover—within his experience of himself and of his life—what he himself really cares about and what will actually satisfy him, although this is the most basic and the most decisive task upon which an intelligent selection of economic goals depends. Exaggerating the moral importance of economic equality is harmful, in other words, because it is alienating. . . .

The mistaken belief that economic equality is important in itself leads people to detach the problem of formulating their economic ambitions from the problem of understanding what is most fundamentally significant to them. It influences them to take too seriously, as though it were a matter of great moral concern, a question that is inherently rather insignificant and not directly to the point, namely, how their economic status compares with the economic status of others. In this way the doctrine of equality contributes to the moral disorientation and shallowness of our time. . . .

II

There are a number of ways of attempting to establish the thesis that economic equality is important. Sometimes it is urged that the prevalence of fraternal relationships among the members of a society is a desirable goal and that equality is indispensable to it. Or it may be maintained that inequalities in the distribution of economic benefits are to be avoided because they lead invariably to undesirable discrepancies of other kinds—for example, in social status, in political influence, or in the abilities of people to make effective use of their various opportunities and entitlements. In both of these arguments, economic equality is endorsed because of its supposed importance in creating or preserving certain noneconomic conditions. Such considerations may well provide convincing reasons for recommending equality as a desirable social good or even for preferring egalitarianism as a policy over the alternatives to it. But both arguments construe equality as valuable derivatively, in virtue of its contingent connections to other things. In neither argument is there an attribution to equality of any unequivocally inherent moral value.

A rather different kind of argument for economic equality, which comes closer to construing the value of equality as independent of contingencies, is based upon the principle of diminishing marginal utility. According to this argument, equality is desirable because an egalitarian distribution of economic assets maximizes their aggregate utility. The argument presupposes: (*a*) for each individual the utility of money invariably diminishes at the margin and (*b*) with respect to money, or with respect to the things money can buy, the utility functions of all individuals are the same. In other words, the utility provided by or derivable from an *n*th dollar is the same for everyone, and it is less than the utility for anyone of dollar ($n - 1$). Unless *b* were true, a rich man might obtain greater utility than a poor man from an extra dollar. In that case an egalitarian distribution of economic goods would not maximize aggregate utility even if *a* were true. But given both *a* and *b*, it follows that a marginal dollar always brings less utility to a rich person than to one who is less rich. And this entails that total utility must increase when inequality is reduced by giving a dollar to someone poorer than the person from whom it is taken.

In fact, however, both *a* and *b* are false. Suppose it is conceded, for the sake of the argument, that the maximization of aggregate utility is in its own right a morally important social goal. Even so, it cannot legitimately be inferred that an egalitarian distribution of money must therefore have similar moral importance. For in virtue of the falsity of *a* and *b*, the argument linking economic equality to the maximization of aggregate utility is unsound.

So far as concerns *b*, it is evident that the utility functions for money of different individuals are not even approximately alike. Some people suffer from physical, mental, or emotional weaknesses or incapacities that limit the satisfactions they are able to obtain. Moreover, even apart from the effects of specific disabilities, some people simply enjoy things more than other people do. Everyone knows that there are, at any given level of expenditure, large differences in the quantities of utility that different spenders derive.

So far as concerns *a*, there are good reasons against expecting any consistent diminution in the marginal utility of money. The fact that the marginal utilities of certain goods do indeed tend to diminish is not a principle of reason. It is a psychological generalization, which is accounted for by such considerations as that people often tend after a time to become satiated with what they have been consuming and that the senses characteristically lose their freshness after repetitive stimulation. It is common knowledge that experiences of many kinds become increasingly routine and unrewarding as they are repeated.

It is questionable, however, whether this provides any reason at all for expecting a diminution in the marginal utility of *money*—that is, of anything that functions as a generic instrument of exchange. Even if the utility of everything money can buy were inevitably to diminish at the margin, the utility of money itself might nonetheless exhibit a different pattern. It is quite possible that money would be exempt from the phenomenon of unrelenting marginal decline because of its limitlessly protean versatility. . . . For there may always remain for [a person], no matter how tired he has become of what he has been doing, untried goods to be bought and fresh new pleasures to be enjoyed.

There are in any event many things of which people do not, from the very outset, immediately begin to tire. From certain goods, they actually derive more utility after sustained consumption than they derive at first. This is the situation whenever appreciating or enjoying or otherwise benefiting from something depends upon repeated trials, which serve as a kind of "warming up" process: for instance, when relatively little significant gratification is obtained from the item or experience in question until the individual has acquired a special taste for it, has become addicted to it, or has begun in some other way to relate or respond to it profitably. The capacity for obtaining gratification is then smaller at earlier points in the sequence of consumption than at later points. In such cases marginal utility does not decline; it increases. Perhaps it is true of everything, without exception, that a person will ultimately lose interest in it. But even if in every utility curve there is a point at which the curve begins a steady and irreversible decline, it cannot be assumed that every segment of the curve has a downward slope. . . .

IV

The preceding discussion has established that an egalitarian distribution may fail to maximize aggregate utility. It can also easily be shown that, in virtue of the incidence of utility thresholds, there are conditions under which an egalitarian distribution actually minimizes aggregate utility. Thus, suppose that there is enough of a certain resource (e.g., food or medicine) to enable some but not all members of a population to survive. Let us say that the size of the population is ten, that a person needs at least five units of the resource in question to live, and that forty units are available. If any members of this population are to survive, some must have more than others. An equal distribution, which gives each person four units, leads to the worst possible outcome, namely, everyone dies. Surely in this case it would be morally grotesque to insist upon equality! Nor would it be reasonable to maintain that, under the conditions specified, it is justifiable for some to be better off only when this is in the interests of the worst off. If the available resources are used to save eight people, the justification for doing this is manifestly not that it somehow benefits the two members of the population who are left to die. . . .

VI

The fundamental error of egalitarianism lies in supposing that it is morally important whether one person has less than another regardless of how much either of them has. This error is due in part to the false assumption that someone who is economically worse off has more important unsatisfied needs than someone who is better off. In fact the morally significant needs of both individuals may be fully satisfied or equally unsatisfied. Whether one person has more money than another is a wholly extrinsic matter. It has to do with a relationship between the respective economic assets of the two people, which is not only independent of the amounts of their assets and of the amounts of satisfaction they can derive from them but also independent of the attitudes of these people toward those levels of assets and of satisfaction. The economic comparison implies nothing concerning whether either of the people compared has any morally important unsatisfied needs at all nor concerning whether either is content with what he has. . . .

In most societies the people who are economically at the bottom are indeed extremely poor, and they do, as a matter of fact, have urgent needs. But this relationship between low economic status and urgent need is wholly contingent. It can be established only on the basis of empirical data. There is no necessary conceptual connection between a person's relative economic position and whether he has needs of any degree of urgency.

It is possible for those who are worse off not to have more urgent needs or claims than those who are better off because it is possible for them to have no urgent needs or claims at all. The notion of "urgency" has to do with what is *important*. Trivial needs or interests, which have no significant bearing upon the quality of a person's life or upon his readiness to be content with it, cannot properly be construed as being urgent to any degree whatever or as supporting the sort of morally demanding claims to which genuine urgency gives rise. From the fact that a person is at the bottom of some economic order, moreover, it cannot even be inferred that he has *any* unsatisfied needs or claims. After all, it is possible for conditions at the bottom to be quite good;

the fact that they are the worst does not in itself entail that they are bad or that they are in any way incompatible with richly fulfilling and enjoyable lives. . . .

VII

What does it mean, in the present context, for a person to have enough? One thing it might mean is that any more would be too much: a larger amount would make the person's life unpleasant, or it would be harmful or in some other way unwelcome. This is often what people have in mind when they say such things as "I've had enough!" or "Enough of that!" The idea conveyed by statements like these is that *a limit has been reached,* beyond which it is not desirable to proceed. On the other hand, the assertion that a person has enough may entail only that *a certain requirement or standard has been met,* with no implication that a larger quantity would be bad. This is often what a person intends when he says something like "That should be enough." Statements such as this one characterize the indicated amount as sufficient while leaving open the possibility that a larger amount might also be acceptable.

In the doctrine of sufficiency the use of the notion of "enough" pertains to *meeting a standard* rather than to *reaching a limit.* To say that a person has enough money means that he is content, or that it is reasonable for him to be content, with having no more money than he has. And to say this is, in turn, to say something like the following: the person does not (or cannot reasonably) regard whatever (if anything) is unsatisfying or distressing about his life as due to his having too little money. In other words, if a person is (or ought reasonably to be) content with the amount of money he has, then insofar as he is or has reason to be unhappy with the way his life is going, he does not (or cannot reasonably) suppose that money would—either as a sufficient or as a necessary condition—enable him to become (or to have reason to be) significantly less unhappy with it.

It is essential to understand that having enough money differs from merely having enough to get along or enough to make life marginally tolerable. People are not generally content with living on the brink. The point of the doctrine of sufficiency is not that the only morally important distributional consideration with respect to money is whether people have enough to avoid economic misery. A person who might naturally and appropriately be said to have just barely enough does not, by the standard invoked in the doctrine of sufficiency, have enough at all.

There are two distinct kinds of circumstances in which the amount of money a person has is enough—that is, in which more money will not enable him to become significantly less unhappy. On the one hand, it may be that the person is suffering no substantial distress or dissatisfaction with his life. On the other hand, it may be that although the person is unhappy about how his life is going, the difficulties that account for his unhappiness would not be alleviated by more money. Circumstances of this second kind obtain when what is wrong with the person's life has to do with noneconomic goods such as love, a sense that life is meaningful, satisfaction with one's own character, and so on. These are goods that money cannot buy; moreover, they are goods for which none of the things money can buy are even approximately adequate substitutes. . . .

It is possible that someone who is content with the amount of money he has might also be content with an even larger amount of money. Since having enough money does not mean being at a limit beyond which more money would necessarily be undesirable, it would be a mistake to assume that for a person who already has enough the marginal utility of money must be either negative or zero. Although this person is by hypothesis not distressed about his life in virtue of any lack of things which more money would enable him to obtain, nonetheless it remains possible that he would enjoy having some of those things. They would not make him less unhappy, nor would they in any way alter his attitude toward his life or the degree of his contentment with it, but they might bring him pleasure. If that is so, then his life would in this respect be better with more money than without it. The marginal utility for him of money would accordingly remain positive. . . .

But how can all this be compatible with saying that the person is content with what he has? What *does* contentment with a given amount of money preclude, if it does not preclude being willing or being pleased or preferring to have more money or even being ready to make sacrifices for more? It precludes his having an *active interest* in getting more. A contented person regards having more money as *inessential* to his being satisfied with his life. The fact that he is content is quite consistent with his recognizing that his economic circumstances could be improved and that his life might as a consequence become better than it is. But this possibility is not important to him. He is simply not much interested in being better off, so far as money goes, than he is. His attention and interest are not vividly engaged by the benefits which would be available to him if he had more money. He is just not very responsive to their appeal. They do not arouse in him any particularly eager or restless concern, although he acknowledges that he would enjoy additional benefits if they were provided to him.

In any event, let us suppose that the level of satisfaction that his present economic circumstances enable him to attain is high enough to meet his expectations of life. This is not fundamentally a matter of how much utility or satisfaction his various activities and experiences provide. Rather, it is most decisively a matter of his attitude toward being provided with that much. The satisfying experiences a person has are one thing. Whether he is satisfied that his life includes just those satisfactions is another. Although it is possible that other feasible circumstances would provide him with greater amounts of satisfaction, it may be that he is wholly satisfied with the amounts of satisfaction that he now enjoys. Even if he knows that he could obtain a greater quantity of satisfaction overall, he does not experience the uneasiness or the ambition that would incline him to seek it. Some people feel that their lives are good enough, and it is not important to them whether their lives are as good as possible. . . .

It may seem that there can be no reasonable basis for accepting less satisfaction when one could have more, that therefore rationality itself entails maximizing, and, hence, that a person who refuses to maximize the quantity of satisfaction in his life is not being rational. Such a person cannot, of course, offer it as his reason for declining to pursue greater satisfaction that the costs of this pursuit are too high; for if that were his reason then, clearly, he would be attempting to maximize satisfaction after all. But what other good reason could he possibly have for passing up an opportunity for more satisfaction? In fact, he may have a very good reason for this: namely, *that he is satisfied with the amount of satisfaction he already has.*

He might still be open to criticism on the grounds that he *should not* be satisfied—that it is somehow unreasonable, or unseemly, or in some other mode wrong for him to be satisfied with less satisfaction than he could have. On what basis, however, could *this* criticism be justified? Is there some decisive reason for insisting that a person ought to be so hard to satisfy? Suppose that a man deeply and happily loves a woman who is altogether worthy. We do not ordinarily criticize the man in such a case just because we think he might have done even better. Moreover, our sense that it would be inappropriate to criticize him for that reason need not be due simply to a belief that holding out for a more desirable or worthier woman might end up costing him more than it would be worth. Rather, it may reflect our recognition that the desire to be happy or content or satisfied with life is a desire for a satisfactory amount of satisfaction and is not inherently tantamount to a desire that the quantity of satisfaction be maximized. . . .

Contentment may be a function of excessive dullness or diffidence. The fact that a person is free both of resentment and of ambition may be due to his having a slavish character or to his vitality being muffled by a kind of negligent lassitude. It is possible for someone to be content merely, as it were, by default. But a person who is content with resources providing less utility than he could have may not be irresponsible or indolent or deficient in imagination. On the contrary, his decision to be content with those resources—in other words, to adopt an attitude of willing acceptance toward the fact that he has just that much—may be based upon a conscientiously intelligent and penetrating evaluation of the circumstances of his life.

TEST YOUR UNDERSTANDING

1. Frankfurt proposes the "doctrine of sufficiency" as an alternative to egalitarianism. Provide a brief statement of the doctrine and how, according to Frankfurt, it differs from egalitarianism.

2. Frankfurt says that a belief in the moral importance of equality "tends to do significant harm." What kinds of harm does he have in mind?

3. Frankfurt says that the utilitarian argument for equality makes two flawed assumptions. What are the assumptions?

4. What does "enough money" mean in the doctrine of sufficiency?

NOTES AND QUESTIONS

1. "There is no necessary conceptual connection between a person's relative economic position and whether he has needs of any degree of urgency." Explain what this statement means and how Frankfurt defends it. Why does he say "no necessary conceptual connection"? (*Hint:* Look at the previous three sentences in the paragraph.) What does he mean by "urgency"?

2. The main idea in Frankfurt's "doctrine of sufficiency" is that, when it comes to the economic assets, "each should have *enough*." According to the doctrine, "If everyone had enough, it would be of no moral consequence whether some had more than others." A simple formulation of the doctrine of sufficiency, then, says:

   > *Sufficiency:* A distribution of economic resources is morally right if and only if each person has enough.

   According to *Sufficiency*, then, changes in the distribution of resources make no moral difference, so long as each person has enough. When some people do not have enough, the situation calls for remedy. The plausibility of *Sufficiency* depends on how we understand what is "enough." Frankfurt offers the following account (focused on having enough money, which is the concern of this article):

   > *Enough:* A person has enough money if and only if the person will not become significantly less unhappy by having more money.

   A person, for example, has enough money if he or she is "suffering no substantial distress or dissatisfaction with his life." More money cannot alleviate this person's unhappiness because the person has no unhappiness to be alleviated.

   Consider, however, the case of Joseph. Joseph is satisfied with his life—he suffers no substantial distress or dissatisfaction—even though he is extremely poor. He is satisfied because he is accustomed from birth to having very little. Having little, he wants little and thinks he does not deserve to have more. He has what are called *adaptive* preferences: his preferences and sense of entitlement have *adapted* to his condition of extreme poverty. Suppose, now, that if Joseph had more money, his preferences would change: perhaps because he is now able to do more, he develops a desire to travel, to see more of his country or more of the larger world. Looking back, Joseph might say that when he was satisfied, he did not have enough money and that it was morally objectionable that he did not have more. He did not have enough because he lacked the resources needed to imagine different ways to live and decide which way is best.

   Do adaptive preferences raise a serious problem for *Enough*? Do they raise troubles for *Sufficiency*? Can you modify *Enough* so that *Sufficiency* can handle the difficulty presented by Joseph?

   For discussion of adaptive preferences, see Jon Elster, *Sour Grapes: Studies in the Subversion of Rationality* (Cambridge University Press, 1983); Amartya Sen, *Development as Freedom* (Oxford University Press, 1999); and Martha Nussbaum, *Women and Human Development* (Oxford University Press, 2000).

3. It follows from *Enough* that a person who has enough may still be very unhappy: that is true when the unhappiness cannot be addressed by more money. But if more money will make a person significantly less unhappy, then the person does not have enough. And if someone does not have enough, then *Sufficiency* tells us that something is not morally right.

Consider now the case of Albert, who has very ambitious goals. He wants to travel often and comfortably, eat at the best restaurants, pilot his own jet, have a large wine cellar with a large stock of the best wines, contribute large amounts of support to worthy causes, have a large family, ensure that all his children attend great schools, have lovely homes in all the places he travels, each filled with Impressionist paintings, and have an opera company on call to perform for him in his personal opera house. Albert already has considerable wealth (let's say he is in the top 0.1 percent in wealth). But because his wealth is not nearly sufficient to achieve his ambitious goals, he retains a very "active interest" (to use Frankfurt's term) in having more. So he is unhappy, and money can help.

Do we need to modify *Enough* or *Sufficiency* to respond to Albert? As stated, *Enough* implies that Albert does not have enough. And then *Sufficiency* tells us that something is morally wrong. Is it morally wrong that Albert does not have what he needs to fulfill his very ambitious goals? If it is not morally wrong, then we need to modify *Enough* so that Albert has enough, despite his discontentment. Or do we need to modify *Sufficiency* so that there is not something morally wrong whenever some people have less than enough? If we modify *Sufficiency*, we give up on Frankfurt's central idea: that everyone is entitled to have enough. So consider some modifications in *Enough* that address the challenge presented by Albert. As a starting point, consider the passages in which Frankfurt says that a person has enough when the person "is (*or ought reasonably to be*) content with the amount of money he has" (emphasis added). Will it help to reformulate *Enough*?

> *Enough**: A person has enough money if and only if the person will not reasonably become significantly less unhappy by having more money.

What makes Albert unreasonable? Do you think Albert is unreasonable? If you do, would you say he is unreasonable because he has a misguided idea of what a good life is or because he is demanding too much of other people?

Albert is an example of a person with *expensive tastes*. For discussion of the problem of expensive tastes, see G. A. Cohen, "Expensive Taste Rides Again," in *Dworkin and His Critics*, ed. Justine Burley (Blackwell, 1994), 3–29, and the response by Dworkin to Cohen in that same volume.

4. Frankfurt's doctrine of sufficiency has been the subject of considerable discussion and has been codified as *sufficientarianism*—a view of distributive justice distinct from *egalitarianism* and *prioritarianism*. For a critical exploration of Frankfurt's view and some of the surrounding literature on sufficientarianism, see Paula Casal, "Why Sufficiency Is Not Enough," *Ethics* 117 (2007): 296–326. On the three "–isms," see the entries in the *Stanford Encyclopedia of Philosophy* on "Equality" (http://plato.stanford .edu/entries/equality/) and on "Justice and Bad Luck" (http://plato.stanford.edu /entries/justice-bad-luck/).

5. In this paper, Frankfurt focuses attention on equality of money. In a later paper, he says that his case for sufficiency applies with equal force to "all egalitarian doctrines." "In rejecting equality as a moral ideal," Frankfurt says, "I intend the scope of my rejection to be entirely unlimited." So it does not matter if the focus is money, or opportunity, or rights, or liberties, or respect. In each case, equality is not an appropriate concern. See "The Moral Irrelevance of Equality," *Public Affairs Quarterly* 14, 2 (2000): 87–103.

How does Frankfurt's central objection to a concern with *economic* equality lead to this completely general conclusion about all forms of equality? His central objection cannot be that "there are goods that money cannot buy." That would not lead to the general conclusion. So what does lead to the general conclusion? (*Hint:* Review Frankfurt's reasons, stated early in the article, for thinking that a concern for equality is harmful.)

Martha Nussbaum (b. 1947)

Nussbaum is Ernst Freund Distinguished Service Professor of Law and Ethics at the University of Chicago, with appointments in the philosophy department, the law school, and the divinity school. She received her PhD from Harvard University in 1975 and taught at Harvard and Brown University before moving to the University of Chicago. Nussbaum has written on an extraordinary range of subjects, including political philosophy, ethics, ancient philosophy, American constitutional law, human emotions, literature, music, Indian religion and politics, feminism, and humanistic education. Her books include *Sex and Social Justice* (1998), *Women and Human Development* (2000), *Frontiers of Justice* (2006), *Not for Profit: Why Democracy Needs the Humanities* (2012), *Political Emotions: Why Love Matters for Justice* (2013), and *The Fragility of Goodness* (2013, second edition). In 2003, she cofounded the Human Development and Capability Association.

POLITICAL EQUALITY

Equality is a cherished political value in modern democracies. It is often associated with the idea of human worth or dignity, and also with questions of political entitlements and rights (including the right to vote, the right to education, and many others). The U.S. Declaration of Independence states, "We hold these truths to be self-evident, that all men are created equal, that they are endowed by their Creator with certain unalienable rights, that among these are life, liberty, and the pursuit of happiness." Most modern constitutions the world over contain similar appeals to human equality.

Such appeals are resonant, but it is not terribly clear what they mean. That all human beings are already equal? (Equal in what respect? Surely not in current resources and opportunities. In basic powers and capacities? In worth or dignity? And how, if at all, might that dignity be related to basic powers and capacities?) That all human beings are such that they ought to be treated equally? (Again, equally in what respect? In respect and self-respect? In political rights and liberties? In economic opportunity? In economic achievement?) And why should human beings be treated equally? Because they are in some other sense already equal?

And who are the human beings who are or ought to be equal? The U.S. founders by and large did not believe that slaves or women were or should be equal: that view was achieved only gradually and with much struggle. South Africa and India, by contrast, assert human equality in their founding documents, announcing the end of an era of racial and caste-based hierarchy. Does any nation, however, fully commit itself to the view that human beings with profound cognitive disabilities are or should be equal? (Are such people given equal voting rights? Equal rights to education?) Despite much recent progress, debates continue in most nations.

Finally, is it only human beings, and not other animals, who are equal and who have the right to "life, liberty, and the pursuit of happiness"? If so, we might want to be told what is special about human beings that allows them the right to establish dominion over other forms of life.

These thorny and intricate questions have not been given any final answer in political philosophy, but tracing the paths among the different types and conceptions of political equality at least helps us think better about our alternatives. First we must understand what it means to think of equality as a distinctively political value. Then, addressing the basis of human equality, we will see why a "minimalist" account is attractive; in the light of this account, the community of equals ranges widely. We can then understand why equality of the relevant kind has wide-ranging political and social implications.

I. Political and Comprehensive

Equality is a political value: a value enshrined in the basic political principles of nations and in their founding documents, and is connected with ideas of political entitlement (including both political and civil rights, such as the right to vote, and social and economic rights, such as the right to education or a right to social security). Equality is also, however, an ethical value, meaning one that people use in the nonpolitical aspects of their lives. Even when we are not thinking about political matters at all, we often talk of the equal worth of people, demanding that others respect it. For example, people condemn racism and sexism, even when they are found within the private sphere or in the bosom of the family, because they insult human equality. Such ethical conceptions of human equality are often rooted in some more comprehensive religious or ethical view, which covers all aspects of life, and not simply politics. The Christian doctrine of the equality of all souls in the eyes of God, for example, has been a major source of ethical equality principles.

But all modern nations contain many different religious and nonreligious views that guide the lives of their members. It therefore seems inappropriate, even disrespectful, to build political principles on any particular religious or metaphysical conception. That seems like a demand that everyone convert to that religion or metaphysical conception, if they want to enjoy full citizen status. (Even the Declaration's reference to a creator God now strikes many people as too sectarian in a nation containing believers and nonbelievers, and in which even many believers do not accept the idea that God created the world.) So the political value of equality should be articulated in a way that does not rely on such divisive or sectarian ideas, ideas that many citizens could not accept without converting. If I live in a Christian nation, I should not feel pressured to convert to Christianity by the role Christian language plays in public debate.

If many of a nation's people belong to a religion that teaches a doctrine of human equality, that may certainly be helpful in leading them to accept that everyone is entitled to equal rights. (In the United States, for example, Christian views helped buttress the new nation's political ideals.) But such widespread doctrines of equality are not necessary for the acceptance of a specifically political ideal. When Mahatma Gandhi asked all Indians to accept the political idea of human equality as the foundation of the new Indian nation, he was not relying on the traditions of the majority religion. Hinduism had long taught the unequal worth of human beings, including the idea of untouchability—a doctrine that the Indian constitution outlawed from the start, because it was incompatible with the political ideal. Despite the fact that many Indians continued to believe privately in human inequality, they accepted political equality— perhaps because their long experience of domination by the British had shown them its worth. Similarly, many people all over the world have not built the equality of women into their overall views of human life, but they can often accept the idea that women are equal for the purpose of framing political entitlements and responsibilities.

Our topic is political equality, not ethical or social equality. Sometimes, then, the best answer to disputed questions about the basis of human equality may be, "Answer them in your own way. So long as you accept the political ideal, nothing more need be said." Often, however, philosophers (and political leaders) have felt that more needs to be said, even to ground political principles. Following some of the major answers and the connections they suggest will help us think—even if we may conclude that some familiar replies (such as the Christian language of the Declaration) are too sectarian for political life in a pluralistic society. The ideas that are good guides may be slight variants on the more problematic ones: simply by omitting the Declaration's reference to a creator God, we have a view that all Americans can probably accept.

II. The Basis of Human Equality

What does it mean to assert that human beings are equal? We might begin by understanding what people who make such claims are reacting against. Feudalism, for example, involved a belief that nature has placed people in different social conditions, that these differences are fixed and immutable, part of people's very nature as human beings, constituting immutably distinct subspecies, and that political differences are rightly grounded on those differences of human worth and status. The Indian caste hierarchy was founded upon similar beliefs—as were American views of racial hierarchy.

To assert, against this, that human beings are equal is, most fundamentally, to assert that all human beings have a worth or dignity that is basically equal, and that they are not inherently, naturally, ranked above and below one another in a hierarchical ordering. The hierarchies we observe are the creation of social forces.

How might one defend such a view, in a world in which human beings, as we encounter them, are already profoundly affected by entrenched social hierarchies?

Some philosophers have thought it important to point out that human beings are all roughly similar in their innate physical and mental powers. Thomas Hobbes, for example, points out that in the "state of nature," meaning a situation without organized political society, people will soon recognize that their powers are pretty similar, since even the physically weakest could kill the strongest by stealth. Adam Smith,[1] similarly, said that the differences we observe between a philosopher and a street porter are not grounded in innate characteristics, but, instead, in social differences: differences, for example, of nutrition, education, and opportunity. Such claims are important because they are true, and because they remind us of the enormous power of social differences in our world. Class differences affect people's height, strength, health, cognitive development, emotions, and expectations in such a way that in many eras, people of different classes, races, or genders believed that they were really different subspecies of human beings.

It is not clear, however, that this is the right way to defend the political claim of equal worth or dignity. For one thing, it encourages us to believe that marked or life-long disabilities, physical and mental, diminish a person's worth as a human being, something that seems both incorrect and repugnant.

Other philosophers (beginning with the ancient Greek Stoics) have thought that the source of our equal worth lies in our power of ethical choice. Even though people may vary to some degree in their ethical skill and virtue, they said, all possess in sufficient measure the ability to rank and evaluate goals and to act in accordance with that ranking, and this sufficient degree of ethical capacity is enough to make them of fully equal worth, wherever they are placed in society (male or female, free or slave, rich or poor). In contemporary philosophy, John Rawls espouses a similar view in *A Theory of Justice*. This way of thinking about the source of equality is much more attractive than the way that alludes to equal physical and intellectual powers, since moral capacity does appear to be a source of worth or dignity, and people of very unequal intellectual development may have it in comparable measure; and yet many will think that it does not make quite enough room for equal respect for people with profound cognitive disabilities. Many of these people may not be able to evaluate and rank goals. But does this mean that we owe them unequal respect and concern, or that it is fine to place "normal" human beings hierarchically above them?

At this point, many people will want to point to some further fact about human beings, such as their relationship to God or their possession of a soul, that makes them equal regardless of their powers, whether physical or moral. This type of reply,

---

1. Adam Smith (1723–1790), a leading Scottish moral philosopher and economist, was the author of *The Theory of Moral Sentiments* (1759) and *The Wealth of Nations* (1776).

however, is more suited to personal ethical choice than to political choice, where we have said that we want to avoid sectarian answers.

We could try, instead, what we might call a thinner or more "minimalist" answer: so long as a living creature is of the human species (born of human parents) and possesses some degree of agency or striving and some consciousness, that being is, for political purposes, the full equal of all other humans in worth and dignity. This reply will include people with profound disabilities, but it may not include people in a persistent vegetative state, or fetuses, or anencephalic infants. It will therefore be controversial, since believers in the soul believe that all these creatures have souls and are full equals of people who have consciousness and agency. Political principles will need to wrestle with the special difficulty of such cases, in a country in which political principles ought to be nonsectarian. Nonetheless, the fact that a view cannot solve all our problems in the most difficult cases is not a strong argument against it. Political life poses many hard questions, and sometimes lines must simply be drawn in the best way one can.

If we give the minimalist answer, we have to face the fact that we are ascribing to bare species membership (plus striving and minimal awareness) a political significance that is hard to defend in a world in which members of other species also have striving and awareness. Why should the fact that creature A is born of two human parents give this creature priority over creature B, who might have very similar physical and mental powers but be born of two chimpanzee or two elephant parents? Isn't the preference for the human species itself a kind of sectarian reply, in a world in which many people believe in the underlying kinship of all life and the worth and dignity of other species?

This question has all too rarely been faced by political philosophy, and more rarely still by real-life politics. One reason for this silence is that most assume that the basis of human equality, whatever it is, resides in some property or properties that raise us above "the beasts." Most of the history of Western philosophy encourages this thought, although Hinduism and Buddhism do not. But the idea of a "ladder of nature," humans occupying the top rung, has little to commend it as a political doctrine. There are many capacities in which at least some animals surpass human beings: strength, speed, spatial perception, auditory sensitivity, sensory memory. If we now say, "But they don't have moral rationality," we may possibly be right, but we tip our hand: we are according to that property a decisive political importance, without any convincing argument. And if we have already taken the minimalist position, thus including people with profound cognitive disabilities as full equals, we cannot take this route without inconsistency. So the political idea of equality seems threatened with either an arbitrary species-ism or a repugnant denial of equal worth to some human beings.

We can respond to this dilemma by saying that for some purposes (cruelty, pain, desperate material conditions), the species boundary is not relevant: laws should protect all creatures from these assaults on their dignity. For others (voting, religious freedom), the species boundary is relevant because these things are good within one species community (the human) but not in another one (the chimp or elephant community). For a human with cognitive disabilities to be denied the equal right to vote is an offense to her human dignity; to deny the vote to a chimp with similar cognitive powers is not a similar offense, because voting is a good within the human community and not the chimp community.

III. Who Is Equal?

Seeing how difficult and potentially divisive the question about the basis of equal worth turns out to be, we might wonder whether we are not better off trying not to answer this question at all, at least in the political realm. When we look at history, however, we can see that we can never quite avoid it, because we always have to answer the question "Who is equal?" in order to give a good political argument for our political arrangements. And to do that in a politically productive way, we must at the very least rule out some unsatisfactory answers.

Why shouldn't we say that people whose skin color differs from our own are political unequals, fit for subordination? We need to have something to say, and we usually say that skin color is not relevant to political entitlement because it does not render people inherently different in basic human worth. Why shouldn't we say that women are unequal to men, fit to be ruled by men? Such views were long held, and some still hold them, so we need to have something to say. Typically, we say that the biological accidents of gender do not affect a person's fundamentally equal human worth: human worth resides elsewhere. Well then, where does it reside? The negative reply prompts a search for some type of positive answer, however vague. Again, why have most societies decided that it is wrong to deem people with physical and mental disabilities politically unequal, lacking equal political entitlements? Well, because they have come to the conclusion that a child with Down syndrome, for example, is of equal worth with a professor of philosophy—even though, unlike Smith's street porter, the child's differences from the philosopher cannot plausibly be said to be entirely due to mere social arrangements. We have come to believe, that is, that the basis of human equality lies elsewhere—in a dignity in which the child and the philosopher equally share.

We should probably continue to offer such negative answers without definitively articulating a positive theory of the basis of equality, apart from the vague minimalist account suggested, given the difficulty of going further in a nonsectarian way. We have to remain prepared, however, to respond to challenges and offer some account of why the hierarchies we assail are unjustified.

IV. Equality and Entitlement

When the framers of the Declaration of Independence affirmed the equal worth of human beings (really, of white males), they did so in order to demonstrate the wrongfulness of Britain's arbitrary rule over the colonies. The thought of equal worth is typically connected to ideas of political obligation. How?

First, we need the view that material and institutional conditions matter deeply for human life. The Stoics affirmed the equal worth of human beings but derived no political conclusions from this thought, because they believed that conditions such as wealth and poverty, political voice and lack of voice, even freedom and slavery, make no difference at all to human beings. The source of our equal worth and dignity is safe within, in our moral capacity, and nothing the world does to it can remove or even damage it.

The Stoic idea is deep. In part we should and do believe it: we don't think that people become less valuable as human beings, or lose their basic human dignity, when they lose political rights, or honor, or money, or freedom. And yet, unlike the Stoics, we typically believe that these conditions matter profoundly, and that certain forms of life insult or offend human dignity. Think of rape: we don't think that a woman who has been raped has lost her human dignity, but we do think that something deep has happened to her that cuts to the very heart of her dignity, or violates it. In a similar way, we often think that respect for equal human worth requires at least protecting people from the direst conditions, those that most deeply assail human dignity.

Second, we need a conception of the job of government, and the U.S. founders had one: governments are "instituted among men" in order "to secure these rights," namely the basic entitlements to "life, liberty, and the pursuit of happiness," entitlements grounded in human beings' equal worth. In other words, according to this widely shared view, government exists to provide at least minimum threshold conditions that enable a life that is worthy of our basic human equality. Human dignity itself is inalienable, as are the rights grounded upon it; but the conduct of George III was an insult to it. A government that behaves like this can rightly be rejected.

This idea is vague and intuitive. Where does it lead us? In most modern nations, it has led to the thought that it is unacceptable for governments to give citizens less than fully equal religious freedom, voting rights, freedom of speech, freedom of association, and other key civil and political liberties. To give one person only half a vote is seen, plausibly, as an insult to the person's equal human dignity. This group of political rights has a particularly intimate connection with human dignity, since these rights seem to lie at the heart of a person's role as a free and equal citizen. Few today would question this conclusion, although it is often not fully honored in practice. (Equal voting rights for people with extreme cognitive disabilities will require not only assistance at the polls but also, in some cases, forms of surrogacy that are not yet accepted.)

The payoff of equality for questions of material entitlement is far more disputed. There is widespread agreement that respect for human equality at least requires that government prevent people from living in desperate conditions, because that type of extreme poverty does seem like an assault on human dignity, as it stops people from developing and unfolding their human powers. (Adam Smith said that children sent to work in factories instead of being able to go to school were being "mutilated and deformed.") Beyond this, however, there is dispute. Some believe that the equal worth of human beings requires full-scale equality in educational provisions, in health care, and at least a rough equality in income and wealth. The U.S. founders were closer to that idea than is commonly supposed. James Madison, the primary architect of the U.S. Constitution, wrote that the new government should prevent "an immoderate, and especially an unmerited, accumulation of riches" and should do so "by the silent operation of laws, which, without violating the rights of property, reduce extreme wealth to a state of mediocrity [i.e., a middle level] and raise extreme indigence toward a state of comfort." Like Thomas Paine and other framers, then, he favored strongly redistributive policies aimed at achieving greater economic equality. But the United States has never given economic and social entitlements the status of constitutional rights. Even to the extent that such entitlements have been protected in legislation, it is typically an ample threshold level of provision that is sought, rather than complete equality. Other modern nations, such as India, South Africa, and the nations of Europe, have done much more to connect the thought of equal human worth to definite ideas of substantial equality in economic entitlement. At the very least, they believe, respect for human equality requires an ample social minimum, plus considerable diminution of inequalities between rich and poor, through redistributive taxation and a wide range of social welfare programs. Even issues that seem like matters of private personal choice, such as the choice to take a rewarding vacation or the choice to enjoy a peaceful day at home, depend in many ways on government policies: maximum-hours laws, bans on child labor, prohibitions on domestic violence, and so forth. The closer we look, the more we can see the need for government to establish legal protections for human equality in every area of life.

However, too much government intrusion into material arrangements may allow too little room for incentives to work hard and to achieve. We can grant that all human beings have fundamentally equal worth without granting that one person should always get the same reward as another. A good teacher will not give the same grades to students regardless of their effort, even though she believes them equal in human worth. Similarly, a just society should preserve a decent space for effort and rewards for effort, while providing all with a decent minimum. And a society that would require all parents to spend the same amount on the education of all children would also be too intrusive, diminishing parents' incentives to achieve—although a decent society should certainly guarantee far more educational equality than most modern societies have managed to attain, particularly given the importance of education for all future opportunities.

Here material entitlements look very different from political entitlements: being a slacker should not remove a person's right to vote or a person's equal freedom of religion. We may be satisfied by "enough" education, where some inequalities remain, but we should not be satisfied by "enough" votes, where some groups have more votes than others.

V. Equality as Goal: Equality of What?

Suppose we have decided that in some areas of social and economic life (health care, education, employment), respect for people as equals requires pursuing equality (or, at least, greater equality) as a political goal. Suppose, that is, we are aiming at making people who are already equals in some underlying sense equal (or more nearly equal) in material living conditions. What is the best way of thinking about that goal? What sort of equality should we be aiming at? We now need to make the concept of equality as political goal more precise.

A first appealing thought is that satisfaction is what we want to equalize—how pleased people feel about their lives. Satisfaction, however, is notoriously malleable and elusive. We know that people can get used to a bad state of affairs, avoiding constant frustration by defining their goals down. So they might feel satisfied in a rather bad condition. Many women did not demand equal political and economic rights, for example, before a process of consciousness raising made them aware of their situation.

Another idea we might try out is that people should be equal (or more nearly equal) in the amount of resources (income and wealth) that they control. That sort of equality is what redistributive policies of taxation typically support, and this makes a good deal of sense, because giving people all-purpose resources allows them freedom to choose how to use them. In a society without any entrenched hierarchies, it may well be the best sort of equality to focus on. But when a society contains long-standing hierarchies, giving members of the dominant and subordinate groups exactly the same amount of resources may not be enough. Getting people out of marginalization and low social status into a position of reasonable equality may require spending more on them. Many developing countries, for example, find that they must spend more to educate girls than boys, because girls face obstacles to education (in their families, their villages) that boys do not.

One might then conclude that the right sort of equality to focus on is equality of what some philosophers call "capabilities": substantial opportunities to choose and act. Income and wealth are sometimes good proxies for these freedoms and opportunities, but where they are not, we should focus on opportunity itself. Philosophers who think this way do not insist that full equality of "capability" is the right goal in every area: in some (e.g., housing), an ample social minimum may be enough. Still, a focus on "capabilities," or substantial opportunities, provides a very attractive way of linking the idea of human freedom and choice with the idea that meaningful freedoms involve a background of government action ensuring substantial opportunity.

TEST YOUR UNDERSTANDING

1. Nussbaum says that appeals to the idea of human equality are common, but it is "not terribly clear what they mean." What are some of the ways she thinks they are unclear?

2. To achieve political equality, is it important, according to Nussbaum, for members of a society to have a common religious outlook that affirms the idea of equality?

3. What is the "minimalist" account of the basis of equal human worth?

4. What is the Stoic view about human dignity? Does Nussbaum think we should accept it? What parts does she agree with? What parts does she disagree with?

NOTES AND QUESTIONS

1. Nussbaum wonders what it means for all human beings to have a "worth or dignity that is basically equal." Formulate the answers she considers in your own words. What problems does she identify in the views she associated with Hobbes and with the Stoics? How does her "minimalist" answer avoid those problems?

   Nussbaum worries that the minimalist view avoids a "repugnant denial of equal worth to some human beings" at the cost of endorsing an "arbitrary species-ism." Explain what she means by "arbitrary species-ism." How does she answer the charge of arbitrary species-ism? Is the answer convincing?

   For discussion of Stoicism, see Nussbaum's *The Therapy of Desire: Theory and Practice in Hellenistic Ethics* (Princeton University Press, 1994), chapters 9–13.

2. Explain the difference between treating equality as an ethical value and as a political value. Why does Nussbaum think it is important to treat equality as a political value?

   a. In support of the political conception of equality, she says it is wrong "to build political principles on any particular religious or metaphysical conception." To do this, she says, is tantamount to "a demand that everyone convert to that religion or metaphysical conception, if they want to enjoy full citizen status." But if the possession of full political and civil rights in a country is not dependent on converting (say, not dependent in England on being a member of the Anglican Church), what does it mean to say that there is a demand to convert as a condition of full citizen status?

   b. If equality is treated as a political value without deeper moral or religious moorings, does that make equality seem arbitrary?

   As background for Nussbaum's account of equality as a political value, see John Rawls, *Political Liberalism*, second edition (Columbia University Press, 2005). Rawls emphasizes the importance of formulating, under conditions of religious, moral, and philosophical pluralism, a political conception of justice that can be endorsed by people with different fundamental convictions.

Robert Nozick (1938–2002)

Nozick was born in Brooklyn, New York. He received his PhD from Princeton University (1963) and taught at Harvard University from 1969 to 2002. Best known for his early work in political philosophy, *Anarchy, State, and Utopia* (1974), Nozick had remarkably broad interests and made original contributions to philosophical discussions of personal identity, knowledge, objectivity, the meaning of life, and rationality. He was the author of *Philosophical Explanations* (1983), *The Examined Life* (1990), *The Nature of Rationality* (1993), *Socratic Puzzles* (1999), and *Invariances* (2001).

DISTRIBUTIVE JUSTICE

from Anarchy, State, and Utopia

The term "distributive justice" is not a neutral one. Hearing the term "distribution," most people presume that some thing or mechanism uses some principle or criterion to give out a supply of things. Into this process of distributing shares some error may have crept. So it is an open question, at least, whether *redistribution* should take place; whether we should do again what has already been done once, though poorly. However, we are not in the position of children who have been given portions of pie by someone who now makes last minute adjustments to rectify careless cutting. There is no *central* distribution, no person or group entitled to control all the resources, jointly deciding how they are to be doled out. What each person gets, he gets from others who give to him in exchange for something, or as a gift. In a free society, diverse persons control different resources, and new holdings arise out of the voluntary exchanges and actions of persons. There is no more a distributing or distribution of shares than there is a distributing of mates in a society in which persons choose whom they shall marry. . . .

The Entitlement Theory

The subject of justice in holdings consists of three major topics. The first is the *original acquisition of holdings,* the appropriation of unheld things. This includes the issues of how unheld things may come to be held, the process, or processes, by which unheld things may come to be held, the things that may come to be held by these processes, the extent of what comes to be held by a particular process, and so on. We shall refer to the complicated truth about this topic, which we shall not formulate here, as the principle of justice in acquisition. The second topic concerns the *transfer of holdings* from one person to another. By what processes may a person transfer holdings to another? How may a person acquire a holding from another who holds it? Under this topic come general descriptions of voluntary exchange, and gift and (on the other hand) fraud, as well as reference to particular conventional details fixed upon in a given society. The complicated truth about this subject (with placeholders for conventional details) we shall call the principle of justice in transfer. (And we shall suppose it also includes principles governing how a person may divest himself of a holding, passing it into an unheld state.)

If the world were wholly just, the following inductive definition[1] would exhaustively cover the subject of justice in holdings.

1. A person who acquires a holding in accordance with the principle of justice in acquisition is entitled to that holding.

---

1. An inductive definition defines an object by reference to itself. For example, an inductive definition of *natural number* says: 0 is a natural number; and every number you get by adding 1 to a natural number is a natural number. Nozick's definition is inductive because a person is entitled to something if he or she gets it according to principles of justice in transfer *from someone who is entitled to it.*

2. A person who acquires a holding in accordance with the principle of justice in transfer, from someone else entitled to the holding, is entitled to the holding.

3. No one is entitled to a holding except by (repeated) applications of 1 and 2.

The complete principle of distributive justice would say simply that a distribution is just if everyone is entitled to the holdings they possess under the distribution. . . .

Not all actual situations are generated in accordance with the two principles of justice in holdings: the principle of justice in acquisition and the principle of justice in transfer. Some people steal from others, or defraud them, or enslave them, seizing their product and preventing them from living as they choose, or forcibly exclude others from competing in exchanges. None of these are permissible modes of transition from one situation to another. And some persons acquire holdings by means not sanctioned by the principle of justice in acquisition. The existence of past injustice (previous violations of the first two principles of justice in holdings) raises the third major topic under justice in holdings: the rectification of injustice in holdings. If past injustice has shaped present holdings in various ways, some identifiable and some not, what now, if anything, ought to be done to rectify these injustices? . . .

The general outlines of the theory of justice in holdings are that the holdings of a person are just if he is entitled to them by the principles of justice in acquisition and transfer, or by the principle of rectification of injustice (as specified by the first two principles). If each person's holdings are just, then the total set (distribution) of holdings is just. To turn these general outlines into a specific theory we would have to specify the details of each of the three principles of justice in holdings: the principle of acquisition of holdings, the principle of transfer of holdings, and the principle of rectification of violations of the first two principles. I shall not attempt that task here. . . .

Historical Principles and End-Result Principles

The general outlines of the entitlement theory illuminate the nature and defects of other conceptions of distributive justice. The entitlement theory of justice in distribution is *historical;* whether a distribution is just depends upon how it came about. In contrast, *current time-slice principles* of justice hold that the justice of a distribution is determined by how things are distributed (who has what) as judged by some *structural* principle(s) of just distribution. A utilitarian who judges between any two distributions by seeing which has the greater sum of utility and, if the sums tie, applies some fixed equality criterion to choose the more equal distribution, would hold a current time-slice principle of justice. As would someone who had a fixed schedule of trade-offs between the sum of happiness and equality. According to a current time-slice principle, all that needs to be looked at, in judging the justice of a distribution, is who ends up with what; in comparing any two distributions one need look only at the matrix presenting the distributions. No further information need be fed into a principle of justice. . . .

Henceforth, we shall refer to such unhistorical principles of distributive justice, including the current time-slice principles, as *end-result principles* or *end-state principles*.

In contrast to end-result principles of justice, *historical principles* of justice hold that past circumstances or actions of people can create differential entitlements or differential deserts to things. An injustice can be worked by moving from one distribution to another structurally identical one, for the second, in profile the same, may violate people's entitlements or deserts; it may not fit the actual history.

Patterning

The entitlement principles of justice in holdings that we have sketched are historical principles of justice. To better understand their precise character, we shall distinguish them from another subclass of the historical principles. Consider, as an example, the principle of distribution according to moral merit. This principle requires that total distributive shares vary directly with moral merit; no person should have a greater share than anyone whose moral merit is greater. (If moral merit could be not merely ordered but measured on an interval or ratio scale, stronger principles could be formulated.) Or consider the principle that results by substituting "usefulness to society" for "moral merit" in the previous principle. Or instead of "distribute according to moral merit," or "distribute according to usefulness to society," we might consider "distribute according to the weighted sum of moral merit, usefulness to society, and need," with the weights of the different dimensions equal. Let us call a principle of distribution *patterned* if it specifies that a distribution is to vary along with some natural dimension, weighted sum of natural dimensions, or lexicographic ordering of natural dimensions. And let us say a distribution is patterned if it accords with some patterned principle. . . . The principle of distribution in accordance with moral merit is a patterned historical principle, which specifies a patterned distribution. "Distribute according to I.Q." is a patterned principle that looks to information not contained in distributional matrices. It is not historical, however, in that it does not look to any past actions creating differential entitlements to evaluate a distribution; it requires only distributional matrices whose columns are labeled by I.Q. scores. The distribution in a society, however, may be composed of such simple patterned distributions, without itself being simply patterned. Different sectors may operate different patterns, or some combination of patterns may operate in different proportions across a society. A distribution composed in this manner, from a small number of patterned distributions, we also shall term "patterned." And we extend the use of "pattern" to include the overall designs put forth by combinations of end-state principles.

Almost every suggested principle of distributive justice is patterned: to each according to his moral merit, or needs, or marginal product,[2] or how hard he tries, or the weighted sum of the foregoing, and so on. The principle of entitlement we have sketched is not patterned. There is no one natural dimension or weighted sum or combination of a small number of natural dimensions that yields the distributions

---

2. In economics, the marginal product is the extra output produced by one additional unit of input.

generated in accordance with the principle of entitlement. The set of holdings that results when some persons receive their marginal products, others win at gambling, others receive a share of their mate's income, others receive gifts from foundations, others receive interest on loans, others receive gifts from admirers, others receive returns on investment, others make for themselves much of what they have, others find things, and so on, will not be patterned. . . .

To think that the task of a theory of distributive justice is to fill in the blank in "to each according to his _____" is to be predisposed to search for a pattern; and the separate treatment of "from each according to his _____" treats production and distribution as two separate and independent issues. On an entitlement view these are *not* two separate questions. Whoever makes something, having bought or contracted for all other held resources used in the process (transferring some of his holdings for these cooperating factors), is entitled to it. The situation is *not* one of something's getting made, and there being an open question of who is to get it. Things come into the world already attached to people having entitlements over them. From the point of view of the historical entitlement conception of justice in holdings, those who start afresh to complete "to each according to his _____" treat objects as if they appeared from nowhere, out of nothing. A complete theory of justice might cover this limit case as well; perhaps here is a use for the usual conceptions of distributive justice.[3]

So entrenched are maxims of the usual form that perhaps we should present the entitlement conception as a competitor. Ignoring acquisition and rectification, we might say:

> From each according to what he chooses to do, to each according to what he makes for himself (perhaps with the contracted aid of others) and what others choose to do for him and choose to give him of what they've been given previously (under this maxim) and haven't yet expended or transferred.

This, the discerning reader will have noticed, has its defects as a slogan. So as a summary and great simplification (and not as a maxim with any independent meaning) we have:

> From each as they choose, to each as they are chosen.

How Liberty Upsets Patterns

It is not clear how those holding alternative conceptions of distributive justice can reject the entitlement conception of justice in holdings. For suppose a distribution favored by

---

3. The "usual conceptions" include distribution according to need, or effort, or contribution. Nozick's point is that these conceptions, unlike his historical entitlement view, may be appropriate in deciding how to distribute goods that appear from nowhere, that were not made by people working with things they own.

one of these nonentitlement conceptions is realized. Let us suppose it is your favorite one and let us call this distribution D_1; perhaps everyone has an equal share, perhaps shares vary in accordance with some dimension you treasure. Now suppose that Wilt Chamberlain is greatly in demand by basketball teams, being a great gate attraction.[4] (Also suppose contracts run only for a year, with players being free agents.) He signs the following sort of contract with a team: In each home game, twenty-five cents from the price of each ticket of admission goes to him. (We ignore the question of whether he is "gouging" the owners, letting them look out for themselves.) The season starts, and people cheerfully attend his team's games; they buy their tickets, each time dropping a separate twenty-five cents of their admission price into a special box with Chamberlain's name on it. They are excited about seeing him play; it is worth the total admission price to them. Let us suppose that in one season one million persons attend his home games, and Wilt Chamberlain winds up with $250,000, a much larger sum than the average income and larger even than anyone else has. Is he entitled to this income? Is this new distribution D_2, unjust? If so, why? There is *no* question about whether each of the people was entitled to the control over the resources they held in D_1; because that was the distribution (your favorite) that (for the purposes of argument) we assumed was acceptable. Each of these persons *chose* to give twenty-five cents of their money to Chamberlain. They could have spent it on going to the movies, or on candy bars, or on copies of *Dissent* magazine, or of *Monthly Review*.[5] But they all, at least one million of them, converged on giving it to Wilt Chamberlain in exchange for watching him play basketball. If D_1 was a just distribution, and people voluntarily moved from it to D_2, transferring parts of their shares they were given under D_1 (what was it for if not to do something with?), isn't D_2 also just? If the people were entitled to dispose of the resources to which they were entitled (under D_1), didn't this include their being entitled to give it to, or exchange it with, Wilt Chamberlain? Can anyone else complain on grounds of justice? Each other person already has his legitimate share under D_1. Under D_1, there is nothing that anyone has that anyone else has a claim of justice against. After someone transfers something to Wilt Chamberlain, third parties *still* have their legitimate shares; *their* shares are not changed. By what process could such a transfer among two persons give rise to a legitimate claim of distributive justice on a portion of what was transferred, by a third party who had no claim of justice on any holding of the others *before* the transfer? To cut off objections irrelevant here, we might imagine the exchanges occurring in a socialist society, after hours. After playing whatever basketball he does in his daily work, or doing whatever other daily work he does, Wilt Chamberlain decides to put in *overtime* to earn additional money. . . .

The general point illustrated by the Wilt Chamberlain example . . . is that no end-state principle or distributional patterned principle of justice can be continuously

---

4. Wilt Chamberlain (1936–1999) was one of the greatest basketball players of all time, and when Nozick wrote his book, Chamberlain was playing center for the Los Angeles Lakers. He once scored 100 points in a single game, and was named Most Valuable Player four times.

5. *Dissent* and *Monthly Review* are both American political magazines, on the political left.

realized without continuous interference with people's lives. Any favored pattern would be transformed into one unfavored by the principle, by people choosing to act in various ways; for example, by people exchanging goods and services with other people, or giving things to other people, things the transferrers are entitled to under the favored distributional pattern. To maintain a pattern one must either continually interfere to stop people from transferring resources as they wish to, or continually (or periodically) interfere to take from some persons resources that others for some reason chose to transfer to them. (But if some time limit is to be set on how long people may keep resources others voluntarily transfer to them, why let them keep these resources for *any* period of time? Why not have immediate confiscation?) . . .

Redistribution and Property Rights

Patterned principles of distributive justice necessitate *re*distributive activities. The likelihood is small that any actual freely-arrived-at set of holdings fits a given pattern; and the likelihood is nil that it will continue to fit the pattern as people exchange and give. From the point of view of an entitlement theory, redistribution is a serious matter indeed, involving, as it does, the violation of people's rights. (An exception is those takings that fall under the principle of the rectification of injustices.) From other points of view, also, it is serious.

Taxation of earnings from labor is on a par with forced labor. Some persons find this claim obviously true: taking the earnings of *n* hours labor is like taking *n* hours from the person; it is like forcing the person to work *n* hours for another's purpose. Others find the claim absurd. But even these, *if* they object to forced labor, would oppose forcing unemployed hippies to work for the benefit of the needy. And they would also object to forcing each person to work five extra hours each week for the benefit of the needy. But a system that takes five hours' wages in taxes does not seem to them like one that forces someone to work five hours, since it offers the person forced a wider range of choice in activities than does taxation in kind with the particular labor specified. . . . Furthermore, people envisage a system with something like a proportional tax on everything above the amount necessary for basic needs. Some think this does not force someone to work extra hours, since there is no fixed number of extra hours he is forced to work, and since he can avoid the tax entirely by earning only enough to cover his basic needs. This is a very uncharacteristic view of forcing for those who *also* think people are forced to do something *whenever* the alternatives they face are considerably worse. However, *neither* view is correct. The fact that others intentionally intervene, in violation of a side constraint against aggression, to threaten force to limit the alternatives, in this case to paying taxes or (presumably the worse alternative) bare subsistence, makes the taxation system one of forced labor and distinguishes it from other cases of limited choices which are not forcings. . . .

What sort of right over others does a legally institutionalized end-state pattern give one? The central core of the notion of a property right in *X*, relative to which other parts of the notion are to be explained, is the right to determine what shall be done with *X*; the right to choose which of the constrained set of options concerning *X* shall be realized or attempted. The constraints are set by other principles or laws operating in the society; in our theory, by the Lockean rights people possess (under the minimal state).[6] My property rights in my knife allow me to leave it where I will, but not in your chest. I may choose which of the acceptable options involving the knife is to be realized. This notion of property helps us to understand why earlier theorists spoke of people as having property in themselves and their labor. They viewed each person as having a right to decide what would become of himself and what he would do, and as having a right to reap the benefits of what he did. . . .

When end-result principles of distributive justice are built into the legal structure of a society, they (as do most patterned principles) give each citizen an enforceable claim to some portion of the total social product; that is, to some portion of the sum total of the individually and jointly made products. This total product is produced by individuals laboring, using means of production others have saved to bring into existence, by people organizing production or creating means to produce new things or things in a new way. It is on this batch of individual activities that patterned distributional principles give each individual an enforceable claim. Each person has a claim to the activities and the products of other persons, independently of whether the other persons enter into particular relationships that give rise to these claims, and independently of whether they voluntarily take these claims upon themselves, in charity or in exchange for something.

Whether it is done through taxation on wages or on wages over a certain amount, or through seizure of profits, or through there being a big *social pot* so that it's not clear what's coming from where and what's going where, patterned principles of distributive justice involve appropriating the actions of other persons. Seizing the results of someone's labor is equivalent to seizing hours from him and directing him to carry on various activities. If people force you to do certain work, or unrewarded work, for a certain period of time, they decide what you are to do and what purposes your work is to serve apart from your decisions. This process whereby they take this decision from you makes them a *part-owner* of you; it gives them a property right in you. Just as having such partial control and power of decision, by right, over an animal or inanimate object would be to have a property right in it.

End-state and most patterned principles of distributive justice institute (partial) ownership by others of people and their actions and labor. These principles involve a shift from the classical liberals' notion of self-ownership to a notion of (partial) property rights in *other* people.

6. Lockean rights are the individual rights that the English philosopher John Locke (1632–1704) emphasizes in his *Second Treatise of Government*. They are rights we would have even if there were no government, including rights to life, liberty, and possessions. The minimal state is a state whose functions are limited to the protection of these basic individual rights.

TEST YOUR UNDERSTANDING

1. What topics are addressed by a theory of justice in holdings?

2. Nozick distinguishes two types of principles of justice. What are the types, and what distinguishes them?

3. What is the main point of Nozick's Wilt Chamberlain story?

4. Does Nozick favor taxation on earnings from work as an alternative to forcing people to work?

NOTES AND QUESTIONS

1. What is the point of the Wilt Chamberlain example? Review Nozick's presentation of it and then consider four variants of the case. In each case, assume (following Nozick's presentation) that the status quo distribution fits a distributional pattern:

> *No Taxation 1*: Each person who attends a basketball game is required, as part of the admission fee, to drop $10 into a Wilt Chamberlain box. At the end of the season, the Chamberlain box has accumulated $10 million. Everything in the box is handed to Chamberlain as a supplement to his salary, with no taxes on this income.

> *No Taxation 2*: Each person who attends a basketball game is required to put $5 into a Wilt Chamberlain box and is given the option of also putting $5 into a Literacy Program box. Attendance is the same as in *No Taxation 1*. At the end of the season, the Chamberlain box has $5 million, which he receives without taxation, and the Literacy Program box has nothing. Chamberlain then gives his $5 million to the literacy program.

> *Taxation 1*: A tax rate of 50 percent is announced before the basketball season starts, and it is announced that the revenues will be spent on funding a literacy program. Chamberlain decides not to play, and so no money is put in the Wilt Chamberlain box. Attendance is 20 percent lower than it would have been, and everyone keeps their $10.

> *Taxation 2*: A tax rate of 50 percent is announced before the season starts, and it is announced that the revenues will be spent on a literacy program. Chamberlain plays, and each person who attends drops $10 into the Wilt Chamberlain box. Once more, $10 million is accumulated in the box. Chamberlain gets $5 million, and the $5 million in taxes goes to the literacy program.

   a. In *Taxation 1* and *Taxation 2*, do we have an intrusion on liberty? Whose liberty is burdened? (Notice that in *Taxation 2*, people willingly pay, and Chamberlain willingly plays.)

    b. How should we think about the use of the money to support the literacy program? Does that spending benefit the liberty of the people who receive the training?

    c. Nozick says "liberty upsets patterns." In which of the four cases has liberty upset the previous pattern?

2. Nozick says "taxation on earnings from labor is on a par with forced labor." To illustrate: Suppose James works 40 hours each week as a lawyer. Assume that it is illegitimate for the law to require James spend 8 of those hours (20 percent of his time) working at a school. (Do you think this assumption is correct, that it is illegitimate?) How, then, could it be legitimate to tax 20 percent of his earnings to support the school? "Seizing the results of someone's labor," Nozick says, "is equivalent to seizing hours from him and directing him to carry on various activities."

    Is Nozick right about this deep connection between taxation and forced labor? List some possible distinctions between being taxed to support the school and being required to work in the school. (Think about your own reactions to being taxed as distinct from being required to work in the school.) After you have a list, review Nozick's discussion of taxation and forced labor to see how it addresses the apparent differences. Is he right that the distinctions do not make a moral difference?

3. Nozick says that patterned conceptions are in conflict with the "classical liberal's notion of self-ownership." Patterned conceptions "institute (partial) ownership by others of people and their actions and labor." Nozick's idea is that each of us belongs fully to himself or herself; none belongs at all to humanity or to our state, church, community, race, ethnicity, or nation, nor to those who brought us into existence, whether the makers be biological parents or God. Because we fully own ourselves, we can sell ourselves into slavery if we wish to or submit to unlimited political authority. Moreover, we are entitled to everything we can get other people to pay for the use of our talents.

    For discussion of the idea of self-ownership in Nozick's theory, see G. A. Cohen, *Self-Ownership, Freedom, and Equality* (Cambridge University Press, 1995), chapters 3 and 4.

4. The place of self-ownership in classical liberalism is a complex issue. John Locke is widely agreed to be a classical liberal, and Nozick presents some of his ideas as having a Lockean inspiration. In chapter 5 of his *Second Treatise of Government*, Locke suggests the idea of self-ownership when he says that each of us "has a property in his own person." See John Locke, *Two Treatises of Government and A Letter Concerning Toleration*, ed. Ian Shapiro (Yale University Press, 2003), section 27 of *Two Treatises*. But Locke's position is founded on natural obligations that are in turn based on natural laws established by God. Those natural laws qualify the rights we have in our own persons in two ways, each of which distinguishes Locke from Nozick. First, the natural laws limit what we are permitted to do to ourselves. We are not permitted, for example, to kill ourselves, enslave ourselves, or submit to an absolute political authority. We are not permitted to because the natural laws limit our authority over ourselves: "A man cannot subject himself to the arbitrary power of another, but only so much as the law of nature gave him for the preservation of himself and the rest of mankind, this is all he doth or can give up to the commonwealth" (*Second Treatise*, section 135). Second, the natural laws require us to assist others in certain cases, and not simply to care for

ourselves: "when [a person's] own preservation comes not in competition, ought he, as much as he can, to preserve the rest of mankind" (*Second Treatise*, section 6). What do you think of Locke's two qualifications?

For an illuminating discussion of Locke's theory of rights and natural obligations, see A. John Simmons, *The Lockean Theory of Rights* (Princeton University Press, 1992).

Susan Moller Okin (1946–2004)

Okin taught at Brandeis University and Stanford University, where she was Marta Sutton Weeks Professor of Ethics in Society. Okin was best known for her work in feminist political theory, including *Women in Western Political Thought* (1979), *Justice, Gender, and the Family* (1989), and her title essay in *Is Multiculturalism Bad for Women?* (1999).

IS MULTICULTURALISM BAD FOR WOMEN?[1]

Until the past few decades, minority groups—immigrants as well as indigenous peoples—were typically expected to assimilate into majority cultures. This assimilationist expectation is now often considered oppressive, and many Western countries are seeking to devise new policies that are more responsive to persistent cultural differences. The appropriate policies vary with context: countries such as England, with established churches or state-supported religious education, find it difficult to resist demands to extend state support to minority religious schools; countries such as France, with traditions of strictly secular public education, struggle over whether the clothing required by minority religions may be worn in the public schools. But one issue recurs across all contexts, though it has gone virtually unnoticed in current debate: What should be done when the claims of minority cultures or religions clash with the norm of gender equality that is at least formally endorsed by liberal states (however much they continue to violate it in their practices)?

In the late 1980s, for example a sharp public controversy erupted in France about whether Magrébin girls could attend school wearing the traditional Muslim head scarves regarded as proper attire for postpubescent young women. Staunch defenders of secular education lined up with some feminists and far-right nationalists against the practice; much of the Old Left supported the multiculturalist demands for flexibility and respect for diversity, accusing opponents of racism or cultural imperialism. At the very same time, however, the public was virtually silent about a problem of vastly greater importance to many French Arab and African immigrant women: polygamy.

---

1. Thanks to Elizabeth Beaumont for research assistance and to Beaumont and Joshua Cohen for helpful comments on an earlier draft. [Okin's note.]

During the 1980s, the French government quietly permitted immigrant men to bring multiple wives into the country, to the point where an estimated 200,000 families in Paris are now polygamous. Any suspicion that official concern over head scarves was motivated by an impulse toward gender equality is belied by the easy adoption of a permissive policy on polygamy, despite the burdens this practice imposes on women and the warnings disseminated by women from the relevant cultures.[2] On this issue, no politically effective opposition galvanized. But once reporters finally got around to interviewing the wives, they discovered what the government could have learned years earlier: that the women affected by polygamy regarded it as an inescapable and barely tolerable institution in their African countries of origin, and an unbearable imposition in the French context. Overcrowded apartments and the lack of private space for each wife led to immense hostility, resentment, even violence both among the wives and against each other's children.

In part because of the strain on the welfare system caused by families with twenty to thirty members, the French government has recently decided to recognize only one wife and to consider all the other marriages annulled. But what will happen to all the other wives and children? Having ignored women's views on polygamy for so long, the government now seems to be abdicating its responsibility for the vulnerability that its rash policy has inflicted on women and children.

The French accommodation of polygamy illustrates a deep and growing tension between feminism and multiculturalist concern for protecting cultural diversity. I think we—especially those of us who consider ourselves politically progressive and opposed to all forms of oppression—have been too quick to assume that feminism and multi-culturalism are both good things which are easily reconciled. I shall argue instead that there is considerable likelihood of tension between them—more precisely, between feminism and multiculturalist commitment to group rights for minority cultures.

A few words to explain the terms and focus of my argument. By *feminism,* I mean the belief that women should not be disadvantaged by their sex, that they should be recognized as having human dignity equal to that of men, and that they should have the opportunity to live as fulfilling and as freely chosen lives as men can. *Multiculturalism* is harder to pin down, but the particular aspect that concerns me here is the claim, made in the context of basically liberal democracies, that minority cultures or ways of life are not sufficiently protected by the practice of ensuring the individual rights of their members, and as a consequence these should also be protected through special *group* rights or privileges. In the French case, for example, the right to contract polygamous marriages clearly constituted a group right not available to the rest of the population. In other cases, groups have claimed rights to govern themselves, to have guaranteed political representation, or to be exempt from certain generally applicable laws.

Demands for such group rights are growing—from indigenous native populations, minority ethnic or religious groups, and formerly colonized peoples (at least when the latter immigrate to the former colonial state). These groups, it is argued, have their own "societal cultures" which—as Will Kymlicka, the foremost contemporary defender of

---

2. *International Herald Tribune,* 2 February 1996, News section. [Okin's note.]

cultural group rights, says—provide "members with meaningful ways of life across the full range of human activities, including social, educational, religious, recreational, and economic life, encompassing both public and private spheres."[3] Because societal cultures play so pervasive and fundamental a role in the lives of their members, and because such cultures are threatened with extinction, minority cultures should be protected by special rights. That, in essence, is the case for group rights.

Some proponents of group rights argue that even cultures that "flout the rights of [their individual members] in a liberal society"[4] should be accorded group rights or privileges if their minority status endangers the culture's continued existence. Others do not claim that all minority cultural groups should have special rights, but rather that such groups—even illiberal ones that violate their individual members' rights, requiring them to conform to group beliefs or norms—have the right to be "left alone" in a liberal society.[5] Both claims seem clearly inconsistent with the basic liberal value of individual freedom, which entails that group rights should not trump the individual rights of its members; thus I will not address the additional problems they present for feminists here.[6] But some defenders of multiculturalism confine their defense of group rights largely to groups that are internally liberal.[7] Even with these restrictions, feminists—everyone, that is, who endorses the moral equality of men and women—should remain skeptical. So I will argue.

Most cultures are suffused with practices and ideologies concerning gender. Suppose, then, that a culture endorses and facilitates the control of men over women in various ways (even if informally, in the private sphere of domestic life). Suppose, too, that there are fairly clear disparities in power between the sexes, such that the more powerful, male members are those who are generally in a position to determine and articulate the group beliefs, practices, and interests. Under such conditions, group rights are potentially, and in many cases actually, antifeminist. They substantially limit the capacities of women and girls of that culture to live with human dignity equal to that of men and boys, and to live as freely chosen lives as they can.

Advocates of group rights for minorities within liberal states have not adequately addressed this simple critique of group rights, for at least two reasons. First, they tend to treat cultural groups as monoliths—to pay more attention to differences between and among groups than to differences within them. Specifically, they accord little or no recognition to the fact that minority cultural groups, like the societies in which they

---

3. Will Kymlicka, *Multicultural Citizenship: A Liberal Theory of Minority Rights* (Oxford University Press, 1995), 89, 76. See also Kymlicka *Liberalism, Community, and Culture* (The Clarendon Press, 1989). It should be noted that Kymlicka himself does not argue for extensive or permanent group rights for those who have voluntarily immigrated. [Okin's note.]

4. Avishai Margalit and Moshe Halbertal, "Liberalism and the Right to Culture," *Social Research* 61, 3 (1994): 491. [Okin's note.]

5. For example, Chandran Kukathas, "Are There Any Cultural Rights?," *Political Theory* 20, 1 (1992): 105–39. [Okin's note.]

6. Okin, "Feminism and Multiculturalism: Some Tensions," *Ethics* 108, 4 (1998): 661–84. [Okin's note.]

7. For example, Kymlicka, *Liberalism, Community, and Culture* and *Multicultural Citizenship* (esp. chapter 8). Kymlicka does not apply his requirement that groups be internally liberal to those he terms "national minorities," but I will not address that aspect of his theory here. [Okin's note.]

exist (though to a greater or lesser extent), are themselves *gendered,* with substantial differences in power and advantage between men and women. Second, advocates of groups rights pay little or no attention to the private sphere. Some of the most persuasive liberal defenses of group rights urge that individuals need "a culture of their own," and that only within such a culture can people develop a sense of self-esteem or self-respect, as well as the capacity to decide what kind of life is good for them. But such arguments typically neglect both the different roles that cultural groups impose on their members and the context in which persons' senses of themselves and their capacities are first formed *and* in which culture is first transmitted—the realm of domestic or family life.

When we correct for these deficiencies by paying attention to internal differences and to the private arena, two particularly important connections between culture and gender come into sharp relief, both of which underscore the force of this simple critique of group rights. First, the sphere of personal, sexual, and reproductive life functions as a central focus of most cultures, a dominant theme in cultural practices and rules. Religious or cultural groups often are particularly concerned with "personal law"—the laws of marriage, divorce, child custody, division and control of family property, and inheritance.[8] As a rule, then, the defense of "cultural practices" is likely to have much greater impact on the lives of women and girls than on those of men and boys, since far more of women's time and energy goes into preserving and maintaining the personal, familial, and reproductive side of life. Obviously, culture is not only about domestic arrangements, but they do provide a major focus of most contemporary cultures. Home is, after all, where much of culture is practiced, preserved, and transmitted to the young. On the other hand, the distribution of responsibilities and power at home has a major impact on who can participate in and influence the more public parts of the cultural life, where rules and regulations about both public and private life are made. The more a culture requires or expects of women in the domestic sphere, the less opportunity they have of achieving equality with men in either sphere.

The second important connection between culture and gender is that most cultures have as one of their principal aims the control of women by men. Consider, for example, the founding myths of Greek and Roman antiquity, and of Judaism, Christianity, and Islam: they are rife with attempts to justify the control and subordination of women. These myths consist of a combination of denials of women's role in reproduction; appropriations by men of the power to reproduce themselves; characterizations of women as overly emotional, untrustworthy, evil, or sexually dangerous; and refusals to acknowledge mothers' rights over the disposition of their children.[9] Think of Athena, sprung from the head of Zeus, and of Romulus and Remus, reared without a human mother. Or Adam, made by a male God, who then (at least according to one of the two biblical versions of the story) created Eve out of part of Adam. Consider

8. See, for example, Kirti Singh, "Obstacles to Womens' Rights in India," in *Human Rights of Women: National and International Perspectives,* ed. Rebecca J. Cook (University of Pennsylvania Press, 1994), 375–96, esp. 378–89. [Okin's note.]

9. See, for example, Arvind Sharma, ed., *Women in World Religions* (SUNY Press, 1987); John Stratton Hawley, ed., *Fundamentalism and Gender* (Oxford University Press, 1994). [Okin's note.]

Eve, whose weakness led Adam astray. Think of all those endless "begats" in Genesis, where women's primary role in reproduction is completely ignored, or of the textual justifications for polygamy, once practiced in Judaism, still practiced in many parts of the Islamic world and (though illegally) by Mormons in some parts of the United States. Consider, too the story of Abraham, a pivotal turning point in the development of monotheism.[10] God commands Abraham to sacrifice "his" beloved son. Abraham prepares to do exactly what God asks of him without even telling, much less asking, Isaac's mother, Sarah. Abraham's absolute obedience to God makes him the central, fundamental model of faith for all three religions.

Although the powerful drive to control women—and to blame and punish them for men's difficulty in controlling their own sexual impulses—has been softened considerably in the more progressive, reformed versions of Judaism, Christianity, and Islam, it remains strong in their more orthodox or fundamentalist versions. Moreover, it is by no means confined to Western or monotheistic cultures. Many of the world's traditions and cultures, including those practiced within formerly conquered or colonized nation-states—which certainly encompasses most of the peoples of Africa, the Middle East, Latin America, and Asia—are quite distinctly patriarchal. They too have elaborate patterns of socialization, rituals, matrimonial customs, and other cultural practices (including systems of property ownership and control of resources) aimed at bringing women's sexuality and reproductive capabilities under men's control. Many such practices make it virtually impossible for women to choose to live independently of men, to be celibate or lesbian, or to decide not to have children.

Those who practice some of the most controversial of such customs—clitoridectomy, polygamy, the marriage of children or marriages that are otherwise coerced—sometimes explicitly defend them as necessary for controlling women and openly acknowledge that the customs persist at men's insistence. In an interview with *New York Times* reporter Celia Dugger, practitioners of clitoridectomy in Côte d'Ivoire and Togo explained that the practice "helps insure a girl's virginity before marriage and fidelity afterward by reducing sex to a marital obligation." As a female exciser said, "[a] women's role in life is to care for her children, keep house and cook. If she has not been cut, [she] might think about her own sexual pleasure."[11] In Egypt, where a law banning female genital cutting was recently overturned by a court, supporters of the practice say it "curbs a girl's sexual appetite and makes her more marriageable."[12] Moreover, in such societies, many women have no economically viable alternative to marriage.

In polygamous cultures, too, men readily acknowledge that the practice accords with their self-interest and is a means of controlling women. As a French immigrant from Mali said in a recent interview: "When my wife is sick and I don't have another, who will care for me? . . . [O]ne wife on her own is trouble. When there are several,

10. See Carol Delaney, *Abraham on Trial: The Social Legacy of Biblical Myth* (Princeton University Press, 1998). Note that in the Qur'anic version, it is not Isaac but Ishmael whom Abraham prepares to sacrifice. [Okin's note.]

11. *New York Times*, 5 October 1996, A4. The role that older women in such cultures play in perpetuating these practices is important but complex and cannot be addressed here. [Okin's note.]

12. *New York Times*, 26 June 1997, A9. [Okin's note.]

they are forced to be polite and well behaved. If they misbehave, you threaten that you'll take another wife." Women apparently see polygamy very differently. French African immigrant women deny that they like polygamy and say that not only are they given "no choice" in the matter, but their female forebears in Africa did not like it either.[13] As for child or otherwise coerced marriage: this practice is clearly a way not only of controlling who the girls or young women marry but also of ensuring that they are virgins at the time of marriage and, often, of enhancing the husband's power by creating a significant age difference between husbands and wives. . . .

While virtually all of the world's cultures have distinctly patriarchal pasts, some— mostly, though by no means exclusively, Western liberal cultures—have departed far further from them than others. Western cultures, of course, still practice many forms of sex discrimination. They place far more importance on beauty, thinness, and youth in females and on intellectual accomplishment, skill, and strength in males. They expect women to perform for no economic reward far more than half of the unpaid work related to home and family, whether or not they also work for wages; partly as a consequence of this and partly because of workplace discrimination, women are far more likely than men to become poor. Girls and women are also subjected by men to a great deal of (illegal) violence, including sexual violence. But women in more liberal cultures are, at the same time, legally guaranteed many of the same freedoms and op- portunities as men. In addition, most families in such cultures, with the exception of some religious fundamentalists, do not communicate to their daughters that they are of less value than boys, that their lives are to be confined to domesticity and service to men and children, and that their sexuality is of value only in marriage, in the service of men, and for reproductive ends. This situation, as we have seen, is quite different from that of women in many of the world's other cultures, including many of those from which immigrants to Europe and North America come.

Group Rights?

Most cultures are patriarchal, then, and many (though not all) of the cultural minorities that claim group rights are more patriarchal than the surrounding cultures. So it is no surprise that the cultural importance of maintaining control over women shouts out to us in the examples given in the literature on cultural diversity and group rights within liberal states. Yet, though it shouts out, it is seldom explicitly addressed.[14]

A paper by Sebastian Poulter about the legal rights and culture-based claims of various immigrant groups and Gypsies in contemporary Britain mentions the roles

13. *International Herald Tribune*, 2 February 1996, News section. [Okin's note.]

14. See, however, Bhikhu Parekh's "Minority Practices and Principles of Toleration," *International Migration Review* (April 1996): 251–84, in which he directly addresses and critiques a number of cultural practices that devalue the status of women. [Okin's note.]

and status of women as "one very clear example" of the "clash of cultures."[15] In it, Poulter discusses claims put forward by members of such groups for special legal treatment on account of their cultural differences. A few are non–gender-related claims; for example, a Muslim schoolteacher's being allowed to be absent part of Friday afternoons in order to pray, and Gypsy children's being subject to less stringent schooling requirements than others on account of their itinerant lifestyle. But the vast majority of the examples concern gender inequalities: child marriages, forced marriages, divorce systems biased against women, polygamy, and clitoridectomy. Almost all of the legal cases discussed by Poulter stemmed from women's or girls' claims that their individual rights were being truncated or violated by the practices of their own cultural groups. . . .

Similarly, the overwhelming majority of "cultural defenses" that are increasingly being invoked in U.S. criminal cases involving members of cultural minorities are connected with gender—in particular with male control over women and children.[16] Occasionally, cultural defenses are cited in explanation of expectable violence among men or the ritual sacrifice of animals. Much more common, however, is the argument that, in the defendant's cultural group, women are not human beings of equal worth but rather subordinates whose primary (if not only) function is to serve men sexually and domestically. Indeed, the four types of cases in which cultural defenses have been used most successfully are: (1) kidnap and rape by Hmong men who claim that their actions are part of their cultural practice of *zij poj niam*, or "marriage by capture"; (2) wife-murder by immigrants from Asian and Middle Eastern countries whose wives have either committed adultery or treated their husbands in a servile way; (3) murder of children by Japanese or Chinese mothers who have also tried but failed to kill themselves, and who claim that because of their cultural backgrounds the shame of their husbands' infidelity drove them to the culturally condoned practice of mother-child suicide; and (4) in France—though not yet in the United States, in part because the practice was criminalized only in 1996—clitoridectomy. In a number of such cases, expert testimony about the accused's or defendant's cultural background has resulted in dropped or reduced charges, culturally based assessments of *mens rea*, or significantly reduced sentences. In a well-known recent case in the United States, an immigrant from rural Iraq married his two daughters, aged 13 and 14, to two of his friends, aged 28 and 34. Subsequently, when the older daughter ran away with her 20-year-old boyfriend, the father sought the help of the police in finding her. When they located her, they charged the father with child abuse and the two husbands and boyfriend with statutory rape. The Iraqis' defense is based in part on their cultural marriage practices.[17] . . .

15. Sebastian Poulter, "Ethnic Minority Customs, English Law, and Human Rights," *International and Comparative Law Quarterly* 36, 3 (1987): 589–615. [Okin's note.]

16. For one of the best and most recent accounts of this, and for legal citations for the cases mentioned below, see Doriane Lambelet Coleman, "Individualizing Justice through Multiculturalism: The Liberals' Dilemma," *Columbia Law Review* 96, 5 (1996): 1093–167. [Okin's note.]

17. *New York Times*, 2 December 1996, A6. [Okin's note.]

Part of the Solution?

It is by no means clear, then, from a feminist point of view, that minority group rights are "part of the solution." They may well exacerbate the problem. In the case of a more patriarchal minority culture in the context of a less patriarchal majority culture, no argument can be made on the basis of self-respect or freedom that the female members of the culture have a clear interest in its preservation. Indeed, they *might* be much better off if the culture into which they were born were either to become extinct (so that its members would become integrated into the less sexist surrounding culture) or, preferably, to be encouraged to alter itself so as to reinforce the equality of women—at least to the degree to which this value is upheld in the majority culture. Other considerations would, of course, need to be taken into account, such as whether the minority group speaks a language that requires protection, and whether the group suffers from prejudices such as racial discrimination. But it would take significant factors weighing in the other direction to counterbalance evidence that a culture severely constrains women's choices or otherwise undermines their well-being.

What some of the examples discussed above illustrate is how culturally endorsed practices that are oppressive to women can often remain hidden in the private or domestic sphere. In the Iraqi child marriage case mentioned above, if the father himself had not called in agents of the state, his daughters' plight might well not have become public. And when Congress in 1996 passed a law criminalizing clitoridectomy, a number of U.S. doctors objected to the law on the basis that it concerned a private matter which, as one said, "should be decided by a physician, the family, and the child."[18] It can take more or less extraordinary circumstances for such abuses of girls or women to become public or for the state to be able to intervene protectively.

Thus it is clear that many instances of private-sphere discrimination against women on cultural grounds are never likely to emerge in public, where courts can enforce the women's rights and political theorists can label such practices as illiberal and therefore unjustified violations of women's physical or mental integrity. Establishing group rights to enable some minority cultures to preserve themselves may not be in the best interests of the girls and women of those cultures, even if it benefits the men.

Those who make liberal arguments for the rights of groups, then, must take special care to look at inequalities within those groups. It is especially important to consider inequalities between the sexes, since they are likely to be less public, and thus less easily discernible. Moreover, policies designed to respond to the needs and claims of cultural minority groups must take seriously the urgency of adequately representing less powerful members of such groups. Because attention to the rights of minority cultural groups, if it is to be consistent with the fundamentals of liberalism, must ultimately be aimed at furthering the well-being of the members of these groups, there can be

---

18. *New York Times*, 12 October 1996, A6. Similar views were expressed on National Public Radio. [Okin's note.]

no justification for assuming that the groups' self-proclaimed leaders—invariably composed mainly of their older and their male members—represent the interests of all of the groups' members. Unless women—and, more specifically, young women (since older women often are co-opted into reinforcing gender inequality)—are fully represented in negotiations about group rights, their interests may be harmed rather than promoted by the granting of such rights.

TEST YOUR UNDERSTANDING

1. How does Okin define "feminism"? How does she define "multiculturalism"?

2. What are the two connections between gender and culture that Okin highlights?

3. Why does Kymlicka think that group rights are so important?

4. Why, according to Okin, have defenders of group rights failed to address adequately the criticism that group rights are "antifeminist"?

NOTES AND QUESTIONS

1. In her opening paragraph, Okin states the general issue that she addresses in her essay: "[W]hat should be done when the claims of minority cultures or religions clash with the norm of gender equality that is at least formally endorsed by liberal states ... ?" Okin's essay was written in 1997. Can you think of current examples of such clashes? Try to think of both cultural and religious examples. What conception of gender equality are you using in your examples? How would Okin resolve the tensions in the cases you are thinking about? Would she resist extending group rights? Do you find her resolution plausible? If not, why not? If so, why?

2. Okin says that "most cultures have as one of their principal aims the control of women by men." Let's call this the *gender-culture thesis*. How does Okin defend the *gender-culture thesis*? Is her defense convincing? Does her argument about tensions between multi-culturalism and women's equality depend on the *gender-culture thesis*? Formulate her argument about tensions between multiculturalism and gender equality using a less strong assumption (try variations on "most cultures" and "principal aims").

3. Okin says that multiculturalism, for her purposes, is the view that "minority cultures or ways of life" should sometimes be protected with "special group rights or privileges." What are some other ways to understand the idea of multiculturalism? Do Okin's arguments raise equally compelling concerns for multiculturalism on these other understandings?

ANALYZING THE ARGUMENTS

1. Rawls describes several ways in which his principles of justice "express an egalitarian conception of justice." Restate the points in your own words. Does an "egalitarian" conception of justice say that all inequalities are unjust? If an egalitarian conception does not condemn all inequalities as unjust, what exactly makes it *egalitarian*? How would Rawls answer this question? What about Nussbaum and Okin?

2. The idea of a patterned conception of distributive justice plays a central role in Nozick's discussion of distributive justice and his criticisms of egalitarian views of distributive justice. His entitlement conception is not patterned, whereas most other conceptions are patterned, he says. Review Nozick's definition of patterned conceptions. (Be sure to understand the differences between patterned conceptions and end-state conceptions of justice.) Is Rawls's conception of justice a patterned conception? What about Frankfurt's sufficiency doctrine? Does Nussbaum endorse patterned principles? Do Nozick's criticisms of patterned views apply with equal force to all of these views?

3. Frankfurt says that a focus on equality—on where you stand relative to others—is a harmful distraction from what matters and "contributes to the moral disorientation and shallowness of our time." Why does he think so? Do you agree? How would Okin—with her specific concern about gender equality—respond to Frankfurt?

4. In his discussion of the basis of equality, of "the features of human beings in virtue of which we are to be treated in accordance with the principles of justice," Rawls asks: "On what grounds . . . do we distinguish between mankind and other living things and regard the constraints of justice as holding only in our relations to human persons?" Rawls's answer—his account of the basis of equality—provides a **sufficient condition** for being owed justice.

    a. What is Rawls's proposed sufficient condition? Would there be troubles if Rawls treated the condition as also necessary? Reformulate Rawls's proposed condition as both necessary and sufficient for being owed justice. Does the answer seem any less plausible?

    b. Rawls says that the sufficient condition is "not at all stringent." Formulate a more stringent and a less stringent condition. Are either of the proposed conditions more plausible?

    c. Rawls says that we do best to assume that the sufficient condition is "always satisfied." What does he mean? And why is that the best thing to do?

    Do you agree with Rawls that considerations of justice apply only to our "relations to human persons"? Do you think he has given a good explanation why?

5. Nussbaum expresses some reservations about Rawls's account of the basis of equality and offers her more "minimalist" account as an alternative. What precisely is the difference

between Rawls's view and Nussbaum's minimalist view? What are her reservations? In addressing these issues, it will help to consider the following questions:

a. Does Nussbaum think that Rawls is offering a necessary condition for being owed justice?

b. Does Nussbaum think that Rawls's condition is too stringent? In what ways is it too stringent?

c. When Rawls says that we do best to assume that his sufficient condition is "always satisfied," does he mean that we should assume it to be satisfied in the cases that Nussbaum is concerned about?

Is Nussbaum's minimalist answer more compelling than Rawls's answer to the question about the basis of equality?

Answers to Test Your Understanding

Chapter 1: Does God Exist?

ANSELM OF CANTERBURY, The Ontological Argument

1. Anselm assumes that some things are greater—closer to perfection—than others. He identifies God with a being that is absolutely perfect: not just the best *actual* thing, but the best *conceivable* thing.
2. When an architect designs a building, the building first exists in her understanding—she is capable of thinking about it. If the building is then built according to her plan, it exists in reality as well.
3. You can't deny that God exists unless you're capable of thinking about God. But if you're capable of thinking about *X*, *X* must exist *in your understanding*. So God must exist in the Fool's understanding.
4. Donald Trump exists, but we can conceive of a world in which he was never born. So he is a thing that can be "thought not to exist." There are no uncontroversial examples of things that cannot be thought not to exist, but Anselm argues that since it is *better* to be a thing that cannot be thought not to exist, a *perfect* being would be a being of this sort. (Philosophers sometimes give other examples. Since we can't conceive of a situation in which $2 + 2 \neq 4$, perhaps the number 4 is a thing that cannot be thought not to exist.)

THOMAS AQUINAS, The Five Ways

1. When a thing starts to move, it goes from being *potentially* in motion to being *actually* in motion. According to Aquinas, when a thing changes from being potentially *F* to being actually *F*, this change must be caused by something that is actually *F*. So everything that starts to move is moved by something else.
2. A "first cause" is a being that causes other things to exist but which is not itself caused to exist.
3. Ordinary things are all contingent. You exist, but if your parents had never met—which could have happened—you would not have existed. A necessary being is a being that could not possibly have failed to exist. There are no uncontroversial examples, but Aquinas thinks that God is an example.
4. False.

WILLIAM PALEY, The Argument from Design

1. Watches and living things *appear to have been designed for a purpose*. Their many parts interact with one another to produce intricate, complex behavior. *Note:* When Paley says that living things exhibit "contrivance" or "design," he is not *assuming* that these things have in fact been designed. That is the conclusion of his argument, not his premise.
2. The challenge is to explain the appearance of design in nature. A child may inherit its "appearance of design" from its parents, who inherited their apparent design from their parents, and so on. But this does not explain why natural things exhibit apparent design at all.
3. False. Rocks do not exhibit apparent design in Paley's sense.
4. False. Paley wrote 60 years before Darwin.

ROGER WHITE, The Argument from Cosmological Fine-Tuning

1. The fundamental laws include certain constants that determine, for example, the masses of various fundamental particles. The claim is that if those constants had been slightly different, life would have been impossible.
2. If a monkey at a typewriter types out "khwgdui2ery," that fact requires no explanation. There doesn't have to be an answer to the question, "Why did she type *that*?" If a monkey types out "I am a philosopher," it would be irrational to regard that fact as inexplicable.
3. If you flip a fair coin 10 times and get THHTTHTHTT, the result is improbable. The chance of getting just this sequence was $\frac{1}{2}^{10}$. But there need be no reason why you got that sequence rather than some other.
4. False. White considers several possible explanations that do not involve a God, including the hypothesis that our universe is one of infinitely many universes, each with its own laws.

LOUISE ANTONY, No Good Reason—Exploring the Problem of Evil

1. The logical argument aims to show that the existence of suffering is logically incompatible with the existence of a perfect God. The evidential argument aims to show that the suffering we see around us *provides strong evidence* that God does not exist.
2. No. The argument includes the premise that "no morally good being would tolerate suffering if she could prevent it." Antony rejects this premise.
3. Parents are not omnipotent. They allow their children to suffer now because they have no better way to prevent greater suffering later on. God is omnipotent: he can protect his creatures from suffering altogether.
4. False. You can't defend an abusive parent by insisting that there *could be* a morally sufficient reason for the abuse. If you can't provide a *plausible* reason, the only rational conclusion is that the parent is not good. Similarly, if the theist cannot provide a plausible reason for God to permit the suffering we see around us, the only rational conclusion is that a perfect God does not exist.

ELEONORE STUMP, The Problem of Evil

1. (4)
2. Hell is "eternal separation from God." It does not involve torture. Instead it involves a "naturally painful state" (like guilt or regret) that arises in a person who has

habitually made bad choices and whose will remains opposed to God's. Heaven is "union with God": an eternal state in which a person's will is aligned with God's will.

3. Ever since the Fall, human beings have been disposed to oppose God's will. This is a defect in our wills. We can't go to heaven unless this defect is repaired. We can't cure it ourselves, and God can't cure it for us unless we freely ask for help. God allows suffering as a way to bring people who are born with a defective will to will that God repair this defect.

4. No. Stump claims only that these assumptions are not known to be false. Her conclusion is that *if* Christian theology is correct on these key points, as it may be, then God has a morally sufficient reason to permit evil.

Chapter 2: Is It Reasonable to Believe without Evidence?

BLAISE PASCAL, The Wager

1. We're betting on the proposition that God exists. You bet on this proposition by believing it or by doing your best to believe it. If you bet on God and win, you get eternal life. If you bet on God and lose (because God does not exist), you get an ordinary, finite life.

2. You "bet" in Pascal's Wager either by choosing to believe in God or by declining to make this choice. No matter what you do, you will do one of these things. So no matter what you do, you will inevitably place a "bet" in Pascal's Wager.

3. An infinite quantity in Pascal's sense is a quantity that cannot possibly be increased. So if you have infinitely many eggs and someone gives you another egg, you have the same number of eggs you had before.

4. True. If you wager for God and lose, you will miss out on "tainted pleasures," but you will be "humble," "grateful," "a good friend," and so on; and these virtues more than compensate for any pleasures you may forgo.

ALAN HÁJEK, Pascal's Ultimate Gamble

1. Hájek follows Pascal in assuming that for any positive finite number n, $n \times \infty = \infty$, and $\infty + n = \infty$. If you assign a probability p to God's existence, then the expected utility of believing in God will be $(p \times \infty) + [(1 - p) \times f_1]$, where f_1 is some finite quantity. Given Hájek's assumptions, that sum will be the same—it will be ∞—so long as p is not zero.

2. False. Hájek argues that given Pascal's assumptions, *every course of action is equally rational*. That's a bizarre result, and Hájek does not endorse it. But he thinks that given Pascal's assumptions, we are not rationally *required* to try to believe in God.

3. Pascal assumes that the only possible God is the Christian God. But we can imagine many Gods—the Greek gods, the Norse gods—each of whom rewards those who worship him with infinite happiness. Given Pascal's framework, the expected utility of worshipping Zeus or Odin will be the same as that of worshipping the Christian God, so there will be no reason to favor Christianity over any other such religion.

4. There is some (perhaps *very* small) probability p that if you tie your shoes, God will reward you with infinite felicity. But then the expected utility of tying your shoes is $p \times \infty$ plus various other finite quantities f. But $(p \times \infty) + f = \infty$. So the expected utility of tying your shoes is infinite.

W. K. CLIFFORD, The Ethics of Belief

1. False. Clifford's thesis is that "it is wrong always, everywhere, and for any one, to believe anything upon insufficient evidence."

2. Each of us has a *duty* to believe what the evidence supports. We have this duty because if we allow ourselves to believe on insufficient evidence, this will have bad consequences for society in the long run. Both shipowners violate this duty even though no one is hurt in the second case.

3. False. If we were allowed to believe only what we can support with evidence we have gathered on our own, scientific progress would be impossible. The fact that an informed expert has told you something is sufficient evidence to believe it.

4. Such beliefs are permissible when they are based on the assumption that "the unknown is like the known." We believe that the sun contains hydrogen because (a) spectroscopes pointed at the sun display certain "spectral lines," and (b) we know from laboratory experiments that such lines indicate the presence of hydrogen.

WILLIAM JAMES, The Will to Believe

1. An option is *live* when both possibilities are things you might actually do given your character and circumstances. The choice whether to finish a paper or go to the movies is a live option for most of us.

   An option is *forced* when it is inevitable that you will choose one of the possibilities. Any option of the form "Do *X* or don't do *X*" is forced.

   An option is *momentous* when you stand to lose something of great value if you choose one of the possibilities. The once-in-a-lifetime option to join an expedition to Antarctica is momentous.

   A question *cannot be resolved on intellectual grounds* when the available evidence does not count decisively in favor of any particular answer. At present, the question whether there is life on other planets can't be resolved on intellectual grounds.

2. True.

3. You're sick with a disease that will probably kill you. However, the evidence suggests that optimistic people—people who are confident that they will survive—have a slightly higher probability of survival, even though survival is still unlikely. For James, it is both rationally and morally permissible for you to believe that you will survive. This is a case in which "faith in the fact can help create the fact."

4. Someone who cared only about believing as many truths as possible would believe everything; someone who cared only about avoiding error would believe nothing. In general, the goal of believing truth pushes us to be bold in forming beliefs that go beyond the evidence; the goal of avoiding error pushes us toward caution.

ALVIN PLANTINGA, Is Belief in God Properly Basic?

1. A belief is basic for a person *S* iff *S* does not hold the belief on the basis of any other beliefs. A *properly* basic belief is a basic belief that *S* is justified in holding.

2. True.

3. Someone who is looking at a rose may have a properly basic belief that she is seeing a rose. She does not derive the belief from other beliefs, so it is basic for her. But her visual experience provides her with a *ground* for the belief. In different circumstances (e.g., circumstances in which there are no roses in the vicinity), the same belief might not be properly basic.

4. The perceptual belief that Jones is talking to me now and the theological belief that God is talking to me now may both be:
   a. basic, in the sense that they are not derived from other beliefs;
   b. properly basic, in the sense that the subject is justified in holding them as basic; and
   c. grounded in the subject's conscious experience: the way things seem or appear to her.

LARA BUCHAK, When Is Faith Rational?

1. False.
2. You have faith that your friend is trustworthy when (a) you want your friend to be trustworthy, (b) your evidence for this is inconclusive, (c) you're willing to trust your friend on some important matter without seeking further evidence of her trustworthiness, and (d) you're willing to continue to trust her even when you receive evidence that she's not trustworthy.
3. True. For Buchak, faith is not a matter of what you believe; it is a matter of how you act. According to Buchak, it can be rational to act as if God exists even if your evidence leads you to doubt that God exists.
4. False. It can be rational for Anna to decide now to marry Bates on Sunday and to follow through on that decision when the time comes, even if in the meantime she acquires evidence that lowers the expected utility of the marriage.

Chapter 3: What Is Knowledge?

PLATO, Meno

1. Someone who has a true belief (but not knowledge) about the way to Larissa.
2. No.
3. The reason is that both correct opinion and knowledge will lead to successful action. According to Socrates, "knowledge is a more valuable thing than correct opinion" (p. 139).
4. No (at least, not in this selection from the *Meno*; earlier in the dialogue, Socrates famously suggests that "being good *is* a kind of knowledge").

EDMUND GETTIER, Is Justified True Belief Knowledge?

1. No.
2. Yes.
3. No.
4. (b)

TIMOTHY WILLIAMSON, Knowledge and Belief

1. No.
2. (c)
3. He means that there is no solution that doesn't mention crimson. The analogy is supposed to show that we should not assume that knowledge can be analyzed.
4. No.

Chapter 4: How Can We Know about What We Have Not Observed?

DAVID HUME, Sceptical Doubts Concerning the Operations of the Understanding, and Sceptical Solution of These Doubts

1. A relation of ideas is a statement whose denial is self-contradictory or impossible. "Triangles have three angles" is a relation of ideas, since it's equivalent to the claim that three-angled polygons have three angles, the denial of which is clearly self-contradictory. A matter of fact claim is a statement whose denial is *not* self-contradictory; for example, "It's raining now in Bangkok."

2. It is not a contradiction to suppose that the future will be very different from the past. Since the denial of the statement is not self-contradictory, the claim is a "matter of fact."

3. Whenever you draw a conclusion about things you haven't experienced from things you have experienced, you assume that the unobserved cases resemble the observed ones. But you didn't reason your way to this assumption. You simply found yourself accepting it. Hume puts this by saying that your inference is the result of "custom, not reasoning."

4. No, Hume never says this. His key claim is that our "inferences from experience" are not the result of deductive reasoning, but rather reflect a non-rational tendency to suppose that the future will be like the past. This tendency is *non-rational*, in the sense that we can imagine rational beings without it, but Hume never says that it is contrary to reason (irrational).

P. F. STRAWSON, The "Justification" of Induction

1. Inductive arguments are arguments from premises about what we have observed to conclusions about things we have not observed. Since it is always *possible* for the unobserved to be quite different from the observed, such arguments will never be deductively valid. The standards for assessing inductive arguments must therefore be different from those for assessing deductive arguments.

2. Anyone who has mastered the English word "reasonable" knows that we apply it to people who follow ordinary inductive procedures. If we met someone who lives in mortal fear that the sun will not rise tomorrow despite having seen it rise every day for years, we would say: "That person is not reasonable." Strawson's idea is that asking why induction is rational is like asking why bachelors are unmarried. We don't *call* something a bachelor unless it's unmarried, and likewise, we don't *call* a person rational unless she goes in for induction.

3. False.

4. No. We have many methods for investigating the world. Meteorologists have methods; doctors have methods. Successful methods of this sort have inductive support, since to call them "successful" is just to say that they have been successful in the past. But there is no single method of inductive reasoning that we apply in every case. So it makes no sense to ask whether "the inductive method" is justified.

NELSON GOODMAN, The New Riddle of Induction

1. A *principle* of inductive reasoning is a general rule that tells us which predictions to make or which generalizations to accept given a body of evidence. Goodman's claim is that general rules of this sort are justified, not because they satisfy some neat logical or mathematical condition, but rather because they conform to the actual practice of scientists and others who make concrete inductive inferences. In this respect, they are like the rules of descriptive grammar, which are justified insofar as they conform to the linguistic behavior of native speakers of the language.

2. An object is grue if and only if it is green and first observed before some specified time *t* or blue and first observed only after *t*. If we let *t* be January 1, 2020, then the grass on the lawn in 2017 was grue, as are the blue skies of 2021.

3. A "lawlike (projectable) hypothesis" is a general claim that is apt for inductive confirmation. "All ravens are black" is a lawlike hypothesis, since we can acquire reason to believe it by observing a large number of ravens and noting that all are black. "All emeralds are grue," on the other hand, is not lawlike. We have in fact observed a large number of emeralds, all of which are grue; but this does not give us reason to believe that emeralds are grue.

4. True.

GILBERT HARMAN, The Inference to the Best Explanation

1. IBE is a form of argument that begins from known facts and some putative explanation of those facts and concludes that the proposed explanation is (probably, roughly) true. For example:

> Known facts: I hear noises in the wall and my cheese is disappearing.
>
> Hypothesis: The best explanation for this fact is that a mouse has come to live with me.
>
> Conclusion: So probably, a mouse has come to live with me.

2. No. It is always *possible* for the premises in an instance of IBE to be true and the conclusion false. There is no guarantee that the best explanation for the observed facts is true.

3. Inductive argument:

> In the past, whenever I flipped the switch, the lights came on. So next time I flip the switch, the lights will come on.

Recast as an example of IBE:

> In the past, whenever I flipped the switch, the lights came on.
>
> The best explanation for this fact is that there is some underlying mechanism connecting the switch to the lights, which ensures that in general, whenever the switch is flipped, the lights come on.
>
> Therefore, there is some underlying mechanism . . . which ensures that whenever the switch is flipped, the lights come on.
>
> Therefore, next time I flip the switch, the light will come on.

4. Any instance of IBE whose conclusion concerns the *unobservable* causes of observable phenomena will do to illustrate the point. For example, biologists notice the many observed facts about heredity and adaptation and conclude that new species emerge as a result of mutation and natural selection (among other causes). This is a classic instance of IBE. We accept the hypothesis because it is the best explanation of the observed facts. But it can't be a case of enumerative induction, since we do not *observe* the emergence of new species.

Chapter 5: How Can You Know Your Own Mind or the Mind of Another Person?

BERTRAND RUSSELL, The Argument from Analogy

1. (c)
2. (b)
3. (a)
4. (b)

SAUL KRIPKE, Wittgenstein and Other Minds

1. (a)
2. (a)
3. It is thinking; equivalently, there is thinking, or some thinking is occurring.
4. No. See pages 225–26.

MAURICE MERLEAU-PONTY, Man Seen from the Outside

1. (c)
2. No.
3. Yes to both.
4. No.

D. M. ARMSTRONG, Introspection

1. (a) There is no sense organ (or at least, not one that we have any control over). (b) The things one person perceives are not the same as the things another person perceives.
2. No.
3. (a)
4. The mind is a substance, a particular thing.

SARAH K. PAUL, John Doe and Richard Roe

1. (b), (c), (d)
2. (b)
3. No.
4. (b), (d)

ALEX BYRNE, Skepticism about the Internal World

1. No.
2. Yes.
3. The objection is that some animals have knowledge of their surroundings by perception but don't have knowledge of their sensory experiences.
4. No to both. The skeptic about the external world argues that *you don't know* you have a hand, and the skeptic about the internal world argues that *you don't know* you see a hand.

Chapter 6: How Can We Know about the External World?

RENÉ DESCARTES, Meditation I: What Can Be Called into Doubt

1. No.
2. Because the hypothesis that he might be dreaming does not show that "arithmetic, geometry and other subjects of this kind" (p. 265) can be doubted, and Descartes is trying to extend doubt as far as possible.

3. No.
4. (a) No. (b) Yes.

DAVID HUME, Of Scepticism with Regard to the Senses

1. No.
2. We (i.e., ordinary people) do not know of any arguments for the conclusion that the objects we perceive have a continued and distinct existence.
3. They think that X has a continued and distinct existence.
4. The philosophical system is the view that although the things we perceive have no continued and distinct existence, there are objects (presumably somehow responsible for our perceptions) that do have a continued and distinct existence. The principles are (1) that the things we perceive have a continued and distinct existence and (2) that the things we perceive have an interrupted existence and are dependent on the mind.

G. E. MOORE, Proof of an External World

1. Yes. See item (2) on page 280.
2. No.
3. Because the conclusions might have been true even if the (relevant) premises had been false.
4. No. See item (1) on page 280.

JONATHAN VOGEL, Skepticism and Inference to the Best Explanation

1. No.
2. (b)
3. An explanatory hypothesis might "say too little" to give a satisfying explanation or it might "say too much" (p. 289), that is, be unnecessarily complicated.
4. The second.

RAE LANGTON, Ignorance of Things in Themselves

1. No. Kant thinks we cannot have knowledge of "things in themselves." According to Langton, this phrase does not mean "things independent of our minds" (see page 293). So, on Langton's interpretation, Kant is not restricting our knowledge to mind-dependent appearances.
2. No. See page 298.
3. No. "[W]e are supposing . . . intrinsic properties are not inert" (p. 300).
4. No. See page 300.

Chapter 7: Is Mind Material?

RENÉ DESCARTES, Meditation II: The Nature of the Human Mind, and How It Is Better Known than the Body, and Meditation VI: . . . The Real Distinction between Mind and Body

1. No. "Thinking," for Descartes, includes desiring, imagining, and perceiving (p. 314).
2. No.
3. (c)
4. No. If Descartes is a "non-extended thing," he has no height at all.

ELISABETH OF BOHEMIA, Correspondence with Descartes

1. Being spatially extended, and being in physical contact with something.
2. Same as (1).

3. Here's one way of doing it:

> P1. If the mind causes the body to move, the mind must either be in physical contact with something (e.g., some part of the brain) or else be spatially extended.
>
> P2. If dualism is true, the mind is not in physical contact with anything, and neither is it spatially extended.
>
> C. If dualism is true, the mind does not cause the body to move.

ANTOINE ARNAULD, Fourth Set of Objections

1. No. He is only arguing that Descartes has not established this.
2. Yes.
3. (b)

GILBERT RYLE, Descartes' Myth

1. (c)
2. Yes.
3. No.
4. No.

J. J. C. SMART, Sensations and the Brain Processes

1. No.
2. No. See the reply to Objection 4.
3. No.
4. No. If Tweedledum and Tweedledee are strictly identical, then Tweedledum = Tweedledee and so there are not two twins, just one person with two names. Tweedledum and Tweedledee are identical in the sense that they are very similar (likewise, you and your classmate might own identical copies of this anthology).

JOHN SEARLE, Can Computers Think?

1. Yes.
2. No.
3. No.
4. No.

Chapter 8: What Is Consciousness?

THOMAS NAGEL, What Is It Like to Be a Bat?

1. No.
2. No.
3. No. "It would be a mistake to conclude that physicalism must be false" (p. 363).
4. Yes. "We can be compelled to recognize the existence of such facts without being able to state or comprehend them" (p. 360).
5. The reduction of lightning to electrical discharges involves describing lightning in terms that do not mention the idiosyncratic "impressions it makes on our senses," or

"a specifically human viewpoint." Similarly for other cases of reduction. The problem is that if this also holds for the reduction of *experience* to (say) brain processes, then reduction seems impossible, because experience (unlike lightning) cannot be separated from "the particularity of our human point of view."

FRANK JACKSON, Epiphenomenal Qualia

1. No.
2. Yes. (See the story of the sea slugs at the end.)
3. No. We need to assume that *we* know that, not Fred.
4. No. "It is hard to see an objection to Physicalism here" (p. 370).

PATRICIA SMITH CHURCHLAND, Are Mental States Irreducible to Neurobiological States?

1. Yes. However, Churchland denies that (A) and (B) are of that general form; instead, they "are analogous to arguments (C) through (E)" (p. 379).
2. Lois doesn't know that Superman works for the *Daily Planet*.
3. The fallacy of equivocation; argument (F).
4. Who knows what will happen? At least, there's no good reason for thinking that Mary will learn something.

DAVID CHALMERS, The Hard Problem of Consciousness

1. Yes.
2. No.
3. (b)
4. No.

MICHAEL TYE, The Puzzle of Transparency

1. (a) yes; (b) yes; (c) no; (d) no.
2. No.
3. Yes.
4. *Being green* and *being cubical*.

Chapter 9: Are Things as They Appear?

BERTRAND RUSSELL, Appearance and Reality

1. No. He thinks that this is only one of many "surprising possibilities" (p. 415).
2. (b)
3. (b)
4. (c)

GEORGE BERKELEY, Three Dialogues between Hylas and Philonous

1. No. See page 417.
2. (c), (b), (e), (a), (d)
3. No. Philonous gets Hylas to admit that the microscope gives a "more close and accurate inspection" than the naked eye, but ultimately he concludes that colors seen under a microscope also have "no existence without the mind."

4. Yes. "Divines and philosophers had proved beyond all controversy, from the beauty and usefulness of the several parts of the creation, that it was the workmanship of God" (p. 425). See also the introduction to Chapter 1 in this anthology, page 6.

5. Yes. "*Hylas:* . . . Ask the fellow, whether yonder tree has an existence out of his mind: what answer think you he would make? *Philonous:* The same that I should myself, to wit, that it doth exist out of his mind" (p. 427).

VASUBANDHU, *Twenty Verses* with Auto-Commentary

1. (d). See "Response to option 2" (p. 433).
2. No. Nothing is mind-independent, according to Vasubandhu.
3. No. See the last part of Verse 17.
4. (d). See Verse 19 and the commentary.

NICK BOSTROM, Are We Living in a Computer Simulation?

1. $p = 0.01$, $i = 0.01$, $N_i = 100$, so $f_{sim} = (0.01 \times 0.01 \times 100)/[(0.01 \times 0.01 \times 100) + 1] \approx 0.0099$.
2. That the average number of ancestor simulations run by such posthuman civilizations is 100. "N_i is extremely large" (p. 447).
3. (c). (1) is false, and (2) is false, so (3) is true; that is, $f_{sim} \approx 1$ (see p. 447). And Bostrom thinks that, assuming (3) is true, the probability that you are living in a simulation is very close to 1 (see section V).
4. (c)

Chapter 10: What Is There?

STEPHEN YABLO, A Thing and Its Matter

1. False. PEN and COP are alike in many respects: same size, shape, location, and so forth. But PEN was made in 1909, whereas COP has existed for millions of years. So they are not alike in every respect.

2. Leibniz's Law says that X and Y are identical if and only if they have *all* of their properties in common. Two widgets from the same assembly line may have many of their properties in common: they may be the same size, shape, and so forth. But they are in different places so they are not identical.

3. The monist says that a human being is identical with her body. But we can argue that a human being is not identical with her body as follows:

   It is possible for me to survive the destruction of my body. If my brain were removed beforehand and transplanted into a new body, I might survive.

   It is not possible for my body to survive the destruction of my body.

   So I am not identical to my body.

   Still, my body and I are in the same place at the same time. So it's possible for two things to be in the same place at the same time.

4. False. Yablo argues that "distinctions do not have to be physically fundamental to be fully real" (p. 466).

PETER UNGER, There Are No Ordinary Things

1. Ordinary things are medium-sized inanimate objects recognized by common sense: tables, rocks, and so forth. They do not include objects posited by physics and other scientific disciplines; for example, atoms, and sharply bounded collections of such things. For present purposes, Unger also excludes living things.

2. Common sense says that:
   (a) Tables exist.
   (b) Tables are made of many atoms (or small microscopic parts).
   (c) If you take a table and remove one atom, the result is still a table.
   These propositions can't all be true, since (a) and (c) entail that there could be a table made from a single atom, and (b) says that that's impossible.

3. If there are tables, it's possible to make one by starting with a single atom and then adding atoms until a table is produced. So start with a single atom and add another atom anywhere you like. A single atom is not a table. And the result of adding a single atom to a non-table is not a table. So you still don't have a table. Now repeat the process as many times as you like. At no stage in this process is a table produced. So it's impossible to make a table by starting with a single atom and adding more atoms. So there are no tables.

4. False. The argument applies only to "ordinary" objects that satisfy a principle of the following sort:

   If you start with an X, then the result of adding or removing one atom is still an X.

   This is compatible with there being large, sharply bounded physical objects, like some particular crystal composed of exactly 10^{23} carbon atoms in a certain arrangement.

GIDEON ROSEN, Numbers and Other Immaterial Objects

1. Numerals are linguistic expressions. Numbers are the objects numerals stand for. The Arabic numeral "9" and the Roman numeral "IX" are clearly different from one another. But according to Rosen, they are names for a single thing: the number nine.

2. Numbers are not physical objects. They do not have physical properties such as mass and velocity, nor are they made of physical "stuff." Physicalism is the thesis that absolutely everything is physical. So if Rosen is right about numbers, physicalism is false.

3. The English sentence "Philosophy is groovy" is a type. Every copy of this book contains a token of this sentence. There are thousands of such tokens, but the type is a single thing.

4. True. The causal theory of knowledge says that knowledge always requires some causal connection between the knower and the things she knows about. Rosen thinks that mathematical knowledge is possible and that numbers don't cause anything. So he rejects the causal theory as a general constraint on knowledge.

PENELOPE MADDY, Do Numbers Exist?

1. If there are three apples on the table, then the apples on the table have *the property of being three*. (*Note:* The claim is not that the individual apples each have this property. The claim is that the apples *collectively* have this property, or alternatively, that the *collection* of apples has this property.)

2. We are making a general claim about the number properties of collections. More specifically, we are saying that if some collection of things has twoness, and some non-overlapping collection has threeness, then the two collections together have fiveness.

3. Ordinary arithmetic concerns the number properties of real things such as (collections of) apples or stars. Since there may be only finitely many such things, these numbers need not go on forever. Idealized arithmetic—the arithmetic mathematicians take for granted—includes the assumption that if n exists, so does $n + 1$.

4. As children, we master a system of numerical expressions that allows us to construct a name for the next number after any given number: "a million" → "a million and one." We have an innate capacity to master this system, and once we have mastered it, we can tell that the system of number *words* can always be extended. This fact about mathematical language then leads us to suppose that the numbers themselves—and not just their names—go on forever.

Chapter 11: What Is Personal Identity?

JOHN LOCKE, Of Identity and Diversity

1. Secretariat in 1970 and Secretariat in 1973 are the same horse, but they are not the same mass of matter, since the matter that composes the first is not the same as the matter that composes the second. An animal such as a horse is made of different matter at different times. So horses are not masses of matter.

2. *Man* is Locke's generic term for a human animal. *Person* is Locke's term for a rational thinking thing that can be responsible for its actions. A man continues to exist so long as it continues to be a living human animal, even if its capacity for rational thought is completely destroyed. A person ceases to be when its capacity for rational thought is destroyed. If Jones is a person on Monday but falls into a permanent coma on Tuesday, the *man* survives but the *person* does not. Similarly, if Smith's body dies on Monday but Smith's soul retains her memories and survives in heaven, then the person survives but the man does not.

3. According to Locke, a later person Y is identical to an earlier person X if and only if X and Y share the same *consciousness*. Locke goes on to explain that X and Y share the same consciousness if and only if Y is capable of remembering—recalling to consciousness—some of X's experiences.

4. Locke thinks so, but with a twist. Locke concedes that if the person can't remember *anything* about the crime, then the person we punish is not the person who did the crime, since the person does not partake of the "same consciousness." Locke nonetheless thinks that our practice of punishing people for what they do when drunk is justified on the ground that it's impossible to tell in practice whether someone *really* can't remember what he did.

RICHARD SWINBURNE, The Dualist Theory

1. No. Swinburne argues that personal identity is unanalyzable. This means that for Swinburne, there is no way of saying in more basic terms what it means for Y to be the same person as X.

2. No. Swinburne thinks that you have a soul, but that you also have a body (at least in this life), and that your body is part of you.

3. You can imagine existing without your body. (Imagine that your body slowly disappears, while you keep thinking, hence existing.) There is nothing incoherent in this supposition. So it is possible for you to exist without your body.

4. True.

DEREK PARFIT, Personal Identity

1. (a) numerically identical; (b) qualitatively identical; (c) numerically identical; (d) numerically identical; (e) qualitatively identical.

2. (a), (b), and (e) are transitive. To see that (f) is not transitive, imagine a sequence of billiard balls lined up in a row, each of which is *slightly but invisibly* larger than its neighbor to the left. Each adjacent pair may be indiscriminable to the naked eye. But the ball at the far right may be visibly bigger than the ball at the far left.

3. Parfit accepts a version of the psychological criterion: X today is the same person as some past person Y if and only if X is psychologically continuous with Y; this continuity has the right kind of cause; and no one *else* at the later time is psychologically continuous with Y.

4. Relation R—psychological continuity with the right kind of cause—is not transitive. Identity is transitive. So relation R cannot be the criterion of personal identity all by itself.

5. Parfit is cagey on this point. It is open to debate whether the causal process involved in teletransportation counts as the "right kind of cause."

BERNARD WILLIAMS, The Self and the Future

1. In the relevant "experiment," information from A's brain is copied into B's brain while information from B's brain is copied into A's brain. We are tempted to describe this as a case in which A and B have "switched bodies." But that is question-begging in the present context. The question we are asking is whether a person is identical to his living body, and this description begs the question against an affirmative answer.

2. The second case is (as it were) half of the first case. In the first case, you are presented with two people at the start and told what will be done to their bodies, and your instinctive reaction is that the people switch bodies. In the second case, you are presented with one body—yours—whose memories will be erased and then replaced with new memories, after which the body will be tortured. In this case, you are tempted to think that the torture lies in your (exceptionally grim) future, no matter what may be happening elsewhere in the lab.

3. Williams is arguing that once we hear the second version of the case, we should reconsider our judgment that in the first case, the people switch bodies. An objector says: "But the two cases are very different. In the second case, my memories and personality are *destroyed* before they are replaced with new ones and I am tortured. In the first case, my memories and personality are *transferred to a new body*, and that makes all the difference." The sequence of cases (i)–(vi) is designed to respond to this objection.

4. False. Williams concludes that the first case favors a psychological criterion of personal identity, while the second case and its variants favor a bodily criterion. He finds himself uncertain about which criterion to adopt.

Chapter 12: What Is Race? What Is Gender?

ANTHONY APPIAH, The Uncompleted Argument: Du Bois and the Illusion of Race

1. No.
2. (d)
3. (b)
4. (a)

SALLY HASLANGER, Gender and Race: (What) Are They? (What) Do We Want Them to Be?

1. (b), (d)
2. No: she thinks that race is a "biological fiction" (p. 566).
3. Haslanger's view (put loosely) is that if someone is a woman, then she will be subject to certain subordinating treatment *because* she is perceived as having female "reproductive features" (p. 566). That subordinating treatment will be *"along some dimension"* (p. 566). It is entirely compatible with being subordinated along some dimension that one is immensely privileged along other dimensions, including one's overall position in society. Thus, there's no reason to think Haslanger would deny that Winfrey is a woman. (And, since she gives a similar account for race, there is no reason to think she would deny that Winfrey is black.)
4. Haslanger thinks that to be a woman is (in part) to be systematically oppressed. Because feminism aims at the eradication of gender-based oppression, if feminism achieves its aims then on Haslanger's view there will be no more women. There will still be adult female humans, but they will not be women because they are no longer oppressed.

QUAYSHAWN SPENCER, Are Folk Races Like Dingoes, Dimes, or Dodos?

1. (b), (c)
2. (b), (d). The human continental populations can be distinguished by their different frequencies of *genetic variants*, many of which won't even be parts of genes.
3. (c)
4. No. Spencer's view is that *some* folk races, specifically OMB races, are real biological entities—not *all*.

ELIZABETH BARNES, The Metaphysics of Gender

1. (a), (c), (d)
2. (a), (b), (d)
3. (b), (c)
4. (b), (c)

Chapter 13: Do We Possess Free Will?

GALEN STRAWSON, Free Will

1. "True and ultimate" responsibility is the sort of responsibility that might justify serious rewards and punishments; for example, eternal punishment in hell or bliss in heaven.

2. To be *causa sui* is to be a cause of oneself. Strawson's claim is that no one can cause his own mental states—the beliefs, desires, and values from which he acts—in a way that would make him responsible for those states.

3. True self-determination would require that your present mental state (desires, values, etc.) be wholly determined by your past free choices. But a past choice is free only if your mental state *then* was wholly determined by prior free choices. And so on. A free choice thus requires an infinite sequence of choices extending backwards into the past in which each choice results from prior mental states that result from prior free choices—and that's impossible.

4. According to Kane, you are responsible for our character if it results from a "self-forming action." Suppose you face a conflict between doing the right thing and promoting your self-interest and that prior factors do not settle what you will do. Kane thinks that you can make the choice freely and thereby *make yourself the sort of person who will be more inclined to do the right thing* (or the wrong thing) in the future.

Strawson replies: If this self-forming action is undetermined by prior factors, then it is a matter of luck that you choose to do it. And a lucky choice can't make you responsible for anything.

RODERICK CHISHOLM, Human Freedom and the Self

1. False. Chisholm holds that a free act is an act that is uncaused by prior events, but which is caused by the agent himself.

2. According to Moore, when I say that:

I could have raised my hand,

what I mean is that

if I had chosen to raise my hand, I would have raised it.

Chisholm replies that these claims are not equivalent. Suppose I am incapable of choosing to raise my hand for whatever reason, but that if I could somehow make that choice, my hand would go up. In that case, the second claim is true but the first is false.

3. *Transeunt* causation occurs when one event causes another, as when the impact of my pool cue with a billiard ball causes the ball to move. *Immanent* causation occurs when a *substance*—for Chisholm, a *person*—causes an event, as when *I* move my hand.

4. I make myself a sandwich. At first I'm hungry for a sandwich—that's a desire—and I know what I have to do to make one: those are beliefs. I am then faced with a practical question: What should I do next? I consider my options in light of my beliefs and desires, and then *I form the intention* to walk into the kitchen to make the sandwich. This intention causes my muscles to contract and my body to move. All of that is transeunt causation. The formation of the intention itself, however, involves immanent causation. It consists in *my* causing a change in my brain that is not caused by prior events.

A. J. AYER, Freedom and Necessity

1. True.

2. False. According to Ayer, you are responsible for an act when your choice to do it was not *constrained*. If you deliberate in the normal way—without compulsion or

interference—your choice is not constrained. So you can be responsible for your act even if you're not responsible for the mental states that caused it.

3. All human actions are caused, but only some are constrained. More specifically, an action is constrained when the agent is compelled by threats to do it or when it is caused by a psychological disorder (kleptomania) or an abnormal causal process (e.g., hypnotism) that bypasses the agent's deliberation altogether. The distinction matters because everyone agrees that we are not responsible if we are constrained to act as we do. Ayer's main thesis is that even if this is so, we can be responsible for actions we are caused to do, since in general, causation is not constraint.

4. To say that Jones could have done otherwise on some occasion is to say that Jones's action was not constrained in the sense defined in the answer to question 3 above.

P. F. STRAWSON, Freedom and Resentment

1. The optimist is roughly the compatibilist: she thinks that the truth of determinism would not undermine our normal practices for holding people responsible for what they do. The pessimist is roughly the incompatibilist: she thinks that if determinism is true, then our normal practices for holding people responsible are unjustifiable.

2. The reactive attitudes are emotional responses to human conduct. The main examples are resentment, indignation, and guilt on the negative side and certain forms of gratitude, admiration, and pride on the positive side. These emotions are all responses, not just to the overt act and its consequences, but to the "quality of will" the act expresses.

3. An act is blameworthy when it merits resentment (or some other negative reactive attitude).

4. False and false. Strawson thinks it is "practically inconceivable" for us to abandon the reactive attitudes, and that we have no good reason to abandon them even if determinism turns out to be true.

HARRY FRANKFURT, Freedom of the Will and the Concept of a Person

1. Sam wants to eat breakfast. That's a first-order desire. Sam does not want to act on his desire to eat breakfast; he would rather act on his desire to get to school on time. These are second-order desires: desires about first-order desires.

2. According to Frankfurt, your *will* is the first-order desire you act on or the desire you would act on if you made a choice. If Sam eats breakfast because he wants to, then his desire to eat breakfast is his will at that time.

3. According to Frankfurt, X is a person if and only if X has *second*-order volitions. Second-order volitions are desires about which of your first-order desires to act on. A creature with first-order desires but no second-order volitions is a *wanton*.

4. A creature has freedom of action iff it is free to act as it wills. (A dog in an open field has freedom of action; if it wants to run, it will run.) A creature enjoys freedom of the will iff it is free to have the *will* it wants. A normal person in normal circumstances has freedom of will: if Sam wants his desire to have breakfast to be his will (the desire he acts on), then it will be his will.

SUSAN WOLF, Sanity and the Metaphysics of Responsibility

1. According to the Deep-Self View, an agent is responsible for an action if and only if the agent's choice is determined by certain relatively stable features of his psychology:

his "deep self." For Frankfurt, the relevant features are the agent's higher-order desires. For Watson, they are the agent's values.

2. JoJo has been raised by his father, a brutal and sadistic dictator, to be a brutal and sadistic dictator. His actions are determined by his "deep self": he acts in accordance with his second-order desires and his values. But intuitively he's not responsible for his actions.

3. Wolf endorses the *sane deep-self view*: An agent is responsible for an action if and only if (a) her choice is determined by her deep self, and (b) her deep self is *sane*.

4. Sanity is roughly the ability to know right from wrong. More exactly, it is the "minimally sufficient" ability to perceive one's environment accurately, to reason soundly, and to know whether some proposed act is right or wrong.

NOMY ARPALY, Why Moral Ignorance Is No Excuse

1. A person acts from *moral ignorance* when she does something wrong (or right) without knowing that it's wrong (right), not because she's mistaken about the non-moral facts, but rather because she holds a mistaken moral view.

2. False. Arpaly holds that *factual* ignorance is often an excuse. If I mistakenly take your coat from the coatroom at a party in the honest belief that it's mine, I'm not blameworthy for taking your coat; my ignorance provides me with an excuse. Her thesis is that *moral* ignorance does not excuse wrongdoing.

3. Gottfried acts from moral ignorance: he believes that his act is wrong when in fact it's right. But he is not thereby "excused" for his good act. He's still praiseworthy. That shows that you can be responsible for what you do even though you acted from moral ignorance.

4. Steve acts from factual ignorance, but he is morally blameworthy nonetheless. He is blameworthy because (a) his factual beliefs are not supported by the evidence, and (b) he holds them anyway, not because he's mentally ill, but rather because he hates Jews so much that he ignores the evidence against his belief.

Chapter 14: What Is the Right Thing to Do?

PETER SINGER, Famine, Affluence, and Morality

1. The initial principle is: If it is in our power to prevent something bad from happening, without thereby sacrificing anything of *comparable* moral importance, we ought, morally, to do it. The qualified principle is: If it is in our power to prevent something *very* bad from happening, without thereby sacrificing *anything morally significant*, we ought, morally, to do it. The initial principle is more demanding. Singer says that while the qualified principle would require one to reduce oneself to the level of marginal utility (the point at which there is no sacrifice one can make that would benefit someone else more than it would cost oneself), the qualified principle would not.

2. Singer thinks that we should not think of helping remote people in dire need as engaging in *charity*—as something that is a wonderful thing to do but *optional*. Rather, we should realize that it is wrong to fail to help them.

3. Singer says it's true that *if* everyone gave a small amount, *then* each of us would only be obligated to give a small amount. But he says that since we are not in that

situation—it is not true that every person is going to give a small amount—that does not tell us what our duties are in our actual situation.

4. Singer holds his claims are perfectly compatible with the claim that governments ought to be acting in these cases. He says that giving privately will not make governments *less likely* to act. And he says that people ought to encourage their governments to act.

ONORA O'NEILL, The Moral Perplexities of Famine and World Hunger

1. (a) and (c)
2. Some utilitarians argue that we ought to engage in foreign aid aimed at famine relief; other utilitarians argue that we ought to refrain from doing so, because foreign aid makes things worse in the long run.
3. No. Both utilitarians and Kantians care about consequences, but O'Neill claims that utilitarians require agents to make their decisions on the basis of detailed knowledge of consequences, which is hard to attain.
4. (c) and (d)

JUDITH JARVIS THOMSON, A Defense of Abortion

1. (b)
2. (b) and (c). Thomson's explicit use of the case is (b) to show that the anti-abortion argument she discusses at the outset will not work. But the paper can also be read as (c) discussing the violinist case as an analogy with pregnancy. Like any analogy, there are some important differences between the two cases. But there is something illuminating about the comparison.
3. (a) and (c). While Thomson does not say (b)—she uses the case of the coats to make a different but related point—it is clear that she would agree with (b).
4. (c). Thomson argues that one might do something with an awareness that a further consequence might result, while taking steps to prevent it from happening, and that if the further consequence does occur, one has not given one's consent to that consequence. She gives the examples of putting bars on one's window to prevent the entrance of people seeds, and walking outside with body guards to prevent one's being kidnapped.

DON MARQUIS, Why Abortion Is Immoral

1. (a)
2. (c)
3. (a)
4. It is wrong to kill people in many cases in which they lack a desire to continue to live: it is wrong to kill the unconscious, the sleeping, those who are tired of life, and those who are suicidal.

ELIZABETH HARMAN, The Moral Significance of Animal Pain and Animal Death

1. She argues that it is false.
2. Harman says that death can also be bad for a person because it deprives her of future life, which would involve some happiness and valuable experiences. Even a person who truly "lives in the moment" and has no plans or desires for the future

is still deprived of some positive experiences by death (if she would have had some positive experiences, had she lived).

3. (b)
4. (c)

CORA DIAMOND, Eating Meat and Eating People

1. Speciesism is supposed to be analogous to racism. Just as racism is an unjustified prejudice against and systematic discounting of the moral significance of a group of people, speciesism is an unjustified prejudice against and systematic discounting of the moral significance of the interests of non-human animals. The term "speciesism" suggests that it is *mere unjustified prejudice* to see animals as counting less, morally, than persons.

2. (a)
3. (a) and (c)
4. (d)

Chapter 15: Do Your Intentions Matter?

G. E. M. ANSCOMBE, Mr Truman's Degree

1. In Anscombe's view, Truman's motive was to end the war by killing innocent people. He intended to kill innocent people as a means to his end. Anscombe holds that if a killing is a case of intending to kill an innocent person—either as one's end or as a means to one's end—then it is murder, and it is always morally wrong.

2. The bombing would be acceptable, according to Anscombe, if the intention is to destroy the factory: if that is the intention, then the deaths of the civilians would merely be unintended side effects. The bombing would be unacceptable if the intention is to kill civilians, and thereby to demoralize the enemy.

3. A farmer is neither engaged in harming anyone nor in providing the means to harm anyone. By contrast, a soldier is engaged in the project of harming and threatening harm, even if at a particular moment he is not harming. Even a soldier who was forced into service is still engaged in harming.

4. (b)

THOMAS M. SCANLON, When Do Intentions Matter to Permissibility?

1. (a)
2. Scanlon holds that differences in intentionality can affect how *morally criticizable* a person is, even if they don't affect the moral permissibility of an action.

   Scanlon says that if a person harms another person unintentionally (she did not realize she would harm him), but she should have known she would harm him, then she has acted impermissibly and she is morally criticizable. A different kind of moral criticism applies to an agent who knows that she will harm someone as a side effect of getting what she wants and yet goes ahead and acts anyway; she harms knowingly and yet she does not aim to harm. Yet a third kind of moral criticism applies to an agent who aims to harm someone.

3. (b)

4. The question asks for two examples, but here are four kinds of cases Scanlon gives in which intention can make a difference to moral permissibility.

First, Scanlon says that sometimes intentions are *predictive* of what will happen if one does something. If your aim is to drive safely, you are more likely to actually drive safely. Second, Scanlon says that some actions are crucially *expressions* of attitudes. Dishonesty is sometimes impermissible, and so these actions may be impermissible. For example, it may be impermissible to pretend to care about one's grandmother's illness when really one just wants to inherit money. Third, Scanlon says that some actions involve problematically creating *expectations* in other people. Like the second category, these actions may be morally wrong because dishonesty can be morally wrong. Finally, Scanlon says that it can be impermissible to carry out certain threats. When one carries out a threat, one performs the threatened action with a certain intention: one does it because the person one threatened refused to comply with one's threat. It may be perfectly permissible to choose not to hire a particular person, and yet it may be wrong to choose not to hire her *because she refused to go on a date with you*, for example.

BARBARA HERMAN, Impermissibility and Wrongness

1. (b)
2. The answer is (a). Contrary to (b), Herman thinks that if people would pay attention to cases of lying and deception, they would realize that impermissibility and wrongness are not equivalent.
3. (a)
4. (b)

MICHELE M. MOODY-ADAMS, Culture, Responsibility, and Affected Ignorance

1. No. Moody-Adams thinks that those claims are *not* enough to show that he is not blameworthy.
2. (d)
3. (a). A person's failure to know something is morally wrong counts as *affected ignorance* if the explanation of *why* he doesn't know it involves the fact that he *doesn't want to know* that it's morally wrong. The explanation might proceed via his avoiding important evidence, or avoiding thinking about the issue too hard, or some other mechanism, but for a person whose ignorance is affected ignorance, it is not true that he *could not* have known the truth that what he is doing is morally wrong.
4. (b)

ANGELA M. SMITH, Implicit Bias, Moral Agency, and Moral Responsibility

1. A person has an implicit bias when her reactions to others and judgments of others are biased systematically against people in certain groups. This may happen although the person disavows the bias in question, and although she has no idea that she is reacting in a biased way. One example of implicit bias might be judging a résumé to be less strong when it has a typically black name on it than when the identical résumé has a typically white name on it; a person might do this despite being personally opposed to racism.
2. Yes. Smith mentions two ways that a person can be morally responsible for something without being blameworthy for it. First, a person might be morally responsible for something that is not a morally bad thing to do: it might be a morally good thing

to do such as helping someone or it might be a morally neutral thing to do such as brushing one's teeth. Second, a person might be morally responsible for something but have an *excuse* for having done it.

3. (b). Smith's view is that a person is morally responsible for something just in case she is morally answerable for it—that is, just in case it is appropriate to ask her to offer reasons that would *justify* it. For a sneeze or an accidental stumble, this demand would not be appropriate; an agent is not morally responsible for a sneeze or a stumble. But for any action that an agent performs intentionally, this demand is appropriate; agents are morally responsible for their intentional actions. Smith argues that agents are also sometimes morally responsible for forgetting to do something or for failing to notice something.

4. Yes. Smith thinks that we are morally answerable for any implicit biases we have, so we are morally responsible for them. And we lack excuses for them, so we are blameworthy for them.

Chapter 16: Which Moral Theory Is Correct?

JOHN STUART MILL, Utilitarianism

1. The answer to both questions is "yes." Mill thinks that there are higher-quality pleasures that are worth some accompanying dissatisfaction.

2. Everyone's happiness counts, and it counts equally. The agent's happiness does not count more than others' happiness, and the happiness of the agent's friends and family does not count more than strangers' happiness, in settling what the agent should do.

3. (b)

4. Mill says that for many types of actions, the expanse of human history has enabled us to learn whether these actions tend to increase or decrease utility. He also says that any fundamental principle about how to act, such as the principle of utility, will have to be supplemented by subordinate principles, which the agent follows in an effort to follow the fundamental principle.

IMMANUEL KANT, Groundwork of the Metaphysics of Morals

1. A categorical imperative is a claim about how a person *ought* to act that applies to everyone, regardless of what she happens to desire. A hypothetical imperative is a claim about how a person *ought* to act that is true only because she desires a certain thing. Here is an example of a hypothetical imperative: "Jane ought to turn her car from Elm Street onto Pine Street." This is true because Jane wants to buy milk on her way home, and the store is on Pine Street. If Jane did not want to buy milk, that imperative would not be true of her.

2. The answer is (a). It's important that Kant thinks the answer is (a), and not (b), because (a) fails his test, given by the Formula of Universal Law, but it's not clear that (b) would fail the test.

3. First, consider the maxim "I will work hard in order to gain a promotion." If everyone worked hard to get promotions, that would be good; I can wish for that possibility. So I can wish that it be a universal law that everyone works hard to get promotions. So, the maxim "I will work hard in order to gain a promotion" does pass the universalization test. Second, consider the maxim "I will kill my boss in order to gain a promotion." Suppose that everyone killed their bosses in order to gain a promotion.

Then, as soon as someone was promoted, she would be killed by someone below her who wanted her job. So, killing one's boss would not actually be a way to gain her job. So it's *impossible* that everyone kills their bosses to get promoted. Therefore, I can't wish that everyone does that. Therefore, the maxim "I will kill my boss in order to gain a promotion" does not pass the universalization test.

4. Kant's Formula of Humanity says that one must act so that one uses humanity, whether one's own humanity or others' humanity, always as an end in itself and never as a means.

ARISTOTLE, Nicomachean Ethics

1. Happiness.
2. (c)
3. (a)
4. (c) and (d)

ROSALIND HURSTHOUSE, Virtue Ethics

1. (c)
2. No. Virtue ethics focuses on what a virtuous agent would do in particular moral situations, considering what virtue—benevolence, courage, generosity, honesty, justice, kindness, loyalty, responsibility, and trustworthiness, for example—would require in those situations.
3. No. On this view, moral expertise is tantamount to moral wisdom, and the morally wise person will see what is really worthwhile, what virtue requires, and will act accordingly.
4. (d)

FRIEDRICH NIETZSCHE, On the Genealogy of Morals, Beyond Good and Evil, and The Gay Science

1. The two basic types are the master morality and slave morality.
2. No. Nietzsche is opposed to social conditions of equality and thinks that people have become too sensitive to pain and suffering.
3. Nietzsche thinks that we need to observe our own strengths and weaknesses and then fit all these qualities into an "artistic plan." What is essential is that we make our own lives into an integrated work of art, with a "single taste" guiding the development of the plan.
4. The pairing good/bad grows from an aristocratic morality, whereas the pairing good/evil grows from slave morality. With an aristocratic morality, the dominant group characterizes its own qualities as good, and the opposite qualities, for which it has contempt, as bad. With the slave morality, the qualities of the powerful are feared and called "evil," whereas the qualities that make people useful—including pity, humility, and industriousness—are called "good."

Chapter 17: Is Morality Objective?

J. L. MACKIE, The Subjectivity of Values

1. For Mackie, moral subjectivism is (b): there are no objective values.
2. A first-order moral view is a position on a question about what a person ought to do. The proposition that you ought to keep your promises expresses a first-order moral

view, as does the proposition that you ought to tell the truth. A second-order moral view is a view about the nature of morality. The thesis that morality is objective is a second-order moral view, as is Mackie's view that there are no objective values.

3. Mackie claims that ordinary moral judgments are assumed to be objective: they "include a claim to objectivity." Mackie argues that this claim to objectivity is wrong; thus ordinary moral judgments are in error.

4. The argument from queerness has a *metaphysical* and an *epistemological* part. The metaphysical part says that objective values, if they existed, would be different from anything else in the universe that we are familiar with. The epistemological part says that our awareness of objective values, if they existed, would require a kind of mental capacity that is different from any other kind of mental capacity that we are familiar with.

R. JAY WALLACE, Moral Subjectivism

1. The best statement of "subjectivism," for Wallace, is (d).

2. The first aspect is metaphysical and concerns the subject matter of moral thought. This metaphysical aspect encourages subjectivism because moral thought uses evaluative and normative concepts, which do not seem to correspond with features of the world. The second aspect is motivational and concerns the connection between moral thought and action. This motivational aspect encourages subjectivism because moral thought motivates our action, whereas thought about objects in the world does not.

3. Simple expressivism holds that moral judgments express our desires. The main problem arises from the fact that we do not always act on our moral judgments, as when we break a promise that we know we ought to have kept. If we break a promise that we know we should have kept, then there is some conflict between our desires (which led us to break the promise) and our moral judgment (which says that we should have kept it). So we need a more complex understanding of the relationship between desires and moral judgments that allows us to understand how desires and moral judgments can conflict.

4. For the constructivist, agents are "already committed" to acting in accordance with the critical standards. For example, the norm of instrumental rationality says that we ought to choose the means that are required for achieving our ends. The constructivist says that agents have goals and that an agent with a goal is already committed to taking the means required for achieving the goal. So agents who do not take the means are violating a critical standard they are already committed to.

THOMAS NAGEL, Ethics

1. Nagel says that a subjectivist view about morality is more plausible because we do not have well-developed and settled methods for reasoning about moral issues, whereas we do have such methods for reasoning about scientific issues.

2. Nagel endorses (d). Disagreements are an invitation to reason about the issues on which we disagree.

3. Prudential rationality requires that we attach the same importance to desires and interests that we have at different times in our lives. I should not, according to the requirement of prudential rationality, attach more importance to satisfying my current desires than to satisfying my future desires.

4. We use practical reason to decide what we should do. The idea, then, is that different people who ask the question about what they should do, and use the same data, should arrive at the same answer. The answer is general, not peculiar to the person who is asking the question.

PHILIP L. QUINN, The Divine Command Theory

1. The theory needs to say which moral statuses are dependent on God, what the nature of the dependence relation is, and which divine act the moral statuses depend on.
2. Quinn says that he is not aiming to provide a deductive argument. Instead, he proposes a "cumulative case argument" that has four parts.
3. The requirement of Christian love is very demanding in that it requires us to love everyone, even our enemies and those we have never met. We do not have any natural emotional tendency to such expansive love. So it is not plausible that people would do this if it were not demanded of them as a matter of divine obligation.
4. According to the anything goes objection, the divine intention theory says that *whatever* God intends is morally required of us. But that means that if God intends us to torture innocent children, we have an obligation to torture innocent children. But it is monstrous to say that we have an obligation to torture innocent children. So the divine intention theory must be wrong.

ELIZABETH HARMAN, Is It Reasonable to "Rely on Intuitions" in Ethics?

1. The first example, from Peter Singer, is about a man walking past a drowning child. The second, from Judith Jarvis Thomson, is about a person who wakes up with his kidneys being used to keep a violinist alive. The third is about a train that is headed for five innocent people.
2. Harman disagrees. An argument that starts from controversial premises can show connections between ideas that are of interest both to those who accept the controversial premises and those who reject them.
3. Two people are epistemic peers if and only if they are roughly as good as one another at arriving at the truth on some issue. A person, for example, who is as likely as you are to get an answer right to a moral question is your epistemic peer about morality.
4. The third epistemological worry is that the examples used in ethical arguments are too strange for us to have reasonable beliefs about them.

SHARON STREET, Does Anything Really Matter or Did We Just Evolve to Think So?

1. When you learn that a belief was implanted through hypnotism, the genealogy undermines your belief. When you remember that you saw a suspicious-seeming character profiled on *America's Most Wanted*, the genealogy of your sense of suspicion strengthens your belief.
2. Metaethics is about the "nature of ethics." Among other things, it is about the nature of value: about what it is for something to be good.
3. For a mind-dependent conception of value, things have value in virtue of our evaluative attitudes to the things. For a mind-independent conception, things have value independent from any of our evaluative attitudes. Street endorses a mind-dependent conception of value.
4. The statement is false. If a mind-independent conception is correct, then evolutionary theory provides an undermining genealogy.

SARAH McGRATH, What Is Weird about Moral Deference?

1. To outsource your moral convictions is to accept the moral conclusions that someone else draws as correct and not to think for yourself about moral issues.
2. One claim is that moral deference is weird—either hard to understand (puzzling) or objectionable (problematic). The second claim is that moral questions have objectively correct answers.

3. The moral ideal in question is to do the right thing for the right reasons. People who are morally deferential may do the right thing. But they will not understand the reasons that account for the rightness of their action, so they will not do it for the right reasons.

4. One route to this conclusion would be to think for ourselves about moral questions and then attribute expertise to people who come to the same conclusions that we come to. (If this is the route to the conclusion, then we are not deferring to them.)

Chapter 18: Why Do What Is Right?

PLATO, The Republic

1. The first type of good is desired "for its own sake," not for the sake of what comes from it. Joy is his example. The second type of good is desired both for itself and for the sake of what it produces. Glaucon gives the example of knowledge. The third type of good is desired solely for the sake of what it produces. Medical treatment is his example.

2. When the ring is turned in a certain direction, it makes the person who has the ring invisible. So the person who has it can do as he or she wishes, without fear of detection.

3. Glaucon describes a perfectly unjust person who appears to be perfectly just and a perfectly just person who appears to be perfectly unjust.

4. Adeimantus says that Socrates needs to praise justice in itself and condemn injustice in itself, and not pay any attention.

JUDITH JARVIS THOMSON, Why Ought We Do What Is Right?

1. (d)
2. No.
3. (d)
4. No.

DAVID HUME, Of the Passions, Of Morals, and Why Utility Pleases

1. (b)
2. Reason can influence our behavior by informing us of the existence of something that we already want, so that we can act to obtain it, or by informing us of the means to something we already want, so that we can take those means in order to obtain it.
3. (a)
4. Hume says that people will react with happiness and approval when they see a happy home, even when it is a home of strangers, and will react with horror and disapproval to hear of people being mistreated, even when they are strangers. He says that even people who are very selfish still feel some sympathy with others and are moved by the fate of others, even if their own situation is unaffected.

IMMANUEL KANT, Groundwork of the Metaphysics of Morals

1. (c)
2. Kant thinks that if a person does the right thing out of sympathy or affection for other people, or just because he feels like doing it, or to make money, then his action has no moral worth.
3. One conforms with duty whenever one does the right thing. One acts *from duty* when one's motive or reason for acting is that one wants to do one's duty. If you write your mother a birthday card in order to get her to lend you her car for the

evening (because her warm appreciation for the card will make her disposed to let you borrow the car), then you have done the right thing, but not because it was your duty; you have conformed with duty but not acted from duty. Suppose you think that you are morally required to tell your friend Anne that Betsy said something mean about her, but in fact, you should not say anything (because it would hurt Anne's feelings); your motive in telling Anne is that you think you are morally required to do so. In this case, you act *from duty*, but you don't do the right thing, so you don't conform with duty.

4. Kant says that one may act only on a principle that one can wish were a *universal law* for everyone. Suppose everyone made a lying promise when in trouble; then no one would believe a promise; so it wouldn't work to make a lying promise when one was in trouble; so it wouldn't be true that everyone made a lying promise when in trouble. We have reached a contradiction: it's not possible for this to be a universal law, and so one can't wish that it be a universal law. Therefore, one may not make a lying promise.

Chapter 19: What Is the Meaning of Life?

RICHARD TAYLOR, The Meaning of Life

1. Sisyphus is condemned by the gods to spend eternity rolling a rock up a hill only to have it roll back down again.
2. Sisyphus does not *will* the goal he pursues or the activity he engages in.
3. True.
4. No, not by themselves. Our achievements are temporary, and viewed from a distance our lives are objectively like the life of Sisyphus. Our lives have meaning for us because we *will* the activities we engage in.

SUSAN WOLF, Meaning in Life and Why It Matters

1. A meaningful life involves (a) loving objects (people, activities) that are (b) worthy of love and (c) engaging with them in a positive way.
2. False. Sisyphus Fulfilled loves what he's doing, but the thing he loves is not worthy of love. So his life is not meaningful.
3. Unless Jones takes satisfaction in some other aspect of his life, the answer is no. His life is objectively good in some ways, but it's not meaningful.
4. Someone who lives a meaningful life must find some aspects of her life fulfilling, but she need not to be happy overall, and she certainly does not need to be happy all the time.

THOMAS NAGEL, The Absurd

1. A situation is absurd when there is a conspicuous clash between "pretension" and "reality," as when you are being knighted (a solemn ceremony) and your pants fall down.
2. One standard argument says that our lives are absurd because we are small and the universe is large. Nagel's reply is that if your life is absurd as it is, it would still be absurd if your were roughly the same size as the universe (i.e., if you were very large or the universe were rather small).
3. We devote extraordinary energy to our jobs, our relationships, and so on. In doing so, we take it for granted that these things *matter*. But when we step back and view

our lives objectively, we can see that our particular commitments are arbitrary; we could easily have cared about other things, people, and so forth. So there is a clash between the seriousness with which we pursue our goals and our recognition that from an objective point of view, we cannot justify commitments.

4. No. The sense of absurdity arises, according to Nagel, when we realize that we cannot *justify* our fundamental commitments. But even if you can't *justify* caring about (say) your family as you do, it may still be the case that your relationship to your family has exactly the kind of importance that you think it has.

SAMUEL SCHEFFLER, Death and the Afterlife

1. The idea that human life will continue on after we die.
2. In the doomsday scenario, the earth will be destroyed 30 days after your death. In *Children of Men*, the human race has become infertile so that the human race will die out much more slowly. The doomsday scenario involves the premature death of everyone you know and love; the *Children of Men* scenario does not.
3. Cancer research, artistic and scholarly pursuits, reading novels, having sex.
4. Many of the things we appear to value for their own sake, including knowledge, art, and participation in various communities and traditions, are in fact valuable for us only on the condition that the human race will continue to exist long after we die.

Chapter 20: How Can the State Be Justified?

ARISTOTLE, Politics

1. The parts of the state are its citizens.
2. A citizen in the strictest sense is a person who participates in the administration of justice and can serve as an officeholder in the state.
3. A constitution is a way to organize the "magistracies" or offices in a state. For example, there are democratic and oligarchic constitutions, depending on whether the people (democratic) or the few (oligarchic) hold the highest offices.
4. The central purpose of the state is not simply to protect life or to ensure peace. The central purpose is to foster the good life, which is a life of noble actions.

THOMAS HOBBES, Leviathan

1. The sources are *competition*, which reflects the scarcity of resources relative to what people desire; *diffidence*, which means "distrust"; and *glory*, which is a desire to be regarded by others as having great value.
2. Each person must subordinate his or her own will and judgment to the will and judgment of an authority, and each must regard himself or herself as authorizing everything the authority decides about issues of peace and security. In effect, each of the individuals says to the authority they are creating: "You decide what is necessary to achieve peace and security, and I will support your decisions." The authority is called the "sovereign."
3. First, the sovereign may not be punished by subjects. Second, the sovereign has the right to decide what people are allowed to say in public gatherings. And third, the sovereign has the right to make foreign policy, including decisions about war and peace.

4. Hobbes thinks that people tend to exaggerate the short-term costs of law and political authority (e.g., the need to pay taxes) and not to give attention to the long-term benefits of law and political authority (achieving peace and security). He thinks that the kind of "moral and civil science" he develops in *Leviathan* will help people to understand and pay more attention to the longer-term benefits. He is providing a telescope instead of a microscope.

JEAN-JACQUES ROUSSEAU, The Social Contract

1. The problem is to figure out what kind of society will use its power to ensure protection of person and property for each member while also enabling each member to be free—to obey only himself or herself.

2. A person is morally free when the person obeys laws that the person has made for himself or herself. This person achieves a kind of self-mastery. Natural freedom is an unlimited right in a situation in which there are no laws. And civil freedom is a matter of having a right to act within the bounds of the law.

3. Each person has an interest in personal security and in the protection of his or her goods. So when Rousseau mentions common interests, he means these interests that everyone shares.

4. Rousseau's social contract is made by individuals with one another, not by individuals with a government or sovereign. Individuals form a sovereign people by making an agreement with one another. Rousseau says that we need "to examine the act by which a people is a people." The social contract is that act.

A. JOHN SIMMONS, Rights-Based Justifications for the State

1. Conventional rights are created by social practices; for example, by laws. Voting rights are conventional rights, defined and created by a constitution or by laws about voting. Moral rights are rights we have that are not created by social practices. For example, the right to defend ourselves is a moral right. The law protects the right to self-defense, but the right is not created by law.

2. The walled space idea reminds us that rights define barriers against aggression by others. It also suggests that rights define barriers against making us act to serve certain valuable social ends: we are free to act as we wish within the walls. And the metaphor also suggests the idea that individuals have dignity and independence, that individuals are not simply parts of a larger whole.

3. First, according to a rights-based justification, states receive their rights to govern from the individuals that they govern (they have "the consent of the governed"). Second, according to a rights-based justification, the authority of states is justified when they provide better protection of the rights of individuals than individuals would receive without a state, in a situation of anarchy.

4. The first Lockean response is that it is possible for individuals to live together outside a state and fully respect each other's rights: that result is not likely, but contrary to the Kantian view, it is possible. The second Lockean response is that the Kantian cannot explain *which* state a person has obligations to. To explain membership, we need, the Lockean argues, individual consent.

CHARLES MILLS, The Racial Contract

1. The Racial Contract is an agreement between and among people who are counted as white. In the compact, they agree to categorize others as "non-white" and to

assign those others a subordinate status. But the others are not themselves parties to the Racial Contract.

2. A racial polity has two main features. First, the "purpose" of the order is to maintain the privileged position of the white members—thus the subordinate position of the non-white members. Second, the responsibilities of citizens are in part to maintain the racial supremacist order. So in a racial polity, there is a close connection between being a good citizen and preserving racial hierarchy.

3. Mills asserts that the Racial Contract is fundamentally about securing economic advantage. The Racial Contract serves both to establish a system of economic exploitation and to justify that system.

4. No, just the opposite. For the participants in the Racial Contract, conditions in the world—especially issues about race itself—are obscured because participants are required to see the world in ways that uphold the system of white supremacy. Part of what participants in the Racial Contract accept or consent to is a view "about what counts as a correct, objective interpretation of the world," and that interpretation justifies racial hierarchy.

Chapter 21: What Is the Value of Liberty?

JOHN LOCKE, A Letter Concerning Toleration

1. Locke says that we need to be clear about the distinction between the responsibility of civil government and the responsibility of religion. Otherwise, the controversies about religious toleration will never end.

2. The main duty of civil government is to ensure that people are secure in the possession of the goods that they are entitled to. Civil government should focus exclusively on goods "of this world."

3. No. Locke argues that the authority of civil government cannot and should not include the salvation of the souls of citizens. Salvation is not one of the goods "of this world."

4. Locke thinks that a person's salvation depends on that person's faith, what he calls "an inner persuasion of mind." But the tools available to civil government involve a use of "outward force." And he says that the use of outward force cannot create the inner persuasion or conviction that salvation requires: "such is the nature of the understanding," he says, "that it cannot be compelled to the belief of any thing by outward force" (p. 1084).

JOHN STUART MILL, On Liberty

1. Mill's principle says that coercion and control, either from law or from public opinion, should be used to restrict a person's liberty only for the purpose of preventing the person from harming others. A person should not be subject to coercion and control in order to promote that person's own good.

2. No. Mill specifically mentions two restrictions. First, he says that the principle does not apply to children or young people below a legally defined age of "manhood or womanhood." Second, he says that his principle does not apply in "backward states of society," but only when people can be persuaded to act differently through discussion.

3. Mill thinks that when people simply and unreflectively follow custom—when they do something simply because it is the custom—they do not use any of the characteristics that are unique to human beings. The alternative to following "custom as custom"

is to make choices. Mill says that when we make choices, we use a wide range of human powers, including perception, judgment, feeling, and reason.

4. The Calvinistic theory, as Mill describes it, is the view that human beings need to be obedient. Our nature is so "radically corrupt" that we should not try to develop in our own ways. Instead, we should follow "the will of God."

PATRICK DEVLIN, Morals and the Criminal Law

1. Immorality, Devlin says, is a matter of what "every right-minded person is presumed to consider to be immoral." It is the moral view of the person on the street, or the view that we expect jurors to agree on after they have discussed the issues.

2. Devlin says that societies are held together by *shared ideas*, including ideas about good and evil.

3. No. Devlin denies that there is such a private sphere that is beyond regulation. We cannot have an inflexible rule that protects private conduct from law.

4. No. Devlin thinks that dislike by a majority is not a good enough reason. People must think that the conduct is in some way unacceptably bad. There must be feelings of indignation at the conduct or a sense of disgust.

AMARTYA SEN, Elements of a Theory of Human Rights

1. For Bentham, all rights are created by the law, so the idea of natural rights—rights that people have outside a legal system—is nonsense. For Hart, human rights provide the basis for new laws: they are the "parents of laws." Sen also thinks that human rights can provide the basis for new laws, but he says that they have wider reach as moral standards that can be used by nongovernmental organizations that do not have lawmaking power.

2. Sen thinks that the freedoms protected by human rights must meet two conditions: they must be important and they must be socially influenceable. He says that the freedoms not to be assaulted and to receive medical care meet both conditions. In contrast, the freedom not to be called up by neighbors you detest is not important enough to be protected by a human right. And the freedom to achieve tranquillity is not socially influenceable enough to be protected by a human right.

3. The feasibility critique assumes that it must be feasible to achieve human rights: to ensure that all the human rights can be fully realized. But it then says that economic and social rights cannot be fully realized under all circumstances: perhaps they require greater resources than are available. So it concludes that we should not include economic and social rights as human rights.

4. Sen thinks that the unobstructed discussion must be global, not simply within a specific society. Defending claims about human rights "demands" that we consider the different points of view of people in different societies and the different practices in those societies. We need to see with "the eyes of the rest of mankind."

Chapter 22: Does Justice Require Equality?

JOHN RAWLS, Two Principles of Justice

1. The idea of fair equality of opportunity is that individuals should have equal chances in life regardless of their social or family background: where they end up should not depend on where they start out. More precisely, people who have the same talents and abilities, and have the same motivation to use their talents and abilities, should have equal chances of success, regardless of where they start out.

2. Democratic equality is an interpretation of the second principle of justice. It combines two elements: fair equality of opportunity and the difference principle. According to fair equality of opportunity, people should have equal chances to succeed, whatever their social background. According to the difference principle, inequalities in income and wealth, as well as powers and positions of authority, should work to the maximum advantage of the least advantaged group in society.

3. No. Rawls thinks that inequality in natural abilities is just a natural fact. It is neither just nor unjust: it simply is. Justice is a matter of how we and our institutions respond to the natural facts.

4. First, moral persons have a conception of the good, which means an organized set of ideas about the goals they are aiming at in their life and how they propose to achieve those goals. Second, moral persons have a sense of justice, which means that they have a view about what justice requires of them and a desire (normally present but perhaps not always acted on) to comply with the standards of justice that they endorse.

HARRY FRANKFURT, Equality as a Moral Ideal

1. According to the doctrine of sufficiency, what is morally important in the distribution of economic resources is that everyone has enough. The doctrine of sufficiency does not pay attention to whether one person has more or less than other people. Egalitarianism, in contrast, is concerned about whether some people have more than others.

2. Frankfurt thinks that a focus on equality leads people to concentrate their attention on whether they have as much money as other people have instead of focusing their attention on figuring out what really matters in life and how they might be able to achieve what really matters. So a focus on equality alienates people from their own lives by encouraging them to focus on the resources that are available to them rather than on the ends they are pursuing.

3. The first flawed assumption is that there is a declining marginal utility of money; that is, the benefit a person gets from having one more dollar is smaller than the benefit to the person from getting the previous dollar. The second assumption is that, with respect to money, the utility functions of all persons are the same.

4. According to the doctrine of sufficiency, a person has *enough money* when he or she is content, or can reasonably be content, with having no more money than he or she now has. So person A might have more than person B, but they both have enough. Or person A might have more than person B, and, while B has enough, A does not.

MARTHA NUSSBAUM, Political Equality

1. Nussbaum thinks that it is not clear whether the idea is that people *are already equal*, and if so in what ways. Or is the idea that people *ought to be treated as equals*, and if so in what ways? In addition, she thinks it is not clear *which people* either are or ought to be treated as equals.

2. No, a common religious outlook is not essential. People in a religiously diverse society might all endorse the idea of equality for their political system, but for very different reasons.

3. According to the minimalist view, all human beings with some degree of consciousness and some degree of agency—of an ability to act—are of equal worth and dignity.

4. According to Nussbaum, the Stoics embraced the idea of equal human dignity. But the Stoics thought that nothing that happens in the world—hunger, slavery, lack of political rights—can have any impact on human dignity. She agrees with the Stoics

that human beings have equal dignity, and she agrees that external conditions cannot deprive people of their basic dignity. But she thinks that external conditions can violate our dignity. So, she claims, the Stoics did not fully appreciate the moral importance of external conditions.

ROBERT NOZICK, Distributive Justice

1. A theory of justice in holdings includes (i) a theory of *original acquisition*, which tells us when someone justly comes to own something that was previously unowned; (ii) a theory of *justice in transfer*, which tells us how a person can justly come to own something that was previously owned by someone else; and (iii) a theory of rectification, which tells us how to correct injustices in holdings; that is, how to correct violations of one of the first two parts of the theory.

2. One type is historical. For a historical principle of justice, the justness of a state of affairs—say, a distribution—depends on its history, on how it came about. The other type is end-state. For an end-state principle, the justness of a state of affairs—say, a distribution—can be determined without having to know the history that produced it. For example, if you believe that goods should be distributed so that total social happiness is maximized, then you will not need to know the history that produced a distribution in order to know if it is right.

3. The basic point is that all end-state principles or patterned principles of justice permit "continuous interference" in people's lives. Continuous interference means that a person's liberty is severely abridged. So the Wilt Chamberlain story is intended to reveal a conflict between a commitment to liberty and a commitment to an end-state or patterned principle of justice.

4. Nozick thinks that taxation on earnings from work is "on a par with" forcing people to work. In the one case, you tell someone what they must do. In the other case, you take the results of what they have done, which means that the person is working for someone else's purpose.

SUSAN MOLLER OKIN, Is Multiculturalism Bad for Women?

1. Feminists affirm that men and women are moral equals. They hold the view, Okin says, "that women should not be disadvantaged by their sex, that they should be recognized as having human dignity equal to that of men, and that they should have the opportunity to live as fulfilling and as freely chosen lives as men." Multiculturalism is the view that members of minority cultures should receive "special group rights or privileges," beyond the rights and privileges accorded to members of the majority culture.

2. First, cultures typically focus on personal, sexual, and reproductive issues. Second, cultures typically are patriarchal, in that they aim to secure men's control of women.

3. According to Kymlicka, some minority cultures need special rights because these cultures would otherwise disappear. But the persistence of the minority culture is essential for the self-respect of the members of the group.

4. Okin suggests two reasons. First, defenders of group rights treat groups as coherent and harmonious: they do not think enough about the internal conflicts within groups. Second, they do not focus their attention on families and domestic life, which is an important focus for the control of women by men.

Glossary

A posteriori Dependent on experience. Person *S* knows *p* a posteriori (or *empirically*) **iff** *S*'s knowledge of *p* depends on her experience. Smith's knowledge that Shakespeare died in 1616 is a posteriori, whether she knows it firsthand (as an eyewitness) or on the basis of testimony. (In the latter case, her knowledge depends on her experience of the testimony.) A **proposition** is a posteriori iff it can only be known a posteriori. An **argument** is a posteriori iff it contains at least one a posteriori premise. The **design argument** is an a posteriori argument for the existence of God.

    See also **a priori.**

A priori Prior to, or independent of, experience. Person *S* knows *p* a priori (or *non-empirically*) iff *S*'s knowledge of *p* does not depend on his experience. Our knowledge of logic and pure mathematics is widely (though not universally) held to be a priori. A **proposition** is a priori iff it can be known a priori. An **argument** is a priori iff all of its premises are a priori.

Abduction See **inference to the best explanation.**

Absolute sovereign See **sovereign.**

Abstract object An object that does not exist in space and lacks causal powers. The existence of abstract objects is controversial, but possible examples include mathematical objects such as the number 17, fictional characters such as Spiderman, abstract **types** such as the Greek letter "α" (as distinct from the concrete inscription of the letter on this page of your copy of this book), and **propositions** such as the proposition that snow is white.

Accident See **essence.**

Actual world See **possible world.**

Agent causation Sometimes called "immanent causation"; an irreducible causal relation between an agent and an **event,** as when Jones directly causes an event in his mind or brain. The existence of agent causation is controversial. Agent causation contrasts with *event causation* (also called "transeunt causation"), the uncontroversial sort of causal relation in which an event is caused by prior events.

    Most statements that seem to cite an agent (or an object) as a cause are really shorthand for claims of event causation. Instead of saying that *the rock* caused the window to break, one could have said more long-windedly that an event involving the rock—for example, the *collision of the rock with the window*—caused the window to break. Proponents of agent causation hold that in certain special cases, there is no shorthand of this sort. To say that John caused his arm to move isn't to say that an event involving John caused the movement, but that John himself was the cause.

Agnosticism In the philosophy of religion, the view that we cannot know whether God exists and should therefore suspend judgment about God's existence. More generally, a person is *agnostic* about a topic if and only if he or she adopts a principled suspense of judgment on that topic. ("Pauline is agnostic about the existence of abstract objects.")

Analogical argument An **argument** of the form:

> P1.   *A* resembles *B* in so-and-so respects.
> P2.   *B* has property *F*.
> Therefore:
> C.   *A* has property *F*.

Analysandum, analysans See **analysis.**

Analysis To analyze a word or a **concept** is to define it in more basic terms. For example, "triangle" can be analyzed as "plane figure with three interior angles." The word or concept to be analyzed (e.g., "triangle") is the *analysandum*; the proposed definition (e.g., "plane figure with three interior angles") is the *analysans*. Philosophical analyses are standardly formulated as general **biconditionals;** for example,

> *X* is a triangle iff *X* is a plane figure with three interior angles.
> *S* knows *p* iff *S* believes *p*, *S*'s belief is **justified,** and *p* is true.

"Analysis" can denote either the process of analyzing words or concepts ("Philosophical analysis is difficult") or the product of this process ("Jill's analysis of the concept *knowledge* was influential").

Analytic and synthetic A sentence is analytic iff it is "true solely in virtue of its meaning," or "true by definition," or "true by virtue of linguistic convention."

Alternatively, a sentence is analytic iff any competent speaker of the language is in a position to recognize its truth simply by virtue of being a competent speaker.

Examples are controversial (on either understanding of "analytic"), but possibilities include:

> An even number is divisible by 2.
> Red is a color.
> Nothing can be red and green all over.
> If *a* is taller than *b*, then *b* is shorter than *a*.

A true sentence that is not analytic is *synthetic.*

Hume's distinction between "relations of ideas" and "matters of fact" is an early precursor of the distinction between analytic and synthetic statements.

Antecedent See **conditional.**

Argument In logic, a list or sequence of **propositions** or *statements*: $p_1, \ldots p_n$, c. (Alternatively, a list of *sentences*: "P_1," … "P_n," "C.") $p_1, \ldots p_n$ are the **premises** and c is the *conclusion*. See also **soundness and validity.**

Argument from evil Sometimes called the *problem of evil* or the *argument from suffering.* An argument against the existence of God that proceeds from the premise that some people and animals suffer unnecessarily. A simple version:

P1. If God exists, then God is omnipotent and perfectly good.
P2. A perfectly good being would prevent unnecessary suffering if it could.
P3. An omnipotent being could prevent unnecessary suffering.
Therefore:
C1. If God exists, there is no unnecessary suffering.
P4. There is unnecessary suffering.
Therefore:
C2. God does not exist.

The argument is sometimes presented as a **proof** that there is no God. In more recent versions, the existence of apparently unnecessary suffering is adduced as powerful *evidence* that there is no God. An attempted answer to the argument from evil is a **theodicy.**

Aristotelian Resembling the views of Aristotle (384–322 BCE). *Aristotelian ethics* is an approach to ethical theory that focuses on the question "What is the best human life?" and explores the virtues that are required for living the best human life; also—in some formulations—it connects the notion of the best human life with an account of human nature.

Aristotelian logic A system of logic due to Aristotle (384–322 BCE) and his followers that attempts a complete catalogue of valid arguments. Aristotelian logic assumes that every assertion contains two terms, a subject "S" and a predicate "P." The subject may be either particular ("Socrates") or general ("human being"); the predicate is always general. An assertion either affirms or denies that the predicate holds of the subject. Assertions are therefore of the form:

S is P.
Every S is P.
Some S is P.
S is not P.
No S is P.
Not every S is P.

Aristotelian logic aims to reduce all valid arguments to sequences of *syllogisms*: two premise arguments involving assertions of this sort, where the premises must have at least one term in common. For example,

No human being is immortal.
Every sailor is a human being.
Therefore:
No sailor is immortal.

The great achievement in this tradition is a complete catalog of the various forms of valid syllogism and a set of techniques for reducing arguments to sequences of syllogisms. The limits of Aristotelian logic were clear by the fourteenth century. For example, the following argument is valid, though not representable as a valid Aristotelian syllogism:

Every horse is an animal.
Therefore:
The head of a horse is the head of an animal.

Modern logic is developed on rather different principles.

Atheism The view that there are no gods.

Autonomy Literally, *self-rule*. In ethics, the capacity of rational agents to act on reflectively endorsed reasons or principles, and not simply in response to non-rational impulses, desires, or feelings.

In political philosophy, the capacity of individuals to determine how they will live. *Private autonomy* is the capacity to determine the course of one's own life. *Public autonomy* is the capacity to decide, along with the others, the basic rules and regulations of public order. A political system designed to promote autonomy will involve limits on coercive interference, but it may also involve legal rules designed to ensure that individual choices are not driven by need or by the domination of others; for example, a system of public assistance funded by taxes.

Axiom Broadly, an assumption; a claim taken for granted without proof or argument. More narrowly, one of a class of privileged statements in the presentation of a formal theory. Classically, an axiom is a proposition that "neither needs nor admits of proof," but which is nonetheless clearly true. For example, "Every natural number has a successor" is an axiom in the standard theory of arithmetic. In modern mathematics, it is common to present a theory by specifying its axioms, and then to study the theory without regard to the truth of its axioms. The *theorems* of a theory are the *logical consequences* (see **entailment**) of its axioms.

Basic belief and knowledge A belief in *p* is *basic* for a person *S* iff *S* believes *p* but has no reasons or evidence (distinct from *p* itself) that supports *p*. A belief in *p* is *properly basic* for *S* iff it is basic for *S* and **justified**. Properly basic **propositions** are those we are justified in believing without further evidence. A belief in *p* is *basic knowledge* for *S* iff it is basic for *S* and *S* knows *p*.

Begging the question and circular arguments An **argument** is *circular* iff its conclusion is also one of its premises. The simplest form of such an argument is "*P*, therefore *P*." Note that there need be no *logical* flaw in a circular argument: "*P*, therefore *P*" is **valid** and may well be **sound**. The problem is that circular arguments cannot justify their conclusions and so cannot provide a rational basis for accepting their conclusions. Circular arguments are unpersuasive because they *beg the question*: anyone who does not already believe the conclusion will not believe one of the premises. More generally, an argument begs the question against person *S* iff *S* regards the justification of a premise of the argument as resting on the truth of the conclusion.

Note that a **cogent** argument may sometimes beg the question against certain people. Consider:

P1. Radiocarbon dating shows these bones to be 60,000 years old.
Therefore:
C. The Earth is more than 6,000 years old and young-Earth creationism is false.

This argument may beg the question against a biblical literalist who maintains that P1 depends for its justification on the assumption that young-Earth creationism is false; and yet the argument is cogent in the sense that a reasonable person might come to accept the conclusion on the basis of it.

More controversially, some philosophers hold that the following argument is cogent.

P1. I have a hand.
Therefore:
C. At least one material object exists.

Yet this argument begs the question against a **skeptic** who doubts the existence of the material world.

Behaviorism In psychology, the view that the proper object of psychological study is behavior, and that explanations of behavior that appeal to internal states and processes are to be avoided. In the philosophy of mind, the view that **mental states** are **dispositions** to behave in such-and-such ways. *Analytical behaviorism* is the view that mental state **concepts** can be **analyzed** in terms of behavior.

Biconditional A statement of the form "*P* if and only if *Q*" or some related form, either in a natural language or a formal logical language. Usually written in symbolic logic as "$P \leftrightarrow Q$."

Burden of proof In law, the burden of proof lies with the party who must prove his case if he is to prevail. (The term is also sometimes used to refer to the standard of certainty with which one's case must be proved if one is to prevail.) More generally, the burden of proof in a debate or controversy lies with the party who must provide positive evidence for his view if it is to be accepted.

Categorical imperative In **Kantian** moral philosophy, an imperative of the form "Do *A* in circumstances *C*" is categorical iff it is binding on all rational agents regardless of their particular desires, plans, or commitments. The phrase is sometimes used for basic principles of ethics that Kant himself deemed categorical, for example:

Act only in accordance with that maxim through which you can at the same time will that it become a universal law. (Kant's "formula of universal law")
So act that you use humanity, whether in your own person or in the person of any other, always at the same time as an end, never merely as a means. (Kant's "formula of humanity")

Category See **property.**

Circular argument See **begging the question and circular arguments.**

Classical foundationalism See **foundationalism.**

Closure principle In epistemology, a principle affirming that knowledge or **justified belief** is "closed" under some form of **entailment.** For example:

If *S* knows *p*, and *p* entails *q*, then *S* knows *q*.

or

If *S* is justified in believing *p*, and *S* knows that *p* entails *q*, then *S* is justified in believing *q*.

Coextensive See **extension.**

Cogent argument An **argument** that genuinely establishes its conclusion. Alternatively, an argument whose premises provide good, though perhaps inconclusive, grounds for accepting its conclusion.

Compatibilism The view that **free will** is compatible with **determinism.** Alternatively, the view that **moral responsibility** is compatible with determinism.

Common good In political philosophy, the good or welfare of a group (e.g., family, nation, team, etc.), as opposed to the good or welfare of individuals.

Concept The meaning of a word or phrase. "Cat" (in English) and "gato" (in Spanish) both mean *cat*; that is, they both express the concept *cat*. Alternatively, concepts are symbols in the brain—perhaps words in some neural language—that are used in thinking.

Conceptual analysis See **analysis.**

Conditional A sentence of the form "If *P*, then *Q*" or some related form, either in a natural language or a formal logical language. "*P*" is the *antecedent* of the conditional and "*Q*" the *consequent*. Some important varieties of conditionals include:

> *Material conditional:* In symbolic logic, usually written as "*P* ⊃ *Q*" or "*P* → *Q*." By definition, the material conditional is false when its antecedent is true and its consequent is false, and it is true in all other cases, even when the antecedent and consequent are entirely unrelated. For example, the following material conditionals are true:
>
> > $2 + 2 = 4$ ⊃ Albany is the capital of New York
> > $2 + 2 = 5$ ⊃ the moon is made of cheese
> > $2 + 2 = 5$ ⊃ Albany is the capital of New York
>
> whereas the following is false:
>
> > $2 + 2 = 4$ ⊃ the moon is made of cheese
>
> *Counterfactual conditional:* A sentence of the form "If it were that *P*, it would be that *Q*" or "If it had been that *P*, it would have been that *Q*."
>
> *Indicative conditional:* A natural language sentence of the form "If *P*, then *Q*" where "*P*" and "*Q*" are in the indicative mood; for example, "If Bob is not in his office, he's at home." Some philosophers hold that indicative conditionals are material conditionals. But consider:
>
> > If Ronald Reagan was a spy, no one knew it.
> > If Ronald Reagan was a spy, he was a spy for the Martians.
>
> The corresponding material conditionals (e.g., "Ronald Reagan was a spy ⊃ no one knew it") are both true, since their antecedents are false, and that is enough to render a material conditional true. But the first conditional seems true and the second false. This suggests that indicative conditionals are not material conditionals.

Conjunction A sentence of the form "*P* and *Q*" or some related form, either in a natural language or a formal logical language. In symbolic logic, usually written as "*P* & *Q*" or "*P* ∧ *Q*." By definition, "*P* & *Q*" is true iff both *conjuncts*—"*P*" and "*Q*"—are true.

Consequent See **conditional.**

Consequentialism The view that the moral rightness of an act depends entirely on the (actual or expected) value of its consequences. Historically, the most important form of consequentialism is **utilitarianism,** but the general framework permits a variety of alternatives.

Consistency A set of sentences (or **propositions**) is consistent iff it is possible for all of the sentences (or propositions) in the set to be true together. For example, the set {"John is happy," "John is rich"} is consistent, since it is possible for someone to be both happy and rich. By contrast, the set {"John is rich," "John is not rich"} is not consistent, since it is impossible for the two sentences to be true together.

Constructivism In moral philosophy, the view that the truth of a moral claim is determined, not by its conformity to mind-independent reality, but rather by the fact that it would be accepted by members of some (perhaps idealized) individual or group after informed reflection.

Content (of a mental state) Some **mental states,** for example *believing that grass is green,* appear to involve **relations** to **propositions**—in this case, the proposition that grass is green. (See **propositional attitudes.**) When a mental state involves a relation to a proposition, the proposition is called the "content" of the state, or sometimes its *representational* or *intentional* content. Thus, the content of the state of believing that grass is green is the proposition that grass is green.

Contextualism In epistemology, the view that the truth or falsity of a **propositional knowledge** attribution—a statement of the form "*S* knows *p*"—depends on the context in which the sentence is uttered. Suppose a student is asked, "Who wrote *Hamlet?*" and answers "Shakespeare." Now consider two utterances of "The student *knows* that Shakespeare wrote *Hamlet,*" one made by her English teacher in an ordinary classroom context, the other made by a scholar during the course of a heated academic debate about whether Shakespeare really wrote the plays attributed to him. According to the contextualist, the first utterance may be true and the second false: the student's belief may count as knowledge *by ordinary standards* but not by the more demanding standards of scholarly debate.

Contingent proposition See **necessity and possibility.**

Contractualism Broadly, the view that moral principles are justified by an actual or hypothetical agreement by members of a society, usually conceived as being forged under fair conditions of choice.

More narrowly, the view that an act is morally right because it is permitted by principles that informed, reasonable people would accept (or would not reject) for the purposes of regulating their conduct in society. See **social contract theory.**

Contrapositive The contrapositive of a **conditional,** "If *P* then *Q,*" is the conditional, "If not-*Q,* then not-*P.*"

Converse of a relation See **relation.**

Cosmological argument An argument for the existence of God that begins from a manifest fact about the natural world—for example, the fact that objects are in motion—and then argues that this fact entails the existence of an **entity** that differs from ordinary objects in fundamental respects: an uncaused cause, or a first mover. Every version of the cosmological argument exploits general principles about causation and explanation; for example, the principle that whatever comes to be comes to be from something else. A simple version:

P1. Some object *X* has come into existence.
P2. Whenever an object comes into existence, its existence is caused by something else.
Therefore:
C1. *X*'s existence is caused by something else, *Y.*
Therefore (from P2 and C1):
C2. If *Y* has come into existence, then its existence was caused by something else, *Z.*
P3. This sequence of causes cannot go on forever or loop round in a circle.

Therefore:

C3. There must be at least one object that has not come into existence.

Cosmological arguments rarely purport to establish the existence of the God of Christianity, Islam, and so forth. Rather, they purport to show that there must be at least one being that differs from ordinary objects (and resembles God) in fundamental metaphysical respects.

Cosmological fine-tuning argument A version of the **design argument** for the existence of God that is based on the alleged fact that if the numerical constants in the fundamental laws of nature had been slightly different, there would have been no organized matter and hence no life anywhere in the universe. This premise is sometimes put as the claim that the basic laws of nature appear "fine-tuned" to support the existence of life.

Counterexample A particular case that refutes a general claim. The discovery of a black swan refutes the general claim that all swans are white and is thus a counterexample to that claim. If the general claim is supposed to be only *contingently* true, as in the example just given, the particular case must actually obtain. If the general claim is meant to be a *necessary* truth, as is common in philosophy, then it can be refuted by a merely *possible* counterexample. (See **necessity and possibility**.) Thus, if a philosopher claims that, necessarily, an act is free only if the agent could have acted differently, her claim can be refuted by describing a merely possible case in which an agent acts freely but could not have acted differently.

Counterfactual conditional See **conditional**.

Counterfactual dependence An event e_2 counterfactually depends on an event e_1 iff e_2 would not have occurred if e_1 had not occurred.

Criterion of personal identity A general specification of the conditions under which a person existing at one time is **numerically identical** to (the very same person as) a person existing at another time. A criterion of personal identity is often given by a principle of the form

> Person A who exists at t_1 = person B who exists at t_2 iff A stands in relation R to B.

where R is specified without using the word "person" or any synonym thereof. For example,

> Person A at t_1 = person B at t_2 iff A's soul at t_1 = B's soul at t_2.

or

> Person A at t_1 = person B at t_2 iff at t_1, B can remember some experience A had at t_1.

Decision theory Also called *rational choice theory*. The effort to state general principles that specify which option a rational agent should choose in any given situation as a function of the agent's preferences or **utilities** and her degrees of confidence.

Demarcation problem The problem of drawing the boundary between science and pseudoscience.

Demonstrative argument See **proof**.

Demonstrative certainty For David Hume and other early modern philosophers, a proposition is demonstratively certain iff it can be known with certainty, but only on the basis of a **proof**.

Demonstrative certainty contrasts with *intuitive certainty*, the certainty of a proposition that can be known without proof or reasoning. For example, the Pythagorean theorem (that the square of the length of the hypotenuse of a right triangle is equal to the sum of the squares of the other two sides) is (at best) demonstratively certain, whereas "$1 = 1$" might be intuitively certain.

Deontology Originally, the part of ethics concerned with duty and obligation. In contemporary usage, the term is normally reserved for non-consequentialist theories of right action, and more specifically for theories according to which the basic principles of ethics consist in highly general non-consequentialist rules of conduct. In this contemporary sense, deontology is an alternative to **consequentialism,** but also to **virtue ethics** and to *particularism*, the view that there are no general rules that specify the conditions under which an act is right.

Design arguments Arguments for the existence of God that begin with the premise that nature exhibits marks of purpose or "apparent design." Design arguments sometimes point to objects that are particularly well suited for certain purposes: the eye for seeing, the hand for grasping. In other cases they point to general marks of design—ordered complexity—whose underlying purpose may not be evident. Design arguments typically proceed by **inference to the best explanation:**

P1. The natural world exhibits such-and-such signs of apparent design.

P2. The best explanation of this apparent design posits a supernatural being.

Therefore:

C. A supernatural being exists.

Determinism Roughly, the thesis that the state of the universe at any one time determines the state of the universe at all future times. In older treatments, determinism is formulated as the claim that every event is determined (or necessitated) by prior causes. In contemporary treatments, determinism is often defined as the thesis that:

For any time *t*, the complete state of the universe at *t* and the laws of nature together entail the state of the universe at every later time.

Indeterminism, the negation of determinism, is the thesis that the laws of nature and the state of the universe at *t* do not in general determine the state of the universe at later times, and so leave room for genuine randomness or chance.

Difference principle In the political philosophy of John Rawls (1921–2002), a principle of justice according to which social and economic inequalities are just only if they arise under a system of rules that works for the maximum benefit of the least well-off members of society.

Disjunction A sentence of the form "*P* or *Q*" or some related form, either in a natural language or a formal logical language. In symbolic logic, usually written as "$P \lor Q$." By definition, "$P \lor Q$" is true iff at least one *disjunct*—"*P*" or "*Q*"—is true.

Disposition In metaphysics, the tendency, power, or propensity of an object to behave in certain ways under certain conditions. Thus, fragility is a disposition (or a dispositional **property**), since it consists in the tendency to break when struck or dropped.

Divine command theory A metaphysical account of what makes actions obligatory, wrong, and permissible. According to the theory, actions are obligatory in virtue of their conformity to God's commands, wrong in virtue of their violation of those commands, and permissible in virtue of their not violating God's commands.

Divine intention theory An account of what makes actions obligatory, wrong, and permissible. According to the theory, actions are obligatory in virtue of their conformity to God's intentions, wrong in virtue of their violation of those intentions, and permissible in virtue of their not violating God's intentions.

Doctrine of double effect In ethics, a principle governing actions that have both good and bad effects, according to which the permissibility of the act depends on whether the bad effect is intended or merely foreseen. Ethicists dispute how it should be formulated (and whether it is correct). One version of the principle states:

> It is permissible to perform an action that foreseeably has both good and bad effects iff:
>
> a. the act itself (apart from its consequences) is not intrinsically immoral;
> b. the agent does not intend the bad effect, either as a means or as an end;
> c. the good effect is not produced by means of the bad effect;
> d. the value of the good effect is sufficiently great to warrant causing the bad effect.

It is also sometimes referred to as the *principle* of double effect or the *law* of double effect.

Dominance reasoning In **decision theory,** a rule according to which it is rational to choose the *dominant act* when one exists. In a choice between actions A and B, action A dominates B when the **utility** of A is at least as great as the utility of B however things turn out, and greater in at least one case. For example, in a choice between an act A that pays $5 if it rains and $10 if it does not rain, and another act B that pays $4 if it rains and $10 if it does not rain, A is the dominant option, since A is better than B in one case and at least as good in every other. Dominance reasoning instructs the agent to choose option A in this situation. *Note:* In many decision problems, there is no dominant act, in which case dominance reasoning is not available.

Doxastic voluntarism The view that our beliefs are sometimes under our direct voluntary control.

Dualism In the philosophy of mind, dualism comes in two varieties.

> *Substance dualism:* The view that there are two fundamentally distinct kinds of **substance:** thinking things and material (or physical) things. This was famously defended by René Descartes (1596–1650) so is often called *Cartesian* dualism. Descartes also held that a thinking thing and its associated material body causally interact, and this is sometimes called Cartesian *interactionism.*
> *Property dualism:* The view that there are two fundamentally distinct kinds of **property:** mental properties (e.g., the property of being in pain) and physical properties (e.g., the property of having a brain with such-and-such neural firing pattern).

Dualists reject **physicalism.**

Efficient cause See **four causes.**

Eliminativism In the philosophy of mind, the view that no one has ever been in any **mental state** (or in a mental state of a certain kind). If that is right, then mentalistic vocabulary should ultimately be eliminated from scientific psychology.

For example, eliminativism about belief is the view that no one has ever believed anything; if so, psychologists should not use the word "belief" any more than biologists should use "Bigfoot." More generally, eliminativism about *F*s—also sometimes called an **error theory** about *F*s—is the view that there are no *F*s, or that nothing has the property of being *F*. Thus, *color eliminativism* is the view that nothing is colored: roses are not red (or any other color), violets are not blue (or any other color), and so on. Eliminativism is opposed to **realism.**

In the philosophy of race, sometimes eliminativism is used for the view that racial terms (e.g., white, Asian, etc.) should no longer be used, rather that no one is white, Asian, and so on. This is related to the more standard sense of eliminativism but should not be confused with it. Only the standard sense figures in this anthology.

Empirical See **a posteriori.**

Empiricism Roughly, the view that all (substantive) knowledge derives from experience, or is **a posteriori. Concept** empiricism is the view that all *concepts* are either acquired from experience or "composed from" concepts that are acquired from experience (as the concept *unicorn* is said to be composed from concepts like *horse* and *horn*). **Epistemological** empiricism is the view that all **synthetic** knowledge is a posteriori. Empiricists typically deny the existence of innate knowledge and the existence of a faculty of reason that yields substantive, a priori knowledge of reality. Prominent empiricists include David Hume (1711–1776) and John Stuart Mill (1806–1873).

Entailment Proposition *p entails* **proposition** *q* iff it is *absolutely impossible* for *p* to be true and *q* false. Equivalently, *p* entails *q* when as a matter of *absolute necessity*, if *p* is true then so is *q*. (See **necessity and possibility.**) Synonyms: *p implies q*; *p necessitates q*; *q* is a *consequence* of *p*. Alternatively: sentence "*P*" entails sentence "*Q*" if and only if it is absolutely impossible for "*P*" to be true and "*Q*" false.

The terminology of "*logical* entailment" and "*logical* consequence" is used more narrowly, and specifically for sentences: "*P*" logically entails "*Q*" iff "*Q*" follows from "*P*" by formal logic alone, or alternatively, iff the argument from the premise "*P*" to the conclusion "*Q*" is *formally valid*. (See **soundness and validity.**)

Entails See **entailment.**

Entity A maximally general term designed to apply to anything whatsoever. Ordinary physical objects are entities. But so are immaterial souls (if they exist), mathematical objects (if they exist), events, properties, relations, facts, propositions, and so on.

Enumerative induction See **induction.**

Epiphenomenalism In the philosophy of mind, the view that a person's psychology or mental life never has any physical effects (although it may have physical causes): wanting pizza never causes the ingestion of pizza, intending to go the lecture never causes attendance at the lecture, and so on. Sometimes more specifically, the view that **qualia** never have physical effects. According to the qualia epiphenomenalist, the distinctive qualia associated with pain do not cause what we naïvely regard as the physical manifestations of pain—wincing, grimacing, and so forth. Rather, physical changes in the brain cause both distinctive pain qualia and these physical manifestations.

Epistemic rationality See **practical vs. theoretical rationality.**

Epistemology Literally, the theory of knowledge. More commonly, the part of philosophy that studies knowledge, rational belief, and the principles governing the rational revision of belief.

Equality of opportunity The requirement that people have equal chances of attaining socially desirable positions or other goods. A more formal idea of equality of opportunity requires that people not face legal obstacles to attaining socially desirable positions. A more substantive idea of equal opportunity, expressed in John Rawls's (1921–2002) idea of *fair equality of opportunity*, requires that people who are equally able and equally motivated have equal chances of attaining desirable social positions.

Error theory The view that our claims about some topic (e.g., color, ethics, mathematics) are completely mistaken because they involve a fundamental error about what the world is like. An error-theoretic view of ethics (see **moral nihilism**) holds that ethical claims are systematically false because *nothing* is right or wrong. (Alternatively, it might be held that ethical claims are meaningless, and so don't even manage to be false.) An error-theoretic view of color holds that color claims ("This rose is red," etc.) are systematically false because, despite appearances, nothing is colored. (See **eliminativism**.)

Alternatively, a theory that explains *why* we are prone to systematic metaphysical error in some area; for example, an account of why we think objects are colored when in fact nothing is.

Essence and accident The *essential properties* of an object are the properties that it cannot possibly fail to possess, or equivalently, the properties the object possesses in every **possible world** in which it exists. Alternatively, an essential property is a property an object possesses *by its very nature*, or *simply in virtue of being the thing that it is*. A property that is not essential is **accidental**. Examples are controversial, but plausible examples include: gold is essentially a metal, but only accidentally rare; Socrates is essentially human, but only accidentally wise.

Evaluative realism The view that some things are objectively valuable or worthwhile independent of our desires, attitudes, and practices.

Event A happening or occurrence, like a baseball game, a lecture, a wedding, a war, or a flash of lightning.

Expected utility See **utility**.

Expressivism The view that moral statements such as "Stealing is wrong" do not express beliefs, which are capable of being true or false, but rather serve to express states of mind that are not capable of truth or falsity. According to the expressivist, a sincere utterance of "Stealing is wrong" does not ascribe a moral property, wrongness, to certain acts. Rather, it expresses the speaker's *disapproval* of stealing, or her *intention* not to steal, or some similar state that can be characterized without invoking moral properties and which cannot be assessed as true or false.

Extension The extension of a word or **concept** is the set of things to which the word or concept applies. For example, the extension of the concept *horse* is the set of horses. The extension of the phrase "man with nine fingers" is the set of nine-fingered men. Terms with the same extension are *coextensional* or *coextensive*. (*Note:* Coextensional terms can be *contingently* coextensional; see **necessity and possibility**.) So if, as a matter of fact, every philosopher is a genius and every genius is a philosopher, then "philosopher" and "genius" have the same extension, despite the fact that there could have been a philosopher who is not a genius and vice versa.

Externalism and internalism about justification In epistemology, *internalism* is (roughly) the view that when a person has a **justified belief,** the facts in virtue of which the belief is justified must be accessible to the subject. *Externalism*, the denial of internalism, is the view that a belief may be justified in virtue of facts that lie beyond the subject's ken. One simple form of internalism holds that a belief is justified in virtue of facts about the subject's conscious experiences, assumed to be accessible to the subject. One simple form of externalism (called *reliabilism*) holds that a belief is justified in virtue of facts about the reliability of the causal process that produced the belief, regardless of whether the subject is in a position to know about this process or its reliability.

Externalism and internalism about the mind In the philosophy of mind, *internalism* is the view that all **mental states** are *intrinsic* states. (See **extrinsic and intrinsic**.) Equivalently, internalism is the view that if two people are perfect duplicates, exactly alike "from the skin in," they must have exactly the same mental states—the same beliefs, desires, intentions, sensory experiences, and so on. *Externalism*, the denial of internalism, is the view that some mental states involve the subject's relation to his or her environment and are thus *extrinsic*. According to an externalist, two people who are identical from the skin in may nevertheless have different beliefs because of differences in their respective environments.

Extrinsic and intrinsic An *intrinsic* **property** is a property a thing possess "on its own," regardless of its relations to other things. Alternatively, an intrinsic property is a property with respect to which *perfect duplicates* cannot differ. (A "perfect duplicate" of a certain dollar bill, say, is an atom-for-atom replica of the dollar bill, indistinguishable from the original by the most powerful microscopes.) For example, the property of being round is intrinsic, since any perfect duplicate of a round thing must be round. A property is *extrinsic* iff it is not intrinsic. For example, the property of *being made in the USA* is extrinsic, since there could be a pair of perfect duplicates—perhaps two copies of this book—one made in the USA, the other made elsewhere.

Fact A truth, a true **proposition.** That the Earth is round is a fact; equivalently, that the Earth is round is true, or is a true proposition.

Alternatively, a fact is something "in virtue of which" a true proposition is true. It is controversial whether there are facts in this alternative sense, but if there are, then they are not true propositions—instead, they "make" true propositions true, or "ground" the truth of propositions.

Falsificationism Narrowly, the view that a theory counts as genuinely scientific only if it can in principle be falsified; that is, shown to be false. More broadly, the view that science proceeds by framing theories and then seeking to falsify them by means of observation and experiment, retaining only those theories that have survived many such tests.

Fatalism The view that future events will occur regardless of what human beings do.

Final cause See **four causes.**

Finite and infinite Literally, "limited" and "unlimited."

Traditionally, a *finite quantity* is a quantity that can be exceeded or increased. For example, if an object weighs 5 grams, then its mass is finite, since it is possible for an object to weigh more than 5 grams. An *infinite quantity*, by contrast, cannot possibly be exceeded. To say that God's wisdom and mercy are infinite is to say that that nothing could possibly have been wiser or more merciful than God. An **entity** is infinite (in some respect) iff some feature of it is infinite. To say that space is infinite, for example, is to say that its size or volume could not possibly be exceeded or increased.

The words are used somewhat differently in mathematics. According to one definition, a set is infinite when the addition of a new member results in a set with the same size as the original. (Two sets are the same size iff they can be placed in one-one correspondence; that is, iff there is a mapping that associates each member of the first with exactly one member of the second, and vice versa.) The set of positive whole numbers $\{1, 2, 3, \ldots\}$ is infinite, since the result of adding a new member to the set—say, 0—yields a set $\{0, 1, 2, 3, \ldots\}$ that is the same size as the original. To see that these two sets are the same size, note that they can be placed in one-one correspondence as follows:

It is a striking fact about infinite sets that some infinite sets are larger than others. For example, the set of real numbers, or points on a line, is larger than the set of whole numbers, though both are infinite. Indeed, for every infinite set, there is a larger infinite set. A set may therefore be infinite in the mathematical sense without being infinite in the traditional sense (unsurpassably large).

Formal cause See **four causes.**

Formal validity See **soundness and validity.**

Foundationalism In epistemology, the view that whenever a person S knows some **proposition** p, S's knowledge of p is either **basic**—independent of his knowledge of other facts—or grounded in his basic knowledge. Alternatively, the view that whenever S is **justified** in believing p, S's justification for p is either basic—independent of his other beliefs—or grounded in his basic justified beliefs. **Classical foundationalism** is the view that whenever S is justified in holding a nonbasic belief, his justification ultimately derives from basic beliefs that are known with perfect certainty.

Four causes Aristotle (384–322 BCE) distinguishes four kinds of cause (or explanatory principle):

> The **material cause** of a thing is the matter that composes it. The material cause of the statue might be a certain quantity of bronze.
>
> The **formal cause** of a thing is the distinctive arrangement of parts that makes it the thing it is and which persists so long as the thing persists, even though its matter changes. The formal cause of a statue is its shape.
>
> The **efficient cause** of an object is the entity or process whose activity brings it into being. The formal cause of the statue is the sculptor, or some capacity of the sculptor, whose activity brings the statue into existence.
>
> The **final cause** of a thing is "that for the sake of which" it exists. The final cause of the statue might be aesthetic contemplation. The final cause of exercise is health.

Contemporary uses of "cause" do not correspond neatly to any of Aristotle's causes, although "efficient cause" comes closest.

Free will Roughly, the power to choose or to act without certain forms of determination or constraint; alternatively, the power of an agent to control or determine her own choices. Some writers define a free choice as a choice that is not determined in any way by prior causes. Other writers define a free choice as a choice that is not *forced* or *substantially constrained*, but which may nonetheless be caused. Free will is usually understood to be a distinctively human capacity. A dog playing in an open field may be free to *act* as he likes, because nothing gets in the way of his acting as he likes, but his choices are determined by his impulses, over which he has no control. A being with free will, by contrast, would possess the capacity to "step back" from his impulses in order to determine for himself whether to act on them.

Free will defense A proposed explanation of why an all-knowing, all-powerful, and all-loving God would permit suffering. God permits suffering because it is good for human beings to have free will, and God cannot prevent humans from inflicting suffering on others without removing their free will.

Function In logic and mathematics, a mapping from one collection (the *domain*) to another (the *range*) that associates each item in the domain with at most one item in the range. Thus, *heart of x* is a function from, say, the set of animals (the domain) to the set of organs (the range), since it associates each animal with at most one organ, its heart. By contrast, *kidney of x* is not a function, since many animals have more than one kidney. Thus, x^2 is a function (from real numbers to real numbers), since every real number has just one square, whereas $\sqrt{x}$ is not a function, since positive real numbers always have two square roots.

Functionalism In the philosophy of mind, the view that **mental states** are defined by their causes and effects, including their causal relations to other mental states. Thus, a functionalist might define *being in pain* as a state that is typically caused by damage to the body, and which typically causes certain behavior (e.g., wincing) and also certain other mental states, including the belief that one is in pain and the desire to change one's state. Functionalism is opposed to **dualism, the identity theory,** and also to **behaviorism,** according to which mental states can be defined in terms of their environmental causes and behavioral effects, without mentioning their relations to other mental states.

Genealogical method A method developed by Friedrich Nietzsche (1844–1900) for casting doubt on a social arrangement or a set of values (e.g., Christian morality) by examining the psychological and historical factors that gave rise to it. More generally, a genealogy explains a concept or practice by tracing it back to its origins. A genealogy in this more general sense need not cast doubt on the concept or practice.

Genealogy of morals See **genealogical method.**

God of the gaps A pejorative term for versions of the **design argument** that proceed by pointing to "gaps"—that is, to facts that current science cannot explain (e.g., the origin of life)—and then insisting that these facts require a supernatural explanation.

Hard problem of consciousness An expression introduced by David Chalmers (1966–). The problem of explaining why certain physical states (e.g., states of the brain) are associated with certain conscious states or with conscious states of any kind. Even if we had a complete account of the *neural correlates of consciousness*, the physical states that in fact underlie conscious states, the hard problem would still arise, since it would remain to say *why* these physical states give rise to conscious experience as they do.

Harm principle In political philosophy, the claim, due to John Stuart Mill (1806–1873), that a law that limits the freedom of citizens can only be justified if it serves to prevent harm to others. The principle precludes purely *paternalistic* laws that are designed to prevent individuals from harming themselves; certain forms of *morals legislation*, designed to deter conduct that may be wrong in itself but which does not cause harm to others; and perfectionist regulations, designed to foster human excellence.

Hedonism The view (sometimes called "ethical hedonism") that pleasure is the only intrinsic good; that is, the only thing worth pursuing for its own sake. Alternatively, the view that a person's level of well-being is determined by the nature, quantity, and distribution of her pains and pleasures.

Humanity, formula of See **categorical imperative**.

Idealism In metaphysics, the view that reality as a whole is in some sense mental or mind-dependent.

Identity Objects *A* and *B* are **numerically identical** iff they are one and the same thing: $A = B$. Mark Twain and Samuel Clemens are numerically identical, as are 2^2 and 4. If *A* and *B* are numerically identical, then the plural "are" is misleading: "they" are not two things, but one. Objects are **qualitatively** identical iff they are alike in all **intrinsic** respects; equivalently, iff they are perfect duplicates of one another. Numerically identical objects are alike in absolutely every respect. Qualitatively identical objects are alike in some respects (e.g., size, shape, chemical composition) though different in others (e.g., location, monetary value, etc.).

Identity theory (of mind) The view that every **mental state** is *numerically identical* (see **identity**) to a physical state; for example, the state of having a brain with such-and-such neural firing pattern.

Iff Abbreviation for "if and only if." See also **biconditional**.

Incompatibilism See **compatibilism**.

Indiscernibility of identicals See **Leibniz's law**.

Induction A form of **argument** in which the premise describes a pattern or regularity in the observed data, and the conclusion extends that regularity to cases that have not yet been examined. The simplest *inductive rule* is the rule of **enumerative induction**:

>   P1.   Every observed *F* is *G*.
>   Therefore:
>   C.   Every *F* is *G*.

Or more cautiously:

>   C*.   The next *F* we examine will be *G*.

More sophisticated inductive rules specify the conditions under which statistics gleaned from observation ("95 percent of *F*s are *G*") support generalizations and predictions about unexamined cases.

Inductive skepticism See **skepticism.**

Inference See **reasoning and inference.**

Inference to the best explanation Also called **abduction.** A form of argument in which the fact that some hypothesis *H* is the best available explanation of the evidence is taken to support the conclusion that *H* is true. In one version:

> P1. *H* is the best available explanation for some fact *F*.
> P2. *H* is a good explanation of *F* (and not just the best of a bad lot).
> Therefore:
> C. *H* is true.

Intentional content See **content (of a mental state).**

Internalism about the mind See **externalism and internalism about the mind.**

Internalism about justification See **externalism and internalism about justification.**

Intersectionality Broadly, the phenomenon of interaction between **categories** (or causal factors). Familiar from the behavioral sciences, and usually narrowly applied to social categories, in particular race, class, and sex/gender. Consider the categories *man* and *dress-wearer*. The effects of being a man and not wearing a dress are not dramatic, neither are the effects of not being a man and wearing a dress, or not being a man and not wearing a dress. However, the effects of being a man *and* wearing a dress *are* dramatic; this is an example of *non-additive effects*, or intersectionality.

Intrinsic See **extrinsic and intrinsic.**

Intuition A confident immediate judgment, often about a specific, hypothetical case, offered in support of a philosophical claim. For example, a philosopher may object to the view that we should always act so as to maximize happiness by citing the "intuition" that it would be wrong to kill John, an innocent person, in order to extract his organs for transplant into James, Joan, Jim, Jack, and Jane, even if this would increase the amount of happiness in the universe.

Intuitive certainty See **demonstrative certainty.**

Invalid See **soundness and validity.**

Justified See **justified belief.**

Justified belief *S* is justified in believing *p* iff *S*'s belief is "rightly held"; for example, *S* believes *p* on the basis of sufficient reasons or evidence for *p*, or adequate grounds. A belief can be true and yet unjustified, as when one makes a lucky guess. Also, a belief can justified but not true, as when one comes to believe that Jones is guilty on the basis of compelling but misleading evidence. (Some philosophers dispute this last claim because they hold that a belief in *p* is only "rightly held" if one knows *p*. Since one can only know *p* if *p* is true, it follows that no false belief is justified.)

Kantian Resembling the views of Immanuel Kant (1724–1804). *Kantian ethics* is a tradition in moral theory that seeks to articulate general **deontological** principles that apply to all rational agents. In epistemology, *Kantian humility* is the view that we cannot know the **intrinsic** properties of things. Ascribed to Kant by Rae Langton (1961–).

Knowledge argument A controversial argument against **physicalism** in the philosophy of mind due to Frank Jackson (1943–). Suppose Mary is an expert color scientist who knows all the physical facts, but who has been raised in a black-and-white environment and so has never seen red. When she sees a red thing for the first time, she learns a new fact. "I never knew that *that's* what it's like to see red!" we can imagine her saying. But she knew all the physical facts in advance. Hence (the knowledge argument concludes), physicalism is false.

Lawlike statement A statement or **proposition** that is suited, by its form and subject matter, to be a *law of nature*; for example,

Water boils at 100°C.
Water boils at 50°C.
$e = mc^2$.
$e = mc^3$.

Any statement that is in fact a law (e.g., the first and third of the above examples) is lawlike. But so are various false statements that are not laws but which might have been laws had the world been different (e.g., the second and fourth examples). Laws that have some tacit "all things equal" qualification, like the first example (water doesn't boil at 100°C on the summit of Mt. Everest) are *ceteris paribus* laws. Lawlike statements are supposed to be general in scope and not to refer to particular individuals. (Thus, the proposition that it snowed yesterday and the proposition that Fred is eating lunch are not lawlike, even if they are true.) Beyond this, there are no clear tests to distinguish lawlike statements from the rest.

Leibniz's law A principle of metaphysics central to the philosophy of Gottfried Leibniz (1646–1716) according to which objects A and B are **numerically identical** if and only if every **property** of A is a property of B, and vice versa. So formulated, the principle combines two principles:

The indiscernibility of identicals: If $A = B$, then every property of A is a property of B, and vice versa.
The identity of indiscernibles: If every property of A is a property of B, and vice versa, then $A = B$.

The indiscernibility of identicals is relatively uncontroversial. The identity of indiscernibles is also uncontroversial if properties such as *being identical to A* are allowed to count as properties. The principle is highly controversial, however, if only qualitative, *intrinsic* properties are allowed to count. So interpreted, the principle entails that no two snowflakes are exactly alike in shape, composition, and so forth, which may be true in fact but is certainly not a law of metaphysics.

Libertarianism In metaphysics, the view that human beings possess free will of a sort that is incompatible with determinism.

In political philosophy, the view that the government is justified in restricting the liberty of individuals only for a very narrow set of purposes; for example, preventing violence, protecting private property, and enforcing contracts. On one formulation, libertarianism is the view that liberty may be restricted only to better protect liberty itself.

Logical consequence See **entailment**.

Material cause See **four causes**.

Materialism In metaphysics, the view that the world is wholly material or physical. The term derives from a period in which the physical sciences focused exclusively on the properties of matter. Since modern physics recognizes many things that would not ordinarily be classified as *material*—for example, space-time and the various fields that pervade it—philosophers now often prefer to speak of **physicalism** (see that entry for a more precise characterization of the view). Materialism is incompatible with the existence of disembodied minds and God as traditionally conceived. It is often held to preclude the existence of **abstract objects**.

Mental state A psychological or mental condition or **property;** for example, *believing that it's sunny, wanting to go swimming, hoping for rain, being angry, having a headache, seeming to see a tomato.* Some philosophers would add states of knowing (e.g., *knowing that it's sunny*) and seeing (e.g., *seeing a tomato*) to this list. Philosophers sympathetic to *internalism* (see **externalism and internalism about the mind**) resist this on the grounds that knowing and seeing involve relations to the external environment.

Metaethics The part of philosophy concerned with the **metaphysics** and **epistemology** of ethics and with the linguistic function of ethical language. Metaethics asks, for example, whether ethical statements aim to describe a domain of ethical facts, and if so, whether those facts obtain objectively, independently of our beliefs about them. It asks whether moral words such as "right" and "wrong" pick out moral properties, and if so, whether they can be defined in more fundamental (non-moral) terms. Metaethics asks whether ethical knowledge is possible, and in particular, whether it requires a special capacity for moral intuition. Metaethics is sometimes contrasted with *normative ethics*, which comprises both *ethical theory* (the effort to formulate and justify general moral principles) and *applied ethics* (the effort to solve relatively concrete moral problems).

Metaphysics The part of philosophy concerned with the nature and structure of reality. Contrasted with, for example, **epistemology,** the part of philosophy concerned with our knowledge of reality.

Mind-body problem The problem of describing the relation between our mental lives and the physical aspects of our brains, bodies, and environments.

Modus ponens and modus tollens Forms of formally valid argument (see **soundness and validity**):

Modus ponens:	If P then Q
	P
	Therefore:
	Q
Modus tollens:	If P then Q
	Not-Q
	Therefore:
	Not-P

Moorean shift (G. E. Moore shift)   A strategy for rebutting philosophical **arguments** whose conclusions clash with common sense, named for the British philosopher G. E. Moore (1873–1958). The strategy is available whenever a premise of the argument is a nonobvious philosophical thesis. In such cases, the Moorean shift consists in treating the argument not as a proof of its conclusion, but rather as a refutation of the philosophical premise. The underlying idea is that given a clash between a philosophical thesis and a core commitment of common sense—sometimes called a *Moorean fact*—the rational option is to retain the commonsense commitment and give up the philosophical thesis. For example, suppose a philosopher argues that you cannot know that you have a body because (a) you can only know this sort of thing if you can prove it from premises about your experience, and (b) your experiences are consistent with the hypothesis that you do not have a body. The Moorean shift is to say: "Since I certainly *do* know that I have a body, at least one of your philosophical assumptions (a) and (b) must be mistaken."

Moral nihilism   The view that there are no moral differences between actions or people. Thus, no actions are right, and none are wrong; no persons are morally good, and none are morally bad. (See **error theory**.) A nihilist does not simply say, as the moral skeptic does, that we cannot *know* which actions are right and which are wrong, or which are good and which are bad. The nihilist denies that there are any moral differences to know about. (See **skepticism**.)

Moral realism   The view that moral statements describe a domain of moral facts, at least some of which obtain independently of our moral beliefs and practices.

Moral responsibility   A person is morally responsible for an action iff she is properly held accountable for it or praised or blamed on the basis of it.

Natural religion   See **natural theology**.

Natural rights   Rights that human beings possess independently of law, government, or any other human convention or institution (e.g., the right to self-defense).

Natural theology (or natural religion)   The effort to establish principles of religion by scientific means, without appeal to revelation or religious experience. Proponents of natural theology typically invoke the **cosmological argument** and/or the **design argument** to establish the existence of a deity and at least some of its key attributes. The **cosmological fine-tuning argument** is a recent innovation in natural theology.

Necessary and sufficient conditions   Being *G* is a *necessary condition* for being *F* iff it is impossible for a thing to be *F* without being *G*. Being *G* is a *sufficient condition* for being *F* iff it is impossible for a thing to be *G* without being *F*. For example, being a poodle is sufficient for being a dog, and being a dog is necessary for being a poodle. One of the chief aims of philosophical **analysis** is to supply nontrivial necessary and sufficient conditions for the application of important words and concepts. An analysis of "knowledge," for example, will supply a set of conditions for the truth of "*S* knows *p*" that are *individually necessary* and *jointly sufficient*.

Necessity and possibility   A **proposition** *p* is *necessary* (or *necessarily true*, or a *necessary truth*) iff *p* could not possibly have been false; *p* is *possible* (or *possibly true*) iff *p* could have been true; *p* is *impossible* iff its **negation,** not-*p*, is necessary; *p* is *contingent* iff both *p* and not-*p* are possible; *p* is *contingently true* iff *p* is both contingent and true.

Another explanation appeals to **possible worlds:** a proposition is possible iff there is a possible world in which it is true; a proposition is necessary iff it is true in all possible worlds. An impossible proposition is true in no possible world, and a contingent proposition is true in some possible worlds but not in others.

A *necessary being* is a being that could not have failed to exist or a being that exists in every possible world. Putative examples include God and the objects of pure mathematics (e.g., numbers). A *contingent being* is a being that exists in some possible worlds but not in others. It is widely thought that ordinary objects—mountains, people—are contingent beings, though some philosophers deny this.

Philosophers distinguish several varieties of necessity and possibility. For example:

A proposition is *absolutely* or *metaphysically* necessary if there is no possible world of any sort in which it is false. (Similarly, a proposition is *absolutely* or *metaphysically impossible* if there is no possible world of any sort in which it is true.) Examples are controversial, but the truths of pure logic and mathematics are widely regarded as metaphysically necessary, as are **analytic** truths (e.g., "Hexagons are six-sided") and truths about the *essential properties* of things (e.g., "Gold is a metal"). (See **essence and accident.**)

A proposition is *nomologically* or *physically necessary* iff it holds in every possible world in which the laws of nature hold. Thus, it is nomologically necessary that massive bodies attract, even though there could have been a world without gravity in which massive bodies do not attract. A proposition is *physically possible* iff it is consistent with the laws of physics.

A proposition is *mathematically* necessary iff it is a logical consequence of the truths of mathematics and *logically* necessary iff it is a consequence of the laws of logic. Thus, it is *mathematically impossible* to tile a rectangle with 17 square tiles and *logically impossible* for an object to be both square and not square at the same time.

Negation A sentence of the form "It is not the case that *P*" or some related form, either in a natural language or a formal logical language. In symbolic logic, usually written as "*~P.*" By definition, "*~P*" is true iff "*P*" is false.

The negation of a **proposition** *p*, *not-p*, is a proposition that, necessarily, is true iff *p* is false.

Non-demonstrative argument (or inference) See **proof.**

Normativity Narrowly, a normative statement is a statement about how things ought to be or about how a person ought to think or act. More broadly, a normative statement is a statement that evaluates or applies a standard. Normative statements in the broad sense include claims about what is good or desirable, claims about virtue and vice, and claims to the effect that an action or mental state is rational or reasonable or justified. Normative statements are contrasted with *descriptive* (better: *nonnormative*) statements. Thus the claim that John *is* eating his vegetables is descriptive; the claim that he *ought* to eat them is normative.

Numerically identical See **identity.**

Object Sometimes used broadly, as interchangeable with **entity**. On a narrower usage, an object is a **particular** that is not an **event**: on this usage, Barack Obama, Jupiter, and (more controversially) the number 17 are objects, while Obama's second inauguration and the First World War are not.

Objective list theory The view that there are many fundamental goods—things worth pursuing for their own sake; for example, knowledge, pleasure, friendship, love, and so forth. Alternatively, the view that an agent's level of utility or well-being depends on many such factors. Objective list theories typically add that at least some fundamental goods or determinants of well-being concern the agent's relations to the world (e.g., knowledge, friendship) and not just her *intrinsic* **mental states** (e.g., pleasure). (See **extrinsic and intrinsic**.) The plurality of goods is given by a *list* because the objective list theorist believes that there is no unifying explanation of what goes on the list.

Occam's razor A methodological principle of parsimony in theorizing, often rendered by the slogan "entities are not to be multiplied beyond necessity," sometimes misattributed to William of Occam (or Ockham) (c. 1287–1347). More generally, the view that when all else is equal, it is reasonable to prefer a simple theory to a more complex one.

Omnibenevolent Perfectly good; morally flawless.

Omnipotent All-powerful; capable of performing any act or bringing about any (possible) state of affairs.

Omniscient All-knowing. An omniscient being knows every true **proposition** and has no false beliefs.

Ontological argument An **a priori** argument for the existence of God that seeks to show that a correct account of God's nature (alternatively, a correct account of the concept *God*) entails that God exists. A simple version:

> P1.   God is, by definition, an absolutely perfect being.
> P2.   Existence is a perfection. (Just as a perfect being must be omniscient and omnipotent, so a perfect being must exist.)
> Therefore:
> C.   God exists.

The premises are meant to be acceptable to the *atheist* (the proponent of **atheism**) who must understand the word "God" if she is to deny that God exists. The argument as a whole is designed to show that just as it is incoherent to deny that God is wise, it is likewise incoherent to deny that God exists. The most widely discussed versions of the argument are due to Anselm of Canterbury (c. 1033–1109).

Ontology The study of being. Ontology seeks to clarify the sense (or senses) in which a thing may be said to be, or to exist, and to provide an account of the most basic categories of being. The *ontology of a theory* is the set of **entities** that exist according to the theory. The ontology of the standard model of particle physics, for example, includes quarks. A theorist is *ontologically committed* to Fs iff her views **entail** that Fs exist. So physicists who accept the standard model are ontologically committed to quarks.

Paradox An apparently **valid argument** with apparently true premises, but with an apparently false conclusion. Faced with a paradox, you have three options: deny one of the premises, deny the validity of the argument, or accept the conclusion. A famous and ancient paradox is the *paradox of the heap*:

P1. Zero grains of sand do not make a heap.

P2. For all numbers n, if n grains of sand do not make a heap, then $n + 1$ grains of sand do not make a heap.

These two (apparently true) premises (apparently) **entail** that 1 grain does not make a heap, that 2 grains do not make a heap, and so on; hence,

C. No number of grains of sand, no matter how large, make a heap.

To *solve* the paradox is to make a compelling philosophical case either for rejecting one of the premises or for denying the validity of the argument.

Particulars and universals A *particular* is an individual, nonrepeatable **object** or **event** (e.g., you, your **token** copy of this book, or your first philosophy lecture). A universal is an item that is (typically) capable of being repeated or multiply instantiated; for example, the **property** of being human (instantiated by you, but also by Socrates); the **relation** of being *smaller than* (instantiated by Woody Allen and Charles Barkley, but also by the moon and the sun); the *Norton Introduction to Philosophy*, understood as a **type** with many tokens; and so on. The word "universal" is sometimes used more narrowly to refer to properties and relations but not to types.

Pascal's wager An argument due to Blaise Pascal (1623–1662) that seeks to show that we have conclusive reasons of self-interest to believe that God exists, even if there is no evidence whatsoever for God's existence. The argument assumes that if there is a God, he rewards believers with infinite happiness. It then treats the decision whether to believe in God as a gamble in which one wagers one's earthly life for the prospect of gaining this infinite happiness. The argument assumes a framework for evaluating gambles that resembles modern **decision theory.** The key feature of the framework is the assumption that a gamble is rational iff its **expected utility** is at least as great as that of any alternative open to the agent. The argument crucially involves the claim that the expected utility of belief in God is infinite, whereas the expected value of disbelief is finite, even if God's existence is improbable.

Perfectionism An ethical outlook that characterizes the human good in terms of certain kinds of excellences à excellence, say, artistic or scientific. According to an *ethical perfectionist*, the best human life is not necessarily the most pleasurable life or the life a person most wants to lead, but a life that achieves these excellences. A *moral perfectionist* holds that the right way to live is the way that achieves these excellences: not simply that it would be good to achieve them but that we ought to achieve them. In politics, perfectionists hold that the right laws and policies foster the excellences that are components of the best human lives.

Persistence In metaphysics, an object is said to persist through an interval of time iff it exists at every moment in the interval. A leaf that turns from green to red persists through the change iff there is a single item that exists at each moment of the process. Some philosophers hold that what we call "change" is really a process in which one object (e.g., the green leaf) is replaced by another (the red leaf). If this is right in general, then strictly speaking nothing persists through change.

Personal knowledge The sort of knowledge we attribute when we say, for example, that Fred knows Mary or that Alice knows London well. See also **procedural knowledge** and **propositional knowledge**.

Phenomenal character See **qualia**.

Phenomenal consciousness A term introduced by Ned Block (1942–). A **mental state** is phenomenally conscious iff there is "something that it is like" to be in that state; that is, iff the mental state has **qualia**. A phenomenally conscious *creature* is a creature who is in a phenomenally conscious state. The states of *feeling pain*, or *seeing green*, or *tasting sweetness* are (at least typically) phenomenally conscious. The states of *believing that there are canals on Mars* or *wanting to go to graduate school* are (at least typically) not phenomenally conscious. We don't know what it's like to perceive insects by bat echolocation (and perhaps we could never know), but if there *is* something it is like to perceive in that way, then bats are often phenomenally conscious.

Phenomenology The study of the objects and structures of consciousness, as they seem from the first-person perspective. Sometimes used in a strict sense for an approach to philosophy pioneered by Edmund Husserl (1859–1938). In contemporary philosophy of mind, used for any attempt to characterize how things appear to us in perception or reflection.

Physical object See **physicalism**.

Physical possibility See **necessity and possibility**.

Physicalism Also known as **materialism**. The view that the world is entirely physical: every **object** a physical object, every **property** a physical property, and so forth. Sometimes given a (weaker) formulation as a **supervenience** thesis: all the **facts** supervene on, or are determined by, the physical facts (roughly, facts expressible in the language of a complete physics). This version of physicalism can also be put as the thesis that any *minimal physical duplicate* of the actual world is a perfect duplicate of the actual world. (A minimal physical duplicate of the actual world is a possible world that exactly resembles the actual world in every physical respect, and which contains nothing more than is needed to be a physical duplicate of it.)

    Physicalism can be restricted to a particular phenomenon: *physicalism about color* is the view that the colors are physical properties, or that the color facts supervene on the physical facts. *Physicalism about the mind* (opposed to **dualism**) is the view that **mental states** are physical states, or that mental facts supervene on the physical facts.

Possibility See **necessity and possibility**.

Possible world A maximally specific way things could have been. Picturesquely, a novel or story that (a) *could have been true* and (b) is *complete* in the sense that for every **proposition** *p*, either *p* or its **negation** is true according to the story. The *actual world* is the maximally specific way things in fact *are*. See also **necessity and possibility**.

Practical vs. theoretical rationality Practical rationality is the sort of rationality that governs choice and action; *theoretical* or *epistemic rationality* is the sort of rationality that governs the revision of belief in response to evidence. (See **theoretical [or epistemic] rationality**.)

    Note: We can ask whether it would be practically rational to form or hold a belief. For example, **Pascal's wager** is designed to show that it is in your interest to believe that God exists even if you have no evidence for God's existence. Some writers therefore hold that our beliefs are governed both by the requirements of theoretical rationality and by the (perhaps conflicting) requirements of practical rationality.

Pragmatist theory of truth Roughly, the view that a **proposition** is true iff it would be useful for practical and scientific purposes to believe it. Associated with William James (1842–1910).

Predicate A linguistic expression that combines with a proper name (or a sequence of proper names) to yield a complete sentence. So, for example, " . . . is tall" and " . . . loves . . ." are predicates, since they yield complete sentences when the blanks are filled in by names. Sometimes we omit the copula (the linking verb), "is," and say that "tall" by itself qualifies as a predicate.

Preference-satisfaction theory In ethics, the view that a person's utility or well-being is determined by the extent to which her preferences are satisfied. An alternative to **hedonism** and the **objective list theory**.

Premise See **argument**.

Primary and secondary qualities A distinction drawn in several ways by philosophers in the early modern period, notably John Locke (1632–1704). *Primary* qualities are qualities (**properties**) possessed by bodies independently of our experience of them and which figure in a correct scientific account of their behavior. Examples include size, mass, and motion. *Secondary* qualities, by contrast, are not possessed by bodies independently of our experience of them, but rather consist in **dispositions** to produce certain sorts of experiences in us, or perhaps in features *of our experiences* that we mistakenly locate in external objects. On this way of using the terminology, it is a controversial thesis that colors (for example) are secondary qualities. Alternatively, secondary qualities are sometimes defined by means of a list including color, taste, and odor, and excluding size, weight, and motion. In this sense, everyone agrees that colors are secondary qualities.

Problem of induction Inductive **reasoning** assumes that the objects we have examined constitute a representative sample of the domain under investigation, or equivalently, that the unexamined parts of the domain resemble the examined parts in relevant respects. Taken narrowly, the problem of induction is the problem of showing how this assumption can be justified. Some philosophers distinguish the *descriptive problem of induction*, which seeks to an explicit formulation of the principles that guide our inductive reasoning, from the *normative problem of induction*: the problem of showing that these principles are justified.

Procedural knowledge The sort of knowledge we attribute when we say, for example, that John knows how to ride a bicycle, or that Samantha knows how to fix the toaster. See also **personal knowledge** and **propositional knowledge**.

Proof A *valid* **argument** that establishes its conclusion with certainty. Alternatively, a *formally valid* argument whose premises are true (or are known to be true). (See **soundness and validity**.) Also known as a *demonstrative argument*. A cogent argument that is not a proof is a *non-demonstrative* argument.

In formal logic, a proof in a formal system is an argument whose premises are **axioms** or *theorems* of the system and whose conclusion follows from the premises according to the rules of the system.

Projectable property A **property** suitable for use in **inductive** reasoning. The fact that every dog so far examined has been found to be warm-blooded gives us reason to believe that all dogs are warm-blooded. The property of *being warm-blooded* is thus projectable. By contrast, the fact that every dog so far examined has been *observed before the year 2100* gives us no reason to believe that all dogs (past, present, and future) have this feature. So the property of *being observed before 2100* is not projectable.

Properly basic belief See **basic belief and knowledge.**

Property A *feature* or *attribute*. Properties are often denoted by abstract nouns, for example, "whiteness," "wisdom," or by complex noun phrases like "(the property of) weighing 2 grams." Unlike **particulars,** properties have *instances.* Many properties have multiple instances—the many white things are all instances of whiteness. But there may be properties with only one instance (*being John Malkovich*) or with no instances at all (*the property of being a round square*). Some philosophers hold that properties literally exist *in* the items that possess them; others hold that properties do not exist in space and are therefore **abstract objects.** Talk of *categories* is interchangeable with talk of properties: having the property *being a cat* is equivalent to being a member of, or being included in, the category *cat.*

Proposition When a French speaker utters the sentence "La neige est blanche" and a German speaker utters "Schnee ist weiß," they have used different words to make the *same* claim or statement, namely *that snow is white.* The content of this shared claim or statement is called a *proposition,* the proposition that snow is white. Propositions can be assessed for truth or falsity: the proposition that snow is white is true, the proposition that snow is purple is false. Propositions are commonly taken to play a number of roles in metaphysics and the philosophy of mind and language. They are said to be:

> The primary bearers of truth and falsity: when a sentence is true, that is because the proposition it expresses is true. When a belief is true, that is because the proposition that is its **content** à content is true.
>
> The meanings of (declarative) sentences: "La neige est blanche" and "Schnee ist weiß" both have the same meaning, the proposition *that snow is white.*
>
> The contents of **propositional attitudes** such as belief and hope: Carlos believes/hopes *that it will rain.*
>
> The objects of certain linguistic acts: Marcus asserted/denied/implied *that Lisa is a lawyer.*
>
> **Facts,** when true: *That the earth is round* is a fact.

It is a matter of controversy whether one kind of thing can play all of these roles.

Propositional attitude A mental state that consists in a relation between a person and a proposition. If Alfred believes that the pope is infallible, then Alfred bears a certain relation—the belief relation—to a certain proposition: the proposition that the pope is infallible. If Elizabeth hopes that the pope is infallible, then Elizabeth bears a different relation—the hope relation—to the same proposition. Believing and hoping are thus propositional attitudes: relations to—or attitudes toward—propositions. Wanting is commonly taken to be another example, but this is not as clear, because the most natural ways of ascribing wants do not employ a "that-clause"; for example, "Alfred wants pizza."

Propositional knowledge *Factual* knowledge, knowledge that something is the case; the sort of knowledge we attribute when we say, for example, that Eleanor knows that Sue is a philosopher. See also **personal knowledge** and **procedural knowledge.**

Psychophysical laws Laws governing the relation between **mental states** and physical states. (See also **lawlike statement.**)

Qualia From Latin, "of what kind" (singular: *quale*). *Seeing green* is a **phenomenally conscious mental state,** and so are *seeing pink, being in pain,* and *tasting bitterness.* However, they are quite different states, in the sense that what it's like to see green is quite different from (for example) what it's like to taste bitterness. Put in the terminology of "qualia," *seeing green* and *tasting bitterness* have different qualia. In an alternative terminology, they have a different *subjective* (or *qualitative* or *phenomenal*) *character.*

In this broad sense of "qualia," only an **eliminativist** about phenomenal consciousness would deny that mental states have qualia. But there is a narrower sense of the term, according to which qualia are (in addition) *nonphysical* **properties** of mental states. In this narrow sense, **physicalists** deny that mental states have qualia.

In yet another sense of the term, qualia are perceptual qualities or properties; for example, colors and tastes. In this sense, qualia are not properties of mental states but (putative) properties of things in our environment, such as cucumbers and coffee.

Qualitative (or subjective) character See **qualia.**

Quantifier Expressions such as "all," "some," "many," "few," and "at least one" that serve to express claims about quantities of things; for example, "All/some/many/few students attended the lecture." "All" and "every" are *universal quantifiers,* written in symbolic logic as "$\forall$." Statements such as "All professors are wise" are *universally quantified statements* or *universal generalizations.* "Some" and "at least one" are *existential quantifiers,* written in symbolic logic as "$\exists$." Philosophers (but not linguists) often classify "there is . . ." and "there are . . ." as existential quantifiers, on the ground that "There are talking dogs" is equivalent to "Some dogs talk."

Realism Realism about Fs is the view that there are Fs, or that some things have the property of being F. Thus, *realism about numbers* is the view that there are numbers, and *realism about color* is the view that some things have the property of being colored. Realism is opposed to **eliminativism.**

Reasoning and inference The psychological process of forming new beliefs on the basis of other beliefs (or suppositions). For example, a detective may form the belief that the butler committed the murder on the basis of her beliefs that the butler had means, motive, and opportunity. Alternatively, the detective might suppose that the gardener committed the murder, but argue that this supposition or assumption leads to absurdity, then conclude that the butler must be the murderer because he is the sole remaining suspect.

Reasoning is often divided into *theoretical reasoning* (*inference*, or reasoning as explained above) and *practical reasoning*, which results in an intention or decision to do something.

Reductio ad absurdum A form of **argument** in which a **proposition** *p* is established by showing that its **negation**, not-*p*, **entails** a contradiction or some other manifestly absurd conclusion.

Reductionism In the philosophy of science, reductionism about a domain of inquiry (e.g., psychology, biology, economics) is the view that every **concept** in the domain can be **analyzed** or defined in terms drawn from a more fundamental science (often physics). The term is sometimes used more broadly for the view that facts in one area (e.g., psychology) can be explained in more fundamental terms, and so amount to nothing "over and above" these more basic facts.

In the philosophy of personal **identity,** reductionism is the view that the facts about personal identity over time are fully determined by facts that can be stated without reference to personal identity; for example, facts about the physical and psychological relations that hold between persons existing at different times.

Reflective equilibrium A method for inquiry in ethics and other areas that begins from our firmly held "considered judgments" about particular cases and candidate general principles. It then assesses whether our general principles are consistent with our judgments about cases and whether the principles explain and illuminate these judgments. Where there is a conflict, the investigator is to revise either the principles or judgments until the two harmonize and the principles helpfully explain and entail a set of considered judgments we regard as reasonable. Proponents of the method hold that when a stable view of this sort (an equilibrium) has been achieved (through reflection), we are justified in accepting it even if we have no independent evidence for its correctness.

"Reflective equilibrium" sometimes denotes the process of harmonizing one's particular judgments and general principles and sometimes denotes the product of this process; that is, the equilibrium point that is sought.

Regularity theory of causation The view that causation is to be analyzed in terms of general regularities. In one version:

Event *C* causes event *E* iff

C is an event of kind *F*.
E is an event of kind *G*.

and

Throughout the universe, events of kind *F* are always followed by events of kind *G*.

Relation A relation is a **universal** instantiated by two or more entities or *terms*. Thus ... *is taller than* ... is a *two-place relation* (also called a *binary relation*), since it relates two terms—John is taller than Sam—whereas ... *is between* ... *and* ... is a *three-place relation*, since it relates three terms: Chicago is between New York and San Francisco. (A more expansive definition counts **properties** as one-place relations.) The terms of a relation are its *relata*.

A binary relation R is *reflexive* iff every object bears R to itself. Examples: **numerical identity,** sameness of height, weight, color.

A binary relation R is *symmetric* iff whenever x bears R to y, y bears R to x. Examples: ... *is married to* ...; ... *lives next door to* ...

A binary relation R is *transitive* iff whenever x bears R to y and y bears R to z, x bears R to z. Examples: ... *is taller than* ...; ... *is exactly the same color as* ...

A binary relation R is an *equivalence relation* iff R is reflexive, symmetric, and transitive. Examples: ... *is the same height as* ...; ... *is parallel to* ...

The *converse* of a binary relation R is the relation R^* such that x bears R to y iff y bears R^* to x. Example: ... *is shorter than* ... is the converse of ... *is taller than* ...

Relations of ideas See **analytic and synthetic.**

Reliabilism See **externalism and internalism about justification.**

Representational content See **content (of a mental state).**

Rule consequentialism See **consequentialism.**

Rule utilitarianism See **utilitarianism.**

Secondary quality See **primary and secondary qualities.**

Self-evident proposition A proposition that can be known immediately, without further reasoning, by anyone who grasps it. Putative examples include basic logical principles (e.g., if $a = b$ then $b = a$), basic mathematical principles (e.g., between any two points exactly one straight line can be drawn), and basic moral principles (e.g., evil is to be avoided). According to the American Declaration of Independence, it is a self-evident truth that all men are created equal.

Sense data The *sense datum theory* holds that in sensory experience, one is immediately or directly aware of *sense data*—patches of color, sounds, odors—that invariably *are* as they *appear*. If you look at the mountains in the distance and they look purple, the *mountains* need not be purple. However, according to the sense datum theory, you *are* aware of a something that *really is* purple; namely, a purple *sense datum*. If there is such a thing, it is not a physical object, since there need be no purple physical object in the vicinity. Some versions of the theory hold that sense data cannot exist unperceived; others hold that they are entirely mind-independent.

Skeptical hypothesis Arguments for **skepticism** often proceed by describing a hypothetical scenario—a skeptical hypothesis—that is alleged to be consistent with our evidence, but in which our beliefs would be radically and systematically mistaken. Famous examples include the *dream hypothesis*, according to which you are currently dreaming; the *brain in a vat hypothesis*, according to which you are a disembodied brain whose sensory receptors are being stimulated by a supercomputer; and the *no past hypothesis* (due to Bertrand Russell [1872–1970]), according to which the physical universe was created 5 minutes ago with all of the traces of an apparent "past" in place.

Skepticism (also spelled "scepticism") The view that nothing is known about a certain subject matter or that we do not have **justified** beliefs about it. *Global skepticism* is the view that there is no knowledge (or justified belief) at all. *Local skepticisms* are (at least to some extent) selective: for example, *moral* skepticism is the view that we have no moral knowledge; *inductive* skepticism is the view that *inductive arguments* (see **induction**) are never **cogent;** *external world* skepticism is the view that we have no knowledge of our environment.

Social contract theory An approach to political philosophy according to which political arrangements are justified iff they could (or, in some formulations, would) have been rationally agreed to by all who are subject to them. Social contract theories are typically hypothetical: they do not claim that people have *actually* agreed to political arrangements, but rather that they would agree under certain conditions— some kind of initial situation—suited to assessing political arrangements. Social contract theorists include Thomas Hobbes (1588–1679), John Locke (1632–1704), Jean-Jacques Rousseau (1712–1778), and John Rawls (1921–2002).

Solipsism The view that there is only one conscious subject, and that reality as a whole exists (or can be known to exist) only insofar as this subject is conscious of it.

Soundness and validity An **argument** is *valid* iff it is absolutely impossible for the premises to be true and the conclusion false. For example:

P1. The book on the table is scarlet.
Therefore:
C. The book on the table is red.

An argument is *formally valid* iff every argument that shares its *form* is valid. Thus the argument just given is not formally valid, but

P1. Simon is a philosopher.
P2. All philosophers are subtle.
Therefore:
C. Simon is subtle.

is a formally valid argument because it is an instance of the valid form

P1. A is F.
P2. All Fs are G.
Therefore:
C. A is G.

A *sound* argument is a *valid* argument with true premises.

P1. If a number is even, then it is divisible by 2.
P2. 8 is even.
Therefore:
C. 8 is divisible by 2.

Sovereign The supreme authority in a territory. In a monarchy, the monarch is sovereign; in a democracy, the people are sovereign. Though the sovereign is the supreme authority, the sovereign's authority need not be unlimited or unconditional. Sovereign authority may be subject to a constitution that defines how the authority is to be exercised and what its limits are. A sovereign whose authority is not limited in this way is *absolute*.

Standard decision theory See **decision theory.**

State of nature In political philosophy, the condition of human beings living outside of a state, not subject to any political authority.

Stuff In metaphysics, a category that includes *water, plastic*, and other items allegedly denoted by (some) *mass nouns*: common nouns that have no plural and cannot be modified by numerical adjectives (like "seven"). Thus "rice" (no plural) is a mass noun, while "chair" is a *count* noun. Many nouns occur in both mass and count forms: there is *some hair* in the soup (mass occurrence of "hair"); there are *three hairs* in the soup (count occurrence).

Subjectivism In ethics, the view that moral statements are to be analyzed as statements about the subjective mental states of the speaker or some group to which the speaker belongs. Thus, the subjectivist might claim that "Stealing is wrong" simply means: "I disapprove of stealing" or "Stealing is prohibited by the moral system that my culture accepts." Subjectivism is to be contrasted with **expressivism,** the view that moral statements *express* (but do not describe) the speaker's mental states. Analogy: Someone who says "Ouch!" expresses his pain; someone who says "I am in pain" describes his pain.

Substance Roughly, an independently existing **entity.** Traditional metaphysics draws a distinction between substances, which exist *in themselves*, and beings of other sorts, which exist only *in* substances, or as modifications of substances. Thus an animal might be a substance, whereas its various **properties,** the species to which it belongs, and its shape, would not be substances. Alternatively, the word is sometimes used for the basic or fundamental entities: items that exist, but not in virtue of the existence of other things. When the word is used in this way, even though Socrates exists and exemplifies various properties, he is not a substance because he exists in virtue of the arrangement of the atoms (or subatomic particles) that compose him. On a view of this sort, elementary particles might qualify as substances.

Sufficient condition See **necessary and sufficient conditions.**

Supererogatory Relating to the performance of morally good actions that go beyond the demands of duty.

Supervenience A relation between one class of facts (the *higher-level* or *supervenient* facts) and a class of more fundamental facts (the *supervenience base*) according to which the higher-level facts are fixed or determined by facts in the base. Thus, the biological facts plausibly supervene on the physical facts in the following sense: two situations that are exactly alike in every physical respect—down to the last atom—must also be alike in every biological respect. More generally, the B-facts supervene on the A-facts iff the B-facts cannot differ unless the A-facts also differ. ("No B-difference without an A-difference.") Supervenience claims are common in philosophy. For example, it is widely held that the moral facts supervene on the purely descriptive, non-moral facts in the following strong sense: if two actions differ in some moral respect (the one good, the other bad, say), then they must also differ in some non-moral respect. Many philosophical doctrines are framed as supervenience theses. Thus, **physicalism** is sometimes formulated as the thesis that all of the facts supervene on the physical facts.

Symmetric relation See **relation.**

Synthetic statement See **analytic and synthetic.**

Theism The view that at least one god exists.

Theodicy A response to the **argument from evil** that seeks to show that evil and suffering in the world are compatible with the existence of a perfect God.

Theoretical (or epistemic) rationality A *theoretical* (or *epistemic*) *reason* for believing that p is a fact that supports the conclusion that p is true. A *practical* (or *pragmatic*) *reason* for believing that p is a reason for thinking that it would be good or beneficial to believe that p regardless of whether p is true. Thus, the fact that the pavement is wet is a theoretical reason to believe that it has rained, while the fact you will be happier if you believe that God exists is a practical, though not an epistemic, reason to believe that God exists.

See also **practical rationality.**

Tokens See **types and tokens.**

Types and tokens In metaphysics, a *type* is a kind or category of which there may be many concrete instances or examples or *tokens*. Thus, a particular inscription of the sentence

The cat sat on the mat.

will contain five word types—"the," "cat," "sat," "on" and "mat"—but six word *tokens*: one token each of "cat," "sat," "on" and "mat," but two distinct tokens of "the." The tokens of a given type are unrepeatable individuals, whereas the types themselves are **universals.**

Another example: The particular copy of the *Norton Introduction to Philosophy* you are currently holding is one of many *tokens* of a single *type*, the only book edited by Rosen, Byrne, Cohen, Harman, and Shiffrin.

Undermining evidence Evidence that weakens the force of evidence previously obtained.

Uniformity of nature John Stuart Mill's (1806–1873) name for the principle that allegedly underlies inductive reasoning. In David Hume's (1711–1776) rough formulation, it is the assumption that *the future will resemble the past*, or more generally: "If, in a large sample, all observed Fs are G, then (probably) all Fs are G." The principle is sometimes put as the thesis that nature is governed by laws (or regularities) that hold in all times and places.

Universal law, formula of See **categorical imperative.**

Universals See **particulars and universals.**

Utilitarianism A form of **consequentialism** according to which an act is morally right if and only if it would produce more net happiness (or pleasure) overall than any other act open to the agent (*act utilitarianism*). Alternatively, the view that an act is right iff it is permitted by a set of rules with which general compliance would maximize happiness (*rule utilitarianism*).

Utility In *ethics*, a term that refers to the well-being of a person and plays an especially important role in **utilitarianism.** Different theories measure utility in different ways. Some, like **hedonism,** focus exclusively on a person's mental states, often placing great emphasis on the duration and intensity of pleasures and pains. Other theories, such as **preference-satisfaction theories** and **objective list theories,** assess a person's utility in terms both of her mental states and aspects of her objective circumstances.

In **decision theory,** a measure of an agent's preferences for different outcomes, the utility of A for an agent is greater than the utility of B for that agent if and only if the agent prefers A to B. The decision-theoretic utility of an outcome is a subjective matter. It is not a function of the outcome's moral value, or its real objective value, or its value to society. It is determined entirely by an agent's desire for the outcome or by his preference for it over other outcomes. In economics it is sometimes assumed, with many caveats, that the utility you attach to an outcome can be measured by determining how much you would be willing to pay to bring it about.

The **expected utility** of an action is the sum of the utilities of the various outcomes the act might produce, each weighted by the probability that the action will produce that outcome. For example, if an action (say, bringing one's umbrella) has a utility of 10 if it rains and a utility of 2 if it does not, then the expected utility of the act is

(10 × the probability that it will rain) + (2 × the probability that it will not rain)

Valid argument See **soundness and validity.**

Validity See **soundness and validity.**

Virtue ethics The view that ethics is mainly concerned with describing various virtues of character and promoting their cultivation. The view is sometimes understood as an alternative to **consequentialism** and **deontology,** according to which the right action is identified, not as the act with the best consequences or the act that conforms to authoritative rules, but rather with the act that a virtuous agent would perform in the agent's circumstances.

Warrant In epistemology, sometimes used loosely as a synonym for "evidence" or "justification." Alternatively, following Alvin Plantinga (1932–), a technical term for whatever must be added to true belief to yield knowledge.

Zombies In the philosophy of mind, hypothetical creatures exactly like human beings in all physical and biological respects but who are never **phenomenally conscious.** If there could have been zombies, then **physicalism** is false.

Credits

Saul A. Kripke. "Wittgenstein and Other Minds" from *Wittgenstein on Rules and Private Language: An Elementary Exposition* (Oxford: Basil Blackwell, 1982). © Saul A. Kripke, 1982. Reprinted by permission of John Wiley & Sons, Inc.

J. L. Mackie. "The Subjectivity of Values" from *Ethics: Inventing Right and Wrong* (Harmondsworth: Penguin Books, 1977), pp. 15–42. Copyright © J. L. Mackie, 1977. Reproduced by permission of Penguin Books Ltd.

Don Marquis. "Why Abortion Is Immoral," *The Journal of Philosophy*, Vol. 86, No. 4 (April 1989), pp. 183–202 (excerpted). Reprinted by permission of *The Journal of Philosophy*.

Maurice Merleau-Ponty. "Man Seen from the Outside" from *The World of Perception*, translated by Oliver Davis. Translation © Routledge, 2004. Reproduced by permission of Taylor & Francis Books UK.

Charles W. Mills. Excerpts from *The Racial Contract* (Ithaca, NY: Cornell University Press, 1997). © 1997 by Cornell University. Reprinted by permission of Cornell University Press.

Michele M. Moody-Adams. "Culture, Responsibility, and Affected Ignorance," *Ethics*, Vol. 104, No. 2 (January 1994). © 1994 by The University of Chicago. Reprinted by permission of The University of Chicago Press.

G. E. Moore. "Proof of an External World" from *G. E. Moore: Selected Writings*, edited by Thomas Baldwin. © 1993 Thomas Baldwin. Reproduced by permission of Taylor & Francis Books UK.

Thomas Nagel. "Ethics" from *The Last Word* (New York: Oxford University Press, 1997), pp.101–12. © 1997 by Thomas Nagel. By permission of Oxford University Press USA.

———. "The Absurd," *The Journal of Philosophy*, Vol. 68, No. 20 (October 1971), pp. 716–27 (excerpted). Reprinted by permission of *The Journal of Philosophy*.

———. "What Is It Like to Be a Bat?" *The Philosophical Review*, Vol. 83, No. 4 (October 1974). Reprinted by permission of the author.

Friedrich Nietzsche. "What Is Noble" from *Beyond Good & Evil: Prelude to a Philosophy of the Future* by Friedrich Nietzsche, translated by Walter Kaufmann. Copyright © 1966 by Penguin Random House LLC. Used by permission of Random House, an imprint and division of Penguin Random House LLC. All rights reserved.

———. Excerpts from *The Gay Science* by Friedrich Nietzsche, translated by Walter Kaufmann. Copyright © 1974 by Penguin Random House LLC. Used by permission of Random House, an imprint and division of Penguin Random House LLC. All rights reserved.

———. Excerpts from *On the Genealogy of Morals and Ecce Homo* by Friedrich Nietzsche, translated by Walter Kaufmann and R. J. Hollingdale, edited with commentary by Walter Kaufmann. Copyright © 1967 by Penguin Random House LLC. Used by permission of Random House, an imprint and division of Random House LLC. All rights reserved.

Robert Nozick. "Distributive Justice" from *Anarchy, State, and Utopia* by Robert Nozick. Copyright © 1974. Reprinted by permission of Basic Books, an imprint of Perseus Books LLC, a subsidiary of Hachette Book Group, Inc.

Susan Moller Okin. "Part I" from *Is Multiculturalism Bad for Women?*, edited by Joshua Cohen, Matthew Howard, and Martha C. Nussbaum (Princeton, NJ: Princeton University Press, 1999). © 1999 by Princeton University Press. Reprinted by permission of Princeton University Press.

Onora O'Neill. "The Moral Perplexities of Famine Relief" from *Matters of Life and Death*, edited by Tom L. Beauchamp and Tom Regan. Reprinted by permission of the author.

William Paley. "The Argument from Design" from *Natural Theology*, edited with an introduction and notes by Matthew D. Eddy and David Knight (Oxford: Oxford University Press, 2008), excerpts from pp. 7–36. By permission of Oxford University Press.

Eleanore Stump. "The Problem of Evil," *Faith and Philosophy*, Vol. 2, No. 4 (October 1985), pp. 392–423 (excerpted). Reprinted by permission of the Society of Christian Philosophers.

Richard Swinburne. "Personal Identity: The Dualist Theory" from *Personal Identity* by Sydney Shoemaker and Richard Swinburne (Oxford: Basil Blackwell, 1984). © Sydney Shoemaker and Richard Swinburne, 1984. Reprinted by permission of John Wiley & Sons, Inc.

Richard Taylor. Excerpted from *Good and Evil* (Amherst, NY: Prometheus Books, 1984), pp. 256–68. Copyright © 1984 by Richard Taylor. All rights reserved. Used with permission of the publisher. www.prometheusbooks.com.

Judith Jarvis Thomson. "A Defense of Abortion," *Philosophy & Public Affairs*, Vol. 1, No. 1 (Autumn 1971), pp. 47–66 (excerpted). © 1971 Blackwell Publishing, Inc. Reprinted by permission of John Wiley & Sons, Inc.

Peter Unger. "There Are No Ordinary Things," *Synthese*, Vol. 41, No. 2 (June 1979). © 1979 by D. Reidel Publishing Co., Dordrecht, Holland, and Boston, U.S.A. With permission of Springer.

Bernard Williams. "The Self and the Future," *Philosophical Review*, Vol. 79, No. 2 (April 1970), pp. 161–80. Reprinted by permission of The Estate of Bernard Williams.

Susan Wolf. "Sanity and the Metaphysics of Responsibility" in *Responsibility, Character and the Emotions: New Essays in Moral Psychology*, edited by Ferdinand Schoeman (Cambridge: Cambridge University Press, 1987). Copyright © Cambridge University Press, 1987. Reprinted by permission of Cambridge University Press.

———. "Meaning in Life and Why It Matters: Lecture I." The Tanner Lectures on Human Values delivered at Princeton University, November 7–8, 2007.

Name Index